PROPERTY LAW
CASES, MATERIALS, AND QUESTIONS

PROPERTY LAW CASES, MATERIALS, AND QUESTIONS

Second Edition

EDWARD E. CHASE
Visiting Professor of Law
Loyola University College of Law, New Orleans
Professor Emeritus
Rutgers, The State University of New Jersey School of Law — Camden

JULIA PATTERSON FORRESTER
Professor of Law
Southern Methodist University
Dedman School of Law

ISBN: 978-08205-7094-5

Library of Congress Cataloging-in-Publication Data

Chase, Edward E. (Edward Earl)
    Property law : cases, materials, and questions / Edward E. Chase, Julia P. Forrester. -- 2nd ed.
    p. cm.
    Includes index.
    ISBN 978-0-8205-7094-5 (hard cover)
    1. Property--United States--Cases. I. Forrester, Julia P. II. Title.
KF560.C45 2010
346.7304--dc22   2010008099

This publication is designed to provide accurate and authoritative information in regard to the subject matter covered. It is sold with the understanding that the publisher is not engaged in rendering legal, accounting, or other professional services. If legal advice or other expert assistance is required, the services of a competent professional should be sought.

NOTE TO USERS
To ensure that you are using the latest materials available in this area, please be sure to periodically check the LexisNexis Law School web site for downloadable updates and supplements at www.lexisnexis.com/lawschool.

Editorial Offices
121 Chanlon Rd., New Providence, NJ 07974 (908) 464-6800
201 Mission St., San Francisco, CA 94105-1831 (415) 908-3200
www.lexisnexis.com

MATTHEW◆BENDER

Dedication

To my daughter Lisa, son-in-law Paul, and granddaughters Lauren and Rachel

— E.C.

To my parents, Don and Dorothy, for their constant love and support
To my children, Emily and Stuart, for the joy they bring to my life
And to Paul for his endless wit, good cheer, and fun

— J.P.F.

Table of Contents

Preface
Acknowledgments

Table of Contents

Table of Contents

Table of Contents

Table of Contents

Table of Contents

Table of Contents

Table of Contents

Table of Contents

Table of Contents

Table of Contents

Table of Contents

Table of Contents

Table of Contents

Preface to the Second Edition

In the second edition, we have updated and have made improvements where we thought they were warranted, but we have continued to focus on the objectives stated in the preface to the first edition. We have emphasized the relationship of Property to Contracts and Torts, and we have continued to place an emphasis on remedies.

In choosing cases, we have selected the most recent available. Property has the reputation of being obscure and stodgy, and we want our students to see the modern relevance of the subject. Where cases in the first edition have proved unsatisfactory in the classroom, we have tried to replace them with recent cases. In our selection of all cases, recent or older, we have taken those that we believe represent the correct view (or at least one of the correct views).

Instead of including lengthy textual introductions to materials, we have continued to rely primarily on cases, with notes and questions to develop the material and flesh out the issues. However, we have included fewer questions than appeared in the first edition. We have tried to streamline the notes and questions where they were too cumbersome. In addition, when a case citation is provided to answer a question, we have provided a parenthetical answer. However, we have left the "thought" questions unanswered.

To make the materials more readable, we have continued using the editorial practices of the first edition. In editing cases and other materials, we have deleted sentences, paragraphs, and citations. We have run together separate paragraphs or parts thereof and separated single paragraphs into two. We have silently corrected grammatical and syntactical errors.

Professor Forrester would like to thank Amanda Burcham, Erin Melsheimer, Matt Enoch, Jessica Sheridan, Jennifer Larson, Kendall Banowsky, and Sean Bellah, students or recent graduates of Southern Methodist University Dedman School of Law, for their excellent research assistance. She would also like to thank Dean John Attanasio and SMU Dedman School of Law for providing research funds to complete this project.

Professor Chase would like to thank Michael Blackwell, Laken Davis, and Geoffrey Garber, all students at Loyola University College of Law in New Orleans, for valuable research assistance. He would also like to thank Dean Brian Bromberger for providing research funds for this project.

Professor Chase joins the foregoing Preface but wishes to state separately that the *really* new and important addition to the book is its co-author, Julie Forrester, and the fresh perspective, expertise, and welcome enthusiasm that she has brought to the project. With her, the book is far stronger than it otherwise would have been, and has been a lot more enjoyable to work on.

Edward E. Chase, Jr.
New Orleans, Louisiana

Julia Patterson Forrester
Dallas, Texas

March, 2010

Preface to the First Edition

Property is a difficult subject for students. It lacks a unifying theme. In Contracts, bargain serves as a theoretical focus (contrasted with reliance and unjust enrichment as alternative sources of obligation) and an organizational device (contracts casebooks consider, more or less in sequence, the formation of a valid bargain, interpretation of its terms, performance, remedies for nonperformance, and the like). In Torts, the concepts of intentional harms, negligently-caused harms, and strict liability provide theoretical focus and organizational structure. In contrast, Property appears to the beginning law student as life did to Frank Ward O'Malley: "just one damned thing after another." And while the subject remains as difficult as it ever was, the students who encounter it nowadays have changed. Although my students today are no less bright than their predecessors of a few years ago, they do come with different skills; in particular, they are less prepared than their predecessors to handle complex texts. It is useless to lament this; it is a fact of our lives as teachers at the graduate level of education.

These two concerns — the complexity of the topic to the newcomer and the changed aptitudes of the newcomers themselves — have caused this book to take the specific shape that it does. Although it is a tall order, I have tried to create materials that are at once accessible enough to allow students to learn some fundamentals on their own, and yet intellectually rigorous enough to allow for the kind of evaluating, questioning, and deepening of analysis that should occur in the classroom. Readers will have to judge whether I have accomplished that worthy goal.

Here are some specifics of the book:

Unity. To counteract the perceived disunity of property law, some books use economic analysis, or philosophy, or something else, as a unifying perspective. The following materials are usable with any such approach. My unifying device (such as it is), however, seeks to be internal to law: wherever possible, I try to familiarize students with the essential concepts of property law by building on ideas with which they are acquainted if not familiar. Thus the heavy emphasis in these materials on the relationship of Property to Contracts and (to a lesser extent) to Torts, the three essential sources of common law rights and duties, and three mainstays of the first-year curriculum. (The chapters on landlord and tenant and on servitudes provide the most obvious, but not the only, candidates for comparison to contract doctrine.)

Cases vs. text. Students seem to get much more from reading cases than from reading explanatory text. Perhaps, as a colleague of mine says, this is because cases present stories — dramatizations of events — to which students respond. In any event, I have tried to avoid or to condense lengthy textual introductions to chapters and sections, preferring to let the Notes and Questions develop the material. Of course, Notes and Questions are text also. But by coming after and dealing specifically with issues opened up by the cases, the Notes and Questions give students a concrete focus that mere explanatory text usually lacks. In the instances in which textual explication, introductory or otherwise, seemed unavoidable, I have tried to make it as clear, and to keep it as brief, as possible.

Case selection. Wherever possible, I have used the most recent cases available. This alone may help to shake some of the obscurity from the subject. I have also tried to avoid

Preface to the First Edition

using cases that get doctrine wrong (a pervasive problem in future interests — where, yes, I have ventured to use a couple of cases — and servitudes): partly this springs from my objection to hide-the-ball pedagogy; in addition, on efficiency grounds, it is a waste of valuable classroom time to expect students to learn some of the law from their own reading only to have them unlearn it in class discussion. Cases that get the law right but still raise timely and discussable questions are the ones I have aimed for.

Focus on remedies. As a descendant of the American Legal Realists, no modern casebook author can (or at least should) write a text that fails to devote much the same kind of rigorous attention to remedies that is devoted to the substantive law. Accordingly, materials on remedies appear at many points in this book. What is perhaps unusual about the coverage of remedies herein is that I have tried to include restitution — currently the subject of a new Restatement project under the Reportership of Professor Andrew Kull — in the discussion of available remedies wherever possible. Raven Red Ash v. Ball, dealing with restitution for an easement holder's misuse of the benefit, is one of the classics of restitution literature, and it appears here in Chapter 6. Edwards v. Lee's Administrator, another classic in the law of restitution, is discussed in the Notes following Marengo Cave Co. v. Ross in Chapter 1. Restitution in its intriguing role as a basis for the recovery of *reliance* expenditures by the disappointed promisee under a contract of lease that is invalid due to the Statute of Frauds also receives attention. Of course, attention is also devoted to damages and equitable remedies for the protection of property rights.

History of Property law. This may be heretical to old-line teachers of Property (I should say *other* old-line teachers), but like the New Critics in literature, I have tried consistently in this book to separate the question of the meaning of the rules of Property law from the question of the historical origin of those rules. I do this neither proudly nor lightly; no one enjoys exploring the historical development of doctrine more than I, and I know that such an exploration can enrich one's understanding of the law immeasurably. But with today's students, excursions into the legal history of doctrine tend to fall either flat or on deaf ears. So — and again, this is solely in the interest of effective pedagogy — knight service, grand serjeantry, common socage, and frankalmoign are not in this book; Quia Emptores and De Donis appear in passing; the Statute of Uses gets a short paragraph; lost grant, a shorter one. Where Property law is most burdened by its history (future interests and servitudes come immediately to mind), I try to present the law as a meaningful *conceptual* system, and doing that does not require extended discussions of legal history.

Questions. More than any other Property casebook of which I am aware, this book provides questions (usually many) after each principal case. (These questions are so integral to the structure and intent of the book that a reference to them is included in its subtitle.) In general, the questions begin with the issues raised in the cases to which the questions are appended, and expand outward from there. Instructors inclined to use all of the questions after each case will find that there is enough material to occupy whatever classroom time the instructor is likely to be willing to devote to the topic at hand. Instructors wishing to devote somewhat less time to a case or topic than the questions call for can do so by selectively assigning the questions. When an instructor disagrees with the line of analysis suggested by the questions (which seasoned instructors may do quite often), *that* disagreement itself can generate valuable classroom discussion.

Weighted coverage of topics. In addition to trying to present a book that is fair to

Preface to the First Edition

students as well as to the subject being presented to them, I have tried to write a book whose coverage and attention to detail reflect the course that I teach, rather than some other course. I have not deemed it wise to try to give the same kind of fulldress treatment to conveyancing, zoning, or regulatory takings that I give, for example, to servitudes, concurrent interests, and landlord-tenant law. My course, like many others, is a one-semester course, and conveyancing, zoning and regulatory takings are not part of it. On the core topics covered herein, I have included material on all aspects of the subjects that I believe anyone would want to cover in class or by outside reading; I have devoted considerable space to my organizing device (comparing the rules of Property, Contract and Tort); I have provided an extensive set of questions for each major case; and I have stated in detail in the Instructor's Manual my thoughts on the questions raised. On topics covered in less detail than the core topics, I have tried simply to give the big picture. This strategy of "weighting" the book's coverage according to the likelihood of the topic being covered in most schools, means that most teachers will have more than enough material to cover on core topics. On the other topics, my materials allow for a quick in-and-out treatment for anyone desiring that approach, and they allow for easy supplementation for any teachers wishing to develop the topics in greater depth than my materials do.

Sequencing. The chapters follow the traditional triadic structure of ownership (Chapters 1-3), transfer (4 and 5) and use (6-8) of land and other resources. But each chapter is intended as a self-contained unit, and an instructor can as well begin with estates (Chapter 2) or landlord and tenant (chapter 4) as with animals or finders. (I have in the past started the course at different points in the materials, and will continue to do so in the future. The opportunity for this kind of re-shuffling of the deck, with the occasional insights afforded thereby, is the one big advantage of the disunity of the subject.)

Editorial practices. Since this book is intended for use as a teaching tool, I have engaged in editorial practices that would be unthinkable in a work designed for different purposes and audiences. The overriding aim of these practices has been to make the materials readable, accomplished through the elimination of distracting editorial intrusions. Accordingly: I have deleted sentences and paragraphs (parts of, or entire) without the usual ellipses so indicating; I have occasionally run together separate paragraphs, or separated single paragraphs. I have silently corrected most grammatical or syntactical errors. And so on. All of the recited practices have aided sense or at least not detracted from it, and all seem self-evident to me. One final practice — whose justification is far from self-evident — is my consistent omission of the case authorities cited in the judicial opinions reprinted herein; I have retained only those case citations identifying a quote or serving some other important purpose. This is a difficult choice because one of the requirements of effective advocacy that we try to instill in our students is that of making authoritative statements in support of the propositions they advance, and what better way to teach it than to show it being done over and over? But the overall savings in space, as well as the relative meaninglessness to students of string citations of authority, more than compensate for the advantage lost.

Like any author, I have incurred academic debts in the preparation of this book. The two largest debts will happily never be paid in full, because the accounts remain active. Professor Craig Oren, a fellow teacher of the basic Property course at Rutgers for many years, has often and in detail shared with me his insights about the substance and the

Preface to the First Edition

pedagogy of Property. Much of whatever virtue there is in the materials on future interests and servitudes is owed to him, and I am grateful. Professor (Emeritus) Hunter Taylor, my longtime good friend, sometime coauthor, and *compadre* of many an academic battle, taught me all the Contracts law I know, and thus made an indelible impression on Chapter 4, the longest in the book. A Renaissance teacher, he also volunteered to teach the book in draft form to a section of evening students, and his insights from that experience have immeasurably improved the final text and the Instructor's Manual. I am indebted to him beyond the power of words to express. I also thank Dean Rayman Solomon for generous financial support in the preparation of this book and, more importantly, for creating an atmosphere at Rutgers that encourages and acknowledges scholarly endeavors.

I owe a debt that transcends academics to my brother Charley, a Presbyterian minister in Dothan, Alabama. For many years, and at every place and turn, he has enlarged my steps so that my feet would not slip. I am eternally grateful to, and for, him.

I thank Professor Glen Weissenberger for helping me to get into this project, as well as for writing two seminal articles in the field of landlord and tenant law that it has been my pleasure to read and profit from. At Anderson Publishing Company, I have had the good fortune to fall into the expert hands of Sean Caldwell, whose incomparable editorial skills and judgment are exceeded only by his patience and tact in dealing with my interminable delays in forwarding material to him.

The following research assistants — present or past students at Rutgers Law School — provided invaluable assistance in the compiling of the manuscript: Jon Batastini, David T. Blonder, Kristie Curtis, Andrew Podolski, and Lynda Searles. (Andrew and Lynda also provided expert assistance in the compilation of tables.) My secretary Debbie Comuso provided her usual superb help on tasks great and small.

This is my first book, and I am acutely aware, having finished it, of what Paul Tillich called "the incompleteness of the completed." Who knows what revisions a deeper understanding of the subject might have prompted, what lines of authority a more searching analysis might have detected, what infelicities of style or content yet another proofreading might have uncovered? But you have to go into production sometime, and I am reasonably satisfied that this book is the one I wanted to and was capable of writing at this time.

Edward E. Chase, Jr.

Acknowledgments

Permission to reproduce excerpts from the following materials is gratefully acknowledged:

American Law Institute, Restatement of Property (1944); Restatement (Second) of Property, Landlord and Tenant (1977); Restatement (Third) of Property, Donative Transfers (2000); Restatement (Third) of Property, Servitudes (2000); Restatement of Contracts (1932); Restatement (Second) of Contracts (1981). Reprinted by permission of the American Law Institute.

Elizabeth Bishop, excerpt from "One Art" from The Complete Poems: 1927-1979, by Elizabeth Bishop. Copyright © 1979, 1983 by Alice Helen Methfessel. Reprinted by permission of Farrar, Straus and Giroux, LLC.

Alfred Conard, The Privilege of Forcibly Ejecting an Amusement Patron, 90 U. Pa. L. Rev. 809 (1942). Reprinted by permission.

John Humbach, The Common-Law Conception of Leasing: Mitigation, Habitability, and Dependence of Covenants, 60 Wash. U.L.Q. 1213 (1983). Reprinted by permission.

Quintin Johnstone, Land Transfers: Process and Processors, 22 Val. U. L. Rev. 493 (1988). Reprinted by permission.

National Conference of Commissioners on Uniform State Laws, Uniform Probate Code (copyright © 1990), Uniform Premarital Agreement Act (copyright © 1983). Reprinted by permission.

Henry Reed, "Naming of Parts," from *Collected Poems*, edited by Jon Stallworthy (1991). Reprinted by permission of Oxford University Press.

William B. Stoebuck & Dale A. Whitman, The Law of Property (3d ed. 2000). Pages 869-70 and 892-93 reprinted from Stoebuck & Whitman, The Law of Property (3d ed. 2000) by permission of the West Group.

John Stone, "The Truck," from *In All This Rain* (1980). Reprinted by permission of the author.

Table of Consanguinity, reproduced from *California Decedent Estate Practice, Volumes 1 & 2*, copyright © 1986, 2000, by the Regents of the University of California. Reproduced with permission of Continuing Education of the Bar–California. (For information about CEB publications, telephone toll free 1-800-CEB-3444 or go to our web site, CEB.com.)

Chapter 1

PROPERTY: AN INTRODUCTION

A. PROPERTY AS THINGS AND AS INTERESTS IN THINGS

If you were asked whether you own any property, you would probably answer that you own a car, or a boat, or even a property casebook. That is, you would understand the question to refer to objects and you would respond, quite appropriately on that understanding, by listing the objects that you own. The usage of the word "property" to refer to things is so pervasive that any attempt we might make to suppress that meaning would be futile.

But it is not the essential meaning that the word "property" has in the law, and consequently in this book. To lawyers, "property" refers not to a thing, but rather to interests that one may have in relation to a thing. I may "own" my house, but the company that holds the mortgage also has an important interest in it. If I lease a room to you, you and I both own important interests in "my" house. Even if I own my house without a mortgage or a tenant, I still cannot regard it as "mine" in a way that focuses only on me and on the soil or the bricks and mortar of the structure on the soil: I cannot open a professional office at home if the declaration of restrictions covering my subdivision forbids it; I cannot open a piggery in my back yard if it would constitute a nuisance to my neighbor; I cannot build a third story if zoning laws do not allow it. (Don't be disturbed by the negatives; each of the previous sentences could be rephrased to emphasize the positive: I may use my land as I choose so long as I don't excessively disturb my neighbor, and so on. Whether stated negatively or positively, any accurate proposition about "my" house will indicate the relativity of my interests to those of others who may assert an interest.)

We needn't multiply examples here; you will see many as the course progresses. The important point is that property consists of a bundle of privileges, rights and duties with respect to things. The metaphor used by generations of law professors is that property consists of a bundle of sticks. The first case below suggests a possible provenance of that metaphor, identifies some of the major sticks in the bundle, and shows the subtlety of analysis that results from thinking about property as a bundle of sticks. The second case shows — quite dramatically — the importance that our legal system places on one of the sticks in the bundle. Neither case need detain us long; they set the stage for much of the remainder of the course.

1. The "Bundle of Sticks" Metaphor

ADAMS v. CLEVELAND-CLIFFS IRON CO.
602 N.W.2d 215 (Mich. Ct. App. 1999)

O'CONNELL, J.

Defendants appeal from a jury verdict awarding damages in trespass for invasions of plaintiffs' property by intrusions of dust, noise, and vibrations. [T]his appeal presents the question whether Michigan recognizes a cause of action in trespass stemming from invasions of these intangible agents. No published decision of an appellate court of this state is directly on point. We conclude that the law of trespass in Michigan does not cover airborne particulate, noise, or vibrations, and that a complaint alleging damages resulting from these irritants normally sounds instead in nuisance.

I. Facts

[T]he Empire Mine, which is operated by defendant Cleveland-Cliffs Iron Company, is one of the nation's largest mines, producing eight million tons of iron ore annually. The mine operates twenty-four hours a day, year round. [P]laintiffs lived near the mine, in the village of Palmer in Marquette County. Cleveland-Cliffs, which also operates the nearby Tilden Mine, employs approximately 2,200 persons, making it the area's largest civilian employer. The mine engages in blasting operations approximately three times a week, year round, and the extraction and processing of the iron ore generates a great deal of airborne dust.

Plaintiffs complain that the blasting sends tremors through their property and that defendants' dust constantly accumulates inside and outside plaintiffs' homes. Plaintiffs assert that these emanations aggravate their need to clean and repaint their homes, replace carpets and drapes, repair cracks in all masonry, replace windows, and tend to cause plumbing leaks and broken sewer pipes. In addition to concerns about the dust, many plaintiffs testified that the noise and vibrations from the blasts caused them to suffer shock, nervousness, and sleeplessness. Finally, several plaintiffs asserted that these conditions diminished the value of their homes, in some cases to the point of rendering them unmarketable.

At the close of proofs, the trial court instructed the jury concerning both trespass and nuisance. The jury was unable to agree on a verdict regarding the nuisance claim, but returned a verdict in favor of these plaintiffs with regard to the trespass claim, awarding damages totaling $599,199. The court denied defendants' posttrial motions for a new trial or judgment notwithstanding the verdict. Defendants did not object on the record that the trial court's instruction improperly recognized a cause of action in trespass where the intrusion complained of consisted of airborne particulate, noise, or vibrations, nor did they initially frame their issue on appeal that way. Nonetheless, in the interests of justice, and because the issue concerns a question of law and all the facts necessary for its resolution have been presented, we will examine the related doctrines of trespass and nuisance and will determine how they bear on the intrusions at issue in this case.

II. Trespass and Nuisance

The general concept of "property" comprises various rights — a "bundle of sticks," as it is often called[6] — which is usually understood to include "[t]he exclusive right of possessing, enjoying, and disposing of a thing." Black's Law Dictionary (6th ed., 1990), p. 1216. As this latter characterization suggests, the right to exclude others from one's land and the right to quiet enjoyment of one's land have customarily been regarded as separate sticks in the bundle. E.g., Lucas v. South Carolina Coastal Council, 505 U.S. 1003, 1044 (1992) (Blackmun, J., dissenting) (addressing as separate "attributes of ownership" the rights of exclusion, alienation, and enjoyment); Biggs v. Comm'r of Internal Revenue, 632 F.2d 1171, 1177 (5th Cir. 1980) ("title to real property is nothing more than a bundle of potential causes of action: for trespass, to quiet title, for interference with quiet enjoyment, and so on"); Livingston, *Public Access to Virginia's Tidelands: A Framework for Analysis of Implied Dedications and Public Prescriptive Rights*, 24 Wm. & Mary L.R. 669, 698 (1983) ("The notion of fee simple ownership carries with it the idea that the owner may exclude all others from his property, shall have the quiet enjoyment of it, and shall be free from unrecorded conflicting interests in it."), citing Cribbet, Principles of the Law of Property (2d ed., 1975), pp. 263-332. Thus, possessory rights to real property include as distinct interests the right to exclude and the right to enjoy, violations of which give rise to the distinct causes of action respectively of trespass and nuisance.[7] Prosser & Keeton, Torts (5th ed.), § 87, p. 622.

A. Historical Overview

"At common law, trespass was a form of action brought to recover damages for any injury to one's person or property or relationship with another." Black's Law

---

[6] Some attribute the origins of this metaphor to a work by Benjamin N. Cardozo, dating from shortly before he ascended to the United States Supreme Court. *See* Cardozo, The Paradoxes of Legal Science, p. 129 ("The bundle of power and privileges to which we give the name of ownership is not constant through the ages. The faggots must be put together and rebound from time to time.").

[7] A.M. Honore likewise distinguished between the rights of exclusion and of use and enjoyment, listing the incidents of ownership as follows:

 (1) the right to *exclusive possession*;

 (2) the right to personal *use and enjoyment*;

 (3) the right to manage use by others;

 (4) the right to the income from use by others;

 (5) the right to the capital value, including alienation, consumption, waste, or destruction;

 (6) the right to security (that is, immunity from expropriation);

 (7) the power of transmissibility by gift, devise, or descent;

 (8) the lack of any term on these rights;

 (9) the duty to refrain from using the object in ways that harm others;

 (10) the liability to execution for repayment of debts; and

 (11) residual rights on the reversion of lapsed ownership rights held by others.

Heller, *The Tragedy of the Anticommons: Property in the Transition from Marx to Markets*, 111 Harv. L. R. 621, 663, n. 187 (1998), citing Honore, *Ownership, in* Oxford Essays in Jurisprudence 107, 112-128 (A.G. Guest ed. 1961) (emphasis added).

Dictionary (6th ed.), p. 1502. This broad usage of the term "trespass" then gave way to a narrower usage, referring to intrusions upon a person's "tangible property, real or personal." Prosser & Keeton, *supra* at § 13, p. 67. Today, the general concept of "trespass" has been refined into several specific forms of trespass, see Black's Law Dictionary (6th ed.), pp. 1502-1504, and related doctrines known by various names. Landowners seeking damages or equitable relief in response to violations of their possessory rights to land now generally proceed under the common-law derivatives of strict liability, negligence, nuisance, or trespass to land. It is the latter two products of this evolution from the general concept of trespass that are at issue in the present case.

Because a trespass violated a landholder's right to exclude others from the premises, the landholder could recover at least nominal damages even in the absence of proof of any other injury. Recovery for nuisance, however, traditionally required proof of actual and substantial injury. Further, the doctrine of nuisance customarily called for balancing the disturbance complained of against the social utility of its cause. Traditionally, trespass required that the invasion of the land be direct or immediate and in the form of a physical, tangible object. Under these principles, recovery in trespass for dust, smoke, noise, and vibrations was generally unavailable because they were not considered tangible or because they came to the land via some intervening force such as wind or water. Instead, claims concerning these irritants were generally pursued under a nuisance theory.

B. Recent Trends

Plaintiffs would have us follow the example of certain courts from other jurisdictions, which have eliminated the traditional requirements for trespass of a direct intrusion by a tangible object, directing the inquiry instead toward the nature of the interest harmed. These courts have permitted recovery in trespass for indirect, intangible invasions that nonetheless interfered with exclusive possessory interests in the land.

The courts that have deviated from the traditional requirements of trespass, however, have consequently found troublesome the traditional principle that at least nominal damages are presumed in cases of trespass. Thus, under the so-called modern view of trespass, in order to avoid subjecting manufacturing plants to potential liability to every landowner on whose parcel some incidental residue of industrial activity might come to rest, these courts have grafted onto the law of trespass a requirement of actual and substantial damages.[11]

We do not welcome this redirection of trespass law toward nuisance law. The requirement that real and substantial damages be proved, and balanced against the usefulness of the offending activity, is appropriate where the issue is interference with one's use or enjoyment of one's land; applying it where a landowner has had to endure an unauthorized physical occupation of the landowner's land, however, offends traditional principles of ownership. The law

---

[11] We are of the opinion that this kind of analysis is generally only required in a nuisance case and that it is better to preserve that aspect of traditional trespass analysis requiring no proof of actual injury because the invasion of the plaintiff's right to exclude was regarded as tortious by itself.

should not require a property owner to justify exercising the right to exclude. To countenance the erosion of presumed damages in cases of trespass is to endanger the right of exclusion itself.

III. Holding

Recovery for trespass to land in Michigan is available only upon proof of an unauthorized direct or immediate intrusion of a physical, tangible object onto land over which the plaintiff has a right of exclusive possession. Once such an intrusion is proved, the tort has been established, and the plaintiff is presumptively entitled to at least nominal damages. Where the possessor of land is menaced by noise, vibrations, or ambient dust, smoke, soot, or fumes, the possessory interest implicated is that of use and enjoyment, not exclusion, and the vehicle through which a plaintiff normally should seek a remedy is the doctrine of nuisance. To prevail in nuisance, a possessor of land must prove significant harm resulting from the defendant's unreasonable interference with the use or enjoyment of the property. Thus, in nuisance, the plaintiff must prove all damages, which may be awarded only to the extent that the defendant's conduct was "unreasonable" according to a public-policy assessment of its overall value. In the present case, because the intrusions of which plaintiffs complained were intangible things, the trial court erred in allowing the jury to award damages in trespass. Instead, any award of damages would have had to proceed from plaintiffs' alternative but (as yet) unsuccessful theory of nuisance.

IV. Conclusion

Because Michigan does not recognize a cause of action in trespass for airborne particulate, noise, or vibrations, we hereby vacate the jury verdict in this matter and remand this case to the trial court for further proceedings consistent with this opinion. We do not retain jurisdiction.

Reversed and remanded.

NOTES AND QUESTIONS

1. **Possession and use.** Which stick in the bundle does a trespass claim involve? Which stick does a nuisance claim involve? Why is it important to unpack these separate interests? *See generally* Osborne M. Reynolds, Jr., *Distinguishing Trespass and Nuisance: A Journey Through a Shifting Borderland*, 44 Okla. L. Rev. 227 (1991).

2. **Examples.** If you are a tenant, who "owns" the premises that you rent for purposes of determining liability for real estate taxes? *See* Wycoff v. Gavriloff Motors, Inc., 107 N.W.2d 820 (Mich. 1961) ("[I]n the absence of an agreement making it the duty of the lessee to pay the taxes, the law ordinarily imposes this obligation upon the lessor."). Who owns the premises for purposes of a cause of action for trespass? *See* AmSouth Bank, N.A. v. City of Mobile, 500 So. 2d 1072, 1075 (Ala. 1986) (holding that landlords had no standing to assert an action for trespass because they had no right to possession and "trespass is a wrong relating to the right of possession"). Who owns the premises for the purposes of paying just

compensation, if the state takes the property in eminent domain? *See* Alamo Land & Cattle Co., Inc. v. Arizona, 424 U.S. 295, 303 (1976) (holding that both landlord and tenant are entitled under the Fifth Amendment to just compensation for value of their interests taken by condemnation).

3. **Another example.** You rent half of a duplex; your landlord lives in the other half. After moving in, you find that the landlord regularly invites all his rowdy friends to his apartment for parties, which go on into the wee hours of the morning, just when you are studying Property. You complain vigorously. The landlord says, "I rented you a unit; you still have it — I haven't done anything to take it back from you." (He also invites you to one of his parties; you decline.) Has the landlord interfered with any of your rights as a tenant? How is the principal case helpful in answering this question?

4. **Another stick in the bundle.** You own Blackacre, situated next to Whiteacre. Your neighbor, owner of Whiteacre, approaches you about running a crushed stone driveway across Blackacre, which will provide more convenient access to her parcel than presently exists. Assuming that you are willing to accommodate your neighbor, must you give her title to the strip in question, or is some other arrangement possible (and desirable)? In Chapter 6, we will study easements, property interests that give the owner thereof a right to use someone else's land.

5. **Airborne particulate.** Other courts have found that airborne particulate can create a physical entry upon land that constitutes a trespass. *See* Stevenson v. E.I. DuPont De Nemours & Co., 327 F.3d 400, 406 (5th Cir. 2003).

6. **Criticism of the metaphor.** The conception of property as a bundle of sticks has come under intense scrutiny by scholars in the last few years. *See* Craig Anthony Arnold, *The Reconstruction of Property: Property as a Web of Interests*, 26 Harv. Envtl. L. Rev. 281 (2002); Hanoch Dagan, *The Craft of Property*, 91 Cal. L. Rev. 1517 (2003); Myrl L. Duncan, *Reconceiving the Bundle of Sticks: Land as a Community-Based Resource*, 32 Envtl. L. 773 (2003); Peter S. Menell & John P. Dwyer, *Reunifying Property*, 46 St. Louis U. L.J. 599 (2002); Adam Mossoff, *What is Property? Putting the Pieces Back Together*, 45 Ariz. L. Rev. 371 (2003).

JACQUE v. STEENBERG HOMES, INC.
563 N.W.2d 154 (Wis. 1997)

WILLIAM A. BABLITCH, JUSTICE.

Steenberg Homes had a mobile home to deliver. Unfortunately for Harvey and Lois Jacque (the Jacques), the easiest route of delivery was across their land. Despite adamant protests by the Jacques, Steenberg plowed a path through the Jacques' snow-covered field and via that path, delivered the mobile home. Consequently, the Jacques sued Steenberg Homes for intentional trespass. At trial, Steenberg Homes conceded the intentional trespass, but argued that no compensatory damages had been proved, and that punitive damages could not be awarded without compensatory damages. Although the jury awarded the Jacques $1 in nominal damages and $100,000 in punitive damages, the circuit court set aside the jury's award of $100,000. The court of appeals affirmed, reluctantly concluding that it could not reinstate the punitive damages because it was bound by precedent establishing that an award of nominal damages will not sustain a punitive damage award. We conclude that when nominal damages are awarded for an intentional trespass to land, punitive damages may, in the discretion of the jury, be awarded. We further conclude that the $100,000 awarded by the jury is not excessive. Accordingly, we reverse and remand for reinstatement of the punitive damage award.

I.

The relevant facts follow. Plaintiffs, Lois and Harvey Jacques, are an elderly couple, now retired from farming, who own roughly 170 acres near Wilke's Lake in the town of Schleswig. The defendant, Steenberg Homes, Inc. (Steenberg), is in the business of selling mobile homes. In the fall of 1993, a neighbor of the Jacques purchased a mobile home from Steenberg. Delivery of the mobile home was included in the sales price.

Steenberg determined that the easiest route to deliver the mobile home was across the Jacques' land. Steenberg preferred transporting the home across the Jacques' land because the only alternative was a private road which was covered in up to seven feet of snow and contained a sharp curve which would require sets of "rollers" to be used when maneuvering the home around the curve. Steenberg asked the Jacques on several separate occasions whether it could move the home across the Jacques' farm field. The Jacques refused. The Jacques were sensitive about allowing others on their land because they had lost property valued at over $10,000 to other neighbors in an adverse possession action in the mid-1980's. Despite repeated refusals from the Jacques, Steenberg decided to sell the mobile home, which was to be used as a summer cottage, and delivered it on February 15, 1994.

On the morning of delivery, Mr. Jacque observed the mobile home parked on the corner of the town road adjacent to his property. He decided to find out where the movers planned to take the home. The movers, who were Steenberg employees, showed Mr. Jacque the path they planned to take with the mobile home to reach the neighbor's lot. The path cut across the Jacques' land. Mr. Jacque informed the movers that it was the Jacques' land they were planning to cross and that Steenberg did not have permission to cross their land. He told them that Steenberg had been refused permission to cross the Jacques' land.

One of Steenberg's employees called the assistant manager, who then came out to the Jacques' home. In the meantime, the Jacques called and asked some of their neighbors and the town chairman to come over immediately. Once everyone was present, the Jacques showed the assistant manager an aerial map and plat book of the township to prove their ownership of the land, and reiterated their demand that the home not be moved across their land.

At that point, the assistant manager asked Mr. Jacque how much money it would take to get permission. Mr. Jacque responded that it was not a question of money; the Jacques just did not want Steenberg to cross their land. Mr. Jacque testified that he told Steenberg to "[F]ollow the road, that is what the road is for."

Steenberg employees left the meeting without permission to cross the land.

At trial, one of Steenberg's employees testified that, upon coming out of the Jacques' home, the assistant manager stated: "I don't give a — — what [Mr. Jacque] said, just get the home in there any way you can." The other Steenberg employee confirmed this testimony and further testified that the assistant manager told him to park the company truck in such a way that no one could get down the town road to see the route the employees were taking with the home. The assistant manager denied giving these instructions, and Steenberg argued that the road was blocked for safety reasons.

The employees, after beginning down the private road, ultimately used a "bobcat" to cut a path through the Jacques' snow-covered field and hauled the home across the Jacques' land to the neighbor's lot. One employee testified that upon returning to the office and informing the assistant manager that they had gone across the field, the assistant manager reacted by giggling and laughing. The other employee confirmed this testimony. The assistant manager disputed this testimony.

When a neighbor informed the Jacques that Steenberg had, in fact, moved the mobile home across the Jacques' land, Mr. Jacque called the Manitowoc County Sheriff's Department. After interviewing the parties and observing the scene, an officer from the sheriff's department issued a $30 citation to Steenberg's assistant manager.

The Jacques commenced an intentional tort action in Manitowoc County Circuit Court, seeking compensatory and punitive damages from Steenberg. The case was tried before a jury on December 1, 1994. At the completion of the Jacques' case, Steenberg moved for a directed verdict. For purposes of the motion, Steenberg admitted to an intentional trespass to land, but asked the circuit court to find that the Jacques were not entitled to compensatory damages or punitive damages based on insufficiency of the evidence. The circuit court denied Steenberg's motion and the questions of punitive and compensatory damages were submitted to the jury. The jury awarded the Jacques $1 nominal damages and $100,000 punitive damages. Steenberg filed post-verdict motions claiming that the punitive damage award must be set aside because Wisconsin law did not allow a punitive damage award unless the jury also awarded compensatory damages. Alternatively, Steenberg asked the circuit court to remit the punitive damage award. The circuit court granted Steenberg's motion to set aside the award. Consequently, it did not reach Steenberg's motion for remittitur.

This case presents [the] issue of whether an award of nominal damages for intentional trespass to land may support a punitive damage award.

Before the question of punitive damages in a tort action can properly be submitted to the jury, the circuit court must determine, as a matter of law, that the evidence will support an award of punitive damages. Steenberg argues that, as a matter of law, punitive damages could not be awarded by the jury because punitive damages must be supported by an award of compensatory damages and here the jury awarded only nominal and punitive damages. The Jacques contend that the rationale supporting the compensatory damage award requirement is inapposite when the wrongful act is an intentional trespass to land. We agree with the Jacques.

First, we consider the individual and societal interests implicated when an intentional trespass to land occurs. Then, we analyze the rationale supporting the rule in light of these interests.

The United States Supreme Court has recognized that the private landowner's right to exclude others from his or her land is "one of the most essential sticks in the bundle of rights that are commonly characterized as property." Dolan v. City of Tigard, 512 U.S. 374, 384 (1994). This court has long recognized "[e]very person['s] constitutional right to the exclusive enjoyment of his own property for any purpose which does not invade the rights of another person." Diana Shooting Club v. Lamoreux, 89 N.W. 880 (Wis. 1902) (holding that the victim of an intentional trespass should have been allowed to take judgment for nominal damages and costs). Thus, both this court and the Supreme Court recognize the individual's legal right to exclude others from private property.

Yet a right is hollow if the legal system provides insufficient means to protect it. Felix Cohen offers the following analysis summarizing the relationship between the individual and the state regarding property rights:

[T]hat is property to which the following label can be attached:

To the world:

Keep off X unless you have my permission, which I may grant or withhold.

Signed: Private Citizen

Endorsed: The state

Felix S. Cohen, *Dialogue on Private Property*, 9 Rutgers Law Review 357, 374 (1954). Harvey and Lois Jacque have the right to tell Steenberg Homes and any other trespasser, "No, you cannot cross our land." But that right has no practical meaning unless protected by the State. And, as this court recognized as early as 1854, a "halfpenny" award does not constitute state protection.

The nature of the nominal damage award in an intentional trespass to land case further supports an exception to [the general rule requiring compensatory damages to support a punitive damages award]. Because a legal right is involved, the law recognizes that actual harm occurs in every trespass. The action for intentional trespass to land is directed at vindication of the legal right. W. Page Keeton, Prosser and Keeton on Torts, § 13 (5th ed. 1984). The law infers some damage from every direct entry upon the land of another. *Id.* The law recognizes actual harm in every trespass to land whether or not compensatory damages are awarded. *Id.* Thus, in the case of intentional trespass to land, the nominal damage award represents the recognition that, although immeasurable in mere dollars, actual harm has occurred.

The potential for harm resulting from intentional trespass also supports an exception to [the general rule]. A series of intentional trespasses, as the Jacques had the misfortune to discover in an unrelated action, can threaten the individual's very ownership of the land. The conduct of an intentional trespasser, if repeated, might ripen into prescription or adverse possession and, as a consequence, the individual landowner can lose his or her property rights to the trespasser. *See* Wis. Stat. § 893.28.

In sum, the individual has a strong interest in excluding trespassers from his or her land. Although only nominal damages were awarded to the Jacques, Steenberg's intentional trespass caused actual harm. We turn next to society's interest in protecting private property from the intentional trespasser.

Society has an interest in punishing and deterring intentional trespassers beyond that of protecting the interests of the individual landowner. Society has an interest in preserving the integrity of the legal system. Private landowners should feel confident that wrongdoers who trespass upon their land will be appropriately punished. When landowners have confidence in the legal system, they are less likely to resort to "self-help" remedies. [O]ne can easily imagine a frustrated landowner taking the law into his or her own hands when faced with a brazen trespasser, like Steenberg, who refuses to heed no trespass warnings.

People expect wrongdoers to be appropriately punished. Punitive damages have the effect of bringing to punishment types of conduct that, though oppressive and hurtful to the individual, almost invariably go unpunished by the public prosecutor. The $30 forfeiture was certainly not an appropriate punishment for Steenberg's egregious trespass in the eyes of the Jacques. If punitive damages are not allowed in a situation like this, what punishment will prohibit the intentional trespass to land? Moreover, what is to stop Steenberg Homes from concluding, in the future, that delivering its mobile homes via an intentional trespass and paying the resulting Class B forfeiture, is not more profitable than obeying the law? Steenberg Homes plowed a path across the Jacques' land and dragged the mobile home across that path, in the face of the Jacques' adamant refusal. A $30 forfeiture and a $1 nominal damage award are unlikely to restrain Steenberg Homes from similar conduct in the future. An appropriate punitive damage award probably will.

In sum, as the court of appeals noted, the [general] rule sends the wrong message to Steenberg Homes and any others who contemplate trespassing on the land of another. It implicitly tells them that they are free to go where they please, regardless of the landowner's wishes. As long as they cause no compensable harm, the only deterrent intentional trespassers face is the nominal damage award of $1, and the possibility of a Class B forfeiture under Wis. Stat. § 943.13. We conclude that both the private landowner and society have much more than a nominal interest in excluding others from private land. Intentional trespass to land causes actual harm to the individual, regardless of whether that harm can be measured in mere dollars. Accordingly, assuming that the other requirements for punitive damages have been met, we hold that nominal damages may support a punitive damage award in an action for intentional trespass to land.

Our holding is supported by respected legal commentary. The Restatement (Second) of Torts supports the proposition that an award of nominal damages will support an award of punitive damages in a trespass to land action:

The fact that the actor knows that his entry is without the consent of the possessor and without any other privilege to do so, while not necessary to make him liable, may affect the amount of damages recoverable against him, by showing such a complete disregard of the possessor's legally protected interest in the exclusive possession of his land as to justify the imposition of punitive in addition to nominal damages for even a harmless trespass, or in addition to compensatory damages for one which is harmful.

Restatement (Second) of Torts § 163 cmt. e (1979). The Restatement reiterates this position under the punitive damages section: nominal damages support an award of punitive damages "when a tort, such as trespass to land, is committed for an outrageous purpose, but no significant harm has resulted." Restatement (Second) of Torts § 908 cmt. c (1979).

Prosser also finds the compensatory damages prerequisite unsupportable:

Since it is precisely in the cases of nominal damages that the policy of providing an incentive for plaintiffs to bring petty outrages into court comes into play, the view very much to be preferred appears to be that of the minority which have held that there is sufficient support for punitive damages.

Page Keeton, et al., Prosser and Keeton on the Law of Torts § 2, at 14 (5th ed. 1984). A minority of other jurisdictions follow this approach. *See* Annotation, Sufficiency of Showing of Actual Damages to Support Award of Punitive Damages — Modern Cases, 40 A.L.R.4th 11, 36 (1985).

[The court concluded that the damages awarded were not excessive.]

In conclusion, we hold that when nominal damages are awarded for an intentional trespass to land, punitive damages may, in the discretion of the jury, be awarded. Accordingly, we reverse and remand to the circuit court for reinstatement of the punitive damage award.

Reversed and remanded with directions.

NOTES AND QUESTIONS

1. **The right to exclude.** In a widely-anthologized case, the New Jersey Supreme Court reversed the trespass convictions of legal aid attorneys who entered an employer's land to counsel migrant farm workers. Here, highly edited, are some of the propositions relied on by the court:

[U]nder our State law the ownership of real property does not include the right to bar access to governmental services and hence there was no trespass within the meaning of the penal statute. Property rights serve human values. They are recognized to that end and are limited by it. Here we are concerned with a highly disadvantaged segment of our society. A man's right in his real property of course is not absolute. [R]ights are relative and there must be an accommodation when they meet. [We] see no legitimate need for a right in the farmer to deny the worker the opportunity for aid available from federal, State, or local services.

State v. Shack, 277 A.2d 369, 371-74 (N.J. 1971). Does the law of trespass, invoked by the landowner in State v. Shack, also serve human values? How does State v. Shack differ from the principal case: what human values were at stake in each case? How are the cases factually distinguishable?

2. **Sequel.** In New Jersey Coalition Against War in the Middle East v. J.M.B. Realty Corp., 650 A.2d 757 (N.J. 1994), the New Jersey Supreme Court held that the owner of a private shopping mall could not bar anti-war protesters from distributing leaflets on the premises, subject to reasonable conditions, based on a right of free speech under the state constitution. The United States Supreme Court has rejected a similar interpretation of the federal Constitution. *See* Pruneyard Shopping Center v. Robins, 447 U.S. 74 (1980).

3. **Method: categories.** In State v. Shack, the defendants argued that the migrant workers should be deemed tenants, and thus entitled to a tenant's right to receive visitors. Although the court invalidated the convictions, it chose not to adopt this argument of the defendants:

> We see no profit in trying to decide upon a conventional category and then forcing the present subject into it. That approach would be artificial and distorting. The quest is for a fair adjustment of the competing needs of the parties, in the light of the realities of the relationship between the migrant worker and the operator of the housing facility [the farm owner, who provided housing for the workers].

Shack, 277 A.2d at 374. That excerpt raises important questions about legal method that will be with us throughout the course. Property law consists of a large number of categories (e.g., tenant, trespasser, real property, personal property, easement, real covenant), and not all courts are as willing as the court in State v. Shack to dispense with those categories in explaining and justifying their decisions. For an excellent article on the role of categories in the law, see Jay M. Feinman, *The Jurisprudence of Classification*, 41 Stan. L. Rev. 661 (1989).

2.   Classification of Property

a.   Real and Personal Property

Reminder: "The word 'property' is sometimes used to denote the thing with respect to which legal relations between persons exist and sometimes to denote the legal relations." Restatement of Property, Introductory Note to Ch. 1, at 3 (1936). In the previous section, we looked briefly at the relational side. Here, we take a brief look at one important distinction on the "thing" side — the difference between real property and personal property. (Continuing the relational point, we might note that the legal relations among persons with respect to things is still the central focus of legal analysis, but those relations may differ, as the case below shows, depending on whether the object of the relations is real or personal property.)

JOHNSON v. HICKS
626 P.2d 938 (Or. Ct. App. 1981)

ROBERTS, JUDGE.

This is a suit in equity for a mandatory injunction. Plaintiff seeks to require defendants to restore an irrigation line to its original position on her property and to refrain from further interference with it. She also seeks $10,000 general damages. Defendants Hicks counterclaim, seeking compensation from plaintiff for her use of the system. The trial court found plaintiff had not proven her right to use of the irrigation system and dismissed all claims. Our review is de novo. We reverse and remand.

The record is replete with indications that this suit arises at least partially from personal animosities. Ronald Dean Johnson, one of the four defendants, is the brother of plaintiff's former husband Hoy Johnson; defendant Maxine Hicks, wife of defendant Neil Hicks, is Hoy Johnson's sister. The property of the Ronald Johnsons and the Hickses abuts plaintiff's on two sides, and the disputed irrigation line runs along that boundary. The facts of the dispute are as follows.

In 1964, plaintiff's former husband and defendant Neil Hicks, his brother-in-law, installed an irrigation system to serve land belonging to plaintiff and her husband and land belonging to defendants Hicks. Costs of installation were divided equally between the two men and labor was shared. The system contained approximately 700 feet of two-inch pipe which, besides crossing property owned by plaintiff and Hoy Johnson, ran along the edge of property owned by Ronald Johnson and defendants Hicks. In addition, the system included 1,500 feet of "moveable" aluminum pipe used to irrigate the pasture owned by plaintiff and her husband. Plaintiff's former husband testified the system was "probably three-fourths underground," but the portion on what later became his wife's property was above ground. After the pipe was installed, maintenance costs were split 50-50 between the two men, as was the cost of the electricity to run the system's water pump.

Plaintiff's former husband testified that his purpose in installing the system was to irrigate the pastureland, on which they apparently raised steers and horses. Mr. Hicks testified he wanted the system to irrigate his yard. Plaintiff's former husband testified the installation was to be permanent and that when he sold the pastureland, he "let the sprinkler system go with it."

On April 1, 1967, at a time when plaintiff and Hoy Johnson were experiencing marital problems, he and Neil Hicks entered into an agreement declaring the irrigation system which included a five-horsepower pump motor and pump house not located on plaintiff's property, and the 700 feet of pipe to be their joint property and declaring "upon the death or incapacity of either of the parties hereto that the property shall be in the ownership and control of the surviving party." Hicks testified that their intent in drawing up the agreement was as follows:

> Well, at the time we made it up Hoy was the one I told Hoy we were going to have trouble because if something happened to him and she was involved in it. You know, we can't get along with her to begin with and he said that

he can see our point and that we'll go to a lawyer and have him write this paper up, you know in case something happened to him or to myself and there wouldn't be no women involved into it.

In 1969, plaintiff and Hoy Johnson were divorced. By a decree dated October 29, 1969, she was awarded the family home and the one-third of an acre on which it was located, her personal property and all furniture and fixtures in the home. Hoy Johnson was awarded two other parcels of land and all other personal property. No disposition was made of the irrigation system. From 1969 until April of 1979, a portion of the irrigation pipe remained on her property, and plaintiff continued to use the water from the system for watering her yard and trees. During this time she neither offered nor was asked to contribute to the expense of operating the system: her ex-husband and Neil Hicks continued to split costs for electricity, repairs and maintenance. Her former husband testified he let her keep using the water because the amount she used was negligible and he had no objection to it. He said Neil Hicks suggested they "cut her off," but he refused. On April 1, 1979, Neil Hicks entered plaintiff's property and moved some 140 feet of irrigation pipe, which was on her property, approximately six feet to the west and north, placing it on his property and on that owned by defendants Ronald and Teresa Johnson, thereby depriving plaintiff of access to water from the county irrigation system. This suit ensued.

Plaintiff's claim of right is by reason of the divorce decree. She maintains that the portion of the irrigation system placed upon her property passed to her as part of the real property settlement because it was a fixture upon the land. In First State Bank v. Oliver, 198 P. 920 (Or. 1921), another suit from Klamath County involving an irrigation system and determining that the system was a fixture, the supreme court set forth the test for determining whether an article on the land is part of the realty or personal property:

> In deciding whether an article used in connection with real property should be considered as a fixture and a part and parcel of the land, as between a grantor and a grantee or mortgagor and mortgagee, the usual tests are: (1) real or constructive annexation of the article to the realty; (2) appropriation or adaptation to the use or purposes of the realty with which it is connected; (3) the intention to make the annexation permanent.

198 P. at 922.

The court went on to say:

> The intention of making the article permanently accessory to the real property is to be inferred from the nature of the article, the relation of the party making or maintaining the annexation, the policy of the law in relation thereto, the structure and mode of annexation, and the purpose and use for which it is made.

> It is the trend of judicial opinion to regard all of those things as fixtures which have been attached, whether physically or constructively to the realty with a view to the purposes for which the real property is held or employed, however slight or temporary the connection between the articles and the land. The important element to be considered is the intention of the party making the annexation. Neither the intention existing at the time of

procuring the article nor that which exists while the same is being transported to the real property where it is designed to be placed, nor the secret plan in the mind of the person making the annexation govern. The controlling intention is that which the law deduces from all of the circumstances of the installation of the article upon the land.

198 P. at 922.

Cases since *First State Bank* have emphasized intent at the time of the attachment of the item to the real property as the controlling factor.

In this case we have the intent of both defendant Neil Hicks and plaintiff's former husband to consider, as well as their April 1, 1967 agreement, which purports to formalize their intent. A written agreement that a chattel already annexed to the soil shall be termed personalty, however, is binding only upon the parties to the agreement and those having notice. Plaintiff had no knowledge of the 1967 agreement. We therefore have to determine the intent of plaintiff's former husband and Neil Hicks with respect to the permanency of the pipe at the time of its installation in 1964. The supreme court also said in *First State Bank*:

> Applying these rules to all the facts and circumstances in the present case, we note that it is apparent that Mr. Reames, or whoever installed the irrigation system on the farm, did so with a view to enhancing the production of the farm, to increase the growth of vegetation thereon. Irrigation in a semi-arid region, like parts of Klamath County, is the very life of the land. It is beyond comprehension that the system was installed for any temporary purpose.

> From the nature of the irrigation system constructed on the farm, the relation and situation of the owner who installed the apparatus, the whole surroundings and mode of the annexation, the evident purpose thereof, and all the facts disclosed by the testimony, we conclude that the owner making the connection and maintaining the system for a long time did so with the intention of making the system accessory to the real estate.

198 P. at 922-23.

We infer Mr. Hicks' intent to be that the system they installed would be used to provide water for the two properties for so long as the Johnsons remained in possession of their parcel. We think it obvious that if Hoy Johnson had remained in possession of the entire three-acre parcel, he would have viewed the irrigation system as a permanent accessory, increasing the value and use of the property. That the parcel of land was later, in effect, subdivided, makes no difference as to his intention at the time of installation or in the status of the pipe at the present time. Further, Mr. Johnson said he had always been content to let plaintiff use the water and had resisted attempts to remove her supply.

It is important to note that we are not here determining water rights of any kind, but only plaintiff's right to continued possession of the irrigation pipe which had been on her property for 15 years and for 10 years in her exclusive possession. We find the pipe installed on plaintiff's property was a fixture and that defendants' removal of the pipe and subsequent possession wrongfully interfered with her rights. The trial court's order denying the mandatory injunction is therefore reversed. The injunction should issue on remand.

We remand to the trial court on the issue of damages. The only evidence in the record is that by the time of trial plaintiff had suffered some $870 in damages to trees, shrubs and lawn on her property due to lack of water after the removal of the irrigation pipe. There is also evidence, however, that there was city water available to her but that she had this hookup removed. We therefore remand to the trial court to ascertain the actual damage to plaintiff's property, and whether she could have mitigated these damages. We express no opinion on defendant Hicks' right to recover for contribution to the repair and maintenance of the system, since, because of the disposition of the case, no evidence was taken on this issue.

Reversed and remanded for further proceedings consistent with this opinion.

NOTES AND QUESTIONS

1. **Real and personal property.** Real property consists of land and improvements like buildings that become permanently attached to the land to the extent that they lose their separate identity. Personal property consists of things not attached to land (such as cars, paintings, and books), and intangible items (like bank accounts, stocks and bonds, and ideas, the latter covered by the law of intellectual property). Civil law legal systems use the terms "immovables" and "movables." Tangible personal property is sometimes referred to as "chattels," etymologically related to "cattle," which were an early form of such non-land wealth.

2. **Fixtures.**   As the principle case indicates, a fixture is an item that was originally a chattel but is treated as part of the realty because of its annexation to or relationship with the realty. Can you think of any other situations in which parties may be concerned with whether an item is a fixture?

3. **Leases.**   Leases earned the oxymoronic label "chattels real" at common law, a phrase that reflects the development of remedies to protect the tenant. Early in common law history, the tenant who was dispossessed by a third party had only what we would now call a contract claim against the landlord (for damages); later, the courts extended a possessory remedy to the tenant, good against the landlord and third parties. *See* William M. McGovern, *The Historical Conception of a Lease for Years*, 23 UCLA L. Rev. 501 (1976). *See generally* 2 Powell on Real Property § 16.02[2] (Michael Allan Wolf ed. 2000).

b.   Intellectual Property

INTERNATIONAL NEWS SERVICE v. ASSOCIATED PRESS
248 U.S. 215 (1918)

MR. JUSTICE PITNEY delivered the opinion of the Court.

The parties are competitors in the gathering and distribution of news and its publication for profit in newspapers throughout the United States. The Associated Press, which was complainant in the District Court, is a co-operative organization, incorporated under the Membership Corporations Law of the state of New York, its members being individuals who are either proprietors or representatives of about 950 daily newspapers published in all parts of the United States. Complainant gathers in all parts of the world, by means of various instrumentalities of its own, by exchange with its members, and by other appropriate means, news and intelligence of current and recent events of interest to newspaper readers and distributes it daily to its members for publication in their newspapers. The cost of the service, amounting approximately to $3,500,000 per annum, is assessed upon the members and becomes a part of their costs of operation, to be recouped, presumably with profit, through the publication of their several newspapers. Under complainant's by-laws each member agrees upon assuming membership that news received through complainant's service is received exclusively for publication in a particular newspaper, language, and place specified in the certificate of membership, that no other use of it shall be permitted, and that no member shall furnish or permit any one in his employ or connected with his newspaper to furnish any of complainant's news in advance of publication to any person not a member. And each member is required to gather the local news of his district and supply it to the Associated Press and to no one else.

Defendant is a corporation organized under the laws of the state of New Jersey, whose business is the gathering and selling of news to its customers and clients, consisting of newspapers published throughout the United States, under contracts by which they pay certain amounts at stated times for defendant's service. It has widespread news-gathering agencies; the cost of its operations amounts, it is said, to more than $2,000,000 per annum; and it serves about 400 newspapers located in the various cities of the United States and abroad, a few of which are represented, also, in the membership of the Associated Press.

The parties are in the keenest competition between themselves in the distribution of news throughout the United States; and so, as a rule, are the newspapers that they serve, in their several districts.

Complainant in its bill, defendant in its answer, have set forth in almost identical terms the rather obvious circumstances and conditions under which their business is conducted. The value of the service, and of the news furnished, depends upon the promptness of transmission, as well as upon the accuracy and impartiality of the news; it being essential that the news be transmitted to members or subscribers as early or earlier than similar information can be furnished to competing newspapers by other news services, and that the news furnished by each agency shall not be furnished to newspapers which do not contribute to the expense of gathering it.

The bill was filed to restrain the pirating of complainant's news by defendant in three ways: First, by bribing employees of newspapers published by complainant's members to furnish Associated Press news to defendant before publication, for transmission by telegraph and telephone to defendant's clients for publication by them; second, by inducing Associated Press members to violate its by-laws and permit defendant to obtain news before publication; and, third, by copying news from bulletin boards and from early editions of complainant's newspapers and selling this, either bodily or after rewriting it, to defendant's customers.

The District Court, upon consideration of the bill and answer, with voluminous affidavits on both sides, granted a preliminary injunction under the first and second heads, but refused at that stage to restrain the systematic practice admittedly pursued by defendant, of taking news bodily from the bulletin boards and early editions of complainant's newspapers and selling it as its own. The court expressed itself as satisfied that this practice amounted to unfair trade, but as the legal question was one of first impression it considered that the allowance of an injunction should await the outcome of an appeal. Both parties having appealed, the Circuit Court of Appeals sustained the injunction order so far as it went, and upon complainant's appeal modified it and remanded the cause, with directions to issue an injunction also against any bodily taking of the words or substance of complainant's news until its commercial value as news had passed away.

The only matter that has been argued before us is whether defendant may lawfully be restrained from appropriating news taken from bulletins issued by complainant or any of its members, or from newspapers published by them, for the purpose of selling it to defendant's clients. Complainant asserts that defendant's admitted course of conduct in this regard both violates complainant's property right in the news and constitutes unfair competition in business. And notwithstanding the case has proceeded only to the stage of a preliminary injunction, we have deemed it proper to consider the underlying questions, since they go to the very merits of the action and are presented upon facts that are not in dispute. As presented in argument, these questions are: (1) Whether there is any property in news; (2) Whether, if there be property in news collected for the purpose of being published, it survives the instant of its publication in the first newspaper to which it is communicated by the news-gatherer; and (3) whether defendant's admitted course of conduct in appropriating for commercial use matter taken from bulletins or early editions of Associated Press publications constitutes unfair competition in trade.

The federal jurisdiction was invoked because of diversity of citizenship, not upon the ground that the suit arose under the copyright or other laws of the United States. Complainant's news matter is not copyrighted. It is said that it could not, in practice, be copyrighted, because of the large number of dispatches that are sent daily; and, according to complainant's contention, news is not within the operation of the copyright act. Defendant, while apparently conceding this, nevertheless invokes the analogies of the law of literary property and copyright, insisting as its principal contention that, assuming complainant has a right of property in its news, it can be maintained (unless the copyright act by complied with) only by being kept secret and confidential, and that upon the publication with complainant's consent of uncopyrighted news of any of complainant's members in a newspaper or upon a bulletin board, the right of property is lost, and the subsequent use of the news by the public or by defendant for any purpose whatever becomes lawful.

In considering the general question of property in news matter, it is necessary to recognize its dual character, distinguishing between the substance of the information and the particular form or collocation of words in which the writer has communicated it. No doubt news articles often possess a literary quality, and are the subject of literary property at the common law; nor do we question that such an article, as a literary production, is the subject of copyright by the terms of the act as it now stands.

But the news element — the information respecting current events contained in the literary production — is not the creation of the writer, but is a report of matters that ordinarily are publici juris; it is the history of the day. It is not to be supposed that the framers of the Constitution, when they empowered Congress "to promote the progress of science and useful arts, by securing for limited times to authors and inventors the exclusive right to their respective writings and discoveries" (Const. art. 1, § 8, par. 8), intended to confer upon one who might happen to be the first to report a historic event the exclusive right for any period to spread the knowledge of it.

We need spend no time, however, upon the general question of property in news matter at common law, or the application of the copyright act, since it seems to us the case must turn upon the question of unfair competition in business. And, in our opinion, this does not depend upon any general right of property analogous to the common-law right of the proprietor of an unpublished work to prevent its publication without his consent; nor is it foreclosed by showing that the benefits of the copyright act have been waived. We are dealing here not with restrictions upon publication but with the very facilities and processes of publication. The peculiar value of news is in the spreading of it while it is fresh; and it is evident that a valuable property interest in the news, as news, cannot be maintained by keeping it secret. Besides, except for matters improperly disclosed, or published in breach of trust or confidence, or in violation of law, none of which is involved in this branch of the case, the news of current events may be regarded as common property. What we are concerned with is the business of making it known to the world, in which both parties to the present suit are engaged. That business consists in maintaining a prompt, sure, steady, and reliable service designed to place the daily events of the world at the breakfast table of the millions at a price that, while of trifling moment to each reader, is sufficient in the aggregate to afford compensation for the cost of gathering and distributing it, with the added profit so necessary as an incentive to effective action in the commercial world. The service thus performed for newspaper readers is not only innocent but extremely useful in itself, and indubitably constitutes a legitimate business. The parties are competitors in this field; and, on fundamental principles, applicable here as elsewhere, when the rights or privileges of the one are liable to conflict with those of the other, each party is under a duty so to conduct its own business as not unnecessarily or unfairly to injure that of the other.

Obviously, the question of what is unfair competition in business must be determined with particular reference to the character and circumstances of the business. The question here is not so much the rights of either party as against the public but their rights as between themselves. And, although we may and do assume that neither party has any remaining property interest as against the public in uncopyrighted news matter after the moment of its first publication, it by no means follows that there is no remaining property interest in it as between themselves. For, to both of them alike, news matter, however little susceptible of ownership or dominion in the absolute sense, is stock in trade, to be gathered at the cost of enterprise, organization, skill, labor, and money, and to be distributed and sold to those who will pay money for it, as for any other merchandise. Regarding the news, therefore, as but the material out of which both parties are seeking to make profits at the same time and in the same field, we hardly can fail to recognize that for this purpose, and as between them, it must be regarded as quasi property, irrespective of the rights of either as against the public.

In order to sustain the jurisdiction of equity over the controversy, we need not affirm any general and absolute property in the news as such. The rule that a court of equity concerns itself only in the protection of property rights treats any civil right of a pecuniary nature as a property right; and the right to acquire property by honest labor or the conduct of a lawful business is as much entitled to protection as the right to guard property already acquired. It is this right that furnishes the basis of the jurisdiction in the ordinary case of unfair competition.

The question, whether one who has gathered general information or news at pains and expense for the purpose of subsequent publication through the press has such an interest in its publication as may be protected from interference, has been raised many times, although never, perhaps, in the precise form in which it is now presented.

Not only do the acquisition and transmission of news require elaborate organization and a large expenditure of money, skill, and effort; not only has it an exchange value to the gatherer, dependent chiefly upon its novelty and freshness, the regularity of the service, its reputed reliability and thoroughness, and its adaptability to the public needs; but also, as is evident, the news has an exchange value to one who can misappropriate it.

The peculiar features of the case arise from the fact that, while novelty and freshness form so important an element in the success of the business, the very processes of distribution and publication necessarily occupy a good deal of time. Complainant's service, as well as defendant's, is a daily service to daily newspapers; most of the foreign news reaches this country at the Atlantic seaboard, principally at the city of New York, and because of this, and of time differentials due to the earth's rotation, the distribution of news matter throughout the country is principally from east to west; and, since in speed the telegraph and telephone easily outstrip the rotation of the earth, it is a simple matter for defendant to take complainant's news from bulletins or early editions of complainant's members in the eastern cities and at the mere cost of telegraphic transmission cause it to be published in western papers issued at least as early as those served by complainant. Besides this, and irrespective of time differentials, irregularities in telegraphic transmission on different lines, and the normal consumption of time in printing and distributing the newspaper, result in permitting pirated news to be placed in the hands of defendant's readers sometimes simultaneously with the service of competing Associated Press papers, occasionally even earlier.

Defendant insists that when, with the sanction and approval of complainant, and as the result of the use of its news for the very purpose for which it is distributed, a portion of complainant's members communicate it to the general public by posting it upon bulletin boards so that all may read, or by issuing it to newspapers and distributing it indiscriminately, complainant no longer has the right to control the use to be made of it; that when it thus reaches the light of day it becomes the common possession of all to whom it is accessible; and that any purchaser of a newspaper has the right to communicate the intelligence which it contains to anybody and for any purpose, even for the purpose of selling it for profit to newspapers published for profit in competition with complainant's members.

The fault in the reasoning lies in applying as a test the right of the complainant as against the public, instead of considering the rights of complainant and defendant, competitors in business, as between themselves. The right of the purchaser of a single newspaper to spread knowledge of its contents gratuitously, for any legitimate purpose not unreasonably interfering with complainant's right to make merchandise of it, may be admitted; but to transmit that news for commercial use, in competition with complainant — which is what defendant has done and seeks to justify — is a very different matter. In doing this defendant, by its very act, admits that it is taking material that has been acquired by complainant as the result of organization and the expenditure of labor, skill, and money, and which is salable by complainant for money, and that defendant in appropriating it and selling it as its own is endeavoring to reap where it has not sown, and by disposing of it to newspapers that are competitors of complainant's members is appropriating to itself the harvest of those who have sown. Stripped of all disguises, the process amounts to an unauthorized interference with the normal operation of complainant's legitimate business precisely at the point where the profit is to be reaped, in order to divert a material portion of the profit from those who have earned it to those who have not; with special advantage to defendant in the competition because of the fact that it is not burdened with any part of the expense of gathering the news. The transaction speaks for itself and a court of equity ought not to hesitate long in characterizing it as unfair competition in business.

The underlying principle is much the same as that which lies at the base of the equitable theory of consideration in the law of trusts — that he who has fairly paid the price should have the beneficial use of the property. Pom. Eq. Jur. § 981. It is no answer to say that complainant spends its money for that which is too fugitive or evanescent to be the subject of property. That might, and for the purposes of the discussion we are assuming that it would furnish an answer in a common-law controversy. But in a court of equity, where the question is one of unfair competition, if that which complainant has acquired fairly at substantial cost may be sold fairly at substantial profit, a competitor who is misappropriating it for the purpose of disposing of it to his own profit and to the disadvantage of complainant cannot be heard to say that it is too fugitive or evanescent to be regarded as property. It has all the attributes of property necessary for determining that a misappropriation of it by a competitor is unfair competition because contrary to good conscience.

The contention that the news is abandoned to the public for all purposes when published in the first newspaper is untenable. Abandonment is a question of intent, and the entire organization of the Associated Press negatives such a purpose. The cost of the service would be prohibited if the reward were to be so limited. No single newspaper, no small group of newspapers, could sustain the expenditure. Indeed, it is one of the most obvious results of defendant's theory that, by permitting indiscriminate publication by anybody and everybody for purposes of profit in competition with the news-gatherer, it would render publication profitless, or so little profitable as in effect to cut off the service by rendering the cost prohibitive in comparison with the return. The practical needs and requirements of the business are reflected in complainant's by-laws which have been referred to. Their effect is that publication by each member must be deemed not by any means an abandonment of the news to the world for any and all purposes, but a publication for limited purposes; for the benefit of the readers of the bulletin or the newspaper as such; not for the purpose of making merchandise of it as news, with the result of depriving complainant's other members of their reasonable opportunity to obtain just returns for their expenditures.

It is to be observed that the view we adopt does not result in giving to complainant the right to monopolize either the gathering or the distribution of the news, or, without complying with the copyright act, to prevent the reproduction of its news articles, but only postpones participation by complainant's competitor in the processes of distribution and reproduction of news that it has not gathered, and only to the extent necessary to prevent that competitor from reaping the fruits of complainant's efforts and expenditure, to the partial exclusion of complainant. and in violation of the principle that underlies the maxim 'sic utere tuo,' etc.

It is said that the elements of unfair competition are lacking because there is no attempt by defendant to palm off its goods as those of the complainant, characteristic of the most familiar, if not the most typical, cases of unfair competition. But we cannot concede that the right to equitable relief is confined to that class of cases. In the present case the fraud upon complainant's rights is more direct and obvious. Regarding news matter as the mere material from which these two competing parties are endeavoring to make money, and treating it, therefore, as quasi property for the purposes of their business because they are both selling it as such, defendant's conduct differs from the ordinary case of unfair competition in trade principally in this that, instead of selling its own goods as those of complainant, it substitutes misappropriation in the place of misrepresentation, and sells complainant's goods as its own.

The decree of the Circuit Court of Appeals will be affirmed.

Mr. Justice Holmes, dissenting.

When an uncopyrighted combination of words is published there is no general right to forbid other people repeating them — in other words there is no property in the combination or in the thoughts or facts that the words express. Property, a creation of law, does not arise from value, although exchangeable. Many exchangeable values may be destroyed intentionally without compensation. Property depends upon exclusion by law from interference, and a person is not excluded from using any combination of words merely because someone has used it before, even if it took labor and genius to make it. If a given person is to be prohibited from making the use of words that his neighbors are free to make some other ground must be found. One such ground is vaguely expressed in the phrase unfair trade. This means that the words are repeated by a competitor in business in such a way as to convey a misrepresentation that materially injures the person who first used them, by appropriating credit of some kind which the first user has earned. The ordinary case is a representation by device, appearance, or other indirection that the defendant's goods come from the plaintiff. But the only reason why it is actionable to make such a representation is that it tends to give the defendant an advantage in his competition with the plaintiff and that it is thought undesirable that an advantage should be gained in that way. Apart from that the defendant may use such unpatented devices and uncopyrighted combinations of words as he likes. The ordinary case, I say, is palming off the defendant's product as the plaintiff's but the same evil may follow from the opposite falsehood — from saying whether in words or by implication that the plaintiff's product is the defendant's, and that, it seems to me, is what has happened here.

Fresh news is got only by enterprise and expense. To produce such news as it is produced by the defendant represents by implication that it has been acquired by the defendant's enterprise and at its expense. When it comes from one of the great news collecting agencies like the Associated Press, the source generally is indicated, plainly importing that credit; and that such a representation is implied may be inferred with some confidence from the unwillingness of the defendant to give the credit and tell the truth. If the plaintiff produces the news at the same time that the defendant does, the defendant's presentation impliedly denies to the plaintiff the credit of collecting the facts and assumes that credit to the defendant. If the plaintiff is later in Western cities it naturally will be supposed to have obtained its information from the defendant. The falsehood is a little more subtle, the injury, a little more indirect, than in ordinary cases of unfair trade, but I think that the principle that condemns the one condemns the other. It is a question of how strong an infusion of fraud is necessary to turn a flavor into a poison. The dose seems to me strong enough here to need a remedy from the law. But as, in my view, the only ground of complaint that can be recognized without legislation is the implied misstatement, it can be corrected by stating the truth; and a suitable acknowledgment of the source is all that the plaintiff can require. I think that within the limits recognized by the decision of the Court the defendant should be enjoined from publishing news obtained from the Associated Press for _____ hours after publication by the plaintiff unless it gives express credit to the Associated Press; the number of hours and the form of acknowledgment to be settled by the District Court.

Mr. Justice McKenna concurs in this opinion.

Mr. Justice Brandeis, dissenting.

News is a report of recent occurrences. The business of the news agency is to gather systematically knowledge of such occurrences of interest and to distribute reports thereof. The Associated Press contended that knowledge so acquired is property, because it costs money and labor to produce and because it has value for which those who have it not are ready to pay; that it remains property and is entitled to protection as long as it has commercial value as news; and that to protect it effectively, the defendant must be enjoined from making, or causing to be made, any gainful use of it while it retains such value. An essential element of individual property is the legal right to exclude others from enjoying it. If the property is private, the right of exclusion may be absolute; if the property is affected with a public interest, the right of exclusion is qualified. But the fact that a product of the mind has cost its producer money and labor, and has a value for which others are willing to pay, is not sufficient to ensure to it this legal attribute of property. The general rule of law is, that the noblest of human productions — knowledge, truths ascertained, conceptions, and ideas — became, after voluntary communication to others, free as the air to common use. Upon these incorporeal productions the attribute of property is continued after such communication only in certain classes of cases where public policy has seemed to demand it. These exceptions are confined to productions which, in some degree, involve creation, invention, or discovery. But by no means all such are endowed with this attribute of property. The creations which are recognized as property by the common law are literary, dramatic, musical, and other artistic creations; and these have also protection under the copyright statutes. The inventions and discoveries upon which this attribute of property is conferred only by statute, are the few comprised within the patent law. There are also many other cases in which courts interfere to prevent curtailment of plaintiff's enjoyment of incorporeal productions; and in which the right to relief is often called a property right, but is such only in a special sense. In those cases, the plaintiff has no absolute right to the protection of his production; he has merely the qualified right to be protected as against the defendant's acts, because of the special relation in which the latter stands or the wrongful method or means employed in acquiring the knowledge or the manner in which it is used. Protection of this character is afforded where the suit is based upon breach of contract or of trust or upon unfair competition.

The knowledge for which protection is sought in the case at bar is not of a kind upon which the law has heretofore conferred the attributes of property; nor is the manner of its acquisition or use nor the purpose to which it is applied, such as has heretofore been recognized as entitling a plaintiff to relief.

NOTES AND QUESTIONS

1. **Property rights.** On what basis does the court find that AP has property rights in its news? Why does AP have a property right in the news as against INS, but not as against the general public? Why do Justices Holmes and Brandeis disagree with the majority opinion?

2. **Relationship with copyright law.** Much of the law governing intellectual property is federal statutory law. In fact, the rule of the principal case, based in state common law, has been applied narrowly to avoid federal preemption by copyright law. *See* National Basketball Association v. Motorola, Inc., 105 F.3d 841, 852 (2d Cir. 1997). The court in that case defined the elements of a claim under *International News Service* as follows:

> (i) the plaintiff generates or collects information at some cost or expense;
> (ii) the value of the information is highly time-sensitive; (iii) the defendant's use of the information constitutes free-riding on the plaintiff's costly efforts to generate or collect it; (iv) the defendant's use of the information is in direct competition with a product or service offered by the plaintiff; (v) the ability of other parties to free-ride on the efforts of the plaintiff would so

> reduce the incentive to produce the product or service that its existence or quality would be substantially threatened.

Motorola, 105 F.3d at 852.

3. **Copyright law.** Copyright law is governed by federal statute pursuant to authority given to Congress by the Constitution.

> Copyright law covers the broad range of literary and artistic expression — including books, poetry, song, dance, dramatic works, computer programs, movies, sculpture, and paintings. Ideas themselves are not copyrightable, but the author's particular expression of an idea is protectable. A work must exhibit a modicum of originality and be fixed in a "tangible medium of expression" to receive protection. Copyright protection attaches as soon as a work is fixed. There is no examination by a governmental authority, although the Copyright Office registers copyrightable works. Such registration is no longer required for validity, but U.S. authors must register their works prior to filing an infringement suit. A copyright lasts for the life of the author plus 70 years, or a total of 95 years in the case of entity authors.

Robert P. Merges, Peter S. Menell & Mark A. Lemley, Intellectual Property in the New Technological Age 29 (Revised 4th ed. 2006).

4. **Patent law.** Like copyright law, patent law is authorized by the Constitution and gives a type of limited monopoly.

> [P]atent law offers the possibility of a limited period of exclusive rights to encourage research and development aimed at discovering new processes, machines, and compositions of matter, and improvements thereof. The public benefits directly through the spur to innovation and disclosure of new technology. After the term of the patent expires, the innovation becomes part of the public domain, freely available to all.
>
> To obtain a utility patent, an inventor must submit an application to the Patent and Trademark Office (PTO) that meets five requirements: patentable subject matter, usefulness, novelty and non-obviousness, and disclosure sufficient to enable others skilled in the art to make and use the invention. . . . If the PTO grants the patent, the inventor obtains exclusive rights to make, use, and sell the innovation for a term of up to 20 years.

Merges, Menell & Lemley, *supra*, at 28. What are some differences between copyright law and patent law?

5. **Trade secret law.** Trade secrets are protected by state rather than federal law. "The basic purpose behind protecting trade secrets is to prevent 'theft' of information by unfair or commercially unreasonable means." Merges, Menell & Lemley, *supra*, at 24.

6. **Other types of intellectual property.** Trademark law is governed by federal statute. The following case introduces trademark law and another intangible property right.

PARKS v. LAFACE RECORDS
329 F.3d 437 (6th Cir. 2003)

HOLSCHUH, DISTRICT JUDGE.

This is a dispute over the name of a song. Rosa Parks is a civil rights icon who first gained prominence during the Montgomery, Alabama bus boycott in 1955. She brings suit against LaFace Records, a record producer, and OutKast, a "rap" (or "hip-hop") music duo, as well as several other named affiliates, for using her name as the title of their song, *Rosa Parks*. Parks contends that Defendants' use of her name constitutes false advertising under § 43(a) of the Lanham Act, 15 U.S.C. § 1125(a), and intrudes on her common law right of publicity under Michigan state law. Defendants argue that they are entitled to summary judgment because Parks has failed to show any violation of the Lanham Act or her right of publicity. Defendants further argue that, even if she has shown such a violation, their First Amendment freedom of artistic expression should be a defense as a matter of law to each of these claims. Parks also contends that Defendants' conduct renders them liable under Michigan law for defamation and tortious interference with a business relationship; Defendants have also denied liability with respect to these claims.

Parks brought this action in a Michigan state court. Defendants subsequently removed the case to the District Court for the Eastern District of Michigan. Following cross-motions for summary judgment, the district court denied Parks' motion for summary judgment and granted summary judgment for Defendants. Parks now appeals the grant of summary judgment for Defendants.

For the reasons hereafter set forth, we believe that, with respect to Rosa Parks' claims under the Lanham Act and under the common law right of publicity, "the evidence is such that a reasonable jury could return a verdict for the nonmoving party." Anderson v. Liberty Lobby, Inc., 477 U.S. 242, 248 (1986). We therefore conclude that the district court erred in granting Defendants' motion for summary judgment on those claims. We conclude, however, that the district court properly granted summary judgment in favor of Defendants on Rosa Parks' state law claims of defamation and tortious interference with a business relationship.

I. BACKGROUND
A. Facts

Rosa Parks is an historical figure who first gained prominence as a symbol of the civil rights movement in the United States during the 1950's and 1960's. In 1955, while riding in the front of a segregated bus in Montgomery, Alabama, she refused to yield her seat to a white passenger and move to the back of the bus as blacks were required to do by the then-existing laws requiring segregation of the races. A 381-day bus boycott in Montgomery flowed from that one event, which eventually became a catalyst for organized boycotts, sit-ins, and demonstrations all across the South. Her single act of defiance has garnered her numerous public accolades and awards, and she has used that celebrity status to promote various civil and human rights causes as well as television programs and books inspired by her life story. She has also approved a collection of gospel recordings by various artists entitled *Verity Records Presents: A Tribute to Mrs. Rosa Parks* (the "*Tribute*" album), released in 1995.

Defendants are OutKast, comprised of recording artists André "Dré" Benjamin and Antwan "Big Boi" Patton; their record producers, LaFace, founded by and named after Antonio "L.A." Reid and Kenny "Babyface" Edmonds; and LaFace's record distributors, Arista Records and BMG Entertainment (collectively "Defendants"). In September 1998, Defendants released the album *Aquemini*. The album's first single release was a song titled *Rosa Parks*, described as a "hit single" by a sticker on the album. The same sticker that contained the name *Rosa Parks* also contained a Parental Advisory warning of "explicit content." Because, as later discussed, the critical issue in this case is a determination of the artistic relevance of the title, *Rosa Parks*, to the content of the song, the lyrics obviously must be considered in their entirety. [The court quoted the song lyrics including the chorus: "Ah ha, hush that fuss. Everybody move to the back of the bus."]

II. DISCUSSION
B. The Lanham Act

Section 43(a) of the Lanham Act creates a civil cause of action against any person who identifies his or her product in such a way as to likely cause confusion among consumers or to cause consumers to make a mistake or to deceive consumers as to association of the producer of the product with another person or regarding the origin of the product or the sponsorship or approval of the product by another person. The language of § 43(a) is broad. It provides:

> (1) Any person who, on or in connection with any goods or services, or any container for goods, uses in commerce any word, term, name, symbol, or device, or any combination thereof, or any false designation of origin, false or misleading description of fact, or false or misleading representation of fact, which —

> (A) is likely to cause confusion, or to cause mistake, or to deceive as to the affiliation, connection, or association of such person with another person, or as to the origin, sponsorship, or approval of his or her goods, services, or commercial activities by another person . . . shall be liable in a civil action by any person who believes that he or she is or is likely to be damaged by such act.

15 U.S.C. § 1125(a).

Plaintiffs often invoke § 43(a) to protect intellectual property rights in "marks," or brand names, of ordinary merchandise, such as apparel, see, e.g., A & H Sportswear, Inc. v. Victoria's Secret Stores, Inc., 237 F.3d 198, 206 (3d Cir.2000) (suit by manufacturer of "Miraclesuit" swimwear against manufacturer of "The Miracle Bra" swimwear), or of services, such as mortgage companies, see Platinum Home Mortgage Corp. v. Platinum Fin. Group, Inc., 149 F.3d 722, 725 (7th Cir.1998) (suit between mortgage service companies using the "Platinum" name).

However, the scope of § 43(a) extends beyond disputes between producers of commercial products and their competitors. It also permits celebrities to vindicate property rights in their identities against allegedly misleading commercial use by others. See Waits v. Frito-Lay, Inc., 978 F.2d 1093, 1110 (9th Cir.1992) (celebrity suit against snack manufacturer for unauthorized use of his distinctive voice in a commercial); Allen v. National Video, Inc., 610 F.Supp. 612, 624-25 (S.D.N.Y.1985) (celebrity suit against a video retailer for use of a celebrity look-alike in its advertisements); Landham v. Lewis Galoob Toys, Inc., 227 F.3d 619, 626 (6th Cir.2000) (actor sued toy company for creating an action figure named after one of his movie characters); Abdul-Jabbar v. Gen. Motors Corp., 85 F.3d 407, 410 (9th Cir.1996) (professional basketball player sued car manufacturer for using his birth name to sell cars). Celebrities have standing to sue under § 43(a) because they possess an economic interest in their identities akin to that of a traditional trademark holder.

In order to prevail on a false advertising claim under § 43(a), a celebrity must show that use of his or her name is likely to cause confusion among consumers as to the "affiliation, connection, or association" between the celebrity and the defendant's goods or services or as to the celebrity's participation in the "origin, sponsorship, or approval" of the defendant's goods or services. See 15 U.S.C. § 1125(a)(1)(A).

Parks contends that Defendants have violated the Lanham Act because the *Rosa Parks* title misleads consumers into believing that the song is about her or that she is affiliated with the Defendants, or has sponsored or approved the *Rosa Parks* song and the *Aquemini* album. She argues that the risk of confusion is enhanced by the fact that her authorized *Tribute* album is in the marketplace alongside Defendants' album featuring the *Rosa Parks* single. As additional evidence for her claim, Parks points to Defendants' concession that they have used the *Rosa Parks* title to advertise and promote both the song and the *Aquemini* album. She also supplies twenty-one affidavits from consumers affirming that they either believed Defendants' song was about Parks or was connected to the *Tribute* album authorized by her.

Defendants respond that Parks' Lanham Act claim must fail for two reasons. First, they claim that Parks does not possess a trademark right in her name and Defendants have not made a trademark use of her name, as allegedly required for a cause of action under the Lanham Act. Second, they contend that even if use of the title posed some risk of consumer confusion, the risk is outweighed by Defendants' First Amendment right to free expression.

1. *Trademark Right In and Trademark Use of Parks' Name*

Defendants contend that Parks' § 43(a) claim must fail because they have made no trademark use of her name. However, Defendants misconceive the legal basis of a Lanham Act claim. It is not necessary for them to make a "trademark" use of Rosa Parks' name in order for her to have a cause of action for false advertising under § 43(a) of the Lanham Act.

Rosa Parks clearly has a property interest in her name akin to that of a person holding a trademark. It is beyond question that Parks is a celebrity. The parties have stipulated to her international fame and to her prior authorization of television programs and books. We have already established, supra, that courts routinely recognize a property right in celebrity identity akin to that of a trademark holder under § 43(a). We find Parks' prior commercial activities and international recognition as a symbol of the civil rights movement endow her with a trademark interest in her name the same as if she were a famous actor or musician.

Therefore, even though Rosa Parks' name might not be eligible for registration as a trademark, and even though Defendants were not selling Rosa Parks-brand CD's, a viable cause of action also exists under § 43(a) if consumers falsely believed that Rosa Parks had sponsored or approved the song, or was somehow affiliated with the song or the album. We turn then to Defendants' second argument, that even if Parks could establish some likelihood of confusion, the First Amendment protects Defendants' choice of title.

[The court discusses at length the Defendants' First Amendment defense and concludes that a genuine issue of material fact exists "that must be resolved by a finder of fact following an evidentiary hearing and not by a judge as a matter of law upon the limited record submitted in support of a motion for summary judgment."]

C. Right of Publicity
1. *Applicable Law*

The right of publicity protects the identity of a celebrity from exploitive commercial use. See Carson v. Here's Johnny Portable Toilets, Inc., 698 F.2d 831, 835 (6th Cir.1983). "The theory of the right is that a celebrity's identity can be valuable in the promotion of products, and the celebrity has an interest that may be protected from the unauthorized commercial exploitation of that identity." *Id.* As such, the common law right of publicity forms a species of property right.

The right of publicity is governed by state law. Michigan has indicated that it would recognize a right of publicity, see Pallas v. Crowley, Milner & Co., 33 N.W.2d 911, 914 (Mich. 1948), and the parties have not questioned that Plaintiff has a right of publicity. The dispute is over its application to the facts of this case.

Parks' right of publicity argument tracks that of her Lanham Act claim. She alleges that Defendants have profited from her fame by using her name solely for a commercial purpose. She supplies much the same evidence in support of her right of publicity claim as she did for her Lanham Act claim: the lyrics of *Rosa Parks*, the "translation," and the press clippings quoting OutKast members. Defendants do not deny that they have used the title *Rosa Parks* commercially, but argue that Parks has produced no evidence that their use was *solely* commercial. Instead, they argue that the choice was also artistic, and that they therefore have a complete defense in the First Amendment.

2. *Analysis*

A right of publicity claim is similar to a false advertising claim in that it grants a celebrity the right to protect an economic interest in his or her name. See *Carson*, 698 F.2d at 835 ("The right of publicity has developed to protect the commercial interest of celebrities in their identities."). However, a right of publicity claim does differ from a false advertising claim in one crucial respect; a right of publicity claim does not require any evidence that a consumer is likely to be confused. All that a plaintiff must prove in a right of publicity action is that she has a pecuniary interest in her identity, and that her identity has been commercially exploited by a defendant.

The parties have stipulated that Parks is famous and that she has used her name to promote other goods and services. She has therefore established an economic interest in her name. Furthermore, Defendants admit that they have used Parks' name as the name of their song, and have used that name to sell the song and their album. They argue, however, that, as with the Lanham Act claim, their First Amendment right of artistic expression should prevail over Parks' claim.

a. *Cognizability of a First Amendment Defense*

Because a plaintiff bears a reduced burden of persuasion to succeed in a right of publicity action, courts and commentators have recognized that publicity rights carry a greater danger of impinging on First Amendment rights than do rights associated with false advertising claims.

We have recognized the importance of a First Amendment defense to right of publicity actions in a recent case. In Ruffin-Steinback v. dePasse, friends and family members of the Motown group, the "Temptations," sued the makers of a televised mini-series for the manner in which they and the former group members were portrayed in the film. 82 F.Supp.2d 723, 726-27 (E.D.Mich.2000), aff'd, 267 F.3d 457 (6th Cir.2001). The plaintiffs alleged that their likenesses were appropriated to endorse a product, the film, without their permission. The court found in that case that the plaintiffs could not overcome the defendant's First Amendment defense, even where the portrayal of the plaintiffs was partly fictionalized, and even where the likenesses of the plaintiffs were used to promote a videocassette version of the mini-series. *Id.* at 730-31.

As with the Lanham Act, then, we must conduct another balancing of interests — Parks' property right in her own name versus the freedom of artistic expression.

[The court discusses the Defendants' First amendment defense and concludes "that Parks' right of publicity claim presents a genuine issue of material fact." Then the court briefly discusses Parks claims for defamation and intentional interference with a business relationship, finding no merit in these claims.]

III. CONCLUSION

We are not called upon in this case to judge the quality of Defendants' song, and whether we personally regard it as repulsive trash or a work of genius is immaterial to a determination of the legal issues presented to us. Justice Holmes, 100 years ago, correctly observed that, "It would be a dangerous undertaking for persons trained only to the law to constitute themselves final judges of the worth of pictorial illustrations, outside of the narrowest and most obvious limits." George Bleistein v. Donaldson Lithographing Co., 188 U.S. 239, 251 (1903). The same is no less true today and applies with equal force to musical compositions. The point, however, is that while we, as judges, do not presume to determine the artistic quality of the song in question, we have the responsibility, as judges, to apply a legal standard of "artistic relevance" in resolving the rights of Rosa Parks concerning the use of her name and the First Amendment rights of the Defendants in the creation and marketing of a musical composition. Application of that standard involves a recognition that Rosa Parks has no right to control her image by censoring disagreeable portrayals. It also involves a recognition that the First Amendment cannot permit anyone who cries "artist" to have *carte blanche* when it comes to naming and advertising his works.

In this case, for the reasons set forth above, the fact that Defendants cry "artist" and "symbol" as reasons for appropriating Rosa Parks' name for a song title does not absolve them from potential liability for, in the words of Shakespeare, filching Rosa Parks' good name. The question of that liability, however, should be determined by the trier of fact after a full evidentiary hearing and not as a matter of law on a motion for summary judgment.

For the reasons stated, as to Rosa Parks' Lanham Act claim and her common law right of publicity claim, the judgment of the District Court is REVERSED and this case is REMANDED for future proceedings not inconsistent with this Opinion. With respect to Rosa Parks' claims of defamation and tortious interference with a business relationship, the judgment of the District Court is AFFIRMED.

NOTES AND QUESTIONS

1. **The rest of the story.** After the court's remand, the parties settled, with Outkast and the record producers and distributors agreeing to pay for educational programs about Mrs. Parks to be distributed to schools. *See Rap Group Settles Rosa Parks Lawsuit,* N.Y. Times, Apr. 15, 2005, at C5.

2. **Reasons for remand.** Why did the court have to remand the case to the lower court? Cases on the right of publicity often raise First Amendment issues. *See, e.g.,* Zacchini v. Scripps-Howard Broadcasting Company, 433 U.S. 562 (1977) (the First Amendment did not give the press a privilege to broadcast as news the entire 15 second performance of the "human cannonball" in violation of the performer's right of publicity).

3. **Extent of the right of publicity.** In the principal case, Rosa Parks had property rights that protected against the unauthorized use of her name, subject to First Amendment rights of the defendants, if any. The existence of a property right in other identifying features of a celebrity may not be so clear. How far should the right of publicity extend? *See* Carson v. Here's Johnny Portable Toilets, Inc., 698 F.2d 831 (6th Cir. 1983) (finding Johnny Carson's right of publicity was invaded by use of the phrase "Here's Johnny"); Midler v. Ford Motor Company, 849 F.2d 460 (9th Cir. 1988) (finding appropriation of Bette Midler's identity where Ford hired a former backup singer for Midler to sing in a commercial and told her

to "sound as much as possible" like Midler).

Vanna White sued Samsung for violation of her right of publicity based on an advertisement which showed a robot with a blond wig, evening gown, and jewelry similar to White's next to a Wheel of Fortune game board. White v. Samsung Electronics America, Inc., 971 F.2d 1395, 1396 (9th Cir. 1992). The court held that the district court had erred by rejecting her right of publicity claim on summary judgment. *Id.* at 1399. A dissenting judge disagreed with the holding as to White's right of publicity, stating:

> The only characteristic in the commercial advertisement that is not common to many female performers or celebrities is the imitation of the "Wheel of Fortune" set. This set is the only thing which might possibly lead a viewer to think of Vanna White. The Wheel of Fortune set, however, is not an attribute of Vanna White's identity. It is an identifying characteristic of a television game show, a prop with which Vanna White interacts in her role as the current hostess. To say that Vanna White may bring an action when another blond female performer or robot appears on such a set as a hostess will, I am sure, be a surprise to the owners of the show.

> The record shows that Samsung recognized the market value of Vanna White's identity. No doubt the advertisement would have been more effective if Vanna White had appeared in it. But the fact that Samsung recognized Vanna White's value as a celebrity does not necessarily mean that it appropriated her identity. The record shows that Samsung dressed a robot in a costume usually worn by television game-show hostesses, including Vanna White. A blond wig, and glamorous clothing are not characteristics unique to the current hostess of Wheel of Fortune. This evidence does not support the majority's determination that the advertisement was meant to depict Vanna White. The advertisement was intended to depict a robot, playing the role Vanna White currently plays on the Wheel of Fortune. I quite agree that anyone seeing the commercial advertisement would be reminded of Vanna White. *Any* performance by another female celebrity as a game-show hostess, however, will also remind the viewer of Vanna White because Vanna White's celebrity is so closely associated with the role. But the fact that an actor or actress became famous for playing a particular role has, until now, never been sufficient to give the performer a proprietary interest in it. I cannot agree with the majority that the California courts, which have consistently taken a narrow view of the right to publicity, would extend law to these unique facts.

971 F.2d at 1405 (Alarcon, dissenting).

4. **Acquiring rights in property.**   Property rights in intellectual property are acquired by creation. How else do property rights arise? This chapter will consider acquisition of property rights by possession (section B) and by gift (section C). In Chapter 2, we will consider acquisition of property rights in real property by conveyance, will, or intestate succession, and in Chapter 5, we will consider in more detail the acquisition of real property by purchase.

B. ACQUIRING INTERESTS IN THINGS: THREE STUDIES IN POSSESSION

Possession is one of the major sticks in the bundle, and a foundational concept in the law of property. It is, directly or indirectly, nearly everywhere in what we shall be studying hereafter. So we must ask: What does possession mean? And why is it important? The following three studies — animals, finders, and adverse possession — give us different and cumulative perspectives on those questions.

1. First Possession: Wild Animals

PIERSON v. POST
3 Cai. R. 175 (N.Y. S. Ct. 1805)

This was an action of trespass on the case commenced in a justice's court, by Post against Pierson. The declaration stated that Post, being in possession of certain dogs and hounds under his command, did, "upon a certain wild and uninhabited, unpossessed and waste land, called the beach, find and start one of those noxious beasts called a fox," and whilst there hunting, chasing and pursuing the same with his dogs and hounds, and when in view thereof, Pierson, well knowing the fox was so hunted and pursued, did, in the sight of Post, to prevent his catching the same, kill and carry it off. A verdict having been rendered for the plaintiff below, the defendant there sued out a *certiorari*, and now assigned for error, that the declaration and the matters therein contained were not sufficient in law to maintain an action.

Tompkins, J., delivered the opinion of the court.

The question submitted by the counsel in this cause for our determination is, whether Lodowick Post, by the pursuit with his hounds in the manner alleged in his declaration, acquired such a right to, or property in, the fox, as will sustain an action against Pierson for killing and taking him away?

The cause was argued with much ability by the counsel on both sides, and presents for our decision a novel and nice question. It is admitted that a fox is an animal *ferae naturae*, and that property in such animals is acquired by occupancy only. These admissions narrow the discussion to the simple question of what acts amount to occupancy, applied to acquiring right to wild animals?

If we have recourse to the ancient writers upon general principles of law, the judgment below is obviously erroneous. Justinian's Institutes, lib. 2, tit. 1, s.13, and Fleta, lib. 3, c.2, p.175, adopt the principle, that pursuit alone vests no property or right in the huntsman; and that even pursuit accompanied with wounding, is equally ineffectual for that purpose, unless the animal be actually taken. The same principle is recognized by Bracton, lib. 2, c.1, p.8.

Puffendorf, lib. 4, c.6, s.2, and 10, defines occupancy of beasts *ferae naturae*, to be the actual corporal possession of them, and Bynkershoek is cited as coinciding in this definition. It is indeed with hesitation that Puffendorf affirms that a wild beast mortally wounded, or greatly maimed, cannot be fairly intercepted by another, whilst the pursuit of the person inflicting the wound continues. The foregoing authorities are decisive to show that mere pursuit gave Post no legal right to the fox, but that he became the property of Pierson, who intercepted and killed him.

It therefore only remains to inquire whether there are any contrary principles, or authorities, to be found in other books, which ought to induce a different decision. Most of the cases which have occurred in England, relating to property in wild animals, have either been discussed and decided upon the principles of their positive statute regulations, or have arisen between the huntsman and the owner of the land upon which beasts *ferae naturae* have been apprehended; the former claiming them by title of occupancy, and the latter *ratione soli*. Little satisfactory aid can, therefore, be derived from the English reporters. Barbeyrac, in his notes on Puffendorf, does not accede to the definition of occupancy by the latter, but, on the contrary, affirms, that actual bodily seizure is not, in all cases, necessary to constitute possession of wild animals. He does not, however, *describe* the acts which, according to his ideas, will amount to an appropriation of such animals to private use, so as to exclude the claims of all other persons, by title of occupancy, to the same animals: and he is far from averring that pursuit alone is sufficient for that purpose. To a certain extent, and as far as Barbeyrac appears to me to go, his objections to Puffendorf's definition of occupancy are reasonable and correct. That is to say, that actual bodily seizure is not indispensable to acquire right to, or possession of, wild beasts; but that, on the contrary, the mortal wounding of such beasts, by one not abandoning his pursuit, may, with the utmost propriety, be deemed possession of him; since, thereby, the pursuer manifests an unequivocal intention of appropriating the animal to his individual use, has deprived him of his natural liberty, and brought him within his certain control. So also, encompassing and securing such animals with nets and toils, or otherwise intercepting them in such a manner as to deprive them of their natural liberty, and render escape impossible, may justly be deemed to give possession of them to those persons who, by their industry and labour, have used such means of apprehending them. Barbeyrac seems to have adopted, and had in view of his notes, the more accurate opinion of Grotius, with respect to occupancy. The case now under consideration is one of mere pursuit, and presents no circumstances or acts which can bring it within the definition of occupancy by Puffendorf, or Grotius, or the ideas of Barbeyrac upon that subject.

The case cited from 11 Mod. 74-130 [Keeble v. Hickeringill, the next principal case below], I think clearly distinguishable from the present; inasmuch as there the action was for maliciously hindering and disturbing the plaintiff in the exercise and enjoyment of a private franchise; and in the report of the same case, (3 Salk. 9) Holt, Ch. J., states, that the ducks were in the plaintiff's decoy pond, and so in his possession, from which it is obvious the court laid much stress in their opinion upon the plaintiff's possession of the ducks, *ratione soli*.

We are the more readily inclined to confine possession or occupancy of beasts *ferae naturae*, within the limits prescribed by the learned authors above cited, for the sake of certainty, and preserving peace and order in society. If the first seeing, starting, or pursuing such animals, without having so wounded, circumvented or ensnared them, so as to deprive them of their natural liberty, and subject them to the control of their pursuer, should afford the basis of actions against others for intercepting and killing them, it would prove a fertile source of quarrels and litigation. However uncourteous or unkind the conduct of Pierson towards Post, in this instance, may have been, yet his act was productive of no injury or damage for which a legal remedy can be applied. We are of opinion the judgment below was erroneous, and ought to be reversed.

LIVINGSTON, J.

My opinion differs from that of the court. Of six exceptions, taken to the proceedings below, all are abandoned except the third, which reduces the controversy to a single question: Whether a person who, with his own hounds, starts and hunts a fox on waste and uninhabited ground, and is on the point of seizing his prey, acquires such an interest in the animal, as to have a right of action against another, who in view of the huntsman and his dogs in full pursuit, and with knowledge of the chase, shall kill and carry him away? This is a knotty point, and should have been submitted to the arbitration of sportsmen, without poring over Justinian, Fleta, Bracton, Puffendorf, Locke, Barbeyrac, or Blackstone, all of whom have been cited; they would have had no difficulty in coming to a prompt and correct conclusion. In a court thus constituted, the skin and carcass of poor *reynard* would have been properly disposed of, and a precedent set, interfering with no usage or custom which the experience of ages has sanctioned, and which must be so well known to every votary of Diana. But the parties have referred the question to our judgment, and we must dispose of it as well as we can, from the partial lights we possess, leaving to a higher tribunal, the correction of any mistake which we may be so unfortunate as to make. By the pleadings it is admitted that a fox is a "wild and noxious beast." Both parties have regarded him, as the law of nations does a pirate, "*hostem humani generis*," and although "*de mortuis nil nisi bonum*," be a maxim of our profession, the memory of the deceased has not been spared. His depredations on farmers and on barn yards have not been forgotten; and to put him to death wherever found, is allowed to be meritorious, and of public benefit. Hence it follows, that our decision should have in view the greatest possible encouragement to the destruction of an animal, so cunning and ruthless in his career. But who would keep a pack of hounds; or what gentleman, at the sound of the horn, and at peep of day, would mount his steed, and for hours together, "*sub jove frigido*," or a vertical sun, pursue the windings of this wily quadruped, if, just as night came on, and his stratagems and strength were nearly exhausted, a saucy intruder, who had not shared in the honours or labours of the chase, were permitted to come in at the death, and bear away in triumph the object of pursuit? Whatever Justinian may have thought of the matter, it must be recollected that his code was compiled many hundred years ago, and it would be very hard indeed, at the distance of so many centuries, not to have a right to establish a rule for ourselves. In his day, we read of no order of men who made it a business, in the language of the declaration in this cause, "with hounds and dogs to find, start, pursue, hunt, and chase," these animals, and that, too, without any other motive than the preservation of Roman poultry; if this diversion had been then in fashion, the lawyers who composed his institutes would have taken care not to pass it by, without suitable encouragement. If any thing, therefore, in the digests or pandects shall appear to militate against the defendant in error, who, on this occasion, was the foxhunter, we have only to say *tempora mutantur*; and if men themselves change with the times, why should not laws also undergo an alteration?

It may be expected, however, by the learned counsel, that more particular notice be taken of their authorities. I have examined them all, and feel great difficulty in determining, whether to acquire dominion over a thing, before in common, it be sufficient that we barely see it, or know where it is, or wish for it, or make a declaration of our will respecting it; or whether, in the case of wild beasts, setting a trap, or lying in wait, or starting, or pursuing, be enough; or if an actual wounding, or killing, or bodily tact and occupation be necessary. Writers on general law, who have favoured us with their speculations on these points, differ on them all; but, great as is the diversity of sentiment among them, some conclusion must be adopted on the question immediately before us. After mature deliberation, I embrace that of Barbeyrac, as the most rational, and least liable to objection. If at liberty, we might imitate the courtesy of a certain emperor, who, to avoid giving offence to the advocates of any of these different doctrines, adopted a middle course, and by ingenious distinctions, rendered it difficult to say (as often happens after a fierce and angry contest) to whom the palm of victory belonged. He ordained, that if a beast be followed with *large dogs and hounds*, he shall belong to the hunter, not to the chance occupant; and in like manner, if he be killed or wounded with a lance or sword; but if chased with *beagles only*, then he passed to the captor, not to the first pursuer. If slain with a dart, a sling, or a bow, he fell to the hunter, if still in chase, and not to him who might afterwards find and seize him.

Now, as we are without any municipal regulations of our own, and the pursuit here, for aught that appears on the case, being with dogs and hounds of *imperial stature*, we are at liberty to adopt one of the provisions just cited, which comports also with the learned conclusion of Barbeyrac, that property in animals *ferae, naturae* may be acquired without bodily touch or manucaption, provided the pursuer be within reach, or have a *reasonable* prospect (which certainly existed here) of taking, what he has *thus* discovered an intention of converting to his own use.

When we reflect also that the interest of our husbandmen, the most useful of men in any community, will be advanced by the destruction of a beast so pernicious and incorrigible, we cannot greatly err, in saying, that a pursuit like the present, through waste and unoccupied lands, and which must inevitably and speedily have terminated in corporal possession, or bodily *seisin*, confers such a right to the object of it, as to make any one a wrongdoer, who shall interfere and shoulder the spoil. The justice's judgment ought therefore, in my opinion, to be affirmed.

Judgment of reversal.

NOTES AND QUESTIONS

1. **Method.** What is the holding of the case? (Be precise: remember that the holding is the answer that the court gives to the issue it frames for review.) What rule of law does the court use to justify its holding? Notice the sources from which the court extracts its rule; why didn't the court rely on cases or statutes?

2. **Forms of argument.**   In addition to citing authorities, does the court make any prudential or instrumental arguments in favor of its result (arguments that take the explicit or implicit form, "our announced rule is good because. . . .")? Might the two forms of argument ("precedent or other authority requires this result," and "good policy requires this result") overlap? When precedent and the court's perception of policy diverge, what are the court's options? What are some relevant policies cited by the court?

3. **Mortal wounding.**   If Post had mortally wounded the fox, would the outcome of the case have been different? Does the court give a decisive answer on this question?

4. **The dissent.**   What rule of capture does the dissent advocate? How would the dissent deal with mortal wounding? Does the dissent rely on authorities, or on instrumental reasoning, or both? What policies support the dissent's result?

5. **The concept of possession.**   A time-honored question put by generations of law professors to their students is this: In Pierson v. Post, did Post lose because he did not have possession, or did he not have possession because he lost? Do you understand the question? Is possession a fact or definition that, if we just master its characteristics or its terms, will allow us to solve all cases easily? Or is it a conclusion that we apply after we decide, on other grounds (of principle or policy), how a case *should* come out?

6. **Custom.**   Which rule (majority or dissent) is more likely to accord with the custom of fox hunters? Should the custom of hunters have been decisive in the case? Do you see any difficulties with basing a rule of law on custom? In Ghen v. Rich, 8 F. 159 (D. Mass. 1881), the plaintiff sued for the market value of a whale that defendant had purchased from the person who found the dead whale on the beach in Brewster, Massachusetts, seventeen miles from where plaintiff shot and killed it with a specially-marked, gun-fired lance, after which the whale sank immediately to the bottom of the bay. The custom on Cape Cod was that a whale killed in such a manner belonged to the person who killed it. The court rendered judgment for the plaintiff, based on the custom:

> [The application of the custom on Cape Cod to decide cases] must necessarily be extremely limited, and can affect but a few persons. It has been recognized and acquiesced in for many years. It requires in the first taker the only act of appropriation that is possible in the nature of the case. Unless it is sustained, this branch of industry must necessarily cease, for no person would engage in it if the fruits of his labor could be appropriated by any chance finder. It gives reasonable salvage [to the finder] for securing or reporting the property. That the rule works well in practice is shown by the extent of the industry which has grown up under it, and the general acquiescence of a whole community interested to dispute it.

Ghen, 8 F. at 162.

7. **Ratione soli.**   Suppose that the hunt in Pierson v. Post had occurred on Post's land rather than on the public beach, and Pierson had still beaten Post to the fox. What result? *See* Restatement of Property § 450 cmt. g (1944) (landowner "not only has power to prevent appropriation by others, but an attempt at appropriation by others may be rendered ineffective by his right to claim the benefit of the

attempt"). What additional policy comes into play in this situation? If you would reach a different result on these facts, would you explain your result as an exception to the rule of Pierson v. Post, or by saying that the landowner possesses wild animals on the owner's land? What is the difference between those two explanations?

8. **Hypotheticals.** All other facts being the same, what result if the fox hunt in Pierson v. Post had occurred on X's land, and Pierson and Post were both trespassers? If the hunt had occurred on X's land, but Post and not Pierson had obtained permission to hunt there? If the hunt had occurred on X's land and Pierson had permission but not Post?

9. **Escape.** Property rights in wild animals are lost when they regain their liberty. *See* Wiley v. Baker, 597 S.W.2d 3, 5 (Tex. Ct. Civ. App. 1980). Animals that are domesticated or that exhibit *animus revertendi*, an intention to return, are exceptions to the rule of escape. *Wiley*, 597 S.W.2d at 6.

10. **Elephants in Iowa.** Suppose that a Bengal tiger escapes from a traveling menagerie in Pennsylvania, and you capture it. Assume (realistically) that the tiger doesn't exhibit *animus revertendi*. In a suit between the owner of the menagerie and you, who wins? What would be the rationale for another exception to the rule of escape? (Hint: think about the policies, if any, that would support a judgment in your favor. Can you find any? What are the policies that are opposed to your recovery?) *See* E.A. Stephens & Co. v. Albers, 256 P. 15, 18 (Colo. 1927) (plaintiff recovered value of pelt of escaped silver fox, not indigenous to the locale, bought by defendant) ("We are loath to believe that a man may capture an elephant in a cornfield in Iowa, or a silver fox on a ranch in Colorado, and snap his fingers in the face of its former owner, whose title had been acquired by a considerable expenditure of time, labor, and money.").

11. **Commentary.** For instructive discussions of the concept of possession, see Carol M. Rose, *Possession as the Origin of Property*, 52 U. Chi. L. Rev. 73 (1985); Richard A. Epstein, *Possession as the Root of Title*, 13 Ga. L. Rev. 1221 (1979). For a recent discussion of the rule of capture, see *Symposium: The Rule of Capture and Its Consequences*, 35 Envtl. L. 647-1106 (2005).

12. **Dealing with cases.** Post "merely" pursued the fox, and lost. The duck hunter in the next case (another famous one), merely pursued the ducks, but won. The skills of legal analysis and argument require not only that you be able to ascertain the meaning(s) of a single case, but also that you be able to compare, distinguish, and synthesize a group of cases that may be relevant to the issue you are working on. (Determining relevance is itself a legal skill.) Your skill at case comparison, developed through analysis of cases such as Pierson v. Post and Keeble v. Hickeringill, will grow as you progress through law school and law practice.

KEEBLE v. HICKERINGILL
11 East 574, 103 Eng. Rep. 1127 (Q.B. 1707)

Action upon the case. Plaintiff [Keeble] declares that he was, on 8th November in the second year of the Queen, lawfully possessed of a close of land called Minott's Meadow, [containing] a decoy pond, to which divers wildfowl used to resort and come: and the plaintiff had at his own costs and charges prepared and procured divers decoy ducks, nets, machines and other engines for the decoying and taking of the wildfowl, and enjoyed the benefit in taking them: the defendant, knowing which, and intending to damnify the plaintiff in his vivary, and to fright and drive away the wildfowl used to resort thither, and deprive him of his profit, did, on the 8th of November, resort to the head of the said pond and vivary, and did discharge six guns laden with gunpowder, and with the noise and stink of the gunpowder did drive away the wildfowl then being in the pond: and on the 11th and 12th days of November the defendant, with design to damnify the plaintiff, and fright away the wildfowl, did place himself with a gun near the vivary, and there did discharge the said gun several times that was then charged with the gunpowder against the said decoy pond, whereby the wildfowl were frighted away, and did forsake the said pond. Upon not guilty pleaded, a verdict was found for the plaintiff and 20 pounds damages.

HOLT, C.J.

I am of opinion that this action doth lie. It seems to be new in its instance, but is not new in the reason or principle of it. For, 1st, this using or making a decoy is lawful. 2dly, this employment of his ground to that use is profitable to the plaintiff, as is the skill and management of that employment. As to the first, every man that hath a property may employ it for his pleasure and profit, as for alluring and procuring decoy ducks to come to his pond. To learn the trade of seducing other ducks to come there in order to be taken is not prohibited either by the law of the land or the moral law; but it is as lawful to use art to seduce them, to catch them, and destroy them for the use of mankind, as to kill and destroy wildfowl or tame cattle. Then when a man useth his art or his skill to take them, to sell and dispose of for his profit; this is his trade; and he that hinders another in his trade or livelihood is liable to an action for so hindering him.

[W]here a violent or malicious act is done to a man's occupation, profession, or way of getting a livelihood, there an action lies in all cases. But if a man doth him damage by using the same employment; as if Mr. Hickeringill had set up another decoy on his own ground near the plaintiff's, and that had spoiled the custom of the plaintiff, no action would lie, because he had as much liberty to make and use a decoy as the plaintiff. This is like the case of 11 H. 4, 47 [the citation refers to a case reported in a volume of cases decided in the eleventh year of the reign of King Henry IV, at page 47]. One schoolmaster sets up a new school to the damage of an ancient school, and thereby the scholars are allured from the old school to come to his new. (The action was held there not to lie.) But suppose Mr. Hickeringill should lie in the way with his guns, and fright the boys from going to school, and their parents would not let them go thither; sure that schoolmaster might have an action for the loss of his scholars. 29 E. 3, 18. A man hath a market, to which he hath toll for horses sold: a man is bringing his horse to market to sell: a stranger hinders and obstructs him from going thither to the market: an action lies, because it imports damage.

There was an objection that did occur to me, though I do not remember it to be made at the bar; which is, that it is not mentioned in the declaration what number or nature of wildfowl were frightened away by the defendant's shooting. Now considering the nature of the case, it is not possible to declare the number, that were frighted away; because the plaintiff had not possession of them, to count them. And when we do know that of long time in the kingdom these artificial contrivances of decoy ponds and decoy ducks have been used for enticing into those ponds wildfowl, in order to be taken for the profit of the owner of the pond, who is at the expense of servants, engines, and other management, whereby the markets of the nation may be furnished; there is great reason to give encouragement thereunto; that the people who are so instrumental by their skill and industry so to furnish the markets should reap the benefit and have their action. But, in short, that which is the true reason is that this action is not brought to recover damage for the loss of the fowl, but for the disturbance. So is the usual and common way of declaring.

NOTES AND QUESTIONS

1. **The duck decoy.** In speaking of a duck "decoy," the court in *Keeble* is not referring to the carved wooden replicas of waterfowl such as those that are now recognized as outstanding examples of folk art and that fetch high prices at auction. Rather, the duck decoy in *Keeble* refers to the market hunter's elaborate apparatus of equipment and personnel, consisting of a pond with one or more tributaries roofed with nets, "tolling dogs" to walk along the shore and lure the inquisitive ducks into the tributaries, dog managers (who pace the dogs while remaining out of sight behind blinds along the shoreline), and helpers to close off the entrance to the tributaries after the ducks have been funneled in. A description, sketch, and photograph of a 20th century version of such a duck decoy (used now to capture birds for banding) may be found in George Reiger's informative book, The Wings of Dawn: The Complete Book of North American Waterfowling 22-25 (2d ed. 1980). Reiger reports that the first such decoy in Britain was constructed in 1665. *See also* A.W. Brian Simpson, Leading Cases in the Common Law 45-75 (1995) (extensive discussion of *Keeble* and of the use of the duck decoy apparatus).

2. **English case reports.** From the early 16th through the late 18th centuries, English cases were reported and marketed by private members of the bar, who transcribed the oral opinions delivered by the judges. The result is considerable "duplication and variance" in the reporting of cases. *See* Miles O. Price, Harry Bitner & Shirley Raissi Bysiewicz, Effective Legal Research §§ 24.5-24.6 (4th ed. 1979). "[I]n determining the authority of one of the old cases, you must evaluate not only the standing of the judges but also the accuracy of the report." A. James Casner & W. Barton Leach, Cases and Text on Property 18 (3d ed. 1984). Casner & Leach report that the East version of Keeble v. Hickeringill is considered the most reliable of the four versions of the case, being based on a copy of the judge's manuscript. *Id.* at 19.

3. **The "private franchise."** What is the basis for the decision in favor of the hunter in *Keeble*? That the defendant took the plaintiff's ducks? Or is it that Hickeringill interfered with the plaintiff's "private franchise" (i.e., his business)? *Keeble* was cited in Pierson v. Post. Did the court in *Pierson* properly distinguish *Keeble*?

4. **A broader principle.** Justice Holt reasons that the duck decoy case is "new in its instance, but is not new in the reason or principle of it," the principle presumably being the "fair competition" principle indicated by the schoolmaster case. Can you use Holt's method to make both the duck decoy *and* the schoolmaster cases instances of a still broader principle, one that is not limited by the private franchise facts? Professor Krier states, "Interference with capture is allowed, but only when it is a kind of interference that promotes capture in the end. When the interference is inconsistent with social welfare, we say it is illegal. But when it is productive, we call it competition." James E. Krier, *Capture and Counteraction: Self-Help by Environmental Zealots*, 30 U. Rich. L. Rev. 1039, 1050 (1996). What result applying your revised, broader principle to the facts of Pierson v. Post?

5. **Application.** Plaintiff's fishing boat draws its net in a circle around a school of mackerel, to the point where, according to the court, it appears "almost certain that the plaintiff would have had possession of the fish," except that the defendant's boat slips through the opening in plaintiff's net and captures the fish before plaintiff can draw the ends of his net together. Should judgment be for plaintiff or defendant? *See* Young v. Hichens, 6 Q.B. 606 (1844).

6. **Buffalos and carrier pigeons.** What are the implications of the rule of capture for animal populations? Does the rule create incentives to conserve, or to take? Do you see why state regulation of the capture of wild animals is important? To take the case of ducks, for example, federal laws (because ducks are migratory) and state laws regulate seasons, bag limits, equipment, hunting locations, number of birds that may be taken daily and possessed, as well as other matters.

7. **Power to regulate: ownership and stewardship.** Does the state have authority to regulate capture because it owns wild animals? *Compare* State ex rel. Visser v. State Fish & Game Comm'n, 437 P.2d 373 (Mont. 1968) (state, as owner, is entitled to recover carcasses of elk shot out of season by defendant landowner), *with* Commonwealth v. Agway, Inc., 232 A.2d 69, 71 (Pa. Super. Ct. 1967) (state is not entitled to sue for value of fish killed by defendant's polluting of navigable stream) ("Neither this court nor the court below nor the Commonwealth has discovered any case which has held that a state has such a property interest in wild game and fish that it could be the subject of a tortious invasion."), Sickman v. United States, 184 F.2d 616, 618 (7th Cir. 1950) (lacking ownership, federal government is not liable for damage to landowner caused by migrating geese), *and* Booth v. State, 83 P.3d 61 (Ariz. Ct. App. 2004) (upholding jury verdict against state for motorist injured in collision with elk on highway on basis that collision was foreseeable and state had taken insufficient precautions). Can the state own wild animals for one purpose but not another? *See* Ray Andrews Brown, The Law of Personal Property § 2.2 (3d ed. Walter B. Rauschenbush 1975).

POPOV v. HAYASHI
2002 WL 31833731 (Cal. Super. Ct.)

McCarthy, J.

In 1927, Babe Ruth hit sixty home runs. That record stood for thirty-four years until Roger Maris broke it in 1961 with sixty-one home runs. Mark McGwire hit seventy in 1998. On October 7, 2001, at PacBell Park in San Francisco, Barry Bonds hit number seventy-three. That accomplishment set a record which, in all probability, will remain unbroken for years into the future.

The event was widely anticipated and received a great deal of attention. The ball that found itself at the receiving end of Mr. Bonds' bat garnered some of that attention. Baseball fans in general, and especially people at the game, understood the importance of the ball. It was worth a great deal of money[1] and whoever caught it would bask, for a brief period of time, in the reflected fame of Mr. Bonds.

With that in mind, many people who attended the game came prepared for the possibility that a record setting ball would be hit in their direction. Among this group were plaintiff Alex Popov and defendant Patrick Hayashi. They were unacquainted at the time. Both men brought baseball gloves, which they anticipated using if the ball came within their reach.

They, along with a number of others, positioned themselves in the arcade section of the ballpark. This is a standing room only area located near right field. It is in this general area that Barry Bonds hits the greatest number of home runs. The area was crowded with people on October 7, 2001 and access was restricted to those who held tickets for that section.

Barry Bonds came to bat in the first inning. With nobody on base and a full count, Bonds swung at a slow knuckleball. He connected. The ball sailed over the right-field fence and into the arcade.

Josh Keppel, a cameraman who was positioned in the arcade, captured the event on videotape. Keppel filmed much of what occurred from the time Bonds hit the ball until the commotion in the arcade had subsided. He was standing very near the spot where the ball landed and he recorded a significant amount of information critical to the disposition of this case.

When the seventy-third home run ball went into the arcade, it landed in the upper portion of the webbing of a softball glove worn by Alex Popov. While the glove stopped the trajectory of the ball, it is not at all clear that the ball was secure. Popov had to reach for the ball and in doing so, may have lost his balance.

Even as the ball was going into his glove, a crowd of people began to engulf Mr. Popov. He was tackled and thrown to the ground while still in the process of attempting to complete the catch. Some people intentionally descended on him for the purpose of taking the ball away, while others were involuntarily forced to the ground by the momentum of the crowd.

---

[1] It has been suggested that the ball might sell for something in excess of $1,000,000.

Eventually, Mr. Popov was buried face down on the ground under several layers of people. At one point he had trouble breathing. Mr. Popov was grabbed, hit and kicked. People reached underneath him in the area of his glove. Neither the tape nor the testimony is sufficient to establish which individual members of the crowd were responsible for the assaults on Mr. Popov.

Mr. Hayashi was standing near Mr. Popov when the ball came into the stands. He, like Mr. Popov, was involuntarily forced to the ground. He committed no wrongful act. While on the ground he saw the loose ball. He picked it up, rose to his feet and put it in his pocket.

Mr. Popov eventually got up from the ground. He made several statements while he was on the ground and shortly after he got up which are consistent with his claim that he had achieved some level of control over the ball and that he intended to keep it. Those statements can be heard on the audio portion of the tape. When he saw that Mr. Hayashi had the ball he expressed relief and grabbed for it. Mr. Hayashi pulled the ball away. Security guards then took Mr. Hayashi to a secure area of the stadium.

LEGAL ANALYSIS

Plaintiff has pled causes of actions for conversion, trespass to chattel, injunctive relief and constructive trust. Conversion is the wrongful exercise of dominion over the personal property of another. There must be actual interference with the plaintiff's dominion. Wrongful withholding of property can constitute actual interference even where the defendant lawfully acquired the property. If a person entitled to possession of personal property demands its return, the unjustified refusal to give the property back is conversion.

The act constituting conversion must be intentionally done. There is no requirement, however, that the defendant know that the property belongs to another or that the defendant intends to dispossess the true owner of its use and enjoyment. Wrongful purpose is not a component of conversion. The injured party may elect to seek either specific recovery of the property or monetary damages.

Trespass to chattel, in contrast, exists where personal property has been damaged or where the defendant has interfered with the plaintiff's use of the property. Actual dispossession is not an element of the tort of trespass to chattel.

In the case at bar, Mr. Popov is not claiming that Mr. Hayashi damaged the ball or that he interfered with Mr. Popov's use and enjoyment of the ball. He claims instead that Mr. Hayashi intentionally took it from him and refused to give it back. There is no trespass to chattel. If there was a wrong at all, it is conversion.

Conversion does not exist, however, unless the baseball rightfully belongs to Mr. Popov. One who has neither title nor possession, nor any right to possession, cannot sue for conversion. The deciding question in this case then, is whether Mr. Popov achieved possession or the right to possession as he attempted to catch and hold on to the ball.

The parties have agreed to a starting point for the legal analysis. Prior to the time the ball was hit, it was possessed and owned by Major League Baseball. At the time it was hit it became intentionally abandoned property. The first person who came in possession of the ball became its new owner.

While there is a degree of ambiguity built into the term possession, that ambiguity exists for a purpose. Courts are often called upon to resolve conflicting claims of possession in the context of commercial disputes. A stable economic environment requires rules of conduct which are understandable and consistent with the fundamental customs and practices of the industry they regulate. Without that, rules will be difficult to enforce and economic instability will result. Because each industry has different customs and practices, a single definition of possession cannot be applied to different industries without creating havoc. This does not mean that there are no central principles governing the law of possession. It is possible to identify certain fundamental concepts that are common to every definition of possession.

Professor Roger Bernhardt has recognized that "[p]ossession requires both physical control over the item and an intent to control it or exclude others from it. But these generalizations function more as guidelines than as direct determinants of possession issues. Possession is a blurred question of law and fact."[21]

Professor Brown argues that "[t]he orthodox view of possession regards it as a union of the two elements of the physical relation of the possessor to the thing, and of intent. This physical relation is the actual power over the thing in question, the ability to hold and make use of it. But a mere physical relation of the possessor to the thing in question is not enough. There must also be manifested an intent to control it."[22]

The task of this court is to use these principles as a starting point to craft a definition of possession that applies to the unique circumstances of this case. We start with the observation that possession is a process which culminates in an event. The event is the moment in time that possession is achieved. The process includes the acts and thoughts of the would-be possessor which lead up to the moment of possession.

The focus of the analysis in this case is not on the thoughts or intent of the actor. Mr. Popov has clearly evidenced an intent to possess the baseball and has communicated that intent to the world. The question is whether he did enough to reduce the ball to his exclusive dominion and control. Were his acts sufficient to create a legally cognizable interest in the ball?

Mr. Hayashi argues that possession does not occur until the fan has complete control of the ball. Professor Brian Gray, suggests the following definition:

> A person who catches a baseball that enters the stands is its owner. A ball is caught if the person has achieved complete control of the ball at the point in time that the momentum of the ball and the momentum of the fan while attempting to catch the ball ceases. A baseball, which is dislodged by incidental contact with an inanimate object or another person, before

---

[21] Real Property in a Nutshell, Roger Bernhardt and Ann M. Burkhart, chapter one, page 3.

[22] Brown, The Law on Personal Property (Callaghan and Company, 3rd Edition, 1975) section 2.6, page 21.

momentum has ceased, is not possessed. Incidental contact with another person is contact that is not intended by the other person. The first person to pick up a loose ball and secure it becomes its possessor.[24]

Mr. Popov argues that this definition requires that a person seeking to establish possession must show unequivocal dominion and control, a standard rejected by several leading cases. Instead, he offers the perspectives of Professor Bernhardt and Professor Paul Finkelman[26] who suggest that possession occurs when an individual intends to take control of a ball and manifests that intent by stopping the forward momentum of the ball whether or not complete control is achieved.

Professors Finkelman and Bernhardt have correctly pointed out that some cases recognize possession even before absolute dominion and control is achieved. Those cases require the actor to be actively and ably engaged in efforts to establish complete control. Moreover, such efforts must be significant and they must be reasonably calculated to result in unequivocal dominion and control at some point in the near future.

This rule is applied in cases involving the hunting or fishing of wild animals or the salvage of sunken vessels. The hunting and fishing cases recognize that a mortally wounded animal may run for a distance before falling. The hunter acquires possession upon the act of wounding the animal not the eventual capture. Similarly, whalers acquire possession by landing a harpoon, not by subduing the animal.

In the salvage cases, an individual may take possession of a wreck by exerting as much control "as its nature and situation permit." Inadequate efforts, however, will not support a claim of possession.

These rules are contextual in nature. They are crafted in response to the unique nature of the conduct they seek to regulate. Moreover, they are influenced by the custom and practice of each industry. The reason that absolute dominion and control is not required to establish possession in the cases cited by Mr. Popov is that such a rule would be unworkable and unreasonable. The "nature and situation" of the property at issue does not immediately lend itself to unequivocal dominion and control. It is impossible to wrap ones arms around a whale, a fleeing fox or a sunken ship.

The opposite is true of a baseball hit into the stands of a stadium. Not only is it physically possible for a person to acquire unequivocal dominion and control of an abandoned baseball, but fans generally expect a claimant to have accomplished as much. The custom and practice of the stands creates a reasonable expectation that a person will achieve full control of a ball before claiming possession. There is no reason for the legal rule to be inconsistent with that expectation. Therefore Gray's Rule is adopted as the definition of possession in this case.

The central tenant of Gray's Rule is that the actor must retain control of the ball after incidental contact with people and things. Mr. Popov has not established by a

---

[24]   This definition is hereinafter referred to as Gray's Rule.

[26]   Professor Finkelman is the author of the definitive law review article on the central issue in this case, *Fugitive Baseballs and Abandoned Property: Who Owns the Home Run Ball?*; Cardozo Law Review, May 2002, Paul Finkelman, (Chapman Distinguished Professor of Law).

preponderance of the evidence that he would have retained control of the ball after all momentum ceased and after any incidental contact with people or objects. Consequently, he did not achieve full possession.

That finding, however, does not resolve the case. The reason we do not know whether Mr. Popov would have retained control of the ball is not because of incidental contact. It is because he was attacked. His efforts to establish possession were interrupted by the collective assault of a band of wrongdoers.

As a matter of fundamental fairness, Mr. Popov should have had the opportunity to try to complete his catch unimpeded by unlawful activity. To hold otherwise would be to allow the result in this case to be dictated by violence. That will not happen.

For these reasons, the analysis cannot stop with the valid observation that Mr. Popov has not proved full possession. The legal question presented at this point is whether an action for conversion can proceed where the plaintiff has failed to establish possession or title. It can. An action for conversion may be brought where the plaintiff has title, possession or the right to possession.

Here Mr. Popov seeks, in effect, a declaratory judgment that he has either possession or the right to possession. In addition he seeks the remedies of injunctive relief and a constructive trust. These are all actions in equity. A court sitting in equity has the authority to fashion rules and remedies designed to achieve fundamental fairness.

Consistent with this principle, the court adopts the following rule. Where an actor undertakes significant but incomplete steps to achieve possession of a piece of abandoned personal property and the effort is interrupted by the unlawful acts of others, the actor has a legally cognizable pre-possessory interest in the property. That pre-possessory interest constitutes a qualified right to possession which can support a cause of action for conversion.

Recognition of a legally protected pre-possessory interest, vests Mr. Popov with a qualified right to possession and enables him to advance a legitimate claim to the baseball based on a conversion theory. Moreover it addresses the harm done by the unlawful actions of the crowd.

It does not, however, address the interests of Mr. Hayashi. The court is required to balance the interests of all parties. Mr. Hayashi was not a wrongdoer. He was a victim of the same bandits that attacked Mr. Popov. The difference is that he was able to extract himself from their assault and move to the side of the road. It was there that he discovered the loose ball. When he picked up and put it in his pocket he attained unequivocal dominion and control.

If Mr. Popov had achieved complete possession before Mr. Hayashi got the ball, those actions would not have divested Mr. Popov of any rights, nor would they have created any rights to which Mr. Hayashi could lay claim. Mr. Popov, however, was able to establish only a qualified pre-possessory interest in the ball. That interest does not establish a full right to possession that is protected from a subsequent legitimate claim.

On the other hand, while Mr. Hayashi appears on the surface to have done everything necessary to claim full possession of the ball, the ball itself is encumbered by the qualified pre-possessory interest of Mr. Popov. At the time Mr. Hayashi came into possession of the ball, it had, in effect, a cloud on its title.

An award of the ball to Mr. Popov would be unfair to Mr. Hayashi. It would be premised on the assumption that Mr. Popov would have caught the ball. That assumption is not supported by the facts. An award of the ball to Mr. Hayashi would unfairly penalize Mr. Popov. It would be based on the assumption that Mr. Popov would have dropped the ball. That conclusion is also unsupported by the facts.

Both men have a superior claim to the ball as against all the world. Each man has a claim of equal dignity as to the other. We are, therefore, left with something of a dilemma. Thankfully, there is a middle ground.

The concept of equitable division was fully explored in a law review article authored by Professor R.H. Helmholz in the December 1983 edition of the Fordham Law Review.[38] Professor Helmholz addressed the problems associated with rules governing finders of lost and mislaid property. For a variety of reasons not directly relevant to the issues raised in this case, Helmholz suggested employing the equitable remedy of division to resolve competing claims between finders of lost or mislaid property and the owners of land on which the property was found. There is no reason, however, that the same remedy cannot be applied in a case such as this, where issues of property, tort and equity intersect.

The concept of equitable division has its roots in ancient Roman law. As Helmholz points out, it is useful in that it "provides an equitable way to resolve competing claims which are equally strong." Moreover, "[i]t comports with what one instinctively feels to be fair."[40]

Although there is no California case directly on point, Arnold v. Producers' Fruit Company, 61 P. 283 (Cal. 1900) provides some insight. There, a number of different prune growers contracted with Producer's Fruit Company to dry and market their product. Producers did a bad job. They mixed fruit from many different growers together in a single bin and much of the fruit rotted because it was improperly treated.

When one of the plaintiffs offered proof that the fruit in general was rotten, Producers objected on the theory that the plaintiff could not prove that the prunes he contributed to the mix were the same prunes that rotted. The court concluded that it did not matter. After the mixing was done, each grower had an undivided interest in the whole, in proportion to the amount of fruit each had originally contributed. The principle at work here is that where more than one party has a valid claim to a single piece of property, the court will recognize an undivided interest in the property in proportion to the strength of the claim.

---

[38] *Equitable Division and the Law of Finders*, (1983) Fordham Law Review, Professor R.H. Helmholz, University of Chicago School of Law. This article built on a student comment published in 1939. *Lost, Mislaid and Abandoned Property* (1939) 8 Fordham Law Review 222.

[40] *Id.* at 315.

Application of the principle of equitable division is illustrated in the case of Keron v. Cashman, 33 A. 1055 (1896). In that case, five boys were walking home along a railroad track in the city of Elizabeth, New Jersey. The youngest of the boys came upon an old sock that was tied shut and contained something heavy. He picked it up and swung it. The oldest boy took it away from him and beat the others with it. The sock passes from boy to boy. Each controlled it for a short time. At some point in the course of play, the sock broke open and out spilled $775 as well as some rags, cloths and ribbons.

The court noted that possession requires both physical control and the intent to reduce the property to one's possession. Control and intent must be concurrent. None of the boys intended to take possession until it became apparent that the sock contained money. Each boy had physical control of the sock at some point before that discovery was made. Because none could present a superior claim of concurrent control and intent, the court held that each boy was entitled to an equal share of the money. Their legal claims to the property were of equal quality, therefore their entitlement to the property was also equal.

Here, the issue is not intent, or concurrence. Both men intended to possess the ball at the time they were in physical contact with it. The issue, instead, is the legal quality of the claim. With respect to that, neither can present a superior argument as against the other.

Mr. Hayashi's claim is compromised by Mr. Popov's pre-possessory interest. Mr. Popov cannot demonstrate full control. Albeit for different reasons, they stand before the court in exactly the same legal position as did the five boys. Their legal claims are of equal quality and they are equally entitled to the ball.

The court therefore declares that both plaintiff and defendant have an equal and undivided interest in the ball. Plaintiff's cause of action for conversion is sustained only as to his equal and undivided interest. In order to effectuate this ruling, the ball must be sold and the proceeds divided equally between the parties.

NOTES AND QUESTIONS

1. **What happened next?** Although the court estimated that the ball might sell for more than $1,000,000, it eventually sold at auction for only $450,000. Hayashi was quoted as saying, "After legal fees, I guess it will be a wash." Ira Berklow, *73rd Home Run Ball Sells for $450,000*, N.Y. Times, June 26, 2003, at D4. Popov's lawyer eventually sued him for legal fees. *See* Triano v. Popov, 2005 Cal. App. Unpub. LEXIS 4594 (Cal. App. 1st Dist.)

2. **Applicability of the rule of capture.** Why does the rule of capture apply in this case? If you inadvertently leave your property book in the classroom today, does its first possessor become the absolute owner of the book? What feature do wild animals share with the baseball in the principle case?

3. **Abandonment.** "Abandonment is shown by proof that the owner intends to abandon the property and has voluntarily relinquished all right, title and interest in the property." *See* Benjamin v. Lindner Aviation, Inc., 534 N.W.2d 400, 406 (Iowa 1995), reprinted in Section B.2. below. Why is abandonment not an issue in the principal case?

4. **Popov v. Hayashi in the literature.** The principal case has generated quite a lot of comment. *See* Peter Adomeit, *The Barry Bonds Baseball Case — An Empirical Approach — Is Fleeting Possession Five Tenths of the Ball?*, 48 St. Louis U. L.J. 475 (2004); Paul Finkelman, *Fugitive Baseballs and Abandoned Property: Who Owns the Home Run Ball?*, 23 Cardozo L. Rev. 1609 (2002); Steven Semeraro, *An Essay on Property Rights in Milestone Home Run Baseballs*, 56 SMU L. Rev. 2281 (2003).

5. **The rule of capture in other contexts.** The rule of capture has been applied in contexts other than wild animals and baseballs. One application has been to minerals like oil and gas that can "migrate" from beneath one tract to another. Oil and gas were called "fugitive" minerals and the rule of capture governed their ownership. The rule encouraged landowners to drill and pump as much and as quickly as possible in order to take the minerals from beneath the lands of neighbors and to prevent their neighbors from taking minerals that migrated from beneath their land. More recently, regulation of drilling has supplanted the rule of capture to a great extent. *See* Bruce M. Kramer & Owen L. Anderson, *The Rule of Capture — An Oil and Gas Perspective*, 35 Envtl. L. 899 (2005).

6. **Real property and the rule of capture?** Consider the following: Johnson purchased land from the Piankeshaw Indians in 1775. M'Intosh later purchased the same land from the United States. A dispute arose between them over who owned the land, which went all the way to the United States Supreme Court. The Court held that M'Intosh had good title; the opinion was delivered by Chief Justice John Marshall:

> The United States [has] unequivocally acceded to that great and broad rule by which its civilized inhabitants now hold this country. They hold, and assert in themselves, the title by which it was acquired. They maintain, as all others [i.e., European nations] have maintained, that discovery gave an exclusive right to extinguish the Indian title of occupancy, either by purchase or by conquest; and gave also a right to such a degree of sovereignty, as the circumstances of the people would allow them to exercise.

> The power now possessed by the government of the United States to grant lands, resided, while we were colonies, in the crown, or its grantees. The validity of the titles given by either has never been questioned in our Courts. It has been exercised uniformly over territory in possession of the Indians. The existence of this power must negative the existence of any right which may conflict with, and control it. An absolute [title] to lands cannot exist, at the same time, in different persons, or in different governments. An absolute title, must be an exclusive title, or at least a title which excludes all others not compatible with it. All our institutions recognise the absolute title of the crown, subject only to the Indian right of occupancy, and recognise the absolute title of the crown to extinguish that right. This is incompatible with an absolute and complete title in the Indians.

Johnson v. M'Intosh, 21 U.S. 543, 587-88 (1823). Query: how could America have been "discovered" by the European nations if it was already occupied by Native

Americans? Was M'Intosh's title really based *exclusively* on conquest, rather than, as the Court suggests, on conquest ancillary to discovery? *See generally* Eric Kades, *History and Interpretation of the Great Case of* Johnson v. M'Intosh, 19 Law & Hist. Rev. 67 (2001); Johnson v. M'Intosh *Reargument*, 9 Kan. J.L. & Pub. Pol'y 846 (2000); David Wilkins, *Quit-Claiming the Doctrine of Discovery: A Treaty-Based Reappraisal*, 23 Okla. City U. L. Rev. 277 (1998).

7. **Possession of property that has a true owner.** In discussing the rules applicable to first possession of abandoned property, the court in Popov v. Hayashi also discusses cases involving property that has not been abandoned by its owner. Does the rule of first possession have any applicability in these cases? The following materials explore this question.

2. Subsequent Possession: Losers and Finders

> The art of losing isn't hard to master;
> so many things seem filled with the intent
> to be lost that their loss is no disaster.
>
> Lose something every day. Accept the fluster
> of lost door keys, the hour badly spent.
> The art of losing isn't hard to master.

Elizabeth Bishop, *One Art, in* The Complete Poems 1927-1979 (1983)*

ARMORY v. DELAMIRIE
93 Eng. Rep. 664 (K.B. 1722)

The plaintiff being a chimney sweeper's boy found a jewel and carried it to the defendant's shop (who was a goldsmith) to know what it was, and delivered it into the hands of the apprentice, who under pretense of weighing it, took out the stones, and calling to the master to let him know it came to three halfpence, the master offered the boy the money, who refused to take it, and insisted to have the thing again; whereupon the apprentice delivered him back the socket without the stones. And now in trover against the master these points were ruled:

1. That the finder of a jewel, though he does not by such finding acquire an absolute property or ownership, yet he has such a property as will enable him to keep it against all but the rightful owner, and consequently may maintain trover.

2. That the action well lay against the master, who gives a credit to his apprentice, and is answerable for his neglect.

3. As to the value of the jewel several of the trade were examined to prove what a jewel of the finest water that would fit the socket would be worth; and the Chief Justice (Pratt, C.J.) directed the jury that unless the defendant did produce the jewel and show it not to be of the finest water, they should presume the strongest against him and make the value of the best jewel the measure of their damages, which they accordingly did.

---

* Excerpt from *One Art* from *The Complete Poems: 1927-1979* by Elizabeth Bishop. Copyright © 1979, 1983 by Alice Helen Methfessel. Reprinted by permission of Farrar, Straus and Giroux, LLC.

NOTES AND QUESTIONS

1. **The finders rule.**   In Armory v. Dalamirie, as in Pierson v. Post, we get a simple rule that proves to be unsuitable to cover the variety of cases that the unruliness of life presents to the courts. What is the rule? Suppose this case: I find a diamond ring and subsequently lose it; you come along and find it. How will the court decide the case under the rule in Armory v. Delamarie? Putting your self-interest aside, who do you think *should* win?

2. **Relativity of rights.**   Even though the sweep in *Armory* is not an original owner, is there nevertheless a sense in which the sweep is "first in time"? In relation to whom? Who is the sweep *not* first in relation to? In the hypothetical in Note 1, do I have the same protection against you that the "true owner" of the diamond ring would have against me? Would you have that same protection against someone who possessed after you?

3. **How possession was acquired.**   Does it matter how the alleged finder acquired possession? Suppose that the sweep in Armory v. Delamarie really had stolen the ring. Should that matter? The leading case for the proposition that (relative) first occupancy is protected by the law, even if wrongful, is Anderson v. Gouldberg, 53 N.W. 636 (Minn. 1892). Plaintiff sued to recover the possession of ninety-three pine logs from the defendant miller who took the logs from plaintiff. Plaintiff, however, had cut the logs from the owner's land without permission. On appeal, the court affirmed a jury verdict for the plaintiff, stating:

> [T]he only question is whether bare possession of property, though wrongfully obtained, is sufficient title to enable the party enjoying it to maintain replevin against a mere stranger, who takes it from him. We had supposed that this was settled in the affirmative as long ago as the early case of Armory v. Delamarie, so often cited on that point. When it is said that to maintain replevin the plaintiff's possession must have been lawful, it means merely that it must have been lawful as against the person who deprived him of it; and possession is good title against all the world except those having a better title. Any other rule would lead to an endless series of unlawful seizures and reprisals in every case where property had once passed out of the possession of the rightful owner.

Anderson, 53 N.W. at 636.

4. **Law and morals.**   Do you find the view expressed by Anderson v. Gouldberg morally repugnant? If plaintiff doesn't win, defendant will; is defendant's conduct more praiseworthy than plaintiff's? Isn't the idea of a rule of law contrary to the might-makes-right concern that troubled the court in *Anderson*? For an astute evaluation of the issues raised in this Note and the preceding one, see R.H. Helmholz, *Wrongful Possession of Chattels: Hornbook Law and Case Law*, 80 Nw. U. L. Rev. 1221 (1986).

5. **Reasons.**   Why does the law decide to protect (relative) first possessors as well as absolute first possessors like the successful hunter in Pierson v. Post?

6. **Jus tertii defense.**   *See* Anderson v. Gouldberg, *supra*, 53 N.W. at 636:

> Counsel [for defendant] says that possession only raises a presumption of title, which, however, may be rebutted. Rightly understood, this is correct; but counsel misapplies it. One who takes property from the possession of

another can only rebut this presumption by showing a superior title in himself, or in some way connecting himself with one who has. One who has acquired the possession of property, whether by finding, bailment, or by mere tort, has a right to retain that possession as against a mere wrongdoer who is a stranger to the property.

NOTE: BAILMENTS

A finder is a type of *bailee*. Under one view, "[a] bailment is an agreement, either express or implied, that one person will entrust personal property to another for a specific purpose and that when the purpose is accomplished the bailee will return the property to the bailor." Pitman v. Pitman, 717 N.E.2d 627, 631 (Ind. Ct. App. 1999). That definition, stressing the contractual origin of the relationship, contends with a broader view of bailment as "the rightful possession of goods by one who is not the owner." Brown on Personal Property § 10.1 at 209, quoting 9 Williston, Law of Contracts 875 (3d ed. 1967). Does the finder have a contract, express or implied, with the true owner of the property?

Bailments are all around; you just haven't known what to call them. Your neighbor who keeps your dog while you go on vacation is a bailee (bailment for the benefit of the bailor, or "gratuitous bailment"); when you borrow your neighbor's lawnmower, you are a bailee (bailment for the sole benefit of the bailee: you); when you take your clothes to the dry cleaner, the cleaning establishment is a bailee (bailment for the mutual benefit of bailor and bailee, or "bailment for hire"). What function do these different categories perform? *See* Pitman v. Pitman, *supra*, 717 N.E.2d at 631:

> The standard of care required of a bailee is determined by the benefit each party derives from the bailment. A bailee need use only slight care when a bailment is for the sole benefit of the bailor, must exercise great care when the bailment is for the sole benefit of the bailee, and must exercise ordinary care when the bailment is for the mutual benefit of the bailor and the bailee. Whether a bailee has complied with the expected standard of care is a question of fact for the trier of fact.

From the standpoint of legal method, much the same kinds of lessons can be learned from the bailment cases as from animals and finders, or from gifts, which are considered later in this chapter. Classification of a transaction as a bailment or something else, or classifying the particular type of bailment, is usually determinative of the outcome of a case:

> In order to achieve desired results the courts may in one type of case hold the transaction a bailment, while in another type the same kind of transaction will be held not a bailment. Again, as is common in other branches of the law, in order to achieve justice in particular types of cases, and at the same time preserve a seeming consistency in the logical apparatus, the courts will declare that the transaction is a "constructive" bailment with the consequences that flow from an actual one, although under any reasonable interpretation of the definition there was no bailment at all. It would be nice if we could abandon the search for the definitions and

elements of bailment, and confine ourselves to a consideration of the various rights and duties which arise when one person has possession of goods which belong to another.

Brown on Personal Property § 10.1 at 209-210. In McGlynn v. Newark Parking Auth., 432 A.2d 99 (N.J. 1981), the court followed Professor Brown's suggested approach in determining whether the operator of an enclosed park-and-lock garage was liable for the theft of property from plaintiff's car. The court rejected an outcome-determinative analysis based on distinctions between a lease, a license, or a bailment, and determined the defendant's liability under the general tort standard of ordinary care under all of the circumstances. *See generally* William V. Vetter, *The Parking Lot Cases Revisited: Confusion at or About the Gate,* 40 Santa Clara L. Rev. 27 (1999).

BENJAMIN v. LINDNER AVIATION, INC.
534 N.W.2d 400 (Iowa 1995)

TERNUS, JUSTICE.

Appellant, Heath Benjamin, found over $18,000 in currency inside the wing of an airplane. At the time of this discovery, appellee, State Central Bank, owned the plane and it was being serviced by appellee, Lindner Aviation, Inc. All three parties claimed the money as against the true owner. After a bench trial, the district court held that the currency was mislaid property and belonged to the owner of the plane. The court awarded a finder's fee to Benjamin. Benjamin appealed and Lindner Aviation and State Central Bank cross-appealed. We reverse on the bank's cross-appeal and otherwise affirm the judgment of the district court.

I. Background Facts and Proceedings.

In April of 1992, State Central Bank became the owner of an airplane when the bank repossessed it from its prior owner who had defaulted on a loan. In August of that year, the bank took the plane to Lindner Aviation for a routine annual inspection. Benjamin worked for Lindner Aviation and did the inspection.

As part of the inspection, Benjamin removed panels from the underside of the wings. Although these panels were to be removed annually as part of the routine inspection, a couple of the screws holding the panel on the left wing were so rusty that Benjamin had to use a drill to remove them. Benjamin testified that the panel probably had not been removed for several years.

Inside the left wing Benjamin discovered two packets approximately four inches high and wrapped in aluminum foil. He removed the packets from the wing and took off the foil wrapping. Inside the foil was paper currency, tied in string and wrapped in handkerchiefs. The currency was predominately twenty-dollar bills with mint dates before the 1960s, primarily in the 1950s. The money smelled musty.

Benjamin took one packet to his jeep and then reported what he had found to his supervisor, offering to divide the money with him. However, the supervisor reported the discovery to the owner of Lindner Aviation, William Engle. Engle insisted that they contact the authorities and he called the Department of Criminal Investigation. The money was eventually turned over to the Keokuk police department.

Two days later, Benjamin filed an affidavit with the county auditor claiming that he was the finder of the currency under the provisions of Iowa Code chapter 644 (1991) [now chapter 556F]. Lindner Aviation and the bank also filed claims to the money. The notices required by chapter 644 were published and posted. No one came forward within twelve months claiming to be the true owner of the money. *See* Iowa Code § 644.11 (if true owner does not claim property within twelve months, the right to the property vests in the finder).

Benjamin filed this declaratory judgment action against Lindner Aviation and the bank to establish his right to the property. The parties tried the case to the court. The district court held that chapter 644 applies only to "lost" property and the money here was mislaid property. The court awarded the money to the bank, holding that it was entitled to possession of the money to the exclusion of all but the true owner. The court also held that Benjamin was a "finder" within the meaning of chapter 644 and awarded him a ten percent finder's fee. *See id.* § 644.13 (a finder of lost property is entitled to ten percent of the value of the lost property as a reward).

Benjamin appealed. He claims that chapter 644 governs the disposition of all found property and any common law distinctions between various types of found property are no longer valid. He asserts alternatively that even under the common law classes of found property, he is entitled to the money he discovered. He claims that the trial court should have found that the property was treasure trove or was lost or abandoned rather than mislaid, thereby entitling the finder to the property.

The bank and Lindner Aviation cross-appealed. Lindner Aviation claims that if the money is mislaid property, it is entitled to the money as the owner of the premises on which the money was found, the hangar where the plane was parked. It argues in the alternative that it [Lindner] is the finder, not Benjamin, because Benjamin discovered the money during his work for Lindner Aviation. The bank asserts in its cross-appeal that it owns the premises where the money was found — the airplane — and that no one is entitled to a finder's fee because chapter 644 does not apply to mislaid property.

II. Standard of Review

Whether the money found by Benjamin was treasure trove or was mislaid, abandoned or lost property is a fact question. 1 Am.Jur.2d Abandoned, Lost, and Unclaimed Property § 41, at 49 (2d ed. 1994) (hereinafter "1 Am.Jur.2d Abandoned Property"). Therefore, the trial court's finding that the money was mislaid is binding on us if supported by substantial evidence.

III. Does Chapter 644 Supercede the Common Law
Classifications of Found Property?

Benjamin argues that chapter 644 governs the rights of finders of property and abrogates the common law distinctions between types of found property. As he points out, lost property statutes are intended "to encourage and facilitate the return of property to the true owner, and then to reward a finder for his honesty if the property remains unclaimed." Paset v. Old Orchard Bank & Trust Co., 378 N.E.2d 1264, 1268 (Ill. Ct. App. 1978) (interpreting a statute similar to chapter 644); accord, Flood v. City Nat'l Bank, 253 N.W. 509, 514 (Iowa 1934) (public policy reflected in lost property statute is "to provide a reward to the finder of lost goods"); Willsmore v. Township of Oceola, 308 N.W.2d 796, 804 (Mich. Ct. App. 1981) (lost goods act "provides protection to the finder, a reasonable method of uniting goods with their true owner, and a plan which benefits the people of the state through their local governments").[2] These goals, Benjamin argues, can best be achieved by applying such statutes to all types of found property.

Although a few courts have adopted an expansive view of lost property statutes, we think Iowa law is to the contrary. In 1937, we quoted and affirmed a trial court ruling that "the old law of treasure trove is not merged in the statutory law of chapter 515, 1935 Code of Iowa." Zornes v. Bowen, 274 N.W. 877, 879 (Iowa 1937). Chapter 515 of the 1935 Iowa Code was eventually renumbered as chapter 644. The relevant sections of chapter 644 are unchanged since our 1937 decision. As recently as 1991, we stated that "[t]he rights of finders of property vary according to the characterization of the property found." Ritz v. Selma United Methodist Church, 467 N.W.2d 266, 268 (Iowa 1991). We went on to define and apply the common law classifications of found property in deciding the rights of the parties. As our prior cases show, we have continued to use the common law distinctions between classes of found property despite the legislature's enactment of chapter 644 and its predecessors.

The legislature has had many opportunities since our decision in *Zornes* to amend the statute so that it clearly applies to all types of found property. However, it has not done so. When the legislature leaves a statute unchanged after the supreme court has interpreted it, we presume the legislature has acquiesced in our interpretation. Therefore, we presume here that the legislature approves of our application of chapter 644 to lost property only. Consequently, we hold that chapter 644 does not abrogate the common law classifications of found property. We note this position is consistent with that taken by most jurisdictions. *See, e.g.,* Bishop v. Ellsworth, 234 N.E.2d 49, 51 (Ill. Ct. App. 1968) (holding lost property statute does not apply to abandoned or mislaid property); Foster v. Fidelity Safe Deposit Co., 174 S.W. 376, 379 (Mo. 1915) (refusing to apply lost property statute to property that would not be considered lost under the common law); Sovern v.

---

[2] The Michigan statute had two provisions lacking in the Iowa lost property statute. The Michigan law provided for registration of a find in a central location so that the true owner could locate the goods with ease. It also required notice to potential true owners. Because Iowa's statute has no central registry and requires only posting and publication of notice, Iowa's law does not accomplish as well the goal of reuniting property with its true owner. Finally, under the Michigan statute, the local government obtains one half the value of the goods. Iowa's law does not include this public benefit.

Yoran, 20 P. 100, 105 (Or. 1888) (same); Zech v. Accola, 33 N.W.2d 232, 235 (Wis. 1948) (concluding that if legislature had intended to include treasure trove within lost property statute, it would have specifically mentioned treasure trove).

In summary, chapter 644 applies only if the property discovered can be categorized as "lost" property as that term is defined under the common law. Thus, the trial court correctly looked to the common law classifications of found property to decide who had the right to the money discovered here.

IV. Classification of Found Property

Under the common law, there are four categories of found property: (1) abandoned property, (2) lost property, (3) mislaid property, and (4) treasure trove. The rights of a finder of property depend on how the found property is classified.

A. *Abandoned property*. Property is abandoned when the owner no longer wants to possess it. Abandonment is shown by proof that the owner intends to abandon the property and has voluntarily relinquished all right, title and interest in the property. Abandoned property belongs to the finder of the property against all others, including the former owner.

B. *Lost property*. "Property is lost when the owner unintentionally and involuntarily parts with its possession and does not know where it is." Ritz v. Selma United Methodist Church, 467 N.W.2d 266, 269 (Iowa 1991). Stolen property found by someone who did not participate in the theft is lost property. Under chapter 644, lost property becomes the property of the finder once the statutory procedures are followed and the owner makes no claim within twelve months. Iowa Code § 644.11 (1991).

C. *Mislaid property*. Mislaid property is voluntarily put in a certain place by the owner who then overlooks or forgets where the property is. It differs from lost property in that the owner voluntarily and intentionally places mislaid property in the location where it is eventually found by another. In contrast, property is not considered lost unless the owner parts with it involuntarily. *See* Hill v. Schrunk, 292 P.2d 141, 143 (Or. 1956) (carefully concealed currency was mislaid property, not lost property). The finder of mislaid property acquires no rights to the property. The right of possession of mislaid property belongs to the owner of the premises upon which the property is found, as against all persons other than the true owner.

D. *Treasure trove*. Treasure trove consists of coins or currency concealed by the owner. *Id.* It includes an element of antiquity. To be classified as treasure trove, the property must have been hidden or concealed for such a length of time that the owner is probably dead or undiscoverable. Treasure trove belongs to the finder as against all but the true owner.

V. Is There Substantial Evidence to Support the Trial Court's
Finding That the Money found by Benjamin Was Mislaid?

We think there was substantial evidence to find that the currency discovered by Benjamin was mislaid property. In Eldridge v. Herman, 291 N.W.2d 319 (Iowa 1980), we examined the location where the money was found as a factor in determining whether the money was lost property. *Accord*, 1 Am.Jur.2d Abandoned Property § 6, at 11-12 ("The place where money or property claimed as lost is found is an important factor in the determination of the question of whether it was lost or only mislaid."). Similarly, in *Ritz*, we considered the manner in which the money had been secreted in deciding that it had not been abandoned.

The place where Benjamin found the money and the manner in which it was hidden are also important here. The bills were carefully tied and wrapped and then concealed in a location that was accessible only by removing screws and a panel. These circumstances support an inference that the money was placed there intentionally. This inference supports the conclusion that the money was mislaid. Jackson v. Steinberg, 200 P.2d 376, 378 (Or. 1948) (fact that $800 in currency was found concealed beneath the paper lining of a dresser indicates that money was intentionally concealed with intention of reclaiming it; therefore, property was mislaid, not lost); Schley v. Couch, 284 S.W.2d 333, 336 (Tex. 1955) (holding that money found buried under garage floor was mislaid property as a matter of law because circumstances showed that money was placed there deliberately and court presumed that owner had either forgotten where he hid the money or had died before retrieving it).

The same facts that support the trial court's conclusion that the money was mislaid prevent us from ruling as a matter of law that the property was lost. Property is not considered lost unless considering the place where and the conditions under which the property is found, there is an inference that the property was left there unintentionally. 1 Am.Jur.2d Abandoned Property § 6, at 12; *see Sovern*, 20 P. at 105 (holding that coins found in a jar under a wooden floor of a barn were not lost property because the circumstances showed that the money was hidden there intentionally); Farrare v. City of Pasco, 843 P.2d 1082, 1084 (Wash. Ct. App. 1993) (where currency was deliberately concealed, it cannot be characterized as lost property). Contrary to Benjamin's position the circumstances here do not support a conclusion that the money was placed in the wing of the airplane unintentionally. Additionally, as the trial court concluded, there was no evidence suggesting that the money was placed in the wing by someone other than the owner of the money and that its location was unknown to the owner. For these reasons, we reject Benjamin's argument that the trial court was obligated to find that the currency Benjamin discovered was lost property.

We also reject Benjamin's assertion that as a matter of law this money was abandoned property. Both logic and common sense suggest that it is unlikely someone would voluntarily part with over $18,000 with the intention of terminating his ownership. The location where this money was found is much more consistent with the conclusion that the owner of the property was placing the money there for safekeeping. *See Ritz*, 467 N.W.2d at 269 (property not abandoned where money was buried in jars and tin cans, indicating a desire by the owner to preserve it);

Jackson, 200 P.2d at 378 (because currency was concealed intentionally and deliberately, the bills could not be regarded as abandoned property); 1 Am.Jur.2d Abandoned Property § 13, at 17 (where property is concealed in such a way that the concealment appears intentional and deliberate, there can be no abandonment). We will not presume that an owner has abandoned his property when his conduct is consistent with a continued claim to the property. Therefore, we cannot rule that the district court erred in failing to find that the currency discovered by Benjamin was abandoned property.

Finally, we also conclude that the trial court was not obligated to decide that this money was treasure trove. Based on the dates of the currency, the money was no older than thirty-five years. The mint dates, the musty odor and the rusty condition of a few of the panel screws indicate that the money may have been hidden for some time. However, there was no evidence of the age of the airplane or the date of its last inspection. These facts may have shown that the money was concealed for a much shorter period of time.

Moreover, it is also significant that the airplane had a well-documented ownership history. The record reveals that there were only two owners of the plane prior to the bank. One was the person from whom the bank repossessed the plane; the other was the original purchaser of the plane when it was manufactured. Nevertheless, there is no indication that Benjamin or any other party attempted to locate and notify the prior owners of the plane, which could very possibly have led to the identification of the true owner of the money. Under these circumstances, we cannot say as a matter of law that the money meets the antiquity requirement or that it is probable that the owner of the money is not discoverable.

We think the district court had substantial evidence to support its finding that the money found by Benjamin was mislaid. The circumstances of its concealment and the location where it was found support inferences that the owner intentionally placed the money there and intended to retain ownership. We are bound by this factual finding.

VI. Is the Airplane Or the Hangar the "Premises" Where the Money Was Discovered?

Because the money discovered by Benjamin was properly found to be mislaid property, it belongs to the owner of the premises where it was found. Mislaid property is entrusted to the owner of the premises where it is found rather than the finder of the property because it is assumed that the true owner may eventually recall where he has placed his property and return there to reclaim it.

We think that the premises where the money was found is the airplane, not Lindner Aviation's hangar where the airplane happened to be parked when the money was discovered. The policy behind giving ownership of mislaid property to the owner of the premises where the property was mislaid supports this conclusion. If the true owner of the money attempts to locate it, he would initially look for the plane; it is unlikely he would begin his search by contacting businesses where the airplane might have been inspected. Therefore, we affirm the trial court's judgment that the bank, as the owner of the plane, has the right to possession of the property as against all but the true owner.

VII. Is Benjamin Entitled to a Finder's Fee?

Benjamin claims that if he is not entitled to the money, he should be paid a ten percent finder's fee under section 644.13. The problem with this claim is that only the finder of "lost goods, money, bank notes, and other things" is rewarded with a finder's fee under Iowa Code § 644.13 (1991). Because the property found by Benjamin was mislaid property, not lost property, section 644.13 does not apply here. The trial court erred in awarding Benjamin a finder's fee.

VIII. Summary.

We conclude that the district court's finding that the money discovered by Benjamin was mislaid property is supported by substantial evidence. Therefore, we affirm the district court's judgment that the bank has the right to the money as against all but the true owner. This decision makes it unnecessary to decide whether Benjamin or Lindner Aviation was the finder of the property. We reverse the court's decision awarding a finder's fee to Benjamin.

Affirmed in part; Reversed in part.

SNELL, JUSTICE (dissenting).

I respectfully dissent. The life of the law is logic, it has been said. *See* Davis v. Aiken, 142 S.E.2d 112, 119 (Ga. Ct. App. 1965) (quoting Sir Edward Coke). If so, it should be applied here. After considering the four categories of found money, the majority decides that Benjamin found mislaid money. The result is that the bank gets all the money; Benjamin, the finder, gets nothing. Apart from the obvious unfairness in result, I believe this conclusion fails to come from logical analysis.

Mislaid property is property voluntarily put in a certain place by the owner who then overlooks or forgets where the property is. The property here consisted of two packets of paper currency totaling $18,910, three to four inches high, wrapped in aluminum foil. Inside the foil, the paper currency, predominantly twenty dollar bills, was tied with string and wrapped in handkerchiefs. Most of the mint dates were in the 1950s with one dated 1934. These packets were found in the left wing of the airplane after Benjamin removed a panel held in by rusty screws.

These facts satisfy the requirement that the property was voluntarily put in a certain place by the owner. But the second test for determining that property is mislaid is that the owner "overlooks or forgets where the property is." *Ritz*, 467 N.W.2d at 269. I do not believe that the facts, logic, or common sense lead to a finding that this requirement is met. It is not likely or reasonable to suppose that a person would secrete $18,000 in an airplane wing and then forget where it was.

Cases cited by the majority contrasting "mislaid" property and "lost" property are appropriate for a comparison of these principles but do not foreclose other considerations. After finding the money, Benjamin proceeded to give written notice of finding the property as prescribed in Iowa Code chapter 644 (1993), "Lost

Property." [N]otices were posted on the courthouse door and in three other public places in the county. In addition, notice was published once each week for three consecutive weeks in a newspaper of general circulation in the county. Also, affidavits of publication were filed with the county auditor who then had them published as part of the board of supervisors' proceedings. After twelve months, if no person appears to claim and prove ownership of the property, the right to the property rests irrevocably in the finder.

The purpose of this type of legal notice is to give people the opportunity to assert a claim if they have one. If no claim is made, the law presumes there is none or for whatever reason it is not asserted. Thus, a failure to make a claim after legal notice is given is a bar to a claim made thereafter. Benjamin followed the law in giving legal notice of finding property. None of the parties dispute this. The suggestion that Benjamin should have initiated a further search for the true owner is not a requirement of the law, is therefore irrelevant, and in no way diminishes Benjamin's rights as finder.

The scenario unfolded in this case convinces me that the money found in the airplane wing was abandoned. Property is abandoned when the owner no longer wants to possess it. The money had been there for years, possibly thirty. No owner had claimed it in that time. No claim was made by the owner after legally prescribed notice was given that it had been found. Thereafter, logic and the law support a finding that the owner has voluntarily relinquished all right, title, and interest in the property. Whether the money was abandoned due to its connection to illegal drug trafficking or is otherwise contraband property is a matter for speculation. In any event, abandonment by the true owner has legally occurred and been established.

I would hold that Benjamin is legally entitled to the entire amount of money that he found in the airplane wing as the owner of abandoned property.

HARRIS and ANDREASEN, JJ., join this dissent.

NOTES AND QUESTIONS

1. **Categories: rationales and operation.** Are the common law categories determinative of the outcome of a case? That is, once you classify the property, do you know who wins? Might it not be preferable for courts to concentrate on the policy considerations raised by lost and found cases rather than on attempting to categorize the items? What additional policies — beyond those considered in our discussion of Armory v. Delamarie — might come into play when the dispute is between the finder and the owner of the place where the find occurs? *See generally* Edward R. Cohen, *The Finders Cases Revisited*, 48 Tex. L. Rev. 1001 (1970).

2. **Mislaid property.** Consider the difference between mislaid and lost property: Is it awkward to base a distinction (that determines an outcome) on the subjective intent of a party who is not before the court? If the focus of inquiry is objective — on the location where the property is discovered — are those circumstances reliable evidence of intent? Are those circumstances perhaps manipulable by the finder of the property? Does the distinction between lost and mislaid property facilitate return of the property to the true owner? Granting that

the property in the principal case is mislaid, what other relevant factors should a court consider before deciding who is entitled to the property? *See* R.H. Helmholz, *Equitable Division and the Law of Finders*, 52 Fordham L. Rev. 313 (1983).

3. **Place of find.** If mislaid property goes to the owner of the place of the find (the so-called locus in quo), we have to identify the relevant "place." Should the money have gone to the bank (owner of the plane) or the service contractor?

4. **The statute.** What is Benjamin's argument for broad construction of the statute? What are the court's reasons for construing the statute to apply only to lost property? Compare the Michigan and Iowa statutes; which one is more likely to fulfill the policies discussed by the court?

5. **Abandoned property.** Recall the discussion of abandoned property in the notes after the *Popov* case. Why did the court in *Benjamin* determine that the money was not abandoned? *See also* In re Seizure of $82,000, 119 F. Supp. 2d 1013, 1019-20 (W.D. Mo. 2000) (money found in gas tank of car forfeited by its owner under federal forfeiture statute was abandoned by drug traffickers who had placed it there and, thus, belonged to purchaser of car as finder of the money through his agent).

6. **Joint finders.** Two boys find a manila envelope in a grocery store parking lot, and seek the advice of an older friend. The envelope contains over $12,000 in cash. Who is entitled to the money? *See* Edmonds v. Ronella, 342 N.Y.S.2d 408, 411 (N.Y. Sup. Ct. 1973) (holding joint finders had equal rights in the money on the basis that "the lost money was not found, in a legal sense, until the [boys and their older friend] had, together, removed it from the parking lot"), discussed in R.H. Helmholz, Note 2 above, at 324-325. *See also* Keron v. Cashman, 33 A. 1055 (N.J. Ch. 1896), discussed in Popov v. Hayashi in the previous section.

7. **Other options.** Notice that the common law categories produce an all-or-nothing result: the finder or the landowner wins. What are some alternative solutions? *See* R.H. Helmholz, Note 2 above and Popov v. Hayashi in Section B.1. Notice the reward provision of the Iowa statute; why does the court refuse to apply it here? Why can't the court implement such an outcome under common law principles?

8. **Return of Boy.** How would you rule in the following case? Kroupa adopted a mixed-breed puppy (named Boy), and trained it to be a hunting dog. Boy ran away five years later and became lost. Kroupa immediately informed his friends and local businesses, and he notified the county humane society. Two weeks later, Morgan found Boy. She called the humane society, which never called her back, and posted notices in stores and parks in the area. Morgan took care of the dog and considered it a pet. Slightly over one year after Morgan found Boy, Kroupa showed up at her house, having been told by a friend that the dog was there. Morgan's boyfriend refused to let Kroupa have Boy, but as Kroupa was preparing to leave, Boy jumped in his truck and rode away with him. Morgan sued in replevin to recover "Max" (a.k.a. Boy). What result would you reach and why? *See* Morgan v. Kroupa, 702 A.2d 630, 633 (Vt. 1997) (finder entitled to the dog):

> [M]odern courts have recognized that pets generally do not fit neatly within traditional property law principles. "[A] pet is not just a thing but occupies a special place somewhere in between a person and a piece of personal property." Corso v. Crawford Dog & Cat Hosp., Inc., 415 N.Y.S.2d

182, 183 (City Civ. Ct. 1979). Ordinary common law or statutory rules governing lost personal property therefore do not provide a useful framework for resolving disputes over lost pets. Instead, courts must fashion and apply rules that recognize their unique status, and protect the interests of both owner and finder, as well as the public. Recognizing the substantial value that society places on domestic animals, it is proper that the law encourage finders to take in and care for lost pets. A stray dog obviously requires care and shelter, and left unattended could pose hazards to traffic, spread rabies, or exacerbate an animal overpopulation problem if unneutered. A rule of decision that made it difficult or impossible for the finder to keep the animal after many months or years of care and companionship might deter these salutary efforts, and would not be in the public interest.

The value of a pet to its human companions has already been noted. Accordingly, apart from providing care and shelter, finders of stray pets should also be encouraged to make every reasonable effort to find the animal's owner. Additionally, owners of lost pets should be enjoined to undertake reasonable efforts to locate their animals by contacting local humane societies and other appropriate agencies, printing and placing notices, or taking out appropriate advertisements. Together these requirements provide an incentive to finders to care for stray pets and attempt to locate their owners, and place the onus on owners to conscientiously search for their pet.

Two justices dissented. *Compare* Conti v. ASPCA, 353 N.Y.S.2d 288, 291 (N.Y. Civ. Ct. 1974) (escaped parrot named "Chester" found to be domesticated animal and returned to owner). *See generally* Eric W. Neilsen, Comment, *Is the Law of Acquisition of Property by Find Going to the Dogs?*, 15 T.M. Cooley L. Rev. 479 (1998).

CORLISS v. WENNER
34 P.3d 1100 (Idaho App. 2001)

SCHWARTZMAN, CHIEF JUDGE.

Gregory Corliss appeals from the district court's orders granting summary judgment in favor of Jann Wenner on the right to possess ninety-six gold coins unearthed by Anderson and Corliss on Wenner's property and in favor of Larry Anderson on a promissory note signed by Corliss. We affirm.

I.
FACTUAL AND PROCEDURAL BACKGROUND
A. The Gold Coins

In the fall of 1996, Jann Wenner hired Anderson Asphalt Paving to construct a driveway on his ranch in Blaine County. Larry Anderson, the owner of Anderson Asphalt Paving, and his employee, Gregory Corliss, were excavating soil for the driveway when they unearthed a glass jar containing paper wrapped rolls of gold coins. Anderson and Corliss collected, cleaned, and inventoried the gold pieces dating from 1857 to 1914. The coins themselves weighed about four pounds. Anderson and Corliss agreed to split the gold coins between themselves, with Anderson retaining possession of all the coins. At some point Anderson and Corliss argued over ownership of the coins and Anderson fired Corliss. Anderson later gave possession of the coins to Wenner in exchange for indemnification on any claim Corliss might have against him regarding the coins.

Corliss sued Anderson and Wenner for possession of some or all of the coins. Wenner, defending both himself and Anderson, filed a motion for summary judgment. The facts, except whether Corliss found all or just some of the gold coins without Anderson's help, are not in dispute. All parties agree that the coins were unearthed during excavation by Anderson and Corliss for a driveway on Wenner's ranch, that the coins had been protected in paper tube rolls and buried in a glass jar estimated to be about seventy years old. Following a hearing on Wenner's motion for summary judgment, the district court declined to grant the motion and allowed approximately five months for additional discovery. Six months later the court held a status conference at which counsel for Wenner and Anderson asked the court to rule on Wenner's motion and counsel for Corliss did not object. No new facts were offered.

The district court then entered a memorandum decision stating that the "finders keepers" rule of treasure trove had not been previously adopted in Idaho, that it was not a part of the common law of England incorporated into Idaho law at the time of statehood by statute, and that the coins, having been carefully concealed for safekeeping, fit within the legal classification of mislaid property, to which the right of possession goes to the land owner. Alternatively, the court ruled that the coins, like the topsoil being excavated, were a part of the property owned by Wenner and that Anderson and Corliss were merely Wenner's employees. Corliss appeals.

III.
LAW APPLICABLE TO DETERMINING THE RIGHTFUL POSSESSOR OF THE GOLD COINS
A. Standard Applicable To Review Of The District Court's Choice Of Law

This is a case of first impression in Idaho, the central issue being the proper rule to apply in characterizing the gold coins found by Corliss and Anderson on Wenner's property. The major distinctions between characterizations of found property turn on questions of fact, i.e., an analysis of the facts and circumstances in an effort to divine the intent of the true owner at the time he or she parted with the property. See generally 1 Am.Jur.2d, Abandoned, Lost and Unclaimed Property §§ 1-14 (1994). The material facts and circumstances surrounding the discovery of the gold coins are not in dispute. However, the characterization of that property, in light of these facts, is a question of law over which we exercise free review. Schley v. Couch, 284 S.W.2d 333, 336 (Tex. 1955) (While the character of property is determined from all the facts and circumstances in the particular case of the property found, the choice among categories of found property is a question of law.); see also Batra v. Batra, 17 P.3d 889, 893 (Idaho Ct. App.2001) (The characterization of an asset as separate or community, in light of the facts found, is a question of law.). With these principles in mind we now discuss, in turn, the choice of categories applicable to the district court's characterization of the gold coins found by Anderson and Corliss, recognizing that the choice of characterization of found property determines its rightful possessor as between the finder and landowner.

B. Choice of Categories

At common law all found property is generally categorized in one of five ways. See Benjamin v. Lindner Aviation, Inc., 534 N.W.2d 400 (Iowa 1995); see also 36A C.J.S. Finding Lost Goods § 5 (1961); 1 Am.Jur.2d, Abandoned, Lost, Etc., § 10 (1994). Those categories are:

ABANDONED PROPERTY — that which the owner has discarded or voluntarily forsaken with the intention of terminating his ownership, but without vesting ownership in any other person. Terry v. Lock, 37 S.W.3d 202, 206 (Ark. 2001);

LOST PROPERTY — that property which the owner has involuntarily and unintentionally parted with through neglect, carelessness, or inadvertence and does not know the whereabouts. *Id.*; Ritz v. Selma United Methodist Church, 467 N.W.2d 266 (Iowa 1991);

MISLAID PROPERTY — that which the owner has intentionally set down in a place where he can again resort to it, and then forgets where he put it. *Terry*, 37 S.W.3d at 206;

TREASURE TROVE — a category exclusively for gold or silver in coin, plate, bullion, and sometimes its paper money equivalents, found concealed in the earth or in a house or other private place. *Id.* Treasure trove carries with it the thought of antiquity, i.e., that the treasure has been concealed for so long as to indicate that the owner is probably dead or unknown. 1 Am.Jur.2d Abandoned, Lost, Etc., § 8 (1994);

EMBEDDED PROPERTY — that personal property which has become a part of the natural earth, such as pottery, the sunken wreck of a steamship, or a rotted-away sack of gold-bearing quartz rock buried or partially buried in the ground. See Chance v. Certain Artifacts Found and Salvaged from the Nashville, 606 F.Supp. 801 (S.D.Ga.1984); Ferguson v. Ray, 77 P. 600 (Or. 1904).

Under these doctrines, the finder of lost or abandoned property and treasure trove acquires a right to possess the property against the entire world but the rightful owner regardless of the place of finding. *Terry*, 37 S.W.3d at 206. The finder of mislaid property is required to turn it over to the owner of the premises who has the duty to safeguard the property for the true owner. *Id.* Possession of embedded property goes to owner of the land on which the property was found. Allred v. Biegel, 219 S.W.2d 665 (Mo. Ct. App. 1949) (citing Elwes v. Brigg Gas Co., 33 Ch. D. 562 (Eng.1886)); 1 Am.Jur.2d Abandoned, Lost, Etc., § 29.

One of the major distinctions between these various categories is that only lost property necessarily involves an element of involuntariness. Campbell v. Cochran, 416 A.2d 211, 221 (Del.Super.Ct.1980). The four remaining categories involve voluntary and intentional acts by the true owner in placing the property where another eventually finds it. *Id*. However, treasure trove, despite not being lost or abandoned property, is treated as such in that the right to possession is recognized to be in the finder rather than the premises owner.

C. Discussion and Analysis

On appeal, Corliss argues that the district court should have interpreted the undisputed facts and circumstances surrounding the placement of the coins in the ground to indicate that the gold coins were either lost, abandoned, or treasure trove. Wenner argues that the property was properly categorized as either embedded or mislaid property.

As with most accidentally discovered buried treasure, the history of the original ownership of the coins is shrouded in mystery and obscured by time. The coins had been wrapped in paper, like coins from a bank, and buried in a glass jar, apparently for safekeeping. Based on these circumstances, the district court determined that the coins were not abandoned because the condition in which the coins were found evidenced an intent to keep them safe, not an intent to voluntarily relinquish all possessory interest in them. The district court also implicitly rejected the notion that the coins were lost, noting that the coins were secreted with care in a specific place to protect them from the elements and from other people until such time as the original owner might return for them. There is no indication that the coins came to be buried through neglect, carelessness, or inadvertence. Accordingly, the district court properly concluded, as a matter of law, that the coins were neither lost nor abandoned.

The district court then determined that the modern trend favored characterizing the coins as property either embedded in the earth or mislaid — under which the right of possession goes to the landowner — rather than treasure trove-under which the right of possession goes to the finder. Although accepted by a number of states prior to 1950, the modern trend since then, as illustrated by decisions of the state and federal courts, is decidedly against recognizing the "finders keepers" rule of treasure trove. See, e.g., Klein v. Unidentified, Wrecked & Abandoned Sailing Vessel, 758 F.2d 1511 (11th Cir.1985) (treasure and artifacts from a sunken sailing ship properly characterized as embedded property); *Ritz*, 467 N.W.2d 266 (silver coins and currency dated prior to 1910 and 1928 gold certificates buried in cans and jars under a garage floor classified as mislaid property); Morgan v. Wiser, 711 S.W.2d 220 (Tenn.Ct.App.1985) (gold coins found buried in an iron pot properly characterized as embedded property).

Corliss argues that the district court erred in deciding that the law of treasure trove should not apply in Idaho. However, the doctrine of treasure trove has never been adopted in this state. Idaho Code § 73-116 provides: "[t]he common law of England, so far as it is not repugnant to, or inconsistent with, the constitution or laws of the United States, in all cases not provided for in these compiled laws, is the rule of decision in all courts of this state." Nevertheless, the history of the "finders keepers" rule was not a part of the common law of England at the time the colonies gained their independence. Rather, the doctrine of treasure trove was created to determine a rightful possessor of buried Roman treasures discovered in feudal times. See Leeanna Izuel, *Property Owner's Constructive Possession of*

Treasure Trove: Rethinking the Finders Keepers Rule, 38 U.C.L.A. L.Rev. 1659, 1666-67 (1991). And while the common law initially awarded the treasure to the finder, the crown, as early as the year 1130, exercised its royal prerogative to take such property for itself. *Id.* Only after the American colonies gained their independence from England did some states grant possession of treasure trove to the finder. *Id.* Thus, it does not appear that the "finders keepers" rule of treasure trove was a part of the common law of England as defined by Idaho Code § 73-116. We hold that the district court correctly determined that I.C. § 73-116 does not require the treasure trove doctrine to be adopted in Idaho.

Additionally, we conclude that the rule of treasure trove is of dubious heritage and misunderstood application, inconsistent with our values and traditions. The danger of adopting the doctrine of treasure trove is laid out in *Morgan*, 711 S.W.2d at 222-23:

> [We] find the rule with respect to treasure-trove to be out of harmony with modern notions of fair play. The common law rule of treasure trove invites trespassers to roam at large over the property of others with their metal detecting devices and to dig wherever such devices tell them property might be found. If the discovery happens to fit the definition of treasure-trove, the trespasser may claim it as his own. To paraphrase another court: The mind refuses consent to the proposition that one may go upon the lands of another and dig up and take away anything he discovers there which does not belong to the owner of the land.
>
> The invitation to trespassers inherent in the rule with respect to treasure-trove is repugnant to the common law rules dealing with trespassers in general. The common-law made a trespass an actionable wrong without the necessity of showing any damage therefrom. Because a trespass often involved a breach of the peace and because the law was designed to keep the peace, the common law dealt severely with trespassers.
>
> Recognizing the validity of the idea that the discouragement of trespassers contributes to the preservation of the peace in the community, we think this state should not follow the common law rule with respect to treasure-trove. Rather, we adopt the rule suggested in the concurring opinion in Schley v. Couch, which we restate as follows: "Where property is found embedded in the soil under circumstances repelling the idea that it has been lost, the finder acquires no title thereto, for the presumption is that the possession of the article found is in the owner of the locus in quo."

Land ownership includes control over crops on the land, buildings and appurtenances, soils, and minerals buried under those soils. The average Idaho landowner would expect to have a possessory interest in any object uncovered on his or her property. And certainly the notion that a trespassing treasure hunter, or a hired handyman or employee, could or might have greater possessory rights than a landowner in objects uncovered on his or her property runs counter to the reasonable expectations of present-day land ownership.

There is no reason for a special rule for gold and silver coins, bullion, or plate as opposed to other property. Insofar as personal property (money and the like) buried or secreted on privately owned realty is concerned, the distinctions between treasure trove, lost property, and mislaid property are anachronistic and of little value. The principle point of such distinctions is the intent of the true owner which, absent some written declaration indicating such, is obscured in the mists of time and subject to a great deal of speculation.

By holding that property classed as treasure trove (gold or silver coins, bullion, plate) in other jurisdictions is classed in Idaho as personal property embedded in the soil, subject to the same limitations as mislaid property, possession will be awarded to the owner of the soil as a matter of law. Thus, we craft a simple and reasonable solution to the problem, discourage trespass, and avoid the risk of speculating about the true owner's intent when attempting to infer such from the manner and circumstances in which an object is found. Additionally, the true owner, if any, will have the opportunity to recover the property.

D. Conclusion

We hold that the owner of the land has constructive possession of all personal property secreted in, on or under his or her land. Accordingly, we adopt the district court's reasoning and conclusion melding the law of mislaid property with that of embedded property and conclude, as a matter of law, that the landowner is entitled to possession to the exclusion of all but the true owner, absent a contract between the landowner and finder.

NOTES AND QUESTIONS

1. **Treasure trove.** "Treasure trove consists essentially of articles of gold and silver, intentionally hidden for safety in the earth or in some secret place, the owner being unknown." Brown on Personal Property § 3.3 at 28. Treasure trove goes to the finder under the common law rule. Do you agree with the court in the principal case that the doctrine of treasure trove leads to an objectionable result where the treasure trove is found on private land? Can you think of any other objections to the doctrine? Suppose the treasure trove has historical significance? *See generally* Forrest Booth, *Who Owns Sunken Treasure? The Supreme Court, the Abandoned Shipwreck Act and the Brother Jonathan,* 11 U.S.F. Mar. L.J. 77 (1998-1999); Peter Tomlinson, Comment, *"Full Fathom Five": Legal Hurdles to Treasure,* 42 Emory L.J. 1099 (1993); Leanna Izuel, Comment, *Property Owners' Constructive Possession of Treasure Trove: Rethinking the Finders Keepers Rule,* 38 UCLA L. Rev. 1659 (1991); Annotation, Modern Status of Rules as to Ownership of Treasure Trove as Between Finder and Owner of Property on Which Found, 61 A.L.R.4th 1180; *cf.* David J. Larezwitz, Note, *Bones of Contention: The Regulation of Paleontological Resources on the Federal Public Lands,* 69 Ind. L.J. 601 (1994).

2. **Embedded property.** What policies or rules of law support the award of embedded property to the landowner?

3. **The trespassing finder.** Suppose the finder trespasses on private property to make the find. Should that influence the result? If so, how is this situation

different from that presented in Anderson v. Gouldberg (Note 3 after Armory v. Delamarie)? *See* Favorite v. Miller, 407 A.2d 974 (Conn. 1978) (awarding to the landowner rather than a trespassing finder a fragment of "gilded lead" from a statue of King George III, broken up by revolutionary era patriots to be cast into bullets).

4. **Employees.** In addition to introducing you to the common law categories of discovered property, the *Benjamin* and *Corliss* cases also raise the question whether the status of the finder — as agent or employee of the landowner — is relevant. A maid employed to clean hotel rooms finds a wad of currency in one of the rooms. Should it belong to the employer or the finder? (If the maid were the employee of an independent cleaning service, we would have the same situation as in *Benjamin* and *Corliss*.) What are the relevant considerations? *See, e.g.,* Jackson v. Steinberg, 200 P.2d 376 (Or. 1948) (discussing categories, hotel's obligation to its guests, and maid's duty to take property left by hotel guest to the desk clerk in awarding the money to the hotel); Terry v. Lock, 37 S.W.3d 202, 209 (Ark. 2001) (holding money hidden above ceiling of motel room and found by renovation workers was mislaid property belonging to motel owner); Kalyvakis v. The Olympia, 181 F. Supp. 32, 36 (S.D.N.Y. 1960) (holding money found by assistant steward on floor of public men's restroom of passenger ship was either lost or abandoned property belonging to steward and rejecting a master-servant exception). Police and soldiers may be treated as employees in finding cases. *See* In re Funds in the Possession of Conemaugh Township Supervisors, 753 A.2d 788 (Pa. 2000) (Police officer who found cash was an agent of the state); United States v. Morrison, 492 F.2d 1219 (Ct. Cl. 1974) (Army sergeant who discovered currency was an agent of the United States.).

PROBLEM 1-A. In Hannah v. Peel, [1945] K.B. 509 (King's Bench 1945), Lance-Corporal Duncan Hannah, quartered in a private home requisitioned by the government, while adjusting a blackout curtain, found in a crevice on the top of a window frame a brooch covered with cobwebs and dirt. The home was owned by Major Hugh E.E. Peel, who bought it in 1938 but had never occupied it; he was paid a yearly sum by the government during the requisition. Hannah found the brooch in August, 1940; the following October he informed his commanding officer, and turned the brooch over to the police. In August, 1942 the police gave the brooch to Peel, who sold it for £66. In October, 1943, Hannah sued Peel for the £66. What arguments would you make for Hannah? For Peel?

3.   Adverse Possession

We studied wild animals to indicate how first possession can be the basis for the acquisition of original ownership of things. In studying finders, we saw that a subsequent possessor, though theoretically subordinate to the claims of a prior true owner (or prior possessor), nonetheless enjoys the next best thing to outright ownership, since true owners or prior possessors often fail to show up. In this, our third, study in possession, we will see possessors acquiring title even though they are not first in time, and even as against true owners who *do* show up to assert their claims. We must ask: What new policies are at work to produce these different results?

Why adverse possession? Rephrasing the question, when and why should the law allow a possessor to acquire ownership as against a prior true owner? Suppose that O has a recorded title to Blackacre, a modestly sized parcel in a semi-rural area. O does not use the parcel and, for one reason or another, never visits the area where Blackacre is located. (If you asked O about this, O might say something like, "Well, I don't need to see it; I know it's mine. Maybe one of these days, after I retire, I'll build a small cabin on it.") Meanwhile A, who owns Whiteacre, decides to build a garage. Lacking suitable space on Whiteacre, A builds his garage entirely on Blackacre, the terrain in any other direction being unsuitable. (A has never seen O, or anyone else, on Blackacre.) Years pass. O retires, visits Blackacre, and finds A's garage occupying her parcel. O sues A in ejectment to recover possession of Blackacre.

Policies. Given the flexibility built into some of the requirements of the doctrine of adverse possession, the result in O's lawsuit is not foreordained, but it may surprise you — it does many beginning law students — to find out that a decision in favor of A, the knowing wrongdoer, is entirely possible. Here are three excerpts offering explanations (some of them repetitive) for a result in favor of A. (The *Mannillo* case is reprinted in full later in the chapter.) From the excerpts, compile your own list of the reasons offered in support of the doctrine of adverse possession. Consider which rationales focus on: the adverse possessor A; the record owner O; the interests of society in general.

(1) Mannillo v. Gorski, 255 A.2d 258, 263 (N.J. 1969):

It must not be forgotten that the foundation of so-called "title by adverse possession" is the failure of the true owner to commence an action for the recovery of the land involved, within the period designated by the statute of limitations. The justifications for the doctrine are aptly stated in 4 Tiffany, Real Property (3d ed. 1939) § 1134, p. 406 as follows:

> The desirability of fixing, by law, a definite period within which claims to land must be asserted has been generally recognized, among the practical considerations in favor of such a policy being the prevention of the making of illegal claims after the evidence necessary to defeat them has been lost, and the interest which the community as a whole has in the security of title. The moral justification of the policy lies in the consideration that one who has reason to know that land belonging to him is in the possession of another, and neglects, for a considerable period of time, to assert his right thereto, may properly be penalized by his preclusion from thereafter asserting such right. It is, apparently, by reason of the demerit of the true owner, rather than any supposed merit in the person who has acquired wrongful possession of the land, that this possession, if continued for the statutory period, operates to debar the former owner of all right to recover the land.

(2) Devins v. Borough of Bogota, 592 A.2d 199, 202 (N.J. 1991):

First, statutes of limitation allow repose and avoid adjudications based on stale evidence. Second, adverse possession promotes certainty of title, *see* Ballantine, *Title by Adverse Possession*, 32 Harv. L. Rev. 135, 135 (1918), and protects the possessor's reasonable expectations, *see* Note, *Developments in the Law: Statutes of Limitations*, 63 Harv. L. Rev. at 1185. Third, allowing adverse possession promotes active and efficient use of land, *see* R. Posner, Economic Analysis of Law 70-71 (3rd ed. 1986); Netter, Hersch & Manson, *An Economic Analysis of Adverse Possession Statutes*, 6 Int'l Rev. of L. & Econ. 217, 219 (1986), and "tends to serve the public interest by stimulating the expeditious assertion of public claims," Eureka Printing Co. v. Department of Labor & Indus., 122 A.2d 345, 347 (N.J. 1956).

(3) Webster's Real Property Law in North Carolina § 286 (1988), quoted in Marlowe v. Clark, 435 S.E.2d 354, 358 (N.C. Ct. App. 1993):

> If persons who own land do not attend it and leave it fallow, and make no attempt to watch after it and use it, it is deemed better for the community and society in general for the title to be shifted after a specified period of time to those who undertake to use it and make it productive.

Effect of running of the statute of limitations. Suppose that A adversely possesses Blackacre for the period of the statute of limitations, and thereafter vacates the land for a short period of time. During A's absence, the record owner, O, resumes possession of Blackacre. Upon returning, A sues O for possession. If the effect of the running of the statute of limitations is simply to bar O from suing A, then O would win. But if the effect of the running of the statute is to vest title in A, then A wins. Which effect does adverse possession doctrine adopt? *See* Devins v. Borough of Bogota, 592 A.2d 199, 201 (N.J. 1991):

> Adverse possession is a method of acquiring title by possessing property in a specified manner for a statutory period. The expiration of that period bars the owner's right to bring an ejectment action and transfers title from the owner to the possessor. Title passes to the adverse possessor when the owner fails to commence an action for recovery of the property within the specified statutory period. In effect, the acquisition of title by adverse possession is based on the expiration of a statute of limitation.

See also 3 A.L.P. § 15.1 at 757-58.

The relation-back doctrine. Suppose that A satisfies the possession and adversity requirements for the period specified in the statute of limitations. We noted that the effect of A's possession is both to bar O's cause of action and to create title in A. There is no *transfer* of title from O to A, "by operation of law or otherwise." 3 A.L.P. § 15.2 at 760-61. A's title is a new title, created by operation of law. *Id.* When does A's new title begin? Under the relation-back doctrine, A's title is dated back to the time that A's adverse possession started. Suppose that A completes the twenty-one year limitations period in June of the year 2000. In September of that year, O sues for possession, and joins a count for the value of A's use and occupation of the land for that portion of A's possession occurring within six years of the filing of the suit. (Six years is the standard statute of limitations for the bringing of contractual or quasi-contractual claims.) We know that O will lose on the possession claim; what result on the restitution claim? What result on each claim if O had sued in January, 2000? *See* J & M Land Co. v. First Union Nat'l Bank, 742 A.2d 583 (N.J. Super. Ct. App. Div. 1999) (landowner who sues before statute of limitations has run is entitled to recover the value of the adverse possessor's use and occupation of the land for six years preceding suit), *rev'd on other grounds*, 766 A.2d 1110.

Adverse possession as a disfavored doctrine? *See* Grace v. Koch, 692 N.E.2d 1009, 1011-12 (Ohio 1998):

> The court of appeals spoke at length about adverse possession being disfavored. We agree. A successful adverse possession action results in a legal titleholder forfeiting ownership to an adverse holder without compensation. Such a doctrine should be disfavored, and that is why the elements of adverse possession are stringent. *See* 10 Thompson on Real Property (Thomas ed. 1994) § 87.05, at 108 ("there are no equities in favor of a person seeking to acquire property of another by adverse holding").

Should adverse possession be a disfavored doctrine? Does the answer depend on which policies underlying the doctrine one emphasizes? For a recent critique that adverse possession doctrine is "dominated by a prodevelopment nineteenth century ideology that encourages and legitimates economic exploitation — and thus environmental degradation — of wild lands," *see* John G. Sprankling, *An Environmental Critique of Adverse Possession*, 79 Cornell L. Rev. 816, 816 (1994). *See also* Jeffrey Evans Stake, *The Uneasy Case for Adverse Possession*, 89 Geo. L.J. 2419 (2001) (discussing whether adverse possession is a doctrine worth keeping).

Adverse possession: composite doctrine. Adverse possession doctrine is a "synthesis of statutory and decisional law." 16 Powell on Real Property § 91.01[1], at 91-4 (2000). Some statutes of limitations are "bare bones" statutes; they provide simply that a person (O) having a cause of action to recover land must assert it within the specified period or else lose it; see the statute in Marengo Cave v. Ross, below. These statutes say nothing about the title-conferring effect of adverse possession, nor do they specify the widely-followed fivefold requirements that A must satisfy and that you will meet shortly. The requirements are judicial interpolations into the statute, and in general they serve to ensure that adverse possession doctrine accomplishes the purposes that we discussed earlier.

Other statutes specify at least some of the elements and consequences of adverse possession; Miss. Code § 15-1-13, for example, provides as follows (emphases added):

> Ten years' *actual* adverse possession by any person *claiming* to be the owner for that time of any land, uninterruptedly, *continued* for ten years by occupancy, *shall vest in every actual occupant* or possessor of such land *a full and complete title.*

Regardless of the exact terms of the statutes, there is widespread agreement on five requirements of adverse possession. In our study, we focus initially on the four "possession" elements, and then on the "adversity" element.

a. Adverse "Possession"

We begin our study of adverse possession doctrine by focusing on the "possession" complex: the requirements that the adverse possessor's occupancy of O's land be (1) actual, (2) open and notorious, (3) exclusive, and (4) continuous for the period of the statute of limitations. *See, e.g.,* Stansbury v. Heiduck, 961 P.2d 977 (Wyo. 1998); Nazarian v. Pascale, 638 N.Y.S.2d 661 (N.Y. App. Div. 1996); Harkins v. Fuller, 652 A.2d 90 (Me. 1995); 16 Powell on Real Property § 91.01[2]. (Later, we will address what it means to say that possession must be "adverse" to the true owner.)

Very often, the facts that satisfy one of the four requirements of possession will also satisfy the others. If A trespasses on O's land, erects a building, and occupies it for the period of the statute of limitations, A will almost certainly have met the "possession" requirements. But, just as a ray of light can be broken into constituent colors by passing it through a prism, it is sometimes the case that the various facets of possession do not overlap and buttress one another, but must be examined separately and more closely. Here is an example, addressed in one of the principal cases below: for the period of the statute of limitations, A occupies a portion of a cave that is under O's land; A's occupancy is actual, exclusive, and continuous, but is it "open and notorious"? (For one answer, see Marengo Cave Co. v. Ross, below.)

SCHULTZ v. DEW
564 N.W.2d 320 (S.D. 1997)

MILLER, CHIEF JUSTICE.

Thomas C. Dew and Denise A. Dew appeal a summary judgment in favor of the claim of adverse possession made by Mark F. Schultz, Pearl E. Pepka, and Mary T. Carter. We affirm.

FACTS

This case concerns ownership of a strip of land, 45.5 feet by 230 feet, which includes Pepka's driveway and runs across the western edge of Dew's property. The undisputed facts are as follows.

On April 11, 1946, Lawrence and Pearl Pepka obtained by warranty deed the residential property described generally as Outlot 37, and a portion of Outlot 40 of Big Stone City. In 1991, the Pepkas conveyed their interest to their children Bernard L. Pepka and Mary T. Carter, reserving for themselves a life estate. Mary then conveyed her remainder interest to Mark F. Schultz on October 15, 1993 by quitclaim deed. Bernard conveyed his remainder interest, also by quitclaim deed, to Mary on December 6, 1993. All instruments were recorded shortly after their execution.

[The neighboring Dew property had been in the Dew family since 1934; the date on which the defendants Thomas C. Dew and Denise A. Dew, husband and wife, received title is not indicated.]

The Pepkas believed their driveway was on their property and never sought consent of Dew to use the property. Lawrence Pepka put gravel on the driveway and later paved it with asphalt. He mowed the lawn up to a line six feet west of the driveway, believing it to be the boundary between his land and Dew's. In the 1960s, Lawrence and his son Bernard planted seven evergreen trees along the driveway in what is now the disputed area. Bernard received the trees as a gift from the local minister when he was an altar boy. Over the years, they watered the trees, mowed the grass, and maintained the driveway in the disputed area.

They did not erect a fence along what they believed to be the western boundary of their property, nor did they post "no trespassing" signs. A separate gravel road also crosses the property, running roughly parallel to the Pepka driveway, which provides access to the city gravel pit. As a city employee, Lawrence Pepka used the gravel road to the city gravel pit regularly until he retired in 1973.

It appears that over the years the Pepkas and Dews had a neighborly relationship. As the Pepkas advanced in age, Tom Dew helped them maintain their property. He mowed and shoveled snow for them on the disputed strip, and Pearl provided him baked goods in exchange. Also, when Pearl wanted the snow fence put in place near the driveway after her husband passed away, she asked Tom to put it up, which he did.[4]

In 1993, Pearl decided to sell her property. It was at that time [that the] Dews asserted ownership of the disputed property. Despite attempts to resolve the matter by offering to purchase the disputed strip or obtain an easement, the Pepkas could not reach an amicable resolution with the Dews. The Pepkas then sued, claiming adverse possession. The trial court found there were no disputed material facts and granted judgment declaring Pepkas to be the owners of the disputed property. The Dews appeal.

ISSUE

Did the trial court err in granting summary judgment on the basis that the Pepkas had adversely possessed the property for twenty years?

The Dews claim that adverse possession was not established because the Pepkas failed to prove that the disputed strip of land was actually possessed by the Pepkas. They claim the facts do not constitute a substantial enclosure or cultivation of the property sufficient to satisfy the requirements of SDCL 15-3-13. On this basis, the Dews claim that the Pepkas failed to establish entitlement to judgment as a matter of law.

"The burden of proving title by adverse possession is upon the one who asserts it." Cuka v. Jamesville Hutterian Mut. Soc., 294 N.W.2d 419, 422 (S.D. 1980). The relevant law governing adverse possession in this case is found in SDCL 15-3-13. That statute provides:

---

4. In the Dews' brief to this Court, they imply they put up the snow fence as evidence they exercised control over the disputed strip of land. However, Pearl Pepka's deposition testimony does not support that inference.

For the purpose of constituting an adverse possession by a person claiming title not founded upon a written instrument, or judgment, or decree, land shall be deemed to have been possessed and occupied in the following cases only:

(1) Where it has been protected by a substantial inclosure; or

(2) Where it has been usually cultivated or improved.

Since these provisions are stated in the disjunctive, a claim of adverse possession may succeed if the claimant establishes either a substantial enclosure or cultivation or improvement. It is the application of these two subsections to the undisputed facts that is at issue here.

First, the Dews claim there was no substantial enclosure sufficient to establish the necessary intent to claim exclusive right to the property. Admittedly, there was no fence. However, natural barriers may also satisfy the requirement of a substantial enclosure. In *Cuka*, we adopted the rationale of courts in Oregon and Florida, which held:

> "The land claimed in the instant case is unfenced, but because of the water boundary the peninsula can be considered for all practical purposes as enclosed," and "the sufficiency of the enclosure is a question of law for the court." We hold, therefore, that under the facts of this case the James River formed a substantial enclosure around the land, the same as if a fence had in fact been erected around it.

294 N.W.2d at 422. Here, the Pepkas claim that the trees planted along the driveway constitute a barrier or enclosure sufficient to satisfy the statute. Their position has logical appeal. If a naturally occurring river, the boundaries of which are susceptible to change over the years (as was established in *Cuka*), may constitute an enclosure, surely natural elements such as trees which are deliberately placed by the person claiming adverse possession may also serve as a boundary. It might be claimed [that] the tree line is not as complete a barrier or enclosure as a river, but as pointed out in *Cuka*, the James River actually provided access (rather than denied it) during the winter months when the river was frozen. Surely, the enclosure need not be absolutely secure to satisfy subsection (1) of the statute. Further, the trees might actually be more in the nature of an enclosure than the river because, although both can be naturally occurring, the tree line is decidedly a more deliberate enclosure because Pepkas intentionally planted and maintained the trees. As a matter of law, then, the tree line does constitute a substantial enclosure.

Next, the Dews claim that the facts do not support the conclusion that the strip of land was "usually cultivated or improved" by the Pepkas. The Dews claim that:

> a continuous planting or a continuous cultivation would be required but was not the case in this instance where it was simply planting seven trees and then allowing them to grow. Some water may have been put on those trees for a few years, but there is no testimony that "usual cultivation" by any stretch of the imagination was performed.

The Pepkas not only planted the trees in the 1960s and encouraged them to grow, but Pearl testified by deposition that they had cleaned debris out of the strip on which the driveway and gravel road exist, and mowed the strip as part of the yard surrounding their house, garage, and shed regularly since the 1940s or 1950s. Even Tom Dew conceded that the Pepkas had mowed the area until 1988. As a matter of law, mowing the strip of land (in a residential area on the outskirts of town) and planting and maintaining trees on the strip constitutes cultivation.

Similarly, the undisputed facts also establish that the Pepkas improved the land. Pepkas initially improved the driveway to their garage by putting gravel over the surface. Later, the surface was upgraded to asphalt or blacktop. These facts are not disputed. The Dews argue that the blacktop had not been sealed or regularly maintained, and thus was not enough of an improvement to satisfy the statute. However, the fact remains that the strip of land is not unimproved; the driveway and landscaping are plain evidence supporting this conclusion. As a matter of law, the gravel and later asphalt driveway, together with landscaping, constitute an improvement to the land, indicating the Pepkas were in possession of the disputed strip of property.

The judgment is affirmed.

NOTES AND QUESTIONS

1. **The principal case.** Are the requirements of actual, open and notorious, and exclusive possession stated in the South Dakota statute? Are some of those requirements perhaps implicit in the statutory requirements? Do you agree with the court in Schultz v. Dew that the Pepkas satisfied both the enclosure and cultivation parts of the statute? (Must the adverse possessor comply with both parts of the statute?) Suppose the land is not suitable for enclosure, cultivation or improvement — for example, a swamp. Can A adversely possess such land under the South Dakota statute? (Does *Cuka*, discussed in Schultz v. Dew, suggest an answer to this question?)

2. **Actual possession.** Suppose that A asserts ownership of Blackacre, and offers the following evidence of her claim: that she had a survey made of Blackacre, and put boundary markers up; paid taxes on the land; and executed deeds to parts of the land. Are those acts sufficient to satisfy the actual possession requirement? *See* 16 Powell on Real Property § 91.03, at 91-15 ("As a starting point, there must be physical possession of some type in order to meet the actual possession requirement."); 3 A.L.P. § 15.3 at 768; Weiss v. Meyer, 303 N.W.2d 765, 770 (Neb. 1981) (payment of taxes by claimant is not determinative of possession; it is only evidence of possession). What is the purpose of the requirement of actual possession? Does the fact that adverse possession is based on the running of the statute of limitations for the recovery of possession of land suggest one answer?

3. **Acts required of the adverse possessor.** The test for actual possession is "the degree of actual use and enjoyment of the parcel of land involved which the average owner would exercise over similar property under like circumstances." 3 A.L.P. § 15.3 at 765. That standard obviously allows for differences due to topography, character of the land, location, and any other relevant variables. *See* Houston v. U.S. Gypsum Co., 652 F.2d 467, 473 (5th Cir. 1981):

> The character of the disputed property is always crucial in determining what degree of control and what character of possession is required to

establish adverse possession. Thus, wild and undeveloped land that is not readily susceptible to habitation, cultivation, or improvement does not require the same quality of possession as residential or arable land, since the usual acts of ownership are impossible or unreasonable.

See also Ewing's Lessee v. Burnet, 36 U.S. (11 Peters) 41 (1837) (adverse claimant's digging of sand and gravel from unimproved lot in Cincinnati, licensing others to dig, and bringing actions of trespass against parties who dug without his permission, held sufficient to establish adverse possession); Acosta v. Nunez, 5 So. 2d 574, 576-77 (La. Ct. App. 1942) (A and his predecessors "actively and systematically" trapped animals on marshland each two- or three-month season from 1927 to 1941, and paid state and local taxes; held, A acquired title by adverse possession); Davis v. Chadwick, 55 P.3d 1267 (Wyo. 2002) (claimant's acts of grazing up to a half-dozen cattle or horses on disputed property when weather and vegetative conditions permitted were sufficient to constitute adverse possession). *See generally* 16 Powell on Real Property § 91.09.

4. **Extent of actual Possession.** A claims title to a portion of O's land on the basis of adverse possession; A's proof is insufficient to establish actual possession of the entire area claimed by A. Does A acquire title to the portion of O's land as to which A's proof is sufficient, or does the adverse possession doctrine impose an all-or-nothing requirement? *See* Harkins v. Fuller, 652 A.2d 90, 91 (Me. 1995) (holding the adverse possessor acquires title to what he can prove he occupies). Another way to define the extent of the adverse possessor's title is by a deed that gives color of title as discussed in Section 3.c. below.

5. **Taxes.** Unless required by statute, payment of taxes by the adverse possessor is not a requirement of adverse possession under claim of right (although for adverse possession under "color of title," considered in Section 3.c below, where the statutory period is typically shorter, payment of taxes is a common statutory requirement). *Compare* Burlingame v. Marjerrison, 665 P.2d 1136, 1140 (Mont. 1983) (adverse possession claim denied because claimant failed to pay taxes as required by statute), *with* Houston v. U.S. Gypsum Co., 652 F.2d 467, 474 (5th Cir. 1981) (applying Mississippi law) ("Payment of taxes is but one incident of property ownership, and whether an adverse possessor has paid property taxes on the land in controversy is not dispositive of his claim."). When payment of taxes *is* required by statute, that requirement exists in addition to the possession and adversity requirements. *See* LeGro v. Saterdalen, 607 N.W.2d 173, 175 n.2 (Minn. Ct. App. 2000) (considering statute requiring payment of taxes for five successive years, with exceptions for boundary line disputes and lands not assessed for taxation).

6. **Open and notorious.** If A uses O's property in the way that an average owner would under the circumstances, A's possession would usually, in addition to being actual, also be open and notorious. But not always. The next case, a casebook favorite, indicates that it is sometimes necessary to examine an admittedly actual possession to determine whether it is open and notorious.

MARENGO CAVE CO. v. ROSS
10 N.E.2d 917 (Ind. 1937)

ROLL, JUDGE.

Appellee [John Ross] and appellant [Marengo Cave Co.] were the owners of adjoining land in Crawford county, Indiana. The opening to a subterranean cavity known as "Marengo Cave" was located on appellant's land. This cave extended under a considerable portion of appellant's land, and the southeastern portion thereof extended under lands owned by appellee. This action arose out of a dispute as to the ownership of that part of the cave that extended under appellee's land. Appellant was claiming title to all the cave and cavities, including that portion underlying appellee's land. Appellee instituted this action to quiet his title. There was a trial by jury which returned a verdict for the appellee. Appellant filed its motion for a new trial which was overruled by the court, and this is the only error assigned on appeal. Appellant assigns as grounds for a new trial that the verdict of the jury is not sustained by sufficient evidence, and is contrary to law. These are the only grounds urged for a reversal of this cause.

The facts as shown by the record are substantially as follows: In 1883 one Stewart owned the real estate now owned by appellant, and in September of that year some young people who were upon that land discovered what afterwards proved to be the entrance to the cavern since known as Marengo Cave, this entrance being approximately 700 feet from the boundary line between the lands now owned by appellant and appellee, and the only entrance to said cave. Within a week after discovery of the cave, it was explored, and the fact of its existence received wide publicity through newspaper articles, and otherwise. Shortly thereafter the then owner of the real estate upon which the entrance was located took complete possession of the entire cave as now occupied by appellant and used it for exhibition purposes, and began to charge an admission fee to those who desired to enter and view the cave, and to exclude therefrom those who were unwilling to pay for admission. This practice continued from 1883, and during the following years the successive owners of the land upon which the entrance to the cave was located advertised the existence of said cave through newspapers, magazines, posters, and otherwise, in order to attract visitors thereto; also made improvements within the cave, including the building of concrete walks, and concrete steps where there was a difference in elevation of said cavern, widened and heightened portions of passageways; had available and furnished guides, all in order to make the cave more easily accessible to visitors desiring to view the same; and continuously, during all this time, without asking or obtaining consent from any one, but claiming a right so to do, held and possessed said subterranean passages constituting said cave, excluding therefrom the whole world, except such persons as entered after paying admission for the privilege of so doing, or by permission.

Appellee has lived in the vicinity of said cave since 1903, and purchased the real estate which he now owns in 1908. He first visited the cave in 1895, paying an admission fee for the privilege, and has visited said cave several times since. He has never, at any time, occupied or been in possession of any of the subterranean passages or cavities of which the cave consists, and the possession and use of the cave by those who have done so has never interfered with his use and enjoyment of the lands owned by him. For a period of approximately 25 years prior to the time appellee purchased his land, and for a period of 21 years afterwards, exclusive possession of the cave has been held by appellant, its immediate and remote grantors.

The cave, as such, has never been listed for taxation separately from the real estate wherein it is located, and the owners of the respective tracts of land have paid the taxes assessed against said tracts.

A part of said cave at the time of its discovery and exploration extended beneath real estate now owned by appellee, but this fact was not ascertained until the year 1932, when the boundary line between the respective tracts through the cave was established by means of a survey made by a civil engineer pursuant to an order of court entered in this cause. Previous to this survey neither of the parties to this appeal, nor any of their predecessors in title, knew that any part of the cave was in fact beneath the surface of a portion of the land now owned by appellee. Possession of the cave was taken and held by appellant's remote and immediate grantors, improvements made, and control exercised, with the belief on the part of such grantors that the entire cave as it was explored and held was under the surface of lands owned by them. There is no evidence of and dispute as to ownership of the cave, or any portion thereof, prior to the time when in 1929 appellee requested a survey, which was approximately 46 years after discovery of the cave and the exercise of complete dominion thereover by appellant and its predecessors in title.

It is appellant's contention that it has a fee-simple title to all of the cave; that it owns that part underlying appellee's land by adverse possession. Section 2-602, Burns' Ann.St.1933, section 61, provides as follows:

> The following actions shall be commenced within the periods herein prescribed after the cause of action has accrued, and not afterward: . . . Sixth. Upon contracts in writing other than those for the payment of money, on judgments of courts of record, and for the recovery of the possession of real estate, within twenty (20) years.

It will be noted that neither appellee nor his predecessors in title had ever effected a severance of the cave from the surface estate. Therefore the title of the appellee extends from the surface to the center but actual possession is confined to the surface. Appellee and his immediate and remote grantors have been in possession of the land and estate here in question at all times, unless it can be said that the possession of the cave by appellant as shown by the evidence above set out has met all the requirements of the law relating to the acquisition of land by adverse possession. A record title may be defeated by adverse possession. All the authorities agree that, before the owner of the legal title can be deprived of his land by another's possession, through the operation of the statute of limitations, the possession must have been actual, visible, notorious, exclusive, under claim of ownership and hostile to the owner of the legal title and to the world at large, and continuous for the full period prescribed by the statute.

The possession must be actual. It must be conceded that appellant in the operation of the "Marengo Cave" used not only the cavern under its own land but also that part of the cavern that underlaid appellee's land, and assumed dominion over all of it.

The possession must be open and notorious. The mere possession of the land is not enough. It is knowledge, either actual or imputed, of the possession of his lands by another, claiming to own them bona fide and openly, that affects the legal owner thereof. Where there has been no actual notice, it is necessary to show that the possession of the disseisor was so open, notorious, and visible as to warrant the inference that the owner must or should have known of it. It must be so conspicuous that it is generally known and talked of by the public. "It must be manifest to the community." Thus, the appellate court said in Philbin v. Carr, 129 N.E. 19, 29 (Ind. App. 1920), that:

> Where the persons who have passed frequently over and along the premises have been unable to see any evidence of occupancy, evidently the possession has not been of the character required by the rule. The purpose of this requirement is to support the principle that a legal title will not be extinguished on flimsy and uncertain evidence. Hence, where there has been no actual notice, the possession must have been so notorious as to warrant the inference that the owner ought to have known that a stranger was asserting dominion over his land. Insidious, desultory, and fugitive acts will not serve that purpose. To have that effect the possession should be clear and satisfactory, not doubtful and equivocal.

The possession must be exclusive. It is evident that two or more persons cannot hold one tract of land adversely to each other at the same time.

> It is essential that the possession of one who claims adversely must be of such an exclusive character that it will operate as an ouster of the owner of the legal title; because, in the absence of ouster, the legal title draws to itself the constructive possession of the land. A possession which does not amount to an ouster or disseisin is not sufficient.

Philbin v. Carr, 129 N.E. at 28.

The facts as set out above show that appellee and his predecessors in title have been in actual and continuous possession of his real estate since the cave was discovered in 1883. At no time were they aware that any one was trespassing upon their land. No one was claiming to be in possession of appellee's land. It is true that appellant was asserting possession of the Marengo Cave. There would seem to be quite a difference in making claim to the Marengo Cave, and making claim to a portion of appellee's land, even though a portion of the cave extended under appellee's land, when this latter fact was unknown to any one. The evidence on both sides of this case is to the effect that the Marengo Cave was thought to be altogether under the land owned by appellant, and this erroneous supposition was not revealed until a survey was made at the request of appellee and ordered by the court in this case.

It seems to us that the following excerpt from Lewey v. H. C. Frick Coke Co., 31 A. 261, 263 (Pa. 1895), is peculiarly applicable to the situation here presented, inasmuch as we are dealing with an underground cavity. It was stated in [that] case:

> The title of the plaintiff extends from the surface to the center, but actual possession is confined to the surface. Upon the surface he must be held to know all that the most careful observation by himself and his employees could reveal, unless his ignorance is induced by the fraudulent conduct of the wrongdoer. But in the coal veins, deep down in the earth, he cannot see. Neither in person nor by his servants nor employees can he explore their recesses in search for an intruder. If an adjoining owner goes beyond his own boundaries in the course of his mining operations, the owner on whom he enters has no means of knowledge within his reach. Nothing short of an accurate survey of the interior of his neighbor's mines would enable him to ascertain the fact. This would require the services of a competent mining engineer and his assistants, inside the mines of another, which he would have no right to insist upon. To require an owner, under such circumstances, to take notice of a trespass upon his underlying coal at the time it takes place, is to require an impossibility; and to hold that the statute begins to run at the date of the trespass is in most cases to take away the remedy of the injured party before he can know that an injury has been done him. A result so absurd and so unjust ought not to be possible.

> The reason for the distinction exists in the nature of things. The owner of land may be present by himself or his servants on the surface of his possessions, no matter how extensive they may be. He is for this reason held to be constructively present wherever his title extends. He cannot be present in the interior of the earth. No amount of vigilance will enable him to detect the approach of a trespasser who may be working his way through the coal seams underlying adjoining lands. His senses cannot inform him of the encroachment by such trespasser upon the coal that is hidden in the rocks under his feet. He cannot reasonably be held to be constructively present where his presence is, in the nature of things, impossible. He must learn of such a trespass by other means than such as are within his own control, and, until these come within his reach, he is necessarily ignorant of his loss. He cannot reasonably be required to act until knowledge that action is needed is possible to him.

Even though it could be said that appellant's possession has been actual, exclusive, and continuous all these years, we would still be of the opinion that appellee has not lost his land. It has been the uniform rule in equity that the statute of limitation does not begin to run until the injured party discovers, or with reasonable diligence might have discovered, the facts constituting the injury and cause of action. Until then the owner cannot know that his possession has been invaded. Until he has knowledge, or ought to have such knowledge, he is not called upon to act, for he does not know that action in the premises is necessary and the law does not require absurd or impossible things of any one.

Here the possession of appellant was not visible. No one could see below the earth's surface and determine that appellant was trespassing upon appellee's lands. This fact could not be determined by going into the cave. Only by a survey could this fact be made known. The same undisputed facts clearly show that appellant's possession was not notorious. Not even appellant itself nor any of its remote grantors knew that any part of the "Marengo Cave" extended beyond its own boundaries, and they at no time even down to the time appellee instituted this action made any claim to appellee's lands.

Appellee did not know of the trespass of appellant, and had no reasonable means of discovering the fact. It is true that appellant took no active measures to prevent the discovery, except to deny appellee the right to enter the cave for the purpose of making a survey, and disclaiming any use of appellee's lands. But in this case nature has supplied the situation which gives the trespasser the opportunity to occupy the recesses on appellee's land and caused the ignorance of appellee which he now seeks to avail himself. We cannot assent to the doctrine that would enable one to trespass upon another's property through a subterranean passage and under such circumstances that the owner does not know, or by the exercise of reasonable care could not know, of such secret occupancy, for 20 years or more and by so doing obtained a fee-simple title as against the holder of the legal title. The fact that appellee had knowledge that appellant was claiming to be the owner of the Marengo Cave, and advertised it to the general public, was no knowledge to him that it was in possession of appellee's land or any part of it. We are of the opinion that appellant's possession for 20 years or more of that part of "Marengo Cave" underlying appellee's land was not open, notorious, or exclusive, as required by the law applicable to obtaining title to land by adverse possession.

We cannot say that the evidence is not sufficient to support the verdict or that the verdict is contrary to law.

Judgment affirmed.

NOTES AND QUESTIONS

1. **Flying the flag.** *See* Darling v. Ennis, 415 A.2d 228, 230 (Vt. 1980) (the adverse possessor "must unfurl his flag on the land, and keep it flying so that the owner may see, if he will, that an enemy has invaded his dominions and planted his standard of conquest"). The open and notorious requirement is "particularly meaningful when the land concerned is of a type concerning which visible acts of possession are normally few and far between, as, for example, open land, timber lands, or hunting and fishing preserves." 16 Powell on Real Property § 91.04[1], at 91-17.

2. **Open and notorious possession.** Must the record owner actually *see* the adverse possessor's flag, that is, must O actually know that A is asserting a claim against O's land? *See* Wheeling Dollar Bank v. City of Delray Beach, 639 So. 2d 113, 115 (Fla. Dist. Ct. App. 1994) (actual knowledge of adverse claim is not necessary under "open and notorious" requirement); Alaska Nat'l Bank v. Linck, 559 P.2d 1049, 1053 (Alaska 1977) ("possession must be 'notorious,' so that if the owner visits the property, he would be put on notice and be able to assert his rights"); Lawrence v. Town of Concord, 788 N.E.2d 546, 552 (Mass. 2003) (rejecting a requirement of actual knowledge). Why might an actual knowledge reading of the open and notorious requirement be objectionable? If the requirement is that O knows or should have known of A's adverse claim, is the decision in the principal case wrong? How did Ross ultimately discover that the

cave encroached beneath his land? Why couldn't Ross have made this discovery earlier? Are you persuaded by the excerpt from the *H.C. Frick Coke Co.* case, which the court relies upon?

3. **Open and notorious: a different view.** Consider the following view of the open and notorious requirement. How does it differ from the view of that requirement expressed in the principal case?

> The implication that there must be notoriety of possession so as to acquaint the owner thereof before the statute starts to run is quite untenable if possession in fact exists, because the owner has the right to maintain ejectment against such possessor, and the statute starts to run as soon as the cause of action accrues.

> The improvement, use and enjoyment of the property in the way in which the average owner would use it, which the law requires in order to establish possession in fact of land, is expressed in these statements that [possession] must be open and notorious so that people living in the neighborhood, as average persons, would regard the possession as that of an owner. Statements that this is for the purpose of giving the owner notice of the adverse claim have no apparent relevancy or effect in the actual decision of cases.

3 A.L.P. § 15.3, at 769-70. Do you agree? If there is a weakness in the argument, where is it?

4. **Property rules and liability rules.** A highly influential article by Guido Calabresi & A. Douglas Melamed, *Property Rules, Liability Rules, and Inalienability: One View of the Cathedral*, 85 Harv. L. Rev. 1089 (1972), introduced the terms "property rules" and "liability rules" into the literature of property law. An entitlement is protected by a property rule when a transfer of the entitlement can occur only with the owner's consent and at a price determined by the owner; an entitlement is protected by a liability rule when the owner can be forced to sell the entitlement at a price determined by the court. The simplest example of a property right protected by a liability rule is offered by the law of eminent domain (see Chapter 8): the government can expropriate Blackacre even if its owner O wants to retain title; the government must compensate O for the forced taking, but the price will be determined by the court rather than by O. How does the law of adverse possession protect O's interest before the statute of limitations has run? How does it protect A's interest after the statute has run? *See* Thomas W. Merrill, *Property Rules, Liability Rules, and Adverse Possession*, 79 Nw. U. L. Rev. 1122 (1984). In Jacque v. Steenberg Homes, Inc. (section A.1. above), did Jacque invoke a property rule in his dealing with the mobile home seller? If so, should the court have converted it to a liability rule?

5. **Economic analysis.** Although the *Marengo Cave* case is arguably wrong on doctrine (see Note 2 above), might the result (in favor of Ross) be right? The situation seems ripe for bargaining: Marengo Cave Co. has the entrance and the expertise, Ross has a portion of the cave. The Coase Theorem asserts that, in the absence of high transaction costs (costs of bargaining), the court's placement of a legal entitlement in plaintiff or defendant is immaterial; the party who values the entitlement most, measured by willingness to pay, will end up with it. (Economic

analysis assumes rational behavior by the parties.) *See* Ronald Coase, *The Problem of Social Cost*, 3 J.L. & Econ. 1 (1960). If Marengo Cave Co. values the right to use Ross's portion of the cave more than Ross values his right to exclude the company, the parties will strike a bargain allowing the company to use Ross's portion; if Ross values his right to exclude more, the court has placed the entitlement where, in economic terms, it belongs. (The same analysis would apply had the court vested the entitlement in the cave company: Ross would buy back the right to exclude if he valued it more than the company.)

High transaction costs, however, can prevent successful bargaining. One source of high transaction costs arises when the parties are in a relationship that economists call *bilateral monopoly*: no other markets being available, the parties are forced to deal with each other. (Can you see why that might generate high costs of bargaining?) Is that a problem in the cave case? Does Ross have a monopoly on his part of the cave? Does the company have a monopoly on the entrance to the cave?

How might an economically minded court in the cave case respond to the risk of high transaction costs? Could the court deny adverse possession but protect Ross's entitlement with a liability rule? *See* Thomas W. Merrill, *Property Rules, Liability Rules, and Adverse Possession*, 79 Nw. U. L. Rev. 1122 (1984); Noel Elfant, Comment, *Compensation for the Involuntary Transfer of Property Between Private Parties: Application of a Liability Rule to the Law of Adverse Possession*, 79 Nw. U. L. Rev. 758 (1984); *cf.* Mannillo v. Gorski, below.

6. **Restitution of benefit obtained by wrongdoing.** In Edwards v. Lee's Adm'r, 96 S.W.2d 1028 (Ky. 1936), the only entrance to a cave was on defendant's land, but one-third of the cave, including some of the most scenic attractions, was located under plaintiff's land. Defendant knew of the encroachment on plaintiff's land. Plaintiff sued to enjoin defendant's trespass, and for an accounting for the *profits* derived by defendant from using the cave as a commercial venture. The court awarded the plaintiff a proportionate share of the defendant's net profits, measured by the ratio of the footage under plaintiff's land to the total footage of the cave. *See* 1 George E. Palmer, The Law of Restitution § 2.5 (1978) (discussing recovery in restitution for trespass to land); § 2.12 (discussing recovery of profits in a restitutionary action).

7. **Dog-in-the-manger law?** The legal analysis of the courts in *Marengo Cave* and *Edwards* assumes that a surface landowner has a property right to that portion of the cave that lies beneath his land (at least before the statute of limitations runs). *See* Edwards v. Sims, 24 S.W.2d 619, 620-21 (Ky. 1929) (earlier decision by Edwards v. Lee's Adm'r court, holding that plaintiff owned the portion of the cave beneath his land; strong dissent). Is that realistic? Is it better for property law to deal with these cases by awarding the entitlement to the cave to the party who owns the entrance? *See* Prosser and Keeton on the Law of Torts 82 (5th ed. 1984) ("Since it is quite apparent that [the plaintiff in Edwards v. Sims] had no slightest practical possibility of access to the cave, either now or in the future, the decision is dog-in-the-manger law, and can only be characterized as a very bad one."). Who has the better argument, the court in Edwards v. Sims or Prosser?

8. **Exclusive possession.** Possession *means* exclusivity of use; does that suggest what the requirement of "exclusivity" means in adverse possession law? *See* Machholz-Parks v. Suddath, 884 S.W.2d 705, 708 (Mo. Ct. App. 1994):

> The element of "exclusive possession" means that the claimant must show that he held possession of the land for himself, as his own, and not for another. To meet this burden, a claimant must prove that he wholly excluded the owner from possession for the required period. This does not mean that mere sporadic use, temporary presence, or permissive visits by others (including the title holder), will defeat a claim of exclusive possession.

See also Gruebele v. Geringer, 640 N.W.2d 454 (N.D. 2002), reprinted in section 3.b; Thornburg v. Haecker, 502 N.W.2d 434, 439 (Neb. 1993) (adverse possession claim denied; record owner "used the disputed property as a garbage dump throughout the claimed period of adverse possession and also ran a sewer line from their residence which emptied onto the property during the same period in which the [adverse claimant] used the property"); Farella v. Rumney, 649 P.2d 185, 187 (Wyo. 1982) (same; both adverse claimant and record title holder used the disputed area during summer grazing seasons); 16 Powell on Real Property § 91.06.

9. **Continuous possession.** With regard to the requirement that possession be continuous or uninterrupted, the court in Howard v. Kunto, 477 P.2d 210, 213-14 (Wash. App. 1970), a case involving possession of a summer home during the summer only, said:

> We reject the conclusion that summer occupancy only of a summer beach home destroys the continuity of possession required by the statute. It has become firmly established that the requisite possession requires such possession and dominion "as ordinarily marks the conduct of owners in general in holding, managing, and caring for property of like nature and condition." Whalen v. Smith, 167 N.W. 646, 647 (Iowa 1918).

> We hold that occupancy of tract B during the summer months for more than the 10-year period by defendant and his predecessors, together with the continued existence of the improvements on the land and beach area, constituted "uninterrupted" possession within this rule. To hold otherwise is to completely ignore the nature and condition of the property.

> We find such rule fully consonant with the legal writers on the subject. In F. Clark, Law of Surveying and Boundaries, § 561 (3d ed. 1959) at 565: "Continuity of possession may be established although the land is used regularly for only a certain period each year." Further, at 566: "It is not necessary that the occupant should be actually upon the premises continually. If the land is occupied during the period of time during the year it is capable of use, there is sufficient continuity."

What is the relevance of the "continued existence of the improvements on the land" to the court's finding of continuous possession? Does this language suggest a reason for the continuity requirement?

10. **Abandonment.** Continuity can be broken by the actions of A, the adverse possessor. Suppose that A grazes cattle on O's land for three years, then ceases

doing so for two years, then resumes thereafter. The legal rule is straightforward, but application can pose difficulties: if A's nonuse amounts to an abandonment of any claim to O's land, the statute of limitations starts over when A resumes adverse possession after the hiatus. *See* 3 A.L.P. § 15.9. What factors might be relevant in determining whether A abandoned the claim to O's land? *See* United States v. Tobias, 899 F.2d 1375. 1379-80 (4th Cir. 1990) (finding possession was not continuous for the statutory period where claimant continuously possessed the property for 12 years, but then made only occasional repairs and visited sporadically).

11.   **Interruption.**   Continuity can also be broken by the actions of O, the record owner. The owner's filing of suit to recover possession interrupts the continuity of A's possession, if the suit is pursued to a successful conclusion. If the suit is withdrawn, what result? If A wins the suit, what result? *See* 3 A.L.P. at 807-08; 16 Powell on Real Property § 91.07[2]. O's reentry into possession also constitutes an interruption, even if O does not dispossess A. 3 A.L.P. at 809. How would you explain that latter result? If you were advising O, would you recommend reentry, or the filing of a suit, to interrupt A's adverse occupancy? *See* Ortmann v. Dace Homes, Inc., 86 S.W.3d 86, 88-89 (Mo. Ct. App. 2002) ("To halt an adverse possession, the record title owner must re-enter the property under circumstances showing his intention to assert dominion against the adverse user.").

NOTE ON TACKING

Suppose that there are a succession of adverse possessors of O's land. Is the last possessor entitled to the benefit of the adverse possession of those predecessors? The answer is that successive adverse possessions may be "tacked" together to satisfy the total period required for adverse possession, if the requisite doctrinal requirements are met.

While abandonment and interruption serve to disrupt the continuity of A's possession, tacking does the opposite: it facilitates continuous possession by allowing A to claim as his own the time logged by earlier adverse possessors. *See* Enzor v. Minton, 472 S.E.2d 376, 378 (N.C. Ct. App. 1996) ("Tacking has long been accepted as a means of aggregating related periods of adverse possession into one for the purpose of satisfying the statutory minimum period necessary to ripen title in the adverse possessor."). *See generally* 16 Powell on Real Property § 91.10[2].

The doctrinal requirement for tacking is "privity" between each successor in the adverse possessor's chain of possession. *See* Sawyer v. Kendall, 10 Cush. (Mass.) 241, 244 (1852):

> To sustain separate successive disseisins [adverse possessions] as constituting a continuous possession and conferring a title upon the last disseisor, there must have been a privity of estate between the several successive disseisors. To create such privity, there must have existed as between the different disseisors, in regard to the estate of which a title by disseisin is claimed, some such relation as that of ancestor and heir, grantor and grantee, or devisor and devisee. In such cases, the title acquired by disseisin passes by descent, deed or devise.

PROBLEM 1-B. Should the court allow tacking in the following cases? Assume a ten-year statute of limitations unless otherwise indicated.

a. A occupies Blackacre for 5 years beginning in 1990. A dies, survived by an heir B, who enters into possession. When does B acquire title by adverse possession? Suppose B is A's devisee?

b. A occupies Blackacre for 5 years beginning in 1990. In 1995, A deeds Blackacre to B, who goes into possession immediately. When does B acquire title by adverse possession?

c. A occupies for 5 years beginning in 1990, before being ousted by B, who occupies for another 5 years. Does B own the land in 2000? *See* 3 A.L.P. § 15.10 at 816.

d. A occupies Blackacre from 1938 until 1950, then ceases to use it. In 1961, B, with A's permission, moves a camper trailer onto the land. In 1990, the record owner of Blackacre sues B for possession. Under a thirty year limitations statute, who should win the case? *See* Crowell Land & Mineral Corp. v. Funderburk, 692 So. 2d 535 (La. Ct. App. 1997).

e. In the preceding case, suppose that B had gone into possession immediately after A vacated, but without any contact with or consent from A. What is the result if O sues for possession in 1970?

NOTES AND QUESTIONS

1. **Privity of possession.** In Baylor v. Soska, 658 A.2d 743 (Pa. 1995), Hanacek built a garage that encroached onto her neighbor's land in an area 165 feet long and 22 feet wide. Hanacek sold her home, including the garage, to Baylor, who continued to occupy the garage area for the remainder of the period of the statute of limitations. The deed from Hanacek to Baylor purported to convey only the land to which Hanacek held record title; it did not include the garage area. When a dispute arose between Baylor and the neighbor, Baylor sued to quiet title to the garage area, claiming title by adverse possession. The Pennsylvania Supreme Court held that Baylor could not tack his possession onto that of Hanacek's: "[T]he only method by which an adverse possessor may convey the title asserted by adverse possession is to describe in the instrument of conveyance by means minimally acceptable for conveyancing of realty that which is intended to be conveyed." *Baylor*, 658 A.2d at 746. How does this case differ from problem 1-B.b. above?

In Thornburg v. Haecker, 502 N.W.2d 434, 438 (Neb. 1993), the court took a different position:

> In the case before us, the Thornburgs cannot claim that privity exists with their grantors as to the land beyond that described in the deed because of the deed alone. "[T]o permit tacking of successive adverse possession of grantees of an area not within the calls of a deed or contract, but contiguous thereto, among the ultimate facts to be established is the intended and actual transfer and delivery of such area to the grantees as successors in ownership, possession and claim." Rentschler v. Walnofer, 277 N.W.2d 548,

554 (Neb. 1979). "Privity means privity of possession. It is the transfer of possession, not title, which is the essential element." Bryan v. Reifschneider, 150 N.W.2d 900, 904 (Neb. 1967). Here, it is clear that possession of the land up to the fence was maintained for the same purposes and by the same persons for at least a 10-year period, even though legal title changed hands in 1973. The necessary privity between the successive possessive interests therefore existed, and the Thornburgs met the 10-year statutory requirement of possession in 1975.

Accord, Ewald v. Hubbard, 737 So. 2d 858 (La. Ct. App. 1999); Stansbury v. Heiduck, 961 P.2d 977 (Wyo. 1998). In light of the policies underlying the adverse possession doctrine, who has the better view on the issue?

2. **What's the issue?** In Brown v. Gobble, 474 S.E.2d 489 (W. Va. 1996), Blevins, defendant's predecessor in title, occupied a fenced two-foot strip of land along the boundary between the plaintiff's and defendant's land from 1937. In 1978, Blevins sold the land to Fletcher, both parties believing that the sale included the disputed strip. In 1985, the defendant purchased the land from Fletcher, likewise believing that the sale included the disputed strip. The deeds from Blevins to Fletcher and from Fletcher to the defendant did not include the disputed strip. In 1989, plaintiff bought the adjoining land; a survey commissioned by the plaintiff in 1989 showed that the disputed strip was part of the plaintiff's land. In plaintiff's suit for possession, defendant claimed title by adverse possession, and sought to tack his nine-and-a-half year occupancy of the strip onto that of his predecessors to satisfy the ten year statute of limitations. Did defendant misunderstand the issue presented by his case? *See Brown*, 474 S.E.2d at 497 n.11. Is tacking the issue in this case?

3. **Succession on O's side.** Suppose that A enters Blackacre adversely in 1980 and remains continuously thereafter. In 1985, O conveys Blackacre to X. In 1987, X conveys Blackacre to Y. Assuming a ten-year limitations period, who owns Blackacre in 1991? In other words, does O's transfer of title during the limitations period affect the running of the statute of limitations? It does not. If A otherwise satisfies the requirements for adverse possession, A owns the property in 1991. What is the reasoning behind this result?

4. **Sale by O after the running of the statutory period.** Suppose that the record owner (O) sells the land to purchaser P after A has completed adverse possession and during a time when A, being absent, could not be observed in possession by P. Does P get a good title? If not, does P have a claim against O? *See* Wright v. Hinnenkamp, 687 P.2d 163, 165 (Or. Ct. App. 1984) (holding that the adverse possessor owns the land and discussing the purchaser's claim for breach of a deed warranty). Deed warranties are discussed in Chapter 5.

NOTE ON DISABILITY

An owner who suffers from a statutorily specified disability when A goes into possession usually gets the benefit of some form of extension of the statutory period required for A to obtain title. *See generally* 16 Powell on Real Property § 91.10[3]. Suppose that your state has a statutory provision identical to the following Ohio statute:

An action to recover the title to or possession of real property shall be brought within twenty-one years after the cause of action accrued, but if a person entitled to bring the action is, at the time the cause of action accrues, within the age of minority or of unsound mind, the person, after the expiration of twenty-one years from the time the cause of action accrues, may bring the action within ten years after the disability is removed.

Ohio Rev. Code Ann. § 2305.04 (Anderson 1998). (The 1623 English statute on which the Ohio statute is modeled provided that "such person, *notwithstanding* the expiration of twenty-one years" could bring the action within 10 years. *See* 16 Powell on Real Property at 91-74.)

Consider two other ways in which disability problems could be handled. First, a statute might provide that the limitations period is tolled — suspended — if O is disabled when the cause of action arises, and begins to run, in full, when the disability is removed. Second, disabilities could be disregarded entirely; A's entry against a competent and an incompetent owner would be treated the same. What can be said on behalf of each of those approaches? Which among the three approaches you have seen do you prefer?

PROBLEM 1-C. Using each of the three approaches to disability discussed above, when does the statute of limitations run in the following situations? In all cases, assume a 21-year statute, that the age of majority is 18, and that A enters adversely in 1970 (actual, open and notorious, exclusive possession), and remains continuously thereafter.

a. In 1970, Blackacre's owner O is mentally incompetent. O becomes competent in 1992.

b. In 1970, O is mentally incompetent. O dies in 1992.

c. In 1970, O is mentally incompetent. O becomes competent in 1972.

d. In 1970, O is 30 years old. In 1985, O becomes mentally incompetent.

e. In 1970, O is 5 years old.

f. In 1970, O is 5 years old. O dies in 1982. O's heir H is then mentally incompetent.

g. In 1970, O is 15 and mentally incompetent. In 1990, O becomes competent.

b. "Adverse" Possession

The requirement of "adversity" is often restated as a requirement that the claimant's possession be "hostile and under claim of right." *See, e.g.*, Garrett v. Holcomb, 627 N.Y.S.2d 113, 114 (N.Y. App. Div. 1995). Hostility does not mean enmity. *See* Elder v. Smith, 474 S.E.2d 590, 592 (W. Va. 1996) ("hostile" means "adverse," and does not require that the claimant show ill will or malevolence toward the true owner). Moreover, despite the conjunctive "and," hostility and claim of right are generally regarded as synonymous. *See* Fulkerson v. Van Buren, 961 S.W.2d 780, 782 (Ark. Ct. App. 1998) ("[f]or possession to be adverse, it is only necessary that it be hostile in the sense that it is under a claim of right"). Granting that adversity, hostility, and claim of right mean the same thing, our question is, what is that meaning? When will a claimant's possession be treated as lacking the element of adversity? The question is frequently litigated, and as the following materials show, there is some perhaps healthy disagreement, as well as some unfortunate confusion, among the cases.

GRUEBELE v. GERINGER
640 N.W.2d 454 (N.D. 2002)

NEUMANN, JUSTICE.

Lawson Geringer appeals from a judgment quieting title in a piece of property owned by Reinhold and Marion Gruebele. We conclude the trial court did not err in finding Geringer failed to establish ownership of the disputed property under the doctrine of adverse possession, and we affirm.

I

Reinhold and Marion Gruebele and Lawson Geringer own adjacent property in Pettibone, North Dakota. On September 18, 2000, the Gruebeles began an action against Geringer to quiet title to a disputed piece of property. The dispute involves ownership of a garage located on the property line between Geringer's property ("Tract 1") and the Gruebeles' property ("Tract 2"). The parties do not dispute that the garage sits on the property line.

The garage was built in 1959 or 1960 by John and Katie Pleines, the owners of Tract 1 at that time. In 1975, Raymond Guthmiller purchased Tract 1 from the Pleines. During Guthmiller's ownership, it was determined the garage sat on the property line. The owners of Tract 2 at that time, John and Elizabeth Guthmiller, gave Raymond Guthmiller permission to keep the garage at its location, and the two adjacent owners shared the garage. Henry Wallenvein purchased Tract 1 from Raymond Guthmiller in 1977. Wallenvein heard rumors the garage was on the property line after he had purchased the property. The Gruebeles purchased Tract 2 in 1994, and stored gardening tools, a boat, and a pickup in the garage. In 1996, Wallenvein sold Tract 1 to Geringer, as the high bidder over the Gruebeles. At the sale, the Gruebeles removed their gardening tools from the garage and informed Geringer the garage was on the property line and would have to be moved. In November 1998, the Gruebeles wrote to Geringer telling him to move the garage.

A trial was held on February 9, 2001. The court found that the garage was determined to be on the boundary line in 1975, and has been shared by the adjacent owners since then, defeating any claim of adverse possession based on a failure to show exclusive and continuous possession of the property. The trial court concluded the Gruebeles are the rightful owners of Tract 2, and ordered title to the property quieted as to Geringer's claims. Geringer appeals.

II

Geringer argues the trial court erred in finding he did not adversely possess the property because his possession was not exclusive and continuous. Geringer claims an adverse claimant's possession does not have to be absolutely exclusive in order to satisfy the exclusivity condition of adverse possession. Geringer contends that a use permitted by neighborly courtesy does not defeat the exclusivity requirement of adverse possession.

To satisfy the elements for adverse possession, the acts on which the claimant relies must be actual, visible, continuous, notorious, distinct, and hostile, and of such character to unmistakably indicate an assertion of claim of exclusive ownership by the occupant. Torgerson v. Rose, 339 N.W.2d 79, 84 (N.D.1983). To constitute an effective adverse possession, all the elements must be satisfied, and if a single element is wanting, the possession will not confer title. See 2 C.J.S. Adverse Possession § 25, at 678 (1972).

The burden is on the person claiming property by adverse possession to prove the claim by clear and convincing evidence, and every reasonable intendment will be made in favor of the true owner. There exists a statutory presumption of possession by the record titleholder under N.D.C.C. § 28-01-07, which provides:

> 28-01-07. Presumption against adverse possession of real estate. In every action for the recovery of real property or for the possession thereof, the person establishing a legal title to the premises must be presumed to have been possessed thereof within the time required by law, and the occupation of such premises by any other person must be deemed to have been under and in subordination to the legal title, unless it appears that such premises have been held and possessed adversely to such legal title for twenty years before the commencement of such action.

Under N.D.C.C. § 28-01-07, Geringer had the burden to prove the owners of Tract 1 adversely possessed the garage for a continuous twenty-year period. The trial court found that Raymond Guthmiller purchased Tract 1 in 1975. During Raymond Guthmiller's ownership of Tract 1, it was determined by the owners that the garage sat on the property line. The trial court found that the owners of Tract 2 at that time, John and Elizabeth Guthmiller, gave Raymond Guthmiller permission to keep the garage at its location, and the parties shared the garage.

To be entitled to a decree of adverse possession, the property of a legal title-owner must be held by hostile possession for the statutorily required time. When possession begins by the true owner granting permission to the claimant, such possession cannot acquire the character of adverse possession until the claimant rebuts the presumption of subservience. 16 Richard R. Powell, Powell on Real Property § 91.05[5][a], at 91-30 (2001). In *Torgerson*, this Court explained:

> Possession, which is permissive in its inception can become adverse only where there is a disclaimer of the true owner's title, or there are acts of such an unequivocal nature on the part of the user, that notice of the hostile character of the possession is brought home to the record owner.

339 N.W.2d at 84. To be effective as a means of acquiring title, an adverse claimant's exclusive possession must be such as to operate as an ouster or disseisin of the owner of legal title, and the owner must be wholly excluded from possession by the claimant. 2 C.J.S. Adverse Possession § 55, at 728 (1972). There was no evidence in the record to indicate any act on Raymond Guthmiller's part to establish hostile and exclusive possession of the garage. Raymond Guthmiller's own testimony indicated shared possession with John and Elizabeth Guthmiller. He testified about a conversation with John Guthmiller in which John stated Raymond could leave the garage on John's property for the time being. Raymond Guthmiller also testified the owners each had their own part of the garage. The evidence supports the trial court's finding that shared possession of the garage existed during Raymond Guthmiller's ownership.

Henry Wallenvein purchased Tract 1 from Raymond Guthmiller in 1977. The trial court found Henry Wallenvein knew the garage was located on the property line after he purchased Tract 1. The trial court also found Wallenvein and the Gruebeles shared the garage throughout Wallenvein's ownership of Tract 1. There was no evidence to indicate Wallenvein possessed the property adversely against the owners of Tract 2. There was also no evidence presented of a hostile act, which is required to overcome the heavy burden created by the permissive use granted by the owners. Exclusive possession, for purposes of establishing title through adverse possession, requires the exclusion of the record owner and third parties as well. 16 Powell, *supra*, § 91.06, at 91-38. The trial court found the Gruebeles stored gardening tools, a boat, and a pickup in the garage during Wallenvein's possession of Tract 1. The evidence presented at trial supports the trial court's finding that shared possession of the garage existed during Wallenvein's ownership of Tract 1.

The first hostile and exclusive act that might rebut the presumption of permissive use was by Geringer after he purchased Tract 1 in December 1996. After Geringer's purchase of Tract 1, the Gruebeles removed their tools stored in the garage, and Geringer maintained exclusive possession of the garage.

While Geringer's acts may satisfy the hostile and exclusive requirements for adverse possession, his claim fails to comply with the twenty-year requirement under N.D.C.C. § 28-01-07. When an original entry is permissive and not adverse, the time will not begin to run against the true owner until the adverse claimant establishes exclusive right in himself. The evidence presented showed shared possession of the garage by Wallenvein and the Gruebeles in 1996. Under these facts, the trial court correctly concluded Geringer's claim failed to trace a period of twenty years where Geringer or his predecessors maintained adverse possession of the property the garage encroaches upon.

Geringer failed to meet his burden to prove adverse possession by clear and convincing evidence. When a claimant fails to prove legal title by adverse possession, the presumption of possession by the legal owner applies. The trial court correctly found the Gruebeles were the rightful owners of the disputed property, and properly quieted title as to any claim by Geringer.

III

Under our standard of review, the trial court did not clearly err in finding a lack of exclusive and continuous possession. We conclude the trial court's findings of fact are supported by the evidence. The judgment is affirmed.

NOTES AND QUESTIONS

1. **Nonconsensual occupancy.** All authorities agree with the principal case that adversity means that the occupant must possess without the permission of the owner; a consensual occupancy is thus not adverse. *See, e.g.,* Grace v. Koch, 692 N.E.2d 1009, 1013 (Ohio 1998) ("The Kochs asked for the Graces' permission before proceeding to mow the [disputed] strip. Mr. Koch conceded that he knew that the strip belonged to Grace and that he never would have used it without permission."); Dickerson Pond Sewage Works Corp. v. Valeria Associates, 647 N.Y.S.2d 268, 270 (N.Y. App. Div. 1996) ("When permission can be implied from the beginning, adverse possession will not arise until there is a distinct assertion of a claim of right hostile to the owner."); Dugan v. Jensen, 510 N.W.2d 313, 313 (Neb. 1994) ("If the railroad's initial use was permissive, the railroad could not have acquired title to the property by adverse possession.").

2. **Tenants, etc.** When the would-be adverse possessor begins occupancy under an agreement with the landowner, the statute of limitations does not begin to run against the owner until the possessor first repudiates the title of the owner. *See* 3 A.L.P. § 15.6 (tenants and licensees); § 15.7 (cotenants and mortgagees). *See also* Walker v. Walker, 739 So. 2d 3 (Ala. 1999) (tenants in common); King Ranch, Inc. v. Chapman, 118 S.W.3d 742 (Tex. 2003) (19th century consent judgment obtained by Richard King against his non-possessory cotenants constituted an ouster that started running of statute of limitations against cotenants). What is the basis for this common law rule? What problems does the rule create?

3. **Adversity and exclusivity.** The court in the principal case discusses both the exclusivity and the adversity of the adverse possessor's use of O's land. What is the relationship between those doctrines? If O does not use the land herself, but consents to A's possession, is A's use exclusive? Is A's use adverse? If O uses the land regularly with A, does the lack of exclusivity of A's possession perhaps indicate an implied permission from O to use the land?

4. **Presumptions, proof and persuasion.** The concept of "burden of proof" consists of two elements: the responsibility of coming forward with evidence — the burden of production — and the responsibility for establishing one's case according to the applicable standard of proof (preponderance of evidence, clear and convincing evidence, proof beyond a reasonable doubt) — the burden of persuasion. In adverse possession disputes, as illustrated by the principal case, some states recognize a presumption that A's possession of O's land is consensual (not adverse). *See* Lawrence v. Town of Concord, 788 N.E.2d 546, 551 (Mass. 2003). In those states, A must initially come forward with evidence on all five of the adverse possession elements; A's failure to do so on any of those elements could result in a directed verdict for O. If A satisfies the burden of production, the burden of production shifts to O, who must introduce evidence to negate the elements claimed by A. After all evidence is in, the risk that the evidence as a

whole does not prove adverse possession according to the applicable standard of proof is on A. Other states take a different approach, saying that if A establishes the possession elements, a presumption arises that A's possession was adverse (nonconsensual). *See* Gillett v. White, 153 P.3d 911 (Wyo. 2007). Whether that means that O thereafter bears the burdens of both production and persuasion on the issue of adversity is not always clear. For a discussion of these matters, see 4 Herbert Thorndike Tiffany, The Law of Real Property § 1144, at 766 (3d ed. 1975).

5. **Sufficiency of evidence.** Of the three standards of proof (preponderance of evidence, clear and convincing evidence, proof beyond a reasonable doubt), which should apply to an adverse possessor's claim? *See* Brown v. Gobble, 474 S.E.2d 489, 493-95 (W. Va. 1996):

> There is a minority view that a preponderance of the evidence is sufficient to establish adverse possession. There is little reason given for adopting this standard other than it is the usual rule in civil cases. On the other hand, the view adopted by a majority of jurisdictions is that adverse possession must be shown by clear and convincing evidence.

> It is appropriate, in our opinion, that adverse possession be proved by a more stringent standard than a mere preponderance of the evidence. [O]n policy grounds there is sound and reasonable justification for the majority view. The function of a standard of proof is to "instruct the factfinder concerning the degree of confidence our society thinks he [or she] should have in the correctness of a factual conclusion for a particular kind of adjudication." In re Winship, 397 U.S. 358, 370 (1970) (Harlan, J. concurring). "The standard [of proof] serves to allocate the risk of error between the litigants and to indicate the relative importance attached to the ultimate decision." Addington v. Texas, 441 U.S. 418, 423 (1979).

> While the preponderance standard applies across the board in civil cases, a higher standard is needed where fairness and equity require more persuasive proof. In Wheeling Dollar Sav. & Trust Co. v. Singer, 250 S.E.2d 369, 374 (W. Va. 1978), this Court stated that "clear and convincing" is the measure or degree of proof that will produce in the mind of the factfinder a firm belief or conviction as to the allegations sought to be established. It should be the highest possible standard of civil proof. The interest at stake in an adverse possession claim is not the mere loss of money as is the case in the normal civil proceedings. Rather, it often involves the loss of a homestead, a family farm or other property associated with traditional family and societal values. To this extent, most courts have used the clear and convincing standard to protect these important property interests. Adopting the clear and convincing standard of proof is more than a mere academic exercise. At a minimum, it reflects the value society places on the rights and interests being asserted.

Accord, Grace v. Koch, 692 N.E.2d 1009, 1012 nn.2 & 3 (citing authority from thirty-three states requiring the clear and convincing standard, and authority from fourteen states requiring only the preponderance standard).

6. **Offer to Buy by A.** Prior to the running of the statute of limitations, the adverse possessor offers to buy the land from the record owner. Should the offer

have any effect on A's adverse possession claim, and if so, on which element of that claim? *See* Garrett v. Holcomb, 627 N.Y.S.2d 113 (N.Y. App. Div. 1995) (claimant failed to establish claim of right "since he conceded that title remained with a record owner prior to the running of the 10-year statutory period" by making two offers to buy the land from the record owner); Provenzano v. Provenzano, 870 A.2d 1085, 1089-1090 (Conn. App. Ct. 2005) (claimants' offer to purchase a lot in its entirety was not acknowledgment of record owner's superior title to disputed portion of the lot that would interrupt adverse possession). Does it matter whether A requests a quitclaim deed from O? (The grantor in a quitclaim deed transfers the title, if any, that the grantor has, without warranting that the grantor has any title.) Compare the majority and dissent in Myers v. Beam, 713 A.2d 61, 62-63 (Pa. 1998) (denying title by adverse possession on the basis that the claimant sought a quitclaim deed from the record owner during the statutory period) (dissent: "While an offer to acquire legal title may constitute recognition of superior right in another and support the inference that use of the property is by permission, an attempt to secure a quitclaim deed does not, in my view, support a similar inference."). *See also* Schultz v. Dew, 564 N.W.2d 320 (S.D. 1997), cited in the following note.

7.   **Disclaimer by A.**   Prior to the running of the statute of limitations, A publicly acknowledges that A lacks title to the land he occupies. Does (should) that disclaimer prevent A from acquiring title by adverse possession? *See* Patterson v. Reigle, 4 Pa. 201 (1846):

> No declaration by [the two adverse possessors] was inconsistent with an intention to hold the land as long as they could, or evincive of a design to give it up before they should be compelled to do so by the appearance of a claimant whom they could not resist. They were conscious they had no title themselves, and they said so; they were conscious they could not resist him who had it, and they said so; but they did not say that they meant not to acquire a title to it for themselves. Whatever they did say, was predicated on the expected appearance of the owner while he continued to be so; for they certainly did not mean to purchase the land from any one else. Shingledecker himself testified that he and Reigle settled on the land "to hold it till a better owner came for it;" but the holder of the title would lose it, and cease to be the better owner at the end of one-and-twenty years. They intended to hold adversely to all the world till the title should be produced to them, and consequently as adversely to the owner before he disclosed himself. The sum of the evidence is that they entered to hold the land as long as they could; and they consequently gained the title to it by the statute of limitations.

Is it significant whether O knows or should know about the disclaimer? *See* 3 A.L.P. § 15.4, at 774-776 (disclaimer is properly based on estoppel of A).

How, if at all, does a disclaimer differ from an offer by A to purchase the land from O, discussed in the preceding Note? *See* Schultz v. Dew, 564 N.W.2d 320, 324-325 (S.D. 1997) (majority: "a disclaimer exists only if it is a knowing relinquishment of an asserted property right and a single act, standing alone, is insufficient to establish a disclaimer"; adverse possessor's "attempts to settle the matter short of litigation can hardly be said" to be a disclaimer) (Saber, J., concurring in the result: claimant's offer to buy during the statutory period "constitutes a disclaimer of title and terminates the running of the requisite twenty-year holding period"). Whether they are related or not, should an offer to buy or a disclaimer that occurs after the statute of limitations has run have any significance? *See generally* William Hayden Spitler, Case Note, *Over a Century of Doubt and Confusion: Adverse Possession in Arkansas, Intent to Hold Adversely and Recognition of Superior Title in* Fulkerson v. Van Buren, 53 Ark. L. Rev. 459 (2000).

8. **A mental element?** Adversity requires that A's occupancy occur without O's consent. The question explored in the remainder of this section is whether the requirement of adversity means anything *more* than a nonconsensual occupancy, specifically, whether it includes any particular state of mind or subjective intent on the part of the adverse possessor.

MANNILLO v. GORSKI
255 A.2d 258 (N.J. 1969)

HANEMAN, J.

Plaintiffs filed a complaint in the Chancery Division seeking a mandatory and prohibitory injunction against an alleged trespass upon their lands. Defendant counterclaimed for a declaratory judgment which would adjudicate that she had gained title to the disputed premises by adverse possession under N.J.S. 2A:14-6, N.J.S.A., which provides:

> Every person having any right or title of entry into real estate shall make such entry within 20 years next after the accrual of such right or title of entry, or be barred therefrom thereafter.

After plenary trial, judgment was entered for plaintiffs. Mannillo v. Gorski, 241 A.2d 276 (N.J. Super. Ct. Ch. Div. 1968). Defendant appealed to the Appellate Division. Before argument there, this Court granted defendant's motion for certification.

The facts are as follows: In 1946, defendant and her husband entered into possession of premises in Keansburg known as Lot No. 1007 in Block 42, under an agreement to purchase. Upon compliance with the terms of said agreement, the seller conveyed said lands to them on April 16, 1952. Defendant's husband thereafter died. The property consisted of a rectangular lot with a frontage of 25 feet and a depth of 100 feet. Plaintiffs are the owners of the adjacent Lot 1008 in Block 42 of like dimensions, to which they acquired title in 1953.

In the summer of 1946 Chester Gorski, one of the defendant's sons, made certain additions and changes to the defendant's house. He extended two rooms at the rear of the structure, enclosed a screened porch on the front, and put a concrete platform with steps on the west side thereof for use in connection with a side door. These steps were built to replace existing wooden steps. In addition, a concrete walk was installed from the steps to the end of the house. In 1953, defendant raised the house. In order to compensate for the resulting added height from the ground, she modified the design of the steps by extending them toward both the front and the rear of the property. She did not change their width.

Defendant admits that the steps and concrete walk encroach upon plaintiffs' lands to the extent of 15 inches. She contends, however, that she has title to said land by adverse possession. Plaintiffs assert contrawise that defendant did not obtain title by adverse possession as her possession was not of the requisite hostile nature. They argue that to establish title by adverse possession, the entry into and continuance of possession must be accompanied by an intention to invade the rights of another in the lands, i.e., a knowing wrongful taking. They assert that, as defendant's encroachment was not accompanied by an intention to invade plaintiffs' rights in the land, but rather by the mistaken belief that she owned the land, and that therefore an essential requisite to establish title by adverse possession, i.e., an intentional tortious taking, is lacking.

The trial court concluded that defendant had clearly and convincingly proved that her possession of the 15-inch encroachment had existed for more than 20 years before the institution of this suit and that such possession was "exclusive, continuous, uninterrupted, visible, notorious and against the right and interest of the true owner." There is ample evidence to sustain this finding except as to its visible and notorious nature, of which more hereafter. However, the judge felt impelled by existing New Jersey case law, holding as argued by plaintiffs above, to deny defendant's claim and entered judgment for plaintiffs. The first issue before this Court is, therefore, whether an entry and continuance of possession under the mistaken belief that the possessor has title to the lands involved, exhibits the requisite hostile possession to sustain the obtaining of title by adverse possession.

The first detailed statement and acceptance by our then highest court, of the principle that possession as an element of title by adverse possession cannot be bottomed on mistake, is found in Folkman v. Myers, 115 A. 615 (N.J. 1921). In [that case], the former Court of Errors and Appeals aligned this state with that branch of a dichotomy which traces its genesis to Preble v. Maine Cent. R. Co., 27 A. 149 (Me. 1893), and has become known as the Maine doctrine. In *Preble*, the court said at p. 150:

> There is every presumption that the occupancy is in subordination to the true title, and, if the possession is claimed to be adverse, the act of the wrongdoer must be strictly construed, and the character of the possession clearly shown. "The intention of the possessor to claim adversely," says Mellen, C.J., in Ross v. Gould, (5 Me. 204), "is an essential ingredient in disseisin." And in Worcester v. Lord, (56 Me. 266) the court says: "To make a disseisin in fact, there must be an intention on the part of the party assuming possession to assert title in himself." Indeed, the authorities all agree that this intention of the occupant to claim the ownership of land not embraced in his title is a necessary element of adverse possession; and in case of occupancy by mistake beyond a line capable of being ascertained this intention to claim title to the extent of the occupancy must appear to be absolute, and not conditional; otherwise the possession will not be deemed adverse to the true owner. It must be an intention to claim title to all land within a certain boundary on the face of the earth, whether it shall eventually be found to be the correct one or not. If, for instance, one in ignorance of his actual boundaries takes and holds possession by mistake up to a certain fence beyond his limits, upon the claim and in the belief that

it is the true line, with the intention to claim title, and thus, if necessary, to acquire "title by possession" up to that fence, such possession, having the requisite duration and continuity, will ripen into title.

If, on the other hand, a party through ignorance, inadvertence, or mistake occupies up to a given fence beyond his actual boundary, because he believes it to be the true line, but has no intention to claim title to that extent if it should be ascertained that the fence was on his neighbor's land, an indispensable element of adverse possession is wanting. In such a case the intent to claim title exists only upon the condition that the fence is on the true line. The intention is not absolute, but provisional, and the possession is not adverse.

This thesis, it is evident, rewards the possessor who entered with a premeditated and predesigned "hostility" — the intentional wrongdoer — and disfavors an honest, mistaken entrant. 3 American Law of Property (Casner ed. 1952), § 104, pp. 773, 785; Bordwell, *Disseisin and Adverse Possession*, 33 Yale L.J. 1, 154 (1923); Darling, *Adverse Possession in Boundary Cases*, 19 Ore. L. Rev. 117 (1940); Sternberg, *The Element of Hostility in Adverse Possession*, 6 Temp. L.Q. 206 (1932); Annotation, Adverse possession involving ignorance or mistake as to boundaries — modern views, 80 A.L.R.2d 1171 (1961).

The other branch of the dichotomy relies upon French v. Pearce, 8 Conn. 439 (Conn. 1831). The court said in *Pearce* on the question of the subjective hostility of a possessor:

> Into the recesses of his (the adverse claimant's) mind, his motives or purposes, his guilt or innocence, no enquiry is made. The very nature of the act (entry and possession) is an assertion of his own title, and the denial of the title of all others. It matters not that the possessor was mistaken, and had he been better informed, would not have entered on the land.

8 Conn. at 442, 445-446.

The Maine doctrine has been the subject of much criticism in requiring a knowing wrongful taking. The criticism of the Maine [doctrine] and the justification of the Connecticut branch of the dichotomy is well stated in 6 Powell [on] Real Property (1969), pp. 725-28:

> Do the facts of his possession, and of his conduct as if he were the owner, make immaterial his mistake, or does such a mistake prevent the existence of the prerequisite claim of right? The leading case holding the mistake to be of no importance was French v. Pearce, decided in Connecticut in 1831. This viewpoint has gained increasingly widespread acceptance. The more subjectively oriented view regards the "mistake" as necessarily preventing the existence of the required claim of right. The leading case on this position is Preble v. Maine Central R.R., decided in 1893. This position is still followed in a few states. It has been strongly criticized as unsound historically, inexpedient practically, and as resulting in better treatment for a ruthless wrongdoer than for the honest landowner. On the whole the law is simplified, in the direction of real justice, by a following of the Connecticut leadership on this point.

Again, 4 Tiffany, Real Property (3d ed. 1939), § 1159, pp. 474-475, criticizes the employment of mistake as negating hostility as follows:

> [T]he introduction of the element of mistake in the discussion of the question of adverse possession is, it is submitted, unnecessary and undesirable. In no case except in that of a mistake as to boundary has the element of mistake been regarded as having any significance, and there is no reason for attributing greater weight thereto when the mistake is as to the proper location of a boundary than when it is a mistake as to the title to all the land wrongfully possessed. And to introduce the element of mistake, and then limit its significance by an inquiry as to the intention which the possessor may have as to his course of action in case there should be a mistake, an intention which has ordinarily no existence whatsoever, is calculated only to cause confusion without, it is conceived, any compensating advantage.

We are in accord with the criticism of the Maine doctrine and favor the Connecticut doctrine for the above quoted reasons. As far as can be seen, overruling the former rule will not result in undermining any of the values which stare decisis is intended to foster. The theory of reliance, a cornerstone of stare decisis, is not here apt, as the problem is which of two mistaken parties is entitled to land. Realistically, the true owner does not rely upon entry of the possessor by mistake as a reason for not seeking to recover possession. Whether or not the entry is caused by mistake or intent, the same result eventuates — the true owner is ousted from possession. In either event his neglect to seek recovery of possession, within the requisite time, is in all probability the result of a lack of knowledge that he is being deprived of possession of lands to which he has title.

Accordingly, we discard the requirement that the entry and continued possession must be accompanied by a knowing intentional hostility and hold that any entry and possession for the required time which is exclusive, continuous, uninterrupted, visible and notorious, even though under mistaken claim of title, is sufficient to support a claim of title by adverse possession.

However, this conclusion is not dispositive of the matter sub judice. Of equal importance under the present factual complex, is the question of whether defendant's acts meet the necessary standard of "open and notorious" possession. In 4 Tiffany, *supra* (Supp.1969, at 291), the character of possession for that purpose, is stated to be as follows:

> [I]t must be public and based on physical facts, including known and visible lines and boundaries. Acts of dominion over the land must be so open and notorious as to put an ordinarily prudent person on notice that the land is in actual possession of another. Hence, title may never be acquired by mere possession, however long continued, which is surreptitious or secret or which is not such as will give unmistakable notice of the nature of the occupant's claim.

Generally, where possession of the land is clear and unequivocal and to such an extent as to be immediately visible, the owner may be presumed to have knowledge of the adverse occupancy. In Foulke v. Bond, 41 N.J.L. 527, 545 (N.J. 1879), the court said:

> Notoriety of the adverse claim under which possession is held, is a necessary constituent of title by adverse possession, and therefore the occupation or possession must be of that nature that the real owner is *presumed to have known* that there was a possession adverse to his title, under which it was intended to make title against him.

(Emphasis supplied.) However, when the encroachment of an adjoining owner is of a small area and the fact of an intrusion is not clearly and self-evidently apparent to the naked eye but requires an on-site survey for certain disclosure as in urban sections where the division line is only infrequently delineated by any monuments, natural or artificial, such a presumption is fallacious and unjustified. The precise location of the dividing line is then ordinarily unknown to either adjacent owner and there is nothing on the land itself to show by visual observation that a hedge, fence, wall or other structure encroaches on the neighboring land to a minor extent. Therefore, to permit a presumption of notice to arise in the case of minor border encroachments not exceeding several feet would fly in the face of reality and require the true owner to be on constant alert for possible small encroachments. The only method of certain determination would be by obtaining a survey each time the adjacent owner undertook any improvement at or near the boundary, and this would place an undue and inequitable burden upon the true owner. Accordingly we hereby hold that no presumption of knowledge arises from a minor encroachment along a common boundary. In such a case, only where the true owner has actual knowledge thereof may it be said that the possession is open and notorious.

It is conceivable that the application of the foregoing rule may in some cases result in undue hardship to the adverse possessor who under an innocent and mistaken belief of title has undertaken an extensive improvement which to some extent encroaches on an adjoining property. In that event the situation falls within the category of those cases of which Riggle v. Skill, 74 A.2d 424 (Ch. Div. 1950), *affirmed* 81 A.2d 364 (N.J. 1951) is typical and equity may furnish relief. Then, if the innocent trespasser of a small portion of land adjoining a boundary line cannot without great expense remove or eliminate the encroachment, or such removal or elimination is impractical or could be accomplished only with great hardship, the true owner may be forced to convey the land so occupied upon payment of the fair value thereof without regard to whether the true owner had notice of the encroachment at its inception. Of course, such a result should eventuate only under appropriate circumstances and where no serious damage would be done to the remaining land as, for instance, by rendering the balance of the parcel unusable or no longer capable of being built upon by reason of zoning or other restrictions.

We remand the case for trial of the issues (1) whether the true owner had actual knowledge of the encroachment, (2) if not, whether plaintiffs should be obliged to convey the disputed tract to defendant, and (3) if the answer to the latter question is in the affirmative, what consideration should be paid for the conveyance. The remand, of course, contemplates further discovery and a new pretrial.

NOTES AND QUESTIONS

1. **Significance of mistaken possession.** When A encroaches across a boundary line, A might know it is a trespass; in cases of mistake as to the location of the boundary, A doesn't know. Under the Connecticut rule, is A's mistake relevant to the question whether A possesses adversely? Is A's mistake relevant under the Maine rule? Suppose A testifies on cross-examination as follows:

> Q. In the building of that fence, you were not going to try to get or you were not claiming property that you did not have a deed for, were you?
>
> A. I was merely building a fence where —
>
> Q. You were not trying to claim property that you did not have a deed for, were you?
>
> A. I was only — are you saying that I —
>
> Q. I asked you a question.
>
> A. I don't know what you want me to say.
>
> Q. Mr. Norman, I am just asking you a question. You did not intend to claim some property that you did not have a deed for but you were just going to build a fence, is that right?
>
> A. Yes, I guess that would be right.

Norman v. Allison, 775 S.W.2d 568, 571 (Mo. Ct. App. 1989). Result under the Connecticut rule? Under the Maine rule?

2. **Counseling.** Think of the interviewing and counseling issues raised by the Maine rule. In the initial interview with your client, what information might you receive that could seriously compromise your ability to present A's case at trial, or in a deposition? Do you need to advise A of the law before you get A's story? Is it ethical to do that?

3. **Comparisons.** What are the advantages of the Connecticut rule over the Maine rule? Whatever else you think of, consider the logic of the Maine rule. Even if O sues after the statutory period, O wins if A, because of mistake, lacked the requisite intent to possess adversely. If A lacks adversity, doesn't that imply that O had no cause of action before the statute ran? If O did have a cause of action before the statute ran, how is it that the statute didn't cut it off after the requisite period of occupancy by A? *See* 3 A.L.P. § 15.5, at 788-89. (Note that the A.L.P. argument is based on the same idea — that adverse possession is based solely on the running of the statute of limitations — provoking the A.L.P. critique of the open and notorious requirement. Is the A.L.P. critique perhaps more persuasive here than it was earlier?) *But see* Lee Anne Fennel, *Efficient Trespass: The Case for "Bad Faith" Adverse Possession*, 100 Nw. U. L. Rev. 1037, 1095 (2006) (arguing in favor of a bad faith requirement for adverse possession in "a dramatic break with the carefully articulated views of leading property scholars, as well as with the modern approaches of courts").

4. **"The intention and not the mistake" is the test.** What intention must the adverse possessor have under the Connecticut rule? *See* 3 A.L.P. § 15.4, at 774 (claimant "must show an intention to appropriate and use the land as his own");

Brown v. Gobble, 474 S.E.2d 489, 496 n.9 (W. Va. 1996) ("the intention [to possess as owner] and not the mistake is the test by which the character of the possession is determined"); Boyle v. Burk, 749 S.W.2d 264, 266 (Tex. App. 1988) ("claim of right" means "that the entry of the claimant must be with the intent to claim the land as his own, to hold it for himself"). Won't that intention be present in almost all cases?

5. **Doctrine.**   Can you see any basis for the Maine rule in the requirement that adverse possession be "hostile"? In Maine rule states, is A required to occupy in bad faith? Does the Connecticut rule require that A be in good faith?

6. **Maine on the Maine rule.**   In 1993, Maine adopted the following statute:

> § 810-A. Mistake of boundary line establishes hostility
>
> If a person takes possession of land by mistake as to the location of the true boundary line and possession of the land in dispute is open and notorious, under claim of right, and continuous for the statutory period, the hostile nature of the claim is established and no further evidence of the knowledge or intention of the person in possession is required.

Is Maine still a Maine rule state?

7. **Another issue — open and notorious.**   Although the would-be adverse possessor in *Mannillo* wins on the intent requirement, she may lose on the open and notorious requirement. What does the court suggest is the meaning of that requirement in cases of a minor encroachment? Do you agree?

8. **Remedies, and another case.**   In Elder v. Smith, 474 S.E.2d 590, 592 (W. Va. 1996), the court agreed with Mannillo v. Gorski that the possessor's mistake as to the true boundary does not vitiate the requirement of adversity. In that case, Mrs. Elder's house encroached four inches onto her neighbor's lot. The court did not address the open and notorious issue, but if Mrs. Elder's possession is not open and notorious, what result? She can't very well cut off four inches of her house, can she? How does the New Jersey court in *Mannillo* suggest that the question might be resolved? Does the New Jersey court protect the record owner's title by a liability rule or a property rule?

CARPENTER v. RUPERTO
315 N.W.2d 782 (Iowa 1982)

McCormick, Justice.

Plaintiff Virginia Carpenter appeals from an adverse decree in her action to quiet title to land adjacent to her residential premises based on a theory of adverse possession. Defendants Charles L. Ruperto, Edith C. Ruperto, and Tom McCormick cross-appeal from a portion of the decree awarding plaintiff limited relief on equitable grounds. We affirm on the merits of the appeal and dismiss the cross-appeal for want of jurisdiction.

The determinative question on the appeal is whether the trial court misinterpreted the law governing the claim of right element in finding plaintiff failed to carry her burden of proof. The determinative question on the cross-appeal is whether it was timely.

Plaintiff and her husband moved in 1951 to a home which they purchased in southeast Des Moines. Plaintiff's husband subsequently died, but plaintiff has lived on the premises continuously. Her lot has a frontage of 40 feet and is 125 feet long. It is legally described as:

> Lot One Hundred Forty-Four (144) in Gray's Subdivision of Lots Fifty (50) and Sixty-Two (62) in BROOKS AND COMPANY, an Addition, now included in and forming a part of the City of Des Moines, Iowa.

A larger undeveloped lot bounded plaintiff's property to the north. It is described as:

> The East 125 Feet of the North 474 Feet of Lot Sixty-Two (62) in BROOKS AND COMPANY'S ADDITION TO THE CITY OF DES MOINES, now included in and forming a part of the City of Des Moines, Iowa.

Defendants and their predecessors have held record title to this lot at all material times.

The property which plaintiff claims to have acquired by adverse possession is the south 60 feet of defendants' lot. Thus, the property in dispute is a 60 by 125 foot parcel adjacent to the north boundary of plaintiff's lot.

When plaintiff and her husband moved into their home in July 1951, the lot north of their property was a cornfield. Although plaintiff was not certain of the location of the northern boundary of her lot, she knew her lot's dimensions, and she knew it did not include the cornfield. In 1952 the corn was not planted as far south on the adjacent lot. Concerned about rats and the threat of fire, and desiring additional yard for their children, plaintiff and her husband cleared several feet of the property to the north, graded it, and planted grass seed on it. Since that time plaintiff has used the land as an extension of her yard. She planted peony bushes on it during the 1950's, installed a propane tank on it approximately 30 feet north of her lot in 1964, constructed a dirt bank on the city right of way to divert water from that parcel in 1965, and put in a driveway infringing five feet onto the land in 1975.

The remainder of defendants' lot was planted in corn until approximately 1957. The lot was owned by Abraham and Beverly Rosenfeld from July 1960 until February 1978. During that period the only use Rosenfelds made of the property was to store junk and debris on it. Except for the strip used by plaintiff, the lot was overgrown with brush and weeds. The Rosenfelds paid all taxes and special assessments on the property. Plaintiff and her husband at one time obtained the Rosenfelds' permission to keep a horse on the lot. On one occasion in the 1960's plaintiff examined the plat of defendants' lot in the courthouse to see if it ran all the way to a street to the north.

When defendant McCormick purchased his interest in the lot in 1978, he was aware of the possibility of a boundary dispute because of the location of plaintiff's propane tank and driveway. He and the other defendants were unsuccessful in their efforts to settle the dispute with plaintiff, who subsequently brought this action.

In seeking to establish her ownership of the disputed parcel, plaintiff alleged she had "for more than thirty (30) years last past been in open, exclusive, hostile, adverse and actual possession under claim of right." The trial court held in part that she did not establish her possession was under a claim of right. The court reasoned that a claim of right must be made in good faith and that plaintiff was not in good faith because she knew someone else had title to the land. Although the court found plaintiff had not proved her claim of adverse possession, it ordered defendants to "do equity" by deeding to her the strip of land her driveway was on and to pay the costs of moving the propane tank to her lot. The appeal and cross-appeal followed.

I. *The appeal.* The doctrine of adverse possession is based on the ten-year statute of limitations for recovery of real property in section 614.1(5), The Code. One claiming title by adverse possession must establish hostile, actual, open, exclusive and continuous possession, under a claim of right or color of title, for at least ten years, by clear and positive proof.

As permitted, plaintiff relied on claim of right rather than color of title. In contending the trial court erred in finding she failed in her proof of this element, she attacks the viability of the principal case relied on by the trial court, Goulding v. Shonquist, 141 N.W. 24 (Iowa 1913). Its facts are analogous to those here.

In *Goulding* the individual also cleared land adjacent to his house. The land was overrun with brush and willows and was frequented by hunters. After clearing it, the individual used the land as a pasture and garden. In finding he did not establish good faith claim of right, the court said:

> When he moved into his present property, the lands in question were objectionable because they were frequented by hunters, and for that reason he and his wife thought they ought to clear them up. He says he supposed they were part of the old river bed or waste land upon which anyone could enter. No other facts are offered by defendant as a reason for entering into the possession of the land at that time. Whether the title to the land was in the state or some other person, the defendant knew that he had no title and that he had no claim of title, and no right whatever to enter into the possession, and his possession was not in good faith for that reason.

141 N.W. at 25. The court quoted a statement from Litchfield v. Sewell, 66 N.W. 104, 106 (Iowa 1896), "that there can be no such thing as adverse possession where the party knows he has no title, and that, under the law, he can acquire none by his occupation."

Plaintiff argues that it is inconsistent to say ownership can be acquired by claim of right as an alternative to color of title and at the same time say ownership cannot be acquired by a person who knows he does not have title. Although we agree it is an overstatement to say ownership cannot be acquired by a person who knows he does not have title, plaintiff is incorrect in her argument that good faith is not an essential component of claim of right. Moreover, we agree with the trial court that plaintiff did not prove this element of her adverse possession claim.

The overbreadth of the statement that title cannot be obtained through adverse possession by one who knows he has no title is demonstrated in *Litchfield*, *Goulding* and subsequent decisions. In *Litchfield* the court rejected the adverse possession claim of a person in possession of land under a quitclaim deed from a squatter. In finding an absence of good faith, the court noted the adverse possession doctrine "has no application to one who actually knows that he has no claim, or title, or right to a title." 66 N.W. at 106. Under this holding a mere squatter or one who claims under a squatter cannot have a good faith claim of right to the property, but mere knowledge by the person that he has no title is not preclusive. A claim of right by a squatter is a false claim. To permit a squatter to assert a claim of right would put a premium on dishonesty. See 4 H. Tiffany, Real Property § 1147 at 792 (3d ed. 1975). One of the main purposes of the claim of right requirement is "to bar mere squatters from the benefits of adverse possession." 7 R. Powell, Real Property, para. 1015 (Rohan ed. 1981).

As in *Litchfield*, the possessor in *Goulding* not only knew that he had no title but that he had no claim of title or any right to enter into possession of the property. He was a mere squatter.

Knowledge of a defect in title is not alone sufficient to preclude proof of good faith:

> One is not deprived of the benefit of the statute of limitations merely because his claim of right is unenforceable or his title is known to be defective. The doctrine of adverse possession presupposes a defective title. It is not based on, but is hostile to, the true title. If the statute were to run only in favor of a valid title, it would serve no purpose. The holder of such a title has no need to invoke the statute. Where bad faith is held to negative an alleged claim of right, it is only another way of saying that such claim has been disproved.

Creel v. Hammans, 13 N.W.2d 305, 307 (Iowa 1944).

Nevertheless, when knowledge of lack of title is accompanied by knowledge of no basis for claiming an interest in the property, a good faith claim of right cannot be established. For example, a mere exchange of quitclaim deeds by persons who know legal title is in another will not support a claim of right:

> It is evident the claim and possession of George C. Abel could not have been in good faith. There was no reason why he and his brother should believe they had any right to divide and apportion between themselves the real estate of their father while he was an insane patient in the state hospital. They must be held to have known the quitclaim deeds they exchanged gave them no title. At best, they proceeded upon what proved to be an unfounded assumption that their father would never be discharged from the adjudication of insanity. No claim of ownership by adverse possession will be sustained upon such a foundation. Plaintiff's position at this point does not appeal to a court of equity.

Abel v. Abel, 65 N.W.2d 68, 75 (Iowa 1954).

We now confirm that good faith, as explained in [the present] case, is essential to adverse possession under a claim of right.

We believe plaintiff failed to prove a good faith claim of right in the present case. She knew her lot did not include the cornfield north of it. She knew someone else had title to it and she had no interest in it or claim to it. This is not a case of confusion or mistake. At the time she entered possession of the disputed land, plaintiff knew she had no legal right to do so. To say that one can acquire a claim of right by merely entering possession would recognize squatter's rights. Possession for the statutory period cannot be bootstrapped into a basis for claiming a right to possession.

We hold that the trial court was right in rejecting plaintiff's claim.

[The court dismissed defendants' cross appeal, which was not filed within the time specified by the Iowa rules of appellate procedure.]

Affirmed on the appeal; dismissed on the cross appeal.

NOTES AND QUESTIONS

1. **Comparisons.** Does the court in *Carpenter* adopt the Connecticut rule, the Maine rule, or something else?

2. **Knowledge of what?** If A mistakenly believes that he has title, is A in good faith? If A knows that he lacks title, is A in bad faith? If not, what else does A have to know to negate good faith?

3. **Reasonableness of belief.** One can be honest, yet unreasonable. Does good faith in adverse possession require that the claimant's belief be reasonable? Some courts have suggested that it does. *See* Wallace v. Magie, 522 P.2d 989, 994 (Kan. 1974) ("the issue in this case is whether the [claimant] had a good faith belief of ownership and whether under the facts and circumstances such a belief was justified").

4. **Sub rosa good faith: an iconoclastic scholarly view.** In a provocative article, Professor Helmholz acknowledges that the great weight of scholarly opinion favors the objective view (dispensing with a good faith requirement), and that the great majority of courts do not state good faith as an affirmative element of adverse possession doctrine. Nevertheless, he argues that the courts in fact do require good faith, by manipulating the possession requirements to deny title to a claimant who appears to be a knowing trespasser. *See* Richard H. Helmholz, *Adverse Possession and Subjective Intent*, 61 Wash. U. L.Q. 331 (1983). A scholarly brouhaha ensued after publication of the article, with each of the two protagonists questioning the other's reading of the cases. *See* Roger A. Cunningham, *Adverse Possession and Subjective Intent: A Reply to Professor Helmholz*, 64 Wash. U. L.Q. 1 (1986); Richard H. Helmholz, *More on Subjective Intent: A Response to Professor Cunningham*, 64 Wash. U. L.Q. 65; Roger A. Cunningham, *More on Adverse Possession: A Rejoinder to Professor Helmholz*, 64 Wash. U. L.Q. 1167 (1986).

5. **Doctrine.** *See* Jasperson v. Scharnikow, 150 F. 571, 572 (9th Cir. 1907):

This idea of acquiring title by larceny does not go in this country. A man must have a bona fide claim, or believe in his own mind that he has got a right as owner, when he goes upon land that does not belong to him, in order to acquire title by occupation and possession.

Do you see a linguistic basis for the requirement of good faith in the formulation that A must possess under a "claim of right"?

6. **Testimony.** Dr. Way owns Lot 42, and occupies up to a fence between Lot 42 and a neighbor's lot. The fence does not straddle the boundary, but encroaches onto the neighbor's land. What is the significance of the following testimony by Dr. Way under the Connecticut rule? Under the Maine rule? In Iowa? *See* Boyle v. Burk, 749 S.W.2d 264, 267 (Tex. App. 1988):

Q. How long was it — When did you discover that there was extra property between your lot and the fence in question?

A. I never discovered that there was any.

Q. You never knew that that was not part of Lot 42?

A. No, I did not.

Q. So, as far as you were concerned, you were just claiming your property? You weren't claiming anybody else's property?

A. Correct.

Q. You weren't holding — didn't think you were holding property adverse to anybody else, did you?

A. Do you mean if they came on there and said they were going to get it, yes.

Q. No. I am saying you didn't intend to be occupying somebody else's property adverse to their rights, did you?

MR. ANDERSON: I object to that. I think he answered the question. Now, it's argumentative, Your Honor.

THE COURT: I overrule the objection.

A. (By the witness) Now, wait a minute. You are getting too many "adverses" on too many sides here. Could you restate that?

Q. Did you intend to claim somebody else's property in addition to your own by your use, or did you think you were just claiming your own property?

A. I was only claiming what was inside the fence which was, as I understood it, my property.

Q. And you thought you had a deed to it?

A. Yes.

Q. (By Mr. Morris) Did you intend to adversely occupy somebody else's property and take it by adverse possession?

A. Not knowingly that it was somebody else's property.

c. Possession Under Color of Title

None of the adverse possessors in our principal cases so far has possessed under a deed describing the property claimed by the possessor. We now look at possessors who do have a paper title to support their claims. As the materials show, it is advantageous for a possessor to claim under "color of title."

LOTT v. MULDOON ROAD BAPTIST CHURCH, INC.
466 P.2d 815 (Alaska 1970)

BONEY, JUSTICE.

This case involves the title to certain real property which appellee claims to have acquired through adverse possession under color of title.

In 1951, appellant, Leo Lott (also known as Leo L. Luckett) came to Alaska; shortly thereafter she married Burnie B. Garland. In September of 1952, appellant acquired in her own name, Leo L. Garland, real property described as the northernmost 75 feet of tract [92] in section 13 [of a government survey].

In 1955, Leo and Burnie Garland were divorced. As part of the property settlement, appellant obtained by a recorded deed an additional 60 feet of lot 92 from Burnie. This property was to the south of and adjacent to the 75 foot parcel acquired by appellant in 1952. The result of this settlement was to divide the lot, which is 330 feet long, into two parcels: the north 135 feet belonging to appellant and the south 195 feet belonging to Burnie Garland.

Some time in 1955 appellant left the State of Alaska. While she was absent from the state, Burnie Garland caused a survey to be made and a plat prepared in which the south 270 feet of the lot was subdivided into three lots. Since Burnie Garland only owned the south 195 feet of the lot, the platted land extended 75 feet on to the portion of the lot owned by appellant. This encroachment included the 60 foot parcel which Burnie had deeded to appellant in the divorce settlement, and a small part of the 75 foot parcel appellant had acquired in her own name. The platted land was designated "Homesite Park Subdivision." The plat contained a certificate of ownership whereby Burnie Garland certified that he owned all of the property described in the plat. The plat was dated June 7, 1958, and filed on August 21, 1958.

On August 8, 1958, Burnie Garland purported to convey the property described in the plat to the Title Insurance and Trust Company, as trustee, under a recorded deed of trust. The deed of trust was to secure a loan to Garland of $3,612 from the City National Bank of Anchorage. On September 12, 1959, Title Insurance and Trust, by a deed of reconveyance conveyed the platted land back to Burnie Garland. This deed was recorded on September 14, 1959, and described the property as Lot 92, of Section 13, Township 13 North, Range 3 West, Seward Meridian except the north sixty feet. At this time actual title to the north 135 feet was still held by appellant.

Some time in 1959 Burnie Garland rented the property for use as a Sunday school to Cecil Owens, a member of the Tribal Baptist Church. On July 7, 1960, Garland entered, with the Eagle River First Baptist Church, into a recorded one-year lease with option to purchase. The property described in the lease was the same as had been described in the deed of trust, deed of reconveyance and the plat, that is, the entire lot 92 except the north 60 feet. The lease provided that the owner "is willing to rent and sell said property to the church in accordance with the terms and provisions of this agreement." The church was to pay $150 per month for one year at which time $900 would be applied to the purchase price of $25,000. The "option" to purchase was to be exercised with thirty days' notice; and in the event it was not exercised, the lease provided that the church could remove its improvements but would reimburse the owner for any expenditures for title insurance. The church took possession immediately, and the church has held services on the property every week since it took possession. Reverend Chron testified that it was the church's understanding that they were really buying the property outright, not leasing it.

Burnie Garland died in California on June 7, 1961. On February 27, 1962, the National Bank of Alaska executed an administrator's deed which purported to convey the same property which was the subject of the "lease with option to purchase." The deed was issued to the appellee Muldoon Road Baptist Church, successor to the Eagle River First Baptist Church.

On July 27, 1967, appellant filed suit to eject appellee from the property and to quiet title to that portion (72 feet) of Homesite Subdivision which is included in the north 135 feet of lot 92. After trial without a jury, a judgment was entered which decreed that appellant had no right to or interest in property. From this judgment, Leo Lott appealed claiming that color of title was not established by the lease with option to purchase, or any other instrument, and that the statute of limitations applying to actions for ejectment of persons without color of title had not run. On appeal the church claims that the superior court correctly determined that the church or its predecessors have held the property under color of title for the required length of time.

Evidence adduced at the trial showed that the earliest act of hostile possession of land in question came at some time in 1958 when Burnie Garland had the land surveyed and platted. Other evidence at the trial was sufficient to allow the court to find that Burnie Garland retained actual possession of all of the land in question. Moreover, there is apparent agreement that the possession by the church and its predecessors has been open, notorious and continuous. Thus the sole question presented in this appeal is whether such possession has been under color of title.

In Alaska the "color of title" doctrine is created by statute; AS 09.25.050 provides: "The uninterrupted adverse notorious possession of real property under color and claim of title for seven years or more is conclusively presumed to give title to the property except as against the state or the United States." "Color of title" as used in this statute has been defined by this court in Ayers v. Day & Night Fuel Co., 451 P.2d 579, 581 (Alaska 1969): "Color of title exists only by virtue of a written instrument which purports, but which may not be effective, to pass title to the claimant."

The function of the doctrine of color of title is to define the exact boundaries of the land which is claimed. When one adversely possesses land under color of title the extent of the land possessed is measured by the terms of the purported instrument giving color of title rather than by the actual physical use by the claimant. The other effect of the doctrine is to shorten the period of prescription from 10 years to 7.[4] The shortened period of prescription is most logically attributable to a belief that a person holding land under color of title will be more likely to make improvements and otherwise commit himself to that land.

The good faith of the claimant is not a relevant issue under our ten-year adverse possession statute. But we must consider whether good faith is a necessary element in order to establish adverse possession under color of title pursuant to AS 09.25.050. This question has not yet been determined in the courts of Alaska. Although several jurisdictions have held that a claim under color of title does not require good faith,[7] we prefer to follow those other states which hold that the good faith of the claimant is a prerequisite to the establishment of his claim under color of title.[8]

In adopting this interpretation, we also favor the concomitant presumption of good faith, in the absence of an express allegation and showing to the contrary.[9] In short, we feel that it would be inequitable to allow a claimant to create color of title in himself by means of a sham conveyance or a reconveyance to himself through a "strawman" transaction. In the circumstances of this case, however, we need not pass upon the details of what constitutes good faith, nor do we have occasion to discuss exactly what would constitute bad faith under AS 09.25.050.[10] The only question is whether the claim here is based on a written instrument which purports to pass title, and which adequately describes the claimed property.

Appellant is correct in asserting that Burnie Garland could not have claimed color of title by virtue of the plat which he filed. This document contained a claim of ownership but did not purport to pass title to Garland. However, the deed of trust from Garland to Title Insurance and Trust Company created color of title in the title company. Although Garland had no title to convey as to the disputed

---

[4] AS 09.10.030 provides:

> No person may bring an action for the recovery of real property, or for the recovery of the possession of it unless commenced within 10 years. No action may be maintained for the recovery unless it appears that the plaintiff, his ancestor, predecessor, or grantor was seized or possessed of the premises in question within 10 years before the commencement of the action.

[7] See for example, McDaniel v. Ramsey's Adm'rs, 204 S.W.2d 953 (Ky. 1947); Shutt v. Methodist Episcopal Church, 218 S.W. 1020 (Ky. 1920); Burns v. Stewart, 78 S.E. 321 (N.C. 1913); Marky Investment, Inc. v. Arnezeder, 112 N.W.2d 211 (Wis. 1961).

[8] O'Reilly v. Balkwill, 297 P.2d 263 (Colo. 1956); Hearn v. Leverette, 99 S.E.2d 147 (Ga. 1957); Branch v. Lee, 26 N.E.2d 88 (Ill. 1940); Bruce v. Cheramie, 93 So. 2d 202 (La. 1957); State v. Davis, 83 S.E.2d 114 (W. Va. 1954).

[9] It should be noted that in almost all of these jurisdictions the requirement of good faith was explicitly written into the statutes. We interpret AS 09.25.050 as creating a presumption of good faith, which presumption can be rebutted by a showing of bad faith on the part of the claimant.

[10] In the present case it must be noted that there has been no allegation made by appellant of fraud or bad faith on the part of Burnie Garland in obtaining color of title. No showing has been made to indicate that any bad faith was in fact involved. Even in the states that require color of title to be held in good faith, it appears that a strong presumption will exist in favor of the person claiming possession under color of title, and that under such a presumption there is a great reluctance to find bad faith or fraud, absent express proof thereof by the opposing party. See, e.g., cases cited note 8 *supra*.

portion of the subdivision, he executed a deed which purported to pass title to a third person.

The deed of reconveyance which Burnie received from the title company on September 12, 1959, was in effect a quitclaim deed,[12] and purported to pass title to the property to Burnie Garland. Again, the deed purported to convey title and the property was described in clear terms. It follows, then, that the deed of reconveyance created color of title in Garland.

We are unable to agree with our dissenting colleague's view that our holding does not accord with the policy of reliance underlying AS 09.25.050. The view of reliance taken in the dissenting opinion amounts to a conclusion that a deed of reconveyance could never suffice to establish color of title under our statute. Such a view unduly restricts the doctrine of color of title and is virtually unsupported in the case law of this or any other jurisdiction. By definition, color of title presupposes invalidity in the instrument purporting to convey title. Yet if we were to adopt the narrow view of reliance advocated in the dissent, the instances would indeed be rare when a person could rely on any instrument not in actuality valid. This result, in terms of color of title, is anomalous and would only serve to render ineffective the color of title provision.

Moreover, we do not think that it requires an inordinate strain of the imagination to find that Burnie Garland could have relied on the deed of reconveyance in committing himself to the land. We start with the assumption that our color of title provision was meant to protect persons unversed in the fundamentals of business and property transactions. Accordingly, in order to find that there might have been reliance here, it is not necessary to conclude that the deed in question was relied upon as absolutely establishing Burnie's claim to the land. Rather we need only point out that Burnie may well have believed that his claim to the land was strengthened by the deed of reconveyance, and he might thereby have been prompted to commit himself to the land to a greater extent. In our view this is the type of reliance contemplated by the policy underlying color of title. Under these circumstances we can see no compelling reason, in the absence of some showing of bad faith, to hold a deed of reconveyance insufficient to establish color of title.

With regard to the deed of trust and the deed of reconveyance, appellant has argued only that these documents do not create color of title because they do not describe the property in dispute. This assertion is erroneous. Apparently, appellant believes that the designation "Parcel 1" and "Parcel 2," that appears in these instruments, had reference to lots 1 and 2 of the subdivision. From an examination of the instruments it is clear that "Parcel 1" referred to property unrelated to any of the property that is the subject of this appeal, and "Parcel 2" refers to the entire Homesite Subdivision.

Appellant has not argued that appellee should not be permitted to tack on its period of possession to that of Burnie Garland. Nor has appellant advanced any other considerations which would preclude our finding that Burnie Garland, from

---

[12] Quitclaim deeds have been held to create color of title in the grantee. Additionally, it has been held that a release deed is sufficient to convey color of title.

the date of the deed of reconveyance, September 12, 1959, adversely possessed the disputed property under color of title, and that appellee, as successor to Garland, may claim title by adverse possession according to AS 09.25.050 for over seven years. Accordingly, we find no error in the decision below, and we affirm the judgment of the superior court.

RABINOWITZ, JUSTICE (concurring in part and dissenting in part).

The court states that the rationale of the shorter seven-year period of AS 09.25.050 "is most logically attributable to a belief that a person holding land under color of title will be more likely to make improvements and otherwise commit himself to that land." In my view, the holding of the majority opinion is inconsistent with this rationale. Without going into any issue of good faith, which I agree should be a prerequisite to establishment of a claim under AS 09.25.050, it appears to me that the gist of the court's holding is that an adverse claimant under color of title can obtain the benefit of the shorter period by means of a conveyance to a third person and reconveyance.

Such a result strikes me as being contrary to the policy reasons for granting an adverse claimant the benefit of the shorter period. For in my view, it is not dispositive of the issue in the case at bar that the form of the instruments used by Burnie Garland and the Title Insurance and Trust Company purported to pass title and adequately described the property in question. The crucial question here is whether the person claiming under color of title would have been more likely to make improvements and otherwise commit himself to the land because of his reliance upon an instrument purporting to create color of title. Given the factual context of this record, I cannot conceive that Burnie Garland made improvements or otherwise further committed himself to the land in question in reliance upon the reconveyance from the Title Insurance and Trust Company. Under the bootstrap circumstances of the case, I fail to discern any persuasive policy reasons for holding that a claimant's color of title under AS 09.25.050 commences from the point in time that he receives a reconveyance of land to which he never previously held the title.

I agree with the court's statement that it is impermissible for a claimant to create color of title in himself through a strawman transaction. But I entertain reservations as to whether the newly adopted "concomitant presumption of good faith" will further this end. In my view, adoption of a presumption of good faith in the circumstances of the case at bar, and in all future similar circumstances, creates a distinction which will prove difficult to administer and will emasculate the good-faith-of-claimant prophylactic under AS 09.25.050.

On the particular facts of this case, I believe that the seven-year period must be measured from the time the Eagle River First Baptist Church exercised its option to purchase. Since the record is silent on this issue, I would remand for further evidence and findings of fact and conclusions of law on this point.

NOTES AND QUESTIONS

1. **Color of title: meaning.**   *See* Marlowe v. Clark, 435 S.E.2d 354, 357 (N.C. Ct. App. 1993):

> Adverse possession under color of title has been defined as "occupancy under a writing that purports to pass title to the occupant but which does not actually do so either because the person executing the writing fails to have title or capacity to transfer the title or because of the defective mode of the conveyance used." Cobb v. Spurlin, 327 S.E.2d 244, 247 (N.C. Ct. App. 1985).

See also Wilson v. Divide County, 76 N.W.2d 896 (N.D. 1956) (buyer at tax foreclosure sale possessed under color of title when deed was invalid due to defective notice to record owner of right to redeem the land after the tax sale).

Contrast color of title with claim of right (or, as it is sometimes called, claim of title), which we saw earlier: "A claim of title has generally been held to mean nothing more than that the disseisor enters upon the land with the intent to claim it as his own." Somon v. Murphy Fabrication and Erection Co., 232 S.E.2d 524, 529 (W. Va. 1977).

2. **Defective deeds.**   In the principal case, why was Burnie's deed to the bank defective? Why was the reconveyance from the bank to Burnie defective?

3. **The principal case.**   Why wasn't Burnie Garland in bad faith? Do the distinctions made in Carpenter v. Ruperto (Section 3.b above) suggest a possible answer? Do you agree with the majority in the *Lott* case, or the dissent?

4. **Advantages of color of title.**   The principal case illustrates one advantage to an adverse possessor of having color of title — it shortens the period of possession necessary to gain title. Another advantage is that it permits acquisition by constructive possession of the entire tract described in the deed when the adverse possessor has actual possession of only a portion thereof. What policies support the doctrine of color of title? In addition to the discussion in the principal case, see Marlowe v. Clark, Note 1 above; Fulkerson v. Van Buren, 961 S.W.2d 780, 782 (Ark. Ct. App. 1998).

5. **Requirements.**   Statutes often require that the claimant under color of title pay taxes on the land. *See, e.g.,* Wilson v. Divide County, supra Note 1 (discussing North Dakota statute requiring payment of taxes by possessor under color of title); DeChambeau v. Estate of Smith, 976 P.2d 922, 925 (Idaho 1999) (same under Idaho statute). Some states require that the deed be recorded in order for the claimant to take advantage of the doctrine of color of title. *See, e.g.,* Ala. Code § 6-5-200(a)(1). Good faith is a common requirement. *See, e.g.,* Joiner v. Janssen, 421 N.E.2d 170, 174 (Ill. 1981) (good faith required under color of title, not claim of right); Gigger v. White, 586 S.E.2d 242, 245 (Ga. 2003) (quitclaim deed from one of four cotenants constituted color of title where adverse possessor had no actual knowledge of grantor's fraud on the other cotenants). All states require that the claimant "satisfy the basic elements of adverse possession in establishing his or her claim." Bentley Family Trust v. Lynx Enterprises, Inc., 658 P.2d 761, 764-65 (Alaska 1983).

PROBLEM 1-D. What result in the following cases?

a. A receives a defective deed to lot 1, consisting of one acre. A goes into possession of the front half of the lot and occupies it for the statutory period (the back half of the lot is a densely wooded area that A never sets foot in). What does A own?

b. A receives a deed that describes three lots. The lots are not contiguous, but all are in the same general area. A goes into possession of a part of one of the lots and remains for the statutory period. What does A own?

c. A receives a deed to lots 1 and 2, which are contiguous, and goes into possession of lot 1, occupying it for the statutory period. Lot 1 is owned by O; lot 2 is owned by X. Does A acquire title by adverse possession to lot 1, lot 2, or both?

d. Under a deed covering all 80 acres of Blackacre, A goes into possession of the back 40 acres; the record owner, O, is in possession of the front 40 acres. What does A acquire after the running of the statute of limitations?

See generally 16 Powell on Real Property § 91.08[2].

MORE NOTES AND QUESTIONS

1. **Review and extensions.** Compare adverse possession to the following doctrines:

a. *Agreed boundaries.* "An oral agreement to fix a property boundary between adjacent landowners is enforceable if there is uncertainty as to the true location of the boundary, the uncertainty is resolved by agreement and the agreement is evidenced by the parties' subsequent actions." Eidman v. Goldsmith, 941 P.2d 1045, 1048 (Or. Ct. App. 1997).

b. *Acquiescence.* "The doctrine of acquiescence allows land to be acquired by adverse possession, without the usual adverse intent, when the true owner has acquiesced in another's possession for a period of twenty years." Arnold v. Robbins, 563 N.W.2d 178, 179 (Wis. Ct. App. 1997). *But see* Lawrence Berger, *Unification of the Doctrines of Adverse Possession and Practical Location in the Establishment of Boundaries,* 78 Neb. L. Rev. 1, 7 (1999) (noting that some courts carefully distinguish between agreed boundaries and acquiescence, while other courts "seem to regard acquiescence merely as evidence establishing that an oral agreement setting a disputed boundary has been made"). *See* 16 Powell on Real Property § 91.05[3] at 91-28.

c. *Estoppel.* "Estoppel is analytically separate [from agreed boundaries and acquiescence]. It involves a representation by one owner to an adjoining owner as to the location of the boundary between them. Title passes when the representation is detrimentally relied upon by the second owner through her construction of encroaching improvements." Berger, *supra,* 78 Neb. L. Rev. at 7.

2. **Adverse possession against the government.** The traditional rule is that an adverse possessor may not gain title to government-owned land. What are the arguments pro and con on allowing a claimant to acquire government land by

adverse possession? A compromise position adopted in some states is to allow adverse possession against land owned by the government in a proprietary capacity, but not in a governmental capacity. *See* Devins v. Borough of Bogota, 592 A.2d 199 (N.J. 1991) (allowing adverse possession of municipally owned land not used for governmental purposes); Nyman v. Anchor Development, LLC, 73 P.3d 357, 360 (Utah 2003) (county's acquisition of land at tax sale was "public purpose" precluding adverse possession); 16 Powell on Real Property § 91.11; Paula R. Latovick, *Adverse Possession of Municipal Land: It's Time to Protect This Valuable Resource*, 31 U. Mich. J.L. Reform 475 (1998).

3. **Government as adverse possessor.** *See* State ex rel. A.A.A. Investments v. City of Columbus, 478 N.E.2d 773, 775-76 (Ohio 1985):

> The prevailing view is that public or governmental entities may acquire title to land by adverse possession. In the case of adverse possession, property is not taken. Rather, once the statutory period has expired, the former titleholder has lost his claim of ownership and the adverse possessor is thereafter maintaining its possession, not taking property. Accordingly, we hold that a municipal corporation can acquire title to private property by adverse possession.

d. Adverse Possession of Personal Property

Stolen personal property presents issues that, perhaps more so than those raised by "stolen" (i.e., adversely possessed) land, defy easy resolution. The relative shortness of statutes of limitation on a claim in replevin for return of personal property, and the easy concealability and moveability of such property, suggest the difficulties that a straightforward adverse possession regime poses for the victim of the theft, and the reasons why a court might be reluctant to use the statute of limitations approach. Yet, more often than not, the dispute over stolen personal property arises not between the innocent owner and the thief, but rather between the owner and an innocent good faith purchaser, the latter also having strong equities on his or her side. How do courts navigate between these competing policy considerations?

O'KEEFFE v. SNYDER
416 A.2d 862 (N.J. 1980)

POLLOCK, J.

This is an appeal from an order of the Appellate Division granting summary judgment to plaintiff, Georgia O'Keeffe, against defendant, Barry Snyder, d/b/a Princeton Gallery of Fine Art, for replevin of three small pictures painted by O'Keeffe. O'Keeffe v. Snyder, 405 A.2d 840 (N.J. Super. Ct. App. Div. 1979). In her complaint, filed in March, 1976, O'Keeffe alleged she was the owner of the paintings and that they were stolen from a New York art gallery in 1946. Snyder asserted he was a purchaser for value of the paintings, he had title by adverse possession, and O'Keeffe's action was barred by the expiration of the six-year period of limitations provided by N.J.S.A. 2A:14-1 pertaining to an action in replevin. Snyder impleaded third party defendant, Ulrich A. Frank, from whom

Snyder purchased the paintings in 1975 for $35,000.

The trial court granted summary judgment for Snyder on the ground that O'Keeffe's action was barred because it was not commenced within six years of the alleged theft. The Appellate Division reversed and entered judgment for O'Keeffe. A majority of that court concluded that the paintings were stolen, the defenses of expiration of the statute of limitations and title by adverse possession were identical, and Snyder had not proved the elements of adverse possession. Consequently, the majority ruled that O'Keeffe could still enforce her right to possession of the paintings.

The dissenting judge stated that the appropriate measurement of the period of limitation was not by analogy to adverse possession, but by application of the "discovery rule" pertaining to some statutes of limitation. He concluded that the six-year period of limitations commenced when O'Keeffe knew or should have known who unlawfully possessed the paintings, and that the matter should be remanded to determine if and when that event had occurred.

We granted certification to consider not only the issues raised in the dissenting opinion, but all other issues. We reverse and remand the matter for a plenary hearing in accordance with this opinion.

I

The record, limited to pleadings, affidavits, answers to interrogatories, and depositions, is fraught with factual conflict. Apart from the creation of the paintings by O'Keeffe and their discovery in Snyder's gallery in 1976, the parties agree on little else.

O'Keeffe contended the paintings were stolen in 1946 from a gallery, An American Place. The gallery was operated by her late husband, the famous photographer Alfred Stieglitz. An American Place was a cooperative undertaking of O'Keeffe and some other American artists identified by her as Marin, Hardin, Dove, Andema, and Stevens. In 1946, Stieglitz arranged an exhibit which included an O'Keeffe painting, identified as Cliffs. According to O'Keeffe, one day in March, 1946, she and Stieglitz discovered Cliffs was missing from the wall of the exhibit. O'Keeffe estimates the value of the painting at the time of the alleged theft to have been about $150. About two weeks later, O'Keeffe noticed that two other paintings, Seaweed and Fragments, were missing from a storage room at An American Place. She did not tell anyone, even Stieglitz, about the missing paintings, since she did not want to upset him.

O'Keeffe testified on depositions that at about the same time as the disappearance of her paintings, 12 or 13 miniature paintings by Marin also were stolen from An American Place. According to O'Keeffe, a man named Estrick took the Marin paintings and "maybe a few other things." Estrick distributed the Marin paintings to members of the theater world who, when confronted by Stieglitz, returned them. However, neither Stieglitz nor O'Keeffe confronted Estrick with the loss of any of the O'Keeffe paintings.

There was no evidence of a breaking and entering at An American Place on the dates when O'Keeffe discovered the disappearance of her paintings. Neither Stieglitz nor O'Keeffe reported them missing to the New York Police Department or any other law enforcement agency. Apparently the paintings were uninsured, and O'Keeffe did not seek reimbursement from an insurance company. Similarly, neither O'Keeffe nor Stieglitz advertised the loss of the paintings in Art News or any other publication. Nonetheless, they discussed it with associates in the art world and later O'Keeffe mentioned the loss to the director of the Art Institute of Chicago, but she did not ask him to do anything because "it wouldn't have been my way." O'Keeffe does not contend that Frank or Snyder had actual knowledge of the alleged theft.

Stieglitz died in the summer of 1946, and O'Keeffe explains she did not pursue her efforts to locate the paintings because she was settling his estate. In 1947, she retained the services of Doris Bry to help settle the estate. Bry urged O'Keeffe to report the loss of the paintings, but O'Keeffe declined because "they never got anything back by reporting it." Finally, in 1972, O'Keeffe authorized Bry to report the theft to the Art Dealers Association of America, Inc., which maintains for its members a registry of stolen paintings. The record does not indicate whether such a registry existed at the time the paintings disappeared.

In September, 1975, O'Keeffe learned that the paintings were in the Andrew Crispo Gallery in New York on consignment from Bernard Danenberg Galleries. On February 11, 1976, O'Keeffe discovered that Ulrich A. Frank had sold the paintings to Barry Snyder, d/b/a Princeton Gallery of Fine Art. She demanded their return and, following Snyder's refusal, instituted this action for replevin.

Frank traces his possession of the paintings to his father, Dr. Frank, who died in 1968. He claims there is a family relationship by marriage between his family and the Stieglitz family, a contention that O'Keeffe disputes. Frank does not know how his father acquired the paintings, but he recalls seeing them in his father's apartment in New Hampshire as early as 1941-1943, a period that precedes the alleged theft. Consequently, Frank's factual contentions are inconsistent with O'Keeffe's allegation of theft. Until 1965, Dr. Frank occasionally lent the paintings to Ulrich Frank. In 1965, Dr. and Mrs. Frank formally gave the paintings to Ulrich Frank, who kept them in his residences in Yardley, Pennsylvania and Princeton, New Jersey. In 1968, he exhibited anonymously Cliffs and Fragments in a one day art show in the Jewish Community Center in Trenton. All of these events preceded O'Keeffe's listing of the paintings as stolen with the Art Dealers Association of America, Inc. in 1972.

Frank claims continuous possession of the paintings through his father for over thirty years and admits selling the paintings to Snyder. Snyder and Frank do not trace their provenance, or history of possession of the paintings, back to O'Keeffe.

As indicated, Snyder moved for summary judgment on the theory that O'Keeffe's action was barred by the statute of limitations and title had vested in Frank by adverse possession. For purposes of his motion, Snyder conceded that the paintings had been stolen. On her cross motion, O'Keeffe urged that the paintings were stolen, the statute of limitations had not run, and title to the paintings remained in her.

II

The Appellate Division accepted O'Keeffe's contention that the paintings had been stolen. However, in his deposition, Ulrich Frank traces possession of the paintings to his father in the early 1940's, a date that precedes the alleged theft by several years. The factual dispute about the loss of the paintings by O'Keeffe and their acquisition by Frank, as well as the other subsequently described factual issues, warrant a remand for a plenary hearing.

In reversing the cross motions for summary judgment, the Appellate Division erred in accepting one of two conflicting versions of material fact: the theft of the paintings in March, 1946 as asserted by O'Keeffe as against the possession of the paintings by the Frank family since the early 1940's. Instead of recognizing the existence of this controversy, the Appellate Division misconstrued Snyder's concession that the paintings had been stolen. That concession was made to enable the trial court to determine Snyder's motion for summary judgment that title had passed by adverse possession. The concession was not available to resolve O'Keeffe's cross motion for summary judgment. Hence, there is an issue of material fact, whether the paintings were stolen, that compels remand for trial.

Without purporting to limit the scope of the trial, other factual issues include whether the paintings were not stolen but sold, lent, consigned, or given by Stieglitz to Dr. Frank or someone else without O'Keeffe's knowledge before he died, and whether there was any business or family relationship between Stieglitz and Dr. Frank so that the original possession of the paintings by the Frank family may have been under claim of right.

III

On the limited record before us, we cannot determine now who has title to the paintings. That determination will depend on the evidence adduced at trial. Nonetheless, we believe it may aid the trial court and the parties to resolve questions of law that may become relevant at trial.

Our decision begins with the principle that, generally speaking, if the paintings were stolen, the thief acquired no title and could not transfer good title to others regardless of their good faith and ignorance of the theft. Proof of theft would advance O'Keeffe's right to possession of the paintings absent other considerations such as expiration of the statute of limitations.

Another issue that may become relevant at trial is whether Frank or his father acquired a "voidable title" to the paintings under N.J.S.A. 12A:2-403(1). That section, part of the Uniform Commercial Code (U.C.C.), does not change the basic principle that a mere possessor cannot transfer good title. Nonetheless, the U.C.C. permits a person with voidable title to transfer good title to a good faith purchaser for value in certain circumstances. N.J.S.A. 12A:2-403(1). If the facts developed at trial merit application of that section, then Frank may have transferred good title to Snyder, thereby providing a defense to O'Keeffe's action. No party on this appeal has urged factual or legal contentions concerning the applicability of the U.C.C. Consequently, a more complete discussion of the U.C.C. would be premature, particularly in light of our decision to remand the matter for trial.

On this appeal, the critical legal question is when O'Keeffe's cause of action accrued. The fulcrum on which the outcome turns is the statute of limitations in N.J.S.A. 2A:14-1, which provides that an action for replevin of goods or chattels must be commenced within six years after the accrual of the cause of action.

The trial court found that O'Keeffe's cause of action accrued on the date of the alleged theft, March, 1946, and concluded that her action was barred. The Appellate Division found that an action might have accrued more than six years before the date of suit if possession by the defendant or his predecessors satisfied the elements of adverse possession. As indicated, the Appellate Division concluded that Snyder had not established those elements and that the O'Keeffe action was not barred by the statute of limitations.

In the present case, none of the parties resides in New York and the paintings are located in New Jersey. On the facts before us, it would appear that the appropriate statute of limitations is the law of the forum, N.J.S.A. 2A:14-1. On remand, the trial court may reconsider this issue if the parties present other relevant facts.

IV

On the assumption that New Jersey law will apply, we shall consider significant questions raised about the interpretation of N.J.S.A. 2A:14-1. The purpose of a statute of limitations is to "stimulate to activity and punish negligence" and "promote repose by giving security and stability to human affairs." Wood v. Carpenter, 101 U.S. 135, 139 (1879). A statute of limitations achieves those purposes by barring a cause of action after the statutory period. In certain instances, this Court has ruled that the literal language of a statute of limitations should yield to other considerations.

To avoid harsh results from the mechanical application of the statute, the courts have developed a concept known as the discovery rule. Prosser, The Law of Torts (4th ed. 1971), § 30 at 144-145; 51 Am.Jur.2d, Limitation of Actions, § 146 at 716. The discovery rule provides that, in an appropriate case, a cause of action will not accrue until the injured party discovers, or by exercise of reasonable diligence and intelligence should have discovered, facts which form the basis of a cause of action. The rule is essentially a principle of equity, the purpose of which is to mitigate unjust results that otherwise might flow from strict adherence to a rule of law.

[W]e conclude that the discovery rule applies to an action for replevin of a painting under N.J.S.A. 2A:14-1. O'Keeffe's cause of action accrued when she first knew, or reasonably should have known through the exercise of due diligence, of the cause of action, including the identity of the possessor of the paintings. *See* N. Ward, *Adverse Possession of Loaned or Stolen Objects: Is Possession Still 9/10 of the Law?*, published in Legal Problems of Museum Administration (ALI-ABA 1980) at 89-90.

In determining whether O'Keeffe is entitled to the benefit of the discovery rule, the trial court should consider, among others, the following issues: (1) whether O'Keeffe used due diligence to recover the paintings at the time of the alleged theft and thereafter; (2) whether at the time of the alleged theft there was an effective method, other than talking to her colleagues, for O'Keeffe to alert the art world; and (3) whether registering paintings with the Art Dealers Association of America, Inc. or any other organization would put a reasonably prudent purchaser of art on constructive notice that someone other than the possessor was the true owner.

V

The acquisition of title to real and personal property by adverse possession is based on the expiration of a statute of limitations. R. Brown, The Law of Personal Property (3d ed. 1975), § 4.1 at 33 (Brown). To establish title by adverse possession to chattels, the rule of law has been that the possession must be hostile, actual, visible, exclusive, and continuous. [P]roblems with the requirement of visible, open, and notorious possession readily come to mind. For example, if jewelry is stolen from a municipality in one county in New Jersey, it is unlikely that the owner would learn that someone is openly wearing that jewelry in another county or even in the same municipality. Open and visible possession of personal property, such as jewelry, may not be sufficient to put the original owner on actual or constructive notice of the identity of the possessor.

The problem is even more acute with works of art. Like many kinds of personal property, works of art are readily moved and easily concealed. O'Keeffe argues that nothing short of public display should be sufficient to alert the true owner and start the statute running. Although there is merit in that contention from the perspective of the original owner, the effect is to impose a heavy burden on the purchasers of paintings who wish to enjoy the paintings in the privacy of their homes.

In the present case, the trial court and Appellate Division concluded that the paintings, which allegedly had been kept in the private residences of the Frank family, had not been held visibly, openly, and notoriously. Notwithstanding that conclusion, the trial court ruled that the statute of limitations began to run at the time of the theft and had expired before the commencement of suit. The Appellate Division reversed the trial court on the theory that the defenses of adverse possession and expiration of the statute of limitations were identical. Nonetheless, for different reasons, the majority and dissenting judges in the Appellate Division acknowledged deficiencies in identifying the statute of limitations with adverse possession. The majority stated that, as a practical matter, requiring compliance with adverse possession would preclude barring stale claims and acquiring title to personal property. The dissenting judge feared that identifying the statutes of limitations with adverse possession would lead to a "handbook for larceny." The divergent conclusions of the lower courts suggest that the doctrine of adverse possession no longer provides a fair and reasonable means of resolving this kind of dispute.

The problem is serious. According to an affidavit submitted in this matter by the president of the International Foundation for Art Research, there has been an "explosion in art thefts" and there is a "worldwide phenomenon of art theft which has reached epidemic proportions."

The limited record before us provides a brief glimpse into the arcane world of sales of art, where paintings worth vast sums of money sometimes are bought without inquiry about their provenance. There does not appear to be a reasonably available method for an owner of art to record the ownership or theft of paintings. Similarly, there are no reasonable means readily available to a purchaser to ascertain the provenance of a painting. It may be time for the art world to establish a means by which a good faith purchaser may reasonably obtain the provenance of a painting. An efficient registry of original works of art might better serve the interests of artists, owners of art, and bona fide purchasers than the law of adverse possession with all of its uncertainties. L. DuBoff, The Deskbook of Art Law at 470-472 (Fed.Pub.Inc.1977). Although we cannot mandate the initiation of a registration system, we can develop a rule for the commencement and running of the statute of limitations that is more responsive to the needs of the art world than the doctrine of adverse possession.

We are persuaded that the introduction of equitable considerations through the discovery rule provides a more satisfactory response than the doctrine of adverse possession. The discovery rule shifts the emphasis from the conduct of the possessor to the conduct of the owner. The focus of the inquiry will no longer be whether the possessor has met the tests of adverse possession, but whether the owner has acted with due diligence in pursuing his or her personal property.

For example, under the discovery rule, if an artist diligently seeks the recovery of a lost or stolen painting, but cannot find it or discover the identity of the possessor, the statute of limitations will not begin to run. The rule permits an artist who uses reasonable efforts to report, investigate, and recover a painting to preserve the rights of title and possession.

Properly interpreted, the discovery rule becomes a vehicle for transporting equitable considerations into the statute of limitations for replevin, N.J.S.A. 2A:14-1. In determining whether the discovery rule should apply, a court should identify, evaluate, and weigh the equitable claims of all parties. If a chattel is concealed from the true owner, fairness compels tolling the statute during the period of concealment. That conclusion is consistent with tolling the statute of limitations in a medical malpractice action where the physician is guilty of fraudulent concealment.

It is consistent also with the law of replevin as it has developed apart from the discovery rule. In an action for replevin, the period of limitations ordinarily will run against the owner of lost or stolen property from the time of the wrongful taking, absent fraud or concealment. Where the chattel is fraudulently concealed, the general rule is that the statute is tolled. 51 Am.Jur.2d, Limitation of Actions, § 124 at 693; 54 C.J.S. Limitations of Actions, § 119 at 23; Annotation, "When statute of limitations commences to run against action to recover, or for conversion of, property stolen or otherwise wrongfully taken," 136 A.L.R. 658, 661-665 (1942); see Dawson, *Fraudulent Concealment and Statutes of Limitation*, 31 Mich.L.Rev. 875 (1933); Annotation, "What constitutes concealment which will prevent running of statutes of limitations," 173 A.L.R. 576 (1948); Annotation, "When statute of limitations begins to run against action for conversion of property by theft," 79 A.L.R.3d 847, § 3 at 853 (1975); see also Dawson, *Estoppel and Statutes of*

Limitation, 34 Mich.L.Rev. 1, 23-24 (1935).

A purchaser from a private party would be well-advised to inquire whether a work of art has been reported as lost or stolen. However, a bona fide purchaser who purchases in the ordinary course of business a painting entrusted to an art dealer should be able to acquire good title against the true owner. Under the U.C.C. entrusting possession of goods to a merchant who deals in that kind of goods gives the merchant the power to transfer all the rights of the entruster to a buyer in the ordinary course of business. N.J.S.A. 12A:2-403(2). In a transaction under that statute, a merchant may vest good title in the buyer as against the original owner. The interplay between the statute of limitations as modified by the discovery rule and the U.C.C. should encourage good faith purchases from legitimate art dealers and discourage trafficking in stolen art without frustrating an artist's ability to recover stolen art works.

The discovery rule will fulfill the purposes of a statute of limitations and accord greater protection to the innocent owner of personal property whose goods are lost or stolen. By diligently pursuing their goods, owners may prevent the statute of limitations from running. The meaning of due diligence will vary with the facts of each case, including the nature and value of the personal property. For example, with respect to jewelry of moderate value, it may be sufficient if the owner reports the theft to the police. With respect to art work of greater value, it may be reasonable to expect an owner to do more. In practice, our ruling should contribute to more careful practices concerning the purchase of art.

The considerations are different with real estate, and there is no reason to disturb the application of the doctrine of adverse possession to real estate. Real estate is fixed and cannot be moved or concealed. The owner of real property knows or should know where his property is located and reasonably can be expected to be aware of open, notorious, visible, hostile, continuous acts of possession on it.

Our ruling not only changes the requirements for acquiring title to personal property after an alleged unlawful taking, but also shifts the burden of proof at trial. Under the doctrine of adverse possession, the burden is on the possessor to prove the elements of adverse possession. Under the discovery rule, the burden is on the owner as the one seeking the benefit of the rule to establish facts that would justify deferring the beginning of the period of limitations.

VI

Read literally, the effect of the expiration of the statute of limitations under N.J.S.A. 2A:14-1 is to bar an action such as replevin. The statute does not speak of divesting the original owner of title. By its terms the statute cuts off the remedy, but not the right of title. Nonetheless, the effect of the expiration of the statute of limitations, albeit on the theory of adverse possession, has been not only to bar an action for possession, but also to vest title in the possessor. There is no reason to change that result although the discovery rule has replaced adverse possession. History, reason, and common sense support the conclusion that the expiration of the statute of limitations bars the remedy to recover possession and also vests title in the possessor.

Professor Brown explains the historical reason for construing the statute of limitations as barring the right of title as well as an action for possession:

> The metamorphosis of statutes simply limiting the time in which an action may be commenced into instrumentalities for the transfer of title may be explained perhaps by the historical doctrine of disseisin which, though more customarily applied to land, was probably originally controlling as to chattels also. By this doctrine the wrongful possessor as long as his possession continued, was treated as the owner and the dispossessed occupant considered merely to have a personal right to recapture his property if he could.

Brown on Personal Property, § 4.1 at 34. *See* 3 American Law of Property § 15.16 at 834.

Before the expiration of the statute, the possessor has both the chattel and the right to keep it except as against the true owner. The only imperfection in the possessor's right to retain the chattel is the original owner's right to repossess it. Once that imperfection is removed, the possessor should have good title for all purposes. Ames, *The Disseisin of Chattels*, 3 Harv.L.Rev. 313, 321 (1890) (Ames). As Dean Ames wrote: "An immortal right to bring an eternally prohibited action is a metaphysical subtlety that the present writer cannot pretend to understand." *Id.* at 319.

Recognizing a metaphysical notion of title in the owner would be of little benefit to him or her and would create potential problems for the possessor and third parties. The expiration of the six-year period of N.J.S.A. 2A:14-1 should vest title as effectively under the discovery rule as under the doctrine of adverse possession.

To summarize, the operative fact that divests the original owner of title to either personal or real property is the expiration of the period of limitations. In the past, adverse possession has described the nature of the conduct that will vest title of a chattel at the end of the statutory period. Our adoption of the discovery rule does not change the conclusion that at the end of the statutory period title will vest in the possessor.

VII

We next consider the effect of transfers of a chattel from one possessor to another during the period of limitation under the discovery rule. Under the discovery rule, the statute of limitations on an action for replevin begins to run when the owner knows or reasonably should know of his cause of action and the identity of the possessor of the chattel. Subsequent transfers of the chattel are part of the continuous dispossession of the chattel from the original owner. The important point is not that there has been a substitution of possessors, but that there has been a continuous dispossession of the former owner.

Professor Ballantine explains:

Where the same claim of title has been consistently asserted for the statutory period by persons in privity with each other, there is the same reason to quiet and establish the title as where one person has held. The same flag has been kept flying for the whole period. It is the same ouster and disseisin. If the statute runs, it quiets a title which has been consistently asserted and exercised as against the true owner, and the possession of the prior holder justly enures to the benefit of the last.

H. Ballantine, *Title by Adverse Possession*, 32 Harv.L.Rev. 135, 158 (1919).

The same principle appears in the Restatement (Second) of Torts: "In some cases, the statute of limitations begins to run before the defendant took possession as when a previous taker converted the chattel and later transferred possession to the defendant." Restatement (Second) of Torts 2d § 899 at 442 (1977).

For the purpose of evaluating the due diligence of an owner, the dispossession of his chattel is a continuum not susceptible to separation into distinct acts. Nonetheless, subsequent transfers of the chattel may affect the degree of difficulty encountered by a diligent owner seeking to recover his goods. To that extent, subsequent transfers and their potential for frustrating diligence are relevant in applying the discovery rule. An owner who diligently seeks his chattel should be entitled to the benefit of the discovery rule although it may have passed through many hands. Conversely an owner who sleeps on his rights may be denied the benefit of the discovery rule although the chattel may have been possessed by only one person.

We reject the alternative of treating subsequent transfers of a chattel as separate acts of conversion that would start the statute of limitations running anew. The majority and better view is to permit tacking, the accumulation of consecutive periods of possession by parties in privity with each other. In New Jersey tacking is firmly embedded in the law of real property. The rule has been applied also to personal property.

Treating subsequent transfers as separate acts of conversion could lead to absurd results. As explained by Dean Ames:

If a converter were to sell the chattel, five years after its conversion, to one ignorant of the seller's tort, the disposed owner's right to recover the chattel from the purchaser would continue five years longer than his right to recover from the converter would have lasted if there had been no sale. In other words, an innocent purchaser from a wrong-doer would be in a worse position than the wrong-doer himself, a conclusion as shocking in point of justice as it would be anomalous in law.

Ames, *supra* at 323.

It is more sensible to recognize that on expiration of the period of limitations, title passes from the former owner by operation of the statute. Needless uncertainty would result from starting the statute running anew merely because of a subsequent transfer. 3 American Law of Property, § 15.16 at 837. It is not necessary to strain equitable principles, as suggested by the dissent, to arrive at a just and reasonable determination of the rights of the parties. The discovery rule permits an equitable accommodation of the rights of the parties without establishing a rule of law fraught with uncertainty.

We reverse the judgment of the Appellate Division in favor of O'Keeffe and remand the matter for trial in accordance with this opinion.

NOTES AND QUESTIONS

1. **Statute.** Section 2-403 of the Uniform Commercial Code, discussed in the principal case, provides as follows:

§ 2-403. Power to Transfer; Good Faith Purchase of Goods; "Entrusting"

(1) A purchaser of goods acquires all title which his transferor had or had power to transfer except that a purchaser of a limited interest acquires rights only to the extent of the interest purchased. A person with voidable title has power to transfer a good title to a good faith purchaser for value. When goods have been delivered under a transaction of purchase the purchaser has such power even though

(a) the transferor was deceived as to the identity of the purchaser, or

(b) the delivery was in exchange for a check which is later dishonored, or

(c) it was agreed that the transaction was to be a "cash sale", or

(d) the delivery was procured through fraud punishable as larcenous under the criminal law.

(2) Any entrusting of possession of goods to a merchant who deals in goods of that kind gives him power to transfer all rights of the entruster to a buyer in ordinary course of business.

(3) "Entrusting" includes any delivery and any acquiescence in retention of possession regardless of any condition expressed between the parties to the delivery or acquiescence and regardless of whether the procurement of the entrusting or the possessor's disposition of the goods have been such as to be larcenous under the criminal law.

The general rule is that a party may transfer no greater interest in property than that party owns. Does the statute provide for that general rule? What exceptions to the general rule does the statute create? What policies does the statute advance?

2. **Sorting out doctrines.** What body of law would determine Snyder's rights if the paintings were stolen? Suppose instead that Dr. Frank bought the paintings from Stieglitz, paying with a bad check; how would that affect Snyder's position? Suppose O'Keeffe had entrusted the paintings to An American Place, which sold them to a bona fide purchaser? To the extent that the bona fide purchaser doctrine is relevant, what does Snyder have to establish to qualify as such a purchaser?

3. **The statute of limitations.** Is there more than one way to determine when the statute of limitations runs on a true owner? Note the differences between the trial court, the appellate division, and the supreme court. Which view is better, given the differences between land and moveable personal property, like paintings?

4. **Discovery rule.** How does the discovery rule differ from the requirement that an adverse possessor hold openly and notoriously? Is it possible for possession of personal property to be open and notorious and yet still not afford the owner a reasonable opportunity to discover where the property is?

5. **Tacking.** Will Snyder have to rely on tacking? Should privity be required? Does privity perform some function unrelated to the conduct of the owner? (Recall our earlier discussion in Section 3.a.)

6. **Stolen property: another view.** In Solomon R. Guggenheim Foundation v. Lubell, 569 N.E.2d 426 (N.Y. 1991), the Guggenheim Foundation demanded in January 1986 that defendant return a Chagall gouache ("The Cattle Dealers") allegedly stolen from the Foundation in the late 1960s. The defendant refused, and the Foundation sued in September 1987 to recover the gouache or its value. The defendant asserted the statute of limitations. The Court of Appeals held that the appropriate rule was demand-and-refusal rather than due diligence: "a cause of action accrues when demand is made upon the possessor and the possessor refuses to return the chattel." *Lubell*, 569 N.E.2d at 428. The court reasoned as follows:

> [T]he facts of this case reveal how difficult it would be to specify the type of conduct that would be required for a showing of reasonable diligence. According to the museum, some members of the art community believe that publicizing a theft exposes gaps in security and can lead to more thefts; the museum also argues that publicity often pushes a missing painting further underground. In light of the fact that members of the art community have apparently not reached a consensus on the best way to retrieve stolen art, it would be particularly inappropriate for this Court to spell out arbitrary rules of conduct that all true owners of stolen art would have to follow to the letter if they wanted to preserve their right to pursue a cause of action in replevin. All owners of stolen property should not be expected to behave in the same way and should not be held to a common standard. The value of the property stolen, the manner in which it was stolen, and the type of institution from which it was stolen will all necessarily affect the manner in which a true owner will search for missing property. We conclude that it would be difficult, if not impossible, to craft a reasonable diligence requirement that could take into account all of these variables and that would not unduly burden the true owner.
>
> Further, our decision today is in part influenced by our recognition that New York enjoys a worldwide reputation as a preeminent cultural center. To place the burden of locating stolen artwork on the true owner and to foreclose the rights of that owner to recover its property if the burden is not met would, we believe, encourage illicit trafficking in stolen art. Three years after the theft, any purchaser, good faith or not, would be able to hold onto stolen art work unless the true owner was able to establish that it had undertaken a reasonable search for the missing art. This shifting of the burden onto the wronged owner is inappropriate. In our opinion, the better rule gives the owner relatively greater protection and places the burden of investigating the provenance of a work of art on the potential purchaser.

Id. at 430-431.

7. **Laches.** Having said that, the New York Court of Appeals noted that the defendant had also raised a laches defense. (The museum "had done nothing for twenty years but search its own premises" for the painting.) "[A]lthough [defendant's] statute of limitations argument fails, her contention that the museum did not exercise reasonable diligence in locating the painting will be considered by the trial judge in the context of her laches defense." *Lubell*, 569 N.E.2d at 431. Query: Does the allowance of the laches defense bring the New Jersey approach in by the back door? What differences can you think of between the laches defense and the New Jersey due diligence approach?

8. **Commentary.** For recent commentary on the law of adverse possession of chattels, see Marilyn E. Phelan, *Scope of Due Diligence Investigation in Obtaining Title to Valuable Artwork*, 23 Seattle U. L. Rev. 631 (2000); Stephan J. Schlegelmilch, Note, *Ghosts of the Holocaust: Holocaust Victim Fine Arts Litigation and a Statutory Application of the Discovery Rule*, 50 Case W. Res. L. Rev. 87 (1999); Laura McFarland-Taylor, Comment, *Tracking Stolen Artworks on the Internet: A New Standard for Due Diligence*, 16 J. Marshall J. Computer & Info. L. 937 (1998); Tarquin Preziosi, Note, *Applying a Strict Discovery Rule to Art Stolen in the Past*, 49 Hastings L.J. 225 (1997); Adina Kurjatko, *Are Finders Keepers? The Need for Uniform Law Governing the Rights of Original Owners and Good Faith Purchasers of Stolen Art*, 5 U.C. Davis J. Int'l L. & Pol'y. 59 (1999); Andrea E. Hayworth, Note, *Stolen Artwork: Deciding Ownership is No Pretty Picture*, 43 Duke L.J. 337 (1993); Paula A. Franzese, *Georgia on My Mind — Reflections on* O'Keeffe v. Snyder, 19 Seton Hall L. Rev. 1 (1989).

C. TRANSFERRING INTERESTS IN THINGS: GIFTS

1. Requirements

SCHERER v. HYLAND
380 A.2d 698 (N.J. 1977)

Per Curiam.

Defendant, the administrator ad litem of the estate of Catherine Wagner, appeals from an Appellate Division decision, one judge dissenting, affirming a summary judgment by the trial court holding that Ms. Wagner had made a valid gift causa mortis of a check to plaintiff. We affirm.

The facts are not in dispute. Catherine Wagner and the plaintiff, Robert Scherer, lived together for approximately fifteen years prior to Ms. Wagner's death in January 1974. In 1970, the decedent and plaintiff were involved in an automobile accident in which decedent suffered facial wounds and a broken hip. Because of the hip injury, decedent's physical mobility was substantially impaired. She was forced to give up her job and to restrict her activities. After the accident, plaintiff cared for her and assumed the sole financial responsibility for maintaining their household. During the weeks preceding her death, Ms. Wagner was acutely depressed. On one occasion, she attempted suicide by slashing her wrists. On

January 23, 1974, she committed suicide by jumping from the roof of the apartment building in which they lived.

On the morning of the day of her death, Ms. Wagner received a check for $17,400 drawn by a Pennsylvania attorney who had represented her in a claim arising out of the automobile accident. The check represented settlement of the claim. Plaintiff telephoned Ms. Wagner at around 11:30 a.m. that day and was told that the check had arrived. Plaintiff noticed nothing unusual in Ms. Wagner's voice. At about 3:20 p.m., decedent left the apartment building and jumped to her death. The police, as part of their investigation of the suicide, asked the building superintendent to admit them to the apartment. On the kitchen table they found the check, endorsed in blank, and two notes handwritten by the decedent. In one, she described her depression over her physical condition, expressed her love for Scherer, and asked him to forgive her "for taking the easy way out." In the other, she indicated that she "bequeathed" to plaintiff all of her possessions, including "the check for $17,400.00." The police took possession of the check, which was eventually placed in an interest-bearing account pending disposition of this action.

Under our wills statute it is clear that Ms. Wagner's note bequeathing all her possessions to Mr. Scherer cannot take effect as a testamentary disposition. A donatio causa mortis has been traditionally defined as a gift of personal property made by a party in expectation of death, then imminent, subject to the condition that the donor die as anticipated. Establishment of the gift has uniformly called for proof of delivery.

The primary issue here is whether Ms. Wagner's acts of endorsing the settlement check, placing it on the kitchen table in the apartment she shared with Scherer, next to a writing clearly evidencing her intent to transfer the check to Scherer, and abandoning the apartment with a clear expectation of imminent death constituted delivery sufficient to sustain a gift causa mortis of the check. Defendant, relying on the principles established in Foster v. Reiss, 112 A.2d 553 (N.J. 1955), argues that there was no delivery because the donor did not unequivocally relinquish control of the check before her death. Central to this argument is the contention that suicide, the perceived peril, was one which decedent herself created and one which was completely within her control. According to this contention, the donor at any time before she jumped from the apartment roof could have changed her mind, re-entered the apartment, and reclaimed the check. Defendant therefore reasons that decedent did not make an effective transfer of the check during her lifetime, as is required for a valid gift causa mortis.

The majority and dissenting opinions in Foster v. Reiss contain thorough analyses of the evolution of the delivery requirement of the gift causa mortis. *See also* Mechem, *The Requirement of Delivery in Gifts of Chattels and of Choses in Action Evidenced by Commercial Instruments*, 21 Ill.L.Rev. 341, 457, 568 (1926); Burton, *The Requirement of Delivery as Applied to Gifts of Choses in Action*, 39 Yale L.J. 837 (1930). For commentary on Foster v. Reiss, *see* Bordwell, *Testate and Intestate Succession*, 10 Rutgers L.Rev. 293, 297 (1955); Note, 10 Rutgers L.Rev. 457 (1955); Note, 54 Mich.L.Rev. 572 (1956). We see no need to retrace that history here.

There is general agreement that the major purpose of the delivery requirement is evidentiary. Proof of delivery reduces the possibility that the evidence of [donative] intent has been fabricated or that a mere donative impulse, not consummated by action, has been mistaken for a completed gift. Since "these gifts come into question only after death has closed the lips of the donor," the delivery requirement provides a substantial safeguard against fraud and perjury. *See* Keepers v. Fidelity Title and Deposit Co., 28 A. 585 (N.J. 1893). In *Foster*, the majority concluded that these policies could best be fulfilled by a strict rule requiring actual manual tradition [delivery] of the subject-matter of the gift except in a very narrow class of cases where "there can be no actual delivery" or where "the situation is incompatible with the performance of such ceremony." 112 A.2d at 559. Justice Jacobs, in his dissenting opinion (joined by Justices Brennan and Wachenfeld) questioned the reasonableness of requiring direct physical delivery in cases where donative intent is "freely and clearly expressed in a written instrument." 112 A.2d at 562. He observed that a more flexible approach to the delivery requirement had been taken by other jurisdictions and quoted approvingly from Devol v. Dye, 24 N.E. 246 (Ind. 1890):

> [G]ifts causa mortis are not to be held contrary to public policy, nor do they rest under the disfavor of the law, when the facts are clearly and satisfactorily shown which make it appear that they were freely and intelligently made. While every case must be brought within the general rule upon the points essential to such a gift, yet, as the circumstances under which donations mortis causa are made must of necessity be infinite in variety, each case must be determined upon its own peculiar facts and circumstances. The rule requiring delivery, either actual or symbolical, must be maintained, but its application is to be militated and applied according to the relative importance of the subject of the gift and the condition of the donor. The intention of a donor in peril of death, when clearly ascertained and fairly consummated within the meaning of well-established rules, is not to be thwarted by a narrow and illiberal construction of what may have been intended for and deemed by him a sufficient delivery.

The balancing approach suggested in Devol v. Dye has been articulated in the following manner:

> Where there has been unequivocal proof of a deliberate and well-considered donative intent on the part of the donor, many courts have been inclined to overlook the technical requirements and to hold that by a "constructive" or "symbolic" delivery is sufficient to vest title in the donee. However, where this is allowed the evidence must clearly show an intention to part presently with some substantial attribute of ownership.

Gordon v. Barr, 91 P.2d 101, 104 (Cal. 1939). In essence, this approach takes into account the purposes served by the requirement of delivery in determining whether that requirement has been met. It would find a constructive delivery adequate to support the gift when the evidence of donative intent is concrete and undisputed, when there is every indication that the donor intended to make a present transfer of the subject-matter of the gift, and when the steps taken by the donor to effect such a transfer must have been deemed by the donor as sufficient to pass the donor's interest to the donee. We are persuaded that this approach, which does not minimize the need for evidentiary safeguards to prevent frauds upon the estates of the deceased, reflects the realities which attend transfers of this kind.

In this case, the evidence of decedent's intent to transfer the check to Robert Scherer is concrete, unequivocal, and undisputed. The circumstances definitely rule out any possibility of fraud. The sole question, then, is whether the steps taken by the decedent, independent of her writing of the suicide notes, were sufficient to support a finding that she effected a lifetime transfer of the check to Scherer. We think that they were. First, the act of endorsing a check represents, in common experience and understanding, the only act needed (short of actual delivery) to render a check negotiable. The significance of such an act is universally understood. Accordingly, we have no trouble in viewing Ms. Wagner's endorsement of the settlement check as a substantial step taken by her for the purpose of effecting a transfer to Scherer of her right to the check proceeds. Second, we note that the only person other than the decedent who had routine access to the apartment was Robert Scherer. Indeed, the apartment was leased in his name. It is clear that Ms. Wagner before leaving the apartment placed the check in a place where Scherer could not fail to see it and fully expected that he would take actual possession of the check when he entered. And, although Ms. Wagner's subsequent suicide does not itself constitute a component of the delivery of this gift, it does provide persuasive evidence that when Ms. Wagner locked the door of the apartment she did so with no expectation of returning. When we consider her state of mind as it must have been upon leaving the apartment, her surrender of possession at that moment was complete. We find, therefore, that when she left the apartment she completed a constructive delivery of the check to Robert Scherer. In light of her resolve to take her own life and of her obvious desire not to be deterred from that purpose, Ms. Wagner's failure manually to transfer the check to Scherer is understandable. She clearly did all that she could do or thought necessary to do to surrender the check. Her donative intent has been conclusively demonstrated by independent evidence. The law should effectuate that intent rather than indulge in nice distinctions which would thwart her purpose. Upon these facts, we find that the constructive delivery she made was adequate to support a gift causa mortis.

Defendant's assertion that suicide is not the sort of peril that will sustain a gift causa mortis finds some support in precedents from other jurisdictions. *See generally* Annot., Nature and validity of gift made in contemplation of suicide, 60 A.L.R.2d 575 (1958). We are, however, not bound by those authorities nor do we find them persuasive. While it is true that a gift causa mortis is made by the donor with a view to impending death, death is no less impending because of a resolve to commit suicide. Nor does that fixed purpose constitute any lesser or less imminent peril than does a ravaging disease. Indeed, given the despair sufficient to end it all, the peril attendant upon contemplated suicide may reasonably be viewed as even more imminent than that accompanying many illnesses which prove ultimately to be fatal. *Cf.* Berl v. Rosenberg, 336 P.2d 975, 978 (Cal. Dist. Ct. App. 1959) (public policy against suicide does not invalidate otherwise valid gift causa mortis). And, the notion that one in a state of mental depression serious enough to lead to suicide is somehow "freer" to renounce the depression and thus the danger than one suffering from a physical illness, although it has a certain augustinian appeal, has long since been replaced by more enlightened views of human psychology. In re Van Wormer's Estate, 238 N.W. 210 (Mich. 1931) (melancholia ending in suicide sufficient to sustain a gift causa mortis). We also observe that an argument that the donor of a causa mortis gift might have changed his or her mind loses much of its force when one recalls that a causa mortis gift, by definition, can be revoked at any time before the donor dies and is automatically revoked if the donor recovers.

Finally, defendant asserts that this gift must fail because there was no acceptance prior to the donor's death. Although the issue of acceptance is rarely litigated, the authority that does exist indicates that, given a valid delivery, acceptance will be implied if the gift is unconditional and beneficial to the donee. The presumption of acceptance may apply even if the donee does not learn of the gift until after the donor's death. Taylor v. Sanford, 193 S.W. 661, 662 (Tex. 1912) (assent to gift of deed mailed in contemplation of death but received after grantor's death should be presumed unless a dissent or disclaimer appears). A donee cannot be expected to accept or reject a gift until he learns of it, and unless a gift is rejected when the donee is informed of it the presumption of acceptance is not defeated. Here the gift was clearly beneficial to Scherer, and he has always expressed his acceptance.

Judgment affirmed.

WOO v. SMART
442 S.E.2d 690 (Va. 1994)

Compton, Justice.

The principal issue in this equity suit is whether the trial court erred in ruling that the donee of three checks is not entitled to the check proceeds as gifts causa mortis.

William D. Yee and the appellant S. Hing Woo, unmarried residents of Chesterfield County, had an intimate relationship for almost 20 years until Yee died intestate in March 1989. During the two days before his death, the decedent handed to Woo three personal checks payable to her order in the amounts of $80,000.00, $42,700.00, and $1,900.00, respectively. The day after decedent's death, she presented the latter two checks and the proceeds were paid to her. The check for $80,000.00 has never been presented for payment.

In May 1989, appellee John S. Smart qualified as administrator of the decedent's estate. In December 1989, the administrator filed a bill of complaint for declaratory judgment against the donee, alleging that the three checks were not effective gifts because they were not presented for payment and paid prior to the decedent's death. Thus, the administrator asked the court to declare that the donee is not entitled to receive any part of the decedent's estate to satisfy the $80,000.00 check. In addition, the administrator asked for judgment against the donee in the amount of $44,600.00 representing the sum of the two checks that were cashed.

Also, the administrator alleged that, in addition to a number of bank accounts, the decedent owned various securities registered in his name alone valued at $53,165.00 and the donee claims entitlement to at least one-half of those funds. The administrator asked the court to declare that the donee has no interest in those securities.

In a second amended answer and cross-bill, the donee admitted receipt of the checks and asked the court to declare that she is entitled to the proceeds of the checks as gifts causa mortis or, alternatively, upon the theory of constructive trust. Also, the donee asked the court to declare that she is entitled to at least one-half of the value of the securities registered in the decedent's name at death due to contributions she made to the stock account during the time of the "confidential relationship" that existed between the pair during decedent's lifetime.

The chancellor received testimonial and documentary evidence during an ore tenus hearing. Subsequently, in a letter opinion, the chancellor ruled that the donee was not entitled to the check proceeds and that the donee had failed to establish entitlement to any portion of the securities or accounts listed in the decedent's name at death. We awarded the donee this appeal from the February 1993 final decree, which provided for judgment against the donee in the amount of $44,600, plus interest. The donee has paid this sum to the administrator pending appeal.

The facts relevant to the transfer of the three checks are virtually undisputed. When there is a conflict, however, we will view the facts in the light most favorable to the administrator, who prevailed below, in accord with settled appellate principles.

Born in China, the decedent and the donee met in connection with the operation of a Richmond-area restaurant that was established by her father in the 1970s. The decedent, age 51 when he died, had a high school education; she, age 39 when he died, had "finished" college.

He became manager of the restaurant and she assisted him in its operation. They were "like husband and wife," occasionally living together, and maintained a close relationship that lasted for 19 years. In 1985, he was diagnosed with coronary heart disease.

The decedent had brothers and sisters living in Hong Kong, Canada, and New York, from some of whom he was estranged. He resided in a small house near the restaurant with a younger brother; she resided with her mother and two brothers at a different location. He trusted her "with all his accounts." When checks were to be drawn on his individual checking accounts, she wrote the checks "and he signed them."

On March 27, 1989, two days before his death, the decedent complained to the donee "that he was feeling terribly bad" and that he believed death was imminent. Against her advice "to stay home and take a rest," he came to the restaurant "to take care of some money in his bank." During the evening, he "gave" her the $42,700.00 check drawn on Signet Bank to "close out" his account there. The "same night," he "gave" her the $80,000.00 check drawn on Central Fidelity Bank to represent the value of "various" savings accounts at that bank. During the next day, March 28, 1989, still "feeling badly," the decedent returned to the restaurant and handed the donee the $1,900.00 check to "close out" his checking account at Central Fidelity Bank. These checks were given to the donee so that she would be "provided for"; the decedent told her that he "wanted" her "to have the money if he died."

The decedent died in a hospital emergency room on March 29, 1989; none of the checks had been cashed. The donee received the proceeds of the two checks on the day after death. The check for $80,000.00 was never presented because it represented funds in savings accounts and there were insufficient funds in the checking account to cover it.

In Virginia, we recognize two kinds of gifts: gifts inter vivos and gifts causa mortis, those made in apprehension of death. Here, the donee claims gifts of the second category, in which the distinctive elements are well settled. First, there must be an intent to make a gift. Second, the gift must be of personal property. Third, the gift must be made while the donor is under the apprehension of imminent death, upon the essential condition that the property shall belong to the donee if the donor dies as anticipated leaving the donee surviving, and the gift is not revoked in the meantime. Fourth, possession of the property given must be delivered at the time of the gift to the donee, or to someone for the donee, and the donee must accept the gift. And, the donee must establish the gift causa mortis by clear and convincing evidence.

In ruling that no valid gifts causa mortis were made, the trial court determined that the donee had established all but one of the essential elements. The court found that the decedent fully intended to make gifts of money to the donee; the evidence clearly showed the decedent wanted to provide for her if he died and the checks were handed to her for that purpose. The court also ruled that the attempted gifts of money (personal property) were made while the decedent was under the apprehension of immediate death and upon condition that the property belong to the donee if the decedent died as expected.

The trial court found, however, that the gifts failed "because delivery of the checks did not constitute delivery of the object of the gifts themselves; that is, the money in the bank." The donee contends that this ruling was erroneous. We disagree.

The narrow question presented is whether possession of the property given (the money) was delivered to the donee at the time of the alleged gift. Stated differently, the inquiry is whether a check can be the proper subject of a gift causa mortis, a question of first impression for this Court.

We adopt the majority rule elsewhere that a donor's own check drawn on a personal checking account is not, prior to acceptance or payment by the bank, the subject of a valid gift causa mortis. *See, e.g.,* Basket v. Hassell, 107 U.S. 602, 613 (1882). *See also* L.S. Tellier, Annotation, *Donor's Own Check as Subject of Gift*, 38 A.L.R.2d 594, 597 (1954). Generally, although there is contrary authority, the determination whether delivery of the donor's own check is such a gift depends upon "whether the transaction is regarded as amounting to an assignment of the portion of the deposit indicated by the check." 38 A.L.R.2d at 596.

The Uniform Commercial Code (U.C.C.) makes clear that transfer of a check does not operate as an assignment of money on deposit. Former Code § 8.3-409(1) (now in substance § 8.3A-408), applicable to this dispute, provided: "A check or other draft does not of itself operate as an assignment of any funds in the hands of the drawee available for its payment, and the drawee is not liable on the instrument until he accepts it." Because the check does not operate as an assignment of the funds, mere delivery of a check does not place the gift beyond the donor's power of revocation and the check simply becomes an unenforceable promise to make a gift.

In addition, the required delivery must be "actual and complete, such as deprives the donor of all further control and dominion." Quarles v. Fowlkes, 137 S.E. 365, 369 (Va. 1927). Until the check is paid, the donor retains control and dominion over the funds and the gift is incomplete; the donor could stop payment or write another check for the funds payable to a third person, or the donor may die, thus revoking the donor-drawer's command to the drawee bank to pay the money. Sturgill v. Virginia Citizens Bank, 291 S.E.2d 207, 209 (Va. 1982) (death of principal terminates agent's authority that is not coupled with an interest).

Accordingly, as the trial court ruled, while three checks were delivered by the decedent to the donee, "no money was delivered." Because no money was delivered, no money successfully can be claimed by the donee as a gift causa mortis.

We reject the donee's contention that the foregoing section of the U.C.C. "was meant to protect banks against a holder of a check, not to address the rights of other non-bank parties as to the funds on deposit in the account." The statute is clear and unambiguous; it is not limited as the donee suggests.

And, contrary to the donee's argument, the Official Comment to the section does not require these gifts to be validated. After noting that "a check or other draft does not of itself operate as an assignment in law or equity," the Comment states that an "assignment may, however, appear from other agreements, express or implied; and when the intent to assign is clear the check may be the means by which the assignment is effected." The donee argues, "If one could never use a check for an assignment, this official comment has no meaning." But it is the statute that would be rendered meaningless if the Comment were applied to authenticate the gifts in this case, in which there is the effort to validate the gratuitous promise of a deceased donor.

Alternatively, the donee argues that even if the trial court correctly concluded "that the requirement of delivery was not met," the court erred in refusing to impose a constructive trust in her favor on funds representing the amounts of the checks. We disagree.

To impose a constructive trust under these circumstances, which certainly present a sympathetic case for equitable relief, would eviscerate the doctrine of gift causa mortis and eliminate delivery as an essential element. Intent to make a gift causa mortis, no matter how clear, cannot overcome the lack of delivery and validate the gift under the guise of imposing a constructive trust.

[W]e hold there is no error in the judgment below and it will be

Affirmed.

NOTES AND QUESTIONS

1. **Gifts inter vivos and causa mortis; requirements.** Both *Hyland* and *Woo* deal with gifts "causa mortis" — gifts made by the donor in contemplation of impending death — as distinguished from inter vivos gifts — the "ordinary present unconditional gifts between living persons." Brown on Personal Property § 7.1, at 77. The requirements for the two types of gifts are the same, but "because of the greater opportunity for fraudulent claims in gifts causa mortis due to the ensuing death of the donor" (*id.* § 7.1, at 77), some courts construe the requirements more strictly in the case of deathbed gifts. What are the requirements for a valid gift? Which requirement was at issue in the two principal cases?

2. **Functions of delivery.** The court in *Hyland* cites Professor Philip Mechem's article for the proposition that the "major purpose" of the delivery requirement is evidentiary. Evidence of what? Suppose a would-be donee claims a watch that is still in the possession of the donor, testifying credibly that the donor said "I want this watch to be yours." Result? Suppose the donor claims a watch back from a donee, testifying that he or she did not intend to make a gift of it. Result?

3. **The "wrench of delivery."** Can you think of any other function(s) that the delivery requirement might perform? Hypothesize an impulsive or imprudent person, who — right now — fully intends to give his watch to his best friend. What service might the delivery requirement perform with regard to such a donor?

4. **Compliance.** Were the reasons for requiring delivery satisfied in *Hyland*? In *Woo*? What policy is achieved by denying the validity of the gift in *Woo*? Are the two cases distinguishable? If not, why do you think that the courts reached different results?

5. **Symbolic and constructive delivery.** An object capable of manual delivery ordinarily must be handed over to the donee to satisfy the delivery requirement. Where manual delivery is impractical, however, courts may permit a substitute delivery, either constructive or symbolic.

> The traditional understanding is that a delivery is constructive if the donor gives the donee the means of obtaining possession or control of the subject of the gift, for example by giving the donee the key to the place where the property is located. The traditional understanding of symbolic delivery is that it is one in which the donor gives the donee an object or item that symbolizes the subject of the gift. The classic example of a symbolic delivery is delivery of an inter vivos donative document to the donee.

Restatement Third of Property — Wills and Other Donative Transfers § 6.2, cmt. g (2003). Some courts make the distinction, while others do not. "In fact, no legal consequence turns on the distinction." *Id.* Was the delivery in *Hyland* actual, symbolic, or constructive? *See generally* Brown on Personal Property § 7.5.

6. **Revocation of a gift causa mortis.** The court in Hart v. Ketchum, 53 P. 931, 931-32 (Cal. 1898) made the following statement about gifts causa mortis:

It is essential to a gift causa mortis that the donor shall confer upon the donee, at the time of the gift, a present title and property in the thing given; and, if the thing given is capable of corporeal delivery, there must be an actual or symbolical delivery of it, or if it is not so capable, the means of obtaining control and possession of the thing must be then given. Unless the property in the thing given vests in the donee, it remains in the donor, and there is only a purpose or intention on his part to make a gift. Such purpose or intention is incapable of enforcement. The law requires a gift causa mortis to be absolute [i.e., complete] at the time it is given, but adds to it the condition that it may be revoked at the will of the donor, and that it is revoked by his recovery; but if, by the terms of the gift, it is not to take effect until after the death of the donor, the disposal is testamentary, and not a gift.

7. **Testamentary transfers.** A will transfers property at the time of the testator's death. Until death, the maker of the will may revise it or revoke it entirely. A will is invalid unless it complies with various statutory requirements such as a writing, signature, and witnesses. *See* Chapter 2, Section A.1.c (discussing requirements for execution of a will).

8. **A case to compare.** In Basket v. Hassell, 107 U.S. 602 (1883), Chaney owned a certificate of deposit, which he indorsed "during his last sickness and in apprehension of death" as follows:

Pay to Martin Basket, of Henderson, Ky.; no one else; then, not till my death. My life seems to be uncertain. I may live through this spell. Then I will attend to it myself.

H. M. CHANEY.

Chaney delivered the CD to Basket and subsequently died from his sickness. In holding the gift invalid, the court stated:

[A] donatio mortis causa must be completely executed, precisely as required in the case of gifts inter vivos, subject to be[ing] divested by the happening of any of the conditions subsequent; that is, upon actual revocation by the donor, or by the donor's surviving the apprehended peril, or outliving the donee, or by the occurrence of a deficiency of assets necessary to pay the debts of the deceased donor. These conditions are the only qualifications that distinguish gifts mortis causa and inter vivos. On the other hand, if the gift does not take effect as an executed and complete transfer to the donee of possession and title, either legal or equitable, during the life of the donor, it is a testamentary disposition, good only if made and proved as a will.

Basket, 107 U.S. at 609-10. How does this case compare to *Hyland*? To *Woo*?

GRUEN v. GRUEN
496 N.E.2d 869 (N.Y. 1986)

SIMONS, JUDGE.

Plaintiff commenced this action seeking a declaration that he is the rightful owner of a painting which he alleges his father, now deceased, gave to him. He concedes that he has never had possession of the painting but asserts that his father made a valid gift of the title in 1963 reserving a life estate for himself. His father retained possession of the painting until he died in 1980. Defendant, plaintiff's stepmother, has the painting now and has refused plaintiff's requests that she turn it over to him. She contends that the purported gift was testamentary in nature and invalid insofar as the formalities of a will were not met or, alternatively, that a donor may not make a valid inter vivos gift of a chattel and retain a life estate with a complete right of possession. Following a seven-day nonjury trial, Special Term found that plaintiff had failed to establish any of the elements of an inter vivos gift and that in any event an attempt by a donor to retain a present possessory life estate in a chattel invalidated a purported gift of it. The Appellate Division held that a valid gift may be made reserving a life estate and, finding the elements of a gift established in this case, it reversed and remitted the matter for a determination of value (104 A.D.2d 171, 488 N.Y.S.2d 401). That determination has now been made and defendant appeals directly to this court from the subsequent final judgment entered in Supreme Court awarding plaintiff $2,500,000 in damages representing the value of the painting, plus interest. We now affirm.

The subject of the dispute is a work entitled "Schloss Kammer am Attersee II" painted by a noted Austrian modernist, Gustav Klimt. It was purchased by plaintiff's father, Victor Gruen, in 1959 for $8,000. On April 1, 1963 the elder Gruen, a successful architect with offices and residences in both New York City and Los Angeles during most of the time involved in this action, wrote a letter to plaintiff, then an undergraduate student at Harvard, stating that he was giving him the Klimt painting for his birthday but that he wished to retain the possession of it for his lifetime. This letter is not in evidence, apparently because plaintiff destroyed it on instructions from his father. Two other letters were received, however, one dated May 22, 1963 and the other April 1, 1963. Both had been dictated by Victor Gruen and sent together to plaintiff on or about May 22, 1963. The letter dated May 22, 1963 reads as follows:

Dear Michael:

I wrote you at the time of your birthday about the gift of the painting by Klimt.

Now my lawyer tells me that because of the existing tax laws, it was wrong to mention in that letter that I want to use the painting as long as I live. Though I still want to use it, this should not appear in the letter. I am enclosing, therefore, a new letter and I ask you to send the old one back to me so that it can be destroyed.

I know this is all very silly, but the lawyer and our accountant insist that they must have in their possession copies of a letter which will serve the purpose of making it possible for you, once I die, to get this picture without having to pay inheritance taxes on it.

Love,

s/Victor.

Enclosed with this letter was a substitute gift letter, dated April 1, 1963, which stated:

Dear Michael:

The 21st birthday, being an important event in life, should be celebrated accordingly. I therefore wish to give you as a present the oil painting by Gustav Klimt of Schloss Kammer which now hangs in the New York living room. You know that Lazette and I bought it some 5 or 6 years ago, and you always told us how much you liked it.

Happy birthday again.

Love,

s/Victor.

Plaintiff never took possession of the painting nor did he seek to do so. Except for a brief period between 1964 and 1965 when it was on loan to art exhibits and when restoration work was performed on it, the painting remained in his father's possession, moving with him from New York City to Beverly Hills and finally to Vienna, Austria, where Victor Gruen died on February 14, 1980. Following Victor's death plaintiff requested possession of the Klimt painting and when defendant refused, he commenced this action.

The issues framed for appeal are whether a valid inter vivos gift of a chattel may be made where the donor has reserved a life estate in the chattel and the donee never has had physical possession of it before the donor's death and, if it may, which factual findings on the elements of a valid inter vivos gift more nearly comport with the weight of the evidence in this case, those of Special Term or those of the Appellate Division. The latter issue requires application of two general rules. First, to make a valid inter vivos gift there must exist the intent on the part of the donor to make a present transfer; delivery of the gift, either actual or constructive to the donee; and acceptance by the donee. Second, the proponent of a gift has the burden of proving each of these elements by clear and convincing evidence.

Donative Intent

There is an important distinction between the intent with which an inter vivos gift is made and the intent to make a gift by will. An inter vivos gift requires that the donor intend to make an irrevocable present transfer of ownership; if the intention is to make a testamentary disposition effective only after death, the gift is invalid unless made by will.

Defendant contends that the trial court was correct in finding that Victor did not intend to transfer any present interest in the painting to plaintiff in 1963 but only expressed an intention that plaintiff was to get the painting upon his death. The evidence is all but conclusive, however, that Victor intended to transfer ownership of the painting to plaintiff in 1963 but to retain a life estate in it and that he did, therefore, effectively transfer a remainder interest in the painting to plaintiff at that time. Although the original letter was not in evidence, testimony of its contents was received along with the substitute gift letter and its covering letter dated May 22, 1963. The three letters should be considered together as a single instrument, and when they are they unambiguously establish that Victor Gruen intended to make a present gift of title to the painting at that time.

But there was other evidence, for after 1963 Victor made several statements orally and in writing indicating that he had previously given plaintiff the painting and that plaintiff owned it. Victor Gruen retained possession of the property, insured it, allowed others to exhibit it and made necessary repairs to it but those acts are not inconsistent with his retention of a life estate. Furthermore, whatever probative value could be attached to his statement that he had bequeathed the painting to his heirs, made 16 years later when he prepared an export license application so that he could take the painting out of Austria, is negated by the overwhelming evidence that he intended a present transfer of title in 1963. Victor's failure to file a gift tax return on the transaction was partially explained by allegedly erroneous legal advice he received, and while that omission sometimes may indicate that the donor had no intention of making a present gift, it does not necessarily do so and it is not dispositive in this case.

Defendant contends that even if a present gift was intended, Victor's reservation of a lifetime interest in the painting defeated it. She relies on a statement from Young v. Young, 80 N.Y. 422 that "[a]ny gift of chattels which expressly reserves the use of the property to the donor for a certain period, or as long as the donor shall live, is ineffectual" (id. at 436, quoting 2 Schouler, Personal Property at 118). The statement was dictum, however, and the holding of the court was limited to a determination that an attempted gift of bonds in which the donor reserved the interest for life failed because there had been no delivery of the gift, either actual or constructive. The court expressly left undecided the question "whether a remainder in a chattel may be created and given by a donor by carving out a life estate for himself and transferring the remainder." Young v. Young, 80 N.Y. at p. 440. We answered part of that question in Matter of Brandreth, 169 N.Y. 437, 441-442, 62 N.E. 563, when we held that "[in] this state a life estate and remainder can be created in a chattel or a fund the same as in real property." The case did not require us to decide whether there could be a valid gift of the remainder.

Defendant recognizes that a valid inter vivos gift of a remainder interest can be made not only of real property but also of such intangibles as stocks and bonds. Indeed, several of the cases she cites so hold. That being so, it is difficult to perceive any legal basis for the distinction she urges which would permit gifts of remainder interests in those properties but not of remainder interests in chattels such as the Klimt painting here. The only reason suggested is that the gift of a chattel must include a present right to possession. The application of *Brandreth* to permit a gift of the remainder in this case, however, is consistent with the distinction, well recognized in the law of gifts as well as in real property law, between ownership and possession or enjoyment. Insofar as some of our cases purport to require that the donor intend to transfer both title and possession immediately to have a valid inter vivos gift, they state the rule too broadly and confuse the effectiveness of a gift with the transfer of the possession of the subject of that gift. The correct test is "whether the maker intended the [gift] to have no effect until after the maker's death, or whether he intended it to transfer some present interest," McCarthy v. Pieret, 281 N.Y. 407, 409, 24 N.E.2d 102. As long as the evidence establishes an intent to make a present and irrevocable transfer of title or the right of ownership, there is a present transfer of some interest and the gift is effective immediately. Thus, in Speelman v. Pascal, 10 N.Y.2d 313, 178 N.E.2d 723, we held valid a gift of a percentage of the future royalties to the play "My Fair Lady" before the play even existed. There, as in this case, the donee received title or the right of ownership to some property immediately upon the making of the gift but possession or enjoyment of the subject of the gift was postponed to some future time.

Defendant suggests that allowing a donor to make a present gift of a remainder with the reservation of a life estate will lead courts to effectuate otherwise invalid testamentary dispositions of property. The two have entirely different characteristics, however, which make them distinguishable. Once the gift is made it is irrevocable and the donor is limited to the rights of a life tenant not an owner. Moreover, with the gift of a remainder title vests immediately in the donee and any possession is postponed until the donor's death whereas under a will neither title nor possession vests immediately. Finally, the postponement of enjoyment of the gift is produced by the express terms of the gift not by the nature of the instrument as it is with a will.

Delivery

In order to have a valid inter vivos gift, there must be a delivery of the gift, either by a physical delivery of the subject of the gift or a constructive or symbolic delivery such as by an instrument of gift, sufficient to divest the donor of dominion and control over the property. As the statement of the rule suggests, the requirement of delivery is not rigid or inflexible, but is to be applied in light of its purpose to avoid mistakes by donors and fraudulent claims by donees. *See* Mechem, *Requirement of Delivery in Gifts of Chattels and of Choses in Actions Evidenced by Commercial Instruments*, 21 Ill.L.Rev. 341, 348-349. Accordingly, what is sufficient to constitute delivery "must be tailored to suit the circumstances of the case." Matter of Szabo, 10 N.Y.2d 94, 98, 176 N.E.2d 395. The rule requires that "[t]he delivery necessary to consummate a gift must be as perfect as the nature of the property and the circumstances and surroundings of the parties will reasonably permit." *Id.*

Defendant contends that when a tangible piece of personal property such as a painting is the subject of a gift, physical delivery of the painting itself is the best form of delivery and should be required. Here, of course, we have only delivery of Victor Gruen's letters which serve as instruments of gift. Defendant's statement of the rule as applied may be generally true, but it ignores the fact that what Victor Gruen gave plaintiff was not all rights to the Klimt painting, but only title to it with no right of possession until his death. Under these circumstances, it would be illogical for the law to require the donor to part with possession of the painting when that is exactly what he intends to retain.

Nor is there any reason to require a donor making a gift of a remainder interest in a chattel to physically deliver the chattel into the donee's hands only to have the donee redeliver it to the donor. As the facts of this case demonstrate, such a requirement could impose practical burdens on the parties to the gift while serving the delivery requirement poorly. Thus, in order to accomplish this type of delivery the parties would have been required to travel to New York for the symbolic transfer and redelivery of the Klimt painting which was hanging on the wall of Victor Gruen's Manhattan apartment. Defendant suggests that such a requirement would be stronger evidence of a completed gift, but in the absence of witnesses to the event or any written confirmation of the gift it would provide less protection against fraudulent claims than have the written instruments of gift delivered in this case.

Acceptance

Acceptance by the donee is essential to the validity of an inter vivos gift, but when a gift is of value to the donee, as it is here, the law will presume an acceptance on his part. Plaintiff did not rely on this presumption alone but also presented clear and convincing proof of his acceptance of a remainder interest in the Klimt painting by evidence that he had made several contemporaneous statements acknowledging the gift to his friends and associates, even showing some of them his father's gift letter, and that he had retained both letters for over 17 years to verify the gift after his father died. Defendant relied exclusively on affidavits filed by plaintiff in a matrimonial action with his former wife, in which plaintiff failed to list his interest in the painting as an asset. These affidavits were made over 10 years after acceptance was complete and they do not even approach the evidence in Matter of Kelly, 33 N.E.2d 62, where the donee, immediately upon delivery of a diamond ring, rejected it as "too flashy." We agree with the Appellate Division that interpretation of the affidavit was too speculative to support a finding of rejection and overcome the substantial showing of acceptance by plaintiff.

Accordingly, the judgment appealed from and the order of the Appellate Division brought up for review should be affirmed, with costs.

NOTES AND QUESTIONS

1. **Present and future.** You learned in Contracts that a *promise* to make a gift in the future is invalid. Why? How does a gift differ from a promise to make a gift?

2. **The principal case.** What exactly did Victor Gruen give to his son Michael? The Klimt painting of course; but how can Victor give it when he in fact kept it in his possession? Why didn't Victor's letters constitute merely an unenforceable promise to give the painting, or an invalid (unwitnessed) will? If Michael got something when Victor delivered the letters, what did he get?

3. **Hypothetical.** Suppose that Victor had changed his mind in Vienna, and had decided that he didn't want Michael to have the Klimt. Could Michael have enforced the gift? Suppose that Victor had sold the painting to a third party; could Michael recover it from the third party?

4. **Delivery.** Once you identify what Michael got, the question of delivery becomes easy, doesn't it? How did Victor accomplish delivery of his gift to Michael?

5. **Symbolic or constructive delivery.** Was the delivery in *Gruen* actual, symbolic, or constructive?

LINDH v. SURMAN
742 A.2d 643 (Pa. 1999)

NEWMAN, JUSTICE.

In this appeal, we are asked to decide whether a donee of an engagement ring must return the ring or its equivalent value when the donor breaks the engagement.

The facts of this case depict a tumultuous engagement between Rodger Lindh (Rodger), a divorced, middle-aged man, and Janis Surman (Janis), the object of Rodger's inconstant affections. In August of 1993, Rodger proposed marriage to Janis. To that purpose, he presented her with a diamond engagement ring that he purchased for $17,400. Rodger testified that the price was less than the ring's market value because he was a "good customer" of the jeweler's, having previously purchased a $4,000 ring for his ex-wife and other expensive jewelry for his children. Janis, who had never been married, accepted his marriage proposal and the ring. Discord developed in the relationship between Rodger and Janis, and in October of 1993 Rodger broke the engagement and asked for the return of the ring. At that time, Janis obliged and gave Rodger the ring. Rodger and Janis attempted to reconcile. They succeeded, and Rodger again proposed marriage, and offered the ring, to Janis. For a second time, Janis accepted. In March of 1994, however, Rodger called off the engagement. He asked for the return of the ring, which Janis refused, and this litigation ensued.

Rodger filed a two-count complaint against Janis, seeking recovery of the ring or a judgment for its equivalent value. The case proceeded to arbitration, where a panel of arbitrators awarded judgment for Janis. Rodger appealed to the Court of Common Pleas of Allegheny County, where a brief non-jury trial resulted in a judgment in favor of Rodger in the amount of $21,200. The basis for the $21,200 award of the trial court was Rodger's testimony that this was the fair market value of the ring. Janis appealed to the Superior Court, which affirmed the trial court in a 2-1 panel decision. Judge Ford Elliott, writing for the majority, held that no-fault principles should control, and that the ring must be returned regardless of who broke the engagement, and irrespective of the reasons. In a dissenting opinion, Judge Schiller criticized the majority opinion for creating what he termed a "romantic bailment" because of its refusal to examine the actions of the donor in breaking the engagement, thereby creating a per se rule requiring the return of an engagement ring in all circumstances. We granted allocatur to answer this novel question of Pennsylvania law.

We begin our analysis with the only principle on which all parties agree: that Pennsylvania law treats the giving of an engagement ring as a conditional gift. *See* Pavlicic v. Vogtsberger, 136 A.2d 127 (Pa. 1957). In *Pavlicic*, the plaintiff supplied his ostensible fiancee with numerous gifts, including money for the purchase of engagement and wedding rings, with the understanding that they were given on the condition that she marry him. When the defendant left him for another man, the plaintiff sued her for recovery of these gifts. Justice Musmanno explained the conditional gift principle:

> A gift given by a man to a woman on condition that she embark on the sea of matrimony with him is no different from a gift based on the condition that the donee sail on any other sea. If, after receiving the provisional gift, the donee refuses to leave the harbor — if the anchor of contractual performance sticks in the sands of irresolution and procrastination — the gift must be restored to the donor.

136 A.2d at 130.

Where the parties disagree, however, is: (1) what is the condition of the gift (i.e., acceptance of the engagement or the marriage itself), and (2) whether fault is relevant to determining return of the ring. Janis argues that the condition of the gift is acceptance of the marriage proposal, not the performance of the marriage ceremony. She also contends that Pennsylvania law, which treats engagement gifts as implied-in-law conditional gifts, has never recognized a right of recovery in a donor who severs the engagement. In her view, we should not recognize such a right where the donor breaks off the engagement, because, if the condition of the gift is performance of the marriage ceremony, that would reward a donor who prevents the occurrence of the condition, which the donee was ready, willing, and eagerly waiting to perform.

Janis first argues that the condition of the gift is acceptance of the proposal of marriage, such that acceptance of the proposal vests absolute title in the donee. This theory is contrary to Pennsylvania's view of the engagement ring situation. In Ruehling v. Hornung, 98 Pa.Super. 535 (1930), the Superior Court provided what is still the most thorough Pennsylvania appellate court analysis of the problem:

> It does not appear whether the engagement was broken by plaintiff or whether it was dissolved by mutual consent. It follows that in order to permit a recovery by plaintiff, it would be necessary to hold that the gifts were subject to the implied condition that they would be returned by the donee to the donor whenever the engagement was dissolved. Under such a rule *the marriage would be a necessary prerequisite* to the passing of an absolute title to a Christmas gift made in such circumstances. We are unwilling to go that far, *except as to the engagement ring*.

Id. at 540 (emphasis added). This Court later affirmed that "[t]he promise to return an antenuptial gift made in contemplation of marriage *if the marriage does not take place* is a fictitious promise implied in law." Semenza v. Alfano, 279 A.2d 29, 31 (Pa. 1971) (emphasis added). Our case law clearly recognizes the giving of an engagement gift as having an implied condition that the marriage must occur in order to vest title in the donee; mere acceptance of the marriage proposal is not the implied condition for the gift.

Janis's argument that Pennsylvania law does not permit the donor to recover the ring where the donor terminates the engagement has some basis in the few Pennsylvania authorities that have addressed the matter. The following language from *Ruehling* implies that Janis's position is correct:

> We think that it [the engagement ring] is always given subject to the implied condition that if the marriage does not take place either because of the death, or a disability recognized by the law on the part of, either party, or by breach of the contract by the donee, or its dissolution by mutual consent, the gift shall be returned.

Ruehling, 98 Pa.Super. at 540. Noticeably absent from the recital by the court of the situations where the ring must be returned is when the donor breaks the engagement. Other Pennsylvania authorities also suggest that the donor cannot recover the ring when the donor breaks the engagement. *See* 7 Summary of Pennsylvania Jurisprudence 2d § 15:29, p. 111 ("upon breach of the marriage engagement by the donee, the property may be recovered by the donor"); 17 Pennsylvania Law Encyclopedia, "Gifts," § 9, p. 118 (citing to a 1953 common pleas court decision, "[i]f, on the other hand, the donor wrongfully terminates the engagement, he is not entitled to return of the ring").

This Court, however, has not decided the question of whether the donor is entitled to return of the ring where the donor admittedly ended the engagement. In the context of our conditional gift approach to engagement rings, the issue we must resolve is whether we will follow the fault-based theory, argued by Janis, or the no-fault rule advocated by Rodger. Under a fault-based analysis, return of the ring depends on an assessment of who broke the engagement, which necessarily entails a determination of why that person broke the engagement. A no-fault approach, however, involves no investigation into the motives or reasons for the cessation of the engagement and requires the return of the engagement ring simply upon the nonoccurrence of the marriage.

The rule concerning the return of a ring founded on fault principles has superficial appeal because, in the most outrageous instances of unfair behavior, it appeals to our sense of equity. Where one fiancee has truly "wronged" the other, depending on whether that person was the donor of the ring or the donee, justice appears to dictate that the wronged individual should be allowed to keep, or have the ring returned. However, the process of determining who is "wrong" and who is "right," when most modern relationships are complex circumstances, makes the fault-based approach less desirable. A thorough fault-based inquiry would not only end with the question of who terminated the engagement, but would also examine that person's reasons. In some instances the person who terminated the engagement may have been entirely justified in his or her actions. This kind of inquiry would invite the parties to stage the most bitter and unpleasant accusations against those whom they nearly made their spouse, and a court would have no clear guidance with regard to how to ascertain who was "at fault." The Supreme Court of Kansas recited the difficulties with the fault-based system:

What is fault or the unjustifiable calling off of an engagement? By way of illustration, should courts be asked to determine which of the following grounds for breaking an engagement is fault or justified? (1) The parties have nothing in common; (2) one party cannot stand prospective in-laws; (3) a minor child of one of the parties is hostile to and will not accept the other party; (4) an adult child of one of the parties will not accept the other party; (5) the parties' pets do not get along; (6) a party was too hasty in proposing or accepting the proposal; (7) the engagement was a rebound situation which is now regretted; (8) one party has untidy habits that irritate the other; or (9) the parties have religious differences. The list could be endless.

Heiman v. Parrish, 942 P.2d 631, 637 (Kan. 1997).

A ring-return rule based on fault principles will inevitably invite acrimony and encourage parties to portray their ex-fiancees in the worst possible light, hoping to drag out the most favorable arguments to justify, or to attack, the termination of an engagement. Furthermore, it is unlikely that trial courts would be presented with situations where fault was clear and easily ascertained and, as noted earlier, determining what constitutes fault would result in a rule that would defy universal application.

The approach that has been described as the modern trend is to apply a no-fault rule to engagement ring cases. *See* Vigil v. Haber, 888 P.2d 455 (N.M.1994). Courts that have applied no-fault principles to engagement ring cases have borrowed from the policies of their respective legislatures that have moved away from the notion of fault in their divorce statutes. *See, e.g., Vigil,* supra (relying on the New Mexico legislature's enactment of the first no-fault divorce statute); Aronow v. Silver, 223 N.J.Super. 344, 538 A.2d 851 (1987) (noting New Jersey's approval of no-fault divorce). As described by the court in *Vigil,* this trend represents a move "towards a policy that removes fault-finding from the personal-relationship dynamics of marriage and divorce." *Vigil,* 888 P.2d at 457. Indeed, by 1986, with the passage by the South Dakota legislature of no-fault divorce provisions, all fifty states had adopted some form of no-fault divorce. Doris Jonas Freed & Timothy B. Walker, *Family Law in the Fifty States: An Overview,* 19 Fam. L.Q. 331, 335 (1986). Pennsylvania, no exception to this trend, recognizes no-fault divorces. *See* 23 Pa.C.S. § 3301(c), (d). We agree with those jurisdictions that have looked towards the development of no-fault divorce law for a principle to decide engagement ring cases, and the inherent weaknesses in any fault-based system lead us to adopt a no-fault approach to resolution of engagement ring disputes.

Having adopted this no-fault principle, we still must address the original argument that the donor should not get return of the ring when the donor terminates the engagement. Such a rule would be consonant with a no-fault approach, it is argued, because it need not look at the reasons for termination of the engagement; if there is proof that the donor ended the relationship, then he has frustrated the occurrence of the condition and cannot benefit from that. In other words, we are asked to adopt a no-fault approach that would always deny the donor return of the ring where the donor breaks the engagement.

We decline to adopt this modified no-fault position,[3] and hold that the donor is entitled to return of the ring even if the donor broke the engagement. We believe that the benefits from the certainty of our rule outweigh its negatives, and that a strict no-fault approach is less flawed than a fault-based theory or modified no-fault position.

We affirm the Order of the Superior Court.

CAPPY, JUSTICE, dissenting.

The majority advocates that a strict no-fault policy be applied to broken engagements. In endorsing this view, the majority argues that it is not only the modern trend but also the approach which will eliminate the inherent weaknesses of a fault based analysis. According to the majority, by adopting a strict no fault approach, we will remove from the courtroom the necessity of delving into the inter-personal dynamics of broken engagements in order to decide which party retains possession of the engagement ring. This view brings to mind the words of Thomas Campbell from *The Jilted Nymph*: "Better be courted and jilted than never be courted at all." As I cannot endorse this approach, I respectfully dissent.

An engagement ring is a traditional token of the pledge to marry. It is a symbol of nuptial intent dating back to AD 860. The engagement ring was to be of a valued metal representing a financial sacrifice for the husband to be. Two other customs regarding the engagement ring were established in that same century: forfeiture of the ring by a man who reneged on a marriage pledge; surrender of the ring by the woman who broke off an engagement. *See* Charles Panati, Extraordinary Origins of Everyday Things (1987). This concept is consistent with conditional gift law, which has always been followed in Pennsylvania. When the marriage does not take place the agreement is void and the party who prevented the marriage agreement from being fulfilled must forfeit the engagement ring.

The majority urges adoption of its position to relieve trial courts from having the onerous task of sifting through the debris of the broken engagement in order to ascertain who is truly at fault and if there lies a valid justification excusing fault. Could not this theory justifying the majority's decision be advanced in all other arenas that our trial courts must venture? Are broken engagements truly more disturbing than cases where we ask judges and juries to discern possible abuses in nursing homes, day care centers, dependency proceedings involving abused children, and criminal cases involving horrific, irrational injuries to innocent victims? The subject matter our able trial courts address on a daily basis is certainly of equal sordidness as any fact pattern they may need to address in a simple case of who broke the engagement and why.

I can envision a scenario whereby the prospective bride and her family have expended thousands of dollars in preparation for the culminating event of matrimony and she is, through no fault of her own, left standing at the altar holding the

---

[3] The modified no-fault position is no more satisfactory than a strict no-fault system because it, too, would create an injustice whenever the donor who called off the wedding had compelling reasons to do so.

caterer's bill. To add insult to injury, the majority would also strip her of her engagement ring. Why the majority feels compelled to modernize this relatively simple and ancient legal concept is beyond the understanding of this poor man.

Accordingly, as I see no valid reason to forgo the established precedent in Pennsylvania for determining possession of the engagement ring under the simple concept of conditional gift law, I cannot endorse the modern trend advocated by the majority. Respectfully, I dissent.

Justices CASTILLE and SAYLOR join this dissenting opinion.

CASTILLE, JUSTICE, dissenting.

I dissent from the majority's opinion because I do not believe that a no-fault policy should be applied to broken engagements and the issue of which party retains the engagement ring. The Restatement of Restitution, § 58 comment c, discusses the return of engagement rings and states that:

> Gifts made in the hope that a marriage or contract of marriage will result are not recoverable, in the absence of fraud. Gifts made in anticipation of marriage are not ordinarily expressed to be conditional and, although there is an engagement to marry, if the marriage fails to occur without the fault of the donee, normally the gift cannot be recovered. If, however, the donee obtained the gift fraudulently or if the gift was made for a purpose which could be obtained only by the marriage, a donor who is not himself at fault is entitled to restitution if the marriage does not take place, even if the gift was money. If there is an engagement to marry and the donee, having received the gift without fraud, later wrongfully breaks the promise of marriage, the donor is entitled to restitution if the gift is an engagement ring, a family heirloom or other similar thing intimately connected with the marriage, but not if the gift is one of money intended to be used by the donee before the marriage.

I believe that the Restatement approach is superior to the no-fault policy espoused by the majority because it allows equity its proper place in the outcome. Here, it is undisputed that appellee twice broke his engagement with appellant. Clearly, appellant was not at fault in the breaking off of the couple's engagement, and there is no allegation that she fraudulently induced appellee to propose marriage to her twice. Fairness dictates that appellant, who is the innocent party in this couple's ill-fated romantic connection, retain the engagement ring, which was given to her by appellee as an unconditional gift. I would therefore reverse the order of the Superior Court.

Justices CAPPY and SAYLOR join this dissenting opinion.

NOTES AND QUESTIONS

1. **Types of conditional gifts.** What similarities are there between gifts in contemplation of marriage, and gifts in contemplation of death; what justifies making both of them conditional? Should it be possible for the donor to make any inter vivos gift conditional?

2. **Fault.** In your view, who has the better argument in the principal case on the relevance of fault to the donor's recovery of a gift in contemplation of marriage? For a case agreeing with the principal case, see Meyer v. Mitnick, 625 N.W.2d 136, 140 (Mich. Ct. App. 2001) (donor entitled to return of $19,500 engagement ring upon termination of engagement no matter who was at fault). For a critique of the principal case, see Andrew Kull, *The Simplification of Private Law*, 51 J. Leg. Ed. 284 (2001). *See also* Cooper v. Smith, 800 N.E.2d 372, 378-79 (Ohio Ct. App. 2003) (surveying approaches to disputes over premarital gifts and concluding that engagement ring was a conditional gift, recoverable by donor regardless of fault, but other premarital gifts, including car, computer, tanning bed, and horses, were irrevocable unless expressly conditioned on occurrence of the marriage).

3. **Land.** Gifts of land made in contemplation of marriage may also be recovered if the marriage does not occur. In Fanning v. Iversen, 535 N.W.2d 770 (S.D. 1995), Fanning, a rancher, proposed to Iversen, a teacher, who at the time of trial had completed her first year of law school. Fanning closed on the purchase of land as an investment a few days after the engagement and requested that the deed include Iverson's name also. Fanning paid the entire purchase price and paid to maintain the property. When Iverson called off the engagement, Fanning sued, requesting title to the property. The court held that the gift of the land was made in contemplation of marriage and that the land should be returned when the donee broke the engagement. *Id.* at 773-75.

2. Declarations of Trust

FARKAS v. WILLIAMS
125 N.E.2d 600 (Ill. 1955)

HERSHEY, JUSTICE.

This is an appeal from a decision of the Appellate Court, which affirmed a decree of the circuit court of Cook County finding that certain declarations of trust executed by Albert B. Farkas and naming Richard J. Williams as beneficiary were invalid and that Regina Farkas and Victor Farkas, as coadministrators of the estate of said Albert B. Farkas, were the owners of the property referred to in said trust instruments, being certain shares of capital stock of Investors Mutual, Inc.

The plaintiffs asked the court to declare their legal rights, as coadministrators, in four stock certificates issued by Investors Mutual Inc. in the name of "Albert B. Farkas, as trustee for Richard J. Williams" and which were issued pursuant to written declarations of trust. The decree of the circuit court found that said declarations were testamentary in character, and not having been executed with the formalities of a will, were invalid, and directed that the stock be awarded to the plaintiffs as an asset of the estate of said Albert B. Farkas. Upon appeal to the Appellate Court, the decree was affirmed. We allowed defendants' petition for leave to appeal.

Albert B. Farkas died intestate at the age of sixty-seven years, a resident of Chicago, leaving as his only heirs-at-law brothers, sisters, a nephew and a niece. Although retired at the time of his death, he had for many years practiced veterinary medicine and operated a veterinarian establishment in Chicago. During a considerable portion of that time, he employed the defendant Williams, who was not related to him.

On four occasions (December 8, 1948; February 7, 1949; February 14, 1950; and March 1, 1950) Farkas purchased stock of Investors Mutual, Inc. At the time of each purchase he executed a written application to Investors Mutuals, Inc., instructing them to issue the stock in his name "as trustee for Richard J. Williams." Investors Mutual, Inc., by its agent, accepted each of these applications in writing by signature on the face of the application. Coincident with the execution of these applications, Farkas signed separate declarations of trust, all of which were identical except as to dates. The terms of said trust instruments are as follows:

> Declaration of Trust — Revocable. I, the undersigned, having purchased or declared my intention to purchase certain shares of capital stock of Investors Mutual, Inc. (the Company), and having directed that the certificate for said stock be issued in my name as trustee for Richard J. Williams as beneficiary, whose address is 1704 W. North Ave. Chicago, Ill., under this Declaration of Trust Do Hereby Declare that the terms and conditions upon which I shall hold said stock in trust and any additional stock resulting from reinvestments of cash dividends upon such original or additional shares are as follows:
>
> (1) During my lifetime all cash dividends are to be paid to me individually for my own personal account and use; provided, however, that any such additional stock purchased under an authorized reinvestment of cash dividends shall become a part of and subject to this trust.
>
> (2) Upon my death the title to any stock subject hereto and the right to any subsequent payments or distributions shall be vested absolutely in the beneficiary. The record date for the payment of dividends, rather than the date of declaration of the dividend, shall, with reference to my death, determine whether any particular dividend shall be payable to my estate or to the beneficiary.
>
> (3) During my lifetime I reserve the right, as trustee, to vote, sell, redeem, exchange or otherwise deal in or with the stock subject hereto, but upon any sale or redemption of said stock or any part thereof, the trust hereby declared shall terminate as to the stock sold or redeemed, and I shall be entitled to retain the proceeds of sale or redemption for my own personal account and use.
>
> (4) I reserve the right at any time to change the beneficiary or revoke this trust, but it is understood that no change of beneficiary and no revocation of this trust except by death of the beneficiary, shall be effective as to the Company for any purpose unless and until written notice thereof in such form as the Company shall prescribe is delivered to the Company

at Minneapolis, Minnesota. The decease of the beneficiary before my death shall operate as a revocation of this trust.

(5) In the event this trust shall be revoked or otherwise terminated, said stock and all rights and privileges thereunder shall belong to and be exercised by me in my individual capacity.

The applications and declarations of trust were delivered to Investors Mutual, Inc., and held by the company until Farkas's death. The stock certificates were issued in the name of Farkas as "trustee for Richard J. Williams" and were discovered in a safety-deposit box of Farkas after his death, along with other securities, some of which were in the name of Williams alone.

The sole question presented on this appeal is whether the instruments entitled "Declaration of Trust — Revocable" and executed by Farkas created valid inter vivos trusts of the stock of Investors Mutual, Inc. The plaintiffs contend that said stock is free and clear from any trust or beneficial interest in the defendant Williams, for the reason that said purported trust instruments were attempted testamentary dispositions and invalid for want of compliance with the statute on wills. The defendants, on the other hand, insist that said instruments created valid inter vivos trusts and were not testamentary in character.

It is conceded that the instruments were not executed in such a way as to satisfy the requirements of the statute on wills; hence, our inquiry is limited to whether said trust instruments created valid inter vivos trusts effective to give the purported beneficiary, Williams, title to the stock in question after the death of the settlor-trustee, Farkas. To make this determination we must consider: (1) whether upon execution of the so-called trust instruments defendant Williams acquired an interest in the subject matter of the trusts, the stock of defendant Investors Mutual, Inc., (2) whether Farkas, as settlor-trustee, retained such control over the subject matter of the trusts as to render said trust instruments attempted testamentary dispositions.

If no interest passed to Williams before the death of Farkas, the intended trusts are testamentary and hence invalid for failure to comply with the statute on wills. But considering the terms of these instruments we believe Farkas did intend to presently give Williams an interest in the property referred to. For it may be said, at the very least, that upon his executing one of these instruments, he showed an intention to presently part with some of the incidents of ownership in the stock. Immediately after the execution of each of these instruments, he could not deal with the stock therein referred to the same as if he owned the property absolutely, but only in accordance with the terms of the instrument. Thus assuming to act as trustee, he is held to have intended to take on those obligations which are expressly set out in the instrument, as well as those fiduciary obligations implied by law. In addition, he manifested an intention to bind himself to having this property pass upon his death to Williams, unless he changed the beneficiary or revoked the trust, and then such change of beneficiary or revocation was not to be effective as to Investors Mutual, Inc., unless and until written notice thereof in such form as the company prescribed was delivered to them at Minneapolis, Minnesota. An absolute owner can dispose of his property, either in his lifetime or by will, in any way he sees fit without notifying or securing approval from anyone and without being held to the duties of a fiduciary in so doing.

It seems to follow that what incidents of ownership Farkas intended to relinquish, in a sense he intended Williams to acquire. It is difficult to name this interest of Williams, nor is there any reason for so doing so long as it passed to him immediately upon the creation of the trust. As stated in 4 Powell, The Law of Real Property, at page 87: "Interests of beneficiaries of private express trusts run the gamut from valuable substantialities to evanescent hopes. Such a beneficiary may have any one of an almost infinite variety of the possible aggregates of rights, privileges, powers and immunities."

An additional problem is presented here, however, for it is to be noted that the trust instruments provide: "The decease of the beneficiary before my death shall operate as a revocation of this trust." The plaintiffs argue that this provision removes the only possible distinction which might have been drawn between these instruments and a will. Being thus conditioned on his surviving, it is argued that the "interest" of Williams until the death of Farkas was a mere expectancy. Conversely, they assert, the interest of Farkas in the securities until his death was precisely the same as that of a testator who bequeaths securities by his will, since he had all the rights accruing to an absolute owner.

Admittedly, had this provision been absent the interest of Williams would have been greater, since he would then have had an inheritable interest in the lifetime of Farkas. But to say his interest would have been greater is not to say that he here did not have a beneficial interest, properly so-called, during the lifetime of Farkas. The provision purports to set up but another "contingency" which would serve to terminate the trust. The disposition is not testamentary and the intended trust is valid, even though the interest of the beneficiary is contingent upon the existence of a certain state of facts at the time of the settlor's death. Restatement of the Law of Trusts, section 56, comment f. In an example contained in the previous reference, the authors of the Restatement have referred to the interest of a beneficiary under a trust who must survive the settlor (and where the settlor receives the income for life) as a contingent equitable interest in remainder.

This question of whether any interest passed immediately is also involved in the next problem considered, namely, the quantum of power retained by a settlor which will cause an intended inter vivos trust to fail as an attempted testamentary disposition. Therefore, much of what is said in the next part of the opinion, as well as the authorities cited, will pertain to this interest question.

In each of these trust instruments, Farkas reserved to himself as settlor [various] powers. Additionally, Farkas reserved the right to act as sole trustee, and in such capacity, he was accorded the right to vote, sell, redeem, exchange or otherwise deal in the stock which formed the subject matter of the trust. It is well established that the retention by the settlor of the power to revoke, even when coupled with the reservation of a life interest in the trust property, does not render the trust inoperative for want of execution as a will.

A more difficult problem is posed, however, by the fact that Farkas is also trustee, and as such, is empowered to vote, sell, redeem, exchange and otherwise deal in and with the subject matter of the trusts. In the case at bar, the power of Farkas to vote, sell, redeem, exchange or otherwise deal in the stock was reserved to him as trustee [rather than as settlor], and it was only upon sale or redemption that he was entitled to keep the proceeds for his own use. Thus, the control reserved is not as great as in those cases where said power is reserved to the owner as settlor. For as trustee he must so conduct himself in accordance with standards applicable to trustees generally. It is not a valid objection to this to say that Williams would never question Farkas' conduct, inasmuch as Farkas could then revoke the trust and destroy what interest Williams has. Such a possibility exists in any case where the settlor has the power of revocation. Still, Williams has rights the same as any beneficiary, although it may not be feasible for him to exercise them. Moreover, it is entirely possible that he might in certain situations have a right to hold Farkas' estate liable for breaches of trust committed by Farkas during his lifetime. In this regard, consider what would happen if, without having revoked the trust, Farkas as trustee had given the stock away without receiving any consideration therefor, had pledged the stock improperly for his own personal debt and allowed it to be lost by foreclosure or had exchanged the stock for another security or other worthless property in such manner as to constitute gross impropriety and gross negligence. In such instances, it would seem in accordance with the terms of these instruments that Williams would have had an enforceable claim against Farkas' estate for whatever damage had been suffered. Contrast this with the rights of a legatee or devisee under a will. The testator could waste the property or do anything with it he wished during his lifetime without incurring any liability to those designated by the will to inherit the property.

Another factor often considered in determining whether an inter vivos trust is an attempted testamentary disposition is the formality of the transaction. Historically, the purpose behind the enactment of the statute on wills was the prevention of fraud. The requirement as to witnesses was deemed necessary because a will is ordinarily an expression of the secret wish of the testator, signed out of the presence of all concerned. The possibility of forgery and fraud are ever present in such situations. Here, Farkas executed four separate applications for stock of Investors Mutual, Inc., in which he directed that the stock be issued in his name as trustee for Williams, and he executed four separate declarations of trust in which he declared he was holding said stock in trust for Williams. The stock certificates in question were issued in his name as trustee for Williams. He thus manifested his intention in a solemn and formal manner.

For the reasons stated, we conclude that these trust declarations executed by Farkas constituted valid inter vivos trusts and were not attempted testamentary dispositions. It must be conceded that they have, in the words of Mr. Justice Holmes in Bromley v. Mitchell, 155 Mass. 509, 30 N.E. 83, a "testamentary look." Moreover, it must be admitted that the line should be drawn somewhere, but after a study of this case we do not believe that point has here been reached.

Reversed and remanded, with directions.

NOTES AND QUESTIONS

1. **Introducing the trust.** A trust divides ownership (the bundle of sticks) by vesting title and management powers in the trustee, and beneficial interests in the beneficiary of the trust. For example, O (the settlor of the trust) might transfer stocks and bonds to the Big Trust Company "in trust, to pay the income to A for life, and at A's death, to turn over the securities, free of trust, to B." The trustee (the trust company) has title to the stocks and bonds, with authority to manage the portfolio on behalf of A, who is entitled to the income (dividends) from the trust property. *See* Paul G. Haskell, Preface to Wills, Trusts and Administration 73-91 (2d ed. 1994) (discussing fundamentals of the trust). You will see more of the trust in Chapter 2.

2. **Methods of creation.** The settlor may create a trust by making a transfer of property to a trustee (see Note 1), *or* by declaring himself or herself trustee; in the latter case, no transfer to a trustee occurs. Which method of creation did the settlor use in the principal case?

3. **The self-declared revocable inter vivos trust.** The revocable inter vivos trust in the principal case is not a means of securing expert management of property by a professional trustee (see Note 1); it is rather a way of avoiding probate of the trust assets. Pending his death, Farkas retains control of the trust assets through the power to revoke the trust. Moreover, the validity of the trust instrument does not depend on compliance with the formalities required for wills. At Farkas's death, ownership of the stock passes to Williams; the stock does not pass through Farkas's estate, where it would be subject to probate delays and expenses. Farkas thus gets the best of both the non-testamentary and testamentary worlds — escape from wills act formalities and lifetime control over the trust assets. The theory underlying avoidance of the requirements for a testamentary transfer in the principal case is that Farkas made a *present* transfer of a property interest to Williams when the trust was created (compare the donor in Basket v. Hassell, in the notes after Woo v. Smart). What interest did Farkas transfer? What did Farkas deliver to Williams? *See* Matter of Brown, 169 N.E. 612, 614 (N.Y. 1930) ("[t]he declaration need not be made to the beneficiary, nor the writing given to him," nor is a writing required for a self-declared trust of personal property). How does Williams' remainder in the principal case differ from Michael Gruen's remainder in Gruen v. Gruen? What would happen if Williams tried to enforce the trust against Farkas?

4. **Avoiding probate; rationale.** Looking behind the court's doctrinal reasoning, is there a policy basis for the court's decision to uphold the Farkas trust? What is the significance of the paragraph near the end of the opinion ("Another factor often considered . . .")? Revocable inter vivos trusts like those in the principal case for many years were invalidated as noncomplying testamentary transfers; Farkas v. Williams is a leading case showing a basis for upholding the trust. Revocable inter vivos trusts are now widely recognized as will substitutes. *See* Restatement Third of Trusts §§ 10, 16, 25 (2003).

5. **Salvaging imperfect gifts.** Suppose that a donor clearly manifests an intent to make an inter vivos gift of property to a donee, but the donor dies before she can make delivery. In a dispute between the estate of the donor and the would-be donee, could the court salvage the imperfect gift by treating the donor as the

settlor of a self-declared revocable inter vivos trust, with the property passing at the donor's death to the intended donee? An early 19th century English case, Ex Parte Pye (1811), treated a donor's intent to give undelivered personal property as a manifestation of the donor's intent to hold the property as a trustee. Subsequent cases repudiated the doctrine in England and it is widely rejected in American law. *See, e.g.*, The Hebrew University Association v. Nye, 169 A.2d 641 (Conn. 1961) (intended gift of rare books and manuscripts relating to the Bible could not be upheld as declaration of trust of the documents). Do you agree? Has the donor in a typical gift case declared an intent to be a trustee? What would happen to the delivery requirement in the law of gifts if a failed gift were converted into an effective declaration of trust? Consider, however, whether a failed gift might be upheld if the donor's intent to hold as a trustee is actual rather than fictional. *See* Sarajane Love, *Imperfect Gifts as Declarations of Trust: An Unapologetic Anomaly*, 67 Ky. L.J. 309 (1979) (pointing out that donor in the *Nye* case, after announcing the gift, refused offers of purchase, saying that the books did not belong to her).

6. **Reconsidering gifts.** On remand from the Connecticut Supreme Court's decision in *Nye* rejecting a declaration of trust theory, the donee argued that the intended gift was effective because the donor had made a constructive delivery of the library: the donor announced her intent to give at a widely attended dinner, in which representatives of the donee were present, and the donor handed over to the donee's representatives a list of the books (recall the delivery of Victor Gruen's letter to his son Michael). The court agreed. *See* The Hebrew University Association v. Nye, 223 A.2d 397 (Conn. Super. Ct. 1966). The *Nye* litigation raises an important question about the law of gifts. If a donor's intent to give an undelivered gift is clear, is it better to invalidate the gift because of non-delivery, or to find a fictional declaration of trust, or to treat non-delivery as harmless error and uphold the gift? The Restatement Third of Property — Wills and Other Donative Transfers § 6.2 cmt. yy (2003), takes the latter position: "a gift of personal property can be perfected on the basis of donative intent alone if the donor's intent to make a gift is established by clear and convincing evidence."

Chapter 2

ESTATES IN LAND AND FUTURE INTERESTS

In Chapter 1, we saw that the concept of possession is fundamental in property law. Posssession is a means of acquiring original ownership of things, and also a way of wresting title from a prior true owner. In addition, the possessor who lacks title nevertheless enjoys the next best thing — protection of possession through remedies to recover possession from a dispossessor. It would be surprising if the law did not devote substantial effort to the elaboration of this fundamental concept, particularly as it applies to the ownership of land — the essential form of wealth during the formative period of the common law.

The estate in land concept. The common law system for organizing and categorizing possessory interests in land is based on the concept of an "estate in land." In the language of the first Restatement of Property § 9 (1936), an estate in land is "a right to possession" of land "measured in terms of duration." Both the possessory and the durational focuses are important.

Possession. Landowners sometimes transfer use rights to a transferee rather than broader possessory rights. For example, if O grants a right-of-way easement across Blackacre to her neighbor A, A has a right to use Blackacre as a passageway to and from her adjoining property. But A has no right to exclude others from using the same area of Blackacre covered by the easement; the right to exclude others is the hallmark of a "possessory" interest in land. Nonpossessory interests in another's land have their own vocabulary and classification system, which we will encounter in Chapters 6 and 7. For present purposes, the important point is simply that the "estate" concept applies only to possessory interests.

Duration. Rights to possession need not be of uniform duration. Take two examples. The first will be familiar to you. Terri and her landlord Lawrence sign a one year lease of Blackacre, effective immediately. While the lease document will no doubt contain a variety of promises (mostly by Terri), the lease also — and more importantly for present purposes — also operates as a kind of deed: it conveys to Terri a right to possess (to exclude others from) Blackacre for the one-year duration of the lease. In the vocabulary of property law, Terri now owns an estate in Blackacre, specifically, a term of years estate.

Now — to take the second, less familiar, example — suppose that Terri and Lawrence agree that Terri is entitled to possession of Blackacre for her life rather than for one year, and Lawrence executes a deed of Blackacre to that effect. Just as in the lease example, Terri owns an estate in Blackacre, one that is called, appropriately enough, a "life estate." Unlike the fixed duration of the term of years estate, however, Terri's life estate ends when she dies, which may turn out to be a shorter (or more likely, a much longer) period than the fixed, one year term of the lease specified in the first example.

The generic concept "estate" thus designates any right to possession measured in terms of duration; the different species of estates, e.g., the term of years and the life estate, indicate different durations of the right to possession. The common law developed (and as you will see, rather jealously guarded) an inventory of six estates, and these have been carried over into American law. These estates (including the two discussed above as examples) are: the fee simple, the fee tail, the life estate, the term of years, the periodic tenancy, and the tenancy at will. Learn the specifics about the way in which each estate ends, and you will have learned nearly half of what you need to know about estates. (Learn how each of the estates is *created*, and you will have learned nearly all of the other half.)

Now go back, for a moment, to our examples. What about Lawrence? If your intuition is that Lawrence is again entitled to possession when the lease or the life estate expires, you are correct. Note then that the effect of the lease or life estate is to divide the right to possession of Blackacre between a present holder of that right (Terri) and a future holder (Lawrence). In this chapter, we deal first with present possessors (people in Terri's position), then we consider future possessors (like Lawrence).

Estates and pedagogy. The two simple examples given, and the bare bones explanation accompanying them, no doubt leave you with many questions. Here are some that may have occurred to you: Before Lawrence transferred to Terri, he must have had an estate (he couldn't transfer something he didn't have); what estate did he have? When Lawrence regains possession after the lease or life estate, will he have an estate, and if so, what is it? If estates measure durations of possession, how long can the longest estate last? What's the shortest estate? And what's a fee tail, anyway?

These are all good questions, but please hold them for now, with this assurance: The system of estates, for all its practical importance, is at bottom a system of definitions and concepts that (more or less) hang together in some kind of coherent way. (Whether the system is too complicated is a separate question, and one that we will address, with specifics, as the chapter proceeds.) Some of the things you need to know to make answers to your questions meaningful, you won't learn until later; you can't learn everything at once, and in this chapter, even more than in others in this book, a linear presentation by us and assimilation by you is important. If you can maintain what the poet and literary theorist Samuel Taylor Coleridge in Biographica Literaria (1817) called a "willing suspension of disbelief" as we go along, it will serve you well.

These things said, let's consider estates.

A. PRESENT ESTATES

1. The Fee Simple (to "A and His Heirs")

If you own a home, or if your parents do, chances are you or they have a fee simple estate. A fee simple, to be as simple as possible about it, is a right to possession that may last forever. It thus differs dramatically from the term of years and the life estate sketched above. Since no person lasts forever, the concept that someone can own a right to possession that may last forever must include some notion that a fee simple owner's right to possession can be inherited at her death, and so on down the line of subsequent possessors. That's exactly how a fee simple operates, as we will see, but it gets us far ahead of our story.

Grants "to A." In fact, the fee simple estate did not exist originally in feudal England, the source of the common law. The earliest recognized estate at common law was the life estate. After acquiring England by force of arms in 1066, William the Conqueror parceled out chunks of land to his chief lieutenants and supporters. These transfers were far from the sales of land for a price with which we are familiar today. Quite the opposite. Instead of being a one-shot transaction after which transferor and transferee parted company for good, the feudal transfer of land kept sovereign and subject together for the duration of the grant, in a close, or at least ongoing, "tenurial" relationship. In return for the (lifetime) grant of the parcel of land, the transferee pledged loyalty to the king, and agreed to render various services related to the military, religious, or political functioning of the kingdom, either on a regular basis or as requested. Loyalty being a central ingredient of the transfer, when the transferee died, ownership of the parcel reverted to the sovereign, who could, but need not, put the land back into the transferee's blood line by a regrant to the decedent's heir, and who would, if he did so, no doubt demand renewed assurances of loyalty from the new grantee.

Thus the earliest transfers of land were in the form "to A," with that phrase designating precisely — on the question of duration — its legal significance: A and A alone enjoyed the right to possess the tract of land, and that right to possession ended with A's death.

It adds only a slight complication to note that the original grantees from the crown — those in A's position in our discussion — might make transfers of a portion of the received lands to *their* supporters; and those second-level transferees might make still further transfers, and so on. Each lower-level transferee's right to possession ended on his death *or* on the death of any higher transferor in the chain of title to that parcel. (The latter qualification follows from the fact that each transferee, having no rights beyond his own lifetime, could not grant more extensive rights to subsequent transferees. In the case of the initial level of transferees, the qualification is unnecessary: the sovereign, as an institution rather than a person, did not die.) Because each parcel of land could be subdivided by these repeated transfers, the feudal system of landholding is usually described as a pyramid, with the king on top, and each level of transferees representing the broadening base.

Grants "to A and his heirs." Authorities on the history of estates tell us that at some point, perhaps when regrants by the sovereign to the decedent transferee's heir became customary, the form of conveyancing language changed. Grants "to A and his heirs" replaced grants "to A." Note that, like the earlier phrase, the grant "to A and his heirs" was precisely descriptive: the king was consenting, in advance of the transfer, that the right to possession of the transferred parcel of land would remain in the grantee's bloodline at the grantee's death. And in a patriarchal culture in which the preferred line of familial authority ran from father to eldest son, the plural "heirs" was significant; there being only one heir in each generation (a system called *primogeniture*), a grant to A "and his heirs" signalled that the land would stay in the grantee's bloodline through the generations. (In the incomparable phrase of Lord Coke, a contemporary of Shakespeare, "the ancestor [A], during his life, beareth in his body (in judgment of law) all his heirs." Coke on Littleton 22b.) Only when the initial grantee's bloodline expired — that is, when any subsequent possessor died without an heir — would the sovereign regain the right to possession, by the legal phenomenon still known as "escheat." *See, e.g.,* Uniform Probate Code § 2-105 (1990) ("If there is no taker under the provisions of this Article [specifying who is entitled to inherit], the intestate estate passes to the state.").

Inheritance, conveyance and devise. In early feudal law, under a grant "to A and his heirs," A's right to possession could not accurately be called a life estate, since the right to possession at A's death passed to A's primogenitary heir, rather than reverting to A's transferor. Instead, A's estate was an incomplete form of what we now call a fee simple estate. Because A might have heirs forever, A's estate might last forever. But A's estate was an incomplete fee simple because, while it had the attribute of inheritability, it as yet lacked the equally important attribute of transferability.

To be more precise, A's estate lacked the feature of transferability by A *so as to bar A's primogenitary heir from inheriting.* Although commerce in land lay in the future, pressure for transferability nevertheless arose early. If A were blessed with ample land and a large family, A might wish to offset the primogenitary heir's privileged position by making transfers of some of his land to his other sons, and to his daughters. By the 13th century, the validity of such transfers was recognized by the courts in D'Arundel's Case (1225) and confirmed by Parliament in the statute Quia Emptores (1290): by transferring a parcel "to B and his heirs," A could divest himself (and his heirs) of all interest in the parcel; thereafter, the property would pass via B's primogenitary bloodline (unless of course, B or some later heir subsequently decided, through exercise of the privilege of conveyance, to relocate the title elsewhere). After 1540, when Parliament allowed transfers of land by will at a landowner's death, A could retain his possessory interest in the land until his death, and defeat his primogenitary heir at that point by a testamentary transfer (devise) to B. As far as the transferability of the right to possession is concerned, the historical development was thus from inheritance, to conveyance, to devise.

Words of purchase, words of limitation. The addition of the power to transfer by conveyance or devise to the earlier recognition of inheritance meant that when the sovereign granted Blackacre "to A and his heirs," A's heirs received absolutely nothing by the transfer. *If* A did not convey the property during his lifetime, and *if* A did not devise it away at his death, then A's primogenitary heir would enjoy his inheritance. And what was true of A in relation to his heirs was true of the heirs of any of A's transferees in relation to those transferees; transferability of the fee simple so as to cut off the transferor's primogenitary heir operated up and down the feudal pyramid. In the vocabulary of property law, we describe this state of affairs by saying that the words "and his heirs" in a transfer operate as words of limitation rather than words of purchase: The words "to A" are words of purchase indicating A as the taker of the right to possession, and the words "and his heirs" are words of limitation, indicating the estate (fee simple) that A takes. "Purchase" in this context does not have the familiar meaning of paying consideration for a transfer. If O *gives* property to A and his heirs, the donee A is a purchaser. To be a "purchaser" simply means to be a designated taker in a conveyance or devise. (Who isn't a purchaser? An heir, who takes by operation of law, through inheritance, rather than by a consensual transaction.)

So, what is a fee simple estate? It is a right to possession that may last forever, which means first, that the right to possession of the land in which the fee simple exists is capable of passing down through the generations so long as A has heirs available to inherit; and it means second, that A or any subsequent holder of the right to possession of the parcel in question is free to transfer the entire fee simple package of rights in that parcel (inheritance, conveyance, devise) to whomever he or she chooses.

Necessity for "and his heirs" language. It is one thing to say that the phrase "and his heirs" *designates* a fee simple estate, and quite another to require it as the canonical way to create that estate in a transferee. After all, a transfer "to A in fee simple" or "to A forever" clearly expresses the transferor's intent to create a fee simple estate, and it expresses that intent much more understandably than does the legal code phrase "to A and his heirs." And it seems odd to require the word "heirs" when the legal reality, as noted above, is that the heirs take nothing by the transfer. Nevertheless, the common law courts imposed a requirement that the words "and his [or her] heirs" be used by the transferor wishing to transfer a fee simple estate, no matter how abundant the other evidence of the transferor's intent. The first principal case below indicates that such formalism remains a feature of the law in at least one American state.

Law and conflict. Conflict is inherent in human relations (Hobbes, Locke) and in human nature (see Shakespeare; later, Freud). Law, among other functions, regulates social conflict, preventing it where possible and channeling it through approved state agencies, chiefly courts, when necessary. The brief history of the fee simple estate traced above highlights social conflict as a force in the development of the law of property. Landowners wanting inheritability of possessory rights by their heirs at death are in conflict with landowners wanting to retain the right to regrant possessory interests anew at each occupant's death. Having achieved inheritability, landowners want broader powers to make lifetime (and deathtime) transfers within the family but outside of the primogenitary heir's line. That desire satisfied, another arises: transferors desiring to establish family dynasties want property to remain in the family bloodline, while others, seeking to *become* part of the landed interests, or (in later times) to acquire land for commercial uses, want free transferability to users outside of the family. The story of conflict does not end with the achievement of the fee simple estate; it rather goes off in new directions, which we will trace below (see the fee tail estate, considered immediately after the fee simple, and future interests, considered in Section B).

a.   Creation of a Fee Simple

McLAURIN v. McLAURIN
217 S.E.2d 41 (S.C. 1975)

PER CURIAM:

The issue to be decided [is] whether a deed to real estate from Mrs. J.M. McLaurin to her husband, J.M. McLaurin, conveyed a fee simple title. This appeal is from an order of the lower court holding that a fee simple title was not conveyed. We affirm the order under appeal and largely follow its language in disposing of the issues.

The deed in question is on a printed form for the conveyance of title to real estate and conforms to the requirements of Section 57-251 of the 1962 Code of Laws. However, the format is such as is customary in printed forms with the various parts being set out as separate paragraphs.

The first part of the deed, comprising page 1, contained the granting clause and the description of the property. In this granting clause, Mrs. McLaurin "granted, bargained, sold and released unto the said J.M. McLaurin" a certain tract of land and a lot with improvements in the Town of McColl. Nothing was contained in the granting clause to indicate that a fee simple title was intended to be conveyed as no words of inheritance were added after the name of the grantee.

The first paragraph on page 2 of the deed adds the customary provision: "Together with all and singular, the Rights, Members, Hereditaments and appurtenances to the said premises belonging, or in anywise incident or appertaining." The form for the habendum clause was printed immediately following this paragraph but was not filled in in any manner. In the completed deed it appears as follows: "TO HAVE AND TO HOLD, all and singular, the said premises before mentioned unto the said _____ Heirs and Assigns forever."

The usual warranty clause followed the habendum and was completely filled in in longhand, except that the word "his" did not appear after the name of J.M. McLaurin, the grantee, and before the words "heirs and assigns."

The deed, therefore, contained no words of inheritance in the granting clause and no completed habendum clause, but did contain words of inheritance in the warranty clause.

The decision in Grainger v. Hamilton, 90 S.E.2d 209 (S.C. 1955), is dispositive of the present issue. The rule of law was there stated that words of inheritance in the granting or habendum clause are necessary to convey a fee and that words of inheritance which appear only in the warranty clause cannot supply the deficiency. This principle applies irrespective of the intention of the grantor because, as stated in *Grainger*, "the intention of the grantor, however, apparent, cannot prevail over a rule of law."

The parties are in agreement that the words of inheritance in the warranty clause are not sufficient to create a fee simple estate and that an estate for the life of the grantee results unless, as contended by defendants (appellants), the uncompleted or blank habendum clause supplied the necessary words of inheritance for the conveyance of a fee simple estate.

The uncompleted habendum clause cannot be considered in determining the nature and extent of the estate conveyed. The deed was on a printed form with blank spaces left so that they could be filled in to conform to the agreement of the parties. The various clauses of the deed became operative as, and to the extent that, the blank spaces were filled in. Therefore, the failure to fill in or complete, in any manner, one of the several clauses of a printed deed form, ordinarily, has the effect of eliminating such uncompleted provision as a part of the completed deed. We have in this case only the deed with the habendum clause left entirely uncompleted.

It is true that the printed form for the habendum clause contains words of inheritance appropriate to the creation of a fee simple estate. However, they were of no effect until the habendum clause was made a part of the conveyance. This was not done and the printed form for the habendum clause was properly not considered in determining the estate conveyed by the deed in question.

The judgment is affirmed.

NOTES AND QUESTIONS

1. **Failure to comply.** What is the consequence of Mrs. McLaurin's failure to transfer a fee simple? Did Mr. McLaurin receive anything by the deed?

2. **Formalism.** Does the inclusion of the *handwritten* phrase "and his heirs" in Mrs. McLaurin's warranty clause reveal her intent to transfer a fee simple estate? Does the phrase "and his heirs" in the habendum clause, although printed rather than handwritten, nevertheless reveal Mrs. McLaurin's intent to transmit a fee simple estate? Isn't the court's decision formalistic in two senses: in requiring "heirs" language and in requiring it in a particular location in the deed?

3. **Purpose of forms.** "Formalism" is widely decried in the legal literature; you have encountered objections to it in the materials in Chapter 1 on gifts, and probably also in your course on Contracts. Is the epithet "formalism" an objection to the law's requirement that parties to a transaction adhere to specified forms? If not, what is the objection? Is it an argument in favor of the South Carolina approach that it requires scriveners to be precise? At what cost? *See generally* Symposium, *Formalism Revisited*, 66 U. Chi. L. Rev. 527 (1999).

4. **Genesis 17:8 (KJV).** God said to Abraham, "And I will give unto thee, and to thy seed after thee, the land wherein thou art a stranger, all the land of Canaan, for an everlasting possession." In feudal England, would Abraham have taken a fee simple? In South Carolina?

5. **Corporation as grantee.** Corporations don't have heirs; the appropriate language is "to the A Corporation, its successors and assigns."

6. **Livery of seisin.** Feudal transfers of interests in land did not occur, as today, by the execution and delivery of a deed, but rather by a process called "livery of seisin" (essentially, symbolic delivery of possession):

The transferor and transferee would go to the land to be transferred, and the transferor would then hand to the transferee a lump of soil or a twig from a tree — all the while intoning the appropriate words of grant, together with the magical words "and his heirs" if the interest transferred was to be a potentially infinite one.

Thomas F. Bergin & Paul G. Haskell, Preface to Estates in Land and Future Interests 11 (2d ed. 1984).

7. **Words of limitation.** Suppose that the deed in the principal case had been "to J.M. McLaurin and his heirs." Assume that Mr. McLaurin wanted to sell the property, but his two sons — his only heirs — objected to the sale. Could McLaurin's heirs prevent the sale?

8. **The history of estates.** The discussion of the development of the fee simple estate given in Section 2.A is scandalously abbreviated. For extensive treatments of the history of estates, see Thomas F. Bergin & Paul G. Haskell, Preface to Estates in Land and Future Interests (2d ed. 1984); A.W.B. Simpson, A History of the Land Law (2d ed. 1986); William Searle Holdsworth, An Historical Introduction to the Land Law (1927).

9. **The next case.** The next case, which stands in striking contrast to *McLaurin*, represents the overwhelming majority view on the question whether any particular language is necessary to transfer a fee simple estate to a transferee. In reading it, you will note that the court refers to a "defeasible" life estate and a "defeasible" fee simple. Ignore the quoted words just now; for present purposes, the issue in the case is whether George Simpson's will created a fee simple or a life estate in his widow Virginia. The critical point, for purposes of comparison with *McLaurin*, is to see why the court decides that issue as it does. (We will return to the concept of defeasibility later on in the chapter.)

DICKSON v. ALEXANDRIA HOSPITAL
177 F.2d 876 (4th Cir. 1949)

BARKSDALE, DISTRICT JUDGE.

The question in the case is the construction of the holographic will of George L. Simpson, formerly a resident of Alexandria, Virginia, who died on April 20, 1907, survived by his widow, Virginia Simpson, and two sons, George Robbins Simpson and French Cameron Simpson, which will is as follows:

I, Geo. L. Simpson, being of sound mind do hereby make this my last will and testament; first I do not wish any appraisement of my estate; Secondly I do not wish my wife Virginia Simpson, whom I appoint my executrix, to give any security; Thirdly, I give to my wife Virginia Simpson, my property on Cameron and Columbus Streets, including furniture and contents of my home. Fourthly I give to each of my boys Geo. Robbins Simpson and French Cameron Simpson, the sum of ten thousand dollars, this money to be paid over to them when Geo. Robbins Simpson shall have reached the age of twenty-five years and when French Cameron Simpson shall have reached the age of twenty-five years. The remainder of my property to go to my wife Virginia Simpson as long as she remains my widow. In the event of her marrying then said remainder of my property is to be equally divided between my sons Geo. Robbins and French Cameron Simpson.

Feb. 13, 1903.

Geo. L. Simpson.

Promptly after the death of George L. Simpson, his will was admitted to probate, and his widow, Virginia Simpson, qualified as his executrix. George Robbins Simpson died intestate and unmarried on August 24, 1934. French Cameron Simpson died January 27, 1940, leaving a will whereby he devised and bequeathed his entire estate to his widow, plaintiff in the district court and appellant here. Virginia Simpson, widow of George L. Simpson, died March 19, 1944, without having remarried, and left a will whereby she appointed appellee, First National Bank, as her executor, and the Bank duly qualified as such. Virginia Simpson left a substantial estate, and by her will, after making numerous specific bequests and establishing a trust fund, left her entire residuary estate to Alexandria Hospital, Inc., after the termination of the trust. Prior to the institution of this action, her executor had paid over to Alexandria Hospital, Inc., all the residue of the estate of Virginia Simpson, deceased.

Plaintiff's contention is that testator created a defeasible life estate in Virginia Simpson, one-half of which, at the death of Virginia Simpson, passed to her, the plaintiff, as sole beneficiary under the will of her deceased husband, French Cameron Simpson. Plaintiff alleges that the First National Bank, as executor, and Alexandria Hospital, Inc., as beneficiary, have refused to pay her the share to which she claims she is entitled, and therefore she instituted this action.

On the other hand, defendants contend that the above quoted language of George L. Simpson's will created a defeasible fee simple in Virginia Simpson, and said Virginia Simpson having died without remarrying, a fee simple title to the residuum passed to them by her will. Thus, the question of whether the above quoted sentences created a defeasible life estate in Virginia Simpson, or whether thereby she took a defeasible fee simple, was squarely presented to the district court. The district court held that Virginia Simpson took a defeasible fee simple estate, which became absolute when she died without having remarried, and dismissed the complaint. We hold that the conclusion reached by the district court was right.

By the common law, words of inheritance were absolutely necessary for the creation of a fee simple estate by deed, and even in a devise of land, words such as "issue," "descendants," "offspring," or the like, showing the intent that the land shall descend in indefinite succession, were necessary if the technical word "heirs" was not used. Under these rules of the common law, it would seem clear that, under the language in the will here under consideration, Virginia Simpson could not possibly have taken a fee simple title. But, for many years, by statute, words of inheritance have not been necessary to create a fee simple title by either deed or will in Virginia. The statute is as follows:

> Where any real estate is conveyed, devised, or granted to any person without any words of limitation, such devise, conveyance, or grant shall be construed to pass the fee simple or other whole estate or interest which the

testator or grantor had power to dispose of in such real estate, unless a contrary intention shall appear by the will, conveyance, or grant.

Sec. 5149, Code of Virginia 1942.

The District Judge was of the opinion that within the four corners of the will, the intention of the testator that his widow should have a fee simple, defeasible only by her remarriage, was apparent. A careful consideration of the will gives strong support to this view. At the beginning of the will here in controversy, which testator himself wrote, he did four things: (1) he provided that there be no appraisement, (2) he appointed his wife his executrix, (3) he provided that she give no security, and (4) he devised to his wife, in fee simple, his residence, including its furniture and contents. He would hardly have provided that there be no appraisement if he had wished his wife to be accountable to his sons for the residuum of his estate. The fact that he appointed her his executrix, without security, and gave her outright his home with all its contents, strongly indicates not only his love for her, but his trust in her loyalty and good judgment. The testator then made specific devises of $10,000.00 to each of his sons, payable to them when they reached the age of twenty-five. This would seem to indicate that it was the testator's intention to give each son $10,000.00 with which to start his business career, and rely upon his wife to make such provision for them from the residuary estate as in her judgment might be wise and proper. In the event of a diversion of her affections by remarriage, the testator specifically provided that the residuum of his estate should go to his sons.

It is therefore our conclusion that the last two sentences of the will created a defeasible fee simple title to the residuum in the widow, Virginia Simpson, which became a fee simple absolute when she died without having remarried. It therefore follows that the decision of the district court will be

Affirmed.

NOTES AND QUESTIONS

1. **Classification.** Virginia Simpson didn't remarry, so she did not suffer a premature loss of whatever estate she acquired by her husband's will. What estate did she have? How does classification of Virginia Simpson's estate as a life estate or fee simple determine the outcome of the case? On what basis might plaintiff have argued for a life estate construction?

2. **Law and equity.** How does the Virginia statutory rule of construction of deeds and wills differ from the rules applicable at common law? Did George Simpson's will reveal a clear intent to transfer *less* than a fee simple estate to his wife?

3. **"Total transfer" statutes.** Most states have statutes creating, as does the Virginia statute, a presumption that a deed or will passes the transferor's entire estate unless the transferor expresses an intent to transfer a lesser estate. *See, e.g.,* N.J.S.A. 46:3-13 ("[U]nless an exception be made therein, [every deed shall] be construed to include all the estate of the grantor, including the fee simple if he had such an estate, and the word 'heirs' shall not be necessary in any deed to effect the conveyance of the fee simple."); N.J.S.A. 3B:3-39 (when a devise omits "heirs and assigns" language, but the will contains no expression of intent to create a life

estate, and no further devise over after death of the devisee, the devise shall be deemed to pass an estate in fee simple to the devisee). When the transferor does not clearly express the intent to transfer less than her entire estate, an important question is whether extrinsic evidence is available to prove such intent. *See, e.g.,* Cain v. Finnie, 785 N.E.2d 1039 (Ill. App. Ct. 2003) (one-line will devising property to testator's wife "so long as she remains my widow" and without a gift over, was ambiguous as to whether testator intended a defeasible life estate or fee simple; on the basis of extrinsic evidence, the court concluded that testator intended a life estate); Oldfield v. Stoeco Homes, Inc., 139 A.2d 291, 297 (N.J. 1958) ("If the four corners of the deed provide a coherent expression of the parties' intent, we need search no further; but if an ambiguity or a reasonable doubt appears from a perusal of the particular symbols of expression our horizons must be broadened to encompass the circumstances surrounding the transaction."). Was extrinsic evidence necessary in the principal case to prove the testator's intent? Would extrinsic evidence have been admissible under the Virginia statute?

4. **"To A and her heirs."** Although words of limitation are not necessary in modern law to transfer a fee simple, do the facts of *Dickson* indicate why it is wise for a scrivener to add "and his heirs" or "in fee simple" (or "for life" in appropriate cases) to clarify the intended estate?

5. **The restriction on remarriage.** Under the Restatement Second of Property (Donative Transfers) § 6.3(1), George Simpson's restraint on his wife's *re*marriage was valid; a restraint imposed by a transferor on the transferee's first marriage, however, is invalid under § 6.1(1). What might be the reason(s) for that distinction? The Restatement deals comprehensively with the validity of the following other restraints on personal conduct: § 7.1 (provisions encouraging separation or divorce); § 7.2 (provisions detrimentally affecting family relationships); § 8.1 (provisions concerning religion); § 8.2 (restrictions on personal habits); § 8.3 (restraints concerning education or occupation); and § 9.1 (restraints on contest of a donative transfer).

b.   Inheritance of a Fee Simple

> Now folks have different
> thoughts it's true about
> death but in general it's
> not like any race for
> example you ever ran
> everyone wanting to come in
>
> last and all
>
> John Stone, "The Truck"[*]

When a person dies with a valid will, his or her property passes to the devisees indicated in the will, according to the decedent's specified wishes. When a person dies without a will, his or her property passes by intestacy to the decedent's heirs. You might think of intestacy as an estate plan provided for you by the state; it

---

[*] Reprinted from *In All This Rain*, LSU Press, 1980, with permission of the author.

operates in default of your specifying your own plan through the execution of a valid will.

Under the common law of England, heirship was based on primogeniture, a system which provided for inheritance by the eldest surviving son of the deceased ancestor, and which proceeded to other possible heirs only after exhausting the male filial line. That system remains in England today as the method of determining the sequence of takers to the throne. It does not exist in American law as the method of inheritance of estates.

The statutory hierarchy of heirship. Instead, all American states have statutes specifying who is entitled to inherit when a decedent dies intestate. The statutes usually create a hierarchy of preferred classes of takers: (1) issue (descendants) of the decedent, e.g., children, grandchildren, great-grandchildren; (2) parents of the decedent; (3) descendants of parents (the decedent's siblings, nieces and nephews, grand-nephews and nieces, and so on); and (4) grandparents or their descendants. Those heirs listed in lower categories do not take unless there is no eligible taker in a higher category. Thus, a parent of the decedent will be excluded if the decedent leaves surviving descendants; a grandparent will be excluded if the decedent leaves descendants, parents, or descendants of parents. In the UPC, this ranking of heirs is clear from the language of the statute. *See, e.g.,* UPC § 2-103(2) ("if there is no surviving descendant, to the decedent's parents"). The reprinted Table of Consanguinity, in conjunction with the reprinted Uniform Probate Code sections, should help you visualize the relationship between the decedent's family tree and the statutory provisions on heirship.

The surviving spouse. Although the surviving spouse of the decedent was not an heir at common law, he or she enjoys that status under most American statutes, usually as a co-taker in the first rank along with issue of the decedent (or under some statutes, in specified circumstances, in place of the decedent's issue). Generalization about the surviving spouse's intestate share is difficult; for purposes of our introductory treatment, we omit the spousal provision in the excerpt from the Uniform Probate Code reprinted below, and we assume, in the Problems, which are based on that statute, that the decedent left no surviving spouse.

"Laughing heirs." It is theoretically possible for anyone related to the decedent to qualify as an heir, assuming that the would-be taker can establish the requisite genealogy. Many states, however, forbid inheritance by a person who is related to the decedent remotely, the so-called "laughing heir" (so called not to identify the sense of humor of the heir, but to indicate that inheritance by such a distant relative is a windfall). Again, the Table of Consanguinity, in conjunction with the Uniform Probate Code provision reprinted below, will help you visualize the cutoff of inheritance past a certain point of relationship to the decedent. When a decedent dies without a statutorily-specified heir, the decedent's property passes to the state, by escheat.

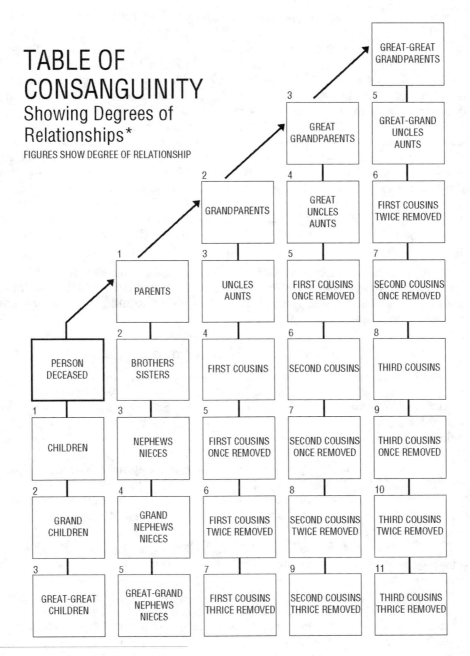

TABLE OF CONSANGUINITY
Showing Degrees of Relationships*
FIGURES SHOW DEGREE OF RELATIONSHIP

*   This material is reproduced from *California Decedent Estate Practice, Volumes 1 & 2*, copyright 1986, 2000, by the Regents of the University of California. Reproduced with permission of Continuing Education of the Bar—California. (For information about CEB publications, telephone toll free 1-800-CEB-3444 or go to our web site, CEB.com.)

Surviving the decedent. An heir must survive the ancestor under all intestacy statutes. *See, e.g.*, Uniform Probate Code § 2-103 (intestate estate passes to designated individuals "who survive the decedent"); Restatement Third of Property (Wills and Other Donative Transfers) § 1.2 (individual who fails to survive the decedent "cannot take as an heir or a devisee"). Survivorship is usually obvious; it is often *not* clear, however, when ancestor and heir die together in a common disaster, such as an automobile wreck or airplane crash. In such cases, the original Uniform Simultaneous Death Act (1940) deemed the ancestor to be the survivor in the absence of "sufficient evidence" that the heir survived. (Think for a moment about what evidence would establish survivorship by the heir in instances of near-simultaneous death. It isn't pleasant.) Taking a different tack, the original Uniform Probate Code (1969) provided that the heir had to survive the ancestor by 120 hours in order to take the ancestor's property; the 1990 revision of the code added the requirement that the 120 hour survival period be established by clear and convincing evidence. *See* UPC § 2-104. The revised UPC provision was subsequently adopted in the revised Uniform Simultaneous Death Act.

In summary: a person qualifies as an heir of a decedent under an intestacy statute if, and only if, that person (1) survives the decedent; (2) is listed in the statute as an eligible taker; and (3) there are no takers in any category having preference over the claimant's category.

NOTES AND QUESTIONS

1. **Vocabulary.** "Even though it happens every year in possibly every law school, it never ceases to shock teachers to discover that some students in the middle of their second year in law school still believe that the heirs of a person who died testate are those who take under the will." Eugene F. Scoles, Edward C. Halbach, Jr., Patricia Gilchrist Roberts & Martin D. Begleiter, Problems and Materials on Decedents' Estates and Trusts 1 (7th ed. 2006). Please do not shock your second-year teachers: a person who takes by inheritance is an *heir*; a person who takes a gift under a will is a *devisee*. A testator might devise his property to those who would be his heirs in the absence of a will, but the testator need not do so; it is not uncommon for a testator who has descendants to devise all of his assets to his surviving spouse.

2. **Escheat.** If the decedent leaves no eligible heir, the decedent's estate escheats to the state. Why do lawmakers prefer the laughing state to the laughing heir?

3. **The constitution and transmission of property at death.** "Rights of succession to the property of a deceased, whether by will or by intestacy, are of statutory creation, and the dead hand rules succession only by sufferance. Nothing in the Federal Constitution forbids the legislature of a state to limit, condition, or even abolish the power of testamentary disposition over property within its jurisdiction." Irving Trust v. Day, 314 U.S. 556, 562 (1942). But in Hodel v. Irving, 481 U.S. 704 (1987), the Court held Section 207 of the Indian Land Consolidation Act unconstitutional, as an uncompensated "taking" of property forbidden by the Fifth Amendment. Section 207 provided that "[n]o undivided fractional interest in any tract of [land] within a tribe's reservation shall descend by intestacy or devise but shall escheat to that tribe if such interest represents 2 per centum or less of the

total acreage in such tract and has earned to its owner less than $100 in the preceding year before it is due to escheat." The Court held that Congress could not constitutionally abolish *both* the descent and devise of property at the owner's death. Whatever the merits of *Hodel*, note that the case protects only a decedent's right to transmit property at his or her death. The decision does not create a constitutional right in an heir or devisee to acquire property from a decedent at his or her death.

4. **The Uniform Probate Code.** Here are some relevant provisions on intestacy from the Uniform Probate Code (1990).

Section 2-101. Intestate Estate.

(a) Any part of a decedent's estate not effectively disposed of by will passes by intestate succession to the decedent's heirs as prescribed in this Code, except as modified by the decedent's will.

Section 2-103. Share of Heirs other than Surviving Spouse.

Any part of the intestate estate not passing to the decedent's surviving spouse under Section 2-102, or the entire intestate estate if there is no surviving spouse, passes in the following order to the individuals designated below who survive the decedent:

(1) to the decedent's descendants by representation;

(2) if there is no surviving descendant, to the decedent's parents equally if both survive, or to the surviving parent;

(3) if there is no surviving descendant or parent, to the descendants of the decedent's parents or either of them by representation;

(4) if there is no surviving descendant, parent, or descendant of a parent, but the decedent is survived by one or more grandparents or descendants of grandparents, half of the estate passes to the decedent's paternal grandparents equally if both survive, or to the surviving paternal grandparent, or to the descendants of the decedent's paternal grandparents or either of them if both are deceased, the descendants taking by representation; and the other half passes to the decedent's maternal relatives in the same manner; but if there is no surviving grandparent or descendant of a grandparent on either the paternal or the maternal side, the entire estate passes to the decedent's relatives on the other side in the same manner as the half.

Section 2-105. No Taker.

If there is no taker under the provisions of this Article, the intestate estate passes to the [state].

PROBLEMS

Who inherits O's property in the following cases under the Uniform Probate Code? Assume in all problems that O leaves no surviving spouse.

2-A. O dies possessed of Blackacre, a car, and a boat. The operative part of O's will provides only as follows: "I give Blackacre to A." Who gets the car and boat? Suppose that O's will provided as follows: "I give Blackacre to A. I leave all the rest, residue and remainder of my property to B." Who gets what? Do you see the advantage of a residuary (catch-all) clause in a will?

2-B. O owns Blackacre in fee simple at death.

a. O dies survived by a son A and two daughters, B and C. Who owns Blackacre under the UPC? Who would have owned Blackacre in feudal England?

b. O dies survived by two children, A and B, and by grandchildren X and Y, the children of O's predeceased child C. Result? If C, along with A and B, had survived O, would C's children X and Y have been heirs of O?

c. O dies survived by one parent P and two nephews N-1 and N-2 (who are the children of O's predeceased brother, B).

d. O dies survived by a brother B, and by nephews N-1 and N-2, the children of O's predeceased sister C.

e. O dies survived by a great uncle. On the Table of Consanguinity, you will see that a great uncle is a descendent of the decedent's *great* grandparents; why is that significant under the UPC?

c.   Devise of a Fee Simple

A decedent may avoid the operation of the intestacy statutes by executing a valid will. As the following case shows, making a valid will is more easily said than done.

STEVENS v. CASDORPH
508 S.E.2d 610 (W. Va. 1998)

PER CURIAM:

The plaintiffs below, Janet Sue Lanham Stevens, Peggy Lanham Salisbury, Betty Jean Bayes, and Patricia Miller Moyers (hereinafter collectively referred to as the "Stevenses"), appeal a summary judgment ruling for the defendants by the Circuit Court of Kanawha County. The Stevenses instituted this action against Patricia Eileen Casdorph and Paul Douglas Casdorph, individually and as executor of the estate of Homer Haskell Miller, for the purpose of challenging the will of Homer Haskell Miller. The circuit court granted the Casdorphs' motion for summary judgment. On appeal, this Court is asked to reverse the trial court's ruling. Following a review of the parties' arguments, the record, and the pertinent authorities, we reverse the decision of the Circuit Court of Kanawha County.

FACTUAL BACKGROUND

On May 28, 1996, the Casdorphs took Mr. Homer Haskell Miller, who was elderly and confined to a wheelchair, to Shawnee Bank in Dunbar, West Virginia, so that he could execute his will. Once at the bank, Mr. Miller asked Debra Pauley, a bank employee and public notary, to witness the execution of his will. After Mr. Miller signed the will, Ms. Pauley took the will to two other bank employees, Judith Waldron and Reba McGinn, for the purpose of having each of them sign the will as witnesses. Both Ms. Waldron and Ms. McGinn signed the will. However, Ms. Waldron and Ms. McGinn testified during their depositions that they did not actually see Mr. Miller place his signature on the will. Further, it is undisputed that Mr. Miller did not accompany Ms. Pauley to the separate work areas of Ms. Waldron and Ms. McGinn.

Mr. Miller died on July 28, 1996. The last will and testament of Mr. Miller, which named Mr. Paul Casdorph, a nephew of Mr. Miller, as executor, left the bulk of his estate to the Casdorphs. Mr. Miller's probated estate exceeded $400,000.00. The will devised $80,000.00 to Frank Paul Smith, a nephew of Mr. Miller. The remainder of the estate was left to the Casdorphs. The Stevenses, nieces of Mr. Miller, filed the instant action to set aside the will. The Stevenses asserted in their complaint that Mr. Miller's will was not executed according to the requirements set forth in W.Va.Code § 41-1-3 (1995). As heirs, the Stevenses would be entitled to recover from Mr. Miller's estate under the intestate laws if his will is set aside as invalidly executed. After some discovery, all parties moved for summary judgment. The circuit court denied the Stevenses' motion for summary judgment, but granted the Casdorphs' motion. From this ruling, the Stevenses appeal to this Court.

DISCUSSION

The Stevenses' contention is simple. They argue that all evidence indicates that Mr. Miller's will was not properly executed. Therefore, the will should be voided. The procedural requirements at issue are contained in W.Va.Code § 41-1-3 (1997). The statute reads:

> No will shall be valid unless it be in writing and signed by the testator, or by some other person in his presence and by his direction, in such manner as to make it manifest that the name is intended as a signature; and moreover, unless it be wholly in the handwriting of the testator, *the signature shall be made or the will acknowledged by him in the presence of at least two competent witnesses, present at the same time; and such witnesses shall subscribe the will in the presence of the testator, and of each other*, but no form of attestation shall be necessary.

(Emphasis added.)

The relevant requirements of the above statute calls for a testator to sign his/her will or acknowledge such will in the presence of at least two witnesses at the same time, and such witnesses must sign the will in the presence of the testator and each other. In the instant proceeding the Stevenses assert, and the evidence supports, that Ms. McGinn and Ms. Waldron did not actually witness Mr. Miller signing his will. Mr. Miller made no acknowledgment of his signature on the will to either Ms. McGinn or Ms. Waldron. Likewise, Mr. Miller did not observe Ms. McGinn and Ms. Waldron sign his will as witnesses. Additionally, neither Ms. McGinn nor Ms. Waldron acknowledged to Mr. Miller that their signatures were on the will. It is also undisputed that Ms. McGinn and Ms. Waldron did not actually witness each other sign the will, nor did they acknowledge to each other that they had signed Mr. Miller's will. Despite the evidentiary lack of compliance with W.Va.Code § 41-1-3, the Casdorphs' argue that there was substantial compliance with the statute's requirements, insofar as everyone involved with the will knew what was occurring. The trial court found that there was substantial compliance with the statute because everyone knew why Mr. Miller was at the bank. The trial court further concluded there was no evidence of fraud, coercion or undue influence. Based upon the foregoing, the trial court concluded that the will should not be voided even though the technical aspects of W.Va.Code § 41-1-3 were not followed.

Our analysis begins by noting that "[t]he law favors testacy over intestacy." In re Teubert's Estate, 298 S.E.2d 456 (W. Va. 1982). However, we clearly held in Black v. Maxwell, 46 S.E.2d 804 (W. Va. 1948), that "[t]estamentary intent and a written instrument, executed in the manner provided by [W.Va.Code § 41-1-3], existing concurrently, are essential to the creation of a valid will." *Black* establishes that mere intent by a testator to execute a written will is insufficient. The actual execution of a written will must also comply with the dictates of W.Va.Code § 41-1-3. The Casdorphs seek to have this Court establish an exception to the technical requirements of the statute. In Wade v. Wade, 195 S.E. 339, 339-340 (W. Va. 1938), this Court permitted a narrow exception to the stringent requirements of the W.Va.Code § 41-1-3:

> Where a testator acknowledges a will and his signature thereto in the presence of two competent witnesses, one of whom then subscribes his name, the other or first witness, having already subscribed the will in the presence of the testator but out of the presence of the second witness, may acknowledge his signature in the presence of the testator and the second witness, and such acknowledgment, if there be no indicia of fraud or misunderstanding in the proceeding, will be deemed a signing by the first witness within the requirement of Code, 41-1-3, that the witnesses must subscribe their names in the presence of the testator and of each other.

See also Brammer v. Taylor, 338 S.E.2d 207, 215 n. 1 (W. Va. 1985) ("[T]he witnesses' acknowledgment of their signatures in the presence of the testator [and in the presence of each other] is tantamount to and will be deemed a 'signing' or 'subscribing' in the presence of those persons.").

Wade stands for the proposition that if a witness acknowledges his/her signature on a will in the physical presence of the other subscribing witness and the testator, then the will is properly witnessed within the terms of W.Va.Code § 41-1-3. In this case, none of the parties signed or acknowledged their signatures in the presence of each other. This case meets neither the narrow exception of *Wade* nor the specific provisions of W.Va.Code § 41-1-3.

CONCLUSION

In view of the foregoing, we grant the relief sought in this appeal and reverse the circuit court's order granting the Casdorphs' cross-motion for summary judgment.

Reversed.

WORKMAN, JUSTICE, dissenting:

The majority once more takes a very technocratic approach to the law, slavishly worshiping form over substance. In so doing, they not only create a harsh and inequitable result wholly contrary to the indisputable intent of Mr. Homer Haskell Miller, but also a rule of law that is against the spirit and intent of our whole body of law relating to the making of wills.

There is absolutely no claim of incapacity or fraud or undue influence, nor any allegation by any party that Mr. Miller did not consciously, intentionally, and with full legal capacity convey his property as specified in his will. The challenge to the will is based solely upon the allegation that Mr. Miller did not comply with the [statutory] requirement that the signature shall be made or the will acknowledged by the testator in the presence of at least two competent witnesses, present at the same time. The lower court, in its very thorough findings of fact, indicated that Mr. Miller had been transported to the bank by his nephew Mr. Casdorph and the nephew's wife. Mr. Miller, disabled and confined to a wheelchair, was a shareholder in the Shawnee Bank in Dunbar, West Virginia, with whom all those present were personally familiar. When Mr. Miller executed his will in the bank lobby, the typed will was placed on Ms. Pauley's desk, and Mr. Miller instructed Ms. Pauley that he wished to have his will signed, witnessed, and acknowledged. After Mr. Miller's signature had been placed upon the will with Ms. Pauley watching, Ms. Pauley walked the will over to the tellers' area in the same small lobby of the bank. Ms. Pauley explained that Mr. Miller wanted Ms. Waldron to sign the will as a witness. The same process was used to obtain the signature of Ms. McGinn. Sitting in his wheelchair, Mr. Miller did not move from Ms. Pauley's desk during the process of obtaining the witness signatures. The lower court concluded that the will was valid and that Ms. Waldron and Ms. McGinn signed and acknowledged the will "in the presence" of Mr. Miller.

In Wade v. Wade, we addressed the validity of a will challenged for such technicalities and observed that "a narrow, rigid construction of the statute should not be allowed to stand in the way of right and justice, or be permitted to defeat a testator's disposition of his property." We upheld the validity of the challenged will, noting that "each case must rest on its own facts and circumstances to which the court must look to determine whether there was a subscribing by the witnesses in the presence of the testator; that substantial compliance with the statute is all that is required." A contrary result, we emphasized, "would be based on illiberal and inflexible construction of the statute, giving preeminence to letter and not to spirit, and resulting in the thwarting of the intentions of testators even under circumstances where no possibility of fraud or impropriety exists."

The majority's conclusion is precisely what was envisioned and forewarned in 1938 by the drafters of the *Wade* opinion: illiberal and inflexible construction, giving preeminence to the letter of the law and ignoring the spirit of the entire body of testamentary law, resulting in the thwarting of Mr. Miller's unequivocal wishes.

The majority strains the logical definition of "in the presence" as used in the operative statute. The legal concept of "presence" in this context encompasses far more than simply watching the signing of the will, which is the technical, narrow interpretation of the word apparently relied upon by the majority. Where the attestation of the will by the witnesses occurred within the same room as the testator, there is, at the very minimum, prima facie evidence that the attestation occurred within the "presence" of the testator. See Annotation, What constitutes the presence of the testator in the witnessing of his will, 75 A.L.R.2d 318 (1961).

In re Demaris' Estate, 110 P.2d 571 (Or. 1941), involved a challenge to a will signed by a very ill gentleman, witnessed in another room by a physician and his wife thirty minutes after the testator signed the will. The court rejected a strict interpretation of the language of the statute, recognizing that the purpose of requiring the presence of the witnesses was to protect a testator against substitution and fraud. [T]he court determined that "presence" did not demand that the witnesses sign within the sight of the testator, if other senses would enable the testator to know that the witnesses were near and to understand what the witnesses were doing. The court concluded that "the circumstances repel any thought of fraud and speak cogently of the integrity of the instrument under review. The signatures of all three persons are conceded. The circumstances of the attestation are free from dispute." To hold the will invalid on a strictly technical flaw would [have been] "to observe the letter of the statute as interpreted strictly, and fail to give heed to the statute's obvious purpose. Thus, the statute would be turned against those for whose protection it had been written." 110 P.2d at 586.

The majority embraces the line of least resistance. The easy, most convenient answer is to say that the formal, technical requirements have not been met and that the will is therefore invalid. End of inquiry. Yet that result is patently absurd. That manner of statutory application is inconsistent with the underlying purposes of the statute. Where a statute is enacted to protect and sanctify the execution of a will to prevent substitution or fraud, this Court's application of that statute should further such underlying policy, not impede it. When, in our efforts to strictly apply legislative language, we abandon common sense and reason in favor of technicalities, we are the ones committing the injustice.

I am authorized to state that Justice MAYNARD joins in this dissent

NOTES AND QUESTIONS

1. **Attested wills: requirements.** All states allow attested (witnessed) wills, and require that the will be in writing, be signed by the testator, and be witnessed by at least two witnesses. However, there is considerable variation among the states on the details of one or more of these three basics, particularly attestation. Suppose testator signs her will in the presence of one witness, who also signs the will, then leaves; shortly thereafter, testator acknowledges her signature to a second witness, who then signs. Has testator authenticated her will in the presence of two witnesses? Have two witnesses signed in the presence of the testator? Has testator complied with the West Virginia statute? *See also* Morris v. West's Estate, 643 S.W.2d 204 (Tex. Ct. App. 1982) (under statute requiring witnesses to sign "in the presence of testator," probate was denied when both witnesses were present when testator signed, but went into another room to do their own signing of the will). In the principal case, had it been argued that Debra Pauley was the agent of Homer Miller, would the will have been signed in the presence of the testator? Would the testator have signed in the presence of the witnesses?

2. **Function of statutory formalities.** The Restatement Third of Property (Wills and Other Donative Transfers) § 3.3 cmt. a (1998) gives the following concise statement of the "four discrete functions" attributed to the statutory formalities for the validity of a will:

> The evidentiary function requires solid evidence of the existence and content of the decedent's directions. The cautionary function requires some indication that the decedent arrived at these directions with adequate awareness. The protective function attempts to assure that the contents and the execution of the will were the product of the decedent's free choice. The channelling function is meant to facilitate a substantial degree of standardization in the organization, language, and content of most wills, so that they can be prepared and administered in a fairly routine manner.

See also Ashbel Gulliver & Catherine Tilson, *Classification of Gratuitous Transfers*, 51 Yale L.J. 1 (1913); John Langbein, *Substantial Compliance with the Wills Act*, 88 Harv. L. Rev. 489 (1975). Despite Homer Miller's failure to comply with the statutory formalities, do you think that his will expressed his deliberate and uncoerced testamentary intent? Does the majority's insistence on strict compliance with the statutory formalities treat the formalities as means to an end, or as ends in themselves?

3. **A model execution procedure.** Statutory formalities differ among the states; testators may own property in different states; slight noncompliance with any state's formalities might invalidate the will in that state. Recognizing these difficulties, the Restatement Second of Property (Donative Transfers) § 33.1 cmt. c, provides a checklist of procedures for a thorough execution ceremony, which are designed to give the will "maximum acceptability in the various States." The checklist includes a recommendation that three witnesses be employed.

4. **Presence: line-of-sight and "conscious" presence.** What meaning of "presence" did the dissent assert in the principal case? *See also* Cunningham v. Cunningham, 83 N.W. 58 (Minn. 1900) (witnesses who signed at a table in the room adjoining testator's bedroom, "a few feet distant, and within easy sound of [testator's] voice," were in testator's presence). Would that argument also have saved the will in Morris v. West's Estate, cited in Note 1?

5. **Avoiding strict compliance: the UPC approaches.** Section 2-502 of the Uniform Probate Code reduces the formal requirements for a valid will; the section requires that a will be in writing, be signed or acknowledged by the testator, and be signed "by at least two individuals, each of whom signed within a reasonable time after he [or she] witnessed either the signing of the will or the testator's acknowledgment of that signature or acknowledgment of the will." Does the UPC require that the witnesses sign in the presence of the testator? Would the procedure followed in the principal case have been sufficient under the UPC provision? In addition to reducing the number of formal requirements, the UPC also addresses the problem of noncompliance with the formalities that remain. Section 2-503 of the Code provides that "a document not executed in compliance with Section 2-502" is nonetheless valid "if the proponent of the document establishes by clear and convincing evidence that the decedent intended the document to constitute the decedent's will." Which of the major formal requirements — writing, signature, attestation — might be dispensed with under

Section 2-503? See generally John H. Langbein, *Excusing Harmless Errors in the Execution of Wills: A Report on Australia's Tranquil Revolution in Probate Law*, 87 Colum. L. Rev. 1, 52-54 (1987).

6. **Unattested (unwitnessed) wills.** Over half of the states, as well as the Restatement Third of Property (Wills and Other Donative Transfers) § 3.2 and UPC § 2-502, permit the testator to transmit property by an unattested (unwitnessed) will, if the will is written and signed in the testator's handwriting (the so-called "holographic" will). Why might a state allow holographic wills? Why might it not?

7. **Lapse.** An heir must survive the ancestor to inherit. So also, a will beneficiary must survive the testator to take a gift under the will. A devise to a beneficiary who dies before the testator lapses (fails). Under common law rules, a lapsed pre-residuary gift falls into the residuary estate and goes to the residuary devisee; a lapsed residuary gift passes by intestacy to the testator's heirs. Widely-adopted "anti-lapse" statutes displace the common law rules, and pass the lapsed gift to the predeceased beneficiary's descendants (by representation) who survive the testator. The testator can displace the common law and statutory rules by naming an alternative taker for the devise ("Blackacre to A if she survives me, and if not, Blackacre to B"). Do you see how the common law rules can defeat the testator's probable intent (had testator anticipated the lapse problem)? Why might a testator's devise to his or her spouse perhaps be more likely to provide an alternative taker than a devise to the testator's child?

d.   Responsibility: Abandonment of a Fee Simple

It is generally allowed that no man ever found the happiness of possession proportionate to that expectation which incited his desire, and invigorated his pursuit.

Samuel Johnson, The Rambler, No. 29 (26 June 1750)

POCONO SPRINGS CIVIC ASSOC., INC. v. MacKENZIE
667 A.2d 233 (Pa. Super. Ct. 1995)

Rowley, President Judge.

The issue in this appeal is whether real property owned by appellants Joseph W. MacKenzie and Doris C. MacKenzie has been abandoned, as they claim. In an order entered January 5, 1995, the trial court granted summary judgment, in the amount of $1,739.82, in favor of appellee Pocono Springs Civic Association, Inc., which argued successfully to the trial court that appellants had not abandoned their property located in appellee's development, and, therefore appellants were still obligated to pay association fees.[1]

---

[1] The covenant upon which appellee relies reads as follows:

> An association of all property owners is to be formed by the Grantor and designated by such name as may be deemed appropriate, and when formed, the buyer covenants and agrees that he, his executors, heirs and assigns, shall be bound by the by-laws, rules and regulations as may be duly formulated and adopted by such association and that they shall be subject to the

The facts are in no manner disputed. Our determination, therefore, is simply whether the trial court erred as a matter of law in finding that appellee's right to summary judgment is clear and free from doubt.

Appellants purchased a vacant lot at Pocono Springs Development, located in Wayne County, on October 14, 1969. In 1987, appellants decided to sell their still-vacant lot. A subsequent offer for the purchase of appellants' lot was conditioned upon the property being suitable for an on-lot sewage system. Upon inspection, the lot was determined to have inadequate soil for proper percolation, and appellants' sale was lost. Believing their investment to be worthless, appellants attempted to abandon their lot at Pocono Springs Development. Appellants claimed that because they successfully abandoned their lot, they are relieved from any duty to pay the association fees sought by appellee. The trial court held, however, that the appellant's abandonment defense is "not a valid defense." We agree with the trial court, and affirm.

Appellants' argument, that they successfully abandoned their lot at Pocono Springs Development, is based upon several actions that they believe disassociate them from the land. First, appellants, after learning that the lot would not meet township sewage requirements, attempted to turn the lot over to appellee. Appellee declined to accept the property. Second, appellants tried to persuade appellee to accept the lot as a gift, to be used as a park-like area for the community. Appellee again declined. Third, in 1986 appellants ceased paying real estate taxes on their lot, and in 1988 the Wayne County Tax Claim Bureau offered the property for sale, due to delinquent tax payments. There were no purchasers. Fourth, in 1990, the lot was again offered for sale by the Tax Claim Bureau. The property again was not sold. The Bureau then placed the lot on its "repository" list. Fifth, appellants signed a notarized statement, mailed to "all interested parties," which expressed their desire to abandon the lot. Sixth, appellants do not accept mail regarding the property. These occurrences, together with appellants having neither visited the lot nor utilized the development's services since 1986, cause appellants to "assert that they do not have 'perfect' title to Lot # 20, in Pocono Springs [Development,] [thus] they can and have abandoned said property back to the sovereign." On the basis of the above, appellants argue that their conduct manifests an intent to abandon, and that their intent to abandon should be a question of fact which precludes summary judgment.

The law of abandonment in Pennsylvania does not support appellants' argument. This Court has held that abandoned property is that:

> to which an owner has voluntarily relinquished all right, title, claim and possession with the intention of terminating his ownership, but without vesting it in any other person and with the intention of not reclaiming further possession or resuming ownership, possession or enjoyment.

Commonwealth v. Wetmore, 447 A.2d 1012, 1014 (Pa. Super. Ct. 1982). However, in the instant case, appellants have not relinquished their rights, title, claim and possession of their lots. They remain owners of real property in fee simple, with a recorded deed and "perfect" title. Absent proof to the contrary, possession is

---

payment of annual dues and assessments of the same.

presumed to be in the party who has record title. As appellants themselves concede, with commendable candor, see Brief for Appellants at 15, no authority exists in Pennsylvania that allows for the abandonment of real property when owned in fee simple with perfect title. Most commonly, abandonment involves personal property or railway lines not owned in fee simple. Additionally, appellants properly admit that neither refusal to pay taxes nor nonuse of real property constitutes abandonment. See Petition of Indiana County, 62 A.2d 3, 5 (Pa. 1948) ("It has frequently been held that abandonment of title is not to be presumed from a mere failure to possess the land or from neglect to pay the taxes thereon; inchoate rights may be abandoned but abandonment is not predictable of perfect titles."). Yet, appellants nonetheless maintain that their nonuse, refusal to pay taxes, and offers to sell create an abandonment, because of a displayed intent to abandon.

But appellants simply do not accept that the record shows that they have retained "perfect" title to their lot. Neither title nor deed has been sold or transferred. Indeed, appellants admit that they are the owners of the lots in question. Perfect title, under Pennsylvania law, cannot be abandoned. O'Dwyer v. Ream, 136 A.2d 90 (Pa. 1957). In *O'Dwyer*, our Supreme Court held that once it is determined that good title exists, then the abandonment theory cannot succeed. See also A.D. Graham & Company, Inc. v. Pennsylvania Turnpike Commission, 33 A.2d 22, 29 (Pa. 1943) (which held that the doctrine of abandonment does not apply to perfect titles, only to imperfect titles). Appellants do not cite, and our own research has not discovered, any more recent cases that would cause us to question the authority of the cited decisions. Absent authority to support their argument, therefore, the appeal cannot be successful for appellants.

Having carefully read the entire deed, we cannot find language that would offset appellants' duty under covenant number 11 [see footnote above], nor any language that would serve as a guide to what appellee's remedies are via the covenant for failure to pay. Thus, appellants, retaining perfect title, albeit reluctantly, and having entered into an agreement with appellee to be subject to certain required payments, have not proven a genuine issue of material fact that would mandate reversal of the trial court's entry of summary judgment for appellee. Therefore, we are constrained to find that appellee is entitled to judgment as a matter of law.

Order affirmed.

NOTES AND QUESTIONS

1. **Perfect title.** MacKenzie's "perfect title" consisted of a recorded fee simple title, which — as the case indicates — cannot be abandoned. (Compare title to an easement, a nonpossessory interest in land that can be abandoned. See Chapter 6.) In some contexts, "perfect title" offers an advantage to the landowner: if possession *could* be abandoned, owners could lose title in less than the period prescribed for adverse possession. Do you see how? The principal case indicates that perfect title is sometimes not an advantage.

2. **Rationale.** Why can an easement be abandoned, but not a fee simple estate? Is there an argument that the two rules, rather than being inconsistent, actually work towards the same end? (The question and the answer will perhaps be more understandable after you study Chapter 6.)

3. **What next?**   What would you advise the MacKenzies to do next?

2.   The (Obsolete) Fee Tail

With the recognition in the thirteenth century of a landowner's power to cut off his primogenitary heir by a conveyance of the land to a third party, the fee simple estate ceased to provide a basis for the creation of landed family dynasties. Any present holder could simply convey the land to whomever he wished (or devise it away, after wills became recognized). Displeased landowners desiring to keep property in their transferees' bloodlines thus changed their verbal formulas in dispositive documents, replacing gifts to A "and his heirs" with gifts "to A and the heirs of his body" (or "to A and her bodily heirs"). These slightly different formulas were intended to create significantly different results: By the new language, O signaled an intent that the right to possession transferred by the gift would roll down the generations, from bodily heir to bodily heir, forever. If the right of inheritance of A's heir (and that heir's heir, and so on) was mandatory, then A, and each successive heir, held in effect a life estate. It followed that no transfer by A, or any successive present interest holder, could transfer more than a right to possession measured by the transferor's lifetime. If A, or any subsequent possessor, died *without* a bodily heir, the right to possession would revert to O (or O's successor), or go to a third person if O had so provided ("to A and her bodily heirs, but if A die without a bodily heir, to B and her heirs").

Such at least were the consequences intended by O. How O fared in the event is stated concisely by the excerpt quoted below. Not to keep you in suspense, we tell you now that this new "fee tail" estate became a dead letter in England within two hundred years of its inception. On our side of the Atlantic, it is recognized in only a handful of states. In the vast majority of American states, statutes rewrite any "heirs of the body" language that appears in a deed or will, replacing the fee tail with some other estate. (It is perhaps a measure of the strength of the dynastic urge that "heirs of the body" language appears, with some frequency, in documents drafted by the laity.) Although the fee tail is thus largely obsolete, and may be passed quickly, you still need to know something about it: you may practice (or have a client with land) in a state that recognizes it; and, when statutes modify something, it is helpful to know what it is they are modifying. The bracketed material in the following excerpt is provided by us:

> Prior to 1285, a gift or devise of real property to a man "and the heirs of his body" constituted a fee simple conditional. The fee was conditioned on the donee having heirs of his body. When this condition was satisfied, the donee had full power of alienation [i.e., power to transfer a fee simple by an inter vivos transfer]. See 2 Richard Powell, The Law of Real Property ¶ 193, at 62 (Patrick J. Rohan ed., 1990). Upon the birth of issue to the donee, the only significant distinction between what the donee held and a fee simple estate was that in the event the donee died without leaving surviving issue and without having alienated the land, the property then reverted to the donor, regardless of the survivorship of collateral heirs. See generally Moynihan, Introduction to the Law of Real Property § 5, at 34 (2d ed. 1988). The power of alienation in the donee was the product of judicial construc-

tion which favored the free alienability of lands. However, the landed nobility of England grew dissatisfied with the result of this judicial construction, which permitted the transfer of lands out of their families. Pressure by the nobility resulted in the enactment of the Statute De Donis Conditionalibus in 1285, which declared, contrary to prior judicial interpretation, that conveyances to a donee and "the heirs of his body" should be strictly construed to convey an estate which would without exception pass to the heirs of the donee's body. See Statute De Donis Conditionalibus, 13 Edw. I (1285). [De Donis: "[T]he will of the giver according to the form in the deed of gift manifestly expressed shall be from henceforth observed, so that they to whom the land was given under such condition shall have no power to aliene the land so given, but it shall remain unto the issue of them to whom it was given after their death, or shall revert unto the giver or his heirs if issue fail."]

Under the Statute De Donis Conditionalibus, the donee was said to hold an estate in fee tail (from the Latin talliatum or "cut out of the fee"). The "fee tail" could be further restricted to a specific class of heirs, such as "heirs male" or "heirs female." In all cases, the estate tail was, by definition, a freehold estate in which there was a fixed line of inheritable succession, limited to the issue of the body of the grantee or devisee, and in which the regular and general succession of statutory heirs was cut off. Thus, under the Statute De Donis Conditionalibus, a donee no longer had a power of alienation.

However, the judicial preference for free alienability of land survived despite the enactment of the Statute De Donis Conditionalibus. English courts began to recognize a fictitious real action known as a "common recovery," whereby a holder of land in fee tail could effectively cut off the interest of the heirs as well as the reversionary interest of the donor [or any interest created in a third party]. After effecting a common recovery, the land holder owned the property in fee simple. The use of the common recovery to convert an estate in fee tail to one in fee simple was commonly referred to as "barring" or "docking the entail."

Robins Island Preservation Fund, Inc. v. Southold Dev. Corp., 959 F.2d 409 (2d Cir. 1992).

NOTES AND QUESTIONS

1. **Future interest.** With the fee tail, we encounter our first "future interest" in land. What happens when A or any subsequent possessor of the fee tail estate dies without a bodily heir? If you answered that the right to possession reverts to the grantor O or O's successor, you are correct. We identify that future right to possession by saying that O, upon transferring the fee tail estate to A, retained a *reversion*. If O had transferred "to A and his bodily heirs, but if A dies without a bodily heir, to B and her heirs," B's future interest would be called a *remainder*, which signifies that the land remains away from O when the present owner dies without a bodily heir.

2. **Disentailing by deed.** "Barring the entail" was an established practice in England by the fifteenth century, and was approved in Taltarum's Case (1472). In the nineteenth century, by statute, England abolished the fine and recovery; thereafter, disentailing could be accomplished by a simple deed from the present interest holder to the transferee. Disentailing by deed is also the proper procedure in those American states that continue to recognize the fee tail (see Note 3). (Disentailing by will is impossible; at the present holder's death, the property automatically passes to the bodily heir.) What is the effect of a disentailing deed on the disentailer's bodily heir? On O's reversion? On any remainder created in B?

3. **Fee tail in four states.** Delaware, Maine, Massachusetts, and (for transfers by deed) Rhode Island recognize the fee tail. In those states, the estate has the characteristics of the fee tail as it existed in the disentailing era. Until disentailed, the fee tail passes down through the generations of bodily heirs; a disentailing deed cuts off bodily heirs as well as the reversioner or remainderman.

4. **Statutes.** In the vast majority of American states, statutes abolish the fee tail and substitute a different configuration of possessory and (sometimes) future interests. These statutes take three main forms:

a. *Fee simple in A.* The most far-reaching statutes convert the fee tail in the first taker (A) into a fee simple absolute. O retains no reversion, and any future interest that O creates in B is cut off by the statute. At A's death, the property passes by A's will or by intestacy. In effect, this type of statute disentails the property in the hands of the first taker, relieving her of the necessity of doing so.

> Any person seized or possessed of an estate in [fee] tail shall be held and deemed to be seized and possessed of the same in fee simple, fully and absolutely, without any condition or limitation whatsoever, to that person, that person's heirs and assigns, forever, and shall have full power and authority to sell or devise the same as such person thinks proper; and such estate shall descend under the same rules as other estates in fee simple.

Tenn. Code § 66-1-102.

b. *Defeasible fee simple in A.* Some states convert the attempted fee tail in A into a fee simple in A (just as in "a" above) *if* O creates no future interest in a third party (B). If O does create a future interest in B, then A takes a defeasible fee simple: B (or B's successor) will take the property if A has no bodily heir at her death; but if A dies with a bodily heir, B's interest fails, and A's fee simple becomes absolute, passing by descent to A's heir or by devise to A's devisee, as the case may be.

> Estates tail have been abolished, and every estate which would be a fee tail shall be a fee simple; and if no valid future estate is limited thereon, a fee simple absolute. Where a future estate in fee is limited on any estate which would be a fee tail, such future estate is valid and vests in possession on the death of the first taker without issue living at the time of his death.

N.Y. EPTL § 6-1.2. *See* Restatement of Property §§ 101-102. (You might see a parallel between A's defeasible estate arising under the New York statute and Virginia Simpson's defeasible fee simple in Dickson v. Alexandria Hospital: had Virginia remarried, she would have lost her fee simple interest; but when she died without having remarried, her defeasible fee simple became absolute at that point, and passed by her will to the Alexandria Hospital.)

c. *Life estate in A.* A few statutes convert the intended fee tail into a life estate in A, with a remainder in fee simple in A's bodily heirs, in effect treating the phrases "heirs of the body" or "bodily heirs" as words of purchase rather than limitation. Under these statutes, O retains a reversion, which takes effect if A dies without a bodily heir. If O creates a remainder ("to A and her bodily heirs, and if A dies without issue, to B and her heirs"), the remainder takes effect in B or B's successor if A dies without a bodily heir.

> In cases when, by common law, any person may become seized in fee tail of any lands or tenements, by virtue of any devise, gift, grant, or other conveyance, the person, instead of being, or becoming, seized thereof in fee tail, shall be adjudged to be, and become, seized thereof for his or her natural life only. The remainder shall pass in fee simple absolute to the person to whom the estate tail would first pass according to the course of the common law by virtue of the devise, gift, grant, or conveyance.

Ark. Code § 18-12-301. *See* Restatement of Property §§ 97-100 (1936). Rhode Island's statute accomplishes the same result by providing that "[n]o person seised in fee simple shall have a right to devise any estate in fee tail for a longer time than to the children of the first devisee." Under this statue, A's child takes as an heir of A, rather than, as in Arkansas, as a purchaser from O. Does that matter? See Thomas F. Bergin & Paul G. Haskell, Preface to Estates in Land and Future Interests 33 (2d ed. 1984) ("unless form is exalted over substance, there should be no difference"). In re-writing only O's attempted *devise* of a fee tail, the Rhode Island statute leaves O free to create a fee tail by deed.

4. **Policy.** Which of the preceding statutes (a) effectuates O's dynastic intent; (b) makes land marketable; (c) protects A's bodily heirs?

5. **Commentary on the fee tail.** See generally John V. Orth, *Does the Fee Tail Exist in North Carolina?*, 23 Wake Forest L. Rev. 767 (1988); Charles D. Spinosa, *The Legal Reasoning Behind the Common, Collusive Recovery: Taltarum's Case (1472)*, 36 Am. J. Legal Hist. 70 (1992).

PROBLEMS

2-C. In a state that recognizes the fee tail, O conveys Blackacre "To A and the heirs of her body." Your client A tells you that she wants to devise Blackacre to F, a family friend (A's children, she says, are well-to-do and don't need Blackacre). Advise A.

2-D. Who has title to Blackacre under each of the statutes reproduced above, in the following situations:

(a) O conveys Blackacre "to A and the heirs of her body." A dies without a bodily heir, survived only by her brother X.

(b) O conveys Blackacre "to A and the heirs of her body." A dies survived by a child, C.

(c) O conveys Blackacre "to A and the heirs of her body, then to B and his heirs." A dies without a bodily heir, survived only by her brother X.

(d) O conveys Blackacre "to A and the heirs of her body, then to B." A dies survived by a child, C.

3.   The Life Estate

As we saw in the introduction to this chapter, the life estate was the earliest estate recognized by the common law. It remains important today as a means of conferring lifetime benefits under a trust: O transfers stocks and bonds to the Provident Bank and Trust Company, to pay the income (dividends, interest) to O's wife A for life, then to distribute the principal to B and C (O's children). *See generally* Paul G. Haskell, Preface to Wills, Trusts and Administration 73-75 (2d ed. 1994) (indicating the managerial and other benefits of placing property in trust).

For reasons that we shall see in connection with our consideration of Long v. Crum below, a *legal* life estate — one created by a transfer directly to the life tenant, without the creation of a trust — is generally inadvisable. Despite this, it appears from *Long* and the other cases in this section (culled from many of the same sort) that the legal life estate remains something of a favorite among the populace.

Life estate pur autre vie. In the absence of a contrary indication in the instrument of transfer, a transfer "to A for life" creates an estate measured by the life of the transferee A. It is possible, however, for A to hold a life estate measured by a life other than A's own. For example, if O transfers "to A for the life of B," A holds a life estate, but it is measured by B's life. The same result follows if O transfers "to B for life" and B then transfers the life estate to A. The technical name for this estate is a life estate *pur autre vie* (which, if you have a little French, means pretty much what it says).

If the measuring life (B) dies before A, the result is clear: A's life estate ends. The converse is not so clear: what happens if A — the tenant in possession — dies before B, the measuring life? The early common law, reflecting rowdier times, left it to a free-for-all; the first occupant after A's death enjoyed the right to possession until B's death. Subsequently, the common law recognized that the balance of the life estate passed upon A's death to A's heirs or devisees, as the case may be. *See, e.g.,* Mass. Gen. Laws, Ch. 190 § 3 ("When a person dies seized of land . . . or of any right thereto . . . in fee simple or for the life of another, not having lawfully devised the same, they shall descend . . . as follows. . . .").

Future interest. We have already met reversions and remainders following the fee tail estate. Reversions and remainders also exist in connection with life estates. If O transfers "to A for life," O retains a reversion in fee simple; the future interest label identifies O's right to future possession of Blackacre when the life estate ends. If O transfers Blackacre "to A for life, then upon A's death to B," B has a remainder in fee simple, indicating that B holds the right to future possession when the life estate ends.

a.   Creation

WILLIAMS v. ESTATE OF WILLIAMS
865 S.W.2d 3 (Tenn. 1993)

REID, CHIEF JUSTICE.

This suit seeks the construction of the last will and testament of G.A. Williams. The will was executed on July 18, 1933, and probated in the Probate Court of McMinn County on November 24, 1944. The testator was survived by nine children, including the three daughters named in the will. The plaintiff, Ethel Williams, who was 92 years of age when the complaint was filed, is the only survivor of the three children named in the will. The defendant Etta Tallent is the only other surviving child of the testator, and the other defendants are lineal descendants of the testator. (There is no statement that the named defendants are all the heirs at law of the testator.) Ethel Williams has maintained possession of the farm since the death of the testator, jointly with Ida Williams and Mallie Williams until their deaths. Apparently none of the three named daughters ever married, though that fact does not affirmatively appear.

The will is as follows:

> I, G.A. WILLIAMS, being of sound mind make this my last will and Testament: At my death I want Ida Williams, Mallie Williams, and Ethel Williams, three of my daughters, to have my home farm where I now live, consisting of one hundred and eighty-eight acres, to have and to hold during their lives, and not to be sold during their lifetime. If any of them marry their interest ceases and the ones that remain single have full control of same. I am making this will because they have stayed at home and taken care of the home and cared for their mother during her sickness, and I do not want them sold out of a home. If any one tries to contest this will I want them debarred from any interest in my estate.

> /s/ G.A. Williams, July the 18, 1933.

The complaint alleged that the interest received by Ethel Williams was a life estate under the will or, in the alternative, a life estate under the will and a "remainder interest" by intestate succession. The latter disposition was adopted by the Chancellor initially, but on rehearing was abandoned for the finding that the devise of a life estate without limitation over indicated an intention that the named daughters have the property in fee simple, which is the position asserted by Ethel Williams on appeal.

The Court of Appeals affirmed the holding of the trial court. It held, on the authority of White v. Brown, 559 S.W.2d 938 (Tenn.1977), that each named daughter owned a one-third undivided interest in fee simple. The record does not support that decision.

The function of a suit to construe a will is to ascertain and effect the intention of the testator. The determinative intention is the predominant purpose expressed by the testator in the will. In the case before the Court, the predominant intention of the testator is clear. Each of the testator's three daughters who had "stayed home" was to have the farm jointly with the other two daughters, so long as they were living and unmarried, as a residence and for their support; after the death or marriage of any of the three daughters, the remaining two daughters would hold jointly until the marriage or death of another; and the remaining unmarried daughter was to hold until she married or died. The statements that the farm was "not to be sold during their lifetime" and "I do not want them sold out of a home" emphasized and re-enforced the predominant intention that each of the three daughters have a residence and support during her life or until she should marry. The testator's statement that he was favoring those children above the others because they had "stayed at home and taken care of their mother" implicitly recognized that each had foregone the opportunity to become self-supporting or be supported by a husband, and limiting the duration of the devise to such time as a daughter should marry, indicates that the devise was intended to be a substitute for support that might otherwise have been available.

The intention of the testator was not to make an absolute gift to all or either of the daughters. The first statement in the will limits the devise "during their lives." The next statement limits the devise to the duration of their unmarried state. The testator devised to the daughters an interest not readily alienable and one that could not be defeated by a suit for partition or sale for partition. His reason for selecting the estate devised is indicated by the statements "not to be sold during their lifetime" and "I do not want them sold out of a home." Upon the death or marriage of the named daughters, the testator's purpose as to them would have been accomplished and the testator's heirs would inherit the property by intestate succession.

The testator recognized that his other heirs would acquire some interest in the property upon his death. The primary emphasis was that the daughters' limited interests not be disturbed by the owners of the interest not devised to the daughters. The severity of his admonition is shown by the provision that any person who should "contest" the will would be "debarred" from any interest, not just in the farm but in his estate.

This case is not controlled by White v. Brown, relied upon by the Court of Appeals. In that case, the following provision was found to constitute the devise of a fee simple: "I wish Evelyn White to have my home to live in and not to be sold. I also leave my personal property to Sandra White Perry. My house is not to be sold." 559 S.W.2d at 938. The majority in *White* based its decision on that portion of what is now T.C.A. § 32-3-101 (1984) which provides: "A will shall convey all the real estate belonging to [the testator], or in which he had any interest at his decease, unless a contrary intention appear by its words in context." That statute does not control the disposition in the case before the Court because, as discussed above, a contrary intention appears from the will. The provision that each daughter's interest would terminate upon her marriage, as well as upon her death, is a further indication that the testator did not intend for the named daughters to have an absolute estate in the farm. As stated in Page on Wills,

> The gift to A may indicate quite clearly that it is a gift for the life of A, as where the gift is to A for life or until her marriage, or a gift to A for life or

during her widowhood. In gifts of this sort, A takes a life estate, since the provision with reference to marriage or widowhood is, at least, not sufficient to overcome the effect of the provisions of the will which show that testator intends to give to A a life estate only.

4 William J. Bowe & Douglas H. Parker, Page on Wills, § 37.22, at 632-634 (4th ed. 1961).

The will as a whole conveys a definite meaning. Though the author obviously was not a skilled legal draftsman, he, also obviously, had a good command of language and was familiar with legal phrases commonly used and understood beyond the legal profession. The testator accurately described the instrument he was writing as his "last will and testament," he asserted that he was "of sound mind," and he employed the traditional words of conveyance — "to have and to hold" — in devising an interest in real estate to the daughters. Even "contest," though perhaps not used accurately in its narrow, technical sense, may indicate an action designed to defeat a testamentary disposition. The conclusion is almost inescapable that, had the testator intended to devise the named beneficiaries an estate in fee, he would have expressed that intention quite clearly. Consequently, the estate devised to the named daughters was less than a fee simple.

The judgment of the Court of Appeals is reversed, and the case is remanded for further proceedings. Costs are taxed to the appellee.

NOTES AND QUESTIONS

1. **Comparisons.** How does the will in the principal case differ from the will in White v. Brown, which the court discusses? In *White*, the majority concluded that testator's holographic will created a fee simple in Evelyn White. The dissenting judge argued strenuously that the underscored phrase "not to be sold" was a caveat addressed to Evelyn; and since that restriction on transfer was inconsistent with a fee simple, testator must have intended for Evelyn to have only a life estate. Does the court's discussion in Williams v. Williams suggest a different reading of the testator's language in White v. Brown?

2. **Estates created.** What estates did G.A. Williams create by his will? Who is entitled to the property after the death of Ethel Williams? Did G.A. Williams die partially intestate?

3. **Leases for life.** A life estate may be created by an instrument of lease, with or without a provision for payment of rent. See Thompson v. Baxter, 119 N.W. 797 (Minn. 1909) (lease "for and during the full term of while he shall wish to live in [the city of] Albert Lea, from and after the first day of December, 1904" created life estate). See also Garner v. Gerrish, in Chapter 4.

b.   Sale by the Life Tenant

Compare two transfers:

- O devises Blackacre "to A for life, then to B."

- O devises Blackacre "to the Provident Bank, in trust, for the benefit of A for life, and upon A's death, the trust is to terminate and Blackacre is to be distributed to B free of trust."

In a trust, the trustee has legal title to the property and is required to manage the property for the benefit of the beneficiaries (here A and B). This power to manage includes a power to sell the trust asset and invest the proceeds in more profitable income-producing property if that is in the best interests of the beneficiaries. Reflecting the origin of the trust in the courts of equity, the beneficiaries under a trust are said to have "equitable" interests; thus, in our second example above, A has an equitable life estate and B has an equitable remainder in fee simple. In the first transfer, the transfer is made outright rather than in trust. A has a legal life estate (distinguished from the "equitable" life estate created by the trust), and B has a legal remainder. Although the number of reported cases suggests that transferors do it regularly, Long v. Crum, which follows, shows the inadvisability of creating a life estate outside of a trust.

LONG v. CRUM
267 N.W.2d 407 (Iowa 1978)

LeGrand, Justice.

This appeal comes to us on an agreed statement of facts. It involves a suit to sell real estate held by plaintiff as life tenant under the will of her husband, Vernon P. Long. Her petition was dismissed and she appeals. We reverse and remand for further proceedings as directed herein.

The undisputed facts are as follows. Vernon P. Long died November 28, 1957. His assets included two parcels of real estate, one situated in Montgomery County and one in Adams County. Although in different counties, the two parcels are contiguous and consist of approximately 342 acres.

At the time of her husband's death, plaintiff was forty-one years old. She is now sixty years of age and remains unmarried. Her two children, Margaret Kathryn and Bernard Wayne, ten and six respectively when their father died, are now twenty-nine and twenty-five years of age. Both are unmarried and childless. Because of severe physical disability, it is unlikely that Margaret will ever have children. Whether Bernard will is, of course, not presently determinable.

The income from the property has been insufficient to maintain and improve the farm. The land is hilly and rough. The soil is thin and subject to considerable erosion, and the buildings and fences are in bad condition. The testimony of two real estate experts fixed the value of the property at approximately $375.00 per acre.

The last will and testament of the decedent contained this provision:

> All the rest residue and remainder of my estate of which I may die seized or to which I may be entitled, I will devise and bequeath to my beloved wife, Ermabeth Long, for her use and benefit during her life time, she to have, collect and use the rents and profits thereof.

Upon the death of my said wife, I will devise and bequeath a life estate only in all the rest, residue and remainder of my estate of which I may die seized or to which I may be entitled, to my beloved children, Margaret Kathryn Long and Bernard Wayne Long, or to the survivor of them, as tenants in common, with remainder over in fee to the heirs of their bodies.

Under the will successive life estates are created, first for the testator's widow, then for his children. Whether the remainder will vest under the will depends on whether either Kathryn or Bernard has a child.

Ermabeth's life estate has already lasted 21 years. The life expectancy of the children makes it probable that theirs will continue for an additional substantial period after Ermabeth's death. They join their mother in asking that the real estate be sold.

Plaintiff's petition asks a sale of the real estate, the appointment [by the court] of a trustee to administer the proceeds on behalf of the life tenants, and preservation of the corpus for the benefit of those who ultimately become entitled to it.

Defendants include Kenneth Crum, a tenant; the two children, Margaret and Bernard; and "all unknown heirs of the body of Margaret Kathryn Long and Bernard Wayne Long and all other unknown potential claimants who may eventually acquire a vested interest in remainder by virtue of being heirs of Vernon P. Long, deceased." A guardian ad litem was appointed to represent all unknown heirs and claimants.

The problem inherent in the foregoing facts arises because the remainder has not vested and, indeed, it is uncertain if it will ever do so. In the meantime an admittedly unproductive farm is held captive for probably more than half a century after decedent's death.

In an effort to resolve this problem, plaintiff seeks authority to sell the land under the following provisions of Iowa Code § 557.9:

[O]n the petition of the life tenant, with the consent of the holder of the reversion, the district court may order the sale of the property in such estate and the proceeds shall be subject to the order of court until the right thereto becomes fully vested. The proceedings shall be as in an action for partition.

The trial court rejected the plaintiff's petition, holding such a sale was prohibited by Traversy v. Bell, 193 N.W. 439 (Iowa 1923). While we agree that Traversy v. Bell would require this result, we do not agree that it is controlling in this case. Our reasons for reaching this conclusion require some discussion of the *Traversy* case and of subsequent legislation, particularly a 1947 amendment to § 557.9.

Factually, *Traversy* is much like the present case. There the life tenants petitioned for a partition [a sale] of real estate, asking that the income from the proceeds be paid to them and the principal preserved for the remaindermen. There were remaindermen then in existence, but the class was still open. The court denied the request for partition on the ground that all parties to a partition action must have present possessory interests in the land, and the holders of a remainder were not present possessors. In affirming the trial court's refusal to allow partition, we [also] said:

> It may be conceded that, under certain circumstances, a court of equity has inherent authority to order the sale of real estate which has been devised by the will of a testator to a life tenant, with remainder over, but the authority so to do is strictly confined within narrow limits. The great weight of authorities is to the effect that such power will not be exercised unless it clearly appears that unless the property is sold and the proceeds invested it will be entirely lost to those entitled thereto. In other words, the court's power in this respect will be invoked only as a matter of extreme necessity, because if exercised under any other circumstances, it would be an unwarranted interference with the express intent of the testator.

193 N.W. at 442. [The *Traversy* court refused to allow sale under the court's inherent equity power because of the lack of any exigency.]

Traversy was decided in 1923. Section 557.9 was first enacted in 1924. It was amended in 1947 to add this language:

> provided that on the petition of the life tenant, with the consent of the holder of the reversion, the district court may order the sale of the property in such estate and the proceeds shall be subject to the order of court until the right thereto becomes fully vested. The proceedings shall be as in an action for partition.

We agree with plaintiff that § 557.9 vested the trial court here with discretionary power to order a sale.

At the time *Traversy* was decided, the equitable action of partition was limited to those owning real estate jointly or as tenants in common. A life tenant could not demand partition against a remainderman because all parties were required to have a present right of possession in the land. This was the rationale of the *Traversy* decision.

The 1947 amendment to § 557.9 worked a significant change in this rule. One of its purposes was to authorize a judicial sale when it would have been virtually impossible to do so otherwise because of the holding in *Traversy*.

Important in our consideration is this statement of legislative purpose at the time the [1947] amendment was enacted:

> The purpose of this bill is to make it possible for a grantor and a life tenant, in cases where contingent remaindermen cannot be determined, to have property sold under proper proceedings, and the proceeds held intact under the jurisdiction of the court until the remaindermen are determined.

The petition before us was filed by Ermabeth as life tenant. The two children, who are entitled to enjoy their own life tenancy on her death, also requested a sale of the real estate. The will provides for the residue to go to the heirs of the body of Margaret and Bernard. This creates a contingent remainder, both because it depends upon the happening of an uncertain event and because, if the event occurs, the persons who will comprise the class are unknown.

The ultimate question is whether these circumstances permit a sale of the property under the terms of § 557.9. The trial court held it had no authority to order a sale because the will created no reversionary interest. As the consent of the holder of the reversion is a condition imposed by the statute on the right to sell, the trial court held § 557.9 not applicable. For the reasons hereafter set out we reach a contrary conclusion.

A reversion is an interest created by law, not by any act of the party. It is simply the interest remaining in the grantor or in a testator when he conveys or devises an interest less than the entire estate which he owns.

In the case now before us, the reversionary interest vested instant[ly] upon the death of Vernon P. Long in Ermabeth, Margaret, and Bernard, the surviving spouse and only children of the decedent. [The court's cryptic statement does not indicate where the reversion came from. Here is the explanation. Vernon Long's will created successive life estates, first in his wife Ermabeth, then in his children Margaret and Bernard. The life estates were followed by a remainder in fee simple in the heirs of Margaret and Bernard. Since the heirs of Margaret and Bernard, if any, will not be determined until the deaths of Margaret and Bernard, the remainder to the heirs is contingent — uncertain to become effective. If Margaret and Bernard are not survived by heirs at their deaths, the contingent remainder will fail. In that event, Vernon's devise in effect will have been "to Ermabeth for life, then to Margaret and Bernard for their joint lives." If Margaret and Bernard have no heirs, what happens to the right to possession after the ending of the second life estate? The grantor — Vernon — retained it. More precisely, Vernon's heirs retained the reversion, since Vernon's will does not become effective until Vernon's death. As the court says, the reversion created by Vernon's will was created instantly upon Vernon's death in Vernon's heirs. Those heirs are his wife and his two children.]

It is quite true that the holders of the reversion might never enjoy the fee because of the conditions created by Vernon's will [because Margaret or Bernard or both may die survived by heirs, who would take fee simple title and divest the reversion in Vernon's heirs]. Nevertheless, they held the right of reversion, an actual estate in praesenti although its enjoyment is postponed to some future time.

The author of 1 American Law of Property § 4.16 gives this example [of a reversion] at p. 435:

> A reversion may [follow a] contingent remainder. Suppose A, owning land in fee simple, conveys it as follows: "To B for life, remainder to the children of B." At the time of the conveyance, B has no children. There is then a reversion in the grantor until a child of B is born, at which time the reversion is extinguished.

Applying these rules to the facts at hand, we hold Ermabeth, Margaret, and Bernard took a reversionary interest in this real estate immediately upon Vernon's death, defeasible if either Margaret or Bernard has children. The only consent necessary to satisfy § 557.9 is theirs, and the trial court had authority to decree a sale of this real estate.

We do not decide whether there should be a sale, only that the trial court has discretionary authority to order one. We remand the case for determination of this question. If a sale is authorized, suitable provisions should be made, of course, for the protection of both the life tenants and those who will ultimately take the fee.

REVERSED AND REMANDED.

NOTES AND QUESTIONS

1. **Statutory and common-law authority.** The court considers three bases for sale of property that is co-owned: (1) statutory partition of assets held by concurrent present owners (sale and division of the proceeds or physical division of the property); (2) the inherent judicial power of a court of equity to order sale of property held by present and future interest holders; and (3) the statutory basis provided by § 557.9, as amended in 1947. Why isn't partition available in the principal case? *See* Maitland v. Allen, 594 S.E.2d 918 (Va. 2004) (present life estate could not be partitioned from a future interest, the interests being successive rather than concurrent). How does the statutory action provided by § 557.9, as amended, differ from the basis for sale discussed in the quote from *Traversy*? Which provides the more stringent test for sale? Which basis for sale does the court in the principal case rely on?

2. **On remand.** Should the trial court order a sale? If the trial court orders a sale, what becomes of the sale proceeds?

3. **Valuation of life estates.** A life estate can be assigned a present value. You need to know the concepts involved in such valuation, but not the math (an accountant with the proper tables can give you the answer). Valuation of present and future interests is based on the concept of *discounting*. If A owes B $100,000 ten years from now, the *present* value of B's right to the money is not $100,000; it is rather the amount of money that, if invested today at a specified interest rate, would equal $100,000 in ten years. Suppose that Blackacre is worth $100,000, and title is divided between a life estate in A and a remainder in B. The present value of B's remainder is the amount of money that, invested today at a specified rate, would equal $100,000 when A dies. The two relevant variables are the duration of A's life and the appropriate interest rate to use in our calculations. A standard mortality table would give us A's remaining life expectancy at any given stage of A's life. The interest rate for discounting would usually be the going rate of return on safe (rather than speculative) investments. If A has a remaining life expectancy of twenty years and the relevant interest rate is 4%, the present value of B's remainder is the amount of money that, invested today at 4%, would create a fund of $100,000 in twenty years. Subtracting the value of B's remainder from $100,000 (the value of Blackacre) gives us the present value of A's life estate. The younger A is when present values are determined, the larger will be A's share of the total value of the underlying asset; the older A is, the less will be A's share. If A held a ten year term of years in Blackacre rather than a life estate, and B held a remainder, the present value of B's remainder would be the present value, as the specified interest rate, of the right to receive $100,000 in ten years.

4. **Second thoughts.** Suppose that O transfers "to A for life, then to B," and A and B agree on a sale. (To what incentives might the remainderman have to

agree?) The property is sold. Before the proceeds can be distributed, the life tenant dies. Can the remainderman set aside the agreement and claim all of the proceeds? *See* Estate of Moore v. Smiley, 714 N.E.2d 675, 678 (Ind. Ct. App. 1999) ("Due to Ruby's untimely death, Janice [the remainderman] may now regret the bargain she made. Nevertheless, she is bound by her agreement.").

PROBLEM 2-E. In Baker v. Weedon, 262 So. 2d 641 (Miss. 1972), John Weedon's will, executed in 1925, provided as follows:

> Second; I give and bequeath to my beloved wife, Anna Plaxico Weedon all of my property both real, personal and mixed during her natural life and upon her death to her children, if she has any, and in the event she dies without issue then at the death of my wife Anna Plaxco Weedon I give, bequeath and devise all of my property to my grandchildren, each grandchild sharing equally with the other.

> Third; In this will I have not provided for my daughters, Mrs. Florence Baker and Mrs. Delette Weedon Jones, the reason is, I have given them their share of my property and they have not looked after and cared for me in the latter part of my life.

On the following facts, taken verbatim from the court's opinion, should the court exercise its equitable jurisdiction to order a sale?

> John Weedon bought Oakland Farm in 1905 and engaged himself in its operation. In 1915 John, who was then 55 years of age, married Anna Plaxico, 17 years of age. This marriage, though resulting in no children, was a compatible relationship. John and Anna worked side by side in farming this 152.95-acre tract of land in Alcorn County. There can be no doubt that Anna's contribution to the development and existence of Oakland Farm was significant. The record discloses that during the monetarily difficult years following World War I she hoed, picked cotton and milked an average of fifteen cows per day to protect the farm from financial ruin.

> While the relationship of John and Anna was close and amiable, that between John and his [two] daughters of his first marriage was distant and strained. He had no contact with Florence Weedon Baker, the mother of Henry Baker, Sarah Baker Lyman and Louise Virginia Baker Heck, the appellants herein. An even more unfortunate relationship existed between John and his second daughter, Delette Weedon Jones. She is portrayed by the record as being a nomadic person who only contacted her father for money, threatening on several occasions to bring suit against him.

> There was no contact between Anna and John Weedon's children or grandchildren from 1932 until 1964. Anna ceased to operate the farm in 1955 due to her age and it has been rented since that time. Anna's only income is $1000 annually from the farm rental, $300 per year from sign rental and $50 per month by way of social security payments. Without contradiction Anna's income is presently insufficient and places a severe burden upon her ability to live comfortably in view of her age and the infirmities therefrom.

In 1964 the growth of the city of Corinth was approaching Oakland Farm. A right-of-way through the property was sought by the Mississippi State Highway Department for the construction of U.S. Highway 45 bypass. The highway department located Florence Baker's three children, the contingent remaindermen by the will of John Weedon, to negotiate with them for the purchase of the right-of-way. Dorothy Jean Jones, the adopted daughter of Delette Weedon Jones, was not located and due to the long passage of years, is presumably dead. A decree pro confesso was entered against her.

Until the notice afforded by the highway department the grandchildren were unaware of their possible inheritance. Henry Baker, a native of New Jersey, journeyed to Mississippi to supervise their interests. He appears, as was true of the other grandchildren, to have been totally sympathetic to the conditions surrounding Anna's existence as a life tenant. A settlement of $20,000 was completed for the right-of-way bypass of which Anna received $7500 with which to construct a new home. It is significant that all legal and administrative fees were deducted from the shares of the three grandchildren and not taxed to the life tenant. A contract was executed in 1970 for the sale of soil from the property for $2500. Anna received $1000 of this sum which went toward completion of payments for the home.

There was substantial evidence introduced to indicate the value of the property is appreciating significantly with the nearing completion of U.S. Highway 45 bypass plus the growth of the city of Corinth. While the commercial value of the property is appreciating, it is notable that the rental value for agricultural purposes is not. It is apparent that the land can bring no more for agricultural rental purposes than the $1000 per year now received.

The value of the property for commercial purposes at the time of trial was $168,500. Its estimated value within the ensuing four years is placed at $336,000, reflecting the great influence of the interstate construction upon the land. Mr. Baker, for himself and other remaindermen, appears to have made numerous honest and sincere efforts to sell the property at a favorable price. However, his endeavors have been hindered by the slowness of the construction of the bypass.

Anna, the life tenant and appellee here, is 73 years of age and although now living in a new home, has brought this suit due to her economic distress. She prays that the property, less the house site, be sold by a commissioner and that the proceeds be invested to provide her with an adequate income resulting from interest on the trust investment. She prays also that the sale and investment management be under the direction of the chancery court.

OGLE v. OGLE

880 S.W.2d 668 (Tenn. 1994)

REID, CHIEF JUSTICE.

This case presents for review the construction of the residuary clause of the last will and testament of General Ogle, who died a resident of Sevier County in March 1984. The trial court construed the will to devise to his widow a life estate in real property. The Court of Appeals reversed. The judgment of the trial court is found to be correct.

The will provided in pertinent part:

> I hereby leave, bequeath and devise the remainder of my estate, including real property and personal or mixed property, to my wife, Loretta Sutton Ogle, *for her lifetime and at her death the remainder, if any at that time*, to be divided equally among my three (3) children, Bobby Ogle, Bonnie Ogle Reagan and Betty Jo Ogle. Said children to share and share alike.

(Emphasis added). After the testator's death, Loretta Ogle executed a warranty deed purporting to convey a fee simple interest in the residence, which had been owned by the testator at the time of his death, to plaintiff Fred Loveday, Loretta Ogle's son by a prior marriage. Ogle and Loveday then instituted this declaratory judgment proceeding against the other persons named in the will, who are the children of the testator by a prior marriage, seeking a declaration that Ogle had acquired under the will a life estate in the real property coupled with an unlimited power of disposition, whereby Ogle could convey the property in fee simple. Defendants answered, admitting that the will gave the widow a life estate, but denying that she obtained the right to convey the fee, and prayed that the warranty deed from Ogle to Loveday be set aside.

The trial court found in favor of the remainder beneficiaries, declaring that the widow took a life estate only. The Court of Appeals reversed, holding that the deed transferred to Loveday a fee simple interest in the residence.

T.C.A. § 66-1-106 provides in pertinent part:

> When the unlimited power of disposition, qualified or unqualified, is given expressly, in any written instrument, to the owner of any particular estate for life or years, such estate is changed into a fee absolute as to [the] right of disposition, but subject to any future estate limited thereon, in [the] event and so far as the power is not exercised or the property sold during the continuation of the particular estate.

Pursuant to this statute, the owner of a life estate with an unlimited power of disposition can convey the fee simple estate, and thus defeat the interest of remaindermen. If the power of disposition is not exercised by the life tenant and if the property is not sold for debts during the continuance of the life estate, the property will pass to the remainder beneficiaries upon the death of the life tenant. This Court, in Hobbs v. Wilson, 614 S.W.2d 328, 330 (Tenn. 1980), summarized these principles of law as follows:

Under the common law of this state, a devise of a life estate coupled with an absolute power of disposition created a fee simple estate in the [life tenant] which effectively defeated the rights of a remainderman, whether the power of disposition was exercised or not. The application of this rule of law often defeated the basic intent of the testator that the remainderman share in that part of the estate not disposed of by the life tenant. To correct this situation, the legislature passed T.C.A. § [66-1-106]. The effect of this statute is to convert a life estate in real property, coupled with the full power to dispose of the property, into a fee simple absolute as to the right of disposition, while saving the rights of a remainderman in property when the power of disposition is not executed.

The determinative issue, therefore, is whether Ogle was expressly given an unlimited power of disposition. In making this determination, several cases are instructive. In Redman v. Evans, 199 S.W.2d 115 (Tenn. 1947), the testatrix devised the residue of her estate to her nephew "to handle as he sees fit during his lifetime and the balance to go to his daughters." The Court found that this language was sufficient to give the life tenant, the nephew, the unlimited power of disposition. Similarly, in Jones v. Jones, 462 S.W.2d 872 (Tenn. 1971), the testator devised all of his property to his wife "to do as she sees fit during her life." As in *Redman*, the Court in *Jones* found that the wife, as the life tenant, had the right to convey the property in fee simple absolute because the phrase " 'to do with as she sees fit' meant just that and when she 'saw fit' to sell, she was carrying out the wishes of the testator and was abiding by the provisions of the will." 462 S.W.2d at 874. *See also* Miller v. Gratz, 3 Tenn. App. 498, 507 (1926) (observing that a life tenant obtains the unqualified right to dispose of property by the use of phrases such as "to do with at pleasure." "to do with at discretion," or "to use and enjoy at pleasure").

Likewise, in Hobbs v. Wilson, *supra*, the testator devised real property to his wife "for life and, having full confidence in her judgment and discretion, I authorize her to use so much of the corpus thereof as she shall find necessary for comfort and maintenance, she being the sole judge of her needs and at her death, whatever remains indisposed of, if any, I will and devise the same in fee simple to my twelve nieces and nephews." This language was also found to have expressly granted the wife the unlimited power to dispose of the property in fee simple. Finally, in Skovron v. Third National Bank in Nashville, 509 S.W.2d 497 (Tenn. Ct. App. 1973), the testator devised his property to his wife "to have and to hold for and during the full term of her natural life, with right to use and employ, all of said property for her use and benefit and upon her death, such of said property as may remain, shall go to and become the property of my brother." The Court of Appeals found that this language evidenced an intent by the testator to give his widow a life estate only.

After reviewing the foregoing case law, the trial court in the present case found as follows:

The Court is persuaded in this case that the testator has not complied with the provisions of the statute, such as to grant to the widow the power of disposition. [T]he Court is constrained to find that the testator did not expressly give the power of disposition to the widow. This is distinguished from those cases that the Court has been referred to and the Court read, wherein there are other wordings, such as, that she may do with it as she sees fit or words to that effect. We don't have that here. And the statute says, that this power must be given expressly. The Court must find and does find that this power of disposition is not expressly given by this provision of the will.

This Court is in agreement with the conclusion reached by the trial court. The testator devised the property to his wife "for her lifetime and at her death the remainder, if any at that time, to be divided equally" among his children. This language does not give the widow the unlimited power of disposition, qualified or unqualified. T.C.A. § 66-1-106 requires that the power of disposition be "expressly given." The most expansive meaning that can be given the words "if any at that time" falls far short of an expressed grant required by the statute. The testator devised a life estate to his widow and a vested remainder to his named children. Therefore, Ogle did not have the power to convey a fee simple estate in the property in question.

The judgment of the Court of Appeals is reversed and that of the trial court reinstated. Costs are assessed against plaintiffs.

DROWOTA, JUSTICE, dissenting.

I respectfully dissent based on my belief that the majority have departed from previous decisions of this Court and have misconstrued the residuary clause of General Ogle's last will and testament.

In Redman v. Evans, [t]he provision before the Court was as follows:

The residue of my estate, including my home and furnishings, to go to my nephew, Fred Watkins Evans, to handle as he sees fit during his lifetime; and the balance to go to his two daughters, Ann and Frances Evans.

The Supreme Court in *Redman* found that the provision in the will was sufficient to give the life tenant the unlimited power of disposition:

Perhaps the most significant expression on the face of this will supporting the view that it was intended that the life tenant might encroach upon the corpus is the reference following the provision authorizing Evans to handle, or use, this property "as he sees fit," to "the balance." It is impossible to avoid the deduction that Mrs. Jackson had in mind that in his handling or use of the estate a part of the principal or corpus would or might be consumed by him, thus leaving a "balance." It is as though she had said to this favorite nephew, "take all that remains of my estate, after payment of my debts and the legacies I have specified, and do with it as you see fit; the balance remaining when you die I want to go to your daughters."

Under the sub-heading "Implied power to sell," many cases are annotated in 2 A.L.R. 1310, 27 A.L.R. 1387, and 69 A.L.R. 835, construing the phrase, following a devise of a life estate, for the use of the life tenant, with a limitation over of "what remains," or "the remainder," as implying a power of disposition, and as indicating a purpose to vest in the remaindermen what is left only. We are unable to make any material distinction between the phrases "the remainder" or "what remains" and "the balance." Both alike clearly imply a power conferred to encroach upon the corpus. It is only the balance, that is, what remains of the estate, that the testator passes by the will to the remainderman. For example, in Young v. Hillier, 103 Me. 17, 67 A. 571, where the will gave to the wife all the testator's estate "for her use during life" and at her death "whatever may remain of said estates" to a daughter, it was held that the use given the wife extended to a sale of the real as well as the personal property as, otherwise, there was no practical significance in the use of the word "remain" in this connection. So here, the use of the phrase "the balance" is meaningless, unless it connotes what is left after the life tenant has handled or used the estate during his lifetime "as he sees fit."

199 S.W.2d at 118.

General Ogle's use of the phrase "if any" following his reference to "the remainder" makes the deduction that he foresaw that his surviving wife might dispose of some or all of the property comprising his residuary estate even more compelling than this Court's deduction in *Redman*.

In the case of Hobbs v. Wilson, the testamentary provision was as follows:

I hereby will and devise unto my said wife, Mrs. Erma Wilson McAuley, all of the remainder of my real estate for life and, having full confidence in her judgment and discretion, I authorize her to use so much of the corpus thereof as she shall find necessary for her comfort and maintenance, she being the sole judge of her needs, and at her death, whatever remains undisposed of, if any, I will and devise the same in fee simple to my twelve nieces and nephews as equal tenants in common, [the remaindermen then are named].

614 S.W.2d at 329. This Court concluded that the foregoing provision gave Mrs. McAuley an unlimited power of disposition and changed her life estate into a fee simple with power of disposition. We went on to hold that it placed in her the power to terminate the interest of the remaindermen by executing the power of disposition in her lifetime.

In *Hobbs*, Mrs. McAuley did sell the real property. The remaindermen argued that a conveyance by a life tenant with power to dispose of property does not cut off their interest but that their interests are merely transferred to the proceeds of the sale. This Court held that if the remaindermen were to take any estate, they must come within the saving provisions of T.C.A. § 66-1-106. The statute saves the remainder interest "in the event and so far as the power is not executed or the property sold during the continuance of the particular estate." Mrs. Ogle executed her power of disposition by selling the real property, which terminated the remainder interest of the defendants.

I would affirm the judgment of the Court of Appeals.

NOTES AND QUESTIONS

1. **Precedent and the principal case.** In *Ogle*, the court relied in part on Redman v. Evans for the proposition that General Ogle's will did not "expressly" give Loretta Ogle the power to transfer a fee simple and cut off the remaindermen. Consider the following excerpt from *Redman:*

> If there is to be found on the face of this bequest of a life estate to Evans, *either expressed, or by necessary implication*, a power of disposition, "qualified or unqualified," [then] in so far as the power is not executed, or the property sold for debts during the continuance of the life estate, the estate will pass to the remaindermen named therein upon the death of the life tenant.

199 S.W.2d at 116-117 (emphasis added). Is Loretta Ogle's power to sell, as the dissent argues, a "deduction" (necessary implication) from the language of General Ogle's will? Is a "deduction" from express language also a kind of "express" provision? Under *Redman's* interpretation of the statute, what is the difference between language giving the life tenant the power "to do with the property as she sees fit" and the language in the principal case giving the remainder "if any" to the remainderman at the life tenant's death? *See generally* David N. Garst, Note, *Estates Coupled With Powers of Disposition in Tennessee*, 15 Mem. St. U. L. Rev. 415 (1985); William F. Fratcher, *Bequests of Orts*, 48 Mo. L. Rev. 475 (1983). ("Orts," Professor Fratcher tells us, are "left-overs, what a person with the powers of disposition and consumption does not dispose of or consume.").

2. **Result.** Although it is likely that General Ogle did not intend for Loretta to be able to divert his house to her children, what is the consequence of the court's holding that Loretta had no power to transfer a fee under the statute? If Loretta needs to mortgage the house to provide funds for her support, can she do so? If not, is that result consistent with General Ogle's intent?

3. **Future interests in consumables.** You have already seen (in Gruen v. Gruen in Chapter 1) that a future interest can be created in a durable item of personal property, such as an art work. And a future interest is commonly created in a trust of income-producing property such as stocks and bonds. Suppose that a testator purports to leave his or her spouse a life estate in the farm and in the associated livestock and farm implements, with remainder to the testator's children. The rule is that a future interest in consumables cannot exist; the life tenant gets outright ownership. *See* Lewis M. Simes, Handbook of the Law of Future Interests § 8 (2d ed. 1966). Suppose the life tenant is given the power to sell the consumables; does that make a difference? *See id.*

PROBLEM 2-F. T's will devises his entire estate to his wife W for her life, "with the right to dispose of any or all of said property as she may deem fit or necessary to do." The will further provides that if any of his property remains at his wife's death, it should be divided equally among testator's five nephews and nieces. Nine months before her death, W sells the family home — the major asset of T's estate — for $180,000; with the proceeds, W buys a condominium for $72,000, taking title in her name individually, and invests $108,000 in a certificate of deposit, taking title as a joint tenant with her niece, one of the five remaindermen under T's will. W's will contains a devise of the condominium. Who is entitled to the condominium and the certificate of deposit under the Tennessee statute at issue in the principal case? Who would be entitled to those assets if the statute did not exist? *See* Caldwell v. Walraven, 490 S.E.2d 384 (Ga. 1997). (It is useful to make a list of the bundle of sticks in a life estate coupled with a power of sale, with and without the Tennessee statute in *Ogle*.)

c.　Division of Benefits and Burdens

The ownership of property carries with it various economic benefits and costs. When ownership of the property is divided between a life tenant and a remainderman, the question naturally arises as to the allocation of these benefits and burdens between the present and future interest holders. As the next case illustrates, the transferor may allocate these rights and responsibilities; and the law provides default rules when the transferor does not make the allocation.

ESTATE OF CAMPBELL
942 P.2d 1008 (Wash. Ct. App. 1997)

KENNEDY, ACTING CHIEF JUDGE.

George Campbell died in 1994, leaving his wife Wilma a life estate in the family home with the remainder over to his six adult children from a previous marriage. The will provided that Wilma was to have undisturbed possession of the property so long as she wished to live there, and required the children to pay all expenses associated with the life estate property. The children appeal the trial court's rulings that Wilma's life estate continues until her death, even if she chooses not to live on the property, and that the provision requiring the children to pay property expenses is valid and enforceable. The children contend that the trial court failed to give effect to every part of the will in determining the testator's intent, and that, as a matter of law, remaindermen cannot be required to pay property expenses of a life estate. We reject both of these contentions and affirm.

FACTS

George Campbell executed his will in September of 1994. He left the majority of his assets to his wife of 13 years, Wilma. George also gave Wilma a life estate in the family home, with the remainder over to his six children from a previous marriage:

I leave to my wife, WILMA J. CAMPBELL, if she survives me, the following:

> 4. All interest in community property, acquired by us during our marriage.

> 5. A life estate in our residence property of approximately 4.7 acres, 15234 Tiger Mt. Rd. SE, Issaquah, King County Tax Acct. No. 242306-9091, including all furniture and furnishings, whether separate or community.

Because there is potential for disagreement between my wife and my children, I wish to make the following provisions regarding the life estate:

A. I wish my wife to have undisturbed possession of the house and land, including all my tools and equipment, our furniture and furnishings, *so long as she wishes to live there.*

B. I give my wife the option, *if she is unable or does not desire to remain on the property,* to require payment from my children of 1/3 of the value of our house and its lot of one acre. The value is to be established by appraisal, if necessary, with my wife and my children jointly to each select one appraiser and those two a third. I give my wife the option to take 1/3 of the assessed value of the buildings and 1/4 of the assessed value of the land, if she so desires. If my children fail to pay my wife the property shall be sold and the receipts divided.

(Emphasis ours). With respect to the life estate, the will required that "all property expenses, except utilities, including maintenance and repair, taxes, and insurance on buildings," be paid by the children, and that any expenses not paid equally by the children be reimbursed to the payor with interest at the legal rate. Wilma Campbell and George's daughter Judith Richardson were named as co-executrices of the estate.

The children filed a petition seeking judicial determination of the parties' rights and obligations under the will. The trial court construed the will in favor of Wilma, ruling that her life estate would not automatically terminate if she were to vacate the property. Instead, the court ruled, Wilma's life estate would continue through-out her lifetime, even if she moved and rented out the life estate property, and would terminate upon the earlier of her death or her exercise of the payout option, which she could do at any time during her lifetime even if she had earlier moved out of the home. Finally, the court ruled that the provision of the will requiring the children to pay costs associated with the life estate property was valid and enforceable.

The children appeal.

DISCUSSION

I

The children first contend that the trial court erred in ruling that Wilma's life estate continues until her death, regardless of whether she vacates the property. They contend that the will provides that Wilma's life estate terminates if she should move from the family home and that the payout option must be exercised within a reasonable time following the move, or be forever lost.

The rule is well established that the holder of a life estate created by will is entitled to all income derived from the estate during his or her tenancy unless the enjoyment of the life estate is specifically limited in terms as clear and decisive as those granting the life estate. This includes the right to sublease the life estate property and collect rents:

The principle is well settled that a life tenant who is the holder of a present estate for life in real property is entitled to the possession and use of the property. Closely associated in legal theory with the life tenant's right of possession is his right to the issues and profits of realty during the duration of the life estate, and his analogous right to the rents received as income from letting possession of the property, for a consideration, to some person.

51 Am.Jur.2d, Life Tenants and Remaindermen, § 32, at 256 (1970). "[A]n estate given in one part of a will in clear and decisive terms will not be taken away or cut down by doubtful language of a subsequent clause, but only by positive provision in words as clear and decisive as those which created the estate." In re Douglas' Estate, 65 Wash.2d at 499, 398 P.2d 7. "[T]he intention which controls is that which is positive and direct, not that which is merely negative or inferential." *Id.*

Applying these rules, we reject the appellants' contentions that the will terminates Wilma's life estate if she should move from the property and that the will requires Wilma to exercise her option to sell the life estate within a reasonable time after moving, or lose that choice entirely. The will grants Wilma a life estate and a payout option in clear and decisive terms, and contains no affirmative limitation in words as clear and decisive as those which created the estate and the option upon her enjoyment of the life estate or upon her exercise of the payout option. As conceded by the children at oral argument for this appeal, as used in the will the word "option" merely means "choice." Accordingly, Wilma may, if she wishes, move from the property, rent it out and enjoy the income, and exercise the payout option if, as and when she might desire to do so, at any time during her lifetime.

II

The children also contend that the portion of the will requiring them to pay all expenses associated with the life estate property is unenforceable as a matter of law. The will provided that the children were to pay the expenses equally, with any expenses not divided equally to be reimbursed to the payor with interest at the legal rate. The trial court found that the children's remainder interest in the life estate property had sufficient value to secure their maintenance obligations. The children do not contest that George intended them to make the payments; instead, they contend that a will cannot impose financial obligations upon heirs without their consent, arguing that it is tantamount to creating a contract based on an offer but no acceptance. We disagree.

In determining whether a legal life tenant or the remaindermen must assume the duty of insuring property or paying the cost thereof, the intention of the creator of the interest, if indicated, will control. 51 Am.Jur.2d, Life Tenants and Remaindermen, § 243, at 524 (1970). Thus, "it is within the power of the creator of interests in property to place the duty of payment of taxes upon the holder of either present or future interest." *Id.*, § 246, at 529. *See also* Annotation, Rights, Duties, and Liabilities of Life Tenant (Legal or Equitable) and Remaindermen in Respect of Property Insurance or Proceeds Thereof, 126 A.L.R. 336, at 337 (1940).

In accordance with this principle, courts from other states have recognized that where a will explicitly so provides, the costs of maintaining life estate property may properly be charged to the remaindermen. Although this apparently is an issue of first impression in Washington, we find no indication in Washington law that a different rule would apply. Indeed, courts must give effect to any lawful intent of the testator, regardless of the reasonableness of conditions imposed. Moreover, a will provision requiring that remaindermen shall pay the expenses of the life estate is not materially different from the statutory provision that devisees of mortgaged property take the property subject to the mortgage, unless the will otherwise provides. *See* RCW 11.12.070. In both situations, obligations created by testators become the obligation of devisees, to the extent of the value of the inherited property, upon acceptance of the inheritance. *Cf.* Higgenbotham v. Topel, 511 P.2d 1365 (Wash. Ct. App. 1973) (devisee of wheatland took title burdened by leases lawfully created by executor where devisee did not reject bequest; devisee liable under lease to extent of value of the inheritance). Because the language of the will in this case clearly indicates George's intent to require the children to pay the cost of the upkeep of the life estate property, and because the children did not reject the bequest of the remainder estate, they are liable for the costs of maintaining the property, to the extent of the value of their respective inheritances. The trial court found that the value of the remainder estate was sufficient to secure the expenses.

Affirmed.

NOTES AND QUESTIONS

1. **Review.** Once again, we have a will that is not drawn as accurately as it might have been. Do you agree with the court that testator intended that Wilma Campbell's life estate not terminate upon her removal from the premises? What drafting would have made that result crystal clear? What provision did George Campbell include in his will that might have been helpful to the life tenants in Baker v. Weedon (Problem 2-E) and Long v. Crum?

2. **Carrying charges.** "The well-established rule states that the life tenant must pay all annual taxes and interest on debts on the land to the extent that he has received profits, rents, or income from the property." George J. Siedel, III, Real Estate Law 117 (1979). Special assessments, such as taxes to finance a permanent public improvement to the land, might be prorated. *Id.* The principal case shows that the "well-established" rules are defaults, which can be changed by the grantor of the life estate.

3. **Insurance.** The law does not allocate insurance payments to either the present or future interest holders, Real Estate Law, *supra*, at 118, but the grantor of the life estate may make an allocation of that responsibility. *See* Banaszak v. Banaszak, 395 N.W.2d 614 (Wis. Ct. App. 1986).

4. **Repairs.** As you might expect, the life tenant bears the responsibility for making ordinary repairs, while the future interest holder is responsible for extraordinary repairs — those that probably increase the value of the reversion or remainder. Real Estate Law, *supra*, at 119. The life tenant's failure to make repairs, or the life tenant's improvements to the property, are addressed under the law of waste, considered below.

5. **Emblements.** *See* Simpson v. McCormmach, 866 P.2d 489, 490-91 (Or. Ct. App. 1994):

In general terms, the doctrine of emblements gives farm tenants certain rights in crops planted by them during their leasehold but that remain unharvested at the termination of the tenancy. At common law, and under the decisional or statutory law of most American jurisdictions that have dealt with the question, the holders of life estates enjoy emblement rights against the holders of remainder interests that correspond to some of the rights that tenant farmers have against their landlords. As Lord Coke explained: "[I]f tenant for life soweth the ground and dieth, his executors shall have the corn, for that his estate was uncertain and determined by the act of God; and the same law is of the lessee for years of the tenant for life." Coke, 1 Commentary upon Littleton 55b.

As the last clause of Coke's Commentary notes, the doctrine of emblements also protects the life tenant's own tenant who sows but doesn't reap before the life tenant's death. *See* Englehart v. Larson, 608 N.W.2d 673 (S.D. 2000).

d.   Responsibility for the Condition of the Premises: Waste

"In using the land, the life tenant is limited by the general rule that he is not allowed to commit waste. Waste is generally defined as destruction of property by the life tenant to the harm of the reversion or remainder." George J. Siedel, III, Real Estate Law 120 (1979). The general standard is one of prudence or good husbandry, the assessment of which requires the sifting of the facts and circumstances of particular cases. One major category is *permissive* waste — inaction by the tenant that diminishes the value of the future interest, illustrated in Moore v. Phillips, which also contains a useful summary of general principles.

MOORE v. PHILLIPS
627 P.2d 831 (Kan. Ct. App. 1981)

PRAGER, JUSTICE PRESIDING.

This is a claim for waste asserted against the estate of a life tenant by remaindermen, seeking to recover damages for the deterioration of a farmhouse resulting from neglect by the life tenant. The life tenant was Ada C. Brannan. The defendant-appellant is her executrix, Ruby F. Phillips. The claimants-appellees are Dorothy Moore and Kent Reinhardt, the daughter and grandson of Ada C. Brannan.

The facts in the case are essentially as follows: Leslie Brannan died in 1962. By his will, he left his wife, Ada C. Brannan, a life estate in certain farmland containing a farmhouse, with remainder interests to Dorothy Moore and Kent Reinhardt. Ada C. Brannan resided in the farmhouse until 1964. She then rented the farmhouse until August 1, 1965, when it became unoccupied. From that point on, Ada C. Brannan rented all of the farmland but nobody lived in the house. It appears that from 1969 to 1971 it was leased to the remaindermen, but they did not live there. It is undisputed that the remaindermen inspected the premises from time to time down through the years. In 1973, Ada C. Brannan petitioned for a voluntary conservatorship because of physical infirmities. In 1976, Ada C. Brannan died testate, leaving her property to others. Dorothy Moore and Kent Reinhardt were not included in Ada's bounty. From the record, it is clear that Ada C. Brannan and her daughter, Dorothy Moore, were estranged from about 1964 on. This estrangement continued until Ada Brannan's death, although there was minimal contact between them from time to time.

After Ada Brannan's death, Dorothy Moore and Kent Reinhardt filed a demand against the estate of Ada Brannan on the theory of waste to recover damages for the deterioration of the farmhouse. The total damages alleged were in the amount of $16,159. Both the district magistrate and the district judge inspected the premises and found deterioration due to neglect by the life tenant. The district court found the actual damages to the house to be $10,433. The executrix of Ada's estate denied any neglect or breach of duty by Ada Brannan as life tenant. She asserted the defenses of laches or estoppel, the statute of limitation, and abandonment. These affirmative defenses were rejected by the district magistrate and the district judge, except the defense of laches or estoppel which the district magistrate sustained. On appeal, the district judge found that the defense of laches or estoppel was not applicable against the remaindermen in this case. Following entry of judgment in favor of the remaindermen, the executrix appealed.

It is important to note that the executrix does not contend that the life tenant was not responsible for deterioration of the farmhouse or that the action is barred by a statute of limitations. The amount of damages awarded is not contested. In her brief, the executrix-appellant asserts four points which essentially present a single issue: Whether the remaindermen, by waiting eleven years until the death of the life tenant before filing any claim or demand against the life tenant for neglect of the farmhouse, are barred by laches or estoppel?

The executrix contends, in substance, that laches and estoppel, although considered to be equitable defenses, are available in an action at law to recover damages. She points out that, under K.S.A. 58-2523, a remainderman may sue to prevent waste during the life of the tenant while the life tenancy is still in existence. She then notes that the remaindermen inspected the premises on numerous occasions during the eleven years the property was vacant; yet they made no demand that the farmhouse be kept in repair. They waited until the death of the life tenant to bring the action, because then they would not be faced with Ada's testimony which might defeat their claim.

The remaindermen, in their brief, dispute certain factual statements made by the executrix. They agree that the remaindermen had very limited contact with the life tenant after the estrangement. They contend that there is evidence to show the vast majority of the damage to the house occurred during the last two or three years of the life tenancy and that Dorothy Moore did, in fact, express concern to her mother about the deterioration of the house 15 to 20 times during the eleven-year period. They contend that mere passage of time does not constitute laches and that, in order to have laches or estoppel, the person claiming the same must show a detrimental change of position or prejudice of some kind. They argue that the executrix has failed to show any prejudice, since the fact of waste and deterioration is clear and undisputed and there is nothing the testimony of the life tenant could have added on that issue had she been at the trial. As to the failure of the remaindermen to file an action in the lifetime of the life tenant, the remaindermen argue that claimants had been advised to avoid contact with Ada Brannan unless it was absolutely necessary and that they did not want to make a claim during her lifetime since it would have only made a bad situation worse. They maintain that they had good reasons to wait until Ada's death to assert the claim.

In order to place this case in proper perspective, it would be helpful to summarize some of the basic principles of law applicable where a remainderman asserts a claim of waste against a life tenant. They are as follows:

(1) A life tenant is considered in law to be a trustee or quasi-trustee and occupies a fiduciary relation to the remaindermen. The life tenant is a trustee in the sense that he cannot injure or dispose of the property to the injury of the rights of the remaindermen, but he differs from a pure trustee in that he may use the property for his exclusive benefit and take all the income and profits.

(2) It is the duty of a life tenant to keep the property subject to the life estate in repair so as to preserve the property and to prevent decay or waste. 51 Am.Jur.2d, Life Tenants and Remaindermen § 259, pp. 546-548. Stated in another way, the law imposes upon a tenant the obligation to return the premises to the landlord or remaindermen at the end of the term unimpaired by the negligence of the tenant.

(3) The term "waste" implies neglect or misconduct resulting in material damages to or loss of property, but does not include ordinary depreciation of property due to age and normal use over a comparatively short period of time.

(4) Waste may be either voluntary or permissive. Voluntary waste, sometimes spoken of as commissive waste, consists of the commission of some deliberate or voluntary destructive act. Permissive waste is the failure of the tenant to exercise the ordinary care of a prudent man for the preservation and protection of the estate. 78 Am.Jur.2d, Waste § 3, p. 397.

(5) The owner of a reversion or remainder in fee has a number of remedies available to him against a life tenant who commits waste. He may recover compensatory damages for the injuries sustained. He may have injunctive relief in equity, or, in a proper case, may obtain a receivership. The same basic remedies are available against either a tenant for years or a life tenant.

(6) By statute in Kansas, K.S.A. 58-2523, "[a] person seized of an estate in remainder or reversion may maintain an action for waste or trespass for injury to the inheritance, notwithstanding an intervening estate for life or years." Thus a remainderman does not have to wait until the life tenant dies in order to bring an appropriate action for waste.

(7) Where the right of action of the remainderman or landlord is based upon permissive waste, it is generally held that the injury is continuing in nature and that the statute of limitations does not commence to run in favor of the tenant until the expiration of the tenancy. Under certain state statutes, it has been held that the period of limitation commences at the time the waste is committed.

(8) There is authority which holds that an action for waste may be lost by laches. 78 Am.Jur.2d, Waste § 38, p. 424. Likewise, estoppel may be asserted as a defense

in an action for waste. The doctrine of laches and estoppel are closely related, especially where there is complaint of delay which has placed another at a disadvantage. Laches is sometimes spoken of as a species of estoppel. Laches is a wholly negative thing, the result of a failure to act; estoppel on the other hand may involve an affirmative act on the part of some party of the lawsuit. The mere passage of time is not enough to invoke the doctrine of laches. Each case must be governed by its own facts, and what might be considered a lapse of sufficient time to defeat an action in one case might be insufficient in another. Laches, in legal significance, is not mere delay, but delay that works a disadvantage to another. The defense of laches may be applied in actions at law as well as in equitable proceedings. [L]aches is an equitable defense and will not bar a recovery from mere lapse of time nor where there is a reasonable excuse for nonaction of a party in making inquiry as to his rights or in asserting them.

The basic question for our determination is whether the district court erred in holding that the defense of laches or estoppel should not be applied in this case. We have concluded that the district court did not commit error in its rejection of the defense of laches or estoppel under the circumstances of this case. In reaching this conclusion, we have noted the following factors: The evidence is clear that the life tenant, Ada Brannan, failed to carry out her duty as life tenant and quasi-trustee to keep the property in reasonable repair. The claim of waste does not arise out of any act on the part of the remaindermen. Preservation of the property was the responsibility of the life tenant. There was evidence to show that the vast majority of the damage to the farmhouse occurred during the last two or three years of the life tenancy. The fact that permissive waste occurred was proved beyond question. If the life tenant had been alive, she could not very well have disputed the fact that the property has been allowed to deteriorate. Hence, any delay in filing the action until after Ada's death could not have resulted in prejudice to her executrix. There is no evidence in the record to support the defense of estoppel.

Furthermore, the evidence was undisputed that the life tenant was an elderly woman who died in August of 1976 at the age of 83. The position of Dorothy Moore was that she did not wish to file an action which would aggravate her mother and take funds which her mother might need during her lifetime. Even though Dorothy Moore was estranged from her mother, the law should not require her to sue her mother during her lifetime under these circumstances. As noted above, it was the tenant's obligation to see that the premises were turned over to the remaindermen in good repair at the termination of the life estate. Under all the circumstances in this case, we hold that the district court did not err in rejecting the defense of laches or estoppel.

The judgment of the district court is affirmed.

NOTES AND QUESTONS

1. **Alternatives.** Ada Brannan apparently had enough assets to justify an administration of her estate. Why, do you suppose, didn't she repair the house? Why didn't she and the remaindermen agree to mortgage the property to acquire funds for repairs? (Were the parties in a bilateral monopoly?) Does the case illustrate, once again, why a trust is preferable to a legal life estate?

2. **Remedies.** As *Moore* says, the usual remedies for waste are damages or injunctive relief. The appointment of a receiver to manage the land is also possible, and was ordered by the court in a case, much like *Moore*, of an elderly life tenant. *See* Beliveau v. Beliveau, 14 N.W.2d 360 (Minn. 1944). Forfeiture (termination) of the life estate for waste is not allowed unless the instrument creating the life estate provides that remedy, *see* Barkacs v. Perkins, 847 N.E.2d 481 (Ohio Ct. App. 2006) (stating the rule; instrument did not provide for forfeiture), or a statute so authorizes, *see* Smith v. Smith, 241 S.W.2d 113 (Ark. 1951) (stating the rule; no relevant statute).

3. **Categories: ameliorative waste.** The court in *Moore* distinguishes voluntary waste (acts of commission that damage the estate) and permissive waste (failure to take prudent action to preserve the estate). But suppose that removal of a building on the premises and replacement with a more modern structure would *increase* the value of the property (so-called "ameliorative" waste)? A leading early case allowing ameliorative waste by the life tenant is Melms v. Pabst Brewing Co., 79 N.W. 738, 739-741 (Wis. 1899):

> Our statutes recognize waste, and provide [for] the recovery of double damages; but they do not define it. In the present case a large dwelling house, expensive when constructed, has been destroyed, and the ground has been graded down, by the owner of the life estate, in order to make the property serve business purposes. [The brewery had purchased the property from the life tenant and thus held a life estate pur autre vie.] That these acts would constitute waste under ordinary circumstances cannot be doubted. [But] the rule that any change in a building upon the premises constitutes waste has been greatly modified, even in England; and it is now well settled that while such change may constitute technical waste, still it will not be enjoined in equity when it clearly appears that the change will be, in effect, a meliorating change, which rather improves the inheritance than injures it.

> The evidence shows that the property became valueless for the purpose of residence property as a result of the growth and development of a great city [Milwaukee]. Business and manufacturing interests advanced and surrounded the once elegant mansion, until it stood isolated and alone, standing upon just enough ground to support it, and surrounded by factories and railway tracks, absolutely undesirable as a residence, and incapable of any use as business property.

> Under all ordinary circumstances the landlord or reversioner, even in the absence of any contract, is entitled to receive the property at the close of the tenancy substantially in the condition in which it was when the tenant received it; but when, as here, there has occurred a complete and permanent change of surrounding conditions, which has deprived the property of its value and usefulness as previously used, the question whether a life tenant, not bound by contract to restore the property in the same condition in which he received it, has been guilty of waste in making changes necessary to make the property useful, is a question of fact for the jury under proper instructions, or for the court, where, as in the present

case, the question is tried by the court. Judgment [for the life tenant] affirmed.

4. **Fast forward.** A modern sequel to *Melms* is Brokaw v. Fairchild, 237 N.Y.S. 6 (Sup. Ct. 1929), *aff'd*, 245 N.Y.S. 402 (App. Div. 1930), *aff'd*, 177 N.E. 186 (N.Y. 1931), a case which was widely criticized at the time for its rejection of the life tenant's proposal to raze an historical mansion on Fifth Avenue and 79th Street — "an exceedingly fine house" — to build an apartment building. The mansion had become surrounded, and the entire immediate vicinity given over to, apartments rather than stately residences. "The law [of waste] intends that the life tenant shall enjoy his estate in such a reasonable manner that the land shall pass to the reversioner or remainderman as nearly as practicable unimpaired in its nature, character and improvements" In *Brokaw*, the court emphasized the testator's wording in creating the life estate — testator referred four times to "my residence" — in support of its view that testator intended the "identical building" to pass from the life tenant to the remaindermen. Couldn't the court have reached the same result without that language? Are *Brokaw* and *Melms* distinguishable? Is *Brokaw* right? What factors might be important in evaluating a waste claim in a case like *Brokaw*?

5. **Aftermath.** The New York legislature reacted to *Brokaw* by enacting N.Y. Real Property Actions and Proceedings Law [RPAPL] § 803. That statute allows a life tenant with a life expectancy of at least five years, or a term tenant with a remaining term of at least five years, to alter or replace structures by complying with statutory requirements, if the change does not reduce the market value of the property. In the end, the forces of modernity won out in *Brokaw* — the mansion was torn down in the 1960s and replaced by a nondescript high-rise apartment building. *See* N.Y. Times, Sept. 17, 1964, at 1, col. 2.

6. **Commentary.** Two recent articles offer comprehensive and insightful treatments of the law of waste. *See* John A. Lovett, *Doctrines of Waste in a Landscape of Waste*, 72 Mo. L. Rev. 1209 (2007); Jedediah Purdy, *The American Transformation of Waste Doctrine: A Pluralist Interpretation*, 91 Cornell L. Rev. 653 (2006).

4.   The Nonfreehold (Landlord and Tenant) Estates

[W]hen we return to that meditation that man is a world, we find new discoveries. Let him be a world, and himself will be the land, and misery the sea. His misery (for misery is his, his own; of the happiness even of this world, he is but tenant, but of misery the freeholder), his misery, as the sea, swells above all the hills, and reaches to the remotest parts of this earth, man.

John Donne, Devotions Upon Emergent Occasions VIII (1624)

Leases will be covered in detail in Chapter 4. Here, we seek simply to identify the types of leases and to show their place in the heirarchy of estates. There are three types of landlord-tenant estates.

Term of years estate. This is a lease for a fixed period: e.g., to A for 25 years, or one year, or six months, or one week. The lease ends when the stated term expires;

neither party needs to give notice to terminate. The remaining lease estates have an indefinite duration.

The periodic tenancy. Common periodic tenancies are the monthly, quarterly, or yearly tenancies, although the parties may agree on any period they wish. Whatever the period, the tenancy continues indefinitely from one period to the next until either the landlord or the tenant gives proper notice to terminate the lease. The common law required six months' notice to terminate a yearly periodic tenancy, and notice equal to the period to terminate the shorter periodic tenancies. Statutory modifications of the amount of notice required are common.

The tenancy at will. In a tenancy at will, as the name indicates, the tenant's right to possession endures so long as both parties wish it to continue. Either party may terminate by communicating to the other an intent to terminate. No minimum amount of notice is required. In addition, the tenancy terminates by operation of law upon the death of either party or upon a transfer by the landlord of his or her interest in the land.

An express tenancy at will is unusual, since it offers neither security of occupancy for the tenant nor of income for the landlord. The category serves largely as a catch-all for leasing arrangements that fail to qualify as a more substantial tenancy. As with the periodic tenancy, statutory modifications of the tenancy at will are common.

Nonfreehold estates. At common law, leases were regarded as "nonfreehold" estates, to distinguish them from the freehold estates we have already considered (the fee simple, fee tail, and life estate). The distinction had significance for purposes of remedies: freeholders had a remedy to recover possession; nonfreeholders originally did not. (Nonfreeholders, however, rebounded with a vengeance: when the possessory remedy of ejectment became available to tenants in the sixteenth century, it proved so efficient that freeholders would allege fictitious leases in order to claim the benefit of the ejectment procedure.)

The nonfreehold estates fall below the freehold estates in the common law hierarchy: thus, for example, a term of years is theoretically shorter than a life estate. While this occasionally makes little practical sense (compare a life estate to a one hundred year term of years estate), it also causes no harm, given the modern irrelevance of the distinction between freehold and nonfreehold estates. The important conceptual point is that all of the common law estates, whether freehold or not, differ from each other in that they come to their respective ends in different ways. Nevertheless, as the excerpt quoted above indicates, the great Jacobean poet and cleric John Donne was able to use the theoretical difference between the longer and shorter freehold and nonfreehold estates to memorable metaphoric effect in his meditation on the predominance of misery in this earthly life.

5.   Qualification of Estates: Defeasibility

The concept of "defeasibility" is easy enough to grasp. Instead of transferring an unqualified fee simple, or life estate, or term of years, a transferor may instead choose to attach strings to the transfer: to provide that if the grantee does something that the grantor prohibits, or fails to do something that the grantor requires, the grantee's estate will come to an end prematurely. Example: you are a tenant on a one year lease; you fail to pay rent; if the lease so provides — as it almost certainly will — you can be evicted for nonpayment even if the lease still has several months left to run.

Please note that we are not here learning new estates, only variations of those that you have already encountered. An estate that may end earlier than the outside duration specified by its typology is a defeasible variant of that basic estate. Hence the defeasible fee simple, the defeasible life estate, and the defeasible term of years estates are all permissible estates. For simplicity, we focus primarily on the defeasible fee; the concepts that you will learn in dealing with that estate by and large apply to the other forms of defeasible estates. The possibility of premature termination is the hallmark of the defeasible variant of any estate.

As for vocabulary, note that what we have been calling up to now a "fee simple" is, more technically, a fee simple absolute. By *absolute*, we mean, simply, nondefeasible — not subject to any restrictions or requirements imposed by the transferor that might cause the estate to end prematurely. A defeasible fee simple *is* a fee simple: it is capable of lasting for as long as there are heirs to inherit it. It is not a fee simple absolute, however, because it may end earlier. (A fee simple absolute is usually called just a "fee simple," or even a "fee" for short. To avoid confusion, when talking about a defeasible fee, you should identify it as such; if the context so requires, you should, even more specifically, indicate the *type* of defeasible fee simple at issue. The types are discussed more fully in the following materials, along with the appropriate vocabulary.)

a.   Creation

Defeasibility can take either of two forms, to be selected by the transferor: upon violation of the restriction imposed by the transferor, the present estate may come to an end *automatically*, or alternatively, only if the transferor *elects* to call a forfeiture of the transferee's estate. Good form requires that the transferor signal in the deed or devise which type of defeasible estate the transferor intends. The volume of litigated cases indicates that transferors often fail to use good form.

FORSGREN v. SOLLIE
659 P.2d 1068 (Utah 1983)

OAKS, JUSTICE.

This appeal concerns the effect of a condition in a deed. After a trial, the district court held that the deed created a fee simple subject to a condition subsequent, and that the grantor had reacquired the fee by reentry upon condition unfulfilled. We affirm.

The facts are essentially uncontested. In February, 1960, the plaintiff (grantor) conveyed 1.4 acres of unimproved property to James H. Sollie. This property had 73 feet of frontage on the west side of Washington Boulevard north of Ogden, and abutted land owned by the grantor on the north and south. The consideration was approximately $1,400, paid in cash. Sollie planned to build a residence on the property, to be used as a church by his small Baptist group until they were able to build a larger building. The warranty deed contained the following provisions:

> This property is conveyed on the condition that the grantee will build a partition fence along the South side of the above described property, being the North line of property now owned by the grantor. That he will have the above described property surveyed at his own expense, and that the survey must have been made, and the fence erected before any construction or placement of improvements on said property.

> This property is conveyed to be used as and for a church or residence purposes only.

Sollie never built the fence, completed the survey, or built anything on the property. He paid no taxes. He left the state sometime in the early 1960s. A portion of the property, the east 71 feet along the frontage, was sold for taxes in May, 1967, and was purchased for and conveyed to the grantor. Shortly thereafter, the grantor reentered the property, which remained unimproved, mowing the weeds annually, doing some fencing, and paying some real estate taxes. (The record is unclear as to the years and the tracts on which the grantor paid taxes.)

In 1972, the defendants LeFleur, who were strangers to the title, purchased the property (except the 71 feet on the frontage) at a tax sale. Thereafter, they paid some of the real estate taxes. In 1978, defendants located Sollie in Georgia. They paid him $1,500 and Sollie and his wife quit-claimed their interest in the property to the defendants LeFleur.

In 1979 and 1980, the grantor excavated and poured concrete for footings for a small building she was constructing on the property. She testified that she dug the footings herself. Observing this, defendants drove a tractor on the property and knocked over the foundations. The grantor then brought this action to quiet her title to the property.

The district court concluded that conditions subsequent for which no time of performance was specified were performable within a reasonable time, failing which the grantor could enforce the right of reentry. Holding that the specified conditions were not performed within a reasonable time and that the grantor had exercised her right of reentry in 1967, the court decreed fee simple ownership in the plaintiff grantor.

On this appeal, defendants rely on the well-settled principles that conditions controlling the use of deeded property are strictly construed against the grantor, and that forfeitures are not favored.[1] Specifically, defendants argue that this deed could not create a condition subsequent because it contained no words indicating a reversion [sic] or forfeiture.

A fee simple subject to a condition subsequent is an interest in which, upon the occurrence or nonoccurrence of a stated event, the grantor or his successor has the

---

[1] The hierarchy of favoritism has been described as follows: "If a choice is between an estate in fee simple determinable and an estate on condition subsequent, the latter is preferred. Where it is doubtful whether a clause in a deed is a covenant or a condition, the former is preferred." Hagaman v. Board of Educ., 285 A.2d 63, 67 (N.J. Super. Ct. App. Div. 1971).

power, at his option, to terminate the estate and reacquire the property. Restatement of Property § 24 (1936).[2] This power of termination is sometimes referred to as a right of reentry, though that terminology is not used in the Restatement. When an estate is conveyed on contingency (condition subsequent or determinable) and no time is specified for the contingency, the law will imply a reasonable time for the event.

A deed provision specifying or limiting the use to which the property is to be put, or stating that the property is conveyed in consideration of a stated specification or limitation of use, does not, by itself, create a condition subsequent. A condition subsequent is normally created by words like "on condition that," "provided that," or phrases of like import, coupled with a provision that if the stated event occurs or does not occur, the grantor "may enter and terminate the estate hereby conveyed" or a phrase of like import. Restatement of Property § 45 comment j (1936). However, the Restatement further states that "the phrase 'upon express condition that' usually indicates an intent to create an estate in fee simple subject to a condition subsequent, even when no express clause for re-entry, termination or reverter accompanies it." *Id.* at comment 1; also see comment n.

Consistent with the Restatement, there are ample instances where a deed provision using the word "condition" has been interpreted as creating a fee simple subject to a condition subsequent even though there was no express provision for reentry or revesting of the estate. As the court stated in Papst v. Hamilton, 66 P. 10 (Cal.1901), all that is necessary is that the language clearly shows the intent of the grantor to make the estate conditional, "and where this is the case, a clause of re-entry is unnecessary."[3]

In determining whether the language of a deed is sufficient to manifest an intent to create a power of termination in the grantor or his successors, the courts have used four factors:

1. The language of the instrument;

2. The nature of the event specified in the condition and its importance to the grantor;

3. The amount of consideration paid for the transfer in proportion to the full value of the estate in fee;[4] and

---

[2] Compare the fee simple determinable, in which the estate terminates automatically upon the stated event, without any exercise of election by the person who will succeed to the interest. Restatement of Property § 23 (1936).

[3] This principle is further emphasized by the fact that some cases declaring that a mere statement of use does not create a condition subsequent explicitly rely on the fact that the deed they are construing does not use the word "condition." Similarly, the word "condition" or a term of similar import is conspicuously missing from many of the cases declaring that forfeitures are not favored or will not be enforced without an express provision for reversion or forfeiture.

[4] "It is a sensible rule that as the worth of the consideration approaches the full market value of the property there is a correspondingly stronger inference that a defeasible fee was not intended." Davis v. St. Joe School Dist., 284 S.W.2d 635, 637 (Ark. 1955).

4. The existence of facts showing the grantor's intent to benefit the adjacent land by the restriction imposed on the conveyed land.[5]

Restatement of Property § 45 comment p (Supp. 1948).

Applying those factors to the provisions before us, we agree with the district court's conclusion that this deed created a fee simple subject to a condition subsequent. (1) In its express language, the deed conveyed the property "on the condition that." Although the sentence structure admits of some doubt, in the context of the trial testimony on why the conveyance was made we interpret the language of condition to apply to the provision on use "for a church or residence purposes only," as well as to the partition fence and the survey. (2) The condition on use was apparently the motivating cause for the grantor's transfer of this property to Sollie. (3) Sollie paid $1,400 for the 1.4 acres. The record is silent on the full value of this property in fee. (4) The conditions on fencing and surveying were obviously intended to benefit the adjacent property, owned by the grantor, but this cannot be said of the condition on use.

All in all, if the conditions specified here were only those pertaining to fencing and surveying, we would be loath to find a condition subsequent, especially in the absence of an express provision for reentry or revesting. But the centrality of the condition on use in the context of this conveyance persuades us that this deed created a fee simple subject to a condition subsequent.

The condition not having been fulfilled within a reasonable time, the grantor exercised her power of termination by reentering the premises and thereby reacquired the property in fee simple. The judgment quieting title in the plaintiff grantor is affirmed. Costs to respondent.

HOWE, JUSTICE, dissenting.

I dissent. I believe this case is governed by the rule of law stated in the majority opinion that a provision in a deed specifying or limiting the use to which property is to be put does not by itself create a condition subsequent. That is exactly what we have here. There was no provision in the deed giving the grantor the right of re-entry and revesting title in her. Moreover, with regard to the use to be put to the property, all we have here is one terse sentence: "This property is conveyed to be used as and for a church or residence purposes only." No words appear which would make a condition subsequent such as "on condition that," "provided that," or "upon express condition that." In the absence of language providing for re-entry and the absence of words which create a condition subsequent, I find no clear showing of intent of the grantor to make the estate which was conveyed conditional.

The majority opinion reaches out to make the condition specified here pertaining to fencing and surveying apply also to the provision in the following paragraph that the property is to be used for a church or residence only. I am unable to make that jump. The majority opinion notes that "if the conditions specified here were only those pertaining to fencing and surveying, we would be loath to find a condition

---

[5] "Such benefit [to adjacent land] is accomplished better by a covenant than by a condition subsequent." Restatement of Property § 45 comment p (Supp. 1948).

subsequent, especially in the absence of an express provision for reentry or revesting." Yet, the opinion has no hesitancy in applying the condition to a later separate paragraph regarding use, to which it is doubtful that it was ever meant to apply. Having made that jump, the majority then reasons that the grantor would have the right of re-entry.

No condition having been clearly expressed, and recognizing the fact that conditions controlling the use of deeded property are strictly construed against the grantor, and that forfeitures are not favored, I am led to conclude that the judgment below should be reversed.

STEWART, J., concurs in the dissenting opinion of HOWE, J.

NOTES AND QUESTIONS

1. **The fee simple on condition subsequent.** The dissent is correct to note that the majority construes the deed generously, both by extending the first paragraph's expressly stated "conditions" of fencing and surveying to the second paragraph's restriction on use, and also by finding a forfeitable estate despite the absence of a re-entry clause. While a re-entry clause may not be theoretically necessary for the creation of a fee simple on condition subsequent, the absence of one could lead a court to find that the transferor did not intend a forfeitable estate. Is it significant in the principal case that the grantor was available to testify about what she intended to create by the language of the disputed deed? *See* Note 6 below.

2. **Fee simple determinable.** The companion estate to the fee simple on condition subsequent is the fee simple determinable, described more fully as follows in Hagaman v. Board of Education, 285 A.2d 63, 65-66 (N.J. Super. Ct. App. Div. 1971):

> An estate in fee simple determinable is an estate in fee simple which automatically determines [terminates] upon the occurrence of a given event. The grantor retains a possibility of reverter upon the occurrence of the stated event. Restatement, Property, § 44 at 121 (1936). Generally, the intent to create such an estate is indicated by the use of words denoting duration of time such as "while," "during," or "so long as." Restatement of Property, § 44, comment l, at 128. "The absence of some one of these phraseologies makes it likely that a court will find a covenant or some other type of interest less drastic in its sanctions." 2 Powell, Real Property, § 187 at 45-47. Words of limitation merely stating the purpose for which the land is conveyed usually do not indicate an intent to create an estate in fee simple determinable although other language in the instrument, the amount of the consideration and the circumstances surrounding the conveyance may indicate such an intent. Restatement, Property, § 44, comment m, at 129-130. When a conveyance contains only a clause of condition or of covenant, such clause does not usually indicate an intent to create a fee simple determinable. Restatement, Property, § 44, comment n, at 130.

3. **Drafting.** You represent O, who wants to give Blackacre to the Church of the Holy Thunder if the church will continue to use it for church purposes. What

language would you insert in the deed in order to give the church (a) a fee simple determinable or (b) a fee simple subject to a condition subsequent? What future interest accompanies each estate? What happens in each instance if the church violates the restriction?

4. **Theory: expiration and divestment.** The theory underlying a present estate that is subject to a special limitation (language of duration) is that the estate expires or ends naturally when the stated restriction occurs. See Griffis v. Davidson County Metropolitan Government, 164 S.W.3d 267, 274 (Tenn. 2005) ("A fee simple determinable estate terminates naturally and automatically when the property is no longer used as required."). In contrast, an estate that is subject to a condition subsequent does not expire; it is "divested" — cut off by the powerholder. In a fee simple subject to a condition subsequent, the holder of the power of termination divests the present interest holder in a real-world sense: the present estate continues after the violation until the holder of the power of termination rises up and reclaims possession. Later, we will see situations in which "divesting" does not require action by the holder of the divesting interest. The important point for now is that you learn to associate "expiration" of an estate with language of special limitation (duration) and "divestment" with language of condition.

5. **Automatic ending and the recalcitrant possessor.** Even if the present estate ends automatically upon the violation of the restriction imposed on it, O will have to file a lawsuit to recover possession if A refuses to vacate. In *that* sense, the holder of the possibility of reverter will have to take action to assert his rights, just as the holder of a power of termination does. Even so, when A's estate ends automatically (fee simple determinable), the law dates the future interest holder's ownership from the time of the violation. In the fee simple subject to a condition subsequent, the future interest holder's ownership dates from the point after the violation at which she rises up to reclaim possession. That in turn can lead to differences in the outcome of cases. See Section A.5.c below.

6. **Covenant compared.** A covenant does not create a defeasible fee. It is rather a promise by the grantee to use, or not to use, the land in a certain way; the covenant is enforced by damages or injunction rather than by forfeiture of the grantee's estate. What language would you use to create a covenant restricting A's use of the land?

7. **Litigation: ambiguous transfers.** Litigation over the question whether a deed or will creates a defeasible fee, and if so, what kind, is common. Courts resolve ambiguities initially by looking at all of the language within the four corners of the disputed document, then by considering, if necessary, circumstantial evidence of O's intent. The relevant factors are listed in *Forsgren*. Do you see any practical problems in proving any of these extrinsic factors? Suppose the litigation arises many years after the transfer? (Was that the case in Forsgren v. Sollie?)

8. **Rules of construction.** Rules of construction attribute an intent to O, based on what the law regards as the likely intent of the average transferor (or on some other policy or policies). A rule of construction operates like a rebuttable presumption of fact; it decides the case unless the party against whom the rule operates can overcome the presumption with admissible evidence. What the *Forsgren* court calls the "hierarchy of favoritism" produces the following

arrangement of constructional rules: when the language allows the choice, the favored construction is for (a) no legal restriction at all over a covenant or defeasible fee, (b) a covenant over either type of defeasible fee; (c) a fee simple on condition subsequent over a fee simple determinable. What policies underlie these constructional rules?

PROBLEM 2-G. The following situations are prototypes of ambiguous drafting that leads to litigation. What causes the ambiguity in each case as to whether the transferor (O) intended a restriction, and if so, the type of restriction? How would you resolve the ambiguity under the rules of construction stated in Forsgren v. Sollie?

a. "To the A School District, its successors and assigns, to be used for school purposes." *See* Station Assoc., Inc. v. Dare County, 513 S.E.2d 789 (N.C. 1999).

b. "To the A School District, on the understanding of the parties that the property is to be used solely for school purposes." *See Hagaman, supra.* If this language does not create a deasible fee, does it impose a covenant restriction on the land?

c. "To the A School District, to be used for school purposes, and when not so used, to revert to O." *See* Mountain Brow Lodge No. 82, Independent Order of Odd Fellows v. Toscano, 64 Cal. Rptr. 816 (Cal. Dist. Ct. App. 1968) (fee simple on condition subsequent). Variation: "to automatically revert" to O. *See* Alby v. Banc One Financial, 128 P.3d 81 (Wash. 2006) (fee simple determinable); Oldfield v. Stoeco Homes, Inc., 139 A.2d 291 (N.J. 1958) (fee simple on condition subsequent).

d. "To the A School District, on condition that it be used for school purposes, and if not, title to revert to O." *See* Griffis v. Davidson County Metropolitan Government, 164 S.W.3d 267, 274 n. 4 (Tenn. 2005) ("provided, however, [that] when said property is abandoned for school purposes said land reverts to" grantor or his successors; although noting that the "uncertain diction and tangled syntax" of the deed "raise a question as to the proper classification of the estate conveyed," the court did not disturb the parties' and lower courts' agreement that the deed created a fee simple determinable).

e. "To the A School District, on condition that the property be used for school purposes." *See* Isanogel Center, Inc. v. Father Flanagan's Boy's Home, 839 N.E.2d 237, 245 (Ind. Ct. App. 2005) (fee simple on condition subsequent not created if no provision for grantor's repossession is included in deed; "clear majority rule").

b. Breach

Regardless of the type of defeasible estate created, the holder of the future interest is not entitled to possession unless the present interest holder breaches the restriction imposed on the use of the land. The judicial bias against forfeiture underlying the rules of construction that limit the *creation* of a defeasible fee operates also to limit the occasions for termination of a defeasible fee by breach.

The next case wrestles with the question whether that strict construction approach, which may operate to frustrate a grantor's intent, should be abandoned in favor of an approach to breach that seeks to effectuate the grantor's discernible intent.

RED HILL OUTING CLUB v. HAMMOND
722 A.2d 501 (N.H. 1998)

HORTON, J.

The defendants, David and Elizabeth Hammond and their son, Robert Hammond, appeal the Superior Court's decision denying them right of re-entry and possession of land they deeded to the plaintiff, Red Hill Outing Club (club), subject to a condition subsequent. We affirm.

David Hammond purchased land in Moultonboro in 1956 known as Red Hill, which was subsequently cleared for use as a ski slope. Hammond installed a rope tow and participated in forming the club for the purpose of operating the ski slope. From 1969 to 1979, the club leased Red Hill. During this period, it operated the rope tow and provided free ski lessons to members and Moultonboro residents.

In 1979, David and Elizabeth Hammond conveyed Red Hill by quitclaim deed to the club for nominal consideration. The deed contained the following condition:

> The Grantee covenants and agrees that the within described premises shall be maintained and made available to residents of Moultonboro as a ski slope in accordance with its now existing by-laws. If the Grantee fails to provide such skiing facilities to Moultonboro residents for a period of two consecutive years then a breach of this covenant has occurred, provided such failure was not caused by reason of an act of God, such as inadequate snowfall. In the event the Grantee breach[es] [this covenant], the Grantor shall have the right to re-enter and take possession of said premises.

From 1979 to the mid-eighties use of the ski slope grew. But the popularity of other ski areas, changing interests of families who had previously frequented the slope, inadequate snowfall in some years, and the waning leadership of the club resulted in a noticeable decline in its use after 1988. Consequently, the club ceased offering free ski lessons after the winter of 1988-1989, and did not obtain a rope tow permit for the ski seasons of 1992-1993 and 1993-1994. Red Hill was closed to all skiing during the winter of 1993-1994.

In October 1994, the defendants filed a notice of re-entry and possession, claiming that the club had breached its condition by failing to provide skiing facilities at Red Hill for two consecutive years. In response, the club brought action against the Hammonds, seeking, inter alia, declaratory judgment regarding the parties' relative rights.

After a bench trial, which included a view, the trial court determined that the condition subsequent should be strictly construed. Therefore, to comply with its obligation to provide Red Hill as "skiing facilities," the club needed only to "maintain and make available the premises as a ski slope." Accordingly, the court found that the club had not substantially breached the condition because it had remained in existence as a club and continued to maintain and offer use of the hill as a ski slope. It found that any failure of the club to provide ski facilities from February 1993 to October 1994 was not sufficient in duration to constitute a breach.

On appeal, the defendants argue that the trial court erred by strictly construing the condition subsequent; finding that the club did not substantially breach the condition subsequent; and refusing to consider evidence of a breach occurring after the club instituted its action.

The defendants first argue that the trial court should have construed the condition subsequent by determining the parties' intent in light of the surrounding circumstances at the time of the conveyance. They contend that by strictly interpreting the condition to refer only to maintaining and making available the ski slope, the trial court ignored the parties' original intent to include the operation of a licensed ski tow and provision of free ski instruction within the club's obligation to provide "skiing facilities." Although the defendants acknowledge that strict construction of conditions subsequent has long been the rule in this state, they urge us to update this rule consistent with the modern trend in contract interpretation.

The construction of deeds is an issue of law for this court. The general rule in interpreting a deed is to determine the parties' intent at the time of conveyance in light of the surrounding circumstances. As the defendants correctly note, formalistic requirements in real estate conveyancing have largely given way to effectuating the manifest intent of the parties, absent contrary public policy or statute. See 4 W. Jaeger, Williston on Contracts § 614, at 584-97 (3d ed. 1961). Thus, for example, when the interests of a changing society persuaded us that restrictive covenants were valuable land use planning devices rather than restraints on the use of land, we discarded the rule of strict construction in favor of ascertaining the parties' intent in light of the surrounding circumstances at the time of a covenant's creation. See Joslin v. Pine River Dev. Corp., 367 A.2d 599, 601 (N.H. 1976).

We are not convinced, however, that we should apply the general rule of construction to conditions subsequent. "The [grantor of a fee simple subject to condition subsequent] shall have his exact legal right, but no more." Emerson v. Simpson, 43 N.H. 475, 478-79 (1862). "[T]o defeat an estate of his own creation, [he] must bring the [grantee] clearly within its letter." *Id.* A fee simple subject to condition subsequent is a conveyance of land in which the grantor expressly retains the right of re-entry upon breach of a stated condition, the exercise of which results in a forfeiture of estate for the grantee. Because of the drastic consequence of a breach, we have traditionally viewed conditions subsequent with disfavor.

The passage of time has failed to increase the social value of conditions subsequent. Unlike restrictive covenants, conditions subsequent continue to be viewed with disfavor because of their potential to cause a forfeiture of land. We disagree with the defendants that the consequences of a forfeiture are "no greater" than those of specific performance of a contract or an attachment on property. A forfeiture by nature is a drastic remedy because in most cases it is widely disproportionate to the breach. See Korngold, *For Unifying Servitudes and Defeasible Fees: Property Law's Functional Equivalents*, 66 Tex. L. Rev. 533, 551 (1988). In addition, restricted use of the land for a potentially indefinite duration substantially diminishes the land's marketability and development, ultimately to the detriment of the community. See Frona Powell, *Defeasible Fees and the Nature of Real Property*, 40 Kan. L. Rev. 411, 418-19 (1992). Neither specific performance, an equitable remedy at the court's discretion, nor attachment, applied to secure payment of judgment should a plaintiff prevail, evokes the hardships associated with a condition subsequent.

The defendants, relying on North Hampton School District v. Congregational Society, 84 A.2d 833 (N.H. 1951), contend that the terms of a defeasible fee should be construed in light of surrounding circumstances. While we agree that *North Hampton* appears to extend the general rule of contract construction to a deed involving a fee simple determinable, we do not read its holding so broadly as to apply to the case before us. *North Hampton* addressed only the issue of the nature of an estate created by language in a deed, not the operation and effect of the particular terms of a forfeiture clause. Here, there is no dispute that the deed contains a condition subsequent. The question before us is the scope of the condition subsequent. *North Hampton* thus addresses aspects of deed construction that do not concern us here.

The overwhelming majority of courts in other jurisdictions also have continued to strictly construe conditions subsequent in deeds with regard to their capacity to work a forfeiture. See, e.g., Wilhite v. Masters, 965 S.W.2d 406 (Mo. Ct. App. 1998). Our position conforms to the great weight of authority from our sister states.

Our decision today does not abrogate the guiding rule that the intent of the parties to a deed is to be determined and effectuated when possible. See Chapin and Wife v. School District, 35 N.H. 445, 451 (1857) (parties' intention is controlling); cf. Div. of Labor Stand. Enf. v. Dick Bullis, Inc., 140 Cal.Rptr. 267, 270 (Cal. Ct. App. 1977) (court will uphold forfeiture where intent clear and terms of contract unambiguous). When it is a condition subsequent that must be construed, however, the rule of strict construction operates to confine the determination of intent to the face of the deed and resolve all ambiguities against forfeiture. We therefore hold that the trial court did not err in construing the club's obligation as limited to maintaining and making the hill available as a ski area. It was not required to import meanings not apparent on the face of the deed, such as obligations to provide a rope tow or ski instruction.

[T]he defendants [also] contend that the trial court erred in finding that the club did not breach the condition. Insofar as they argue that the court was required to consider extrinsic evidence of the parties' intent, we disagree in light of the principles of deed construction set forth above. We address the defendants' remaining arguments separately.

The trial court correctly found that the club's substantial compliance with the express language in the deed would satisfy the terms of the condition. Substantial compliance will avoid a breach of a condition subsequent. "To constitute a breach of a condition subsequent in a deed relating to maintenance or use of the land conveyed, there must be such neglect to comply as to indicate an intention to disregard the condition." City of Lincoln v. Townhouser, Inc., 534 N.W.2d 756, 759 (Neb. 1995).

"We will not substitute our own judgment for that of the trier of fact if it is supported by the evidence, especially when he has been assisted in reaching his conclusions by a view." Heston v. Ousler, 398 A.2d 536, 537 (N.H. 1979). Here, evidence showed that Red Hill was cleared in the fall from 1991 to 1993 during club work sessions in preparation for skiing, that people skied on the property for a few days in February 1993, and that current facilities at Red Hill include a rope tow, clubhouse, storage shed, lights, and snow-packing equipment. Although it is true the club failed after 1991 to operate a rope tow with a permit in compliance with statutory requirements, see RSA 225-A:14 (1989), that fact is not dispositive of whether it provided ski facilities under the plain terms of the deed. Since we hold that the club was not required under the deed to provide a tow, its failure to obtain a permit to operate one may have violated a statute but did not breach the condition. Ample evidence in the record supports the trial court's conclusion that the club did not abandon the property and thus substantially complied with the condition subsequent.

Lastly, the defendants assert that by refusing to consider evidence of a breach that occurred after the suit filed by the club commenced, the trial court wrongfully estopped them from claiming the full period of the club's alleged breach of the condition. We disagree. A grantor may not offer evidence of a breach of condition subsequent when that evidence occurred after the grantor brought action to re-enter and terminate the grantee's estate. A grantor who exercises his right to terminate the grantee's estate is deemed to have taken legal possession of the property. The grantee's obligations under the deed are in effect suspended until the court orders otherwise or makes a final determination that the conditions have not been breached.

Here, the defendants took legal possession of Red Hill upon commencing legal action in October 1994 to re-enter the property, thereby relieving the club of its obligations under the deed. Further, the defendants' claim of breach was based on alleged acts or omissions occurring up to that time. Additional acts or omissions by the club that occurred after October 1994 are irrelevant to the breach already alleged. The defendants' argument therefore must fail.

Affirmed.

NOTES AND QUESTIONS

1. **Jumping the gun.** Instead of suing when he did, might Hammond have been wiser to wait out another ski season before electing to terminate the present estate?

2. **Creation and breach.** The court distinguishes the questions of creation of a restriction on land use and breach of that restriction, and applies different standards to the two questions. What standard does the court use for each question? Is the distinction sensible?

3. *Forsgren* **again.** The majority and dissent in Forsgren v. Sollie, *supra*, disagreed on the question of breach of the restriction by the present interest holder. Here are the two discussions.

a. The majority:

We also agree with the district court's conclusion on the content of the condition on use and sustain its finding that the condition had been breached. [W]hen property is conveyed on condition that it be used only for a particular type of building the grantee has an obligation to build the building within a reasonable time, failing which the grantor has a power of termination. That interpretation serves the purpose of requiring that property restricted as to use be put to that use within a reasonable time or be freed from the restriction by being restored to the grantor or his successors.

b. The dissent:

[T]he majority holds that when property is conveyed on condition that it be used only for a particular type of building, the grantee has an obligation to build the building within a reasonable time, failing which the grantor has a power of termination. However, in the instant case all we have is the naked statement that the property conveyed is to be used as and for a church or residence purposes only. This could be nothing more than an attempt on the part of the grantor to prevent the property from being used for commercial or industrial purposes which would interfere with her enjoyment in residing on her remaining property. It does not appear to affirmatively require that a church or residence ever be built.

Under the rule of strict construction, who has the better argument? Is the majority's interpretation justified on the ground that rules of construction are relevant only in the absence of determinative evidence of the grantor's intent?

4. **School purposes.** A restriction that land is to be used for "school purposes" is ambiguous. For an excellent and comprehensive treatment of that common restriction, see Griffis v. Davidson County Metropolitan Government, 164 S.W.3d 267, 272-273 (Tenn. 2005):

We vacate the Court of Appeals' holding that "school purposes" and the "cause of education" require classroom instruction alone. We hold that these limitations permit any use that directly benefits and enhances the process of learning and instruction or that directly advances the objective of instructing, training, and rearing. Further, we hold that in a fee simple determinable where the term "abandon" is not otherwise defined, the common law definition of abandonment applies; a complainant therefore must show both intent to abandon for the stated limitations and some external act or omission by which the intent to abandon is effectuated. Whether abandonment has occurred is predominantly a factual determination based upon all the relevant circumstances.

PROBLEM 2-H. Under the rule of strict construction, what result would you urge in the following cases:

a. The deed provides that the property shall revert "in the event [it] should be abandoned or should not be used for a public park or recreational purposes." Grantee does nothing with the property for six years except plant a few trees. Breach? *See* Leslie Enterprises, Inc. v. Metropolitan Dade County, 293 So. 2d 73 (Fla. Dist. Ct. App. 1974).

b. A deed to the church provides that "should this land or premises at any time be used for any purpose other than" church purposes, the transfer shall be "null and void" and "the title to said land and premises shall go back to" the grantor and his heirs. After eight years of continuous use, the church ceases to use it for eighteen months prior to trial, due to lack of funds. Breach? *See* Williams v. Box Church Baptist Church, 75 S.W.2d 134 (Tex. Ct. App. 1934).

c. In the *Box Church* case, *supra*, the church allowed a traveling show to use the premises for two nights, splitting the proceeds and allowed a community play to be held in the building, again dividing the proceeds. In addition, "on rare occasions not more often than once every two years local candidates for political offices had been permitted to make their announcements in the church building, at which time they were afforded an opportunity to contribute to the support of the church." Breach? *See also* Dehart v. Ritenour Consolidated School Dist., 663 S.W.2d 332 (Mo. Ct. App. 1983) (temporary cessation of classes by school). How is the issue here different from that in "b" above?

d. "The condition of this deed is that the county commissioners of said Kimball county shall erect and maintain a county courthouse on said block." The county erected the courthouse and used it for twenty years, but then built a new courthouse on a different site and moved the county offices. Breach? *See* Isanogel Center, Inc. v. Father Flanagan's Boy's Home, 839 N.E.2d 237 (Ind. Ct. App. 2005) (alternative holding: over fifty years' compliance by the defeasible fee owner constituted substantial performance terminating the restriction); Mildram v. Town of Wells, 611 A.2d 84 (Me. 1992) (city used property in accordance with restriction for 82 years); City of Caspar v. J.M. Carey & Bros., 601 P.2d 1010 (Wyo. 1979) (deed in 1918 required the city to use the property as a city hall and public park; city discontinued use as a city hall and demolished the building, but continued using the property as a park).

e. The deed requires the city to use the property as a city park. *See* City of Caspar v. J.M. Carey & Bros., *supra* ("Public parks in the center of cities are desirable and essential. It is hard to conceive of a time span which would satisfy a condition subsequent dedicating land for public park purposes in the center of a thriving, active and growing city.").

f. In Gleghorn v. Smith, 62 S.W. 1096 (Tex. Ct. App. 1901), in which the deed conveyed to A "solely for purpose of gin site, and to be used solely and only used for a gin site, and in event not so used, to revert," court held that no forfeiture could be declared by grantor so long as the gin site was operated on premises, even though portions of the tract were used for other purposes. Query: what about the word "solely"? Might the case have been better reasoned on the ground that minor nonconforming uses do not justify forfeiture?

g. Is there a difference between a grant "on condition that the grantee not use" the premises for the sale of alcohol and a grant "on condition that the property not be used" for the sale of alcohol? Who can breach the former? The latter?

NOTES ON DEFEASIBLE FEES WITH EXECUTORY INTERESTS

1. **Two more types: defeasible fees with third-party future interests.** A transferor may create a defeasible fee in A and provide that upon violation of the restriction, title passes to a third party rather than to the transferor:

(a) O transfers "to A and her heirs so long as A never sells alcohol on the premises and when A does sell alcohol on the premises, the property is to go to B and her heirs."

(b) O transfers "to A and her heirs on condition that A never sell alcohol on the premises, and if A does sell alcohol on the premises, to B and her heirs."

B's future interest in both cases is called an executory interest, and in both cases it takes effect (becomes a present possessory estate) automatically upon the present interest holder's violation of the restriction imposed on the land. An election by B is not required; an executory interest operates like a possibility of reverter, not like a power of termination. However, while there is no distinction between automatic and elective forfeiture in these two defeasible estates, they do have different consequences on some questions. We address these different consequences in Section A.5.c below.

2. **Terminology.** Example (b) is called a *fee simple subject to an executory limitation. See* Restatement of Property § 46 (1936). Some authorities also call example (a) a fee simple subject to an executory limitation; others do not. *See id.* § 47 ("fee simple with an executory limitation creating an interest which takes effect at the expiration of a prior interest"). To highlight, again, that defeasible fees created by language of duration and by language of condition have different consequences, we shall follow the Restatement Second of Property and call example (a) a *fee simple determinable with an executory interest. See* Restatement Second of Property (Donative Transfers) § 1.5 cmt. b.

c. Consequences

We now turn to the question, what difference does it make whether a defeasible fee is made defeasible through language of duration (fee simple determinable; fee simple determinable with an executory limitation) or language of condition (fee simple subject to a condition subsequent; fee simple subject to an executory limitation)? You remain free (and are urged) to question, as we go through the various consequences, whether the identified differences justify the rather complex classification scheme that exists for defeasible estates, and if not, what should be done about it.

The principal case deals with a defeasible fee, with the future interest (actually a succession of future interests) created in third parties; it is an example of a fee simple determinable with an executory interest, that is, the first Restatement's § 47 estate. As background, it is useful to know that under Shelley v. Kraemer, 334 U.S. 1 (1948), the racial restriction contained in Jack Adams's will — a private document — was not unconstitutional, but judicial *enforcement* of the restriction would have constituted state action in violation of the Equal Protection Clause of the Fourteenth Amendment. For all practical purposes, *Shelley* renders ineffective the insertion of invidiously discriminatory restrictions in private documents. The distinction between language of duration and language of condition is irrelevant to the constitutional issue, and for reasons you will see, the court in *Hermitage Methodist Homes* did not decide the constitutional issue. The court, however, does indicate that an important difference exists between a restriction phrased as a special limitation (the situation in the *Hermitage* case), and one phrased as a condition subsequent.

HERMITAGE METHODIST HOMES v. DOMINION TRUST CO.
387 S.E.2d 740 (Va. 1990)

COMPTON, JUSTICE.

We consolidated three appeals arising from a single suit brought by the trustee of a charitable, testamentary trust. The trustee sought the trial court's aid and guidance in administration of the trust and in construction of certain racially discriminatory trust provisions applicable to private educational institutions. The provisions allegedly are unconstitutional and unenforceable.

In 1956, Jack Adams, a resident of Lynchburg, executed his will establishing the trust in question. In 1964, the testator executed a codicil to the will. In 1968, Adams died testate. The will and codicil, drafted by a Lynchburg attorney, were duly probated.

Article IV of the codicil provides that the residuum of Adams's estate be held in trust and the income therefrom be distributed pursuant to clause (a). The clause provides, in part:

> So long as Prince Edward School Foundation, Prince Edward Co., Virginia, admits to any school, operated or supported by it, only members of the White Race, my said Trustee shall pay the net income to the Trustees (or other governing body) of such Foundation, to be expended by them for the benefit of any of said schools.

The clause further provides:

> In the event that the said Foundation should cease to operate for one year, or should at any time permit to matriculate in any of the schools operated or supported by it any person who is not a member of the White Race, no further payment of income shall be made to the said Foundation; but all income accruing after such date shall be paid to the Trustees of the Miller School, situated in Albemarle County, so long as said School admits only members of the White Race; said income shall be expended by such Trustees for the payment of the expenses of maintaining and operating said School.

The clause further provides for successive gifts over first to Seven Hills School, Inc., located in Lynchburg, and then to Hampden-Sydney College, in the event of the occurrence of the same contingencies. The final beneficiary of the successive gifts over is Hermitage Methodist Homes of Virginia, Inc., without the limitation of the described contingencies.

In 1987, appellee Dominion Trust Company filed the present suit naming as parties defendant the income beneficiaries. Asserting that it was the successor trustee of the Adams Trust, the trustee alleged that it had paid over the income to Prince Edward School Foundation since the creation of the trust. It stated that "a determinable event" as described in Article IV may have occurred with respect to the school administered by the Foundation. (Counsel represented at the bar of this Court that subsequent to creation of the trust each educational beneficiary had enrolled black students in its schools.)

The trustee sought advice and guidance on "whether the determinative event or contingency [was] legal, valid and enforceable." Therefore, the trustee asserted, it was "uncertain as to the proper income beneficiary of said trust" and asked the court to construe and interpret the will to determine the rights of the parties.

In its answer, Prince Edward, stating that it does not discriminate in the admission of students to the school, asserted that the discriminatory provisions of Article IV of the will "are illegal, invalid and unenforceable," and that the proper interpretation of the disputed provisions requires "the continued payment of the trust income to the Prince Edward School Foundation without interruption or diminution." In its answer, the Hermitage Methodist Homes of Virginia, Inc., asked the court to construe the will and trust, stating that it employs no racially discriminatory conditions upon the admission of persons into its homes for the aging and that it would "accept all sums which may be due it under the will and trust," if the court found it so entitled.

Prince Edward filed a motion for summary judgment [asking] the court to strike the discriminatory language from the will, give effect to the primary charitable intent of the testator to promote the education of children by the Prince Edward School Foundation, and order the trustee to pay it all trust income. Hermitage also filed a motion for summary judgment. It asserted that the trust is valid and that the language should be given its plain meaning to carry out the testator's intent. When this is done, according to Hermitage, a "determinable event has occurred with regard to each" income beneficiary, resulting in the final beneficiary, Hermitage, "being entitled under the terms of the trust to receive all future trust income payments as they become due."

The trial court granted Prince Edward's motion and denied Hermitage's motion. The court found, "All racially discriminatory conditions of the Trust are unconstitutional and void." The court further determined that Prince Edward "shall continue as the principal and sole beneficiary of the Trust, as long as the school remains in operation."

The assignments of error [by Hermitage] present the following issues on appeal. First, are the discriminatory provisions of Article IV valid, or are they unconstitutional and invalid? Second, if such provisions are invalid, is the primary educational bequest of the trust nevertheless valid, or must it fail, requiring future income to be paid to Hermitage?

Because of the view we take of the second issue, based on principles of real property law, we will agree with Prince Edward on the first issue for purposes of this decision. Whether the discriminatory provisions are valid or void, the result is the same, as we will demonstrate below. Thus, we will assume, without deciding, that the trial court correctly ruled that the racially discriminatory provisions are unconstitutional and void. This brings us to the second issue, that is, whether the educational trust is otherwise valid.

Asserting that the restrictive language provides for an illegal condition subsequent, Prince Edward relies on Meek v. Fox, 88 S.E. 161 (Va. 1916), to sustain the trial court's ruling that the racially discriminatory condition is void, but the gift is valid. *Meek* involved the proper construction of a will regarding the testator's devise to his daughter, Julia Anne. [After devising one-third shares of his land to his son and another daughter], the testator made the following provision for Julia Anne: "Also to my daughter, Julia Anne, I desire that she shall have her equal share laid off, also according to quality and quantity, and she shall have it forever, except she should marry, then at her death I desire that it shall revert to her legal heirs."

This Court held that the devise to Julia Anne transferred to her a fee simple estate in the land. The Court further held that the added provision of the devise, "except she should marry, then at her death I desire that it revert to her legal heirs," was a condition subsequent and was in restraint of marriage, and void. Therefore, the Court struck the condition, "and the estate thus became absolute and free from condition."

Drawing on the rationale of *Meek*, Prince Edward contends that because the discriminatory condition is void, its "interest in the income from the Trust remains vested" and "a subsequent beneficiary's interest will vest only in the event that Prince Edward ceases operation of a school." We disagree.

The principle of striking the offending condition subsequent and thereby creating an absolute estate, as applied in *Meek*, does not control this case because the provision at issue here is not a condition subsequent. Rather, this provision is a special limitation. Professor Minor explains that "special limitations are created by such words as 'while,' 'during,' 'as long as,' [or] 'until.' Thus, a grant to A until Z returns from abroad [or] to a woman while she remains a widow, or during widowhood are special limitations and not conditions subsequent." 1 Minor on Real Property § 525 at 690 (Ribble ed. 1928). "Limitations differ from conditions subsequent in this: A limitation marks the utmost time of continuance of an estate; a condition marks some event, which, if it happens in the course of that time, is to defeat the estate." *Id.*, quoted in *Meek*, 88 S.E. at 162.

In the granting clauses of Adams's will, he repeatedly specified that each educational beneficiary's right to receive income extended only "so long as" the beneficiary complied with the restrictive provision. But, if an educational beneficiary violated the restrictive provision by the matriculation of a black student, that beneficiary's interest would terminate, and the gift would devolve to successive educational beneficiaries who had not violated the provision. Further, Adams makes his intent clear in clause (b) that the educational beneficiaries' rights to receive income "shall be determinable" upon the happening of the contingency and that "all rights" of those institutions, successively to receive income from the trust "shall automatically terminate." Clearly this is language of limitation and not condition.

Although [*Meek*] did not address the issue of what happens when a gift subject to a special limitation offends constitutional considerations, the essential nature of a limitation as described by the Court in *Meek* points to the decision of the issue in this case. In the words of Minor, a limitation marks the utmost time of continuance of the estate. And, a limitation cannot be altered to extend "beyond that period without violating the terms of the devise." *Meek*, 88 S.E. at 162. If a condition subsequent is unlawful, a court can merely excise the offending language and leave the remaining estate intact. But, where a gift or estate subject to a limitation is unlawful, in order to cure the defect the court must terminate the entire gift or estate.

Therefore, unlike in *Meek*, the interests of the educational charities fail completely. [W]e strike the entire gift to Prince Edward and the gifts to the other educational beneficiaries because the offending language cannot be stricken from the provision without changing the essential nature and quality of the estate.

It necessarily follows from the foregoing that, while the gifts to all the beneficiaries of Adams's charitable educational trust must fail, the executory interest of Hermitage survives. Adams did not place any unconstitutional limitations upon Hermitage's interest. And, as all prior estates have been declared invalid, Hermitage has the only valid, remaining interest. The trial court erred in holding to the contrary.

Because we find that the provision is a limitation, the same final result would be reached if we found that the trust's provisions were constitutional, as we have said earlier. By the natural operation of this limitation, if it were valid, upon the matriculation of a black student into Prince Edward, the school's interest terminated. And, because as counsel have represented, the educational institutions have all admitted black students, their respective interests in the trust proceeds can never vest into possession. Hermitage would be the ultimate beneficiary since no limitations are placed on its interest.

For these reasons, we will reverse the ruling that the trust income will be paid to Prince Edward. Instead, we will enter final judgment here ordering the trustee to pay all retained trust income and future trust income to Hermitage.

NOTES AND QUESTIONS

1.   **Invalidity of the restriction or of the future interest.**   One difference — perhaps the most important current one — between a defeasible fee that is subject to language of special limitation (language of duration) and one that is subject to language of condition is the outcome when the restriction on the present estate is invalid, or when the future interest is invalid.

a. *Invalid restriction.* In the principal case, each successive future interest holder except the last one (Hermitage Methodist Home) held a determinable estate. What is the consequence of invalidity of the restriction on a determinable estate? What result if Adams had transferred "to the Prince Edward School Foundation, but if the school admits any student other than a member of the white race, then to the Hermitage Methodist Home"? Would these consequences have been the same had Adams created a fee simple determinable (retaining a possibility of reverter) or a fee simple on condition subsequent (retaining a power of termination)?

b. *Invalid future interest.* Suppose that O transfers "to the A School District so long as the property is used for school purposes" and further provides that the land is to go to B, a third party, if the restriction is violated. The restriction on the present interest holder (A) is valid, unlike the restriction in *Hermitage Methodist.* However, under some circumstances, the future interest that O attempts to create in B might be invalid. If so, different outcomes result, depending on whether A's estate was determinable or subject to a condition subsequent. A common reason for invalidity of the future interest is a violation of the Rule Against Perpetuities, which we will study in detail in Section B of this chapter. For now, the important point is that language of duration and language of condition produce different results, whether the restriction on the present holder is invalid (as in the principal case) *or* whether the future interest in a third party is invalid.

2. **Breach: statutes of limitation.** The distinction between expiration (automatic ending) of a present estate and elective ending (divestment) carries potential consequences for the running of the statute of limitations upon breach of the restriction by the present interest holder.

a. *Statutes silent as to powers of termination.* Suppose that the local statute of limitation provides that "a person having a right to possession shall assert it within 10 years, or lose it thereafter." Assume that A violates the restriction imposed by a defeasible fee in 1990. When does the statute of limitations begin to run against the holder of a possibility of reverter and against the holder of a power of termination? *See* Metropolitan Park Dist. v. Unknown Heirs of Rigney, 399 P.2d 516, 517-519 (Wash. 1965):

> [S]o far as the law of adverse possession be concerned, it is not conceptually logical for the grantee of a fee simple subject to a condition subsequent to acquire an indefeasible estate simply by remaining in possession of the property following breach of the condition. His continued possession does not become adverse to any possessory estate of the grantor until the latter or his heirs elect to declare a forfeiture. This is not to say, however, that the holder of a right of entry, following a continuing breach of condition, is entitled to endlessly sit by refusing to declare a forfeiture, and thus control the use of the property indefinitely. An appropriate rule to meet such a contingency is succinctly propounded in Simes & Smith, The Law of Future Interests § 258, p. 310, as follows: "[T]hat the statute of limitations begins to run in favor of the grantee on the grantor's election to forfeit and not on the grantee's breach is no argument for the proposition that the grantor's power to forfeit should last forever. Such a legal club over the grantee would tend to discourage any productive use of the land. [A]ll policy considerations which justify the imposition of statutes of limitation would justify limiting the time within which an election could be made after breach of a condition. [I]t is submitted that the sound rule is as follows: *The grantor has a reasonable time after breach within which to declare a forfeiture or to elect not to declare a forfeiture; if he fails to declare a*

forfeiture within that time, his power to do so has expired." The condition in this case has been in continuous breach since sometime prior to 1905. We cannot say that the delay in claiming a forfeiture has been either reasonable or warranted. The time in which the election should have been made has long since passed, and the condition has expired. The decree quieting title in [the park district] is affirmed.

(Italics by the court.) How long is "unreasonable" delay? What would happen to the differences indicated in *Metropolitan Park* if a court decided to standardize results in these kinds of cases by defining "reasonable delay" as a period equal to the statute of limitations for actions to recover land?

b. *Statutes that address powers of termination.* When would the statute of limitations begin to run against O if the statute provided that "[a]ny person or persons entitled to possession or having a right of entry to recover possession of land shall assert such right or make such entry no later than twenty one years after the title or right of entry accrued, or be forever barred therefrom." How does this statute differ from the one supposed in Note 2.a? *See* Knights and Ladies of Samaria v. Board of Ed. of Charles County, 688 A.2d 933 (Md. Ct. Spec. App. 1997). Suppose the applicable statute of limitations provided that "[a]n action to recover the title to or possession of real property shall be brought within twenty-one years after the cause thereof accrued"? How might it be construed to apply equally to the holder of a possibility of reverter or power of termination?

c. *Executory interests.* If the present interest holder commits a breach, when does the statute of limitations begin to run against the holder of an executory interest?

4. **Transferability of future interests following defeasible fees.** A future interest, like a present interest, is susceptible to transfer in either of three ways: by inter vivos transfer (alienation), by devise (transmission via a valid will) and descent (inheritance under an intestacy statute). The holder of a future interest following a defeasible fee does not always enjoy the benefit of all three methods of transfer.

a. *Possibility of reverter.* The first Restatement of Property (1936) provides that a possibility of reverter is transferable by all methods: devise (§ 165); descent (§ 164); and alienation (§ 159).

b. *Power of termination.* The Restatement provides that a power of termination is devisable (§ 165) and descendible (§ 164), but notes that it is alienable only if it "supplements a reversionary interest also held in the same land by the owner of such power." (§ 161(c). The landlord's power of termination incident to the landlord's reversion is such a supplementary power. A "bare" power of termination, such as the one held by the grantor of a fee simple subject to a condition subsequent, is inalienable. What is the reason for the Restatement's exception to alienability for a supplementary power of termination? If a landlord transfers the reversion in leased property to X, would it effectuate the parties' likely intent to say that the transfer doesn't carry the power of termination?

c. *Executory interest.* Under the Restatement, the executory interest is like the possibility of reverter: alienable, devisable, descendible. See the citations given above.

d. *Different rules.* Some states maintain more restrictive rules than those of the Restatement. *See, e.g.*, Mahrenholz v. County Board of School Trustees, 417 N.E.2d 138 (Ill. App. Ct. 1981) (neither possibility of reverter nor power of termination is alienable or devisable); Purvis v. McElveen, 106 S.E.2d 913 (S.C. 1959) (neither interest is descendable); South Carolina Dept. of Parks v. Brookgreen Gardens, 424 S.E.2d 465 (S.C. 1992) (possibility of reverter is not alienable, and not devisable to non-heirs; no discussion of powers of termination on the same questions). It is also possible for a state to be more liberal than the Restatement, and allow transferability of the power of termination by alienation even when it is not incident to a reversion. These variations indicate that it is important to know the local rules for each type of future interest, and to know how to classify the interest with which you are dealing. See Section B.1.a below.

e. *Exceptions.* If a possibility of reverter or power of termination is not transferable under the local rule, the holder of the interest may nevertheless *release* the future interest to the present interest holder. *See* Restatement of Property § 161(a). The release unites in the same person the present and future interests, which then merge into a fee simple absolute. *See Brookgreen Gardens*, Note 4.d above (O's possibility of reverter was released to A, creating a fee simple absolute in A). What sensible policy is served by this exception to alienability?

5. **Leases.** In most states, a tenant who defaults on obligations owed to the landlord can be evicted in a summary (expedited) proceeding, in contrast to the ordinary and time-consuming action in ejectment. In New York, the landlord is entitled to use the summary eviction process against a tenant who fails to pay rent or who use the premises for illegal purposes, whether the landlord has made the lease defeasible on those events or not. *See* N.Y. Real Prop. Acts § 711(2), (5). For other breaches, the landlord is entitled to use summary process only if the tenant "continues in possession of any portion of the premises after the expiration of his term." *Id.* § 711(1). Under subsection (1) of the statute, does it matter if the tenant holds a term of years determinable or one subject to a condition subsequent? *See* Beach v. Nixon, 9 N.Y. 35 (1853) ("The [landlord's] case is subject to a fatal objection in this, that the provision in the lease upon which he has proceeded creates a condition merely, and not a [special] limitation. The lessor upon breach is not to be in immediately of his former estate, but at his option the hiring and the relation of landlord and tenant are to cease, and are of course to continue until he shall otherwise elect."). We return to the question of the interplay between summary process and lease provisions in Chapter 4.C.1.

6. **Ambiguity and consequences.** When a deed or devise is ambiguous, the court must classify the intended transfer before application of any of the different consequences noted above. Notice the possibility of result-oriented classification: the court might first decide which of the possible consequences it prefers, *then* classify the ambiguous instrument so as to produce the preferred outcome. Transferors, of course, can avoid this — by avoiding ambiguity.

d.   Statutory Restrictions

Transferability of the future interests that accompany defeasible fees — particularly their inheritability — may result in considerable fragmentation of the title among many holders. Classroom hypotheticals to show the nightmarish title problems caused by defeasible fee estates pale in comparison to the infamous case of Brown v. Independent Baptist Church of Woburn, 91 N.E.2d 922 (Mass. 1950). In 1849, Sarah Converse devised a parcel of land to her church in fee simple determinable. The church disbanded in 1939, violating the requirement that it "continue a church." The court held that the land or the proceeds of sale should go to the residuary legatees named in Converse's will or their successors in interest. Professor Leach reported that

> [a] receiver sold Sarah Converse's land for $34,000 under a court order. By 1939 all of Sarah's ten residuary legatees and twenty-five heirs (as of 1849) had been dead for decades. There had been three or four devolutions of the fractional shares in Sarah's possibility of reverter, with split-ups into subfractions and sub-subfractions. As a consequence of the litigation the court awarded a total of $9,091.25 for counsel fees and disbursements, $1,500 for the genealogist, $4,017.50 for a receiver, and divided the balance into more than one hundred shares ranging from $774.20 to $6.25.

W. Barton Leach, *Perpetuities in Perspective: Ending the Rule's Reign of Terror*, 65 Harv. L. Rev. 721, 743-45 (1952). The following case deals with a statutory attempt to reduce the title problems caused by a case like that of Sarah Converse.

LUDINGTON & NORTHERN RAILWAY v. EPWORTH ASSEMBLY
468 N.W.2d 884 (Mich. Ct. App. 1991)

MAHER, JUDGE.

Defendant appeals from a circuit court judgment, entered following a bench trial determining the parties' respective interests in [four] adjoining strips of land. [T]he trial court held that plaintiff had acquired a fee interest and that any possibility of reverter possessed by defendant was extinguished pursuant to 1968 P.A. 13, M.C.L. § 554.61 et seq.; M.S.A. § 26.49(11) et seq. In this appeal as of right, defendant contends that 1968 P.A. 13 is unconstitutional or, alternatively, that it is inapplicable. We affirm.

The parcels of land at issue in this case are adjoining fifty-foot-wide strips of land upon which plaintiff's railroad track is located. These strips of land pass through the land of defendant, a Michigan corporation comprised of owners of resort cottages situated northwest of Ludington, Michigan, along the shores of Lake Michigan. The operation of plaintiff's railroad has been a source of controversy between plaintiff and defendant for over seventy years. Twice, their disputes have reached our Supreme Court. *See* Epworth Assembly v. Ludington & N.R. Co., 194 N.W. 562 (Mich. 1923), and Epworth Assembly v. Ludington & N.R. Co., 211 N.W. 99 (Mich. 1926). Originally, defendant desired a railroad to service its members, providing them with transportation to its grounds. Plaintiff's interest in the four strips of land was acquired pursuant to four conveyances from defendant to plaintiff which were executed in 1916. [Three] of the strips were conveyed pursuant to quitclaim deeds stating that the conveyance was "for railroad purposes only." [The remaining] strip of land was conveyed pursuant to a quitclaim deed containing the following language: "[I]f, for any reason the property premises or land above described shall, for one year or longer, cease to be used for railroad purposes, in that case all of the land herein described shall revert to the Epworth Assembly."

On March 8, 1988, plaintiff commenced the instant action, seeking money damages, an injunction to prevent defendant from constructing barricades, and a declaration of the interests of the parties in the strips of land. Defendant responded, contending that the operation of the railroad constituted a nuisance. Prior to trial, defendant brought a motion challenging the constitutionality of M.C.L. § 554.61 et seq.; M.S.A. § 26.49(11) et seq., which provides for the extinguishment of certain reversionary interests in land. The trial court ruled that the act was constitutional. After plaintiff agreed to waive its claim for money damages, a bench trial was held on May 3 and 4, 1989.

At trial, plaintiff's general manager, Bernard Sterk, testified that fifteen derailments occurred on plaintiff's tracks between 1976 and 1980, but that in 1977 plaintiff spent approximately $170,000 to rebuild portions of the track so that it could accommodate larger railroad cars. Nevertheless, by the end of 1978, plaintiff's board of directors began considering the possibility of abandoning the railroad because of the loss of customers. Thereafter, business continued to decline. [A]lthough trains have not run since [February 1981], plaintiff has continued to derive revenue from investments and the rental of its cars.

In 1982, Sterk had a letter hand-delivered to defendant, asking it to restore a portion of the track which it had removed when a water line was put in. The letter also informed defendant that plaintiff had no intention of abandoning the railroad and that it hoped to use the track again when the business climate improved.

Kenneth Howell, one of plaintiff's superintendents, testified that ever since the train stopped operating he has walked the track probably once a month making inspections. There was also testimony that in 1983 plaintiff replaced some railroad ties that had been removed by defendant when the water line was installed, and that in 1984 plaintiff hired laborers to clear the entire length of the track of weeds.

Defendant's general manager, William Karlson, testified that derailments would occur three or four times a month from 1975 on, often blocking traffic for an average of two hours. He believed these derailments posed a hazard to the people who lived there because of the heavy equipment needed to correct a derailment. Residents of the Assembly also testified regarding the disruptive nature of the derailments and the loud screeching noises that occurred when the trains negotiated the track's curves.

Karlson testified that the several alterations defendant made to the strips of land subsequent to February 1982 were made pursuant to the Board of Trustees' purported belief that the land had reverted back to defendant one year after trains had ceased running.

After the parties submitted written closing arguments, the trial court found that the title received by plaintiff pursuant to the conveyances consisted of a fee simple determinable interest, but that defendant's possibility of reverter in each of the strips of land had been extinguished pursuant to 1968 P.A. 13, since defendant never recorded a written notice indicating its desire to preserve such interests. M.C.L. § 554.65; M.S.A. § 26.49(15). Thus, the court declared plaintiff the fee simple owner of the four strips of land and enjoined defendant from interfering with plaintiff's use of the property.

II

By enacting 1968 P.A. 13, which became effective March 29, 1968, our Legislature sought "to limit the duration of possibilities of reverter and rights of entry in conveyances of real property in certain cases." Section 3 of the act, M.C.L. § 554.63; M.S.A. § 26.49 (13), provides:

> A right of termination under a terminable interest which was created prior to the effective date of this act is unenforceable if the specified contingency does not occur within 30 years after the terminable interest was created or within 1 year after the effective date of this act, whichever is later.

The act defines "terminable interest" as a possessory or ownership interest in real property which is subject to termination by a provision in a conveyance or other instrument which either creates a right of reversion to a grantor or his heirs, successors, or assigns or creates a right of entry on the occurrence of a specified contingency. M.C.L. § 554.61(a); M.S.A. § 26.49(11)(a). A "specified contingency" is defined as the event described in a conveyance or other instrument creating a terminable interest, the occurrence of which requires or permits the divesting of the terminableinterest. M.C.L. § 554.61(b); M.S.A. § 26.49(11)(b).

A saving provision is contained in § 5 of the act, M.C.L. § 554.65; M.S.A. § 26.49 (15), which provides that a person desiring to preserve a right of termination may do so by recording a written notice of such intent within a period of not less than twenty-five nor more than thirty years after the creation of the terminable interest or within one year after the effective date of the act, whichever is later. Thereafter, a right of termination may be continually preserved by recording another written notice every thirty years.

In this case, it is undisputed that defendant never recorded a written notice indicating its desire to preserve its possibilities of reverter. Notwithstanding, defendant argues that these interests were not lost because 1968 P.A. 13 is either inapplicable or unconstitutional. We disagree.

Defendant's first constitutional challenge of 1968 P.A. 13 is that the abolition of its reversionary interests constitutes an impermissible impairment of a contract right, contrary to our state and federal constitutions. The Michigan Constitution, art. 1, § 10 provides that "[n]o law impairing the obligation of contract shall be enacted," while the United States Constitution, art. I, § 10, provides that "[n]o State shall pass any Law impairing the Obligation of Contracts." Legislation challenged on a constitutional basis is clothed in a presumption of constitutionality, and every reasonable presumption must be indulged in favor of the statute's constitutionality.

Legislation adjusting the rights and responsibilities of contracting parties must be upon reasonable conditions and serve a legitimate public purpose. When adjudicating impairment claims, the first inquiry should be whether the act has, in fact, operated as a substantial impairment of the contract relationship; the severity of the impairment determines the height of the hurdle the act must clear. While minimal alteration of contractual obligations may end the inquiry at its first stage, severe impairment will push the inquiry to a careful examination of the nature and purpose of the state legislation.

The public purpose served by 1968 P.A. 13 is the reduction of impairments of the marketability of title caused by possibilities of reverter and rights of entry of ancient origin and duration. 1968 P.A. 13 does not provide for the automatic extinguishment of possibilities of reverter and rights of entry, but merely requires periodic recording in order for these interests to be preserved in excess of thirty years. [S]uch recording cannot be considered to be a "high" hurdle, yet it furthers the state's interests in reducing impairments of the marketability of title. We believe that by requiring periodic recording, once every thirty years, and by providing for a one-year grace period in order to preserve those interests created more than thirty years before the effective date of the act, the state's methods are reasonable.

Defendant points to Biltmore Village, Inc. v. Royal Biltmore Village, Inc., 71 So.2d 727 (Fla. 1954), which held unconstitutional a Florida statute canceling reverter provisions in deeds which had been in effect for more than twenty-one years. The decision in that case was premised upon the fact that the saving clause, which gave a holder one year to enforce his right, afforded no remedy to those whose right had not yet accrued, because the condition upon which the right was limited had not yet occurred. However, the saving provision in 1968 P.A. 13 is different, because it specifically affords a remedy to those whose right of termination had not yet accrued by allowing them to record a written notice preserving such right. Therefore, *Biltmore* is distinguishable. On the other hand, several states have upheld statutes similar to 1968 P.A. 13 in the face of similar constitutional challenges. Cline v. Johnson Co. Bd. of Ed., 548 S.W.2d 507 (Ky. 1977); Presbytery of Southeast Iowa v. Harris, 226 N.W.2d 232 (Iowa 1975); Brookline v. Carey, 245 N.E.2d 446 (Mass. 1969); Trustees of Schools of Twp. No. 1 v. Batdorf, 130 N.E.2d 111 (Ill. 1955). *Contra*, Board of Ed. of Central School Dist. No. 1 v. Miles, 207 N.E.2d 181 (N.Y. 1965).

Accordingly, we hold that 1968 P.A. 13 does not unconstitutionally impair the obligation of contract.

Defendant further argues that 1968 P.A. 13 is unconstitutional because it constitutes a deprivation of property without due process of law. First, defendant argues that the act is unreasonable and does not constitute a proper exercise of the state's police power. To overcome the presumption of constitutionality, defendant must establish either that no public purpose is served by the act or that no reasonable relationship exists between the remedy adopted and the public purpose sought to be achieved. [D]efendant argues that no public purpose is served because plaintiff does not serve the public personally and because the land in the hands of plaintiff would not benefit the public. However, because, as indicated previously, the purpose served by the act is the avoidance of impairment of the marketability of title caused by ancient reversionary interests, a finding of public purpose is neither dependent upon nor related to the actual use of the land. Thus, defendant has not shown that a public purpose is not involved.

Furthermore, [a]s we have held previously, 1968 P.A. 13 is a reasonable method of dealing with the problem caused by the continued and unlimited existence of "fleeting and amorphous" interests. While there may exist other methods of achieving the same objective, the existence of other possible means does not render the act unconstitutional.

Finally, we summarily reject defendant's argument that 1968 P.A. 13 is unconstitutional because it does not provide for legally adequate notice; the act itself provides sufficient notice of its recording requirements.

[W]e affirm the trial court's judgment declaring plaintiff the owner, in fee simple absolute, of the four strips of land for the reason that defendant's failure to record a written notice of its desire to preserve its possibilities of reverter in those parcels rendered such interests unenforceable; we further conclude that 1968 P.A. 13 does not violate the constitutional protections against impairment of contract, nor does the act unconstitutionally deprive defendant of property without due process of law.

Affirmed.

NOTES AND QUESTIONS

1. **Validity of statutes.** How does the statute in the principal case differ from the Florida statute invalidated by the court in *Biltmore Village*? The Illinois court held constitutional a statute cutting off possibilities of reverter and powers of termination forty years after the creation of the interest, even as applied to interests in being at the effective date of the statute. *See* Trustees of Schools of Twp. No. 1 v. Batdorf, 130 N.E.2d 111 (Ill. 1955). Can you think of arguments to justify the *Batdorf* view?

2. **Abolition of the fee simple determinable.** At least two states by statute provide that language sufficient to create a fee simple determinable creates a fee simple subject to a condition subsequent instead. *See* Cal. Civ. Code § 885.020; Ky. Rev. Stat. Ann. § 381.218. The statutes are reminiscent of statutes, considered above, that rewrite fee tail language appearing in deeds and wills.

3. **Interviewing and counselling.** If O approaches you to draft documents transferring Blackacre to the local school district subject to certain restrictions, what questions would you want to ask O, and what means of accomplishing O's wishes would you discuss?

6.   Restraints on Alienation

Future interests, which restrict the alienability of property, are policed primarily by the Rule Against Perpetuities, considered in Section B.5 below. The major device for the regulation of restrictions limiting the marketability of present estates in property is the rule (or rules) against restraints on alienation.

ALBY v. BANC ONE FINANCIAL
128 P.3d 81 (Wash. 2006)

JOHNSON, J.

The issue in this case is whether a restriction in a deed, which provides that the deeded property automatically reverts to the grantor if the property is mortgaged or encumbered during the life of the grantor, is a valid restraint on alienation. We find the clause to be reasonable and justified by the interests of the parties and, therefore, valid. We affirm the Court of Appeals.

FACTS

In 1992, Eugene and Susan Alby sold part of their family farm to their niece, Lorri Brashler, and her husband, Larry Brashler. Although the property's market value was $100,000, the parties agreed to a purchase price of $15,000. The contract and the deed contained nearly identical clauses providing for automatic reverter to the Albys if the property were subdivided, mortgaged, or otherwise encumbered during either of the Albys' lifetimes. The restriction at issue provided: "RESERVATION in favor of the Grantors, their heirs and assigns, an automatic reverter, should the property conveyed herein ever be mortgaged or encumbered within the life time of either Grantor."

The parties included these restrictions as a means of ensuring that the land remained within the family during the Albys' lifetimes.[1] Additionally, the real estate contract provided that if Lorri and Larry Brashler ever divorce, the property would remain Lorri Brashler's because the property was in essence a gift to her as separate property. The parties recorded the real estate contract on April

---

[1] Susan Alby's uncontested affidavit states:

Because this piece of property had been in the ALBY family for several generations, GENE and I wanted to make sure that the property always stayed in the family. After several discussions with LORRI about what she and her husband, LARRY R. BRASHLER, could afford to pay for the home, my husband GENE and I decided that $15,000.00 was what LORRI and her husband could afford, even though we believed the property and home was of considerably greater valued [sic]. Since we were so concerned about the property staying in the family, we consulted with an attorney to make a contract with the proper and appropriate language so that LORRI and her husband could not do three things:

1. Sell the property to someone who was not a member of the family;

2. Divide the property in any way; and

3. Encumber the property with a mortgage or deed of trust.

We even told LORRI that we would buy the property back from her and her husband should they ever decide that they did not want it.

My husband GENE ALBY, now deceased, received this property from his mother. His father had received part of this property from his father who immigrated to the United States from Norway. This property has been in the ALBY family for all these generations and *for this reason*, my husband and I had the [attorney] place the necessary language in the real estate contract and deed that should LORRI and her husband attempt to do any of the above mentioned acts, the property would automatically revert back to us.

(emphasis added) (Although neither the contract nor the deed contains restrictions on selling the property to someone who is not a member of the family, the Albys reserved a right of first refusal in the contract).

28, 1992. After the Brashlers satisfied their obligations under the contract, the warranty deed was recorded on September 27, 1996.

Notwithstanding the restrictions, the Brashlers obtained a loan for $92,000 from First Union Mortgage Corporation by executing a deed of trust for the property on February 26, 1999. This loan was recorded on March 3, 1999. The Brashlers executed a second deed of trust to obtain a second loan for $17,250 from CIT Group on March 31, 1999. This loan was recorded on April 2, 1999. CIT Group assigned the loan to petitioner, Banc One Financial (Banc One). The Brashlers defaulted on their payments on their first loan and the lender held a trustee's sale on October 27, 2000. Banc One purchased the property at the sale for $100,822.16 and recorded the trustee's deed on November 2, 2000.[2]

On April 18, 2002, Susan Alby filed a quiet title action in Stevens County Superior Court against Banc One, arguing [that] the title to the property automatically reverted to her when the Brashlers encumbered the property.[3] On competing motions for summary judgment, the trial court quieted title in Banc One and declared the clause void [and] against public policy as an unreasonable restraint on alienation. The Court of Appeals reversed, concluding that the clause is valid because it is not a restraint on alienation and even if it were, the restraint is reasonable. Alby v. Banc One Financial, 82 P.3d 675 (Wash. Ct. App. 2003). We granted review to determine whether the clause is a restraint on alienation, and if so, whether it is reasonable.

ANALYSIS

The first step in resolving the dispute in this case is to identify the type of interest conveyed. Banc One and Susan Alby agree that the interest conveyed to the Brashlers is a fee simple determinable. A "fee simple determinable" is an estate that will automatically end and revert to the grantor if some specified event occurs. Black's Law Dictionary 649 (8th ed.2004). We agree that the Albys conveyed a fee simple determinable interest to the Brashlers because the estate would revert to the Albys if the property were mortgaged or encumbered during their lifetimes.

Though we conclude the transferred estate is a fee simple determinable estate, that conclusion does not end the analysis. Fee simple determinable estates are subject to the rule against restraints on alienation, which prohibits undue or unreasonable restraints on alienation. Black's Law Dictionary defines a "restraint on alienation" as "[a] restriction, usu[ally] in a deed of conveyance, on a grantee's ability to sell or transfer real property; a provision that conveys an interest and that, even after the interest has become vested, prevents or discourages the owner from disposing of it at all or from disposing of it in particular ways or to particular persons." Black's, s *upra*, at 1340.

---

[2] Because the deed containing the restrictions had been recorded, Banc One had actual or constructive notice of the reversion that was created when the Brashlers mortgaged the property.

[3] Eugene Alby died after the Brashlers purchased the property and before Susan Alby filed this action.

Here we have a restraint on alienation because the clause prevented the Brashlers from disposing of the property in a particular way: they could not mortgage or encumber the property without the property automatically reverting to the Albys. Additionally, though the clause did not directly prevent the Brashlers from selling the property, it limited the property's marketability because it prevented potential buyers from financing the purchase of the property.

Because we find the prohibition on mortgaging or encumbering to be a restraint on alienation, we must next determine the validity of the restraint. Washington follows the reasonableness approach to restraints on alienation. "Unreasonable restraints on alienation of real property are . . . invalid; reasonable restraints on alienation . . . are valid if justified by the *legitimate interests of the parties.*" McCausland v. Bankers Life Ins. Co., 757 P.2d 941 (Wash. 1988) (emphasis added). In determining whether a restraint is reasonable, we balance the utility of the purpose served by the restraint against the injurious consequences that are likely to flow from its enforcement.[4] See Restatement (Third) of Property § 3.4, at 440 (2000). Whether a restraint is limited in scope or time is often highly significant. 17 William B. Stoebuck & John W. Weaver, Washington Practice: Real Estate: Property Law § 1.26, at 50 (2d ed.2004). In addition to the scope and duration of the restraint, we look at the purpose of the restraint and whether the restraint is supported by consideration.

The balance in this case is between the operation of a free market in land and the right to maintain property in family ownership for a limited time period. Family ownership is not always subordinated to immediate and free alienability. The fact that restraints may negatively affect marketability does not necessarily render them unreasonable. The Albys conveyed a restrained interest in long-held family property to their niece and her husband for a substantially reduced price with the purpose of maintaining family ownership of the property through the Albys' lifetimes. This restraint prevents the property from being mortgaged or encumbered but does not restrict the right to sell or transfer the property. The restraint has a limited scope of preventing only mortgaging or encumbering, a limited duration of the Albys' lifetimes, and a legitimate purpose of keeping the property in the family. The restraint is also supported by the consideration apparent in the significantly reduced purchase price. The recorded deed provides notice to potentially affected parties. Balancing the relevant factors, we conclude that the potentially injurious consequences of not mortgaging or encumbering the property and reducing its marketability are outweighed by the utility of enforcing the limited restraint to keep the property in the family for the Albys' lifetimes.

We next consider the legitimate interests of the parties. The Albys have a legitimate interest in keeping the property in the family and in preventing the property from being lost through foreclosure. The Brashlers have a legitimate

---

[4] Restraints on alienation of land are used for a variety of legitimate purposes: retaining land in families; preserving affordable housing; furthering conservation, preservation, and charitable purposes to which land is devoted; and facilitating land investment and creating investment opportunities. Potentially harmful consequences that may flow from restraints on alienation include impediments to the operation of a free market in land, limits on the prospects for improvement, development, and redevelopment of land, and limits on the mobility of landowners and would-be purchasers. Restatement (Third) of Property § 3.4 cmt. c at 442 (2000).

interest in realizing the right to freely dispose of their property. However, the Brashlers' interest in free alienation is limited by the fact that they agreed to the restraint in consideration for the substantially reduced price. Enforcement of the restraint still provides the Brashlers with a legitimate interest in owning the property with every aspect of absolute ownership except the right to mortgage or encumber the property. Both parties also have legitimate interests in enforcing the terms of their contract.

When evaluating the reasonableness of any agreement placing a restraint on alienation, courts should be reluctant to invoke common law principles disfavoring restraints to invalidate a bargained for contract freely agreed to by the parties. The parties here contracted to transfer property with the purpose of keeping the family farm in the family during the lifetimes of the grantors. We find nothing unreasonable about this purpose. We conclude that the restraint, which prevents the Brashlers from mortgaging or encumbering the property, is reasonable and justified by the legitimate interests of the parties. Accordingly, we affirm the Court of Appeals and remand to superior court with directions to enter summary judgment in favor of and quieting title in Susan Alby.

OWENS, SANDERS, FAIRHURST, and J.M. JOHNSON, JJ., concur.

ALEXANDER, C.J. (dissenting).

I disagree with the majority's determination that Susan Alby placed a valid restraint on alienation of her niece's property and that the Court of Appeals should be affirmed. While I agree that a reasonableness test applies to restraints on alienation, I would hold that the restraint in this case was not reasonable because the cherished value that our state places on free alienability outweighs the value to the Alby family of maintaining the property in family ownership.

We determine whether a restraint on alienation is reasonable or unreasonable based on "factual determinations and consideration of the equities," *Morris v. Woodside*, 682 P.2d 905 (Wash. 1984), and on an assessment of the "legitimate interests of the parties." *Erickson v. Bank of Cal.*, 643 P.2d 670 (Wash. 1982). Determining reasonableness also requires "weighing the utility of the restraint against the injurious consequences of enforcing the restraint." Restatement (Third) of Property § 3.4, at 440 (2000). Thus, we first consider the "legitimate interests of the parties." Eugene and Susan Albys' interest was keeping the property in the Alby family. Lorri and Larry Brashlers' interest, on the other hand, was that of realizing the right of a property owner to freely dispose of his or her property interest, which, as this court has recognized, is among the "fundamental attribute[s] of property ownership." *Manufactured Hous. Cmtys v. State*, 13 P.3d 183 (Wash. 2000). As has been observed in the Restatement (Second) of Property,

> [i]f the full benefits which flow from the freedom to alienate an interest in property are to be obtained, the owner of such interest must be able to take advantage of any of the existing methods of transferring property. Any restraint which interferes with the power to alienate in some manner, though it leave the owner of the estate free to alienate in other ways, may substantially hinder him in disposing of the property.

Restatement (Second) of Property § 4.2 cmt. n at 183 (1983).

According to Susan Alby, the parties here "freely contracted for the exchange," with full knowledge and after an opportunity to freely negotiate the terms of their bargain. She argues that, although the Brashlers' right to exercise one of the incidents of property ownership was limited by the terms of the deed, this limitation was reflected in the selling price of the property as they paid significantly below market price.

However, nothing in the record supports the claim that the Albys and the Brashlers bargained for a reduction in price in exchange for an estate that did not include the full right of alienation or that the reduction in price was consideration for conveyance of a reduced estate. The real estate contract that the parties signed indicated that the Albys considered the sale of the property to Lorri Brashler to be "in essence a gift to her." Indeed, Susan Alby's own affidavit reflects that the property was sold to the Brashlers at a reduced price, not in exchange for agreeing to a lesser estate, but as a favor to Lorri Brashler. She stated that "[a]fter several discussions with LORRI about what she and her husband, LARRY R. BRASHLER, could afford to pay for the home, my husband GENE, and I decided that $15,000.00 was what LORRI and her husband could afford, even though we believed the property and home was of considerably greater valued [sic]." Susan Alby's affidavit also suggests that the Albys placed the restraint on alienation into the contract and deed *after* having agreed with the Brashlers on a selling price. For the foregoing reasons, I believe that the sale of the property at a reduced price was not a bargained-for exchange in consideration for the conveyance of a reduced estate.

Susan Alby notes that the restraint imposed on the alienability of the property in this case was limited both in scope and duration because it was a restriction on mortgaging or encumbering only and expired upon the death of both of the grantors. However, this limitation effectively rendered the property unalienable during the life of the grantors. The duration of the restriction is unknown; it could be a significant period of time, depending on Susan Alby's longevity.[2] During this period, the Brashlers would effectively be relegated to the status of leaseholders of the property, with the right of possession only. Furthermore, the restriction "runs with the land" and therefore limits the rights of not only the Brashlers, the immediate purchasers of the property, but all subsequent purchasers, for the lifetime of the grantor.

The utility of maintaining property in family ownership has been viewed in the law as subordinate to the value of free alienability of property. 3 John A. Borron, Jr. Simes & Smith, The Law of Future Interests § 1117 (3d ed.2004). The doctrine of restraints on alienation and other common law doctrines such as the rule against perpetuities arose, in large part, to ensure that the desire of individuals to retain ownership of property within their family did not harm the economic interests of the nation by destroying the free market for property. *Id.* Despite the long history

---

[2] Over 14 years have elapsed since the relevant language was placed in the real estate contract and deed. Because Susan Alby is now only 66 years of age, the restriction, if not void, could be in effect for many more years.

of this principle, the majority asserts that "[f]amily ownership is not always subordinated to immediate and free alienability." It cites no authority for this assertion, which dismisses the doctrine recognized in Simes & Smith that society has a stronger interest in the free alienability of property than in fostering family dynasties.

Maintaining the property within the Alby family no doubt has certain value, to Susan Alby individually and to her family. Continued ownership of the property would allow them to maintain possession over land to which they no doubt have an emotional attachment. However, allowing Susan Alby to limit the alienability of the property for the sole purpose of maintaining it in the Alby family has injurious consequences both to the Brashlers and to the general public. The Brashlers are deprived of their right to freely dispose of their property, a right recognized as being one of the "fundamental attribute[s] of property ownership." Manufactured Hous. Cmtys., 13 P.3d 183 (Wash. 2000). Further, the property is effectively removed from the marketplace, causing economic consequences affecting society as a whole.

For the foregoing reasons, I would hold that the clause in the Alby/Brashler deed providing for automatic reversion of the property if it is mortgaged or encumbered during the life of either grantor is unreasonable and, therefore, void. Accordingly, I would reverse the Court of Appeals and remand to the superior court for reinstatement of the summary judgment in favor of Banc One.

MADSEN and BRIDGE, JJ., concur.

CHAMBERS, J. (dissent).

I respectfully dissent. Restraints on alienation are generally unenforceable as against public policy favoring the free alienability of land. The [disputed] clause clearly qualifies. I part company with my colleagues because the encumbrance clause at issue in this case was, in my view, an unreasonable restraint on alienation because it prevented Lorri and Larry Brashler, or their successors, from transferring their interest in the property in a particular and very common way: by way of mortgage or encumbrance. The encumbrance clause also had the effect of seriously discouraging disposition of the property by limiting the ability of a potential buyer to finance the purchase primarily through a mortgage.

It is, however, primarily the majority and Chief Justice Alexander's discussion of reasonableness with which I take issue. Given the nature of the estate and the restraint, I would hold that the restraint was per se unreasonable. It was only after the real estate contract was satisfied and the warranty deed vesting title to the property in the Brashlers had been recorded, that the Brashlers attempted to obtain a loan by executing a deed of trust for the property. After the Brashlers had paid the $15,000 purchase price and recorded the warranty deed, the automatic reverter restraint was, in my view, per se unreasonable and so holding would clarify the law.[1]

---

[1] Assuming that the goal of the Albys was to convey an estate which would keep the whole parcel of land in the family for their lifetimes, there are better ways they could have accomplished this. For

Restraints on alienation fall into two categories: direct and indirect. 3 John A. Borron, Jr., Simes & Smith, The Law of Future Interests § 1112, at 3 (3d ed. 2004) (Simes & Smith). Direct restraints are those provisions in an instrument which, by their terms or implications, "purport[ ] to prohibit or penalize the exercise of the power of alienation" of property. 3 Simes & Smith § 1112, at 3.

Direct restraints take one of three forms: promissory, disabling, or forfeiture. 3 Simes & Smith § 1131, at 14. A promissory restraint is an agreement by the holder of an interest not to alienate, with contractual liability if the agreement is breached. A disabling restraint is a provision in the document creating the interest that renders void any attempt to alienate the interest. Black's Law Dictionary 494 (8th ed.2004) (a disabling restraint places "[l]imits on the alienation of property"); cf. 17 William B. Stoebuck & John W. Weaver, Washington Practice: Real Estate: Property Law § 1.26, at 50 (2d ed.2004) ("restraint [that] is stated in the form of a prohibition; the transferor in some way forbids the transferee from alienating."). A forfeiture restraint is a condition that terminates the fee upon an attempt to alienate. 3 Simes & Smith § 1131, at 14. Such a restraint exists when "an instrument of conveyance provides that if the grantee attempts to alienate, the land shall go to the grantor by way of possibility of reverter or right of entry or to a third person by way of executory interest." 17 Stoebuck & Weaver § 1.26, at 50; see also Restatement (Second) of Property § 3.2, at 147 (1983).

The automatic reverter clause here is a direct forfeiture restraint. Although there are no Washington decisions on point, the general rule is that even limited forfeiture restraints that interfere with the alienability of property if unreasonable, are void. 17 Stoebuck & Weaver § 1.26, at 51; 3 Simes & Smith § 1131, at 14.

It is desirable that the law be clear, understandable, and predictable. The reasonableness test embraced by the majority and dissent does not promote predictability. To send every contested restraint to a court hearing to balance the interests sought to be protected by the restraint against the benefits of alienability serves neither clarity nor predictability. I would hold that where, as here, the condition of payment has been satisfied and a warranty deed is transferred and recorded, a direct and automatic reverter upon the attempt to alienate is unreasonable as a matter of law. I therefore respectfully dissent.

NOTES AND QUESTIONS

1. **Restraints on alienation and on use.** A direct restraint on alienation is a provision in a deed or will that forbids or penalizes the transferees's attempt to transfer the property. Direct restraints are governed by the rule (or rules) against restraints on alienation, discussed in Note 2, which tend to be restrictive. An indirect restraint on alienation is one which, in practical effect although not in so many words, restricts alienability. A restriction on the *use* that the grantee may make of the transferred property, as in a defeasible fee, is an indirect restraint on alienation; purchasers wanting to use the land for purposes forbidden by the restriction will not buy the land. Restrictions on use are not governed by the rules

---

example, they could have given the Albys [Brashlers?] fee simple and retained for themselves a life estate.

on direct restraints. *See* Restatement Second of Property (Donative Transfers) § 3.4. Suppose O conveys land "to the Odd Fellows Lodge, subject to the condition that said property is restricted for the use and benefit of the lodge only; and in the event the property fails to be used by the lodge, or in the event of sale or transfer by the lodge, the same is to revert to the grantor, his successors or assigns." Does the deed language impose a direct or indirect restraint on alienation? *See* Mountain Brow Lodge No. 82 v. Toscano, 64 Cal. Rptr. 816 (Cal. Dist. Ct. App. 1968).

2. **Types of direct restraints.** As Justice Chambers notes, a direct restraint may be a *disabling restraint* ("to A, and any transfer by A shall be null and void"), a *forfeiture restraint* ("to A on condition that if A conveys his interest without O's consent, the grantor may terminate the estate"), or a *promissory restraint* ("to A, who covenants not to transfer without O's consent"). *See* Restatement Second, *supra*, §§ 3.1 (disabling restraint); 3.2 (forfeiture restraint); 3.3 (promissory restraint). The Restatement Second offers the following rules for each type:

a. A disabling restraint that makes transfer "impossible for any period of time" from the creation of the restriction is invalid if imposed on any estate. *Id.* § 4.1(1). A disabling restraint that allows transfer "in some manner" is valid "if, and only if, under all the circumstances of the case and considering the purpose, nature, and duration of the restraint, the legal policy favoring freedom of alienation does not reasonably apply." *Id.* § 4.1(2) and cmt. e.

b. A forfeiture restraint on a life estate or term of years estate is valid. *Id.* § 4.2(1). A forfeiture restraint on a fee simple that makes transfer "impossible" is invalid. *Id.* § 4.2(2), while other forfeiture restraints (presumably those that allow transfer in some manner) are valid, "if and only if" the restraint is reasonable in the following (non-exclusive) ways: the restraint is limited in duration; allows a variety of types of transfers; is limited in the number of persons to whom transfer is prohibited; tends to increase the value of the subject property; is imposed on an interest that is not otherwise readily marketable; or is imposed on property that is not readily marketable. *Id.* § 4.2(3)(a) through (f).

c. A promissory restraint is valid "if, and only if," a comparable forfeiture restraint would be valid. *Id.* § 4.3.

Although the Restatement Second deals with donative transfers, its rules, "to the extent that they permit restraints on alienation, are equally permissive in regard to non-donative transfers." *Id.*, introductory note, at 144.

3. **The basis for the prohibition.** Why does the law restrict direct restraints on alienation? *See* 6 A.L.P. § 26.2 (A. James Casner ed. 1952) (noting disincentive to landowners to make improvements, and exclusion of landowner's creditors from access to the restricted property); White v. White, 251 A.2d 470 (N.J. Super. Ct. Ch. Div. 1969) (invalidating will provision requiring grandnephew, "if he shall sell the house within fifteen years" after testator's death, to divide the sale proceeds with another grandnephew and grandniece of testator). *See generally* Richard A. Epstein, *Why Restrain Alienation?*, 85 Colum. L. Rev. 970 (1985).

4. **The principal case: method and result.** Under the Restatement Second approach (Note 2), decisions about the validity of a restraint are reached on the basis of the estate that is restricted and the kind of restraint imposed on it. Within that framework, the Restatement offers some black-letter rules. In *Alby*, the court

simply asks whether the restraint is reasonable. Although the court's approach may forecast a trend, it is worth noting that the court's citations to the "Restatement Third" for its reasonableness approach are to the Restatement's treatment of servitudes, not fee transactions like those in *Alby. See* Restatement Third of Property (Servitudes) § 3.4 (servitude imposing direct restraint on alienation "is invalid if the restraint is unreasonable," which is determined "by weighing the utility of the restraint against the injurious consequences of enforcing the restraint"). The Restatement provisions dealing with fee simple transfers, cited correctly by the dissenters, are in the Restatement Second of Property. Had you been on the court in *Alby,* would you have sided with the majority or the dissent? Why?

5. **The repugnancy doctrine.** In Sterner v. Nelson, 314 N.W.2d 263 (Neb. 1982), Oscar Wurtele's will devised his entire estate to his wife Mary,

> to be her property absolutely with full power in her to make such dispositions of said property as she may desire; conditioned, however, that if any of said property is remaining upon the death of said Mary Viola Wurtele, such of said property as remains shall vest in my foster daughter Gladys Pauline Sterner and her children.

None of Oscar's property devised to Mary was in her estate in kind when she died, although she did own some property that may have been purchased with the proceeds of sale of the devised property. In the dispute between Gladys and Mary's second husband, the court might have ruled simply that Mary's estate contained no "orts" (leftovers from Oscar's estate; see Note 1 after Ogle v. Ogle in the life estate materials), and that Oscar did not intend for Gladys to be entitled to the proceeds of any of his property sold by Mary. (Does the language of the will support this argument?) Instead, the court took broader ground, concluding that the first clause of Oscar's will created a fee simple absolute in Mary, that the added language of condition was repugnant to (an invalid restraint on) the fee simple created by the first clause, and that Gladys therefore received no interest at all under the terms of Oscar's will. Is that what Oscar intended?

Are the choices to construe Mary's estate either as a fee simple absolute or a life estate (the options stated by the court) or is there a third possibility? *See* Hall v. Hall, 604 S.W.2d 851 (Tenn. 1980) (deed to grantor's wife, "with full control and power" over the property "just so long as she lives my widow but if she should ever marry any other man then this deed becomes void to her and the above described property shall fall to my children" held to be "clear and unequivocal" expression of intent to create fee simple subject to an executory limitation). Can you surmise what kind of language might tempt a court to employ repugnancy doctrine and what language might lead the court instead to search for the transferor's intent in the whole document, as the court did in Hall v. Hall? *See* Epting v. Mayer, 323 S.E.2d 797 (S.C. Ct. App. 1984) (devise to testator's daughters A and B "in fee simple absolute," with additional language giving the property to the survivor of the two and further giving the property to the testator's sons if either daughter should die without issue, *held* to create a fee simple in the surviving daughter, the other language being struck as "repugnant" to the fee created by the first language). A cardinal rule of construction is that the court should determine the transferor's intent from the language of the entire document. Does the repugnancy doctrine ignore that rule? *See generally* Lewis M. Simes, Handbook of the Law of Future Interests § 118 (2d ed. 1966) (repugnancy is an "extraordinary rule, totally indefensible"); Fox v. Snow, 76 A.2d 877, 878 (N.J. 1950) (vigorous and famous dissent by Chief Justice Vanderbilt, offering a strong doctrinal and jurisprudential critique of the repugnancy doctrine); Jesse Dukeminier, *Cleansing the Stables of Property: A River Found at Last*, 65 Iowa L. Rev. 151 (1982) (discussing malpractice liability as a way to rid property law of archaic doctrines).

B.   FUTURE INTERESTS

Today we have naming of parts. Yesterday,
We had daily cleaning. And tomorrow morning,
We shall have what to do after firing. But today,
Today we have naming of parts. Japonica
Glistens like coral in all of the neighboring gardens,
    And today we have naming of parts.
This is the lower sling swivel. And this
Is the upper sling swivel, whose use you will see,
When you are given your slings. And this is the piling swivel,
Which in your case you have not got. The branches
Hold in the gardens their silent, eloquent gestures,
    Which in our case we have not got.
This is the safety-catch, which is always released
With an easy flick of the thumb. And please do not let me
See anyone using his finger. You can do it quite easy
If you have any strength in your thumb. The blossoms
Are fragile and motionless, never letting anyone see
    Any of them using their finger.
And this you can see is the bolt. The purpose of this
Is to open the breech, as you see. We can slide it
Rapidly backwards and forwards: we call this
Easing the spring. And rapidly backwards and forwards
The early bees are assaulting and fumbling the flowers
    They call it easing the Spring.
They call it easing the Spring: it is perfectly easy
If you have any strength in your thumb: like the bolt,
And the breech, and the cocking-piece, and the point of balance,
Which in our case we have not got; and the almond-blossom
Silent in all of the gardens and the bees going backwards and forwards,
    For today we have naming of parts.

Henry Reed, "Naming of Parts," in *Collected Poems* (1991)*

We turn now to a study of future interests. You have already met future interests in passing, as we studied their attendant possessory estates. In the pages that follow, we add detail and system to our exposition.

When does a future interest exist? Every present estate other than a fee simple absolute will have one or more future interests associated with it. Thus, a defeasible fee simple will be accompanied by a future interest. So will a fee tail, a

---

* From Henry Reed: *Collected Poems* edited by Jon Stallworthy (1991). Reprinted by permission of Oxford University Press.

life estate, a leasehold estate, or any defeasible variant of those estates. When a future interest exists, you must be careful to identify and name it. The rules discussed in Sections B.1 and B.2 below will help you to do that.

A present right to future possession. What is "future" about a future interest is only the enjoyment of possession; *that* is delayed until the ending of the present possessory estate, but in all other aspects, the future interest has present significance. In the transfer "to A for life, then to B," B is not entitled to possession until A dies; but from the beginning (the effective date of the transfer), B has a *right* to possession upon A's death, a right that is transferable and that is protected by various remedies against A to insure that A will not deplete the asset before B's time for possession arrives. (Recall the discussion of Michael Gruen's remainder in Gruen v. Gruen in Chapter 1, and the discussion of waste in this chapter.) We might accurately describe a future interest as a present right to future possession.

Why? As you will see shortly (if you haven't already been warned by your upperclass friends), future interests are the bane (one of them, anyway) of the first-year property student's existence. Much pain, some (we hope) gain. You are well within your rights to ask why we impose future interests on you. There are several reasons, in addition to the obvious one, that the future interests are simply *there*. First, something may turn on the classifications we will examine. We have already seen, for example, that different transferability rules might apply to possibilities of reverter and powers of termination connected with a defeasible fee simple. We will see that the answers to some other questions also require that we classify future interests. Second, knowledgeable writers in the field use the terminology of the system of future interests that we study herein. That terminology is part of basic literacy in the field of property law, necessary for you to read intelligently and converse accurately. Third, future interests "are the basic building blocks for estate plans," Roger W. Anderson, Understanding Trusts and Estates 205 (2d ed. 1999), and you will use them constantly — and therefore should use them knowingly — if you engage in an estate planning practice. Finally, and perhaps most important, Professor Anderson offers the following insight about the study of estates and the study of law in general:

> A broader reason for studying this material stems from law schools' mission of training people to analyze legal problems, irrespective of the particular subject matter. The law is full of densely tangled topics. Learning how to handle them takes practice. The law of present and future interests provides an excellent opportunity for getting that practice: this law is complicated; it represents unfamiliar terminology; and it requires attention to detail. At the same time, however, a basic understanding of the topic's core concepts is manageable within the confines of a law school course. Consider this topic as affording a chance to develop skills useful for your professional lifetime. As they say of New York, if you can make it here, you can make it anywhere.

Id. at 206.

While these reasons justify a serious study of future interests, they do not justify a continuation of what we might call an orthodox approach to future interests. The orthodox study of future interests focuses entirely, and usually in detail, on *classification* of the various types of interests and on the *consequences* that apply to the different classes of future interests. We reject this orthodox approach for two reasons. First, some classifications are irrelevant because in modern law they produce no consequences except in a very few states; these classifications are of historical and local interest only. Second, a focus exclusively on classification and consequences omits some of the more important questions that *do* matter in the law of future interests today; we would shortchange you if we failed to advert to (without at all trying to be exhaustive about) some of these important questions. In short, our goal is to condense the irrelevant and to expand (if ever so slightly) the relevant questions that arise under the law of future interests.

That said, we caution you that, while our approach caters to the modern significance of future interests, it does not intend casualness. Even in our modernized and streamlined study of future interests, you will be encountering quite a bit of new terminology. Correct naming of parts is essential, as you will see when you are given the parts. Helpful recent discussions with suggestions for reform are Benjamin Barros, *Toward a Model Law of Estates and Future Interests*, 66 Wash. & Lee L. Rev. 3 (2009), and T.P. Gallanis, *The Future of Future Interests*, 60 Wash. & Lee L. Rev. 513 (2003). An earlier, essential article is Lawrence W. Waggoner, *Reforming the Structure of Estates: A Proposal for Legislative Action*, 85 Harv. L. Rev. 729 (1972).

1.   Classification by Party

There are five future interests: the reversion, possibility of reverter, power of termination, remainder, and executory interest. The first three are retained by or created in the transferor, and collectively are called "reversionary" future interests. The remainder and executory interest are created in a transferee, and are called, collectively, "nonreversionary" future interests. The time of creation of a future interest is the effective date of the document that creates the interest: a deed is effective upon execution and delivery of the document (see Chapter 5, section C.1); a will is effective at the testator's death, not at the time of execution of the will.

a.   Interests in the Transferor: Reversionary Future Interests

There are three future interests that may be held by a transferor who creates a present estate and a future interest. You have already encountered all of them.

Reversion. A reversion represents the undisposed-of interest that a transferor retains when she transfers out an estate of lesser quantum (shorter duration) than she owns. Thus, O retains a reversion if she owns a fee simple and transfers a fee tail, a life estate, or a leasehold estate. For purposes of determining whether O has transferred a lesser estate — and thus retained a reversion — defeasibility is ignored; a defeasible variant of any estate has the same potential outside duration as the basic estate, and the future interest following it is not a reversion. Thus, if O owns a fee simple absolute and transfers a defeasible fee, O does not retain a reversion. See the discussion of the possibility of reverter, below.

The examples given in the preceding paragraph are the most obvious and the most common reversions. However, a transferor also retains a reversion if, holding *any* estate in the hierarchy below a fee simple absolute, she transfers an estate of lesser duration. Thus, a tenant with five years remaining on the lease retains a reversion if she transfers to X for four years; the state of the title in that case would be: term of years (for four years) in X; reversion in T for a term of years of one year; reversion in fee simple in O, the landlord. In Chapter 4 you will see that the most common way of determining whether a tenant's transfer creates an assignment or a sublease is by asking whether the tenant retained a reversion.

Possibility of reverter. O retains a possibility of reverter when O transfers an estate of the same potential duration as O has and subjects the transferee to a special limitation, which is signified by language of duration. You are already familiar with the most common instance of a possibility of reverter, which exists when O, owning in fee simple absolute, creates a fee simple determinable in the transferee.

Possibilities of reverter and reversions are much alike; to classify accurately, you must focus on the difference between them. A possibility of reverter arises when O transfers out an estate of the *same* potential duration as O has, and makes the transferred estate determinable; a reversion arises when O transfers any lesser estate, even one that is subject to premature ending. (Problem 2-I.a below, and the discussion that will attend it, should provide further explanation.)

Power of termination. O has a power of termination when O transfers any estate, whether of the same or a lesser quantum, and imposes a restriction on the transferee's use in the form of a condition subsequent, with a power to reclaim possession in case of violation of the restriction. The most common powers of termination are those created in connection with a defeasible fee, which you have already seen, and the landlord's power of termination for the tenant's breach of any specified promises in the lease.

State of the title. In the following Problems, and throughout our discussion of future interests, you will be asked to give the "state of the title" after specified transfers are made. To give the state of the title is to identify all present and future interests that are created in each transfer. The convention for stating the title is to start with the present estate, to identify subsequent future interests in sequence, and to identify every future interest by type *and* by estate. For example, if O transfers Blackacre "to A for life," the state of the title to Blackacre is life estate in A (the present estate), reversion (the type of future interest) in O in fee simple (the estate that O will hold when she resumes possession after A's death).

PROBLEM 2-I. Give the state of the title in each of the following transfers. Assume that O holds in fee simple absolute immediately prior to the stated transfers.

a. O conveys "to A for A's life so long as A does not drink alcohol." (Be careful with this one; review the distinction between reversions and possibilities of reverter discussed above.)

b. O conveys "to A for life, but if A drinks alcohol, O retains the right to reenter and terminate A's estate." Does O hold two future interests? If so, does each signify a different *way* in which possession will or may return to O?

c. O conveys "to A for 2 years, on condition that the property be used for residential purposes only, and if used for other purposes, O retains the right to reenter and terminate A's estate."

d. O transfers "to T for five years." With four years remaining on her lease, T transfers "to X for four years so long as X does not sell alcohol on the premises."

b.   Interests in a Transferee: Nonreversionary Future Interests

If O creates a future interest in a third party, the future interest is either a remainder or an executory interest. Except perhaps in a very few states (see Section B.3 below), nothing in modern law turns on the distinction between those two interests. *See* Jesse Dukeminier, *Contingent Remainders and Executory Interests: A Requiem for the Distinction*, 43 Minn. L. Rev. 13 (1958). To avoid belaboring the obsolete, we treat the distinction between them quickly. You should not be surprised if your instructor simply assigns the following brief discussion, then moves directly to Problem 2-J, where you have the opportunity to apply what we explain below.

A nonreversionary future interest will be created to follow a defeasible fee, a defeasible life estate or terms of years, or a nondefeasible life estate or term of years. A classification rule of thumb accompanies each of these possibilities.

Rule 1: nonreversionary interests following defeasible fees. *A nonreversionary future interest following a defeasible fee simple is always an executory interest, never a remainder.* We saw this already in discussing defeasible fee estates: B's interest following a defeasible fee simple in A is an executory interest whether A's estate is subject to a special limitation (language of duration) or a condition subsequent (language of condition).

Rule 2: nonreversionary interests following defeasible particular estates. A "particular" estate is a life estate or a term of years estate. *If A's particular estate is subject to a special limitation, the nonreversionary future interest taking effect on violation of the restriction is a remainder; if A's particular estate is subject to a condition subsequent, the nonreversionary future interest is an executory interest.* This rule associates remainders with defeasible particular estates that "expire" (those subject to a special limitation, i.e., language of duration); it associates executory interests with defeasible particular estates that are cut off or "divested" (those subject to a condition subsequent).

(Now might be a good time to summarize the concept of "divesting." A power of termination "divests" the present estate in a meaningful sense: the powerholder must rise up and reclaim title. An executory interest following an estate subject to a condition subsequent "divests" the present interest in the formal sense that it takes effect upon the happening of a restriction that is stated in the form of a condition subsequent rather than a special limitation. An executory interest following a present estate that is determinable (subject to a special limitation, i.e., language of duration) does not divest A's interest in either sense: B does not have to reclaim title because title passes to B automatically upon the present holder's breach; and B's interest does not follow an estate that is subject to a condition subsequent. In the fee simple determinable with an executory interest, B's interest is an executory interest simply because the first rule of thumb given above trumps the second one.)

Rule 3: nonreversionary interests following nondefeasible particular estates. If A's particular estate is not subject to early ending, our third rule of construction applies. *B's interest following a nondefeasible particular estate is a remainder if it is capable of becoming possessory immediately upon the ending of A's estate; if B's interest will not become possessory immediately upon the ending of A's estate, it is an executory interest.*

Sometimes B's future interest is certain to become possessory in B or B's successor immediately upon the ending of A's particular estate ("to A for life, then to B"). In other cases, B's interest is subject to a contingency (e.g., "to A for life, then to B if B reaches 21"), which might or might not happen before A's life estate ends. In the latter cases, it is possible, but not certain, that B will be entitled to possession upon A's death. That possibility is enough; B's interest is classified as a remainder in such cases. Finally, in some cases, B's interest is certain *not* to become possessory immediately upon the ending of A's particular estate ("to A for life, then one day after A's death, to B if B is then living"); in these cases, B's interest is an executory interest.

PROBLEM 2-J. Give the state of the title in the following transfers. It will help you to classify the nonreversionary future interests if you first identify whether the present interest held by A is a defeasible fee, a defeasible particular estate, or a nondefeasible particular estate. Once you do that, you can then apply the appropriate rule of thumb discussed above. All transfers are made by O, who owns in fee simple absolute immediately before the transfer.

a. "To A for life, but if B marries C during A's lifetime, immediately to B and her heirs."

b. "To A for life so long as B is not married to C, and upon A's death or B's marriage to C, to B and her heirs."

c. "To A and her heirs so long as A does not operate a tavern on the land, then to B and her heirs."

d. "To A for life, then to B if B graduates from law school."

e. "To A for life, then one day after A's death, to B if B is then living."

c. Distinguishing reversionary and nonreversionary interests

Whether a future interest is reversionary or nonreversionary is important. One major rule in American law — the Rule Against Perpetuities — applies only to nonreversionary interests. Fortunately, whether a future interest is held by the transferor (and thus is reversionary), or created in a transferee (and thus is nonreversionary) is usually obvious. But consider two potentially troublesome situations.

Post-creation transfers. The appropriate focus in classification of future interests is on the time of creation of the interest. Subsequent transfers of a future interest by its holder do not change the initial classification of the interest.

(1) O conveys Blackacre "to A for life." This transfer leaves O with a reversion. Subsequently O conveys all of her interest in Blackacre to B. B holds a reversion. The state of the title is life estate in A, reversion in B in fee simple.

(2) O conveys Blackace "to A for life." O dies during A's lifetime, with a will devising all of her property to B. B holds a reversion in Blackacre, acquired by O's will. The same result would follow if O died intestate, survived by an only heir B. In addition, if O conveyed Blackacre "to A for life, then to B," and B transferred her interest to O during A's lifetime, the state of the title would be life estate in A, remainder in O in fee simple.

Future interests created in a residuary clause. Future interests created by the residuary clause in a will are a potential source of confusion. If O devises Blackacre "to A for life, then to B," B's interest is clearly a remainder. What about the following:

(3) O devises Blackacre "to A for life." The residuary clause of O's will devises the rest of O's property to B. What is B's interest?

You may be tempted in example (3) to reason that O retained a reversion when creating the life estate in A, then transferred that reversion to B through the residuary clause. If so, reconsider. Isn't the will one single dispositive instrument, transferring all interests at once (the moment of O's death)? Compare examples (1) and (2); each of them consisted of *two* transactions: one in which O's interest was created, and another in which O's interest was transferred. If B gets his interest in (3) in one transaction, at the same time as A, isn't example (3) exactly like a transfer "to A for life, then to B"?

2.   Conditions and Classification: Contingent and Vested Future Interests

We have been classifying future interests on the basis of the party in whom the interest is created — transferor or transferee. A second, overlapping, system classifies on the basis of whether the future interest is contingent or vested. An interest is vested or contingent depending on whether the interest is subject to a condition and if it is, on how the condition is stated. To illustrate the new concepts that are at play when we ask whether a future interest is vested or contingent, we will use remainders. The focus on whether the remainder is subject to a condition yields the following sensible order of treatment: a remainder that is subject to a condition precedent is a *contingent remainder*; a remainder subject to a condition subsequent is *vested subject to divestment*; a remainder that is subject to no condition at all is *indefeasibly vested*; and a *vested remainder subject to open* is in some aspects unconditional (like an indefeasibly vested remainder) and in some respects subject to a condition subsequent (like a vested remainder subject to divestment). For ease of reference, we continue with consecutive numbering of examples as our discussion proceeds through future interests.

a.   Condition Precedent: Contingent Remainders

Transferors often impose conditions on the holder of a future interest.

(4) "To A for life, then if B survives A, to B."

(5) "To A for life, then to the heirs of B." B is alive at the effective date of the transfer.

In example (4), O has expressly imposed a condition to B's taking: B must survive A or B will not be entitled to take the property. In (5), what O has provided is tantamount to an express condition: because a living person has no heirs (recall our earlier discussion of intestacy), the takers of the remainder, if any, are undetermined at the time of the transfer. In effect, the remainder, like the one in example (4), is subject to the condition that B produce at least one heir to take the remainder at A's death. (Save whatever questions these and the next few examples suggest to you; Problem 2-K will give you a chance to consider those questions. Here we want to focus only on the existence of a condition to the remainderman's taking of the interest given by the transferor.)

(6) "To A for life, then if B survives A, to B, and if B fails to survive A, to C."

In example (6) B has a contingent remainder; B must survive A to take. C also has a contingent remainder; C's remainder is subject to the condition that B *not* survive A. In examples (4) through (6), something must happen *before* the remainderman is entitled to possession: B must survive to take, or B must fail to survive for C to take, or B must die survived by heirs.

A remainder is contingent (a) if it is subject to a condition precedent or (b) if the remainderman is unascertained at the time of the creation of the remainder, or both. See Thomas F. Bergin & Paul G. Haskell, Preface to Estates in Land and Future Interests 73 (2d ed. 1984). Although, as explained above, the "unascertained person" variant of a contingent remainder also contains a condition precedent, maintaining it as a separate element of the definition provides a useful aid in identifying this common type of contingent remainder — one given to the heirs of a living person.

Reversions following contingent remainders. In example (4), suppose that B failed to survive A. Who would be entitled to possession upon A's death? If O retained a reversion in that example, does it fit within the definition of a reversion that we gave earlier (i.e., an undisposed-of interest)? In example (5), who would be entitled to possession upon A's death if B died before A, with no heirs?

The "technical" reversion. From the standpoint of O's retention of an interest, note how example (6) differs from examples (4) and (5). In example (6), B will take upon A's death if B is alive, and if not, C or C's successor will take. O seems to have left no gap in the disposition to be filled by a reversion. However, in feudal law, it was possible for A's life estate to end by forfeiture before A died, for example, if A made a "tortious foeffment" (a purported transfer to X of a fee simple) or when A committed treason. If A's life estate ended by forfeiture prior to A's death, neither B nor C was entitled to possession: B had neither outlived A nor failed to do so.

The reversion filled the real gap that existed between A's loss of the life estate (by forfeiture) and A's death (which, in the case of treason, might not have been a long wait). In modern law, the possibility of A's loss of the life estate before A's death is negligible. Nevertheless, we still say, in example (6), that O retains a reversion. It is called a "technical" reversion to reflect its insignificant status. Nevertheless, identifying a technical reversion has this very practical consequence: if you develop the habit of identifying a technical reversion whenever O's last stated disposition is a contingent remainder, you will avoid missing a "real" reversion when one exists. From this discussion, we can derive a handy generalization: if the transferor's last stated disposition is a contingent remainder, the transferor retains a reversion (which may be either technical or substantive).

b.   Condition Subsequent: Vested Remainders Subject to Divestment

A remainder is contingent if it is subject to a condition precedent. A remainder that is subject to a condition *subsequent* is not a contingent remainder; it is rather vested subject to divestment — by the happening of the event specified by the condition.

(7) "To A for life, then to B, but if B fails to survive A, to C."

Compare this transfer with example (6) above — "to A for life, then if B survives A, to B, and if B fails to survive A, to C." In both examples, B will be entitled to possession if B survives A; if B fails to survive A, then C will be entitled to possession. In each, something must happen before the remainderman is entitled to possession. But B's interest in (7) is a vested remainder subject to divestment rather than a contingent remainder. There is a condition to B's taking, but it is a condition subsequent, not a condition precedent.

To see why B's remainder is vested subject to divestment, you must focus on *form*. There is a difference in form between examples (6) and (7) — a difference in the way in which the transferor has stated the condition — although you may (justifiably) find the difference subtle. In example (7), the transferor has stated the condition as a condition subsequent rather than a condition precedent. The transfer is not "if B survives A, to B" or even "to B if B survives A." Rather, the gift to B is stated fully ("to B"), and then, following that gift and set off from it by the comma, the condition is tacked on — "but if B fails to survive A," the property is to go to C at A's death.

How do we tell whether a condition is in form either precedent or subsequent? For economy of statement, no one has improved on the answer given by Professor John Chipman Gray, in his classic work The Rule Against Perpetuities § 108 (4th ed. 1942):

> Whether a remainder is vested [subject to divestment] or contingent depends upon the language employed. If the conditional element is incorporated into the description of, or into the gift to, the remainderman, then the remainder is contingent; but if, after words giving a vested interest, a clause is added divesting it, the remainder is vested [subject to divestment].

Using Professor Gray's terms, explain why the remainders in examples (4) through (6) are contingent, and why the remainder in example (7) is vested subject to divestment. In which examples is the condition "incorporated into" either the description of the remainderman or the identification of the gift? In which does the transferor add a divesting condition to an interest that, standing alone, looks vested? In example (7), what is C's interest called? Note that it follows B's *vested* interest in fee simple.

The constructional preference for vested interests. "In general, it can be said that the courts will construe a provision as not imposing a condition precedent if they can do so without contradicting the express language of the instrument, *i.e.*, where there is sufficient ambiguity in the language to permit what might be called an even choice." Lawrence W. Waggoner, Gregory S. Alexander & Mary Louise Fellows, Family Property Law: Cases and Materials on Wills, Trusts, and Future Interests 948 (2d ed. 1997). The following are examples; determine in each one why the language of the transfer presents an "even choice" between a vested and a contingent remainder.

(8) O conveys "to A for life, then to B if he reaches 21; provided, however, that if he die before 21, then the land shall go to C." When A dies, B is under 21.

The question is whether B is entitled to possession immediately upon A's death, subject to losing his interest if he fails to reach 21, or whether B has to reach 21 *before* he is entitled to possession. The classification difficulty arises because the transferor stated the age condition twice, first as a condition precedent then again as a condition subsequent. The example is based on the famous case of Edwards v. Hammond, 83 Eng. Rep. 614 (Common Pleas 1683), which held that B's interest was a vested remainder subject to divestment; B therefore was entitled to possession upon A's death even though B at that time was under 21. (The Edwards v. Hammond rule of construction may apply only to *age* conditions stated twice, or it may apply to any condition stated twice if the vested remainder construction is necessary to prevent a gap in possession between the life estate and the remainder. If the rule applied to all conditions stated twice, it would tend to prevent the creation of alternative contingent remainders.)

(9) O transfers "to T in trust to pay the income to O for life, and on O's death to pay the principal to B." O retains the right to revoke the trust.

B's remainder is classified as vested subject to divestment. The divesting event is O's exercise of the power to revoke the trust. *See, e.g.*, Williams's remainder in the revocable trust at issue in Farkas v. Williams in Chapter 1. *See also* Tennant v. John Tennant Memorial Home, 140 P. 242 (Cal. 1914) (in deed of land to grantee, grantor reserved life estate and power to revoke the deed; held, the reserved power to revoke "did not restrict the effect of the deed as a present conveyance of a future vested interest," but "merely afforded a means whereby such vested future estate could be defeated and divested before it ripened into an estate in possession").

(10) O conveys "to A for life, then to B for life, then to C and her heirs." Having only a life estate, B must survive A in order for that life estate to become possessory, but B's remainder for life is vested (subject to defeasance) rather than

contingent. *See* Lawrence W. Waggoner & Thomas P. Gallanis, Estates and Future Interests in a Nutshell 57 (3d ed. 2005).

PROBLEM 2-K. Give the state of the title in each of the following transfers. All transfers are made by O, who owns in fee simple absolute immediately before the transfer.

a. "To A for life, then to B if B reaches 21." B is 15 at the time of the conveyance. (After classification, you should ask yourself who would be entitled to possession at A's death: if B reached 21 during A's lifetime; if B died before A at age 18; if B was 18 when A died?)

b. "To A for life, then to B's heirs." B is living and has a child Bart, aged 18. (You can think of comparable post-creation events here also.)

c. "To A for life, then to B if B reaches 21, otherwise to C." B is under 21.

d. "To A for life, then to B, but if B dies without reaching 21, to C." In addition to the difference in form, is there a difference in substance between "c" and "d"? What happens in each if B is under 21 when A dies?

c.   Unconditional Remainders: Indefeasibly Vested

A remainder that is subject to a condition precedent is contingent; one subject to a condition subsequent is vested subject to divestment. Now we move on. If the remainder is subject to no condition at all, it is indefeasibly vested.

(11) O transfers Blackacre "to A for life, then to B and her heirs."

Here, B's remainder is not simply vested (in an identified person and subject to no condition precedent); it is indefeasibly vested (subject to no condition at all, precedent or subsequent).

Perhaps you are thinking, wait a minute: in example (11), if B dies before A, *B* will never enjoy the remainder; so isn't B subject to an *implied* condition of survival of A, even though O hasn't stated one expressly? The answer is "no." B's remainder in fee simple has the same characteristics at B's death (inheritability and devisability) that a *present* estate in fee simple in B would have.

No implied condition of survival. When the transferor O does not state a condition of survival, the applicable rule of construction is this: there is no implied condition of survival in remainders (1) to a single individual ("to A for life, then to B"); (2) or in a remainder to several individuals ("to A for life, then to B, C, and D"); or (3) in a remainder to a single generation class ("to A for life, then to A's children"). *See* In re Bomberger's Estate, 32 A.2d 729, 731 (Pa. 1943) ("The condition of survival to a fixed time is never implied. Such a condition must appear plainly, manifestly and indisputably."). In fact, it is only because of the absence of a condition — express or implied — that we can classify a remainder as indefeasibly vested at all. A transferor can always preclude an indefeasibly vested remainder, by imposing a condition of survival on the remainderman; the law could preclude indefeasibly vested remainders by imposing an implied requirement of survival on all future interest holders, but it does not do so.

Why doesn't the law imply a condition of survival in the above examples? Suppose O conveys in trust "to A for life, then to B, C, and D." Assume (realistically) that the life tenant A is O's spouse, and that the remaindermen are their children. Now suppose that child B dies before A, survived by B's own children, and that C and D also survive A. If B were required to survive A, what result? Would B's children (testator's grandchildren) take B's share? Should we assume that the testator intended to cut off his line of descent through B, or should we instead require O to make such an unusual intent explicit? *See* Edward C. Halbach, *Future Interests: Express and Implied Conditions of Survival (Part I)*, 49 Cal. L. Rev. 297, 299-307 (1961).

Vesting in interest and vesting in possession. No vested remainder — whether indefeasibly vested or vested subject to divestment — is vested in possession so long as it remains a future interest; it vests in possession only when it becomes a present possessory estate. An indefeasibly vested remainder is *certain* to vest in possession in the remainderman or her successor in interest. A vested remainder subject to divestment — "to A for life, then to B, but if B fails to reach 21, to C" — is vested in interest (identifiable person, no condition precedent) but it is *not* certain to vest in possession in the remainderman or her successor, because B could die before A and under 21 years of age. The distinction between vesting in interest and vesting in possession is important: real estate practitioners sometimes have to deal with it in litigation (see the *Tennent* case in example (9) above, and Problem 2-L below), and it is fundamental in the analysis of problems arising under the Rule Against Perpetuities (see Section B.4 below).

As an aside, we should say that the above brief excursion into conditions of survivorship illustrates one of the important modern questions about future interests, mentioned in our introduction to Section B, that we think you should know about. In your practice, it will rarely be important for you to classify B's interest as a remainder or an executory interest; it is vital in all cases that you know whether B has to survive A in order to get the benefit of the future interest.

PROBLEMS

2-L. Katie Coleman executed a will in which she gave her daughter Shirleeta a life estate in certain real property. The will further provided that "[u]pon termination of said life estate all the rest and residue of my estate I give as follows: One half in fee simple absolute to my daughter, Ms. Verdonda Coleman. One half divided equally between [my] daughter, Shirleeta Coleman, and my son Melvin Coleman." Katie Coleman died in 1992. Shirleeta died intestate in 1994, unmarried and without any children, leaving her father Leroy Coleman as her sole heir. Verdonda and Melvin Coleman filed a petition against Leroy Coleman, seeking a determination of the ownership of the remainder interest devised to Shirleeta. Who owns the remainder? Was Shirleeta's remainder vested in interest or vested in possession? If a remainder is indefeasibly vested, does it matter that the remainderman is also the life tenant? *See* Coleman v. Coleman, 500 S.E.2d 507 (Va. 1998).

2-M. O conveys "to A for life, then to A's issue." A dies survived by children X and Y, and by grandson S, the son of Z, a predeceased child of A. Z's will leaves all of her estate to her husband H. What result? The meaning of "issue" in a transfer such as this one, and its meaning in the law of intestacy, is the same (O not having provided any other relevant statement of what he means by "issue"); reviewing your study of intestacy, you will probably be able to arrive at the appropriate answer to this problem. How is this transfer different from one "to A for life, then to A's children"?

d.   Vested Remainders Subject to Open: Class Gifts

We now come to the last of our types of remainders. A remainder that is vested subject to open is a remainder created in a class of takers; common examples are remainders to such single-generation classes as children, grandchildren, nieces, nephews. Class gifts are common in estate planning, and they come with a considerable body of lore, most of which can safely be deferred until you take an upperclass course in Trusts and Estates. Here, we say just enough to allow you to compare this vested remainder with others that are vested, and to answer some of the questions we have found to be popular with students.

(12) "To A for life, remainder to A's children." At the time of the transfer, A has a child A-1.

Initially, notice that the remainder in A's children is vested in interest: it is held by an ascertained person (A-1), and it is not subject to any stated or implied condition precedent. But while the remainder is vested, it is something of a hybrid, combining elements of an indefeasibly vested remainder and one that that is vested subject to divestment.

Indefeasibility: death of a class member before distribution. The vested remainder subject to open is like an indefeasibly vested remainder in that the interest of each remainderman is not cut off by that remainderman's death before the life tenant. In example (12), if A-1 died before the life tenant, A-1's interest in the remainder would pass to her heirs or devisees.

Defeasibility: class opening. Although the remainderman's entitlement to a share is indefeasible, the *amount* of the share is subject to divestment (partial reduction) by the birth of additional members of the class. In example (12), if A subsequently has a second child A-2, that child joins the remainder as an equal member, entitled to a one-half share. The effect of A-2's birth is that the existing remainderman A-1 is divested down from her previous whole interest in the remainder to a one-half interest. If A has a third child A-3, that third child will join the class as an equal member, holding a one-third share; in order to accommodate A-3's share, A-1 and A-2 are cut down from their former one-half shares to one-third shares. The process of divestment of the size of a remainderman's share will continue so long as A has children. As the class grows ("opens") each existing class member's share shrinks.

Because the share of each remainderman in a class gift is subject to reduction by the birth of additional members of the class, a vested remainder subject to open is sometimes called a *vested remainder subject to partial divestment*. The interest of any unborn member of the class is an executory interest. (The classification of the unborn class member's interest will be important for Rule Against Perpetuities purposes, as we will see shortly.)

Class closing. If the class of remaindermen consists of the children of the life tenant A, all members of the class will be determined no later than A's death: the physiological closing of the class (A's death) coincides with the date of distribution of the remainder. But if the class consists of the children of some living person other than the life tenant, additional class members could be conceived and born after the life tenant dies. For example:

(13) "To A for life, then to the children of B." At the effective date of the transfer, B is alive and has children B-1 and B-2.

In (13), it is possible that B might survive A, and produce children after A's death. If that were to happen, what distribution should we make to B-1 and B-2 at A's death? Do we distribute one-half of the remainder to each of them, subject to recall of a portion if B later produces an additional child or children? (To make that work, we would probably also have to require that B-1 and B-2 post security — a bond — to guarantee a fund for any such repayment.) Do we hold back something, giving B-1 and B-2 less than a one-half share each at A's death (and if so, how much do we hold back)? Or do we distribute nothing at A's death, and wait until B's death to determine the fractional shares of the remainder (which seems to violate the transferor's indication that B's children are to take immediately upon the ending of the life estate)?

The law answers these questions by the *rule of convenience*. A class that is not physiologically closed at the life tenant's death nevertheless closes at the life tenant's death if one or more takers is available at that time. In example (13), if B-1 and B-2 are living at A's death, the class closes, B-1 and B-2 each get a one-half share of the remainder, and any child of B conceived after A's death is excluded. If either B-1 or B-2 died *before* A, that child's share would pass to his successors in interest (heirs or devisees). If there is no class taker (or successor to a taker) alive at the life tenant's death, *then* the class stays open until it closes physiologically by the death of the progenitor of the class, here B.

PROBLEM 2-N. O conveys "to A for life, then to the children of B." What is the state of the title if B has no children when the transfer takes effect? If B has a child C during A's lifetime? If B has another child, D, during A's lifetime? Suppose child C dies during A's lifetime, survived by a child C-1; then A dies, survived by C-1, D, and B. What distribution is made? If B has no children during A's lifetime, what happens if B survives A? If B dies before A?

An interesting and revealing case. The following case gives us an opportunity to try out the classifications of remainders that we have just studied. It also (which is the main reason it is included) allows us to go further and ask whether classification of the interest was necessary to the outcome of the case. Classification is *necessary* when some issue turns on the classification of the interest; otherwise, classification is a matter of good form (not to be underestimated at all, but still a different matter).

CANOY v. CANOY
520 S.E.2d 128 (N.C. Ct. App. 1999)

HUNTER, JUDGE.

Roger Terry Canoy ("plaintiff") instituted this declaratory judgment action on 14 March 1996 wherein he requested that the court construe the last will and testament of his mother Myrtle G. Canoy ("testatrix") and declare his interest in certain real property devised to him. Item IV of the testatrix's will provides, in pertinent part:

> Subject to the life estate of Glenn Canoy in Item III preceding, I will and devise all of my farm consisting of all of my real estate in Randolph County to my son, Roger Canoy, for the term of his natural life, and at his death, in ten (10) equal shares to my ten children, and for any that are deceased, to their issue, if any.

The trial court found that each of the testatrix's ten children survived her. The trial court's conclusions relevant to this appeal were that "the class of remaindermen to take pursuant to Item IV of the will consists of the brothers and sisters of plaintiff who survive upon the death of plaintiff or the issue of any deceased brother or sister of plaintiff." While the court stated that only those siblings who survived the plaintiff would take a remainder share, the court did not declare the remainder to be "contingent" or "vested." However, the parties, in their briefs, have addressed the order as if the court found the remainder to be contingent.

Plaintiff and defendant guardian ad litem for the unborn heirs of testatrix contend that the trial court erred in determining that the remainder devised to testatrix's ten children was "contingent" upon their survival of plaintiff. These parties argue that the remainder was "vested" at the death of the testatrix and therefore each child did not have to survive plaintiff in order to inherit his or her one-tenth share of the subject property. We disagree with this contention.

There are three types of vested remainders: indefeasibly vested remainders, remainders vested subject to partial defeasance (subject to open) and remainders subject to complete defeasance (subject to a condition subsequent). A remainder interest is not vested, but is contingent, when it is "*either* subject to a condition precedent (in addition to the natural expiration of prior estates), *or* owned by unascertainable persons, *or both*." Thomas F. Bergin & Paul G. Haskell, Preface to Estates in Land and Future Interests 73 (2d ed. 1984). Therefore, a person who holds a contingent remainder has no immediate fixed right of future enjoyment because whether or not his remainder will vest, or what portion he is to take, is unknown at the time of the devise.

The testatrix in the present case devised the subject property at plaintiff's death, "in ten (10) equal shares to my ten children, and for any that are deceased, to their issue." While she did not specifically name each child in the devise in question, the devise indicates that she is referring to ten individuals, rather than a class, who will each take a one-tenth share of the property if they are alive at the death of the plaintiff life tenant. If the testatrix had not intended the devise to be to specific individuals who would inherit their share only upon surviving the plaintiff, testatrix would not have divided the remainder into shares and included the alternate devise to each child's issue in case the subject child did not survive plaintiff. [I]f a child is deceased at the death of plaintiff life tenant, the testatrix devises the child's share to his or her issue. This clearly indicates that a child takes no estate unless he or she lives past the death of plaintiff life tenant. Thus, a child's survival is a condition precedent to the vesting of the remainder. It is clear that the testatrix intended a condition of survival in the present case. Therefore, each child's remainder is contingent.

Assuming arguendo that each child's remainder is vested at the time of the devise, we note that if a vested remainder is subject to a condition subsequent and that condition is not met, the remainder becomes completely defeated. The devise in question clearly implies that a condition subsequent to vesting must be met in order for each child to come into possession of his or her share — he or she must survive the life tenant. Accordingly, the remainder here [if it is vested] is a vested remainder subject to complete defeasance instead of an indefeasibly vested remainder. The result under such scenario is that a remainderman would actually take possession of his or her one-tenth share only if he or she met the condition of surviving the plaintiff.

We note that the testatrix provided a remainderman share for plaintiff, even though she certainly knew that plaintiff could not survive his own death. While this devise appears confusing upon first glance, it reveals a specific plan that plaintiff's issue, if any, would take just as the issue of any of the other nine children who predeceased plaintiff. It does not indicate that the testatrix intended the plaintiff's remainder to be indefeasibly vested. The devise illustrates that it was the intent of the testatrix that upon the death of her youngest child, the property was to pass to her surviving children and the issue of predeceased children. Because plaintiff was the youngest child and a life estate preceded plaintiff's life estate, the testatrix must have known at the time the will was made that it was very possible that none of her children would survive plaintiff. The testatrix, in making this particular devise, formulated a plan for ensuring that the subject property remain within her family after the death of her youngest child while being divided equally into one-tenth shares, one for each child, or alternatively, the child's issue. Additionally, a review of the entire document reveals that in numerous instances, the testatrix made devises to her children, but provided that if they were deceased, the property was to pass to their issue. Because the testatrix included the identical provision in her will numerous times, it is unlikely that she did not intend for each child's remainder to be contingent on his or her survival of plaintiff. Nothing in the will before us indicates a contrary intent, and to hold otherwise would go against the cardinal rule of will construction that "[t]he paramount aim in the interpretation of a will is to ascertain if possible the intent of the testator." Entwistle v. Covington, 108 S.E.2d 603, 606 (N.C. 1959).] Therefore, the order of the trial court is

Affirmed.

NOTES AND QUESTIONS

1. **Classification.** The court indicates that the remainder to Myrtle's children was not a class gift because Myrtle divided the remainder into ten fixed shares, one for each of her children, each share worth one-tenth of the value of the property given. Could the remainder have been classified as indefeasibly vested (recall that each child had to survive the life tenant to take his or her share)? If the remainder was subject to a condition, was it a contingent remainder or a vested remainder subject to divestment? Would Gray's rule or the constructional preference for vested interests have applied?

2. **Conditions precedent and subsequent.** "It is clear that the testatrix intended a condition of survival in the present case. Therefore, each child's remainder is contingent." Canoy v. Canoy. The first sentence is correct; the second sentence is not. Why? Can a vested remainderman be subject to a condition of surviving the life tenant? See example (7) above (as to B's interest). Can a contingent remainderman be free of such a condition? See example (6) (as to C's interest).

3. **Consequences.** Although initially expressing its preference for the contingent remainder construction, the court notes that the case comes out the same way if the remainder is vested subject to divestment. If so, classification is not relevant to the outcome of the case. What is the relevant question in the case, and what is the answer to it?

4. **Testator's intent.** Roger Canoy was testator's *youngest* child. Does that suggest why testator gave him a life estate and also created a share of the remainder for his issue, if any?

5. **Reversion?** What would happen to the share of any remainderman who died without issue surviving the life tenant? Does it matter whether the gift of the farm was in the residuary clause or not?

6. **The "classificatory mystique."** Canoy v. Canoy illustrates what Professor Lawrence Waggoner has called the *classificatory mystique*, which is "the notion indulged by some courts that classifying the interests solves what is in fact a straightforward problem of construing the meaning of the dispositive language [of a deed or will]." Lawrence W. Waggoner, Gregory S. Alexander, Mary Louise Fellows & Thomas P. Gallanis, Family Property Law: Cases and Materials on Wills, Trusts, and Future Interests (4th ed. 2006). *See also* Lawrence W. Waggoner, *Reformulating the Structure of Estates: A Proposal for Legislative Action*, 85 Harv. L. Rev. 729, 732 (1972). In connection with *Canoy*, perhaps it would be more accurate to say that the case illustrates that *lawyers* easily fall victim to the classificatory mystique and then urge classifications on the court unnecessarily; note in *Canoy* that the trial court didn't classify the remainder, and that the appellate court did so at the urging of counsel.

PROBLEM 2-O. In the following situations, the testator, as in *Canoy*, creates an express condition of survival. Focus carefully on the language of each disposition; what is the relevant question in each case?

a. O devises "to A for life, and upon A's death, to my [O's] then surviving children." At O's death, O has children B and C. B dies before A, leaving successors in interest. Who is entitled to the property upon A's death? Suppose the devise had been "to A for life, remainder to my [O's] surviving children." B dies before A, leaving successors in interest. Who is entitled to the property on A's death?

b. O devises "to W for life, remainder to my daughter A, but if A should die without issue, then to my sons X and Y." A dies before W *with* issue, and a will leaving all of her property to her husband H. Who is entitled to the remainder at A's death? *See* In re Krooss, 99 N.E.2d 222 (N.Y. 1951) (divesting conditions are construed strictly). Do you see any parallel between A's interest in this Problem and A's interest in Problem 2.D(e), dealing with New York's statutory treatment of the fee tail?

ADDITIONAL NOTES ON FUTURE INTERESTS

1. **Other vested and contingent future interests.** We have used remainders to consider the impact of conditions on the classification of future interests. As it turns out, that was a good choice because only remainders are classified with the terminology we identified in discussing vested and contingent remainders. Stated more broadly, the point is that, in classifying future interests, we have only eight labels to work with. If a future interest is held by or created in a transferor, it will be (1) a reversion, (2) a possibility of reverter, or (3) a power of termination; if the future interest is created in a transferee, it will be (4) a contingent remainder, (5) a vested remainder subject to divestment, (6) an indefeasibly vested remainder, (7) a vested remainder subject to open, or (8) an executory interest. There is, for example, no such formally classifiable interest as a "contingent executory interest" or an "executory interest subject to open."

Nevertheless, future interests other than remainders may be vested or contingent in substance. In a transfer "to A for life, then to B if B survives A," the reversion held by O is subject to the condition of B's survival of A: if B fails to survive A, O will own Blackacre upon A's death; if B survives A, B will own Blackacre and O's interest will be cut off. O's interest is classified simply as a reversion; substantively, however, O's reversion is vested subject to divestment, by B's survival of A. (Reversions are deemed vested, which is why O's reversion is not contingent.) Similarly, in a transfer "to A for life, then one day after A's death, to the children of A," the children of A have an executory interest, and it is subject to open, although we simply identify it as an executory interest rather than an "executory interest subject to open." Being versed in the concepts of vestedness and contingency, and how those concepts may determine consequences in particular cases, is important. See Section 2.B.3 below on the consequences of classification.

2. **Multiple classifications.** O conveys "to A for life, then to A's children, but if no child of A survives A, then to B." At the effective date, A has one child, A-1. The remainder in A-1 is vested subject to open (partial divestment), and also vested subject to complete divestment. What is the divesting event?

3. **Merger.** In this chapter, we have spent quite a bit of time on the deconstruction, so to speak, of the fee simple absolute estate, and on the labeling of the various component parts — present and future interests — into which it can be split. You may be happy to learn that a fee simple estate, once fragmented into present and future interests, can thereafter be reconstituted, through the doctrine

of merger. "Merger is the absorption of a lesser estate by a greater estate, and takes place when two distinct estates of greater and lesser rank meet in the same person or class of persons at the same time without any intermediate estate." Elmore v. Austin, 59 S.E.2d 205, 213 (N.C. 1950); Lewis M. Simes, Handbook of the Law of Future Interests 35 (2d ed. 1966) ("two consecutive, vested, legal estates").

(21) O conveys Blackacre "to A for life." Subsequently, O releases her reversion to A.

The same person (A) now holds the life estate and the reversion in fee simple; the two estates merge (the shorter life estate is swallowed up into the reversion in fee); A now owns Blackacre in fee simple absolute. The same result would follow if A conveyed the life estate to O, or if both A and O conveyed their interests to X.

(22) O conveys Blackacre "to A for life, then to B for life, then to C and his heirs." C transfers his remainder to A while B is alive; does merger occur? Suppose that after the transfer, B dies. Does merger occur then?

3.   Consequences: Why Classification Matters (or Mattered)

Proper classification brings whatever satisfaction comes from putting something where it belongs. But in the history of the common law, classification had momentous consequences: it determined the outcome of several important questions. We list below six common law rules whose applicability depended on classification of a future interest as either reversionary or nonreversionary; or as a remainder or an executory interest; or as a vested or contingent interest. (Some of the rules required the use of more than one of the classification pairings.)

Of the six rules, the *Rule Against Perpetuities* remains of major, albeit not unquestioned, influence in modern law. *Acceleration* is an issue that you will probably encounter in an estate planning practice, and perhaps also in a real estate practice. The others — *destructibility of contingent remainders*, the *rule in Shelley's Case;* the *doctrine of worthier title*, and *inalienability of contingent interests* — exist in only a handful of states; they are unlikely to trouble you after admission to the bar, and thus deserve only brief textual treatment. The abolition of any of these doctrines may be prospective only, and a pre-abolition transfer requiring classification might still come before the courts. But with the passage of time — recall the title-clearing function of adverse possession, particularly in its color of title version — we consider this an increasingly negligible possibility. *See, e.g.*, Estate of Hendrickson, 736 A.2d 540 (N.J. Super. Ct. Ch. Div. 1999) (court considered the application of *Shelley* to a pre-abolition devise, but construed the will to avoid application of the rule).

Our approach to destructibility, *Shelley*, worthier title, and inalienability is to state the substance and rationale of each rule, and to give a simple example of each — that is, to indicate what, at a minimum, you should know as a literate property lawyer, and what you might appropriately be asked to divulge on a final examination. Then, on the basis of the latest empirical study, we identify the few states in which the rule or doctrine might still exist. With that, we leave it to your instructor, or to you, to pursue any desired additional issues or details appropriate to the local law at your place of study or practice. Two valuable resources on such additional details are Lawrence W. Waggoner & Thomas P. Gallanis, Estates and Future Interests in a Nutshell (3d ed. 2005) and Thomas F. Bergin & Paul G. Haskell, Preface to Estates in Land and Future Interests (2d ed. 1984).

1. **The Rule Against Perpetuities.** The Rule applies only to contingent nonreversionary interests, including the executory interest of unborn members of a class of remaindermen holding a vested remainder subject to open. It remains of major significance today, and we break it out for detailed treatment in Section B.4.

2. **Acceleration into possession.** In example (8), we saw that at common law, a vested remainder subject to divestment, unlike a contingent remainder, accelerated into possession (subject to later divestment), if the life tenant died before the vested remainderman. A vested remainder subject to divestment also accelerated into possession if the life tenant disclaimed (refused to accept) the life estate. *See* Restatement (First) of Property § 233 (when a prior interest is disclaimed, "a succeeding interest is not accelerated so long as a condition precedent to such succeeding interest continues unfulfilled"). Disclaimers are usually motivated by tax considerations, and the topic is considered in advanced courses in estate planning. The point here is that common law doctrine tied acceleration to classification of the remainder as vested or contingent. Modern courts do not: the "vested" form of a remainder is not regarded as a conclusive indication that the transferor intended acceleration; instead, a court may deny acceleration of a vested remainder if it finds evidence of the donor's contrary intent in the language and circumstances of the transfer. *See, e.g.,* Linkous v. Candler, 508 S.E.2d 657 (Ga. 1998) (acceleration denied; "the indication of the testator's contrary intent need not be express, but may be implied from the provisions and language of the trust").

3. **Destructibility of contingent remainders.** This rule provides that *a legal contingent remainder in land that does not vest by the time the preceding life estate ends is destroyed.* A "legal" contingent remainder is one that is not created in a trust.

a. O transfers Blackacre "to A for life, then to B if B reaches 21." Thereafter, A dies when B is 17. B's remainder is destroyed, and O or O's successor takes via the reversion. B's remainder would also be destroyed, *before* A's death, by merger, if the life estate and the reversion became united in the same holder. Destructibility is a rule of law, not of construction (meaning that it applies even if O states an intent that it not apply).

b. The rule was probably motivated by the feudal requirement that there be no gaps in "seisin" (possession under a freehold estate), on which liability for feudal taxes depended. The holder of a remainder dependent on an unresolved contingency at the life tenant's death could not take possession at that time; destructibility passed the possession on to the next ready freeholder (the remainderman or reversioner), killing off the contingent remainder while preserving the integrity of the fisc.

c. Being easily avoided by adroit drafting, the rule serves its policy goals poorly. Why doesn't destructibility apply in the following transfers: "to A for life, then to

B, but if B fails to reach 21, the property is to return to the grantor," or "to A for life, then one day after A's death, to B if B is then living"?

d. The rule of destructibility of contingent remainders is widely abolished in modern law by judicial decision or statute. *See, e.g.,* Abo Petroleum Corp. v. Amstutz, 600 P.2d 278 (N.M. 1979) ("a relic of the feudal past, which has no justification or support in modern society"); 765 Ill. Comp. Stat. § 340/1 ("No future interest shall fail or be defeated by the determination [termination] of any precedent estate or interest prior to the happening of the event or contingency on which the future interest is limited."). Abolition of the rule means that the future interest holder who satisfies the contingency imposed on the interest is entitled to possession even if the contingency is satisfied after the ending of the life estate; in the interim, the reversioner holds a defeasible fee simple.

e. On the current viability of the rule of destructibity, see T.P. Gallanis, *The Future of Future Interests*, 60 Wash. & Lee L. Rev. 513, 530-532 (2003) (destructibility rule "seems to thrive in its traditional form only in Florida"; it exists in modified form in Mississippi, Missouri, and New Mexico, and is supported by old precedents of doubtful validity in New Hampshire, Pennsylvania, and New Jersey).

4. **The rule in Shelley's Case.** The rule in Shelley's Case provides that *a remainder in land to the heirs or bodily heirs of the life tenant is void; it is replaced by a remainder in the life tenant.*

a. O transfers "to A for life, then to A's heirs." *Shelley* converts the contingent remainder in A's heirs into an indefeasibly vested remainder in A in fee simple. The doctrine of merger then produces a fee simple absolute in A. The rule in Shelley's Case is a rule of law, not of construction. Merger is a separate doctrine, subject to its own rules; see examples (21) and (22) above.

b. Avoidance of the feudal equivalent of inheritance taxes is a plausible explanation for the rule. *See* John V. Orth, *Requiem for the Rule in Shelley's Case,* 67 N.C. L. Rev. 681 (1989) ("it closed a tax loophole"). Without the rule, A's heirs in the example given above would take an interest in Blackacre from the original grantor by purchase (via the contingent remainder), not from A by inheritance. With the rule, A's heirs will take, if they take at all, by inheritance (a taxable event) when A dies possessed of the fee simple created by the application of the rule and merger doctrine.

c. In states abolishing the rule — the great majority — a transfer takes effect exactly as the transferor states it: as a life estate, a contingent remainder in the life tenant's heirs, and a reversion in the grantor.

d. *See* T.P. Gallanis, *supra,* at 534-542 (2003) (*Shelley* is abolished by statute or decision in 43 states; it is partially abolished in Indiana (as to trusts, but not wills), New Hampshire (as to wills, but not inter vivos trusts), and Oregon (wills but not inter vivos trusts); the rule applies without limitation in Colorado, Utah, Arkansas and Delaware, "thriving" in the last two named states). *See also* William A. Reppy, Jr., *Judicial Overkill in Applying the Rule in Shelley's Case,* 73 Notre Dame L. Rev. 83 (1997).

5. **The doctrine of worthier title.** This doctrine provides that *a remainder conveyed to the grantor's heirs is void; it is replaced with a reversion in the grantor.* The doctrine applies to remainders created in deeds (the so-called inter vivos branch of the doctrine), not wills (the testamentary branch, which is obsolete).

a. O conveys "to A for life, then to the heirs of the grantor." The doctrine of worthier title replaces the contingent remainder in O's heirs with a reversion in O, in effect rewriting the conveyance to mean "to A for life." If O's heirs take the property, they will do so at O's death, by inheritance, rather than as purchasers under the terms of O's conveyance. The feudal courts regarded title by inheritance as worthier than title by purchase. (In light of the preceding notes on destructibility and *Shelley*, can you surmise why?)

b. In an influential case, Justice Cardozo treated the doctrine of worthier title as a rule of construction rather than of law, in effect giving it the status of a rebuttable presumption. *See* Doctor v. Hughes, 122 N.E. 221 (N.Y. 1919). Treating worthier title as a rule of construction requires the informed grantor to say the same thing twice ("To A for life, then to O's heirs, and I intend by this transfer to create a remainder in my heirs"). It also subjects all but the most expertly-drafted conveyances to litigation. *See* Hatch v. Riggs National Bank, 361 F.2d 559 (D.C. Cir. 1966) ("recognition of the doctrine as a rule of construction is pernicious"). New York finally abolished the doctrine of worthier title by statute, as have many other states. *See* Restatement Second of Property (Donative Transfers) § 30.2 (1988) (listing the states abolishing the doctrine); Uniform Probate Code § 2-710 (1990) (doctrine abolished as rule of law and rule of construction).

c. *See* T.P. Gallanis, *supra*, at 543-548 (2003) (listing Washington, Mississippi, New Jersey, and Virginia as states in which the doctrine remains alive as a rule of construction, and Iowa, in which it is supported by dicta from the state supreme court). Where the doctrine exists as a rule of construction, its scope is expanded: it applies to remainders and executory interests, both legal and equitable, and both in land and personal property. *See* Lawrence W. Waggoner & Thomas P. Gallanis, Estates and Future Interests in a Nutshell 172 n. 7 (3d ed. 2005).

6. **Alienability.** "Alienability" has a technical meaning: it refers to an inter vivos transfer.

a. The common law originally ruled against the alienability of all contingent future interests. Vested interests, including those subject to divestment, were (are) freely transferable. Classification of the future interest as vested or contingent therefore determined its alienability. The trend in modern law is toward the recognition of free transferability of contingent interests, thus putting those interests on a par with vested interests. *See* T.P. Gallanis, *supra*, at 515-519 (inalienability rule rejected in forty states; it is still followed in Arkansas, Colorado, Illinois, Maryland, New Jersey, South Carolina, Tennessee, Virginia, and Maine; Alaska has no precedent or statute on the question). Even when the common law rule of inalienability of a contingent interest is followed, it is subject to exceptions for the *release* of the interest to the holder of the present interest and to assignments of the interest for adequate consideration.

b. Whether a future interest is devisable or inheritable at the holder's death does *not* depend on classification of the future interest as vested or contingent. Transmissibility of a future interest at the holder's death depends on whether the interest is subject to a condition of survival (usually to the point of distribution at the life tenant's death), not on whether the survival requirements is stated as a condition precedent or subsequent. (Recall Canoy v. Canoy.) If O transfers "to A for life, then to B if B survives A, and if not, to C," what result if B dies before A? If C dies before A? Answer those same questions if the transfer is "to A for life, then to B, but if B fails to survive A, to C." *See* Restatement of Property §§ 164 (1936) (any future interest "which is not so restricted in duration that it ceases on [the holder's] death" is inheritable), 164 (same as to devisability of the interest).

4.   The Rule Against Perpetuities

The Rule Against Perpetuities overshadows all of the other common law rules affecting the creation or the classification of nonreversionary future interests. Either in its common law form or with modifications, the Rule Against Perpetuities exists today in all but a handful of states, and must be anticipated by the adroit drafter of documents. The Rule has survived for more than 300 years as the chief means of preventing the dead hand of past generations from controlling the disposition of property too far into the future, and of keeping property marketable. You may encounter the Rule again in an upperclass course in trusts and estates; or you may not. Its importance requires that we give it a relatively good look at this stage in your study of the law of property.

As always, we begin with basics and move forward. The case of City of Klamath Falls v. Bell offers a simple illustration of a violation of the Rule in the familiar context of an executory interest following a defeasible fee simple in land. Problem 2-S after *Klamath Falls* allows you to consider the application of the Rule to typical dispositions creating future interests in a trust of personal property; that application of the Rule is of central concern to estate planners. Finally, the case of Ferrero Construction Co. v. Dennis Rourke Corp., returns us to the impact of the rule on land transfers outside of trust; the case deals with the applicability of the Rule to an option to buy land, a common device in modern commercial real estate transactions.

If, during or after our study, you wish to do some outside reading, you can do no better than to start with a classic in the field, W. Barton Leach, *Perpetuities in a Nutshell*, 51 Harv. L. Rev. 638 (1938), and then, time or inclination permitting, go on to a trove of articles by the late Professor Jesse Dukeminier. *See* Jesse Dukeminier, *A Modern Guide to Perpetuities*, 74 Calif. L. Rev. 1867 (1986); Jesse Dukeminier, *Perpetuities: The Measuring Lives*, 85 Colum. L. Rev. 1648 (1985); Jesse Dukeminier, *Perpetuities: The New Empire*, 77 Yale L.J. 159 (1967).

a.   Introduction to the Rule

Be forewarned that what we say here by way of "introduction" will not make nearly as much sense to you now as it will when you apply our remarks to concrete cases. You thus will probably want to refer to the following brief comments periodically as we work through the Rule.

We begin with Gray's classic statement of the Rule provided in the *Klamath Falls* case, reprinted below: "No interest is good unless it must vest, if at all, not later than twenty-one years after some life in being at the creation of the interest."

1. **"No interest" — applicability of the Rule.** The Rule applies only to nonreversionary future interests: contingent remainders, executory interests (which are usually contingent), and vested remainders subject to open (in which the interest in unborn members of the class is a divesting executory interest). The Rule does not apply to reversionary interests, a result sometimes sought to be justified on the ground that "reversions, possibilities of reverter and powers of termination are inherently vested in nature." Mountain Brow Lodge No. 82 v. Toscano, 64 Cal. Rptr. 816, 818 n. 3 (Cal. Dist. Ct. App. 1968).

2. **"Unless it must vest, *if at all*" — the Rule question.** The Rule doesn't require vesting. A contingent future interest might vest or it might fail to vest. The Rule is indifferent on that question. What the Rule requires is that the question *whether* the interest will vest or fail be resolved within the perpetuities period. Example: "To A for life, then to B if B reaches 21." If B reaches 21, his interest vests; but if B dies before reaching 21, his interest will fail. Although *B* cares whether his interest vests or not, the Rule doesn't care; it wants to know whether we will get the answer to the question of vesting or failing to vest within the perpetuities period. In the example, we will; it is impossible for B's interest to vest or fail any later than B's lifetime.

3. **"Unless it *must* vest, if at all" — certainty is required.** The only acceptable answer to the question posed by the Rule — will the future interest vest or fail within the perpetuities period? — is certainty of vesting or failing to vest. If the future interest will necessarily vest or fail within the perpetuities period, it is valid. If there is any scenario — however improbable — under which the question of vesting might not be resolved within the perpetuities period, the interest is invalid. In the above example ("to B if B reaches 21"), is there any possible way in which the question — whether B reaches 21 or not — can be resolved any later than B's death? If not, B qualifies as a validating life for the validity of his interest.

4. **Certainty when?** The time for asking the question about the certainty of vesting or failing to vest is the date of creation of the future interest. The future interest will either be created in a deed or a will. A deed becomes effective upon execution (signing and delivery), a will upon the testator's death. Under the Rule, you position yourself at the date of creation of the future interest and ask: is it certain, right now, that the future interest will necessarily vest or fail to vest no later than the end of the perpetuities period? If so, the interest is valid; if not, it is invalid, even if the interest were to vest in fact one year after its creation.

5. **The perpetuities period: some life in being, plus 21.** The perpetuities period is the lifetime of some person in being when the future interest is created, plus twenty-one years after that person's death. (The Rule allows a transferor to provide for those persons known to the transferor and for the minority of any person thereafter.) This is surely the most difficult part of the Rule to comprehend, and you should expect to gain confidence with it only as you work through a number of examples. What we are looking for is a validating life; someone about whom we can say this: the contingency affecting the future interest will be resolved

one way or the other no later than 21 years after that person's death. We only need to identify one person as a validating life. If one person works as a validating life and another person doesn't, the interest is valid. The one person we have identified makes it impossible for the future interest to vest or fail outside of "*some* life in being" (as opposed to "all lives in being"). The measuring life, if there is one, will be someone who can affect the vesting of the future interest being evaluated under the Rule. Often, this will be someone named in the transfer or implied by the terms of the transfer (e.g., in a gift "to A for life, remainder to A's grandchildren," A's children, although not named as takers, are relevant candidates to serve as a validating life because those children will be the parents of any takers of the remainder).

6. **"No interest is good" — consequence of a Rule violation.** If a future interest violates the Rule, it is void from the outset, and treated as though it had not been written. The rest of the transfer takes effect as stated. If, for example, the contingent remainder following a life estate is invalid, the effective part of the transfer is the life estate, and the transferor retains a reversion in the property subject to the life estate.

The following case presents an easily-understood Rule violation.

CITY OF KLAMATH FALLS v. BELL
490 P.2d 515 (Or. Ct. App. 1971)

SCHWAB, CHIEF JUDGE.

In 1925, a corporation conveyed certain land to the city of Klamath Falls as a gift for use as the site for a city library. The deed provided, among other things, that the city should hold the land "so long as" it complied with that condition with regard to its use.

In 1969, the city terminated the use of the land for a library, and the question presented by this appeal is, "Does the title to the land remain in the city or did the termination of use as a library cause title to pass to the descendants of the shareholders of the donor-corporation (now dissolved)?"

The issue was presented to the trial court in the form of an agreed narrative statement: the donor-corporation was known as the Daggett-Schallock Investment Company; the corporate deed provided that if at any time the city ceased to use the land for library purposes, title to the land should pass to Fred Schallock and Floy R. Daggett, their heirs and assigns; on September 19, 1927, the corporation was voluntarily dissolved, all creditors paid, and all assets (which we interpret as including the rights of the corporation, if any, in the land in question) were distributed in accordance with law to the sole shareholders Schallock and Daggett.

The city of Klamath Falls built a library on the land in 1929 in compliance with the conditions set out in the deed. The library continued in use from that date until July 1, 1969, when the books were moved to the County Library Building. Since that time, the city library services have been provided by Klamath County on a contract basis. The City Library building has not been used for any other purpose and now stands vacant.

After the library closure, the city of Klamath Falls filed a complaint against all the heirs of Schallock and Daggett for declaratory judgment, asking the court to adjudicate the respective rights of the parties under the deed. The city joined Constance F. Bell, the sole heir of Fred Schallock, and Marijane Flitcraft and Caroline Crapo, the sole heirs of Floy R. Daggett, along with George C. Flitcraft, the husband of Marijane Flitcraft, and Paul Crapo, the husband of Caroline Crapo, as all the necessary parties to the suit.

The defendants Constance F. Bell, Caroline Crapo, and Paul Crapo conveyed their interests in the real property to the defendant Marijane Flitcraft in May and June 1970.

The trial court found that title to the real property was vested in the city of Klamath Falls. Its decision was based on a finding that the gift over to Fred Schallock and Floy R. Daggett was void under the rule against perpetuities.

The deed, in pertinent part, is as follows:

> KNOW ALL MEN BY THESE PRESENTS That Daggett-Schallock Investment Company a corporation organized and existing under the laws of the State of Oregon, for and as a gift and without any consideration, does hereby give, grant and convey unto the City of Klamath Falls, Oregon, so long as it complies with the conditions hereinafter set forth, and thereafter unto Fred Schallock and Floy R. Daggett, their heirs and assigns, the following described parcel of real estate, in Klamath County Oregon, to-wit:

> To have and to hold the same unto the said City of Klamath Falls, Oregon (and to any other municipal corporation which may lawfully succeed it) so long as it complies with the conditions above set forth, and thereafter unto Fred Schallock and Floy R. Daggett, their heirs and assigns forever.

I

We conclude that the estate that passed to the city under this deed was a fee simple determinable. The "magic" words "so long as" have generally been held to create such an estate. Simes and Smith, The Law of Future Interests § 287 at 345 (2d ed. 1956), states:

> The words of duration "so long as" will almost certainly be judicially recognized as the distinctive insignia of such an estate, and, if coupled with a provision which clearly calls for an automatic termination of the estate granted, there is little room for construction.

One of the features of the fee simple determinable thus created is that it terminates automatically upon breach of condition [the court uses "condition" here generically, meaning "restriction"].[2]

---

[2] There would be a different result if the interests of the city of Klamath Falls were characterized as

II

Upon breach of the condition, the deed provided for a gift over to Fred Schallock and Floy R. Daggett or their heirs and assigns. This gift over was an attempt to grant an executory interest since only an executory interest can follow an earlier grant in fee simple.

The rule against perpetuities applies to executory interests. Gray's classic statement of the rule is as follows:

NO INTEREST IS GOOD UNLESS IT MUST VEST, IF AT ALL, NOT LATER THAN TWENTY-ONE YEARS AFTER SOME LIFE IN BEING AT THE CREATION OF THE INTEREST.

Gray, The Rule Against Perpetuities § 201, at 191 (4th ed. 1942).

One of the main characteristics of a defeasible fee simple estate is that the first grantee might continue in possession in perpetuity. The city of Klamath Falls could have maintained a library on the site for an indefinite time in the future, or even forever. Therefore, the trial judge correctly found that the gift over to Fred Schallock and Floy R. Daggett, their heirs and assigns, was void ab initio under the rule against perpetuities.

III

The trial court's conclusion does not, however, dispose of the case at bar. Just because the gift over is invalid, it does not follow that the city of Klamath Falls now has an absolute interest in the property in question. There remains the question of whether under the deed a possibility of reverter remained in the grantor corporation.

When a deed reveals an unquestionable intent to limit the interest of the first grantee (here the city of Klamath Falls) to a fee simple on a special limitation, the courts of the United States do not create an indefeasible estate in the first grantee when a subsequent executory interest (here that of Schallock and Daggett) is void under the rule against perpetuities. Instead, the grantor (here the corporation) retains an interest known as a possibility of reverter.[3] The general rule has been stated to be [as follows]: "[W]hen an executory interest, following a fee simple interest in land is void under the rule against perpetuities, the prior interest becomes absolute unless the language of the creating instrument makes it very clear that the prior interest is to terminate whether the executory interest takes effect or not." Simes and Smith, The Law of Future Interests § 827 at 316, 318 (2d ed. 1956).

---

a fee simple on a condition subsequent. When such an estate is created, there is no forfeiture until the grantor exercises his right of re-entry.

[3] It is well settled that the rule against perpetuities does not apply to possibilities of reverter. This historical anomaly has been criticized for allowing "dead hand rule" and creating "appalling practical results" when a possibility of reverter does fall in many years after the original grant. Leach, *Perpetuities in Perspective: Ending the Rule's Reign of Terror*, 65 Harv.L.Rev. 721, 739 (1952); Leach, *Perpetuities: The Nutshell Revisited*, 78 Harv.L.Rev. 973, 980 (1965).

All the jurisdictions in the United States which have dealt with a determinable fee and an executory interest void under the rule against perpetuities have followed this rule. Fletcher v. Ferrill, 227 S.W.2d 448, 449, 16 A.L.R.2d 1240 (Ark. 1950); Brown v. Independent Baptist Church of Woburn, 91 N.E.2d 922 (Mass. 1950); Leonard v. Burr, 18 N.Y. 96 (1858); Yarbrough v. Yarbrough, 269 S.W. 36 (Tenn. 1924). This conclusion is favored by Restatement of Property §§ 228, 229.

V

[T]he Oregon statutes make it clear that corporate assets no longer escheat or revert to the original grantor upon dissolution. In this case, the parties agree that the corporation was lawfully dissolved, all the creditors paid, and that Daggett and Schallock, the sole shareholders of the corporation, were statutorily entitled to and did receive all of the remaining assets of the corporation. One such asset was the possibility of reverter of the land in question. The parties further agree that the defendants in this case were all of the heirs of Daggett and Schallock. [T]here is no Oregon decision on the issue of the descendability of the possibility of reverter. However, the weight of authority recognizes that such an interest is descendable. Restatement of Property § 164 cmt. a, at 606; 3 Simes § 707 (1936). We discern no sound policy considerations which lead us to a contrary conclusion. Marijane Flitcraft acquired all rights to the property when the other defendants conveyed their interests to her in 1970.

Reversed.

NOTES AND QUESTIONS

1. **What might happen.** Suppose that the city in the principal case had violated the restriction ten years after the future interest was created. At that time, the city's right to possession would have ended, and the executory interest would have vested (in interest and possession) in Shallock and Dagget — well within the perpetuities period. In a suit by the city against the future interest holders at that time, what result? Would we have known in 1925 (the date of the gift to the city) when the violation would occur?

2. **The Rule violation.** Perhaps you are thinking, "Surely there must have been *some* life in being in 1925 who was still alive when the violation occurred!" Can you point to such a person? Take the survivor of Shallock or Dagget: is it *necessarily* the case that the violation would occur within 21 years of the survivor's death? If not, is it possible to point to any other living person in 1925 who stood in any better position as a validating life? *See* Brown v. Independent Baptist Church of Woburn, 91 N.E.2d 922, 923 (Mass. 1950) (holding invalid the executory interest following a gift to the testator's church "so long as they shall maintain and promulgate their present religious belief and faith and shall continue a Church"):

> [T]he determinable fee might not come to an end until long after any life or lives in being and twenty-one years, and in theory at least might never come to an end, and for an indefinite period no clear title to the entire estate could be given.

Notice that the contingency in City of Klamath Falls v. Bell was not related to any life event, such as a requirement that a beneficiary survive someone, or do something. Compare a transfer "to A for life, then to B if B survives A." Or a transfer "to A for life, then to B if B goes to law school." Does B's interest violate the Rule in either case? Explain.

3. **Consequences of the Rule violation.** Different results follow from the invalidity of the executory interest following a defeasible fee, depending on the wording of the present interest. If A's present estate is determinable ("To A and her heirs so long as the property is not used for the sale of alcohol, and if so used, to B and his heirs"), the invalidity of B's interest leaves A with a fee simple determinable and O (or O's successor) with a possibility of reverter. *See* First Universalist Soc'y v. Boland, 29 N.E. 524, 524 (Mass. 1892):

> Where there is an invalid limitation over [i.e., an executory interest], the general rule is that the preceding estate is to stand, unaffected by the void limitation. The [preceding] estate becomes vested in the first taker, *according to the terms in which it was granted or devised.* Since the estate of the [First Universalist Society] may determine, and since there is no valid limitation over, it follows that there is a possibility of reverter in the original grantor.

If B's invalid future interest follows a present estate subject to a condition subsequent ("To A and her heirs, but if the property is ever used for the sale of alcohol, to B and his heirs"), the invalidity of the executory interest leaves the present interest holder with a fee simple absolute instead of a defeasible fee. *See* Proprietors of the Church in Brattle Square v. Grant, 69 Mass. (3 Gray) 142 (1855). *See generally* William H. Agnor, *A Tale of Two Cases*, 17 Vand. L. Rev. 1427 (1964). The court in *Klamath Falls* says that this difference in result effectuates O's intent. How so? *See* Griffis v. Davidson County Metropolitan Government, 164 S.W.3d 267, 274 (Tenn. 2005) ("Termination is automatic [in the fee simple determinable] because the limitation forms part of the estate's very nature."); Lynch v. Bunting, 29 A.2d 155 (Del. 1942) ("the special limitation marks the cessation of the estate of the grantee, and upon the happening of the event the estate of the grantee is absolutely concluded"). How sound is the argument? If O had thought about the possibility of a Rule violation, wouldn't O have drafted the document to avoid violating it? If O inadvertently violated the Rule, how likely is it O understood the consequences of the distinction between a special limitation and a condition subsequent?

When an executory interest following a defeasible fee is invalid, the Restatement Second of Property leaves the present interest holder with a fee simple absolute in all cases, whether the present estate was determinable or subject to a condition. *See* Restatement Second of Property (Donative Transfers) § 1.5 cmts. b & c. Does that result frustrate any legitimate expectations of O's successors? If A were a charitable organization or a school district, would there by any advantage to leaving A with a fee simple absolute? What is the comparable solution when the restriction on the present estate, rather than the future interest, is invalid (as in our earlier case of Hermitage Methodist Homes v. Dominion Trust Co.)?

4. **Exemption of reversionary interests from the Rule.** Is it good policy to exempt reversionary future interests from the Rule? Is O's power of termination or possibility of reverter following a determinable fee any less objectionable than B's executory interest following a defeasible fee? If reversionary future interests are to be excluded from the Rule, shouldn't the law at least limit their permissible duration? (See the statutes to that effect in Section A.5 above.)

5. **Drafting: two deeds.** You represent O, who wants to give land to the city with a perpetual restriction to specified city uses, and to give the land over to B or B's successors should the city ever violate the restriction. *City of Klamath Falls* shows that you can't accomplish O's wishes with one deed. How might you do it with two deeds? What does this easy circumvention of the Rule suggest about the wisdom of exempting reversionary interests from the Rule?

PROBLEM 2-R. Do the following executory interests violate the Rule? Do the transfers accomplish what O wanted to accomplish in Note 5?

a. O transfers "to A and her heirs so long as liquor is not sold on the premises during A's lifetime, and if it is, to B and her heirs."

b. O transfers "to the A Church in fee simple so long as the property is used for church purposes, and when it shall cease to be so used, to B and his heirs if B is then living." Does the property remain subject to the limitation after B's death?

c. O transfers "to the A Church in fee simple so long as the property is used for church purposes for 20 years, and if it ceases to be so used during that 20 years, to B and his heirs."

ADDITIONAL EXERCISES ON THE RULE

PROBLEM 2-S. The following transfers are more likely to be made in trusts of personal property than in outright devises or conveyances of land. In each problem, identify the future interests and determine whether those interests satisfy or violate the Rule Against Perpetuities. For any interests that violate the Rule, indicate the impact of the violation on the other interests created by the transfer. (Questions posed with the examples are intended to help you reason to a correct answer. Now would also be a good time to review the introductory comments to the discussion of the Rule at the beginning of Section B.4.)

a. O transfers "to A for life, then to the first child of A to reach 21." A is alive and childless. On the same facts, suppose the gift were to "the first child of A to reach 25"? *See generally* Sharona Hoffman & Andrew P. Morriss, *Birth After Death: Perpetuities and the New Reproductive Technologies*, 38 Ga. L. Rev. 575 (2004).

b. O transfers "to A for life, then to B if B reaches 25." B is a living person. How does B's remainder differ from the remainder "to the first child of A to reach 21" in the Problem 2-S.a?

c. O transfers "to A for life, then to the first child of A to reach the age of 30." A is alive and has two children, B (age 28) and C (age 27). A is alive at the effective date of the gift. Is it possible for some child of A *other* than B or C to take the gift?

Suppose the transfer had been "to A's first child, if that child reaches 30"?

d. O devises "to A for life, then to A's first grandchild." A is alive and has a child B, but no grandchildren. Different result if A had predeceased O?

e. O transfers "to A for life, then to the children of A for life, and upon the last survivor's death, to the grandchildren of A in fee simple." A is alive and has two children and one grandchild. (The common law rule is that a class gift violates the Rule if any member of the class might be determined outside of the perpetuities period.)

f. O transfers "to A for life, then to my descendants who are living 21 years after the deaths of B, C, D, E, F, G, H, I, and J (9 healthy babies picked at random). *See* Leach, *supra*, 51 Harv. L. Rev. at 642.

g. O devises "to A for life, then to O's descendants who are living 21 years after the deaths of all people listed in the Philadelphia phone directory who are alive at O's death." Is the logic of the Rule satisfied? What about administrative convenience — will O's trustee be able to locate and pay the remaindermen?

h. O transfers "to A 30 years from now." Is A subject to a requirement of survival to the time of distribution? If not, why does that cause a violation of the Rule? Just as reversions are deemed vested, executory interests are frequently deemed contingent; is this one contingent? Suppose the gift had been "to A 30 years from now, if A is then living"?

i. O devises "to A for life, then to A's children for their lives, then to B and his heirs." Is B's interest subject to the Rule? Will B's interest vest in possession within the perpetuities period?

ADDITIONAL NOTES ON THE RULE

1. **The "charity on a charity" exemption.** O transfers "to the A Cancer Society in fee simple until a cure for cancer is found, then to the Society for the Prevention of Cruelty to Animals." *See* W. Barton Leach, *Perpetuities in a Nutshell*, 51 Harv. L. Rev. 638, 669 (1930) ("Where there is a gift to the A charity, with a gift over to the B charity upon a remote contingency, the disposition is wholly valid. But if either the first or second of those gifts is to a noncharity the second gift fails."); Restatement Second of Property (Donative Transfers) § 1.6. Suppose O transfers "to A and his heirs until a cure for cancer is found, then to the American Cancer Society." Is the Society's executory interest good? Why do you suppose the law recognizes the charity-on-a-charity exemption from the Rule?

2. **Three classic traps under the Rule.** The following technical violations, caused by the Rule's "what might happen" methodology, earned sobriquets in Professor W. Barton Leach's classic article, *Perpetuities in a Nutshell*, 51 Harv. L. Rev. 638 (1938).

a. *The fertile octogenarian.* In Problem 2-S.e, suppose that A is a woman and is 70 years old at the effective date; is the future interest good or bad? *See* Louis J. Sirico, Jr., *Future Interest Haiku*, 67 N.C. L. Rev. 171, 175 (1988) ("Sarah laughing at eighty / morning nausea").

b. *The unborn widow.* O transfers "to A for life, then to A's widow for life, then to A's first child if he is then living." A is married but has no children. *See* Dickerson v. Union National Bank of Little Rock, 595 S.W.2d 677, 680 (Ark. 1980) (remainder to life tenant's heirs living at death of life tenant's "widow" was invalid under Rule: the life tenant "might marry an 18-year-old woman twenty years after [testator's] death, have additional children by her, and then die. [The life tenant's] young widow, however, might live for another 40 or 50 years, after which the [remainder] interests would finally vest."); Lawrence W. Waggoner & Thomas P. Gallanis, Estates in Land and Future Interests in a Nutshell 126 (3d ed. 2005) (renamed "the after-born spouse").

c. *The administrative contingency.* O devises "to my grandchildren, born before or after my death, who are living upon final distribution of my estate." Will O's estate necessarily be wound up within the perpetuities period?

3. **Saving clauses.** To protect against inadvertent technical violations of the Rule, experienced estate planning attorneys always insert a saving clause into the wills and trusts they draft (real estate lawyers handling a *Klamath Falls* transaction should do the same). In substance, a saving clause provides that the trust will terminate, if it has not terminated earlier by its terms, no later than 21 years after the death of the last survivor of a specified group who are living at the creation of the trust (e.g., the descendants of the settlor of the trust). *See* Thomas L. Shaffer & Carol Ann Mooney, The Planning and Drafting of Wills and Trusts 175 (3d ed. 1991). How does such a provision avoid a Rule violation?

4. **Reform: Wait-and-See.** The most important modification of the common law Rule Against Perpetuities is the wait-and-see variation. Under wait-and-see, interests that satisfy the common law Rule are valid. Interests that violate the common law Rule are not void; instead, those interests are invalid only if, as events unfold, they do not vest within the common law perpetuities period — some life in being plus 21 years. Rather than asking "what might happen," we wait to see what does in fact happen. Notice that to apply the common law wait-and-see modification, it is necessary to identify a measuring life. If wait-and-see had applied in *Klamath Falls*, what result? Who would have been the measuring life? *See generally* Jesse Dukeminier, *Perpetuities: The Measuring Lives*, 85 Colum. L. Rev. 1648 (1985).

5. **Wait-and-see under USRAP.** The Uniform Statutory Rule Against Perpetuities (1986) adopts a variant of the wait-and-see approach. Interests that satisfy the common law Rule are valid; but the waiting period for interests that violate the Rule is a fixed period of 90 years rather than a period measured by a life in being. When states adopting the conventional and USRAP versions of wait-and-see are combined, wait-and-see represents the majority view in this country. The pros and cons of the USRAP and conventional versions of wait-and-see are aired respectively in Lawrence W. Waggoner, *The Uniform Statutory Rule Against Perpetuities: The Rationale of the 90-Year Waiting Period*, 73 Cornell L. Rev. 157 (1988), and Jesse Dukeminier, *The Uniform Statutory Rule Against Perpetuities: Ninety Years in Limbo*, 34 UCLA L. Rev. 1023 (1987). If USRAP were applied to *Klamath Falls*, what result? For a proposed variation of USRAP, which dispenses with the initial determination of validity under the common law test and validates an interest if it in fact vests in 90 years, see Frederick R. Schneider, *A Rule*

Against Perpetuities for the Twenty-First Century, 41 Real Prop., Prob. and Tr. J. 743, 805 (2007) ("A Rule that waits to see how actual events develop, without encouraging an initial determination of invalidity, will save the time and money that would have been spent on reaching the initial determination.").

6. **Abolition of the Rule; dynasty trusts.** Trust business — which generates trustee's fees and administrative charges — is good for banks that handle trusts. Aware of that, legislatures in an increasing number of states have abolished or curtailed the Rule Against Perpetuities to entice out-of-state trust business. When the Rule is not a limit on the vesting of interests in a trust, a transferor may create a perpetual succession of life income interests in succeeding generations ("to A for life, then to A's children for life, then to A's grandchildren," etc.). Federal tax law creates some disincentive to such arrangements through the so-called "generation-skipping tax," but that tax exempts transfers that (as of 2009) do not exceed $3.5 million. In states that abolish or curtail the Rule, the federal tax exemption establishes the amount that a transferor can devise in a perpetual or "dynasty" trust. A recent list indicates eighteen states that "appear" — some statutes are unclear — to allow dynasty trusts either by abolishing the Rule, or maintaining it as a default rule (allowing for opt-outs) rather than as a rule of law. *See* Jesse Dukeminier, Stanley M. Johanson, James Lindgren & Robert H. Sitkoff, Wills, Trusts and Estates 719 (7th ed. 2005). *See generally* Jesse Dukeminier & James E. Krier, *The Rise of the Perpetual Trust*, 50 U.C.L.A. L. Rev. 1303 (2003); Joshua C. Tate, *Perpetual Trusts and the Settlor's Intent*, 53 U. Kan. L. Rev. 595 (2005).

b. The Rule and Commercial Transactions

The Rule Against Perpetuities originated as a device to control the transmission of family wealth from one generation to another. The next case considers the controversial question whether the Rule should apply to commercial transactions.

FERRERO CONSTRUCTION CO. v. DENNIS ROURKE CORP.
536 A.2d 1137 (Md. 1988)

ELDRIDGE, JUDGE.

The principal question in this case is whether the Rule Against Perpetuities applies to a right of first refusal to purchase an interest in property.

The pertinent facts are as follows. On April 27, 1981, the plaintiff Dennis Rourke Corp. and the defendant Ferrero Construction Co. entered into a contract for the purchase of two lots on Mercy Court in Montgomery County, Maryland. This contract contained the following clause:

> In consideration of this contract, the Seller [Ferrero] agrees to extend to the Purchaser [Rourke] a first right of refusal on the future sale of any of the seven lots remaining on Mercy Court.

Rourke never recorded this contract. Settlement under the contract apparently occurred in May 1981.

On March 12, 1984, Ferrero notified Rourke by mail of a third party offer to purchase Lot 27, one of the remaining lots on Mercy Court. The letter contained the terms of the third party's offer and afforded Rourke the opportunity "to submit a contract" by March 21, 1984, for it "to be considered." Rourke immediately stated that it was exercising its right of first refusal and requested that Ferrero provide a copy of the third party's offer so that Rourke could prepare a contract with identical terms and conditions. On March 21, 1984, Rourke received a copy of the third party's offer. The next day, Rourke submitted a contract that in its essential terms conformed to the third party's offer. Subsequently, Rourke stated that it was prepared to settle on April 24, 1984. Ferrero responded that it had decided to reject both offers and that it would not appear at settlement. Ferrero in fact did not appear at the settlement and, on April 26, 1984, returned both offers, unsigned.

Rourke brought this action for specific performance in the Circuit Court for Montgomery County. In its amended complaint, Rourke claimed that it was entitled to a conveyance of Lot 27 by virtue of its exercise of the right of first refusal. At trial, after the conclusion of Rourke's case, the trial court granted Ferrero's motion for judgment, ruling that Rourke's right of first refusal violated the Rule Against Perpetuities and was, consequently, void.

The Court of Special Appeals reversed on the ground that the Rule Against Perpetuities was inapplicable and that the right of first refusal was valid. See 498 A.2d 689 (1985). [W]e granted Ferrero's petition for a writ of certiorari.[4]

I.

Subject to a few statutory exceptions, the common law Rule Against Perpetuities remains in effect in Maryland.

A.

The vast majority of courts and commentators have held that rights of first refusal, which are more commonly known as "preemptive rights," are interests in property and not merely contract rights. This is so because, if the property owner attempts to sell to someone other than the owner of the right of first refusal ("the preemptioner"), the latter may have a court of equity enter a decree of specific performance ordering that the property be conveyed to him. Thus, the preemptioner acquires an equitable interest, which will vest only when the property owner decides to sell. *See* Note, *Real Property — Preemptive Right or Right of Refusal — Violative of The Rule Against Perpetuities?*, 40 Mo.L.Rev. 389, 391-392 (1975) (a right of first refusal "is in the nature of a springing executory interest").

---

[4] From the outset of this case, both parties and both courts below have proceeded as though Rourke would be entitled to specific performance if the right of first refusal in the 1981 contract did not violate the Rule Against Perpetuities. Thus, the parties and the lower courts assumed that Ferrero had made an actual decision to sell Lot 27 so as to activate Rourke's right of first refusal. Moreover, the parties and the lower courts assumed that the right of first refusal required Rourke to submit a bid that equaled a third party's offer rather than market price. For purposes of this case, we shall proceed as though these assumptions are valid.

As rights of first refusal are interests in property, the great majority of American jurisdictions have applied the Rule Against Perpetuities to such rights. In addition, the Restatement has adopted the majority position. Restatement of Property § 413 comment e (1944). *See also* Note, 40 Mo.L.Rev. at 391-392; 5A Powell on Real Property, ¶ 771[2] (1987) ("Options to purchase or to repurchase land, unconnected with a lease, commonly denominated options in gross, have generally been held bad under the common law rule against perpetuities, when not restricted in duration so as to comply with the permissible period under that rule") (collecting right of first refusal cases); L. Simes & A. Smith, The Law of Future Interests, § 1154, at 61 (2d ed. 1956) (rights of first refusal are "normally subject to the rule against perpetuities").

In light of this widespread acceptance of the majority view, we should hesitate before attempting to fashion an exception to the Rule Against Perpetuities for rights of first refusal. In this area of property law, vested rights and settled expectations are at stake. A departure from settled law might introduce doubt as to the value of vested rights. Moreover, the contours of an exception for rights of first refusal might prove difficult to define. Consequently, the policies favoring certainty and stability strongly support our following the majority of courts and applying the Rule Against Perpetuities to rights of first refusal.

A right of first refusal is a type of option. 4 Restatement of Property § 413 comment b (rights of first refusal are "analogous to options on a condition precedent"). Again, the majority rule, in England as well as in this country, is that the Rule Against Perpetuities generally applies to options. 4 Restatement of Property § 393. In the area of options, courts in the 300 years since the High Court of Chancery decided the Duke of Norfolk's Case, 3 Ch. Cas. 1, 22 Eng.Rep. 931 (1681), have developed exceptions to the Rule Against Perpetuities. The Rule does not apply to a lessee's option to renew a lease, Restatement of Property § 395(b). It does not apply to a lessee's option to purchase all or part of the leased premises, Restatement of Property § 395(a). *See generally*, 5A Powell on Real Property, ¶ 771[2]. All options may violate the Rule Against Perpetuities. Nevertheless, courts have justified these narrow exceptions because these types of options yield social benefits that offset the consequences of that violation.

In urging us to exempt rights of first refusal from the Rule Against Perpetuities, Rourke would have us undertake such a balancing process. Again, however, it is significant that a majority of courts have struck the balance against creating the exception Rourke seeks.

B.

We recognize that a minority of courts have held the Rule Against Perpetuities inapplicable to certain rights of first refusal. This minority view appears to stem from a law review article written in 1935 by Professor Merrill I. Schnebly. Schnebly, *Restraints Upon the Alienation of Legal Interests: III*, 44 Yale L.J. 1380, 1390-1395 (1935). Professor Schnebly was the editor of the section of the American Law of Property which relates to this issue and which adopts the same view. 6 American Law of Property, § 26.67 (1952). The Court of Special Appeals in the present case, and many of the other cases reaching the same conclusion, rely on

Professor Schnebly's writings. In fact, the relatively few cases espousing the minority view all arose after the publication of Professor Schnebly's article in 1935. We reiterate that, in this area of the law, where certainty and stability are important values, it is undesirable to adopt such a recent and minority position.

The Court of Special Appeals in the present case and other courts adopting the minority view reach their conclusion by assuming that the sole policy underlying the Rule Against Perpetuities is the elimination of restraints on alienation. Thus, in effect, the minority view postulates that an interest should not be subject to the Rule unless the interest constitutes a restraint on alienation. The minority view then distinguishes rights of first refusal from ordinary options. As stated in 6 American Law of Property, § 26.64, at 507:

> An option creates in the optionee a power to compel the owner of property to sell it at a stipulated price whether or not he be willing to part with ownership. A pre-emption does not give to the pre-emptioner the power to compel an unwilling owner to sell; it merely requires the owner, when and if he decides to sell, to offer the property first to the person entitled to the pre-emption, at the stipulated price. Upon receiving such an offer, the pre-emptioner may elect whether he will buy. If he decides not to buy, then the owner of the property may sell to anyone.

Based on this distinction, the minority view contends that, unlike ordinary options, at least some rights of first refusal do not restrain alienation; consequently, the minority view concludes that such rights of first refusal should not be subject to the Rule Against Perpetuities. 6 American Law of Property, § 26.67, at 511-512.

Even assuming the validity of the distinction between rights of first refusal and other options, the minority view errs in assuming that an interest should not be subject to the Rule unless the interest constitutes a restraint on alienation. In making this assumption, courts adopting the minority view confuse the Rule Against Perpetuities with the rule against unreasonable restraints on alienation. Admittedly, both rules belong to "a family of related rules that regulate the devolution of wealth from generation to generation." R. Lynn, The Modern Rule Against Perpetuities 9 (1966). These two rules are nonetheless distinct. The Rule Against Perpetuities prevents property interests from vesting remotely. The rule against restraints on alienation, on the other hand, prevents grantors from unreasonably depriving grantees of the power to alienate their estates.

The policies underlying these two rules are likewise not identical. Obviously, the rule against restraints on alienation serves to facilitate the alienability of property. Similarly, one of the purposes of the Rule Against Perpetuities is to facilitate the alienability of property. Contrary to the minority view, however, the Rule Against Perpetuities is not simply a rule against restraints on alienation. Instead, the Rule Against Perpetuities is concerned with restrictions that render title uncertain. Without the Rule Against Perpetuities, it would be possible at some distant point for a remotely vesting future interest to divest the current owner's estate. Because of this threat of divestment, the owner might be deterred from making the most effective use of the property, even if he never has any desire to alienate his estate. Thus, by voiding certain remotely vesting future interests, the Rule Against Perpetuities eliminates this deterrent both for owners who wish to alienate their estates and for owners who have no intention of ever doing so. Consequently, from the standpoint of the Rule Against Perpetuities, it is irrelevant whether a particular future interest imposes a light burden, a heavy burden, or no burden at all upon the alienability of property.

C.

Even if the minority view were correct that an interest should not be subject to the Rule Against Perpetuities unless that interest constitutes a restraint on alienation, we would disagree that rights of first refusal should not be subject to the Rule. In our opinion, rights of first refusal do restrain the alienability of property. In this respect, however, it is necessary first to distinguish among the various types of rights of first refusal.

Some rights of first refusal permit the right's owner to purchase property at a fixed price if the property owner, his heirs, or assigns should ever desire to sell. Plainly a right of first refusal at a fixed price inhibits alienability. Often, with the passage of time, the fixed price will bear no relationship to the property's actual market value. *See, e.g.*, Peele v. Wilson Co. Bd. of Ed., 289 S.E.2d 890 (N.C. Ct. App. 1982) (property owner had received bid at $4,300, while right of first refusal would have permitted heirs to pay only $50). Because the owner must often offer the property to the preemptioner at an artificially low price, the owner is deterred from selling the property or from increasing its value by making improvements. Consequently, even the minority view acknowledges that the Rule Against Perpetuities should apply to rights of first refusal at a fixed price. 6 American Law of Property, § 26.67, at 510.

A second type of right of first refusal permits the preemptioner to purchase the property at "market value" if the owner, his heirs or assigns should ever desire to sell. Some authorities would find the Rule Against Perpetuities inapplicable to such a right. 6 American Law of Property, § 26.67, at 511. Nevertheless, a right of first refusal to purchase at market value also effects a substantial restraint on alienability. A potential purchaser's offer might, in the preemptioner's opinion, exceed market value. The preemptioner could then contend that he need pay only some lesser amount. Fearing that a determination of the parties' rights would have to await the uncertain outcome of litigation, a prospective purchaser might be deterred from ever making an initial offer.

The third type of right of first refusal permits the preemptioner to purchase the property at a price equal to any bona fide offer that the owner, his heirs or assigns desire to accept. In this situation, however, many prospective purchasers, recognizing that a matching offer from the preemptioner will defeat their bids, simply will not bid on the property. This in turn will depress the property's value and discourage the owner from attempting to sell. Moreover, even a right of first refusal tied to a bona fide offer may constitute an unreasonable restraint on alienation if the right is of unlimited duration. See Restatement of Property § 406 comment i.[6]

---

[6] The Court of Special Appeals concluded that Rourke's right of first refusal did not constitute an unreasonable restraint on alienation under Restatement of Property § 406. Section 406, the general rule on unreasonable restraints on alienation, expressly states that its provisions are subject to Restatement

Similarly, if, as in this case, the right of first refusal is unrecorded, the task of ascertaining and locating the holder of the preemptive right at some remote point in the future might also become so difficult that the right of first refusal could constitute an unreasonable restraint on alienation.

Thus, contrary to the minority view, we conclude that rights of first refusal restrain alienation.

For all of the foregoing reasons, we hold that the Court of Special Appeals erred in adopting the minority view in this case. We choose to follow the majority of courts that apply the Rule Against Perpetuities to rights of first refusal.

E.

It remains to assess the validity of Rourke's right of first refusal under the Rule Against Perpetuities.

We first observe that Rourke's right of first refusal was not limited to a term of years but was of unlimited duration. Moreover, in this case, the right was conveyed between two corporations, which theoretically have a perpetual existence. Thus, under the conveyance as drafted, the right of first refusal might vest well beyond the period of some life in being plus twenty-one years that is prescribed in the Rule.[7] Consequently, the circuit court correctly held that the right of first refusal in this case violated the Rule Against Perpetuities and, therefore, was unenforceable.

JUDGMENT OF THE COURT OF SPECIAL APPEALS REVERSED, AND CASE REMANDED TO THAT COURT WITH DIRECTIONS TO AFFIRM THE JUDGMENT OF THE CIRCUIT COURT FOR MONTGOMERY COUNTY. RESPONDENT TO PAY COSTS.

COLE, Judge, dissenting.

The underlying policies of the Rule Against Perpetuities are to "preserve the freedom of alienation, and to prevent restrictions on the circulation of property." Ryan v. Ward, 64 A.2d 258, 260 (Md. 1949). In other words, if a remotely vesting property interest hinders a property's alienability, marketability, or development, the interest should be subject to the Rule Against Perpetuities.

In determining if the Rule applies, it is important to distinguish rights of first refusal from options, and to recognize that different types of rights of first refusal exist. The majority suggests that a right of first refusal is a type of option. An option, however, gives the holder the immediate right to tender the purchase price and force the owner to sell. A right of first refusal, on the other hand, does not give the holder the power to require the owner to sell at any time, but instead only requires the owner to offer the property to the holder once the owner has decided

---

of Property § 413. Section 413 provides that a right of first refusal is not an unreasonable restraint on alienation "unless it violates the rule against perpetuities." Thus, § 413 and not § 406 contains the final word as to the reasonableness of rights of first refusal. Nevertheless, the Court of Special Appeals did not assess Rourke's right of first refusal under § 413.

[7] Corporations such as Rourke and Ferrero cannot be used as measuring lives for purposes of the Rule Against Perpetuities.

to sell. 6 American Law of Property § 26.64 (1952). In addition, the operative document creating a right of first refusal normally dictates whether the holder will exercise the right at a fixed price or a price which reflects true market value. While a fixed price will normally have a negative impact on the alienability of the land, a price reflecting true market value will not.

In this case, the right of first refusal could be exercised only if Rourke agreed to match an acceptable third party offer for the land. As this price should reflect true market value, the alienability and marketability of land is unaffected. Accordingly, although the right may not vest within the time constraints of the Rule Against Perpetuities, there is no need to void the right because such action does not further the policies of the Rule.

The majority argues that the policies underlying the Rule Against Perpetuities are furthered by voiding this right of first refusal. It asserts that although one of the purposes of the Rule Against Perpetuities is to facilitate the alienability of property, the Rule is also concerned with any restrictions that render title uncertain and unmarketable. However, the majority fails to distinguish between these two concerns and does not provide any evidence as to how this right of first refusal renders Ferrero's title uncertain or unmarketable.

The majority states that the great majority of American jurisdictions have applied the Rule Against Perpetuities to rights of first refusal. I believe that several of the cases cited to support this position are distinguishable. In particular, no less than eight of the cases cited involve rights to purchase at a fixed price. As previously stated, when the price is fixed, the alienability of the land is clearly affected. However, when the price to be paid is the market value of the land, alienability is no longer affected. Since this case arises from a granting clause which mandates that the selling price shall be equivalent to an acceptable offer from a third party, cases where the selling price is fixed are inapposite.

[T]he modern trend is to limit application of the Rule Against Perpetuities, particularly in commercial transactions. Lives in being have no significance in commercial transactions, nor has the period of twenty-one years. Moreover, in accordance with standard perpetuities doctrine, when an option is held to be too remote the entire option is struck down, instead of only the excess beyond some permissible shorter period. This is unduly punitive on one party to the advantage of another who may be equally at fault. The usual case involves an option which the option-holder attempts to exercise within a very short period; the Rule Against Perpetuities is seized upon by the owner to escape from his contract on the ground that the option-holder might have exercised the option too remotely — a situation which does not appeal to the common sense of business men or the ethical sense of anyone. Like the late lamented Statute of Frauds, the Rule becomes a destroyer of bargains which in all conscience ought to be performed. Morris and Leach, The Rule Against Perpetuities, p. 217 (1956).

There is substantial authority supporting the proposition that the Rule Against Perpetuities should not apply to [invalidate] rights of first refusal. A right of first refusal is impotent to put property outside the stream of commerce. The holder of a right of first refusal cannot force the owner to sell the property. Nor can the holder prevent a sale once the owner has decided to sell. The holder of the right is limited to either accepting or rejecting the offer when the owner desires to sell. Moreover, because the right of first refusal in this case is not to be exercised at a fixed price, but is instead based on a price the owner is willing to accept from a third party, the right does not discourage the owner from placing improvements on the property, and the owner is assured of getting the fair market value for his land and added improvements.

Ferrero argues, and the majority agrees, that the outstanding right of first refusal "could discourage prospective developer purchasers from spending time and money for architectural and engineering services, to arrange financing and to negotiate a complicated real estate sales contract, knowing that preemption is possible." The majority concludes that the right restrains the alienability of the land. I disagree.

Prospective buyers always face the risk that their investigatory efforts will be wasted due to unavoidable market forces. A prospective developer might study the property and then conclude that a purchase would not be wise. The prospective buyer might also make an offer that the owner finds too low. Finally, another buyer may come along and offer a higher price. Thus, the risk of investigatory costs being wasted is present in every property acquisition. To the extent that a right of first refusal heightens this risk, I find it to be de minimis.

In sum, I believe that a right of first refusal does not hinder the alienability, marketability, or development of property and therefore conclude that the rule against perpetuities should not apply. I therefore dissent.

Judge M c AULIFFE has authorized me to state that he concurs with the views expressed herein.

NOTES AND QUESTIONS

1. **Options under the Rule.** Both options and rights of first refusal (preemptive options) are interests created by contract rather than by conveyance or devise; why is either one subject to the Rule Against Perpetuities? Why does Rourke's right of first refusal violate the Rule? The *Ferrero* court says that Maryland follows the common law Rule; would Rourke's right of first refusal have been valid under the wait-and-see modification of the Rule? *See* SEPTA v. Philadelphia Transp. Co., 233 A.2d 15 (Pa. 1967) (option that was exercised within 21 years of its creation was valid under the wait-and-see modification of the Rule).

2. **Should the Rule apply to options?** There is authority (1) for applying the Rule to options and rights of first refusal, which is the majority view, according to the principal case; (2) for exempting rights of first refusal from the Rule, discussed as a minority view in the principal case; and (3) for exempting both options and rights of first refusal from the Rule and policing them instead under the doctrine of restraints on alienation, which is the position taken in the Uniform Statutory Rule Against Perpetuities § 4(1). In evaluating these possibilities, consider that both types of options occur most frequently in commercial, arms-length transactions, and are intended to be and in fact are exercised well within the perpetuities period if no fixed time for exercise is set by the parties. Is an option of either type objectionable when it is exercisable at a fixed price? Is either type objectionable if

it is exercisable at market price at the time of exercise? In policing options by the *time* of exercise, does the Rule focus on the relevant question?

3. **Restraints on alienation.** Would it be better to police options and rights of first refusal under the rule against restraints on alienation instead of the Rule Against Perpetuities? How about legislation restricting the duration of options to a fixed period, for example, ten years? *See* Louisiana Civil Code art. 2628 (options or pre-emptive options may not be granted for a term longer than ten years; longer terms are reduced to ten years; leases creating such options are excluded).

4. **Options in gross and options appendant.** Courts generally agree that an option to buy or right of first refusal granted to a tenant is valid under the Rule Against Perpetuities. In Citgo Petroleum Corp. v. Hopper, 429 S.E.2d 6 (Va. 1993), Hopper leased to the oil company for 15 years, with options to renew, and with an option in the tenant to purchase the leased premises "at any time during the term of this lease or any renewal or extension thereof." When Citgo sought to exercise the option to purchase, Hopper refused, claiming that the option was void under the Rule Against Perpetuities. (What is the argument for that conclusion?) Judgment for Hopper was reversed on appeal:

> The rule against perpetuities, which invalidates interests that vest too remotely, exists to further the public policy of preventing excessive restraints or limitations upon the alienation of real property. Nearly 70 years ago, we applied the rule to options in gross, or independent options. However, we have not previously considered whether the rule should apply to an option that is appendant to a long-term commercial lease and exercisable during the term of the lease.
>
> Courts in a majority of other jurisdictions have held that the rule does not apply to such options. Many of these courts have concluded that an option appendant to a lease is consistent and in harmony with the policy objectives of the rule. They reason that such an option stimulates improvement of the property and fosters full use thereof by the lessee. This, in turn, benefits the lessor, the lessee, and the community at large.
>
> We agree that an option to purchase that is appendant to a long-term commercial lease and exercisable during the term of the lease actually fosters the purpose of the rule. We think that there is a real and valid distinction to be drawn between an option in gross and an option appendant to a long-term commercial lease. Thus, consistent with the majority view, we hold that the rule does not apply to Citgo's option to purchase because the option is appendant to a long-term commercial lease and exercisable within the term of the lease.

429 S.E.2d at 7-8.

5. **Classification.** Suppose O's deed of Blackacre to A specifies certain uses that A must make of the land, and then provides as follows: "In the event that at any time hereafter such specified uses enumerated above shall be abandoned so that the said land is not used for the specified uses, the grantor or his successors in interest shall be entitled to repurchase the land upon payment to the grantee of the purchase price paid by grantee to grantor." Is this an option, or a power of termination exempt from the Rule? *See* Central Delaware County Auth. v.

Greyhound Corp., 588 A.2d 485 (Pa. 1991) (option, held invalid under wait-and-see because interest did not vest within 21 years of its creation). *Compare* Trailsend Land Co. v. Virginia Holding Corp., 321 S.E.2d 667 (Va. 1984) (power of termination, but court applied rule of strict construction and found no breach of the restriction).

6. **Leases to begin in the future.** Options are not the only commercial arrangements susceptible to analysis under the Rule. Suppose that L (a corporation) leases space to T in a shopping center, the lease term to begin when L completes construction of the main building of the center. The lease agreement creates an executory interest in the tenant. Is the lease valid under the common law Rule Against Perpetuities? In the leading case of Wong v. DiGrazia, 386 P.2d 817 (Cal. 1968), the court held that the lease was valid; the court interpreted the parties' intent to be that the building be completed within a reasonable time, and it interpreted a reasonable time to be no more than 21 years from the date of the agreement. Is that approach appropriate for options to purchase and rights of first refusal that do not specify a time for exercise?

Chapter 3

CONCURRENT INTERESTS

With concurrent interests, we continue our study of divided ownership. In the chapter on estates, we analyzed transfers that divided the right to possession temporally, between a present owner and a future owner:

O → to A for life, then to B.

In this chapter, we focus on transfers that confer concurrent (contemporaneous) possessory interests on two (or sometimes more) persons. The concurrent interests may be present or future interests:

O → to A and B.

O → to X for life, then to A and B.

As concurrent owners, A and B share the right to possession of the whole of Blackacre; neither owns a discrete portion of the land. *See* William B. Stoebuck & Dale A. Whitman, The Law of Property § 5.8 at 203 ("all are entitled to possession of all parts of the land at all times"); 2 Herbert Thorndike Tiffany, The Law of Real Property § 417, at 195 (3d ed. Basil Jones 1939) (cotenants "have no separate rights as regards any distinct portion of the land, but each is interested according to the extent of his share, in every part of the whole"). In contrast, if A owned the west half of Blackacre, and B the east half, each would own *in severalty*, as distinguished from the "undivided" ownership enjoyed by A and B as cotenants. The fractional share of each cotenant mentioned by Tiffany is important; it represents the amount of net profit to which the cotenant is entitled if the property is used productively, and the share of the ongoing costs of ownership (taxes, mortgage payments) that each cotenant must shoulder regardless of the use of the property — matters that are taken up more fully below.

A. TYPES OF CONCURRENT INTERESTS

We are concerned with three forms of concurrent ownership: the joint tenancy, the tenancy in common, and the tenancy by the entirety. Any two or more people can be joint tenants or tenants in common. Only spouses can hold as tenants by the entirety. We treat the joint tenancy and the tenancy in common first, both for their more generalized availability, and to prepare the way for the somewhat more complex marital tenancy.

The tenancy in common. In the *tenancy in common*, each cotenant's interest is transferable not only inter vivos, but also at the cotenant's death. Thus, if A and B are tenants in common of Blackacre and A devises his interest to X, upon A's death, X will join B as a tenant in common. B's interest is likewise devisable. Should A or

B die intestate still owning an interest in the cotenancy, that interest will pass to the heirs of the decededent cotenant.

The joint tenant's right of survivorship. In contrast, the interest of a *joint tenant* is not devisable or inheritable at the cotenant's death. If A and B are joint tenants of Blackacre and A dies, leaving heirs or devisees, Blackacre is owned by B in severalty; no interest in Blackacre passes to A's successors. (The right of survivorship would likewise entitle A to sole possession were cotenant B to die first.) The doctrinal explanation is that each joint tenant is considered to own not just a share, but also the whole, so that the death of any joint tenant confers nothing on the surviving joint tenants. *See* Estate of Phillips v. Nyhus, 874 P.2d 154, 156-57 (Wash. 1994) (since joint tenants "together own but one estate," the survivor "takes no title by survivorship but holds under the deed by virtue of which he was originally seised of the whole").

The four unities. One of the more arcane features of the joint tenancy is the concept of the four unities applicable to it. At common law, parties could not hold as joint tenants unless they received their interests (1) at the same time and (2) by the same document (deed or will), giving them (3) equal shares and (4) an equal right to possess the entire land. In contrast, the tenancy in common requires only the unity of possession — the "undivided" possessory interest in each cotenant (as opposed to ownership in severalty) that we noted earlier.

Severance of the joint tenancy. A right of equal importance with the right of survivorship is the right of any joint tenant to emancipate her interest from the survivor-take-all regime, by a transfer that effectively severs her interest from that of the other cotenants. Thus if A and B are joint tenants, and A conveys to X, the transfer severs A's one-half interest. X steps into the cotenancy with B as a tenant in common, and both X and B have transmissible interests when they die. The doctrine of severance follows from the doctrine of the four unities; in our example, X acquires title at a different time and by a different title than does B. *See* Harms v. Sprague, 473 N.E.2d 930 (Ill. 1984) (four unities "are fundamental to both the creation and the perpetuation" of joint tenancy).

You may have noticed that for purposes of survivorship, the joint tenant is regarded as owner of the whole, but that for purposes of severance, a joint tenant owns a fractional share. *See* Jezo v. Jezo, 127 N.W.2d 246, 249 (Wisc. 1964) ("Joint tenants are said to be seised of the entire estate for purposes of survivorship, but of only a particular part or interest for the purpose of immediate alienation; whereas tenants in common, having no right of survivorship, hold separate estates in the whole."). In the law French of the early common law, joint tenants were said to own *per my et per tout*, while tenants in common held *per my et non per tout*.

Severance requires an inter vivos transfer by the joint tenant; a will won't sever, because at the moment of the decedent tenant's death, her interest ceases. We will consider severance more fully below.

Advantages of a joint tenancy. In states in which the tenancy by the entirety is not available, spouses often elect the joint tenancy form of ownership to avoid the costs and delays of probate. To see this advantage, consider first the tenancy in common. If A and B own Blackacre as tenants in common, and A dies, A's interest in Blackacre, since it is inheritable and devisable, is an asset of A's probate estate. A's executor or administrator must gather and inventory A's assets, see that A's creditors are paid, and then distribute the net estate to A's devisees or heirs. This takes time, and costs money: court costs and fees of the executor or administrator and the attorney representing the estate. Because A's interest in Blackacre is involved in probate, the fee simple title is tied up during the winding up of A's estate.

Compare the joint tenancy. When A dies, B owns outright, freed of A's participation in the ownership of the property. Nothing passes from A to B with respect to the former joint tenancy property; B's title is an original title from the transferor of the joint tenancy, not a title derived from or through A in any sense. Recalling Chapter 2, we can say that each joint tenant is a *purchaser* from the grantor of the cotenancy, not an heir or transferee of the decedent cotenant. Since the cotenancy property is not involved in the probate of A's estate, the surviving joint tenant B can immediately transfer good title to the property to a prospective purchaser, simply by furnishing a copy of A's death certificate. Indeed, so important is this advantage of the joint tenancy that the Washington legislature has stated it as a statutory preamble to its recognition of the cotenancy. *See* Wash. Rev. Code Ann. § 64.28.010 ("Whereas joint tenancy with right of survivorship permits property to pass to the survivor without the cost or delay of probate proceedings, there shall be a form of co-ownership of property, real and personal, known as joint tenancy.").

The joint tenancy also offers the advantage of simplifying the administration of estates and trusts when two or more persons are appointed as executors or trustees, and one of them dies. Joint tenancy ownership of the trust or estate assets allows the surviving fiduciary to continue to perform the duties of the office without interruption; the trust or estate property is not involved in the deceased fiduciary's own estate proceedings. An earlier version of the same phenomenon — centralization of ownership — prompted the common law courts to establish a presumption in favor of the joint tenancy over the tenancy in common. In feudal times, when significant services or payments were required as the return to the grantor for the grantee's right to possess, it was important that the obligor be readily identifiable at all times. Unlike the inheritable tenancy in common, the joint tenancy *reduces* the number of cotenants as deaths among the coowners occur, thus simplifying the identification of the obligor.

Disadvantages of a joint tenancy. The benefits of the joint tenancy, however, come at a cost to the cotenants and to society. First, in the case of joint tenants who furnish consideration for the taking of title, the right of survivorship can lead to an unanticipated loss of investment for the cotenant who dies first, because there is no disposable interest to pass to the decedent's devisees or heirs. To dramatize: suppose that A and B buy Blackacre, each furnishing half of the $100,000 purchase price, and take title as joint tenants; A dies several years later. A's $50,000 investment (or more realistically, A's share of the equity that has accumulated as A and B have paid down the loan they took to buy the property) is lost, and B is correspondingly enriched. (Severance, of course, allows A to avoid that loss, *if* A is careful to act during his or her lifetime.)

Second, joint tenancies are hazardous for creditors of a cotenant. If A is involved in an automobile accident with X, for which X gets a $50,000 judgment in excess of A's insurance, A's interest in the joint tenancy is property that X can levy on (force a sale of) to satisfy the judgment if A does not pay it. If the execution sale is completed before A dies, the purchaser acquires an indefeasible interest in the underlying property as a tenant in common. However, were A to die before completion of the execution process, the surviving joint tenant would take the property free of the judgment creditor's lien. *See* Jamestown Terminal Elevator, Inc. v. Knopp, 246 N.W.2d 612 (N.D. 1976) (judgment lien on joint tenancy property expired when debtor cotenant died before execution sale).

Abolition of joint tenancy; presumptions. Perhaps in response to these difficulties, and the entire feudal aroma surrounding the joint tenancy, a few states have abolished it, which is probably a draconian approach given the usefulness of this form of cotenancy. Most states continue to recognize the joint tenancy, but they also create a presumption that a transfer to multiple grantees creates a tenancy in common unless the grantor expresses the intent to create a joint tenancy in the deed or will. The presumption is often stated in a statute, and the statutes sometimes exempt husband and wife grantees or transfers to trustees or executors, situations in which, as noted above, a right of survivorship is advantageous. When not aided by statute, courts on their own have adopted a presumption favoring a tenancy in common construction of an unspecific or ambiguous instrument. *See, e.g.,* Choman v. Epperley, 592 P.2d 714 (Wyo. 1979) (deed "unto Mary Choman, for her natural life, remainder to Mike Choman and Joe Choman, their heirs and assigns forever" created tenancy in common of the remainder).

1.   Creation of the Joint Tenancy

Two problems might plague the transferor who seeks to transfer a joint tenancy to transferees. First, because the modern presumption favors the tenancy in common, the transferor must affirmatively express his or her intent to create a joint tenancy with sufficient clarity to overcome the presumption. Second, in states where the ancient four unities requirement still exists, the drafter must take steps to comply with it. By statute or judicial decision, a transferor may be excused from the common law four unities requirement. There is no relief, nor should there be, from the requirement that the transferor affirmatively express his or her intent to create a joint tenancy.

a.   Intent: Clarity and Extrinsic Evidence

If A transfers Blackacre "to A and B," with no other relevant language in the document, a tenancy in common will almost surely result. The transferor has expressed no intent whatsoever for a joint tenancy, and the language would not overcome the common statutory requirement that the transferor's intent to create a joint tenancy be "expressed in" the deed or will. Beyond that, generalizations are risky. Language that, in the abstract, seems sufficient to create a joint tenancy ("to A and B as joint tenants and not as tenants in common") might not do so, and language that seems insufficient ("to A and B jointly") might be held to create a joint tenancy. The outcome of any case depends on several variables: (1) the language of the statute setting out the presumption in favor of a tenancy in common, (2) the availability of extrinsic evidence of the parties' intent, and perhaps (3) the hostility that some courts seem to have for the joint tenancy. The myriad formulations of careless drafters (some of whom, unfortunately, are lawyers) provide grist for litigation that could and should have been avoided. Ambiguity here, as in defeasible estates, can be fatal, and, to complicate matters, courts differ on whether particular language *is* ambiguous.

HOOVER v. SMITH
444 S.E.2d 546 (Va. 1994)

CARRCO, CHIEF JUSTICE.

The question for decision in this case is whether a deed conveying land to grantees creates an estate with survivorship. The trial court answered the question in the affirmative. Finding that the trial court erred, we reverse.

The question arose from a deed dated November 1, 1928, conveying to Add Shoemaker and Bessie Shoemaker, his wife, one acre of land on Gap Road, near Peak Mountain, in Rockingham County. The deed contained this provision: "It is hereby mutually understood and agreed, that the grantees herein named are to have and to hold the said land and tenements as joint tenants, and not as tenants in common."

Add Shoemaker died intestate in 1951, survived by his wife, Bessie, and several children. Bessie passed away in 1984. During her lifetime, but subsequent to Add's death, she conveyed to Wilmer A. Shoemaker, one of her sons, what purported to be the entire interest in a 0.542-acre portion of the land she and Add Shoemaker had acquired by the 1928 deed.

Wilmer died testate some time before 1988 and, in his will, devised the 0.542-acre tract to Shelby Jean Moubray. By deed dated January 28, 1988, Moubray conveyed the tract to David Martin Smith and Vivian Secrist Smith.

On February 19, 1992, the complainants, Susan M. Shoemaker Hoover, Catherine G. Shoemaker Smith, Sarah P. Shoemaker Pennington, and Margie C. Shoemaker Hoover (collectively, the Hoovers), all children of Add and Bessie Shoemaker, filed a bill of complaint against Alvin Leon Shoemaker, Nellie Craun, and Charles Shoemaker, also children of Add and Bessie Shoemaker. Named as defendants in addition were Shelby Moubray and David and Vivian Smith (collectively, the Smiths), the parties to the 1988 deed.

The bill alleged that by virtue of the provisions of Code §§ 55-20 and 55-21, *infra*, and the language of the 1928 deed, Add and Bessie Shoemaker became "joint tenants of such real estate having only those rights of a tenant in common" and, accordingly, "each obtained by such conveyance a one-half moiety in such real estate." As a result, it was alleged, upon the death of Add Shoemaker, his one-half moiety passed by intestate succession to his surviving children, who had never conveyed away any interest in the moiety. The bill alleged that the real estate was not susceptible of convenient partition in kind and prayed for its sale, with a division of the proceeds among those entitled as their respective interests may appear.

Shelby Moubray filed a demurrer to the bill of complaint, and David and Vivian Smith demurred separately. In each demurrer, it was alleged that the bill of complaint failed to state a cause of action because, as a matter of law, the 1928 deed established in Add and Bessie Shoemaker a joint tenancy with the right of survivorship. After argument, the trial court sustained the demurrers and, in a final decree, dismissed the case with prejudice as it concerned the 0.542-acre tract conveyed by Moubray to David and Vivian Smith in 1988. We awarded the Hoovers this appeal.

Code §§ 55-20 and 55-21 are at the heart of the controversy. Formerly §§ 5159 and 5160 of the Code of 1919, respectively, they read now as they did at the time of the 1928 deed. Section 55-20 provides as follows:

> § 55-20. Survivorship between joint tenants abolished. — When any joint tenant dies, before or after the vesting of the estate, whether the estate is real or personal, or whether partition could have been compelled or not, his part shall descend to his heirs, or pass by devise, or go to his personal representative, subject to debts or distribution, as if he had been a tenant in common. And if hereafter any estate, real or personal, is conveyed or devised to a husband and his wife, they shall take and hold the same by moieties in like manner as if a distinct moiety had been given to each by a separate conveyance.

Section 55-21 provides as follows:

> § 55-21. Exceptions to § 55-20. — Section 55-20 shall not apply to any estate which joint tenants have as executors or trustees, nor to an estate conveyed or devised to persons in their own right when it *manifestly appears* from the tenor of the instrument that it was intended [that] the part of the one dying should then belong to the others. Neither shall it affect the mode of proceeding on any joint judgment or decree in favor of or on any contract with two or more one of whom dies.

(Emphasis added.) The crucial inquiry, therefore, is whether it manifestly appears from the tenor of the 1928 deed that it was intended that Add and Bessie Shoemaker would hold the one-acre tract with the right of survivorship. The Hoovers maintain that the deed does not manifest an intention to create a survivorship estate; the word "survivorship" is never mentioned, nor is there any statement to the effect that the part of the one dying should then belong to the other.

On the other hand, the Smiths argue that the statement in the deed, "and not as tenants in common," does manifest the necessary intention to establish a survivorship estate. The Smiths point out that, at common law, three characteristics distinguished joint tenants from tenants in common, namely, (1) joint tenants were required to convey to each other by release rather than deed, (2) they could only sue and be sued jointly, and (3) they enjoyed the right of survivorship. (The first of these common law distinctions, conveyance by release, has been abolished by statute. See Code §§ 55-5 and 55-6.)

The Smiths state that the words, "and not as tenants in common," were added to the deed "for some reason." The Smiths then ask, was it so that Add and Bessie Shoemaker would have to make conveyances by release? Was it because they wanted to make sure one could not participate in court proceedings without the other? "Or were they trying to encompass" the "doctrine of survivorship"?

The Smiths argue that "[t]his last point, the common law distinction of survivorship, is the only meaningful reason to call special attention to the fact that parties are taking title as joint tenants and specifically not as tenants in common." And the Smiths conclude with the admonition that "[t]he parties gave us directions and we are obligated to follow them."

We are not obligated to follow directions, however, that are unclear, that are derived from language that is susceptible of more than one meaning. It is true that "[n]o particular words are necessary" to create a survivorship estate. Wallace v. Wallace, 190 S.E. 293, 298 (Va. 1937). Also, it may well be that the parties to the 1928 deed did intend to create such an estate.

However, they used uncertain language to accomplish their purpose. And for all that the language tells us, the parties may have had a different intention. There still does exist such an estate as a joint tenancy without survivorship, and if the parties, for whatever reason, desired to create such an estate, they might have thought they could accomplish that purpose with precisely the same language they employed in the 1928 deed.

Code § 55-21 requires only that the intention to create a survivorship estate be made manifest. To satisfy this requirement, parties need only use language that passes a simple test, one inherent in the meaning of the word "manifest." According to Black's Law Dictionary 962 (6th ed. 1990), manifest means "obvious to the understanding, evident to the mind, not obscure or hidden, and is synonymous with open, clear, visible, unmistakable, indubitable, indisputable, evident, and self-evident." We think the language of the 1928 deed wholly fails this test and is insufficient, as a matter of law, to create a survivorship estate.

Accordingly, we will reverse the judgment of the trial court and remand the case for further proceedings consistent with the views expressed in this opinion.

Reversed and remanded.

NOTES AND QUESTIONS

1. **Consequences.** Trace the chain of title from the 1928 deed down to the time of litigation. Why did it matter to the outcome of the case whether the 1928 deed to Add and Bessie Shoemaker created a right of survivorship in Add and Bessie or not?

2. **To A and B "as joint tenants and not as tenants in common."** Might the disputed deed in Hoover v. Smith have created a joint tenancy under the following statute (N.J. Stat. Ann. § 46:3-17)?

> [N]o estate shall be considered and adjudged to be an estate in joint tenancy, except it be expressly set forth in the grant or devise creating such

estate that it was or is the intention of the parties to create an estate in joint tenancy and not an estate in tenancy in common.

See Lipps v. Crowe (Section A.1.b below). In *Hoover*, the court reads the Virginia statutes to create three categories of concurrent estates: tenancy in common; joint tenancy with right of survivorship; and joint tenancy without survivorship. How does the court distinguish a joint tenancy without survivorship from a tenancy in common? Do the differences suggest why anyone would want to create a joint tenancy without survivorship? Can the Virginia statutes be construed as a statement, however inartful, of the typical statutory presumption in favor of a tenancy in common, with an exception for documents that express an intent for survivorship rights? What is the argument that the deed in Hoover v. Smith expressed the parties' intent to create survivorship rights?

3. **To A and B "as joint tenants."** *See* Downing v. Downing, 606 A.2d 208 (Md. 1992) (transfer "to A and B as joint tenants" creates joint tenancy under statute providing that a transfer creates a tenancy in common "unless the deed, will, or other written instrument expressly provides that the property granted is to be held in joint tenancy"). Even if the phrase "as joint tenants" is made acceptable by the local statute or case law, and especially when that question hasn't been resolved, what might you add to the instrument of transfer to make the transferor's intent clear?

4. **To A and B "jointly."** Is the word "jointly" ambiguous? *See* Montgomery v. Clarkson, 585 S.W.2d 483 (Mo. 1979) ("jointly" is not "express declaration" of joint tenancy as required by statute). Does it matter whether the document is drawn up by a lawyer? *See* Overheiser v. Lackey, 100 N.E. 738, 739 (N.Y. 1913) (word "jointly" in will prepared by layman created a tenancy in common); Householter v. Householter, 164 P.2d 101 (Kan. 1945) (word "jointly," used five times in a will prepared by individual who had served one term as a probate judge, created joint tenancy). Suppose the deed is "to A and B jointly and not as tenants in common"? *See* Kurpiel v. Kurpiel, 271 N.Y.S.2d 114 (N.Y. Sup. Ct. 1966) (joint tenancy). Is a transfer "to A and B jointly" sufficient to create a joint tenancy under the following statute (Vt. Stat. Ann. Tit. 27, § 2)?

§ 2. Estate in common preferred to joint tenancy.

Conveyances and devises of lands, whether for years, for life or in fee, made to two or more persons, shall be construed to create estates in common and not in joint tenancy, unless it is expressed therein that the grantees or devisees shall take the lands jointly or as joint tenants or in joint tenancy or to them and the survivors of them. This provision shall not apply to devises or conveyances made in trust or made to husband and wife or to conveyances in which it manifestly appears from the tenor of the instrument that it was intended to create an estate in joint tenancy.

5. **To A and B "and their heirs" as joint tenants, etc.** If the *other* language of the deed or will is sufficiently clear to create a joint tenancy, does the phrase "and their heirs" create an ambiguity? Some courts have thought so. *See* Kipp v. Chips Estate, 732 A.2d 127 (Vt. 1999) (clause granting land "to Erwin N. Chips and June Kipp, joint tenants, and their heirs and assigns forever" was ambiguous because of the inclusion of the "heirs" language; extrinsic evidence was not

admissible to clarify the parties' intent). Why is the *Kipps* analysis of the "heirs" language — with which you may be tempted to agree — wrong? At common law, how would a grantor transfer a joint tenancy *in fee simple* if "heirs" language, which was mandatory to create a fee, is inconsistent with a joint tenancy? How should a court construe the "heirs" language? *See* Downing v. Downing, 606 A.2d 208, 212 n.5 (Md. 1992) ("and his heirs" are words of limitation, not words of purchase); Maxwell v. Saylor, 58 A.2d 355, 356 (Pa. 1948) (same).

6. **To A and B "as joint tenants, with right of survivorship, and not as tenants in common."**   In Hoover v. Smith, and under most statutes, the inclusion of survivorship language in the deed or will should create a joint tenancy in fee simple. *See* Cunningham v. Hastings, 556 N.E.2d 12 (Ind. Ct. App. 1990) (deed to A and B "as joint tenants with the right of survivorship, and NOT as tenants in common" was "unequivocal language" to create a joint tenancy) (emphasis in original). In some states, however, survivorship language might create a concurrent life estate in the grantees with a remainder to the survivor. *See* Section A.2.d below. That, as we will see, is a much more formidable estate than a joint tenancy in fee simple.

7. **Statutes.**   The current statutory law on the creation of a joint tenancy is usefully summarized in 4 Thompson on Real Property § 31.06(d) (David A. Thomas ed. 1994).

CAMP v. CAMP
260 S.E.2d 243 (Va. 1979)

COMPTON, JUSTICE.

In this appeal, we must construe a deed to determine the title acquired by a mother and son to real property conveyed to them "as tenants in common with the right of survivorship as at common law."

The issue arose in the following manner, as revealed by the pleadings and a summary statement of the facts prepared by the trial judge. In 1955, Robert Camp, Jr., unmarried, and appellee Tincy Camp, his mother, agreed to purchase a house and lot located in the City of Richmond. Tincy Camp consulted a Richmond attorney who, at her request, drew the deed in question, which was duly executed and admitted to record.

The deed contained the usual formal parts. The premise included the names of the three grantors as "parties of the first part" and the son and mother as "parties of the second part." The next paragraph contained the consideration, the recital of payment of purchase money, and the granting clause (there was no habendum), as follows:

> That for and in consideration of the sum of Ten ($10.00) Dollars, receipt whereof is hereby acknowledged, and other good and valuable consideration, the said parties of the first part do grant and convey with general warranty of title unto the said parties of the second part, as tenants in common with the right of survivorship as at common law, the following [described] real estate.

Then the deed provided for assumption by the grantees of the obligations of two prior deeds of trust on the property.

Robert Camp, Jr., married appellant Hilda Camp in 1956. He died in 1966 survived by his widow, six children (who are also appellants), and by his mother. Thereafter, a dispute arose between the mother and the widow as to the ownership of the property in question.

Subsequently, the widow, in her own name and on behalf of her children, filed the instant petition for declaratory judgment in equity against the mother asserting that the property was conveyed to mother and son as tenants in common and seeking a declaration that the widow and children had "a one-half legal interest in said property." In response, the mother maintained she was a joint tenant under the deed and, because she survived her son, had a fee simple interest in the property.

The chancellor received the ore tenus testimony of the attorney who drew the deed and, after considering argument of counsel for the parties, decided in favor of the mother. The trial court found that when the deed was drafted, the intention of the mother and son was to have the real estate conveyed to them as joint tenants with the right of survivorship as at common law. The court also found that the attorney "was in error as to the correct terminology to be used to create survivorship between the parties," that "tenants in common" was intended to be "joint tenants," and "that it manifestly appear[ed] to the court from the tenor of the deed and from the evidence in the case, that it was intended that the part of the first to die should then belong to the other." Consequently, the court below ruled that the real estate passed by operation of law to the mother, Tincy Camp, in fee simple. We think the trial court erred.

Initially, several fundamental rules for the construction of deeds should be reviewed. The prime consideration, as with any writing, is to determine the intention of the parties executing the instrument. The intention, including a finding as to the estate conveyed, should be ascertained from the language used in the deed, if possible. If the language is explicit and the intention is thereby free from doubt, such intention is controlling, if not contrary to law or to public policy, and auxiliary rules of construction should not be used. If, on the other hand, the instrument is uncertain and ambiguous, oral evidence may be received to show all the attendant circumstances existing at the time the deed was executed, including the situation of the parties and their relationship. But "parol contemporaneous evidence is, in general, inadmissible to contradict or vary the terms of a valid written instrument because the writing is the only outward and visible expression of the meaning of the parties, and to allow it to be varied or contradicted by verbal testimony of what passed at or before its making, would be to postpone the more certain and reliable mode of proof, to the more precarious and less trustworthy; to prefer the less good to the best evidence." 2 J. Minor, Institutes of Common and Statute Law 1059 (4th ed. 1892). Finally, where two clauses are irreconcilably repugnant in a deed, the first prevails. Mills v. Embrey, 186 S.E. 47, 49 (Va. 1936). The foregoing rule is to be applied, however, only in the case of "rigorous necessity" and when the two clauses are absolutely incapable of reconciliation.

Against this background, we now turn to the facts of this case. The attorney who drew the deed, testifying 22 years after the event, stated that he recalled talking to

Tincy Camp about preparing the deed. She told counsel, he said, that her son was to buy the property for her and that the son wanted her to live there for the remainder of her life. The attorney stated the mother said the "longer liver" of the mother and son was "to get all of the property." Counsel testified he had never before drawn a deed between "tenants by the entireties" except when a husband and wife were involved and, because of this, he consulted other attorneys about the problem. They told him, he testified, that he should use the phrase "tenants in common" instead of "tenants by the entireties" when the deed did not involve husband and wife. The attorney further testified that the grantees intended to receive the property "with the right of survivorship between them."

It is manifest from the trial court's ruling that the chancellor considered all of the foregoing evidence dehors the deed in reaching his decision. Yet, as we have noted, the terms of a valid deed may not be varied or contradicted by testimonial evidence of that which passed at or before its making. Consequently, the trial court should not have relied on the attorney's statements dealing with the intention of the parties. Thus, we shall cast aside that evidence and examine the deed, uncertain in meaning, in the light of the circumstances under which it was written.

The remaining evidence merely shows that residential urban property was to be purchased by a mother and her unmarried son, and that the mother consulted counsel with reference to the purchase. No definitive conclusion can be drawn from those meager facts as to the parties' intention with reference to the nature of the title to be acquired. Turning to the provisions of the instrument as contained within its four corners, we likewise obtain little, if any, guidance as to the parties' intention, except as revealed by the disputed provision. We do know from the deed that the mother and son became obligated to pay the unpaid balances on prior encumbrances affecting the property. But that fact may not be the basis for a positive judgment as to the parties' intention. Such an obligation would just as likely be incurred by tenants in common as by joint tenants.

Consequently, we are left with the disputed provision of the deed as the sole means to ascertain the parties' intention about the title to be acquired. The language "as tenants in common" is totally repugnant to the words "with the right of survivorship as at common law." The two portions are absolutely incapable of being reconciled. Accordingly, we are left with no alternative but to hold, applying the foregoing rule of repugnant clauses to this situation, that the portion first appearing in the deed controls, and that the mother and son were conveyed the property as tenants in common, not as joint tenants. The effect of this holding is, of course, to treat the latter portion of the disputed provision as surplusage. This is a case of "rigorous necessity" in which the harsh common-law rule must be applied if the deed is to have some effect rather than being a nullity.

For these reasons, the order appealed from will be reversed and final judgment will be entered here decreeing that Robert Camp. Jr. and Tincy Camp took the property as tenants in common under the 1955 deed.

Reversed and final judgment.

POFF, JUSTICE, dissenting.

I respectfully dissent. The majority's conclusion results from a mechanistic application of an arbitrary rule devised for other cases and offends the spirit, if not the letter, of statutes enacted by the General Assembly.

Under Code § 55-20, the interest of a "joint tenant" passes at death "as if he had been a tenant in common." Yet, the legislature has not abolished the estate of joint tenancy; § 55-21 states that:

> The preceding section [§ 55-20] shall not apply to an estate conveyed or devised to persons in their own right when it manifestly appears from the tenor of the instrument that it was intended the part of the one dying should then belong to the others.

Thus, the fundamental issue in this case is whether "it manifestly appears from the tenor of the instrument that it was intended the part of the one dying should then belong to the others." I believe such an intent so appears from the face of this deed.

While it is true that a tenant in common has no right of survivorship, it is also true that a survivorship interest is the interest distinguishing a joint tenancy from a tenancy in common. The use of the phrase "as tenants in common with the right of survivorship as at common law" was obviously an attempt, albeit inartful, to create a joint tenancy by appending a right of survivorship to a tenancy in common. Why would the words "with the right of survivorship as at common law" be used except to create a right of survivorship? In my view, the language the majority considers "surplusage" is the very language that manifests the intent that "the part of the one dying should then belong to the survivor."

Since the two parts of the phrase in dispute are reconcilable, the rule of Mills v. Embrey, 186 S.E. 47 (Va. 1936), designed for cases involving two irreconcilably repugnant clauses, does not apply. Adhering to the rule prescribed by the legislature, I would affirm the chancellor's construction of the deed.

HARRISON and COCHRAN, JJ., join in dissent.

NOTES AND QUESTIONS

1. **Is the deed language ambiguous?** What is the argument that the deed language in Camp v. Camp was reasonably clar? *See* Germaine v. Delaine, 318 So. 2d 681 (Ala. 1975) (deed to grantees "jointly, as tenants in common and to the survivor thereof" created joint tenancy because of the language of survivorship); Gagnon v. Pronovost, 71 A.2d 747, 750 (N.H. 1949) (dissenting opinion) (survivorship language appeared in the *payment* clause of the deed rather than in the granting or habendum clauses; according to the dissent: "It may be conceded that the deed in dispute is not a model form to create a joint tenancy and that the notary public who prepared it was not a model draftsman. That is not fatal, however, if it can be fairly said that the intent was expressed in reasonably clear terms."). What is the argument for the ambiguity of the language in *Camp*?

2. **Ambiguity and extrinsic evidence.** The court in Camp v. Camp stated that extrinsic evidence is admissible to resolve the meaning of an ambiguous

document, but then excluded the scrivener's testimony about Tincy Camp's intent, because parol (oral) evidence is inadmissible to "contradict or vary the terms of a valid written agreement." How can extrinsic evidence "contradict or vary" an *unclear* meaning? *See* W.W.W. Associates, Inc. v. Giancontieri, 566 N.E.2d 639 (N.Y. 1990) ("A familiar and eminently sensible proposition of law is that, when parties set down their agreement in a *clear*, complete document, their writing should as a rule be enforced according to its terms.") (emphasis added). In *Camp*, didn't the scrivener's testimony help to resolve the contradiction that the court finds in the language of the deed? How did the court deal with the inconsistency between the tenancy in common language and the survivorship language in the deed? If the relevant deed phrase — "as tenants in common with right of survivorship" — contains a repugnancy, why not strike the tenants in common language?

3. **Exclusion of extrinsic evidence.**   Some cases hold that extrinsic evidence is inadmissible in joint tenancy cases, even though the document contains a relevant ambiguity. *See, e.g.*, Kipp v. Chips Estate, 732 A.2d 127, 132 (Vt. 1999) ("Even if the extrinsic evidence was overwhelming that the parties to the deed in this case intended to create a joint tenancy, that intent was inadequately expressed to allow us to find such a property interest."). In Gagnon v. Pronovost, 71 A.2d 747, 750-751 (N.H. 1949; rehearing op. 1950), the court explained the exclusion of extrinsic evidence this way:

> It is true generally that in this state, the interpretation of any grant consists in the ascertainment of intention and that the question of intention is one of fact to be determined upon all the competent evidence available. However, if R.L., c. 259, § 17 [the joint tenancy statute] means anything, it must necessarily mean that to create a joint-tenancy the grantor or testator must not only intend to create such an estate, he must [also] express this intention in his deed or will, either by the use of the words set out in said section, or by using other words clearly expressing his intention. [The New Hampshire statute provides that "Every conveyance or devise of real estate made to two or more persons shall be construed to create an estate in common and not in joint tenancy, unless it shall be expressed therein that the estate is to be holden by the grantees or devisees as joint tenants, or to them and the survivor of them, or unless other words are used clearly expressing an intention to create a joint tenancy."].
>
> [I]n the opinion of a majority of the Court the admission of evidence as to the facts and circumstances existing at the time of and surrounding the drawing of this deed, no matter how crystal clear it may be as to the grantor's intent to create a joint tenancy, would serve no useful purpose in this case, for it cannot alter the fact that he failed to express this intention in the deed in clear language as required by said § 17. If he had there would be no need for extraneous evidence to determine what kind of estate the deed creates.

Compare the Virginia statute (*see* Hoover v. Smith), the Vermont statute at issue in Kipps v. Chips Estate (Note 4 after Hoover v. Smith) and the New Hampshire statute at issue in Gagnon v. Pronovost. Do any of the statutes seem to compel the exclusion of extrinsic evidence, and if so, which?

NOTES ON REFORMATION

1. **Mistake and extrinsic evidence.** Estate of Vadney, 634 N.E.2d 976 (N.Y. 1994), was a case much like Camp v. Camp: the lawyer who drafted the disputed deed testified that the parties (mother and son) intended to create a joint tenancy, although the deed was apparently in the form "to A and B," without any further expression of the grantor's intent. After the mother's death, the son claimed that the deed created a joint tenancy; his three siblings contended that the deed created a tenancy in common. The son sued for *reformation* of the deed, contending that "the absence of survivorship language in the instrument of conveyance was contrary to the grantor's intent and due solely to a scrivener's error." The trial court ruled that extrinsic evidence of the grantor's intent would not be received to vary the terms of the deed; the Appellate Division reversed and granted the petition. The Court of Appeals affirmed:

> Petitioner has met his burden of proving by clear and convincing evidence that decedent intended to create a joint tenancy rather than a tenancy in common, and that language manifesting such an intent was mistakenly omitted from the instrument of conveyance by the scrivener. Petitioner's uncontroverted evidence consisted of testimony of the attorney who drafted the deed indicating that he had received oral instructions from decedent to prepare a deed conveying the subject property to herself and petitioner as joint tenants, that he neglected to include survivorship language in the deed through his own oversight, and that neither he nor the grantor noticed the omission at the time of the execution of the instrument. The drafting attorney also produced a copy of his notes taken during a preliminary meeting with decedent which indicate that decedent desired the co-ownership interest created by the deed to include the "right of survivorship." The attorney's wife, who was present during the execution of the deed and who witnessed decedent's contemporaneously executed will, testified that decedent stated at that time that she wanted petitioner to have the house. Indeed, unless decedent intended to remove that property from the estate assets that were to pass by the contemporaneously executed will, the execution of a deed conveying the property to herself and petitioner would have been unnecessary. Accordingly, petitioner has met his high burden of proving that the instrument as written did not accurately reflect decedent's intent to include a right of survivorship, and the deed should be reformed to include the omitted language.

If Tincy Camp had added a count for reformation in her case, might she have won under the standard announced in Estate of Vadney? Notice her position had she joined the two claims: if the deed were ambiguous, the extrinsic evidence should have been admitted; if the deed were unambiguous, it should have been reformed. Was Tincy Camp perhaps the victim of double malpractice — in the 1955 drafting of the deed, and again in the 1970s litigation over the meaning of the deed?

2. **Mistaken joint tenancy.** Massicotte v. Matuzas, 738 A.2d 1260 (N.H. 1999), presents the opposite mistake from *Vadney*: inadvertent *creation* of a joint tenancy. Josephine Massicotte asked her attorney to draw up a deed placing her residence in the names of herself and her second husband, and providing that upon their deaths, her three children would receive title. The attorney drafted a deed

conveying title to Josephine, her husband, and her three children as joint tenants with right of survivorship. When the mistake was discovered, Josephine requested quitclaim deeds from the children; two complied, but defendant Anthony Matuzas refused. In Josephine's suit to compel Matuzas to convey his interest to her, the trial court ordered the conveyance. On Matuzas's appeal, the order was vacated and the case remanded:

> The defendant argues that the trial court's order should have conformed with the plaintiff's intent at the time she executed the 1981 deed. Therefore, the court erred by [not] reforming the deed and conveyance to preserve for the defendant a remainder interest in the property. We agree.

> The trial court found that instead of the remainder interest she intended, the plaintiff mistakenly conveyed a present interest to her three children. Once the court determined that the defendant would be unjustly enriched by the plaintiff's mistake, and therefore [that] the circumstances warranted reforming the conveyance, established principles of equity should have controlled the reformation. Thus, the plaintiff was entitled to have the court reform the conveyance to correct the mistake and grant that which she intended to convey. Instead of reforming the deed to reflect the plaintiff's intent at the time of the conveyance, however, the court canceled the conveyance in its entirety. In doing so, the trial court erred.

Massicotte reveals an important point about the remedy of reformation: when available, it gives the reformer what she originally intended; it does not allow her to change her mind. What document(s) would you have drafted to accomplish Josephine Massicotte's original wishes? On remand, should the trial court also cancel the quitclaim deeds from Anthony's siblings, restoring them to their shares of the remainder?

NOTES ON MULTIPLE-PARTY BANK ACCOUNTS

1. **Different types of joint accounts.** Suppose that A deposits money in a bank and includes B's name on the account. In creating a joint account, A may intend any of three substantively different consequences. *See generally* William M. McGovern, *The Payable on Death Account and Other Will Substitutes*, 67 Nw. U. L. Rev. 7 (1972); Donald Kepner, *Five More Years of the Joint Bank Account Muddle*, 26 U. Chi. L. Rev. 376 (1959).

a. A *payable on death* account is listed in A's name, "POD to B." B has neither present possessory rights nor withdrawal powers during A's life; B is only entitled to the balance, if any, remaining in the account at A's death. The form of the account accurately expresses the depositor's intent, which is to transfer funds to B only at the depositor's death, and only those funds in the account at that time. Courts initially invalidated POD accounts as unattested testamentary transfers; such accounts are widely authorized today by statute. *See* UPC §§ 6-101, 6-201 et seq. (1989). Where not so authorized, the earlier view of invalidity may apply; note, however, that the objection to the account is not that the donor expressed her intent unclearly, but rather than the donor did not express her intent in proper testamentary form.

b. A *joint tenancy account* will also usually be stated clearly; the bank card or application papers will say that the account belongs "to A and B as joint tenants with right of survivorship." As in the case of joint tenancies of land, the cotenants have present ownership interests in the account as well as a right of survivorship in any balance existing when one of the cotenants dies. (In disputes between the cotenants themselves, the cotenant who withdraws more than his or her proportionate share of the funds has to account to the other. Our concern is with disputes arising after one cotenant's death, between the family of the deceased cotenant and the surviving cotenant.) The problem raised by these express joint tenancy accounts is that the depositor may not intend a joint tenancy account, but may intend instead a convenience account.

c. A *convenience account* is one in which the depositor A adds B's name to the account to authorize B to withdraw money for A's benefit or at A's direction. B is an agent. B's power to withdraw funds is solely for A's convenience; B has no present ownership of funds in the account during A's life, nor a right of survivorship in the funds remaining in the account at A's death.

2. **Bank offerings.** When POD accounts are recognized, a bank may offer both it and the joint tenancy account to a prospective depositor seeking a joint account. Banks probably won't offer what is designated above as a convenience account: death of the principal (depositor) revokes an agency, and the bank might be liable for payments made after the principal's death.

3. **Extrinsic evidence and joint accounts.** Courts in the bank account cases generally allow the depositor's successors to introduce extrinsic evidence showing that the depositor intended a convenience account rather than the joint tenancy account indicated by the form of the bank card. *See, e.g.*, Franklin v. Anna Nat'l Bank, 488 N.E.2d 1117 (Ill. App. Ct. 1986) (bank card specified joint tenancy with right of survivorship; extrinsic evidence admitted to show depositor's intent for convenience account); Zink v. Stafford, 509 S.E.2d 833 (Va. 1999) (same). However, at least one court has held that an express joint tenancy account cannot be shown by extrinsic evidence offered after the death of the depositor to be a convenience account; after the depositor's death, the funds in the account belong to the surviving joint tenant. Robinson v. Delfino, 710 A.2d 154 (R.I. 1998). Why might a court, as in Franklin v. Anna National Bank, be more liberal in admitting extrinsic evidence in bank account cases than in land ownership cases? Why might a court, as in Robinson v. Delfino, conclusively presume that a surviving joint tenant is entitled to the remaining funds in the account after the death of the depositor?

b.   The Four Unities

Having considered the difficulties posed by a grantor's lack of clarity in stating his or her intent to create a joint tenancy, we now consider the obstacle posed by the requirement of the four unities. Clarity of intent and the four unities are cumulative, not alternative, problems. In states that require satisfaction of the four unities, a noncomplying transfer will create a tenancy in common, no matter how clearly the grantor has expressed the intent to create a joint tenancy. *See* Anson v. Murphy, 32 N.W.2d 271, 272 (Neb. 1948) ("The deeds presently before us do not create a joint tenancy for the reason that they lacked the unity of time and title necessary to create such an estate. It may be that the grantors intended to create a joint tenancy and not a tenancy in common, but for failure to comply with controlling rules of law, their expressed intention could not be given effect."). Likewise, a transfer that satisfies the four unities will nevertheless create a tenancy in common if the grantor has not expressed the intent for a joint tenancy with the requisite clarity. *See* Choman v. Epperley, 592 P.2d 714, 715 (Wyo. 1979):

> Plaintiff contends that if the four unities of time, possession, title and interest are present, a joint tenancy results from that fact alone. This reasoning is faulty in the same manner as would be the reasoning that since wood is necessary to construct a wooden chair, all items constructed with wood are *ipso facto* chairs. Historically, the four unities have been a requirement for a joint tenancy, but not a definition of such. The presence of the four unities, therefore, does not *ipso facto* create the joint tenancy.

The four unities rule is outdated and unjustified, but it continues to exist in an uncertain number of states. *See* Therrien v. Therrien, 46 A.2d 538 (N.H. 1946) (rule exists "in several jurisdictions"); Jesse Dukeminier, James E. Krier, Gregory S. Alexander & Michael H. Schill, Property 276 (6th ed. 2006) (four unities are required "[a]t common law and in many states today"). Where the rule exists, it is easy to evade by a skilled drafter, but it is a trap for the unwary. Forewarned is forearmed.

LIPPS v. CROWE
28 N.J. Super. 131, 100 A.2d 361 (N.J. Super. Ct. Ch. Div. 1953)

FREUND, J.S.C.

On August 16, 1926 the plaintiff, Edward J. Lipps, executed a deed conveying to Margaret Howard an "undivided one-half interest as joint tenant" in premises owned by him. The habendum clause provided that she was to have and to hold the premises "as joint tenant with the party of the first part [the plaintiff], and not as tenant in common." The grantee died intestate on July 28, 1943, and the defendant Denis Crowe, one of her heirs-at-law, claims an interest in the property, contending that the tenancy was in common and not joint. The plaintiff claims title as surviving joint tenant and seeks summary judgment to quiet title. The question for determination is whether or not the aforesaid deed effectively created a joint tenancy.

The essential characteristics of a joint tenancy are the four unities of interest, title, time and possession, and their co-existence, for, if any is lacking there is no joint tenancy.

> The requirement of the four unities expresses in an artificial way the basic idea that cotenants hold as a unity with a community of interest between them, since if they take as one they must take at the same time, by the same deed or feoffment, and must have interests which are identical. The requirement of the four unities necessarily arose as a result of the basic concept rather than as prerequisites to the creation of the estate.

2 American Law of Property (1952), § 6.1, at 4 and 5.

The defendant argues that since the plaintiff had acquired title through a prior deed and subsequently conveyed an undivided one-half interest directly to Margaret Howard, two requisites for a joint tenancy — the unities of interest and time — are lacking. He urges that the interests of joint tenants must be acquired by one and the same conveyance.

At the early common law such a contention would have been meritorious. 2 Blackstone's Commentaries, § 180 and § 181. If the plaintiff had executed a deed to an intermediary who in turn conveyed to the plaintiff and Margaret Howard as joint tenants, unquestionably the title would have been vested in them as such tenants. Until comparatively recent days the cautious conveyancer would resort to the use of a conduit whenever a change was being made in the nature of a grantor's estate. [T]oday there is hardly any need to use an intermediary. "It is now being held that such a circuitous procedure is outmoded and that a direct conveyance is permissible, the ancient unities to the contrary notwithstanding." 2 American Law of Property (1952), § 6.2, page 9. The trend of modern cases is to regard the creation of a joint tenancy or tenancy by the entirety just as valid if made directly between grantor and grantees as it would be if made through a third person.

If a joint tenancy can be created between or among persons by means of a conveyance through third persons, it can be created by direct conveyance. Indeed, our Legislature in 1950 enacted a statute to that effect, N.J.S.A. 46:3-17.1, which reads as follows:

> Any conveyance of real estate, hereafter made, by the grantor therein, to himself and another or others, as joint tenants shall, if otherwise valid, be as fully effective to vest an estate in joint tenancy in such real estate in the grantees therein named, including the grantor, as if the same had been conveyed by the grantor therein to a third party and by such third party to said grantees.

However, this statute does not apply to the facts here, because both the conveyance and the death of Margaret Howard occurred before its effective date and it is prospective in operation. But it is indicative of the legislative intent that a joint tenancy may be vested in the grantor and a grantee by direct conveyance.

In the instant case the deed expressly set forth that the plaintiff was conveying an interest which was owned by him and was to be held by him and his grantee as joint tenants and not as tenants in common. The grant and habendum are clear and specific as to the intention of the grantor. To hold, as the defendant urges, that a tenancy in common was created by the deed would not be in accord with, but in direct opposition to, the expressed intention of the plaintiff.

Here, until the execution and delivery of the deed, the plaintiff was the sole owner in fee, and it was not until the execution and delivery of his deed and by means of it that any interest was vested in Margaret Howard. Therefore, the tenancy between the plaintiff and Margaret Howard was created at the same time and through the same instrument, and, accordingly, the unities essential for a joint tenancy are to be found from the facts and construction of the deed. Upon the death of Margaret Howard, title vested in the plaintiff as surviving joint tenant.

Judgment accordingly.

NOTES AND QUESTIONS

1. **Explanation; justification?** As the American Law of Property (quoted in the principal case) notes, the four unities requirement has a conceptual explanation: the unities result from the courts' somewhat pedantic teasing out of the full implications of the notion that the joint tenants "take as one." The requirement persists today, at least in some states, "although no attempt is made to justify either its present or its past existence." Therrien v. Therrien, 46 A.2d 538, 539 (N.H. 1946).

2. **Direct conveyances: two time and title violations.** The four unities requirement is violated when the grantor transfers to himself and another (A transfers "to A and B" as joint tenants, etc.); the common law rule that a grantor cannot transfer an interest to himself means that A gets nothing in that transfer, and therefore has an interest acquired at a different (earlier) time and by a different (earlier) title than B's interest. See Dolley v. Powers, 89 N.E.2d 412, 415 (Ill. 1950) ("Edward Powers could not convey any interest to himself as a joint tenant, and for that reason he could not by the same instrument convey to his son, Thomas Edward Powers, in joint tenancy."); Stuehm v. Mikulski, 297 N.W. 595 (Neb. 1941); Strout v. Burgess, 68 A.2d 241 (Me. 1949); Robert G. Natelson, Modern Law of Deeds to Real Property § 1.2, at 8 (1992) (after transfers by deed replaced livery of seisin, the "metaphor of transfer [requiring two parties to make a transfer] did not die").

The principal case illustrates a second way in which the unities of time and title can be violated: the grantor transfers an undivided one-half interest to another (A conveys "to B, an undivided one-half interest as joint tenant and not as tenant in common"). B alone receives an interest by that transfer; A's interest preexists B's. Cf. In re Walker's Estate, 16 A.2d 28 (Pa. 1940) (deed from husband conveying undivided half interest to his wife violated time and title unities and created tenancy in common rather than tenancy by the entirety).

3. **Satisfying the four unities: the "strawman" procedure.** Both of the four unities violations in Note 2 can be avoided with the assistance of a strawman: the grantor A transfers to X (an office worker or law partner), who by prearrangement transfers "to A and B" by a deed containing the appropriate words to create a joint tenancy. See William A. Stoebuck & Dale A. Whitman, The Law of Property § 5.3, at 187; Downing v. Downing, 606 A.2d 208 (Md. 1992) (facts illustrate use of strawman). What problems do you find with the need for a strawman to create a joint tenancy?

4. **Abolishing the strawman: intent.** By judicial decision (as in the principal case) or statute, some states have eliminated the need for a strawman. In these states, a transfer that fails to satisfy the four unities nevertheless creates a joint tenancy if the parties sufficiently express the intent for that cotenancy. See, e.g., Miller v. Riegler, 419 S.W.2d 599 (Ark. 1967) (bank account); Switzer v. Pratt, 23 N.W.2d 837 (Iowa 1946) (land); N.J. Stat. Ann. § 46:3-17.1 (cited in the principal case); Ohio Rev. Code § 5302.18 ("A deed in which a grantor is also a grantee is effective to convey the interest in the title of the grantor or grantors to all of the grantees in the proportion and manner indicated in the deed."). See generally Ellen Carle Lilly, The Creation of Joint Tenancies — Common Law Technicalities vs. the Grantor's Intent, 82 W. Va. L. Rev. 335 (1979); 4 Thompson on Real Property

§ 31.06(c) (discussion of statutes affecting some or all of the four unities). Do the New Jersey and Ohio statutes, which are typical, remove the need for a strawman in both types of direct conveyances in Note 2? If not, how would you argue that the statutes should be construed to apply to both types of transfer?

5. **Satisfying the four unities: creative interpretation.** In addition to emphasizing the grantor's intent to create a joint tenancy, did the court in the principal case also conclude that Lipps' deed did not violate the four unities? Is that claim easier to make when A transfers an undivided one-half interest to B as a joint tenant than when A transfers to herself and B as joint tenants? *See* Curtis v. Smithers, 134 A.2d 576, 579 (Conn. Super. Ct. 1957) (deed from A "to A and B as joint tenants and not as tenants in common, with right of survivorship" satisfied the four unities: "where a sole owner conveys property to another and himself as joint tenants, he is intending to create a new estate in himself as well as in the other person, and consequently in such a case the unities of time and of title are in fact present, since their title comes into existence by such conveyance"). Did the court in *Curtis* implicitly reject the common law rule forbidding a transfer to oneself? Is such a rejection necessary in the transfer at issue in Lipps v. Crowe?

6. **Unity of interest.** Joint tenants cannot share a unity of interest unless they hold equal fractional shares in the land. The question of the significance of unequal shares often arises in suits to partition (abolish) the cotenancy, when one party claims more than an equal fractional share of the land or proceeds of sale on the ground that he or she contributed more than a proportionate part of the purchase price. Partition is considered in Section 3.a below. At this point, consider whether, in the following transfers, the parties share a unity of interest:

a. O conveys "to A in fee simple, and to B for life, remainder to C, as joint tenants and not as tenants in common." *See* 2 Tiffany on Real Property, § 418, at 197.

b. O conveys "a one-half undivided interest to A and a one-half undivided interest to B, as joint tenants with right of survivorship and not as tenants in common." This one is tricky; *see* 2 A.L.P. § 6.1, at 4-5 (A.J. Casner ed. 1952). By specifying a fractional share for each cotenant separately, is O violating the requirement of unity of interest, or simply stating (in part) the consequences of a joint tenancy? (Recall that for some purposes — severance and sharing of benefits and burdens — joint tenants have separate fractional shares.)

2. Severance of the Joint Tenancy

Now that we know what one has to do to get into a joint tenancy, we consider what one has to do to get out. As noted at the beginning of the chapter, the doctrine of severance follows from the doctrine of the four unities. If A and B are joint tenants, and A conveys to X, the unities of time and title do not exist between X and B; as a result, X and B hold as tenants in common.

Severance requires an inter vivos transfer by the severing cotenant; a will does not sever. That leaves open the question, what counts as a severing inter vivos transfer? The following cases indicate the troublesome issues involved in answering that question. An excellent article by Professor Helmholz offers a thorough review of these issues. *See* R.H. Helmholz, *Realism and Formalism in the Severance of Joint Tenancies*, 77 Neb. L. Rev. 1 (1998).

a.   Severance by Conveyance

IN RE KNICKERBOCKER
912 P.2d 969 (Utah 1996)

HOWE, JUSTICE.

Plaintiff Bradford E. Knickerbocker and Christine Cannon Knickerbocker married on July 2, 1984. On July 22, 1991, Mrs. Knickerbocker filed a divorce action against her husband. The trial court awarded her exclusive temporary use of the house that she owned in joint tenancy with Mr. Knickerbocker and issued a temporary restraining order prohibiting him from contacting her. On August 7, 1991, the court issued another order prohibiting the parties from "selling, encumbering or mortgaging" their assets. Thereafter, Mr. Knickerbocker left the state and did not return to Utah until after Mrs. Knickerbocker's death on December 7, 1991. The divorce action was pending at that time.

About the time she filed for divorce, Mrs. Knickerbocker learned that she was suffering from a potentially life-threatening disease, diagnosed after her death as malignant intravascular lymphomatosis, a rare blood disease. As Mrs. Knickerbocker's condition worsened, she expressed concern about the welfare of her two [minor] children [from a prior marriage] to her attorney, Joseph Henriod, her mother, Elaine Cannon, and her brother, James Q. Cannon. In an effort to preserve her assets for her children, she decided to establish an inter vivos trust for their benefit, execute a will naming them as her beneficiaries, and appoint James Q. Cannon as her attorney-in-fact. On August 21, 1991, while she was a patient at the University of Utah Medical Center, she executed (1) a declaration of trust and agreement establishing a trust for the benefit of her children and naming herself, Anthony J. Cannon, and Elaine Cannon as trustees; (2) her last will and testament naming James Q. Cannon as the personal representative of her estate; and (3) a durable power of attorney naming Mr. Cannon as her attorney-in-fact.

A few days before executing these documents but after the trial court had prohibited Mr. and Mrs. Knickerbocker from "selling, encumbering or mortgaging" their assets, Mrs. Knickerbocker executed a quitclaim deed "as a Joint Tenant," conveying to herself "as a Tenant in Common" her interest in the house. The deed was promptly recorded. After establishing the trust, she executed a deed conveying her one-half interest in the house to the trustees. Mrs. Knickerbocker died the next day.

Mr. Knickerbocker filed an action against James Q. Cannon challenging the severance of the joint tenancy in the house. Mr. Knickerbocker moved for partial summary judgment on the joint tenancy issue. The court granted this motion, holding that Mrs. Knickerbocker's attempt to sever the joint tenancy in the house was legally ineffective because (1) she did not effectively convey the property to a third party, and (2) it violated the August 7, 1991, order prohibiting the parties from "selling, encumbering or mortgaging" their assets.

James Q. Cannon, Anthony J. Cannon, and Elaine Cannon cross-appeal, asserting that the trial court erred in ruling that Mrs. Knickerbocker failed to sever the joint tenancy in the house.

A. The Unilateral Severance

Historically, a joint tenant could unilaterally terminate a joint tenancy by destroying one of the four unities essential to joint tenancy — time, title, interest, and possession. 2 American Law of Property § 6.2, at 8-9 (1952). However, a joint tenant could not terminate a joint tenancy by executing a unilateral self-conveyance because such a conveyance had no legal effect and could not destroy any of the four unities.

A substantial number of jurisdictions have now recognized that a severance may be accomplished by a unilateral self-conveyance. While it is true that, as Mr. Knickerbocker points out, many states have not abolished the need to convey to a strawman to sever a joint tenancy, we find that the reasoning of those that have abolished it is more convincing.

The reasoning of the Illinois Court of Appeals in Minonk State Bank v. Grassman, 432 N.E.2d 386, at 389 (Ill. App. Ct. 1982), is particularly persuasive. In that case, after pointing out that the Illinois legislature had already abolished the strawman requirement for the creation of joint tenancies, the court observed that "adherence to a rule which would make it more difficult to destroy joint tenancies than to create them, runs contrary to the basic concept of joint tenancy." *Minonk State Bank*, 432 N.E.2d at 389 (citing 2 American Law of Property § 6.2 (1952)). The court reasoned that if a person can create a joint tenancy by granting to himself and another person, a tenant should also be able to sever the joint tenancy by conveying his interest to himself. In addition, the court stated that the key to determining whether a joint tenancy has been severed is the intent of the parties rather than the four unities. The court held that a joint tenant clearly demonstrates an intent to sever by making a unilateral self-conveyance and courts should not frustrate that intent by refusing to recognize the severance.

We agree with that analysis. Like the Illinois legislature, the Utah legislature has recognized that the use of a strawman to create a joint tenancy is unnecessary. Utah Code Ann. § 57-1-5. More than half of the states have statutorily eliminated the need to employ a strawman for the creation of a joint tenancy. 4 Thompson on Real Property 16 (David A. Thomas ed. 1994). Continuing to require the use of a strawman to sever a joint tenancy would create a lopsided body of law wherein property owners are required to perpetrate legal fictions for one purpose but not for another. There is substantial support for the concept that it is the intent of the parties, not the destruction of one of the four unities, that should govern. Samuel M. Fetters, *An Invitation to Commit Fraud: Secret Destruction of Joint Tenant Survivorship Rights*, 55 Fordham L.Rev. 173, 186-89 (1986) [hereinafter Fetters]. A unilateral, recorded self-conveyance sufficiently demonstrates an intent to sever.

We also note that other courts have asserted that it is contrary to sound public policy to prohibit a party from doing directly what that party could do indirectly through the use of a strawman. We agree and hold that a joint tenant may sever a joint tenancy by executing a unilateral self-conveyance and recording the deed.

In contending that this court should continue to require strawman conveyances to terminate joint tenancies, Mr. Knickerbocker asserts that such conveyances will ensure that one joint tenant cannot defraud the other by conducting a secret severance transaction. He points out that when one joint tenant secretly severs the joint tenancy, he is free to treat the tenancy as a tenancy in common for his own purposes and if the other tenant dies first, he may destroy any evidence of the severance transaction and become the sole owner of the property. Thus, he argues, a secret severance transaction allows the severing joint tenant to "have his cake and eat it too." Fetters, *supra*, at 179.

Although an unrecorded and unwitnessed unilateral transaction may allow one joint tenant to defraud the other, that is not at issue in this case. Here, Mrs. Knickerbocker severed the joint tenancy by conveying her interest to herself and promptly recording the deed. Not only did recording the deed eliminate the possibility of fraud, but it provided a clear indication of Mrs. Knickerbocker's intent to sever and it afforded Mr. Knickerbocker a reasonable opportunity to discover the severance. Fetters, *supra*, at 179-89. In these respects, Mrs. Knickerbocker's recorded self-conveyance is equal to a recorded strawman transaction, and it is superior to an unrecorded one. A joint tenant does not eliminate the possibility of fraud by executing an unrecorded strawman transaction because he may destroy all evidence of the transaction by disposing of the two deeds. Further, a joint tenant who fails to record a strawman transaction has not clearly demonstrated the intent to sever because he has reserved the opportunity to destroy evidence of the transaction. Finally, the nonsevering joint tenant does not have a reasonable opportunity to discover the unrecorded strawman transaction. He is completely dependent upon the severing joint tenant or the "strawman" to inform him of the transaction. Thus, sound reasons support our holding that a joint tenant may effectively sever a joint tenancy by executing and recording a unilateral self-conveyance.

B. The Order in the Divorce Proceeding as Applied to the Unilateral Severance

[The court held that Christine Knickerbocker's conveyance to herself did not violate the trial court's restraining order because the conveyance did not result in the removal of the assets from the state: "it merely changed the form in which Mr. and Mrs. Knickerbocker held title to their residence. Therefore, the severance was valid, and the residence was held in tenancy in common at Mrs. Knickerbocker's death."]

Reversed.

NOTES AND QUESTIONS

1. **Policy: should severance by unilateral transfer be allowed?**   Is it a valid objection to Christine Knickerbocker's severance that she acted unilaterally, without Bradford's consent? Or is it that she severed secretly? Do the *Knickerbocker* court's requirements for a self-severance adequately address the potential problems of a secret severance? *See* Samuel M. Fetters, *An Invitation to*

Commit Fraud: Secret Destruction of Joint Tenant Survivorship Rights, 55 Fordham L. Rev. 173 (1986). *See also* Taylor v. Canterbury, 92 P.3d 961 (Colo. 2004) (allowing severance of a joint tenancy by a unilateral self-conveyance).

2. **Severance of what?** A, B, and C own Blackacre in joint tenancy; A conveys "to X." What is the relationship among X, B and C? *See* Remax of Blue Springs v. Vajda & Co., 708 S.W.2d 804, 806 (Mo. Ct. App. 1986) ("A conveyance by a cotenant destroys the unity of title and converts the joint tenancy into a tenancy in common insofar as the interest of the particular joint tenant is concerned."). Suppose that A and B are joint tenants and A conveys "to X." What is the relationship between X and B? Why the difference between the two situations? Suppose that A and B are joint tenants and A conveys her interest "to A and X." What interests are created? *See* Johnson v. MacIntyre, 740 A.2d 599 (Md. 1999) (X has a 25% interest in the property). In *Johnson*, does B remain a joint tenant with A, or are A, B, and X tenants in common?

3. **Joint tenancy and divorce.** Divorce does not sever a joint tenancy between the former spouses, unless the divorce decree or a statute so provides. *See* William B. Stoebuck & Dale A. Whitman, The Law of Property § 5.5, at 192 (3d ed. 2000); Mamalis v. Bornovas, 297 A.2d 660 (N.H. 1972) (parties' stipulation to "divide the equity" in their home, incorporated into the decree of divorce, severed the joint tenancy on the effective date of the divorce); Mich. Comp. Laws Ann. § 552.102 (judgment of divorce converts joint tenants into tenants in common). If severance were based on intent rather than the four unities, shouldn't a divorce convert a joint tenancy into a tenancy in common without a stipulation or decree to that effect? *See* Mamalis v. Bornovas, *supra*, 297 A.2d at 663:

> [H]usbands and wives ordinarily take title to their homestead as joint tenants because they are married, intend to remain so, and intend that in the event of the death of one of them the survivor should take full title to the homestead in the capacity of surviving spouse. When the marriage is dissolved, the basic condition and consideration involved in the original decision to create the mutual survivorship rights — the marriage itself — is expressly, actively, and publicly terminated. The majority of persons severing their marital relationship very probably intend at least intuitively to simultaneously separate their respective property interests. A rule which would pass to the survivor after a divorce the half of the property belonging to the deceased ex-spouse would often vest the bulk of the estate in the survivor and would ordinarily be in direct contravention of the intent of the deceased.

4. **Severance by will?** Indisputable proof of a joint tenant's intent to sever is not a substitute for an inter vivos conveyance; a will does not sever. See Nicholas v. Nicholas, 83 P3d 214 (Kan. 2004) (ill joint tenant clearly expressed her intent to sever joint tenancy holdings with her spouse, through writings and other transactions, but failed to execute a conveyance before death; will purporting to sever joint tenancy was ineffective to do so); Harbin v. Harbin, 582 S.E.2d 131 (Ga. Ct. App. 2003) (husband's will devising his share of joint tenancy property to his children did not sever joint tenancy; surviving spouse owned the joint tenancy property in fee simple); Colo. Rev. Stat. § 15-15-102 ("No will of one of the owners in joint tenancy of real or personal property shall destroy or affect the joint

tenancy or prevent the entire title and interest owned by the joint tenants from becoming vested upon his death in the joint tenants who shall have survived him.").

b.   Severance by Mortgage

A joint tenant sometimes makes unilateral conveyances that are not fully-executed transfers of her entire interest in the joint tenancy property. The transferor may execute a contract to sell in advance of the actual conveyance of the property, which will occur at a later date; or she may lease the property, rather than sell or donate it in fee, to a third party; or she may execute a mortgage on the property to secure a loan. The question arises whether any of these other transfers effects a severance of the joint tenancy. The principal case deals with a mortgage executed by one joint tenant without the participation of the other. We deal with leases and contracts to sell in problems after the principal case.

PEOPLE v. NOGARR
330 P.2d 858 (Cal. Dist. Ct. App. 1958)

NOURSE, JUSTICE PRO TEM.

This appeal presents but one question: Is a mortgage upon real property executed by one of two joint tenants enforceable after the death of that joint tenant?

The facts are not in dispute. The appellant, Elaine R. Wilson, and Calvert S. Wilson, were husband and wife. On April 10, 1950, they acquired the real property in question as joint tenants and the record title remained in them as joint tenants until the death of Calvert [in 1955]. In July 1954 Elaine and Calvert separated. On October 11, 1954, Calvert executed his promissory note to his parents, the respondents, Frank H. and Alice B. Wilson. This note was in the sum of $6,440. At the same time he executed and delivered to respondents a mortgage upon the real property in question. Elaine did not have knowledge of or give her consent to the execution of this mortgage. On June 23, 1955, Calvert died. On May 8, 1956, the People of the State of California commenced an action to condemn the subject real property. By its complaint the condemner alleged that Elaine R. Wilson was the owner of the subject real property and that respondents were mortgagees thereof. By her answer Elaine alleged that she was the owner of the property, that respondents had no right, title or interest therein. Respondents by their answer alleged that they were the owners and holders of the mortgage executed by Calvert and prayed that the mortgage be satisfied from the proceeds of the condemnation award.

By agreement the fair market value of the property was fixed at $13,800 and that amount together with interest was paid into court by the condemner. Thereafter trial was had as to the rights and interests of Elaine and the respondents. [B]y a memorandum ruling the court found that there was owing to respondents the sum of $6,440 upon the promissory note executed by Calvert and secured by the mortgage and ordered that sum plus interest disbursed to respondents out of 50 per cent of the funds remaining in the hands of the trustee (the county clerk) after the payment of certain liens which were concededly a charge upon the joint estate. Judgment was entered accordingly. As a practical matter this resulted in distribution of 50 per cent of said balance to respondents, as the amount found due them was in excess of one-half of the balance remaining after the payment of other liens.

It is [Elaine's] contention that execution of the mortgage by Calvert did not operate to terminate the joint tenancy and sever his interest from that of Elaine but that the mortgage was a charge or lien upon his interest as a joint tenant only and that therefore upon his death his interest having ceased to exist the lien of the mortgage terminated and that Elaine was entitled to the distribution of the entire award exclusive of the sums distributed to other lienholders.

We have reached the conclusion that [Elaine's] contention must be sustained. In order that a joint tenancy may exist four unities are required; unity of interest, unity of title, unity of time and unity of possession. So long as these unities exist the right of survivorship is an incident of the tenancy and upon the death of one joint tenant the survivor becomes the sole owner in fee by right of survivorship and no interest in the property passes to the heirs, devisees or personal representatives of the joint tenant first to die.

It is undisputed in the present case that a joint tenancy in fee simple existed between Elaine and Calvert at the time of the execution of the mortgage, that at that time there existed all of the four unities, that consequently Elaine upon the death of Calvert became the sole owner of the property in question and to the entire award in condemnation, unless the execution by Calvert of the mortgage destroyed one of the unities and thus severed the joint tenancy and destroyed the right of survivorship.

Under the law of this state a mortgage is but a hypothecation of the property mortgaged. It creates but a charge or lien upon the property hypothecated without the necessity of a change of possession and without any right of possession in the mortgagee and does not operate to pass the legal title to the mortgagee. Civ.Code § 2920. Inasmuch as the mortgage was but a lien or charge upon Calvert's interest and as it did not operate to transfer the legal title or any title to the mortgagees or entitle the mortgagees to possession it did not destroy any of the unities and therefore the estate in joint tenancy was not severed and Elaine and Calvert did not become tenants in common. It necessarily follows that as the mortgage lien attached only to such interest as Calvert had in the real property, when his interest ceased to exist the lien of the mortgage expired with it.

Respondents have directed our attention to decisions of other jurisdictions which they assert support their contention that a joint tenant has a right to mortgage his interest and that this operates to sever the joint tenancy. Examination of each of the cases relied upon by respondents discloses that all except one of them were rendered in jurisdictions where a mortgage operated not merely as a lien or charge upon the mortgagor's interest but as a transfer or conveyance of his interest, the conveyance being subject to defeasance upon the payment of the mortgage debt. It is evident that in those jurisdictions where a mortgage operates to convey title to the mortgagee the unity of title is destroyed and in those jurisdictions where it operates not only to transfer title but the right of possession to the mortgagee both the unity of title and of possession are destroyed and that in either case there is a severance of the joint tenancy.

There is nothing inequitable in holding that the lien of respondents' mortgage did not survive the death of the mortgagor. Their note was payable upon demand and they could have enforced the lien and mortgage by foreclosure and sale prior to the death of the mortgagor and thus have severed the joint tenancy. If they chose not to do so but to await the contingency of which joint tenant died first they did so at their own risk. Under that event the lien that they had expired. If the event had been otherwise and the mortgagor had been the survivor the security of their lien would have been doubled.

The judgment is reversed.

NOTES AND QUESTIONS

1. **Mortgages.** A mortgage creates a security interest in real property, granted by the borrower (*mortgagor*) to the lender (*mortgagee*). The borrower signs a promissory note (a contract) promising to repay the loan, and grants the mortgage to secure the debt. The mortgage enhances the lender's position as a promisee. If the borrower defaults, a judgment for the lender on the contract would simply put the lender among the borrower's general (unsecured) creditors, and the lender would have to settle for a pro-rata recovery against the borrower. The mortgage gives the lender a specific asset — the mortgaged real property — available to sell in satisfaction of the debt (by the process of *foreclosure* on the mortgage).

2. **Severance by mortgage: title and lien theories.** Whether A's execution of a mortgage in favor of lender X severs A's joint tenancy with B depends, under present law, on the state's theory of how a mortgage operates. Under the *title theory*, the borrower's execution of a mortgage severs the joint tenancy; the mortgage conveys what is in effect a defeasible fee to the mortgagee, thus dissolving at least three of the four unities. *See* Downing v. Downing, 606 A.2d 208, 213 (Md. 1992) (recognizing that "a mortgage by a single joint tenant destroy[s] the joint tenancy," but holding that severance doesn't occur "where all joint tenants join in the mortgage"). However, the great majority of states follow the *lien theory* of mortgages, under which title remains in the mortgagor, but is encumbered with the lien created in favor of the mortgagee. In lien theory states, as the principal case indicates, the *granting* of the mortgage does not work a severance. Severance does not occur until the debtor defaults, the lender forecloses, the property is sold at execution sale, and the debtor's right of redemption expires. *See* Jackson v. Lacy, 97 N.E.2d 839 (Ill. 1951) (severance does not occur upon conveyance of the property to the foreclosure purchaser, but only upon expiration of the debtor's period for redemption of the property after sale). Is the current law's linking of severance of a joint tenancy to the state's mortgage theory an example of faulty analysis? Doesn't a lien mortgage arguably alter at least one of the four unities between A and B? *See generally* B. Taylor Mattis, *Severance of Joint Tenancies by Mortgages: A Contextual Approach,* 1977 S. Ill. U. L.J. 27; B. Taylor Mattis, *Notice of Severance: Mortgages and Survivorship,* 7 N. Ill. U. L. Rev. 41 (1987).

3. **Severance and policy: the debtor's intent and expectations.** Should execution of a mortgage under either theory constitute a severance? A right of survivorship is valuable; does the debtor cotenant grant the mortgage intending to sever the cotenancy (and destroy his right of survivorship), or because he needs the money and the lender won't give it without the mortgage? If the debtor cotenant paid off the mortgage and survived the nondebtor cotenant, might he be surprised to find that he had to share the property with the nondebtor's heirs or devisees?

4. **Policy: protection of mortgagees.** In title theory states, severance is based on concepts (the four unities and the state's classification of mortgages), but title theory also serves the policy of protecting mortgagees (lenders). Upon the mortgagor's execution of the mortgage, the mortgagee has a security interest against a one-half interest in the mortgaged property, which cannot be defeated should the mortgagor default and die before completion of the foreclosure process. Lien theory doesn't protect mortgagees, but mortgagees can live with it: institutional lenders will require the other cotenant to sign the note and mortgage, or will require the borrowing cotenant to sever the cotenancy before getting the loan. Occasionally, an institutional lender acts imprudently. *See* Texas American Bank v. Morgan, 733 P.2d 864 (N.M. 1987) ("[A]t the time [the debtor joint tenant] executed the mortgage, the Bank was on constructive notice, by reason of recordation, that [the debtor] was merely a joint tenant. The Bank did not require [the other joint tenant's] approval of the mortgage, and we will not do for the Bank what it failed to do for itself."). But the lenders most at risk under lien theory (the vast majority position) are unprofessional lenders (who are often relatives or friends of the borrower), as in the principal case and in Harms v. Sprague, 473 N.E.2d 930 (Ill. 1984) (joint tenant mortgaged his share of cotenancy property to secure a loan allowing his friend to buy other property).

5. **Survival of the mortgage.** Why put any lender at risk? If lien theory states were to say that the mortgage remains effective against the mortgaging joint tenant's share of the land after the mortgagor's death, mortgage law would protect the expectations of the borrower who grants the mortgage (Note 3 above) and would also protect the interests of the lender when the debtor dies (Note 4). The effect would be to require the surviving joint tenant to assume or pay off the mortgage, or participate in a cotenancy with the buyer at the foreclosure sale, or undergo a partition action. Are any of those results unfair to the surviving joint tenant? *See* Estate of Gulledge, 673 A.2d 1278, 1281 (D.C. App. 1996):

> Bernis and Clayton agreed to the creation of a joint tenancy. Bernis was bound by the legal consequences of that estate. One of these consequences was that, if Clayton transferred his interest to a third party, a tenancy in common would be created. The occurrence of that eventuality did not deny Bernis any legitimate expectation or infringe upon his rights in any way.

6. **Competing policy.** Still, courts don't take the tack suggested in Note 5, either in mortgage or judgment lien cases. See Harms v. Sprague, 473 N.E.2d 930 (Ill. 1984) (mortgage executed by decedent joint tenant was not effective against surviving joint tenant); Irvin L. Young Foundation, Inc. v. Damrell, 511 A.2d 1069, 1070 (Me. 1986) (judgment creditor's lien against debtor husband's interest in joint

tenancy ended when husband died before the execution sale). The *Irving L. Young* court offered this explanation:

> The nature of a joint tenancy requires that we reject the plaintiff's argument that the debtor-joint tenant's interest in the property must continue after his death in order to protect the creditor's interest in the property. [T]he law regarding joint tenancy dictates that the debtor's interest in the property terminates upon his death. Since the debtor's interest is extinguished on his death, there is no surviving interest to which the real estate attachment can adhere.

Although the principal case ("It necessarily follows . . ."), and *Irving L. Young* ("the law dictates that . . ."), treat their decisions as axiomatic, isn't the ineffectiveness of the mortage against the surviving cotenant best explained as a sensible policy choice? Often the judgment or mortgage lien will encumber the interest of a debtor spouse in the marital home, and the cotenant is the surviving spouse. Can the law protect unsophisticated creditors without running the risk of harming family values? Can the law protect the family home without risking harm to some unsophisticated creditors? The view that the mortgage lien doesn't survive the debtor's death protects the family home; would you change that?

7. **A resurgence of family lending?** The issues canvassed in the preceding Notes may acquire renewed significance in the current economic climate. A recent article in the Week in Review section of the New York Times notes that "Suddenly, it's not so easy to borrow." Floyd Norris, *The Loan Comes Due*, August 5, 2007, Section 4, page 1, column 1. In the last few years, professional lenders (banks and savings and loan companies) have enticed borrowers with "subprime" mortgages (made to poor credit risks, in return for higher interest rates), and with "adjustable rate" mortgages (in which the interest rate is not fixed but varies according to a referenced index) to those without income or savings to make the conventional 10% or 20% down payment on a home purchase. *See generally* Julia P. Forrester, *Still Mortgaging the American Dream: Predatory Lending, Preemption, and Federally-Supported Lenders*, 74 U. Cin. L. Rev. 1303, 1310-1311 (2006). Overextended, those borrowers are now defaulting in large numbers. The result? Floyd Norris again: "Home buyers are likely to pay more for mortgages, and some with less-than-pristine credit or an inability to come up with a down payment may find they no longer can borrow at all." At least, the prospective home buyer won't be able to borrow from institutional lenders. Faced with a drying-up market for professional loans, borrowers will have to forego a piece of the American Dream — or turn to family and friends for loans.

PROBLEMS

3-A. Improvident Bank loans cotenant A $100,000, secured by a mortgage on Blackacre, which A owns in joint tenancy with B, who is not a party to the loan or mortgage. Subsequently, A conveys his interest in Blackacre to B. A defaults and the Bank forecloses. After satisfaction of a prior mortgage, the proceeds of sale of A's interest are insufficient to cover Bank's mortgage. Is the bank entitled to force a sale of B's interest as well? See Texas American Bank v. Morgan, 733 P.2d 864 (N.M. 1987) (no). Under the trial court's ruling in *Nogarr*, did Calvert's parents recover the outstanding balance on their mortgage?

3-B. Joint tenant A leases the cotenancy property to T for five years. What result if A dies two years later, and cotenant B demands possession from T? *See* Tenhet v. Boswell, 554 P.2d 330 (Cal. 1976) (unilateral lease does not sever a joint tenancy, but the lease expires on the death of the lessor joint tenant). Is the lease situation any different than the case in which one joint tenant mortgages his or her interest?

3-C. After a contract to sell land is executed, but before the actual conveyance of title, the law regards the seller's interest as personal property (the right to the money), and the buyer's interest as an equitable interest in the land. (This doctrine of "equitable conversion" is discussed more fully in Chapter 5.) If A and B are joint tenants, and A executes a contract to sell A's interest to X, does (should) a severance result from the contract? Suppose that A and B together execute a contract to sell Blackacre to X? *See* Estate of Phillips v. Nyhus, 874 P.2d 154 (Wash. 1994) (joint tenancy is not severed when all of the joint tenants join in the contract to sell; good review of the authorities).

c. Unconventional Severance: Homocide and Common Disasters

Felonious killing, like joint tenancy, often occurs between parties who are married or related. What should happen when a joint tenant murders his or her cotenant? Should the law overlook the crime and allow the felon to own the entire estate in severalty? *See* 2 Tiffany on Real Property § 430, at 219 ("It would seem that the right of survivorship would depend upon the fact and not the manner of the other tenant's death."). Or, going to the opposite end, should the felonious joint tenant forfeit all interest in the property — the decedent's *and* his own share — on the moral principle that one should not profit from his own wrongdoing? *Cf.* Riggs v. Palmer, 22 N.E. 188 (N.Y. 1889) (denial of legacy to grandson who killed his grandfather to prevent revocation of the grandfather's will). There are other possibilities, indicated by the principal case below and the notes following it. To arrive at your own answer, you will have to unpack the joint tenancy bundle of sticks, and think carefully about the "profit" that one cotenant derives from killing the other.

BRADLEY v. FOX
129 N.E.2d 699 (Ill. 1955)

DAVIS, JUSTICE.

Lawrence Fox and Matilda Fox were married on May 6, 1949, and resided near Rockford, in Winnebago County. On April 18, 1950, they purchased with their individual funds the property in controversy, which they held in joint tenancy. Lawrence Fox murdered his wife on September 14, 1954, and three days later conveyed the premises, then valued at $20,000, to his attorney. Fox was convicted of murder on November 26, 1954, and sentenced to the State Penitentiary. [Matilda Fox's daughter, along with the administrator and her estate, sued to impose a constructive trust on the former joint tenancy property. (See Note 1 after the case for discussion of the constructive trust remedy.)] The circuit court of Winnebago County allowed defendants' motion to dismiss the complaint, and rendered judgment against plaintiffs, from which they have appealed directly to this court.

The issue of whether a murderer may acquire or increase his property rights by the fruits of his crime is not a novel legal question. It has arisen in three principal categories of cases: where the beneficiary or heir under a life insurance policy murders the assured to acquire the proceeds of the policy; or where a devisee or distribute feloniously kills the testator or intestate ancestor; and, as in the instant case, where one joint tenant murders the other and thus creates survivorship rights.

In the insurance cases the courts, practically with unanimity, construe the insurance policy in the light of the fundamental common-law maxim that no man shall profit by his own wrong. In conformity therewith, the Illinois courts [have] construed contracts as though the public policy and this common-law maxim were part of the contract, and denied recovery on the policy to the murderer or his heirs.

There has not been the same unanimity in the case law, however, with reference to the right of a devisee or distributee who feloniously kills his ancestor to inherit from the decedent in the absence of a statute. The New York courts have consistently followed the case of Riggs v. Palmer, 22 N.E. 188 (N.Y. 1889), and have construed the statutes of descent to preclude the murderer from inheriting from his victim, on the ground that all laws, as well as contracts, may be controlled in their operation and effect by the fundamental maxim of the common law that no one shall be permitted to acquire property by his own crime or iniquity.

The Illinois court, however, in Wall v. Pfanschmidt, 106 N.E. 785 (Ill. 1914), allowed a murderer to inherit from his victim on the theory that the statutes did not preclude murderers from inheriting property, therefore the legal title which passed to the murderer must be deemed indefeasible. The Illinois [intestacy] statute, however, was modified in 1939 and provides in substance that a person who is convicted of the murder of another shall not inherit from the murdered person or acquire as surviving spouse any interest in the estate of the decedent by reason of the death. Similar statutes have been enacted in most states, incorporating in effect the aforementioned common-law maxim as to the devolution of property. Wade, *Acquisition of Property by Wilfully Killing Another — A Statutory Solution*, 44 Harv.L.Rev. 715.

Defendants have questioned the constitutionality of the Illinois statute on the ground that it offends the constitutional prohibition against forfeiture of estate. Inasmuch as similar statutes in other states have been uniformly sustained on the theory that they do not deprive the murderer of his property, but merely prevent him from acquiring additional property in an unauthorized and unlawful way, there is ample authority for sustaining the validity of the Illinois law, and defendant's argument must be rejected.

However, the validity of that statutory provision is not determinative of the issue in the instant case, but at most indicates the broad policy of the state to prohibit a murderer from enjoying by descent the fruits of his crime, since at the time of the commission of the murder defendant held, not merely an expectation of an inheritance, but a joint tenancy with the deceased, and his rights arise largely from the original instrument under which he had a right of survivorship, rather than by descent.

In this category of cases the courts have differed as to whether the murderer should be allowed his survivorship rights. Those courts which hold that he is entitled to the entire property as surviving joint tenant predicate their conclusion on the legal fiction [that] each tenant is deemed to hold the entire estate from the time of the original investiture, and reason that the murderer acquired no additional interest by virtue of the felonious destruction of his joint tenant, of which he can be deprived. Other courts, however, concerned with the equitable principles prohibiting a person from profiting from his own wrong, and with the realities of the situation, have abandoned the common-law fictions, and have either divested the killer of the entire estate, or have deprived him of half the property, or have imposed a constructive trust on the entire estate held by the murderer for the benefit of the heirs of the victim, or a constructive trust modified by a life interest in half the property.

The imposition of a constructive trust in this class of cases has been urged by legal scholars and is advocated by the Restatement of Restitution. Section 188b thereof provides in substance that when there are two joint tenants, and one of them murders the other, the murderer takes by survivorship the whole legal interest in the property, but he can be compelled to hold the entire interest upon a constructive trust for the estate of his cotenant, except that his is entitled to one half the income for life.

From the foregoing analysis of the entire issue as considered in the related insurance policy and descent cases, and in the analogous joint tenancy cases, as well as by legal scholars and lawmakers, certain conclusions follow. Contracts and other instruments creating rights should properly by construed in the light of prevailing public policy evidenced in the statutes. The Illinois statute prohibiting the devolution of property to a convicted murderer from his victim, while not determinative of the rights of the parties in this situation, does evince a legislative policy to deny the convicted murderer the fruits of his crime. That policy would be thwarted by a blind adherence to the legal fiction that a joint tenant holds the entire property at the date of the original conveyance, and acquires no additional interest by virtue of the felonious death of his cotenant, since that rationale sanctions in effect the enhancement of property rights through murder. For legal fictions cannot obscure the fact that before the murder, defendant, as a joint tenant, had to share the profits of the property, and his right to complete ownership, unfettered by the interests of a joint tenant, was contingent upon surviving his wife; whereas, after, and because of, his felonious act that contingency was removed, and he became the sole owner of the property, no longer sharing the profits with any one nor fearing the loss of his interest. We cannot disregard these realities and apply a legal fiction which operates to increase the estate of one who murders his joint tenant.

In joint tenancy the contract that the survivors will take the whole necessarily presupposes that the death of either will be in the natural course of events and that it will not be generated by either tenant murdering the other. One of the implied conditions of the contract is that neither party will acquire the interest of the other by murder. It is fundamental that four coexisting unities are necessary and requisite to the creation and continuance of a joint tenancy; namely, unity of interest, unity of title, unity of time, and unity of possession. Any act of a joint tenant which destroys any of these unities operates as a severance of the joint tenancy and extinguishes the right of survivorship. It is our conclusion that Fox by his felonious act destroyed all rights of survivorship and lawfully retained only the title to his undivided one-half interest in the property in dispute as a tenant in common with the heir-at-law of Matilda Fox, deceased.

Reversed and remanded, with directions.

NOTES AND QUESTIONS

1. **Constructive trust.** A constructive trust is not a trust, and is not a source of duties imposed on the constructive trustee; it is rather an equitable restitutionary remedy, based on duties imposed by the substantive law of unjust enrichment. When the defendant holds title to real property that in equity and good conscience belongs to the plaintiff, the court can declare the defendant to be a "trustee," and order the defendant to convey the property to plaintiff. In the principal case, Lawrence Fox acquired his wife's one-half interest by unlawful act, and transferred it to his attorney. Both were appropriate defendants in the civil suit for imposition of the constructive trust. *See* Pope v. Garrett, 211 S.W.2d 559 (Tex. 1948) (two of decedent's heirs prevented decedent from executing a will; constructive trust imposed on the innocent and the culpable heirs who took decedent's estate by intestacy). The constructive trust remedy has always been available to the plaintiff victimized by fraud or breach of a confidential relationship; more recently it has become available, as in the principal case, for other kinds of wrongdoing by the defendant. *See generally* 1 George E. Palmer, The Law of Restitution § 1.4 (1978) (introductory discussion; for citations to the use of constructive trust for various defaults by the defendant, see the extensive index entry under "constructive trust" in volume 4).

2. **The killer's profit.** Under the *Bradley* view, the killer, by manipulating the order of deaths, forfeits the right of survivorship that would otherwise entitle him to full ownership. That view identifies the killer's profit as the half interest of the victim. *See* Estate of Garland, 928 P.2d 928 (Mont. 1996) (adopting *Bradley* view that murder automatically severs the joint tenancy); Uniform Probate Code § 2-803(c)(2) (same). Is that the only benefit? Does treating the homicide as an automatic severance do for the killer what the killer didn't do for himself? *See* Restatement Third of Property (Wills and Other Donative Transfers) § 8.4 & cmt. 1 (2003) (the blackletter section states the principle that "A slayer is denied any right to benefit from the wrong," and the comment states a presumption that the killer "retains only the right to half of the income from the property for life"); Restatement of Restitution § 188 & cmt. b (1937) (murderer is entitled to one half the income for life). Is a joint tenant's right to half of the income for the duration of the joint tenancy affected by the order of the joint tenants' deaths?

3. **Riggs v. Palmer.** In Riggs v. Palmer, cited in the principal case, the court denied the murderer his entire legacy under the victim's will. Is that result correct — what is the "profit" in that situation? *See* UPC § 2-803(c)(1) (felonious and intentional killing by a will beneficiary revokes the legacy to the killer). Suppose

that an heir murders his father, who dies intestate, survived by the murderer and another child; does the murderer take an intestate share as a "descendant" of the decedent? *See* UPC § 2-803(b) (heir who feloniously and intentionally kills the ancestor is treated as having predeceased the ancestor). Under the UPC view, are the children of the murderer barred from taking an intestate share of the ancestor's estate by representation?

4. **Law as rule and principle.** *Riggs* is a famous case. It occupies center stage in Professor Ronald Dworkin's critique of the positivist view that law consists of rules promulgated by the sovereign; the wills statute in *Riggs* was such a rule, and it contained no exception barring a murdering devisee from taking under the victim's will. Against the positivists, Dworkin argued that the law also consists of principles (such as the principle that one should not profit by his wrong), which have *weight* rather than the directive force of rules, and which often contain moral precepts. *See* Ronald Dworkin, Taking Rights Seriously 22 (1978). Dworkin's view of law is elaborated in his books Law's Empire (1986) and Justice in Robes (2006). A collection of essays, Exploring Law's Empire: The Jurisprudence of Ronald Dworkin (Scott Hershovitz ed. 2006), is usefully reviewed, along with *Justice in Robes*, in Brian Leiter, *Book Review*, 56 J. Legal Ed. 675 (2006).

5. **The common disaster.** The original Uniform Simultaneous Death Act (1940) provided that, if joint tenants died simultaneously, their joint property would be divided half as though one survived (that is, it would go to that survivor's heirs or devisees), and half as though the other survived. By its terms, however, the Act's sensible result — division of the property among the decedents' successors — did not apply if there was proof establishing that the parties did not die simultaneously — that one joint tenant survived the other. The result: numerous cases litigated on the basis of often fallible and always gruesome proof of the order of the parties' deaths. Section 2-702(a) of the 1990 Uniform Probate Code offers an easier-to-administer rule. It provides that "an individual who is not established by clear and convincing evidence to have survived an event, including the death of another individual, by 120 hours is deemed to have predeceased the event." If neither A nor B survives the other for 120 hours, "one-half of the [co-owned] property passes as if one [cotenant] had survived by 120 hours and one-half as if the other had survived by 120 hours." *Id.* § 2-702(b). The USDA was subsequently amended to adopt the UPC provisions. Both UPC § 2-702 and the comparable USDA provision apply to other situations in which ownership depends on survival. Thus heirs, devisees, and life insurance and pension beneficiaries, must all survive their respective benefactors for 120 hours to claim their benefits under the statutes. Under both acts, the governing instrument — will, insurance policy, or pension contract — may require survival for a longer or shorter period than 120 hours, or may dispense with the requirement of survival. These UPC and USDA provisions have not been adopted in all states.

d. Indestructible Rights of Survivorship

So far we have considered joint tenancies in fee simple, which carry a destructible right of survivorship. By way of comparison, we now briefly consider a related, but altogether more formidable, interest: an *indestructible* right of survivorship.

ALBRO v. ALLEN
454 N.W.2d 85 (Mich. 1990)

BOYLE, JUSTICE.

On October 14, 1977, certain commercial property in Macomb County was conveyed to Carol Allen and Helen Albro "as joint tenants with full rights of survivorship." On April 23, 1987, Carol Allen entered into a purchase agreement with Steven Kinzer, in which she agreed to convey her interest in the property to Kinzer by quitclaim deed.

On May 12, 1987, Helen Albro instituted an action to enjoin sale of Allen's interest. Both Allen and Kinzer were named as defendants. [The trial court granted the requested injunction. The court of appeals affirmed. Both courts ruled that the proposed sale would defeat Albro's right of survivorship. Kinzer appealed to the state supreme court.]

Michigan law recognizes two forms of joint tenancies. The first is of the type typically recognized in various jurisdictions. The principal characteristic of [this] joint tenancy is the right of survivorship. Upon the death of one joint tenant, the surviving tenant or tenants take the whole estate. In the standard joint tenancy, the right of survivorship may be destroyed by severance of the joint tenancy. If one joint tenant conveys his interest to a third party, then the remaining joint tenant and the grantee become tenants in common, thus destroying the element of survivorship.

The "joint tenancy" involved in this case, while unfortunately sharing the same appellation as the typical joint tenancy, is an interest of a different nature. It is created by express words of survivorship in the granting instrument in addition to those creating a joint tenancy, such as "and to the survivor of them," "to them and the survivor of them," "with right of survivorship," or "with full rights of survivorship."

At the crux of this case is the distinction between the "joint tenancy with full rights of survivorship" and the ordinary joint tenancy. The "joint tenancy with full rights of survivorship" is comprised of a joint life estate with dual contingent remainders. While the survivorship feature of the ordinary joint tenancy may be defeated by the act of a cotenant, the dual contingent remainders of the "joint tenancy with full rights of survivorship" are indestructible. A cotenant's contingent remainder cannot be destroyed by an act of the other cotenant.

The Court of Appeals correctly recognized that the interest held by Allen and Albro was a "joint life estate followed by a contingent remainder in fee to the survivor," but it erred when it applied the rules governing ordinary joint tenancies to this case. Were this an ordinary joint tenancy, conveyance of one party's interest would indeed convert the tenancy into a tenancy in common, thus destroying the survivorship element of the joint tenancy. However, where the interest held is a joint life estate with dual contingent remainders, the principles governing ordinary joint tenancies are not controlling. Instead, we should apply the principles which normally govern the component parts of the joint life estate with dual contingent remainders.

[We] conclude that a person sharing a joint life estate with dual contingent remainders may convey his interest in the joint life estate, without destroying the cotenant's contingent remainder. Of course, a cotenant in a joint life estate cannot convey an estate which will extend beyond his own estate. The interest which Allen held in the joint life estate was limited by the dual contingent remainders; the joint life estate would terminate upon the death of Allen or Albro, whichever occurred sooner. If Allen predeceases Albro, then, upon Allen's death, Albro's contingent remainder will be realized and she will acquire title to the land in fee. If Albro predeceases Allen, then Allen's contingent remainder, which was transferred to Kinzer, will be realized and Kinzer will acquire the land in fee.

We reverse the portion of the Court of Appeals decision which would preclude transfer of a cotenant's interest in a joint life estate, and remand the case to the trial court to modify its order of permanent injunctive relief pursuant to this decision.

NOTES AND QUESTIONS

1. **Effect of survivorship language.** *See also* Hunter v. Hunter, 320 S.W.2d 529 (Mo. 1959) (will devising "unto my mother, Mrs. D.R. Hunter, and unto my sister, Virginia Hunter, as joint tenants with the right of survivorship" created life estate between the devisees and a remainder in the survivor). When the transferor doesn't *expressly* create a concurrent life estate and a remainder to the survivor (or a concurrent fee simple with an executory interest in the survivor), what effect should language of survivorship have? *Compare* Coolidge v. Coolidge, 287 A.2d 566, 568 (Vt. 1971) (words of survivorship "add nothing to the quality or quantum of the joint estate, but merely more particularly describe it"), *with* 2 Tiffany, Real Property § 425, at 208 ("The right of survivorship is merely one incident of a joint tenancy. Another incident of such tenancy is that any one of the tenants can destroy it, with the incidental right of survivorship. [W]hen one makes a gift to two or more with the right of survivorship, it appears to be a reasonable conclusion that he has in mind an indestructible right of survivorship.").

2. **Wisdom of indestructible survivorship rights.** Is the recognition of an indestructible right of survivorship a good idea? Does it depend on whether the grantees are spouses? Which would you prefer: a rule of law barring the creation of indestructible survivorship rights (thus preventing a grantor from expressly using the life estate and remainder formulation or its equivalent); a rule of construction that indestructible survivorship rights will not be implied and must be expressly created; or the rule of Albro v. Allen? Before deciding, read the next Note.

3. **Statutory abolition (and judicial resurrection) of the joint tenancy.** The predecessor of current Or. Rev. Stat. § 93.180 provided as follows:

> **Tenancy in common, when created; joint tenancy abolished.** Every conveyance or devise of lands, or interest therein, made to two or more persons, other than to executors or trustees, as such, creates a tenancy in common unless it is expressly declared in the conveyance or devise that the grantees or devisees take the lands as joint tenants. Joint tenancy is

abolished and all persons having an undivided interest in real property are to be deemed and considered tenants in common.

The Oregon Supreme Court reconciled the stark contrast between the first and second sentences of the statute by treating language of survivorship in a transfer as an indication of the grantor's intent to create a concurrent life estate with an indestructible remainder to the survivor. That is the only way to effectuate survivorship language if the joint tenancy in fee simple is unavailable. *See* Halleck v. Halleck, 337 P.2d 330 (Or. 1959). The Oregon court, however, also expressed its doubt about the wisdom of a statute that forces transferors into the creation of indestructible survivorship rights. *See* Holbrook v. Holbrook, 403 P.2d 12, 14 (Or. 1965) ("There seems to be no reason for forbidding the creation of the common law joint tenancy. However, the legislature has seen fit to abolish it and we have found no way to read out of the statute the express declaration that 'joint tenancy is abolished.' It would appear that there is need for legislation on the subject."). Here is the current version of the statute:

> **Tenancy in common, when created; joint tenancy abolished.** Every conveyance or devise of lands, or interest therein, made to two or more persons, other than to a husband and wife, as such, or to executors or trustees, as such, creates a tenancy in common unless it is in some manner clearly and expressly declared in the conveyance or devise that the grantees or devisees take the lands with right of survivorship. Such a declaration of a right to survivorship shall create a tenancy in common in the life estate with cross-contingent remainders in the fee simple. Joint tenancy is abolished and the use in a conveyance or devise of the words "joint tenants" or similar words without any other indication of an intent to create a right of survivorship shall create a tenancy in common.

Did the Oregon legislature respond to the state supreme court's concern?

4. **The nature of a concurrent life estate.** When a contingent remainder is held by the survivor of two concurrent life tenants, does characterization of the life estate as a joint tenancy or tenancy in common matter? Would it matter in the following transfers?

a. "To A and B as joint tenants and not as tenants in common for the life of the survivor of them, then to X." B dies, survived by heirs.

b. "To A and B as tenants in common for the life of the survivor of them, then to X." B dies, survived by heirs.

c. "To A and B for life, then to X." *See* Briggs v. Briggs, 950 S.W.2d 710 (Tenn. Ct. App. 1997).

5. **Review.** What result in *Knickerbocker* (severance by unilateral conveyance) and Bradley v. Fox (severance by homicide) if the joint tenants in those cases had held concurrent life estates with a contingent remainder in the survivor?

PROBLEM 3-D. A deed from Mary Murphy, George Murphy, and Bernard Murphy, all unmarried, conveyed Blackacre to Mary Murphy, George Murphy, Bryan Murphy, Margaret Murphy, and Theresa Murphy "as joint tenants and not as tenants in common, their assigns, the survivor of said parties, and the heirs or assigns of the survivor forever." The habendum clause stated "To have and to hold the above described premises unto the said grantees, their assigns, the survivor of said parties, and the heirs and assigns of the survivor." The heirs of deceased grantees claimed an interest in the property against Theresa Murphy, who claimed ownership in severalty as the sole surviving grantee. In holding that Theresa was entitled to the property, the court reasoned as follows: (1) The statute allowing a grantor to convey to himself was not retroactive, so the four unities rule applied. (2) The deed violated the unities of time and title, and therefore created a tenancy in common rather than a joint tenancy, even if the grantors intended to create a joint tenancy. (3) "In view of the fact that a survivorship clause was not necessary if a joint tenancy had been properly created, the grantors must have intended that survivorship exist whatever the estate actually conveyed might be. The sole question remaining therefore, is whether a survivorship provision can properly be attached to a tenancy in common. We think that it can. . . . A survivorship attached to a tenancy in common is indestructible except by the voluntary action of all the tenants in common to do so." Anson v. Murphy, 32 N.W.2d 271, 272, 273 (Neb. 1948). The court specifically excluded the possibility "that the addition of a survivorship clause to a joint tenancy by appropriate language might eliminate the destructibility to which it was subject as an incident to a properly created joint tenancy, a matter which we do not here decide." *Id.* at 272. Instead of recognizing a tenancy in common with survivorship, could the court have reached its result by an easier — and less startling — route? (Notice that this Problem brings us full circle: in Hoover v. Smith, we saw a joint tenancy in fee with no right of survivorship; in Anson v. Murphy we see an equally unusual tenancy in common in fee *with* a right of survivorship.)

3.   The Cotenant's Rights and Duties

a.   Partition

Partition is in effect a cotenants' divorce: the parties exit the co-ownership regime, and each former cotenant either assumes individual ownership in severalty of a portion of the property (partition in kind), or pockets his or her fractional share of the net proceeds from the sale of the property (partition by sale). *See* William B. Stoebuck & Dale A. Whitman, The Law of Property § 5.13 (3d ed. 2000). Although statutes frequently express a preference for partition in kind, partition by sale is by far the more common method of partition today. *Id.* at 223; Note, *Partition in Kind: A Preference Without Favor,* 7 Cardozo L. Rev. 855 (1986). *See generally* Thomas J. Miceli & C.F. Sirmans, *Partition of Real Estate; Or, Breaking Up Is Not Hard to Do,* 29 J. Legal Stud. 783 (2000) (the article "develops an economic standard for choosing between partition and forced sale based on the objective of maximizing the aggregate value of the land"). Real property that is improved with buildings does not lend itself to partition in kind, as unimproved land does.

When the parties agree to partition, they can implement their agreement by jointly deeding a specified portion of the land to each individual cotenant, or by deeding the land to a third party and sharing the sale proceeds. When the parties cannot agree, partition is supervised by the court. A court of equity has inherent jurisdiction to entertain a partition action, but statutes confirming and detailing the partition action exist in all states. *See* Stoebuck & Whitman, The Law of Property § 5.11; 2 Tiffany on Real Property §§ 468-472 (voluntary partition); §§ 473-483 (compulsory partition).

As in marital break-ups, disputes among cotenants about partition are common.

CUNNINGHAM v. HASTINGS
556 N.E.2d 12 (Ind. Ct. App. 1990)

BAKER, JUDGE.

Plaintiff-appellant, Joan L. Cunningham (Cunningham), appeals a judgment entered on her partition action in which the trial court credited defendant-appellee, Warren R. Hastings (Hastings), for the purchase money he provided to obtain certain real estate.

We reverse and remand.

On August 30, 1984, Harold and Juanita Carlton conveyed by warranty deed certain real estate to Cunningham and Hastings. The deed referred to Cunningham and Hastings "as joint tenants with the right of survivorship, and NOT as tenants in common" (original emphasis), and was prepared at Hastings' direction. Cunningham and Hastings were unmarried and occupied the property jointly. After the relationship ended and Hastings took sole possession of the property, Cunningham filed a complaint seeking partition of the real estate.

The trial court conducted a hearing after which it determined that Cunningham and Hastings were joint tenants in the property, each with an undivided interest in the whole. Based on its determination that the property was not susceptible of partition, the trial court ordered the sale of the property. The trial court further ordered that the proceeds of the sale be applied first to cover the costs of the partition proceedings, and that the next $45,000 be paid to Hastings as a refund of the purchase price he paid out of his own funds. The remainder of the proceeds, if any, were ordered to be divided equally between the parties. Cunningham appeals the trial court's $45,000 award to Hastings in recognition of the purchase price he paid.

Cunningham presents for our review the following single issue: Whether the trial court's judgment was contrary to law when it attempted to equalize the partition by awarding one joint tenant credit for the purchase price.

There is some discussion in the parties' briefs regarding whether Hastings made an inter vivos gift of the real estate to Cunningham. This discussion is not necessary to the disposition of this appeal because the decisive issue involves the determination of what interest Cunningham acquired in the real estate when her name was included on the deed as a joint tenant.

The parties do not dispute that the unequivocal language of the deed created a joint tenancy in the real estate. When a joint tenancy is created, each tenant acquires "an equal right to share in the enjoyment of the land during their lives." Richardson v. Richardson 98 N.E.2d 190, 192 (Ind. Ct. App. 1951). A joint tenancy relationship confers equivalent legal rights on the tenants that are fixed and vested at the time the joint tenancy is created. 48A C.J.S. Joint Tenancy § 21 (1981).

This court's decision in Becker v. MacDonald, 488 N.E.2d 729 (Ind. Ct. App. 1986), is instructive on the extent of Cunningham's interest in the property. *Becker* involved a joint tenancy between three parties consisting of a sister, a brother, and the brother's wife. This court and the trial court denied the sister's claim that she was sole owner of the property. This court stated that once a determination of joint tenancy was made in the partition action, the next question was whether the sister owned a one-half or one-third interest. Based on *Becker*, the determination of the parties' interests in the present case is simple. There are only two parties involved in the joint tenancy. Once a joint tenancy relationship is found to exist between two people in a partition action, it is axiomatic that each person owns a one-half interest.

Based on the reasoning in *Becker*, we find that the trial court erred in allowing Hastings a $45,000 credit for the purchase price he paid. Regardless of who provided the money to purchase the land, the creation of a joint tenancy relationship entitles each party to an equal share of the proceeds of the sale upon partition. Equitable adjustments to cotenants' equal shares are allowed when the cotenants hold the property as tenants in common, not when they hold as joint tenants. The deed in the case before us unequivocally states that the parties held the property as joint tenants, not as tenants in common. The equitable adjustment of their equal shares, therefore, was improper.

The trial court's judgment is reversed and the case remanded with instructions to order the proceeds of the sale be divided equally between the joint tenants without credit given for the purchase price.

Ratliff, Chief Judge, concurring.

I concur in the majority opinion, and, in so doing, agree that the very nature of joint tenancies involves equal rights on the part of the joint tenants. However, I do not agree with the majority's statement that the inter vivos gift issue is not relevant. The fact that Hastings made a valid inter vivos gift to Cunningham is the foundation of the joint tenancy. The joint tenancy was created when Hastings, by having the real estate placed in joint tenancy, made a valid and completed inter vivos gift of an undivided one-half interest, in joint tenancy, to Cunningham. By so doing, he gave away one-half of his contribution of the purchase price and may not revoke his gift and recover back the purchase price. When the property is sold and the net proceeds are divided equally between the two joint tenants, Hastings will receive all he is entitled to receive.

NOTES AND QUESTIONS

1. **Concepts: partition and severance.** How does partition of a joint tenancy differ from severance of a joint tenancy?

2. **Gift.** Is the majority correct to say that gift analysis is unnecessary to its resolution of the case? If Joan Cunningham didn't pay for a half interest in the

property, but gets to keep it, wasn't that half interest necessarily a gift from Hastings? *See* Wright v. Mallett, 894 A.2d 1016 (Conn. App. Ct. 2006) (male cotenant who brought partition action was denied share of proceeds of sale of property held as tenancy in common with woman with whom he was romantically involved but not married or engaged; man failed to prove that the woman intended a gift to him); Zink v. Stafford, 509 S.E.2d 833, 835-836 (Va. 1999) ("[B]ecause the daughter did not purchase an interest in any of the [promissory] notes [that funded the joint account], the only manner in which she could have become a joint tenant with her father was for him to have made a gift to her of an interest in the notes before his death."). Is there evidence that Hastings intended a gift to Cunningham? If Hastings intended a gift, was the gift necessarily irrevocable or indefeasible? *See* Fanning v. Iversen, 535 N.W.2d 770 (S.D. 1995) (party who paid for cotenancy property and put title in tenancy in common was entitled to return of donee's half interest when donee called off the engagement); Boydstun v. Loveless, 890 P.2d 267 (Colo. Ct. App. 1995) (party who paid for cotenancy property and put title in joint tenancy intended a conditional gift in contemplation of marriage; title quieted in paying cotenant when marriage didn't occur).

3. **Other possibilities: resulting trust; revocable or defeasible gift.** When one party buys property and directs that title be placed in the name of another party, the latter is usually presumed to hold the property on a "purchase money resulting trust" for the benefit of the payor. *See* George T. Bogert, Trusts § 74 (6th ed. 1987); Restatement Third of Trusts § 9 (2003). The presumption of a resulting trust does not arise, however, if the title holder is a member of the payor's family; in that case, the opposite presumption, that a gift was intended, prevails. George T. Bogert, *supra*, at 271. *See* Bowen v. Bowen, 575 S.E.2d 553 (S.C. 2003) (terms of prenuptial agreement rebutted both presumption of gift and of resulting trust; under the agreement, former wife was entitled to a half interest in jointly-held property for which former husband contributed the entire purchase price). Shouldn't these dueling presumptions of resulting trust or gift have framed the issue in the principle case? If Hastings didn't intend to make a gift to Cunningham of a half interest in the property, shouldn't Cunningham have held her half interest on a resulting trust for Hastings? Did Hastings intend to make a gift to Cunningham?

4. **"It is axiomatic."** The court in *Cunningham* says that an equitable adjustment — to adjust for unequal contributions to the purchase of concurrently-titled land — is allowed in the partition of tenancies in common but not joint tenancies; in the latter, it is "axiomatic" that each cotenant has an equal share. It is not axiomatic to all courts; in some states, the unity of interest is treated as a rebuttable presumption in a partition action. *See* Moat v. Ducharme, 555 N.E.2d 897, 898 (Mass. App. Ct. 1990) ("When their long-term relationship evolved from meaningful to just plain mean," the parties sought partition; presumption of equal shares is rebuttable because partition must be "just and equitable"); Jezo v. Jezo, 127 N.W.2d 246, 250 (Wis. 1964) (rebuttable presumption). Is the conclusive presumption of equal shares, as in the principal case, another example of the logic of joint tenancy overriding sound policy?

5. **Equitable distribution.** If Hastings and Cunningham had married and bought the home before their relationship soured, their interests in the joint tenancy would have been subject to equitable distribution upon their divorce. *See*

Section B.1 below. Equitable distribution generally applies only to property acquired during the marriage; each spouse's separate property remains his or hers. Under equitable distribution, would (should?) Hastings's contribution to the purchase price be regarded as his separate property? *Cf.* Utsch v. Utsch, 581 S.E.2d 507 (Va. 2003) (after marriage, husband retitled his residence from his name solely to himself and his wife as tenants by the entirety; held, the residence was marital property: the unambiguous deed conclusively established husband's intent to give a half interest to his wife).

6. **Other cases and issues.** When unmarried cohabitants break up, theories of recovery in addition to partition may be available. *See* Watts v. Watts in Section B.3 below. For a case applying partition and accounting principles on the breakup of a same-sex couple, when the house they occupied was titled in the name of only one of them, see Ireland v. Flanagan in Section B.3.

PROBLEM 3-E. Should the court order partition in the following cases?

a. Cotenant A holds a fee simple interest in an undivided two-thirds of the cotenancy property and a life estate in the remaining one-third. Is A entitled to partition? *See* Treiber v. Citizens State Bank, 598 N.W.2d 96 (N.D. 1999).

b. Cotenant A conveys a portion of the joint tenancy property, described by metes and bounds, to X. On partition, is X entitled to the portion described in the deed from A? See Johnson v. MacIntyre, 740 A.2d 599 (Md. 1999).

c. H and W own their marital home as joint tenants. C gets a judgment against H and buys H's interest at the execution sale. The house is worth $100,000 and is subject to an unassignable $75,000 mortgage at 8%. Is C entitled to partition by sale? What potential loss might the nondebtor spouse incur if sale were allowed? *See* Harris v. Crowder, 322 S.E.2d 854 (W. Va. 1984).

d. A and B are cotenants of Blackacre, which is undeveloped and consists of one 4 acre parcel worth $40,000 and another 6 acre parcel worth $60,000, divided by a navigable river. The parties want partition in kind; how might that be accomplished fairly? *See* Stoebuck & Whitman, The Law of Property § 5.13, at 223.

e. There are 10 cotenants of Blackacre, a one-acre parcel. Should partition be in kind or by sale? *See id.* at 222-23.

f. Cotenant A has worked and lived on the family farm for many years. A's interest in the farm is 15%; other shares are owned by more distant relatives who have various fractional shares. Another cotenant, who owns a 1/37 share, sells that share to X, a realtor. X petitions for partition, and argues that, because the farm cannot be divided conveniently, the court should order partition by sale. Should the court order partition? *See* Thomas W. Mitchell, *From Reconstruction to Deconstruction: Undermining Black Landownership, Political Independence, and Community Through Partition Sales of Tenancies in Common*, 95 Nw. U. L. Rev. 505 (2001); Phyllis Craig-Taylor, *Through a Colored Looking Glass: A View of Judicial Partition, Family Land Loss, and Rule Setting*, 78 Wash. U. L.Q. 737 (2000); John G. Casagrande, Jr., Note, *Acquiring Property Through Forced Partitioning Sales: Abuses and Remedies*, 27 B.C. L. Rev. 755 (1986).

b.   Accounting and Contribution

Suppose that the cotenancy property is leased out to a third party, who pays rent to one of the cotenants. Or suppose that one cotenant occupies the cotenancy property herself. What are the rights of the noncollecting or nonoccupying cotenants? *See generally* Lawrence Berger, *An Analysis of the Economic Relations Between Cotenants*, 21 Ariz. L. Rev. 1015 (1979).

MARTIN v. MARTIN
878 S.W.2d 30 (Ky. Ct. App. 1994)

JOHNSTONE, JUDGE.

Garis and Peggy Martin appeal from a judgment of the Pike Circuit Court which required them to pay rent to the cotenants of certain real estate. Reluctantly, we reverse.

Garis and Peggy own an undivided one-eighth interest in a tract of land in Pike County. This interest was conveyed to Garis by his father, Charles Martin, in 1971. Appellees, Charles and Mary Martin, own a life estate in the undivided seven-eighths of the property for their joint lives, with remainder to appellants.

In 1982, Charles Martin improved a portion of the property and developed a four lot mobile home park which he and Mary rented. In July of 1990, Garis and Peggy moved their mobile home onto one of the lots. It is undisputed that Garis and Peggy expended no funds for the improvement or maintenance of the mobile home park, nor did they pay rent for the lot that they occupied.

In 1990, Garis and Peggy filed an action which sought an accounting of their claimed one-eighth portion of the net rent received by Charles and Mary from the lots. The accounting was granted, however, the judgment of the trial court required appellants to pay "reasonable rent" for their occupied lot. It is that portion of the judgment from which this appeal arises.

The sole issue presented is whether one cotenant is required to pay rent to another cotenant. Appellants argue that absent an agreement between cotenants, one cotenant occupying premises is not liable to pay rent to a co-owner. Appellees respond that a cotenant is obligated to pay rent when that cotenant occupies the jointly owned property to the exclusion of his co-owner.

Appellants and appellees own the subject property as tenants in common. The primary characteristic of a tenancy in common is unity of possession by two or more owners. Each cotenant, regardless of the size of his fractional share of the property, has a right to possess the whole.

The prevailing view is that an occupying cotenant must account for outside rental income received for use of the land, offset by credits for maintenance and other appropriate expenses. The trial judge correctly ordered an accounting and recovery of rent in the case sub judice.

However, the majority rule on the issue of whether one cotenant owes rent to another is that a cotenant is not liable to pay rent, or to account to other cotenants respecting the reasonable value of the occupancy, absent an ouster or agreement to pay. 51 A.L.R.2d 413 § 8.

The trial court relied erroneously on Smither v. Betts, 264 S.W.2d 255 (Ky. 1954), for its conclusion that appellants were "obligated to pay seven-eighths of the reasonable rental for the use of the lot they occupy." In *Smither*, one cotenant had exclusive possession of jointly owned property by virtue of a lease with a court-appointed receiver and there was an agreement to pay rent. That clearly is not the case before us. There was no lease or any other agreement between the parties.

The appellees reason that the award of rent was proper upon the premise that Garis and Peggy ousted their cotenants. While the proposition that a cotenant who has been ousted or excluded from property held jointly is entitled to rent is a valid one, we are convinced that such ouster must amount to exclusive possession of the entire jointly held property. We find support for this holding in Taylor v. Farmers and Gardeners Market Assoc., 173 S.W.2d 803, 807-808, in which the court stated:

> [R]unning throughout all the books will be found two essential elements which must exist before the tenant sought to be charged is liable. These are: (a) that the tenant sought to be charged and who is claimed to be guilty of an ouster must assert *exclusive* claim to the property in himself, thereby necessarily including a denial *of any* interest or any right or title in the supposed ousted tenant; (b) he must give notice to this effect to the ousted tenant, or his acts must be so open and notorious, positive and assertive, as to place it beyond doubt that he is claiming the *entire* interest in the property.

We conclude that appellants' occupancy of one of the four lots did not amount to an ouster. To hold otherwise is to repudiate the basic characteristic of a tenancy in common that each cotenant shares a single right to possession of the entire property and each has a separate claim to a fractional share.

Accordingly, the judgment of the Pike Circuit Court is reversed as to the award of rent to the appellees.

NOTES AND QUESTIONS

A. Accounting for Profits

1. **Profits: third-party rental value.** Why were Charles and Mary Martin required to account for the rents they collected from the rental of the three mobile home lots? For how much of the received rent did they have to account?

2. **Mesne profits: occupancy value.** Why didn't Garis and Peggy Martin have to account for the rental value of the lot *they* occupied? Which rule do you prefer, one requiring the resident cotenant to account to the nonresident cotenants for the value of the occupancy, or one allowing the resident cotenant to occupy rent free?

3. **Ouster: quicksand.** When the occupying cotenant possesses under circumstances that amount to an ouster of the other cotenant, all states require an accounting. *See* Cox v. Cox, 71 P.3d 1028 (Idaho 2003) (tenant in common was

entitled to a one-half share of the fair rental value of the house occupied by her brother, who told her he was putting the house up for sale and that she "had better find a place to live"); Parker v. Shecut, 562 S.E.2d 620 (S.C. 2002) (occupying cotenant's acts of changing locks and refusing to give other cotenant a working key constituted ouster).

If A and B are cotenants of Blackacre, and A occupies the property, is there an ouster in the following cases:

(a) B inquires about the possible rental out of Blackacre, and A denies that B has any title to the property? *See* Estate of Duran, 66 P.3d 326 (N.M. 2003) (possessing cotenant's silence and evasive answers to questions about his intentions towards the property did not constitute ouster; possessing cotenant "never expressly told [the other cotenants] that he claimed to own their portions of the property").

(b) B seeks to use a portion of Blackacre and A prevents B?

(c) B requests one-half of the fair rental value of Blackacre from A, and A refuses to pay? *See* Von Drake v. Rogers, 996 So. 2d 608, 610 (La. Ct. App. 2008) (ouster requires demand for occupancy, not for rent: "[a] co-owner in exclusive possession may be liable for rent, but only beginning on the date another co-owner has demanded occupancy and been refused.").

(d) Blackacre is a single-family home and A and B are recently divorced or separated? *See* Hertz v. Hertz, 657 P.2d 1169 (N.M. 1983) (applying concept of "constructive ouster"); Wood v. Collins, 812 P.2d 951 (Alaska 1991); Seesholts v. Beers, 270 So. 2d 434 (Fla. Dist. Ct. App. 1972).

See generally Evelyn Alicia Lewis, *Struggling With Quicksand: The Ins and Outs of Cotenant Possession Value Liability and a Call for Default Rule Reform*, 1994 Wis. L. Rev. 331.

4. **Staging ouster.** Can the ouster doctrine be manipulated by parties represented by counsel? In the principal case, what could Charles have done to set up an ouster? What could Garis have done in response, to avoid a finding of ouster? If the finding of ouster is subject to manipulation by the parties, does that suggest that ouster is an inappropriate doctrine to determine an occupying cotenant's liability to account?

5. **Agreement.** If the default rule were that an occupying cotenant had to account for the fair rental value of the occupancy, the cotenant in possession would need to secure an agreement for rent-free occupancy from the other cotenants. If the rule were that accounting is not required, the nonpossessing cotenants would need to secure an agreement for payment. Should the occupying cotenant's liability to account depend on agreement alone, without regard to ouster? If so, on whom would you put the burden of getting an agreement?

B. Contribution for Expenditures

6. **Carrying charges.** A cotenant who pays more than his or her proportionate share of taxes or mortgage payments is entitled to contribution from the other cotenants. The claim for contribution may be brought as an independent lawsuit, or joined as a claim in an action for partition or for an accounting. *See*

Stoebuck & Whitman, The Law of Property § 5.9.

7. **Repairs.** A cotenant who pays more than his or her fractional share of the cost of repairs is entitled to contribution from the other cotenants, but there is dispute among the cases on proper procedure: whether the repairing cotenant is entitled to maintain an independent action for contribution, or (the apparent majority view) is only entitled to assert the claim in an action for partition or for an accounting. *See* Stoebuck & Whitman, The Law of Property § 5.9. As to the availability of an independent action for contribution, can you think of any reason to distinguish carrying charges from repairs?

8. **Improvements.** A cotenant who makes improvements to the cotenancy property without the consent of the other cotenants is entitled to contribution only in the final accounting rendered in a partition action; the recovery is limited to the lesser of the cost of the improvement or the value that the improvement adds to the property. As an alternative to contribution, the court may award the improved portion to the improver if that is feasible. See Stoebuck & Whitman, The Law of Property § 5.9, at 208. Can you think of reasons for these limitations on a cotenant's right to contribution for improvements made to the common property? *See generally* Johnie L. Price, *The Right of a Cotenant to Reimbursement for Improvements to the Common Property*, 18 Baylor L. Rev. 111 (1966).

9. **Back-door accounting?** Suppose that cotenant A occupies Blackacre, without ouster, and seeks contribution from B for B's share of the costs of the carrying charges on the property (taxes, mortgage, and insurance payments). In some states following the view that an occupying cotenant has no duty to account for his or her occupancy, A is not entitled to recover contribution from B unless B's proportionate share of those expenses exceeds the value of A's occupancy of the property. Is that logical? Is it fair? *See* Barrow v. Barrow, 527 So. 2d 1373, 1377 (Fla. 1988).

4.   The Tenancy by the Entirety

The tenancy by the entirety is a concurrent estate that can exist only between spouses. It is like the joint tenancy in that it carries a right of survivorship; but it differs from the joint tenancy in that neither cotenant can sever the cotenancy by a unilateral transfer. In other words, the right of survivorship of each spouse is indestructible. *See* Jones v. Conwell, 314 S.E.2d 61, 64 (Va. 1984):

> It is settled that tenancies by the entirety are based upon the same four unities that support joint tenancies. However, it is also settled that tenancies by the entirety are supported by a fifth unity which they do not share with any other tenancy: the unity of marriage. That unity embodies the legal fiction that husband and wife are one. And it leads to the result that neither husband nor wife can by his or her sole act defeat the survivorship interest of the other spouse.

See also Sitomer v. Orlan, 660 So. 2d 1111 (Fla. Dist. Ct. App. 1995) (bank account).

Although heavily imbued with medieval legal and social theory, the tenancy by the entirety also serves important modern policy goals. "Tenancies by the entirety, although originally based on the unity of husband and wife at common law, survive as a means of protecting marital assets during coverture and as a security for one spouse on the death of the other." Freda v. Commercial Trust Co., 570 A.2d 409, 414 (N.J. 1990). How, and how well, the tenancy by the entirety performs these protective functions is a central topic of the following materials.

a. Creation of the Tenancy by the Entirety

Presumptions. States recognizing the tenancy by the entirety usually create a presumption that a transfer to "A and B, husband and wife," creates the marital tenancy. *See, e.g.,* Constitution Bank v. Olson, 620 A.2d 1146 (Pa. Super. Ct. 1993) (bank account). Some states, however, specifically include husband and wife in the statutory presumption in favor of a tenancy in common, thus requiring the would-be grantor of a tenancy by the entirety to clearly express the requisite intent. The Mississippi statute illustrates:

> All conveyances or devises of land made to two or more persons, including conveyances or devises to husband and wife, shall be construed to create estates in common and not in joint tenancy or entirety, unless it manifestly appears from the tenor of the instrument that it was intended to create an estate in joint tenancy or entirety with the right of survivorship. But an estate in joint tenancy or entirety with the right of survivorship may be created by such conveyance from the owner or owners to himself, themselves or others, or to himself, themselves and others.

Miss. Code Ann. § 89-11-7, quoted in Estate of Childress v. Long, 588 So. 2d 192, 198-99 (Miss. 1991) (dissenting opinion).

Unmarried grantees. All states require that the grantees be married at the time of the creation of the tenancy by the entirety. If the parties aren't married, the transfer might create a joint tenancy or a tenancy in common. *See* Lopez v. Lopez, 243 A.2d 588, 599 (Md. 1968) (deed "to Alejo Lopez and Helen Lopez, his wife" created joint tenancy):

> Generally, in the case of a deed conveying property to grantees as husband and wife who are in fact not married, there is a presumption favoring tenancies in common, but this presumption will yield to the showing of a contrary intent. In the instant case, we regard Alejo's attempt to take title as tenants by the entirety as a sufficient showing of his intention to create a right of survivorship, and the presumption favoring a tenancy in common must yield to a joint tenancy.

See also Funches v. Funches, 413 S.E.2d 44 (Va. 1992) (deed to unmarried parties purporting to create tenancy by the entirety, with words of survivorship, created a joint tenancy because of the express survivorship language); Smith v. Stewart, 596 S.W.2d 346 (Ark. Ct. App. 1980) (deed "to Wesley Shaw and Dixie Shaw, his wife" failed to create tenancy by the entirety because the parties weren't married, and failed to create a joint tenancy under statutory requirement of an express declaration of a joint tenancy with right of survivorship), *aff'd*, 601 S.W.2d 837 (Ark. 1980) (per curiam); Annotation, 9 ALR4th 1189 (discussion of estate created by deed to parties described as husband and wife but not legally married). The subsequent marriage of the cotenants does not retroactively validate an attempted tenancy by the entirety. *See* Lopez v. Lopez, *supra*. The requirement of marriage, however, is satisfied by a common-law marriage in those states recognizing that relationship. *See generally* Donald Kepner, *The Effect of Attempted Creation of an Estate by the Entirety in Unmarried Grantees*, 6 Rutgers L. Rev. 550 (1952).

The other four unities. Wherever the four unities are required, a deed from one spouse to herself and the other spouse, or a deed of an undivided interest from one spouse to the other, will usually fail to create a tenancy by the entirety even with a clearly expressed intent. *See* In re Walker's Estate, 16 A.2d 28, 29 (Pa. 1940) (deed from husband to wife, conveying undivided half interest and reciting purpose to create tenancy by the entirety, created tenancy in common: "The grantor conveyed only a half interest. He did not divest himself of the other half; [h]e did not impress that half with any other title than that by which he had always held."); Pegg v. Pegg, 130 N.W. 617 (Mich. 1911) (same). *But see* Matter of Klatzel, 110 N.E. 181 (N.Y. 1915) (deed from husband to himself and wife created tenancy by entirety because it was a conveyance to a separate entity consisting of husband and wife); Annotation, 1 ALR2d 242 (discusses cases salvaging transfers in violation of four unities by construing them to create concurrent life estates with a remainder in the survivor). What exemptions from the four unities requirement are created for tenancies by the entirety in the Mississippi statute quoted in *Estate of Childress*? Does the Ohio statute quoted in Note 5 following Lipps v. Crowe, *supra*, apply to tenancies by the entirety? Does the New Jersey statute quoted in *Lipps*?

PROBLEM 3-F. What is the state of the title in each of the following transfers. Assume that O holds in fee simple absolute immediately prior to the transfsers.

    a. O conveys "to A and B, husband and wife, as joint tenants."

    b. O conveys "to A and B, husband and wife." A and B aren't married.

    c. O transfers Blackacre "to A and B, husband and wife, and C and D, husband and wife, as joint tenants and not as tenants in common, with right of survivorship."

    d. O transfers "to James C. Miller, being unmarried, and Dmitri Katsowney and Elfena Katsowney, his wife, as joint tenants and not as tenants in common." *See* Fulton v. Katsowney. 174 N.E.2d 366 (Mass. 1961).

b.   Consequences of the Tenancy by the Entirety

In the 19th century, most American states enacted Married Women's Property Acts, under which the property of a woman owned at the time of her marriage, as well as the property acquired by her after her marriage, remains or becomes her separate property. (One example of the MWPA is quoted in the principal case below.) More than half of the states adopting the MWPA regarded the tenancy by the entirety as inconsistent with the Act and hence abolished by it. In the remaining twenty-odd states, the Act was considered to have altered rather than abolished the tenancy by the entirety. Not all of the states that continued to recognize the tenancy, however, saw the Act as altering it in precisely the same way. As a result, there is not one tenancy by the entirety, but rather three, each version reflecting a somewhat different collection of sticks in the bundle. As you work through the following materials, ask yourself how well each of the different views serves to implement the policy of spousal and family protection underlying the tenancy by the entirety.

KING v. GREENE
153 A.2d 49 (N.J. 1959)

BURLING, J.

In 1913, plaintiff Marie King acquired the title to three lots on Patterson Avenue in the Borough of Shrewsbury, New Jersey. In 1931 her husband, Philip King, brought an action against her in the Court of Chancery which resulted in a degree being entered that plaintiff owed him $1,225. It was further ordered that plaintiff execute a conveyance of the three lots to herself and her husband as tenants by the entirety.

In 1932 execution was issued to satisfy the 1931 money judgment and a sheriff's deed was made to John V. Crowell of all plaintiff's right, title and interest in the property. In 1933 Philip King conveyed his right, title and interest in the three lots to Martin Van Buren Smock. John V. Crowell and his wife joined in the deed to Smock, conveying their interest acquired by virtue of the sheriff's deed. Philip King died in 1938. In 1946 Smock conveyed his interest to defendants Joseph and Mabel Greene.

In 1957 plaintiff, as surviving spouse of Philip King, instituted the present action for possession, contending that she is the sole owner of the property and that the 1932 sheriff's deed conveyed only one-half the rents, issues and profits of the property during the joint lives of the spouses and did not convey her right of survivorship. She alleges that when her husband died in 1938 the life estate for the joint lives of the spouses terminated and she became entitled to the fee. Defendants' contention is that the sheriff's deed conveyed plaintiff's right of survivorship as well as a life interest.

The trial court concluded that the sheriff's deed did not include the right of survivorship and entered a summary judgment for plaintiff which declared that she is the present holder of a fee simple in the premises; that a mortgage upon the premises held by defendant Margaretta Harrison and given by the defendants Joseph and Mabel Greene is discharged; that defendants John and Elaine Cusick, the Greenes' tenants, must vacate the premises and that plaintiff is entitled to mesne profits for six years prior to the commencement of this action.

The question at issue is whether the purchaser at an execution sale under a judgment entered against the wife in a tenancy by the entirety acquires the wife's right of survivorship. Involved are two fundamental problems: (A) the nature of an estate by the entirety at common law, and (B) the effect upon the estate by the entirety of the Married Women's Act (L.1852, p. 407, now N.J.S.A. 37:2-12 et seq.).

A. Estates by the Entirety at Common Law.

The unique form of concurrent ownership at common law, labeled estates by the entirety, may be traced into antiquity at least as far back as the 14th and 15th

Centuries. 3 Holdsworth, History of the English Law (3d ed. 1923), 128. The estate was unique because of the common-law concept of unity of husband and wife and the positing of that unity in the person of the husband during coverture. Putnam, "The Theory of Estates by the Entirety," 4 Southern L.Rev. 91 (1879). A husband and wife cannot hold by moieties or in severalty, said Littleton, "and the cause is, for that the husband and wife are but one person in law." Coke on Littleton, sec. 291. Blackstone, in his judicial capacity, noted:

> This estate differs from joint-tenancy, because joint-tenants take by moieties, and are each seised of an undivided moiety of the whole, per my et per tout, which draws after it the incident of survivorship or jus accrescendi, unless either party chooses in his life-time to sever the jointure. But husband and wife, being considered in law as one person, they cannot, during the coverture, take separate estates; and therefore upon a purchase made by them both, they cannot be seised by moieties, but both and each has the entirety. They are seised of their respective moieties, but both and each has the entirety. They are seised per tout, and not per my.

Green v. King, 96 Eng.Rep. 713, 714 (C.P. 1777).

[T]he husband was the dominant figure in the marital unity. Thus, in an estate by the entirety the husband had absolute dominion and control over the property during the joint lives. The husband was entitled to the rents, issues and profits during the joint lives of himself and his wife, with the right to use and alienate the property as he desired, and the property was subject to execution for his debts. As stated by the court in Washburn v. Burns, 34 N.J.L. 18, 20 (Sup. Ct. 1869):

> [T]he husband has an interest which does not flow from the unity of the estate, and in which the wife has no concern. He is entitled to the use and possession of the property during the joint lives of himself and wife. During this period the wife has no interest in or control over the property. It is no invasion of her rights, therefore, for him to dispose of it at his pleasure. The limit of this right of the husband is, that he cannot do any act to the prejudice of the ulterior rights of the wife.

The remaining question is, could the husband unilaterally alienate his right of survivorship at common law? Our study of the authorities convinces us that he could. The entire thrust of the authorities on the common law is to the effect that the only distinction between a joint tenancy and a tenancy by the entirety at common law was that survivorship could not be affected by unilateral action in the latter estate.

It was settled in England as early as the 14th Century that the husband could not defeat the wife's right of survivorship. In that case, reported in 2 Coke on Littleton, sec. 291, William Ocle was found guilty of treason (he murdered Edward II) and his estate was forfeited. Edward III granted the forfeited lands (owned by Ocle with his wife) to someone else. It was held that the husband's act of treason could not deprive the wife of her right of survivorship. But to say that the husband cannot by his voluntary or involuntary act defeat the wife's right of survivorship is not to say that his own right of survivorship, subject to wife's right of survivorship, should he predecease her, cannot be alienated. No prejudice would result to the wife's interests at common law by the husband's alienation of his right of survivorship. If he predeceased her, she would take a fee. If she predeceased him, her interests were cut off anyway. During his lifetime she had no interest in the estate.

Most courts and commentators have taken the position that at common law the husband's right of survivorship was alienable, so that the purchaser or grantee would take the entire fee in the event the wife predeceased the husband and the interest was subject to execution for his debts. *See, e.g.,* Bordwell, "Real Property," 8 Rutgers L. Rev. 141 (1953); Ritchie, "Tenancy by the Entirety in Real Property," 28 Va. L. Rev. 608, 609 (1941). It is our view that the husband could, at common law, alienate his right of survivorship, or, more properly, his fee simple subject to defeasance.

B. Effect of the Married Women's Act of 1852 (N.J.S.A. 37:2-12) upon Estates by the Entirety.

N.J.S.A. 37:2-12 provides:

> The real and personal property of a woman which she owns at the time of her marriage, and the real and personal property, and the rents, issues and profits thereof, of a married woman, which she receives or obtains in any manner whatever after her marriage, shall be her separate property as if she were a feme sole.

[P]resently tenancy by the entirety does not exist in 29 states [because of the view that the Married Women's Act, having destroyed the spousal unity, destroyed the foundation upon which estates by the entirety rested]. In the absence of legislation abolishing or altering estates by the entirety, our role, in light of the settled precedent that they do exist in New Jersey, is merely to define their incidents. The Court of Errors and Appeals in Buttlar v. Rosenblath, 9 A. 695 (N.J. 1887), settled the question of the effect of the Married Women's Act upon estates by the entirety. After holding that the act does not destroy the estate, it was held that the effect and purpose of the act was to put the wife on a par with the husband (9 A. at 698):

> There is nothing in the married woman's act which indicates an intention to exclude this estate wholly from its operation. I think, therefore, that the just construction of this legislation, and the one in harmony with its spirit and general purpose, is that the wife is endowed with the capacity, during the joint lives, to hold in her possession, as a single female, one-half of the estate in common with her husband, and that the right of survivorship still exists as at common law.

Subsequent decisions have confirmed that presently husband and wife, by virtue of the Married Women's Act, hold as tenants in common for their joint lives; that survivorship exists as at common law and is indestructible by unilateral action; and that the rights of each spouse in the estate are alienable, voluntarily or involuntarily, the purchaser becoming a tenant in common with the remaining spouse for the joint lives of the husband and wife.

It is clear that the Married Women's Act created an equality between the spouses in New Jersey, insofar as tenancies by the entirety are concerned. If, as we have previously concluded, the husband could alienate his right of survivorship at common law, the wife, by virtue of the act, can alienate her right of survivorship. And it follows, that if the wife takes equal rights with the husband in the estate, she must take equal disabilities. Such are the dictates of complete equality. Thus, the judgment creditors of either spouse may levy and execute upon their separate rights of survivorship.

It might be argued that the involuntary sale of a right of survivorship will not bring a fair price. However, the creditor can receive a one-half interest in the life estate for the joint lives. It seems to us that if this interest were coupled with the debtor spouse's right of survivorship the whole would command a substantially higher price and the creditor may thereby realize some present satisfaction out of the debtor spouse's assets. Moreover, to hold that a sheriff's deed does not pass the debtor-spouse's right of survivorship compels the creditor to maintain a constant vigilance over the estate. This is particularly true where the purchaser at execution sale of the debtor-spouse's life interest is someone other than the judgment creditor. There is, in short, no compelling policy reason why a judgment creditor should be inordinately delayed, or, in some instances completely deprived of his right to satisfaction out of the debtor spouse's assets.

The judgment appealed from is reversed and the cause is remanded for the entry of a judgment in accordance with the views expressed in this opinion.

WEINTRAUB, C.J. (dissenting).

The estate by the entirety is a remnant of other times. It rests upon the fiction of a oneness of husband and wife. Neither owns a separate, distinct interest in the fee; rather each and both as an entity own the entire interest. Neither takes anything by survivorship; there is nothing to pass because the survivor always had the entirety. To me the conception is quite incomprehensible. The inherent incongruity permeates the problem before us.

Presumably the estate by the entirety was designed to serve a social purpose favorable to the parties to the marriage. We are asked to recognize incidents more compatible with present thinking. Specifically, we are asked to subject a spouse's interest in the fee to execution sale. I am not sure that I can identify just what is being sold. In theory there is no right of survivorship; nothing accrues on death. And during coverture neither spouse has a separate interest in the fee. Whatever the nature of the "fee" interest a purchaser receives, he can do nothing with it except wait and hope. What he buys is the chance that the non-debtor spouse will expire before the judgment debtor.

I do not seriously urge such academic difficulties; indeed, one cannot confidently make deductions from a premise that is fictional. My objection is a practical one, that so long as we adhere to the concept of an estate by the entirety, an execution sale will result in the sacrifice of economic interests. Since the purchaser at the sale does not acquire a one-half interest in the fee with a right to partition the fee, the execution sale can be but a gambling event, yielding virtually nothing to the debtor, or for that matter to the creditor either unless he is the successful wagerer at the sale and in the waiting game to follow.

I concede that earlier decisions recognizing a right to sell the life interest of the debtor presented the same problem in theory, but the practical consequences were negligible. I think it has been the general experience of the bar that judgments obtained against a spouse have not been followed by execution sales of the life interest. And in bankruptcy proceedings the interest of the debtor regularly has been sold for a nominal sum to the other spouse or a representative of both. The general assumption, I believe, has been that the fee was not involved; and the life interest for one reason or another was not regarded by outsiders as sufficiently attractive. But if the purchaser at an execution or bankruptcy sale may one day reap the harvest of a full title, there will be an invitation to speculators.

If public policy demands that a creditor's interest be respected (I have no quarrel with the thought), the basis should be just to both the creditor and the debtor. It cannot be unless what is offered for sale is a non-contingent, non-speculative one-half interest which would support a partition suit. In that setting, bidders would know what is being sold and the sale could yield a fair price. An equitable solution can be achieved only by a statute abolishing the estate by the entirety in favor of a joint tenancy, or at least entitling the purchaser at an involuntary sale to have partition. In my judgment, a half-way approach will prove unjust. It will appreciably turn against the husband and wife a fictional concept that doubtless was originated for their benefit.

The impact upon the free movement of property in the marketplace may also be noted. In effect, the purchaser at the involuntary sale becomes a member of the entity for title purposes. In the hands of a husband and wife, property will be sold when the common economic interests of the family will be furthered. But when the power to alienate the whole is divided between a spouse and a stranger with unrelated economic motivations, property will not be moved unless those diverse interests can come to terms. Neither can compel a sale. In practical effect, there is a new restraint upon alienability to the disservice of the public interest.

I accordingly vote to affirm.

NOTES AND QUESTIONS

A. Transferability of Entirety Interests

1. **The principal case.** What rights to possession and enjoyment of the three lots in question did the Greenes acquire, through intermediate conveyances, from Philip King? What rights did they acquire through intermediate conveyances from Marie King?

2. **Current views on the tenancy by the entirety.** The following excerpt from Sawada v. Endo, 561 P.2d 1291, 1294-1295 (Hawai'i 1977), offers a useful categorization of the different views on the nature of the tenancy by the entirety. (Group I is the common law position, discussed in King v. Greene, which provides necessary background for the other views; it is no longer followed in any state.)

In the [former] Group I states (Massachusetts, Michigan, and North Carolina) the estate is essentially the common law tenancy by the entireties, unaffected by the Married Women's Property Acts. As at common law, the possession and profits of the estate are subject to the husband's exclusive dominion and control. [A]s at common law, the husband may convey the entire estate subject only to the possibility that the wife may become entitled to the whole estate upon surviving him. As at common law, the obverse as to the wife does not hold true.

In the Group II states (Alaska, Arkansas, New Jersey, New York, and Oregon) the interest of the debtor spouse in the estate may be sold or levied upon for his or her separate debts, subject to the other spouse's contingent right of survivorship. Alaska, which has been added to this group, has provided by statute that the interest of a debtor spouse in any type of estate, except a homestead as defined and held in tenancy by the entirety, shall be subject to his or her separate debts.

In the Group III jurisdictions (Delaware, District of Columbia, Florida, Indiana, Maryland, Missouri, Pennsylvania, Rhode Island, Vermont, Virginia, and Wyoming) an attempted conveyance by either spouse is wholly void, and the estate may not be subjected to the separate debts of one spouse only.

In Group IV, the two states of Kentucky and Tennessee hold that the contingent right of survivorship appertaining to either spouse is separately alienable by him and attachable by his creditors during the marriage. The use and profits, however, may neither be alienated nor attached during coverture.

The *Sawada* court placed Hawai'i in Group III, which is the majority view among states that recognize the tenancy by the entirety. By statute, New Jersey may now be a Group III state. *See* N.J.S.A. § 46:3-17.4 ("Neither spouse may sever, alienate, or otherwise affect their interest in the tenancy by the entirety during the marriage or upon separation without the written consent of both spouses."). *See generally* John V. Orth, *Tenancy by the Entirety: The Strange Career of the Common-Law Marital Estate*, 1997 B.Y.U. L. Rev. 35.

3. **Indestructible right of survivorship.** Despite the intramural differences sketched in Note 1, all states recognizing the tenancy by the entirety agree that neither spouse's right of survivorship can be defeated by the unilateral action of the other spouse. In Group III states, an effective unilateral transfer by either spouse is not possible. In Groups II and IV, each spouse has a transferable interest and can make effective unilateral transfers of what he or she has. But a transfer of either spouse's interest to a third party does not destroy the right of survivorship of the nontransferring spouse; the transfer simply places the transferring spouse's right of survivorship in the transferee. In Group II states, the transferee gets the transferor's present possessory rights and the right of survivorship; in Group IV states, the transferee gets only the transferor's right of survivorship. In a Group II or IV state, what happens to the interest of a purchaser if the transferring spouse survives the other spouse? What happens if the transferring spouse dies before the other spouse?

4. **Creditors' rights: exposition.** Even if allowed to do so, most spouses probably don't go around unilaterally transferring their interests in entirety property. But the unilateral transfer rules are important, because they define the

scope of creditors' claims, and creditors aren't shy about pursuing those claims. The general rule as to creditors' claims is that assets that a person may voluntarily transfer may also be involuntarily transferred (seized and sold) to satisfy the claim. Thus, in Group II and IV states, the creditor of either spouse may force a sale of whatever interest the debtor spouse can voluntarily transfer; in Group III states, the entirety asset is immune from the claims of either spouse's individual creditors. If H and W are *joint* debtors on an obligation, the creditor is entitled to force the sale of entirety property to satisfy the debt in all entirety states. *See* Rogers v. Rogers, 512 S.E.2d 821 (Va. 1999) (recognizing the stated rule, but refusing to apply it on behalf of a creditor who had judgments against the wife and the husband based on separate causes of action). *See generally* Richard G. Huber, *Creditors' Rights in Tenancies by the Entireties*, 1 B.C. Ind. & Comm. L. Rev. 197 (1960).

5. **Same: critique.**   Is it good policy to allow a creditor of one spouse to reach the debtor spouse's interest in entirety property? Assume an entirety property worth $100,000. Will a sale of H's interest to satisfy a $50,000 debt generate enough to satisfy the debt? Does it matter whether the property is located in a Group II or Group IV state? Is it good policy to divide decisionmaking about the property between the nondebtor spouse and the purchaser at the execution sale? Is that a problem in both Group II and Group IV states? How well do the various groups protect marital assets and provide security to the surviving spouse? In groups that don't fully honor those protective policies, what other policies are involved?

6. **Federal tax liens.**   One creditor that is unaffected by the local entirety rules is the United States, at least with regard to delinquent taxpayers. A federal tax lien attaches to the delinquent taxpayer's interest in entirety property. *See* United States v. Craft, 535 U.S. 274 (2002) (although husband in Group III state — Michigan — lacks the power of unilateral transfer of his interest in entirety real property, that power is not an essential element of the bundle of sticks; husband's other interests in the tenancy constituted sufficient "property" under federal statute creating tax lien on "all property and rights to property" belonging to a delinquent taxpayer). Justices Scalia and Thomas dissented:

> [T]he Court nullifies (insofar as federal taxes are concerned, at least) a form of property ownership that was of particular benefit to the stay-at-home spouse or mother. She is overwhelmingly likely to be the survivor that obtains title to the unencumbered property; and she (as opposed to her business-world husband) is overwhelmingly unlikely to be the source of the individual indebtedness against which a tenancy by the entirety protects. It is regrettable that the Court has eliminated a large part of this traditional protection retained by many States.

7. **Fraudulent transfers.**   "It is a fraudulent transfer for an insolvent debtor to give property away or sell property for less than reasonably equivalent value. It is also a fraudulent transfer for anyone to transfer property on any terms with actual intent to hinder his creditors." Douglas Laycock, Modern American Remedies: Cases and Materials 689 (3d ed. 2002). *See generally* Uniform Fraudulent Transfers Act (1984). Suppose Creditor gets a judgment against H for tort or breach of contract, and attaches H's interest in entirety property. Before execution on the judgment lien, H and W transfer the entirety property to their

children. May the creditor set aside the transfer? Does it matter whether the state is a Group III state? *See* Sawada v. Endo, *supra* Note 1 (conveyance by spouses of entirety property to debtor's children was not fraudulent conveyance where debtor's interest could not be unilaterally transferred and thus could not be reached by a creditor); Stop 35, Inc. v. Haines, 543 A.2d 1133 (Pa. Super. Ct. 1988) (same). Suppose that after notification of a federal tax lien, the delinquent taxpayer and his spouse together transfer the entirety property to her for one dollar. After United States v. Craft (Note 5), is that a fraudulent transfer?

8. **Divorce.** Divorce usually converts the tenancy by the entirety into a tenancy in common. *See, e.g.*, Mich. Comp. Laws Ann. § 552.102 ("Every husband and wife owning real estate as joint tenants or as tenants by entireties shall, upon being divorced, become tenants in common, unless the ownership thereof is otherwise determined by the decree of divorce"). In a few states, the tenancy becomes a joint tenancy upon divorce. *See, e.g.*, Estate of Childress v. Long, 588 So. 2d 192, 200 (Miss. 1991) (disenting opinion, noting majority and minority rules; Mississippi follows the minority rule). Suppose that X buys a debtor husband's interest in a tenancy by the entirety at a forced sale; subsequently the debtor and his spouse divorce. Is X now a tenant in common in fee simple with the nondebtor spouse in Group II and Group IV states? (Identify the sticks in H's bundle in each of those groups, and consider which stick held by X would justify treating X as a tenant in common with the other spouse.) *See* Newman v. Chase, 359 A.2d 474, 482 (N.J. 1975) (concurring and dissenting opinion: "Should the debtor spouse survive the other spouse, the purchaser [at the forced sale] would then become the owner of the property. If the marriage is terminated by divorce, the purchaser would then own an undivided one-half interest in the property as a tenant in common.").

9. **Felonious killing: the slayer and entirety property.** If one spouse murders the other; what impact does the crime have on the ownership of the former spouse's entirety property? *Compare* Restatement Third of Property § 8.4 & cmt. l (2003) (presumption that killer retains only one-half interest for life); Restatement of Restitution § 188 cmt. b (1937) (killer retains only a one-half interest in the property for life; deceased spouse's estate is entitled to a constructive trust on everything else); Neiman v. Hurff, 93 A.2d 345 (N.J. 1952) (reaches Restatement of Restitution's result), *with* UPC § 2-803(c)(2) (1990) ("The felonious and intentional killing of the decedent severs the interests of the decedent and killer in property held by them at the time of the killing as joint tenants with the right of survivorship, transforming the interests of the decedent and killer into tenancies in common."); UPC§ 1-201(26) (" 'Joint tenants with the right of survivorship' includes co-owners of property held under circumstances that entitle one or more to the whole of the property on the death of the other or others").

10. **Change in form.** A home held by H and W as tenants by the entirety is destroyed by fire. After the spouses receive the insurance proceeds on a policy covering the home, H dies. Is W entitled to all of the insurance proceeds? *See* Regnante v. Baldassare, 448 N.E.2d 775 (Mass. App. Ct. 1983); *cf.* Finley v. Thomas, 691 A.2d 1163 (D.C. 1997) (involving creditor's claim to proceeds from sale of property held by spouses as tenancy by the entirety in Group III jurisdiction).

B. Partition and Accounting

11. **Partition.** In a Group II state, a buyer of either spouse's interest becomes a tenant in common with the other spouse for the life of the marriage. Although tenancies in common are partible, as are life estates, the court in Newman v. Chase, 359 A.2d 474 (N.J. 1975), refused to allow a purchaser of the husband's interest at a bankruptcy sale to partition the life estate; the asset in question was the spouse's single-family home, occupied by the bankrupt spouse, his wife, and their two small children:

> Although a debtor's interest in property held as tenant by the entirety may be reached by his or her creditors, the remedy of partition is not automatically available to a purchaser at execution sale or to a grantee of a trustee in bankruptcy such as the plaintiff in this action. [P]artition is an ancient head of equity jurisdiction, an inherent power of the court independent of statutory grant. In the exercise of this power our courts of equity have not hesitated to exercise discretion as to the particular manner in which partition is effected between the parties. Just as the homestead exemptions [see Section C below — Eds.], effect a balance between two competing social policies — on the one hand, that a debtor's assets should be available to his creditors; on the other, that the family of a debtor should not become a charge upon the state — so can an equitable treatment of the rights of a purchaser of one spouse's interest in a tenancy by the entirety serve to achieve a similar balance. The life interest in residential real property for the joint lives of two spouses is a speculative asset, likely to bring only a low price and hence to be of little avail to a creditor seeking satisfaction of a spouse's debt. This consideration alone might not operate to deny to a purchaser the right of partition, especially as it has long been held that life estates are partible. But when the creditor's interest in the dwelling is weighed against that of the debtor's family, equitable principles persuade us that the creditor should not, as of right, be granted such minimal relief at the cost of dispossessing the family of its home. We do not go so far as to hold that a purchaser at an execution sale or from a receiver or trustee in bankruptcy may never be entitled to partition. There is no limit to the value of real property which can be held by husband and wife as tenants by the entirety. Were partition to be automatically denied, there might well be situations in which a debtor would thus be afforded "opportunity to sequester substantial assets from just liabilities." Way v. Root, 140 N.W. 577, 579 (Mich. 1913). But where, as in the present case, a bankrupt husband lives with his young family in a modest home, we hold that it is within the equitable discretion of the court to deny partition to a purchaser of the husband's interest, leaving the creditor to resort to some other remedy.

359 A.2d at 479-480. In what situations does the court suggest that partition of the life estate might be available? If partition is available, explain in your own words exactly what is available for partition, and the consequences of partition.

12. **Accounting and contribution.** Although Mrs. Chase's life estate with Newman was not partible under the court's ruling, the court further held that

Newman *was* entitled to an accounting from her, and that she was entitled to contribution from him:

> As a general rule, since each cotenant has an undivided interest in the whole estate, each is entitled to occupy the entire property. Thus, absent ouster of the other cotenants, a cotenant in possession is not required to account to them for the value of use and occupation. We think, however, that where one cotenant, with her family, remains in possession of a one-family house which is not susceptible of joint occupancy, and refuses to accede to plaintiff's demands for access to the property, such conduct clearly constitutes an ouster. Mrs. Chase is thus accountable to Mr. Newman for one-half the imputed rental value of the house. This conclusion does not end the calculation, however, for the property is encumbered by a mortgage the principal amount of which was $24,150.98 on January 1, 1973. Mrs. Chase asserts that since then she has been making mortgage, tax, and insurance payments and undertaking necessary repairs to the house. Absent ouster, a cotenant in possession is entitled to contribution from cotenants out of possession for payments made to preserve the common property. When, as here, there has been an ouster but the ousted cotenant receives an accounting based on the value of the use and occupation by the cotenant in possession, equity requires that appropriate payments made by the cotenant in possession be credited in calculating what is due the cotenant out of possession.

Newman v. Chase, 359 A.2d 474, 480-481 (N.J. 1975). Suppose that, as a result of the accounting, Mrs. Chase owes Mr. Newman money and doesn't pay it. What remedy does Mr. Newman have? Under the court's decision, is the modest marital home necessarily protected? In separate dissents, Justices Sullivan and Pashman argued that plaintiff should have been denied both partition and an accounting. By denying that the purchaser obtained any present possessory interests in the entirety property, they in effect argued that New Jersey should adopt a Group IV position, at least as to the position of a bankruptcy sale purchaser who buys the debtor-spouse's interest in the marital homestead.

B.   OTHER MARITAL PROPERTY ISSUES

In common law property states (as distinguished from community property states, discussed briefly below), spouses can take advantage of the co-tenancies that we have studied: tenancies in common, joint tenancies, and (if recognized in the jurisdiction) tenancies by the entirety. Property not held in some form of concurrent ownership is owned in severalty and controlled by the spouse in whose name title is taken. However, whether a spouse owns his or her assets in severalty or as a cotenant with the other spouse, special issues arise about the allocation of those assets when the parties divorce, as discussed in Section 1 below. Special issues also arise when the spouse who owns the bulk of the assets acquired during the marriage fails to provide adequately by will for the other spouse, considered in Section 2. Because the division of property upon divorce is a standard topic in Family Law, and division upon death in Trusts and Estates, we provide only an introductory consideration of each topic.

1.   Divorce: Equitable Distribution of Assets

When spouses in a common law property state divorce, the logic of title allows for unequal distribution of assets accumulated during the marriage: property after divorce would continue to belong to the party in whose name it was acquired (typically, the spouse who earned the money to pay for the property). Since the 1970s, however, inequality of ownership between the spouses has been reduced if not eliminated by the adoption in all common law property states of a system of "equitable distribution," under which the court supervising the parties' divorce allocates the marital assets by considerations of fairness rather than title. Equitable distribution is pretty much what it sounds like: the court supervising the divorce considers all equities, usually according to broad statutory guidelines, in determining who is entitled to what portion of the assets acquired by the spouses during the marriage. Thus, a spouse may be required to transfer his or her interest in individually-owned property, or his or her interest in any cotenancy property, to the other spouse in order to arrive at an equitable sharing of marital assets. There is continuing controversy in the law about what assets should be subject to equitable distribution (e.g., assets that a spouse owned prior to marriage?), about what counts as an "asset" (e.g., the value of a degree earned by a spouse during marriage?), and of course the abiding question about how "equitable" the distribution really is in fact.

Among the more interesting consequences of the mandate of equitable distribution is a renewed focus on the meaning of "property." Specifically, as noted and as the next case shows, litigation has frequently involved the question whether a professional degree or a professional career counts as "property" for purposes of equitable distribution.

ELKUS v. ELKUS
572 N.Y.S.2d 901 (N.Y. App. Div. 1991)

ROSENBERGER, JUSTICE.

In this matrimonial action, the plaintiff, Frederica von Stade Elkus, moved for an order determining, prior to trial, whether her career and/or celebrity status constituted marital property subject to equitable distribution. The parties have already stipulated to mutual judgments of divorce terminating their seventeen year marriage and to joint custody of their two minor children. The trial on the remaining economic issues has been stayed pending the outcome of this appeal from the order of the Supreme Court, which had determined that the enhanced value of the plaintiff's career and/or celebrity status was not marital property subject to equitable distribution. Contrary to the conclusion reached by the Supreme Court, we find that to the extent the defendant's contributions and efforts led to an increase in the value of the plaintiff's career, this appreciation was a product of the marital partnership, and, therefore, marital property subject to equitable distribution.

At the time of her marriage to the defendant on February 9, 1973, the plaintiff had just embarked on her career, performing minor roles with the Metropolitan

Opera Company. During the course of the marriage, the plaintiff's career succeeded dramatically and her income rose accordingly. In the first year of the marriage, she earned $2,250. In 1989, she earned $621,878. She is now a celebrated artist with the Metropolitan Opera, as well as an international recording artist, concert and television performer. She has garnered numerous awards, and has performed for the President of the United States.

During the marriage, the defendant travelled with the plaintiff throughout the world, attending and critiquing her performances and rehearsals, and photographed her for album covers and magazine articles. The defendant was also the plaintiff's voice coach and teacher for ten years of the marriage. He states that he sacrificed his own career as a singer and teacher to devote himself to the plaintiff's career and to the lives of their young children, and that his efforts enabled the plaintiff to become one of the most celebrated opera singers in the world. Since the plaintiff's career and/or celebrity status increased in value during the marriage due in part to his contributions, the defendant contends that he is entitled to equitable distribution of this marital property.

The Supreme Court disagreed, refusing to extend the holding in O'Brien v. O'Brien, 66 N.Y.2d 576, 489 N.E.2d 712, in which the Court of Appeals determined that a medical license constituted marital property subject to equitable distribution, to the plaintiff's career as an opera singer. The court found that since the defendant enjoyed a substantial life style during the marriage and since he would be sufficiently compensated through distribution of the parties' other assets, the plaintiff's career was not marital property.

There is a paucity of case law and no appellate authority in New York governing the issue of whether a career as a performing artist, and its accompanying celebrity status, constitute marital property subject to equitable distribution. The plaintiff maintains that since her career and celebrity status are not licensed, are not entities which are owned like a business, nor are protected interests which are subject to due process of law, they are not marital property. In our view, neither the Domestic Relations Law, nor relevant case law, allows for such a limited interpretation of the term marital property.

Domestic Relations Law § 236[B][1][c] broadly defines marital property as property acquired during the marriage "regardless of the form in which title is held." In enacting the Equitable Distribution Law (L.1980, ch. 281, § 9), the Legislature created a radical change in the traditional method of distributing property upon the dissolution of a marriage. By broadly defining the term "marital property," it intended to give effect to the "economic partnership" concept of the marriage relationship. It then left it to the courts to determine what interests constitute marital property.

Things of value acquired during marriage are marital property even though they may fall outside the scope of traditional property concepts (O'Brien v. O'Brien, *supra*; Florescue, *"Market Value," Professional Licenses and Marital Property: A Dilemma in Search of a Horn*, 1982 NY St Bar Assn Fam L Rev 13 [Dec.]). The statutory definition of marital property does not mandate that it be an asset with an exchange value or be salable, assignable or transferable. (Freed, Brandes and Weidman, *What is Marital Property?*, NYLJ, December 5, 1990, p. 3, col. 1). The property may be tangible or intangible (*Id.*).

Medical licenses have been held to enhance the earning capacity of their holders, so as to enable the other spouse who made direct or indirect contributions to their acquisition, to share their value as part of equitable distribution (O'Brien v. O'Brien, *supra*). A Medical Board Certification (Savasta v. Savasta, 146 Misc.2d 101, 549 N.Y.S.2d 544 (Sup.Ct. Nassau Co.)), a law degree (Cronin v. Cronin, 131 Misc.2d 879, 502 N.Y.S.2d 368 (Sup.Ct. Nassau Co.)), an accounting degree (Vanasco v. Vanasco, 132 Misc.2d 227, 503 N.Y.S.2d 480 (Sup.Ct. Nassau Co.)), a podiatry practice (Morton v. Morton, 130 A.D.2d 558, 515 N.Y.S.2d 499), the licensing and certification of a physician's assistant (Morimando v. Morimando, 145 A.D.2d 609, 536 N.Y.S.2d 701), a Masters degree in teaching (McGowan v. McGowan, 142 A.D.2d 355, 535 N.Y.S.2d 990) and a fellowship in the Society of Actuaries (McAlpine v. McAlpine, 143 Misc.2d 30, 539 N.Y.S.2d 680 (Sup.Ct. Suffolk Co.)) have also been held to constitute marital property.

Although the plaintiff's career, unlike that of the husband in *O'Brien*, is not licensed, the *O'Brien* court did not restrict its holding to professions requiring a license or degree. In reaching its conclusion that a medical license constitutes marital property, the *O'Brien* court referred to the language contained in Domestic Relations Law § 236 which provides that in making an equitable distribution of marital property,

> the court shall consider: (6) any equitable claim to, interest in, or direct or indirect contribution made to the acquisition of such marital property by the party not having title, including joint efforts or expenditures and contributions and services as a spouse, parent, wage earner and home-maker, and *to the career or career potential* of the other party [and] (9) the impossibility or difficulty of evaluating any component asset or any interest in a business, corporation or profession.

(Domestic Relations Law § 236[B][5][d][6], [9] (emphasis added). The court also cited § 236[B][5][e] which provides that where, equitable distribution of marital property is appropriate, but "the distribution of an interest in a business, corporation or profession would be contrary to law," the court shall make a distributive award in lieu of an actual distribution of the property (O'Brien v. O'Brien, *supra*, 66 N.Y.2d at 584, 489 N.E.2d 712).

The Court of Appeals' analysis of the statute is equally applicable here. "The words mean exactly what they say: that an interest in a profession or professional career potential is marital property which may be represented by direct or indirect contributions of the non-title-holding spouse, including financial contributions and nonfinancial contributions made by caring for the home and family" (O'Brien v. O'Brien, *supra* at 584, 498 N.Y.S.2d 743, 489 N.E.2d 712). Nothing in the statute or the *O'Brien* decision supports the plaintiff's contention that her career and/or celebrity status are not marital property. The purpose behind the enactment of the legislation was to prevent inequities which previously occurred upon the dissolution of a marriage. Any attempt to limit marital property to professions which are licensed would only serve to discriminate against the spouses of those engaged in other areas of employment. Such a distinction would fail to carry out the premise upon which equitable distribution is based, i.e., that a marriage is an economic partnership to which both parties contribute, as spouse, parent, wage earner or homemaker.

In Golub v. Golub, 139 Misc.2d 440, 527 N.Y.S.2d 946 (Sup.Ct. New York Co.), the Supreme Court agreed with the defendant husband that the increase in value in the acting and modeling career of his wife, Marisa Berenson, was marital property subject to equitable distribution as a result of his contributions thereto. Like Ms. von Stade, Ms. Berenson claimed that since her celebrity status was neither "professional" nor a "license," and, since her show business career was subject to substantial fluctuation, it should not be considered "marital property."

The court disagreed, concluding at p. 447, 527 N.Y.S.2d 946 that "the skills of an artisan, actor, professional athlete or any person whose expertise in his or her career has enabled him or her to become an exceptional wage earner should be valued as marital property subject to equitable distribution." As the *Golub* court found, it is the enhanced earning capacity that a medical license affords its holder that the *O'Brien* court deemed valuable, not the document itself. There is no rational basis upon which to distinguish between a degree, a license, or any other special skill that generates substantial income.

As further noted by the *Golub* court, there is tremendous potential for financial gain from the commercial exploitation of famous personalities. While the plaintiff insists that she will never be asked to endorse a product, this is simply speculation. More and more opportunities have presented themselves to her as her fame increased. They will continue to present themselves to her as she continues to advance in her career. The career of the plaintiff is unique, in that she has risen to the top in a field where success is rarely achieved.

Like the parties here, after Joe Piscopo and his wife married in 1973, they focused on one goal — the facilitation of his rise to stardom (Piscopo v. Piscopo, 231 N.J.Super. 576, 555 A.2d 1190, *aff'd*, 232 N.J.Super. 559, 557 A.2d 1040, *certification denied*, 117 N.J. 156, 564 A.2d 875). The defendant wife claimed that her husband's celebrity goodwill was a distributable asset and that she was entitled to a share in his excess earning capacity to which she contributed as homemaker, caretaker of their child, and sounding board for his artistic ideas.

Rejecting Mr. Piscopo's argument that celebrity goodwill is distinguishable from professional goodwill since professional goodwill has educational and regulatory requirements while celebrity goodwill requires ineffable talent, the court held that "it is the person with particular and uncommon aptitude for some specialized discipline whether law, medicine or entertainment that transforms the average professional or entertainer into one with measurable goodwill" (Piscopo v. Piscopo, *supra*, 231 N.J.Super., at 580-581, 555 A.2d, at 1191). We agree with the courts that have considered the issue, that the enhanced skills of an artist such as the plaintiff, albeit growing from an innate talent, which have enabled her to become an exceptional earner, may be valued as marital property subject to equitable distribution.

The plaintiff additionally contends that her career is not marital property because she had already become successful prior to her marriage to the defendant. As noted above, during the first year of marriage, the plaintiff earned $2,250. By

1989, her earnings had increased more than 275 fold. Further, in Price v. Price, 69 N.Y.2d 8, at 11, 503 N.E.2d 684, the Court of Appeals held that "under the Equitable Distribution Law an increase in the value of separate property of one spouse, occurring during the marriage and prior to the commencement of matrimonial proceedings, which is due in part to the indirect contributions or efforts of the other spouse as homemaker and parent, should be considered marital property (Domestic Relations Law § 236[B][1][d][3])." In this case, it cannot be overlooked that the defendant's contributions to plaintiff's career were direct and concrete, going far beyond child care and the like, which he also provided.

While it is true that the plaintiff was born with talent, and, while she had already been hired by the Metropolitan Opera at the time of her marriage to the defendant, her career, at this time, was only in the initial stages of development. During the course of the marriage, the defendant's active involvement in the plaintiff's career, in teaching, coaching, and critiquing her, as well as in caring for their children, clearly contributed to the increase in its value. Accordingly, to the extent the appreciation in the plaintiff's career was due to the defendant's efforts and contributions, this appreciation constitutes marital property.

In sum, we find that it is the nature and extent of the contribution by the spouse seeking equitable distribution, rather than the nature of the career, whether licensed or otherwise, that should determine the status of the enterprise as marital property.

Accordingly, the order of the Supreme Court, New York County (Walter M. Schackman, J.), entered September 26, 1990, which determined that the plaintiff's career and/or celebrity status was not "marital property" subject to equitable distribution, should be reversed, on the law, without costs, and the matter should be remitted to the Supreme Court for further proceedings.

All concur.

NOTES AND QUESTIONS

1. **Equitable distribution: rationale.** See Rothman v. Rothman, 320 A.2d 496, 501-02 (N.J. 1974):

> The statute we are considering authorizes the courts, upon divorce, to divide marital assets equitably between the spouses. The public policy sought to be served is at least twofold. Hitherto future financial support for a divorced wife has been available only by grant of alimony. Such support has always been inherently precarious. It ceases upon the death of the former husband and will cease or falter upon his experiencing financial misfortune disabling him from continuing his regular payments. This may result in serious misfortune to the wife and in some cases will compel her to become a public charge. An allocation of property to the wife at the time of the divorce is at least some protection against such an eventuality. In the second place the enactment seeks to right what many have felt to be a grave wrong. It gives recognition to the essential supportive role played by the wife in the home, acknowledging that as homemaker, wife and mother she should clearly be entitled to a share of family assets accumulated

during the marriage. Thus the division of property upon divorce is responsive to the concept that marriage is a shared enterprise, a joint undertaking, that in many ways it is akin to a partnership. Only if it is clearly understood that far more than economic factors are involved, will the resulting distribution be equitable within the true intent and meaning of the statute.

2. **The principal case.** New York occupies the distinct minority position on the question litigated in the principal case. Most courts take the position that a professional degree is not marital property. *See, e.g.,* In re Marriage of Graham, 574 P.2d 75 (Colo. 1978). Some of the courts holding that a professional degree is not property do, however, allow the supporting spouse "reimbursement alimony," explained by the New Jersey court as follows:

> To provide a fair and effective means of compensating a supporting spouse who has suffered a loss or reduction of support, or has incurred a lower standard of living, or has been deprived of a better standard of living in the future, the Court now introduces the concept of reimbursement alimony into divorce proceedings. The concept properly accords with the Court's belief that regardless of the appropriateness of permanent alimony or the presence or absence of marital property to be equitably distributed, there will be circumstances where a supporting spouse should be reimbursed for the financial contributions he or she made to the spouse's successful professional training. Such reimbursement alimony should cover all financial contributions towards the former spouse's education, including household expenses, educational costs, school travel expenses and any other contributions used by the supported spouse in obtaining his or her degree or license.

Mahoney v. Mahoney, 453 A.2d 527, 534 (N.J. 1982). *See also* In re Marriage of Olar, 747 P.2d 676 (Colo. 1987) (although professional degree is not marital property subject to equitable distribution, trial court in determining maintenance award should consider any unfairness that results from wife sacrificing her own educational goals to support her spouse through school).

3. **Rationale.** Why isn't a professional degree property? *See* Martinez v. Martinez, 818 P.2d 538, 541-42 (Utah 1991):

> The recipient of an advanced degree obtains that degree on the basis of his or her innate personal talents, capabilities, and acquired skills and knowledge. Such a degree is highly personal to the recipient and has none of the traditional characteristics of property. "It does not have an exchange value or any objective transferable value on an open market. It is personal to the holder. It terminates on death of the holder and is not inheritable. It cannot be assigned, sold, transferred, conveyed, or pledged." In re Marriage of Graham, 574 P.2d 75, 77 (Colo. 1978). The time has long since passed when a person's personal attributes and talents were thought to be subject to monetary valuation for commercial purposes. In short, we do not recognize a property interest in personal characteristics of another person such as intelligence, skill, judgment, and temperament, however characterized.

Is that a satisfactory rationale do you think? *See generally* Susan Etta Keller, *The Rhetoric of Marriage, Achievement, and Power: An Analysis of Judicial Opinions Considering the Treatment of Professional Degrees as Marital Property*, 21 Vt. L. Rev. 409 (1996).

4. **Other arguments.** Is a stronger argument against treating a professional degree as property the difficulty of placing a value on the degree? Or that to consider the degree as property would be to "treat the parties as though they were strictly business partners, one of whom has made a calculated investment in the commodity of the other's professional training, expecting a dollar for dollar return"? DeWitt v. DeWitt, 296 N.W.2d 761, 767 (Wis. Ct. App. 1980).

5. **Double counting?** Suppose in New York that the divorced educated spouse, whose degree is included in the marital estate and valued by that spouse's increased lifetime earning capacity, remarries. If the educated spouse's earnings during the second marriage are included in the second marital estate without deduction for amounts included in the first marital estate, does this make the educated spouse pay twice for the same thing? *See* J. Thomas Oldham, *Putting Asunder in the 1990s*, 80 Cal. L. Rev. 1091, 1121 (1992).

6. **Goodwill as property.** Unlike a professional degree, professional goodwill *is* property subject to equitable distribution upon divorce in many states. *See* Dugan v. Dugan, 457 A.2d 1, 6 (N.J. 1983) (goodwill of a solo law practice):

> Future earning capacity per se is not goodwill. However, when that future earning capacity has been enhanced because reputation leads to probable future patronage from existing and potential clients, goodwill may exist and have value. When that occurs the resulting goodwill is property subject to equitable distribution.
>
> After divorce, the law practice will continue to benefit from that goodwill as it had during the marriage. Much of the economic value produced during an attorney's marriage will inhere in the goodwill of the law practice. It would be inequitable to ignore the contribution of the non-attorney spouse to the development of that economic resource. An individual practitioner's inability to sell a law practice does not eliminate existence of goodwill and its value as an asset to be considered in equitable distribution. Obviously, equitable distribution does not require conveyance or transfer of any particular asset. The other spouse, in this case the wife, is entitled to have that asset considered as any other property acquired during the marriage partnership.

The court discussed several ways in which the value of goodwill might be calculated. *But see* Prahinski v. Prahinski, 582 A.2d 784 (Md. 1990) (goodwill of a solo law practice is not subject to equitable distribution; good discussion of the authorities).

7. **Premarital agreements.** To what extent are spouses entitled to agree before marriage on the distribution of property in the event of divorce? Although the common law traditionally was hostile to such prenuptial agreements, the trend today is toward recognition of them. The Uniform Premarital Agreement Act § 6(a)(1983), provides as follows:

§ 6. Enforcement.

(a) A premarital agreement is not enforceable if the party against whom enforcement is sought proves that:

(1) that party did not execute the agreement voluntarily; or

(2) the agreement was unconscionable when it was executed and, before execution of the agreement, that party:

(i) was not provided a fair and reasonable disclosure of the property or financial obligations of the other party;

(ii) did not voluntarily and expressly waive, in writing, any right to disclosure of the property or financial obligations of the other party beyond the disclosure provided; and

(iii) did not have, or reasonably could not have had, an adequate knowledge of the property or financial obligations of the other party.

Note the conjunctive in § 6(a)(2); shouldn't either unconscionability *or* nondisclosure be a basis for upsetting a prenuptial agreement?

2.   The Surviving Spouse's Elective Share

At common law, a surviving spouse was not an heir of the decedent spouse. In place of an intestate share of the decedent spouse's estate, the surviving spouse was traditionally eligible for dower (if a widow) or curtesy (if a widower). Dower and curtesy gave the surviving spouse a life estate in part or all of the inheritable real estate that the decedent spouse owned during the marriage. (If H owned Blackacre as a joint tenant with X, W would have no dower interest in H's share of the cotenancy, since that share is not an inheritable interest.) By providing a life estate rather than fee simple ownership of a portion of the marital assets, dower and curtesy focused on the *support* of the surviving spouse rather than on the equal sharing of assets that a modern partnership theory of marriage would dictate. In almost all common law property states, dower and curtesy have been replaced by statutes allocating a larger share of the decedent's assets to the surviving spouse. These statutes are of two types.

First, in most states, the surviving spouse is recognized as an heir of the decedent, entitled to inherit a specified portion of the decedent's assets passing by intestacy. States differ on the size of the survivor's portion, but the clear trend is towards enlarging it. *See* UPC § 2-102(1) (decedent's spouse takes entire estate if no descendant or parent survives the decedent, or if all of decedent's descendants are also descendants of the surviving spouse and surviving spouse has no other descendants). Whatever the extent of those rights, however, they apply only to the decedent spouse's *intestate* estate. What happens if, for whatever reason, the decedent spouse leaves a will that makes no provision, or a meager one, for his or her spouse? Although one suspects that such "disinheritance" of the surviving spouse is a relatively rare occurrence, the question is one of profound philosophical significance, going as it does to the heart of what it means to treat marriage as a partnership.

Second, if the decedent's estate passes by a will, the surviving spouse has rights under "elective share" statutes, which exist in all but one or two states. Under elective share statutes, the surviving spouse has an election (choice), exercisable during the administration of the decedent's estate, either to take what the will gives him or her, or to take "against the will" the elective share (typically 1/3) of the decedent's estate provided in the statute. Under the wording of traditional elective share statutes, the surviving spouse's elective share is applied against the decedent's "estate" or "probate estate." The decedent's probate estate consists of all property of the decedent that passes *at the decedent's death*. And therein lies a possible loophole for the decedent spouse bent on disinheriting his or her surviving spouse. By making lifetime transfers that deplete his or her estate, the decedent spouse could so arrange affairs as to leave the survivor with the election to take from an empty estate.

It is against human nature that a decedent spouse would make such lifetime transfers if the result were to impoverish herself or himself. But recall from Chapter 1 the remarkable revocable trust device; under such a trust, the settlor gets to transmit property outside of probate, while retaining substantial lifetime control over the assets in the trust. The principal case below, a leading one, indicates various ways in which courts have managed to bring this particular nonprobate transfer within the reach of elective share statutes.

SULLIVAN v. BURKIN
460 N.E.2d 572 (Mass. 1984)

WILKINS, JUSTICE.

Mary A. Sullivan, the widow of Ernest G. Sullivan, has exercised her right, under G.L. c. 191, § 15, to take a share of her husband's estate. By this action, she seeks a determination that assets held in an inter vivos trust created by her husband during the marriage should be considered as part of the estate in determining that share. A judge of the Probate Court for the county of Suffolk rejected the widow's claim and entered judgment dismissing the complaint. The widow appealed, and, on July 12, 1983, a panel of the Appeals Court reported the case to this court.

In September, 1973, Ernest G. Sullivan executed a deed of trust under which he transferred real estate to himself as sole trustee. The net income of the trust was payable to him during his life and the trustee was instructed to pay to him all or such part of the principal of the trust estate as he might request in writing from time to time. He retained the right to revoke the trust at any time. On his death, the successor trustee is directed to pay the principal and any undistributed income equally to the defendants, George F. Cronin, Sr., and Harold J. Cronin, if they should survive him, which they did. There were no witnesses to the execution of the deed of trust, but the husband acknowledged his signatures before a notary public, separately, as donor and as trustee.

The husband died on April 27, 1981, while still trustee of the inter vivos trust. He left a will in which he stated that he "intentionally neglected to make any provision for my wife, Mary A. Sullivan and my grandson, Mark Sullivan." He directed that, after the payment of debts, expenses, and all estate taxes levied by reason of his death, the residue of his estate should be paid over to the trustee of the inter vivos trust. The defendants George F. Cronin, Sr., and Harold J. Cronin were named coexecutors of the will. The defendant Burkin is successor trustee of the inter vivos trust. On October 21, 1981, the wife filed a claim, pursuant to G.L. c. 191, § 15, for a portion of the estate. [The statute gives the surviving husband or wife the right to elect to take a one-third portion "of the estate of the deceased."]

Although it does not appear in the record, the parties state in their briefs that Ernest G. Sullivan and Mary A. Sullivan had been separated for many years. We do know that in 1962 the wife obtained a court order providing for her temporary support. No final action was taken in that proceeding. The record provides no information about the value of any property owned by the husband at his death or about the value of any assets held in the inter vivos trust. At oral argument, we were advised that the husband owned personal property worth approximately $15,000 at his death and that the only asset in the trust was a house in Boston which was sold after the husband's death for approximately $85,000.

As presented in the complaint, and perhaps as presented to the motion judge, the wife's claim was simply that the inter vivos trust was an invalid testamentary disposition and that the trust assets "constitute assets of the estate" of Ernest G. Sullivan. There is no suggestion that the wife argued initially that, even if the trust were not testamentary, she had a special claim as a widow asserting her rights under G.L. c. 191, § 15. If the wife is correct that the trust was an ineffective testamentary disposition, the trust assets would be part of the husband's probate estate. In that event, we would not have to consider any special consequences of the wife's election under G.L. c. 191, § 15, or, in the words of the Appeals Court, "the present vitality" of Kerwin v. Donaghy, 59 N.E.2d 299 (Mass. 1945).

We conclude, however, that the trust was not testamentary in character and that the husband effectively created a valid inter vivos trust. Thus, whether the issue was initially involved in this case, we are now presented with the question (which the executors will have to resolve ultimately, in any event) whether the assets of the inter vivos trust are to be considered in determining the "portion of the estate of the deceased" (G.L. c. 191, § 15) in which Mary A. Sullivan has rights. We conclude that, in this case, we should adhere to the principles expressed in Kerwin v. Donaghy, supra, that deny the surviving spouse any claim against the assets of a valid inter vivos trust created by the deceased spouse, even where the deceased spouse alone retained substantial rights and powers under the trust instrument. For the future, however, as to any inter vivos trust created or amended after the date of this opinion, we announce that the estate of a decedent, for the purposes of G.L. c. 191, § 15, shall include the value of assets held in an inter vivos trust created by the deceased spouse as to which the deceased spouse alone retained the power during his or her life to direct the disposition of those trust assets for his or her benefit, as, for example, by the exercise of a power of appointment or by revocation of the trust.

We consider first whether the inter vivos trust was invalid because it was testamentary. A trust with remainder interests given to others on the settlor's death is not invalid as a testamentary disposition simply because the settlor retained a broad power to modify or revoke the trust, the right to receive income, and the right to invade principal during his life. We believe that the law of the Commonwealth is correctly represented by the statement in Restatement (Second) of Trusts § 57, comment h (1959), that a trust is "not testamentary and invalid for failure to comply with the requirements of the Statute of Wills merely because the settlor-trustee reserves a beneficial life interest and power to revoke and modify the trust. The fact that as trustee he controls the administration of the trust does not invalidate it."

We come then to the question whether, even if the trust was not testamentary on general principles, the widow has special interests which should be recognized. Courts in this country have differed considerably in their reasoning and in their conclusions in passing on this question. See 1 A. Scott, Trusts § 57.5 at 509-511 (3d ed. 1967 & 1983 Supp.). The rule of Kerwin v. Donaghy, 317 Mass. at 571, 59 N.E.2d 299, is that

> [t]he right of a wife to waive her husband's will, and take, with certain limitations, "the same portion of the property of the deceased, real and personal, that she would have taken if the deceased had died intestate" (G.L. [Ter.Ed.] c. 191, § 15), does not extend to personal property that has been conveyed by the husband in his lifetime and does not form part of his estate at his death. In this Commonwealth a husband has an absolute right to dispose of any or all of his personal property in his lifetime, without the knowledge or consent of his wife, with the result that it will not form part of his estate for her to share under the statute of distributions (G.L. [Ter.Ed.] c. 190, §§ 1, 2), under his will, or by virtue of a waiver of his will. That is true even though his sole purpose was to disinherit her.

In the *Kerwin* case, we applied the rule to deny a surviving spouse the right to reach assets the deceased spouse had placed in an inter vivos trust of which the settlor's daughter by a previous marriage was trustee and over whose assets he had a general power of appointment. The rule of Kerwin v. Donaghy has been adhered to in this Commonwealth for almost forty years and was adumbrated even earlier. The bar has been entitled reasonably to rely on that rule in advising clients. In the area of property law, the retroactive invalidation of an established principle is to be undertaken with great caution. We conclude that, whether or not Ernest G. Sullivan established the inter vivos trust in order to defeat his wife's right to take her statutory share in the assets placed in the trust and even though he had a general power of appointment over the trust assets, Mary A. Sullivan obtained no right to share in the assets of that trust when she made her election under G.L. c. 191, § 15.

We announce for the future that, as to any inter vivos trust created or amended after the date of this opinion, we shall no longer follow the rule announced in Kerwin v. Donaghy. There have been significant changes since 1945 in public policy considerations bearing on the right of one spouse to treat his or her property as he or she wishes during marriage. The interests of one spouse in the property of the other have been substantially increased upon the dissolution of a marriage by divorce. We believe that, when a marriage is terminated by the death of one spouse, the rights of the surviving spouse should not be so restricted as they are by the rule in Kerwin v. Donaghy. It is neither equitable nor logical to extend to a divorced spouse greater rights in the assets of an inter vivos trust created and controlled by the other spouse than are extended to a spouse who remains married until the death of his or her spouse.

The rule we now favor would treat as part of "the estate of the deceased" for the purposes of G.L. c. 191, § 15, assets of an inter vivos trust created during the marriage by the deceased spouse over which he or she alone had a general power of appointment, exercisable by deed or by will. This objective test would involve no consideration of the motive or intention of the spouse in creating the trust. We would not need to engage in a determination of "whether the [spouse] has in good faith divested himself [or herself] of ownership of his [or her] property or has made an illusory transfer" (Newman v. Dore, 275 N.Y. 371, 379, 9 N.E.2d 966 [1937]) or with the factual question whether the spouse "intended to surrender complete dominion over the property" (Staples v. King, 433 A.2d 407, 411 [Me.1981]). Nor would we have to participate in the rather unsatisfactory process of determining whether the inter vivos trust was, on some standard, "colorable," "fraudulent," or "illusory."

The question of the rights of a surviving spouse in the estate of a deceased spouse, using the word "estate" in its broad sense, is one that can best be handled by legislation. See Uniform Probate Code, §§ 2-201, 2-202, 8 U.L.A. 74-75 (1983). See also Uniform Marital Property Act, § 18 (1983), which adopts the concept of community property as to "marital property." But, until it is, the answers to these problems will "be determined in the usual way through the decisional process." Tucker v. Badoian, 376 Mass. 907, 918-919, 384 N.E.2d 1195 (1978) (Kaplan, J., concurring).

We affirm the judgment of the Probate Court dismissing the plaintiff's complaint.

So ordered.

NOTES AND QUESTIONS

1. **Validity of the revocable trust.** Why might Ernest Sullivan's revocable trust have been regarded as a testamentary transfer? If it had been so regarded in the principal case, why would it have been invalid? In concluding that Sullivan's revocable trust was not an invalid testamentary transfer, did the court essentially agree with Farkas v. Williams in Chapter 1?

2. **The issue.** If the issue in the principal case is not the validity of the revocable trust, what is it? What approaches does the court consider in determining whether to treat the trust assets as part of the decedent's estate for purposes of the surviving spouse's elective share? What approach does the court adopt? What advantages does the court's approach have over the alternatives?

3. **Traditional statutes: the fractional share and the focus on the decedent's property.** A depleted estate is not the only problem posed for the surviving spouse by traditional elective share statutes. Even if all of the decedent's assets were in his estate at his death, troublesome divisions of property could arise under the statutes. See Problem 3-G below.

4. **The 1990 UPC.** In an attempt to avoid the difficulties posed by conventional elective share statutes, and to make elective share law approximate the partnership theory underlying community property systems, the 1990 UPC completely overhauled the surviving spouse's elective share. First, the Code replaced the surviving spouse's fixed statutory percentage of the decedent's estate, which was adopted in the 1969 Code, with a sliding scale, in which the spouse's percentage increases with the length of the marriage (up to a maximum 50% share when the marriage has lasted 15 years). *See* UPC § 2-202(a). Second, the Code applied the elective share to the "augmented estate of the decedent spouse," as had the 1969 Code, but the 1990 Code enlarged the composition of the augmented estate. *See* UPC § 2-203. Third, to reduce when possible the impact of the elective share on the decedent's estate plan, the Code applied the surviving spouse's own assets to the elective share claim, leaving the decedent's property liable only when there is a deficiency. *See* UPC § 2-209.

PROBLEM 3-G. Assume that the decedent spouse made no provision for the survivor in his or her will, and that the elective share statute gives the survivor a 1/3 share of the decedent's estate. At H's death, he and W have $600,000 worth of net assets, all acquired during the marriage.

a. All of the assets are titled in H's name. What is W's elective share? *200 k*

b. Half of the assets are titled in H's name, the other half in W's name. What is W's elective share? *100 k , 400 k total*

c. Only $200,000 of the assets are titled in H's name. What is W's elective share? *UPC*

See Uniform Probate Code, Part 2, General Comment, at 58-60 (1998).

NOTES ON COMMUNITY PROPERTY

1. **Numbers and influence.** It is important to know something about community property. The eight community property states (Louisiana in the south, Texas in the southwest, and California and several other western states) comprise a quarter of the population of the United States. Moreover, community property notions — notice the sharing and support connotations of the word "community" — have influenced the non-community property states in the latter's development of the elective share and the concept of equitable distribution. In addition, couples migrate, and so even eastern lawyers need to understand community property to properly advise their clients.

2. **Shared ownership of marital assets.** Under community property, the earnings of either spouse during marriage, and the assets acquired during marriage, are deemed to belong to both spouses, who each hold an undivided one-half interest. Property brought into the marriage, and property acquired by gift, inheritance, or devise to an individual spouse during the marriage, is separate property. A spouse's share in a joint tenancy or tenancy in common is also separate property; the tenancy by the entirety is not recognized in community property states.

If the parties divorce, each spouse in a community property state is entitled to his or her share of the community. (Due to the strong presumption favoring community property, it is likely that most of the assets acquired during the parties' marriage will *be* community assets.) When one spouse dies, his or her share of the community may be devised as the decedent spouse chooses; there is no right of survivorship in community property states. A spouse's share of the community is also inheritable by the decedent's heirs; in some community property states, the decedent's issue inherit the decedent's share, while in others, the decedent's spouse is the heir.

The major difference between common law and community property systems lies in the default rule applicable to earnings and assets acquired during the parties' marriage. In community property states, those earnings and assets are presumptively community property; as noted, the presumption is strong, and to avoid the community property allocation, the parties must clearly agree to confer separate ownership of any asset on one of the spouses. In effect, community property systems treat marriage as a partnership, in which the contribution to the marriage of any spouse who does not work is valued equally with the contribution of the spouse who works. In common law property states, earnings or assets accumulated during the marriage belong to the spouse who earns or acquires them, unless the parties indicate an agreement to hold them in some form of concurrent ownership. As noted above, common law property systems have turned to equitable distribution and the elective share to eliminate or lessen the differences between common law and community property states.

UMPA. The Uniform Marital Property Act (1983) adopts the community property approach to assets acquired during the spouses' marriage. Each spouse enjoys a present, vested interest in property acquired during the marriage. Each spouse's share is disposable by that spouse, and there is no right of survivorship. Wisconsin adopted the Act in 1986, *see* Wis. Stat. Ann. §§ 766.001 through 766.979, effectively adding a ninth state to the roster of commuity property states.

3.   Unmarried Cohabitants

Should legislative systems for the division of marital property upon divorce or death apply to unmarried parties who cohabit and then break up? If not, what other remedies might the contributing partner in such a relationship have? The following well-crafted opinion exhaustively canvasses the issues raised by those questions, in a dispute between an unmarried man and woman. The case after it considers the rights upon separation of a same-sex couple. For a break from the usual regimen, and because both opinions are clear and comprehensive, we venture no commentary or questions.

WATTS v. WATTS
405 N.W.2d 303 (Wis. 1987)

SHIRLEY S. ABRAHAMSON, JUSTICE.

This case involves a dispute between Sue Ann Evans Watts, the plaintiff, and James Watts, the defendant, over their respective interests in property accumulated during their nonmarital cohabitation relationship which spanned 12 years and produced two children. The case presents an issue of first impression and comes to this court at the pleading stage of the case, before trial and before the facts have been determined. [The trial court dismissed the plaintiff's complaint for failure to state a claim on which relief could be granted.]

The plaintiff asked the circuit court to order an accounting of the defendant's personal and business assets accumulated between June 1969 through December 1981 (the duration of the parties' cohabitation) and to determine plaintiff's share of this property. The circuit court's dismissal of plaintiff's amended complaint is the subject of this appeal. The plaintiff rests her claim for an accounting and a share in the accumulated property on the following legal theories: (1) she is entitled to an equitable division of property under sec. 767.255, Stats. 1985-86; (2) the defendant is estopped to assert as a defense to plaintiff's claim under [that statute] that the parties are not married; (3) the plaintiff is entitled to damages for defendant's breach of an express contract or an implied-in-fact contract between the parties; (4) the defendant holds the accumulated property under a constructive trust based upon unjust enrichment; and (5) the plaintiff is entitled to partition of the parties' real and personal property pursuant to the partition statutes, secs. 820.01 and 842.02(1), 1985-86, and common law principles of partition.

The circuit court dismissed the amended complaint, concluding that sec. 767.255, Stats. 1985-86, authorizing a court to divide property, does not apply to the division of property between unmarried persons. Without analyzing the four other legal theories upon which the plaintiff rests her claim, the circuit court simply concluded that the legislature, not the court, should provide relief to parties who have accumulated property in nonmarital cohabitation relationships. The circuit court gave no further explanation for its decision.

We agree with the circuit court that the legislature did not intend sec. 767.255 to apply to an unmarried couple. We disagree with the circuit court's implicit conclusion that courts cannot or should not, without express authorization from the legislature, divide property between persons who have engaged in nonmarital cohabitation. Courts traditionally have settled contract and property disputes between unmarried persons, some of whom have cohabited. Nonmarital cohabitation does not render every agreement between the cohabiting parties illegal and does not automatically preclude one of the parties from seeking judicial relief, such as statutory or common law partition, damages for breach of express or implied contract, constructive trust and quantum meruit where the party alleges, and later proves, facts supporting the legal theory. The issue for the court in each case is whether the complaining party has set forth any legally cognizable claim.

I.

The plaintiff commenced this action in 1982. The plaintiff's amended complaint alleges the following facts, which for purposes of this appeal must be accepted as true. The plaintiff and the defendant met in 1967, when she was 19 years old, was living with her parents and was working full time as a nurse's aide in preparation for a nursing career. Shortly after the parties met, the defendant persuaded the plaintiff to move into an apartment paid for by him and to quit her job. According to the amended complaint, the defendant "indicated" to the plaintiff that he would provide for her.

Early in 1969, the parties began living together in a "marriage-like" relationship, holding themselves out to the public as husband and wife. The plaintiff assumed the defendant's surname as her own. Subsequently, she gave birth to two children who were also given the defendant's surname. The parties filed joint income tax returns and maintained joint bank accounts asserting that they were husband and wife. The defendant insured the plaintiff as his wife on his medical insurance policy. He also took out a life insurance policy on her as his wife, naming himself as the beneficiary. The parties purchased real and personal property as husband and wife. The plaintiff executed documents and obligated herself on promissory notes to lending institutions as the defendant's wife.

During their relationship, the plaintiff contributed childcare and homemaking services, including cleaning, cooking, laundering, shopping, running errands, and maintaining the grounds surrounding the parties' home. Additionally, the plaintiff contributed personal property to the relationship which she owned at the beginning of the relationship or acquired through gifts or purchases during the relationship. She served as hostess for the defendant for social and business-related events. The amended complaint further asserts that periodically, between 1969 and 1975, the plaintiff cooked and cleaned for the defendant and his employees while his business, a landscaping service, was building and landscaping a golf course.

From 1973 to 1976, the plaintiff worked 20-25 hours per week at the defendant's office, performing duties as a receptionist, typist, and assistant bookkeeper. From 1976 to 1981, the plaintiff worked 40-60 hours per week at a business she started with the defendant's sister-in-law, then continued and managed the business herself after the dissolution of that partnership. The plaintiff further alleges that in 1981 the defendant made their relationship so intolerable that she was forced to move from their home and their relationship was irretrievably broken. Subsequently, the defendant barred the plaintiff from returning to her business.

The plaintiff alleges that during the parties' relationship, and because of her domestic and business contributions, the business and personal wealth of the couple increased. Furthermore, the plaintiff alleges that she never received any compensation for these contributions to the relationship and that the defendant indicated to the plaintiff both orally and through his conduct that he considered her to be his wife and that she would share equally in the increased wealth.

The plaintiff asserts that since the breakdown of the relationship the defendant has refused to share equally with her the wealth accumulated through their joint efforts or to compensate her in any way for her contributions to the relationship.

II.

The plaintiff's first legal theory to support her claim against the property accumulated during the cohabitation is that the plaintiff, defendant, and their children constitute a "family," thus entitling the plaintiff to bring an action for property division under sec. 767.02(1)(h), Stats. 1985-86,[2] and to have the court "divide the property of the parties and divest and transfer the title of any such property" pursuant to sec. 767.255, 1985-86.[3]

The plaintiff asserts that the legislature intended secs. 767.02(1)(h) and 767.255, which usually govern division of property between married persons in divorce or legal separation proceedings, to govern a property division action between unmarried cohabitants who constitute a family. The plaintiff points out that secs. 767.02(1)(h) and 767.255 are part of chapter 767, which is entitled "Actions Affecting the Family," and that in 1979 the legislature deliberately changed the title of the chapter from "Actions Affecting Marriage" to "Actions Affecting the Family."[4] The legislature has failed to provide any definition for "family" under ch. 767, or for that matter under any chapter of the Family Code.

The plaintiff relies on Warden v. Warden, 676 P.2d 1037 (Wash. Ct. App. 1984), to support her claim for relief under secs. 767.02(1)(h) and 767.255. In *Warden*, the Washington court of appeals held that the statute providing guidelines for property division upon dissolution of marriage, legal separation, etc., could also be applied to divide property acquired by unmarried cohabitants in what was "tantamount to a marital family except for a legal marriage." *Warden*, 676 P.2d at 1039. *Warden* is remarkably similar on its facts to the instant case. The parties in *Warden* had lived together for 11 years, had two children, held themselves out as husband and wife, acquired property together, and filed joint tax returns. On those facts, the Washington court of appeals held that the trial court correctly treated the parties as a "family" within the meaning of the Washington marriage dissolution statute. In addition, the trial court had considered such statutory factors as the length and purpose of the parties' relationship, their two children, and the contributions and future prospects of each in determining their respective shares of the property.

Although the *Warden* case provides support for the plaintiff's argument, most courts which have addressed the issue of whether marriage dissolution statutes provide relief to unmarried cohabitants have either rejected or avoided application of a marriage dissolution statute to unmarried cohabitants. See, e.g., Marvin v. Marvin, 557 P.2d 106 (Cal. 1976).[6]

---

[2]　Sec. 767.02(1)(h), Stats. 1985-86, provides that "Actions affecting the family are: (h) For property division."

[3]　Sec. 767.255 provides in relevant part: "Upon every judgment of annulment, divorce or legal separation, or in rendering a judgment in an action under § 767.02(1)(h), the court shall divide the property of the parties and divest and transfer the title of any such property accordingly."

[4]　In a supplemental submission, and at oral argument, the plaintiff analogized its interpretation of sec. 767.255 to this court's adoption of a broad definition of "family" in the context of zoning and land use. See, e.g. Crowley v. Knapp, 288 N.W.2d 815 (Wis. 1980), in which this court stated that a "family" in that context "may mean a group of people who live, sleep, cook, and eat upon the premises as a single housekeeping unit." In *Crowley*, the court adopted a definition of "family" serving that public policy favoring the free and unrestricted use of property. By contrast, the plaintiff here has failed to convince us that extending the definition of "family" in this case to include unmarried cohabitants will further in any way the expressed public policy of ch. 767 to promote marriage and the family.

[6]　For a discussion of whether cohabitation should be viewed as analogous to marriage, see Fineman,

[W]e conclude that the legislature did not intend sec. 767.255 to extend to unmarried cohabitants. When the legislature added what is now sec. 767.255 in 1977 as part of the no fault divorce bill, it stated that its "sole purpose" was "to promote an equitable and reasonable adjudication of the economic and custodial issues involved in *marriage* relationships." (Emphasis supplied.) Moreover, the unambiguous language of sec. 767.255 and the criteria for property division listed in sec. 767.255 plainly contemplate that the parties who are governed by that section are or have been married.[9]

Furthermore, the Family Code emphasizes marriage. The entire Family Code, of which ch. 767 is an integral part, is governed generally by the provisions of sec. 765.001(2), which states in part that "[i]t is the intent of chs. 765 to 768 to promote the stability and best interests of *marriage* and the family. *Marriage* is the institution that is the foundation of family and of society. Its stability is basic to morality and civilization, and of vital interest to society and the state." (Emphasis supplied.) Section 765.001(3) further states that "[c]hapters 765 to 768 shall be liberally construed to effect the objectives of sub. (2)." The conclusion is almost inescapable from this language in sec. 765.001(2)(3) that the legislature not only intended chs. 765-768 to protect and promote the "family," but also intended "family" to be within the "marriage" context.

The statutory prohibition of marriages which do not conform to statutory requirements, sec. 765.21, Stats. 1985-86,[11] further suggests that the legislature intended that the Family Code applies, for the most part, to those couples who have been joined in marriage according to law.

On the basis of our analysis of sec. 767.255 and the Family Code which revealed no clear evidence that the legislature intended sec. 767.255 to apply to unmarried persons, we decline the invitation to extend the application of sec. 767.255 to unmarried cohabitants. We therefore hold that the plaintiff has not stated a claim for property division under sec. 767.255.

III.

The plaintiff urges that the defendant, as a result of his own words and conduct, be estopped from asserting the lack of a legal marriage as a defense against the plaintiff's claim for property division under sec. 767.255. As support for her

---

Law and Changing Patterns of Behavior: Sanctions on Non-Marital Cohabitation, 1981 Wis.L.Rev. 275, 316-32.

[9] Some of the criteria listed under § 767.255 are as follows:

> (1) The length of the *marriage*.

> (2) The property brought to the *marriage* by each party.

> (3) The contribution of each party to the *marriage*, giving appropriate economic value to each party's contribution in homemaking and child care services.

> (11) Any written agreement made by the parties before or during the *marriage* concerning any arrangement for property distribution."

(Emphasis supplied.)

[11] Common law marriages were abolished in 1917. Laws of 1917, ch. 218, sec. 21. Sec. 765.21 provides that marriages contracted in violation of specified provisions of ch. 765 are void.

position, the plaintiff cites a 1905 Tennessee case and two law review articles that do no more than cite to the Tennessee case law.[12] Although the defendant has not discussed this legal theory, we conclude that the doctrine of "marriage by estoppel" should not be applied in this case. We reach this result primarily because we have already concluded that the legislature did not intend sec. 767.255 to govern property division between unmarried cohabitants. We do not think the parties' conduct should place them within the ambit of a statute which the legislature did not intend to govern them.

IV.

The plaintiff's third legal theory on which her claim rests is that she and the defendant had a contract to share equally the property accumulated during their relationship. The essence of the complaint is that the parties had a contract, either an express or implied in fact contract, which the defendant breached.

Wisconsin courts have long recognized the importance of freedom of contract and have endeavored to protect the right to contract. A contract will not be enforced, however, if it violates public policy. A declaration that the contract is against public policy should be made only after a careful balancing, in the light of all the circumstances, of the interest in enforcing a particular promise against the policy against enforcement. Courts should be reluctant to frustrate a party's reasonable expectations without a corresponding benefit to be gained in deterring "misconduct" or avoiding inappropriate use of the judicial system.

The defendant appears to attack the plaintiff's contract theory on three grounds. First, the defendant apparently asserts that the court's recognition of plaintiff's contract claim for a share of the parties' property contravenes the Wisconsin Family Code. Second, the defendant asserts that the legislature, not the courts, should determine the property and contract rights of unmarried cohabiting parties. Third, the defendant intimates that the parties' relationship was immoral and illegal and that any recognition of a contract between the parties or plaintiff's claim for a share of the property accumulated during the cohabitation contravenes public policy.

The defendant rests his argument that judicial recognition of a contract between unmarried cohabitants for property division violates the Wisconsin Family Code on Hewitt v. Hewitt, 394 N.E.2d 1204, 3 A.L.R. 4th 1 (Ill. 1979). In *Hewitt* the Illinois Supreme Court concluded that judicial recognition of mutual property rights between unmarried cohabitants would violate the policy of the Illinois Marriage and Dissolution Act because enhancing the attractiveness of a private arrangement contravenes the Act's policy of strengthening and preserving the integrity of marriage. The Illinois court concluded that allowing such a contract claim would

---

[12] Plaintiff cites to Smith v. North Memphis Savings Bank, 89 S.W. 392 (Tenn. 1905), which is one of the more "recent" in a series of Tennessee cases to apply "marriage by estoppel." The plaintiff also cites Comment, *Property Rights Upon Termination of Unmarried Cohabitation*: Marvin v. Marvin, 90 Harv.L.Rev. 1708, 1711-12 (1977); and Weyrauch, *Informal and Formal Marriage — An Appraisal of Trends in Family Organization*, 28 U.Chi.L.Rev. 88, 105 (1960). Weyrauch cites to Tennessee law, and the comment cites to Weyrauch.

weaken the sanctity of marriage, put in doubt the rights of inheritance, and open the door to false pretenses of marriage. *Hewitt*, 394 N.E.2d at 1211.

We agree with Professor Prince and other commentators that the *Hewitt* court made an unsupportable inferential leap when it found that cohabitation agreements run contrary to statutory policy and that the *Hewitt* court's approach is patently inconsistent with the principle that public policy limits are to be narrowly and exactly applied.[14]

Furthermore, the Illinois statutes upon which the Illinois supreme court rested its decision are distinguishable from the Wisconsin statutes. The Illinois supreme court relied on the fact that Illinois still retained "fault" divorce and that cohabitation was unlawful. By contrast, Wisconsin abolished "fault" in divorce in 1977 and abolished criminal sanctions for nonmarital cohabitation in 1983.[15]

The defendant has failed to persuade this court that enforcing an express or implied in fact contract between these parties would in fact violate the Wisconsin Family Code. The Family Code is intended to promote the institution of marriage and the family. We find no indication, however, that the Wisconsin legislature intended the Family Code to restrict in any way a court's resolution of property or contract disputes between unmarried cohabitants.

The defendant also urges that if the court is not willing to say that the Family Code proscribes contracts between unmarried cohabiting parties, then the court should refuse to resolve the contract and property rights of unmarried cohabitants without legislative guidance. The defendant asserts that this court should conclude, as the *Hewitt* court did, that the task of determining the rights of cohabiting parties is too complex and difficult for the court and should be left to the legislature. We are not persuaded by the defendant's argument. Courts have traditionally developed principles of contract and property law through the case-by-case method of the common law. While ultimately the legislature may resolve the problems raised by unmarried cohabiting parties, we are not persuaded that the court should refrain from resolving such disputes until the legislature gives us direction. Our survey of the cases in other jurisdictions reveals that *Hewitt* is not widely followed.

We turn to the defendant's third point, namely, that any contract between the parties regarding property division contravenes public policy because the contract is based on immoral or illegal sexual activity. The defendant does not appear to make this argument directly. It is not well developed in the brief, and at oral argument defendant's attorney indicated that he did not find this argument persuasive in light of the current community mores, the substantial number of

---

[14] Prince, *Public Policy Limitations in Cohabitation Agreements: Unruly Horse or Circus Pony*, 70 Minn.L.Rev. 163, 189-205 (1985).

[15] Both Illinois and Wisconsin have abolished common law marriages. In our view this abolition does not invalidate a private cohabitation contract. Cohabitation agreements differ in effect from common law marriage. There is a significant difference between the consequences of achieving common law marriage status and of having an enforceable cohabitation agreement. In Latham v. Latham, 547 P.2d 144, 147 (Or. 1976), the Oregon supreme court found that the Legislature's decriminalization of cohabitation represented strong evidence that enforcing agreements made by parties during cohabitation relationships would not be contrary to Oregon public policy.

unmarried people who cohabit, and the legislature's abolition of criminal sanctions for cohabitation. Although the parties in the instant case cohabited at a time when cohabitation was illegal, the defendant's counsel at oral argument thought that the present law should govern this aspect of the case. Because illegal sexual activity has posed a problem for courts in contract actions, we discuss this issue even though the defendant did not emphasize it.

Courts have generally refused to enforce contracts for which the sole consideration is sexual relations, sometimes referred to as "meretricious" relationships. See In Matter of Estate of Steffes, 290 N.W.2d 697 (Wis. 1980), citing Restatement of Contracts Section 589 (1932). Courts distinguish, however, between contracts that are explicitly and inseparably founded on sexual services and those that are not. This court, and numerous other courts, have concluded that "a bargain between two people is not illegal merely because there is an illicit relationship between the two so long as the bargain is independent of the illicit relationship and the illicit relationship does not constitute any part of the consideration bargained for and is not a condition of the bargain." Steffes, supra, 95 Wis.2d at 514, 290 N.W.2d 697.

While not condoning the illicit sexual relationship of the parties, many courts have recognized that the result of a court's refusal to enforce contract and property rights between unmarried cohabitants is that one party keeps all or most of the assets accumulated during the relationship, while the other party, no more or less "guilty," is deprived of property which he or she has helped to accumulate.

The Hewitt decision, which leaves one party to the relationship enriched at the expense of the other party who had contributed to the acquisition of the property, has often been criticized by courts and commentators as being unduly harsh.[18] Moreover, courts recognize that their refusal to enforce what are in other contexts clearly lawful promises will not undo the parties' relationship and may not discourage others from entering into such relationships. A harsh, per se rule that the contract and property rights of unmarried cohabiting parties will not be recognized might actually encourage a partner with greater income potential to avoid marriage in order to retain all accumulated assets, leaving the other party with nothing. See Marvin v. Marvin, supra, 557 P.2d at 122.

One Wisconsin case which requires discussion in this context is Smith v. Smith, 38 N.W.2d 12 (Wis. 1949). In Smith, one of the parties to a common law marriage discovered that such marriages were not legal, demanded that the defendant marry her, was refused, and sought equitable property division. The court denied her claim. Although we find the harsh result in Smith troubling, we need not overrule it because Smith is distinguishable from the instant case.

The plaintiff in Smith was seeking equitable property division under the marriage dissolution statutes. Like the court in Smith, we have decided that those statutes are unavailable to an unmarried person. The plaintiff in this case,

---

[18] See Prince, *Public Policy Limitations on Cohabitation Agreements: Unruly Horse or Circus Pony*, 70 Minn.L.Rev. 163, 189-205 (1985); Oldham & Caudill, *A Reconnaissance of Public Policy Restrictions upon Enforcement of Contracts between Cohabitants*, 18 Fam.L.Q. 93, 132 (Spring 1984); Comment, Marvin v. Marvin: *Five Years Later*, 65 Marq.L.Rev. 389, 414 (1982).

however, rests her claim on theories of recovery other than those of the plaintiff in *Smith*. The *Smith* court ruled that the plaintiff had based her claim for property division solely on the fact of the couple's illegal common law marriage. *Smith*, 255 Wis. at 100, 38 N.W.2d 12. In other words, the plaintiff in that case had not alleged facts necessary to find that the couple had agreed to share their property, independent from their sexual relationship.

In *Smith*, the problem was inadequate pleading by the plaintiff. In this case, the plaintiff has alleged many facts independent from the parties' physical relationship which, if proven, would establish an express contract or an implied in fact contract that the parties agreed to share the property accumulated during the relationship.

The plaintiff has alleged that she quit her job and abandoned her career training upon the defendant's promise to take care of her. A change in one party's circumstances in performance of the agreement may imply an agreement between the parties. *Steffes, supra*, 95 Wis.2d at 504, 290 N.W.2d 697.

In addition, the plaintiff alleges that she performed housekeeping, childbearing, childrearing, and other services related to the maintenance of the parties' home, in addition to various services for the defendant's business and her own business, for which she received no compensation. Courts have recognized that money, property, or services (including housekeeping or childrearing) may constitute adequate consideration independent of the parties' sexual relationship to support an agreement to share or transfer property. *Steffes, supra*, 95 Wis.2d at 501, 290 N.W.2d 697.[19]

According to the plaintiff's complaint, the parties cohabited for more than twelve years, held joint bank accounts, made joint purchases, filed joint income tax returns, and were listed as husband and wife on other legal documents. Courts have held that such a relationship and "joint acts of a financial nature can give rise to an inference that the parties intended to share equally." Beal v. Beal, 577 P.2d 507, 510 (Or. 1978). The joint ownership of property and the filing of joint income tax returns strongly implies that the parties intended their relationship to be in the nature of a joint enterprise, financially as well as personally.

Having reviewed the complaint and surveyed the law in this and other jurisdictions, we hold that the Family Code does not preclude an unmarried cohabitant from asserting contract and property claims against the other party to the cohabitation. We further conclude that public policy does not necessarily preclude an unmarried cohabitant from asserting a contract claim against the other party to the cohabitation so long as the claim exists independently of the sexual relationship and is supported by separate consideration. Accordingly, we conclude that the plaintiff in this case has pleaded the facts necessary to state a

---

[19] Until recently, the prevailing view was that services performed in the context of a "family or marriage relationship" were presumed gratuitous. However, that presumption was rebuttable. See *Steffes*, 290 N.W.2d at 703-704. In *Steffes*, we held the presumption to be irrelevant where the plaintiff can show either an express or implied agreement to pay for those services, even where the plaintiff has rendered them "with a sense of affection, devotion and duty." 290 N.W.2d at 703-704. For a discussion of the evolution of thought regarding the economic value of homemaking services by cohabitants, see Bruch, *Property Rights of De Facto Spouses Including Thoughts on the Value of Homemakers' Services*, 10 Fam.L.Q. 101, 110-14 (Summer 1976).

claim for damages resulting from the defendant's breach of an express or an implied in fact contract to share with the plaintiff the property accumulated through the efforts of both parties during their relationship. Once again, we do not judge the merits of the plaintiff's claim; we merely hold that she be given her day in court to prove her claim.

V.

The plaintiff's fourth theory of recovery involves unjust enrichment. Essentially, she alleges that the defendant accepted and retained the benefit of services she provided knowing that she expected to share equally in the wealth accumulated during their relationship. She argues that it is unfair for the defendant to retain all the assets they accumulated under these circumstances and that a constructive trust should be imposed on the property as a result of the defendant's unjust enrichment. In his brief, the defendant does not attack specifically either the legal theory or the factual allegations made by the plaintiff.

Unlike claims for breach of an express or implied in fact contract, a claim of unjust enrichment does not arise out of an agreement entered into by the parties. Rather, an action for recovery based upon unjust enrichment is grounded on the moral principle that one who has received a benefit has a duty to make restitution where retaining such a benefit would be unjust. Because no express or implied in fact agreement exists between the parties, recovery based upon unjust enrichment is sometimes referred to as "quasi contract," or contract "implied in law" rather than "implied in fact." Quasi contracts are obligations created by law to prevent injustice.[20]

In Wisconsin, an action for unjust enrichment, or quasi contract, is based upon proof of three elements: (1) a benefit conferred on the defendant by the plaintiff, (2) appreciation or knowledge by the defendant of the benefit, and (3) acceptance or retention of the benefit by the defendant under circumstances making it inequitable for the defendant to retain the benefit.

The plaintiff has cited no cases directly supporting actions in unjust enrichment by unmarried cohabitants, and the defendant provides no authority against it. This court has previously extended such relief to a party to a cohabitation in Estate of Fox, 190 N.W. 90, 31 A.L.R. 420 (Wis. 1922). In *Fox*, the plaintiff was a woman who had believed in good faith that she was married to the decedent, when in fact she was not. The court found that the decedent "husband" had "by fraudulent representations induced the plaintiff to enter into the illicit relationship." Fox, *supra*, 178 Wis. at 372, 190 N.W. 90. Under those circumstances, the court reasoned that it was "just and logical" to infer "from the nature of the transaction" that "the supposed husband [can be] held to have assumed to pay [for services rendered by his 'spouse'] because in point of law and equity it is just that he should pay." *Id.*

---

[20] For a discussion regarding the relationship between express, implied-in-fact, and implied-in-law contracts, see *Steffes, supra*, 95 Wis.2d at 497 & n. 4, 290 N.W.2d 697.

In *Fox*, the court expressly refused to consider whether the same result would necessarily follow in other circumstances. Thus, *Fox* does not supply explicit support for the plaintiff's position here where she does not claim that she thought the parties were actually married.

The *Steffes* case, however, does provide additional support for the plaintiff's position. Although *Steffes* involved a claim for recovery in contract by an unmarried cohabitant for the value of services she performed for the decedent, the same equitable principles that governed that case would appear to apply in a case where the plaintiff is seeking recovery based upon unjust enrichment. In *Steffes*, the court cited with approval a statement by the trial judge that "[t]he question I have in mind is why should the estate be enriched when that man was just as much a part of the illicit relationship as she was and not let her have her fair dues. I don't understand that law that would interpret unjust enrichment that way and deprive one and let the other benefit and do it on the basis that there was an illicit relationship but not equally held against the both." *Steffes*, *supra*, 95 Wis.2d at 508, 290 N.W.2d 697.

As part of his general argument, the defendant claims that the court should leave the parties to an illicit relationship such as the one in this case essentially as they are found, providing no relief at all to either party. For support, the defendant relies heavily on Hewitt v. Hewitt, *supra*, and the dissent in *Steffes*, to argue that courts should provide no relief whatsoever to unmarried cohabitants until the legislature provides specifically for it. See *Steffes*, *supra*, 95 Wis.2d at 521-22, 290 N.W.2d 697 (Coffey, J., dissenting).

As we have discussed previously, allowing no relief at all to one party in a so-called "illicit" relationship effectively provides total relief to the other, by leaving that party owner of all the assets acquired through the efforts of both. Yet it cannot seriously be argued that the party retaining all the assets is less "guilty" than the other. Such a result is contrary to the principles of equity. Many courts have held, and we now so hold, that unmarried cohabitants may raise claims based upon unjust enrichment following the termination of their relationships where one of the parties attempts to retain an unreasonable amount of the property acquired through the efforts of both.

In this case, the plaintiff alleges that she contributed both property and services to the parties' relationship. She claims that because of these contributions the parties' assets increased, but that she was never compensated for her contributions. She further alleges that the defendant, knowing that the plaintiff expected to share in the property accumulated, "accepted the services rendered to him by the plaintiff" and that it would be unfair under the circumstances to allow him to retain everything while she receives nothing. We conclude that the facts alleged are sufficient to state a claim for recovery based upon unjust enrichment.

As part of the plaintiff's unjust enrichment claim, she has asked that a constructive trust be imposed on the assets that the defendant acquired during their relationship. A constructive trust is an equitable device created by law to prevent unjust enrichment. To state a claim on the theory of constructive trust the complaint must state facts sufficient to show (1) unjust enrichment and (2) abuse of a confidential relationship or some other form of unconscionable conduct. The latter element can be inferred from allegations in the complaint which show, for example, a family relationship, a close personal relationship, or the parties' mutual trust. These facts are alleged in this complaint or may be inferred. Therefore, we hold that if the plaintiff can prove the elements of unjust enrichment to the satisfaction of the circuit court, she will be entitled to demonstrate further that a constructive trust should be imposed as a remedy.

VI.

The plaintiff's last alternative legal theory on which her claim rests is the doctrine of partition. The plaintiff has asserted in her complaint a claim for partition of "all real and personal property accumulated by the couple during their relationship according to the plaintiff's interest therein and pursuant to Chapters 820 and 842, Wis.Stats."

Chapter 820, Stats. 1985-86, provides for partition of personal property. Sec. 820.01 states in part: "When any of the owners of personal property in common shall desire to have a division and they are unable to agree upon the same an action may be commenced for that purpose." Sec. 820.01 thus states on its face that anyone owning property "in common" with someone else can maintain an action for partition of personal property held by the parties. This section codifies a remedy long recognized at common law. See Laing v. Williams, 115 N.W. 821 (Wis. 1908) (courts of equity have general jurisdiction to maintain actions for partition of personalty and to provide any kind of relief necessary to do justice).

Ch. 842, Stats. 1985-86, provides for partition of interests in real property. Sec. 842.02(1) states in relevant part: "A person having an interest in real property jointly or in common with others may sue for judgment partitioning such interest unless an action for partition is prohibited elsewhere in the statutes." Sec. 842.02(1) also codifies an action well known at common law. See Kubina v. Nichols, 6 N.W.2d 657 (Wis. 1942) (partition of real property is an equitable action).

In Wisconsin partition is a remedy under both the statutes and common law. Partition applies generally to all disputes over property held by more than one party. This court has already held, in Jezo v. Jezo, 119 N.W.2d 471 (Wis. 1963), that the principles of partition could be applied to determine the respective property interests of a husband and wife in jointly owned property where the divorce law governing property division did not apply. Because the action was not incident to divorce, separation, or annulment, the *Jezo* court rejected the parties' claim for property division under the divorce law, but did hold that a circuit court should apply the principles of partition to settle the parties' property dispute. The court stated that the "determination of the issues relating to the property of the parties to this action is to be made on the basis of those legal and equitable principles which would govern the rights to property between strangers." Thus, *Jezo* appears to say that persons, regardless of their marital status, may sue for partition of property.

Apart from citing the partition statutes, the plaintiff relies heavily on Carlson v. Olson, 256 N.W.2d 249, 255 (Minn. 1977), in which the Minnesota supreme court approved the application of common law partition principles to augment partition statutes on facts very similar to those in this case.[22] *Carlson* is one of a number of cases similar to the fact situation in the case at bar in which the court used the partition remedy to protect the interests of both parties to a nonmarital cohabitation relationship in the property acquired during their relationship. See, e.g., Carroll v. Lee, 148 Ariz. 10, 14, 712 P.2d 923 (1986) (partition allowed where parties acquired property in joint title through joint common effort and for a common purpose and parties had implied partnership or joint enterprise agreement).

The defendant refutes the plaintiff's claim for partition on two grounds. First, the defendant cites generally to Slocum v. Hammond, 346 N.W.2d 485, 494-95 (Iowa 1984), a case involving nonmarital cohabitation in which the Iowa supreme court denied the plaintiff's partition claim. *Slocum* is inapposite. In *Slocum* the court denied partition simply because the woman had failed to establish through evidence the requisite "joint venture," not because the partition action was an improper remedy in nonmarital cohabitation cases. *Slocum* was recently distinguished in Metten v. Benge, 366 N.W.2d 577, 579-80 (Iowa 1985), in which the Iowa supreme court upheld the trial court's application of equitable partition principals to settle a dispute over property by unmarried cohabitants.

Second, as we have previously said, the defendant, relying on *Hewitt*, groups all of the plaintiff's claims together, including the partition claim, labels them "marriage-like claims," and argues that the court should not grant relief relating to the parties' accumulated property in cases of nonmarital cohabitation. We have already discussed the defendant's position and concluded that we are not persuaded by it.

In this case, the plaintiff has alleged that she and the defendant were engaged in a joint venture or partnership, that they purchased real and personal property as husband and wife, and that they intended to share all the property acquired during their relationship. In our opinion, these allegations, together with other facts alleged in the plaintiff's complaint (e.g., the plaintiff's contributions to the acquisition of their property) and reasonable inferences therefrom, are sufficient under Wisconsin's liberal notice pleading rule to state a claim for an accounting of the property acquired during the parties' relationship and partition. We do not, of course, presume to judge the merits of the plaintiff's claim. Proof of her allegations must be made to the circuit court. We merely hold that the plaintiff has alleged sufficient facts in her complaint to state a claim for relief statutory or common law partition.

In summary, we hold that the plaintiff's complaint has stated a claim upon which relief may be granted. We conclude that her claim may not rest on sec. 767.255, Stats. 1985-86, or the doctrine of "marriage by estoppel," but that it may rest on contract, unjust enrichment or partition. Accordingly, we reverse the judgment of

---

[22] In *Carlson*, as in the instant case, the parties held themselves out to be married. The parties filed joint income tax returns and maintained joint bank accounts. The major difference between *Carlson* and the instant case is that in *Carlson*, the plaintiff's contribution was limited to homemaking and childcare. That contribution was found sufficient to imply an agreement to share all the property accumulated during the parties' relationship. In this case, the plaintiff allegedly contributed business services and personal property as well as homemaking and childcare services.

the circuit court, and remand the cause to the circuit court for further proceedings consistent with this opinion.

The judgment of the circuit court is reversed and the cause remanded.

IRELAND v. FLANAGAN
627 P.2d 496 (Or. Ct. App. 1981)

WARREN, JUDGE.

Plaintiff brought this suit in equity seeking: (1) an award of a one-half interest in a house held in the name of defendant and occupied by the parties during the period of their relationship; and (2) an accounting from defendant for her exclusive use of the property from the time the parties ceased living together. The basis of her complaint was that the parties, during their period of cohabitation, had an express oral agreement whereby they agreed to pool all of their assets for their joint benefit. Defendant generally denied plaintiff's allegations and counterclaimed for payment of plaintiff's share of certain debts, which were allegedly jointly incurred during their relationship, and for recovery of an article of defendant's personal property. The trial court denied any relief; only plaintiff appeals.

The facts of this case are sharply contested. Regarding the parties' financial arrangement, plaintiff testified:

> A. After we moved in together, we sat down and discussed financial things and decided, for convenience sake and because, in essence, we were going to have a long relationship together and a marriage, we would pool our resources.
>
> Q. Did you expressly agree in those terms?
>
> A. Yes, we did.
>
> Q. What did you mean by pooling your resources?
>
> A. Whatever I had was hers; whatever she had was mine. And that included, money, cars, furniture, whatever it was.

In obtaining the $7,000 down payment for the purchase of the house, plaintiff testified that defendant secured a $5,000 loan from her credit union and plaintiff sold her automobile for $2,000.

On direct examination, plaintiff testified that they planned to purchase the house in both names if at all possible and that it was not until they went to sign the closing papers at the escrow office that they discovered that both names did not appear on the contract. Nevertheless, they decided that defendant should sign the papers as written and that they would be corrected at another time. Thereafter, the parties on numerous occasions discussed changing title to both names, but, as plaintiff put it, they "never got around to doing it." On cross-examination, however, an excerpt from plaintiff's May 14, 1979, deposition was read into the record in which plaintiff had testified that, near to the time they purchased the house, they decided to take title solely in defendant's name in order to provide her with a tax shelter for her higher wages.

Defendant's testimony regarding the nature of the parties' agreement as to the house was punctuated with inconsistencies. The essence of her testimony was that the parties had an express oral agreement to pool their resources, each paying fifty percent of everything, and if plaintiff contributed her fifty percent of the house payments, then when the house was sold, plaintiff would get fifty percent of the equity. At one point in her testimony, defendant admitted that plaintiff had contributed $2,000 from the sale of plaintiff's automobile toward the $7,000 down payment on the house; at another point, defendant stated that plaintiff had contributed nothing to the house and that the automobile which allegedly was sold by plaintiff for her $2,000 contribution was not owned by plaintiff, but by defendant.

Several witnesses, including mutual friends of the parties, the escrow agent who prepared the papers on the house and the seller of the house, corroborated plaintiff's testimony that the parties bought the house together. One witness testified that defendant had expressly stated that the house was owned by both parties and that, in the event plaintiff's and defendant's relationship terminated, the house and other jointly-owned property would "be split right down the middle."

Both parties testified to the fact that they maintained a joint checking account, a joint savings account and a safety deposit box and that they had joint loans and two joint credit cards. They testified that their practice was to deposit their paychecks into their joint checking account and from this account to pay their bills, including the house payment. Defendant, moreover, admitted that plaintiff had in fact made most of the numerous, substantial household improvements plaintiff had claimed.

Upon the termination of their relationship, defendant moved out of the house in August, 1978. However, in October, 1978, defendant returned after plaintiff had vacated the premises.

The trial court made findings of fact: (1) both plaintiff and defendant are unreliable witnesses whose testimony is false in parts and is unreliable in parts unless corroborated by other evidence; (2) they agreed to pool their assets for their joint use during the period of their relationship, which terminated on August 31, 1978; (3) on about March 1, 1977, defendant purchased a house and assumed the mortgage; (4) plaintiff contributed $2,000 toward the total down payment for the property of $7,000; (5) pursuant to their agreement the property was used by the parties jointly during their relationship; (6) plaintiff occupied the premises with defendant until August 31, 1978; (7) during her occupancy, plaintiff expended some labor in improvements to the premises and some money was jointly expended by the parties for materials and labor for these improvements; (8) debts for these improvements were incurred in the name of defendant only; and (9) the relationship of the parties, as construed by the parties themselves, imposed upon them a moral obligation to provide for the other, similar to the relationship of husband and wife.

The trial court concluded that the law presumes that plaintiff's contributions toward defendant's purchase and improvement of the residence were gifts from plaintiff to defendant; that this presumption may be overcome only by evidence of the most convincing and satisfactory kind; that plaintiff's evidence failed to overcome the presumption of a gift; that plaintiff did not sustain her burden of proving that defendant promised to convey any legal or equitable interest in said real property to plaintiff, other than the right to use the property jointly with defendant during the time of their relationship; that defendant is not estopped to deny plaintiff's claims; that defendant is not legally required to account to plaintiff for her use of the property after the termination of their relationship; and that plaintiff does not owe defendant any of the sums alleged in defendant's counterclaims. Thereupon, the court denied relief to either party.

Although the trial court held that plaintiff failed to overcome the legal presumption that her contributions toward the purchase and improvements to the house were gifts from plaintiff to defendant, neither party pleaded or argued that plaintiff's contributions were gifts. Instead, this theory was proffered gratuitously by the trial court. It has no applicability here. The general rule is, rather, that a party seeking to establish the existence of a gift must prove its existence by clear and convincing evidence. An exception applies when there is a transfer of property from a parent, or one standing in loco parentis, to a child; such a transfer is presumptively a gift. There is obviously no parent/child relationship here, and defendant's argument that in loco parentis cases are applicable is unpersuasive.

In untangling the affairs of the parties and effecting a division of assets and liabilities between cohabitants, the paramount question is to discern the intent of the parties. As the Supreme Court stated in Beal v. Beal, 282 Or. 115, 122, 577 P.2d 507 (1978):

> We believe a division of property accumulated during a period of cohabitation must be begun by inquiring into the intent of the parties, and if an intent can be found, it should control that property distribution. While this is obviously true when the parties have executed a written agreement, it is just as true if there is no written agreement. The difference is often only the sophistication of the parties. Thus, absent an express agreement, courts should closely examine the facts in evidence to determine what the parties implicitly agreed upon.

The parties in *Beal* purchased a house after they were divorced. The purchase contract listed both parties' names and as husband and wife. Mr. Beal paid $500 of the $2,000 down payment and Mrs. Beal paid the balance of $1,500. While she paid the first monthly payment, he made all subsequent payments. After the purchase, the parties lived together in the house. They maintained a joint savings account, but had separate checking accounts. They made improvements to the property, paid for in part by Mrs. Beal and in part from their joint savings account. Family expenses were paid from Mrs. Beal's income. Mrs. Beal moved out of the house after they had lived together for two years. Mr. Beal remained and paid all monthly house payments.

The Supreme Court concluded:

> [T]he record supports the position that *the parties intended to pool their resources for their common benefit during the time they lived together.* This conclusion is supported by the defendant's testimony that she contributed her entire income to maintenance of the household. Further,

she testified that she gave money on one occasion to the plaintiff to make the house payment. *Neither party made any effort to keep separate accounts or to total their respective contributions for reimbursement purposes*, and, although they had separate checking accounts, they had a joint savings account. Finally, the living arrangement itself is evidence that the parties intended to share their resources. Since the parties intended to pool their funds for payment of their obligations, they should be considered equal cotenants, except that Barbara is entitled to an offset of $500, representing the amount she paid over and above one-half of the down payment.

Beal v. Beal, *supra* 282 Or. at 122-23, 577 P.2d 507. (Emphasis supplied.)

Similarly, in the present case we find that during the parties' relationship they intended to pool their resources for their mutual benefit. In purchasing the house, the parties intended joint ownership. Title was taken in defendant's name for the sole purpose of providing her with a tax shelter. Thus, we conclude that the parties should be considered equal co-tenants. Although the parties here are members of the same sex, we believe that the principles articulated in *Beal* are equally applicable. Because defendant contributed an amount greater than one-half of the down payment, she is entitled to an offset of $1,500.

As in *Beal*, we further find that since October 1, 1978, plaintiff has not contributed toward the house payments. Therefore, defendant is entitled to reimbursement by plaintiff for 50% of the house payments made by defendant after October 1, 1978. Moreover, because defendant's occupancy of the property excluded plaintiff's use and enjoyment thereof, plaintiff as a co-tenant is entitled to recover one-half of its fair rental value from October 1, 1978. The evidence was that the fair rental value of the property as of August 1, 1978, was $275 per month and that its fair rental value as of August 1, 1979, was $325 per month. Plaintiff is entitled to recover from defendant one-half of the reasonable rental value of the premises, less a credit of $1500 and a credit for one-half of the mortgage payments made by the defendant since October 1, 1978.

Reversed and remanded for entry of a decree in conformity with this opinion.

C. PROPERTY AND PROTECTION: THE HOMESTEAD EXEMPTION

One's assets may provide a base for support (for example, land can be farmed, rented out, or lived on), or a base for obtaining credit (land or other assets can be pledged as security for a loan). Since the early nineteenth century, ownership (particularly of land) has also served, to some extent, as a base for protection from the claims of creditors.

MICHELS v. KOZITZA
610 N.W.2d 368 (Minn. Ct. App. 2000)

RANDALL, JUDGE.

Appellant challenges a district court order denying his motion for an injunction barring a sheriff's execution sale of appellant's real property. Appellant asserts that the district court erroneously interpreted the homestead exemption when it concluded that a parcel of his land that is noncontiguous with the parcel on which his home is situated is not covered by the exemption. We affirm.

FACTS

Appellant David Michels and his brother previously co-owned a 40-acre parcel of land, which they stipulated to partitioning in 1998. Michels received the southern 20 acres of the property, and his brother received the northern 20 acres. On April 30, 1999, respondent James Kollman, the Nicollet County Sheriff, levied and attached the 20 acres owned by Michels in satisfaction of a judgment owed to respondents Lucy Kozitza and the Kozitza Family Partnership (the Kozitzas). The execution sale was scheduled for July 15, 1999.

Michels moved for an injunction to stop the sale, contending that his 20 acres was subject to the homestead exemption. The district court denied Michels's motion. In rejecting the motion, the district court examined precedent indicating that Michels was not entitled to the homestead exemption for his 20 acres because his residence is not situated on land that is contiguous with this acreage. The district court determined that Michels was unlikely to succeed on the merits of his argument.

ISSUE

Does the homestead exemption protect noncontiguous parcels of property that are homesteaded for property tax purposes?

ANALYSIS

Michels asserts that the district court erred in its interpretation of the statute granting the homestead exemption.

Statutory construction is a legal question reviewed de novo on appeal. If a statute is unambiguous, its plain meaning is applied. State by Beaulieu v. RSJ, Inc., 552 N.W.2d 695, 701 (Minn. 1996); see also Minn.Stat. § 645.16 (1998) ("When the words of a law in their application to an existing situation are clear and free from all ambiguity, the letter of the law shall not be disregarded under the pretext of pursuing the spirit.").

The statute at issue is the homestead exemption, which states:

> The house owned and occupied by a debtor as the debtor's dwelling place, together with the land upon which it is situated to the amount of area and

value hereinafter limited and defined, shall constitute the homestead of such debtor and the debtor's family, and be exempt from seizure or sale under legal process on account of any debt not lawfully charged thereon in writing.

Minn.Stat. § 510.01 (1998); see also Minn. Const. art. I, § 12 (providing "reasonable amount of property shall be exempt from seizure or sale for the payment of any debt or liability"). The homestead may include up to 160 acres outside of any city. Minn.Stat. § 510.02 (1998).

Michels asserts that the homestead exemption should be construed to apply to noncontiguous land that is homesteaded for property tax purposes. See Minn.Stat. § 273.124, subd. 14 (Supp.1999) (permitting owner of certain noncontiguous parcels located within four townships and/or cities of owner's home to classify such property as agricultural homestead for property tax purposes). He contends that the district court's determination that the homestead exemption does not apply to 20 acres of his property that is noncontiguous with the land on which his home is situated "is outdated and does not square with the present realities of the modern farmer."

There have been no Minnesota appellate decisions considering this issue for over 90 years. In 1907, the Minnesota Supreme Court held that two parcels of land that touched, although only at a corner, and were occupied and cultivated as one homestead, qualified for the homestead exemption, despite the fact that the residence and other buildings stood on only one of the parcels. Brixius v. Reimringer, 112 N.W. 273, 273-74 (Minn. 1907).[1] The fact that the two parcels were contiguous, meaning joined at some point, was the essential fact. The court observed that the parcels "should be so connected that they can be used as one tract" and stated: "The essential thing to constitute a quantity of land within the homestead law is that it shall be occupied and cultivated as one piece or parcel of land, on some part of which is located the residence." Id. at 273; cf. Hommerding v. Travelers Ins. Co., 393 N.W.2d 389, 391 (Minn. App. 1986) (recognizing in dicta that agricultural property does not qualify for homestead exemption if parties' home is not situated on property). No Minnesota appellate decision has held that the homestead exemption applies to noncontiguous parcels of land.

A federal bankruptcy court recently addressed an issue similar to the issue in this case. In In re Priebe, 69 B.R. 100, 101 (1987), farmers who lived in a home on 80 acres attempted to claim an additional, noncontiguous 80-acre parcel as part of their homestead exemption. The bankruptcy court recognized that the nature of farming has changed such that farmers can economically farm tracts of land noncontiguous to the homestead. Id. at 102. The court additionally noted that because only contiguous land qualifies for the exemption, "a large group of the class that the statute is intended to protect are arbitrarily excluded from that protection." Id. at 103. After recognizing this fact, however, the court went on to state that "the statute is clear, and the matter is the proper subject for the legislature, not the

---

[1] The supreme court was interpreting a predecessor to the current homestead exemption, which exempted "any quantity of land not exceeding eighty acres, and the dwelling house thereon, and its appurtenances." *Brixius*, 101 Minn. at 348, 112 N.W. at 273.

Courts." *Id.* The court further observed: "It is not for the Courts to define the rural homestead and thereby fashion the Minnesota rural homestead exemption entitlement. To allow the Debtors' claim of exemption entitlement to stand for the noncontiguous 80 acres in this case would be to engage in legislation by judicial decree." *Id.*

Like the bankruptcy court's observations in *Priebe,* we conclude that Michels has a valid point when he asserts that by precluding the application of the homestead exemption to noncontiguous parcels, certain farmers are at a disadvantage. However, the language of the statute is unambiguous. See State ex rel. Coduti v. Hauser, 17 N.W.2d 504, 507-08 (Minn. 1945) (observing legislature may ignore logic and perpetrate injustice as long as it does not violate constitution; absent ambiguity, remedy must be by amendment and not construction). The exemption specifically states that the home is exempt "together with *the land upon which it is situated.*" Minn.Stat. § 510.01 (emphasis added).

Michels concedes that the 20 acres in dispute is noncontiguous with the land on which his home is situated. Thus, we are compelled to conclude that although he may be able to "homestead" the property for property tax purposes under Minn.Stat. § 273.124, subd. 14, the homestead exemption from judgments and foreclosures does not apply to noncontiguous property. The plain language of the statute precludes the application of the homestead exemption to Michels's 20 acres. The district court properly interpreted the statute. Michels's commonsense argument is suited for presentation to the legislature, but we cannot change the statute by judicial fiat.

DECISION

The statute defining the homestead exemption is unambiguous. It does not include land that is noncontiguous to the land on which the home is situated, even if that land is classified as homestead for property tax purposes. Because the district court did not resolve the merits of this issue in the partition-action proceedings, collateral estoppel did not bar respondents from asserting the inapplicability of the homestead exemption in this action. The district court's finding that Michels is unlikely to succeed on the merits of his argument was proper. The district court did not abuse its discretion by refusing to grant Michels's motion for an injunction barring the sheriff's sale of his property.

Affirmed.

NOTES AND QUESTIONS

1. **The Minnesota homestead.** The following pertinent statutory provisions appear in the Minnesota homestead law:

§ 510.02. Area and value; how limited

The homestead may include any quantity of land not exceeding 160 acres, and not included in the laid out or platted portion of any city. If the homestead is within the laid out or platted portion of a city, its area must not exceed one-half of an acre. The value of the homestead exemption, whether the exemption is claimed jointly or individually, may not exceed $200,000 or, if the homestead is used primarily for agricultural purposes, $500,000, exclusive of the limitations set forth in section 510.05.

§ 510.05. Limitations

Such homestead exemption shall not extend to any mortgage lawfully obtained thereon, to any valid lien for taxes or assessments, to a claim filed pursuant to section 256B.15 [dealing with medical assistance for needy persons] or section 246.53 [dealing with claims for care provided by public institutions] or to any charge arising under the laws relating to laborers or material suppliers' liens.

2. **Policy.** See John E. Cribbet & Corwin W. Johnson, Principles of the Law of Property 92-93 (3d ed. 1989):

Homestead represents a policy decision designed to give protection to the family unit by granting a certain exemption to the head of a family against the claims of creditors. The basic idea is simple enough. Many a householder, through circumstances beyond his control, falls on evil days and creditors, seeking to collect their due, strip him to the bone, taking the very roof from over the heads of his family. To prevent a disruption of the home, society grants him an exemption defined in money value, area, or both, and creditors can then reach only the value or area which is in excess of the exemption.

3. **Taxes and creditors.** A homestead exemption reduces the beneficiary's real estate taxes and also provides an exemption from the claims of general creditors. What is the distinction drawn in the Minnesota homestead system between the tax-exemption and the debtor-protection aspects of the homestead? Is there a rational basis for the distinction?

4. **Limitations.** What do you suppose is the rationale for the limitations on the homestead exemption stated in § 510.05 of the Minnesota statute? *See also* Maki v. Chong, 75 P.3d 376 (Nev. 2003) (homestead exemption did not protect debtor from judgment in favor of creditor from whom debtor fraudulently obtained the funds to buy the homestead property, even though fraud was not listed as one of the specific statutory exceptions to the homestead's exemption); Knolls Condominium Assoc. v. Harms, 781 N.E.2d 261 (Ill. 2002) (homestead exemption was not a defense to a condominium association's suit for possession against a unit owner who defaulted on the obligation to pay maintenance charges).

5. **Homestead and marital property.** The homestead exemption, although it often works to the advantage of a married householder, is not limited to that situation; an unmarried person with a dependent is entitled to claim the exemption. *See* Cribbet & Johnson, *supra* Note 2, at 93. Survivors of the party entitled to the homestead exemption may also be entitled to some interest in the homestead property. *See* George L. Haskins, *Homestead Rights of a Surviving Spouse*, 37 Iowa L. Rev. 36, 37-38 (1951). Note that in some states, the policy may be broader than that suggested in Note 2. *See, e.g.*, Public Health Trust of Dade County v. Lopez, 531 So. 2d 946 (Fla. 1988) (under constitutional amendment granting homestead to "a natural person" rather than "head of a family," a decedent's homestead exemption may be claimed by decedent's adult children, whether

dependent on decedent or not, and whether living in the home or not; dissent would have denied the exemption to heirs not living in the home).

6. **Homestead and tenancy by the entirety.** Family protection undergirds the tenancy by the entirety as well as homestead laws. However, unless the legislature periodically reviews the homestead exemption to keep it abreast of increases in property values, spouses will continue to augment homestead protection with the shield provided by the tenancy by the entirety (at least in Group III states). Has the Minnesota legislature kept the homestead exemption current?

7. **Homestead and joint tenancy.** In Kipp v. Sweno, 683 N.W.2d 259 (Minn. 2004), the Minnesota Supreme Court, in a case of first impression, held that a debtor's homestead property, owned in joint tenancy with his nondebtor spouse, could not be unilaterally severed through an execution sale at the behest of a judgment creditor of the debtor spouse. Does such a decision in effect give a married joint tenant the equivalent of a Group III tenancy by the entirety with regard to creditor's claims?

8. **Statutes.** For discussion of and citations to homestead statutes, see Restatement Second of Property (Donative Transfers) § 34.1, Statutory Note 17, at 193; 1 A.L.P. §§ 5.75-5.120.

Chapter 4

LEASES: PROPERTY AND CONTRACT

The title of this chapter is intended to state its emphasis, not to deny that other perspectives are important. Much of the current law of landlord and tenant governing residential leases originated in a series of state and federal court decisions from the early 1970s through the 1980s. Almost without exception, courts that issued pathbreaking decisions in those years framed the specific legal issues in broader terms of rejecting the outmoded concept of the lease as a conveyance and moving to a more responsive contractual paradigm. *See* Gerald Korngold, *Whatever Happened to Landlord-Tenant Law?*, 77 Neb. L. Rev. 703, 705 (1998) ("notion of the lease as a contract formed the basis for many of the courts' key decisions"). However, because several of the important rules have no obvious counterpart in contract law (despite what the courts say), some academic commentators believe that the new landlord-tenant law is based more on status than contract. *See* Charles Donahue, Jr., *Change in the American Law of Landlord and Tenant*, 37 Mod. L. Rev. 242 (1974). Again, because state legislatures have frequently supplemented what the courts have started, and sometimes have originated where the courts have hesitated, other commentators argue that landlord-tenant law reflects a belated shift from private ordering of the parties' relationship to public regulation. *See* Mary Ann Glendon, *The Transformation of American Landlord-Tenant Law*, 23 B.C. L. Rev. 503 (1982). These viewpoints are important, and they receive attention in what follows.

Nevertheless, case law is as important in this area as it is elsewhere in the law of property. And it remains true that whenever the judiciary has been responsible for reformation of the law, it has relied heavily on the property-contract dichotomy to explain and justify its results. So we do not go wrong if we take what the courts say seriously (though not uncritically). There is the added advantage of this chapter's focus that you either have had or are now taking the course in Contracts.

Most discussions of the property-contract theme in cases and commentary indicate that it is relevant to issues of performance and remedy. Is a warranty of habitability, akin to the UCC's warranty of merchantability, implied in a lease? When the landlord commits a material breach, may the tenant terminate the lease? When the premises are destroyed by fire, may the tenant be excused from paying rent under the doctrine of frustration of purpose? If the tenant abandons the premises before the lease ends, must the landlord seek to mitigate damages by trying to find a replacement tenant? These questions are important, and will be addressed in this chapter. (A preview of how the conveyance view of the lease affects these and other questions is provided in Section A.4 below.) However, as the following materials seek to show, the property-contract theme pervades the whole body of landlord-tenant law. It is as relevant to questions of lease formation as it is to issues of performance, breach and remedy.

A. ISSUES IN LEASE FORMATION

The following materials provide data for the discussion of several important questions of lease formation: (1) What types of leases are recognized at common law and under fairly widespread statutory modifications and what are their consequences? (2) Under what circumstances are oral leases enforceable? (3) How is a lease different from similar arrangements relating to land, such as licenses and servitudes? (4) How is a lease like, and how different from, an ordinary bilateral contract?

1.   The Types of Tenancies

You have already seen the estate concept, which is a genus for classifying possessory interests in land according to their duration. *See* Restatement of Property § 9 (1936) ("ownership measured in terms of duration"). A fee simple absolute lasts forever; a life estate ends when the life tenant dies. A lease also conveys an estate to the tenant. *See* Restatement of Property §§ 19-21. The lease estates differ from the fee simple and life estate, and from each other, in that they endure for different segments of time.

There are three landlord-tenant estates: the term of years, the periodic tenancy, and the tenancy at will. (A fourth common law category, the occupancy at sufferance, denotes a former tenant who remains in possession after the tenancy has ended; what happens to the occupant at sufferance is determined by the holdover doctrine, which is considered in Section C.3 dealing with the landlord's rights and remedies.)

a.   The Term of Years Tenancy

The first Restatement of Property § 19 indicates that a term of years is an estate "the duration of which is fixed in units of a year or multiples or divisions thereof." The emphasis is on the word "term," not "years." A tenancy for two weeks and one for fifty years are both term leases. The essential requirement of a "fixed" tenancy is definiteness of duration, which is satisfied under the first Restatement if the duration "is either precisely stated or can be exactly computed at the time when the estate becomes possessory." *Id.* cmt. a. The Restatement Second of Property, Landlord and Tenant (1977), continues the same idea, designating the term of years as a "lease for a fixed or computable period of time." Restatement Second § 1.4. The following are term of years tenancies: to T for one year, beginning January 1, 1998; to T until L's daughter reaches the age of 21 years.

At common law, there is no limit on the length of the term. Some states have statutes imposing a limit, generally on specified kinds of tenancies (e.g., agricultural tenancies). *See* Restatement Second § 1.4, Statutory Note, at 20-21.

The death of either the landlord or the tenant does not terminate the lease; the duty to provide possession and to pay rent continues as an obligation to be performed by the respective parties' executor or administrator. Some states have provided statutory exceptions for the tenant's death and related problems. *See, e.g.*, N.J.S.A. §§ 46:8-9.1 (residential tenancy of one year or more terminates forty days after landlord's receipt of notice of death of tenant or spouse); 46:8-9.2 (same, upon "disabling accident or illness" befalling tenant or spouse; various procedural and notice requirements specified); N.Y. Real Prop. Law § 236 (in premises used for residential use, or partly for residential and professional use, tenant's executor may request landlord's consent to an assignment or sublease; if landlord unreasonably refuses, the lease and tenant's rent obligation end on the last day of the month in which the request for transfer was made; tenant's rights cannot be modified by lease terms). *See also* Kelly v. Alstores Realty Corp., 613 A.2d 1163 (N.J. 1992) (dissolution of corporation does not terminate term of years lease held by the corporation).

It follows from the requirement of certainty that no notice is required to terminate the term of years tenancy; it ends, just as the parties agreed, when the term expires. *See* Minor v. Hicks, 180 So. 689 (Ala. 1938).

Since parties to a lease often do not draft with the precise common law categories in mind, disputes can arise over whether a transaction creates a term of years or some other leasehold estate. The requirement of certainty can be a trap for parties whose bargain may be otherwise unobjectionable, as the principal case illustrates.

STANMEYER v. DAVIS
53 N.E.2d 22 (Ill. App. Ct. 1944)

MATCHETT, JUSTICE.

On January 4, 1943, [Stanmeyer] sued in forcible entry and detainer to recover possession of premises in the City of Chicago. Defendants appeared, answered and demanded trial by jury. Plaintiffs moved for summary judgment. The motion was supported by the affidavit of plaintiff Stanmeyer. The affidavit showed defendants went into possession under a written lease to the Hupmobile-Illinois Company, dated December 31, 1937, by which the premises were demised to the lessee for a period of five years, commencing January 1, 1938; that Hupmobile took possession under the lease and was succeeded in possession by Willys-Illinois Company, of which Davis was president, and Willys in turn by S.L. Davis, doing business as Davis Motors; that by the terms of the lease rent for the first year of the term was to be $900 per month, second year $950 per month, third year $975 per month, and thereafter $1,000 per month until the end of the term; that the full amount of the rent was not at any time paid because of business conditions; that negotiations for another written lease for a new term at a lower rental were not successful; that on November 25, 1942, plaintiffs served notice on Davis, as president of the corporations and doing business as Davis Motors, terminating the lease on December 31, 1942, and that he refused to give possession pursuant thereto.

Defendants, in opposition to the motion for summary judgment, filed affidavits by Davis, which in substance averred that on March 17, 1942, and in May, 1942, plaintiffs made an oral lease of the premises to Davis for $500 per month, "for the duration of the war and until automobiles are again produced" and "until defendant receives twenty-five automobiles in any one month." The trial judge was of the opinion that this oral lease was no more than a tenancy at will, or from month to month, the terms being so uncertain as to make it unenforceable. [D]efendants appeal.

The question to be determined is whether a verbal leasing of the premises "for the duration of the war and until automobiles are again produced" and "until defendant receives twenty-five automobiles in any one month" creates a leasehold estate for a term of years, or whether it is void for uncertainty of the term and, therefore, gives only an estate at will. The affidavits for defendant are to the effect that the parties by verbal conversations agreed to such a leasing at a rental of $500 per month. Plaintiffs do not raise any issue of fact but rely on the rule of law that a lease for years must have a definite and certain time at which it begins and ends, and that where the end of the term is indefinite and uncertain the agreement creates not a valid and legal lease for a term of years but merely a tenancy at will.

It has long been the law that a lease for a term of years must have a certain beginning and a certain ending. It was so held in Say v. Smith, 1 Plow. Rep. 269, decided A.D. 1530 in the sixth year of the reign of Elizabeth. Blackstone says: "For every such estate must have a certain beginning and a certain end. But id certum est, quod certum reddi potest (that is certain which can be made certain)." Cooley's Blackstone, 4th Ed., p. 546. Coke Lit. 45 B, says: "Albeit, there appear no certainty of years in the case, yet if by reference to a certainty it may be made certain, it is sufficient."

This is the rule in this state. It is believed to be the prevailing general rule. Tiffany on Real Property, 3rd Ed., Vol. 1, § 85, p. 130, states the rule as to certainty thus:

> The lease need not, however, actually name the period during which the tenancy is to endure, but it may fix such period by reference to some collateral fact or event, if the reference is such as to enable the duration of the term to be ascertained at any time. So a lease for as many years as a person named has in other property, or "during the minority of B," a living person whose age is ascertainable, or until certain fixed yearly payments amount to a sum named, operates to create an estate for years

On the contrary, [some] cases seem to hold that a lease for a term to expire upon an event reasonably sure to happen, even though the date of the happening of the event to be is neither certain nor can be made certain until the event actually happens, is a lease for a definite and fixed period. This is not the law. It is not the certainty of the happening of the event but the certainty of the date on which the termination of the lease will take place that is the determinative factor.

Defendant relies much on Great Northern Ry. Co. v. Arnold, Times Law Reports, Vol. 33, p. 114, and cases that follow that decision. The lease there was "for the period of the war." The rent was payable weekly. The lessor sued for possession. The trial judge said that Say v. Smith [*supra*] tended to support the plaintiff's contention and that the contention "might be right." The court, however, said: "By hook or crook, the defendant should have what he bargained for."

We find nothing in the terms of this alleged verbal lease from which any certain time can be inferred when it will terminate. If the phrase "for the duration of the war" be regarded as within the rule that that is certain which may be rendered certain, there would remain the uncertainty as to when automobiles would again be in production, and the further uncertainty as to when defendant should receive twenty-five automobiles in any month. This last provision is objectionable not only on account of uncertainty but also for the reason that the time of happening of the uncertain event might easily depend solely upon the will of the tenant. There is nothing in the record which shows defendant will be required to receive twenty-five automobiles at any particular time or in any particular month of any future year.

If we could regard the end of the war as a certainty, this alleged agreement would still leave us in doubt for the reason that it does not refer to any particular war of the several in which we are engaged. When the alleged agreement was made war existed between Japan and the United States, Germany and the United States and Italy and the United States. There is nothing in the language of the alleged oral lease from which there can be a reasonable certainty of the date upon which it was the intention of the parties that the oral lease should come to an end. Under the former lease, when automobiles were in production, the rent was to be as high as $1,000 per month. Under the new verbal arrangement it is to be only $500 per month. It would seem that in any valid leasing the lessor would be informed when such a lease, made under such circumstances at such a rental, would end. The affidavits of defendant do not disclose any fact from which the duration of the term can be ascertained prior to its end. In the absence of any statute modifying the rule, we think the trial judge correctly held that the alleged verbal lease created no more than a tenancy at will.

Affirmed.

NOTES AND QUESTIONS

1. **Certainty and intent.** What meaning of certainty does the *Great Northern* case (discussed in *Stanmeyer*) adopt, and why? *Cf.* UCC § 2-204(3) ("Even though one or more terms are left open a contract for sale [of goods] does not fail for indefiniteness if the parties have intended to make a contract and there is a reasonably certain basis for giving an appropriate remedy."); Restatement (Second) of Contracts § 33(2) & cmt. b (1981). Davis sought a decree of specific performance. Which terms in the contract have to be certain — rent, duration, location — for specific performance to be granted? *See* Restatement Second § 1.1 (landlord-tenant relationship "exists only with respect to a lease that is intended to have a fixed location for the duration of the lease").

2. **Formalism and intent.** A lease can be made defeasible — subject to a special limitation, condition subsequent, or executory interest — by the parties' agreement. See Restatement Second of Property (Landlord and Tenant) § 1.7 & cmts. d and e; Restatement of Property § 19 cmt. c (1936). How would you draft a defeasible term of years lease to avoid the problem in Stanmeyer v. Davis? How different is your work product from the actual lease in *Stanmeyer*? Is the position of the court in *Stanmeyer* formalistic? *See generally* 2 Powell on Real Property § 16.03[4] (Michael Allan Wolf ed. 2000).

3. **Numerus clausus.** Within the limits of public policy, parties may make contracts as they wish. Property law is different. Parties seeking to create a

possessory interest in land must fit their transaction into one of the recognized types of estates. Customizing isn't allowed; a lease "for the duration of the war" is not one of the leasehold estates. There is an impressive literature, both pro and con, on this "numerus clausus" (closed number) principle. *See* Thomas W. Merrill & Henry E. Smith, *Optimal Standardization in the Law of Property: The Numerus Clausus Principle*, 110 Yale L.J. 1 (2000) (duration of the war leases are discussed on pp. 11-12 and 35); Henry Hansman & Reiner Kraakman, *Property, Contract, and Verification: The Numerus Clausus Problem and the Divisibility of Rights*, 31 J. Legal Studies 373 (2000); Lawrence W. Waggoner & Thomas P. Gallanis, Estates and Future Interests in a Nutshell § 1.2 (3d ed. 2005) (discussing numerus clausus as a "limit on fragmentation" of property interests). Other recent articles discuss numerus clausus as part of broader discussions of the nature of property rights. *See* Hanoch Dagan, *The Craft of Property*, 91 Calif. L. Rev. 1517 (2003); Michael A. Heller, *The Boundaries of Private Property*, 108 Yale L.J. 1163 (2000). *See also* Brendan Edgeworth, *The Numerus Clausus Principle in Contemporary Australian Property Law*, 32 Monash U.L. Rev. 387 (2006).

4. **Meaning and validity.** If certainty of happening of an event is sufficient for a lease, the other problems flagged by *Stanmeyer* can be solved by interpretation or construction of the agreement. *See* Darnall v. Day, 37 N.W.2d 277, 279-80 (Iowa 1949) (landlord breached agreement to improve the leased premises within one year "after the war has ended" by not repairing within one year of cessation of fighting: "War, in the practical and realistic sense in which it is commonly used, refers to the period of hostilities and not to a technical state of war which may exist after the fighting has ended [and before ratification of a peace treaty]. The parties did not contract in terms of diplomatic parlance."). Following *Darnall*, how might a court resolve the ambiguity about *which* war (in the European or the Pacific theater) the parties meant?

5. **The automobile acceptance provision.** How does the automobile-acceptance provision, which also troubled the court in *Stanmeyer*, differ from the "duration of the war" provision? (The significance of Davis's discretion to perform or not is considered in Section A.1.b below.)

6. **Uncertain beginning.** A term of years lease must also have a certain beginning. Certainty for that purpose is determined by the Rule Against Perpetuities: unless the tenant's interest is certain to vest or fail within a life in being plus 21 years, the lease is invalid. As noted in Chapter 2, courts tend to uphold leases to begin upon the future construction of buildings on the leased land either by interpreting the agreement to require such construction within a reasonable time, and by construing "reasonable" to not exceed 21 years from the date of the parties' agreement, *see* Wong v. DiGrazia, 386 P.2d 817 (Cal. 1963), or by finding that the lease grants the tenant an interest in the underlying land, *see* Wonderfair Stores, Inc. v. Walgreen Drug Co., 511 F.2d 1206, 1213 (9th Cir. 1975) (also adopting, alternatively, the Wong v. Di Grazia rationale). If courts can tolerate uncertain beginnings in commercial leases, why not uncertain endings, as in *Stanmeyer*?

b.   The Periodic Tenancy

The periodic tenancy is an estate that continues from period to period until either the landlord or the tenant gives the proper notice to terminate the tenancy. Although any period can be established by the agreement of the parties, the usual periods are monthly, quarterly and yearly. Courts developed the periodic tenancy from the tenancy at will. Hunter v. Frost, 49 N.W. 327, 328 (Minn. 1891), is instructive on this judicial development:

> It was determined very anciently by the common law, upon principles of justice and policy, that estates at will were equally at the will of both parties, and neither of them was permitted to exercise his will in a wanton manner, and contrary to equity and good faith, but that they could only be terminated by notice for a longer or shorter period, depending usually upon the nature of the original demise. At first there was no other rule but that the notice should be a reasonable one. Because of the uncertainty of this rule, the courts early adopted, as far as possible, some fixed period [of notice] as being reasonable.

The notice rule for periodic tenancies crystallized into a two-part formula at common law: a specified amount of notice was required to terminate the tenancy; and the tenancy could only be terminated at the end of a rent period, not in mid-period. The notice required at common law to terminate a yearly periodic tenancy was six months, for quarterly tenancies, one quarter, and for monthly tenancies, one month. To illustrate: assuming a monthly periodic tenancy beginning on January 1, a notice by either party given on March 15 purporting to terminate the tenancy on April 15 would be ineffective to terminate at the specified time. The amount of notice given (one month) is sufficient, but the tenancy cannot be terminated in mid-month; nor could the notice given on March 15 terminate the tenancy on March 31, since that would not provide the required month's notice. To terminate at the end of the March period, notice would have to be given no later than the end of February. *See* PMS Realty Co. v. Guarino, 312 A.2d 898, 899-900 (N.J. D. Ct. 1973):

> In computation of time, when a legal requirement fixes a number of days from a date or an event for the doing of an act, the computation is made by excluding the first date and including the last. [I]f the tenancy begins on the first day of the month, the tenant is entitled to a full and complete month's notice, from midnight of the night before the first day to midnight of the last day of the particular month, thereby making any notice served on the first day of a month for possession on the first day of the following month fatally defective.

The periodic tenancy terminates by notice alone; it is not ended by the death of either party, or transfers by either party, or abandonment of the premises by the tenant. *See* 2 Powell on Real Property § 16.04[3]. In those regards, it resembles the term of years. Nor is there a requirement that either the landlord or the tenant have good cause to terminate the tenancy; termination is constrained only by the notice requirement.

Keep in mind that the common law rules of notice and termination are default rules, subject to contractual modification by the parties.

Although periodic tenancies are frequently created expressly (e.g., the parties agree on a monthly letting), they are also regularly created by implication from the circumstances surrounding the agreement; courts infer a monthly tenancy when the parties agree on a lease and provide for monthly or other periodic rent, but fail to specify a duration for the lease. Periodic tenancies are created by operation of law in some states when the tenant holds over after the original tenancy has ended and the landlord elects to impose a new term on the tenant. *See* Section C.3 below.

NOTES AND QUESTIONS

1. **Defective notice.** In PMS Realty Co. v. Guarino, *supra*, the court indicated that an improper notice to terminate a periodic tenancy was "fatally defective." That view was subsequently rejected by the New Jersey Supreme Court. *See* Harry's Village, Inc. v. Egg Harbor Twp., 446 A.2d 862 (N.J. 1982) (notice naming improper termination date is effective at next proper termination date). The "fatal error" view is also rejected by the Restatement Second § 1.5 cmt. f, although the Reporter's Note states that the weight of authority supports the doctrine. *Id.* at 36. *See generally* 2 Powell on Real Property § 16.04[3].

2. **Renewal or extension?** In a periodic tenancy, is each successive period a new tenancy, implied from the failure of the parties to terminate, or is each successive period simply an extension of the original lease, which continues until terminated by either party? It can matter. *See, e.g.*, Lambur v. Yates, 148 F.2d 137 (8th Cir. 1945) (landlord's overcharging rent in violation of World War II price regulations was new offense each month); Restatement Second § 17.1 comment i (under rule imposing tort liability on landlord for nondisclosed dangerous defects existing at outset of lease, periodic tenancy is new tenancy each month instead of continuous tenancy); *id.* § 1.5, cmt. c (on all questions other than landlord's tort liability, the periodic tenancy is a continuation, unless the parties specify otherwise).

3. **Statutory modifications of the periodic tenancy.** A typical statutory modification of the periodic tenancy shortens the amount of notice required (e.g., three months instead of six for a yearly periodic tenancy; one month for a quarterly periodic tenancy). A less typical modification alters the timing requirement to allow termination in mid-period if the proper amount of notice is given. *See* Restatement Second § 1.5, Statutory Note, at 30-33. The Second Restatement takes the position that a month's notice prior to the end of the period is sufficient in all periodic tenancies, except farming or grazing leases. *Id.* § 1.5 cmt. f, at 25. What do you suppose is the basis for the exception for farming and grazing leases?

PROBLEMS

4-A. What type of tenancy is created in the following problems? Give reasons for your conclusions.

a. L leases to T without specifying a term, at "an annual rent of $3600, payable $300 per month on the first day of each month." *See* Restatement Second § 1.5 cmt.

d, illus. 3 (adopting reservation-of-rent basis for establishing periodic tenancy).

b. L leases to T without specifying a term, at a rental based on the number of barrels of beer sold on the premises by T, payable on demand by L.

c. L and T agree on a monthly periodic tenancy, beginning September 1. On the following November 15, T notifies L that she is terminating effective November 30, and moves out on that date. After diligent efforts to find a new tenant, L leases the property effective the following March 1. L sues T for rent for December through February. What is T's liability? *See* S.D.G. v. Inventory Control Co., 429 A.2d 394 (N.J. Super. Ct. App. Div. 1981).

d. L leases to T "for one year beginning January 1, 1991, and from year to year thereafter." Is notice required to end the tenancy at the end of the initial fixed year? Can the lease be terminated at the end of the fixed term, or no earlier than the end of the first period? *See* Restatement Second § 1.5 cmt. i & Reporter's Note, at 36.

e. L leases to T "beginning on December 12, 1980, through May 30, 1981. This agreement may be terminated by a 30 day notice to vacate, given by either party." T vacates on May 30, 1981, without notice to L, who refuses to return the security deposit, claiming a right to apply it to rentals accruing after T vacated. T sues for the deposit. Result? *See* LaPonsie v. Kumorek, 453 A.2d 1294 (N.H. 1982).

f. Is oral notice to terminate a periodic tenancy effective? Is it wise? Is written notice effective upon receipt or mailing? If the latter, and L or T is a corporation, is notice "received" when it is delivered to the corporation's place of business, or at some later time? *Cf.* UCC § 1-201(27).

4-B. If the landlord wants to increase the rent in a monthly periodic tenancy, is a notice of rent increase sufficient, or must the landlord also notify the tenant of termination of the tenancy in the event that the tenant does not agree to the rent increase? *See Harry's Village*, Note 1 above. What result if the tenant receives a valid notice of rent increase and remains in possession without objection? See id. Suppose the tenant objects, but remains in possession? *See* Welk v. Bidwell, 73 A.2d 295 (Conn. 1950).

c.   The Tenancy at Will

As the name suggests, a tenancy at will is an estate that continues so long as both parties desire it to continue. *See* Restatement § 21; Restatement Second § 1.6. Either party may terminate the tenancy by notifying the other; no set amount of notice is required, which distinguishes the tenancy at will from the periodic tenancy. The tenancy at will also terminates by operation of law upon the death of either the landlord or tenant, and also upon the landlord's transfer of the property, features which distinguish it from both the term of years and the periodic tenancies. *See* 2 Powell on Real Property § 16.05[2]. In respects other than the granting of possession, the tenancy at will is analogous to a nonpossessory license to use land. *See* Section A.3 below, and Chapter 6.

Since such a frail tenancy fails to provide security of income for the landlord or of occupancy for the tenant, the express creation of a tenancy at will, though possible, is probably rare. The tenancy operates rather as a residual, catch-all category, covering agreements for possession that cannot be pigeonholed into one of the other categories. *See* Stanmeyer v. Davis, *supra* (invalid term of years lease; held, tenancy at will); Restatement Second § 1.6, cmt. b, illus. 2 (L allows friend T to occupy an apartment rent-free, with nothing said about duration; tenancy at will is created).

Suppose the parties agree on a lease that is expressly terminable at the will of only one of the parties to the lease. What is created by these unilateral at-will agreements? This casebook and textbook favorite, which raises interesting questions of doctrine and policy, is considered in the following case.

GARNER v. GERRISH
473 N.E.2d 223 (N.Y. 1984)

WACHTLER, JUDGE.

The question on this appeal is whether a lease which grants the tenant the right to terminate the agreement at a date of his choice creates a determinable life tenancy on behalf of the tenant or merely establishes a tenancy at will. The courts below held that the lease created a tenancy at will permitting the current landlord to evict the tenant. We granted the tenant's motion for leave to appeal and now reverse the order appealed from.

In 1977 Robert Donovan owned a house located in Potsdam, New York. On April 14 of that year he leased the premises to the tenant Lou Gerrish. The lease was executed on a printed form and it appears that neither side was represented by counsel. The blanks on the form were filled in by Donovan who provided the names of the parties, described the property and fixed the rent at $100 a month. With respect to the duration of the tenancy the lease provides it shall continue "for and during the term of quiet enjoyment from the first day of May, 1977 which term will end — Lou Gerrish has the privilege of termination [sic] this agreement at a date of his own choice." [Some of the quoted provision consisted of handwritten and typed additions to the printed lease form.] The lease also contains a standard reference to the landlord's right to reentry if the rent is not timely paid, which is qualified by the handwritten statement: "Lou has thirty days grace for payment."

Gerrish moved into the house and continued to reside there, apparently without incident, until Donovan died in November of 1981. At that point David Garner, executor of Donovan's estate, served Gerrish with a notice to quit the premises. When Gerrish refused, Garner commenced this summary proceeding to have him evicted. Petitioner contended that the lease created a tenancy at will because it failed to state a definite term. In his answering affidavit, the tenant alleged that he had always paid the rent specified in the lease. He also contended that the lease granted him a tenancy for life, unless he elects to surrender possession during his lifetime.

The County Court granted summary judgment to petitioner on the ground that the lease is "indefinite and uncertain as regards the length of time accorded respondent to occupy the premises. Although the writing specifies the date of commencement of the term, it fails to set forth the duration of continuance, and the date or event of termination." The court concluded that the original landlord leased the premises to the tenant "for a month-to-month term and that petitioner was entitled to terminate the lease upon the death of the lessor effective upon the expiration of the next succeeding monthly term of occupancy." In support of its decision the court quoted the following statement from our opinion in Western Transp. Co. v. Lansing, 49 N.Y. 499, 508: "A lease for so long as the lessee shall please, is said to be a lease at will of both lessor and lessee." The Appellate Division affirmed for the same reasons in a brief memorandum. 99 A.D.2d 608, 471 N.Y.S.2d 717.

On appeal to our court, the parties concede that the agreement creates a lease. The only question is whether it should be literally construed to grant to the tenant alone the right to terminate at will, or whether the landlord is accorded a similar right by operation of law.

At early common law according to Lord Coke, "when the lease is made to have and to hold at the will of the lessee, this must be also at the will of the lessor." 1 Co.Litt., § 55a. This rule was generally adopted in the United States during the 19th century and at one time was said to represent the majority view. However, it was not universally accepted, and has been widely criticized, particularly in this century, as an antiquated notion which violates the terms of the agreement and frustrates the intent of the parties. 1 Tiffany, Real Property (3d ed.), § 159; 1 American Law of Real Property (Casner ed., 1952), § 3.30; Schoshinski, American Law of Landlord and Tenant, § 2:7; see also Restatement, Property 2d, Landlord and Tenant, § 1.6.

It has been noted that the rule has its origins in the doctrine of livery of seisin, which required physical transfer of a clod of earth, twig, key or other symbol on the premises in the presence of witnesses, to effect a conveyance of [a] land interest. Although this ceremony was not required for leases, which were generally limited to a specified term of years, it was necessary to create a life tenancy which was viewed as a freehold interest. Thus, if a lease granting a tenant a life estate was not accompanied by livery of seisin, the intended conveyance would fail and a mere tenancy at will would result. The corollary to Lord Coke's comment is that the grant of a life estate would be enforceable if accompanied by livery of seisin and the other requisites for a conveyance. Because such a tenancy was terminable at the will of the grantee, there was in fact no general objection at common law to a tenancy at the will of the tenant. The express terms of a lease granting a life tenancy would fail, and a tenancy at will would result, only when livery of seisin, or any other requirement for a conveyance, had not been met.

Because livery of seisin, like the ancient requirement for a seal, has been abandoned, commentators generally urge that there is no longer any reason why a lease granting the tenant alone the right to terminate at will, should be converted into a tenancy at will terminable by either party. The Restatement adopts this view and provides the following illustration: "L leases a farm to T 'for as long as T desires to stay on the land'. The lease creates a determinable life estate in T, terminable at T's will or on his death." Restatement, Property 2d, Landlord and Tenant, § 1.6, Comment g, Illustration 6.

In the case now before us the lease does not provide for renewal, and its duration cannot be said to be perpetual or indefinite. It simply grants a personal right to the named lessee, Lou Gerrish, to terminate at a date of his choice, which is a fairly typical means of creating a life tenancy terminable at the will of the tenant. Restatement, Property 2d, § 1.6, Illustration 6. Thus the lease will terminate, at the latest, upon the death of the named lessee. The fact that it may be terminated at some earlier point, if the named tenant decides to quit the premises, does not render it indeterminate. Leases providing for termination upon the occurrence of a specified event prior to the completion of an otherwise fixed term, are routinely enforced even when the event is within the control of the lessee.

In sum, the lease expressly and unambiguously grants to the tenant the right to terminate, and does not reserve to the landlord a similar right. To hold that such a lease creates a tenancy terminable at the will of either party would violate the terms of the agreement and the express intent of the contracting parties.

Accordingly, the order of the Appellate Division should be reversed and the petition dismissed.

NOTES AND QUESTIONS

1. **Common law and the Restatements.** At common law, a lease at the will of either party was a tenancy at will; the courts implied a reciprocal termination privilege in the other party. The first Restatement of Property modified the common law by treating a lease at the will of the tenant as a determinable life estate, while retaining the tenancy at will classification for leases terminable only at the will of the landlord. *See* Restatement of Property § 21 cmt. a (1936). The Restatement Second provides that a lease terminable at will by either the landlord or the tenant creates a defeasible freehold estate. *See* Restatement Second § 1.6 cmt. g, at 40.

2. **Old rule, new reasons: unconscionability.** Is a lease such as that in *Garner* an unconscionable agreement? Does it matter whether the termination privilege is held by the landlord or the tenant? If unconscionability is a concern, shouldn't that be handled on a case-by-case basis rather than through the adoption of general rules of construction? *See* Restatement Second § 1.6 cmt. g (unilateral at-will lease may "under all the circumstances" present an unconscionable arrangement). If the lease is unconscionable, what tenancy is created?

3. **Illusory promise.** Is a unilateral at-will lease invalid for lack of consideration (sometimes posed as the problem of the absence of "mutuality of obligation")? *See* Dwyer v. Graham, 457 N.E.2d 1239, 1241 (Ill. 1983) (lease providing that tenant "is to have use of rental agreement as long as desired" held to create, at most, a tenancy at will: "We judge that really no tenancy was created. There was no real undertaking or promise by the defendants under the 'rental agreement.' The option given the defendants was unlimited, and the claimed promise was only illusory."). To solve the problem identified in *Dwyer*, might an obligation to give reasonable notice before terminating been imposed on the tenant? In Stanmeyer v. Davis, what interpretation of the automobile acceptance provision might have been urged on the court to save the agreement from the illusory promise objection?

4. **Statutory tenancies at will compared.** Oklahoma has the following statute:

> Thirty days' notice in writing is necessary to be given by either party before he can terminate a tenancy at will, or from one period to another, of three months or less; but where in any case rent is reserved, payable at intervals of less than thirty days, the length of notice need not be greater than such interval between the days of payment.

Suppose that rent is payable on the first of each month. On March 3, the tenant receives a notice from the landlord to vacate on the following April 5. When does the tenancy terminate: (a) if it is a periodic tenancy, and (b) if it is a tenancy at will? *See* Kester v. Disan Engineering Corp., 591 P.2d 344 (Okla. Ct. App. 1979) (discussion of the statute). If there is a difference under the statute between the tenancy at will and the periodic tenancy, is it likely that the opportunity to apply the distinction will arise frequently? If the parties agree on a monthly rent and fail to expressly create a tenancy at will, how is a court likely to classify the lease?

5. **Termination by operation of law.** Does the statute quoted in the previous Note address whether a tenancy at will ends other than by the giving of notice — on the death of either party, or when the landlord sells the property, or the tenant attempts to transfer his interest? Should a statute which provides a notice period for termination of a tenancy at will be read to assimilate the tenancy at will to the monthly periodic tenancy in all respects? *See* 2 Powell on Real Property § 16.05[3]. *See also* Bech v. Cuevas, 534 N.E.2d 1163 (Mass. 1989) (assuming that termination for tenant's waste was allowed at common law, landlord could not terminate without compliance with statutory notice requirements).

6. **Occupancy at sufferance.** The occupancy at sufferance is not an estate, but a status. The term applies to a former tenant who remains in possession after the ending of the lease, and who is subject either to removal or to the imposition of a new lease, at the landlord's option. *See* Section C.3 (addressing landlord's remedies against the holdover).

2.   The Statute of Frauds

> An [oral] contract isn't worth the paper it's printed on.

Samuel Goldwyn

a.   Coverage: Leases "Within" the Statute

All states have a statute (or statutes) of frauds, requiring that specified types of transactions be in writing — for example, sales and leases of land, sales and leases of personal property, contracts in general. For many of the specified categories, the statute states or implies that some oral agreements are permissible. The typical contracts provision of the statute requires a writing for "agreements not to be performed within one year of the making thereof," which implies that an agreement that *can* be performed within one year of its making is enforceable. The same is true of the typical provision that "leases exceeding one year" must be in writing: an oral lease for a term of one year or less would be valid. *See* Restatement Second of Property (Landlord and Tenant) § 2.1 ("landlord-tenant relationship can be created orally if the duration of an oral lease does not exceed the period specified in the controlling Statute of Frauds"). Do not, however, confuse permissibility with prudence; an oral agreement is never a good idea, because the terms of the agreement depend on the vagaries of oral testimony.

In statute of frauds parlance, an agreement that is required to be in writing is said to be "within" the statute, while an agreement that is enforceable even though it is oral is outside of or excluded from the statute. The underlying idea behind the statutory pattern of covered and excepted transactions is that parties should not be locked into a burdensome agreement unless the best evidence of the terms of that agreement — a writing — exists. That said, there is obviously room for legislative judgment as to the location of the line dividing agreements that can permissibly be oral and those that are burdensome enough to require written proof of their existence. See, e.g., Restatement of Property (Landlord and Tenant) § 2.1, Statutory Note at 68-71 (citing statutes requiring a writing for leases in excess of one year, in excess of three years, and in excess of three years from the date on which the lease is made).

Notice a fundamental tension in statute of frauds analysis. By requiring specified transactions to be in writing, the statute prevents a devious party from foisting an alleged agreement onto another party on the basis of fabricated testimony. But the statute also prohibits the enforcement of bargains that are actually made, if those bargains fall within the statute and are not reduced to writing. If a promisor's repudiation of an actual but unwritten bargain is also regarded as a kind of devious conduct (evidence of this sentiment abounds in the cases, typically in statements that the statute of frauds is intended to prevent, and should not be used to perpetuate, frauds), the statute has the paradoxical effect of seeking to prevent, yet also encouraging, fraud. The judiciary has tended to resolve this tension through interpretations of the statute of frauds that restrict its area of operation.

PROBLEM 4-C. Shortly after January 1, 2007, L sues T for possession, asserting that T's lease expired on the previous December 31, and that T is wrongfully holding over. T's answer alleges an oral lease for one year, beginning January 1, 2007, entered into between the parties in October of 2006. Before trial, L moves for judgment on the pleadings, asserting that T's answer raises no meritorious defense. The relevant statute of frauds provides as follows:

> No action shall be brought in any court in the following cases, unless the promise or agreement upon which such action shall be brought, or some memorandum thereof, shall be in writing and signed by the parties to be charged therewith, or by some person by him thereunto lawfully authorized:
>
> 1. upon an agreement which is not to be performed within the space of one year from the making thereof;
>
> 2. upon an agreement for the leasing for a longer period than one year, or for the sale of real property, or of an interest therein; and such agreement, if made by an agent of the party sought to be charged, is invalid, unless the

authority of the agent is in writing, subscribed by the party sought to be charged.

What result? Does it depend on whether section 1 or 2 of the statute applies? If so, which section should apply? *See* Bell v. Vaughn, 53 P.2d 61 (Ariz. 1935) (applying the specific lease section rather than the general contract section of the statute); Restatement Second of Property § 2.1 cmt. f ("[w]hile a lease has substantial contractual aspects, it is sufficiently dissimilar from a contract to justify excluding the lease from" the contract section of the statute). *See generally* 2 Powell on Real Property § 16.03[2][a]. Is the Restatement argument in the comment to Section 2.1 necessary? What rule of statutory construction argues against application of the contract section of the statute of frauds to leases to begin in the future? What policy argument supports the claim that application of the contract section is inappropriate — would you suspect that the creation of leases to begin in the future is a common practice?

b.   Compliance: The Required Writing

When a lease is within the statute — required to be in writing — the "writing" must include the elements that are specified in the statute. The Restatement Second of Property (Landlord and Tenant) § 2.2 provides that a writing is sufficient, unless the local statute prescribes additional requirements, if the writing "(1) identifies the parties; (2) identifies the premises; (3) specifies the duration of the lease; (4) states the rent to be paid; and (5) is signed by the party to be charged."

Many statutes require only a written "memorandum" of essential terms rather than a writing setting out the entire agreement. In either event:

> [t]he statute of frauds does not require the [agreement or memorandum of essential terms] to be in one document. It may be pieced together out of separate writings, connected with one another either expressly or by the internal evidence of subject-matter and occasion. None of the terms of the contract are supplied by parol [oral evidence]. All of them must be set out in the various writings presented to the court, and at least one writing, the one establishing a contractual relationship between the parties, must bear the signature of the party to be charged, while the unsigned document must on its face refer to the same transaction as that set forth in the one that was signed. Parol evidence — to portray the circumstances surrounding the making of the memorandum — serves only to connect the separated documents and to show that there was assent, by the party to be charged, to the contents of the one unsigned.

Crabtree v. Elizabeth Arden Sales Corp., 110 N.E.2d 551, 553 (N.Y. 1953). *See also* Babdo Sales, Inc. v. Miller-Wohl Co., 440 F.2d 962 (2d Cir. 1971) (New York law allows statute of frauds to be satisfied with a "confluence of memoranda").

c. Noncompliance: Avoiding the Statute

A lease within the statute of frauds may fail to satisfy the statute because it is oral, or because the writing submitted by the party seeking to enforce the agreement is insufficient (usually because it is not signed by the party against whom enforcement of the lease is sought). Such a lease is invalid (perhaps more precisely, unenforceable). The Restatement Second of Property (Landlord and Tenant) addresses the consequences of noncompliance as follows:

§ 2.3 Effect of an Invalid Lease

A lease made invalid by the Statute of Frauds will be given no effect unless:

(1) possession is taken, in which case a tenancy at will is created;

(2) possession is taken and rent is paid and accepted as provided under the lease, in which case, without more, a periodic tenancy is created with all the terms of the lease except duration; or

(3) the parties to the lease undertake substantial performances which are clearly referable to the terms of the lease, in which case the lease is given full effect.

The quoted Restatement provision offers an orderly approach to leases that fail to comply with the statute of frauds. The basic proposition is that a noncomplying lease agreement, without more, is ineffective. If, however, there are additional relevant facts, an enforceable lease may be found to exist.

Creation of a "smaller" lease by conduct. If the additional facts consist of the tenant's taking possession of the premises, or taking possession and paying rent, the Restatement Second indicates that an enforceable lease is created, but it is either a tenancy at will or a periodic tenancy, created by the parties' subsequent conduct, rather than the unenforceable term of years lease that the aggrieved party claims was initially agreed upon. These are the subsection (1) and (2) cases under the Restatement Second.

When a periodic tenancy results from the tenant's possession and payment of rent — Section 2.3(2) cases under the Restatement — the majority view of the cases is that the tenancy is yearly. Other approaches are to determine the duration of the tenancy by the intervals at which the rent is reserved or paid; an unsigned document "reserving a rent of $4800 per year, payable in monthly installments of $400," would produce a yearly periodic tenancy if the reservation provision were deemed central, and a monthly tenancy if the payment provision were deemed central. *See* Prescott v. Smits, 505 A.2d 1211 (Vt. 1985) (agreement for annual rent, payable monthly, held to create yearly periodic tenancy requiring six months' notice to terminate, because of the yearly rent calculation and the agricultural nature of the tenancy). The Restatement Second provides a novel solution, an escalating period not to exceed one year: "The initial period is determined by the interval between the rent payments specified in the invalid lease. Where successive periodic payments of rent aggregate the length of one of the traditional periods [monthly, quarterly, yearly], the tenancy acquires the notice protections of the longer period, although rent continues to be paid in accordance with the invalid lease." Restatement Second § 2.3 cmt. d.

Cases falling under subsections (1) and (2) of the Restatement are consistent with the statute of frauds: the lease being enforced under these subsections is not the lease that is rendered unenforceable by the statute, but rather the "smaller" lease — tenancy at will or periodic tenancy — created by the additional facts of possession and payment of rent.

Avoiding the statute: part performance. Under § 2.3(3), if the additional facts show that one party rendered a performance that is "clearly referable to [i.e., evidentiary of] the terms of the [agreed-upon] lease," that agreed-upon lease "is given full effect." Subsection (3) states the widely-followed judicial doctrine of "part performance." Giving "full effect" to the lease under part performance means that the party seeking to enforce the lease is entitled to specific performance of it. If the agreement was for a five-year term, and the defendant's statute of frauds defense fails because the plaintiff rendered part performance, the plaintiff gets the five-year lease.

Avoiding the statute: estoppel. The doctrine of estoppel also allows enforcement of a noncomplying lease, at least to the extent of the recovery of the plaintiff's reliance losses (the money spent by the plaintiff in reliance on the contract). There are two versions of estoppel in statute of frauds cases: equitable and promissory estoppel. The first is widely recognized, though available only in limited factual situations; the latter, which would allow for enforcement of the transaction in a greater number of factual situations, is far more controversial.

Restitution. If the plaintiff under an unenforceable lease cannot get the statute of frauds issue out of the case through the doctrines of part performance or estoppel, the lease claimed by the plaintiff "will be given no effect," as the initial clause of Restatement Second § 2.3 says. However, the plaintiff is still entitled to the remedy of restitution of any benefits conferred on the defendant by the plaintiff. A restitutionary cause of action is not inconsistent with the statute of frauds: the plaintiff in restitution is not seeking to recover damages for breach of the lease by the defendant, but is instead seeking to prevent the unjust enrichment that would result if the defendant could repudiate the contract and retain benefits conferred on her under it.

With this brief preview in place, we begin our consideration of noncompliance issues with a pair of Problems. Then we consider two cases: Crossman v. Fountainebleau Hotel Corp., which applies the doctrine of part performance, and Farash v. Sykes Datatronics, Inc., in which the court confuses, or at least fails adequately to distinguish, all three of the doctrines that may come into play when an agreement violates the statute of frauds — part performance, promissory estoppel, and restitution of benefits.

PROBLEMS

4.-D. L and T orally agree on a 5 year lease, to begin the next January 1.

a. Prior to January 1, L repudiates the agreement. Does T have a claim for breach? What result if T repudiated before January 1?

b. On the same facts, what result if T had given L a security deposit?

4-E. T enters on January 1 under an oral two year lease, rent reserved by the year, payable by the month. T remains one month before vacating and pays no rent because of a one month's rent concession agreed to by L.

a. Is T liable for any rent after the first month?

b. Assume no rent concession. On January 1, T takes possession and pays the first month's rent. In the middle of June, T tells you that she wants to get out because she has found a new roommate and a more suitable place. How would you advise T?

CROSSMAN v. FONTAINEBLEAU HOTEL CORP.
273 F.2d 720 (5th Cir. 1959)

Wisdom, Circuit Judge.

The plaintiff-appellant, Florence Lustig Crossman, operates women's dress shops in Miami Beach, Palm Beach, and Bal Harbour, Florida, in New York City, and in other places. The defendant-appellee is the Fontainebleau Hotel Corporation of Miami, Florida. The Fontainebleau Hotel opened for business in December 1954.

Lustig filed suit for a declaratory judgment against Fontainebleau October 19, 1959, in the Southern District of Florida asserting that she was the assignee of a lessee's interest in a lease for shop space in the hotel, and that the lease had a renewal clause. She attached to the complaint a long, unsigned, and unwitnessed writing, said to represent the lease. The complaint seeks to enjoin any unlawful detainer or dispossessory action in the state courts of Florida to oust her from possession of the premises pending a determination of her rights.

Fontainebleau Hotel moved to dismiss on the ground that the lease was not executed in compliance with the Florida Statute of Frauds. In reply, Lustig contends that possession, payment of the rent, and expenditure of $50,000 for improvements take the contract out of the Statute of Frauds. The district court granted the motion to dismiss for failure to state a claim entitling the plaintiff to relief, and Lustig appeals from the order of dismissal.

The Court is of the view that the judgment should be reversed and the case remanded.

I.

The complaint alleges the following facts. January, 1955, about a month after the Fontainebleau Hotel opened, Florence Lustig and her husband, Crossman, who was also her manager, were staying at the hotel. They were approached by a Mr. Ben Jaffe, an officer, director, and large stockholder of the hotel, who was handling the leasing of store space in the hotel. Jaffe told Lustig that the lower lobby, where all of the shops were to be located, had not been completed and that the management was anxious to have tenants in promptly; it was the height of the season in Florida. Jaffe, Lustig, and Crossman agreed orally on the terms of a lease. Then, in order to expedite the opening of the shopping area in the Fontainebleau, so that the hotel guests would have the benefit of complete facilities, at Jaffe's request Lustig agreed to move in immediately and to take possession of the premises for the operation of a fine dress shop before formal execution of any lease. Based on the oral agreement and on Jaffe's assurances that all would be satisfactory, Lustig took possession of the premises. Using the hotel's architect and general contractor, she spent $50,000 on fixtures and improvements, a part of which was not removable. To bind the transaction Lustig gave the hotel $5,000 as a good faith deposit, an amount still held by the hotel.

After Lustig commenced construction of the improvements, the hotel presented a lease that allegedly was not in accordance with the original understanding of the parties. Lustig, through her husband, Crossman, and the hotel, through Jaffe, made pencilled corrections in the lease to reflect the original understanding. All of these changes were approved by Jaffe and Crossman. Jaffe then stated that the lease would be redelivered to the hotel's attorneys to be redrafted in accordance with the pencil notations. No redrafted lease was ever submitted to Lustig.

The lease shows the lessee to be Florence Lustig of New York, Inc., a New York corporation authorized to do business in Florida. The plaintiff is the sole stockholder, a director, and dominant party in that corporation. All of the rights of the corporation in the lease were transferred to her. She has occupied the premises and paid the rent since March 1, 1955, when the shop opened as "Florence Lustig."

On July 20, 1958, Lustig notified the lessor in writing of her election to exercise the option to renew the lease. In August 1958 the hotel's attorneys' letter to the corporation denied that there was any option to renew the lease. In July 1959 a letter from the hotel demanded possession of the premises no later than September 1, 1959. In September Lustig wrote the hotel tendering a check for $2,000 for the rent for the first month of the alleged new five-year term. The check was returned. The lessor again demanded possession of the premises, but extended the deadline for removal to October 31, 1959.

Florence Lustig alleges that she took possession of the leased premises and paid the rent. The shop was operated under her name. Prior to raising the issue of an alleged invalid assignment, as a defense in this case, the hotel had done nothing to indicate disapproval of Florence Lustig as a tenant.

The Florida Statute of Frauds provides:

> No estate or interest of freehold, or for a term of more than one year, or any uncertain interest of, in or out of any messuages, lands, tenements or hereditaments shall be created, made, granted, transferred or released in any other manner than by instrument in writing, signed in the presence of two subscribing witnesses by the party creating, making, granting, conveying, transferring or releasing such estate, interest, or term of more than one year.

F.S.A. § 689.01.

A statute of frauds makes no exception in favor of a plaintiff who has rendered his own performance in part or in full. But by a course of judicial development, it has become established law for equity courts to hold the statute inapplicable when a contracting party has partially performed his share of the bargain. Corbin states the general principle as follows:

> Nevertheless, it is established law that, after certain kinds of part performance by a purchaser, the court will specifically enforce the vendor's promise to convey land. Part performance of a contract for the transfer of land does not take the case out of the statute; but it may be of such a character that it will take the statute out of the case. The part performance doctrine applies to a contract for any of the lesser interests in land; and cases are numerous in which it has been applied to oral leases of land, even though they are for so long a period as to be clearly within the one-year clause of the statute as well as within the land clause.

2 Corbin, Contracts § 420 (1950).

The lessee concedes that the writing relied on here does not meet the formal requirements called for in the statute for a valid five-year lease. She contends that possession as lessee for five years, coupled with payment of the rent for that time and expenditures for substantial improvements she made on the premises, take the agreement out of the statute and give her the right to specific performance according to the provable terms of her contract.

Under Florida law a lease invalid because of the Statute of Frauds will be enforced in equity, if the lessee has taken possession in reliance upon the instrument. In Pedrick v. Vidal, 116 So. 857 (Fla. 1928), Vidal and another agreed to buy a grocery business from Bush if they could secure a five-year lease from the owner of the building, Pedrick. Pedrick agreed to execute and deliver a lease. Vidal and his partner bought the business, went into possession, spent $500 on improvements and $1500 for additional equipment, all with the knowledge of Pedrick. They remained in possession and complied with the terms of the agreement. Pedrick refused to execute the lease and notified them to vacate. The court granted the lessees specific performance of the agreement to execute the lease, stating that usually possession and payment are sufficient to show the lessee's performance but that the payment for the improvements strengthened the lessee's claim to equitable relief.[2]

Other Florida cases are in agreement that part performance takes the case out of the Statute of Frauds and allows specific performance of an oral lease or an instrument not in conformity with the Statute. Similarly, a number of Florida cases hold that part performance will take a contract to sell land out of the Statute of

---

[2]

    The great weight of authority is to the effect that a court of equity will specifically enforce an oral agreement for the execution of a lease of real estate when the lessee has been put into possession and has paid rent and the lessor has accepted it, under the terms agreed on, where such terms are clearly and definitely alleged and proven. In this case there was another element that strengthens the claim to equitable relief; that is, the making of improvements on the property with the lessor's knowledge and acquiescence. But the putting of the lessees in possession and acceptance of payment of rents as orally agreed on is usually sufficient to take the case out of the statute of frauds.

Pedrick v. Vidal, 116 So. 857 (Fla. 1928).

Frauds and entitle the performing party to specific performance. The considerations allowing equitable relief to a person who has taken possession and partly performed under a contract to sell land that is invalidly executed are equally applicable in a lease situation.

If the case is taken out of the Statute of Frauds by part performance of the lessee, then parol evidence is properly admissible to prove the terms of the agreement relied on by the lessee. And if part performance will take the case out of the statute, a fortiori complete performance will do so — if at the trial the facts show that the primary term expired.

The acts relied on to prove performance taking the case out of the statute must be referable, of course, to the contract. As we see it, there is no great problem in referability. [T]he [tenant's] possession, payment of rent, and expenditures for improvements [all] referred to the contract. It is a fair inference also that the expenditure of as much as $50,000 for improvements was necessarily in contemplation of renewal of the lease. If there is a serious question of referability it is better resolved at a trial on the merits than on a motion to dismiss.

The district court's order dismissing the complaint is reversed and the case is remanded for further proceedings not inconsistent with this opinion.

NOTES AND QUESTIONS

1. **Part performance: rationale.** "The basis of the doctrine is that certain acts refer unequivocally to the existence of a lease and involve such change of position by one of the parties that to allow the defense of nonconformance with the statute would result in irreparable harm." Robert S. Schoshinski, American Law of Landlord and Tenant § 2:6, at 38 n.38 (1980). *See generally* 2 Powell on Real Property § 16.03[2][c].

2. **Part performance: acts "referable to the lease."** Should possession plus payment of rent by the tenant constitute part performance, as stated in the Pedrick v. Vidal dictum quoted in footnote 2 of the principal case? Does the tenant's possession and payment of rent "refer unequivocally to" — furnish unambiguous evidence of — the term of years lease claimed by Florence Lustig in the principal case? Would a tenant who takes possession and pays rent suffer irreparable harm if the lease were not enforced? What additional conduct by the tenant in *Crossman* (and in *Pedrick*) amounted to part performance? Suppose the tenant takes possession and pays rent for several months in accordance with an unsigned writing providing a detailed scheme for computing rents based on a percentage of the tenant's gross sales; might *that* constitute part performance? *See* Carlyle Record Warehouses Corp. v. Scherlo, 404 N.Y.S.2d 530 (Civ. Ct. of City of New York 1978); Restatement Second § 2.3 cmt. e & illus. 10 (adopting *Carlyle*).

3. **Limitation of part performance doctrine to equity.** Part performance doctrine originated in equity, and is generally confined to suits by the plaintiff for specific performance or an injunction. See Restatement Second of Contracts § 129 ("Action in Reliance; Specific Performance"); Trollope v. Koerner, 470 P.2d 91 (Ariz. 1970) (landlord could not assert part performance in his suit against tenant to recover expense of remodeling the premises; court suggested that the landlord might recover in restitution, which is discussed in Note 5 after the next principal

case). Is a tenant who makes substantial improvements to the premises likely to seek damages or enforcement of the lease? Does the Restatement Second of Property § 2.3 confine part performance to equity?

4. **Other possibilities.** When part performance is unavailable, the plaintiff must find some other doctrine to remove the statute of frauds issue from the case, or must limit herself to a recovery in restitution. The next case (a 4-2 decision) explores these possibilities.

FARASH v. SYKES DATATRONICS, INC
452 N.E.2d 1245 (N.Y. 1983)

COOKE, CHIEF JUDGE.

Plaintiff [Max Farash, the landlord] claims that he and defendant entered an agreement whereby defendant would lease a building owned by plaintiff, who was to complete its renovation and make certain modifications on an expedited basis. Defendant, however, never signed any contract and never occupied the building. Plaintiff commenced this litigation, and defendant unsuccessfully moved to dismiss for failure to state a cause of action. [T]he Appellate Division reversed. 456 N.Y.S.2d 556 (App. Div. 1982). For the reasons that follow, we now modify.

Plaintiff pleaded three causes of action in his complaint. The first was to enforce an oral lease for a term longer than one year. This is clearly barred by the Statute of Frauds, General Obligations Law, § 5-703(2). The third cause of action is premised on the theory that the parties contracted by exchanging promises that plaintiff would perform certain work in his building and defendant would enter into a lease for a term longer than one year. This is nothing more than a contract to enter into a lease; it is also subject to the Statute of Frauds. Hence, the third cause of action was properly dismissed.

Plaintiff's second cause of action, however, is not barred by the Statute of Frauds. It merely seeks to recover for the value of the work performed by plaintiff in reliance on statements by and at the request of defendant. This is not an attempt to enforce an oral lease or an oral agreement to enter a lease, but is in disaffirmance of the void contract and so may be maintained. That defendant did not benefit from plaintiff's efforts does not require dismissal; plaintiff may recover for those efforts that were to his detriment and that thereby placed him in a worse position. See Kearns v. Andree, 139 A. 695 (Conn. 1928). "The contract being void and incapable of enforcement in a court of law, the party rendering the services in pursuance thereof, may treat it as a nullity, and recover the value of the services." Erben v. Lorillard, 19 N.Y. 299, 302 (1859).

The dissent's primary argument is that the second cause of action is equivalent to the third, and so is also barred by the Statute of Frauds. It is true that plaintiff attempts to take the contract outside the statute's scope and render it enforceable by arguing that the work done was unequivocally referable to the oral agreement. This should not operate to prevent recovery under a theory of quasi contract as a contract implied by law, which "is not a contract at all but an obligation imposed by law to do justice even though it is clear that no promise was ever made or intended." Calamari and Perillo, Contracts (2d ed.) § 1-12, p. 19. Obviously, the party who seeks both to enforce the contract that is unenforceable by virtue of the Statute of Frauds and to recover under a contract implied in law will present contradictory characterizations. This, however, is proper in our courts where pleading alternative theories of relief is accepted. Moreover, the existence of any real promise is unnecessary; plaintiff's attempt to make his acts directly referable to the unenforceable contract simply is irrelevant.

The authorities all recognize that a promisee should be able to recover in the present situation. [P]laintiff may recover for those expenditures he made in reliance on defendant's representations, and that he otherwise would not have made. The Restatement provides that an injured party who has not conferred a benefit may not obtain restitution, but he or she may "have an action for damages, including one for recovery based on reliance." Restatement (Second) of Contracts § 370, comment a.

> [T]he injured party has a right to damages based on his reliance interest, including expenditures made in preparation for performance or in performance, less any loss that the party in breach can prove with reasonable certainty the injured party would have suffered had the contract been performed.

Id. § 349. The Restatement recognizes an action such as is involved here. See §§ 139, 349, comment b.

The dissent relies on Bradkin v. Leverton, 257 N.E.2d 643 (N.Y. 1970) and Miller v. Schloss, 113 N.E. 337 (N.Y. 1916) for the proposition that plaintiff can recover only if there is an actual benefit to the defendant. Those cases do not state that there can be no recovery for work performed in the absence of any real benefit to defendant. As stated by Professor Williston, 12 Williston, Contracts (3d ed.), pp. 282-284, 286-297:

> [W]here the defendant is a wrongdoer the plaintiff may well be preferred, and if a complete restoration of the status quo or its equivalent is impossible, the plaintiff should at least be replaced in as good a postion as he originally was in, although the defendant is thereby compelled to pay more than the amount which the plaintiff's performance has benefited him. That is, the law should impose on the wrongdoing defendant a duty to restore the plaintiff's former status, not merely to surrender any enrichment or benefit that he may unjustly hold or have received.

A lesson in this area can be taken from Professors Calamari and Perillo:

> The basic aim of restitution is to place the plaintiff in the same economic position as he enjoyed prior to contracting. Thus, unless specific restitution is obtained in Equity, the plaintiff's recovery is for the reasonable value of services rendered, goods delivered, or property conveyed less the reasonable value of any counter-performance received by him. The plaintiff recovers the reasonable value of his performance whether or not the defendant in any economic sense benefitted from the performance. The quasi-contractual concept of benefit continues to be recognized by the rule that the defendant must have received the plaintiff's performance; acts

merely preparatory to performance will not justify an action for restitution. "Receipt," however, is a legal concept rather than a description of physical fact. If what the plaintiff has done is part of the agreed exchange, it is deemed to be "received" by the defendant.

Calamari and Perillo, Contracts (2d ed.) § 15-4, p. 574; see also *id.*, § 19-44; Perillo, Restitution in a Contractual Context, 73 Col. L. Rev. 1208, 1219-1225.

We should not be distracted by the manner in which a theory of recovery is titled. On careful consideration, it becomes clear that the commentators do not disagree in result, but only in nomenclature. Whether denominated "acting in reliance" or "restitution," all concur that a promisee who partially performs (e.g., by doing work in a building or at an accelerated pace) at a promisor's request should be allowed to recover the fair and reasonable value of the performance rendered, regardless of the enforceability of the original agreement.

Accordingly, the order of the Appellate Division should be modified, with costs to appellant, by reinstating plaintiff's second cause of action and, as so modified, affirmed.

JASEN, Judge (dissenting).

The majority hold that [plaintiff's second] cause of action is not barred by the Statute of Frauds as it "merely seeks to recover for the value of the work performed by plaintiff in reliance on statements by and at the request of defendant" and does not "attempt to enforce an oral lease or an oral agreement to enter [into] a lease." Inasmuch as the record before us on this motion for summary judgment clearly demonstrates that this cause of action is barred by the Statute of Frauds, I must dissent.

Plaintiff alleges that "in reliance on statements made [by] the defendant," he performed certain work and provided labor and material to the defendant. In his affidavit in support of this claim, he sets forth the substance of those statements — "Timing is critical and we would like to have you go ahead with the work. Don't worry about the lease, it will be signed and the work should not wait for the actual signing of the lease" and "We need two floors for immediate occupancy on June 1. We will pay rent for the entire building as soon as we move in and then you can proceed with the other floors after the first two floors are ready." [P]laintiff is merely engaging in a blatant attempt to circumvent the proscriptions of the Statute of Frauds. The only claim plaintiff has alleged and supported with evidentiary facts is that he performed work in reliance on defendant's alleged promise to enter into a two-year lease of the Neisner Building and suffered damages when defendant subsequently refused to rent the premises. However his claim is worded, it should be beyond dispute that plaintiff is seeking damages for defendant's breach of an oral contract to enter into a two-year lease. Since this type of contract is barred by the Statute of Frauds, plaintiff should not be allowed to do indirectly what he cannot do directly.

The majority fails to specify the theory of recovery upon which it bases its conclusion that "plaintiff may recover for those efforts that were to his detriment and that thereby placed him in a worse position." Insofar as this conclusion is based upon quasi contract, it is incorrect for the well-established rule in this State is that in order for a plaintiff to recover under such a cause of action, he must demonstrate that the defendant was unjustly enriched by his efforts. The rule has been clearly set forth by this court and consistently followed:

> [a] quasi or constructive contract rests upon the equitable principle that a person shall not be allowed to enrich himself unjustly at the expense of another. In truth it is not a contract or promise at all. It is an obligation which the law creates, in the absence of any agreement, when and because the acts of the parties or others have placed in the possession of one person money, or its equivalent, under such circumstances that in equity and good conscience he ought not to retain it, and which ex aequo et bono belongs to another.

Bradkin v. Leverton, 257 N.E.2d 643, 645 (N.Y. 1970), quoting Miller v. Schloss, 113 N.E. 337, 339 (N.Y. 1916). Since, as the majority correctly points out, defendant did not benefit from plaintiff's efforts, no recovery under quasi contract may be had.

The "lesson" provided by Professors Calamari and Perillo is inapposite to the case before us because section 15-4 of their text deals exclusively with actions based on breach while plaintiff does not allege in his second cause of action that defendant breached any agreement. Additionally, I note that insofar as this statement would allow recovery by the plaintiff under a theory of restitution, even though the defendant has not been benefited by any of plaintiff's efforts, such is not the law in New York. The majority itself concedes this point in stating, "an injured party who has not conferred a benefit may not obtain restitution." Moreover, assuming arguendo the accuracy of the legal principle stated by Calamari and Perillo, this principle does not accord relief to the plaintiff in the instant appeal. As the two professors correctly note, "the defendant must have received the plaintiff's performance; acts merely preparatory to performance will not justify an action for restitution." [P]laintiff's acts in renovating his building were "merely preparatory to performance" of the alleged oral contract whereby plaintiff and defendant agreed to enter into a two-year lease. Thus, even if section 15-4 were applicable, plaintiff would not be entitled to the relief which the majority is offering.

Similarly, the Restatement lends no support to the majority's view. While it is true that section 370 would allow a party to maintain "an action for damages, including one for recovery based on reliance," a reading of the entire section, including its cite to section 349 as the sole authority for this proposition, makes clear that such an action is based strictly on a theory of promissory estoppel, a theory which has never been asserted by the parties and which this court has heretofore declined to adopt.

The majority also mistakenly relies on a quote from section 349 of the Restatement of Contracts, Second:

> [T]he injured party has a right to damages based on his reliance interest, including expenditures made in preparation for performance or in performance, less any loss that the party in breach can prove with reasonable certainty the injured party would have suffered had *the contract* been performed.

(Emphasis supplied.) This passage, by its very terms, deals solely with remedies available where a party has breached an existing contract.

It appears that the majority, in holding that plaintiff can recover the value of his efforts expended in reliance on defendant's alleged statements, is recognizing a cause of action sounding in promissory estoppel. This is implicit in its reference to the Restatement of Contracts, Second, section 139. Section 139 is quite simply one of the estoppel sections of the Restatement.

While the doctrine of promissory estoppel has been recognized and applied in certain cases, to do so here, where the issue has not been pleaded or addressed in the parties' affidavits and has neither been argued nor briefed, is ill-advised. Moreover, we are not presented here with an inexperienced or unsophisticated plaintiff who is unable to protect his own financial interests. To the contrary, Max Farash is a "prominent and successful [real estate] developer," see Farash v. Smith, 453 N.E.2d 537 (N.Y. 1983), who owns thousands of residential housing units in Monroe County and at least eight commercial buildings in downtown Rochester. Surely a sophisticated businessman such as Max Farash knew that he could have easily insured that defendant would pay for the extensive renovation work plaintiff performed on his own building merely by obtaining defendant's promise to that effect. Plaintiff's failure to obtain such a promise leads inevitably to the conclusion that defendant never intended to pay for such renovation and, thus, never agreed to do so. Nevertheless, the majority unnecessarily provides plaintiff with an opportunity to go before a jury and request that the defendant, who received nothing from the plaintiff, be ordered to pay for the improvements made on plaintiff's own building. Nothing in logic or existing law supports such a result.

In the absence of either a contract requiring defendant to pay for plaintiff's renovation or some evidence that defendant was unjustly enriched, thus allowing plaintiff to recover under a cause of action sounding in quasi contract, defendant should not be held potentially liable to plaintiff for such renovation costs. Accordingly, I would affirm the order of the Appellate Division.

JONES, WACHTLER, and MEYER, JJ., concur with COOKE, C.J. JASEN, J., dissents and votes to affirm in a separate opinion in which SIMONS, J., concurs.

NOTES AND QUESTIONS

1. **The problem.** When a contract is enforceable, a promisee whose expectancy damages are uncertain may recover reliance losses (out-of-pocket expenses) from the breaching party. Reliance losses consist of the claimant's cost of performance and costs of preparation to perform. *See* Restatement Second of Contracts § 349. If the contract is unenforceable, the promisee can recover in restitution for any benefit conferred on the defendant. *Id.* § 375. The problem in *Farish* is to justify the landlord's recovery of reliance losses in an unenforceable contract. The court's result is unobjectionable: the expenditures were wasted (they benefitted neither party), and there is little to be said for allowing the loss to fall on the party who made the expenditures rather than the party who induced them. But the court failed to articulate a clear rationale for its holding, and each of the available doctrinal possibilities has limits that the court ignored. *See generally* 2

George E. Palmer, The Law of Restitution § 6.3 (1978); Douglas Laycock, Modern American Remedies 629-637 (3d ed. 2002).

2. **Why not part performance?** Even if a part performance claim were available in suits at law (see Note 5 after the *Fontainebleau* case), might it be deemed inapplicable when the *landlord* asserts it as a basis for enforcement of the lease? What is the evidentiary value of a landlord's improvements to his own property, as in *Farash*? *See* Laycock, *supra* Note 1.

3. **Promissory estoppel to assert the statute of frauds.** The doctrine of promissory estoppel to assert the statute of frauds supports the result in *Farish*. *See* Restatement Second of Contracts § 139(1): "A promise which the promisor should reasonably expect to induce action or forbearance on the part of the promisee . . . and which does induce the action or forbearance is enforceable notwithstanding the Statute of Frauds if injustice can be avoided only by enforcement of the promise. The remedy granted for breach is to be limited as justice requires." The last sentence is an invitation to courts to award reliance damages rather than to give full effect to the contract. But New York courts have insisted that "the doctrine of promissory estoppel may not be used to preclude the raising of the Statute of Frauds as an affirmative defence to the enforcement of an oral lease." Cohen v. Brown, Harris, Stevens, Inc., 475 N.E.2d 116, 118 (N.Y. 1984). Are there traces of promissory estoppel doctrine in *Farash*? Does the court distinguish reliance recovery in enforceable contracts (which is standard doctrine) from reliance recovery in unenforceable contracts (as in *Farash*)?

4. **Equitable estoppel.** The doctrine of equitable estoppel to assert the statute of frauds is available when the defendant assures plaintiff that no writing is necessary, or that defendant has executed or intends to execute a writing, or that the defendant does not intend to invoke the statute of frauds to deny enforcement of the contract. How does this doctrine differ from promissory estoppel to assert the statute? *See* E. Allan Farnsworth, Contracts 417 (3d ed. 1999) (equitable estoppel is not available when a party "simply relies on a promise by the other party that [comes] within the statute of frauds"). Is equitable estoppel arguably more consistent with the policy underlying the statute of frauds than promissory estoppel? Both promissory and equitable estoppel may be asserted at law or in equity. *See* Restatement Second of Contracts § 139 (unlike § 129, this section does not distinguish between specific performance and damages). Do you see any basis in *Farash* for assertion of the claim of equitable estoppel? Did the court — majority or dissent — explore that possibility?

5. **Restitution.** In restitution, plaintiff recovers the benefit — usually money or other property — conferred on the defendant under the unenforceable contract. (a) Did the defendant in *Farish* receive money or other property from the plaintiff? (b) The defendant requested improvements, and the landlord provided them. Some courts have treated a performance rendered or a request satisfied by the plaintiff as a "benefit" to the defendant. *See, e.g.*, Kearns v. Andree, 139 A. 695 (Conn. 1928) (seller of house recovered the reasonable cost of buyer's requested alterations to the house; the changes reduced the fair market value of the house); Minsky's Follies v. Sennes, 206 F.2d 1 (5th Cir. 1953) (landlord recovered cost of liquor license, salary of night watchman, counsel fees in preparing a lease, long distance telephone calls, "and the like," requested by the tenant). (c) However, some cases allowing recovery for plaintiff's performance exclude recovery for preparation to

perform. *See, e.g.,* Boone v. Coe, 154 S.W. 900 (Ky. 1913) (Kentucky sharecroppers were denied recovery of expenses of moving to Texas when the defendant repudiated the oral lease: moving to Texas was preparation; performance consisted of farming the land). The distinction is hard to draw and some courts don't try to draw it. *See* Riley v. Capital Airlines, 185 F. Supp. 165 (S.D. Ala. 1960) (plaintiff recovered in restitution the costs of purchasing tanks for storage of water methanol that defendant contracted to buy under unenforceable contract). *See also* John P. Dawson, *Restitution without Enrichment*, 61 B.U. L. Rev. 563 (1981) (arguing that the purpose of restitution in cases such as *Kearns* and *Minsky's Follies* is to reverse transactions and restore the status quo ante, rather than to force the defendant to disgorge benefits). Did the court in *Farish* distinguish performance from preparation to perform? Did the court adopt Professor Dawson's theory of restitution?

6. **Gaps in doctrine.** Imagine a nightmare scenario for a landlord in a case like *Farash*: the supreme court in the landlord's state rejects (as do the dissenters in *Farash*) a restitution claim when the plaintiff's partial performance has not conferred an actual benefit on the defendant; the court also rejects promissory estoppel to assert the statute of frauds on the ground that it is fundamentally inconsistent with the legislative policy embodied in the statute of frauds; and on the facts of the case, the landlord cannot point to any statements by defendant that might support a claim of equitable, rather than promissory, estoppel. In that situation, a meritorious claim would go uncompensated. Doctrines, and their limitations, matter.

3. Leases and Licenses

A lease conveys an estate — a possessory interest in land — to the tenant. *See* Restatement Second of Property (Landlord and Tenant) § 1.2 (landlord-tenant relationship exists "only if the landlord transfers the right to possession of the leased property"). But land or buildings are frequently occupied under arrangements that resemble leases but give the occupant only a right to *use* rather than to possess (i.e., exclude others from) the land. The question whether an occupant is a tenant under a lease, or has a different interest, such as a license, arises in a variety of situations, among them the following: (a) the supplier of coin-operated washers and dryers (or of jukeboxes) installs and maintains the machines on the owner's premises; (b) the proprietor of an advertising sign maintains a sign on the owner's building; (c) an optician operates a stall in a large department store (or a kiosk in a shopping mall); (d) an employee resides on the employer's premises; (e) a sharecropper farms the owner's land in return for a portion of the crop. *See generally* 1 American Law of Property §§ 3.3-3.38 (A.J. Casner ed. 1952). The question we consider here is, what are the distinguishing features of a transaction that result in the courts' designation of it as a lease rather than some other interest?

WEIMAN v. BUTTERMAN
260 N.E.2d 321 (Ill. App. Ct. 1970)

MURPHY, JUSTICE.

This is an action based on a written agreement under which plaintiff installed coin-operated washers and dryers in the laundry room of an apartment building. Defendant subsequently purchased the building and plaintiff's machines, after being disconnected, were displaced by similar machines installed by another company. Plaintiff contended the original agreement was a lease, and defendant asserted the agreement was a license. In a nonjury trial, the court found for plaintiff and judgment was entered for $2,775 damages.

On appeal defendant contends that the agreement was a mere license and not binding upon a subsequent purchaser of the building. [The defendant also appealed the lower court's award of damages. The portion of the court's opinion discussing and affirming that award is omitted.]

On December 18, 1962, plaintiff entered into an agreement with A. Goldsmith, owner of the premises at 725 North Central Avenue in Chicago, covering the installation and operation of coin-operated washers and dryers. The agreement, which was entitled "Lease," contained the following terms:

> This lease entered into this 18th day of December, 1962, by and between 725 N. Central Building, hereinafter known as Lessor, and E. Weiman d/b/a Metered Laundry Company, hereinafter known as Lessee.
>
> 1. The Lessor hereby rents and leases to said Lessee the premises known as the laundry-room located at the north central section of ground floor being a room approximately 18x40, located in the building commonly known as 725 N. Central Ave., Chicago, Ill., for the purpose of installing and operating coin-operated washers and dryers.
>
> 2. The term of this lease shall be for five (5) years, beginning the 18th day of December, 1962, and ending the 17th day of December, 1967, with an option on the part of the lessee to renew said lease for an additional period of five (5) years under the same terms and conditions as are contained herein. Lessee is to exercise this option by mail, to the last known address of the Lessor, a minimum of thirty (30) days prior to the expiration of this lease.
>
> 3. The Lessee agrees to pay to the Lessor as and for the rental of the above described premises a sum equal to 25 percent of the gross receipts from the operation of the washers and dryers which will be from time to time operated at said premises. Said Lessee further agrees to pay said amount every six months, beginning the 15th day of January, 1963.
>
> 4. Lessor agrees to furnish the Lessee without charge to said Lessee, all necessary electricity, heat, gas and water, both hot and cold, for the continued operation of the washers and dryers installed or to be installed on said premises.

5. Lessor agrees that the title to all washers, dryers and all other equipment necessary for the operation and maintenance of said washers and dryers shall remain in the Lessee at all times, and said Lessee may remove same at the termination of this lease. Lessor further agrees that the Lessee may assign this lease without the consent, either written or oral, of the Lessor.

6. Lessor agrees that for and in consideration of Lessee's rental of the premises above described, Lessor will not during the term of this lease, allow any other coin-operated washer or dryer to be installed or operated in the above described premises.

IN WITNESS WHEREOF, the parties have caused this lease to be executed under their seals on the date first above written.

Thereafter, plaintiff installed two washers and one dryer with coin boxes in the laundry room, ran an electrical line, a gas line, and made water openings in the laundry room. A sign with plaintiff's name and telephone number was posted in the laundry room close to the equipment. Plaintiff had no key to the laundry room and the door was customarily open day and night.

Defendant purchased the premises from Goldsmith on September 1, 1966. The contract of sale listed as tenants only the apartment dwellers and did not list plaintiff. Plaintiff never spoke to defendant prior to the sale of the building and defendant did not see the agreement between plaintiff and Goldsmith until a number of weeks following defendant's purchase of the building. However, before the purchase, defendant inspected the premises and saw the washers and dryers, but made no inquiry as to their ownership. After the building was sold, plaintiff's machines were replaced by those of a competitor.

Defendant initially contends that the agreement between plaintiff and Goldsmith was a mere license, and hence not binding on a subsequent purchaser of the realty. He principally relies on two New York cases involving a similar question. In Wash-O-Matic Laundry Co. v. 621 Lefferts Ave. Corp., 191 Misc. 884, 82 N.Y.S.2d 572 (1948) (trial court), the contract of purchase of the building containing the washing machines made no reference to the agreement concerning the installation of the machines, and the agreement was not recorded. In holding for defendant, the court stated (82 N.Y.S.2d p. 575):

> On all the evidence I hold that the defendant did not have actual or constructive notice of the existence of the agreement when it purchased the property. In the absence of such notice the defendant was not bound by the agreement. The agreement here did not confer upon plaintiff exclusive possession of any definite space as against the owner of the property; it merely granted a license to install and maintain certain laundry equipment in space designated on a diagram as "washing machine room." This is not a sufficient delineation of any identifiable space so as to create a grant thereof. It may not be said that by virtue of this agreement the owner of the building could not require the plaintiff to move the machines to another part of the basement, if necessary.

In Kaypar Corp. v. Fosterport Realty Co., 1 Misc.2d 469, 69 N.Y.S.2d 313, affirmed 272 App.Div. 878, 72 N.Y.S.2d 405 (1947), the question was whether the plaintiff could claim the protection of the New York Rent Control Law. The court stated (69 N.Y.S.2d p. 316):

> The main object of the agreement is to procure for the tenants of defendant a laundering service. The plaintiff agrees to furnish the service. The plaintiff, through its installations, is granted a license or privilege to occupy the land for the purpose of performing its contract of furnishing this laundry service to the tenants. The plaintiff has no ownership of the space allotted to its equipment in the sense that usually obtains in the relationship of landlord and tenant. In a lease the tenant is the owner of the premises for the term therein specified. The rent is the purchase price for outright ownership for the duration of the term. In the instant matter, all that is granted by the terms of the contract, properly read, is a license to use the designated space for the installation and maintenance of its machines. If the occupation of the land is in connection with a service to be rendered to the landlord, then the possession continues to be that of the landlord.

Defendant further argues that this type of situation is similar to a concession where the concessionaire operates an enterprise upon realty and pays a stipulated rental based upon profits derived from the concession. He notes that these are construed as licenses and not leases. Day v. Luna Park Co., 174 Ill.App. 477 (1912).

Defendant finally argues that even if the agreement was a lease, plaintiff did not record and defendant had no notice of the agreement as provided by the Recording Act (Ill.Rev.Stat., Ch. 30, § 29). He points out that possession of realty, in order to constitute "notice" under the Act must be open, visible, exclusive and unambiguous, such as is not liable to be misunderstood. Millikin Trust Co. v. Gregory, 10 N.E.2d 853 (Ill. App. Ct. 1937); Mack v. McIntosh, 54 N.E. 1019 (Ill. 1899).

We are not persuaded that defendant's authorities apply here. In 24 I.L.P., Landlord and Tenant, § 26, p. 272, it is said:

> No particular words are necessary to create a lease, and in determining whether a particular instrument amounts to a lease, greater regard should be had to the clear intent of the parties than to any particular words which may have been used in the expression of that intent. It has been stated to be the rule in Illinois that the only essentials to the creation of a valid lease are a definite agreement as to the extent and bounds of the property leased, a definite and agreed term, and a definite agreement as to the price of rental and the time and manner of payment.

In Bournique v. Williams, 225 Ill.App. 12 (1922), it is said (p. 20):

> Under the authorities, to create a valid contract of lease, but few points of mutual agreement are necessary: First, there must be a definite agreement as to the extent and bounds of the property leased; second, a definite and agreed term; and third, a definite and agreed price of rental, and the time and manner of payment. These appear to be the only essentials. This is the rule in Illinois.

In the instant case the intention of the parties is clearly shown. The instrument is entitled "Lease," refers to the parties as "Lessor" and "Lessee," and gives plaintiff the exclusive right to operate its machines in a specified area for a definite term. Also, the provision that plaintiff could not assign the contract without the consent of the lessor is a provision inconsistent with licensing agreements. We find the agreement here was a lease and is to be so viewed in litigation regarding it.

Next considered is whether defendant had notice of the lease so as to prevent him from being a protected party under the Recording Act. Generally, actual notice of possession is immaterial if the facts were sufficient to put a purchaser on inquiry. "It is well settled that whatever is sufficient to put a party upon inquiry is notice of all facts which pursuit of such inquiry would lead to, and without such inquiry no one can claim to be an innocent purchaser as against him whose possession raises the inquiry." Bryant v. Lakeside Galleries, Inc., 84 N.E.2d 412, 418 (Ill. 1949).) Here, defendant inspected the laundry room and saw the two washers and dryer with coin slot machines in them. Although he denied seeing it, the evidence shows that a sign with plaintiff's name was prominently displayed on one of the walls of the laundry room. In our opinion this was sufficient to put defendant on inquiry and sufficient for the trial court to find that defendant had notice of plaintiff's possession and interest in the premises.

For the reasons given, the judgment is affirmed.

NOTES AND QUESTIONS

1. **Possession and use.** If you were negotiating the agreement for placement of laundry machines on O's premises on behalf of the supplier (S), what terms would you place in the agreement to support a lease construction? Is the designation of the agreement as a "lease" conclusive? What on-site practices pursuant to the agreement would support a lease construction? *See, e.g.,* Restatement Second of Property (Landlord and Tenant) § 1.1 (landlord-tenant relation exists "only with respect to a space that is intended to have a fixed location for the duration of the premises").

2. **Issues.** The question in the principal case was whether Butterman was bound by the agreement between Weiman and Goldsmith, or was entitled to terminate it before the end of the definite term specified in the agreement. Another recurring question is whether the premises owner, if entitled to terminate an occupancy, must use statutory procedures that are designed to protect tenants. *See, e.g.,* Bourque v. Morris, 460 A.2d 1251 (Conn. 1983) (transient occupant of hotel was subject to lockout); Poroznoff v. Alberti, 391 A.2d 984 (N.J. Super. Ct. Law Div. 1978) (lodger in YMCA was not a tenant, could be evicted without cause); Grant v. Detroit Assoc. of Women's Clubs, 505 N.W.2d 254 (Mich. 1993) (employee receiving apartment as sole compensation for employment was evicted by lockout; summary judgment for employer on on question whether employee was entitled to thirty-day notice to quit was improper); Bernet v. Rogers, 519 N.W.2d 808 (Iowa 1994) (live-in companion was licensee not tenant at will, and was subject to being dispossessed without three-day notice of the proceeding). *See also* Cook v. University Plaza, 427 N.E.2d 405 (Ill. App. Ct. 1981) (students in private dormitory were not tenants, and were not entitled to protections of security deposit law).

Classification of the transaction as a lease in these cases usually helps the occupant.

3. **Other issues; classification.** On some issues, classification of the arrangement as a lease rather than a license could be unfavorable to the occupant. In the principal case, if the tenant had removed the machines and abandoned the premises before the end of the specified term, would the owner have had a duty to mitigate damages by seeking a replacement supplier of laundry machines? *See* Heckel v. Griese, 171 A. 148 (N.J. 1934) (lease; mitigation by landlord not required). If the plaintiff had remained past the ending of the agreement, could the owner have imposed a new term on the tenant? *See* Brooklyn Dock & Terminal Co. v. Bahrenburg, 120 N.Y.S. 205 (N.Y. App. Div. 1909) (lease; holdover doctrine applicable). If the premises had been destroyed by fire before the end of the term, would the tenant have continued to owe rent? *See* Roberts v. Lynn Ice. Co., 73 N.E. 523 (Mass. 1905) (lease, not license; tenant owed rent after destruction of premises). The modern law of abandonment (Section C.2), holding over (C.3) and destruction of the premises (C.4.b) is discussed below; changes in the formerly unfavorable rules applicable to leases would reduce the significance of the differences indicated in this paragraph.

4. **Not a lease.** If a disputed transaction is *not* a lease, it is not necessarily a license. Occupant A could hold an easement (a nonpossessory interest) in the owner's premises, or could be the beneficiary of a covenant that runs with the burdened party's land. Litigants and courts tend frequently, and unfortunately, to pose issues such as those stated in Notes 2 and 3 above solely in binary terms (lease versus license). We pick up the question of a more suitable methodology in Chapter 7.

4.   Leases and Bilateral Contracts

As noted in the introduction to this chapter, "contract or conveyance" is a recurring theme in the law of landlord and tenant. It has assumed particular prominence since the 1970s, when courts in the vanguard of what many call a "revolution" in the law looked to contract doctrine for solutions to problems that were supposedly foreclosed by the law of conveyances. The following case is atypical for its time in treating a lease overtly as a bilateral contract, and particularly instructive in expressing the contract approach to one particularly vexing question: if one party to the lease breaches an obligation, may the other party terminate the agreement and be excused from further performance? You will see this question (are lease promises independent or dependent?) recurring regularly in the remaining materials in this chapter.

UNIVERSITY CLUB OF CHICAGO v. DEAKIN
106 N.E. 790 (Ill. 1914)

COOKE, J.

The University Club of Chicago, brought suit in the municipal court of Chicago against Earl H. Deakin, to recover rent alleged to be due under a lease. A trial was had before the court without a jury and resulted in a judgment for $2,007.66.

Deakin prosecuted an appeal to the Appellate Court for the First District, where the judgment of the municipal court was affirmed. A writ of certiorari having been granted by this court, the record has been brought here for review. [Throughout the opinion, including this first paragraph, the court refers to Deakin, who was the the defendant in the landlord's suit, as the "plaintiff in error" (the appellant) and University Club as the "defendant in error" (the appellee). For ease of reading and clarity, we refer to the parties by their names, without inserting brackets to show the change.]

On March 31, 1909, University Club leased to Deakin, for a term of one year, a storeroom in its building at the corner of Michigan avenue and Monroe street, in the city of Chicago, at a rental of $5,000 for the year. The lease provided that Deakin should use the room for a jewelry and art shop and for no other purpose. It also contained the following clause, numbered 12: "Lessor hereby agrees during the term of this lease not to rent any other store in said University Club building to any tenant making a specialty of the sale of Japanese or Chinese goods or pearls."

Shortly after this lease was made University Club leased to one Sandberg, for one year, a room in the University Club building, two doors from the corner at a rental of $2,500. The following provision was inserted in the Sandberg lease: "It is further distinctly understood and agreed by and between the parties hereto that at no time during the term of this lease will the lessee herein use the demised premises for a collateral loan or pawnshop or make a specialty therein of the sale of pearls."

On May 1, 1909, being the first day of the term of the lease, Deakin took possession of the premises and thereafter paid the rent, in monthly installments, for May and June. During the latter part of June, Deakin, through his attorney, sought to obtain from University Club a cancellation of his lease on the ground that by leasing a room in the University Club building to Sandberg and permitting him to display and sell pearls therein defendant in error had violated the provision of Deakin's lease above quoted, and that for such violation Deakin was entitled to terminate the lease. University Club refused to cancel the lease, and on June 30th, Deakin vacated the premises, surrendered the keys, and refused to pay any further installments of rent. This suit was brought to enforce payment of subsequent installments of rent accruing under the lease for the time the premises remained unoccupied after June 30th.

The evidence offered by Deakin tended to show that Sandberg had made a specialty of the sale of pearls in connection with the conduct of his general jewelry business ever since he took possession of the room leased to him, and that Deakin vacated the premises and surrendered possession because of the failure of University Club to enforce the twelfth clause of his lease. The evidence offered by University Club tended to prove that Sandberg had not made a specialty of the sale of pearls, and that when Deakin first made known his desire to assign or cancel his lease he gave as his only reason that his health was failing and that he had been advised by his physician to leave the city of Chicago.

Propositions were submitted to the court by both parties to be held as the law of the case. The court held, at the request of Deakin, that the lease sued upon was a bilateral contract, and upon a breach of an essential covenant thereof by the lessor the lessee had a right to refuse further to be bound by its terms and to surrender possession of the premises, and that a breach of the twelfth clause of the lease would be a good defense to an action for rent if the tenant surrendered possession of the premises within a reasonable time after discovery of the breach. The court refused to hold as law propositions submitted by University Club stating the converse of the propositions so held at the request of Deakin.

The court properly held that the lease in question was a bilateral contract. It was executed by both parties and contained covenants to be performed by each of them. The propositions so held with reference to the effect of a breach of the twelfth clause of the lease also correctly stated the law. By holding these propositions the court properly construed the twelfth clause as a vital provision of the lease and held that a breach of that provision by the lessor would entitle the lessee to rescind. Where there is a failure to comply with a particular provision of a contract and there is no agreement that the breach of that term shall operate as a discharge, it is always a question for the courts to determine whether or not the default is in a matter which is vital to the contract. While there was no provision in this contract that Deakin should have the option to terminate it if the terms of the twelfth clause were not observed, it is apparent that it was the intention of the parties to constitute this one of the vital provisions of the lease. It was concerning a matter in reference to which the parties had a perfect right to contract, and it will be presumed that Deakin would not have entered into the contract if this clause had not been made a part of it. It is such an essential provision of the contract that a breach of it would warrant Deakin in rescinding the contract and surrendering possession of the premises.

The following proposition was submitted by University Club and held by the court as the law of the case: "That University Club performed all the obligations imposed upon it by its covenant that it would not rent any other store in its building to a tenant making a specialty of the sale of pearls, by incorporating in its lease to the second tenant that said second tenant should not make a specialty of the sale of pearls in the demised premises."

From a consideration of all the propositions of law held and refused, it appears that the judgment of the trial court was reached from the application of the proposition just quoted to the facts in the case. The court erred in holding this proposition as the law. By covenanting with Deakin not to rent any other store in this building during the term of Deakin's lease to any tenant making a specialty of the sale of pearls, University Club assumed an obligation which could not be discharged by simply inserting in the contract with the second tenant a covenant that such tenant should not make a specialty of the sale of pearls. It was incumbent upon it to do more than to insert this provision in the second lease. By the terms of its contract with Deakin it agreed that no other portion of its premises should be leased to any one engaged in the prohibited line of business, and, if it failed to prevent any subsequent tenant from engaging in the business of making a specialty of the sale of pearls, it did so at the risk of Deakin terminating his lease and surrendering possession of the premises.

It is idle to say that an action for damages for a breach of contract would afford Deakin ample remedy. He contracted with University Club for the sole right to engage in this specialty in its building, and, if University Club saw fit to ignore that provision of the contract and suffer a breach of the same, Deakin had the right to terminate his lease, surrender possession of the premises, and refuse to further perform on his part the provisions of the contract.

For the errors indicated, the judgment of the Appellate Court and the judgment of the municipal court are reversed, and the cause is remanded to the municipal court for a new trial.

Reversed and remanded.

NOTES AND QUESTIONS

A. Bilateral Contracts and Leases

1. **Promises and conditions.** University Club promised not to lease to a competitor of Deakin, but the parties did not say whether University Club's breach of the promise allowed Deakin to terminate the lease. For that purpose, a *condition* rather than a promise was required. Promises create duties; conditions specify events that qualify or eliminate the duties that promises create. *See* S. Williston, A Treatise on the Law of Contracts § 665, at 132 (3d ed. W. Jaeger 1961). Did the court *imply* a condition in the lease?

2. **Implied conditions: three views.** (a) The common law's earliest view was that promises are unconditional (independent) unless expressly made dependent by the terms of the agreement; under this view, without an express condition, the promisee's performance was not excused, no matter how serious the promisor's breach. *See, e.g.,* Paradine v. Jane, 82 Eng. Rep. 897 (K.B. 1647). (b) The Restatement Second of Contracts § 232 (1981) is diametrically opposed: promises in bilateral contracts are presumed to be dependent in all cases, "unless a contrary indication is clearly manifested" by the parties; the implied condition of performance is satisfied if the promisor renders substantial performance of her promises, but the condition fails, excusing the promisee, if the promisor commits a material breach and the promisee elects to terminate the contract. (c) *Deakin* employs an intermediate approach, probably typical of contract law at the time: the court distinguishes "vital" (dependent) promises in a contract from those that are non-essential (independent); breach of the former allows termination despite the absence of an express condition. See, e.g., Jacob & Youngs, Inc. v. Kent, 129 N.E. 889 (N.Y. 1921) (Cardozo, J.) (some promises are "plainly dependent," some "plainly independent," and some "though dependent and thus conditions where there is a departure in point of substance, will be viewed as independent and collateral when the departure is insignificant"); Kingston v. Preston, 99 Eng. Rep. 437 (K.B. 1773) (landmark contracts case, rejecting the *Paradine* requirement of an express condition in all cases; forerunner of cases like Jacob & Youngs v. Kent). Notice that Justice Cardozo in *Jacob & Youngs* refers to a breached promise that does not authorize termination by the promisee as an "independent" promise. That terminology is harmless *if* one does not confuse it with the true independency view

of *Paradine*, which requires an express condition in all cases, even when a vital promise is breached.

The parties in the principal case did not state an express condition excusing Deakin in the event that University Club breached the noncompetition promise. Would Deakin have been entitled to terminate under *Paradine*? Under the Restatement Second of Contracts?

3. **Terminology.** A condition that a court discovers by scrutinizing the nature and importance of the parties' promises, as in *Deakin*, is an implied-in-fact condition — one that the parties have agreed upon and simply failed to expressly state. The condition imposed by the Second Restatement of Contracts is an implied-in-law or "constructive" condition, which is based on considerations of fairness and efficiency. Some implied-in-law terms (promises and conditions) are *default terms*, which the parties can change by their agreement, such as the constructive condition of performance in the Restatement Second of Contracts § 232. Other implied-in-law terms are *mandatory*, meaning that they cannot be modified by the parties. The landlord's implied warranty of habitability (Section B.3 below) is, in most states, a mandatory (non-waivable) promise.

4. **Leases and independency.** The landlord in *Deakin* submitted "converse propositions" to those submitted by the tenant. Traditional doctrine states that lease promises are independent. Williston attributed independency to the common law view that a lease is primarily a conveyance rather than a contract. *See* 6 Williston, *supra* § 890. *See also* Sagamore Corp. v. Willcutt, 180 A. 464 (Conn. 1935) (a lease is "primarily a conveyance of an interest in land, and its execution by the lessor may be said to constitute performance on his part, making the instrument, when considered as a contract, a unilateral agreement with no dependency of performance"); Fowler v. Bott, 6 Mass. 63 (1809) (a "lease for years is a sale of the demised premises for the term"). What does the conveyance view suggest about the *time* in the transaction at which the landlord renders substantial performance? What does the conveyance view suggest is the essential *subject-matter* of the lease transaction?

5. **The conveyance view: other issues.** In all of the following instances, assume that the lease does not specifically address the question presented. What result is suggested by the conveyance view of the lease?

a. The landlord breaches a promise to repair, and the premises become uninhabitable. Is the tenant entitled to terminate the lease? *See* Section B.2.b (discussing landlord's breach of repair covenant as basis for tenant's termination of the lease); Wright v. Lattin, 38 Ill. 293 (1865) (if landlord fails to repair, "[the tenant's] possession remains undisturbed, the breach of covenant only hindering the more commodious enjoyment of the term").

b. The tenant fails to pay rent. May the landlord terminate the lease? (Recall Chapter 2.A.4, dealing with defeasible estates.) *See* Section C.1.b (addressing landlord's power to terminate without lease provision); Brown's Adm'rs v. Bragg, 22 Ind. 122 (1864) (tenant's failure to pay rent does not "work a forfeiture" unless it "be so expressed" in the lease).

c. The lease includes land and a building, which the tenant uses. If the building is destroyed by fire without the tenant's fault, is the tenant excused from further performance? *See* Section C.4 (addressing doctrine of frustration of purpose in leases); Paxson & Comfort Co. v. Potter, 30 Pa. Super. 615, 616 (1906) ("the tenant is still in possession of the soil on which the building was located," and "may use the land for some purpose and may reconstruct the building"); 1 A.L.P. § 3.103, at 397 (A.J. Casner ed. 1952) ("the lease being a conveyance of an interest in land and not a contract, there is no failure of consideration for the lessee has received his estate on execution of the lease").

d. If land is the essence of the lease agreement, are implied warranties as to the condition of buildings on the land necessary? *See* Section B.3 (addressing the modern implied warranty of habitability in leases); Franklin v. Brown, 23 N.E. 126 (N.Y. 1889) (tenant of real property "must run the risk of its condition, unless he has an express agreement on the part of the lessor covering that subject"); 1 A.L.P. § 3.45 ("the tenant is the purchaser of an estate in land, subject to the doctrine of *caveat emptor*").

e. The tenant abandons the premises before the end of the term. Must the landlord try to mitigate damages by seeking a replacement tenant? *See* Section C.2.b (addressing landlord's duty to mitigate); Gruman v. Investors Diversified Services, Inc., 78 N.W.2d 377 (Minn. 1956) ("a lease is a conveyance of an interest in real property and, when a lessor has delivered the premises to his lessee, the latter is bound to him by privity of estate as well as by privity of contract").

f. The tenant abandons, and the landlord would like to recover damages rather than rent for the remainder of the term. Does the doctrine of anticipatory breach apply? *See* Section C.2.b (addressing availability of anticipatory breach in lease cases); Sagamore Corp. v. Willcutt, 180 A. 464 (Conn. 1935) (lease "is primarily a conveyance of an interest in land, and its execution by the lessor may be said to constitute performance on his part, making the instrument, when considered as a contract, a unilateral agreement with no dependency of performance which would make an anticipatory breach possible"; the court, however, rejected the stated view and allowed recovery based on anticipatory breach).

B. Contracts to Lease

6. **Leases and contracts to lease.** As a conveyance, a lease is a partly-executed transaction as of the time of the parties' agreement. It differs from a contract to make a lease, which is entirely executory: all performances lie in the future. Both create binding obligations, although the contract to make a lease is sometimes confused with nonbinding preliminary negotiations and agreements not to be bound until a later formal document is executed. *See* Feeley v. Michigan Avenue National Bank, 490 N.E.2d 15 (Ill. App. Ct. 1986) (landlord argued contract to lease, apparently meaning an unenforceable agreement; the court concluded that the parties had passed the stage of preliminary negotiations and had created a lease). *See generally* E. Allan Farnsworth, Contracts § 3.8 (3d ed. 1999); Alan Schwartz & Robert E. Scott, *Precontractual Liability and Preliminary Agreements*, 120 Harv. L. Rev. 661 (2007). On the issue litigated in Weiman v. Butterman (Section A.3), a successor with notice is subject to the rights of both a tenant and a promisee under a contract to lease. *See* Robert S. Schoshinski, American Law of Landlord and Tenant § 8:3, at 539-40 (1980) (lease), *id.* § 1.8, at

25 (contract to lease). On some questions, outcomes may differ. A lease, like a deed, is ineffective until delivery of the lease document to the tenant; a contract to lease may not require delivery. *See* 219 Broadway Corp. v. Alexander's, Inc., 387 N.E.2d 1205 (N.Y. 1979) (lease: delivery required; question of delivery of a contract to make a lease raised, but not decided); *cf.* UCC § 2-201 cmt. 5 ("It is not necessary that the writing [a written contract for the sale of goods] be delivered to anybody."). In some states today, a landlord may not be subject to a duty to mitigate, but that duty applies in a contract to make a lease. *See* Wright v. Baumann, 398 P.2d 119 (Or. 1965). *See generally* 2 Powell on Real Property § 16.02[5]. There is much to be said for treating leases and contracts to lease alike on all issues.

B.   TENANT'S RIGHTS AND REMEDIES

In this Section, we consider the tenant's rights and remedies against the landlord with respect to a core set of tenant's concerns: possession of the leased premises (access to all of the leased area, both at the start of the lease and during its continuation), enjoyment of that possession (e.g., as against interference by the landlord or noisy neighbors), and habitability of the premises (as against dilapidations thereof).

1.   Delivery of Possession

Is the tenant entitled to possession at the beginning of the lease? The question seems either obvious ("yes, of course") or foolish (what would it mean to talk about a lease — a possessory estate — in which the tenant did not receive possession?). But there is possession and there is possession or, stated differently (and recalling the bundle of sticks metaphor), there is a legal right to possession and there is actual possession (possession in fact). Must the landlord deliver only the legal right to possession, or also actual possession? And when the landlord fails to perform whatever obligation is required, what are the tenant's remedies? The principal case, Hannan v. Dusch, which has been edited down to essentials from its ponderous length in the original, remains one of the best discussions of these questions.

Introducing the covenant of quiet enjoyment. On the question of delivery, as on all questions in Section B relating to the tenant's possession and enjoyment of the leased premises, we will be examining in detail the landlord's express or implied covenant of quiet enjoyment, which until the 1970s and 1980s was the most important source of the tenant's rights and remedies against the landlord. The story of attempts to expand the meaning of the covenant in the increasingly industrialized and urbanized America of the 19th century, and the successes and failures of that attempt, is a significant theme in the law of tenant's rights and remedies. But, not to get ahead of ourselves, we begin with statements from English and American cases reflecting the prevalent understanding of the covenant during much of the 19th century:

> [I]t is clear that from the word "demise" in a lease [or the word "let" or any equivalent words], the law implies a covenant for title to the estate merely,

that is, for quiet enjoyment against the lessor. [T]he estate of the lessor is all the lessor impliedly warrants. [T]here is no implied warranty on a lease of a house, or of land, that it is, or shall be, reasonably fit for habitation or cultivation. The implied contract relates only to the estate, not to the condition of the property.

Hart v. Windsor, 12 M. & W. 67 (1843). *See also* Cleves v. Willoughby, 7 Hill 83, 86 (N.Y. 1845) ("[T]he common-law doctrine as to implied covenants and warranties has a very limited application to a lease for years, and in every case has reference to the title, and not to the quality or condition, of the property."). Our immediate questions are these: what does it mean to say that the landlord warrants only the tenant's "estate," and what impact does that view have on the landlord's obligation to deliver possession to the tenant?

HANNAN v. DUSCH
153 S.E. 824 (Va. 1930)

PRENTIS, C.J.

The declaration filed by the plaintiff, Hannan, against the defendant, Dusch, alleges that Dusch had on August 31, 1927, leased to the plaintiff certain real estate in the city of Norfolk, Virginia, therein described, for fifteen years, the term to begin January 1, 1928, at a specified rental; that it thereupon became and was the duty of the defendant to see to it that the premises leased by the defendant to the plaintiff should be open for entry by him on January 1, 1928, the beginning of the term, and to put said petitioner in possession of the premises on that date; that the petitioner was willing and ready to enter upon and take possession of the leased property, and so informed the defendant; yet the defendant failed and refused to put the plaintiff in possession or to keep the property open for him at that time or on any subsequent date; and that the defendant suffered to remain on said property a certain tenant or tenants who occupied a portion or portions thereof, and refused to take legal or other action to oust said tenants or to compel their removal from the property so occupied. Plaintiff alleged damages which he had suffered by reason of this alleged breach of the contract and deed, and sought to recover such damages in the action. There is no express covenant as to the delivery of the premises nor for the quiet possession of the premises by the lessee.

The defendant demurred to the declaration [on the ground that] "under the lease the right of possession was vested in said plaintiff and there was no duty upon the defendant to see that the premises were open for entry by said plaintiff."

The single question of law presented in this case is whether a landlord, who without any express covenant as to delivery of possession leases property to a tenant, is required under the law to oust trespassers and wrongdoers so as to have it open for entry by the tenant at the beginning of the term — that is, whether without an express covenant there is nevertheless an implied covenant to deliver possession. For an intelligent apprehension of the precise question it may be well to observe that some questions somewhat similar are not involved.

It seems to be perfectly well settled that there is an implied covenant in such cases on the part of the landlord to assure to the tenant the legal right of possession — that is, that at the beginning of the term there shall be no legal obstacle to the tenant's right of possession. This is not the question presented. Nor need we discuss in this case the rights of the parties in case a tenant rightfully in possession under the title of his landlord is thereafter disturbed by some wrongdoer. In such case the tenant must protect himself from trespassers, and there is no obligation on the landlord to assure his quiet enjoyment of his term as against wrongdoers or intruders. Of course, the landlord assures to the tenant quiet possession as against all who rightfully claim through or under the landlord.

The discussion then is limited to the precise legal duty of the landlord in the absence of an express covenant [to deliver possession], in case a former tenant, who wrongfully holds over, illegally refuses to surrender possession to the new tenant. This is a question about which there is a hopeless conflict of the authorities.

The English rule is that in the absence of stipulations to the contrary, there is in every lease an implied covenant on the part of the landlord that the premises shall be open to entry by the tenant at the time fixed by the lease for the beginning of his term. King v. Reynolds, 67 Ala. 229, has been said to be the leading case in this country affirming the English rule. In that case, after citing some of the cases which affirm the American rule, this is said:

> [O]ne who accepts a lease expects to enjoy the property, not a mere chance of a lawsuit. A lease for a year, or term of years, is not a freehold. It is a chattel interest. The prime motive of the contract is, that the lessee shall have possession; as much so as if a chattel were the subject of the purchase. Delivery is one of the elements of every executed contract. When a chattel is sold, the thing itself is delivered. Formerly parties went upon the land, and there symbolical delivery was perfected. Now the delivery of the deed takes the place of this symbolical delivery. Still, it implies that the purchaser shall have possession; and without it, it would seem the covenant for quiet enjoyment is broken. Up to the time the lessee is entitled to possession under the lease, the lessor is the owner of the larger estate, out of which the lease-hold is carved, and ownership draws to it the possession, unless someone else is in actual possession. The moment the lessor's right of possession ceases by virtue of the lease, that moment the lessee's right of possession begins. There is no appreciable interval between them, and hence there can be no interregnum or neutral ground between the two attaching rights of possession, for a trespasser to step in and occupy. If there be actual, tortuous occupancy, when the transition moment comes, then it is a trespass or wrong done to the lessor's possession. If the trespass or intrusion have its beginning after this, then it is a trespass or wrong done to the lessee's possession; for the right and title to the property being then in the lessee for a term, it draws to it the possession, unless there is another in the actual possession.

As to the suggestion in that opinion that such a lease is a chattel, we think that it should be also observed that it is not a mere chattel which passes by delivery, but a chattel real. The lease here involved is for a fifteen year term, which cannot be created in this State except by deed, and therefore the title of the lessee, Hannan, and his right of possession became perfect without more when the deed was delivered. The suggestion in the opinion that there is no appreciable interval between the expiration of the term of the former tenant and the beginning of the term of the new tenant does not seem to be significant, because just as soon as the first tenant's term ended the new tenant's term began, and there is no instant of time when the lessor had any right of possession because his tenants always had that right, and so the trespass or wrong done by the first tenant is to the lessee directly rather than to the lessor.

Another case which supports the English rule is Herpolsheimer v. Christopher, 107 N.W. 382 (Neb. 1906), 111 N.W. 359 (Neb. 1907). In that case the court gave these as its reasons for following the English rule:

> Whether or not a tenant in possession intends to hold over or assert a right to future term may nearly always be known to the landlord, and is certainly much more apt to be within his knowledge than within that of the prospective tenant. Moreover, since in an action to recover possession against a tenant holding over, the lessee would be compelled largely to rely upon the lessor's testimony in regard to the facts of the claim to hold over by the wrongdoer, it is more reasonable and proper to place the burden upon the person within whose knowledge the facts are most apt to lie. We are convinced, therefore, that the better reason lies with the courts following the English doctrine, and we therefore adopt it, and hold that, ordinarily, the lessor impliedly covenants with the lessee that the premises leased shall be open to entry by him at the time fixed in the lease as the beginning of the term.

[U]nder the American rule, where the new tenant fails to obtain possession of the premises only because a former tenant wrongfully holds over, his remedy is against such wrongdoer and not against the landlord — this because the landlord has not covenanted against the wrongful acts of another and should not be held responsible for such a tort unless he has expressly so contracted. This accords with the general rule as to other wrongdoers, whereas the English rule appears to create a specific exception against lessors. It does not occur to us now that there is any other instance in which one clearly without fault is held responsible for the independent tort of another in which he has neither participated nor concurred and whose misdoings he cannot control.

There are some underlying fundamental considerations. Any written lease, for a specific term, signed by the lessor and delivered is like a deed signed, sealed and delivered by the grantor. This lease for fifteen years is, and is required to be, by deed. It is a conveyance. During the term the tenant is substantially the owner of the property, having the right of possession, dominion and control over it. Certainly, as a general rule, the lessee must protect himself against trespassers or other wrongdoers who disturb his possession. The English rule seems to have been applied only where the possession is disturbed on the first day, or perhaps more fairly expressed, where the tenant is prevented from taking possession on the first day of his term; but what is the substantial difference between invading the lessee's right of possession on the first or a later day? To apply the English rule you must imply a covenant on the part of the landlord to protect the tenant from the tort of another, though he has entered into no such covenant. This seems to be a unique exception, an exception which stands alone in implying a contract of insurance on the part of the lessor to save his tenant from all the consequences of the flagrant wrong of another person. Such an obligation is so unusual and the prevention of such a tort so impossible as to make it certain, we think, that it should always rest upon an express contract.

We are confirmed in our view by the Virginia statute, providing a summary remedy for unlawful entry or detainer. The adequate, simple and summary remedy for the correction of such a wrong provided by the statute was clearly available to this plaintiff. It specifically provides that it shall lie for one entitled to possession "in any case in which a tenant shall detain the possession of land after his right has expired without the consent of him who is entitled to possession."

The plaintiff alleges in his declaration as one of the grounds for his action that the defendant suffered the wrongdoer to remain in possession, but the allegations show that he it was who declined to assert his remedy against the wrongdoer, and so he it was who permitted the wrongdoer to retain the possession. Just why he valued his legal right to the possession so lightly as not to assert it in the effective way open to him does not appear. Whatever ethical duty in good conscience may possibly have rested upon the defendant, the duty to oust the wrongdoer by the summary remedy provided by the unlawful detainer statute clearly rested upon the plaintiff. The law helps those who help themselves, generally aids the vigilant, but rarely the sleeping, and never the acquiescent.

Affirmed.

EPES, J., concurring:

I concur in the conclusions reached by the chief justice in the opinion in this case, because of the fact that under the provisions of the law of Virginia, a lessor, having made a lease to take effect immediately upon termination of an expiring lease, appears to have been left without power or process to himself evict a tenant under the expiring lease, who tortiously holds over on the day succeeding the termination of his lease, and therefore the power to evict being denied by law to the lessor, no covenant to put the new tenant into possession should or can be properly implied.

But I am further of the opinion that what is stated to be the English rule in the opinion of the chief justice is the law under the common law, and that in the absence of a statute which by express provision or necessary implication changes this common law, it is the law of Virginia on the subject. If at any time the statutes of Virginia be so amended as to permit the lessor after the moment of the expiration of the prior lease to evict his tenant tortiously holding over under the expiring lease, I am of opinion that the English rule, the rule of the common law, will again become the law of the land in Virginia.

NOTES AND QUESTIONS

A. The Tenant's Right to Possession

1. **Landlord's duties regarding possession.** In both American and English rule states, the landlord breaches the covenant of quiet enjoyment if (a) the landlord prevents the incoming tenant from taking possession; (b) a prior tenant or third party is in possession with the landlord's consent; or (c) the incoming tenant is prevented from taking occupancy by the holder of a superior title (e.g., the landlord defaults on his mortgage and the purchaser at the foreclosure sale takes possession before the incoming tenant's lease begins). *See* 1 American Law of Property § 3.37 (A.J. Casner ed. 1952); 2 Powell on Real Property § 16B.02[1][a]; 2401 Pennsylvania Ave. Corp. v. Federation of Jewish Agencies, 489 A.2d 733 (Pa. 1985) (landlord's extension of prior tenant's lease into the first three months of incoming tenant's lease constituted breach of covenant of quiet enjoyment). In what additional situation is the landlord in breach only in an English rule jurisdiction?

2. **Explanations: quiet enjoyment and other rationales.** The leading article on delivery of possession attributes the American rule primarily to the courts' "misplaced reliance on the covenant of quiet enjoyment." Glen Weissenberger, *The Landlord's Duty to Deliver Possession: The Overlooked Reform*, 46 U. Cinn. L. Rev. 937, 947 (1977). How might the covenant of quiet enjoyment — assuming it to be the only relevant covenant — be said to exclude a duty on the landlord to deliver actual possession? Does King v. Reynolds — a leading English rule case, discussed in Hannan v. Dusch — treat the landlord's failure to deliver actual possession as a breach of the covenant of quiet enjoyment? Is quiet enjoyment the only source of a duty on the landlord to deliver actual possession? *See* Dieffenbach v. McIntyre, 254 P.2d 346 (Okla. 1952) (English rule is based on "an implied covenant to place lessee in actual possession").

3. **Explanations: summary eviction statutes.** The American rule is also based on "a slavishly literal reading" of summary eviction statutes. Weissenberger, Note 2, at 951. All states have statutes authorizing the summary (speedy) removal of a tenant who wrongfully holds over after the lease is over. (You will see these statutes several times in this chapter.) If the local summary eviction statute provides that the party "entitled to possession" may sue to get the premises from a holdover tenant, as in the principal case, American rule states read that as a statutory authorization for the incoming tenant, but not the landlord, to sue the holdover. Why is that a "slavishly literal" reading of the statute? Does the concept of relativity of property rights from Chapter 1 suggest an argument that the landlord is also a party "entitled to possession" as against the wrongful holdover? *See* Restatement Second § 14.1 & cmt. a (either landlord or incoming tenant is entitled to sue holdover tenant for possession); Uniform Residential Landlord and Tenant Act § 2.103 (same). If the landlord sued the holdover for possession, would the holdover have a defense that the incoming tenant was the proper party plaintiff? *See* Eells v. Morse, 101 N.E. 803 (N.Y. 1913) (defense denied).

4. **Policy.** Notes 2 and 3 suggest that legal doctrine is sufficiently flexible to allow a court to adopt either the English or American rule, depending on the court's assessment of the underlying policies. What policies support the English

rule? *See* Restatement Second of Property, Note 1 above, Reporter's Note at 236-237. The American rule? Among other things, Hannan v. Dusch notes the absence of instances "in which one clearly without fault is held responsible for the independent tort of another in which he has neither participated nor concurred and whose misdoings he cannot control" as a justification for the American rule. Is there a flaw in that argument? Has the court begged the question (i.e., assumed the answer to the question under discussion)? Is the landlord "clearly without fault" when the premises remain occupied by a holdover tenant?

5. **Knowledge by the tenant.** Suppose that when the lease is executed, the tenant knows that a holdover is likely to interfere with the tenant's possession. Make an argument that such knowledge should (a) have no effect, (b) abrogate the landlord's implied promise under the English rule, (c) extend the time for the landlord's removal of the holdover. *See* Restatement Second § 6.2 cmt. d, at 241.

B. Remedies

6. **Termination.** When the landlord breaches the English rule, the tenant is entitled to terminate the lease. *See* Harley v. Jobe, 249 P.2d 468, 470 (Okla. 1952) (delivery of possession "is necessary to the obligation of the [tenant] to pay rent, and is a condition precedent to the right of the landlord to demand such payment"). Termination excuses the tenant from the duty to pay rent. 2 Powell on Real Property § 16B.02[1][b]; Restatement Second § 6.2(1). The tenant also has a cause of action against the landlord for any damages resulting from the landlord's breach. Does Harley v. Jobe signify that the landlord's promise to deliver actual possession is a "vital" covenant in the lease? See the discussion in Section A.4 above on termination of the lease for breach of "vital" promises.

7. **Damages.** The Restatement Second, Landlord and Tenant, § 10.2 provides a useful listing of the elements of damages available to the tenant when the landlord breaches the lease.

§ 10.2 Damages

If the tenant is entitled to recover damages from the landlord for his failure to fulfill his obligations under the lease, absent a valid agreement as to the measure of damages, damages may include one or more of the following items as may be appropriate so long as no double recovery is involved:

(1) if the tenant is entitled to terminate the lease and does so, the fair market value of the lease on the day he terminates the lease;

(2) the loss sustained by the tenant due to reasonable expenditures made by the tenant before the landlord's default which the landlord at the time the lease was made could reasonably have foreseen would be made by the tenant;

(3) if the tenant is entitled to terminate the lease and does so, reasonable relocation costs;

(4) if the lease is not terminated, reasonable additional costs of substituted premises incurred by the tenant as a result of the landlord's default while the default continues;

(5) if the use of the leased property contemplated by the parties is for business purposes, loss of anticipated business profits proven to a reasonable degree of certainty, which resulted from the landlord's default, and which the landlord at the time the lease was made could reasonably have foreseen would be caused by the default;

(6) if the tenant eliminates the default, the reasonable costs incurred by the tenant in eliminating the default; and

(7) interest on the amount recovered at the legal rate for the period appropriate under the circumstances.

On the market measure, § 10.2(1), *see* Foreman & Clark Corp. v. Fallon, 479 P.2d 362 (Cal. 1971) (market value of lease established by battle of experts); *cf.* Allen v. Scott, Hewitt and Mize, L.L.C., 186 S.W.3d 782, 786-787 (Mo. Ct. App. 2006) ("Value is a matter of opinion — not fact — resulting in conjecture. Property values depend on multiple variables, and a property's value can increase or decrease following sale."); UCC § 2-713 (buyer's market measure of recovery when seller breaches contract for sale of goods). The tenant's recovery of lost profits is subject, as § 10.2(5) notes, to the requirements of certainty (which is a general requirement of the law of damages) and foreseeability. *See* Restatement Second of Contracts §§ 351 (unforeseeability); 352 (certainty); Dieffenbach v. McIntyre, 254 P.2d 346 (Okla. 1952) (certainty: tenant who had operated beauty parlor at another location denied recovery of profits at new location when landlord failed to deliver possession); Fera v. Village Plaza, Inc., 242 N.W.2d 372 (Mich. 1976) (certainty: rejecting the new business rule and awarding the incoming tenant $200,000 lost profits for the landlord's failure to deliver possession). Punitive damages are not available for breach of contract unless the breach is accompanied by tortious conduct. *Id.* § 355.

8. **Affirmance.** Instead of terminating the lease, the tenant may choose to affirm it. In that case, rent is suspended while the tenant is out of possession, and the tenant is entitled to recover possession by suing the landlord or the holdover. *See* Restatement Second § 6.2 (suspension of rent); *id.* § 14.1 (tenant may sue either landlord or holdover); Soffer v. Beech, 409 A.2d 337 (Pa. 1979) (recovery of possession from landlord). The tenant who affirms is entitled to recover damages for partial rather than total breach; thus, if the tenant loses market value or profits, recovery is measured by the time the tenant is out of possession rather than by the duration of the lease.

9. **Legal possession and remedies.** If the landlord cannot deliver legal possession because of an outstanding paramount title, what remedies should the tenant have? Can the tenant affirm the lease?

PROBLEMS

4-F. (a) The incoming tenant, T, is unable to gain possession because of the presence of a holdover tenant, H. In an English rule state, may T terminate the lease immediately, or does L have a reasonable time to cure the defective delivery by evicting H? *See* John G. Sprankling, Understanding Property Law § 16.04[C][1], at 248 (2d ed. 2007) (under the English rule, "when T discovers X still in possession of Greenacre on July 1 [the first day of the lease], he may either terminate his lease or recover damages from L"); Restatement Second of Property (Landlord and Tenant) § 6.2(1) (tenant may terminate "if a third person is improperly in possession of the leased property on the date the tenant is entitled to possession and the landlord does not act promptly to remove him and does not in fact remove him within a reasonable period of time"). *Cf.* UCC § 2-601 (buyer may reject the goods "if the goods or the tender of delivery fail in any respect to conform to the contract"); UCC § 2-508 (seller has right to cure defective tender before time for performance expires); § 2-608 (after acceptance, buyer may revoke only if the nonconformity "substantially impairs" value of the performance to the buyer). The question of termination on day one of the lease is rarely litigated, probably because most tenants give the landlord some time to remove the holdover; why might the tenant do so? What are some relevant factors in determining whether the landlord has removed the holdover within a reasonable time, if that is the test?

(b) T intends to use the premises — a building consisting of four units of several rooms each, two upstairs and two downstairs — to operate a beauty parlor. At the beginning of T's lease, one of the units is available and suitable for T to use as intended, but the other three units remain occupied by holdover tenants. Under the English rule, is L in breach, justifying termination of the lease by T? How does this situation differ from that in (a)? *See* Dieffenbach v. McIntyre, 254 P.2d 346, 348 (Okla. 1953) (partial delivery: "[the landlord] contends that the breach was only a partial breach since it did not interfere with the operation of the beauty parlor by [the tenant], but we think it was a complete breach, since it forced the [tenant] either to bring ouster proceedings against tenants holding over, or to continue to pay $500 a month rent for a portion of the premises only"). Why couldn't T pay partial rent for partial possession?

4-G. In an English rule state, L breaches by failing to deliver possession and T properly terminates the lease. The lease calls for rent of $500 per month. T is unable to find comparable premises in the immediate vicinity at that price, but does find a reasonably comparable rental unit in a nearby location at $575 per month. If the fair market value of the leased premises on the date of breach is $550 per month, what is T entitled to recover as general damages from L? *See* Restatement Second of Property (Landlord and Tenant) § 10.2, cmt. d, at 343 ("an increase in rental for a comparable new location" is included under the "reasonable relocation costs" allowed to the tenant). *Cf.* UCC § 2-714 (cover authorized as alternative to market measure). The cover measure requires the availability of goods that are fungible with those that were bought by the buyer; are residential apartments in the typical apartment building unique? *Cf.* Centex Homes Corp. v. Boag, 320 A.2d 194 (N.J. Super. Ct. Ch. Div. 1974) (denying specific performance of a contract to sell a high rise condominium unit, because the unit "has no unique quality but is one of hundreds of virtually identical units being offered for sale to the public").

4-H. A residential tenant in New York is unable to take possession at the start of the lease because of the presence of a holdover tenant. The state has the following statute, N.Y. Real Prop. Law § 223-a:

> In the absence of an express provision to the contrary, there shall be implied in every lease of real property a condition that the lessor will

deliver possession at the beginning of the term. In the event of breach of such implied condition the lessee shall have the right to rescind the lease and to recover the consideration paid. Such right shall not be deemed inconsistent with any right of action he may have to recover damages.

What are the tenant's remedies against the landlord? *See* Atlantic Bank of New York v. Sutton Assocs., Inc., 321 N.Y.S.2d 380, 381 (N.Y. App. Div. 1971) (per curiam) ("[Section 223-a of the Real Property Law], which implies in all leases a condition of delivery of premises at the beginning of a term, provides only the remedies of rescission and repayment for failure to deliver; plaintiff [tenant] seeks only money damages thereunder, and the cause may not stand."). If *Atlantic Bank* is correct, what is the meaning of the last sentence of the statute? Does the New York distinction between a promise and a condition provide a useful halfway house between the absolutes of the English rule (tenant may terminate and claim damages against the landlord) and the American rule (tenant may not terminate and has a claim only against the holdover)? *See* URLTA § 4.102 (tenant may terminate upon 5 days' written notice to the landlord, or affirm "and recover the damages actually sustained" from the landlord or the holdover); Weissenberger, *supra* Note 2 (URLTA view characterized as "modified English").

2.   Possession and Enjoyment During the Lease Term

In this section, we continue our concern with the tenant's access to the premises (Section 2.a), but we also broaden the focus to include the tenant's now well-established companion right to *enjoyment* of the leased space (Section 2.b). Whatever the role of the covenant of quiet enjoyment on the question of delivery of possession at the outset of the lease, it occupies a central role once the lease term begins.

a.   Access: Actual Eviction

In actual eviction cases, the tenant acquires physical possession of the premises at the outset of the lease, only to be turned out thereafter. In rowdier times, the landlord might have committed an actual eviction by going around to the leased premises with his henchmen and throwing the tenant off. The modern version is usually a lockout of the tenant. As you might suspect, landlords doesn't usually choose to lock the tenant out capriciously. Rather, the landlord might, in good faith, think that the tenant has committed a breach, that the breach justifies the landlord's termination of the lease, and that self-help is an available remedy for the breach. But if the landlord is wrong on any one of those beliefs, the landlord's lockout constitutes an actual eviction of the tenant, and a breach of the covenant of quiet enjoyment.

Total eviction. The tenant's remedies when the landlord commits an actual eviction during the lease term are the same as those available when the landlord fails to deliver possession. The tenant may terminate the lease and recover appropriate damages, or affirm the lease and recover possession as well as any appropriate damages. The damages measures discussed after Hannan v. Dusch are applicable here. *See* 2 Powell on Real Property § 16B.03[3]; 1 A.L.P. § 3.51; Restatement Second § 6.1. Even if the tenant has committed a breach justifying termination of the lease by the landlord, the landlord's lockout of the tenant may violate a state's ban on the use of self-help remedies by the landlord to recover possession, thus opening up the possibility of augmented damages (usually a multiple of the tenant's actual damages). *See* Cruz v. Molina, 788 F. Supp. 122 (D.P.R. 1992) (landlord's lockout of tenant violated both the covenant of quiet enjoyment and the statutory ban on self-help evictions, but tenant who was in process of moving out at time of landlord's breach suffered no damages). *See also* Section C.3 below. Clearly, a lockout is not a step to be undertaken lightly by the landlord.

Partial actual eviction. Smith v. McEnany is a brief and leading case on the curious common law doctrine of *partial* actual eviction, which offers a powerful, if questionable, remedy to the tenant.

SMITH v. McENANY
48 N.E. 781 (Mass. 1897)

HOLMES, J.

This is an action [by the landlord, Clara A. Smith, against the tenant, Thomas McEnany] upon a lease for rent and for breach of a covenant to repair. The defense is an eviction. The land is a lot in the city of Boston, the part concerned being covered by a shed which was used by the defendant to store wagons. The eviction relied on was the building of a permanent brick wall for a building on adjoining land belonging to the plaintiff's husband, which encroached 9 inches, by the plaintiff's admission, or, as his witness testified, from measurements, 13 1/2 inches, or, as the defendant said, 2 feet, for 34 feet along the back of the shed. The wall was built with the plaintiff's assent, and with knowledge that it encroached on the demised premises. The judge ruled that the defendant had a right to treat this as an eviction determining [i.e., terminating] the lease. The plaintiff asked to have the ruling so qualified as to make the question depend upon whether the wall made the premises "uninhabitable for the purpose for which they were hired, materially changing the character and beneficial enjoyment thereof." This was refused, and the plaintiff excepted. [T]he only question before us is the one stated, and we have stated all the facts which are necessary for its decision.

The refusal was right. It is settled in this state, in accordance with the law of England, that a wrongful eviction of the tenant by the landlord from a part of the premises suspends the rent under the lease. The main reason which is given for the decisions is that the enjoyment of the whole consideration is the foundation of the debt and the condition of the covenant [to pay rent], and that the obligation to pay cannot be apportioned. [T]he traditional doctrine [is] that the rent issues out of the land, and that the whole rent is charged on every part of the land. But the same view naturally would be taken if the question arose now for the first time. The land is hired as one whole. If by his own fault the landlord withdraws a part of it he cannot recover either on the lease or outside of it for the occupation of the residue.

It follows from the nature of the reason for the decisions which we have stated that, when the tenant proves a wrongful deforcement by the landlord from an appreciable part of the premises, no inquiry is open as to the greater or less importance of the parcel from which the tenant is deforced. Outside the rule de minimis, the degree of interference with the use and enjoyment of the premises is important only in the case of acts not physically excluding the tenant, but alleged to have an equally serious practical effect, just as the intent is important only in the case of acts not necessarily amounting to an entry and deforcement of the tenant. The inquiry is for the purpose of settling whether the landlord's acts had the alleged effect; that is, whether the tenant is evicted from any portion of the land. If that is admitted, the rent is suspended because, by the terms of the instrument as construed, the tenant has made it an absolute condition that he should have the whole of the demised premises, at least as against willful interference on the landlord's part.

We must repeat that we do not understand any question, except the one which we have dealt with, to be before us. An eviction like the present does not necessarily end the lease, or other obligations of the tenant under it, such as the covenant to repair.

Exceptions overruled.

NOTES AND QUESTIONS

1. **No rent, no restitution, no possession.** "[T]he plaintiff [landlord] could not recover on the express contract [for rent] because he had not furnished the stipulated consideration, and he could not recover upon an implied one for the benefit actually received because the failure to furnish the whole was due to his own willful fault." Moore v. Mansfield, 65 N.E. 398 (Mass. 1902) (Holmes, J.). Because the tenant does not owe rent so long as the encroachment continues, the landlord is not entitled to recover possession for the tenant's nonpayment of rent. *See* Ravet v. Garelick, 190 N.W. 637 (Mich. 1922) ("Unless the tenant could make the defense [of partial actual eviction] at this time [in the landlord's suit for possession for nonpayment of rent], his remedy would be of no avail."). When available, partial actual eviction doctrine is a powerful doctrine for the tenant.

2. **The test of partial actual eviction.** When is a claim of partial actual eviction available? The court says that the landlord commits a partial actual eviction by encroaching on an "appreciable" part of the tenant's space. How is an "appreciable" eviction determined? If the area reclaimed by the landlord is of no particular use to the tenant, does that matter? (Was that the situation in Smith v. McEnany?)

3. **The contract explanation.** Justice Holmes explains the ancient metaphor that rent "issues out of the land" as a primitive form of contract reasoning. The lease contract is "entire" rather than divisible — the tenant bargained to pay full rent for full possession, not part rent for part possession. Is that a convincing explanation for the result in actual eviction cases? Did the tenant bargain to get substantial possession for nothing? Or is that the point: possession is so important a stick in the bundle that any interference beyond de minimis *is* a material breach by the landlord? If so, shouldn't the tenant still have to choose within a reasonable time either to terminate the lease (and vacate the premises) for the material breach or affirm (and pay rent, reduced by damages for the eviction)?

4. **Modifications and rejections of the rule.** How do the following approaches to partial actual eviction differ from the standard doctrine announced in Smith v. McEnany?

a. Dussin Inv. Co. v. Bloxham, 157 Cal. Rptr. 646, 651 (Cal. Dist. Ct. App. 1979):

We are persuaded by our analysis of the California cases that a tenant is not relieved entirely of the obligation to pay rent by an actual partial eviction unless the eviction is from a substantial portion of the premises and that in determining the question of substantiality, the court may and should consider the extent of the interference with the tenant's use and enjoyment of the property.

b. Warren v. Wagner, 75 Ala. 188 (1883):

When the landlord enters and dispossesses the tenant of a part of the premises, a discharge of the entire rent will not result unless it be shown that the tenant surrendered or abandoned possession entirely. The rent is discharged only *pro tanto*, to the extent of the value of the use and occupation of the part of the premises of which the tenant is dispossessed, if he remains in undisturbed possession of the residue.

c. Restatement Second of Property (Landlord and Tenant) § 6.1 (in cases of partial actual eviction, T may terminate the lease if the eviction is substantial, or affirm the lease and recover damages to reflect the diminished value of the premises with the encroachment).

5. **Termination.** Under Smith v. McEnany, is the tenant entitled to terminate the lease for an "appreciable" partial actual eviction? Why would the tenant ever *want* to terminate for the landlord's breach, given the rent suspension remedy? Under what circumstances might an encroachment be significant enough to allow termination?

6. **Partial actual eviction by paramount title.** "If the eviction is the act of a stranger by force of paramount title, the rent will be apportioned, and a recovery permitted for the value of the land retained"). Fifth Ave. Bldg. Co. v. Kernochan, 117 N.E. 579, 580 (N.Y. 1917) (lease included a basement containing a vault area held by the landlord under a revocable license from the city; during the lease, the city revoked the license and excluded the tenant from the vault; opinion by Cardozo, J.).

b. Enjoyment: "Constructive" Eviction

In the delivery and actual eviction cases, the landlord's conduct interferes with the tenant's *possession* of the premises — i.e., the tenant's estate in the land — which is the essence of the lease bargain from the perspective of a lease understood as a conveyance. However, suppose that the tenant's estate remains intact — the tenant still has access to, and the right to exclude others from, the leased space — but the *enjoyment* of that space is significantly reduced because of activity by or attributable to the landlord; in that case, might the landlord still be guilty of a breach of the covenant of quiet enjoyment, and what remedies does the tenant have for that breach? We address those questions here.

Sometimes the tenant wants to respond to the landlord's interference with the tenant's enjoyment of possession by vacating the premises, terminating the lease, and recovering any applicable damages. In that situation, the appropriate analysis is "constructive" eviction. Sometimes the tenant would prefer to affirm the lease, despite the landlord's interference with enjoyment, and seek relief by way of damages or an injunction. In that situation, "eviction" is not a proper analysis, because the tenant remains in possession. The tenant who seeks either to terminate or to affirm the lease when the landlord breaches the covenant of quiet enjoyoment encounters important doctrinal obstacles to the chosen remedy. We explore those obstacles in the materials that follow.

Although the implied warranty of habitability and its associated remedies (see Section B.3 below) have displaced the covenant of quiet enjoyment as the central source of a residential tenant's protection from landlord misconduct, the covenant of quiet enjoyment remains important: the warranty of habitability does not apply to residential tenants in a few states, to commercial tenants in most states, and to some conditions existing on the premises even in states recognizing the warranty. To emphasize their continuing importance, we offer in the principal cases and notes a thorough review of the lineaments and limitations of the covenant of quiet enjoyment and the remedies available for its breach.

ECHO CONSULTING SERVICES, INC. v. NORTH CONWAY BANK
669 A.2d 227 (N.H. 1995)

BROCK, CHIEF JUSTICE.

The plaintiff, Echo Consulting Services, Inc., sued its landlord, North Conway Bank, claiming constructive eviction, partial actual eviction, breach of an implied covenant of quiet enjoyment, and breach of the lease. Echo appeals the decision of the Superior Court denying all of Echo's claims after a bench trial. We affirm in part, reverse in part, and remand.

Pursuant to a written lease dated March 15, 1986, Echo leased premises on the downstairs floor of a building in Conway, together with "common right of access" thereto. When the bank purchased the building from Echo's prior landlord, it assumed the lease and became Echo's landlord.

The bank undertook a series of renovations to make the building suitable for a branch banking business on the main, street-level floor. These renovations, occurring on and off through 1987, created noise, dirt, and occasional interruptions of electric service. The construction work also made the rear parking lot inaccessible. During most of 1987, therefore, many of Echo's employees used the street-level parking lot in front of the building; they gained access to Echo's downstairs office by first using the main, street-level access to the building and then walking downstairs. On October 13, the bank changed the locks on the main floor access door for security reasons, and Echo's employees were no longer able to get in or out of the building through that door after regular business hours. At that point, Echo's only means of access after hours was through the rear door, and

Echo presented testimony that even that access was obstructed and difficult at times. The parties disagree as to the extent of these interferences, and as to the damage that they caused to Echo's permissible uses of its leasehold.

On appeal, Echo argues that the trial court erred by: (1) confusing the legal standards for constructive eviction and partial actual eviction; (2) finding that locking the street-level access doors did not constitute a partial actual eviction; (3) ruling that there was no constructive eviction; and (4) applying the wrong legal standard to determine the quiet enjoyment issue.

This case involves a commercial, as distinguished from a residential, lease. Since we have not addressed in the commercial context all of the issues raised here, we will draw some insight from residential lease cases, even though the applicable law may be more protective in the residential context.

In any lease, along with the tenant's possessory interest, the law implies a covenant of quiet enjoyment, which obligates the landlord to refrain from interferences with the tenant's possession during the tenancy. There are several ways in which a landlord might breach that covenant, each giving rise to a different claim by the tenant. The landlord's actual physical dispossession of the tenant from the leased premises constitutes an actual eviction, either total or partial, as well as a breach of the covenant. "Interferences by the landlord that fall short of a physical exclusion but that nevertheless substantially interfere with the tenant's enjoyment of the premises, causing the tenant to vacate, are actionable by the tenant as 'constructive' evictions." 2 Powell on Real Property § 16B.03[1], at 16B-34. The landlord's general breach of the covenant of quiet enjoyment, even if not "substantial" enough to constitute a constructive eviction, nevertheless entitles the tenant to damages. We turn now to addressing each of Echo's claims separately.

I. Partial Actual Eviction

A partial actual eviction occurs when the landlord deprives the tenant of physical possession of some portion of the leased property, including denial of access to the leased premises. A landlord cannot apportion a tenant's rights under a lease. See Smith v. McEnany, 48 N.E. 781 (Mass. 1897). Thus, the bank cannot apportion Echo's rights to choose which door to enter if the lease gives Echo a right to two different doors for access.

Echo, however, was not physically deprived of any portion of the property leased to it, nor of any appurtenant rights given to it under the lease. For its claim of partial actual eviction, Echo relies on the following language in the lease: "approximately 1,890 square feet of floor area, together with common right of access thereto, and common use of the parking lot." Echo argues that this language gives it a right of access through the main, street-level door, since that door is the only door that was actually used in common by both the bank and Echo. We disagree.

The word "common" in Echo's lease modifies the phrase "right of access." Thus it plainly means only that the tenant's right to access is not an exclusive right; it is in "common" with the landlord's. The lease is not ambiguous; it cannot reasonably be construed to afford Echo the right in "common" to use the street-level door simply because that is the door which the bank chose actually to use. We interpret the trial court's finding that "Echo employees had access to their offices through at least one door at all times" to be a determination that such access was reasonable. That is all that is required under the language of this lease.

The trial court apparently applied the standard for constructive eviction in ruling on the actual eviction claim. Even though this was error, we affirm its decision on this issue because it reached the correct result and there are valid alternative grounds to reach that result. Since Echo was not physically deprived of any portion of the premises to which it had a right under the lease, the partial actual eviction claim was properly denied.

II. Constructive Eviction

A constructive eviction is similar to a partial actual eviction except that no actual physical deprivation takes place. A constructive eviction occurs when the landlord so deprives the tenant of the beneficial use or enjoyment of the property that the action is tantamount to depriving the tenant of physical possession. The bank argues that a constructive eviction claim will not lie unless the landlord intends that its actions (1) render the premises unfit for occupancy or (2) permanently interfere with the tenant's beneficial use or enjoyment of the premises. We disagree.

It is well established that "the landlord's conduct, and not his intentions, is controlling." Blackett v. Olanoff, 358 N.E.2d 817, 819 (Mass. 1977); cf. Restatement (Second) of Property § 6.1 (1976 & Supp.1995) (not mentioning any requirement that the landlord intend to evict the tenant). The bank mistakenly relies on one prior case to support its view that intent is required for a constructive eviction. See Thompson v. Poirier, 420 A.2d 297 (N.H. 1980). Although *Thompson* contains allegations of intentional conduct on the landlord's part, intent was not a necessary element of our decision, and the prevailing view is to the contrary. For example, even though no intent was or could have been found, courts have found a constructive eviction where a nuisance outside the leased premises — such as excessive noise from neighboring tenants — was attributable to, though not affirmatively undertaken by, the landlord. See, e.g., *Blackett*, 358 N.E.2d at 819; Gottdiener v. Mailhot, 431 A.2d 851, 854 (N.J. Super. Ct. App. Div. 1981).

The focus of the inquiry in a constructive eviction case is not on intent but on the extent of the interference, i.e., whether, in the factual circumstances of the case, the interference is substantial enough that it is tantamount to depriving the tenant of physical possession. The law regarding this substantiality requirement has moved over the years "in the direction of an increase in the landlord's responsibilities." 2 Powell, *supra*, § 16B.03[1], at 16B-35. Even without any affirmative activity on the landlord's part, courts have found a constructive eviction where the landlord fails to perform a lease covenant, fails to perform statutory obligations, or fails to perform a duty that is implied from the circumstances. Sierad v. Lilly, 22 Cal.Rptr. 580, 583 (Cal. Dist. Ct. App. 1952) (deprivation of use of parking space impliedly included in the lease); Cherberg v. Peoples Nat. Bank of Washington, 564 P.2d 1137, 1142 (Wash. 1977) (landlord's failure to repair outside wall rendering it unsafe).

As we held in connection with the partial actual eviction claim, the lease here did not grant Echo a right to use the particular door of its choosing. The lease provision was satisfied since, as the trial court found, Echo employees had access to their offices through at least one door at all times. Likewise, the trial court found "the interruptions and noise [from construction activities] were intermittent and temporary and did not substantially interfere or deprive Echo of the use of the premises."

There was conflicting testimony on these points, but the credibility of witnesses and the weight to be given to testimony are questions of fact for the trial court to resolve. We will not disturb the trial court's findings of fact on the constructive eviction issue since the evidence in the record was sufficient to support its conclusion.

III. The Covenant of Quiet Enjoyment

A breach of the covenant of quiet enjoyment occurs when the landlord substantially interferes with the tenant's beneficial use or enjoyment of the premises. Even if not substantial enough to rise to the level of a constructive eviction, such interference may constitute a breach of the covenant of quiet enjoyment entitling the tenant to damages. See Restatement (Second) of Property § 5 (changes in the physical condition of the premises which make them unsuitable for the use contemplated by the parties), § 6 (conduct by the landlord, or by a third party under the landlord's control, which interferes with the tenant's permissible use of the premises).

The trial court concluded that quiet enjoyment only protects a tenant's possession against repossession by the landlord or one claiming title superior to the landlord. Although our prior cases have not addressed any other basis for a claim that the covenant of quiet enjoyment has been breached, they have not rejected such a claim either. We do not believe such a view of the covenant of quiet enjoyment constitutes good law today; many other courts have extended the covenant beyond mere denial of actual possession. See, e.g., Pollock v. Morelli, 369 A.2d 458, 461 n.1 (Pa. Super. Ct. 1976).

When reasons of public policy dictate, "[c]ourts have a duty to reappraise old doctrines in the light of the facts and values of contemporary life — particularly old common law doctrines which the courts themselves created and developed." Kline v. Burns, 276 A.2d 248, 251 (N.H. 1971). Our society has evolved considerably since the tenurial system of property law was created by the courts. The complexities, interconnectedness, and sheer density of modern society create many more ways in which a landlord or his agents may potentially interfere with a tenant's use and enjoyment of leased premises. Even without rising to the level of a constructive eviction and requiring the tenant to vacate the premises, such interferences may deprive the tenant of expectations under the lease and reduce the value of the lease, requiring in fairness an award of compensatory damages. Moreover, under modern business conditions, there is "no reason why a lessee, after establishing itself on the leased premises, should be forced to await eviction by the lessor or surrender the premises, often at great loss, before claiming a breach of the covenant for interference with the use and possession of the premises" that is not substantial enough to rise to the level of a total eviction. Tenn-Tex Properties v. Brownell-Electro, Inc., 778 S.W.2d 423, 428 (Tenn.1989). Likewise, the landlord's greater level of knowledge of and control over the leased premises and the surrounding property militates in favor of a more modern view of the covenant of quiet enjoyment than the trial court adopted.

Since the trial court understandably, but erroneously, believed the implied covenant of quiet enjoyment protected only Echo's possession of the property, the court did not consider Echo's claim that the bank's construction activities breached the covenant by depriving Echo of the beneficial use of the premises. There was conflicting testimony as to whether such a breach occurred, and, if so, the damages caused thereby. These are questions of fact for the trial court to determine in the first instance. Accordingly, we reverse the trial court's conclusion on this issue and remand the quiet enjoyment claim for further proceedings consistent with this opinion.

We note, however, that our holding as to the definition of a covenant of quiet enjoyment effects a change in the common law in New Hampshire, and that others might have relied on the view of the covenant that our older cases had set forth. We decline, therefore, to make this change retroactive. Instead, for anyone who is not a party to the instant action, we will only apply this new interpretation prospectively.

Affirmed in part; reversed in part; remanded.

NOTES AND QUESTIONS

1. **Review: partial actual eviction.** In the principal case, how did the trial court confuse the standards for actual and constructive eviction? Why wasn't the landlord guilty of a partial actual eviction? *See* Barash v. Pennsylvania Terminal Real Estate Corp., 256 N.E.2d 707 (N.Y. 1970) (denying claim of tenant — a lawyer working late hours — that he had suffered a partial actual eviction and was excused from the further payment of rent because of landlord's breach of a promise to provide after-hours ventilation: "There must be a physical expulsion or exclusion.").

A. Constructive Eviction: Origin of the Doctrine

2. **Dyett v. Pendleton.** In Dyett v. Pendleton, 8 Cow. 727 (N.Y. 1826), the landlord sued the tenant for rent accruing after the tenant vacated the premises. The tenant pleaded eviction, and at trial offered to prove that the landlord brought "lewd women or prostitutes," as well as other men, into the house, and that the parties thus assembled, including the landlord, "were accustomed to make a great deal of indecent noise and disturbance, the said women or prostitutes often screaming extravagantly, and so as to be heard throughout the house, and by the near neighbors." The trial and intermediate appellate courts refused to admit the tenant's proferred evidence. On further appeal, those decisions were reversed and the case remanded for a new trial. The main opinion, reduced to essentials, announced two propositions: (a) The landlord's express covenant that the tenant shall have "peaceable, quiet and indisputable possession" of the premises was "in its nature, a condition precedent to the payment of rent; and whether the

possession was peaceable and quiet, was clearly a question of fact for the jury. Such conduct of the lessor as was offered to be proved in this case, went directly to that point." (b) The doctrines of actual and partial actual eviction provided the basis for a doctrine of "constructive" eviction. The opinion found the doctrine of partial actual eviction to be a particularly apt analogy:

> [Partial actual eviction] is a case where actual entry and physical eviction are not necessary to exonerate the tenant from the payment of rent; and if the principle be correct as applied to a part of the premises, why should not the same principle equally apply to the whole property demised, where there has been an obstruction to its beneficial enjoyment, and a diminution of the consideration of the contract, by the acts of the landlord, although those acts do not amount to a physical eviction? If physical eviction be not necessary in the one case, to discharge the rent of the part retained, why should it be essential in the other, to discharge the rent of the whole? If I have not deceived myself, the [cases] referred to [settle] the principle for which the [tenant] contends, that there may be a constructive eviction produced by the acts of the landlord.

One of the dissenters objected that the new doctrine of "constructive" eviction would "introduce a new and very extensive chapter in the law of landlord and tenant." Fortunately, that prediction turned out to be correct.

Are you persuaded by the analogy to partial actual eviction as a basis for the extrapolated doctrine of "constructive" eviction? On what basis might one conclude that Dyett v. Pendleton "reads much like a contract case"? William B. Stoebuck & Dale A. Whitman, The Law of Property § 6.32, at 283 (3d ed. 2000). Is quiet enjoyment a "vital" promise in the lease? *Dyett* is a landmark case in landlord-tenant law. It is discussed extensively and insightfully in Michael Weinberg, *From Contract to Conveyance: The Law of Landlord and Tenant, 1800-1920* (Part I), 1980 S. Ill. U. L.J. 29.

3. **From possession to enjoyment.** What new meaning does the majority in *Dyett* add to the covenant of quiet enjoyment — what else does the covenant protect besides the tenant's access to the premises? Is the majority's view of the covenant suited to the increasing urbanization occurring in the 19th century? Is the view that the covenant protects possession — and thus is not breached unless the landlord evicts the tenant — suited to a predominantly agricultural society?

4. **Law and morality.** References to the immorality of the landlord's conduct permeate several of the opinions in Dyett v. Pendleton. Shouldn't the case have come out the same anyway: the landlord's morality may have bothered the tenant, but wasn't it the incessant loud noise that kept him awake at night?

5. **Tort remedies.** In *Dyett*, the tenant had a tort remedy against the disturbing tenants (and the landlord); is that remedy sufficient to protect the tenant's interests? Might the lease expire before the tenant's tort remedies can be pursued to judgment? If not, what future relationship with the landlord might a tenant expect if the tenant instigates a civil action against the landlord?

B. Scope of the Covenant of Quiet Enjoyment: Landlord's Acts and Omissions

6. **Landlord's acts; further examples.** The landlord might breach the covenant of quiet enjoyment by active interference with the tenant's enjoyment of possession, such as renovating the premises, as in *Echo Consulting*; or constructing additions to a shopping center, *see* Pollock v. Morelli, 369 A.2d 458 (Pa. Super. Ct. 1976) (additions blocked off the former visibility of the tenant's store from the mall parking lot); or harassing the tenant, *see* Chapman v. Brokaw, 588 N.E.2d 462 (Ill. App. Ct. 1992) (male landlord harassed female residential tenant); Thompson v. Poirier, 420 A.2d 297 (N.H. 1980) (commercial lease: landlord shut off tenant's electricity during business hours and verbally abused tenant and tenant's employees and customers). The landlord's remodeling or adding to commercial premises is a common occurrence; for examples of drafting of the lease to avoid or minimize a tenant's potential claim of breach of the covenant of quiet enjoyment, see Stinson, Lyons, Gerlin and Bustamante, P.A. v. Brickell Building 1 Holding Co., 923 F.2d 810 (11th Cir. 1991); Fitzwilliam v. 1220 Iroquois Venture, 598 N.E.2d 1003 (Ill. App. Ct. 1992).

7. **Failure to act in general: implied and statutory duties.** The landlord's *failure* to act is also a basis for a constructive eviction claim, if the landlord is under a duty to act. The court's list in *Echo Consulting* of relevant failures includes the landlord's breach of statutory duties and duties implied from the circumstances of the leasing. On statutory duties, see Tallman v. Murphy, 24 N.E. 716 (N.Y. 1890) (alternative holdings: landlord's failure to maintain noisy water tower atop leased building breached statutory duty of maintenance as well as implied duty to maintain areas within the landlord's control in good repair). As the alternative holding in *Tallman* indicates, the landlord's control over the area causing disturbance to the tenant is the main circumstantial factor leading to the imposition of a duty to act. *See* Cherberg v. Peoples Nat. Bank, 564 P.2d 1137, 1141-1142 (Wash. 1977) (alternative holdings: constructive eviction based on landlord's failure to repair a structurally defective outside wall over which the landlord had expressly retained control in the lease, and on breach of the landlord's implied duty to make repairs mandated by competent government authority; the court also noted the landlord's implied duty to maintain common areas of the leased premises in good repair). In the few situations in which the courts prior to the 1970s found an implied warranty of habitability (*see* Note 7 after the *Javins* case, below), breach of the warranty justified the tenant in terminating the lease. *See* Ingalls v. Hobbs, 31 N.E. 286 (Mass. 1892); Young v. Povich, 116 A. 26 (Me. 1922).

The landlord's implied duty to make repairs ordered by governmental authority, considered in *Cherberg*, does not exist if the lease excuses the landlord or shifts that duty onto the tenant. For discussions of the interpretation of relevant lease clauses, see Dennison v. Marlowe, 744 P.2d 906 (N.M. 1987); Scott v. Prazma, 555 P.2d 571 (Wyo. 1976).

8. **Landlord's implied duty to control the conduct of tenants.** When tenant A is substantially disturbed by the rowdy conduct of tenant B occurring in common areas of the leased premises, the landlord's failure to suppress the disturbing conduct provides a basis for tenant A's claim of constructive eviction. See Note 7 above and Phyfe v. Dale, 130 N.Y.S. 231 (S. Ct. App. T. 1911) (landlord

"had the complete power to abate" the nuisance). Whether the landlord has a duty to prevent disturbing conduct occurring in tenant B's own apartment, however, remains controversial. *Compare* Stewart v. Lawson, 165 N.W. 716 (Mich. 1917) (despite lease clause prohibiting conduct that disturbed other tenants, landlord's failure to correct the "intolerably offensive" conduct and language of a tenant was not a breach of duty owed to the disturbed tenants), *with* Blackett v. Olanoff, 358 N.E.2d 817 (Mass. 1977) (the "late evening and early morning music and disturbances coming from nearby premises which the landlord leased to others for use as a bar or cocktail lounge" constituted a constructive eviction), *and* Restatement Second of Property (Landlord and Tenant) § 6.1 cmt. d, at 226 and Reporter's Note, at 232 (*Blackett* is preferable rule, but "the weight of authority is contra").

Is *Blackett* objectionable because it creates a slippery slope: isn't the landlord almost always in a better position than his residential tenants to enjoin nearby nuisances, even if the tortfeasor isn't a tenant of the landlord? Is the case objectionable because it creates a "moral hazard" — an opportunistic tenant might try to exit a bad bargain by magnifying the extent of a neighboring nuisance? What about a comparison to the landlord's duty to deliver possession: can a state consistently adopt the English rule on delivery of possession *and* Stewart v. Lawson on constructive eviction?

9. **Express promises and independency.** *Echo Consulting* also lists the landlord's "failure to perform express covenants" in the lease as a relevant failure to act that allows the tenant to claim a constructive eviction. We have already seen that the landlord's breach of the covenant of quiet enjoyment — express or implied — allows the tenant to terminate the lease, under a claim of either actual or constructive eviction. The covenant of quiet enjoyment is in effect a dependent covenant. See 1 A.L.P. § 3.11, at 204 (constructive eviction "serves as a substitute for dependency of covenants"); Restatement of Contracts § 290 (1932) (lease covenants are independent except to the extent that "the law of property governing the effect of eviction of the grantee or of waste by him provides."). *Echo Consulting* indicates that the landlord's breach of *other* covenants in the lease might allow the tenant to claim constructive eviction. Suppose the landlord breaches a covenant to repair the leased premises, and the effect is that the tenant's enjoyment is disturbed?

a. *See* Wright v. Lattin, 38 Ill. 293 (Ill. 1865):

There seems to be no analogy between an eviction, or an act of the landlord which amounts to an eviction, and the breach of a covenant of the landlord to repair the premises. [H]aving entered upon the term and received possession, [the tenant] can not abandon the lease and refuse to pay rent for the breach of any other covenant except for quiet enjoyment. [H]is possession remains undisturbed, the breach of covenant [to repair] only hindering the more commodious enjoyment of the term, whilst in case of an eviction the term is gone, or the property so situated that it ceases to be useful for the purpose for which the term was obtained.

See also Surplice v. Farnsworth, 135 Eng. Rep. 232 (1844) ("No authority has been cited to shew that [the landlord's] contract to repair implies . . . a condition [excusing the tenant from the obligation to pay rent]. Where it is intended that a covenant shall operate as a condition, there is always an express covenant to that effect.").

b. *See* Dolph v. Barry, 148 S.W. 196 (Mo. Ct. App. 1912):

> The common law imposes no duty upon the landlord to make repairs during the term of the lease, but, if by a stipulation in the lease the lessor agrees to do so, of course, the obligation is cast upon him. It may be that the premises demised become untenantable because of the want of such repairs as the landlord has agreed to make. In such circumstances the breach of the covenant touching repairs, of course, not only operates to impair the consideration for the lease, but operates as well to breach the implied covenant for the quiet enjoyment of the premises, which permits the defendant to abandon the premises and escape the further payment of rent therefor.

See also 1 A.L.P. § 3.51, at 281 ("Perhaps the most significant cases on constructive eviction are those involving breach of an express covenant or a statutory duty to repair or to furnish heat or services."). Why is the repair covenant important in *Dolph*? Why is the covenant of quiet enjoyment important?

10. **Is independency dead?** If the landlord's substantial breach of *any* lease promise provides a basis for a tenant's constructive eviction claim, independency of promises in leases is a dead letter. Are material breach (contract) and constructive eviction (property) identical substantive doctrines simply decked out in different language, or do they differ? What do the following two cases suggest?

a. Brigham Young University v. Seman, 672 P.2d 15 (Mont. 1983) (landlord breached a promise in the lease to accept any reasonable assignment or sublease proposed by tenant; landlord breached, and the tenant vacated the premises):

> [T]he refusal by BYU to consent to the sublease was not an interference by the landlord with the leasehold estate of the lessee which would justify a cancellation of the lease by the lessee. No power to terminate the lease by the lessee is provided by the lease agreement, and even where the lessor unreasonably withholds consent contrary to a specific provision of the written lease, the consent clause has been construed to be an independent clause, not mutually dependent on other clauses in the lease. A substantial breach of the independent covenant not to withhold consent unreasonably to a sublease does not excuse the lessee from further performance of his duties under the lease.

Why wasn't the landlord's breach an interference with the tenant's "estate"? How does a repair covenant (Dolph v. Barry) differ from the landlord's covenant in *Brigham Young*? *See* Edward Chase & E. Hunter Taylor, Jr., *Landlord and Tenant: A Study in Property and Contract*, 30 Vand. L. Rev. 571, 602-605 (1985) (suggesting that "premises" covenants — covenants by the landlord that secure the tenant's enjoyment of physical possession — are dependent via the doctrine of constructive eviction expressed in Dolph v. Barry, while economic covenants are independent).

b. Wesson v. Leone Enterprises, 774 N.E.2d 611 (Mass. 2002) (landlord's breach of a covenant to repair in a commercial lease did not constitute a constructive eviction, but did constitute a material breach justifying termination by the tenant):

> The requirements of the rule we have adopted today [dependency of lease promises] are different from the requirements necessary to demonstrate a constructive eviction. For example, the rule does not require that the premises be untenantable for the purpose for which they were used, in order for the tenant to terminate the lease and vacate the premises. It is sufficient for the tenant to demonstrate the landlord's failure, after notice, to perform a promise that was a significant inducement to the tenant's entering the lease in the first instance. Here that substantial benefit was a dry space necessary to safely conduct the high technology printing business for which the landlord knew the premises were to be used. In other cases, it might include promises having little to do with the condition of the premises, such as an agreement not to lease space in the same building to competing businesses.

See also Ringwood Associates, Ltd. v. Jack's of Route 23, Inc., 398 A.2d 1315 (N.J. Super. Ct. App. Div. 1979) (same covenant as in *Brigham Young* held to be dependent, allowing tenant to terminate for material breach); University Club v. Deakin, section A.4 above (tenant entitled to terminate for landlords' breach of noncompetition covenant); Restatement Second of Property (Landlord and Tenant) § 7.1 (termination allowed for breach of noncompetition promise); *id.* § 7.2 (termination allowed when landlord fails to perform any promise that causes tenant to be "deprived of a significant inducement to the making of the lease"; section 7.2 provided the basis for both *Ringwood* and *Wesson*). If *Brigham Young* and *Wesson* suggest that the property and contract approaches to the termination question differ, how might a court achieve a unified doctrine on that question? Is the covenant of quiet *enjoyment* necessarily limited to enjoyment of possession?

C. Perfecting the Constructive Eviction Claim

11. **Requirements.** Whether the tenant's constructive eviction claim is based on the landlord's acts or failures to act, successful assertion of the claim requires that the tenant (a) notify the landlord of the interference (unless — as in *Dyett* — the landlord already knows); (b) give the landlord a reasonable opportunity to cure — cease or correct — the offending situation; and (c) vacate within a reasonable time after the landlord is in default. *See* 2 Powell on Real Property § 16B.03[3][b]; Restatement Second of Property (Landlord and Tenant) § 6.1 ("prompt" action by the landlord to correct the condition is required); Reste Realty Corp. v. Cooper, 251 A.2d 268 (N.J. 1969) (continuous flooding of tenant's basement offices; previous landlord had always responded to complaints; tenant's nine-month delay in vacating was not unreasonable); Automobile Supply Co. v. Scene-in-Action Corp., 172 N.E. 35 (Ill. 1930) (landlord's failure to supply heat was continuing breach each month, but tenant waived the breaches by remaining in possession for unreasonable period after latest breach).

12. **Risks of a constructive eviction claim.** What risks does a tenant who vacates under a claim of constructive eviction run? To avoid those risks, the tenant might seek, before vacating, a declaratory judgment that the landlord's conduct

constitutes a basis for the claim. *See* Charles E. Burt, Inc. v. Seven Grand Corp., 163 N.E.2d 4 (Mass. 1959). What limitations do you see on the widespread use of the *Burt* remedy? Are the risks faced by the tenant who claims constructive eviction unique, or do they also exist in general contract law? *See, e.g.,* Walker & Co. v. Harrison, 81 N.W.2d 352 (Mich. 1957) (lessee of 18' by 8' advertising sign terminated the lease when, "[s]hortly after the sign was installed, someone hit it with a tomato," and the lessor delayed one month in coming out to clean it off; relying on an acceleration clause in the lease, lessor sued for and recovered the entire rental due for the term):

> Repudiation [termination] is one of the weapons available to an injured party in the event the other contractor has committed a material breach. But the injured party's determination that there has been a material breach, justifying his own repudiation, is fraught with peril, for should such determination, as viewed by a later court in the calm of its contemplation, be unwarranted, the repudiator himself will have been guilty of material breach and himself have become the aggressor, not an innocent victim.

Instead of (precipitously) terminating the contract, what might Harrison have done?

13. Defense and claim for damages. Constructive eviction furnishes both a defense to the landlord's suit for rent accruing after the tenant vacates, and a cause of action for any damages sustained by the tenant. *See* 2 Powell on Real Property § 16B.03[3][a]; Restatement Second of Property (Landlord and Tenant) § 10.2 (listing elements of damages).

D. Quiet Enjoyment and the Tenant in Possession

14. "No breach without eviction." The statement recurs in cases that the covenant of quiet enjoyment is not "breached" unless the tenant is evicted. *See, e.g.,* Petroleum Collections Inc. v. Swords, 122 Cal. Rptr. 114, 117 (Cal. Dist. Ct. App. 1975). After Dyett v. Pendleton, isn't the tenant's vacating of the premises a remedial choice rather than an element of the landlord's breach of the covenant? The better view is that an eviction is necessary when the tenant seeks to terminate the lease and be excused from the tenant's own remaining obligations, but not when the tenant affirms the lease and seeks damages or injunctive relief. A leading case is Moe v. Sprankle, 221 S.W.2d 712, 715 (Tenn. Ct. App. 1948), allowing the tenant to affirm and recover damages:

> It is a modern practice to lease property for business purposes for long terms and there occurs to us no reason why a lessee, after establishing his business on the leased premises, should be forced to await eviction by the lessor or surrender the premises, often at great loss, before claiming a breach of the covenant for interference with his use and possession of the premises falling short of total eviction.

Accord, Hosmer v. Avayu, 636 P.2d 875 (Nev. 1982). *See* Note, *Landlord and Tenant — Covenant for Quiet Enjoyment in a Lease — Breach Without Eviction,* 3 Vand. L. Rev. 333 (1950). *See also* Winchester v. O'Brien, 164 N.E. 807 (Mass. 1929) (tenant entitled to enjoin present interference with quiet enjoyment); Hannan v. Harper, 208 N.W. 255 (Wis. 1926) (tenant entitled to enjoin landlord from renting upstairs unit of duplex to a college fraternity); Restatement Second of Property (Landlord and Tenant) § 6.1 (tenant may affirm and obtain equitable relief). What view of the no-breach-without-eviction issue does the *Echo Consulting* court take?

15. **Summary dispossess statutes as a limit on tenant's affirmance.** All states have statutes, passed in the 19th century, giving the landlord an expedited procedure to remove a tenant who holds over after the lease has expired, and usually to remove a tenant who fails to pay rent or commits some other significant breach of the lease prior to the ending of the term. The statute may be called a "summary dispossess" or "summary eviction" or "forcible entry and detainer" statute. However styled, the summary proceeding differs from the ordinary and usually slow civil action in ejectment: time limits for pleading are shortened; discovery is omitted; triable issues may be limited; jury trials may not be allowed; and the judgment for possession if the landlord is successful can be enforced quickly. Conventional doctrine stated that the tenant could not withhold rent and successfully assert the landlord's breach in the landlord's suit for possession under a summary eviction statute. Courts attributed that result to the independency of lease covenants and the policy of summary dispossession statutes to provide a speedy recovery for a landlord faced with a tenant who wasn't paying rent. *See* Arnold v. Krigbaum, 146 P. 423 (Cal. 1915) (leading case). Might the tenant withhold rent, then sue to enjoin the landlord from seeking to dispossess the tenant? *See* Darnall v. Day, 37 N.W.2d 277 (Iowa 1949) (granting the injunction; vigorous dissent). We will return to the roles of doctrine and policy regarding the tenant's withholding and abatement remedy in the habitability materials, below. For present purposes, we might just note that independency performs a different function in Arnold v. Krigbaum than it does in the question addressed in Notes 9 and 10 above; how so?

16. **Partial constructive eviction?** If the landlord interferes with the tenant's enjoyment of a part of the leased space, should the tenant's rent be suspended (as in partial actual eviction), or partially suspended, or should the doctrine of partial constructive eviction be rejected entirely? Lower courts in New York have said all of the above, and the status of the doctrine of partial constructive eviction is unclear. *See* Robert S. Schoshinski, American Law of Landlord and Tenant § 3:6, at 101 (1980) (doctrine is "far from settled"). Query: Although distinguishable (how?), does *Barash* (Note 1 above) suggest that partial constructive eviction — at least as a total preclusion of the landlord's recovery of rent — is not a tenable claim?

17. **Review.** Make a list of the limitations, from the tenant's standpoint, of the covenant of quiet enjoyment and the doctrines of actual and constructive eviction.

3.   Condition of the Premises

By the 1970s, a series of social and legal events — the civil rights movement, consumer protection legislation, the war on poverty, the rise of the legal services movement, to name some of the most influential — had brought tenants' rights to the forefront of legal consciousness. The result was a widespread judicial recognition of a duty on the part of landlords to furnish habitable premises to residential tenants, and to maintain the premises in that condition throughout the term of the lease. While the doctrine that emerged did not *require* the landlord to perform the habitability duties, it did give the tenant an effective remedy for the landlord's nonperformance, a remedy that, as you will see, amounted essentially to a judicial reformation of the rent term in the lease to reflect the substandard premises that urban residential tenants were receiving for their rental dollars.

The doctrinal story is one of the creation of new rights and new remedies rather than the recasting of older doctrines. We have seen that, except for common areas and other areas under the landlord's control, the covenant of quiet enjoyment imposed no duty on the landlord to repair the leased premises. While the covenant of quiet enjoyment could have been extended to incorporate a general duty on the landlord to furnish and maintain habitable premises, the courts did not take that route. Perhaps the strong association of the covenant of quiet enjoyment with the doctrine of constructive eviction, or the "no breach without eviction" fallacy, or the Arnold v. Krigbaum negation of a withholding remedy, stood in the way. In any event, all of these were *old* doctrines, and in the spirit of the times, the courts in the 1970s and 1980s were more inclined to strike out in new directions (or to appear to do so) rather than to refurbish the covenant of quiet enjoyment and its associated remedies. *See* Lemle v. Breeden, 462 P.2d 470, 475 (Hawai'i (1969) ("[T]o search for gaps and exceptions in a legal doctrine such as constructive eviction which exists only because of the somnolence of the common law and the courts is to perpetuate further judicial fictions when preferable alternatives exist."). The result was the new implied warranty of habitability and the tenant's rent withholding and abatement remedy.

a.   The Implied Warranty of Habitability

Although one or two earlier decisions can be read to have imposed an implied warranty of habitability on the landlord in residential tenancies, the following case is generally regarded as the seminal decision on recognition of the warranty. By the end of the 1970s, most state supreme courts had adopted the result of the case, and much of the rationale stated by Judge Skelly Wright. In breadth of reasoning and in the influence it has exerted on other courts, *Javins* is truly a landmark decision in landlord-tenant law.

JAVINS v. FIRST NATIONAL REALTY CORP.
428 F.2d 1071 (D.C. Cir. 1970)

J. Skelly Wright, Circuit Judge.

These cases present the question whether housing code violations which arise during the term of a lease have any effect upon the tenant's obligation to pay rent. The Landlord and Tenant Branch of the District of Columbia Court of General Sessions ruled proof of such violations inadmissible when proffered as a defense to an eviction action for nonpayment of rent. The District of Columbia Court of Appeals upheld this ruling. Saunders v. First National Realty Corp., 245 A.2d 836 (1968).

Because of the importance of the question presented, we granted appellants' petitions for leave to appeal. We now reverse and hold that a warranty of habitability, measured by the standards set out in the Housing Regulations for the District of Columbia, is implied by operation of law into leases of urban dwelling units covered by those Regulations and that breach of this warranty gives rise to the usual remedies for breach of contract.

I

The facts revealed by the record are simple. By separate written leases, each of the appellants rented an apartment in a three-building apartment complex in Northwest Washington known as Clifton Terrace. The landlord, First National Realty Corporation, filed separate actions in the Landlord and Tenant Branch of the Court of General Sessions on April 8, 1966, seeking possession on the ground that each of the appellants had defaulted in the payment of rent due for the month of April. The tenants, appellants here, admitted that they had not paid the landlord any rent for April. However, they alleged numerous violations of the Housing Regulations as "an equitable defense or claim by way of recoupment or set-off in an amount equal to the rent claim," as provided in the rules of the Court of General Sessions.[3]

Tenants offered to prove

> that there are approximately 1500 violations of the Housing Regulations of the District of Columbia in the building at Clifton Terrace, where Defendant resides, some affecting the premises of this Defendant directly, others indirectly, and all tending to establish a course of conduct of violation of the Housing Regulations to the damage of Defendants.

Settled Statement of Proceedings and Evidence, p. 2 (1966). Appellants conceded at trial, however, that this offer of proof reached only violations which had arisen since the term of the lease had commenced. The Court of General Sessions refused appellants' offer of proof and entered judgment for the landlord. The District of Columbia Court of Appeals affirmed, rejecting the argument made by appellants that the landlord was under a contractual duty to maintain the premises in compliance with the Housing Regulations.

II

Since, in traditional analysis, a lease was the conveyance of an interest in land, courts have usually utilized the special rules governing real property transactions to resolve controversies involving leases. However, as the Supreme Court has noted in another context, "the body of private property law, more than almost any other

---

[3] Rule 4(c) of the Landlord and Tenant Branch of the Court of General Sessions provides:

In suits in this branch for recovery of possession of property in which the basis of recovery of possession is nonpayment of rent, tenants may set up an equitable defense or claim by way of recoupment or set-off in an amount equal to the rent claim. No counterclaim may be filed unless plaintiff asks for money judgment for rent. The exclusion of prosecution of any claims in this branch shall be without prejudice to the prosecution of any claims in other branches of the court.

branch of law, has been shaped by distinctions whose validity is largely historical." Jones v. United States, 362 U.S. 257, 266 (1960). Courts have a duty to reappraise old doctrines in the light of the facts and values of contemporary life — particularly old common law doctrines which the courts themselves created and developed. As we have said before, "The continued vitality of the common law depends upon its ability to reflect contemporary community values and ethics." Whetzel v. Jess Fisher Management Co., 282 F.2d 943, 946 (D.C. Cir. 1960).

The assumption of landlord-tenant law, derived from feudal property law, that a lease primarily conveyed to the tenant an interest in land may have been reasonable in a rural, agrarian society; it may continue to be reasonable in some leases involving farming or commercial land. In these cases, the value of the lease to the tenant is the land itself. But in the case of the modern apartment dweller, the value of the lease is that it gives him a place to live. The city dweller who seeks to lease an apartment on the third floor of a tenement has little interest in the land 30 or 40 feet below, or even in the bare right to possession within the four walls of his apartment. When American city dwellers, both rich and poor, seek "shelter" today, they seek a well known package of goods and services[9] — a package which includes not merely walls and ceilings, but also adequate heat, light and ventilation, serviceable plumbing facilities, secure windows and doors, proper sanitation, and proper maintenance.

Professor Powell summarizes the present state of the law:

> The complexities of city life, and the proliferated problems of modern society in general, have created new problems for lessors and lessees and these have been commonly handled by specific clauses inserted in leases. This growth in the number and detail of specific lease covenants has reintroduced into the law of estates for years a predominantly contractual ingredient. In practice, the law today concerning estates for years consists chiefly of rules determining the construction and effect of lease covenants.

2 R. Powell, Real Property ¶ 221(1) at 179 (1967).

Ironically, however, the rules governing the construction and interpretation of "predominantly contractual" obligations in leases have too often remained rooted in old property law.

Some courts have realized that certain of the old rules of property law governing leases are inappropriate for today's transactions. In order to reach results more in accord with the legitimate expectations of the parties and the standards of the community, courts have been gradually introducing more modern precepts of contract law in interpreting leases. Proceeding piecemeal has, however, led to confusion where "decisions are frequently conflicting, not because of a healthy disagreement on social policy, but because of the lingering impact of rules whose policies are long since dead."[12] In our judgment the trend toward treating leases as contracts is wise and well considered. Our holding in this case reflects a belief that

---

[9] See, e.g., National Commission on Urban Problems, Building the American City 9 (1968). The extensive standards set out in the Housing Regulations provide a good guide to community expectations.

[12] Kessler, *The Protection of the Consumer Under Modern Sales Law*, 74 Yale L.J. 262, 263 (1964).

leases of urban dwelling units should be interpreted and construed like any other contract.[13]

III

Modern contract law has recognized that the buyer of goods and services in an industrialized society must rely upon the skill and honesty of the supplier to assure that goods and services purchased are of adequate quality. In interpreting most contracts, courts have sought to protect the legitimate expectations of the buyer and have steadily widened the seller's responsibility for the quality of goods and services through implied warranties of fitness and merchantability. Thus without any special agreement a merchant will be held to warrant that his goods are fit for the ordinary purposes for which such goods are used and that they are at least of reasonably average quality. Moreover, if the supplier has been notified that goods are required for a specific purpose, he will be held to warrant that any goods sold are fit for that purpose. These implied warranties have become widely accepted and well established features of the common law, supported by the overwhelming body of case law. Today most states as well as the District of Columbia have codified and enacted these warranties into statute, as to the sale of goods, in the Uniform Commercial Code.

Implied warranties of quality have not been limited to cases involving sales. The consumer renting a chattel, paying for services, or buying a combination of goods and services must rely upon the skill and honesty of the supplier to at least the same extent as a purchaser of goods. Courts have not hesitated to find implied warranties of fitness and merchantability in such situations. In most areas product liability law has moved far beyond "mere" implied warranties running between two parties in privity with each other.

The rigid doctrines of real property law have tended to inhibit the application of implied warranties to transactions involving real estate. Now, however, courts have begun to hold sellers and developers of real property responsible for the quality of their product. For example, builders of new homes have recently been held liable to purchasers for improper construction on the ground that the builders had breached an implied warranty of fitness. In other cases courts have held builders of new homes liable for breach of an implied warranty that all local building regulations had been complied with. And following the developments in other areas, very recent decisions and commentary suggest the possible extension of liability to parties other than the immediate seller for improper construction of residential real estate.

---

[13] This approach does not deny the possible importance of the fact that land is involved in a transaction. The interpretation and construction of contracts between private parties has always required courts to be sensitive and responsive to myriad different factors. We believe contract doctrines allow courts to be properly sensitive to all relevant factors in interpreting lease obligations. We also intend no alteration of statutory or case law definitions of the term "real property" for purposes of statutes or decisions on recordation, descent, conveyancing, creditors' rights, etc. We contemplate only that contract law is to determine the rights and obligations of the parties to the lease agreement, as between themselves. The civil law has always viewed the lease as a contract, and in our judgment that perspective has proved superior to that of the common law. See 2 M. Planiol, Treatise on the Civil Law § 1663 et seq. (1959); 11 La.Stat.Ann., Civil Code, Art. 2669 (1952).

Despite this trend in the sale of real estate, many courts have been unwilling to imply warranties of quality, specifically a warranty of habitability, into leases of apartments. Recent decisions have offered no convincing explanation for their refusal; rather they have relied without discussion upon the old common law rule that the lessor is not obligated to repair unless he covenants to do so in the written lease contract. In our judgment, the old no-repair rule cannot coexist with the obligations imposed on the landlord by a typical modern housing code, and must be abandoned in favor of an implied warranty of habitability.[29] In the District of Columbia, the standards of this warranty are set out in the Housing Regulations.

IV

A. In our judgment the common law itself must recognize the landlord's obligation to keep his premises in a habitable condition. This conclusion is compelled by three separate considerations. First, we believe that the old rule was based on certain factual assumptions which are no longer true; on its own terms, it can no longer be justified. Second, we believe that the consumer protection cases discussed above require that the old rule be abandoned in order to bring residential landlord-tenant law into harmony with the principles on which those cases rest. Third, we think that the nature of today's urban housing market also dictates abandonment of the old rule.

The common law rule absolving the lessor of all obligation to repair originated in the early Middle Ages. Such a rule was perhaps well suited to an agrarian economy; the land was more important[31] than whatever small living structure was included in the leasehold, and the tenant farmer was fully capable of making repairs himself.[32] These historical facts were the basis on which the common law constructed its rule; they also provided the necessary prerequisites for its application.

Court decisions in the late 1800's began to recognize that the factual assumptions of the common law were no longer accurate in some cases. For example, the common law, since it assumed that the land was the most important part of the leasehold, required a tenant to pay rent even if any building on the land was destroyed. See Paradine v. Jane, 82 Eng. Rep. 897 (K.B. 1947); 1 American Law of Property, § 3.103. Faced with such a rule and the ludicrous results it produced, in 1863 the New York Court of Appeals declined to hold that an upper story tenant was obliged to continue paying rent after his apartment building burned down. Graves v. Berdan, 26 N.Y. 498 (1863). The court simply pointed out that the urban

---

[29] Although the present cases involve written leases, we think there is no particular significance in this fact. The landlord's warranty is implied in oral and written leases for all types of tenancies.

[31] The land was so central to the original common law conception of a leasehold that rent was viewed as "issuing" from the land: "The governing idea is that the land is bound to pay the rent. We may almost go to the length of saying that the land pays it through (the tenant's) hand." 2 F. Pollock & F. Maitland, The History of English Law 131 (2d ed. 1923).

[32] Many later judicial opinions have added another justification of the old common law rule. They have invoked the timeworn cry of caveat emptor and argued that a lessee has the opportunity to inspect the premises. On the basis of his inspection, the tenant must then take the premises "as is," according to this reasoning. As an historical matter, the opportunity to inspect was not thought important when the rule was first devised.

tenant had no interest in the land, only in the attached building.

Another line of cases created an exception to the no-repair rule for short term leases of furnished dwellings. See 1 American Law of Property § 3.45, at 267-268, and cases cited therein. The Massachusetts Supreme Judicial Court, a court not known for its willingness to depart from the common law, supported this exception, pointing out:

> [A] different rule should apply to one who hires a furnished room, or a furnished house, for a few days, or a few weeks or months. Its fitness for immediate use of a particular kind, as indicated by its appointments, is a far more important element entering into the contract than when there is a mere lease of real estate. One who lets for a short term a house provided with all furnishings and appointments for immediate residence may be supposed to contract in reference to a well-understood purpose of the hirer to use it as a habitation. It would be unreasonable to hold, under such circumstances, that the landlord does not impliedly agree that what he is letting is a house suitable for occupation in its condition at the time.

Ingalls v. Hobbs, 31 N.E. 286 (1892).

These cases demonstrate that some courts began some time ago to question the common law's assumptions that the land was the most important feature of a leasehold and that the tenant could feasibly make any necessary repairs himself. Where those assumptions no longer reflect contemporary housing patterns, the courts have created exceptions to the general rule that landlords have no duty to keep their premises in repair. It is overdue for courts to admit that these assumptions are no longer true with regard to all urban housing.

Today's urban tenants, the vast majority of whom live in multiple dwelling houses, are interested, not in the land, but solely in a house suitable for occupation. Furthermore, today's city dweller usually has a single, specialized skill unrelated to maintenance work; he is unable to make repairs like the "jack-of-all-trades" farmer who was the common law's model of the lessee. Further, unlike his agrarian predecessor who often remained on one piece of land for his entire life, urban tenants today are more mobile than ever before. A tenant's tenure in a specific apartment will often not be sufficient to justify efforts at repairs. In addition, the increasing complexity of today's dwellings renders them much more difficult to repair than the structures of earlier times. In a multiple dwelling repair may require access to equipment and areas in the control of the landlord. Low and middle income tenants, even if they were interested in making repairs, would be unable to obtain any financing for major repairs since they have no long-term interest in the property.

Our approach to the common law of landlord and tenant ought to be aided by principles derived from the consumer protection cases referred to [in Part III] above. In a lease contract, a tenant seeks to purchase from his landlord shelter for a specified period of time. The landlord sells housing as a commercial businessman and has much greater opportunity, incentive and capacity to inspect and maintain the condition of his building. Moreover, the tenant must rely upon the skill and bona fides of his landlord at least as much as a car buyer must rely upon the car manufacturer. In dealing with major problems, such as heating, plumbing, electrical or structural defects, the tenant's position corresponds precisely with "the ordinary consumer who cannot be expected to have the knowledge or capacity or even the opportunity to make adequate inspection of mechanical instrumentalities, like automobiles, and to decide for himself whether they are reasonably fit for the designed purpose." Henningsen v. Bloomfield Motors, Inc., 161 A.2d 69, 78 (N.J. 1960).[42]

Since a lease contract specifies a particular period of time during which the tenant has a right to use his apartment for shelter, he may legitimately expect that the apartment will be fit for habitation for the time period for which it is rented. We point out that in the present cases there is no allegation that appellants' apartments were in poor condition or in violation of the housing code at the commencement of the leases. Since the lessees continue to pay the same rent, they were entitled to expect that the landlord would continue to keep the premises in their beginning condition during the lease term. It is precisely such expectations that the law now recognizes as deserving of formal, legal protection.

Even beyond the rationale of traditional products liability law, the relationship of landlord and tenant suggests further compelling reasons for the law's protection of the tenants' legitimate expectations of quality. The inequality in bargaining power between landlord and tenant has been well documented. Tenants have very little leverage to enforce demands for better housing. Various impediments to competition in the rental housing market, such as racial and class discrimination and standardized form leases, mean that landlords place tenants in a take it or leave it situation. The increasingly severe shortage of adequate housing further increases the landlord's bargaining power and escalates the need for maintaining and improving the existing stock. Finally, the findings by various studies of the social impact of bad housing has led to the realization that poor housing is detrimental to the whole society, not merely to the unlucky ones who must suffer the daily indignity of living in a slum.

Thus we are led by our inspection of the relevant legal principles and precedents to the conclusion that the old common law rule imposing an obligation upon the lessee to repair during the lease term was really never intended to apply to residential urban leaseholds. Contract principles established in other areas of the law provide a more rational framework for the apportionment of landlord-tenant responsibilities; they strongly suggest that a warranty of habitability be implied into all contracts[49] for urban dwellings.

B. We believe, in any event, that the District's housing code requires that a warranty of habitability be implied in the leases of all housing that it covers. The

---

[42] Nor should the average tenant be thought capable of "inspecting" plaster, floorboards, roofing, kitchen appliances, etc. To the extent, however, that some defects are obvious, the law must take note of the present housing shortage. Tenants may have no real alternative but to accept such housing with the expectation that the landlord will make necessary repairs. Where this is so, caveat emptor must of necessity be rejected.

[49] We need not consider the provisions of the written lease governing repairs since this implied warranty of the landlord could not be excluded. See Henningsen v. Bloomfield Motors, Inc., supra. See also Note 58, *infra*.

housing code — formally designated the Housing Regulations of the District of Columbia — was established and authorized by the Commissioners of the District of Columbia on August 11, 1955. Since that time, the code has been updated by numerous orders of the Commissioners. The 75 pages of the Regulations provide a comprehensive regulatory scheme setting forth in some detail: (a) the standards which housing in the District of Columbia must meet; (b) which party, the lessor or the lessee, must meet each standard; and (c) a system of inspections, notifications and criminal penalties. The Regulations themselves are silent on the question of private remedies.

Two previous decisions of this court, however, have held that the Housing Regulations create legal rights and duties enforceable in tort by private parties. In *Whetzel v. Jess Fisher Management Co.*, 282 F.2d 943 (D.C. Cir. 1960), we followed the leading case of *Altz v. Leiberson*, 134 N.E. 703 (N.Y. 1922), in holding (1) that the housing code altered the common law rule and imposed a duty to repair upon the landlord, and (2) that a right of action accrued to a tenant injured by the landlord's breach of this duty. As Judge Cardozo wrote in *Lieberson*:

> We may be sure that the framers of this statute, when regulating tenement life, had uppermost in thought the care of those who are unable to care for themselves. The Legislature must have known that unless repairs in the rooms of the poor were made by the landlord, they would not be made by any one. The duty imposed became commensurate with the need. The right to seek redress is not limited to the city or its officers. The right extends to all whom there was a purpose to protect.

134 N.E. at 704. Recently, in *Kanelos v. Kettler*, 406 F.2d 951, 953 (D.C. Cir. 1968), we reaffirmed our position in *Whetzel*, holding that "the Housing Regulations did impose maintenance obligations upon [the landlord] which he was not free to ignore."

The District of Columbia Court of Appeals gave further effect to the Housing Regulations in *Brown v. Southall Realty Co.*, 237 A.2d 834 (1968). There the landlord knew at the time the lease was signed that housing code violations existed which rendered the apartment "unsafe and unsanitary." Viewing the lease as a contract, the District of Columbia Court of Appeals held that the premises were let in violation of Sections 2304[53] and 2501 of the Regulations and that the lease, therefore, was void as an illegal contract. In the light of *Brown*, it is clear not only that the housing code creates privately enforceable duties as held in *Whetzel*, but that the basic validity of every housing contract depends upon substantial compliance with the housing code at the beginning of the lease term.

The *Brown* court relied particularly upon Section 2501 of the Regulations which provides:

> Every premises accommodating one or more habitations shall be maintained and kept in repair so as to provide decent living accommodations for

---

[53] "No person shall rent or offer to rent any habitation, or the furnishings thereof, unless such habitation and its furnishings are in a clean, safe and sanitary condition, in repair, and free from rodents or vermin."

the occupants. This part of this Code contemplates more than mere basic repairs and maintenance to keep out the elements; its purpose is to include repairs and maintenance designed to make a premises or neighborhood healthy and safe.

By its terms, this section applies to maintenance and repair during the lease term. Under the *Brown* holding, serious failure to comply with this section before the lease term begins renders the contract void. We think it untenable to find that this section has no effect on the contract after it has been signed. To the contrary, by signing the lease the landlord has undertaken a continuing obligation to the tenant to maintain the premises in accordance with all applicable law.

This principle of implied warranty is well established. Courts often imply relevant law into contracts to provide a remedy for any damage caused by one party's illegal conduct. In a case closely analogous to the present ones, the Illinois Supreme Court held that a builder who constructed a house in violation of the Chicago building code had breached his contract with the buyer:

> The law existing at the time and place of the making of the contract is deemed a part of the contract, as though expressly referred to or incorporated in it.
>
> The rationale for this rule is that the parties to the contract would have expressed that which the law implies "had they not supposed that it was unnecessary to speak of it because the law provided for it." Consequently, the courts, in construing the existing law as part of the express contract, are not reading into the contract provisions different from those expressed and intended by the parties, as defendants contend, but are merely construing the contract in accordance with the intent of the parties.[56]

We follow the Illinois court in holding that the housing code must be read into housing contracts. The duties imposed by the Housing Regulations may not be waived or shifted by agreement if the Regulations specifically place the duty upon the lessor.[58] Criminal penalties are provided if these duties are ignored. This regulatory structure was established by the Commissioners because, in their judgment, the grave conditions in the housing market required serious action. Yet official enforcement of the housing code has been far from uniformly effective.

---

[56] Schiro v. W.E. Gould & Co., 18 Ill.2d at 544, 165 N.E.2d at 290. As a general proposition, it is undoubtedly true that parties to a contract intend that applicable law will be complied with by both sides. We recognize, however, that reading statutory provisions into private contracts may have little factual support in the intentions of the particular parties now before us. But, for reasons of public policy, warranties are often implied into contracts by operation of law in order to meet generally prevailing standards of honesty and fair dealing. When the public policy has been enacted into law like the housing code, that policy will usually have deep roots in the expectations and intentions of most people. See Costigan, *Implied-in-Fact Contracts and Mutual Assent*, 33 Harv.L.Rev. 376, 383-385 (1920).

[58] Any private agreement to shift the duties would be illegal and unenforceable. The precedents dealing with industrial safety statutes are directly in point: "The only question remaining is whether the courts will enforce or recognize as against a servant an agreement express or implied on his part to waive the performance of a statutory duty of the master imposed for the protection of the servant, and in the interest of the public, and enforceable by criminal prosecution. We do not think they will. To do so would be to nullify the object of the statute." Narramore v. Cleveland, C., C. & St. L.Ry. Co., 96 F. 298, 302 (6th Cir. 1899). See W. Prosser, Torts § 67 at 468-469 (3d ed. 1964) and cases cited therein.

Innumerable studies have documented the desperate condition of rental housing in the District of Columbia and in the nation.

In view of these circumstances, we think the conclusion reached by the Supreme Court of Wisconsin as to the effect of a housing code on the old common law rule cannot be avoided:

> The legislature has made a policy judgment — that it is socially (and politically) desirable to impose these duties on a property owner — which has rendered the old common law rule obsolete. To follow the old rule of no implied warranty of habitability in leases would, in our opinion, be inconsistent with the current legislative policy concerning housing standards.[60]

We therefore hold that the Housing Regulations imply a warranty of habitability, measured by the standards which they set out, into leases of all housing that they cover.

V

In the present cases, the landlord sued for possession for nonpayment of rent. Under contract principles,[61] however, the tenant's obligation to pay rent is dependent upon the landlord's performance of his obligations, including his warranty to maintain the premises in habitable condition. In order to determine whether any rent is owed to the landlord, the tenants must be given an opportunity to prove the housing code violations alleged as breach of the landlord's warranty.[62]

At trial, the finder of fact must make two findings: (1) whether the alleged violations[63] existed during the period for which past due rent is claimed, and (2) what portion, if any or all, of the tenant's obligation to pay rent was suspended by the landlord's breach. If no part of the tenant's rental obligation is found to have been suspended, then a judgment for possession may issue forthwith. On the other hand, if the jury determines that the entire rental obligation has been extinguished by the landlord's total breach, then the action for possession on the ground of nonpayment must fail.[64] The jury may find that part of the tenant's rental obligation

---

[60] Pines v. Perssion, 111 N.W.2d 409, 412-413 (Wis. 1961).

[61] In extending all contract remedies for breach to the parties to a lease, we include an action for specific performance of the landlord's implied warranty of habitability.

[62] To be relevant, of course, the violations must affect the tenant's apartment or common areas which the tenant uses. Moreover, the contract principle that no one may benefit from his own wrong will allow the landlord to defend by proving the damage was caused by the tenant's wrongful action. However, violations resulting from inadequate repairs or materials which disintegrate under normal use would not be assignable to the tenant. Also we agree with the District of Columbia Court of Appeals that the tenant's private rights do not depend on official inspection or official finding of violation by the city government. Diamond Housing Corp. v. Robinson, 257 A.2d 492, 494 (1969).

[63] The jury should be instructed that one or two minor violations standing alone which do not affect habitability are de minimis and would not entitle the tenant to a reduction in rent.

[64] As soon as the landlord made the necessary repairs rent would again become due. Our holding, of course, affects only eviction for nonpayment of rent. The landlord is free to seek eviction at the termination of the lease or on any other legal ground.

has been suspended but that part of the unpaid back rent is indeed owed to the landlord. In these circumstances, no judgment for possession should issue if the tenant agrees to pay the partial rent found to be due. If the tenant refuses to pay the partial amount, a judgment for possession may then be entered.

The judgment of the District of Columbia Court of Appeals is reversed and the cases are remanded for further proceedings consistent with this opinion.[67]

So ordered.

NOTES AND QUESTIONS

A. The Tenant's Right to Habitable Premises

1. **Sources of the warranty.** Did the court in *Javins* recognize a warranty of habitability because (a) the parties expressly or impliedly created one; (b) modern common law requires such a warranty; (c) the District's housing code requires the implication of the warranty into all housing covered by the code, or (d) all of the above? Is the landlord responsible for the condition of the leased premises only at the outset of the lease or also during the term of the lease?

2. **Content of the implied warranty.** What are the advantages and disadvantages of each of the following ways of giving content to the implied warranty of habitability?

a. Winchester Management Corp. v. Staten, 361 A.2d 187 (D.C. Ct. App. 1976) (abatement of rent allowed for the landlord's failure to provide hot water, but not air conditioning; lease contained promise by landlord to supply both):

> *Javins* held that "a warranty of habitability, measured by the standards set out in the Housing Regulations for the District of Columbia, is implied by operation of law into leases." We do not stray from nor expand upon that holding. We define habitable housing as those dwelling units which substantially comply with the standards detailed in the Housing Regulations. We are satisfied that the housing code represents the legislative evaluation of the requirements of habitability, and that the requirements

---

[67] Appellants in the present cases offered to pay rent into the registry of the court during the present action. We think this is an excellent protective procedure. If the tenant defends against an action for possession on the basis of breach of the landlord's warranty of habitability, the trial court may require the tenant to make future rent payments into the registry of the court as they become due; such a procedure would be appropriate only while the tenant remains in possession. The escrowed money will, however, represent rent for the period between the time the landlord files suit and the time the case comes to trial. In the normal course of litigation, the only factual question at trial would be the condition of the apartment during the time the landlord alleged rent was due and not paid. As a general rule, the escrowed money should be apportioned between the landlord and the tenant after trial on the basis of the finding of rent actually due for the period at issue in the suit. To insure fair apportionment, however, we think either party should be permitted to amend its complaint or answer at any time before trial, to allege a change in the condition of the apartment. In this event, the finder of fact should make a separate finding as to the condition of the apartment at the time at which the amendment was filed. This new finding will have no effect upon the original action; it will only affect the distribution of the escrowed rent paid after the filing of the amendment.

set forth therein are both strict and comprehensive. Moreover, they provide accessible and objective criteria by which to judge the landlord's satisfaction of his warranty.

b. Green v. Superior Court, 517 P.2d 1168 (Cal. 1974):

The recent case of Academy Spires, Inc. v. Brown, 268 A.2d 556, 559 (N.J. Super. Ct. 1970), gives a good indication of the general scope of the warranty of habitability. In that case, a tenant in a multi-story apartment building complained of a series of defects, including (1) the periodic failure to supply heat and water, (2) the malfunctioning of an incinerator, (3) the failure in hot water supply, (4) several leaks in the bathroom, (5) defective venetian blinds, (6) cracks in plaster walls, (7) unpainted condition of walls and (8) a nonfunctioning elevator. The *Academy Spires* court held: "Some of these clearly go to the bare living requirements. In a modern society one cannot be expected to live in a multi-storied apartment building without heat, hot water, garbage disposal or elevator service. Failure to supply such things is a breach of the implied covenant of habitability. Malfunction of venetian blinds, water leaks, wall cracks, lack of painting, at least of the magnitude presented here, go to what may be called 'amenities.' Living with lack of painting, water leaks and defective venetian blinds may be unpleasant and aesthetically unsatisfying, but does not come within the category of uninhabitability. Such things will not be considered in diminution of the rent." In most cases substantial compliance with those applicable building and housing code standards which materially affect health and safety will suffice to meet the landlord's obligations under the common law implied warranty of habitability we now recognize.

c. Park Hill Terrace Associates v. Glennon, 369 A.2d 938 (N.J. Super. Ct. App. Div. 1977) (abatement allowed for landlord's failure to provide air conditioning):

[The] landlord argues that air conditioning in this case was but an amenity and that "air conditioning is but a luxury." We do not deem it controlling that the leasing contract contemplated the providing of air conditioning and that the rentals were higher because of it. There are many instances of breaches of the leasing agreement which would not affect habitability and thus would not be relevant in a dispossess action although they might very well be a proper basis for a separate cause of action for breach of contract.

See also Timber Ridge Town House v. Dietz, 338 A.2d 21 (N.J. Super. Ct. Law Div. 1975) (new upscale townhouse: abatement allowed for mud overflowing tenant's patio but not for delay in construction of playground and pool; patio, pool, and playground were all highlighted in landlord's rental brochures).

3. **Waiver.** Under *Javins*, are waivers of the warranty of habitability allowed? The Restatement Second of Property (Landlord and Tenant) § 5.6 allows waivers, unless they "are unconscionable or significantly against public policy." In P.H. Investment v. Oliver, 818 P.2d 1018, 1021-1022 (Utah 1991), the court adopted what it called a "workable compromise" between these positions: waivers must be express, and any waiver is effective only as to the specific defects listed as waived. The court said that its approach would "invalidate boilerplate language, eliminate any duty of inspection [by the tenant], and protect against uninformed waivers of

any latent defects"; the requirement of an express waiver "should have the advantage of preventing much of the case-by-case litigation on the subject of implied waivers which may be generated by adherence to the Restatement approach."

4. **Comparisons: warranty of merchantability and warranty of habitability.** Under the implied warranty of merchantability established by the Uniform Commercial Code for the sale of goods, the warranty can be disclaimed by the seller, except that disclaimers of liability for personal injuries resulting from defective goods are limited. *See* UCC §§ 2-316, 2-302, 2-719(3). The implied sales warranty is a representation that the goods are merchantable at the time of sale; it does not include a promise to repair defects that do not exist when the goods are sold but that arise after purchase. *See generally* Samuel Abbott, *Housing Policy, Housing Codes and Tenant Remedies: An Integration*, 56 B.U. L. Rev. 1 (1976). Do these differences from the implied warranty of habitability suggest that courts are treating the landlord-tenant relationship as a status to which certain incidents apply rather than as a contract in which the parties determine their own bargain?

5. **The statutory warranty.** In some states, the warranty of habitability is provided by a statute of statewide applicability. For extensive discussions, see Roger A. Cunningham, *The New Implied and Statutory Warranties of Habitability in Residential Leases: From Contract to Status*, 16 Urb. L. Ann. 3 (1979); 2 Powell on Real Property § 16B.04[3]; Robert S. Schoshinski, American Law of Landlord and Tenant §§ 3:30-3:45 (1980).

6. **The minority view.** The courts in a few states have rejected the implied warranty of habitability. *See* 2 Powell on Real Property § 16B.04[2][a], at 16B-50 & n.43 (citing cases from Alabama, Colorado, Kentucky, South Carolina, and Wyoming, but noting that South Carolina subsequently adopted the implied warranty by statute).

7. **Common law exceptions.** Before the 1970s, courts recognized exceptions to the no-warranty rule, finding an implied warranty of habitability in (a) a lease of furnished premises for a short term, *see* Ingalls v. Hobbs, 31 N.E. 286 (Mass. 1892), and (b) a lease of premises under construction when the lease was entered into, *see* J.D. Young Corp. v. McClintic, 26 S.W.2d 460 (Tex. Civ. App. 1930). *See generally* 2 Powell on Real Property § 16B.04[1]. These exceptions should remain available in those states that reject the general warranty developed in *Javins*. What rationale(s) support these exceptions?

8. **Notice and cure.** Under *Javins*, must the tenant notify the landlord of any defective conditions as a prerequisite to exercising any of the remedies provided by the implied warranty? Does the landlord have a reasonable time after notice or knowledge of the defect to correct the defect? *See* 2 Powell on Real Property § 16B.04[2][e].

B. Remedies

9. **Withholding and abatement: policy.** Rent withholding is the procedure by which the tenant asserts his or her damages claim for the landlord's breach of the warranty of habitability; abatement is the amount of reduction of the tenant's monthly rent liability to reflect those damages. How does a tenant implement the withholding and abatement remedy provided by *Javins*? If tenants can litigate

habitability claims in summary eviction proceedings, the proceedings will be less summary. Is that a problem? The court in Green v. Superior Court, 517 P.2d 1168, 1181 (Cal. 1974), thought not:

> In the first place, while the state does have a significant interest in preserving a speedy repossession remedy, that interest cannot justify the exclusion of matters which are essential to a just resolution of the question of possession at issue. Certainly the interest in preserving the summary nature of an action cannot outweigh the interest of doing substantial justice. To hold the preservation of the summary proceeding of paramount importance would be analogous to the tail wagging the dog.

> Second, we believe the landlord's contention greatly exaggerates the detrimental effect of the recognition of this defense on the summary unlawful detainer procedure. [D]efendants in unlawful detainer actions have long been permitted to raise those affirmative defenses — both legal and equitable — that are directly relevant to the issue of possession; over the years, the unlawful detainer action has remained an efficient, summary procedure. We see no reason why the availability of a warranty of habitability defense should frustrate the summary procedure when the availability of these other defenses has not. Indeed, the landlord's dire forecast fades in the light of the host of recent out-of-state decisions which, in adopting a warranty of habitability, have explicitly permitted the issue to be raised in summary dispossession proceedings. In addition, several "model" landlord-tenant codes, recently drafted under the auspices of highly regarded legal bodies, have also recommended the recognition of this defense in such summary actions. See Uniform Residential Landlord-Tenant Act (1972) § 4.105; Model Residential Landlord-Tenant Code (Tent. Draft 1970) §§ 2-203(1), 3-210. As these authorities recognize, this development accords with "[t]he salutary trend toward determination of the rights and liabilities of litigants in one, rather than multiple proceedings." Jack Spring, Inc. v. Little, 280 N.E.2d 208, 213 (Ill. 1972).

> Moreover, sound procedural safeguards suffice to protect the landlord's economic interests without depriving the tenant of a meaningful opportunity to raise the breach of warranty issue. [The trial court, at the request of either party, may require the tenant to pay rent at the contract rate while the tenant remains in possession.] Such a procedure can serve as a fair means of protection of landlords from potential abuses of the proposed warranty of habitability defense.

Does *Javins* require the "sound procedural safeguard" (escrow of the withheld rent) identified by the court in *Green*? Should it be required? Is it a good practice anyway — what happens if the tenant doesn't pay whatever rent remains due after the tenant's damages for the habitability violation are subtracted from rent? Is a tenant who claims a habitability defense and fails to escrow money acting in bad faith, and raising a frivolous claim?

10. **Withholding and dependency of promises.** *Javins* identifies dependency of promises as the rationale for the withholding remedy, as do almost all post-*Javins* cases. That rationale suffers from a major theoretical weakness. In

contract law, dependency is relevant to a contracting party's termination of the contract for the other party's material breach; a party who affirms a contract following such a breach continues to owe his own performance. The tenant who remains in possession affirms the lease and consequently still owes rent, and summary dispossession statutes usually provide that nonpayment of rent is a basis for eviction. *See* John A. Humbach, *The Common-Law Conception of Leasing: Mitigation, Habitability, and Dependence of Covenants*, 60 Wash. U. L.Q. 1213, 1276-1281 (1983). More persuasive rationales for withholding and abatement might have been found elsewhere: perhaps in public policy (see Notes 9 and 12) or *state* constitutional limits on summary dispossession statutes (compare Note 11), or (as Professor Humbach argues), in expansion of the traditional equitable limitations on the forfeiture of property interests, or perhaps in the recognition of a narrower withholding remedy. *See* UCC § 2-717 (when goods are defective, buyer may withhold amount of damages from future installments of the purchase price); Jack Spring, Inc. v. Little, 280 N.E.2d 208, 222 (Ill. 1972) (dissenting opinion of Justice Ryan: tenant who remains in occupancy after breach of warranty of habitability "must tender an amount of rent equal to the reasonable rental value of the premises in the unrepaired condition; and if this amount is refused by the landlord and a forcible detainer action instituted, the tenant should in his answer be permitted to plead the breach of the covenant to repair and the reduced rental value caused by the breach"). Whatever its merits, the linkage of the withholding and abatement remedy to dependency doctrine is a *fait accompli* in residential habitability cases; the question of rationale remains important, however, where the remedy is controversial, as in commercial leases. *See* Section B.3.b below.

11. **Due process.** The Supreme Court has held that a tenant's inability to raise the landlord's breach of contract in a summary dispossession proceeding (an inability which the Court attributed to independency doctrine) is not unconstitutional as a denial of due process; the tenant can bring a separate suit for damages for breach of the covenant of quiet enjoyment, and get a full hearing in that suit on the question of the landlord's breach. *See* Lindsey v. Normet, 405 U.S. 56 (1972). Is that rationale more plausible in a commercial lease than in a residential one? Shouldn't parties to a contract — or all wronged parties for that matter — be entitled to a *practical* remedy?

12. **Rent and possession?** In some states, the landlord can recover past due rent as well as possession in the summary proceeding. Is it fair to allow the landlord to settle all accounts with the tenant in one proceeding, but to relegate the tenant to a separate proceeding to recover damages? Is it efficient?

13. **Abatement; other breaches of contract.** Suppose that the landlord promises the tenant something that, from a habitability standpoint, would be classified as an "amenity," not entitling the tenant to the withholding and abatement remedy under habitability principles. Is the withholding and abatement remedy available (should it be) for breaches other than breach of the warranty of habitability? For a negative answer, see Winchester Management Corp. v. Staten (Note 2 above) (abatement for landlord's failure to provide promised air conditioning denied):

> In our view the mutuality of the contractual relationship between tenant and landlord properly is seen as the payment of rent in exchange for the

providing and maintaining of a livable dwelling. [S]ince the tenant's liability for the rent is predicated upon the receipt of habitable housing, only the breach, in whole or in part, of the landlord's covenant to provide habitable housing abrogates the tenant's responsibility for rent. To hold otherwise could have the potentially devastating effect of depriving the landlord of the rental income needed to maintain the premises and correct any defective conditions about which the tenants complain.

See also Timber Ridge Town House v. Dietz, Note 2 above.

14. **Tenant remedies: summary.** The list of common law remedies potentially available to the tenant for the landlord's breach of the warranty of habitability (statutory remedies are discussed in Cunningham, Note 5, *supra*) is as follows:

a. *Termination* of the lease. Why is this unlikely to be appealing to the tenant?

b. *Damages.* The tenant's abatement of rent is calculated by deducting the tenant's damages from the withheld rent. The cases announce different formulas for computing damages: the difference between the premises as warranted and the premises as is, *cf.* UCC § 2-714; the difference between the agreed rent and the fair rental value of the defective premises; the "proportion of the rent which the fair rental value after the event giving the right to abate bears to the fair rental value before the event." Restatement Second § 11.1. In Timber Ridge Town House v. Dietz, 338 A.2d 21 (N.J. Super. Ct. Law Div. 1975), the opinion stated that "the court has little to guide the admeasurement of damages other than the application of equitable principles"; the judge viewed the premises, and ordered a 15% abatement. What are the problems with each of these measures of damages?

c. *Repair and deduct.* The tenant is entitled to make necessary repairs and deduct the cost of those repairs from future installments of rent. *See* Marini v. Ireland, 265 A.2d 526 (N.J. 1970). What are the legal and practical limitations of the repair-and-deduct remedy?

d. *Specific performance.* Would you expect a court to be receptive to a tenant's action to compel the landlord to bring the premises up to the required standard of habitability? *See* 2 Powell on Real Property § 16B.04[2][e]. What would be the impact on rentals if repair of the premises were required?

e. *Punitive damages.* In Hilder v. St. Peter, 478 A.2d 202 (Vt. 1984), the court indicated that egregious conduct by the landlord in failing to perform the warranty could be the basis for a claim of punitive damages. The tenant, however, had not pursued the question on appeal.

See generally James Charles Smith, *Tenant Remedies for Breach of Habitability: Tort Dimensions of a Contract Concept*, 35 Kan. L. Rev. 505 (1987) (detailed examination of tenant's remedies for landlord's breach of the warranty of habitability, other than remedies for personal injury).

PROBLEMS

4-I. The facts are these:

> The plaintiff Jane Doe is a tenant of the defendant New Bedford Housing Authority. She lives at the Shawmut Village public housing project in New Bedford, owned and operated by the defendant and consisting of 170 units in "two-story garden apartments." The plaintiff Jane Roe is also a tenant of the defendant. She lives at the Satellite Village public housing project in New Bedford, owned and operated by the defendant and consisting of 146 units in "two-story garden apartments."

> Both housing developments are plagued by unlawful drug activity which occurs in external common areas of the developments. The record reflects that those persons involved in the drug activity on the premises are both tenants and nontenants. The record further reflects that the defendant has attempted, pursuant to a standard provision in its leases, to evict those tenants who are involved in drug activity. The record reveals little or no action on the part of the defendant to remove nontenants. Police patrols in the area are infrequent.

Is the landlord in breach of duties owed to the tenants under the implied warranty of habitability? The covenant of quiet enjoyment? Must the landlord provide around the clock security or other police services? *See* Doe v. New Bedford Housing Authority, 630 N.E.2d 248 (Mass. 1994) (answers: no, yes, no).

4-J. T, a residential tenant, is a handyman. L offers to lease the premises to T for $500 per month with a warranty of habitability, or $400 per month "as is." T agrees and signs a lease containing a disclaimer of the implied warranty of habitability. T later defaults in making rent payments, and L sues for possession. May T raise L's breach of the warranty in L's suit? *See* Foisy v. Wyman, 515 P.2d 160 (Wash. 1976). Should it be relevant whether T has a spouse and children?

4-K. Suppose that evidence were available in a habitability case to show the following: the fair rental value of the premises as warranted under the implied warranty of habitability is $150 per month; the fair rental value of the premises in their defective condition is $100 per month; the stipulated rent is $100 per month. How much of an abatement is T entitled to?

4-L. (a) The lease term expires before T asserts a habitability claim. May T sue to recover her damages from the landlord's breach of the warranty of habitability? *See* Wade v. Jobe, 818 P.2d 1006 (Utah 1991); Berzito v. Gambino, 308 A.2d 17 (N.J. 1973).

(b) The rent is $300 per month. The premises are in violation of the warranty of habitability from January through April. T withholds rent in March and April. In the summary dispossession trial in April, the court determines that T is entitled to a 25% rent abatement. How much of an offset against the withheld rent does T receive? What is the issue? *See* 2 Powell on Real Property § 16B.04[2][e], at 62-63. If T cannot offset her damages for the months of January and February from the withheld rent, what is T's remedy, if any, for L's breach during those months? *See* C.F. Seabrook Co. v. Beck, 417 A.2d 89 (N.J. Super Ct. App. Div. 1980).

b. Habitability in Commercial Leases.

The implied warranty is widely adopted in cases involving residential leases, but not commercial leases. The following case is exceptional.

DAVIDOW v. INWOOD NORTH PROFESSIONAL GROUP
747 S.W.2d 373 (Tex. 1988)

SPEARS, JUSTICE.

This case presents the question of whether there is an implied warranty by a commercial landlord that the leased premises are suitable for their intended commercial purpose. Respondent Inwood North Professional Group — Phase I sued petitioner Dr. Joseph Davidow for unpaid rent on medical office space leased by Dr. Davidow. The jury found that Inwood materially breached the lease agreement and that the defects rendered the office space unsuitable for use as a medical office. The trial court rendered judgment that Inwood take nothing. The court of appeals reversed the trial court judgment and rendered judgment that Inwood recover unpaid rents for the remainder of the lease. See 731 S.W.2d 600.

Dr. Davidow entered into a five-year lease agreement with Inwood for medical office space. The lease required Dr. Davidow to pay Inwood $793.26 per month as rent. The lease also required Inwood to provide air conditioning, electricity, hot water, janitor and maintenance services, light fixtures, and security services. Shortly after moving into the office space, Dr. Davidow began experiencing problems with the building. The air conditioning did not work properly, often causing temperatures inside the office to rise above eighty-five degrees. The roof leaked whenever it rained, resulting in stained tiles and rotting, mildewed carpet. Patients were directed away from certain areas during rain so that they would not be dripped upon in the waiting room. Pests and rodents often infested the office. The hallways remained dark because hallway lights were unreplaced for months. Cleaning and maintenance were not provided. The parking lot was constantly filled with trash. Hot water was not provided, and on one occasion Dr. Davidow went without electricity for several days because Inwood failed to pay the electric bill. Several burglaries and various acts of vandalism occurred. Dr. Davidow finally moved out of the premises and discontinued rent payments approximately fourteen months before the lease expired.

Inwood sued Dr. Davidow for the unpaid rent and costs of restoration. Dr. Davidow answered by general denial and the affirmative defenses of material breach of the lease agreement, a void lease, and breach of an implied warranty that the premises were suitable for use as a medical office. The jury found that Inwood materially breached the lease, that Inwood warranted to Dr. Davidow that the lease space was suitable for a medical office, and that the lease space was not suitable for a medical office. One month after the jury returned its verdict, but before entry of judgment, the trial court allowed Dr. Davidow to amend his pleadings to include the defense of constructive eviction. The trial court then rendered judgment that Inwood take nothing and that Dr. Davidow recover $9,300 in damages.

With one justice dissenting, the court of appeals reversed the trial court judgment and rendered judgment in favor of Inwood for unpaid rent. The court of appeals held that because Inwood's covenant to maintain and repair the premises was independent of Dr. Davidow's covenant to pay rent, Inwood's breach of its covenant did not justify Dr. Davidow's refusal to pay rent. The court of appeals also held that the implied warranty of habitability does not extend to commercial leaseholds and that Dr. Davidow's pleadings did not support an award of affirmative relief.

Inwood contends that the defense of material breach of the covenant to repair is insufficient as a matter of law to defeat a landlord's claim for unpaid rent. In Texas, the courts have held that the landlord's covenant to repair the premises and the tenant's covenant to pay rent are independent covenants. Thus, a tenant is still under a duty to pay rent even though his landlord has breached his covenant to make repairs.

This theory of independent covenants in leases was established in early property law prior to the development of the concept of mutually dependent covenants in contract law. At common law, the lease was traditionally regarded as a conveyance of an interest in land, subject to the doctrine of caveat emptor. The landlord was required only to deliver the right of possession to the tenant; the tenant, in return, was required to pay rent to the landlord. Once the landlord delivered the right of possession, his part of the agreement was completed. The tenant's duty to pay rent continued as long as he retained possession, even if the buildings on the leasehold were destroyed or became uninhabitable. The landlord's breach of a lease covenant did not relieve the tenant of his duty to pay rent for the remainder of the term because the tenant still retained everything he was entitled to under the lease — the right of possession. All lease covenants were therefore considered independent.

In the past, this court has attempted to provide a more equitable and contemporary solution to landlord-tenant problems by easing the burden placed on tenants as a result of the independence of lease covenants and the doctrine of caveat emptor. In Kamarath v. Bennett, 568 S.W.2d 658 (Tex.1978), we reexamined the realities of the landlord-tenant relationship in a modern context and concluded that the agrarian common-law concept is no longer indicative of the contemporary relationship between the tenant and landlord. The land is of minimal importance to the modern tenant; rather, the primary subject of most leases is the structure located on the land and the services which are to be provided to the tenant. The modern residential tenant seeks to lease a dwelling suitable for living purposes. The landlord usually has knowledge of any defects in the premises that may render it uninhabitable. In addition, the landlord, as permanent owner of the premises, should rightfully bear the cost of any necessary repairs. In most instances the landlord is in a much better bargaining position than the tenant. Accordingly, we held in *Kamarath* that the landlord impliedly warrants that the premises are habitable and fit for living. We further implicitly recognized that the residential tenant's obligation to pay rent is dependent upon the landlord's performance under his warranty of habitability.

When a commercial tenant such as Dr. Davidow leases office space, many of the same considerations are involved. A significant number of commentators have recognized the similarities between residential and commercial tenants and concluded that residential warranties should be expanded to cover commercial property. See, e.g., Chused, *Contemporary Dilemmas of the Javins Defense: A Note on the Need for Procedural Reform in Landlord-Tenant Law*, 67 Geo.L.J. 1385, 1389 (1979); Greenfield & Margolies, *An Implied Warranty of Fitness in Nonresidential Leases*, 45 Albany L.Rev. 855 (1981); Levinson & Silver, *Do Commercial Property Tenants Possess Warranties of Habitability?*, 14 Real Estate L.J. 59 (1985); Note, *Landlord-Tenant — Should a Warranty of Fitness be Implied in Commercial Leases?*, 13 Rutgers L.J. 91 (1981); see also Restatement (Second) of Property § 5.1 reporter's note at 176 (1977).

It cannot be assumed that a commercial tenant is more knowledgeable about the quality of the structure than a residential tenant. A businessman cannot be expected to possess the expertise necessary to adequately inspect and repair the premises, and many commercial tenants lack the financial resources to hire inspectors and repairmen to assure the suitability of the premises. Note, *supra*, at 111. Additionally, because commercial tenants often enter into short-term leases, the tenants have limited economic incentive to make any extensive repairs to their premises. Levinson & Silver, *supra*, at 68. Consequently, commercial tenants generally rely on their landlords' greater abilities to inspect and repair the premises. *Id.*

There is no valid reason to imply a warranty of habitability in residential leases and not in commercial leases. Although minor distinctions can be drawn between residential and commercial tenants, those differences do not justify limiting the warranty to residential leaseholds. Therefore, we hold there is an implied warranty of suitability by the landlord in a commercial lease that the premises are suitable for their intended commercial purpose. This warranty means that at the inception of the lease there are no latent defects in the facilities that are vital to the use of the premises for their intended commercial purpose and that these essential facilities will remain in a suitable condition. If, however, the parties to a lease expressly agree that the tenant will repair certain defects, then the provisions of the lease will control.

We recognized in *Kamarath* that the primary objective underlying a residential leasing arrangement is "to furnish [the tenant] with quarters suitable for living purposes." *Kamarath*, 568 S.W.2d at 661. The same objective is present in a commercial setting. A commercial tenant desires to lease premises suitable for their intended commercial use. A commercial landlord impliedly represents that the premises are in fact suitable for that use and will remain in a suitable condition. The tenant's obligation to pay rent and the landlord's implied warranty of suitability are therefore mutually dependent.

The existence of a breach of the implied warranty of suitability in commercial leases is usually a fact question to be determined from the particular circumstances of each case. Among the factors to be considered when determining whether there has been a breach of this warranty are: the nature of the defect; its effect on the tenant's use of the premises; the length of time the defect persisted; the age of the structure; the amount of the rent; the area in which the premises are located; whether the tenant waived the defects; and whether the defect resulted from any unusual or abnormal use by the tenant.

The jury found that Inwood leased the space to Dr. Davidow for use as a medical office and that Inwood knew of the intended use. The evidence and jury findings further indicate that Dr. Davidow was unable to use the space for the intended purpose because acts and omissions by Inwood rendered the space unsuitable for use as a medical office. The jury findings establish that Inwood breached the implied warranty of suitability. Dr. Davidow was therefore justified in abandoning the premises and discontinuing his rent payments.

For the reasons stated, the court of appeals' judgment awarding Inwood damages for unpaid rent and attorney's fees is reversed and judgment is here rendered that Inwood take nothing.

NOTES AND QUESTIONS

1. **Is _Davidow_ an appropriate case for the warranty?** Make an argument that the _Davidow_ case really raises only a garden variety constructive eviction claim.

2. **The warranty in commercial leases.** Most courts that have considered the question have rejected the warranty in commercial leases. Authorities are collected in Paula C. Murray, _The Evolution of Implied Warranties in Commercial Real Estate Leases_, 28 U. Rich. L. Rev. 145 (1994); Anthony J. Vlatas, _An Economic Analysis of Implied Warranties of Fitness in Commercial Leases_, 94 Colum. L. Rev. 658, 667 (1994). The common law exception for premises under construction when the lease is executed (Note 7 after _Javins_) presumably is available to a commercial tenant. _Should_ a warranty of habitability be implied in commercial leases? If so, which ones?

3. **Waiver.** In Gym-N-I Playgrounds, Inc. v. Snider, 220 S.W.3d 905 (Tex. 2007), one clause in the lease provided that the tenant accepted the premises "as is," and that the landlord "has not made and does not make any representations as to the commercial suitability" of the premises. Another clause stated that the tenant "covenants and agrees, at Tenant's sole cost and expense, to perform all maintenance and repairs of the Premises." The landlord argued that those provisions constituted a waiver of the _Davidow_ warranty. The tenant argued that _Davidow_ allowed a waiver only when the lease made the tenant responsible for specifically enumerated defects. The court agreed with the landlord:

> In Prudential Inv. Co. v. Jefferson Associates, Ltd., 896 S.W.2d 156 (Tex. 1995), we held that the "sole cause of a buyer's injury [when the buyer agrees to purchase property 'as is'], by his own admission, is the buyer himself. He has agreed to take the full risk of additional compensation. Rather than pay more, a buyer may choose to rely entirely upon his own

determination of the condition and value of his purchase. In making this choice, he removes the possibility that the seller's conduct will cause him damage." We did not address what effect, if any, an "as is" provision would have on a claim for breach of the implied warranty of suitability, as this warranty applies only to commercial leases and *Prudential* involved a sale of commercial property. Today, we squarely address whether an express disclaimer may waive the implied warranty of suitability in a commercial lease.

Davidow noted that the provisions of the lease would control if the parties expressly agreed that the tenant would repair certain defects. *Prudential* stands for the proposition that an "as is" provision can waive claims based on a condition of the property. Taken together, these cases lead to one logical conclusion: the implied warranty of suitability is waived when, as here, the lease expressly disclaims that warranty. We hold, therefore, that as a matter of law, Gym-N-I waived the implied warranty of suitability. Our conclusion is also supported by public policy. Texas strongly favors parties' freedom of contract. Freedom of contract allows parties to bargain for mutually agreeable terms and allocate risks as they see fit. A lessee may wish to make her own determination of the commercial suitability of premises for her intended purposes. By assuming the risk that the premises may be unsuitable, she may negotiate a lower lease price that reflects that risk allocation. Alternatively, the lessee is free to rely on the lessor's assurances and negotiate a contract that leaves the implied warranty of suitability intact.

We recognize that our holding today stands in contrast to the implied warranty of habitability, which "can be waived only to the extent that defects are adequately disclosed." Centex Homes v. Buecher, 95 S.W.3d 266, 274 (Tex. 2002). The implied warranty of habitability "applies in almost all jurisdictions only to residential tenancies" while commercial tenancies are "excluded primarily on the rationale that the feature of unequal bargaining power justifying the imposition of the warranty in residential leases is not present in commercial transactions." 2 Richard R. Powell, Powell on Real Property § 233[2][b] (Patrick J. Rohan, ed., 1991). The fact that the lessor impliedly warrants suitability in Texas ensures that, when the warranty is waived, the parties focus their attention on who is responsible for discovering and repairing latent defects, and they may allocate the risk accordingly. We see no compelling reason to disturb that market transaction here.

The court did not decide the "preliminary question" mandated by *Prudential* — whether an "as is" clause is enforceable — because neither party had appealed the lower court's finding of enforceability, 220 S.W.3d at 912 n. 10; the court also left open the question "whether an 'as is' clause lacking express disclaimer language would effectively waive the implied warranty of suitability," *id.* at 910 n. 7.

3. **Significance of waiver.** Assuming equal bargaining power between the parties, how might the possibility of waiver of the warranty of habitability benefit the commercial tenant? If the parties have unequal bargaining power, should the tenant's waiver be valid?

4. **Fraud compared.** Fraud consists of an intentional misrepresentation about the condition of the leased premises or about some other important aspect of the lease transaction; breach of warranty is based on an innocent misrepresentation. Lacking general access to the warranty of habitability, commercial tenants often try to fit their complaints into a fraud cause of action. Fraud is difficult to prove. Among the obstacles: (a) scienter (knowledge of the misrepresentation rather than, say, negligence in making the misrepresentation) may be required; (b) opinions (puffing), as opposed to statements of fact, are not actionable; (c) nondisclosure (as opposed to affirmative misstatement or active concealment of a condition) may not be actionable; (d) the required reliance by the tenant on the misrepresentation will not exist if the tenant has a reasonable opportunity to inspect the property; and (e) the tenant may, after discovering the misrepresentation, unintentionally waive the cause of action. *See, e.g.,* Herring-Marathon Master Partnership v. Boardwalk Fries, Inc., 979 F.2d 1326 (8th Cir. 1992) (under Arkansas law, landlord had no affirmative duty to disclose declining sales experienced by other food court lessees); Anderson Drive-In Theatre v. Kirkpatrick, 110 N.E.2d 506 (Ind. Ct. App. 1953) (in absence of warranty in lease as to suitability of land for tenant's intended use, allegation of landlord's failure to disclose condition of the premises did not state cause of action); Flair Fashions, Inc. v. SW CR Eisenhower Drive, Inc., 427 S.E.2d 56 (Ga. Ct. App. 1993) (tenant waived fraud and ratified lease by silence and payment of rent after falsity of landlord's representations became apparent). For a case in which the tenant successfully made out a case of fraud, with a good discussion of the requirements, see Roberts v. United New Mexico Bank at Roswell, 14 F.3d 1076 (5th Cir. 1994) (bank's statements regarding productivity and quality of water on leased farm were misrepresentations rather than opinions, on which tenants justifiably relied).

5. **Remedies.** If the warranty of habitability were available to a commercial tenant, one would expect the tenant to have the associated remedy of rent withholding and abatement. It is possible, however, that the warranty might be rejected and the commercial tenant *still* be allowed a withholding remedy for the landlord's breach of an express promise, at least one relating to the condition or use of the premises.

RICHARD BARTON ENTERPRISES, INC. v. TSERN
928 P.2d 368 (Utah 1996)

STEWART, ASSOCIATE CHIEF JUSTICE.

Defendants John F. Tsern and the Tsern Family Trust (collectively "Tsern") appeal a judgment awarding plaintiffs Richard Barton and Richard Barton Enterprises (collectively "Barton") a rent abatement under a commercial lease and the cost of repairing an elevator. We affirm.

I. FACTS

On November 21, 1991, Barton and Tsern entered into an agreement titled "Earnest Money Receipt and Offer to Lease," and on November 27, 1991, the parties executed a lease pursuant thereto for the first and second floors of a commercial building in downtown Salt Lake City. Barton agreed to pay rent at the rate of $3,000 per month for the one-year lease. The lease required Tsern to deliver possession of the premises to Barton on December 1, 1991. On November 27, Barton paid Tsern $9,000, covering the first and last months' rent and a $3,000 security deposit. Barton also paid an additional $3,000 as earnest money for an option to purchase the entire building.

The terms of the earnest money agreement were expressly incorporated into the lease. The lease provided, "[T]he 'Earnest Money Receipt and Offer to Lease' dated November 21, 1991, shall be attached to this lease as an addendum. All terms and conditions are binding to [sic] both parties." Added to the terms of the printed earnest money form were the typed words, "Other than stated in lines 32 and 33, Tenant shall accept the building in 'As Is' condition." The language on lines 32 and 33 required Tsern to repair the building's leaky roof and the freight elevator to "good working order."

Barton's purpose in leasing the building was to establish an antiques dealership. The business inventory included large architectural pieces that, because of the dropped ceiling of the main floor and other limitations, had to be stored on the second floor. For that reason Barton required a freight elevator to transport the large, heavy pieces to the second floor. Barton's need for the elevator was communicated to Tsern repeatedly, both prior to signing the earnest money agreement, when Barton became aware that the elevator was inoperable, and after the lease was executed and Barton took occupancy of the leased premises.

Barton took possession of the ground floor on December 1, 1991, but could not obtain possession of the second floor until December 20, when a holdover tenant finally vacated the floor. The elevator was wholly inoperable, and Tsern had neither repaired the elevator nor entered into a contract to have it repaired. Moreover, the roof had not been repaired. The elevator remained inoperable until January 9, 1992, when Kimball Elevator Co., pursuant to a time and materials contract with Tsern, made certain repairs to the elevator. On Tsern's instructions, however, Kimball made only those repairs necessary to make the elevator operational in the sense that it would "go up and down." Tsern strictly limited the amount of money he would pay Kimball for repairs to $5,000 and expressly refused to authorize a number of repairs that Kimball stated were necessary to make the elevator operate reliably and safely. The strict limitations placed on Kimball's repairs and the failure to authorize additional needed repairs were not communicated to Barton. In fact, Tsern instructed Kimball not to mention those limitations to Barton.

The elevator operated from January 9, 1992, until January 24, 1992, when a city inspector ordered it shut down. After Kimball made an additional repair required by the city inspector on February 13, the elevator again operated until March 14. On April 10, a state elevator inspector found that the elevator was not in compliance with state law, directed Tsern to correct nine violations, and ordered the elevator shut down until it could pass a state safety inspection. Apparently believing that Barton intended to exercise its option to purchase the building, Tsern refused to spend the $5,552 to make those repairs. During the term of the lease, Barton continually demanded that the elevator be properly repaired. It never was and did not operate at all after March 14, 1992.

On December 10, 1991, Barton and Tsern each sent the other a communication concerning the possibility of a rent abatement. As already noted, at that point Barton had not yet obtained occupancy of the second floor because of a holdover tenant, the leaky roof still had not been repaired, and the elevator was inoperable. Barton suggested a rent abatement because of the difficulties. Independent of that request, Tsern on his own suggested a 50% rent abatement, but Barton never accepted his proposal. The parties never agreed on a rent abatement amount, nor did they specify which of Barton's claims would give rise to an abatement.

Barton tendered less than the full rent for the months of January and February, and Tsern cashed the checks but maintained that he was entitled to the full rent of $3,000 for each month. Because the elevator operated during the latter part of January and the early part of February, Barton tendered full rent for February on February 1, minus a minor offset for something unrelated to the elevator. On April 15, 1992, Barton filed a complaint for a declaratory judgment to establish Tsern's legal duty to repair the elevator. Tsern counterclaimed with a three-day notice to pay the rent in full or quit the premises. The counterclaim was dismissed for reasons not now pertinent. Mr. Barton later gave notice that he was exercising his option to purchase, and to cure any possible rental defaults, he deposited $19,000 with the court on October 29, 1992. On November 30, 1992, the court ruled that Barton could exercise the option to purchase prior to the conclusion of the bench trial on his declaratory judgment claim.

In its final judgment, the court found that the elevator had not been repaired to "good working order" as required by the lease, and entered judgment against Tsern for the cost of repairing the elevator to that standard. Citing Wade v. Jobe, 818 P.2d 1006 (Utah 1991), the court also ruled that although Barton and Tsern had never agreed on the amount of a rent abatement, Barton was entitled to have the rent abated to $2,000 a month and, in addition, that Barton's damages plus accrued interest should be deducted from the purchase price of the building.

On this appeal, Tsern asserts that Barton's covenant to pay rent was independent of all Tsern's covenants and that the trial court erred in awarding Barton a rent abatement.

II. RENT ABATEMENT UNDER A COMMERCIAL LEASE

In Wade v. Jobe, 818 P.2d 1006 (Utah 1991), we observed that the reality of modern residential leases is that lessees bargain for the use of the structures, facilities, and services attached to the land rather than the land itself, so that the appurtenances to the land are the more important feature of the lease. We held that a contract concept of implied warranty should be extended to residential leases in the form of an implied warranty of habitability and that the covenant to pay rent was dependent on the lessor's compliance with the implied warranty of habitability. The ruling in *Wade* is consistent with the positions taken on similar issues in a majority of states.

We find that the principles announced in *Wade* in the context of residential leases are equally applicable to the commercial context. In addition, several other states have held that under certain circumstances, commercial lessees may withhold rent. One group of states, which includes Texas and New Jersey, holds that covenants in commercial leases are mutually dependent. Texas offers the most expansive protection for commercial leases; it extends to commercial lessees all protections available to residential lessees, including an implied warranty of suitability that the leased premises are suitable "for their intended commercial purpose." Davidow v. Inwood North Professional Group, 747 S.W.2d 373, 377 (Tex. 1988). The court in *Davidow* reasoned that a commercial lessee should have the same protections as those accorded a residential lessee and that contract principles rather than medieval property principles should apply. Although it stopped short of providing the same broad protections as Texas, the New Jersey Supreme Court held that "fair treatment for tenants with respect to latent defects remediable by the landlord require[s] imposition on [the landlord] of an implied warranty against such defects." Reste Realty Corp. v. Cooper, 251 A.2d 268, 273 (N.J. 1969). A New Jersey appellate court thereafter noted that the state supreme court's decision heralded "the demise of the doctrine of independent covenants." Ringwood Assocs. v. Jack's of Route 23, Inc., 398 A.2d 1315, 1319 (N.J. Super. Ct. App. Div. 1979).

A second group of states does not recognize implied warranties in commercial leases but nevertheless holds that covenants in commercial leases may be mutually dependent. Massachusetts and Indiana hold that the covenant to pay rent and the covenant to repair may be mutually dependent. Erhard v. F.W. Woolworth Co., 372 N.E.2d 1277 (Mass. 1978). The Supreme Court of Pennsylvania has held that a covenant to pay rent is dependent on all covenants that were significant inducements to the making of the lease. Teodori v. Werner, 415 A.2d 31 (Pa. 1980).

Both groups of cases recognize that the covenant to pay rent under a commercial lease is dependent on the lessor's compliance with those covenants necessary to provide the lessee with the benefits that were the essence of the bargain as reflected in the lease. This approach relieves a lessee of the obligation to abandon the premises, as is necessary under the fiction of a constructive eviction. By making the lessee's covenant to pay rent dependent on the lessor's performance of essential covenants, the legal analysis can focus, as it should, on the essential elements and purposes of the bargain between the lessor and the lessee. By employing contract principles, a court's analysis of a dispute between a lessor and a lessee should provide a more fair, realistic, and forthright analysis of whether a lessee may abate rent. The result reached on such an analysis should better comport with modern leasing practices and expectations than the result under an analysis based on the principle of independent covenants as modified by the doctrine of constructive eviction.

Not all breaches of covenants by a lessor, however, justify a lessee in withholding rent. Only a significant breach of a covenant material to the purpose for which the lease was consummated justifies a lessee in abating rent. Temporary or minor breaches of routine covenants by a lessor do not. Thus, if a breach has little effect on the essential objectives of the lessee in entering into the lease, the lessee may not withhold rent. Restatement (Second) of Property § 7.1, cmt. c (1977) states that a covenant is not a significant inducement if "the landlord's failure to perform his promise has only a peripheral effect on the use of the leased property by the tenant." A significant inducement means the "performance of [a] promise [that has] a significant impact on the benefits the tenant anticipated he would receive under the lease." Restatement (Second), § 7.1 cmt. c. Thus, in assessing whether a lessor's breach is sufficient to justify the withholding of rent, a lessee first and a court later, if necessary, must gauge the materiality of the breach in light of the lessee's purpose in leasing the premises. Relevant to that determination may be whether the breach has a significant effect on the rental value of the premises. In sum, we hold that the lessee's covenant to pay rent is dependent on the lessor's performance of covenants that were a significant inducement to the consummation of the lease or to the purpose for which the lessee entered into the lease.

Holding Barton liable for the full amount of rent when a significant part of the leased premises was practically unusable for the purpose for which the premises were leased would be tantamount to requiring that Barton pay for something he could not use in the manner intended when the lease was executed, given the nature of his business and the nature of the building. Tsern knew that an operable elevator was essential to Barton's use of the second floor and that the lack of an operable elevator was not simply a matter of inconvenience. Tsern's promise to repair the elevator was a significant inducement to Barton to enter into the lease. Indeed, on several occasions before the lease was signed, Barton explicitly told Tsern that the business required an operable elevator. The absence of an operable and safe elevator had more than a peripheral effect on Barton's use of the premises; it impaired Barton's ability to conduct its business on the premises. It follows that Tsern was entitled to receive rent equal to the value of the premises without an operable freight elevator.

Under [the formula set out in Wade v. Jobe], the lessee is entitled to abate rent by an amount equal to the reduced value of the premises due to the lessor's breach.

[Affirmed.]

NOTES AND QUESTIONS

1. **Commentary.** For a critical discussion of the principal case, see Rena Ashauer-Miller, Note, *Dependent Covenants and Commercial Leases after Barton v. Tsern: Rhetoric of Reform Claims an Easy Victory in Utah*, 1997 Utah L. Rev. 807.

2. **Two questions.** Why might a court be inclined to deny an implied warranty in a commercial lease, yet allow the withholding and abatement remedy for breach of a landlord's express warranty or promise?

3. **An unsettled question.** Whether a commercial tenant is entitled to the remedy of withholding and abatement when the landlord breaches an express promise is far from settled. The principal case, and Teodori v. Werner, cited therein, are important decisions allowing the remedy. *Teodori* allowed it for the landlord's breach of a noncompetition covenant. However, it is likely that more cases would agree with Schulman v. Vera, 166 Cal. Rptr. 620, 626 (Cal. Dist. Ct. App. 1980), in which the court distinguished Green v. Superior Court, 517 P.2d 1168 (Cal. 1974) (see Notes 2 and 9 after *Javins*), and concluded that a commercial tenant is not entitled to the withholding and abatement remedy for the landlord's breach of a covenant of repair:

While the cases, probably because of the historical sources of the rules of law, have discussed the issue at hand in terms of dependence or independence of the parties' covenants, the real issue in determining whether a lessor's breach of covenant may be litigated by a lessee in defense of an unlawful detainer action is whether the need for litigating that matter in the unlawful detainer action is so vital as to overcome the public policy underlying the summary nature of unlawful detainer. [I]f lessees had been permitted to litigate their claim of damages from lessors' breach of covenant to repair, the summary nature of the unlawful detainer procedure would have been destroyed. There would have been injected into the action issues of whether or not lessees properly notified the lessors of the need for repairs, whether the repairs were in fact needed, whether or not lessors failed to repair within a reasonable time, the nature and extent of the damages resulting from the failure to repair, whether or not lessees took proper measures to mitigate damages, the reasonable cost of making the required repairs, and whether or not lessees had the means to have the repairs made themselves. By contrast, no reason appears why lessees' alternative remedies to recover damages for lessors' alleged breach were inadequate.

Green might be distinguishable on the question whether to imply a warranty in a commercial lease. However, unless a commercial tenant's assertion of the withholding remedy would delay the summary proceeding more than a residential tenant's assertion of it would, didn't *Green* settle the question of the availability of the withholding remedy in a summary eviction suit?

4. **Waiver and disclaimer.** If a commercial tenant has the withholding and abatement remedy, may that remedy be disclaimed or waived? *Cf.* Bomze v. Jaybee Photo Suppliers, Inc., 460 N.Y.S.2d 862 (N.Y. App. T. 1983) (lease provision barring commercial tenant's counterclaim in any suit for rent by landlord upheld); Middletown Plaza Associates v. Dora Dale of Middletown, Inc., 621 F. Supp. 1163 (D. Conn. 1985) (same; applying New York law).

5. **Repair and deduct.** In Westrich v. McBride, 499 A.2d 546 (N.J. Super. Ct. Law Div. 1984), the court allowed a tenant (an optometrist) who operated a small professional office to deduct the cost of renting space heaters to compensate for the landlord's failure to perform an express promise in the lease to supply heat. Is the case distinguishable from Schulman v. Vera?

6. **Partial constructive eviction (again).** In Dennison v. Marlowe, 744 P.2d 906 (N.M. 1987), the landlord failed to comply with regulations requiring the installation of sprinklers in the upper floor of the commercial premises rented to the tenant, and state inspectors closed that floor. The tenant stopped paying rent, and the landlord sued for possession. The court reversed the lower court judgment for the landlord:

> Lessees contend that because of lessor's breach of the covenant of quiet enjoyment, the payment of the rental should have been suspended in total. An actual eviction by the landlord, even though it is partial, "suspends the entire rent because the landlord is not permitted to apportion his wrong." Fifth Ave. Bldg. Co. v. Kernochan, 117 N.E. 579, 580 (N.Y. 1917). Under constructive eviction cases, however, the tenant must abandon the pre-

mises in order to sustain his claim of eviction. Here, lessees were compelled to vacate the second floor because of lessor's failure to install the sprinkler system. Because lessees were not deprived of the beneficial use of the first floor of the premises, there was no constructive eviction regarding this portion of the premises. Thus, lessees had an obligation to continue paying a fair rental value for use of the first floor. They cannot recover damages for breach of covenant of quiet enjoyment regarding this portion of the building. We hold, therefore, that lessor's failure to install the sprinkler system in accordance with the safety code amounted to a partial constructive eviction, greatly diminishing the value of the premises in comparison to the consideration for rent. Thus, under these circumstances, it is equitable that the rent owed to the lessor be offset by the extent of the diminished facilities.

Is partial constructive eviction in *Dennison* an exact parallel to partial actual eviction? Would *Dennison*'s version of partial constructive eviction have worked in *Barton*? *See generally* Robert S. Schoshinski, American Law of Landlord and Tenant § 3:6, at 101 (1982) (partial constructive eviction "holds some attraction" for a residential or commercial tenant "who is deprived in part of his use of the premises and unable for economic reasons to relocate to a different property").

PROBLEM 4-M. The landlord in a commercial lease breaches obligations of repair and heating owed to the tenant under the lease. The tenant withholds rent. The landlord sues for possession and does not join a claim for rent. The state summary eviction statute provides as follows:

> If the landlord elects to make a claim for unpaid rent, the court shall consider any defense, claim, or counterclaim by the tenant which offsets or reduces the amount owed to the plaintiff. If the court finds that the landlord is entitled to possession on the ground of nonpayment of rent, it shall also award the landlord a money judgment. If the court determines that the amount owed by the landlord to the tenant, as a result of set-off or counterclaim exceeds or equals the amount of rent and other lawful charges owed by the tenant to the landlord, judgment in the possessory action shall be granted in favor of the tenant. If the court finds that the tenant's counterclaim exceeds the amount of the nonpayment, a money judgment shall issue in favor of the tenant.

Another provision of the statute provides a defense to a possessory action in "any premises leased or rented for residential purposes, other than for vacation or recreation," if the premises are in substantial violation of "standards of fitness for health and safety" that "materially affects the habitability of the premises." Is the tenant entitled to assert the landlord's breach of the repair and heating obligations in the summary eviction proceeding? *See* Matte v. Shippee Auto, Inc., 876 A.2d 167 (N.J. 2005) (tenant argued dependency of promises, which the court rejected).

c.   The Landlord's Tort Liability

As we have seen, the landlord's duty to provide and maintain habitable premises has caused a major change in the *contractual* relationship between the parties to the residential lease, and to a lesser extent, to the commercial lease. Tenants of either sort (and their invitees), have not fared so well when the question is the landlord's *tort* liability for the condition of the premises. The traditional rule of the common law, still followed in many states, is that the landlord is not responsible to the tenant or the tenant's guests for injuries resulting from the condition of the leased premises, subject to a handful of exceptions. Skeptical of the wisdom of the rule-and-exceptions approach and the dubious immunity it confers on the landlord, some courts have opted for a rule of general negligence: the landlord's tort liability should be akin to that of any other defendant, based on the standard of reasonable care under all of the circumstances. The most radical, and controversial, approach has appeared in cases which have rejected fault entirely — whether as the basis for exceptions to a general rule of nonliability or as the basis for treating the landlord like any other potential tortfeasor. In these courts, the landlord has been held to a standard of strict liability. The principal case airs these various approaches to the question of the landlord's tort liability; the articles by Professor Jean Love and Professor Olin Browder cited in the principal case provide comprehensive treatments of the topic.

ORTEGA v. FLAIM
902 P.2d 199 (Wyo. 1995)

GOLDEN, CHIEF JUSTICE.

A social guest of landlord's tenant sustained personal injuries after falling down stairs at the tenant's residential dwelling. The social guest sued landlord for damages. Relying on the common law's general rule of landlord's immunity from liability, however, the district court granted landlord's motion for summary judgment. The social guest appealed, presenting this court with the primary issue of whether Wyoming will abandon the common law rules governing landlord liability as set forth in Restatement (Second) of Torts §§ 356-362 (1965) and adopt a duty of reasonable care. Alternatively, if the court does not impose a duty of reasonable care, appellant social guest invites this court to attach liability based on theories of implied warranty of habitability, strict liability, and nuisance. Having carefully considered the questions before us, we decline to abrogate the common law rule or attach liabilities under the presented alternative theories.

We affirm the grant of summary judgment.

FACTS

In 1981, Appellee Guido Flaim (landlord) purchased seven homes, sight unseen, by contract for deed and received the warranty deeds on August 6, 1990. One of those properties, a residential home located at 324 "O" Street in Rock Springs, Wyoming, was orally leased to Dan and Becky Stroud (tenants). The oral lease was a bare bones commitment by the tenants to pay rent of $200.00 per month in return for landlord's surrender of possession. The parties did not discuss or make any agreements regarding repairs, express warranties of habitability, landlord's right to reenter or landlord's retention of any control over the premises. Tenants received exclusive possession and control.

Appellant Jackie Ortega (Ortega) was a social guest of the tenants on the evening of July 17, 1992. Ortega had visited at the house before and knew the house contained an interior stairway descending to the basement. In the early morning hours of July 18, 1992, Ortega told several people she was going to the bathroom and left the kitchen. A few seconds later others heard a crash and found an injured Ortega at the bottom of the staircase. Ortega filed suit against landlord alleging a defective staircase caused her injuries and discovery followed.

Discovery revealed essential material facts of this case were undisputed, although the parties disputed whether the tenants had previously complained to the landlord that the stair system was dangerous because it was too steep, its treads too narrow and it did not have a handrail. Under the law applicable to landlord liability, this factual dispute was relevant only to the issue of whether the defects were patent or latent. Accepting the tenants' contention they had complained only indicated any defects of the staircase were patent.

Following discovery, landlord moved for summary judgment based upon depositions indicating the material facts were undisputed and the question faced was a legal question of whether the law attached liability to a landlord. The district court held the common law rule of landlord nonliability applied and although exceptions to the general rule existed, none applied to these facts. The district court summarily rejected the other liability theories as being without merit. The landlord's motion for summary judgment was granted and this appeal followed.

DISCUSSION

Landlord Liability

In the landlord and tenant relationship, Wyoming follows the common law rules. Under those rules, a landlord owes no greater duty to a tenant's guests than the landlord owes to the tenant himself. Generally, that duty is nonexistent since landlords enjoy immunity from tort liability, being one of the few classes of defendants who can invoke caveat emptor.

The common law rule as applied today actually originated during 16th century feudalism when a tenant leased to acquire land. Buildings were simple and their living conditions of little concern to the tenant. Tenants' rights were best protected by the common law view that a landlord's lease to a tenant was a conveyance of the premises for the term of the lease.[1] From that view, the tenant was the owner and occupier subject to all the responsibilities of one in possession and burdened with maintaining the premises in a reasonably safe condition to protect persons who came upon the land. Borders v. Roseberry, 532 P.2d 1366, 1368-69 (Kan. 1975). As a general rule, the landlord owed no duty to the tenant or the tenant's guests for dangerous or defective conditions of the premises. See Restatement (Second) of Torts §§ 335, 356 (1965).

---

[1] Jean C. Love, *Landlord's Liability for Defective Premises: Caveat Lessee, Negligence, or Strict Liability?*, 1975 Wis. L. Rev. 19, 26 (1975).

Over time, the courts created exceptions to the rule of landlord nonliability, some of which have been recognized in Wyoming:

1. Undisclosed conditions known to lessor and unknown to the lessee which were hidden or latently dangerous and caused an injury.

2. The premises were leased for public use and a member of the public was injured.

3. Part of the premises was retained under the lessor's control, but was open to the use of the lessee.

4. Lessor had contracted to repair the premises.

5. Negligence by lessor in making repairs.

See also Restatement (Second) of Torts §§ 356-362 (1965).

In order for social guest Ortega to succeed in imposing landlord liability in this case, Wyoming's adherence to the common law rule must be abandoned. She points to Sargent v. Ross, 308 A.2d 528 (N.H. 1973), in which the court did abandon the common law rule and impose a duty of reasonable care on landlords. Similar to this case, *Sargent* involved a fall down the stairs, but the fall was caused by the landlord's negligent construction of the stairs. The resulting defective stairs caused a child to fall to her death. The tenants in *Sargent* had no authority to alter or remedy the defective stairs and the court considered that the steepness of the stairway could be considered a hidden defect or secret danger in the case of a child since the danger and risk may have been obvious to an adult but may have been imperceptible to a child. Despite the possibility that this hidden defect exception applied, the court chose to abandon the general rule of landlord nonliability and apply ordinary negligence principles.

Sargent's conclusion that the nonliability rule must be abandoned followed the court's examination of the reasons for the landlord nonliability rule. Determining [that] those reasons should be reevaluated in light of current needs and principles of law from related areas, the court found that stare decisis must yield to the need for responsible growth and change in rules that have failed to keep pace with modern developments.

Other states, either judicially or through legislation, have accepted the contention that tenants in today's modern society are primarily concerned with acquiring a place to live rather than acquiring land to farm and have abrogated the common law rule. New Hampshire's lead in the adoption of an independent negligence doctrine for landlords has been followed by several other states. Pagelsdorf v. Safeco Ins. Co., 284 N.W.2d 55 (Wis. 1979); Young v. Garwacki, 402 N.E.2d 1045 (Mass. 1980); Mansur v. Eubanks, 401 So.2d 1328 (Fla.1981); Stephens v. Stearns, 678 P.2d 41 (Idaho 1984); Turpel v. Sayles, 692 P.2d 1290 (Nev. 1985); Favreau v. Miller, 591 A.2d 68 (Vt. 1991); Newton v. Magill, 872 P.2d 1213 (Alaska 1994). Other states have construed statutes, contracts, or an implied warranty of habitability as imposing tort liability upon landlords. Since the 1970s, this legal trend has resulted in the majority of states abrogating the common law rule of landlord nonliability under various legal theories. See Olin L. Browder, *The*

Taming of a Duty — The Tort Liability of Landlords, 81 Mich. L. Rev. 99, 112-13 (Nov. 1982).

Presently, Wyoming has no legal basis for landlord tort liability as it has not enacted legislation on this issue, has not judicially recognized an implied warranty of habitability for rental premises and has not judicially altered the common law rule. Social guest Ortega asserts Wyoming should abandon the common law rule and adopt landlord liability under both an independent negligence doctrine and an implied warranty of habitability. Landlord argues that when the tenant knows of dangerous conditions and is in control of the premises, the tenant is in the best position to at least warn social guests of the danger.

The common law "is but the accumulated expressions of the various judicial tribunals in their efforts to ascertain what is right and just between individuals with respect to private disputes." *Newton*, 872 P.2d at 1217-18. By this definition, the common law is dynamic and a court can modify it to meet changing conditions. This court has modified or abandoned the common law on the issues of interspousal tort immunity, parental tort immunity, recovery for loss of spousal and parental consortium, negligent infliction of emotional distress, off-premises liability of a lessee, and classifications of tort plaintiffs in landowner liability cases.[2]

Where this court has considered whether a duty should be imposed based on a particular relationship, numerous factors have been balanced to aid in determining whether a duty should be imposed.[3] Social guest Ortega does not analyze these factors or provide a record for our analysis, but offers only the decision of Sargent as argument that modern trends demand abrogation of the common law in this instance. We believe such a change cannot be based solely upon a trend, but rather must be based upon relevant data and analysis which supports the legal, social and/ or economic theories behind abrogating the common law.

---

[2] Tader v. Tader, 737 P.2d 1065 (Wyo.1987) (abrogating common law rule of interspousal tort immunity); Dellapenta v. Dellapenta, 838 P.2d 1153 (Wyo.1992) (abrogating common law rule of parental tort immunity); Weaver v. Mitchell, 715 P.2d 1361 (Wyo.1986) (rejecting common law rule denying recovery for loss of spousal consortium); Nulle v. Gillette-Campbell Fire Bd., 797 P.2d 1171 (Wyo.1990) (rejecting common law rule denying recovery for claim for loss of parental consortium); Gates v. Richardson, 719 P.2d 193 (Wyo.1986) (rejecting common law rule denying a family member recovery of damages for the negligent infliction of emotional distress); Mostert v. CBL & Assoc., 741 P.2d 1090 (Wyo.1987) (rejecting common law rule that a landowner has no duty to warn an invitee of risks off the landowner's premises); and Clarke v. Beckwith, 858 P.2d 293 (Wyo.1993) (rejecting the common law classifications of invitee and licensee and ruling that landowners owed a duty of reasonable care).

[3] In *Mostert*, the court analyzed the factors below in concluding movie theater lessees owed an affirmative duty to business invitees to warn of off-premises danger: (1) the foreseeability of harm to the plaintiff, (2) the closeness of the connection between the defendant's conduct and the injury suffered, (3) the degree of certainty that the plaintiff suffered injury, (4) the moral blame attached to the defendant's conduct, (5) the policy of preventing future harm, (6) the extent of the burden upon the defendant, (7) the consequences to the community and the court system, and (8) the availability, cost and prevalence of insurance for the risk involved. The factors have been succinctly summarized in a landlord liability case as: Factors to consider in imposing a duty on a landlord include weighing the relationship of the parties against the nature of the risk and the public interest in the proposed solution, as well as the likelihood of injury, the magnitude of the burden of guarding against it, and the consequences of placing that burden on a defendant. C.S. v. Sophir, 368 N.W.2d 444, 446 (Neb. 1985).

Although most states have judicially recognized some type of landlord liability without relevant data, this recognition appears to have been driven by a desire to further the social policy of improving living conditions. See Restatement (Second) of Property, Landlord and Tenant, § 17.6 (1977). In our opinion this is a matter for the legislature, and we decline to abrogate the common law in this instance without a proper record and insightful analysis of whether conditions in Wyoming warrant a change regarding residential leases.

Having held the common law will not be abrogated in this case, we apply it to the facts. Generally, when real property is leased to a tenant, the landlord's duty as a landowner shifts to the tenant as soon as the landlord surrenders possession and control of the premises to the tenant. Although the tenants had complained to the landlord the staircase was dangerous because it was too steep, the treads too narrow and it did not have a handrail, this evidence only indicates the defects were patent rather than latent. Absent a contractual provision to repair, a landlord has no duty to repair patent defects. The landlord owed no duty to social guest Ortega and summary judgment was properly granted.

Implied Warranty of Habitability

In Wyoming, an implied warranty of habitability attaches only to a sale of improved property by the builder. Barlage v. Key Bank of Wyoming, 892 P.2d 124, 126 (Wyo.1995). The warranty is to be honored by the builder even as to remote purchasers, but is not applicable in sales between a non-builder vendor and a vendee.

Social guest Ortega contends that Wyoming should join the majority of states in adopting the implied warranty of habitability for rental premises and then impose a tort duty upon landlords. See Restatement (Second) of Property, Landlord and Tenant § 17.6 (1977). For the same reasons discussed above, the rule of an implied warranty of habitability will not be extended to rental premises under these facts. *Barlage*, 892 P.2d at 126.

Nuisance

Social guest Ortega contends the stairs posed a private nuisance as defined in Restatement (Second) of Torts § 821 (1965). Landlord contends application of this rule of nuisance requires that social guest Ortega have standing to assert this claim. Citing to Restatement (Second) of Torts § 821E, he claims recovery at law for damages or in equity for injunctive relief is limited to those who have property rights and privileges with respect to the use and enjoyment of the land affected. Landlord identifies those persons as including possessors, owners of easements and profits and owners of nonpossessory estates in the land who are detrimentally affected by interferences with its use and enjoyment.

Relying on this authority, landlord contends a social guest is a licensee with no property interest in the land and cannot maintain an action for private nuisance; social guest Ortega does not address the issue of standing. Although this particular section of the Restatement has not been adopted by this court, she does not provide argument or authority for its application. This court has generally limited nuisance actions to those situations described in Restatement (Second) of Torts § 371 (1965):

> A possessor of land is subject to liability for physical harm to others outside of the land caused by an activity carried on by him thereon which he realizes or should realize will involve an unreasonable risk of physical harm to them under the same conditions as though the activity were carried on at a neutral place.

Timmons v. Reed, 569 P.2d 112, 124 (Wyo.1977). Without argument or analysis to support a nuisance action on these facts, social guest Ortega's claim for nuisance must be rejected as a matter of law. Summary judgment is affirmed on this issue.

Strict Liability

Social guest Ortega contends landlord is strictly liable to her under the rule of Restatement (Second) of Torts § 402A (1965), adopted by this court in Ogle v. Caterpillar Tractor Co., 716 P.2d 334 (Wyo.1986). Section 402A applies strict liability in product liability actions. She asserts the California decision of Becker v. IRM Corp., 698 P.2d 116 (Cal. 1985), extending strict liability to landlords should be applied in Wyoming because there is no significant difference between current Wyoming law and the rule in *Becker*. In *Becker*, a tenant injured by broken, untempered glass from his shower door recovered from the landlord under § 402A's strict liability rule. The *Becker* court determined the untempered shower door glass was a latently defective product since one viewing the glass could not distinguish it from tempered glass. The court considered shower door glass a product which the landlord had placed in the stream of commerce and, for policy reasons, the court extended strict liability to the landlord.

In adopting a strict liability cause of action for injuries caused by defective products, this court adopted the Restatement (Second) of Torts § 402A (1965) definition of product liability:

Special Liability of Seller of Product for Physical Harm to User or Consumer

(1) One who sells any product in a defective condition unreasonably dangerous to the user or consumer or to his property is subject to liability for physical harm thereby caused to the ultimate user or consumer, or to his property, if

(a) the seller is engaged in the business of selling such a product, and

(b) it is expected to and does reach the user or consumer without substantial change in the condition in which it is sold.

(2) The rule stated in Subsection (1) applies although

(a) the seller has exercised all possible care in the preparation and sale of his product, and

(b) the user or consumer has not bought the product from or entered into any contractual relation with the seller.

The court's expressed policy reason for adopting product liability was to permit recovery by plaintiffs who would not recover under a negligence theory and distribute the damages among those most able to prevent future occurrences or who would pass on the loss to all customers. This policy is effectuated by strict liability's focus on the product itself, and, in the absence of fault, holding a seller or distributor liable for injury or loss resulting from a defective product that entered the stream of commerce.

Wyoming adopted product liability to afford a cause of action against manufacturers or suppliers of defective mass-produced products. To extend product liability to a landlord for a leased residential dwelling, or to an integral component of that dwelling, does not serve those policy reasons. See generally American Law of Products Liability, Part 11, § 38:15, p. 31, § 38:16, pp. 33-34 (Supp.1995) (collecting cases holding buildings are not products and holding strict liability against landlords does not serve policy of § 402A); and see generally Boddie v. Litton Unit Handling Systems, 455 N.E.2d 142, 147-49 (Ill. App. Ct. 1983) (considering when components parts of buildings are products within the definition of § 402A). Summary judgment is affirmed on this issue.

CONCLUSION

The common law rule that a landlord owes no duty to the social guest of a tenant unless the injury was caused by a latent defect or the landlord has retained control applies in this case and no duty was owed to social guest Ortega. A duty was not created by virtue of any contractual relationship. Without duty, summary judgment was properly granted to landlord in social guest Ortega's action for negligence. No other legal basis for recovery for her personal injuries exists in Wyoming. The grant of summary judgment is affirmed.

NOTES AND QUESTIONS

1. **Strict liability.** In Peterson v. Superior Court, 899 P.2d 905 (Cal. 1995), the court overruled Becker v. IRM Corp. (Cal. 1985) (cited in *Ortega*), its earlier decision imposing strict liability on the landlord. What are the arguments for and against strict liability?

2. **The Restatement Second of Property.** The Restatement Second of Property (Landlord and Tenant) §§ 17.1 through 17.7 list the exceptions to the general common law rule of the landlord's nonliability that are cited in the principal case. The Restatement also includes, however, an exception for the landlord's failure to exercise reasonable care to repair a "dangerous" condition existing before or after the tenant's possession if the condition is in violation of an implied warranty of habitability or a duty created by statute or administrative regulation. *Id.* § 17.6 (1) and (2). A tort action based on the landlord's breach of the implied warranty sounds in negligence, not strict liability.

3. **The non-merchant landlord.** A college professor going on sabbatical leases her house to a student, who is injured as a result of a defective condition of the premises. Should the student have a cause of action in tort against the landlord? Does (should) it matter whether breach of the warranty of habitability creates strict liability rather than liability in negligence? *See generally* Jane P.

Mallor, *The Implied Warranty of Habitability and the "Non-Merchant" Landlord*, 22 Duquesne L. Rev. 637 (1984).

4. **Tort and crime.** Should the landlord be liable if the tenant or a guest suffers personal injury resulting from a criminal assault on the leased premises? Among the important questions: Is it relevant that the injuries in such cases result from the independent activity of the criminal? Should the landlord's duty, if one exists, be limited to injuries sustained in common areas of the premises? Should it be limited to reasonably foreseeable injuries? Are prior incidents of criminal activity *in* the landlord's premises (versus in the neighborhood) necessary to establish foreseeability? Does the occurrence of larcenies and thefts on the premises make personal assault foreseeable? *See* Professor Browder's article, cited in the principal case, 81 Mich. L. Rev. at 144-155 (discussing landlord's liability for crimes); Kline v. 1500 Massachusetts Ave. Corp., 439 F.2d 477 (D.C. Cir. 1970) (assault of tenant in common area was foreseeable to landlord; landllord was aware of conditions which created the likelihood of such attacks). *See generally* Robert S. Schoshinski, American Law of Landlord and Tenant §§ 4:14 through 4:15 (1980).

5. **Exculpatory clauses.** If valid, a clause in the lease exculpating the landlord from liability in tort will be strictly construed. *Should* an exculpatory clause be valid? Does it matter whether the lease is residential or commercial? *See generally* Robert S. Schoshinski, *supra*, §§ 4:10 through 4:13.

4.   Security of Possession: The Tenant's Protections Against Retaliatory and Discriminatory Conduct and Eviction Without Cause

a.   Retaliatory Eviction

Suppose that the tenant in a monthly periodic tenancy notifies the landlord of a defective condition on the premises and withholds rent, as authorized by the local law on habitability. Instead of suing for possession based on the tenant's nonpayment of rent (the cause of action asserted by the *Javins* landlord), the landlord gives the tenant the proper one month's notice to terminate the periodic tenancy, then sues for possession on the basis that the tenant is a wrongful holdover. It may go without saying that, if this ploy by the landlord is successful, the implied warranty of habitability will be of little use to many of the residential tenants who most need it. Although the *Javins* court limited its holding to eviction for nonpayment of rent, and noted that the landlord "is free to seek eviction at the termination of the lease or on any other legal ground," 428 F.2d 1071, 1083 n. 64, the court had earlier eliminated the potential loophole under consideration. *See* Edwards v. Habib, 397 F.2d 687 (D.C. Cir. 1968) (opinion by Wright, J.) (landlord cannot terminate tenancy in retaliation for tenant's reporting of housing code violations; the tenant may raise such "retaliatory eviction" as a defense to the landlord's summary suit for possession).

From its beginnings as a protection for the tenant who reports housing code violations and receives a notice of termination, the doctrine generally has been expanded to cover other tenant activities (for example, the tenant's assertion of common-law rights to habitability, and the tenant's joining of a tenant's union) and other landlord responses to that conduct (for example the landlord's cutting off or reduction of the tenant's utilities). The doctrine is sometimes covered by statute, and the statute may or may not be construed by the courts to preempt common-law development of the scope of retaliatory eviction law. For a comprehensive review of retaliatory eviction, see Robert S. Schoshinski, American Law of Landlord and Tenant §§ 12:1 through 12:13 (1980).

b.   Protection Against Discrimination: Fair Housing Issues

At common law, the landlord was free to rent to whomever he or she pleased, and also to impose such terms and conditions of renting as the landlord pleased. *See, e.g.*, Lamont Bldg. Co. v. Court, 70 N.E.2d 447 (Ohio 1946) (landlord's restriction against occupancy of premises by tenants with children upheld). This common law right is substantially eroded in modern law by federal and state statutes that prohibit discrimination in renting on a variety of grounds. These statutes are discussed below. The common law rule, however, retains vitality in cases not covered by the statutes. *See, e.g.*, Kramarsky v. Stahl Management, 401 N.Y.S.2d 943 (N.Y. Sup. Ct. Special Term 1977) (landlord's common-law freedoms are still in effect except as modified by statute; landlord may refuse to rent to a lawyer or other intelligent person who might give landlord trouble, since statute contained no restriction on refusals to rent based on occupation).

Whether a particular ground for refusal to rent is covered by a statute depends on how broadly the court is willing to read the statutory prohibition against discrimination. In Marina Point, Ltd. v. Wolfson, 640 P.2d 115 (Cal. 1982), the state statute expressly prohibited discrimination on the basis of race, religion, national origin or gender. The court held that the landlord could not discriminate against families with minor children; the court treated the statute as the source of a general anti-discrimination principle prohibiting any discrimination. The *Marina Point* situation — discrimination against tenants with minor children — is now covered by the 1988 amendments to the federal Fair Housing Act, discussed below, which added "family status" to the prohibited bases of discrimination. Had those amendments existed at the time of the *Marina Point* litigation, a federal cause of action would have been available along with the state cause of action recognized by the court.

Federal statutes. Two federal statutes limit discrimination by the landlord in the leasing of property: the 1968 Fair Housing Act (and its subsequent amendments) and the Civil Rights Act of 1866.

THE FAIR HOUSING ACT
42 U.S.C. §§ 3601 et seq.

§ 3601. Declaration of policy

It is the policy of the United States to provide, within constitutional limitations, for fair housing throughout the United States.

§ 3603. Effective dates of certain prohibitions

(a) Application to certain described dwellings

[T]he prohibitions against discrimination in the sale or rental of housing set forth in section 3604 of this title shall apply: [to dwellings owned, operated, or financed by the federal government] and to all other dwellings except as exempted by subsection (b) of this section [and by section 3607 of this title, which exempts religious organizations and private clubs under specified circumstances, and which provides that the ban on discrimination based on familial status does not apply to housing for older persons].

(b) Exemptions

Nothing in section 3604 of this title (other than subsection (c)) shall apply to —

(1) any single-family house sold or rented by an owner: *Provided*, That such private individual owner does not own more than three such single-family houses at any one time: *Provided further*, That in the case of the sale of any such single-family house by a private individual owner not residing in such house at the time of such sale or who was not the most recent resident of such house prior to such sale, the exemption granted by this subsection shall apply only with respect to one such sale within any twenty-four month period: *Provided further*, That such bona fide private individual owner does not own any interest in, nor is there owned or reserved on his behalf, under any express or voluntary agreement, title to or any right to all or a portion of the proceeds from the sale or rental of, more than three such single-family houses at any one time: *Provided further*, That after December 31, 1969, the sale or rental of any such single-family house shall be excepted from the application of this subchapter only if such house is sold or rented (A) without the use in any manner of the sales or rental facilities or the sales or rental services of any real estate broker, agent, or salesman, or of such facilities or services of any person in the business of selling or renting dwellings, or of any employee or agent of any such broker, agent, salesman, or person and (B) without the publication, posting or mailing, after notice, of any advertisement or written notice in violation of section 3604(c) of this title; but nothing in this proviso shall prohibit the use of attorneys, escrow agents, abstractors, title companies, and other such professional assistance as necessary to perfect or transfer the title, or

(2) rooms or units in dwellings containing living quarters occupied or intended to be occupied by no more than four families living independently of each other, if the owner actually maintains and occupies one of such living quarters as his residence.

§ 3604. Discrimination in the sale or rental of housing and other prohibited practices

As made applicable by section 3603 of this title and except as exempted by sections 3603(b) and 3607 of this title, it shall be unlawful —

(a) To refuse to sell or rent after the making of a bona fide offer, or to refuse to negotiate for the sale or rental of, or otherwise make unavailable or deny, a dwelling to any person because of race, color, religion, sex, familial status, or national origin.

(b) To discriminate against any person in the terms, conditions, or privileges of sale or rental of a dwelling, or in the provision of services or facilities in connection therewith, because of race, color, religion, sex, familial status, or national origin.

(c) To make, print, or publish, or cause to be made, printed, or published any notice, statement, or advertisement, with respect to the sale or rental of a dwelling that indicates any preference, limitation, or discrimination based on race, color, religion, sex, handicap, familial status, or national origin, or an intention to make any such preference, limitation, or discrimination.

(d) To represent to any person because of race, color, religion, sex, handicap, familial status, or national origin that any dwelling is not available for inspection, sale, or rental when such dwelling is in fact so available.

(e) For profit, to induce or attempt to induce any person to sell or rent any dwelling by representations regarding the entry or prospective entry into the neighborhood of a person or persons of a particular race, color, religion, sex, handicap, familial status, or national origin.

(f)(1) To discriminate in the sale or rental, or to otherwise make unavailable or deny, a dwelling to any buyer or renter because of a handicap of —

(A) that buyer or renter;

(B) a person residing in or intending to reside in that dwelling after it is so sold, rented, or made available; or

(C) any person associated with that buyer or renter.

(2) To discriminate against any person in the terms, conditions, or privileges of sale or rental of a dwelling, or in the provision of services or facilities in connection with such dwelling, because of a handicap of —

(A) that person; or

(B) a person residing in or intending to reside in that dwelling after it is so sold, rented, or made available; or

(C) any person associated with that person.

(3) For purposes of this subsection, discrimination includes —

(A) a refusal to permit, at the expense of the handicapped person, reasonable modifications of existing premises occupied or to be occupied by such person if such modifications may be necessary to afford such person full enjoyment of the premises except that, in the case of a rental, the landlord may where it is reasonable to do so condition permission for a modification on the renter agreeing to restore the interior of the premises to the condition that existed before the modification, reasonable wear and tear excepted.

(B) a refusal to make reasonable accommodations in rules, policies, practices, or services, when such accommodations may be necessary to afford such person equal opportunity to use and enjoy a dwelling; or

(C) in connection with the design and construction of covered multifamily dwellings for first occupancy after the date that is 30 months after September 13, 1988, a failure to design and construct those dwellings in such a manner that —

(i) the public use and common use portions of such dwellings are readily accessible to and usable by handicapped persons;

(ii) all the doors designed to allow passage into and within all premises within such dwellings are sufficiently wide to allow passage by handicapped persons in wheelchairs; and

(iii) all premises within such dwellings contain the following features of adaptive design:

(I) an accessible route into and through the dwelling;

(II) light switches, electrical outlets, thermostats, and other environmental controls in accessible locations;

(III) reinforcements in bathroom walls to allow later installation of grab bars; and

(IV) usable kitchens and bathrooms such that an individual in a wheelchair can maneuver about the space.

(4) Compliance with the appropriate requirements of the American National Standard for buildings and facilities providing accessibility and usability for physically handicapped people (commonly cited as "ANSI A117.1") suffices to satisfy the requirements of paragraph (3)(C)(iii).

CIVIL RIGHTS ACT OF 1866
42 U.S.C. § 1982

§ 1982. Property rights of citizens

All citizens of the United States shall have the same right, in every State and Territory, as is enjoyed by white citizens thereof to inherit, purchase, lease, sell, hold, and convey real and personal property.

NOTES, QUESTIONS, AND PROBLEMS

1. **Is state action required?** In Jones v. Alfred H. Mayer Co., 392 U.S. 409 (1968), the Court held that § 1982 bars racial discrimination in the sale or rental of public and private property. To what extent is private housing covered by the 1968 Fair Housing Act?

2. **Discriminatory intent or effect?** In Village of Arlington Heights v. Metropolitan Hous. Dev. Corp., 429 U.S. 252 (1977), the Court held that the plaintiff must prove discriminatory purpose or motive to establish an equal

protection violation, but suggested that discriminatory effect is sufficient for federal statutory violations, unless Congress provides otherwise. The lower courts were initially divided, *compare* Boyd v. Lefrak Organization, 509 F.2d 1110 (2d Cir. 1975), *with* Robinson v. 12 Lofts Realty, Inc., 610 F.2d 1032 (2d Cir. 1979), but the disparate effect test now seems to predominate. *See, e.g.,* Charleston Housing Auth. v. U.S. Dept. of Agriculture, 419 F.3d 729 (8th Cir. 2005) ("disparate impact"); Tsombanidis v. West Haven Fire Dept., 352 F.3d 565 (2d Cir. 2003) (same).

3. **Comparisons.** Make a comparison of the Fair Housing Act (FHA) and the Civil Rights Act of 1866. Some relevant questions: If a landlord refuses to rent to an unmarried heterosexual couple, or to a gay couple, does the landlord violate either the FHA or the Civil Rights Act? Does either the FHA or the Civil Rights Act apply to discrimination in commercial transactions? Within its coverage, does the Civil Rights Act contain any exclusions?

4. **Remedies.** The Fair Housing Act specifies a comprehensive set of administrative and judicial remedies. *See* 42 U.S.C. § 3610 (within one year of an alleged discriminatory act, an aggrieved person may file a complaint with the Secretary of Housing and Urban Development, which may lead to a conciliation agreement, or to a further referral to the Attorney General or to a state or local public agency for prosecution as a civil action); § 3612 (Secretary may present complaints to an administrative law judge or file suit in court; judicial remedies are the same as those provided in § 3613); § 3613 (within two years after the occurrence or termination of an alleged discriminatory practice, the aggrieved party may file suit in the appropriate federal district court; if the court finds that a discriminatory practice has or is about to occur, the court may award actual and punitive damages, and may grant permanent or temporary injunctive relief; the court may also allow the prevailing party other than the United States a reasonable attorney's fee); § 3614 (in cases of a "pattern or practice of resistance to the full enjoyment of any rights provided by" the Act, the Attorney General may file a civil action in the appropriate federal district court; court may award injunctive relief, monetary damages to the person aggrieved, and level fines of $50,000 for a first violation and $100,000 for any subsequent violation, and attorney's fees to the prevailing party other than the United States).

The Civil Rights Act of 1866 does not provide administrative remedies. Courts have held that equitable and legal remedies are available, including punitive damages.

5. **State statutes.** Many states have statutes prohibiting discrimination in renting. *See* Restatement Second § 3.1 at 95-117 (1977) (comprehensive listing of statutes). These statutes are useful as potential sources of rights and remedies in addition to those provided by federal law, particularly with regard to discriminatory practices not covered by the federal acts. *See* McCready v. Hoffius, 586 N.W.2d 723 (Mich. 1998), *vacated and remanded,* 593 N.W.2d 545 (Mich. 1999) (dealing with landlord's refusal to rent to unmarried couples on religious grounds); Attorney General v. Desilets, 636 N.E.2d 233 (Mass. 1994) (same).

6. **Literature.** *See generally* James A. Kushner, *The Fair Housing Amendments Act of 1988: The Second Generation of Fair Housing,* 42 Vand. L. Rev. 1049 (1989); James A. Kushner, Fair Housing: Discrimination in Real Estate,

Community Development and Revitalization (2d ed. 1995); Robert S. Schoshinski, American Law of Landlord and Tenant §§ 11:1 through 11:12 (1980); 2 Powell on Real Property § 16B.09.

PROBLEMS

4-N. The following facts are edited, but otherwise taken verbatim from Jancik v. Department of Housing and Urban Development, 44 F.3d 553 (7th Cir. 1995):

> Stanley Jancik owns Building No. 44 in King Arthur's Court, a large housing complex in the Chicago suburb of Northlake. King Arthur's Court houses people of all ages, including children, and although all of the apartments in Jancik's building have only one bedroom, they are large enough to house more than one occupant under local codes. Jancik placed this ad in a local suburban newspaper: "NORTHLAKE deluxe 1 BR apt, a/c, newer quiet bldg, pool, prkg, mature person preferred, credit checked. $395." The Investigations Manager for the Chicago Leadership Council for Metropolitan Open Communities decided to "test" the property. In that process, "testers" bearing fictitious identities pose as potential renters in order to check for discriminatory practices. In this instance, [the investigations manager] chose to use volunteer testers Cindy Gunderson, who is white, and Marsha Allen, who is African American, for the task.
>
> Gunderson spoke with Jancik by telephone on the evening of September 7, 1990. She subsequently related that after asking Gunderson her age and learning that she was 36, Jancik told her "that was good — he doesn't want any teenagers in there." Jancik also asked Gunderson her name and, upon hearing it, inquired "what kind of name" it was. Learning that the name was Norwegian, Jancik asked whether "that's white Norwegian or black Norwegian" and repeated the question a second time after Gunderson failed to answer. Gunderson asked Jancik whether he was inquiring as to her race and, after he responded affirmatively, told him that she was white. Gunderson then asked to view the apartment and the two arranged for her to do so the following morning.
>
> Marsha Allen spoke with Jancik two hours later the same evening. Jancik asked Allen her occupation, income, age, marital status, race and whether she had any children or pets. Allen did not reveal her race, but in response to that question asked Jancik why he needed this information. He responded, in her words, "that he had to screen the applicants because the tenants in the building were middle-aged and he did not want anyone moving in who was loud, made a lot of noise and had children or pets." When Allen told Jancik that she did not have any children or pets he said "wonderful," and the two arranged for Allen to see the apartment the next morning. Both testers arrived the next morning at approximately 10:00, and Jancik's rental manager separately informed each that the apartment had been rented earlier that morning.
>
> Based on the reports filed by Gunderson and Allen, the Leadership Council filed an administrative complaint with HUD [in] May, 1991.

[handwritten: 3604(a) a statement relating to race]

(a) What discriminatory practices might the landlord have committed? (b) If the "testers" had been actually seeking apartments, would any additional discriminatory practices have been involved? (c) Could the Leadership Council, or even the testers, have filed the lawsuit instead of referring the case to HUD? *See* Havens Realty Corp. v. Coleman, 455 U.S. 363 (1982); Ragin v. Harry Macklowe Real Estate Co., 6 F.3d 898 (2d Cir. 1993). (d) If Jancik had been renting a room in his house, would your answer to (a) and (b) change?

[handwritten: No, actually rented]
[handwritten: c) both could sue]
[handwritten: statute N/A except for discrim stmts]
[handwritten: (a) does not change]

4-O. Does "a complaint [against a corporation that publishes a newspaper] alleging a violation of section 3604(c) based on the single publication of an advertisement which uses a small number of all-white models . . . state a cognizable claim under section 3604(c) as a matter of law (i.e., so as to withstand a motion to dismiss for failure to state a cause of action)"? If not, what additional allegations might be necessary? Is it relevant that the advertiser uses a large number of models in the ad, or places numerous ads with a particular publisher? *See* Housing Opportunities Made Equal, Inc. v. Cincinnati Enquirer, Inc., 943 F.2d 644 (6th Cir. 1991); Ragin v. The New York Times Co., 923 F.2d 995 (2d Cir. 1991).

[handwritten: No, it was just 1 ad, but if multiple yes]

4-P. Which of the following activities of the landlord might constitute a violation of the FHA's prohibition against discrimination based on "family status"? What evidence of discriminatory impact might be relevant in each case?

    a. Landlord maintains an apartment building containing studio, one-bedroom, and two-bedroom apartments. Landlord's regulations contain the following statement: "Occupancy shall be limited to not more than two persons for studio and one-bedroom apartments, and to not more than three persons for two-bedroom apartments." Tenants, a married couple with a three year old child, apply to rent one of the landlord's studio apartments, and are turned down by the landlord. *See* United States v. Tropic Seas, Inc., 887 F. Supp. 1347 (D. Ct. D. Hawai'i 1995).

[handwritten: discriminatory to restrict studio]

    b. The landlord's printed "Pool and Building Rules" contain the following provisions:

        Rule 4. All unnecessary noise, running, jumping, screaming, loud talking, or dangerous behavior will not be tolerated at any time in or around the pool or building areas.

        Rule 7. No toys, inner tubes, balls or any other objects whatsoever will be allowed in or around the pool area or inside the building area at any time.

        Rule 8. Children will not be allowed to play or run around inside the building area at any time because of disturbance to other tenants or damage to building property. Bikes, carriages, strollers, tricycles, wagons, etc., must be kept inside apartments or in garage area and not left outside.

On deposition, the manager of the apartments testified that she prefers to rent apartments with second-floor entries to families without small children, and that she has told prospective children with small children that they should rent an apartment with a first-floor entry because the second-floor entry units were "dangerous." After 15 months of occupancy, Tenant vacated a first-floor apartment after being served with a notice threatening eviction because her son had been admonished by the manager not to splash in the pool, not to bounce a basketball, and not to ride his bicycle. Tenant, joined by the local chapter of the Fair Housing Congress, sued the apartment landlord and manager for discrimination. What statements or actions by the manager might constitute violations of the FHA, and of which sections? *See* Fair Housing Congress v. Weber, 993 F. Supp. 1286 (C.D. Cal. 1997). *See also* United States v. Grishman, 818 F. Supp. 21 (D. Me. 1993).

4-Q. On discrimination against the handicapped, consider the following:

a. Tenant is confined to a wheelchair and unable to enter or exit the Landlord's building without assistance. Tenant alleges that the lack of a wheelchair ramp or lift on the building violates the Fair Housing Act. The building was constructed in 1910. Estimates for the cost of modification to the building to accomodate tenant range from $25,000 to $55,000. Landlord has lost money in the operation of the building for the previous three years. Rodriguez v. 551 West 157th St. Owners Corp., 992 F. Supp. 385 (S.D.N.Y. 1998).

b. The local housing authority's lease form contains a no-pets provision. The authority refuses to allow tenant, who is deaf in both ears, to keep a dog as a hearing assistance animal unless tenant proves that the dog has been trained by a certified animal assistance trainer or at least by a highly skilled individual. Does the landlord's requirement violate the Fair Housing Act? *See* Green v. Housing Auth. of Clakamas County, 994 F. Supp. 1253 (D. Or. 1998). *See also* Prindable v. Association of Apartment Owners of 2987 Kalakaua, 304 F. Supp. 2d 1245 (D. Hawai'i 2003) (further discussion of dogs as service animals, in situation in which the plaintiff's disability is mental rather than physical).

c. A city ordinance prohibits facilities that serve recovering alcoholics and drug addicts from locating within residential areas of the city. Does the ordinance violate the FHA? *See* Jeffrey O. v. City of Boca Raton, 511 F. Supp. 2d 1339 (S.D. Fla. 2007).

4-R. Landlord owns a six-bedroom residential property that she rents to six unrelated students, each of whom occupies a separate bedroom, and who collectively share common areas of the house. Turnover among tenants in the residence is high. The tenants generally assume responsibility for publicizing vacancies and seeking prospective tenants. The landlord's role in the selection of new tenants is limited; she does not involve herself in the tenant selection process, nor has she ever rejected any applicant who has been accepted by her current tenants. The lease does, however, give landlord the authority either to accept or reject the candidates who are chosen by the tenants. May the landlord be held liable for the discriminatory acts of her tenants in the selection process? Are the tenants liable? *See* Marya v. Slakey, 190 F. Supp. 2d 95 (D. Mass. 2001).

c.   Good Cause for Termination or Nonrenewal

The current widespread prohibitions on the landlord's retaliatory and discriminatory conduct prevent the landlord who has a bad motivation from terminating leases with his tenants. That leaves open the question whether, in the absence of a provable retaliatory or discriminatory motivation, the landlord is free today, as at common law, to terminate or refuse to renew a tenancy without cause — "for any reason or no reason" (but not for a bad reason) as it is sometimes said.

The answer today in most jurisdictions is that the common law prevails. The landlord is not required to have good cause to terminate an indefinite tenancy or to refuse to renew a term tenancy. *See* 2 Powell on Real Property § 16B.05.

There are exceptions. In housing maintained or financed by the federal government, the landlord cannot terminate a tenancy without good cause. *See, e.g.,* Joy v. Daniels, 479 F.2d 1236 (4th Cir. 1973). By statute, New Jersey requires landlords in most residential settings to have good cause for terminating or failing to renew a tenancy. *See* N.J.S.A. § 2A:18-61.1:

2A:18-61.1. Removal of residential tenants; grounds

No lessee or tenant may be removed by the Superior Court from any house, building, mobile home or land in a mobile home park or tenement leased for residential purposes, other than owner-occupied premises with not more than two rental units or a hotel, motel or other guest house or part thereof rented to a transient guest or seasonal tenant except upon establishment of one of the following grounds as good cause:

a. The person fails to pay rent due and owing under the lease whether the same be oral or written.

b. The person has continued to be, after written notice to cease, so disorderly as to destroy the peace and quiet of the occupants or other tenants living in said house or neighborhood.

c. The person has willfully or by reason of gross negligence caused or allowed destruction, damage or injury to the premises.

d. The person has continued, after written notice to cease, to substantially violate or breach any of the landlord's rules and regulations governing said premises, provided such rules and regulations are reasonable and have been accepted in writing by the tenant or made a part of the lease at the beginning of the lease term.

e. (1) The person has continued, after written notice to cease, to substantially violate or breach any of the covenants or agreements contained in the lease for the premises where a right of reentry is reserved to the landlord in the lease for a violation of such covenant or agreement, provided that such covenant or agreement is reasonable and was contained in the lease at the beginning of the lease term. (2) In public housing under the control of a public housing authority or redevelopment agency, the person has substantially violated or breached any of the covenants or agreements contained in the lease for the premises pertaining to illegal uses of controlled dangerous substances, or other illegal activities, whether or not a right of reentry is reserved to the landlord in the lease for a violation of such covenant or agreement, provided that such covenant or agreement conforms to federal guidelines regarding such lease provisions and was contained in the lease at the beginning of the lease term.

f. The person has failed to pay rent after a valid notice to quit and notice of increase of said rent, provided the increase in rent is not unconscionable and complies with any and all other laws or municipal ordinances governing rent increases.

. . . .

i. The landlord or owner proposes, at the termination of a lease, reasonable changes of substance in the terms and conditions of the lease, including specifically any change in the term thereof, which the tenant, after written notice, refuses to accept.

. . . .

m. The landlord or owner conditioned the tenancy upon and in consideration for the tenant's employment by the landlord or owner as superintendent, janitor or in some other capacity and such employment is being terminated.

Does the New Jersey statute in effect convert every residential lease covered by the statute into a determinable life estate (or determinable fee simple, if the tenant's right to security of tenure is transmissible at her death), or do the types of tenancies (term of years, etc.) remain relevant under the statute? *Should* a right to security of possession — a right to remain in possession until the landlord has cause to evict — be recognized as part of the common law of tenants' rights, on a par with the widely-recognized right to habitable premises? *See generally* Deborah Hodges Bell, *Providing Security of Tenure for Residential Tenants: Good Faith as a Limitation on the Landlord's Right to Terminate*, 19 Ga. L. Rev. 483 (1985); Kenneth Salzberg & Audrey A. Zibelman, *Good Cause Eviction*, 21 Willamette L. Rev. 61 (1985).

C. LANDLORD'S RIGHTS AND REMEDIES

In this Section, we consider the tenant's duties with respect to a core set of the landlord's concerns: the tenant who doesn't pay rent; the tenant who abandons the premises before, or who holds over after, the term ends; the tenant who uses the premises improperly; and the tenant who injures the leased premises. No less than the landlord, the tenant is subject to a variety of obligations imposed by law to deal with those concerns. According to the Restatement Second, "[t]he obligations of the tenant inherent in the landlord-tenant relationship which arise without the aid of any express promise by the tenant are to pay the rent reserved, not to commit waste, and not to use the leased property for an illegal purpose." Restatement Second of Property (Landlord and Tenant), Introductory Note to Ch. 12, at 383 (1977). In modern parlance, the duties specified in the Restatement are default rules, which the parties may modify by their agreement. In addition, the lease will almost invariably contain express promises by the tenant that buttress or expand the tenant's implied-in-law obligations, and that add others, thus putting a contractual overlay on the underlying property relationship. Whether the tenant has committed a breach of any duty depends on the content of that duty, which may be specified in the parties' agreement, and where not, will be determined by applicable rules of construction.

When the tenant *does* breach a duty owed to the landlord, questions of remedy arise: Under what circumstances may the landlord terminate the lease? When the landlord affirms, is specific performance available? In either event, what damages may the landlord recover?

1.   Rent and Rental Value

The parties to a lease usually specify a sum that is due to the landlord as rent. The *form* of the provision for rent varies: the tenant may "promise" (or "agree" or "covenant") to pay rent or the landlord may "reserve" rent. Even without an express stipulation for rent (promise or reservation), the tenant might owe the landlord for the fair rental value of the premises.

Rent. Rent is the compensation specified by the parties for the tenant's use of the landlord's premises. *See* Application of Rosewell, 387 N.E.2d 866, 870 (Ill. App. Ct. 1979). The compensation is usually, although it need not be, a sum of money. *See* Grant v. Detroit Assoc. of Women's Clubs, 505 N.W.2d 254 (Mich. 1993) ("[tenant's] consideration for the use and occupancy of the apartment was his labor"). When the compensation is money, it need not be a fixed sum. For example, an agreement that rent is to consist of a percentage of the gross sales made by the tenant is a common feature of commercial leases (often in conjunction with a provision providing a fixed minimum rental that is due regardless of sales). *See generally* 1 American Law of Property §§ 3.64 through 3.74 (A.J. Casner ed. 1952); 2 Powell on Real Property § 17A.01[2][a]; Robert S. Schoshinski, American Law of Landlord and Tenant §§ 5:34 through 5:50 (1980).

Promise and reservation. Early leases were agricultural, and the landlord's compensation depended on the success of the tenant's crop. In the days before bilateral contracts, the medieval legal mind developed a property theory of rent (which we saw in Smith v. McEnany in Section B.2.a). Rent "issued out of the land," and was due not because the tenant promised to pay it, but because the landlord "reserved" a rent, as an owner might reserve a right of way easement across land transferred to a grantee. *See* John A. Humbach, *The Common-Law Conception of Leasing: Mitigation, Habitability, and Dependence of Covenants,* 60 Wash. U. L.Q. 1213, 1126-1129 (1980):

> The tenant's obligation to pay rent can be interpreted to result from a purely "property" interest in the land, in this case a property interest held by the landlord. Unlike the tenant's possessory property interest, the landlord's property interest in the rent is not possessory, but [is] rather an "incorporeal" interest in the land, similar to an easement or profit a prendre. These interests are referred to as "incorporeal" because they do not carry a right to possession.
>
> The incorporeal property interest called rent is created by a so-called "reservation" in the lease. In making a lease, the landlord does not have to part with the entirety of the ownership interest. The landlord may hold back or "reserve" part of the ownership. For example, the landlord may reserve a right of passage across the land, or a right to sever timber. Comparably, a landlord may reserve a right to receive a stipulated monetary amount out of the benefits that the land is deemed to yield during specific time periods, for example $500 per month for each month of the

lease term. Like other incorporeal interests, rent is a property interest in the land itself, reserved and held by the landlord, and this reserved property right to share in the benefits of possession exists irrespective of any express contractual promise by the tenant to pay rent.

Under common law pleading, an action in debt was the appropriate form of action for enforcing the duty to pay. The gist of this action was that the defendant held a sum of money belonging to the plaintiff.

The important point is that a sum of money could become due, and the action in debt was available, even if the tenant never, even impliedly, promised or contracted to pay a penny. The landlord's right to the rent payments could exist purely as a property interest whenever, by "reserving" a rent, he withheld from the tenant a part of the total interest that he held in the land.

Instead of (or in addition to) a reservation, the parties might state the rent obligation in the form of a promise by the tenant to pay rent. The distinction between promised and reserved rent (and thus the importance of classification when the parties express themselves ambiguously) is important in the law of assignment and sublease: a tenant who promises to pay rent remains liable after assigning the lease if the assignee does not pay; if the tenant's obligation to the landlord is based on a reservation, the assignment terminates the tenant's liability. *See* Section D.3.

Fair rental value. Fair rental value is not the same thing as rent, although some courts mistakenly call it that. The theory of the tenant's obligation to pay fair rental value is suggested by the Restatement Second of Property (Landlord and Tenant) § 12.1 cmt. b:

> *Effect if no rent reserved in the lease.* If no rent is reserved [or promised] in the lease, the tenant is not under any obligation to pay rent. It is a question of fact in each case whether the landlord intended to make a gift to the tenant of the use of the leased property. If he did not, the tenant is liable for the reasonable worth of his use and occupation and the landlord is entitled to recover in an appropriate action the amount owed by the tenant. This amount is not rent, and hence the landlord's rights thereto are not the rights he has with respect to rent.

See also Uniform Residential Landlord and Tenant Act § 1.401(b) (in absence of agreement, tenant shall pay fair rental value for use and occupation); Beacom v. Daley, 81 N.W.2d 907 (Neb. 1957) (discussing occupant's duty to pay fair rental value). The landlord's cause of action for the recovery of fair rental value is restitutionary; the theory is that the tenant, if not a donee, would be unjustly enriched without the duty to account for the fair rental value of the occupied premises. The existence of a parent-child or other close relationship might support an inference of a gift.

One common situation in which a tenant owes fair rental value is when the tenant holds over after the expiration of the lease term. The tenant becomes an occupant at sufferance, and owes the fair rental value of his possession until the landlord elects to impose a new lease or to terminate the possession. *See* Section C.3 below.

A tenant who occupies under an illegal lease also owes fair rental value for the period of occupancy. *See* Section C.3 below.

a.   Suits for Rent

The Second Restatement § 12.1(2) provides that "the landlord may recover from the tenant the amount of the rent that is due" when the tenant fails to pay. While that sounds simple enough, there are complications, particularly in long-term commercial leases, as the following short but important case shows.

FIRST NATIONAL BANK OF OMAHA v. OMAHA NATIONAL BANK
214 N.W.2d 483 (Neb. 1974)

McCOWN, JUSTICE.

[The tenant under a fifty year lease stopped paying rent ($833.34 per month), as well as taxes and insurance, all of which the tenant was required to pay by the terms of the lease. The landlord sued and got a judgment for the sums that had accrued up to the date of trial. A few months later, the landlord applied to the trial court for recovery of the rent, insurance premiums and taxes that had accrued since the original judgment. The trial court entered judgment for the landlord as to these accrued sums. The judgment also provided that the court would retain jurisdiction and that the judgment "shall mature and become effective as to each unmatured installment of rent, taxes and insurance on the day after said installment or payments are due and execution may then issue at the instance of the Plaintiff to satisfy the same." The tenant appealed, arguing that the trial court lacked jurisdiction to enter a judgment for future unmatured installments of rent, taxes, and insurance. The lease did not contain an acceleration clause.]

Rent, as such, is not payable until it falls due under the terms of a lease, and no suit can be brought for future rent in the absence of a clause permitting acceleration. Here there is no abandonment, nor has the lessor retaken possession, and there is no acceleration clause. The granting of judgment for unmatured installments of rent, taxes, and insurance was improper. That conclusion is reinforced in this case by the fact that any judgment for sums to become due in the future must, of necessity, be uncertain and indefinite in amount. The amounts of future taxes and insurance are obviously subject to variation, and therefore the specific amount cannot be determined in advance. Any judgment for future rent is likewise uncertain in that destruction of the building might terminate the liability for rent. The entry of such judgments for indefinite and variable amounts to mature and become payable in the future also shifts the basic burden of proof from the lessor to the lessee.

That portion of the judgment here which pertains to matured installments of rent, taxes, and insurance and provides for the retention of jurisdiction by the District Court should be affirmed. That part of the judgment which provides for the entry of judgment and the issuance of execution as to any unmatured installments of rent, taxes, and insurance should be vacated. The judgment should be modified to provide that upon application and showing to the court from time to time, after due notice to all parties, judgment or judgments as to any installments of rent, taxes, or insurance then matured may be entered. As so modified, the judgment of the District Court is affirmed. Costs are assessed to plaintiff appellee, First National Bank of Omaha.

Affirmed in part, and in part vacated and remanded with directions for modification.

NOTES AND QUESTIONS

1. **Time of payment.** If you are a tenant, take a look at your lease. Does it state that rent is "payable in advance on the first of each month" or words to that effect? What result without the quoted language?

2. **No installment judgments.** In the principal case, the district court's judgment provided that it would become effective as to each unmatured installment of rent "on the day after said installment [is] due, and execution may *then* issue at the instance of the Plaintiff to satisfy the same" (emphasis added). What procedure did that judgment make available to the landlord? In reversing that judgment, what procedure did the Nebraska Supreme Court require?

3. **Importance of acceleration clauses.** How often will the plaintiff in the *First National Bank* case have to go back to court? Note that the lease was for 50 years; is the statute of limitations a relevant consideration for the plaintiff's lawyer? Does the case indicate why an acceleration clause is important in long-term leases?

4. **Operation of acceleration clauses.** How do acceleration clauses operate, and what are their limits? *See* Restatement Second § 12.1 cmt. k at 394:

> *Rent acceleration clause as expansion of landlord's remedies.* The parties may provide in the lease that if the tenant defaults in the payment of rent or fails in some other way to perform his obligations under the lease, the total amount of rent payable during the term of the lease shall immediately become due and payable. If the acceleration clause is enforced, the landlord cannot terminate the lease for the tenant's default that generated the rent acceleration, nor can the landlord terminate the lease for any other default of the tenant, without reimbursing the tenant for the rent he has paid in advance, less any damages the landlord is entitled to collect from the tenant for such default.
>
> If the rent acceleration clause does not provide for any discount as to the rent for the remaining term that will be paid in advance as a result of the enforcement of the clause, its enforcement has the effect of increasing the total amount of the rent that would otherwise be payable under the lease. It may be unconscionable to enforce the clause without a discount, particularly in the case of a lease that has a substantial number of years to run at the time the acceleration takes place. If it is determined that the enforcement of the clause without a discount would be unconscionable, the clause may be enforced with an appropriate discount being allowed.

A rent acceleration clause may be unconscionable if it provides for rent acceleration on a default by the tenant without first requiring a demand by the landlord that the tenant eliminate the default, which demand allows the tenant a reasonable time to comply. If it is determined that the enforcement of a rent acceleration clause without a demand would be unconscionable, the clause may be enforced after a demand has been made, if the tenant has not complied.

See also Horizon Medical Group v. City Center of Charlotte County, Ltd., 779 So. 2d 545 (Fla. Dist. Ct. App. 2001) (landlord cannot collect accelerated rent from tenant and also retain proceeds from reletting premises).

5. **No abandonment.** The court in the principal case notes that the tenant had not abandoned the premises. For a consideration of the landlord's options had the tenant abandoned, see Section C.2 below. Should the landlord in the principal case — who failed to recover future rent — next sue for *possession* of the premises on the basis of the tenant's nonpayment? For a consideration of potential obstacles on that question (apart from the possible application of the doctrine of election of remedies), see the next principal case.

b.   Termination of the Lease and Recovery of Possession

A major remedy in the landlord's arsenal is the power to terminate the lease and evict the tenant when the tenant defaults on the obligation to pay rent. As the following materials indicate, the existence and effective use of the power to terminate may depend on careful drafting of the lease by the landlord's lawyer. And although our immediate focus is on the landlord's recovery of possession for the tenant's failure to pay rent, the concepts discussed are applicable to the tenant's breach of any other important obligations imposed by the lease.

CAIN PARTNERSHIP, LTD. v. PIONEER INVESTMENT SERVICES CO.
914 S.W.2d 452 (Tenn. 1996)

REID, JUSTICE.

This case presents for review the decision of the trial court granting summary judgment to the defendant/lessee in an unlawful detainer action to recover possession of certain commercial property leased to the defendant by the plaintiff. The award of summary judgment is reversed, and the case is remanded to the trial court.

I

The facts and circumstances which form the context for the questions of law presented are not disputed. In 1974, the Cain Partnership LTD (Cain), a limited partnership, leased a tract of commercial real property located in Knox County for a term of 20 years and granted the lessee the right to extend the lease for three terms of 20 years each and an additional term of 15 years. In 1987, the lease was assigned to a subsidiary of the defendant, Pioneer Investment Services Co. (Pioneer), and later transferred to Pioneer.

The provisions of the lease relevant to the issues are:

> In consideration of the lease aforesaid the Lessee contracts and agrees to pay for the aforesaid premises an annual rental of $18,000.00, payable at the rate of $1,500.00 per month in advance, the first said monthly payment to be due on the 1st day of January, 1975. The rental shall be paid at the office of the general partner of Lessor in Knoxville, Tennessee, promptly when due and without demand either upon the premises or elsewhere.
>
> As further consideration for said lease, and in addition to the monthly payment provided for herein, the Lessee shall pay all real property taxes assessed against said property by taxing authorities during the term of this lease and any renewal thereof. Said taxes shall be paid promptly when due during the entire term.

The lease contains no language regarding defaults in payment or performance, forfeiture, or remedies for breach of the terms of the lease, except for a provision allowing the recovery of attorneys' fees in the event Cain should be required to take legal action to enforce the terms of the lease.

On November 12, 1991, this suit was commenced [by the landlord]. The complaint alleges unlawful detainer [under] Tenn.Code Ann. § 29-18-104 (1980), and seeks possession of the leased premises, incidental damages, and attorney's fees. The plaintiff contends that the lease automatically terminated upon the defendant's failure to pay the taxes when due, and, in the alternative, that the defendant persisted in its failure to comply with the provisions of the lease for the payment of taxes after the receipt of adequate notice and an opportunity to cure the default.

The trial court accepted Pioneer's argument that the lease could not be judicially terminated because it contains no provision for termination, and dismissed the complaint. The Court of Appeals affirmed the trial court's dismissal of the suit. For the purposes of this appeal, the record supports the trial court's finding that the lessee failed to pay the taxes assessed against the property, and that failure was a breach of a material provision of the lease.

II

The only issue before the Court is the relief available to the lessor. Consequently, the issue presented is a question of law. Questions of law are reviewed de novo with no presumption of correctness.

III

The principles defining the rights and obligations of the parties to a lease of real property developed as part of the common law and arise from both property and contract law. A short review regarding the evolvement of these principles is helpful in determining the rights and obligations of the parties in this case.

Lease as Conveyance

Under the theory that the lease conveys the property for a term of years, the tenant is the owner of the leased property for the term and, therefore, the landlord need not concern himself with the property, but only with his damages under the lease; thus, the nonpayment of rent or taxes would result, not in an effort to regain possession of the property by forfeiture, but in a suit for payment of the rent, interests and costs.

> From the premise that a lease is a conveyance there were some consequences. When a landlord conveyed — executed and delivered a lease to a tenant — he had done all he had to. From then on the tenant was on his own. Landlord need not repair. Nor need he render any services to tenant. If the house burned down it did not matter. The lease continued, as well as tenant's liability for rent and other obligations.

> There was also an important consequence to the landlord. By conveying to the tenant for a specified term, landlord parted with all possessory rights until the time specified in the lease for its expiration. Neither nonpayment of rent nor breach of covenant by tenant divested the estate so created or revested landlord with a right to possession. His remedy was to sue for rent or for breach of covenant, but with no right to dispossess. This has been changed generally in this country by statutes that give a landlord possessory remedies for nonpayment of rent, and by statutes and lease provisions that extend possessory remedies to breach of covenant and to other circumstances as well.

1 Milton R. Friedman, Friedman on Leases, § 1.1 (1990).

Detainer and Re-entry Law

The Tennessee statute creates a right to bring a cause of action for a writ of possession when a lessee remains on the leased property after the lease has been terminated. The statute provides:

> Unlawful detainer is where the defendant enters by contract, either as tenant or as assignee of a tenant, or as personal representative of a tenant, or as subtenant, or by collusion with a tenant, and, in either case, willfully and without force, holds over the possession from the landlord, or the assignee of the remainder or reversion.

Tenn.Code Ann. § 29-18-104 (1980). However, the detainer statute by itself does not address the problem of the tenant who breaches the provisions of the lease which has not by its terms expired. Thus, at common law, the landlord had to specifically provide for forfeiture of the lease upon a breach of the terms in the lease itself.

This harsh result has been changed in many instances by statute:

> At common law, if the lease simply imposed a promissory obligation on the tenant and nothing more, a breach of the obligation gave the landlord an action for breach of contract, but no power to terminate the lease. In order to have the power to terminate at common law, the landlord had to couple

the covenant with an express provision for forfeiture of the lease upon breach of the covenant. The common law approach has now been widely changed by statutes which give the landlord, in the absence of a lease forfeiture clause, the power to terminate the lease for at least the most serious kinds of tenant defaults, such as failure to pay rent.

2 Richard R. Powell, Powell on Real Property § 17.02[1][a][i].

> It is generally recognized that a strict adherence to viewing the lease as a conveyance in property should yield to contract law in the situation of the tenant who fails to pay rent. The Uniform Residential Landlord and Tenant Act explicitly recognizes the landlord's remedy of termination of the lease in cases of "material noncompliance by the tenant with the rental agreement." Accordingly, under the Uniform Act, the landlord's remedy of termination, subject to proper notice to the tenant, is recognized regardless of whether the landlord has specifically reserved the right to terminate in the lease. The Restatement (Second) of Property § 13.1 takes substantially the same position, allowing the landlord to terminate the lease for the tenant's failure to perform a promise within a reasonable time after being requested by the landlord to do so where as a result of the failure "the landlord is deprived of a significant inducement to the making of the lease." Upon the tenant's failure to leave voluntarily after failure to correct the breach, the landlord may pursue whatever remedies are provided under local law to recover property from a holdover tenant.

Id. § 17.02[1][a][ii]. *Cf.* Tenn.Code Ann. § 66-28-505 (1993) (providing for termination of a lease governed by the Tennessee Uniform Residential Landlord and Tenant Act — "[i]f rent is unpaid when due and the tenant fails to pay, written notice by the landlord of nonpayment is required" before termination of a residential lease). However, the Tennessee statute is limited to residential leases and does not by its terms control the rights and liabilities of the parties to a lease of non-residential property.

IV

Prior decisions of this Court have followed the common law concept that a lease is a conveyance of an interest in real property and the rights of the parties are determined by property law. Historically, the chief distinction between a condition and a covenant in an instrument of conveyance pertains to the remedy available to the grantor; breach of a condition subjects the grantee's estate to forfeiture, breach of a covenant subjects the grantor to an action for damages only.

This common law concept, which is based on the technical characteristics of conditions, covenants, and limitations, see 2 Powell on Real Property at § 17.02[1][a][i], has been replaced in most jurisdictions by statutes which provide the landlord a summary procedure whereby the tenant may be evicted after a default in the payment of rent, whether or not the lease has a clause terminating the lease on failure to pay rent. Restatement Second of Property (Landlord and Tenant) § 12.1 (1977); 2 Powell on Real Property at § 17.02[1][a][ii]. However, Tennessee has no such statute applicable to non-residential leases.

The positions of the parties in this case demonstrate the failure of these traditional common law rules of property law to accommodate present business conditions. Cain's position is that Pioneer "irrevocably breached" the lease by failing to pay the taxes, thereby allowing Cain to terminate the lease at its will. Cain contends that the commencement of the unlawful detainer suit constituted its election to terminate the lease. Pioneer, on the other hand, contends that a leasehold estate in non-residential property "cannot be terminated" in the absence of a clearly stated condition subsequent, and proof of breach, notice and re-entry. Pioneer contends that Cain's only remedy for Pioneer's failure to pay the taxes (or any other breach or default) was an action, or perhaps successive actions, against Pioneer for damages. The history of this case is ample evidence of the inadequacy of these common law rules of property.

In the case before the Court, the lessee's obligation to pay the taxes is stated in the same language and in the same context as the obligation to pay the rent. The instrument evidences the intention that these obligations, which are "in consideration of the lease," are of equal significance. In analyzing the issues in this case, there is no basis on which to distinguish between a covenant and a condition. The terms of the lease are unambiguous in providing that both rent and taxes were to be paid by the lessee. It is recognized that, "[t]he covenant of a tenant to pay taxes, like a covenant to pay rent, involves the payment of a sum of money which is ascertained, or readily ascertainable." Dreisonstok v. Dworman Bldg. Corp., 284 A.2d 400, 404 (Md. 1971). The consequences of the tenant's failure to pay taxes may be more detrimental to the lessor than the failure to pay rent.

The intention of the parties is not given expression in the technical differences between covenants and conditions. The parties' rights and liabilities should turn on an interpretation of the lease, the conduct of the parties, and rules which are consistent with modern business practice. The timely evolution of the common law requires that this result be accomplished.

The provisions of the Restatement of Property (Second) § 13.1 (1977) reflect the principles of mutuality and fairness which should govern the determination and enforcement of the legal rights at issue in this case. Consequently, the resolution of the issues presented will be according to that section, which states:

§ 13.1 Nonperformance of Tenant's Promise — Remedies Available

Except to the extent the parties to a lease validly agree otherwise, if the tenant fails to perform a valid promise contained in the lease to do, or to refrain from doing, something on the leased property or elsewhere, and as a consequence thereof, the landlord is deprived of a significant inducement to the making of the lease, if the tenant does not perform his promise within a reasonable period of time after being requested to do so, the landlord may:

(1) terminate the lease and recover damages; or

(2) continue the lease and obtain appropriate equitable and legal relief, including

(a) recovery of damages, and

(b) recovery of the reasonable cost of performing the tenant's promise.

[Our] decision requires that the case be remanded to the trial court for further proceedings. The parties may be allowed to amend their pleadings if necessary to address all of the issues relevant to the resolution of their rights and obligations under the lease.

The costs are assessed against the appellants and appellees equally.

NOTES AND QUESTIONS

A. Termination for Breach: Common Law, Statutes, and Lease Clauses

1. **Common law.** What is the common law rule regarding the landlord's power to terminate the lease when the tenant commits a breach? The rule is based on the distinction between a covenant (promise) and a condition (recall defeasible estates from Chapter 2); can you also explain it in terms of the doctrine of independency of promises? Why did the court reject the common law rule?

2. **Authorities.** Although *Cain* might augur a trend in the common law, it is at present a minority view: in general, the tenant's failure to pay rent, or to perform any other duty imposed by law or expressed in the agreement, is not a basis for the landlord's termination of the lease unless the lease or a statute (see Note 3) expressly provides for termination. *See, e.g.*, Kennamer Shopping Center, Inc. v. Bi-Low Foods, Inc., 571 So. 2d 299 (Ala. 1990) (tenant's failure to pay rent; statute providing for termination of lease upon "default of any terms of the lease" did not "of itself provide an independent right of re-entry or power of termination upon failure of terms of the leasehold agreement in the absence of a provision therefor in the agreement itself"); Schlegel v. Hansen, 570 P.2d 292 (Idaho 1977) (rent; right to forfeiture for tenant's breach must be "clearly stipulated"); Churchwell v. Coller & Stoner Bldg. Co., 385 N.E.2d 492 (Ind. App. Ct. 1979) (no-pets clause; tenant's breach of covenant "generally" does not allow termination without express clause); Rubin v. Josephson, 478 A.2d 665 (Me. 1984) (rent); Olson v. Pedersen, 231 N.W.2d 310 (Neb. 1975) (various breaches alleged by landlord); Couch v. ADC Realty Corp., 268 S.E.2d 237, 241 (N.C. Ct. App. 1980) ("Unless there is an express provision for a forfeiture in a lease, a breach of covenant does not work a forfeiture.").

3. **Summary eviction statutes.** All summary dispossess statutes have procedural significance: when applicable, they establish a streamlined process for the landlord to recover possession from a tenant, in place of the cumbersome common law or statutory action in ejectment. Unlike the Tennessee statute, many statutes also have substantive significance: they provide the landlord with a cause of action to recover possession for specified breaches by the tenant, even though the landlord has not expressly provided in the lease for such termination. Statutory provisions for summary eviction when the tenant fails to pay rent are widespread; generalization about other breaches is difficult. The following New York statute illustrates the substantive significance of summary eviction statutes:

§ 711. Grounds where landlord-tenant relationship exists

A tenant shall not be removed from possession except in a special proceeding. A special proceeding may be maintained under this article upon the following grounds:

1. The tenant continues in possession of any portion of the premises after the expiration of his term, without the permission of the landlord.

2. The tenant has defaulted in the payment of rent, pursuant to the agreement under which the premises are held, and a demand of the rent has been made, or at least three days' notice in writing requiring, in the alternative, the payment of the rent, or the possession of the premises, has been served upon him as prescribed in section 735.

5. The premises, or any part thereof, are used or occupied as a bawdy-house, or house or place of assignation for lewd persons, or for purposes of prostitution, or for any illegal trade or manufacture, or other illegal business.

N.Y. Real Prop. Acts § 711 (McKinney).

Under the New York statute, when is the landlord entitled to use summary eviction proceedings if the lease does not provide a termination clause? Would the *Cain Partnership* landlord have been entitled to summarily evict the tenant under the terms of the New York statute? In *Cain Partnership*, why didn't the holdover provision allow the landlord to use the summary eviction statute without a termination clause? (Apart from remaining in possession after the lease term has run its course, how does a tenant "hold over the possession" from the landlord?) After *Cain Partnership*, does a Tennessee landlord need to include a termination clause to summarily evict a tenant who fails to pay rent, or taxes?

4. **Express termination clauses: obstacles to enforcement.**

(a) When the lease *does* contain an express termination clause, the clause will be strictly construed. *See, e.g.*, Housing Authority of City of Mansfield v. Rovig, 676 S.W.2d 314 (Mo. Ct. App. 1984) (termination denied for tenant's violation of no pets clause, which was not listed among the examples of "good cause" for termination stated in another clause of the lease).

(b) In addition, the Contracts hornbook rule that an express condition — unlike an implied in law ("constructive") condition — must be literally rather than substantially performed is likely to be ignored in lease cases, as it is in contract cases generally. *See* Kiriakides v. United Artists Communications, Inc., 440 S.E.2d 364 (S.C. 1994) (tenant's substantial performance bars termination under express lease clause); Foundation Development Corp. v. Loehmann's, Inc., 788 P.2d 1189 (Ariz. 1990) (same); Friedrich Kessler, Grant Gilmore & Anthony T. Kronman, Contracts: Cases and Materials 985-86 (3d ed. 1986) ("The academic consensus is that the courts will continue to decide condition questions according to their own ideas of materiality and will not be overborne by a nice choice of words in the contract."). *Kiriakides* overruled several cases, including Beard v. Ryder/P-I-E Nationwide, Inc., 355 S.E.2d 872 (S.C. Ct. App. 1987), which had allowed the landlord to terminate the lease because of the tenant's corporate reorganization, even though the reorganized corporation posed no threat of insolvency.

(c) Finally, the landlord's acceptance of a rent payment with knowledge of a breach by the tenant will usually be considered as a "waiver" of the condition, even if the lease contains an anti-waiver clause. *See* Chadwick v. Winn, 421 P.2d 890 (Ariz. 1966) (waiver of condition by acceptance of late rent payment); Winslow v. Dillard Department Stores, Inc., 849 S.W.2d 862 (Tex. App. 1993) (by acceptance of rent, landlord waived anti-waiver clause in lease). Apart from an anti-waiver clause, how might a landlord make a qualified acceptance of rent so as to preserve a right to declare a forfeiture?

B. Self-Help Repossession

5. **Is self-help allowed?** Once the landlord terminates the lease (other than pursuant to a summary dispossession statute), may the landlord recover possession by self-help, such as locking the tenant out? *See* Berg v. Wiley, 264 N.W.2d 145 (Minn. 1978):

> Minnesota has historically followed the common-law rule that a landlord may rightfully use self-help to retake leased premises from a tenant in possession without incurring liability for wrongful eviction, provided two conditions are met: (1) The landlord is legally entitled to possession, such as where a tenant holds over after the lease term or where a tenant breaches a lease containing a reentry clause; and (2) the landlord's means of reentry are peaceable. Under the common law rule, a tenant who is evicted by his landlord may recover damages for wrongful eviction where the landlord either had no right to possession or where the means used to remove the tenant were forcible.

Although it states the common law rule allowing peaceable self-help evictions, the court in *Berg* concluded that *any* attempt at self help by the landlord would be nonpeaceable as a matter of law; the landlord must go to court to recover possession. How would you justify that view? On that point, *Berg* represents the clear trend of the decisions, and some statutes expressly so provide. *See* Robert S. Schoshinski, American Law of Landlord and Tenant § 6.9 (1980). Some of the courts and statutes prohibiting self-help evictions, however, apply only to residential leases; commercial landlords remain free to use peaceable means of recovering possession without going to court. Is that a sound distinction on the self-help question? *See* Simpson v. Lee, 499 A.2d 889, 893-94 (D.C. App. 1985) ("Interest and desire for commercial properties, particularly those in prime locations, as here, are sufficiently keen to result in violence when self-help is permitted."); Spinks v. Taylor, 266 S.E.2d 857, 861 (N.C. Ct. App. 1980), *aff'd in part and remanded*, Spinks v. Taylor, 278 S.E.2d 501 (N.C. 1981) (modern policy of alternative dispute resolution supports lawful self-help remedies: "[T]he courts cannot resolve every dispute between persons or between persons and the state.").

6. **Forcible entry and detainer statutes.** FED statutes have an ancient lineage, and provide remedies to the person forcibly *dispossessed* or forcibly *excluded* from possession. In that guise, the statutes are a remedy intended primarily for the tenant. When 19th century legislators undertook to give the landlord a summary possessory remedy as an alternative to the action in ejectment, some states simply amended their FED statutes to add (or enlarge) a cause of action for unlawful detainer; the landlord's suit for possession in *Cain*

Partnership was a proceeding in unlawful detainer. Some states provide different landlord's and tenant's statutes. *See, e.g.,* N.J. Stat. Ann. § 2A:18-53 (summary eviction); N.J. Stat. Ann. § 2A:39-6 (forcible entry and detainer).

7. **Remedies.** Forcible entry and detainer statutes usually seek to deter forcible evictions by giving the dispossessed tenant a cause of action to recover possession, as well as a claim for augmented (e.g., treble) damages against the landlord. In Spinks v. Taylor, above, the North Carolina Supreme Court held, in the case of a particularly egregious exercise of self-help by the landlord, that the punitive damages and attorney's fees available under the state statute prohibiting unfair and deceptive trade practices were available in an action under the FED statute. Are the remedies and penalties available for the victim of a forcible recovery of possession a relevant factor on the question whether peaceable self-help entries should be allowed?

C. Judicial Proceedings

7. **Summary eviction.**   If self-help isn't allowed or is impractical, the landlord who wants to recover possession must go to court, using the local summary eviction statute, or an action in ejectment. For an extensive discussion of the issues and procedures involved in the landlord's summary eviction of the tenant, see Robert S. Schoshinski, American Law of Landlord and Tenant §§ 6:10-6:20 (1980); Randy Gerchick, *No Easy Way Out: Making the Summary Eviction Process a Fairer and More Efficient Alternative to Landlord Self-Help*, 41 UCLA L. Rev. 759 (1994).

PROBLEM 4-S.

(a) L leases to T, a commercial tenant, for 10 years, ending December 31, 2007. The lease obligates T to pay real estate taxes on the property, and further provides that "In the event that the tenant fails to pay taxes as provided herein, the landlord may re-enter and terminate the tenant's estate." T complies with the lease throughout the ten-year term. After December 31, 2007, T remains in possession, without L's consent, and tenders rent, which L refuses. Is L entitled to evict T in a summary proceeding under the New York statute or the Tennessee statute, both considered in connection with *Cain Partnership*, above? How does this Problem differ from the facts of *Cain Partnerhip*?

(b) Same facts, except that, about halfway through the lease, T stops paying taxes. L wants to terminate the lease. Is L entitled to terminate the lease and use the Tennessee summary eviction statute to recover possession? (Might L signal the election to terminate by the act of filing the summary suit for possession?) Would L be entitled to use summary proceedings under § 711(1) of the New York statute, considered after *Cain Partnership*? *See* Beach v. Nixon, 9 N.Y. 35 (1853) (landlord may use summary eviction statute only when the termination provision creates a term of years determinable, not when it creates a term of years subject to a condition subsequent). How would you draft a lease to satisfy the Beach v. Nixon interpretation of the New York statute? *See* Ross, *Converting Nonpayment to Holdover Summary Proceedings: The New York Experience with Conditional Limitations Based on Nonpayment of Rent*, 15 Fordham Urb. L.J. 289 (1986-

1987). Without reading Ross's article, can you surmise what a "conditional limitation" is?

c.　Security Deposits

The tenant's security deposit provides protection for the landlord against various tenant defaults. Because nonpayment of the last month's rent is one such typical default, we consider security deposits here, at the earliest possible location, just as we considered the availability of summary eviction for nonpayment of rent. The modern law of security deposits in residential leases is widely governed (and changed) by legislation. The following case offers typical statutory provisions for study, and canvasses some of the difficulties facing the landlord who runs afoul of the tenant-protection bent of those statutes. The court ultimately concludes, however, that the landlord was not in breach or committed only a minor breach of the relevant statutory provisions.

NEIHAUS v. MAXWELL
766 N.E.2d 556 (Mass. App. Ct. 2002)

COHEN, J.

The plaintiff, Alexander Neihaus, rented his single family house to the defendants, Mitchell and Tiffani Maxwell, for $2,450 per month, under a written lease covering the period from September 1, 1997, to August 31, 1998. What began as a mutually convenient arrangement — Neihaus had a one-year overseas job assignment, and the Maxwells needed temporary housing while their new home was under construction — degenerated into litigation when the Maxwells refused to vacate the house after Neihaus's return and the expiration of the lease term.

On September 25, 1998, Neihaus brought a summary process action against the Maxwells who, in turn, filed a counterclaim alleging violations of GL c. 186 § 15B, and G.L. c. 93A. After trial, a judge of the Worcester Housing Court entered judgments for Neihaus on both his complaint and the Maxwells' counterclaim. The present appeal is by the Maxwells from the disposition of their counterclaim. At issue is whether Neihaus and his agent complied with those subsections of G.L. c. 186 § 15B, as amended through St.1992, c. 133, § 522, which govern the receipt, holding, and return of tenant security deposits by residential landlords.

The pertinent facts may be summarized as follows. At the inception of the lease, the Maxwells paid Neihaus's agent, Hunneman Residential Services, $2,450 representing the last month's rent and another $2,450 as a security deposit against damage to the premises. Hunneman deposited that money into its "Security Deposit Account," a single account at a Massachusetts bank, in which Hunneman held security deposits and last months' rents for all of Hunneman's residential landlord clients. Hunneman used an internal accounting system which, the trial judge found, was adequate to track the various deposits that were placed in the pooled Security Deposit Account. Hunneman also maintained a separate landlords' operating account into which it deposited the rent received on behalf of Neihaus and from which it paid the expenses associated with Neihaus's property, such as the mortgage, property taxes, water and sewer charges, and repair and maintenance costs.

Although the Maxwells remained in possession after the expiration of the lease and paid rent for August, they failed to make a monthly rent payment for September, 1998. Hunneman, therefore, withdrew the last month's rent from the Security Deposit Account and used it as payment for the Maxwells' use and occupancy of the property during September. The following month, by court order, the Maxwells made a rent payment of $2,450 for October, as a condition of obtaining a continuance of the summary process trial. On October 22, 1998, the judge ordered that judgment for possession of the property enter for Neihaus; he ruled against the Maxwells on their counterclaims; and he required Neihaus to return the Maxwells' security deposit with interest and to pay the Maxwells interest on the last month's rent that they had advanced at the inception of the lease. It is undisputed that Neihaus promptly made these payments.

The Maxwells' primary contention is that their security deposit was illegally commingled with funds belonging to Neihaus and exposed to claims by Neihaus's creditors, in violation of § 15(B)(1)(e),[2] and not held in an appropriate, separate bank account, in violation of § 15(B)(3)(a),[3] thereby entitling them to an award of three times the security deposit plus interest, costs and attorney's fees, pursuant to §§ 15B(6) and 15B(7).[4] We agree with the trial judge that the Maxwells' claim is without merit, because Hunneman's method of holding the security deposit for Neihaus did not run afoul of the statute.

The security deposit provisions of G.L. c. 186, § 15B are designed to insure that tenant monies are protected from potential diversion to the personal use of the landlord, earn interest for the tenant, and are kept from the reach of the landlord's creditors.[5] These objectives were met in this case. The deposit was placed in a bank account that was maintained separately from the landlord's operating account containing Neihaus's own funds; the accounting system utilized by Hunneman kept track of the deposit, distinguished it from other funds in the account and enabled a

---

[2] "A security deposit shall continue to be the property of the tenant making such deposit, shall not be commingled with the assets of the lessor, and shall not be subject to the claims of any creditor of the lessor or of the lessor's successor in interest, including a foreclosing mortgagee or trustee in bankruptcy; provided, however, that the tenant shall be entitled to only such interest as is provided for in subsection (3)(b)." G.L. c. 186, § 15B(1)(e).

[3] "Any security deposit received by such lessor shall be held in a separate, interest-bearing account in a bank, located within the commonwealth under such terms as will place such deposit beyond the claim of creditors of the lessor, including a foreclosing mortgagee or trustee in bankruptcy, and as will provide for its transfer to a subsequent owner of said property." G.L. c. 186, § 15B(3)(a).

[4] "The lessor shall forfeit his right to retain any portion of the security deposit for any reason, or, in any action by a tenant to recover a security deposit, to counterclaim for any damage to the premises if he: (a) fails to deposit such funds in an account as required by subsection (3)." G.L. c. 186, § 15B(6).

"If the lessor or his agent fails to comply with clauses (a), (d), or (e) of subsection 6, the tenant shall be awarded damages in an amount equal to three times the amount of such security deposit or balance thereof to which the tenant is entitled plus interest at the rate of five per cent from the date when such payment became due, together with court costs and reasonable attorney's fees." G.L. c. 186, § 15B(7).

[5] The statute is not without benefit to the landlord, as well, since the landlord is entitled to use the funds if the tenant has damaged the premises or has vacated without paying due rent. G.L. c. 186, § 15B(4).

proper computation of the interest due to the Maxwells; and, because the security deposit was separately designated in this manner, it could not be attached: a creditor could not make the requisite showing that these separately identified funds were due to Neihaus absolutely and without contingency. See G.L. c. 246 § 24; Goodspeed's Book shop, Inc. v. State Street Bank & Trust Co., 391 N.E.2d 1262 (Mass. App. Ct. 1979).

Although the Maxwells are correct that last months' rents are, with certain limitations, the property of the landlord, not the tenant,[6] in the circumstances of this case Hunneman's placement of security deposits in a pooled account along with last months' rents did not constitute prohibited commingling. We do not underestimate the importance of the statutory prohibition on commingling, which is often the first step towards personal use of entrusted funds, whether by accident or design. But, in this case, whether it was required to do so or not, Hunneman kept last months' rents unavailable for use by or on behalf of the landlord until due and owing, at which time they were transferred out of the Security Deposit Account. Thus, the risk inherent in commingling — that a landlord might intentionally or inadvertently use tenant funds when accessing the commingled account to pay operating or other personal expenses — simply did not exist here.

The Maxwells also claim that Neihaus was required to return their security deposit within thirty days of the expiration of the written lease on August 31, 1998, even though they remained in possession of the property until the end of October. This, they argue, was a violation of G.L. c. 186, § 15B(6)(e).[7] Again, we agree with the trial judge that Neihaus's obligation to return the Maxwells' security deposit within thirty days did not arise at the expiration of the written lease but, rather, when they relinquished possession.

An important purpose of security deposits is "to provide a source of funds for the payment of the cost of repairs for which a tenant is responsible." Jinwala v. Bizzaro, 505 N.E.2d 904 (Mass. App. Ct. 1987). It would not be in keeping with this purpose were the statute interpreted to require return of a security deposit before the tenant vacates the premises. It also would be incongruous to confer upon tenants at sufferance, like the Maxwells, greater rights than accrue to tenants at will, who are not due their security deposits until thirty days after the termination of their occupancy of the premises.

---

[6] The landlord is not required to set aside the tenant's last month's rent or to place it in a bank account; however, he is required to pay interest on it at five per cent or any lesser rate paid by the bank, if the money is, in fact, deposited. The landlord must give the tenant an annual statement of interest earned and either remit the interest at the end of each year of tenancy or permit the tenant to deduct the interest from the next rental payment. If the tenancy is terminated before its anniversary date, the landlord must pay the accrued interest within thirty days of the termination to avoid exposure to liability for treble damages, costs, and attorney's fees. G.L. c. 186, § 15B(2)(a).

[7] "The lessor shall forfeit his right to retain any portion of the security deposit for any reason, or, in any action by a tenant to recover a security deposit, to counterclaim for any damage to the premises if he: . . . (e) fails to return to the tenant the security deposit or balance thereof to which the tenant is entitled after deducting therefrom any sums in accordance with the provisions of this section, together with any interest thereon, within thirty days after termination of the tenancy." G.L. c. 186, § 15B(6). Also pertinent is § 15B(4): "The lessor shall, within thirty days after the termination of occupancy under a tenancy-at-will or the end of the tenancy as specified in a valid written lease agreement, return to the tenant the security deposit or any balance thereof."

Finally, the Maxwells contend that Neihaus is liable under G.L. c. 93A for alleged multiple violations of G.L. c. 186, § 15B and regulations promulgated by the Attorney General that designate various security deposit transgressions as unfair and deceptive acts and practices. See 940 Code Mass. Regs. § 3.17 (1993). It may be that Neihaus and Hunneman were not fully in compliance with law in one respect: neither provided the Maxwells with the name or location of the account containing the Maxwells' security deposit, as required by G.L. c. 186 § 15B(3)(a) and 940 Code Mass. Regs. § 3.17(4)(d). Even if c. 93A otherwise provides a remedy for this misstep, and we need not so decide, Neihaus nevertheless cannot be liable under that statute, because he was not engaged in trade or commerce with respect to the isolated rental of his home while he was temporarily living overseas. The mere fact that he used a professional real estate agent to assist him with the rental did not convert what was patently a personal, private transaction into a business activity.

The judgment for Neihaus on the Maxwells' counterclaim is therefore affirmed.

NOTES AND QUESTIONS

1. **Security deposit statutes and consumer protection laws.** In Wallace v. Pastore, 742 A.2d 1090 (Pa. Super. Ct. 1999), the landlord failed to return the tenants' security deposit within thirty days after termination of the lease; in cases of noncompliance, the state's security deposit law required the landlord to pay double the amount of the deposit, minus the actual amount of damage to the premises caused by the tenant. The court affirmed a judgment awarding the tenants their security deposit of $600, treble damages of $1,800, and attorney's fees of $4,980, the latter two sums being based on the state's Unfair Trade Practices and Consumer Protection Law. "In the present case, the trial court found that Pastore engaged in a deceptive business practice because he misrepresented the existence and extent of damage to the apartment. Such a misrepresentation is actionable under the UTPCPL. Accordingly, we find no merit to Pastore's contention that the UTPCPL does not apply herein."

2. **Another security device: the landlord's lien.** By common law, statute, or contractual agreement, the landlord might acquire a lien on the tenant's goods to secure payment of the tenant's rent obligation. To the extent that the common law and statutory liens authorize seizure of the tenant's property prior to judgment on the underlying claim of rent default, and upon the ex parte application of the landlord, they may deny the tenant due process under the Supreme Court's checkered course of decisions dealing with comparable pre-judgment seizures. *Compare* Sniadach v. Family Finance Corp., 395 U.S. 337 (1969) (prejudgment wage garnishment statute violated due process), *and* Fuentes v. Shevin, 407 U.S. 67 (1972) (prejudgment replevin procedure authorizing sheriff to seize property held by debtor under conditional sales contract violated due process), *with* Mitchell v. W.T. Grant Co., 416 U.S. 600 (1974) (statute authorizing prejudgment seizure of property sold under conditional sales contract did not violate due process because of protections of the debtor written into the statute), *and* North Georgia Finishing, Inc. v. Di-Chem, Inc., 419 U.S. 601 (1975) (pre-judgment garnishment procedure lacking the protections of the statute in *Mitchell* violated due process). For full discussion of the constitutional issue, as well as of the scope of the common law, statutory and contractual landlord's lien, see Robert S. Schoshinski, American Law

of Landlord and Tenant §§ 6:21 through 6:26 (1980).

2.   Remedies Against the Abandoning Tenant

When the tenant wrongfully abandons the premises before the end of the term, the traditional common law view is that the landlord is entitled to recover from the tenant the full rentals provided in the lease, without any offset for rentals that the landlord could have received by reletting the premises to a new tenant. The landlord has no "duty to mitigate." (We will use prevailing terminology throughout our remaining discussion of this topic, without quotation marks. Be aware, however, that mitigation is not a true duty: the landlord who fails to mitigate does not commit a breach entitling the tenant to damages and possible termination of the lease. Rather, the rule is one of avoidable consequences: the landlord is unable to recover for losses that the landlord could have avoided by seeking a new tenant or accepting the tenant's preferred reasonable substitute; the corollary is that the landlord is not barred, despite failure to mitigate, from recovering losses that could not have been mitigated.)

Today there is a trend away from the common law rule, and towards imposition of a duty to mitigate on the landlord. But there continue to be adherents to the common law rule. We therefore first address, in Section C.2.a, the question of whether a duty to mitigate should be recognized in lease cases, and if so, the subsidiary questions that arise when a duty to mitigate exists.

Even if a state refuses to recognize a duty to mitigate, landlords may not wish to take advantage of the no-mitigation in its extreme manifestation. Although the landlord is entitled to sit back and do nothing as rent accrues against the abandoning tenant, vacant premises are a headache for the landlord (and society), and the prudent landlord might well want to install a new tenant and look to the abandoning tenant only if the new tenant's payments fail to cover the old tenant's obligations, or the new tenant himself defaults. Traditional doctrine allows the landlord to install a new tenant in the abandoned premises, but encumbers it with some rather important, and not always obvious, restrictions. We consider the landlord's options in a no-mitigation state in Section C.2.b.

Two excellent articles on the topic of abandonment and surrender are Glen Weissenberger, *The Landlord's Duty to Mitigate Damages on the Tenant's Abandonment: A Survey of Old Law and New Trends*, 53 Temple L.Q. 1 (1980), and Sarajane Love, *Landlord's Remedies When the Tenant Abandons: Property, Contract, and Leases*, 30 Kan. L. Rev. 533 (1982).

a.   Duty to Mitigate or Not?

SOMMER v. KRIDEL
378 A.2d 767 (N.J. 1977)

Pashman, J.

We granted certification in these cases to consider whether a landlord seeking damages from a defaulting tenant is under a duty to mitigate damages by making reasonable efforts to re-let an apartment wrongfully vacated by the tenant. Separate parts of the Appellate Division held that, in accordance with their respective leases, the landlords in both cases could recover rents due under the leases regardless of whether they had attempted to re-let the vacated apartments. Although they were of different minds as to the fairness of this result, both parts agreed that it was dictated by Joyce v. Bauman, 174 A. 693 (N.J. 1934). We now reverse and hold that a landlord does have an obligation to make a reasonable effort to mitigate damages in such a situation. We therefore overrule Joyce v. Bauman to the extent that it is inconsistent with our decision today.

I

A.

Sommer v. Kridel

This case was tried on stipulated facts. On March 10, 1972, the defendant, James Kridel, entered into a lease with the plaintiff, Abraham Sommer, owner of the "Pierre Apartments" in Hackensack, to rent apartment 6-L in that building.[1] The term of the lease was from May 1, 1972 until April 30, 1974, with a rent concession for the first six weeks, so that the first month's rent was not due until June 15, 1972.

One week after signing the agreement, Kridel paid Sommer $690. Half of that sum was used to satisfy the first month's rent. The remainder was paid under the lease provision requiring a security deposit of $345. Although defendant had expected to begin occupancy around May 1, his plans were changed. He wrote to Sommer on May 19, 1972, explaining

> I was to be married on June 3, 1972. Unhappily the engagement was broken and the wedding plans cancelled. Both parents were to assume responsibility for the rent after our marriage. I was discharged from the U.S. Army in October 1971 and am now a student. I have no funds of my own, and am supported by my stepfather.
>
> In view of the above, I cannot take possession of the apartment and am surrendering all rights to it. Never having received a key, I cannot return same to you.

---

[1] Among other provisions, the lease prohibited the tenant from assigning or transferring the lease without the consent of the landlord. If the tenant defaulted, the lease gave the landlord the option of re-entering or re-letting, but stipulated that failure to re-let or to recover the full rental would not discharge the tenant's liability for rent.

I beg your understanding and compassion in releasing me from the lease, and will of course, in consideration thereof, forfeit the 2 month's rent already paid.

Please notify me at your earliest convenience.

Plaintiff did not answer the letter.

Subsequently, a third party went to the apartment house and inquired about renting apartment 6-L. Although the parties agreed that she was ready, willing and able to rent the apartment, the person in charge told her that the apartment was not being shown since it was already rented to Kridel. In fact, the landlord did not re-enter the apartment or exhibit it to anyone until August 1, 1973. At that time it was rented to a new tenant for a term beginning on September 1, 1973. The new rental was for $345 per month with a six week concession similar to that granted Kridel.

Prior to re-letting the new premises, plaintiff sued Kridel in August 1972, demanding $7,590, the total amount due for the full two-year term of the lease. Following a mistrial, plaintiff filed an amended complaint asking for $5,865, the amount due between May 1, 1972 and September 1, 1973. The amended complaint included no reduction in the claim to reflect the six week concession provided for in the lease or the $690 payment made to plaintiff after signing the agreement. Defendant filed an amended answer to the complaint, alleging that plaintiff breached the contract, failed to mitigate damages and accepted defendant's surrender of the premises. He also counterclaimed to demand repayment of the $345 paid as a security deposit.

The trial judge ruled in favor of defendant. Despite his conclusion that the lease had been drawn to reflect "the 'settled law' of this state," he found that "justice and fair dealing" imposed upon the landlord the duty to attempt to re-let the premises and thereby mitigate damages. He also held that plaintiff's failure to make any response to defendant's unequivocal offer of surrender was tantamount to an acceptance, thereby terminating the tenancy and any obligation to pay rent. As a result, he dismissed both the complaint and the counterclaim. The Appellate Division reversed in a per curiam opinion, and we granted certification.

B.
Riverview Realty Co. v. Perosio

This controversy arose in a similar manner. On December 27, 1972, Carlos Perosio entered into a written lease with plaintiff Riverview Realty Co. The agreement covered the rental of apartment 5-G in a building owned by the realty company at 2175 Hudson Terrace in Fort Lee. As in the companion case, the lease prohibited the tenant from subletting or assigning the apartment without the consent of the landlord. It was to run for a two-year term, from February 1, 1973 until January 31, 1975, and provided for a monthly rental of $450. The defendant took possession of the apartment and occupied it until February 1974. At that time he vacated the premises, after having paid the rent through January 31, 1974.

The landlord filed a complaint on October 31, 1974, demanding $4,500 in payment for the monthly rental from February 1, 1974 through October 31, 1974. Defendant answered the complaint by alleging that there had been a valid surrender of the premises and that plaintiff failed to mitigate damages. The trial court granted the landlord's motion for summary judgment against the defendant, fixing the damages at $4,050 plus $182.25 interest.

The Appellate Division affirmed the trial court, holding that it was bound by prior precedents, including Joyce v. Bauman, 174 A. 693 (App. Div. 1976). Nevertheless, it freely criticized the rule which it found itself obliged to follow. We granted certification.

II

As the lower courts in both appeals found, the weight of authority in this State supports the rule that a landlord is under no duty to mitigate damages caused by a defaulting tenant. This rule has been followed in a majority of states, and has been tentatively adopted in the American Law Institute's Restatement of Property. Restatement (Second) of Property [§ 12.1(3)]. The majority rule is based on principles of property law which equate a lease with a transfer of a property interest in the owner's estate. Under this rationale the lease conveys to a tenant an interest in the property which forecloses any control by the landlord; thus, it would be anomalous to require the landlord to concern himself with the tenant's abandonment of his own property.

Yet the distinction between a lease for ordinary residential purposes and an ordinary contract can no longer be considered viable. As Professor Powell observed, evolving "social factors have exerted increasing influence on the law of estates for years."

2 Powell on Real Property (1977 ed.), sec. 221(1) at 180-81.

This Court has taken the lead in requiring that landlords provide housing services to tenants in accordance with implied duties which are hardly consistent with the property notions expressed in [earlier cases]. See Braitman v. Overlook Terrace Corp., 346 A.2d 76 (N.J. 1975) (liability for failure to repair defective apartment door lock); Berzito v. Gambino, 308 A.2d 17 (N.J. 1973) (construing implied warranty of habitability and covenant to pay rent as mutually dependent); Marini v. Ireland, 265 A.2d 526 (N.J. 1970) (implied covenant to repair); Reste Realty Corp. v. Cooper, 251 A.2d 268 (N.J. 1969) (implied warranty of fitness of premises for leased purpose).

Application of the contract rule requiring mitigation of damages to a residential lease may be justified as a matter of basic fairness.[4] Professor McCormick first commented upon the inequity under the majority rule when he predicted in 1925 that eventually:

---

[4] We see no distinction between the leases involved in the instant appeals and those which might arise in other types of residential housing. However, we reserve for another day the question of whether a landlord must mitigate damages in a commercial setting.

the logic, inescapable according to the standards of a "jurisprudence of conceptions" which permits the landlord to stand idly by the vacant, abandoned premises and treat them as the property of the tenant and recover full rent, while yield to the more realistic notions of social advantage which in other fields of the law have forbidden a recovery for damages which the plaintiff by reasonable efforts could have avoided.

McCormick, *The Rights of the Landlord Upon Abandonment of the Premises by the Tenant*, 23 Mich. L. Rev. 211, 221-22 (1925).

The pre-existing rule cannot be predicated upon the possibility that a landlord may lose the opportunity to rent another empty apartment because he must first rent the apartment vacated by the defaulting tenant. Even where the breach occurs in a multi-dwelling building, each apartment may have unique qualities which make it attractive to certain individuals. Significantly, in Sommer v. Kridel, there was a specific request to rent the apartment vacated by the defendant; there is no reason to believe that absent this vacancy the landlord could have succeeded in renting a different apartment to this individual.

We therefore hold that antiquated real property concepts which served as the basis for the pre-existing rule, shall no longer be controlling where there is a claim for damages under a residential lease. Such claims must be governed by more modern notions of fairness and equity. A landlord has a duty to mitigate damages where he seeks to recover rents due from a defaulting tenant.

If the landlord has other vacant apartments besides the one which the tenant has abandoned, the landlord's duty to mitigate consists of making reasonable efforts to re-let the apartment. In such cases he must treat the apartment in question as if it was one of his vacant stock.

As part of his cause of action, the landlord shall be required to carry the burden of proving that he used reasonable diligence in attempting to re-let the premises. We note that there has been a divergence of opinion concerning the allocation of the burden of proof on this issue. While generally in contract actions the breaching party has the burden of proving that damages are capable of mitigation, here the landlord will be in a better position to demonstrate whether he exercised reasonable diligence in attempting to relet the premises.

III

The Sommer v. Kridel case presents a classic example of the unfairness which occurs when a landlord has no responsibility to minimize damages. Sommer waited 15 months and allowed $4658.50 in damages to accrue before attempting to re-let the apartment. Despite the availability of a tenant who was ready, willing and able to rent the apartment, the landlord needlessly increased the damages by turning her away. While a tenant will not necessarily be excused from his obligations under a lease simply by finding another person who is willing to rent the vacated premises, see, e.g., Reget v. Dempsey-Tegler & Co., 216 N.E.2d 500 (Ill. App. Ct. 1966) (new tenant insisted on leasing the premises under different terms); Edmands v. Rust & Richardson Drug Co., 77 N.E. 713 (Mass. 1906) (landlord need not accept insolvent tenant), here there has been no showing that the new tenant would not have been suitable. We therefore find that plaintiff could have avoided the damages which eventually accrued, and that the defendant was relieved of his duty to continue paying rent. Ordinarily we would require the tenant to bear the cost of any reasonable expenses incurred by a landlord in attempting to re-let the premises, but no such expenses were incurred in this case.

In Riverview Realty Co. v. Perosio, no factual determination was made regarding the landlord's efforts to mitigate damages, and defendant contends that plaintiff never answered his interrogatories. Consequently, the judgment is reversed and the case remanded for a new trial.

In assessing whether the landlord has satisfactorily carried his burden, the trial court shall consider, among other factors, whether the landlord, either personally or through an agency, offered or showed the apartment to any prospective tenants, or advertised it in local newspapers. Additionally, the tenant may attempt to rebut such evidence by showing that he proffered suitable tenants who were rejected. However, there is no standard formula for measuring whether the landlord has utilized satisfactory efforts in attempting to mitigate damages, and each case must be judged upon its own facts. Compare Hershorin v. La Vista, Inc., 138 S.E.2d 703 (Ga. Ct. App. 1964) ("reasonable effort" of landlord by showing the apartment to all prospective tenants); Carpenter v. Wisniewski, 215 N.E.2d 882 (Ind. Ct. App. 1966) (duty satisfied where landlord advertised the premises through a newspaper, placed a sign in the window, and employed a realtor); Re Garment Center Capitol, Inc., 93 F.2d 667 (2d Cir. 1938) (landlord's duty not breached where higher rental was asked since it was known that this was merely a basis for negotiations); Foggia v. Dix, 509 P.2d 412, 414 (Or. 1973) (in mitigating damages, landlord need not accept less than fair market value or "substantially alter his obligations as established in the pre-existing lease"); with Anderson v. Andy Darling Pontiac, Inc., 43 N.W.2d 362 (Wis. 1950) (reasonable diligence not established where newspaper advertisement placed in one issue of local paper by a broker); Scheinfeld v. Muntz T.V., Inc., 214 N.E.2d 506 (Ill. App. Ct. 1966) (duty breached where landlord refused to accept suitable subtenant); Consolidated Sun Ray, Inc. v. Oppenstein, 335 F.2d 801, 811 (8th Cir. 1964) (dictum) (demand for rent which is "far greater than the provisions of the lease called for" negates landlord's assertion that he acted in good faith in seeking a new tenant).

IV

The judgment in Sommer v. Kridel is reversed. In Riverview Realty Co. v. Perosio, the judgment is reversed and the case is remanded to the trial court for proceedings in accordance with this opinion.

NOTES AND QUESTIONS

A. Duty to Mitigate

1. **Policy.** The Texas Supreme Court recently adopted the rule requiring mitigation, offering the following policies in support of the requirement:

First, requiring mitigation in the landlord-tenant context discourages economic waste and encourages productive use of the property. Second, a mitigation rule helps prevent destruction of or damage to the leased property. Third, the mitigation rule is consistent with the trend disfavoring contract penalties. Courts have held that a liquidated damages clause in a contract must represent a reasonable estimate of anticipated damages upon breach. Similarly, allowing a landlord to leave property idle when it could be profitably leased and forc[ing] an absent tenant to pay rent for that idled property permits the landlord to recover more damages than it may reasonably require to be compensated for the tenant's breach. This is analogous to imposing a disfavored penalty upon the tenant. Finally, the traditional justifications for the common law rule have proven unsound in practice. Proponents of the no-mitigation rule suggest that the landlord-tenant relationship is personal, and that the landlord therefore should not be forced to lease to an unwanted tenant. Modern lease arrangements, however, are rarely personal and are usually business arrangements between strangers. Edwin Smith, Jr., Comment, *Extending the Contractual Duty to Mitigate Damages to Landlords when a Tenant Abandons the Lease*, 42 Baylor L. Rev. 553, 559 (1990). Further, the landlord's duty to make reasonable efforts to mitigate does not require that the landlord accept replacement tenants who are financial risks or whose business was precluded by the original lease. Note, *Landlord and Tenant — Mitigation of Damages*, 45 Wash. L. Rev. 218, 225 (1970).

Austin Hill Country Realty, Inc. v. Palisades Plaza, Inc., 948 S.W.2d 293 (Tex. 1997). *Accord*, Frenchtown Square Partnership v. Lemstone, Inc., 791 N.E.2d 417 (Ohio 2003). The duty to mitigate is now statutory in Texas. *See* Tex. Prop. Code § 91.006.

2. **Duty to mitigate: limited and broad versions.** Sommer v. Kridel requires the landlord to accept a suitable replacement if one is offered by the tenant, and otherwise to seek out a new tenant. Might the court have adopted a more limited version of mitigation?

3. **Anti-assignment clauses.** If the lease contains no clause prohibiting transfers by the tenant without the landlord's consent, the tenant can avoid the problem presented by the principal case by assigning the lease to a substitute (if one is available). When the lease does contain such a clause, the traditional view is that the landlord may arbitrarily refuse consent to a proposed transfer by the tenant. The more modern approach is to read into the anti-assignment clause a (true) duty on the landlord to act reasonably in refusing a proposed substitute tenant; for breach of that duty, some courts allow the tenant to terminate the lease. *See* Robert S. Schoshinski, American Law of Landlord and Tenant §§ 8:15-8:17 (1980). When the abandoning tenant proposes a reasonable substitute, what is the difference between an assessment of the landlord's response under a mitigation analysis and under the implied duty to agree to reasonable transfers?

4. **Reasonable conduct by landlord.** Under Sommer v. Kridel, what actions by the landlord satisfy the duty to mitigate?

5. **The lost volume problem.** If the landlord rents the tenant's unit anew, must the landlord credit the abandoning tenant with the rent payments received from the new tenant? (Assume the landlord has other vacant units.) *Cf.* UCC § 2-

708(2) ("lost volume" seller who resells goods when the buyer breaches may keep the resale price and recover from the breaching buyer the profit that the seller would have made on the sale had the buyer not breached). The lost volume rule assumes fungible goods. Why? Are apartments, unlike goods, unique rather than fungible?

6. **Burden of proof.** Failure to mitigate is usually an affirmative defense. Does the court in *Sommer* treat it so? Other cases applying the rule of avoidable consequences to leases disagree with *Sommer* on this point. *See, e.g.*, Austin Hill Country Realty, Note 1 above; Hailey v. Cunningham, 654 S.W.2d 392 (Tenn. 1983).

7. **Commercial leases.** Should mitigation be required in commercial leases: is the avoidable consequences rule based on inequality of bargaining power or the inefficiency of letting a productive resource lie fallow? *See* McGuire v. City of Jersey City, 593 A.2d 309 (N.J. 1991) (extending the rule of avoidable consequences to commercial leases). Might the distinction between residential and commercial leases nevertheless be relevant in fashioning some of the subsidiary rules of mitigation law, such as (a) the imposition of a broad or narrow duty on the landlord (Note 2 above); (b) the determination of reasonable conduct by the landlord (Note 4); (c) the allocation of the burden of proof (Note 6)?

B. No Duty to Mitigate

8. **Arguments for.** In Stonehedge Square Limited Partnership v. Movie Merchants, Inc., 715 A.2d 1082 (Pa. 1998), the court rejected the rule of avoidable consequences:

> First, this rule [no duty to mitigate] is firmly established in Pennsylvania. Business decisions and structured financial arrangements have been made with the expectation that this rule, which has been the law, will continue to be the law. Second, the established rule has the virtue of simplicity. If the landlord is required to relet the premises, there is unlimited potential for litigation initiated by the tenant concerning the landlord's due diligence, whether the landlord made necessary repairs which would be required to rent the premises, whether the landlord was required to borrow money to make repairs, whether the landlord hired the right agents or a sufficient number of agents to rent the premises, whether the tenants who were refused should have been accepted, and countless other questions in which the breaching tenant is permitted to mount an assault on whatever the landlord did to mitigate damages, alleging that it was somehow deficient. This potential for complexity, expense, and delay is unwelcome and would adversely affect the existing schema utilized to finance commercial development. Third, the Landlord and Tenant Act of 1951, 68 P.S. § 250.101 et seq., which is a comprehensive regulatory scheme governing the landlord and tenant relationship, does not modify the landlord's duty to mitigate damages as it had been established in our cases. Fourth, there is a fundamental unfairness in allowing the breaching tenant to require the nonbreaching landlord to mitigate the damages caused by the tenant. This unfairness takes the form of depriving the landlord of the benefit of his bargain, forcing the landlord to expend time, energy and money to respond

to the tenant's breach, and putting the landlord at risk of further expense of lawsuits and counterclaims in a matter which he justifiably assumed was closed. Fifth, in this case, the tenant was in a position to mitigate his own damages. [Under the assignment and subletting clause in the lease], the tenant could have provided the landlord with a sublessee and the landlord had a duty not to unreasonably withhold consent. It seems self-evident that in choosing between requiring the non-breaching party and the breaching party to mitigate damages, the requirement, if any, should be placed on the breaching party, as it has been for centuries.

See also Holy Properties Ltd., L.P. v. Kenneth Cole Productions, Inc., 661 N.E.2d 694 (N.Y. 1995) (when tenant abandoned, "the landlord was within its rights under New York law to do nothing and collect the full rent due under the lease."); Restatement Second of Property (Landlord and Tenant) § 12.1(3) & cmt. i (1977) (adopting the no-duty view: "[a]bandonment of property is an invitation to vandalism, and the law should not encourage such conduct by putting a duty of mitigation of damages on the landlord"). What answers would you make to each of the *Stonehedge* court's arguments?

9. **The (overlooked) sales analogy: doctrine and policy.** If a buyer of goods repudiates the contract of sale before delivery, or wrongfully rejects the goods upon delivery, the seller's claim for damages is measured either by the excess of the contract price over the market price of the goods at the date of breach, or the excess of the contract price over the resale price if the seller finds another buyer. *See* UCC § 2-708(1) (market price); § 2-706 (resale price). Notice that these measures build in a mitigation feature — the buyer receives an offset against the price for the fair market value or the resale price of the goods. However, if the buyer breaches *after* acceptance, the seller is entitled to recover the full price from the buyer under UCC § 2-709. In lease cases, abandonment typically occurs after the tenant's term begins. What result under the UCC's rules? What result under the Code's *policy* — why might the UCC limit the aggrieved seller to damages before acceptance by the buyer, but allow recovery of the full price when the buyer breaches after delivery and acceptance? Who is in the best position to dispose of the goods in the two situations? *See* James J. White & Robert S. Summers, Uniform Commercial Code § 7-3 at 296-97 (3d ed. 1988).

10. **Tenant's defenses.** The defense of failure to mitigate is often asserted by the tenant in tandem with other defenses. *See, e.g.*, First Wisconsin Trust Co. v. L.Wiemann Co., 286 N.W.2d 360 (Wis. 1980) (in landlord's suit for rent, tenant asserted defenses of constructive eviction and landlord's failure to mitigate); Berg v. Wiley, *supra* (landlord changed locks while tenant was away from, but had not abandoned, the premises; in landlord's suit for rent, tenant asserted defenses of eviction and failure to mitigate).

b.   No Duty to Mitigate: Landlord's Remedies

Under the no-mitigation view, the landlord has several possible remedies. We sketch them here, and elaborate them in the Notes following the principal cases. (1) The landlord may leave the premises vacant, and collect all of the remaining rents due under the lease, either as they fall due, or in advance under an acceleration clause. This is the *Stonehedge* remedy. See Note 8 after Sommer v.

Kridel, above and Notes 1 and 2 following the *Maida* case below. (2) The landlord may re-rent the premises and recover from the abandoning tenant any rent deficiencies that result. This "tenant's account" theory is applied in *Maida*. (3) The landlord may accept the tenant's surrender of the lease, and discharge the tenant from any further liability. Such an acceptance of surrender may be an express, intentional act on the landlord's part. There is also, however, a doctrine of "surrender by operation of law," illustrated by Richard v. Broussard, reprinted below, which visits the consequences of an intended, express surrender on conduct that the court finds to constitute an implied acceptance of surrender. The doctrine is a trap for the unwary landlord (usually a landlord who acts before seeking legal advice). (4) In some states, the landlord has the option of an immediate suit to recover *damages* rather than rent when the tenant abandons, under the theory that the tenant has breached the lease by anticipatory repudiation, as discussed in Hawkinson v. Johnson, below.

MAIDA v. MAIN BUILDING OF HOUSTON
473 S.W.2d 648 (Tex. Civ. App. 1971)

Tunks, Chief Justice.

This is a suit by a landlord, The Main Building of Houston, against its tenant, S. J. Maida, Sr., d/b/a Houston Shoe Hospital. The suit is on the lease agreement.

By the lease in question the landlord leased to the tenant space in a building called The Main Building of Houston. The lease was for a 10 year term beginning July 1, 1963, and ending June 30, 1973. The rent was fixed at $550.00 per month. The tenant vacated the premises in the latter part of February of 1968, being in arrears in the rent due for the months of December, 1967, and January and February of 1968. The landlord took possession when the tenant vacated.

The lease included the following paragraph:

> If the demised premises be abandoned or vacated by Lessee, or if this lease is terminated under the provisions of Article Eighth hereof, Lessor shall have the right, but not the obligation, to relet the same for the remainder of the period covered hereby; and if the rent received through such reletting is not at least equal to the rent provided for hereunder, Lessee shall pay and satisfy any deficiencies between the amount of the rent called for and that received through reletting, and all expenses incurred by any such reletting, including, but not limited to, the cost of renovating, altering and decorating for a new occupant. Nothing herein shall be construed as in any way denying Lessor the right, in case of abandonment, vacation of premises, or other breach of this contract by Lessee, to treat the same as an entire breach and at Lessor's option immediately sue for the entire breach of this contract and any and all damages occasioned Lessor thereby.

The tenant did not have the right of subleasing except with consent of the landlord.

In 1968 the landlord leased the premises to another tenant for a three year term beginning February 1, 1969, and ending January 31, 1972. The rent provided by this second lease was $800.00 per month. By the terms of the second lease the tenant was given an option to extend for a term of two years. The premises remained vacant from the time the defendant vacated them until they were occupied by the second tenant on February 1, 1969. The second tenant had, up to the time of the trial, remained in occupancy and had paid the $800 monthly rental.

This case was tried on March 2, 1971. The recovery sought by the landlord in its trial pleading was for $7,700.00, which represents the $550 monthly rental for the 14 months beginning with December, 1967, and ending with January, 1969, during which the premises were vacant; for $3,493.81 alleged to be the expenses necessarily incurred in renovating the premises incident to reletting them to the second tenant; for items of $166.53 and $39.35, representing utilities furnished defendant during the last three months of his occupancy; and for attorney's fees as provided for in the lease contract. The landlord did not seek any recovery on the theory of anticipatory breach, for any rents to accrue under the lease after the date of the trial.

Both parties have recognized that the landlord's taking possession of the premises after the tenant vacated them was in the exercise of the landlord's contractual right provided in the first sentence of the above quoted paragraph of the lease.

The pleadings of the plaintiff landlord clearly show that this is a suit on the lease contract and not a suit for the breach of it. The unusual fact situation that gives rise to the questions that have arisen is in the fact that the premises, after the tenant vacated, were relet at a rental which, if it continues to accrue and to be paid until June 30, 1973, will produce more income to the landlord than the landlord would have received under the original lease.

The findings of fact and conclusion of law filed by the trial judge include findings that the defendant tenant was indebted to the landlord plaintiff for $1858.59, the amount of rent and utility payments that had accrued and were unpaid at the date the tenant vacated the premises, and for $2,094.22 the amount found by the trial judge to represent the renovating expense necessarily incurred as an incident to releting the premises. These two items make up the $3,952.81 award in the judgment rendered. There is no complaint as to the trial judge's findings of fact. Rather it is the contention of the appellant tenant that the trial court applied an erroneous measure of recovery.

Under the language of the usual lease contract there are a number of alternatives available to a landlord when the tenant, without justification, abandons the leased premises and stops paying the rent due. The landlord may decline to retake possession of the premises and sue for the rent provided by the lease as such rent becomes due. In such case his suit is on the contract and the measure of his recovery is the contractual rental.

He may elect to treat the conduct of the tenant as an anticipatory breach of contract, retake possession, and, without reletting the premises, sue for damages for such anticipatory breach. In such case his measure of damages is the present value of the rentals to accrue under the lease contract less the reasonable cash market value of the lease for the unexpired term. He may retake possession, relet the premises and sue for anticipatory breach. In such case his measure of damages usually is the contractual rental provided in the lease less the amount realized from the reletting. [W]here the landlord retakes possession and relets the premises for only a portion of the unexpired term the measure of damages for that period of the lease term as to which there has been no reletting is contractual rental less the market value of the lease for such period.

He may declare the lease forfeited which will relieve the lessee of obligation to pay future rent.

The appellant tenant contended in the trial court, and contends here, that his liability for rents under the lease contract should be credited with not only the rent that has accrued and been paid under the second lease, but also with an assumed payment of rent at the rate of $800 per month for the remainder of the term of the second lease (eleven months) and an assumed value of $800 per month for that portion of the unexpired term of his lease not covered by the second lease. If such contention were sustained the tenant would owe nothing because the credit thus allowed him would exceed his liability under the lease contract. The appellant's principal authority for such contention is White v. Watkins, 385 S.W.2d 267 (Tex. Civ. App. 1964).

The *White* case is not authority for the appellant's contentions. There the landlord's suit was treated as a suit for breach of contract. He sought recovery for not only the rent that had accrued up to the date of the trial, but also for that to accrue in the future. The Court of Civil Appeals, in its opinion, clearly recognized that a different measure of recovery is applicable to a suit for breach of contract than would be applicable to a suit on the contract.

The facts in this case seem to be more nearly analogous to those in a case where the landlord, without retaking possession and reletting, elects to sue on the contract for rent as it accrues, as in Western Flavor-Seal Company v. Kallison, 389 S.W.2d 521 (Tex. Civ. App. 1965). Here, too, the landlord sued only for rent accrued together with necessary costs incurred as an incident to reletting. The difference between this case and Kallison is that this landlord, having retaken possession and having relet, as authorized by the lease contract, was obliged to credit the defaulting tenant with rents that had been collected under the second lease up to the time of the trial.

It is apparent that the trial judge determined the amount of recovery by computing the rent that had accrued under the defendant's lease and crediting it with the rent that had been paid under the second lease. The time from the date that the defendant abandoned the premises and the plaintiff retook possession to the date of trial was 36 months. At $550 a month $19,800 of rent accrued during that period. At the date of the trial, the second lease had been in force for 25 months. $20,000 of rent had been paid under that lease. (The accrued and unpaid rent during the last three months of the defendant's occupancy were the subject of a separate item in the trial court's findings and need not be considered in this computation.)

A number of questions exist under the facts of this case that need not be answered. The trial court credited the rent paid under the second lease against that which accrued under the first lease before the term of the second lease began as well as that which accrued under the first lease and during the term of the second. Should the court have credited rent paid under the second lease only to that under the first lease which accrued after the second lease began? The appellee here has not complained of such credit, by cross-point or otherwise, so that we need not answer that question. There was an excess of $200 in the rent paid under the second lease over that which had accrued under the first lease after the defendant's abandonment and up to the time of the trial. Should that excess have been credited against the cost of renovating incurred as an incident to reletting? Appellant's brief does not so present that question as to require that it be answered.

Appellant vigorously urges that he should have had credited against any liability that he had at the date of the trial the excess over his contractual rental of the rent to be paid in the future under the second lease as well as the excess in the value of the possession of the premises after the primary term of the second lease ends (which value he says is shown to be $800 per month) over his contractual rent. For a number of reasons that contention is overruled. While the landlord had a right to retake and relet the premises, it owed the tenant no duty to do so. It could have, if it wished, permitted the premises to remain vacant and thus brought about a situation wherein the tenant would have had nothing to credit against his contractual liability for rent. It would seem inconsistent to hold that the landlord, having no duty to create a credit in the first place, should be required to speculate and assume the responsibility for the fact that such credit created would continue to exist in the future.

Also, it is to be remembered that the landlord did not sue for the tenant's anticipatory breach of the contract to pay rent in the future. If he had done so, as noted above, his measure of recovery would have been the excess, if any, of the present value of the rent to accrue in the future over the value of the possession of the property for the rest of the term. The trial court in this case did not make any finding as to the value of the lease (or the possession of the property) for that portion of its term which lay in the future, and was not requested to do so. The fact that the second tenant leased the property for $800 a month for part of the unexpired term of the first lease did not necessarily establish that such unexpired term had a value of $800 a month. The second tenant may not continue to pay $800 a month for the entire term of the second lease. The conduct of the defendant in this case demonstrates that possibility. The second tenant's primary term does not cover the entire unexpired term of the first lease. There is a possibility that at the end of the second lease the property will remain vacant for a time, as it remained vacant for eleven months after this tenant vacated. The evidence shows that the second tenant, at her own expense, did considerable alteration of the premises to adapt it to a special use, a beauty parlor. If the second tenant vacates the premises the landlord may well be put to the expense of remodeling, or be restricted to leasing the premises to another beauty parlor. The trial court could well have found that the value of the unexpired term of the first lease did not exceed the amount of the rent to be paid under it. If such a finding were necessary to the judgment rendered it would be presumed that the trial judge so found.

The judgment of the trial court is affirmed.

NOTES AND QUESTIONS

A. Recovery of Full Rent From the Tenant

1. **Affirming the lease.** Under the *Stonehedge* theory (Note 8 after Sommer v. Kridel), is the landlord affirming the lease (recognizing its continuing existence) or terminating it? Why does it matter insofar as the tenant's liability for rent is concerned?

2. **Timing of suit.** Without a valid acceleration clause (*see* Note 4 following *First National Bank of Omaha* in Section C.1.a above), the landlord is entitled to recover from the tenant "the full rentals due under the lease *as and when they become due.*" Gruman v. Investors Diversified Services, Inc., 78 N.W.2d 377, 379 (Minn. 1956) (emphasis added). What is the significance of the italicized language? If the lease has not expired before trial, what is the landlord entitled to recover at the time of trial? Is the landlord entitled to recover future rentals? Is the landlord entitled to an installment judgment? (Recall *First National Bank of Omaha.*) What is the impact of the statute of limitations on the timing of the landlord's suit?

B. The Tenant's Account Theory

3. **Reletting on the abandoning tenant's account: doctrine and policy.** Instead of letting the premises stand idle and suing for rent as it falls due, the landlord might choose to find a replacement tenant. Doing so generates cash flow, avoids vandalism, helps the abandoning tenant by reducing that tenant's liability for unpaid rent, and is good for society in that it puts a productive resource to use. How does the theory differ from the recognition of a duty to mitigate? How does it differ from the *Stonehedge (*do nothing) theory? Under the tenant's account theory, does the landlord keep the lease in effect, or terminate it? *Cf.* UCC § 2-709 (seller's suit for the price).

4. **The principal case.** Make sure you understand how the trial court in the principal case established the tenant's account, and how the appellate court responded. (For this purpose, it is helpful to draw a time line, showing the periods when the premises were vacant and when occupied by another tenant.) What questions did the appellate court identify but not resolve? What should the answer to those questions be?

5. **Surrender by operation of law.** The landlord who elects either the *Stonehedge* (do nothing) theory or the tenant's account theory is vulnerable to the tenant's defense of surrender by operation of law. That doctrine is discussed in Richard v. Broussard, the next principal case.

6. **Duty to mitigate in Texas.** *Maida* is a Texas case, decided before the state supreme court's imposition of a duty to mitigate on landlords. See Note 1 after Sommer v. Kridel. Which of the landlord's options discussed in *Maida* is no longer available to a Texas landlord when a tenant abandons the premises?

PROBLEM 4-T. Suppose that rent is $1000 per month. At the time of T's abandonment, the premises have a fair rental value of $900 per month. After T abandons, L relets to his daughter and son-in-law for $500 per month. What is L entitled to recover from T under the tenant's account theory: $100 per month; $500 per month; nothing? Suppose instead that L rents to a second tenant at $875 per month and sues T for the $125 monthly deficiencies. Tenant introduces expert testimony that the fair rental value of the premises is $900 per month. Does L recover $125 per month from T or only $100 per month? How does the issue here differ from that in the first variation of the problem?

RICHARD v. BROUSSARD
495 So. 2d 1291 (La. 1980)

LEMMON, JUSTICE.

The issue in this case is whether the lessors of immovable property, upon abandonment of the property by the lessees during the term of the lease, are entitled to occupy the premises for their own business purposes for the remainder of the term and also to collect from the lessees the contractual rent for the same period. We conclude that the lessors are not entitled to recover rent from the lessees after the date the lessors occupied the premises for their own business purposes.

Plaintiffs-lessors leased a building to defendants-lessees on November 20, 1981 for a period of twenty-four months at a monthly rental of $3,250 per month. Plaintiffs had previously operated a restaurant on the premises, but had retired from the restaurant business. Defendants leased the property for the purpose of operating a similar seafood restaurant business. The lessees paid the rent from November 20, 1981 until July, 1982, at which time the lessees abandoned the premises and informed the lessors that they were unable to operate the unsuccessful business any longer.

The lessors immediately began advertising for a new tenant. When they failed to secure a new rental contract, the lessors occupied a portion of the premises and began a seafood take-out business, with about two tables. They also proceeded to renovate the premises with the idea of making it more attractive for rental purposes. Eventually the lessors occupied the entire premises with their seafood business and continued to operate the business on the premises beyond the remainder of the term of the original lease.

In the meantime the lessors filed this action in December, 1982 to recover accelerated rents, [and] costs. The trial court rendered a judgment in favor of the lessors for $42,272.05 in accelerated rent, costs and expenses. The court of appeal affirmed the judgment. 482 So.2d 729. We granted the lessees' application for certiorari.

Generally, when a lessee defaults on a lease agreement, the lessor has two options available: he may sue to *cancel* the lease and to recover accrued rentals due, or he may sue to *enforce* the lease and to recover both accrued rentals and future accelerated rentals (if the lease contains an acceleration clause). These remedies are mutually exclusive. Comment, *The Louisiana Law of Lease*, 39 Tul.L.Rev. 798, 860 (1965); V. Palmer, Leases, The Law in Louisiana § 5-19 (1982). If the lessor elects to *cancel* the lease, the lease is terminated and the lessor is entitled to return into possession, but he forfeits the right to all future rentals. On the other hand, if the lessor elects to *enforce* the lease, he may obtain a money judgment against the lessee based on the terms of the lease agreement, but the lease remains in effect and the lessee retains the right of occupancy for the remainder of the term of the lease. However, when the lessee breaches the lease by abandoning the premises, the lessor has the right to take possession of the premises as agent for the lessee and to relet the premises to a third party without canceling the lease or relieving the lessee of his obligations under the lease contract. In the present case, the lease contract incorporated all of these remedies. Paragraph XXIII(C) of the lease provided:

> "*If the demised premises shall be deserted or abandoned during the term of this lease* or should the LESSEES begin to remove personal property or goods to the prejudice of the LESSORS liens, or if the LESSEES shall be evicted from said premises by a summary proceedings, or otherwise, or upon the happening of any event or default, *LESSORS may, at its election re-enter the same by force or otherwise*, without being liable for prosecution therefore, *and may relet said premises at any time as agent of LESSEES*, applying any monies collected first, to costs, fees and expenses of collection, second, to the expense of obtaining possession and redecoration and/or altering the premises, third, to the payment of the rent and all other sum owing and to become owing LESSORS, and paying any surplus thereof to the LESSEES, and such re-entry and reletting shall not discharge LESSEES from liability for rent nor from any other covenant of this lease by it or to be kept and performed" (emphasis supplied).

Accordingly, when the lessees abandoned the premises in this case, the lessors had the right to reenter the premises for the purpose of reletting the property to a third person, with the lessees receiving the benefit of any rent collected from the third person (after recovery by the lessors of costs, fees and expenses of collection, and the expense of redecorating or altering the premises) but remaining liable for their obligations under the lease. The purpose of this paragraph was to permit the lessors, faced with the undesirable situation of having empty rental premises because of the lessees' abandonment, to reduce their damages without incurring any liability and without releasing the lessees from their obligation to pay rent. The lessors, however, did more than simply reenter the premises for the purposes of reletting to a third party. The critical issue is the legal effect of their reentry after abandonment by the lessees and their proceeding to utilize the premises in the operation of a personal business.

The court of appeal noted that the lease contract did not expressly grant the lessors the right upon abandonment to reenter the premises and operate a business, but stated that no Louisiana case has addressed the issue whether such action constituted a termination of the lease. The court concluded that the lessors never intended to cancel the lease and discharge the lessees, but intended only to reduce the damages for the benefit of all parties. The court emphasized that the lessors made every effort to relet the premises, although under no obligation to do so, before finally reestablishing a business on the premises in a good faith effort to mitigate their damages after the lessees had failed to fulfill their contractual obligations. In the court's view, these actions constituted a mere reentry "for the purpose of preserving the property and enhancing its leasing value" which did not impair the lessors' rights against the lessees under the lease contract.[2] We disagree.

When the lessors sued to recover the accelerated rent, the lessees retained the right to occupy the premises. However, the lessors thereafter usurped this right from the lessees by occupying the premises themselves to the exclusion of the lessees.[3] Although the lessors may have mentally reserved the intention not to dispossess the lessees, their physical actions effected this result.[4] A lessor simply cannot physically dispossess the lessee by extrajudicial action and then recover a money judgment for the future rentals which would have accrued if the lessee had continued to enjoy the right of occupancy.[5] Moreover, the lessors' argument that they were forced into taking possession when the lessees left them "holding the bag" ignores the reality that every lessor finds himself involuntarily in this situation when the lease is breached.

Accordingly, the lessors are not entitled to recover from the lessees the rent which otherwise would have been due during the period that the lessors occupied the premises by operating their own business. The lessors' election to occupy the premises for their own business use effectively terminated the lease, regardless of

---

[2] The court of appeal referred by analogy to cases dealing with the types of activities a lessor may engage in without evidencing an intent to cancel. For example, in Shaw v. Knight, 16 La.App. 474, 134 So. 286 (2nd Cir.1931), the lessor hired a caretaker to watch over the property, and the court held that the lessor had the right to take possession of the abandoned leased premises for the purpose of protection and conservation. The lessor's actions in *Shaw*, of course, are clearly distinguishable for the lessors' actions in the present case. Although hiring a caretaker is an act of preservation and conservation, operating a business on the property goes far beyond either preservation or conservation.

[3] The lessors contend that the premises were available for the lessees during the entire term in the sense that the lessees could have reoccupied but declined to do so. Of course, the lessors would have been even more delighted if the lessees had never abandoned the premises and made all rent payments timely. In point of fact, however, the lessors after the abandonment elected to exercise the right of occupancy, a right which the lessors could only acquire by terminating the lease (or by enforcing the lease and obtaining a judgment against the lessees and then seizing the lessees' right of possession as an asset in the execution of the judgment, as pointed out in note 5).

[4] The lessors' actions in this case were more analogous to a sale. In Weil v. Segura, 178 La. 421, 151 So. 639 (1933), this court held that the sale by the lessor of the abandoned premises to a third party terminated the lessee's right of occupancy and that the lessor therefore forfeited all future rents accruing after the date of the sale. In arriving at this conclusion, this court reasoned as follows:

> "When plaintiff resumed possession of the leased premises after they had been abandoned by defendant, he was acting for his tenant, and his possession was that of his tenant, and he was required to account to his tenant for any rent he received from the property. But, when plaintiff sold the property . . . he conveyed to the vendee full dominion, including the exclusive right of possession, of the property which he owned. Plaintiff's possession for account of his tenant was converted necessarily into possession for his own account for the purpose of making the sale. Thereafter it is clear that defendant could not reoccupy the premises, nor could defendant, nor plaintiff for defendant's account, sublease to another or sell the right of occupancy from the proceeds of which defendant might extinguish or diminish his obligation to plaintiff." *Id.* 151 So. at 641.

[5] A lessor in this situation is generally not without a remedy. Upon default, a lessor may obtain a judgment against the lessee for the accelerated rent due for the remainder of the period and then execute on that money judgment by seizing the lessee's right of occupancy under the lease as an asset belonging to the lessee. See Comment, *The Louisiana Law of Lease*, 39 Tul.L.Rev. 798, 860, n. 520 (1965). Of course, that remedy may not have been practical in the present case because of the short period remaining under the lease, unless the lessees had failed to contest the action to recover the future rentals.

the lessors' good faith motivation or their intent that the lease should continue in effect.[6]

The remaining issue involves the determination of the amount due to the lessors between the abandonment and the time they reoccupied the premises. The record established that the lessors reoccupied the premises in early October of 1982 and began gradually to reestablish their business. This business operation on the premises continued until after November, 1983, the termination date of the lease. The lessors are not entitled to collect rent after October, 1982, but are entitled to recover the rent due for the period between July, 1982, the date the lessees discontinued rental payments, and the end of September, 1982, the date the lessors reoccupied the premises and began using the property for operation of a personal business.[7]

For these reasons, the judgment of the court of appeal is amended to decrease the amount of the rent recovery to $6,500. As amended, the judgment is affirmed. Costs in all courts are assessed to the lessees.

NOTES AND QUESTIONS

1. **Express acceptance of surrender.** The landlord and tenant can always expressly agree on a surrender of the lease. The surrender ends the tenancy and terminates the parties' obligations. In property terms, the surrender amounts to a reconveyance by the tenant of the remaining term of the lease; in contract terms, the agreement constitutes a mutual cancellation of the contractual obligations of the lease. If the remaining lease term at the time of surrender exceeds the permissible duration of oral leases, the statute of frauds requires the surrender agreement to be in writing, subject to the doctrines of part performance and extoppel that we examined earlier. Under what circumstances might the landlord be willing to let the tenant go without further recourse?

2. **Surrender by operation of law and the *Stonehedge* theory.** The doctrine of surrender by operation of law is an extrapolation from the doctrine of express surrender: if the landlord "takes possession for his own use or in his own interest," a court will conclude that an acceptance of surrender has occurred by operation of law, which bars the landlord from recovery against the tenant from the time of acceptance. Restatement Second § 12.1, Reporter's Note 8, at 425. *See* John L. Cutler Ass'n. v. De Jay Stores, 279 P.2d 700 (Utah 1955) (landlord allowed a third party to store furniture on the premises free of charge, without notifying tenant; surrender); Coffin v. Fowler, 483 P.2d 693 (Alaska 1971) (rural property; landlord placed a family in possession without rental payments for the purposes of caring for the property; no surrender). What is the basis of the doctrine, as indicated in

---

[6] Of course, the lessors and lessees could have agreed that the lessors would occupy the premises after the abandonment and operate the business, with the lessees remaining liable under the lease but receiving some benefits for their consenting to forego their right of occupancy.

[7] In D.H. Overmeyer Co., Inc. v. Blakeley Floor Cover, Inc., 266 So.2d 925 (La.App. 4th Cir.1972), the lessor relet the leased premises at a higher rental six weeks after an abandonment. The lessee asserted that the additional increment of rent should be credited retroactively. The court disagreed and held the lessee liable for the rent during the six weeks the premises were vacant, reasoning that the property was available to the lessee for use during this time.

the principal case? Does the court in the principal case indicate agreement with either *John L. Cutler* or *Coffin*?

3. **Acceleration clauses.** What impact did the landlord's acceptance of surrender in the principal case have on its recovery under the acceleration clause?

4. **Surrender by operation of law and the tenant's account theory.** If the landlord pursues the tenant's account theory, the test of surrender by operation of law is whether the landlord in seeking to relet acts "ostensibly as the tenant's agent" or acts on his own behalf. Restatement Second § 12.1, Reporter's Note, at 426. Why must the landlord who relets the premises act as the tenant's agent? (Recall that the tenant's account theory assumes that the lease remains in effect.) Some courts hold that any reletting is an acceptance of surrender unless the terms of the lease authorize the landlord to act as the tenant's agent; others say that an acceptance of surrender occurs unless the landlord notifies the tenant at the time of reentry that he is acting on the tenant's behalf; the most liberal view (for the landlord) finds an acceptance only if the landlord at the time of reletting intended a surrender, as determined from the surrounding facts and circumstances. *See* McGrath v. Shalett, 159 A. 633 (Conn. 1932). Recalling the advantages that follow from the landlord's finding of a new tenant, *should* the doctrine of surrender by operation of law apply when the landlord elects the tenant's account theory?

5. **The second Restatement.** Section 12.1(3) of the second Restatement adopts the doctrine of surrender by operation of law? *See id.* cmt. i, illustration 9 (L's reletting without notice to T, "who was readily available," is acceptance of surrender, relieving T of liability for the difference between his rent and the new tenant's rent).

6. **Consequences.** The conventional view is that the landlord's acceptance of a surrender by operation of law terminates the tenant's liability for rent accruing after the acceptance, and also for damages for any future losses that the landlord suffers. The doctrine therefore completely releases the tenant — the breaching party — from liability. The landlord's recovery of damages for future losses requires adoption of the doctrine of anticipatory breach, which landlord-tenant law has traditionally rejected. If state law allows the tenant to assert an anticipatory breach claim — Hawkinson v. Johnston below is an example — the landlord is entitled to recover damages representing rental losses that will occur in the future. The classic article arguing against the conventional view and for the theory adopted in Hawkinson v. Johnston is Charles T. McCormick, *The Rights of the Landlord Upon Abandonment of the Premises by the Tenant*, 23 Mich. L. Rev. 211 (1925).

7. **Counseling and drafting.** What should the landlord do to avoid surrender by operation of law, both at the drafting and reentry stages?

HAWKINSON v. JOHNSTON
122 F.2d 724 (8th Cir. 1941)

JOHNSEN, CIRCUIT JUDGE.

Two principal questions are presented for determination: (1) Whether a repudiation of a lease and an abandonment of the premises, accompanied by a default in the payment of an installment of rent, may constitute a total breach of the contract of lease, under the law of Missouri; and (2), if so, whether, for such a breach of a 99 year lease, having a remaining term of 67 years, the trial court erred in fixing the determinable or predictable period of damages, under the evidence in this case, at ten years.

The lease covered a vacant lot located at 1331 Walnut Street, in the city of Kansas City, Missouri. It was made in 1909, for a period of 99 years, between plaintiff's devisor, as owner, and defendant and his brother, as lessees. The lease provided for rent for the unexpired term was $1,600 per annum. The lessees also were obligated to pay all taxes upon the property for the period of the lease.

The lessees occupied the property and apparently paid the rent and taxes to June 30, 1940. On June 14, 1940, they notified plaintiff in writing of their intention to surrender and abandon his interest in the premises on June 30, 1940. The next quarterly instalment of rent was due on July 1, 1940. Plaintiff promptly replied that a surrender would not be accepted and that he expected to hold the lessees liable for their full term. On June 25th, the lessees repeated their notice of intention to surrender on June 30th. On June 28th, plaintiff again advised the lessees that he would not accept a surrender, which he termed "inexcusable on any ground," and declared that he would enforce his legal rights against them. On June 30th, the lessees posted a notice on the property that they had surrendered and abandoned the premises to plaintiff. On July 3rd, plaintiff made demand for his share of the quarterly rent instalment due July 1st. The lessees denied liability for any further rent, and reasserted that they had surrendered and abandoned the property on June 30th.

On August 2, 1940, plaintiff brought this action, alleging that it was certain and determinable that "performance of the terms of said lease could and would have been possible for a period of not less than thirty years from and after June 30, 1940," and that during that period, except for the repudiation, plaintiff would have received his $1,600 share of the annual lease rental and the benefit of the payment of the taxes upon the property. The prayer of the petition was for damages in the amount of the difference between [the rent due under the lease] for a thirty year period, and the reasonable rental value of [of the premises] during such period, commuted to its present value of the taxes which, it was claimed, the lessees would, with reasonable certainty, have been obliged to pay during that period.

The case was tried to the court without a jury. The trial court held that the repudiation constituted a total breach of the contract of lease, and that, under the evidence, damages were determinable or predictable with reasonable certainty for a period of ten years, and that plaintiff was accordingly entitled to recover an amount equal to [the rent obligation] for a ten year period, less the reasonable rental value of the property during such period, commuted to its present value at four per cent compound interest, and, by reason of the failure to pay taxes, a further sum equal to the taxes which the lessees with reasonable certainty would have been required to pay during such ten year period, similarly commuted to its present value. Judgment was entered against defendant [accordingly], from which he has appealed generally; and plaintiff has appealed from the refusal of the trial court to fix the determinable or predictable period of damages at more than ten years.

The first and principal question is whether, under the law of Missouri, a repudiation of a lease and an abandonment of the premises, accompanied by a refusal to pay an accrued instalment of rent, can constitute a total breach of the contract of lease. The courts of Missouri do not appear to have passed upon the precise point. The general doctrine of anticipatory breach by repudiation has, however, been clearly recognized in that state. A majority of the courts in this country that have passed upon the question have applied the doctrine of total breach to an anticipatory repudiation or other unjustified refusal to perform some material, permeating provision of a contract of lease, and the trial court held that, since there was nothing contrary to such a view in the expressions of the Missouri courts on the subject of anticipatory repudiation, it was proper to assume that Missouri would follow the general law.

The general common law rule as to anticipatory repudiation that has emerged from its evolutionary crystallization, in its here applicable portion, is set out in the Restatement as follows:

> Except in the cases of a contract originally unilateral and not conditional on some future performance by the promisee, and of a contract originally bilateral that has become unilateral and similarly unconditional by full performance by one party, any of the following acts, done without justification by a promisor in a contract before he has committed a breach under the rules stated in Secs. 314-315, constitutes an anticipatory repudiation which is a total breach of contract: (a) A positive statement to the promisee or other person having a right under the contract, indicating that the promisor will not or cannot substantially perform his contractual duties.[11]

The Missouri courts have used substantially equivalent language.

The Restatement does not purport to except contracts of lease from the operation of the general rule which it sets out, either by its language or in its comments, if they are otherwise within the conditions and qualifications prescribed, nor is there anything in the expressions of the Missouri courts to indicate such an intention. As a matter of sound practicality, and ignoring the spirit of mere legalistic negation and artificial differentiation, there is no reason to attempt to draw a distinction. The rationale underlying the rule as declared in Hochster v. De La Tour, 22 L.J.Q.B. 455, 458, 2 El. & Bl. 678 (1853), certainly is as fairly applicable to contracts of lease as to other general contracts:

> The man who wrongfully renounces a contract into which he has deliberately entered cannot justly complain if he is immediately sued for a compensation in damages by the man whom he has injured: and it seems reasonable to allow an option to the injured party, either to sue immediately, or to wait till the time when the act was to be done, still holding it as

---

[11] Restatement, Contracts Sec. 318.

prospectively binding for the exercise of this option, which may be advantageous to the innocent party, and cannot be prejudicial to the wrongdoer.

The real sanctity of any contract rests only in the mutual willingness of the parties to perform. Where this willingness ceases to exist, any attempt to prolong or preserve the status between them will usually be unsatisfactory and mechanical. Generally speaking, it is far better in such a situation, for the individuals and for society, that the rights and obligations between them should be promptly and definitely settled, if the injured party so desires, unless there is some provision in the contract that, as a matter of mutual intention, can be said to prevent this from being done. The commercial world has long since learned the desirability of fixing its liabilities and losses as quickly as possible, and the law similarly needs to remind itself that, to be useful, it too must seek to be practical.

We hold that, within the conditions and qualifications of the rule applied to general contracts under the Missouri decisions, the doctrine of total breach by anticipatory repudiation is applicable to contracts of lease in that state. This is sufficient to sustain plaintiff's right to sue in the present case. The contract of lease here was in part still executory on the part of plaintiff, since he was obligated by specific and continuing covenants to assure the quiet enjoyment of the premises during the term of the lease, and, also, at all times to defend the title. These covenants were in a sufficient sense interdependent with the lessees' obligation to pay rent, since the payment of rent at any particular time necessarily was conditional on their continued performance. By the provisions of the lease, this obligation of the original lessor was specifically made to devolve upon plaintiff as assignee or devisee.

While the trial court properly disposed of the case on the strict theory of anticipatory repudiation, it might perhaps have adopted a broader applicable theory, which is recognized by the Restatement, by Williston, and by some of the decisions. The original repudiation and abandonment here constituted, of course, purely an anticipatory breach, since there was at the time apparently no default under the contract. When on July 1st, however, the lessees refused to pay the installment of rent that became due, and still adhered to and repeated their repudiation, there then existed more than a technical anticipatory breach.[14]

The rule applied by the Restatement and by Williston to such a situation is that, except in the case of a unilateral contract, or a bilateral contract that has been wholly performed on one side, for the payment of money instalments or for the performance of other acts, not connected with one another by a condition having reference to more than one of them or otherwise, any breach of a contract is total if it is accompanied by a positive repudiation of the entire contractual obligation.[15] While the observation has been made that there would appear to be no "controlling

---

[14] Strictly an anticipatory breach is one committed before the time has come when there is a present duty of performance." New York Life Insurance Co. v. Viglas, 297 U.S. 672 (Cardozo, J.). See also Restatement, Contracts, Sec. 318, Comment (b).

[15] Restatement, Contracts, Secs. 316, 317, 318; 5 Williston on Contracts, Revised Edition, Sec. 1317, pp. 3714-3716.

distinction"[16] between the two classes of cases, both the Restatement and Williston imply a more liberal interpretation and application of the rule relating to an actual breach in performance accompanied by a repudiation, than of the rule involving a technical anticipatory repudiation alone. But it is not necessary here to deal further with this distinction.

The second question for consideration is whether the trial court erred in fixing the determinable or predictable period, for damage purposes, at ten years. We think not. There was competent evidence from which it could be inferred with reasonable certainty or probability that the rental value of the property and the amount of taxes payable under community conditions and locational situation for the next ten years could be expected to remain fairly stable. The rental returns for a long period of years, the taxes assessed against the property for the preceding eight years, community conditions and locational situation, together with the opinions of experts, were all before the court. The parties expressly stipulated that the present reasonable rental value of plaintiff's interest in the property did not exceed $450. In this situation, the question as to the amount of the damages was properly a matter for the judgment of the trial court, under all the evidence, just as it would have been for a jury; and we think the evidence warranted the conclusion which the court reached. The interest rate adopted in computing the present value of the amount of the recovery was sufficiently supported by the evidence, and no specific complaint is made on this point.

It will of course generally be argued in a case of this character, as it is here, that any period of definite forecast or certain predictability attempted to be fixed by the trial court is arbitrary and excessive. But the rule for determining the damages in such a situation is no different than in any other case. The damages are not speculative merely because they cannot be computed with mathematical exactness, if under the evidence they are capable of reasonable approximation. Obviously there is not, nor can there be a fixed, uniform period for which damages should be allowed in every case of total breach of a long term lease, but the period for which the damages can be reasonably forecast or soundly predicted in such a situation must depend upon the circumstances and evidence of the particular case.

Plaintiff argues on his cross-appeal that, under the testimony of the expert witnesses which he produced, and to which defendant offered no opposing experts, the court should have fixed the predictable damage period at not less than fifteen years. But the trial court was not required to accept at face value the opinion of the expert witnesses as to future rental returns and tax valuations. The weight to be given purely opinion evidence is always a matter for the appraisal and judgment of the trial court or jury, in the light of all the circumstances of the particular situation.

Defendant argues that plaintiff's actions in the situation amounted to an acceptance of surrender, and so precluded a suit for repudiation. We find nothing in the evidence that compels or merits this construction. Plaintiff, from the start, had notified the lessees that he would not accept a surrender, and had advised them in effect that their inexcusable attempt to abandon the premises and their unjustifiable refusal further to perform the obligations of the lease would be regarded as a

---

[16] Per Fuller, C.J., in Roehm v. Horst, 178 U.S. 1, 19.

repudiation. He had informed defendant, after the abandonment, that he would be willing to work out some arrangement to lease the premises in order to minimize the damages, but that "any such arrangement will, of course, be with full reservation of his rights against you." Such an arrangement was finally agreed upon, for a leasing of the premises to a third party, "without waiver of the respective rights of the parties." There is nothing in any of these actions, or in the institution of a suit for damages in harmony with them, that must or can be held to have consummated a surrender, as a matter of necessary legal implication. Plaintiff's whole course, on the contrary, was a studied effort to preserve his legal rights on the contract, and to avoid any act that could be declared to be inconsistent with them.

The judgment of the trial court should be and is affirmed.[23]

NOTES AND QUESTIONS

1. **Anticipatory breach.** (a) Under the theory of anticipatory breach, does the landlord keep the lease in effect, or terminate it? (b) Does the landlord sue for rent or for damages? (c) Is the landlord entitled to sue immediately after the breach? (d) Is the landlord entitled to recover all of his allowable losses in that one suit? (e) In a long-term lease, is the landlord entitled to recover the full rent accruing after the tenant abandons?

2. **Applicability of anticipatory breach to leases.** The *Stonehedge* (do nothing) and tenant's account remedies were widely accepted at common law. Anticipatory breach — in either of the versions discussed in the principal case — was not, because of a widely-recognized exception to that doctrine:

> A positive statement to the promisee that the promisor will not perform his contract constitutes an anticipatory repudiation which is a total breach of contract, except in cases of a contract originally unilateral and not conditional on some future performance by the promisee and of a contract originally bilateral that has become unilateral and similarly unconditional by full performance by one party. There must be some dependency of performance in order to make anticipatory breach possible. A lease is primarily a conveyance of an interest in land, and its execution by the lessor may be said to constitute performance on his part, making the instrument, when considered as a contract, a unilateral agreement with no dependency of performance which would make an anticipatory breach possible.

---

[23] To the writer it would logically seem that, where a lease gives full control of the property to the lessee, and so contemplates that the lessor shall be relieved of the supervisory burden which ownership otherwise naturally imposes, the obligation which is thereby implied on the part of the lessee, and the obvious detriment which repudiation and abandonment will produce to the lessor, should be treated as making the contract more than a mere obligation for the payment of instalments of rent monies, and that the lessor should accordingly be permitted to sue for total breach on such an abandonment and repudiation and a default in payment of rent, regardless of whether there is any executory obligation remaining on his part that will bring the situation within the technical application of the general doctrine of total breach by anticipatory repudiation discussed above. In the present case, however, the situation properly is within the conditions of the general rule announced by the Missouri courts, and there is, of course, no need or right to go farther.

Sagamore Corp. v. Willcutt, 180 A. 464 (Conn. 1935). *See* E. Allan Farnsworth, Contracts §§ 8.18, 8.20 (3d ed. 1999). Does the writer of the *Hawkinson* opinion think that the dependency limitation on anticipatory breach is valid? *See* footnote 23.

3. **Contracts: applicability of anticipatory breach to installment contracts.** A widely-followed rule in contract law is that "contracts to pay money in installments are breached one installment at a time." Quick v. American Steel & Pump Corp., 397 F.2d 561 (2d Cir. 1968). In Phelps v. Herro, 137 A.2d 159 (Md. 1957), Herro agreed to sell stock and realty to Phelps for $37,000. Phelps paid $5,000 down, and signed a promissory note for the remainder, payable in installments. Herro transferred the stock and realty; Phelps then repudiated the obligation to pay the installments. Can Herro sue immediately for the balance due on the note or does the case fall under the exception stated in Note 2? In what way is Herro's position like that of a landlord whose tenant abandons possession and repudiates the lease?

4. **Measure of damages.** In Maida v. Main Bldg., the court discussed two measures of recovery when the landlord pursues an anticipatory breach theory: if the landlord leases to a new tenant, the recovery is the difference between the abandoning tenant's rental and the rental recovered by the landlord on the "resale." *Cf.* UCC § 2-706 (resale measure of damages). If the landlord does not get a new tenant (for example, the landlord uses the premises for the landlord's own purposes), the recovery is the difference between the abandoning tenant's rent and the fair rental value of the premises. *Cf.* UCC § 2-708(1) (market value measure). That distinction is helpful in keeping doctrines straight: the landlord's reletting of the premises does not necessarily commit the landlord to the tenant's account theory. What should the landlord who relets the premises do to signal the intent to proceed under anticipatory breach (where available), or on the tenant's account theory?

5. **Surrender by operation of law.** Should a defense of surrender by operation of law apply to the landlord's cause of action for anticipatory breach? Is the landlord's termination of the lease inconsistent with the remedy sought by the landlord under anticipatory breach theory? *See* Winshall v. Ampco Auto Parks, Inc., 417 F. Supp. 334 (E.D. Mich. 1976).

3.   Remedies Against the Holdover Tenant

The law of abandonment and surrender deals with the tenant who wrongfully leaves early. The tenant who wrongfully stays late — after the agreed-upon right to occupancy is over — is governed by the holdover doctrine.

A tenant who holds over after the expiration or valid termination of the lease becomes an occupant at sufferance. *See* 2 Powell on Real Property § 16.06. As that name suggests, the former tenant's position is determined by the landlord, who may choose either to evict the tenant, or — and this is the unusual part — to impose a new tenancy on the tenant. The justification for the rule allowing the imposition of a new tenancy is that it deters tenants from holding over and thus assures possession to the incoming tenant; the rule penalizes the individual holdover tenant for the good of tenants as a class. *See* A.H. Fetting Mfg. Jewelry

Co. v. Waltz, 152 A. 434 (Md. 1930). That rationale, of course, assumes that the would-be holdover knows the doctrine. The fallacy of the deterrence rationale is clear; holdover doctrine is a trap for unwary tenants, and is not favored by the courts.

The rules in holdover cases are relatively clear. The landlord has an election to evict or to impose a new tenancy on the tenant. The election is the landlord's: the landlord may evict a tenant who wants to remain, and impose a new tenancy on a tenant who wants to get out. *See* Restatement Second of Property (Landlord and Tenant) § 14.4 (unilateral right of landlord). The election, once made, is irrevocable. The landlord's election for a new tenancy results in most states in a periodic tenancy; in the rest, it results in a term of years lease. The duration of the period or term is usually determined by the original lease: when the holding over occurs after an original lease of a year or greater, the new lease is a yearly periodic tenancy or one-year term of years; some courts, however, specify the length of the period by the way rent is reserved or paid. *See* Restatement Second § 14.4 cmt. f (holdover periodic tenancy depends on way rent is computed; maximum tenancy is yearly periodic tenancy). All the provisions of the previous lease, except duration and type of tenancy, apply to the holdover tenancy. *See generally* Robert S. Schoshinski, American Law of Landlord and Tenant §§ 2:23-2:24 (1980).

The rules stated above are default rules, which the parties may modify by appropriate provisions in the lease. Whether and to what extent lease provisions modify the holdover doctrine is not always clear, as the principal case shows.

GYM-N-I PLAYGROUNDS, INC. v. SNIDER
220 S.W.3d 905 (Tex. 2007)

CHIEF JUSTICE JEFFERSON delivered the opinion of the Court.

Commercial real estate landlords [in Texas] impliedly warrant that their premises are suitable for the tenants' intended commercial purposes. In this case, however, the tenants expressly disclaimed that warranty. We must decide whether the disclaimer precludes the tenants' suit against the landlord for breach of the warranty. We also decide whether the tenants' agreement to lease the commercial building "as is" prevents them from suing the landlord for other claims based on the property's condition. We answer both questions "yes" and affirm the court of appeals' judgment.

Background

In 1981, Ron Snider founded Gym-N-I Playgrounds, Inc., a playground equipment manufacturing company. The business grew rapidly. In 1983, Snider purchased six acres of land in New Braunfels and subsequently constructed a 20,075 square foot building for the business. By the late 1980s, Gym-N-I employed about twenty people, including Bonnie Caddell and Patrick Finn, to whom Snider later sold the business. Caddell was Gym-N-I's bookkeeper; Finn performed miscellaneous jobs including assembling and installing playgrounds, maintaining machinery, purchasing supplies, and managing human resources.

The City of New Braunfels' fire code requires owners to install sprinkler systems for any building exceeding 20,000 square feet if the building contains certain combustible materials. GymN-I's building exceeded that threshold, and the fire marshal recommended, but did not require, that the building have a sprinkler system. Both Caddell and Finn knew that the fire marshal's recommendation was never implemented.

Eventually, Finn and Caddell purchased the business, and Snider leased them the building. Each party was represented by counsel during the lease negotiations. Finn and Caddell decided not to inspect the premises before leasing because, as Caddell testified, they "knew more about the building" than anyone else. The lease provided that Gym-N-I would accept the building "as is," expressly waiving all warranties. The lease also contained a holdover provision [stating that "[a]ny holding over without written consent of Landlord shall constitute a lease from month-to-month, under the terms and provisions of this Lease to the extent applicable to a tenancy from month-to-month"]. The lease was signed on September 30, 1993, and the original term expired in September of 1996. The parties did not execute a new instrument, but Gym-N-I continued to pay and Snider continued to accept monthly rent checks. On August 10, 2000, a fire destroyed the building.

Procedural History

Snider's insurer, American Economy Insurance Company, paid him approximately $400,000 for the loss of the building. Gym-N-I received nearly $1,000,000 under its insurance policy covering the building's contents and business interruption. Thereafter, American Economy brought a subrogation suit against Gym-N-I, which filed cross-claims against American Economy and third-party claims against Snider. Ultimately, all parties other than Gym-N-I and Snider were dismissed prior to this appeal.

Gym-N-I's suit against Snider alleged that defective electrical wiring and the lack of a sprinkler system caused the fire. Snider's summary judgment motion argued that all of Gym-N-I's claims, except the breach of contract claim, were barred by the "as is" clause and warranty disclaimer. The parties settled the contract claim, and the trial court granted Snider a final summary judgment. In the court of appeals, Gym-N-I argued that the "as is" clause was no longer in effect after the original lease term ended in 1996, and that even if it was, the clause was unenforceable. The court of appeals affirmed the trial court's judgment. 158 S.W.3d 78. We granted Gym-N-I's petition for review.

Discussion

Gym-N-I argues that the "as is" provision did not survive when the lease's original term expired. Gym-N-I contends that because it never exercised the lease's renewal options, and the lease expired almost four years before the fire, the parties "shared a simple month-to-month, landlord-tenant relationship under the 'holding over' clause of the original lease" when the fire occurred. Citing Bockelmann v. Marynick, 788 S.W.2d 569 (Tex. 1990), Gym-N-I argues that the holdover tenancy is a "new tenancy" to which the terms of the original lease do not apply. Snider responds that, under the written lease, the "as is" clause, along with all other terms of the lease, governs during any holdover month-to-month tenancy. The court of appeals held that the "as is" clause survived the original lease term's expiration. We agree.

Gym-N-I and Snider allowed the original lease agreement to expire without executing a new instrument. Because Gym-N-I continued to occupy the premises, it was a holdover tenant. The parties agree that their relationship was best characterized as a month-to-month tenancy as contemplated by the holdover clause in the lease. That clause provides that "[a]ny holding over without written consent of Landlord shall constitute a lease from month-to-month, *under the terms and provisions of this Lease* to the extent applicable to a tenancy from month-to-month." (Emphasis added.) Although Gym-N-I argues that the tenancy is not governed by the lease's terms, we cannot ignore the plain and ordinary meaning of the phrase "under the terms and provisions of this Lease." We hold that "under the terms and provisions of this Lease" means just that: the lease governed the month-to-month tenancy. Thus, the "as is" clause was in effect when the fire occurred.

Furthermore, Gym-N-I's reliance on *Bockelmann* is misplaced. In that case, Brenda and Hermann Bockelmann, husband and wife, were cotenants in a residential lease. Ten days before the lease expired, Brenda separated from Hermann and vacated the residence. Hermann remained on the premises after the lease expired, triggering the lease's holdover provision, which provided that "[s]hould Tenant remain in possession of the demised premises after the natural expiration of this lease, a new tenancy from year to year shall be created between Lessor and Tenant which shall be subject to all the terms and conditions hereof." Subsequently, Hermann ceased paying rent and the landlord sued both Hermann and Brenda to recover the unpaid rent.

The issue before us was whether Brenda was liable for the rent that accrued while Hermann was a holdover tenant. Holding that Brenda was not liable, we said that "under the express terms of the lease, [Hermann's] holdover tenancy was a new tenancy rather than an extension or renewal of the original lease." Thus, Hermann's holdover tenancy was not a continuation of the original cotenancy, but rather a new tenancy for which only Hermann was liable. Our use of the term "new tenancy" came directly from the holdover provision of the lease. We did not say that the terms and provisions of the original lease would not apply. To the contrary, we gave effect to the lease stating that "this new tenancy would be subject to the same terms and conditions as the original tenancy." The difference between the original and new tenancies involved the parties who were bound, not the tenancy's terms and conditions. At least one court of appeals has recognized this important distinction. Clark v. Whitehead, 874 S.W.2d 282 (Tex. App. 1994, writ denied) (rejecting holdover tenant's argument that *Bockelmann* supports a finding that guarantees contained in the original lease did not apply to the holdover tenancy). *Bockelmann* stands for the proposition that a cotenant who does not holdover is not liable for unpaid rent incurred when the other cotenant holds over; thus, it does not support Gym-N-I's argument that the original lease terms did not apply to the holdover tenancy.

Having concluded that the "as is" provision was still in effect when the fire occurred, we next address whether it waives some or all of Gym-N-I's claims. [The court concluded that the waiver was effective, and affirmed the appellate court's decision.]

NOTES AND QUESTIONS

1. **What's new?** In what sense is the tenancy created under common law holdover doctrine a new tenancy? In what sense is it not a new tenancy?

2. **Common law and holdover clauses.** If the situation in the principal case had been governed by common law rules, what would have been the duration of Gym-N-I's holdover tenancy? Did the lease provision change the common law on that question? Under the common law rules, would the "as is" provision have applied to the holdover tenancy? Under the lease provision would it have applied?

3. **Precedent.** The issue in *Bockelmann*, as the court in that case recognized, is controversial. Some courts hold that both cotenants are holdovers unless the out of possession cotenant notifies the landlord that he or she no longer is in possession. Other courts hold that the tenancy created under the holdover doctrine is a continuation of the old one rather than a new tenancy, thus binding the out of possession cotenant to the rent during the holdover tenancy. Still other courts hold that one tenant cannot be involuntarily bound to a new tenancy by the acts of another. *Bockelmann* adopted the last view, adding these remarks:

> Under the common law holdover rule, a landlord may elect to treat a tenant holding over as either a trespasser or as a tenant holding under the terms of the original lease. The lease incorporated this rule of holdover, providing that, if the landlord consents, a "new tenancy" would be created if the tenant remained in possession beyond expiration of the lease. The lease stated that this new tenancy would be subject to the same terms and conditions as the original tenancy, except that the holdover tenancy would be "from year to year terminable by 60 days notice." Thus, under the express terms of the lease, this holdover tenancy was a new tenancy rather than an extension or renewal of the original lease. The idea that a holdover tenancy might constitute a continuation of the prior tenancy is inconsistent with both the fact that the former lease has expired and the rule that the holdover tenancy is imposed by law without regard to the tenant's intention. 1 American Law of Property § 3.35 (1952). Therefore, Hermann's holdover tenancy was not, as the court below held, a continuation of the original tenancy he held jointly with Brenda, but was rather a new tenancy for which he alone was liable.

> The court of appeals bound Brenda to this new tenancy by presuming that a holding over by Hermann was also a holding over by Brenda, absent notice to the contrary. However, [t]he relationship of cotenancy exists only so long as the parties own rights in common property. At the moment the original lease expired, neither Hermann nor Brenda had any legal right to possession of the duplex, and their relationship as cotenants was extinguished. Because they were no longer cotenants, there was no basis from which to presume a joint holding over. Moreover, under Texas law, "each

owner in a co-tenancy acts for himself and no one is the agent of another or has any authority to bind him merely because of the relationship." Lander v. Wedell, 493 S.W.2d 271, 274 (Tex. Ct. App. 1973, writ refused). Thus, where a lease contains an option to renew, one tenant may not unilaterally exercise that option and bind nonconsenting cotenants. *Id.* Since Texas does not permit Hermann to renew the lease for another term on Brenda's behalf, it similarly should not presume that he was authorized to hold over on her behalf.

4. **Statutes.** Statutes modifying the common law holdover rules are not unusual, but statutory treatment is "quite varied." Robert S. Schoshinski, American Law of Landlord and Tenant § 2:23, at 75 (1980). The most important modifications are a rejection of the landlord's unilateral option to create a new tenancy, and a limitation of the duration of the new holdover tenancy to a monthly tenancy rather than a term of years tenancy. *Id.*

PROBLEM 4-U.

a. The tenant's two-year lease expires on December 31, 2006. The lease provides for "rent of $1200 per year, payable $100 per month on the first of each month." T remains in possession in January 2007 and tenders rent for January, which L accepts, intending to create another tenancy under the holdover doctrine. On November 30, 2007, T notifies L that he will vacate at the end of December, and on December 31, 2007, T vacates. Is T liable to L for any rentals accruing in January, 2008 and thereafter? If T is liable, what did T need to do to prevent such liability?

b. A two-year lease expires on December 31, 2007. Suppose that T remains in possession on January 1, 2008 and tenders a check for January's rent to L with the following letter: "Because my new premises will not be available until February 1, 2008 or thereafter, I wish to remain as a month to month tenant. I am of course willing to pay the same rental as previously. Enclosed please find my check for January rental." What result if L cashes the check? If L wants to invoke the holdover doctrine, what response should L make to T's letter?

c. T is ill in December 2007, and on the advice of his doctor is confined to bed. T remains in possession until the end of January 2008, then vacates. May L invoke the holdover doctrine? *See* Restatement Second § 14.4 (holdover doctrine not available to landlord when "equitable considerations justify giving the tenant an extension of time to vacate the leased property and the tenant vacates the leased property before the end of the extended period").

d. After the end of the original tenancy, T installs fixtures or otherwise expends money on the premises; L knows what T is doing and doesn't object. L thereafter gets a better offer for rental and seeks to evict T. Result?

e. T remains in possession after a term ending in December and tenders one month's rent in January. L does not respond and does not cash the check. L sues for possession on January 31. Has L elected to create another tenancy? Suppose instead that L sues 45 days, or two months, after the holding over? What is the issue in all of these cases?

f. At the end of T's term in December, 2007, the parties are negotiating over a new lease. The negotiations continue through mid-January, then collapse. Is T a holdover? If not, what is T's status? *See* Donnelly Advertising Corp. v. Flaccomio, 140 A.2d 165 (Md. 1958).

g. X has a security interest in property owned by L. L leases the property to T; L expressly promises to maintain the building's plumbing system and to restore the premises after any damage. L defaults on the mortgage; X forecloses and buys the property at the foreclosure sale. T remains in possession and tenders the same rent, which X accepts. A ruptured water pipe causes a flood that damages T's personal property. T sues X for damages, asserting (1) that X breached duties imposed by the lease contract and (2) that X was negligent. X moves for a directed verdict on X's contract count. Result? *See* First Interstate Bank v. Tanktech, Inc., 864 P.2d 116 (Colo. 1993) (trial court's denial of X's motion reversed: "We have found no cases in which a third party, not party to the original lease, was bound to the terms of a lease of which it might not be aware and which it had no power to negotiate.").

4.   Use and Condition of the Premises

To what uses may the tenant put the leased premises? However the tenant uses the premises, to what extent is the tenant liable for their upkeep, and what limitations exist on uses by the tenant that cause damage to the premises? In keeping with our usual practice, we consider the default rules that apply to these questions when the parties have not addressed them in the lease, and also the possibilities and limits of contractual modification of the default rules.

a.   Use

The tenant pays rent for the right to possess the premises for the duration of the lease. Does the tenant have a *duty* to possess and use the premises? The question usually arises in a shopping center lease, when a major retailer decides, for economic reasons, to close a location but to retain the premises, paying the minimum specified lease rental, in order to keep the location out of the hands of a competitor. Other questions about the use rights or duties of the tenant are covered in the notes following the principal case.

MERCURY INVESTMENT CO. v. F.W. WOOLWORTH CO.
706 P.2d 523 (Okla. 1985)

Opala, Justice.

The issue on certiorari is whether in a landlord's suit to terminate a shopping center lease for failure of consideration — based on the alleged breach of an implied covenant diligently to operate the business so as to trigger the percentage rental provisions — the trial court erred in granting summary judgment for the tenant. We answer in the negative and vacate the Court of Appeals' opinion that reaches a contrary conclusion.

FACTS

In 1958 Mercury Investment Co. built a multi-tenant shopping center in Sand Springs, Oklahoma and leased space to F.W. Woolworth Co. in early 1959. Their agreement, printed on a form drafted by Woolworth, provided for an original term of fifteen years and allowed five successive options, each to extend for five years. Woolworth agreed to pay Mercury an "annual minimum rent" of $19,350 for the first fourteen years and $17,425 annually for the remainder of the term. The lease also called for additional rent in the form of a percentage of gross receipts. The percentage rent was to be triggered by annual sales in excess of $387,000 for the first fourteen years and $348,500 thereafter. These sales' levels were never reached, and hence no percentage rent was ever paid.

Late in 1981 Mercury brought a termination suit for failure of consideration based on Woolworth's alleged breach of an implied covenant diligently to operate its business in such a manner as to generate percentage rentals and to attract customers to the shopping center for the benefit of the other tenants as well.

Woolworth sought summary judgment in its favor on two grounds: (a) the landlord's claim relied on inadmissible parol evidence of oral negotiations which occurred prior to the execution of the lease, and (b) the action was barred by the statute of limitations. On review of the summary judgment for Woolworth, the Court of Appeals reversed and remanded the cause for further proceedings. We now reinstate the trial court's summary judgment.

THE COURT OF APPEALS' DECISION

The Court of Appeals held that: (a) because of the interdependent nature of the relationships created among all the tenants by the shopping center's leasing plan, the lease agreement on its face indicates that Woolworth, as an "anchor tenant," owes the obligation diligently to pursue its operations in a manner to "secure a fair and adequate return to the Lessor"; (b) the "asserted covenant" does not come within the parol evidence rule because it was so clearly within the contemplation of the parties that they deemed it unnecessary to express it; (c) questions of fact remain as to (1) the manner in which Woolworth presently operates its business, and (2) the adequacy of the minimum monthly payment; and (d) in determining whether the "minimum monthly payments" were intended as adequate rental, the court may look into the circumstances surrounding the inception of and performance under the lease agreement.

THE PERTINENT LEASE PROVISIONS

Mercury contends the face of the lease demonstrates that Woolworth was intended to be an "anchor tenant" of the shopping center and its function was to generate traffic, to attract patronage to the shopping center for the mutual benefit of all retail tenants and, as a consequence, to generate substantial and adequate percentage rentals, all as anticipated by the parties to the lease. This is gleaned in part, Mercury asserts, from a common merchandising plan, as shown by the lease terms that provide for a common parking area and contemplate the presence of three other principal tenants — i.e., a supermarket, a drug store and a clothing store. If the three tenants were not in operation by a certain date, Woolworth could exercise its option of terminating the lease or of having its rent abated until the other tenants were doing business in their respective locations. The lease also contained a restrictive covenant in favor of Woolworth which prohibited occupancy of the shopping center by another "variety" or "junior" department store. According to the Court of Appeals, the physical relationship of the tenants and the "interdependent nature" of the leasing plan demonstrate that the parties contemplated Woolworth would operate in such a manner "as to satisfy its obvious function" in the shopping center.

Woolworth, on the other hand, contends that the terms of the lease agreement are clear and explicit as to its obligations. The contract, Woolworth argues, required it to pay a minimum base rental, with additional percentage rentals due only if sales reached a certain volume. Furthermore, Woolworth asserts that the lease agreement expressly excluded any warranty by Woolworth with respect to the volume of sales it would generate upon the premises.[2] This, along with the other provisions,[3] Woolworth argues, negates any obligation on its part to operate its business under some amorphous standard of "commercial prudence." Additionally, Woolworth contends that the parties specifically contemplated that Woolworth was not to be compelled to operate its business at all, but could vacate the premises, cease its operations and simply continue paying the stated rental for the remainder of the term.[4] Mercury, viewing this provision in a different light, asserts that implicit therein is the understanding by the parties that the "annual minimum rent" was neither substantial nor adequate, for the space and other facilities provided to Woolworth by the shopping center.

BASIS FOR IMPLYING A COVENANT IN LEASE AGREEMENT

Mercury's failure-of-consideration argument is based on (1) an inference from a four-corners' examination of the lease that Woolworth promised diligently to conduct its business so as to generate percentage rentals — a condition that was within the contemplation of the parties when they entered into the agreement but

---

[2] Article 5A of the lease agreement provided [that] "the Tenant makes no representation or warranty as to the sales which it expects to make in the demised premises."

[3] Article 26 of the lease agreement provided in part:

This lease is and shall be considered to be the only agreement between the parties hereto; all negotiations and oral agreements acceptable to both parties are included herein. The Landlord by the execution hereof acknowledges full performance to the date hereof of all covenants required to be performed by the Tenant under all prior leases, contracts and agreements of every kind and nature whatsoever affecting the demised premises or the property of which the demised premises are a part. The Landlord further releases the Tenant from the performance of any and all obligations of every kind and nature whatsoever under said leases, contracts and agreements (except such obligations as are expressly included in the herein lease), all of which are hereby cancelled and terminated.

[4] Article 5A of the lease agreement provided in part:

Should the Tenant at any time vacate its store in the demised premises then anything in this lease to the contrary notwithstanding, it is hereby mutually agreed that the Tenant shall pay to the Landlord annually during the remainder of the term of this lease, in addition to the annual rent a sum equal to one-third (1/3) of the additional rent (if any) paid by the Tenant to the Landlord pursuant to the provisions of this article for the three (3) calender years next preceding the vacating of said store. (Emphasis added.)

which they failed to include within the express terms of the lease and (2) after-developed facts that show consideration failed during the lease term because of Woolworth's lack of diligence to operate its business in a commercially prudent manner. In short, the asserted failure of consideration is sought to be rested on a two-part test: (a) an implied covenant to be inferred from the terms of the agreement[14] and (b) extrinsic evidence to show that the implied covenant was breached.

As a general rule implied covenants are not favored in the law. This view owes its force to the presumption that when the parties have entered into a written agreement that embodies their obligations, they have expressed all of the conditions by which they intend to be bound. Courts are reluctant to imply covenants where the obligations sought to be imposed on the contracting parties are not expressed in the written text. Absent illegality, contracting parties are free to bargain as they see fit. When the bargained-for agreement is reduced to writing, a court may not make a new contract for the parties or rewrite the existing contract.

This does not mean that covenants may never be implied from written agreements. Because the courts are reluctant to tamper with the parties' written contract, certain conditions are imposed before a covenant will be inferred from the language used. There are many decisions, mostly from other jurisdictions, laying down well defined rules that govern implied covenants in lease contracts, where as here, there is a provision for a guaranteed minimum rent and a further provision for a percentage rental. The general rule enunciated in these decisions is that (1) the obligation must arise from the presumed intention of the parties as gathered from the language used in the written instrument itself or it must appear from the contract as a whole that the obligation is indispensable in order to give effect to the intent of the parties; and (2) it must have been so clearly within the contemplation of the parties that they deemed it unnecessary to express it.

Recognized as a corollary to the general rule governing covenants that could be inferred from a written instrument is the principle that when the rental reserved in a lease is based upon a percentage of the gross receipts of a business and a guaranteed substantial minimum rent, a covenant would not be implied; but if the minimum rental is so low as to be nominal, or where there is no minimum rental, then a covenant might be implied.

---

[14] Covenants are of two types — express or implied. Express covenants are created by the words in an agreement. Implied covenants are generally grouped into two categories: implied-in-fact and implied-in-law. A covenant implied-in-law — i.e., a constructive covenant — is presumed from the relation of the parties and the object to be achieved by the agreement. Public policy supplies the basis of such covenant without regard to the intention of the parties. In other words, it is but a legal duty imposed by law and created otherwise than by assent and without any words or conduct that are interpreted as promissory. Public policy extends to freedom of contract insofar as private dealing is restricted by law for the good of the community. A covenant implied-in-fact, in contrast, is deemed to be more akin to the nature of an express covenant because it is raised by inference from words used in the agreement to effect the intention of the parties. See 3 Corbin on Contracts § 562 (1960); 1 Tiffany, The Law of Real Property § 89 (1936); 1 Friedman on Leases § 6.9 (1983).

NO COVENANT MAY BE INFERRED FROM THE LEASE AGREEMENT

A

Keeping in mind the rules so far articulated, we find nothing in the language employed in the lease to support the conclusion that there was an implied covenant by which Woolworth could be required to conduct its business in what in some case law is referred to as a "commercially prudent manner." Nor is there anything in the nature of the transaction to justify a finding that the implied covenant was indispensable to effectuate the intention of the parties. An examination of the agreement shows that its terms are clear, definite and unambiguous.

Under the agreed rental terms Woolworth was obligated to pay a "minimum base rental" and additional percentage only if sales passed a certain threshold level. The lease does not contain any express covenant by which Woolworth promises to so operate its business as to generate percentage rentals and to accelerate customer traffic flow for the benefit of the other tenants. The express provisions of the lease agreement clearly negate the covenant sought to be implied against Woolworth. In Article 5A of the lease Woolworth expressly declined to guarantee any level of sales expected to be generated by its business upon the leased premises. An express covenant on a given subject-matter excludes the possibility of an implied covenant of a different or contradictory nature. Furthermore, the lease terms found in Article 26 make it clear that the contract embodied all the pre-contract negotiations and contained all the obligations that were to be performed by Woolworth. This is further borne out by the explicit provisions that govern liability after vacation of the premises during the lease term. In the event of pre-termination abandonment Woolworth must pay the base rent for the remainder of the term and one-third of the percentage rentals, "if any," that had been generated during the three-year period last preceding the vacation.

Furthermore, the conduct Woolworth would be required to pursue in order to satisfy the asserted implied covenant is articulable by Mercury in most amorphous terms. The court would have great difficulty in determining whether Woolworth's breach had in fact occurred. Enforcement of the implied covenant that is sought to be imposed would violate the time-honored principle that a covenant may not be implied unless it is so clearly within the contemplation of the parties that they deemed it unnecessary to express it. In short, a covenant calling for a performance the parties themselves cannot define in clear and certain terms will not be implied.

The lease is cast in the form of a highly sophisticated document employing clear, precise and unambiguous language that covers a myriad of details regarding the parties' relationship as landlord vis-a-vis tenant. In the face of its comprehensive terms, this court is powerless to add a covenant requiring Woolworth to generate sales that would subject it to liability for percentage rentals. The parties could have inserted an explicit termination clause to be triggered by continued failure of Woolworth to reach some agreed level of gross receipts within a specified period. To now imply the covenant pressed for by Mercury would be to rewrite the parties' agreement. We should be loath to hold Woolworth to any greater level of business productivity than Mercury itself was able to exact from a willing tenant.

B

Neither can we infer from our four-corners' examination of the lease that — at the time it was set — the guaranteed minimum rent was so low as to be merely nominal and thus warrant an implied covenant requiring Woolworth to generate sales which create a liability for percentage rentals. No basis exists for this assumption. The lease under consideration was not a renewal of a prior lease. There was here no established period of past experience by which the parties could be guided in determining the minimum rental. Woolworth was entering upon a new venture, and neither party was capable of accurately projecting the potential gross receipts from the business to be conducted on the premises. Under these circumstances, it can only be concluded that the parties considered the stipulated minimum rent to be in itself fair and adequate, and any additional sum was in the nature of a bonus Woolworth was to pay if its sales were to rise above the stipulated figures.

In short, from a four-corners' examination of the lease we find nothing to warrant a conclusion that the base rental, sans any part of the percentage rental, would result in a failure of consideration. Consideration may be said to have failed when consideration that was bargained for does not pass to the promisor, either in whole or in part. This is not the case here. Neither is there any latent ambiguity that would authorize parol testimony to elucidate the meaning of the words used or the intention of the parties from circumstances that surrounded the transaction.

C

In the absence of fraud, accident or mistake, oral testimony cannot be used to vary or contradict the terms of a written contract. When parol evidence is sought to be admitted to show failure of consideration, the law draws a distinction between the terms "failure of consideration" and "want of consideration." Failure of consideration has been defined as the neglect, refusal, or failure of one of the parties to perform or furnish the consideration agreed upon. The phrase "want or absence of consideration" has been defined as a total lack of any valid consideration for a contract. A plea of want of consideration amounts to a contention that the instrument did not become a valid obligation in the first place. Parol or extrinsic evidence is generally held to be admissible, at least as between the parties themselves, to show that there was an absence or want of consideration. Such evidence does not contradict any particular term of the writing but attacks its existence as a contract and is therefore admissible.

Where the statement in the contract as to the consideration is of a contractual nature — as where the consideration consists of the mutual promises of the parties — the statement constitutes a term of the contract which may not be varied by parol testimony attempting to show that the consideration was other than as stated in the written instrument. Thus it is not permissible by extrinsic evidence to insert into the contract a condition or provision for its termination which is not expressed therein.

It is clear that in this case Mercury's claim is not based on absence or want of consideration. The contract did provide for contractual consideration in the form of a guaranteed annual amount. Rather, Mercury's claim to failure of consideration, while appearing to be premised on after-developed facts — i.e., lost percentage rentals during the term of the lease because of poorly managed operations — was in fact based on conditions — i.e., Mercury's right to claim percentage rentals and Woolworth's duty diligently to produce them — which were dealt with and contemplated by the parties when they entered into the agreement. This is borne out by an examination of the lease agreement: (a) the lease contained a provision that disclaimed any obligation on Woolworth's part to produce a certain level of percentage rentals and (b) the absence of any other term in the contract that would allow termination of the instrument because percentage rentals were not generated. Thus, while the very foundation of Mercury's failure-of-consideration theory is its claim to percentage rentals, its right to them must be regarded as a condition that was not only within the contemplation of the parties but one that was expressly dealt with in the lease. In short, failure of consideration cannot be inferred from continued nonpayment of percentage rentals.

SUMMARY

Woolworth's inability to bring its sales within the range of lease-created liability for percentage rentals constituted neither a default in performance that was Mercury's due nor a failure of consideration legally essential to maintain Woolworth's status as lessee. No duty stood imposed upon Woolworth, qua tenant, to generate any specific amount of receipts — and none may be rested upon it in this lawsuit by inference from the four corners of the lease. Nay, the existence of the duty Mercury now seeks to have us infer here is plainly and conclusively contradicted by the parties' agreement whose face refutes its presence in clear and unambiguous terms. No breach of promise to Mercury — express or implied — can hence arise from Woolworth's nonpayment of percentage rentals.

Because a breach from nonpayment of percentage rentals cannot be said to have been within the contemplation of the parties, there was no default in Woolworth's performance. The sufficiency of minimum or base rentals as a principal consideration for the lease is not a fit subject for judicial scrutiny. Courts do not possess a gauge for measuring or weighing the adequacy of an agreed quid pro quo. If, as here, consideration appears to have been a bargained-for benefit to the promisor and a detriment to the promisee, it must be deemed to have been accepted as more than just nominal. It is hence sufficient in law to support the promise.

The lease is written in plain, clear and unambiguous language. There is hence no room for construction. Summary denial of lease termination decree for failure of consideration is entirely free from legal error.

The Court of Appeals' opinion is vacated and the trial court's judgment reinstated.

NOTES AND QUESTIONS

A. Duty to Use

1. **Another case.** See Thompson Dev., Inc. v. Kroger Co., 413 S.E.2d 137, 140-42 (W. Va. 1991):

> The majority of jurisdictions refuses to imply a covenant of continuous operation in leases when that implied covenant contradicts or is inconsistent with an express term or when the fixed base rent is substantial. In addition to the existence of an inconsistent express term or a substantial fixed base rent, other factors utilized by courts include whether there is a provision giving the tenant free assignability of the lease without the consent of the landlord. Also, courts consider whether the lease is found to have been actively negotiated between the parties. If the lease was actively negotiated between the parties, then implying a covenant is disallowed since the parties were free to include whatever provisions they wished. Finally, some courts consider whether the lease contains a noncompetitive clause in determining whether to imply a covenant of continuous operation.

2. **Percentage rent.** "Courts have recognized the uniqueness of a percentage lease and have generally implied therefrom an obligation on the part of the lessee to occupy the property and to use reasonable diligence in operating the business in a productive manner. 1 American Law of Property, § 3.66, p. 321 (1952)." Dover Shopping Center, Inc. v. Cushman's Sons, Inc., 164 A.2d 785, 791 (N.J. Super. Ct. App. Div. 1960). Why is the implication of a covenant of continuous operation sensible when the landlord's compensation is based *exclusively* on a percentage of the gross sales made by the tenant? *See* Wood v. Lucy, Lady Duff-Gordon, 118 N.E. 214 (N.Y. 1917) (Cardozo, J.) (under contract giving plaintiff the exclusive right to market defendant's fashion designs, plaintiff was subject to an implied obligation to use best efforts to market defendant's creations; obligation to use best efforts constituted consideration, making contract enforceable by plaintiff). If the lease provides a minimum base rent with a "percentage override" — the percentage rent coming into play only if it exceeds the base rent — should a continuous operation covenant be implied? Does it matter whether the minimum rent is substantial or not? *See* East Broadway Corp. v. Taco Bell Corp., 542 N.W.2d 816 (Iowa 1996) (covenant implied when rent is fixed "exclusively or primarily" on the basis of a percentage of tenant's gross revenues).

3. **Express covenant required.** Unlike the principal case and *Thompson Dev. Co.*, some courts refuse to entertain the landlord's claim of an *implied* covenant of continuous operation; an express clause is necessary. *See* Sampson Investments v. Jondex Corp., 499 N.W.2d 177 (Wis. 1993).

4. **"To be used for specified purposes only."** The denial of an implied covenant of continuous use puts pressure on the landlord whose lease lacks an explicit continuous use clause to argue that other lease provisions impose that requirement. Does a lease clause providing that "the premises shall be occupied and used only" for a specified purpose constitute an express covenant by the tenant to use the premises? *See* Sampson Investments v. Jondex Corp., Note 3 above (clause allows the tenant either to refrain from using the premises at all, or to use the premises as a retail warehouse store, to which the tenants were restricted

under the lease); Serfecz v. Jewel Food Stores, 67 F.3d 591 (7th Cir. 1995) (lease provision for grocery-store-use only did not prohibit tenant from leaving the store vacant). These cases rely on a widely-recognized distinction that often eludes students of this area of the law. *See* Dickey v. Philadelphia Minit-Man Corp., 105 A.2d 580, 581 (Pa. 1954) ("a provision in a lease that the premises are to be used only for a prescribed purpose imports no obligation on the part of the lessee to use or continue to use the premises for that purpose; such a provision is a covenant against a noncomplying use, not a covenant to use"). Although economy in drafting is a virtue, there is a danger in trying to say too much with a few words. For the landlord, how would you draft a lease so as to both restrict the tenant to a particular use of the premises and *also* require that the tenant operate the specified business continuously during the term of the lease? *See Dover Shopping Center* (Note 2) (example of an effective continuous operation covenant).

5. **Anchor tenant.** Should an "anchor tenant" be subject to an implied obligation to operate continuously? *See* Ingannamorte v. Kings Super Markets, Inc., 260 A.2d 841 (N.J. 1970) (economic dependence of landlord and other tenants on anchor tenant's continuous operation justified imposition of implied covenant). *Contra*, Walgreen Arizona Drug Co. v. Plaza Center Corp., 647 P.2d 643 (Ariz. Ct. App. 1982) ("New Jersey seems to stand alone for this proposition"). Suppose the anchor tenant ceases operations ("goes dark"); has the *landlord* breached any duties owed to satellite tenants under the covenant of quiet enjoyment by failing to expressly require that the anchor tenant operate continuously throughout its lease? *See* Fuller Market Basket Co. v Gillingham & Jones, Inc., 539 P.2d 868 (Wash. Ct. App. 1975).

6. **Specific performance.** Specific performance isn't available unless the claimant's legal remedy is inadequate. A court might also refuse specific performance for institutional reasons, such as the difficulty of supervision of the court's order. *See Dover Shopping Center* (Note 2):

> [T]he gravamen of the [landlord's] complaint here is not only the possible loss of additional income by way of a percentage of defendant's increased gross sales, but the difficulty in measuring the harm that would come from the withdrawal of one of the members of a semi-cooperative enterprise like a shopping center. Plaintiff's damages cannot therefore be accurately ascertained, and remedy by way of damages at law would be impractical and unsatisfactory. We turn to defendant's argument that relief should have been denied because of the necessity of continued superintendence on the part of the court. Equity will not ordinarily order specific performance where the duty to be enforced continues over a long period of time and is difficult of supervision. However, the modern tendency is to grant specific performance in the case of a clear breach, where the difficulties of enforcement are not great, particularly when compared with the inadequacy of damages at law.

> The specific performance granted by the court was directed at certain covenants simple of performance and supervision. The judgment expressly provided that except as specifically set forth therein, the court would "make no direction with respect to the method of operating the defendant's business on the demised premises or to the quality of the products sold and

services rendered by the defendant therein." Since the court was careful to limit its order, defendant's objection to it on the ground of required continued supervision is without persuasive force. The judgment as it stands is not so difficult of enforcement that it can be said that the difficulties of supervision outweigh the importance of granting specific performance because of the inadequacy of the remedy of damages at law.

164 A.2d at 791.

B. Illegal Use of Premises by the Tenant

7. **Illegal uses in general.** The Restatement Second of Property (Landlord and Tenant), discussed in the introduction to Section C, lists the obligation "not to use the leased property for an illegal purpose" as one of the implied obligations of the tenant. For breach of that obligation, the landlord is entitled to terminate the lease, or affirm it and get legal and equitable relief. *Id.* § 12.5(1). *See generally* Robert S. Schoshinski, American Law of Landlord and Tenant §§ 5:12 through 5:15 (1980).

8. **Illegal drug use: one strike and you're out.** In the Anti-Drug Abuse Act of 1988, as amended, Congress required public housing agencies to include a provision in all leases that "any criminal activity that threatens the health, safety, or right to peaceful enjoyment of the premises by other tenants or any drug-related criminal activity on or off such premises, engaged in by a public housing tenant, any member of the tenant's household, or any guest or other person under the tenant's control, shall be cause for termination of tenancy." 42 U.S.C. § 1437d(*l*)(6). In Department of Housing and Urban Development v. Rucker, 535 U.S. 125, 122 S. Ct. 1230 (2002), the Supreme Court held that the act authorized the eviction of a tenant for illegal activity committed by a member of the tenant's household or a guest of which the tenant was unaware. The act "unambiguously requires lease terms that vest local public housing authorities with the discretion to evict tenants for the drug-related activity of household members and guests whether or not the tenant knew, or should have known, about the activity." 122 S. Ct. at 1233. *See also* Phillips Neighborhood Housing Trust v. Brown, 564 N.W.2d 573 (Minn. Ct. App. 1997) (eviction of mother, who didn't know of son's possession of crack cocaine in the apartment, was not improper: "eviction is a harsh remedy," but is the landlord's "most effective, if not its only effective, means of eliminating drugs and providing a safe environment").

9. **Other violations.** Is the Anti-Drug Abuse Act, cited in Note 8, limited to criminal activity in violation of drug laws? *See* In re Featherstone, 742 N.E.2d 607 (N.Y. 2000) (Housing Authority lawfully terminated tenant because of teenage son's violent behavior).

10. **Termination clauses.** In *Rucker*, the lease contained an express termination clause. *See also* Burke v. Bryant, 128 A. 821 (Pa. 1925) (landlord's power to terminate was implied by Volstead Act's provision permitting termination of lease for possession of alcohol on leased premises); Restatement Second of Property (Landlord and Tenant) § 12.5(1) (landlord may terminate lease for tenant's illegal activity; express clause not required). *But see* Ross v. Gulf Oil Corp., 522 A.2d 97 (Pa. Super. Ct. 1987) (termination refused for tenant's illegal discharge of sewage into abandoned coal mine under premises: "If a lease is silent

as to the consequence of unlawful activity, neither party should be able to point to the violation to support their voiding the lease unless a statute or ordinance so provides"; the court distinguished Burke v. Bryant, above). How does Ross v. Gulf Oil differ from *Cain Partnership* (Section C.1.b)?

11. **Illegality: distinctions.** Distinguish the question of the tenant's *illegal activity on the leased premises*, discussed above, from that of a *lease for an illegal purpose*. If the landlord and tenant agree on a lease for an illegal purpose — e.g., manufacture of illegal drugs — the lease is invalid and unenforceable by either party. *See* Restatement Second §§ 9.1, 12.4 ("property leased for illegal purpose"); 1 American Law of Property § 3.43 (A.J. Casner ed. 1952); Brown v. Southall Realty Co., 237 A.2d 834 (D.C. App. 1968) (violations of the local housing code existing at the outset of the lease rendered the agreement illegal, barring the landlord from evicting the tenant who refused to pay rent); Diamond Housing Corp. v. Robinson, 257 A.2d 492 (D.C. App. 1969) (minor code violations; no illegality); Saunders v. First National Realty Corp., 245 A.2d 836 (D.C. App. 1968) (defects arising during the lease term; no illegality); William J. Davis, Inc. v. Slade, 271 A.2d 412 (D.C. App. 1970) (tenant occupying under illegal lease owes fair rental value). *See generally* R. Schoshinski, American Law of Landlord and Tenant § 3:15 (1980). (The line of authority basing illegality on the defective condition of the premises has been superseded by the modern development of the implied warranty of habitability. Do you see why?) Distinguish also illegal activity and illegal-purpose leases from the situation of a lease for a purpose that is initially legal, but that becomes illegal as a result of legislation; the question whether this is a *supervening event* terminating the tenant's obligation to pay rent is considered in Section C.4.b below.

C. Contractual Restrictions on Use

12. **Constructional techniques.** If the lease imposes no restrictions on use, the tenant is entitled to use the premises for any purpose that is not illegal, against public policy, or in contravention of any applicable zoning restrictions. Landlords usually narrow the ambit of that broad default rule by restricting the tenant's use (e.g., to "residential purposes only" or "for the specified commercial purposes only"). Restrictions on use are disfavored and hence strictly construed. Cases on use restrictions are legion; a useful review of the issues is provided in Robert S. Schoshinski, American Law of Landlord and Tenant §§ 5:6-5:11 (1980).

The following subsidiary rules of construction, discussed in Turman v. Safeway Stores, 317 P.2d 302, 306-307 (Mont. 1957), suggest the kinds of traps that await the careless drafter: *Implied restrictions on use* are not favored, and will be found "only upon the ground of legal necessity arising from the terms of a contract or the substance thereof." Therefore, the fact that the parties contemplated a particular use by the tenant at the time the lease was entered into does not raise an implied agreement not to use it for any other purpose. *Descriptions are permissive:* words that identify the character of the premises (e.g., "residence," "commercial building") are not construed as restrictions confining the tenant to the particular use expressed in the description. *Statements of intended use are permissive:* statements that the premises are "to be used as a residence" or "to be used for commercial purposes," allow, but do not restrict the tenant to, the use specified.

Compare "to be used as a residence only." Review: if the lease provides that the premises are "to be used as a residence only," is the tenant required to occupy the premises?

b.   Condition of the Premises

We introduced waste in Chapter 2, in connection with the life tenant's duty to maintain and repair the subject property. The doctrine of waste also applies to a tenant under a term of years lease, a periodic tenancy, or a tenancy at will.

BRIZENDINE v. CONRAD
71 S.W.3d 587 (Mo. 2002)

LAURA DENVIR SMITH, JUDGE

David Brizendine brought suit for treble damages under Missouri's anti-waste statute, Section 537.420, against Nora Lee Conrad, his former tenant under a written lease-purchase agreement ("Agreement"). Ms. Conrad appeals the trial court's $33,760.35 judgment in favor of Mr. Brizendine, alleging that a $15,000 liquidated damages clause in the Agreement was his only remedy and that it waived Mr. Brizendine's right to sue for waste under the statute.

This Court affirms the judgment for Mr. Brizendine. Section 537.420 provides for treble damages for waste committed by a tenant for a term of years, such as Ms. Conrad, unless the tenant is given a special license in writing to commit waste. Neither the liquidated damages provision nor other provisions of the Agreement constituted a special license to commit waste. To the contrary, the Agreement required Ms. Conrad to return the property in good condition, absent ordinary wear and tear, and did not permit improvements or changes to the property by Ms. Conrad. Consequently, Mr. Brizendine was entitled to sue under the statute for treble damages for waste. Ms. Conrad was not entitled to a set-off of the $15,000 deposit she made with the Agreement because she did not plead set-off below, include it in her motion for new trial, or ask for such relief in her point relied on, and cannot request such relief for the first time on appeal.

FACTUAL AND PROCEDURAL BACKGROUND

Ms. Conrad and Mr. Brizendine entered into the Agreement by which he leased to her, for 12 months, a low-income apartment-office-storage complex building in the central business district of Jefferson City beginning on October 1, 1997, and expiring on September 30, 1998. The sale of the property was to be concluded at the end of the lease. Paragraph 5 of the Agreement required Ms. Conrad to pay $15,000 at the execution of the Agreement, which would be credited against the purchase price when the sale was completed and all conditions under the Agreement were satisfied. The Agreement obligated Ms. Conrad to assume several duties, such as to manage the property by collecting rents, to provide all trash pickup for the premises, to use the property as residential and commercial property unless otherwise authorized by the written consent of Mr. Brizendine, to keep the grass "neatly mowed," to maintain the premises in good condition and to surrender it "in the same condition as received," and to arrange for and pay for all utilities.

In paragraphs 3(c) and (f) of the Agreement, Ms. Conrad also covenanted and agreed to maintain and repair the property as follows:

(c) To maintain in good condition all interior and exterior surfaces and to do all interior decorating and maintenance at her own expense. It is agreed that all costs for maintenance and repair of the premises and mechanical apparatus located thereon (including replacement) shall be borne by the Lessee during the term of this Agreement. After execution, all costs of maintenance shall be at the Lessee's expense.

(f) If for any reason Lessee fails to purchase the property, she agrees to surrender it to Lessor in the same condition as received, ordinary wear and tear excepted.

Paragraph 14 of the Agreement provided that the $15,000 that Ms. Conrad gave to Mr. Brizendine at the beginning of the lease term would be retained as liquidated damages if Ms. Conrad failed to fulfill her obligations under the Agreement:

14. In the event Lessor shall perform his part of this agreement or shall tender performance thereof, and Lessee fail to perform her part, then the sum of Fifteen Thousand Dollars ($15,000) paid herewith shall be retained by Lessor as liquidated damages, it being agreed that actual damages are difficult, if not impossible, to ascertain. However, Lessor reserves the right to seek specific performance of this agreement.

At the end of the lease term, Ms. Conrad advised Mr. Brizendine that she had decided not to purchase the property because it was "too much maintenance, too much upkeep." Mr. Brizendine informed Ms. Conrad that the property was not in acceptable condition under the Agreement because it had extensive damage, not merely normal wear and tear. While Ms. Conrad contested Mr. Brizendine's claims about the condition of the property, he presented evidence of a dozen instances of damage, ranging from damage to the floors, walls, and ceilings to damage to heating units, plumbing, and common ways. He also discovered that many units were infested with roaches.

At the time the parties entered into the Agreement, the purchase price agreed to was $140,000. When the property was tendered back to Mr. Brizendine, the cost to repair the damage done to it was $30,335. Mr. Brizendine indicated that, rather than investing this sum of money to repair the property, and then trying to sell it again, he took an offer of $90,000 for the property from a new buyer and then filed suit against Ms. Conrad under a variety of theories of damage. Ultimately, he dismissed all claims except the one for statutory waste. Ms. Conrad filed a counterclaim.

At trial, Mr. Brizendine presented evidence that Ms. Conrad mismanaged the property by failing to screen tenants, failing to repair the property and keep it clean, and otherwise failing to actively manage the property. The trial court heard all the evidence, found in favor of Mr. Brizendine and awarded damages for waste in the amount of $11,253.45, based on the cost of repair, which the court then trebled to $33,760.35 pursuant to Section 537.420. Following opinion by the Court of Appeals, this Court granted transfer.

ANALYSIS

A Liquidated Damages Clause Does Not Automatically Waive a Claim for Statutory Waste

Mr. Brizendine submitted his case under Section 537.420, which states: "If any tenant, for life or years, shall commit waste during his estate or term, of anything belonging to the tenement so held, *without special license in writing so to do, he shall be subject to a civil action for such waste,* and shall lose the thing wasted and *pay treble the amount* at which the waste shall be assessed" (emphasis added). Section 537.420 thus "mandates the trebling of damages for waste when a tenant for life or years commits waste to the tenement." Greeson v. Ace Pipe Cleaning, Inc., 830 S.W.2d 444, 448 (Mo. Ct. App. 1992). "[T]he measure of damages is generally the difference between the fair market value of the realty at the end of the lease, had no waste occurred, and the fair market value of the property in its damaged condition." Brown v. Midwest Petroleum Co., 828 S.W.2d 686, 687 (Mo. Ct. App. 1992).

A tenant is not liable for waste under the statute, however, if the tenant has been given a "special license" in writing to commit waste. Ms. Conrad does not contend that she was specifically given a special license to commit waste, but rather contends that the existence of a special license can be implied from the presence in the lease of the $15,000 liquidated damages clause. As noted earlier, that clause states, "[i]n the event Lessor shall perform his part of this agreement and Lessee fail to perform her part, then the sum of [$15,000] shall be retained by the Lessor as liquidated damages, it being agreed that actual damages are difficult, if not impossible, to ascertain."

Ms. Conrad argues that this clause constituted a waiver of the right to sue for statutory treble damages for waste. Alternatively, she argues, by electing to retain the $15,000 she deposited with him at the beginning of the lease period, Mr. Brizendine elected to enforce his right to liquidated damages, and that he cannot be permitted to recover again for the same wrong by suing for damages for waste under the statute. In support, she cites Warstler v. Cibrian, 859 S.W.2d 162 (Mo. Ct. App. 1993) for the point that "[l]iquidated and actual damages generally may not be awarded as compensation for the same injury." *Id.* at 165. Moreover, she argues, had Mr. Brizendine desired to exclude waste damages from the operation of the liquidated damages clause he could have simply included language in the Agreement to that effect.

The terms of the Agreement do not support Ms. Conrad's position. The statute is clear that a landlord is entitled to damages for waste unless the tenant has a special license to commit waste. It was not incumbent on Mr. Brizendine, therefore, to include a provision in the Agreement that statutory damages for waste were not waived; rather, it was Ms. Conrad's burden to show that the Agreement, or some other document, expressly or impliedly gave her a special license to commit waste.

While Ms. Conrad says the liquidated damages clause served this function, she cites no case holding that a liquidated damages clause constitutes a special license to commit waste. Cases finding such a license have either interpreted documents, such as a will, that expressly waived damages for waste, *see, e.g.*, Frey v. Huffstutler, 748 S.W.2d 59, 62, 63-64 (Mo. Ct. App. 1988) or were cases in which permission to commit waste could be implied from the terms of the lease, such as where the lease permitted substantial improvements and changes to the property by the lessee.

Here, by contrast, there are multiple reasons why the terms of the Agreement do not support finding that the liquidated damages clause constituted a special license for waste. First, the liquidated damages clause does not mention waste, although it could easily have done so, just as did the will provision at issue in *Huffstutler*. Second, Ms. Conrad was required under the lease to forfeit the $15,000 she had already paid to Mr. Brizendine whether or not waste occurred, for paragraph 5 provided that the money was to be retained by him even if the purchase fell through, and paragraph 14 provided that the money would be paid as liquidated damages for *any* breach of the Agreement, not merely for waste.

Third, far from giving Ms. Conrad a license to commit waste, paragraph 3 and its subparts specifically obligated Ms. Conrad, as the tenant, to repair and maintain the premises, to provide trash removal, and to keep the grass "neatly mowed." The Agreement also specifically stated that the tenant could not "make any renovation of the interior or exterior of the premises which would permanently alter such interior or exterior" without the written consent of the lessor, and further required "all improvements must be approved by Lessor." The Agreement also restricted the uses to which the tenant could put the property, stating that unless written consent of the Lessor were first obtained, Ms. Conrad could only "use the premises as residential and commercial rental property and for no other purpose." Finally, the Agreement provided that, if the purchase were not consummated, Ms. Conrad was to surrender the property "in the same condition as received, ordinary wear and tear excepted." Ms. Conrad's claim that the exception for ordinary wear and tear is an express license to commit waste flies in the face of the ordinary meaning of those terms. " 'Ordinary wear and tear' includes any usual deterioration from use of the premises during the lease period." 49 Am.Jur.2d, Landlord and Tenant Section 893. It means "normal depreciation." *Id. See also* Black's Law Dictionary 1593 (6th ed. 1990) (" 'Natural wear and tear' means deterioration or depreciation in value by ordinary and reasonable use of the subject-matter."). Waste, on the other hand, "is the failure of a lessee to exercise ordinary care in the use of the leased premises or property that causes material and permanent injury thereto over and above ordinary wear and tear." McLane v. Wal-Mart Stores, Inc.,10 S.W.3d 602, 605 (Mo. Ct. App. 2000).

Read as a whole, these provisions of the Agreement refute Ms. Conrad's claim that the parties intended the presence of the $15,000 liquidated damages clause to constitute a "special license" to commit waste. Nothing in the Agreement suggests such a license; to the contrary, the Agreement provided that no damage or alterations were to be made to the property and it was to be returned in good condition. Therefore, the fact the Agreement contained a liquidated damages clause does not preclude Mr. Brizendine from recovering from his tenant, Ms. Conrad, for waste under section 537.420.

CONCLUSION

For all of the foregoing reasons, the judgment of the trial court is affirmed.

NOTES AND QUESTIONS

A. Waste

1. **Repairs at common law.** Subject to exceptions covered in Section B.3 above (areas under the landlord's control and government-ordered repairs), the common law imposed on the landlord neither an implied warranty of habitability at the outset of the lease, nor an implied promise by the landlord to make repairs during the term. The only implied obligation covering the leased premises was imposed on the *tenant*, under the law of waste. Waste might consist of the tenant's affirmative acts of destruction (voluntary or commissive waste), or the tenant's failure to act (permissive waste). The tenant's duty to avoid permissive waste imposed a limited obligation to make repairs; Suydam v. Jackson, 54 N.Y. 450, 453-454 (1873) discusses the scope of that common law duty:

> [T]he lessee was under an implied covenant from his relation to his landlord, to make what are called "tenantable repairs." The lessee was not bound to make substantial, lasting or general repairs, but only such ordinary repairs as were necessary to prevent waste and decay of the premises. If a window in a dwelling should blow in, the tenant could not permit it to remain out and the storms to beat in and greatly injure the premises without liability for permissive waste; and if a shingle or board thereof should blow off or become out of repair, the tenant could not permit the water, in time of rain, to flood the premises, and thus injure them, without a similar liabililty. He being present, a slight effort and expense on his part could save a great loss, and hence the law justly casts the burden upon him.

As that quotation suggests, the common law duty requires the tenant to make minor repairs that are necessary to preserve the leased premises; it excludes a duty to reverse ordinary wear and tear, except when failure to do so "would result in progressive and rapid decay of the premises." Robert S. Schoshinski, American Law of Landlord and Tenant § 5:18, at 271 (1980). What is the rationale for the common law rule? Is it likely that the tenant's common law duty to repair is still good law in states adopting the landlord's implied warranty of habitability in residential leases? *See* Schoshinski, § 5:19; Anthony J. Fejfar, *Permissive Waste and the Warranty of Habitability in Residential Tenancies*, 31 Cumb. L. Rev. 1 (2000-2001). What about the continued viability of the tenant's duty to avoid commissive (active) waste in a residential lease?

2. **Termination of the lease for waste.** If the lease or a statute so provides, the tenant who commits waste may be evicted. Did the statute in the principal case so provide? In the absence of a contractual or statutory provision, the landlord's power to terminate raises the *Cain Partnership* question: is the landlord's performance of the duty to protect the tenant's possession dependent on the tenant's substantial performance of the obligation to avoid waste? *See* Creekmore

v. Redman Industries, Inc., 671 P.2d 73 (Okla. Ct. App. 1983) (no termination without statute); Restatement of Contracts § 290 (1932) (without express condition, nonperformance of promise by the landlord or the tenant "does not excuse the other party from performing his covenants further than the law of property governing the effect of eviction of the grantee or of waste by him provides").

B. Tenant's Covenant to Repair

3. **Drafting and construction of covenants.** What effect, if any, might a lease clause requiring the tenant to keep the premises "in repair," or "in good repair," or to make "necessary repairs," or to return the premises after the lease "in as good a condition as when received," have on the tenant's common law duty to repair? Would any of those clauses require the tenant to make structural repairs, or to rebuild the premises if they are destroyed by fire or other casualty? *See* Schoshinski, *supra*, § 5:20 (discussion of the quoted phrases). *See also* Fortune Funding, LLC v. Ceridian Corp., 368 F.3d 985 (8th Cir. 2004) (applying Minnesota law: under covenant obligating tenant to "make all structural and nonstructural, foreseen and unforeseen and ordinary and extraordinary repairs which may be required to keep all parts of the [building] in good repair and condition (including, glass), ordinary wear and tear excepted," tenant was not obligated to repair a glass curtain wall and elevator system).

NOTES ON FRUSTRATION OF PURPOSE AND IMPOSSIBILITY OF PERFORMANCE IN LEASES

1. **Destruction of the leased premises.** At common law, "if the demised premises became, during the term, wholly untenantable by destruction thereof by fire, flood, tempest or otherwise, the lessee still remained liable for the rent unless exempted from such liability by some express covenant in his lease." Suydam v. Jackson, 54 N.Y. 450, 453 (1873). The courts stated various rationales for that result: (1) Promissory obligations are absolute unless expressly made conditional. *See* Paradine v. Jane, 82 Eng. Rep. 897 (K.B. 1647) (tenant dispossessed by foreign army; landlord's judgment for rent accruing thereafter affirmed). (2) A lease is a sale with the risk of loss on the buyer. *See* Fowler v. Bott, 6 Mass. 63 (1809). (3) The tenant still possesses the soil on which the building was located, and "may use the land for some purpose and may reconstruct the building." Paxson & Comfort Co. v. Potter, 30 Pa. Super. 615, 616 (1906). An exception allowed the tenant to terminate the lease and be excused from further payment of rent when the tenant leased a *part* of a building from the landlord and the entire building was destroyed. *See* 1 A.L.P. § 3.103, at 397-398. Which of the common law rationales might justify this exception? Which of the three common-law rationales remains persuasive today? *See* UCC § 2-509 (risk of loss "passes to the buyer when the goods are duly so tendered as to enable the buyer to take delivery"); § 2-709 (seller may recover price of destroyed goods after risk of loss has passed to buyer); Krell v. Henry, 2 K.B. 740 (King's Bench 1903) (leading contracts case; tenant of rooms rented to view coronation was excused when parade was cancelled because of monarch's illness); Albert M. Greenfield & Co. v. Kolea, 380 A.2d 758 (Pa. 1977) (applying frustration of purpose to excuse tenant from further liability for rent upon destruction of building on leased premises). The common law view is widely

changed by statute. *See* 1 A.L.P. § 3.103, at 398.

2. **Supervening illegality.** If the tenant's intended use of the premises is initially legal but subsequently becomes illegal, the cases are split on whether the tenant may terminate the lease and escape further lease obligations; those that deny termination emphasize that the risk of loss is on the tenant. If the tenant is entitled to make another use of the premises, the prevailing view denies termination altogether, either on the risk of loss or the *Paxson & Comfort* rationale. *See* 1 A.L.P. § 3.44; Robert S. Schoshinski, American Law of Landlord and Tenant § 5:16 (1980). The Restatement Second § 9.2 allows termination when another use of the premises is available, if it "would be unreasonble to place on the tenant the burdens of the lease after converting to the other use." *Id.* § 9.2(2).

3. **Supervening government regulation.** If the tenant's use is restricted rather than made illegal by supervening government activity, the traditional view is that the tenant is not excused, usually on the basis of one or more of the rationales discussed in Note 1. *See* Schoshinski, *supra*, § 5:17. *But see* Restatement Second § 9.3 ("tenant's rights when intended use frustrated by governmental action"; termination allowed if the government regulation was unforeseeable at the time of contracting). Even when the doctrine of frustration of purpose is applied to leases, the standard of frustration remains high, as it is in contract law. *See* Restatement Second of Property (Landlord and Tenant) § 9.3, Reporter's Note at 322 (tenant's intended use must be frustrated; total or nearly total frustration of use is required; supervening event must not have been reasonably foreseeable); Lloyd v. Murphy, 153 P.2d 47 (Cal. 1944) (leading case; doctrine requires "extreme hardship"; September, 1941 lease for automobile dealership was not frustrated by foreseeable subsequent wartime restrictions on automobile production; landlord also waived the lease restriction on tenant's permissible uses of the premises). *See also* Cook v. Deltona Corp., 753 F.2d 1552 (11th Cir. 1985) (by recognizing the supervening event defense "as a sort of 'escape hatch' from the self-made chamber of contractual duty, the courts have recognized that absolute contractual liability is economically and socially unworkable").

On the unpredictability of results generated by the unforeseeability requirement, compare North American Capital Corp. v. McCants, 510 S.W.2d 901 (Tenn. 1974) (lease restricting tenant to use of premises as savings and loan association not frustrated by governmental denial of permit, despite preliminary informal approval by government inspector), with Smith v. Roberts, 370 N.E.2d 271 (Ill. App. Ct. 1977) (owners of clothing store leased landlord's adjoining first floor and basement, intending to connect the areas into one store; lease contained a casualty clause addressing destruction of the leased premises; fire that destroyed tenant's own premises was a "remote contingency to provide for in a lease"; tenant excused from further payment of rent). If a risk is foreseeable, does it necessarily follow that the tenant cannot claim frustration of purpose? In *McCants*, isn't there an explanation for the tenant's failure to raise the question of permit denial in bargaining and to get an express condition regarding that possibility?

4. **Supervening events and the landlord.** The landlord leases a large theatre to a rock impresario to stage a concert. If the theatre is destroyed by fire after execution of the lease but before the concert, is the landlord liable for the tenant's lost anticipated profits (assuming the profits can be proved with

reasonable certainty)? *See* Taylor v. Caldwell, 122 Eng. Rep. 310 (Q.B. 1863) (contract is subject to "an implied condition that the parties shall be excused in case, before breach, performance becomes impossible from the perishing of the thing without default of the contractor"). Impossibility of performance (Taylor v. Caldwell) is frequently confused with frustration of purpose (Lloyd v. Murphy, Note 2 above); how do they differ? Is impossibility of performance the appropriate claim for the tenant in cases of supervening illegality (Note 2)? How does the implied ("constructive") condition in frustration and impossibility cases differ from the condition implied in *Cain Partnership* (Section C.1.b) — does the party asserting frustration or impossibility claim excuse based on the other party's breach, or something else? *See* Taylor v. Caldwell, above.

D. RUNNING PROMISES IN LEASES: ASSIGNMENT AND SUBLEASE

In Chapter 7, we will encounter the legal phenomenon of "promises running with the land." These are promises made between landowners A and B that, under certain conditions, have the capacity to "run" to — i.e., bind and benefit — successor owners of the land held by A and B. Example: In an unzoned area of the city, landowner A promises neighbor B that A will use his land only for residential purposes. If A subsequently transfers his land to X, the latter may be bound by A's promise; if B transfers her land, the transferee, Y, may get the benefit of the residential-use-only promise. Running promises are unique because they entail the creation of rights and liabilities in parties who did not agree to the creation of the rights and duties to which they succeed.

The same phenomenon of running promises exists in leases. The tenant promises the landlord to pay a specified rent; the tenant subsequently transfers the leased premises to X, who makes no promise to the landlord regarding the payment of rent. Under certain circumstances — those specified in the doctrines constituting the law of running promises in leases — X will owe rent to L despite the absence of a promise by X to pay.

Leases provide a familiar context to introduce you to the topic of running promises. As befits that introductory role, we concentrate on basics here, consigning additional or more complex concepts regarding running promises to our treatment in Chapter 7. Further befitting an introductory treatment, we employ principal cases dealing with transfers by the tenant, rather than the landlord, and we focus only on the running of the tenant's obligation to pay rent, rather than other obligations. Initially, we consider the circumstances under which the tenant is authorized to transfer his or her interest to a third party (Section D.1). When the tenant makes an effective transfer, we then ask whether that transfer is an assignment or a sublease (Section D.2), a distinction that determines the property-based rights and liabilities of all parties — the landlord, tenant, and the tenant's transferee. Finally, we look at the different consequences of an assignment and a sublease, and consider the impact that the transferee's agreement to be bound makes on the allocation of rights and liabilities conferred by property law (Section D.3). Rest assured that, if you understand the concepts involved in determining the liabilities and rights of the tenant and the tenant's transferee, you will be equipped to extrapolate these to the landlord's side.

1.   Power to Transfer Lease Interests

As an interest in land, a leasehold interest falls under the general principle, considered in Chapter 2, that the law favors the free transferability of property interests. In leases, however, free transferability, of the tenant's interest at least, is rarely the fact: landlords, as they are allowed to do, usually impose restrictions on the tenant's power to transfer the leasehold interest. The following case considers, and reinterprets in a way that is becoming increasingly common, a standard lease provision preventing transfers by the tenant without the landlord's consent.

KENDALL v. ERNEST PESTANA, INC.
709 P.2d 837 (Cal. 1985)

BROUSSARD, JUSTICE.

This case concerns the effect of a provision in a commercial lease that the lessee may not assign the lease or sublet the premises without the lessor's prior written consent. The question we address is whether, in the absence of a provision that such consent will not be unreasonably withheld, a lessor may unreasonably and arbitrarily withhold his or her consent to an assignment. This is a question of first impression in this court.

I.

The allegations of the complaint may be summarized as follows. The lease at issue is for 14,400 square feet of hangar space at the San Jose Municipal Airport. The City of San Jose, as owner of the property, leased it to Irving and Janice Perlitch, who in turn assigned their interest to respondent Ernest Pestana, Inc. Prior to assigning their interest to respondent, the Perlitches entered into a 25-year sublease with one Robert Bixler commencing on January 1, 1970. The sublease covered an original five-year term plus four 5-year options to renew. The rental rate was to be increased every 10 years in the same proportion as rents increased on the master lease from the City of San Jose. The premises were to be used by Bixler for the purpose of conducting an airplane maintenance business.

Bixler conducted such a business under the name "Flight Services" until, in 1981, he agreed to sell the business to appellants Jack Kendall, Grady O'Hara and Vicki O'Hara. The proposed sale included the business and the equipment, inventory and improvements on the property, together with the existing lease. The proposed assignees had a stronger financial statement and greater net worth than the current lessee, Bixler, and they were willing to be bound by the terms of the lease.

The lease provided that written consent of the lessor was required before the lessee could assign his interest, and that failure to obtain such consent rendered the lease voidable at the option of the lessor.[5] Accordingly, Bixler requested consent from the Perlitches' successor-in-interest, respondent Ernest Pestana, Inc. Respondent refused to consent to the assignment and maintained that it had an absolute right arbitrarily to refuse any such request. The complaint recites that respondent demanded "increased rent and other more onerous terms" as a condition of consenting to Bixler's transfer of interest.

The proposed assignees brought suit for declaratory and injunctive relief and damages seeking, inter alia, a declaration "that the refusal of ERNEST PESTANA, INC. to consent to the assignment of the lease is unreasonable and is an unlawful restraint on the freedom of alienation." The trial court sustained a demurrer to the complaint without leave to amend and this appeal followed.

II.

The law generally favors free alienability of property, and California follows the common law rule that a leasehold interest is freely alienable. Contractual restrictions on the alienability of leasehold interests are, however, permitted. "Such restrictions are justified as reasonable protection of the interests of the lessor as to who shall possess and manage property in which he has a reversionary interest and from which he is deriving income." (Schoshinski, American Law of Landlord and Tenant (1980) § 8:15, at pp. 578-579).

The common law's hostility toward restraints on alienation has caused such restraints on leasehold interests to be strictly construed against the lessor. This is particularly true where the restraint in question is a "forfeiture restraint," under which the lessor has the option to terminate the lease if an assignment is made without his or her consent.

Nevertheless, a majority of jurisdictions have long adhered to the rule that where a lease contains an approval clause (a clause stating that the lease cannot be assigned without the prior consent of the lessor), the lessor may arbitrarily refuse to approve a proposed assignee no matter how suitable the assignee appears to be and no matter how unreasonable the lessor's objection. The harsh consequences of this rule have often been avoided through application of the doctrines of waiver and estoppel, under which the lessor may be found to have waived (or be estopped from asserting) the right to refuse consent to assignment.

The traditional majority rule has come under steady attack in recent years. A growing minority of jurisdictions now hold that where a lease provides for assignment only with the prior consent of the lessor, such consent may be withheld

---

[5] Paragraph 13 of the sublease between the Perlitches and Bixler provides:"Lessee shall not assign this lease, or any interest therein, and shall not sublet the said premises or any part thereof, or any right or privilege appurtenant thereto, or suffer any other person (the agents and servants of Lessee excepted) to occupy or use said premises, or any portion thereof, without written consent of Lessor first had and obtained, and a consent to one assignment, subletting, occupation or use by any other person, shall not be deemed to be a consent to any subsequent assignment, subletting, occupation or use by another person. Any such assignment or subletting without this consent shall be void, and shall, at the option of Lessor, terminate this lease. This lease shall not, nor shall any interest therein, be assignable, as to the interest of lessee, by operation of alaw [sic], without the written consent of Lessor."

only where the lessor has a commercially reasonable objection to the assignment, even in the absence of a provision in the lease stating that consent to assignment will not be unreasonably withheld. For the reasons discussed below, we conclude that the minority rule is the preferable position.

III.

The impetus for change in the majority rule has come from two directions, reflecting the dual nature of a lease as a conveyance of a leasehold interest and a contract. The policy against restraints on alienation pertains to leases in their nature as conveyances. Numerous courts and commentators have recognized that in recent times the necessity of permitting reasonable alienation of commercial space has become paramount in our increasingly urban society.

One commentator explains as follows:

> The common-law hostility to restraints on alienation had a large exception with respect to estates for years. A lessor could prohibit the lessee from transferring the estate for years to whatever extent he might desire. It was believed that the objectives served by allowing such restraints outweighed the social evils implicit in the restraints, in that they gave to the lessor a needed control over the person entrusted with the lessor's property and to whom he must look for the performance of the covenants contained in the lease. Whether this reasoning retains full validity can well be doubted. Relationships between lessor and lessee have tended to become more and more impersonal. Courts have considerably lessened the effectiveness of restraint clauses by strict construction and liberal applications of the doctrine of waiver. With the shortage of housing and, in many places, of commercial space as well, the allowance of lease clauses forbidding assignments and subleases is beginning to be curtailed by statutes.

(2 Powell on Real Property, ¶ 246[1], at pp. 372.97-372.98.)

The Restatement Second of Property adopts the minority rule on the validity of approval clauses in leases: "A restraint on alienation without the consent of the landlord of a tenant's interest in leased property is valid, but the landlord's consent to an alienation by the tenant cannot be withheld unreasonably, unless a freely negotiated provision in the lease gives the landlord an absolute right to withhold consent." (Rest.2d Property, § 15.2(2) (1977).[14] A comment to the section explains: "The landlord may have an understandable concern about certain personal qualities of a tenant, particularly his reputation for meeting his financial obligations. The preservation of the values that go into the personal selection of the tenant justifies upholding a provision in the lease that curtails the right of the tenant to put anyone else in his place by transferring his interest, but this justification does not go to the point of allowing the landlord arbitrarily and without reason to refuse to allow the tenant to transfer an interest in leased property." (Id., com. a.) Under the

---

[14] This case does not present the question of the validity of a clause absolutely prohibiting assignment, or granting absolute discretion over assignment to the lessor. We note that under the Restatement rule such a provision would be valid if freely negotiated.

Restatement rule, the lessor's interest in the character of his or her tenant is protected by the lessor's right to object to a proposed assignee on reasonable commercial grounds. (*See id.*, reporter's note 7 at pp. 112-113.) The lessor's interests are also protected by the fact that the original lessee remains liable to the lessor as a surety even if the lessor consents to the assignment and the assignee expressly assumes the obligations of the lease.

The second impetus for change in the majority rule comes from the nature of a lease as a contract. "In every contract there is an implied covenant that neither party shall do anything which will have the effect of destroying or injuring the right of the other party to receive the fruits of the contract." (Universal Sales Corp. v. Cal. Mfg. Co. (1942) 20 Cal.2d 751, 771, 128 P.2d 665.) "[W]here a contract confers on one party a discretionary power affecting the rights of the other, a duty is imposed to exercise that discretion in good faith and in accordance with fair dealing." (California Lettuce Growers v. Union Sugar Co. (1955) 45 Cal.2d 474, 484, 289 P.2d 785.) Here the lessor retains the discretionary power to approve or disapprove an assignee proposed by the other party to the contract; this discretionary power should therefore be exercised in accordance with commercially reasonable standards.[15]

reasoning

Under the minority rule, the determination whether a lessor's refusal to consent was reasonable is a question of fact. Some of the factors that the trier of fact may properly consider in applying the standards of good faith and commercial reasonableness are: financial responsibility of the proposed assignee; suitability of the use for the particular property; legality of the proposed use; need for alteration of the premises; and nature of the occupancy, i.e., office, factory, clinic, etc.

Denying consent solely on the basis of personal taste, convenience or sensibility is not commercially reasonable. (Rest.2d Property, § 15.2, reporter's note 7 at pp. 112-113.) Nor is it reasonable to deny consent in order that the landlord may charge a higher rent than originally contracted for. This is because the lessor's desire for a better bargain than contracted for has nothing to do with the permissible purposes of the restraint on alienation — to protect the lessor's interest in the preservation of the property and the performance of the lease covenants. "[T]he clause is for the protection of the landlord in its ownership and operation of the particular property — not for its general economic protection." (Ringwood Associates v. Jack's of Route 23, Inc., *supra*, 379 A.2d 508 at p. 512.)

In contrast to the policy reasons advanced in favor of the minority rule, the majority rule has traditionally been justified on three grounds. Respondent raises a fourth argument in its favor as well. None of these do we find compelling.

First, it is said that a lease is a conveyance of an interest in real property, and that the lessor, having exercised a personal choice in the selection of a tenant and

---

[15] Some commentators have drawn an analogy between this situation and the duties of good faith and reasonableness implied in all transactions under the Uniform Commercial Code. (U.Com.Code §§ 1-203, 2-103(b); see also U.Com.Code § 1-102, com. 1 [permitting application of the U.Com.Code to matters not expressly within its scope]. See Comment, *The Approval Clause in a Lease: Toward a Standard of Reasonableness, supra*, 17 U.S.F.L.Rev. 681, 695; see also Levin, *Withholding Consent to Assignment: The Changing Rights of the Commercial Landlord* (1980) 30 De Paul L.Rev. 109, 136.)

1, provided that no substitute shall be acceptable without prior consent, is under no obligation to look to anyone but the lessee for the rent. This argument is based on traditional rules of conveyancing and on concepts of freedom of ownership and control over one's property. A lessor's freedom at common law to look to no one but the lessee for the rent has, however, been undermined by the adoption in California of a rule that lessors — like all other contracting parties — have a duty to mitigate damages upon the lessee's abandonment of the property by seeking a substitute lessee. Furthermore, the values that go into the personal selection of a lessee are preserved under the minority rule in the lessor's right to refuse consent to assignment on any commercially reasonable grounds. Such grounds include not only the obvious objections to an assignee's financial stability or proposed use of the premises, but a variety of other commercially reasonable objections as well. (See, e.g., Arrington v. Walter E. Heller Int'l Corp. (Ill. App. Ct. 1975), 333 N.E.2d 50 [desire to have only one "lead tenant" in order to preserve "image of the building" as tenant's international headquarters]; Warmack v. Merchants Nat'l Bank of Fort Smith (Ark.1981) 612 S.W.2d 733 [desire for good "tenant mix" in shopping center]; List v. Dahnke (Col.Ct.App.1981) 638 P.2d 824 [lessor's refusal to consent to assignment of lease by one restauranteur to another was reasonable where lessor believed proposed specialty restaurant would not succeed at that location].) The lessor's interests are further protected by the fact that the original lessee remains a guarantor of the performance of the assignee.

2, The second justification advanced in support of the majority rule is that an approval clause is an unambiguous reservation of absolute discretion in the lessor over assignments of the lease. The lessee could have bargained for the addition of a reasonableness clause to the lease (i.e., "consent to assignment will not be unreasonably withheld"). The lessee having failed to do so, the law should not rewrite the parties' contract for them. [I]n light of the increasing number of jurisdictions that have adopted the minority rule in the last 15 years, the assertion that an approval clause "clearly and unambiguously" grants the lessor absolute discretion over assignments is untenable. It is not a rewriting of a contract, as respondent suggests, to recognize the obligations imposed by the duty of good faith and fair dealing, which duty is implied by law in every contract.

3, The third justification advanced in support of the majority rule is essentially based on the doctrine of stare decisis. It is argued that the courts should not depart from the common law majority rule because many leases now in effect covering a substantial amount of real property and creating valuable property rights were carefully prepared by competent counsel in reliance upon the majority viewpoint. As pointed out above, however, the majority viewpoint has been far from universally held and has never been adopted by this court. Moreover, the trend in favor of the minority rule should come as no surprise to observers of the changing state of real property law in the 20th century. The minority rule is part of an increasing recognition of the contractual nature of leases and the implications in terms of contractual duties that flow therefrom. (See Green v. Superior Court (Cal. 1974), 517 P.2d 1168.) We would be remiss in our duty if we declined to question a view held by the majority of jurisdictions simply because it is held by a majority.

A final argument in favor of the majority rule is advanced by respondent and stated as follows: "Both tradition and sound public policy dictate that the lessor has a right, under circumstances such as these, to realize the increased value of his property." Respondent essentially argues that any increase in the market value of real property during the term of a lease properly belongs to the lessor, not the lessee. We reject this assertion. One California commentator has written:

> [W]hen the lessee executed the lease he acquired the contractual right for the exclusive use of the premises, and all of the benefits and detriment attendant to possession, for the term of the contract. He took the downside risk that he would be paying too much rent if there should be a depression in the rental market. Why should he be deprived of the contractual benefits of the lease because of the fortuitous inflation in the marketplace[?] By reaping the benefits he does not deprive the landlord of anything to which the landlord was otherwise entitled. The landlord agreed to dispose of possession for the limited term and he could not reasonably anticipate any more than what was given to him by the terms of the lease. His reversionary estate will benefit from the increased value from the inflation in any event, at least upon the expiration of the lease.

(Miller & Starr, Current Law of Cal. Real Estate (1977) 1984 Supp., § 27:92 at p. 321.)

Respondent here is trying to get more than it bargained for in the lease. A lessor is free to build periodic rent increases into a lease, as the lessor did here. Any increased value of the property beyond this "belongs" to the lessor only in the sense, as explained above, that the lessor's reversionary estate will benefit from it upon the expiration of the lease. We must therefore reject respondent's argument in this regard.[17]

IV.

In conclusion, both the policy against restraints on alienation and the implied contractual duty of good faith and fair dealing militate in favor of adoption of the rule that where a commercial lease provides for assignment only with the prior consent of the lessor, such consent may be withheld only where the lessor has a commercially reasonable objection to the assignee or the proposed use. Under this rule, appellants have stated a cause of action against respondent Ernest Pestana, Inc.

The order sustaining the demurrer to the complaint is reversed.

NOTES AND QUESTIONS

1. **Freedom to transfer.** In the absence of a restriction in the lease, the tenant is free to transfer his or her interest. When a restriction is stated in the lease, it is strictly construed: a restriction on assignment without the landlord's

---

[17] Amicus Pillsbury, Madison & Sutro request that we make clear that, "whatever principle governs in the absence of express lease provisions, nothing bars the parties to commercial lease transactions from making their own arrangements respecting the allocation of appreciated rentals if there is a transfer of the leasehold." This principle we affirm; we merely hold that the clause in the instant lease established no such arrangement.

consent does not forbid subleasing; a restriction on subleasing does not forbid assignment; a restriction on assignment and subleasing does not forbid the tenant's transfer of nonpossessory interests in the leased premises. *See* 2 Powell on Real Property § 17.04[1][b]; Restatement Second of Property (Landlord and Tenant) § 15.1. In light of these default rules, was the anti-transfer clause in the principal case carefully drafted?

2. **No-transfer clauses; sole discretion clauses.** How does the court's reading of the standard "no transfer without consent" clause differ from the traditional common law reading of such clauses? Would (should) a lease provision allowing the landlord to arbitrarily withhold consent be valid (e.g., "tenant shall neither assign, sublease, nor otherwise transfer any interest in the leased premises, without the consent of the landlord, which consent may be given or withheld in the sole discretion of the landlord")?

3. **Reasonable and unreasonable action by the landlord.** See Brigham Young University v. Seman, 672 P.2d 15, 18 (Mont. 1983):

> Arbitrary considerations of personal taste, sensibility or convenience are not proper criteria for the landlord's consent, nor is personal satisfaction the sole determining factor. The financial responsibility of the proposed sublessee, the character of his business, its suitability for the building, the legality of the proposed use, and the nature of the occupancy are among the proper criteria.

4. **Remedies.** If the tenant transfers without the landlord's consent, in violation of a lease clause, the landlord is entitled to equitable relief and damages. *See* 1 A.L.P. § 3.58, at 307. Is the landlord entitled to terminate for the breach? Does it matter whether the lease reserves a power in the landlord to terminate for the tenant's breach of lease covenants? See Healthco, Inc. v. W & S Associates, 511 N.E.2d 579 (Mass. 1987). Suppose the landlord accepts rent from the transferee; what impact does that have on the landlord's remedies? *See* 1 A.L.P. § 3.58, at 304.

5. **Dumpor's Case.** A restriction in a lease forbidding transfers without the landlord's consent is a running covenant; assignees of the tenant are obligated to get the consent of the landlord before making further transfers over to another tenant. An oddity of the common law is the Rule in Dumpor's Case, 76 Eng. Rep. 1110 (K.B. 1578), which holds that a landlord's unqualified consent to one assignment "waives" the no-transfer clause, in effect freeing the lease estate from the restriction thereafter. The rule does not apply to the landlord's consent to a subleasing, nor to a waiver made by the landlord's acceptance of rent after an unauthorized assignment. *See* Restatement Second § 16.1, Reporter's Note 7, at 136. The rule is a trap for the unwary drafter and is rejected in the Restatement. *Id.* cmt. g, at 125. Was the lease in the principal case carefully drafted to avoid Dumpor's Case?

6. **Implied no-assignment clauses?** In Rowe v. Great Atlantic & Pacific Tea Co., 385 N.E.2d 566 (N.Y. 1978), the court refused to find an implied-in-fact agreement between the parties restricting the tenant's freedom to transfer. The landlord was "an experienced attorney and businessman," the percentage rental provided in the lease was not out of line with comparable leasings in the vicinity, and the lease had been the subject of extensive negotiations. Would you expect a

have to have an econ reason to deny Sublease

court to recognize an implied-in-law restriction on transfers by either party to the lease?

2. Assignment or Sublease?

A lease creates "privity of estate" — a property relationship — between the landlord and the tenant: the tenant holds the present possessory estate, and the landlord holds the reversion in fee simple. An assignment of the lease from T to X creates no new lease; it simply substitutes X in privity of estate with the landlord on the existing lease. A sublease between T and X creates a second lease; T remains in privity of estate with the landlord under the main lease, and becomes the landlord of the sublessee under the sublease. In a sublease, X does not step into privity of estate with, and has no liability to, the landlord; the tenant remains (exclusively) liable for the performance of the tenant's obligations.

How do we know whether T's transfer to X is an assignment or sublease? The following excerpt states the two main tests for making the distinction:

> If the instrument purports to transfer the lessee's estate for the entire remainder of the term it is an assignment, regardless of its form or of the parties' intention. Conversely, if the instrument purports to transfer the lessee's estate for less than the entire term — even for a day less — it is a sublease, regardless of its form or of the parties' intention. In some states, notably Massachusetts, it has been held that if the [tenant] reserves a right of re-entry for nonpayment of rent this is a sufficient reversionary estate to make the instrument a sublease. Dunlap v. Bullard, 131 Mass. 161; Davis v. Vidal, 151 S.W. 290 (Tex. 1912). But even these decisions have been criticized on the ground that at common law a right of re-entry was a mere chose in action instead of a reversionary estate.

Jaber v. Miller, 239 S.W.2d 760, 761, 763 (Ark. 1951). (As discussed below, the court rejected both of the common law rules in favor of an intent test.)

NOTES AND QUESTIONS

1. **The Restatement.** The Restatement Second § 16.1 cmt. e adopts the Massachusetts and Texas test discussed in Jaber v. Miller: an assignment occurs only if the tenant transfers the "entire balance" of the lease term *and* retains "no reversionary interest." *See also id.* cmt. f; sec. 15.1 cmt. i. The Restatement's explanation is noteworthy:

> It is usually in the landlord's interest to keep the tenant of his choice in the position of primary liability on the obligations under the lease. If the tenant makes an assignment, rather than a sublease, the tenant's liability on the obligations under the lease becomes secondary [to the assignee's primary liability] or is eliminated [if the landlord releases the tenant from further liability]. Thus it is usually in the landlord's interest to treat a transfer by the tenant as a sublease whenever that is possible.

Id. § 15.1 cmt. i. Is that a sound argument? Suppose that the tenant is insolvent? Is the tenant's secondary liability in an assignment a disadvantage to the landlord, or does it give the landlord two potential defendants? How might the landlord exercise control over whether the tenant's liability is "eliminated"?

2. **An intent test.** In Jaber v. Miller, the court rejected both the majority and minority tests:

> A lawyer trained in common law technicalities can prepare either instrument [an assignment or sublease] without fear that it will be construed to be the other. But for the less skilled lawyer or for the layman the common law rule is simply a trap that leads to hardship and injustice by refusing to permit the parties to accomplish the result they seek. For these reasons we adopt as the rule in this state the principle that the intention of the parties is to govern in determining whether an instrument is an assignment or a sublease.

Jaber provides a useful opportunity for evaluation of the three tests. Is an intent test necessary for sophisticated parties? If the parties are unsophisticated, and do not express their intent with clarity, what factors will a court consider in determining what the parties (might have) intended? Which of the three tests is the easiest for a court to administer?

3. **Partial assignment.** Suppose that the leased premises consist of a house and detached garage. The tenant transfers the right to use the garage to X for the remainder of the term. Is X an assignee or sublessee of the garage? *See* Restatement Second § 15.1 cmt. i, illus. 16 (assignment). Or suppose that the tenant assigns a one-half interest in all of the premises to X; assignment or sublease? *See id.* § 16.1 cmt. e, illus. 19 (L and T "are in privity of estate with respect to an undivided one-half interest" and L and X "are in privity of estate with respect to the other undivided one-half interest").

PROBLEM 4-V. Which of the following transfers from T to X is an assignment and which a sublease under the tests discussed in Jaber v. Miller? Assume that the lease between L and T ends on December 31, 2007. (a) T transfers "to X, through December 31, 2007." (b) T transfers "to X through December 31, 2007, but if X fails to pay the rent owed, T has the power to re-enter and terminate X's estate." (c) T transfers "to X through November 30, 2007." (d) T transfers "to X through December 30, 2007." Why might the tenant want to retain a power to terminate the lease in a situation like (b)?

3.   Consequences of Transfer

Knowing now when transfers by the tenant are permissible, and whether those transfers constitute assignments or subleases, we next (and last) ask about the consequences of a transfer. Some consequences follow simply from the existence of privity of estate between the tenant's transferee and the landlord. Additional consequences follow if the transferee assumes the obligations of the tenant's lease, which puts the transferee in privity of contract with the landlord. Finally, having considered the transferee's liability, we address the question of the tenant's continuing liability to the landlord after making an assignment or sublease.

FIRST AMERICAN NATIONAL BANK v. CHICKEN SYSTEM OF AMERICA, INC.
616 S.W.2d 156 (Tenn. Ct. App. 1980)

LEWIS, JUDGE.

This case arose out of a lease entered into on May 28, 1968, between plaintiff First American National Bank and defendant Chicken System of America, Inc.. The lease contained a provision which expressly prohibited any assignment or subletting without the written consent of First American. The lease was for a term of 180 months from May 28, 1968, at a rental of $1049.08 per month, and in addition Chicken System was required to pay premiums on all insurance and to pay all real estate taxes. Chicken System entered and took possession of the premises under the lease and paid all obligations to and including the month of April, 1969. On April 30, 1969, the President of defendant Performance Systems, Inc., (PSI) wrote to C.H. Wright of Wriking Foods/Beverage Systems, Inc., the parent company of Chicken System. We set out the pertinent parts of that letter:

> This will confirm our mutual agreement for the purchase by us at March 30, 1969, of the Minnie Pearl's Chicken retail outlets owned by your subsidiaries at Murfreesboro Road and Nolensville Road, Nashville, Tennessee, for the sum of $137,329, plus $24,895.00. We will assume the contract payable to the Third National Bank, Nashville, Tennessee for the Nolensville Road Store, together with the rent deposit note to us on Murfreesboro Road per schedule attached. At the time of closing you will discharge your equipment note to Nashco Equipment and Supply Company in the amount of $24,895.00. For the price mentioned above and the assumption of these liabilities, we will acquire from you all inventories, store equipment, rent deposits and your franchise to operate these outlets.

> You understand and agree that other liabilities relating to the operation of these stores incurred by you are for your account, except that the real estate and sign leases are our responsibility after April 30, 1969.

On May 5, 1969, First American was advised by Gale Smith & Company of insurance cancellations on the leased property and was informed of Gale Smith's understanding that the business had been purchased by PSI. Prior to that time First American had no knowledge of any agreement or possible agreement between Chicken System and PSI.

On May 8, 1969, First American's counsel wrote PSI in regard to the insurance coverage and also informed PSI that the premises could only be subleased with the written consent of First American. On June 6, 1969, First American's counsel wrote to all concerned parties. Pertinent portions of that letter are as follows:

> Under Section 24 of the lease agreement there may be no assignment or sub-letting without the written consent of the lessor. I wish to make it plain that as of this time no such consent has been given, nor will any such consent be given unless there is a formal request in writing, requesting same. Upon our receipt of such a written request, we will submit the

proposal to those three individuals who have guaranteed performance of the lease by Chicken System of America, Inc., and if they have no objection to the assignment or sub-letting and will continue bound on their guaranty agreement, the Bank will probably have no objection to consenting to a sub-lease or assignment.

The guarantors did not at any time agree to remain bound on their guaranty agreement if the premises were sublet or assigned to PSI. The guarantors were originally defendants in this suit, but prior to trial a nonsuit as to them was taken by First American. There were several letters written by plaintiff's counsel and PSI's counsel regarding subletting or assignment, but at no time did First American ever consent to an assignment of the lease from Chicken System to PSI.

PSI entered the premises and took possession and from May 1, 1969, through October, 1970, paid rent to First American. On November 1, 1970, PSI defaulted in payment of the rent and vacated the premises. Thereafter, First American filed suit in the Chancery Court for Davidson County against Chicken System and PSI and sought rent, insurance, taxes, and maintenance under the terms of the lease agreement due and owing until September 1, 1972. PSI's primary defense was that First American had withheld consent, that absent consent by First American the "assignment" from Chicken System to PSI was invalid and PSI was merely a tenant at sufferance, and that when PSI vacated the premises in November, 1970, its obligations and rights under the lease were suspended.

The Chancellor held that the lack of consent could be waived by First American and could not be raised by PSI as a defense, that PSI's surrender of the premises in November, 1970, did not terminate privity of estate between it and First American, and that PSI was liable to First American for obligations of the lease running with the land, including the obligation to pay rent. PSI appealed, and the Supreme Court affirmed the Chancellor. First American National Bank v. Chicken System of America, Inc., 510 S.W.2d 906, 908 (Tenn. 1974). The Court stated: "[t]here is privity of estate between an original lessor and a subsequent assignee that makes the assignee fully responsible to the lessor for the lease provisions." The Court remanded to the Chancery Court for the purpose of ascertaining damages. The damages were stipulated, but the Chancellor allowed interest on the recovery. PSI again appealed to the Supreme Court which again affirmed the Chancellor. Performance Systems, Inc. v. First American National Bank, 554 S.W.2d 616 (Tenn. 1977).

Following PSI's default in the payment of rent in November, 1970, First American, along with PSI, made efforts to find another tenant for the premises and received some ten proposals. PSI wrote First American and granted approval for First American to enter the premises in the interest of subleasing the land and permanent improvements. On June 1, 1971, PSI wrote First American again and stated: "It is important that we place a tenant in the property at the earliest possible time." First American, without consulting PSI or requesting PSI's consent, entered into a lease with Rodney E. and Melanie Fortner, d/b/a Sir Pizza of Madison, for a term of 60 months beginning the first day of September, 1972, at a rental of $600 per month. The Sir Pizza lease was renewed effective September 1, 1977, for a rental of $1000 per month.

First American has brought this suit for the deficiency in the rent and other obligations occurring after September 1, 1972, the date of the Sir Pizza lease. This case was presented to the Trial Court on stipulated facts, and the Chancellor found that First American was entitled to recover $47,384.27 from PSI. PSI has appealed. While both PSI and First American have set forth issues, we are of the opinion that answering only the following question is necessary to resolve this case. Is PSI liable to First American under either privity of estate or privity of contract?

PRIVITY OF ESTATE

Three legal factors arise to create a liability running from the assignee of a leasehold to the lessor: (a) privity of estate (b) covenants in the lease running with the land and (c) actual assumption of the covenants of the lease by the assignee. An assignee of a lease is bound by privity of estate to perform the express covenants which run with the land, but, in the absence of express agreement on his part, he is liable only on such covenants as run with the land and only during such time as he holds the term.

3A Thompson on Real Property § 1216 (1959).

An assignee, unless he has personally assumed the obligation of the lease, may absolve himself from further liability by an act which terminates his privity of estate. [The assignee] has the benefit and the burden of all covenants running with the land as long as he holds the estate. Liability of the assignee to the lessor, being based solely on privity of estate, does not continue after he transfers his interest to another. The assignee may thus put an end to his liability by making a further assignment, and this although the second assignee is financially irresponsible.

1 American Law of Property (A. Casner ed. 1952) § 3.61.

In accord with this rule is McLean v. Caldwell, 64 S.W. 16, 16-17 (Tenn. 1901), in which the court stated:

As a general rule, the assignee of a lease is only liable for rents while in possession, provided he reassigns the lease to the lessor or any other person; and it does not matter that such assignment is made to a beggar, a minor, a married woman, a prisoner, or an insolvent, or to one hired to take the assignment, or made expressly to rid himself of liability. The reason is that such reassignment and surrender of possession terminate the privity of estate existing between him and the landlord.

A.D. Juilliard & Co. v. American Woolen Co., 32 A.2d 800 (R.I. 1943), is closely akin in facts to the case at bar. There the landlord leased premises to a lessee which, in turn, assigned the lease to the defendant. Thereafter, the defendant reassigned to a third party. The defendant assignee there, as here, had not expressly assumed the lease. The lessor there, as First American here, contended "that the assignee of a lease of real property is liable for the payment of the stipulated rent for the entire unexpired term, notwithstanding that the assignee did not agree to assume such obligation and assigned the lease before the expiration of the term." *Id.* at 801. The court in *Juilliard* stated:

> This contention is contrary to the overwhelming weight of authority both in England and this country. [T]he courts in this country have consistently held that, in the absence of the assumption by the assignee of the obligations of the lease, the liability of such assignee to the lessor rests in privity of estate, which is terminated by a new assignment of the lease made by the assignee.

With this rule, First American says it "has no quarrel." It insists, however, that the rule has no relevance to the case at bar since there was not a reassignment by PSI but a reletting of the premises by First American for the benefit of PSI. This contention is a distinction without difference. While mere abandonment by PSI without reassignment of the lease would not have terminated privity of estate, there was a reletting of the premises on September 1, 1972, by First American. When First American relet the premises to Sir Pizza, PSI's possessory rights to the premises terminated just as if PSI had reassigned the lease. Privity of estate terminated, and PSI had no further leasehold interest in the premises.

An assignee who has not assumed the lease "stands in the shoes" of the original lessee only for covenants that run with the land and then only during privity of estate. If this were not so, then the "dumping" of an unfavorable lease would not be possible. Tennessee clearly recognizes that an assignee who has not assumed the lease may "dump it."

PRIVITY OF CONTRACT

First American contends that the following stipulated facts "demonstrate that PSI assumed the obligations of the Chicken System lease thereby placing it in privity of contract with First American":

1. An agreement was entered into between Chicken System of America, Inc. and Performance Systems, Inc., which is reflected in a letter dated April 30, 1969, from Edward G. Nelson, President of Performance Systems, Inc., to C.H. Wright of Wriking Food/Beverage Systems, Inc., the parent company of Chicken System of America, Inc.

2. The letter, as it related to PSI's purchase of the Nolensville Road store, provided in relevant part that "You understand and agree that other liabilities relating to the operation of these stores incurred by you are for your account, except that the real estate and sign leases are our responsibility (PSI) after April 30, 1969."

3. After April 30, 1969, neither Chicken System of America, nor its parent corporation paid any rent on the property. Rent on the property was paid by PSI from May 1, 1969 through October, 1970, and PSI was in possession of the premises during that time.

In Hart v. Socony-Vacuum Oil Co., 50 N.E.2d 285 (N.Y. 1943), several years after an oral assignment of the lease the assignee signed a modification agreement in regard to the insurance requirements of the lease. The modification agreement contained the following provision: "It is further mutually understood and agreed that except as herein expressly modified, all other provisions and covenants contained in said lease shall remain in full force and effect." In rejecting the lessor's argument that this agreement was a personal assumption of the covenants of the lease on the part of the assignee, the Court stated:

> There is strong authority which says that to hold liable an assignee under a lease, after he has given up the lease and vacated the premises, there must be produced an express promise by him to perform the covenants of the lease. [S]uch an express covenant is never assumed to have been made; it must always be proven. It is not every reference to, or mention of, the covenants of a lease, by an assignee, that amounts to an assumption by him. Even where he covenants that his assignment is to be "subject" to the terms of the lease, that language, without more definite words of promise, does not make him liable as by privity of contract.

Id. at 286-87.

In Consolidated Coal Co. v. Peers, 46 N.E. 1105 (Ill. 1896), there was a written assignment to the assignee which said, according to plaintiff's declaration, that the lease was assigned "together with all the rights, privileges, and appurtenances thereunto appertaining or belonging, as the same were conveyed by the said lease, and subject to the agreements therein mentioned to be performed by said lessee." The court, in holding that the words, "subject to the agreements therein," inserted in the assignment did not import a covenant on the part of the assignee personally to pay the rents, said:

> [I]t is the duty of a party who intends by a deed to bind another by a covenant in a former formal instrument to insert such covenant in the deed in such distinct and intelligible terms as that the party to be bound cannot be deceived, and not called upon the courts to infer such a covenant from equivocal words.

Id. at 1109.

In Meyer v. Alliance Investment Co., 87 A. 476, 477 (N.J. 1913), the court stated:

> The claim of the plaintiffs to recover rent of the defendant rests upon the words of the [lessor's] consent, "subject to all the terms, conditions and covenants contained in said lease." These are words of qualification and not of contract. The case is similar to a conveyance of land subject to a mortgage. The grantee is not personally bound unless there are words equivalent to an assumption of the mortgage.

Before there is privity of contract between the assignee and the lessor, there must be an actual assumption of the lease. In the case at bar there was not an actual assumption, only a mere acceptance of an assignment.

In Johnson v. First National Bank, 187 S.E. 300 (Ga. Ct. App. 1936), the lessor attempted to impute privity to an assignee bank because of its conduct subsequent to an assignment. The court there said: "It is contended by the [lessor] that the conduct of the [assignee] shows that it recognized it was bound to the same extent as the original lessee with whom the contract was made, but the record fails to disclose that the [assignee] ever executed a writing assuming the lease." Further, the court stated:

> The assignment to the defendant was a "naked assignment," and the assignee having assumed no contract obligation cannot be sued on a contract. The same rule applies even though the assignee holds under a lease which provides that its covenants shall bind the lessee and his assigns, where there has been no express assumption of the lease.

Id. at 302.

"The mere acceptance of an assignment is not an assumption. Every assignment requires acceptance, yet an assignee who does not assume the performance of the covenants of the lease holds the lease merely under a privity of estate." Packard-Bamberger & Co. v. Maloof, 89 N.J.Super. 128, 214 A.2d 45, 46-47 (1965).

While no contention is made that there was a written contract between PSI and First American, First American argues, nevertheless, that certain statements made by PSI to other parties after the assignment by Chicken System to PSI created privity of contract between First American and PSI. First American cites Crow v. Kaupp, 50 S.W.2d 995 (Mo. 1932), in support of this contention. Crow is readily distinguishable from the case at bar. In *Crow* the assignee assumed the lease by written assignment which provided, in pertinent part: "[T]he second parties hereby further bind and obligate themselves, their heirs and assigns, to assume the payment of all rent to the said owner, it being understood that the second parties hereto assume the above mentioned contract, together with all liabilities and obligations created thereby." *Id.* at 996-97. The assignee in *Crow* made a complete and detailed assumption of the lease. In the case at bar, the assignment to PSI by Chicken System was oral, and PSI made no promise at any time to be bound to First American.

We are of the opinion that privity of estate between First American and PSI terminated upon PSI's abandonment of the premises and the reletting of the premises to Sir Pizza by First American. We further hold that there was no privity of contract between PSI and First American.

The judgment of the Chancellor is reversed, and this cause is dismissed with costs to First American.

OPINION ON PETITION TO REHEAR

Lewis, Judge.

Plaintiff has filed a courteous and forceful Petition to Rehear. Plaintiff argues that under our Opinion a lessor might be discouraged from reletting premises and that this would be a detriment to a lessee. No such construction is warranted. We simply hold that under facts such as in the case at bar where only privity of estate exists between the original lessor and the assignee of the original lessee, the assignee is no longer liable for rent when the assignee gives up possession and the lease is reassigned either to the lessor or to some other person.

Plaintiff does correctly point out that this court considered only the liability of Performance Systems, Inc. So there can be no misunderstanding, we amend our Opinion by deleting the last paragraph, and substituting the following:

> The judgment of the Chancellor as to Performance Systems, Inc. is reversed and dismissed with costs to First American. The case is remanded to the Chancery Court for collection of costs and any other necessary proceedings.

We otherwise adhere to our original opinion. Costs are taxed to First American.

NOTES AND QUESTIONS

A. Liability of Transferees

1. **Sublessees: no privity of estate.** A sublessee is not in privity of estate with the landlord and escapes liability based on such privity. In some states, the landlord may have a statutory cause of action against a sublessee for rents accruing during the sublease. *See, e.g.,* N.J. Stat. Ann. § 2A:42-4. And the landlord, by lease provision or statute, will usually have the power to terminate the main lease if rent is not paid or other obligations performed. To prevent being dispossed by the tenant's failure to pay rent to the landlord, the sublessee might bargain with the tenant for the right to pay rent directly to the landlord.

2. **Privity of estate: content of the assignee's liability.** Is an assignee liable to perform *all* of the tenant's express promises to the landlord? Is an assignee liable to the landlord for the performance of any *other* obligations of the tenant? *See* Reid v. Weissner & Sons Brewing Co., 40 A. 877, 877 (Md. 1898) (assignee is liable "upon all covenants that run with the land, such as covenants for the payment of rent and the like"); Amco Trust Co. v. Naylor, 317 S.W.2d 47, 50 (Tex. 1958) (assignee "is liable for the rent reserved in the lease *and* for the performance of covenants which run with the land") (emphasis added). For further discussion of the requirements for an express covenant to "run with the land" to a successor, see Chapter 7. For the Restatement Second's list of the tenant's implied-in-law (privity of estate) obligations, see Chapter 4.C.1. If T assigns a one-half interest in the leased premises to X, what is X's liability on a promise of the tenant that runs with the land?

3. **Privity of estate: duration of the assignee's liability.** When does an assignee's liability based on privity of estate end?

4. **The principal case.** Why was PSI an assignee of the Chicken System lease, rather than a sublessee? Did PSI escape liability to First American for rent deficiencies after September 1, 1972 because PSI assigned the premises over to Sir Pizza (through the agency of the landlord), or because First American accepted a surrender by operation of law from PSI?

5. **Privity of contract; the principal case.** What is the consequence of an agreement by the tenant's transferee (X) to assume the liabilities that the tenant owes to the landlord? Why did the court in the principal case conclude that PSI did not assume Chicken System's obligations to the landlord?

B. Transferor's Liability After Transfer

6. **Privity of estate and contract.** An assignment ends privity of estate between the landlord and tenant, but not privity of contract; the tenant remains liable to the landlord on any express promises that the tenant has made. If the tenant's promise runs with the land to an assignee, the tenant's continuing contractual liability after assignment is secondary. The tenant is a surety for the assignee's performance. The landlord may sue the tenant, the assignee, or both; if the landlord recovers from the tenant, the tenant is entitled to recover from the assignee. *See* 2 Powell on Real Property § 17.04[2], p. 17-63; Restatement Second § 16.1(1). The tenant's continuing contractual liability after transfer to an assignee (X) is based on the same principal as the assignee's continuing liability after re-assignment to another party when X has assumed the tenant's obligations to the landlord. *See* Note 5 above.

7. **Express promises; implied-in-law promises.** The tenant remains liable after an assignment on a *promise* to pay rent, but not on a *reservation* of rent. *See* Samuels v. Ottinger, 146 P. 638 (Cal. 1915) (finding a promise based on wording of lease); Robert S. Schoshinski, American Law of Landlord and Tenant § 5:34, at 331-32 (1980) (noting the "clearly established difference in legal theory — and in legal effect — between a mere reservation of rent in a lease and an express covenant to pay rent"). The distinction between an express promise to pay rent (T "agrees," "covenants," or "promises" to pay monthly rent of $100) and a reservation (L leases to T, "reserving a rent of $100 per month") is a trap for the unwary and a source of litigation over ambiguous language; typical are leases "at" or "subject to" a specified rent, or a specified sum "payable" monthly or yearly, all discussed in Samuels v. Ottinger. A better distinction perhaps would be between all stipulated rentals (promise or reservation) and an occupant's quasi-contractual liability for fair rental value, with the tenant escaping liability after assignment only on the latter.

8. **Release; novation.** The tenant's privity of contract liability continues until the obligation is discharged. An assignment does not discharge the tenant, unless the lease so provides. *See* Shadeland Dev. Corp. v. Mech, 489 N.E.2d 1192 (Ind. App. Ct. 1986). Nor does the landlord's consent to an assignment or acceptance of rent from the assignee discharge the tenant. *See* Restatement Second § 16.1, Reporter's Note 5, at 134 ("there must be a release distinct from the assignment itself"); 1 A.L.P. §§ 310-11. A release is usually included as part of a three-party transaction in which the landlord agrees to release the tenant and to accept the assignee in the tenant's place (a novation), and the assignee agrees to assume the tenant's obligations to the landlord. However, if the landlord and the assignee agree on any material changes in the obligations due under the lease (for example, an increase in rent), the result is usually an implied novation. For a useful discussion of novation, see Jedco Dev. Co. v. Bertsch, 441 N.W.2d 664 (N.D. 1989).

9. **Colorable assignments.** As the *Chicken Systems* case notes, the tenant or a subsequent assignee may "dump" the lease onto an assignee and escape further liability based on privity of estate, even if the new assignee is insolvent. (What can the landlord do to protect himself from this?) Colorable assignments, however, do not break privity of estate and the obligations that it imposes. *See* National Bank of Commerce v. Dunn, 78 P.2d 535, 543-48 (Wash. 1938) (individual tenant's

assignment of lease to a corporation in which he held most of the stock did not terminate individual's privity with landlord).

PROBLEM 4-W. L leases to T for ten years. T promises to pay a rental of $1000 per month. With 5 years remaining on the lease, T transfers all of the remaining term to X, who "accepts the assignment and agrees to pay rent of $1000 per month to T." After occupying for two years, X transfers the remaining three years to Z. Z fails to pay rent for two months. Z is insolvent. Who is liable to L for the two months' rent? How would your answer differ if the arrangement between T and X stated that X "accepts the assignment and agrees to perform T's obligations owed to L"? How would your answer differ if T's obligation to pay rent had been based on a reservation of rent, rather than a promise?

Chapter 5

REAL ESTATE TRANSACTIONS: SALES

In this chapter we look at the doctrines and processes involved in the typical sale of a residence or other real property. We begin with an overview (Section A.1) that presents the chronological steps in a real estate transaction and that outlines the major documents generated in the process from the initial contract between buyer and seller to the closing, when the seller conveys title and the buyer pays the purchase price. We also consider the relationship between the seller and the real estate broker (Section A.2) and the application of the Statute of Frauds (Section A.3). Following these preliminary matters, we shift to a thematic presentation, looking in Section B at selected issues arising between the contract of sale and the closing that may prevent the sale from going through, in Section C at the closing itself, and in Section D at selected issues that bring the parties back together as contestants in a lawsuit after they have gone their separate ways.

A. PRELIMINARIES

1. An Overview of the Process

Theoretically you could purchase real property in the same way that you purchase items from a garage sale. You could approach the owner, bargain over the price, and hand him the purchase price in cash in exchange for a deed to and possession of the property. Purchases of real property rarely occur in this manner, however, for a multitude of reasons. First, a purchaser would rarely have cash on hand to pay for real estate. She must arrange to borrow funds for the purchase. Second, the purchaser will probably want to have the improvements on the property inspected for physical defects. Third, the purchaser will likely want to undertake some type of investigation as to defects in the seller's title and obtain some type of title assurance. In addition, a seller is not typically able to hand over possession of real property without some preparation.

Therefore, parties who wish to purchase real estate typically enter into a contract under the terms of which the seller agrees to sell the property for the agreed purchase price and the purchaser agrees to buy the property subject to certain conditions. The closing of the sale, when the deed is delivered and the purchase price paid, typically occurs some period of time after the parties enter into the contract. During the "gap" period between the execution of the contract and the closing, the buyer will typically arrange financing, have the property inspected for defects in its physical condition, obtain information about the seller's title, and in some cases determine whether the property is in compliance with law. Let's look at a typical sale of a residence in more detail.

Most residential sellers use a broker to find a buyer for a home. The seller will typically enter into a listing agreement with the broker which specifies the terms on which the seller is willing to sell and provides for a commission to be paid to the broker. Buyers often use a broker as well to help in locating a suitable home. (Today a buyer often has a broker acting as the buyer's agent. In the past, the broker who worked with the buyer was more likely an agent of the seller.) When a buyer finds a home in which she is interested, she will make an offer through her broker, often on a contract form provided by the broker and approved by the state bar, the state real estate commission, or both. The seller will counter-offer through his broker, and this will continue until the parties reach an agreement (if they do). When the parties reach an agreement, the buyer will pay an earnest money deposit to be applied to the purchase price at the time of closing. Although there are many reasons to recommend that both buyers and sellers consult an attorney in the negotiation of the contract, they rarely do in most states. See generally Michael Braunstein, *Structural Change and Inter-Professional Competitive Advantage: An Example Drawn from Residential Real Estate Conveyancing*, 62 Mo. L. Rev. 241 (1997) (discussing the decreased role of attorneys in residential real estate sales).

After the parties have a contract, the buyer will apply for financing. The buyer may have obtained pre-approval for financing based on her income and credit report, but the lender will still want information about the house before becoming obligated to fund a loan secured by the house.

The buyer will probably arrange to have the property inspected for physical defects and will probably have a right to terminate the contract if the inspector discovers major defects that the seller is not willing to correct. The seller may be obligated by the terms of the contract to correct minor defects.

The buyer usually receives a title commitment and survey as a means of obtaining information about the seller's title to the property. (As we will discover in Section D.3, the use of the title commitment as a title report may cause problems for the buyer.) In the past, a buyer might have obtained a title opinion from an attorney in order to get title information, but because most lenders now require title insurance, it is the predominant method of title assurance today. Lenders also typically require a survey of the property; thus, the buyer will have the information provided by a survey. The contract will likely give the buyer a right to terminate if there are title defects not contemplated by the contract and which the seller is unwilling or unable to cure before the date of closing.

If the seller's title and property condition are satisfactory and the buyer obtains her financing, the parties will be ready for a closing. The closing will occur at the offices of the lender, the title company, or an attorney, depending on local custom. At the closing, the seller will sign the deed and a closing statement and will deliver these documents to an escrow agent for the closing. The buyer will pay the purchase price (most of which is typically delivered by the buyer's lender) and will sign many documents including a promissory note payable to the lender, a mortgage or deed of trust securing payment of the promissory note, a closing statement, and other documents required by the lender, the title company, and by federal and state law. Once again, many reasons exist for both buyers and sellers to have a lawyer's assistance in preparing for and attending the closing, but in many states, the parties are rarely represented by an attorney in the purchase or sale of a home. After the escrow agent has received all of the required documents and all of the parties' conditions of closing are met, closing funds will be distributed and the deed and mortgage or deed of trust will be recorded. The contract will provide for the transfer of possession to the buyer, which often occurs at the time of closing.

2.   Sellers and Brokers

QUINTIN JOHNSTONE,
LAND TRANSFERS: PROCESS AND PROCESSORS
22 Val. U. L. Rev. 493, 494-99 (1988)

The major services provided by real estate brokers are bringing buyers and sellers together, assisting them to make informed decisions on whether or not to enter into sales contracts, and assisting them with the terms of any such agreements. Most brokered real estate sales are of single family residences and one or both parties to these sales agreements usually know little about land transfer procedures and often know little about the housing market. Furthermore, the buyers usually have a limited capacity to evaluate the merits of the properties being purchased. Thus, in these residential transactions, brokers commonly assume important educational and advisory roles in relation to the parties. In sales of commercial, industrial, large multi-unit residential, and most large agricultural land parcels, the parties normally are far more knowledgeable. While brokers in these transactions also may have educational and advisory roles, they operate in a context of far greater buyer and seller expertise. Although most real estate sales are made with the assistance of brokers, a small, but possibly growing, minority are made by owners without the participation of brokers.

Real estate brokers for their sales work almost universally are paid on a commission basis, commonly six percent of the contract price, and estimates indicate that gross commissions nationally can total as much as $10 billion per year. The commission is earned only if a willing buyer is found, a contract to purchase is entered into, or the sales transaction is closed and a deed delivered. The broker's contract with his principal, usually the seller, often expressly states how far the transaction must proceed before the broker's commission is earned. Irrespective of how much time and money the broker invests in trying to effectuate a sale, the broker normally receives nothing for his efforts unless a qualified buyer is produced and a sale is made or some other specified stage in the transaction is reached. Real estate brokers' commission rates are not set by statute or government regulation, but by contract between brokers and their principals.

Broker-principal contracts vary as to the exclusiveness of the broker's right to sell. What brokers prefer and often obtain from their principals is an exclusive right-to-sell listing, one in which only the broker may attempt to sell the property. If another broker or the seller arranges for the sale, the exclusive right-to-sell broker is entitled to the contracted-for commission. Another listing format is the exclusive agency, under which the broker receives a commission if another broker sells, but not if the sale is effectuated by the seller. Still another format is the open listing, one entitling the broker to a commission only if he makes the sale, not if it is made by another broker or by the seller's efforts. Listing agreements often expressly set an expiration date for the listing, and if no such date appears in the agreement, a reasonable time is usually implied.

The typical real estate brokerage firm is a small, local operation serving primarily the small town or section of the metropolitan area in which its office is located. A minority of firms in metropolitan areas expand their effective service coverage by maintaining two or more offices, each in a different suburban or central city area. Almost all communities are served by conveniently located real estate brokers' offices, and a considerable number of competing offices exist in most areas.

In most communities, marketing of single-family residences is greatly enhanced by a form of cooperative venture among brokers, the multiple listing service (MLS). The MLS device, well-established in the United States since at least the 1920s, is a pooled marketing arrangement, functioning somewhat like a stock or commodities exchange, in which listings of properties for sale made with any participating broker are circulated to all other brokers participating in the scheme. Prospective buyers who contact any participating broker then are informed of the types of available properties that are listed through the exchange. If a listed property is sold, the sales commission is split between the listing broker, the one with whom the property was originally listed, and the so-called selling broker, the one who finds a buyer. The split often is even, half to each. Commonly, participating MLS brokers require exclusive right-to-sell listings from their clients with the further understanding that the exclusive right extends to sales efforts by all other brokers participating in the MLS scheme. In many communities, most brokers operating in an area are members of a multiple listing service and each service usually covers a substantial local area, such as an entire trading area or a large section of one. Some brokers belong to more than one MLS, thereby attaining even more expansive coverage.

Real estate brokers have a powerful trade association network of local and state boards affiliated with the National Association of Realtors (NAR). The NAR has approximately 700,000 members, including both brokers and sales persons. Realtors, a copyrighted term, are broker-members of the NAR. About one-third of the NAR members are realtors; the others, mostly salespersons, are realtor-associates. Many multiple listing services are administered by local real estate boards and the trade association network is active in educating members, developing ethical standards for the occupation, lobbying, and litigating regulatory issues.

Sales of industrial and commercial properties are a specialty and most individuals doing this kind of work devote all their time to either the commercial or industrial side of the business with some specializing in a particular subcategory of one of these types of properties. Other brokerage firms concentrate exclusively on industrial or commercial properties, and many larger brokerage firms have a separate commercial or industrial department. Customers of commercial and industrial brokers include both prospective users and equity investors. Many customers are also interested in long-term leasing as a possible alternative to purchasing. The amount of background knowledge and experience required in commercial or industrial brokerage generally is greater than that required for the residential side of the business. This is because commercial and industrial properties are more varied, with more diverse use possibilities, and because transactions transferring interests in these properties are more complex and less standardized than is typical of residential properties. Among other significant respects in which commercial and industrial brokerage differs from residential brokerage are that in the former the percentage of part-time sales personnel is far smaller. Moreover, commission rates are usually lower, but commission payments usually higher, because property values typically are higher. Finally, individual brokerage firms tend to operate over larger geographic areas because their markets tend to be spread out more; multiple listing services are much less frequently relied on although interfirm cooperation and resultant commission splits commonly do take place.

Compared to many occupations, real estate brokers are not extensively regulated by government. Real estate brokers are licensed, although license acquisition is relatively easy to obtain; and real estate brokers are, of course, subject to the limitations of antitrust law and to laws restricting performance of many law-related services to lawyers. There are few other significant regulatory restrictions on them of much significance. Every state licenses brokers, but the requirements vary somewhat from state to state. Generally, an examination is required along with evidence of good moral character. Licenses are subject to revocation for improper conduct. Some classes of persons may engage in real estate brokerage activities without being licensed; commonly, persons selling properties they own, lawyers, and financial institutions acting as fiduciaries. Salespersons, those persons working for a broker as employees or independent contractors, are separately licensed, although the examination and other prerequisites for these licenses ordinarily are less demanding than for broker licenses. A high percentage of licensed salespersons work only part-time at selling real estate. Many hold other jobs full-time and moonlight at selling real estate. Some are housewives or retired persons without other employment. In periods when sales activity is slow, there is a tendency for the part-timers to put in less effort on their real estate work or to withdraw entirely pending market revival. The usual compensation of salespersons, both full- and part-time, is a portion of the sales commission going to the broker.

Over the years, real estate brokers have become embroiled in serious controversies over their alleged violations of antitrust laws and the proscriptions on unauthorized practice of law. In each of these regulatory spheres, there has been considerable litigation involving real estate brokers, and judicial opinions have resolved some of the troublesome questions as to what is permissible and what is not. Most of the antitrust cases have focused on uniformity of commission rates or limiting access to multiple listing services. Agreements to fix commission rates are illegal under the antitrust laws whether express or implied from conduct of the parties, but the fact that brokers in a community charge uniform rates is not by itself sufficient to show illegal collusion. Additional evidence of collusion is necessary, and without evidence of an express agreement, this collusion can be difficult to prove no matter how suspicious one may be that collusion is contributing to the uniformity. A recent report asserts that the uniformity may be noncollusive and may result from a holdover of rates prevalent prior to 1950 when express rate-fixing arrangements were common and thought legal. The report also asserts that the uniformity may result from the belief of brokers that rate cutting would be pointless as rival firms would promptly respond by cutting their rates in order to maintain market share. These arguments are unconvincing, but fully adequate explanations for the uniformity are not apparent. In addition, the multiple listing service has allegedly been used as a contributing device for illegal price fixing by such means as refusing MLS access to brokers who might cut prices, threatening MLS expulsion of brokers who depart from fixed prices, boycotting by selling brokers of cut-rate listing brokers, and exchanging price information with the objective of freezing prices generally. Courts have held blatant instances of this sort to be in violation of the antitrust laws, mostly state laws, but distinguishing legitimate from illegitimate conduct can be difficult. This results in considerable inconsistency in the case law, particularly as to what conditions may validly be imposed on broker access to multiple listing services.

On unauthorized practice of law issues, the brokers have been somewhat more successful against their opponents, usually bar associations. Conflict has centered on which land transfer documents, if any, brokers may draft. This is a matter of state law and courts have quite universally held that brokers may fill in standard form sales contracts for the parties because this type of activity is incidental to the brokers' primary function of bringing buyers and sellers together. There is less consensus among the states as to the right of brokers to draft post-contract-of-sale documents, such as deeds, purchase money mortgages, and instruments curing title defects. Some states permit brokers to prepare these documents, others do not. Even though they usually make no separate charge for instrument preparation, brokers commonly desire to do this type of work because their customers look favorably on what is seen as a free accommodation service. The practice saves time and parties are often in a hurry, and broker instrument preparation eliminates the risk that if lawyers become involved they may upset the deal by finding fault with the business merits of the transaction. However, even if they are legally authorized to do so, brokers are chary of preparing complicated conveyancing instruments, especially those requiring considerable original phrasing by the drafter, due to risks of liability for drafting defective or ill-suited documents.

3.   Statute of Frauds

SHATTUCK v. KLOTZBACH
14 Mass. L. Rptr. 360 (Mass. Super. 2001)

Ernest B. Murphy, Justice.

The plaintiff brought this action to enforce a contract for the sale of real estate and residential dwelling located at 5 Main Street, Marion, Massachusetts ("the property"), and to recover damages arising out of an alleged breach of that contract. This matter is before the court on the defendants' motion to dismiss. For the reasons set forth below, the defendants' motion to dismiss is DENIED.

In April 2001, the plaintiff and the defendants began discussions concerning the sale of the property. On April 9, 2001, the plaintiff sent an e-mail to the defendants which contained an offer of $2,000,000 for the property. On April 10, 2001, the defendant, David Klotzbach, responded via e-mail by expressing his appreciation for a reasonable offer, and stated that he would be willing to accept $2,250,000. The defendant further stated that he and his wife Barbara "have been praying for a man such as [the plaintiff] that would love the property as much as [the defendants] do." The defendant concluded by stating that e-mail is the "preferred" manner of communication during their negotiations.

On or about April 20, 2001, the plaintiff and the defendants entered into a purchase and sale agreement concerning the property which was signed by all parties. The agreement provided a $2,200,000 purchase price along with other contingencies. The plaintiff furnished the defendants with the deposit which was held in escrow. Prior to the closing, however, the defendants were unable to procure a "wharf license" as called for in the purchase and sale agreement. Accordingly, the parties terminated the April 20 purchase and sale agreement, and the defendants returned the plaintiff's deposit.

Nevertheless, commencing in July 2001, the parties again began communicating via e-mail concerning the sale of the same property. In an e-mail sent July 24, 2001, the plaintiff wrote to the defendant that he was increasing his offer to $1.825 million. The e-mail also addressed various other details such as the defendants' requests for a closing to take place in less than 30 days and that there be no contingencies.

The defendant, Dave Klotzbach, responded later that day via e-mail stating that he would decrease the price to $2,000,000 as his counter offer. He further stated that if the plaintiff agreed to his counter offer he would ask for "no contingencies that might tie up the property." The defendant specifically stated that any home inspection should take place within 5 days of the signing of the purchase and sale agreement, and there would be no financing contingency. The defendant conceded that "other standard contingencies are fine."

On August 31, 2001, the defendant again sent an e-mail to the plaintiff which stated that the defendants "still have NOT sold" the property, and "if you are still interested in a clean deal at $1.825 mil [sic] let me know."

On September 2, 2001, the plaintiff sent the defendants an e-mail that stated he was still interested in doing a "clean deal" for $1,825,000. He asked if he could make a "request" that he be able to perform a "quick walk-through inspection" and if no big flaws were apparent then he would be allowed to sign a simple purchase and sale agreement "containing only the usual boiler plate language, no financing contingency, [and] no other contingencies at all."

Finally, on September 10, 2001, the plaintiff sent the defendant an e-mail which stated that the plaintiff's attorney had told him there were no complications and the attorney would draft a very standard purchase and sale agreement for $1,825,000 "with no usual contingencies." The defendant responded the same day by e-mail stating "[o]nce we sign the P & S we'd like to close ASAP. You may have your attorney send the P & S and deposit check for 10% of purchase price ($182,500) to my attorney." The e-mail concluded by stating that "I'm looking forward to closing and seeing you as the owner of '5 Main Street,' the prettiest spot in Marion village."

All e-mails detailed above contained a salutation at the end which consisted of the type written name of the respective sender.

G.L.c. 259, § 1 provides that "no action shall be brought upon a contract for the sale of lands unless the promise, contract or agreement upon which such action is brought, or some memorandum or note thereof, is in writing and signed by the party to be charged therein or by some person thereunto still lawfully authorized." The defendants contend that there is no signed written memorandum sufficient to satisfy the Statute of Frauds. Specifically, the defendants argue that the e-mails in question were not signed and thus cannot satisfy the Statute of Frauds.

Where the defendant pleads the statute of frauds, the burden is on the plaintiff to prove the existence of a memorandum complying with the statute's requirements. "A memorandum is signed in accordance with the statute of frauds if it is signed by the person to be charged in his own name, or by his initials, or by his Christian name alone, or by a printed, stamped or typewritten signature, if signing in any of these methods he intended to authenticate the paper as his act." Irving v. Goodimate Co., 320 Mass. 454, 458-59 (1946). Here, all e-mail correspondences between the parties contained a typewritten signature at the end. Taken as a whole, a reasonable trier of fact could conclude that the e-mails sent by the defendant were "signed" with the intent to authenticate the information contained therein as his act.

Moreover, courts have held that a telegram may be a signed writing sufficient to satisfy the statute of frauds. See Hansen v. Hill, 340 N.W.2d 8, 13 (Neb.1983) (intent to authenticate by signature demonstrated by name typed on telegram). This court believes that the typed name at the end of an e-mail is more indicative of a party's intent to authenticate than that of a telegram as the sender of an e-mail types and sends the message on his own accord and types his own name as he so chooses. In the case at bar, the defendant sent e-mails regarding the sale of the property and intentionally and deliberately typed his name at the end of all such e-mails. A reasonable trier of fact could conclude that the e-mails sent by the defendant regarding the terms of the sale of the property were intended to be authenticated by the defendant's deliberate choice to type his name at the conclusion of all e-mails.

The defendants finally contend that the e-mails, even if sufficiently authenticated, do not contain the essential terms. A memorandum sufficient to satisfy the statute of frauds need not be a formal document intended to serve as a memorandum of the oral contract, but must contain the essential terms of the contract agreed upon: in the case of an interest in real estate, the parties, the locus, the nature of the transaction, and the purchase price. Multiple writings relating to the subject matter may be read together in order to satisfy the memorandum requirement so long as the writings, when considered as a single instrument, contain all the material terms of the contract and are authenticated by the signature of the party to be charged. The writings may, but need not, incorporate each other by reference.

In the case at bar, the e-mails contain terms for the sale of 5 Main Street, Marion Village, Marion, Massachusetts. The e-mails further refer to a purchase price of $1,825,000 and the defendant explicitly asked the plaintiff to send a "deposit check for 10% of [the] purchase price ($182,500)." Finally, the multiple e-mails demonstrate the parties to the sale, to wit the plaintiff and the defendants. Thus, a reasonable trier of fact could conclude that the parties had formed an agreement as to the essential terms of a land sale contract; the parties, the locus, the nature of the transaction, and the purchase price.

For the foregoing reasons, it is hereby ORDERED that the defendants' motion to dismiss be DENIED.

NOTES AND QUESTIONS

1. **The principal case.** What does the court say is required to satisfy the statute of frauds for an agreement for the transfer of an interest in real property? Does the court decide that the parties' e-mails constitute a memorandum sufficient to satisfy the statute of frauds?

2. **A separate issue.** An issue apart from the statute of frauds is whether a contract was formed, i.e., whether the parties intended to be bound. Based on the e-mails, do you think that the parties in this case intended to be bound?

3. **Electronic transactions.** The vast majority of states have adopted the Uniform Electronic Transactions Act, which provides:

SECTION 7. LEGAL RECOGNITION OF ELECTRONIC RECORDS, ELECTRONIC SIGNATURES, AND ELECTRONIC CONTRACTS

    (a)   A record or signature may not be denied legal effect or enforceability solely because it is in electronic form.

    (b)   A contract may not be denied legal effect or enforceability solely because an electronic record was used in its formation.

    (c)   If a law requires a record to be in writing, an electronic record satisfies the law.

    (d)   If a law requires a signature, an electronic signature satisfies the law.

In addition, in 2000 Congress enacted the Electronic Records in Global and National Commerce Act ("E-Sign") which contains similar provisions applicable to "any transaction in or affecting interstate or foreign commerce." 15 U.S.C. § 7001.

4. **Part performance.** Courts have found exceptions to the statute of frauds which permit enforcement of an oral agreement for the transfer of an interest in real property. As discussed in Chapter 4, section A.2, part performance can take a contract out of the statute of frauds. In the context of a contract for the sale of real estate, the acts of part performance that a court looks for are full or partial payment, possession by the buyer, and substantial improvements on the property by the buyer. Courts require from one to three of these acts, but generally would

not find part performance where the only act is payment. *See* William B. Stoebuck & Dale A. Whitman, The Law of Property § 10.2 at 718-19 (3d ed. 2000). Most courts require that the acts unequivocally refer to the existence of a contract. *Compare* Crossman v. Fontainebleau Hotel Corp. (Chapter 4, Section A.2.c). If acts of part performance unequivocally refer to the existence of the contract, for what function of the statute of frauds do they substitute?

5. **Estoppel.** Some courts have also found estoppel as a basis for taking a contract for the sale of property out of the statute of frauds. *See, e.g.,* Hickey v. Green, 442 N.E.2d 37 (1982). The Restatement (Second) of Contracts, § 129, provides:

> A contract for the transfer of an interest in land may be specifically enforced notwithstanding failure to comply with the Statute of Frauds if it is established that the party seeking enforcement, in reasonable reliance on the contract and on the continuing assent of the party against whom enforcement is sought, has so changed his position that injustice can be avoided only by specific enforcement.

Comment d to that section adds:

> Where specific enforcement is rested on a transfer of possession plus either part payment of the price or the making of improvements, it is commonly said that the action taken by the purchaser must be unequivocally referable to the oral agreement. But this requirement is not insisted on if the making of the promise is admitted or is clearly proved. The promisee must act in reasonable reliance on the promise, before the promisor has repudiated it, and the action must be such that the remedy of restitution is inadequate. If these requirements are met, neither taking of possession nor payment of money nor the making of improvements is essential.

Restatement (Second) of Contracts, § 129, comment d (1981).

B.   THE GAP PERIOD: FROM CONTRACT TO CLOSING

If, after preliminary negotiations, the buyer and seller reach agreement, they will usually execute a contract of sale. The contract of sale is first and foremost a contract; the parties have moved past the preliminary negotiations stage and are committing themselves to render their respective performances, or to pay for any losses suffered by the aggrieved party if the contract is not performed. What you learned in your Contracts course about the requirements for the formation of a valid contract — offer and acceptance, consideration, and the like — is applicable here, and for the most part need not be repeated. Our emphasis rather is on the provisions in the sales contract that are unique or especially important to the buyer and the seller of real estate.

The buyer will want to make sure that certain protections are written into the contract (Section B.1). One such protection is a provision conditioning the buyer's duty to proceed with the sale on the receipt of mortgage financing; another is a provision requiring the seller to transfer marketable title at the closing. The contract of sale is important not only because it states the respective obligations of the parties, but also because, under the doctrine of equitable conversion (Section B.2), it changes the nature of the parties' relation to the property being sold; for some purposes, the buyer is regarded as the owner of the property prior to the closing. If either buyer or seller breaches the contract, the question of remedies becomes important (Section B.3).

1.   Conditions in the Contract of Sale

a.   Financing

LUTTINGER v. ROSEN
316 A.2d 757 (Conn. 1972)

LOISELLE, ASSOCIATE JUSTICE.

The plaintiffs contracted to purchase for $85,000 premises in the city of Stamford owned by the defendants and paid a deposit of $8500. The contract was "subject to and conditional upon the buyers obtaining first mortgage financing on said premises from a bank or other lending institution in an amount of $45,000 for a term of not less than twenty (20) years and at an interest rate which does not exceed 8½ per cent per annum." The plaintiffs agreed to use due diligence in attempting to obtain such financing. The parties further agreed that if the plaintiffs were unsuccessful in obtaining financing as provided in the contract, and notified the seller within a specific time, all sums paid on the contract would be refunded and the contract terminated without further obligation of either party.

In applying for a mortgage which would satisfy the contingency clause in the contract, the plaintiffs relied on their attorney who applied at a New Haven lending institution for a $45,000 loan at 8¼ percent per annum interest over a periold of twenty-five years. The plaintiffs' attorney knew that this lending institution was the only one which at that time would lend as much as $45,000 on a mortgage for a single-family dwelling. A mortgage commitment was obtained for $45,000 with "interest at the prevailing rate at the time of closing but not less than 8¾%." Since this commitment failed to meet the contract requirement, timely notice was given to the defendants and demand was made for the return of the down payment. The defendants' counsel thereafter offered to make up the difference between the interest rate offered by the bank and the 8½ percent rate provided in the contract for the entire twenty-five years by a funding arrangement, the exact terms of which were not defined. The plaintiffs did not accept this offer and on the defendants' refusal to return the deposit an action was brought. From a judgment rendered in favor of the plaintiffs the defendants have appealed.

The defendants claim that the plaintiffs did not use due diligence in seeking a mortgage within the terms specified in the contract. The unattacked findings by the court establish that the plaintiffs' attorney was fully informed as to the conditions and terms of mortgages being granted by various banks and lending institutions in and out of the area and that the application was made to the only bank which might satisfy the mortgage conditions of the contingency clause at that time. These findings adequately support the court's conclusion that due diligence was used in seeking mortgage financing in accordance with the contract provisions. The defendants assert that notwithstanding the plaintiffs' reliance on their counsel's knowledge of lending practices, applications should have been made to other lending institutions. This claim is not well taken. The law does not require the performance of a futile act.

The remaining assignment of error briefed by the defendants is that the court erred in concluding that the mortgage contingency clause of the contract, a condition precedent, was not met and, therefore, the plaintiffs were entitled to recover their deposit. "A condition precedent is a fact or event which the parties intend must exist or take place before there is a right to performance." Lach v. Cahill, 138 Conn. 418, 421, 85 A.2d 481, 482. If the condition precedent is not fulfilled the contract is not enforceable. In this case the language of the contract is unambiguous and clearly indicates that the parties intended that the purchase of the defendants' premises be conditioned on the obtaining by the plaintiffs of a mortgage as specified in the contract. From the subordinate facts found the court could reasonably conclude that since the plaintiffs were unable to obtain a $45,000 mortgage at no more than 8½ percent per annum interest "from a bank or other lending institution" the condition precedent to performance of the contract was not met and the plaintiffs were entitled to the refund of their deposit. Any additional offer by the defendants to fund the difference in interest payments could be rejected by the plaintiffs. There was no error in the court's exclusion of testimony relating to the additional offer since the offer was obviously irrelevant.

There is no error.

NOTES AND QUESTIONS

1. **The financing condition.** Why is the condition of financing important to the buyer in a contract of sale? What is the buyer's obligation without the condition?

2. **The principal case.** In Luttinger v. Rosen, what were the terms of the financing condition in the contract? Why didn't the mortgage offered to the buyer by the New Haven lending institution satisfy the condition? Why didn't the lending institution's loan plus the seller's offer to cover the difference satisfy the condition? Is it that express conditions in a contract always have to be literally performed, or that this particular kind of contract condition is so important that *it* must be literally performed? *See* E. Allan Farnsworth, Contracts § 8.3, at 526-27 (3d ed. 1999); Stoebuck & Whitman § 10.11, at 772 & n.28.

3. **Best efforts by the buyer.** If the seller had been able to establish that the buyer did not use best efforts to obtain financing, what would have been the result? What would the seller have had to show? Why couldn't the seller show it? Are "best efforts" and "good faith" synonymous? *See* Stoebuck & Whitman § 10.11, at 769 & n.16.

4. **Whose condition?** Suppose in the principal case that the seller had become disenchanted with the sale. Despite being unable to obtain the financing specified in the contract, the buyer is able to borrow money from a relative to make up the shortfall and wants to proceed with the sale. Is the seller entitled to assert

the failure of the express condition as a basis for cancelling the sale?

5. **Seller's retention of the deposit.** Notice that the seller in the principal case refused to return the buyer's 10% deposit. What do you think the seller's argument for retaining the deposit was?

b.   Marketable Title

LOHMEYER v. BOWER
227 P.2d 102 (Kan. 1951)

PARKER, JUSTICE.

This action originated in the district court of Lyon county when plaintiff filed a petition seeking to rescind a contract in which he had agreed to purchase certain real estate on the ground title tendered by the defendants was unmerchantable. The defendants Bower and Bower, husband and wife, answered contesting plaintiff's right to rescind and by cross-petition asked specific performance of the contract. The defendant Newcomer answered, stating he was an escrow agent under terms of the agreement, that he had no interest in the action except in that capacity and that he would abide and be governed by whatever decision was rendered by the court. The case was tried upon the pleadings and stipulated facts by the trial court which rendered judgment for the defendants generally and decreed specific performance of the contract. The plaintiff appeals from that judgment.

Plaintiff agreed to purchase Lot 37 in Berkley Hills Addition in the city of Emporia. [A]fter execution of the agreement it came to his attention that the house on the real estate therein described had been placed there in violation of Section 5-224 of the Ordinances of the city of Emporia in that the house was located within approximately 18 inches of the north line of such lot in violation of the ordinance providing that no frame building should be erected within 3 feet of a side or rear lot line. It [also] came to plaintiff's knowledge [that] the dedication of the Berkley Hills Addition requires that only a two story house should be erected on the lot described in the contract whereas the house located thereon is a one story house. [A]fter becoming aware of such violations plaintiff notified the defendants in writing thereof, demanded that he be released from his contract and that defendants refused such demand.

Pertinent provisions of the contract, entered into between the parties, essential to disposition of the issues raised by the pleadings, read:

> Witnesseth, That in consideration of the stipulations herein contained, and the payments to be made by the second party as hereinafter specified, the first party hereby agrees to sell unto the second party for following described real estate, situated in the County of Lyon, State of Kansas, to-wit:

> Lot numbered Thirty-seven (37) on Berkley Road in Berkley Hills Addition to the City of Emporia, according to the recorded plat thereof.

and to convey the above described real estate to the second party by Warranty Deed with an abstract of title, certified to date showing good merchantable title or an Owners Policy of Title Insurance in the amount of the sale price, guaranteeing said title to party of the second part, free and clear of all encumbrances except special taxes subject, however, to all restrictions and easements of record applying to this property, it being understood that the first party shall have sufficient time to bring said abstract to date or obtain Report for Title Insurance and to correct any imperfections in the title if there be such imperfections.

That the first party cannot deliver title as agreed, the earnest money paid by the second party shall be returned to said second party and this contract cancelled.

From what has been heretofore related, since resort to the contract makes it clear [that] appellees agreed to convey the involved property with an abstract of title showing good merchantable title, free and clear of all encumbrances, it becomes apparent the all decisive issue presented by the pleadings and the stipulation is whether such property is subject to encumbrances or other burdens making the title unmerchantable and if so whether they are such as are excepted by the provision of the contract which reads "subject however, to all restrictions and easements of record applying to this property."

Decision of the foregoing issue can be simplified by directing attention early to the appellant's position. Conceding he purchased the property, subject to all restrictions of record he makes no complaint of the restrictions contained in the declaration forming a part of the dedication of Berkley Hills Addition nor of the ordinance restricting the building location on the lot but bases his right to rescission of the contract solely upon presently existing violations thereof. This, we may add, limited to restrictions imposed by terms of the ordinance, relating to the use of land or the location and character of buildings that may be located thereon, even in the absence of provisions in the contract excepting them, must necessarily be his position for we are convinced, although it must be conceded there are some decisions to the contrary, the rule supported by the better reasoned decisions, indeed if not by the great weight of authority, is that municipal restrictions of such character, existing at the time of the execution of a contract for the sale of real estate, are not such encumbrances or burdens on title as may be availed of by a vendee to avoid his agreement to purchase on the ground they render his title unmerchantable.

On the other hand there can be no question the rule respecting restrictions upon the use of land or the location and type of buildings that may be erected thereon fixed by covenants or other private restrictive agreements, including those contained in the declaration forming a part of the dedication of Berkley Hills Addition, is directly contrary to the one to which we have just referred. Such restrictions, under all the authorities, constitute encumbrances rendering the title to land unmerchantable.

In the instant case assuming the mere existence of the restrictions imposed by the provisions of section 5-224 of the ordinances of the city of Emporia do not constitute an encumbrance or burden and that the dedication restrictions fall within the exception clause of the contract providing Lot 37 was to be conveyed subject to all restrictions and easements of record applying thereto there still remains the question whether, under the stipulated facts, the restrictions imposed by such ordinance and/or the dedication declaration have been violated and if so whether those violations make the title to such property unmerchantable.

[W]e are convinced that on the date of the execution of the contract the house on the real estate in controversy was a one story frame dwelling which had been moved there in violation of section 2 of the dedication restrictions providing that any residence erected on Lot 37 should be of the height of a two story residence and that it had been placed within 18 inches of the side or rear lot line of such lot in violation of section 5-224, *supra*, prohibiting the erection of such building within three feet of such line.

There can be no doubt regarding what constitutes a marketable or merchantable title in this jurisdiction. This court has been called on to pass upon that question on numerous occasions. See our recent decision in Peatling v. Baird, 213 P.2d 1015, 1016 (Kan. 1950), and cases there cited, wherein we held:

> A marketable title to real estate is one which is free from reasonable doubt, and a title is doubtful and unmarketable if it exposes the party holding it to the hazard of litigation.

> To render the title to real estate unmarketable, the defect of which the purchaser complains must be of a substantial character and one from which he may suffer injury. Mere immaterial defects which do not diminish in quantity, quality or value the property contracted for, constitute no ground upon which the purchaser may reject the title. Facts must be known at the time which fairly raise a reasonable doubt as to the title; a mere possibility or conjecture that such a state of facts may be developed at some future time is not sufficient.

Under the rule just stated, and in the face of facts such as are here involved, we have little difficulty in concluding that the violation of section 5-224 of the ordinances of the city of Emporia as well as the violation of the restrictions imposed by the dedication declaration so encumber the title to Lot 37 as to expose the party holding it to the hazard of litigation and make such title doubtful and unmarketable. It follows, since, as we have indicated, the appellees had contracted to convey such real estate to appellant by warranty deed with an abstract of title showing good merchantable title, free and clear of all encumbrances, that they cannot convey the title contracted for and that the trial court should have rendered judgment rescinding the contract. This, we may add is so, notwithstanding the contract provides the conveyance was to be made subject to all restrictions and easements of record, for, as we have seen, it is the violation of the restrictions imposed by both the ordinance and the dedication declaration, not the existence of those restrictions, that renders the title unmarketable. The decision just announced is not without precedent or unsupported by sound authority.

In Moyer v. De Vincentis Const. Co., 164 A. 111 (Pa. Super. 1933), involving facts, circumstances, and issues almost identical to those here involved, so far as violation of the ordinance is concerned, the plaintiff (vendee) sued to recover money advanced on the purchase price pursuant to the agreement on the ground that violation of a zoning ordinance had made title to the property involved under its terms unmarketable. The court upheld the plaintiff's position and in the opinion said:

> We are of the opinion that a proper construction of the agreement of sale supports the position of appellant, the vendee in the agreement. The vendor agreed to furnish a good and marketable title free from liens and incumbrances, excepting existing restrictions and easements, if any. As applied to the facts of the case in hand, vendee agreed to purchase the premises subject to the zoning ordinance, but not to purchase the premises, when the house was built in violation of the terms of that ordinance.
>
> The facts lend weight to the force of this construction. It appears from the pleadings that the premises to be conveyed embraced not only the bare land, but an entire parcel of real estate which included a semidetached dwelling. The description is not by metes and bounds but by house number. The vendee could not take possession without immediately becoming a violator of the law and subject to suit, with a penalty of $25 for every day the building remained in position overlapping the protected area.
>
> The title was not marketable, not because of an existing zoning ordinance, but because a building had been constructed upon the lot in violation of that ordinance.

164 A. at page 112.

To the same effect is 66 C.J. 912 § 592, where the following statement appears: "Existing violations of building restrictions imposed by law warrant rejection of title by a purchaser contracting for a conveyance free of encumbrances. The fact that the premises to be conveyed violate tenement house regulations is ground for rejection of title where the contract of sale expressly provided against the existence of such violations."

With respect to covenants and restrictions similar to those involved in the dedication declaration, notwithstanding the agreement — as here — excepted restrictions of record, see Chesebro v. Moers, 134 N.E. 842 (N.Y. 1922), holding that the violation by a property owner of covenants restricting the distance from front and rear lines within which buildings may be placed renders the title to such property unmarketable.

See, also, Hebb v. Severson, 201 P.2d 156 (Wash. 1948), which holds, that where a contract provided that building and use restrictions general to the district should not be deemed restrictions, the purchaser's knowledge of such restrictions did not estop him from rescinding the contract of purchase on subsequent discovery that the position of the house on the lot involved violated such restrictions. At page 162 of 201 P.2d it is said:

> Finally, the fact that the contract contains a provision that protective restrictions shall not be deemed encumbrances cannot aid the respondents. It is not the existence of protective restrictions, as shown by the record, that constitutes the encumbrances alleged by the appellants; but, rather, it

is the presently existing violation of one of these restrictions that constitutes such encumbrance, in and of itself. The authorities so hold, on the
rationale, to which we subscribe, that to force a vendee to accept property
which in its present state violates a building restriction without a showing
that the restriction is unenforceable, would in effect compel the vendee to
buy a lawsuit.

Finally appellees point to the contract which, it must be conceded, provides they
shall have time to correct imperfections in the title and contend that even if it be
held the restrictions and the ordinance have been violated they are entitled to time
in which to correct those imperfections. Assuming, without deciding, they might
remedy the violation of the ordinance by buying additional ground the short and
simple answer to their contention with respect to the violation of the restrictions
imposed by the dedication declaration is that any changes in the house would
compel the purchaser to take something that he did not contract to buy.

Conclusions heretofore announced require reversal of the judgment with directions to the trial court to cancel and set aside the contract and render such
judgment as may be equitable and proper under the issues raised by the pleadings.

It is so ordered.

NOTES AND QUESTIONS

1. **Source of the obligation.** The law implies that the seller's title must be
marketable if the contract is silent on the question. Can you see why? *See* 3
American Law of Property § 11.47 (A.J. Casner ed. 1952). Is the law-imposed
requirement of marketable title a promise by the seller, or a condition, or both?
Why does it matter? *See* Stoebuck & Whitman § 10.12, at 776.

2. **What is marketable title?** Definitions of marketable title vary and are
slippery in any event. Here is one:

> A marketable title is a title which is free from encumbrances and any
> reasonable doubt as to its validity, and such as a reasonably intelligent
> person, who is well informed as to the facts and their legal bearings, and
> ready and willing to perform his contract, would be willing to accept in the
> exercise of ordinary business prudence.

Clarke v. Title Guaranty Co., 353 P.2d 1002, 1007 (Haw. 1960).

3. **Examples.** Rather than dealing with definitions of marketable title, it is
more useful to consider categories of defects that can render the seller's title
unmarketable (or not).

a. Encumbrances. One major category consists of encumbrances on the land.
"An encumbrance on a title to land is any right to or interest in the land, subsisting
in a third person, to the diminution of the value of the land, though consistent with
the passing of the fee by conveyance." Wright v. Hinnenkamp, 687 P.2d 163, 165
(Or. Ct. App. 1984).

> All encumbrances may be classed as either (1) a pecuniary charge against
> the premises, such as mortgages, judgment liens, tax liens or assessments,
> or (2) estates or interests in the property less than the fee, like leases, life

estates or dower rights, or (3) easements or servitudes on the land, such as rights of way, restrictive covenants and profits.

Frimberger v. Anzellotti, 594 A.2d 1029, 1032 (Conn. App. Ct. 1991). Cases on encumbrances are legion.

b. Restrictive covenant/violation thereof. As the principal case indicates, the existence of a restrictive covenant usually renders title unmarketable, but a contract may except restrictions of record. Even if the contract does except restrictive covenants, an existing violation of a restriction renders title unmarketable.

c. Existence/violation of zoning ordinance. "[M]arketability of title is concerned with impairments on title to a property, i.e., the right to unencumbered ownership and possession, not with legal public regulation of the use of the property. Accordingly, a zoning ordinance, existing at the time of the contract, which regulates only the use of the property, generally is not an encumbrance making the title unmarketable." Voorheesville Rod & Gun Club, Inc. v. E.W. Tompkins Co., 626 N.E.2d 917, 920 (N.Y. 1993). While the existence of a zoning ordinance does not render title unmarketable, most courts hold that a zoning violation existing at the execution of the contract of sale is a breach of the seller's promise of marketable title as indicated in the principal case. See also Stoebuck & Whitman § 10.12, at 783. Why the difference? See John G. Sprankling, Understanding Property Law § 20.06[B][4][b] (2d ed. 2007). Suppose that the subject property is in violation of a zoning ordinance, and that neither buyer nor seller is aware of that fact. Apart from marketable title, might the buyer have another ground for avoiding the sale? See Bar-Del, Inc. v. Oz, Inc., 850 S.W.2d 855 (Ky. Ct. App. 1993); Ger v. Kammann, 504 F. Supp. 446 (D. Del. 1980); Dover Pool & Racquet Club, Inc. v. Brooking, 322 N.E.2d 168 (Mass. 1975).

d. Housing/building codes. Most courts hold that the violation of a housing or building code does not render title unmarketable. See Stoebuck & Whitman § 10.12, at 782; Sprankling, Understanding Property Law § 20.06[B][4][b], at 332 (rationale for the rule "is not well defined"). What argument(s) might distinguish housing code violations from zoning violations?

e. Visible and beneficial easements. Some courts say that if easements are "visible, open and notorious, a buyer is presumed to purchase the land subject to them." In re Ilana Realty, Inc., 154 B.R. 21, 25 (S.D.N.Y. 1993). Courts may require that the easement be of benefit to the subject property in order to apply this exception.

f. Encroachments and protrusions. If a neighbor's improvements encroach on the subject property, most courts find title unmarketable. See, e.g., Azat v. Farruggio, 875 A.2d 778 (Md. App. 2005). Similarly, if improvements on the subject property protrude onto neighboring property, courts may find title unmarketable. See, e.g., Bethurem v. Hammett, 736 P.2d 1128 (Wyo. 1987). Assume a buyer's survey reveals that a fence and patio on the subject property encroaches 9.3 feet onto adjoining property, and that the swimming pool on the property violates the side yard setback requirement of local zoning ordinances. Upon being notified, seller obtains a setback variance from the municipality, and an easement from the contiguous property owner for the patio and fence encroachment. *See* DeJong v. Mandelbaum, 505 N.Y.S.2d 659 (N.Y. App. Div. 1986). Is title now unmarketable?

g. Liens. A lien on property makes title unmarketable; however, sellers often plan to discharge liens at the time of closing out of closing proceeds. See note 5 below regarding the time at which title must be marketable. Suppose that a title search reveals that the property is subject to an undischarged $12,000 mortgage, but the statute of limitations for assertion of a claim on the mortgage has run. *See* Lovell v. Jimal Holding Corp., 512 N.Y.S.2d 138 (N.Y. App. Div. 1987) (finding title marketable). *See also* G/GM Real Estate Corp. v. Susse Chalet Motor Lodge of Ohio, Inc., 575 N.E.2d 141 (Ohio 1991) (lapsed lease did not render title unmarketable).

h. Lack of access. Buyers establish that the premises lack access to a public road. Does this render title unmarketable? *See* Barasky v. Huttner, 620 N.Y.S.2d 121 (N.Y. App. Div. 1994) (title held unmarketable); *but see* Sinks v. Karleskint, 474 N.E.2d 767 (Ill. App. Ct. 1985) (title not unmarketable where buyers had notice of the problem).

i. Hazardous waste or environmental hazard. Seller uses the property as a motor vehicle repair shop. After the contract of sale is signed, buyer discovers that an underground oil storage tank constitutes a potential environmental hazard. Is buyer entitled to rescind the contract? *See* Vandervort v. Higginbotham, 634 N.Y.S.2d 800 (N.Y. App. Div. 1995) (finding title was marketable). *See generally* J. David Reitzel, *CERCLA and Marketable Title: Is Toxic Contamination a Cloud?*, 26 Real Est. L.J. 253 (1998).

j. Adverse possession. If a third party has obtained title by adverse possession to the subject property, then the seller obviously does not have marketable title. But what if the seller's title is based on adverse possession? Most courts hold that the seller's title is not marketable. *See, e.g.*, Bartos v. Czerwinski, 34 N.W.2d 566 (Mich. 1948). The risk of a lawsuit from the record title holder is an unreasonable risk of litigation to impose on a buyer. *But see* Conklin v. Davi, 388 A.2d 598 (N.J. 1978) (permitting the seller to prove title by adverse possession and thus marketability of title in the lawsuit with the buyer if the record title holder could not succeed and there is "no real likelihood" that a claim will be asserted). Some contracts may require that the seller provide "record title" in addition to "marketable title."

k. Defeasible fee. Suppose the seller holds a defeasible fee rather than a fee simple absolute; is seller's title marketable? *See* First Universalist Soc'y v. Boland, 29 N.E. 524 (Mass. 1892) (seller's suit for specific performance denied when seller owned fee simple determinable).

l. Lack of corporate authority. Suppose that the seller acquired title from a corporation or partnership, and the sale does not comply with the partnership agreement or by-laws of the corporation? *See* Gentile v. Kim, 475 N.Y.S.2d 631 (N.Y. App. Div. 1984) (seller purchased property from partnership; no sale of real property by partnership was valid unless 70% of holders of capital assets consented; seller's title was unmarketable).

m. Unreasonable risk of litigation. "A purchaser of property entitled to a 'marketable title' may not be required to accept a conveyance if the title is in such condition that he may be required to [defend] litigation challenging his possession and interest." Bartos v. Czerwinski, 34 N.W.2d 566, 568 (Mich. 1948). "It is not necessary that the title be actually bad in order to render it unmarketable. It is sufficient if there is such a doubt or uncertainty as may reasonably form the basis of litigation." *Id.*

4. **Contractual modifications.** Whatever defects render the seller's title unmarketable under the law-imposed requirement of marketable title, buyer and seller remain free to impose a greater or lesser obligation on the seller by the express terms of the contract. As in the principal case, the contract of sale will usually except certain encumbrances of record from the requirement that marketable title be delivered. *See also* Ziskind v. Bruce Lee Corp., 307 A.2d 377 (Pa. Super. Ct. 1973) (under contract requiring seller to convey title "clear of all encumbrances" buyer could rescind for seller's failure to expunge easements before closing, even though buyer knew of the easements at time of contracting).

5. **Marketable title: when?** Since the seller does not have to convey until the closing, the seller is required to have marketable title at that time rather than on the date of the contract of sale. *See* Powell v. Bagley, 862 S.W.2d 412 (Mo. Ct. App. 1993).

6. **Insurable title.** Sometimes a contract will require that the seller's title be both "marketable and insurable." "[I]nsurable title is not a substitute for marketable title. Insurable title means that property is capable of being insured, not that the title is good or marketable." Brown v. Yacht Club of Coeur D'Alene, Ltd., 722 P.2d 1062, 1065 (Idaho Ct. App. 1986). Can you think of a situation in which title is insurable but not marketable? *See* Kipahulu Investment Co. v. Seltzer Partnership, 675 P.2d 778 (Haw. Ct. App. 1983). Which is the more demanding standard for the seller to satisfy?

7. **Undiscovered defects in title.** One way in which a defect in the seller's title may come to light is through a title search conducted by the buyer. However, some defects are not easily discoverable by a title search, and some defects are not in fact discovered by the searcher although they should be. Often these defects come to light after the buyer and seller have closed the sale, when the holder of an adverse interest asserts a claim against the buyer in possession. Because of the doctrine of merger (Section C.3 below), the buyer's claim against the seller after closing must be based on covenants of title in the deed rather than on promises in the contract of sale. We defer consideration of title search and title defects to Section D dealing with disputes that arise after closing.

8. **Another deferred question: condition of the premises.** In a large majority of states, sellers of new housing are held to an implied warranty of habitability, and in most states, the buyer also has protections regarding the condition of the premises under the law of fraud and nondisclosure. The condition of the premises, of course, is not revealed by a title search. If the buyer, by paying for a home inspection or otherwise, discovers such defects prior to closing, the buyer may have an "out" based on a condition in the contract. Even without a condition, a seller's fraud or breach of warranty provides the buyer with a basis for rescission of the contract. However, the buyer who does not take possession or pay for a home inspection between the contract of sale and the closing is likely to discover fraud or breach of the implied warranty of habitability only after the

closing. Consequently, we consider the seller's responsibility for the condition of the property with our consideration of other post-closing disputes between the parties (Section D.4). One question that can be raised here: Is a condition in the contract of sale allowing the buyer to have an inspection made by an expert and specifying the parties' obligations in the event of an unsatisfactory inspection report a good idea?

2.   Equitable Conversion

For some purposes, the buyer is treated as the owner even before the closing, under the doctrine of equitable conversion.

HOLSCHER v. JAMES
860 P.2d 646 (Idaho 1993)

SILAK, JUSTICE.

Curtis and Brenda James signed an agreement to purchase a cabin and five acres of land from Ernest and Abbielena Holscher. Before the closing date, the Jameses insured the cabin by entering into an insurance binder[1] with State Farm General Insurance Co. through one of its agents. The Jameses then took possession of the premises. Thereafter, but also prior to closing, the cabin was destroyed by fire. The parties disputed who should bear the loss of the cabin. The district court entered judgment in favor of the Holschers, concluding that State Farm was obligated to pay the insurance proceeds to the Jameses pursuant to the insurance binder, and that equitable principles required the Jameses to pay the Holschers the value of the cabin. As set forth below, we reverse that portion of the district court's judgment which held the Jameses liable for the loss of the cabin, and we affirm the judgment against State Farm, although on different grounds, concluding that the Holschers are entitled to recover directly against State Farm as third-party beneficiaries of the James/State Farm insurance binder.

FACTS AND PROCEDURAL BACKGROUND

On March 29, 1989, the Jameses and Holschers entered into a purchase agreement whereby the Jameses agreed to purchase from the Holschers a cabin and five acres. Under the terms of the purchase agreement, the Jameses deposited $500 as earnest money towards the purchase price of $50,000. The purchase agreement specified May 1, 1989, as the closing date for the transaction. Paragraph 13 of the purchase agreement also provided that "[s]hould the premises be materially damaged by fire or other causes, prior to closing this sale, this agreement shall be voidable at the option of the Buyer."

---

[1] An insurance binder is a contract for insurance in the form of "[a] written memorandum of the important terms of contract of insurance which gives temporary protection to insured pending investigation of risk by insurance company or until a formal policy is issued." Black's Law Dictionary 169 (6th ed. 1990).

On April 5, 1989, the Jameses entered into an insurance binder with State Farm to insure the cabin. The insurance binder provided $50,000 coverage on the cabin and $35,000 coverage on the contents of the cabin. A section of the binder form entitled "other int[erests]" provided for the listing of parties other than the named insured who, by virtue of some interest in the covered property, would have a beneficial interest in the insurance. In this section of the binder, the State Farm agent listed the name and address of Ernest Holscher. The binder stated that its effective date was April 5, 1989, and the Jameses made their first premium payment that same day. The amount of the premium was calculated to pay for coverage beginning on April 5th. The Holschers did not themselves purchase any insurance coverage for the cabin.

Also on April 5, 1989, pursuant to the purchase agreement, the Jameses took possession of the property and began moving their personal belongings into the cabin. On April 11, the Jameses moved more of their belongings into the cabin. At about 5 p.m. or 6 p.m. on the 11th, the cabin caught fire and was destroyed. The district court found that the fire was not the fault of either party, and the parties do not dispute that finding. Prior to May 1, the date set for closing, the Jameses notified the Holschers that, because the cabin had been destroyed, they were exercising their option under paragraph 13 to void the purchase agreement.

The Holschers subsequently sued the Jameses and State Farm seeking to recover the value of the cabin. At trial, two issues were submitted to the jury for determination: (1) whether the Holschers were intended beneficiaries of the insurance binder between the Jameses and State Farm, and (2) the fair market value of the cabin at the time it was destroyed. The jury returned a verdict finding that the Holschers were not intended beneficiaries of the insurance binder, and that the fair market value of the cabin was $36,125. The district court entered judgment on the jury's verdict in favor of State Farm, concluding that the Holschers were not third-party beneficiaries, and therefore that they had no claim under the James/State Farm insurance binder.

Two equitable issues were tried to the court: (1) whether the purchase agreement should be reformed, based on mutual mistake, to provide that the Jameses bore the risk of loss prior to closing, and (2) whether the doctrine of equitable conversion applied to shift the pre-closing risk of loss to the Jameses. The district court concluded that reformation of the purchase agreement was inapplicable in this case based on its finding that there was no mutual mistake regarding allocation of the risk of loss or the obligation to insure the property prior to closing because the parties never even considered, much less reached an agreement upon, those issues. The district court did not determine the second issue, whether equitable conversion applied to shift the risk of loss to the Jameses.

However, the district court entered judgment in favor of the Holschers based on two other conclusions: (1) that State Farm was liable to the Jameses for the value of the cabin, and (2) that the Jameses were liable to the Holschers for the value of the cabin. The court concluded that State Farm was liable to the Jameses by applying the doctrine of equitable conversion to determine that the Jameses had an insurable interest in the cabin, and therefore, under the insurance binder, they were entitled to the insurance proceeds after the cabin was destroyed. The court reached its second conclusion, that the Jameses were liable to the Holschers for the value of the cabin, based on its construction of paragraph 13 of the purchase agreement. The court construed paragraph 13 to mean that if the premises were materially damaged prior to closing, the Jameses were entitled to seek equitable rescission of the contract from the court. From this the district court reasoned that the Jameses could not avail themselves of the equitable remedy of rescission unless they restored the Holschers to their pre-contract position. Based on its two conclusions, the district court ordered State Farm to pay the Jameses the proceeds of the insurance on the cabin, and then ordered that the Jameses pay the insurance proceeds to the Holschers before they could void the purchase agreement.

ISSUES ON APPEAL

The appeal and cross-appeal of the parties require us to address [two] issues: (1) whether the district court erred in its application of the doctrines of equitable conversion and equitable rescission; [and] (2) whether the district court erred in entering judgment on the jury's finding that the Holschers were not third-party beneficiaries of the James/State Farm insurance binder.

ANALYSIS

I. Applicability of Equitable Conversion and Equitable Rescission.

The parties raise three issues regarding the application of equitable conversion and rescission. The Holschers assert that the district court erred by not applying equitable conversion to conclude that the risk of loss was on the Jameses at the time of the fire. State Farm asserts that the district court erred because it did apply equitable conversion to conclude that the Jameses had an equitable, and thus insurable, interest in the cabin at the time of the fire. Finally, the Jameses claim that the district court erred by applying the doctrine of equitable rescission to conclude that they were liable to the Holschers for the value of the cabin.

A. Whether the District Court Should Have Applied Equitable Conversion to Conclude that the Jameses Bore the Risk of Loss Prior to Closing.

This Court has explained the doctrine of equitable conversion as follows:

> The doctrine of equitable conversion is a fiction resting upon the fundamental rule of equity that equity regards that as done which ought to be done. Under the doctrine, an equitable conversion takes place when a contract for the sale of real property becomes binding on the parties. The purchaser is then treated in equity as having an interest in realty, and the vendor an interest in personalty, that is, the right to receive the purchase money.

First Security Bank of Idaho v. Rogers, 429 P.2d 386, 389 (Idaho 1967). Thus, when equitable conversion applies, the contract purchaser is deemed the equitable owner of the realty, and assumes the risk of loss on the property. The Holschers assert that the district court should have applied equitable conversion to place the risk of loss of the cabin on the Jameses, as purchasers and equitable owners of the property. For the following reasons, we disagree.

The doctrine of equitable conversion applies only if "nothing in the contract states otherwise." *Rush v. Anestos*, 661 P.2d 1229, 1233 (Idaho 1983). Thus, equitable conversion does not apply if the effect would be to shift the risk of loss to a buyer contrary to the terms of the parties' agreement. In this case, paragraph 13 of the parties' purchase agreement provided: "Should the premises be materially damaged by fire or other causes, prior to closing this sale, this agreement shall be voidable at the option of the Buyer." We construe this provision as placing the risk of loss prior to closing on the Holschers. In a factually similar case, Georgia's Supreme Court held that when a provision in a purchase agreement allows the buyer to cancel the agreement if the premises are destroyed prior to closing, the effect of that provision is to allocate to the seller the risk of loss prior to closing. *Phillips v. Bacon*, 267 S.E.2d 249 (Ga. 1980). The same reasoning applies here. Paragraph 13 absolved the Jameses from assuming the risk of any material damage to the property prior to closing, leaving that risk upon the Holschers. It would be inconsistent and illogical to say that the Jameses had the right to void the purchase agreement if the premises were materially damaged prior to closing, but also hold them responsible to pay for any pre-closing damages to the property. Such a construction would essentially take away the very right conferred upon the Jameses by paragraph 13. Because we construe paragraph 13 of the parties' purchase agreement as placing the pre-closing risk of loss on the Holschers, we hold that the district court did not err in refusing to apply the doctrine of equitable conversion to shift the pre-closing risk of loss to the Jameses.

B. Whether the District Court Erred by Applying Equitable Conversion to Conclude that the Jameses had an Insurable Interest in the Cabin Prior to Closing.

State Farm challenges the district court's conclusion that it was liable to the Jameses under the insurance binder, contending that the Jameses lacked an insurable interest in the cabin at the time of the loss, and I.C. § 41-1806 prohibits any person from enforcing a contract of insurance against an insurer unless that person has an insurable interest in the insured property. By applying the doctrine of equitable conversion, the district court concluded that the Jameses had equitable ownership of, and thus an insurable interest in, the cabin at the time of the loss. The arguable lack of an insurable interest in the Jameses is not conclusive, however, under I.C. § 41-1806, for it is the Holschers, not the Jameses, who are seeking to enforce the insurance contract against State Farm. The Holschers assert coverage in their own right as intended third-party beneficiaries of the insurance binder, not as derivative beneficiaries of the Jameses' rights under the binder. State Farm has not asserted that the Holschers lacked an insurable interest in the property at the time of the loss. Because the Jameses are not seeking to enforce the insurance contract against State Farm, we need not decide whether they had an insurable interest in the cabin at the time of the loss.

C. Whether the District Court Erred in Applying Equitable Rescission to Conclude that the Jameses were Liable for the Value of the Cabin.

The district court construed paragraph 13 of the purchase agreement as giving the Jameses the right to seek equitable rescission of the contract from the court in the event that the premises were materially damaged prior to closing. Based on this determination, the district court concluded that the Jameses could not "equitably rescind" the purchase agreement unless they restored the Holschers to their pre-contract position. The legal meaning and effect of contract terms are questions of law which we review freely.

Paragraph 13 gave the Jameses the right under the contract to void the contract at their option if the premises were materially damaged prior to closing. They did not need to apply to the court and prove the elements essential to a decree of equitable rescission before they could void the contract. Once the premises were materially damaged, the Jameses' right to void the contract was "at law," under the terms of the contract. They could simply refuse to close. A right provided by contract is, by definition, legal and not equitable. Equitable remedies are not dependent upon contractual authorization, but apply precisely because there is no adequate remedy at law under the contract's terms, and because sufficient grounds to invoke equity, such as mutual mistake, fraud, or impossibility, are present. We hold that under paragraph 13 of the parties' purchase agreement the Jameses had the legal right to void the contract once the premises were materially damaged, and their choice to exercise that right was not dependent on their satisfaction of the elements required for the application of equitable rescission. Accordingly, the district court erred in concluding that the Jameses were obliged to restore the value of the cabin to the Holschers.

II. Third-party Beneficiary Status of the Holschers under the James/State Farm Insurance Binder.

At trial, the Holschers submitted as evidence a copy of the insurance binder between the Jameses and State Farm to show that they were intended third-party beneficiaries of that agreement. The Holschers asserted that the listing of Ernest Holscher in the section of the binder entitled "other interests" unambiguously demonstrated that they were intended beneficiaries of the insurance coverage, and therefore no extrinsic evidence was admissible to prove otherwise. The district court, however, over the Holschers' objection, allowed the insurance agent who executed the insurance binder to testify that he did not intend the Holschers to be beneficiaries of the binder prior to closing. The agent testified that he listed Ernest Holscher on the binder under the section entitled "other interests" only because he was told the Holschers would become mortgagees at the time of closing and he wanted to have their name and address so he could send them a copy of the policy insuring their mortgagee interest after the transaction closed. The district court concluded that the insurance binder was ambiguous as to the Holschers' beneficiary status at the time of the loss, and submitted the issue to the jury for resolution. The jury found that the Holschers were not intended beneficiaries of the insurance binder, and the district court entered judgment on that verdict. The Holschers contend that the district court should not have submitted this issue to the jury, but should have ruled as a matter of law that they were intended beneficiaries of the insurance binder.

In Stewart v. Arrington Construction Co., 446 P.2d 895 (Idaho 1968), the Court stated that the contract itself must express an intent to benefit the third party.

"This intent must be gleaned from the contract itself unless that document is ambiguous, whereupon the circumstances surrounding its formation may be considered." *Id.* at 901. The insurance binder in this case was executed on a form contract. A section of the binder provided for the listing of persons, other than the contracting party, who were to have a beneficial interest in the insurance. In addition to space for writing the name and address of the person with the other beneficial interest, this section provided three possible categories of beneficial interests which the person might have: as a mortgagee, a loss payee, or a named additional insured. In this case, the insurance agent listed Ernest Holscher as a person with a beneficial interest under the binder, but the agent did not mark any of the three boxes to indicate which type of beneficial interest Holscher had. The effective date of coverage as stated on the face of the binder was April 5, 1989. State Farm calculated the insurance premium to begin coverage on April 5th, and the Jameses paid State Farm the assessed premium on that date.

State Farm does not dispute that Ernest Holscher was intended to have a beneficial interest in the insurance, only whether he was intended to have a beneficial interest prior to closing. State Farm asserts that it intended to insure only the Holschers' "mortgagee" interest in the property, which the Holschers would not have acquired until closing on May 1. However, State Farm, as drafter of the binder, may not now create an ambiguity by asserting that it did not intend for the Holschers to become beneficiaries until May 1, when the face of the binder clearly states that the Holschers were to have a beneficial interest in coverage effective on April 5th. State Farm gave no indication on the binder that it intended to limit the time of the Holschers' beneficial interest contrary to the effective date specified on the binder. State Farm's agent did not mark the box indicating that the nature of the Holschers' beneficial interest was to be that of mortgagee, nor did the agent add any written words expressly limiting the time of the Holschers' beneficial interest to after closing.

Because the insurance binder listed the Holschers as having a beneficial interest in the insurance with April 5, 1989, as the effective date of coverage, and because the binder contained no words limiting the coverage either to the Holschers' mortgagee interest in the property or to their post-closing losses, we hold that the insurance binder unambiguously provided the Holschers with a beneficial interest in the insurance to cover whatever insurable interest they had in the property as of April 5, 1989. We will not read into the binder a time or nature-of-interest limitation which State Farm did not deem important enough to write into the binder. We hold as a matter of law that the Holschers were third-party beneficiaries under the insurance binder, and that this beneficial interest was limited only to the extent of their insurable interest in the cabin under I.C. § 41-1806.

The district court therefore erred in submitting this issue to the jury and in admitting the parol evidence of the insurance agent. Because the Holschers' insurable interest in the cabin at the time of the loss — as legal owners and risk-of-loss bearers — encompassed the full value of the cabin, the Holschers were entitled to recover from State Farm insurance proceeds up to the full value of the cabin. Therefore, we modify the district court's judgment to hold that State Farm is directly liable to the Holschers under the insurance binder.

CONCLUSION

We hold that the parties' purchase agreement placed the pre-closing risk of loss on the Holschers, and allowed the Jameses to void the agreement at their option once the premises were materially damaged prior to closing. Accordingly, we reverse the district court's judgment holding the Jameses liable to the Holschers. We further hold that the Holschers were intended third-party beneficiaries of the insurance binder between the Jameses and State Farm, and therefore the Holschers are entitled to judgment against State Farm for the proceeds of that insurance. We remand the case to the district court for modification of the judgment with respect to State Farm and for further proceedings consistent with this opinion.

NOTES AND QUESTIONS

1. **Other views.** Some courts reject the doctrine of equitable conversion entirely. *See* Skelly Oil Co. v. Ashmore, 365 S.W.2d 582 (Mo. 1963). Others apply it only when the buyer is in possession prior to closing. *See, e.g.,* Potwin v. Tucker, 259 A.2d 781 (Vt. 1969). What can be said in support of those views?

2. **Seller as insured party.** Suppose the seller carries casualty insurance on the subject premises during the interval between the contract of sale and the closing and the buyer does not. If the building is destroyed by fire, is the seller entitled to retain the insurance proceeds and force the buyer to go through with the sale?

3. **Drafting.** Equitable conversion is a default rule. It yields to the parties' stated intent that the doctrine not apply. A well-drafted contract of sale will address the question of destruction of or injury to the subject property before closing, and will specify the parties' respective responsibilities. Care in drafting of course is essential. *See* Bryant v. Willison Real Estate Co., 350 S.E.2d 748, 750-52 (W. Va. 1986):

> The trial court was of the view that the contract language stating that "the owner is responsible for said property until the Deed has been delivered to said purchasers" was not sufficient to cast the responsibility on the vendors. This conclusion was based, in part, on testimony of the sales agent for the vendor that this language pertained only to vandalism. We disagree with this conclusion. The contract was on a printed form and the language is free from ambiguity. To permit this language to be restricted to acts of vandalism cuts across the plain meaning of its wording and would be contrary to the general rule that forecloses oral modification of contract language which is free from ambiguity.

> Apparently, the trial court also relied on language in the sales contract which provided: "Purchaser to carry enough fire insurance to protect Self." We do not believe that this provision can be read to place the risk of loss on the purchasers. [It] is nothing more than an acknowledgment of the general rule that both parties to an executory contract for the sale of real property have an insurable interest.

> The trial court also referred to the sentence in the contract that "this contract is also subject to 'As Is' condition" as indicating an intention not to

deliver the building in a specific condition. [W]e do not agree that this language can be read to remove the risk of loss from the vendors. The purpose of this type of provision is not to shift the risk of loss in the event the building is damaged without fault on the part of either party. Rather the use of an "as is" provision in a real estate sales contract is generally intended to negate the existence of any warranty as to the particular fitness or condition of the property. This type of clause simply means that the purchaser must take the premises covered in the real estate sales contract in its present condition as of the date of the contract.

4. **The principal case.** Do you think that the result in the principal case is correct?

5. **Other issues.** Characterization of property as real or personal is often important. Equitable conversion, if applicable, decides such characterization questions. Courts do not always apply the doctrine. Consider the following:

a. Testator devises all his personal property to his spouse, and all his real property to his children from a former marriage. Subsequently, testator enters into a contract to sell Blackacre to Buyer. Before closing, testator dies. When the sale of Blackacre is completed (by testator's executor), do the sales proceeds belong to the testator's spouse or the testator's children? Does it matter if the contract of sale is entered into by testator's guardian or agent (testator having become incompetent since making the will) rather than by testator? *See* Funk v. Funk, 563 N.E.2d 127 (Ind. Ct. App. 1990). Does it matter if the will is made *after* the contract of sale? *See* Stoebuck & Whitman § 10.13, at 788-89.

b. Seller contracts to sell Blackacre to Buyer. After the contract of sale, Creditor obtains a tort judgment against Seller. "In most states a judgment becomes, by statute, a lien on the defendant's real property in the county where it is docketed." Stoebuck & Whitman § 10.13, at 790. Does the creditor's lien apply to the seller's interest in Blackacre? *See id.*; Cannefax v. Clement, 786 P.2d 1377 (Utah Ct. App. 1990).

6. **When does equitable conversion occur?** Equitable conversion is based on specific performance; the buyer who is the owner for purposes of specific performance is treated as the owner for other purposes as well. In Note 5(a) above, suppose that the contract of sale was not subject to specific performance at the testator's death because a defect in title had not been corrected at that point; does equitable conversion apply? *See* Coe v. Hays, 614 A.2d 576 (Md. 1992). *Cf.* Woodland Realty, Inc. v. Winzenried, 262 N.W.2d 106, 108 (Wis. 1978) (condition of financing is condition precedent, which "operates to delay the enforceability of the contract until the condition precedent has taken place").

3. Remedies for Breach of Contract

Since a contract of sale is a contract, it offers the same remedies that are available for breaches of other contracts.

Judicial remedies upon breach of contract fall into three general categories: restitution, compensatory damages and performance. Separate concepts undergird each of these remedial provisions. The rationale for restitution is to return the innocent party to his status before the contract was executed [by giving back to the innocent party any benefits conferred on the breaching party]. Compensatory damages are intended to recompense the injured claimant for losses due to the breach, that is, give the innocent party the benefit of the bargain. Performance is to effect a result, essentially other than in terms of monetary reparation, so that the innocent party is placed in the position of having had the contract performed.

Donovan v. Bachstadt, 453 A.2d 160, 165 (N.J. 1982). With reference to compensatory damages, contract law distinguishes two interests that an award of damages might protect. The expectation interest is the promisee's interest "in having the benefit of his bargain, by being put in as good a position as he would have been in had the contract been performed." Restatement Second of Contracts § 344. The reliance interest is the promisee's interest in being "put in as good a position as he would have been in had the contract not been made." *Id.* These damages, and restitution, are considered in Section 3.a.

Although specific performance, as you may recall from your course in Contracts, is theoretically subordinate to the damages remedy, specific performance is readily available to the aggrieved party in a contract for the sale of land (Section 3.b). The theory is that land is unique; no "cover" purchase is possible, so damages are inadequate compensation. For an excellent review of the remedies available for breach of real estate contracts, and a defense of the thesis that the remedy of expectation damages "could be shaped to approach the goal of full compensation while promoting economic efficiency, thereby challenging the strongest argument that the proponents of specific performance invoke," see Lawrence V. Berkovich, *To Pay or To Convey?: A Theory of Remedies for Breach of Real Estate Contracts*, 1995 Ann. Surv. Am. L. 319.

a.   Money Awards: Damages and Restitution

WOLOFSKY v. BEHRMAN
454 So. 2d 614 (Fla. Dist. Ct. App. 1984)

DOWNEY, JUDGE.

In a suit for breach of a contract to sell a condominium apartment, the trial court awarded appellant-purchaser as damages only a return of the purchaser's deposit money plus interest. Contending that he was entitled to damages for loss of his bargain, the purchaser has perfected this appeal.

In developing a condominium complex, appellant, Wolofsky, sold one of the apartments to appellees, Harold and Elaine Behrman. The Behrmans intended to move into the apartment when they were successful in selling their single family residence. When the residence did not sell the Behrmans decided to sell the condominium instead. After some futile efforts to sell the apartment, Behrman accepted Wolofsky's offer to buy it for $73,000 and a memorandum contract was signed. Although Wolofsky was not interested in the furnishings therein, his sales agent agreed to try to sell them for the Behrmans for $4,000. Behrman delivered the keys to the apartment to the agent, who was able to obtain an offer of only $3,000, which Behrman refused. A few weeks before the closing was due, Behrman visited the apartment and found evidence that someone had been staying there without his permission. The electricity was on; he found a T.V. and radio, bedclothes on the bed, food in the kitchen, and a few clothes in a closet. Behrman testified he was very upset; he was outraged; he felt violated. As a consequence, he advised Wolofsky that there could be no further relationship between them and he returned the deposit and refused to close. Apparently, Wolofsky had obtained a purchaser for the apartment for $100,000 and the sales agent had allowed that purchaser to stay briefly in the apartment.

Wolofsky sued the Behrmans for specific performance and damages. The former claim was abandoned and the case went to trial on the claim for damages and Behrmans' counterclaim for trespass. The final judgment states that the Behrmans admit they breached the contract and admit they are liable therefor. However, they denied they acted in bad faith. The trial court accepted Behrmans' contention and found no showing of bad faith.

Before discussing the applicable legal principles, we think it advisable to point out that a) the Behrmans never lived in this apartment, nor did they ever intend to after contracting with Wolofsky, b) while Wolofsky did not have permission to allow anyone to occupy the apartment, the contract between the parties was silent as to possession, c) Wolofsky offered to compensate the Behrmans for the use of the apartment, d) under the doctrine of equitable conversion the equitable title was in Wolofsky and any loss or destruction to the property would fall upon him, and e) the closing was only a few weeks away.

There are numerous Florida cases involving the measure of damages for breach of a contract to sell realty. Florida has long since aligned itself with the English rule announced in Flureau v. Thornhill, 2 W.Bl. 1078, 96 Eng.Rep. 635, to the effect that, except where a vendor has acted in bad faith, his liability for breach of a land sale contract is limited to the amount of the deposit paid by the purchaser, with interest and reimbursement for expenses in investigating title to the property. However, absent good faith, he is liable for full compensatory damages, including the loss of his bargain, which is the difference between the value of the property and the contract price.

In Key v. Alexander, 108 So. 883 (Fla. 1926), the Supreme Court of Florida quoted from Sutherland on Damages as follows:

> If the person selling is in default — if he knew or should have known that he could not comply with his undertaking; if he, being an agent, contracted in his own name, depending on his principal to fulfill his contract merely because he had power to negotiate a sale; if he has only a contract of the owner to convey, or a bond for a deed; if his contract to sell requires the signature of his wife to bar an inchoate right of dower, or the consent of a third person to render his deed effectual; if he makes his contract without title in the expectation of subsequently being able to acquire it and is unable to fulfill by reason of cause so known the want of concurrence of other persons; or *if he has title and refused to convey*, or disables himself from doing so by conveyance to another person — in all such cases he is

beyond the reach of the principle of Flureau v. Thornhill, and is liable to full compensatory damages including those for the loss of the bargain.

108 So. at 885 (emphasis added).

In analyzing the good faith-bad faith dichotomy, which pertains to this rule, Professor McCormick suggests that the present refinements of the rule seem to lean heavily on the requirement that the vendor must "do his best" by reasonable efforts or expenditures to complete the conveyance. McCormick on Damages, § 179, p. 189.

The Behrmans had legal title to the property in question but refused to convey. Thus it is clear to us that the Behrmans did not "do their best" to complete the conveyance. While they may be justified in not acceding to someone's living in the apartment until closing, that is an inadequate reason for refusing to close. The trial court was correct in finding that refusing to close for the reason given constituted a breach of the contract; he erred in finding that it did not demonstrate a failure to exercise the good faith required to preclude full compensatory damages. The inability of a vendor to close for reasons beyond his control, does not necessarily mean the vendee should recover the loss of his bargain. In each of the cited cases the vendor wanted to close but was precluded by factors beyond his control. Here, there were no factors beyond the Behrmans' control except their excessive pique over the unauthorized brief use of their apartment without their consent. Thus, they not only did not do their best, they did nothing to effectuate the completion of the contract. This constitutes lack of good faith. Thus, under the applicable rules, they were liable for full compensatory damages.

Accordingly, the judgment appealed from is reversed and the cause is remanded for further proceedings consistent with this opinion.

NOTES AND QUESTIONS

1. **The English rule.** In states that follow it, the rule of Flureau v. Thornhill, 96 Eng. Rep. 635 (C.P. 1776), is usually applied in cases where the seller is unable to convey satisfactory title to the buyer. *See* Stoebuck & Whitman § 10.3, at 726. If the seller lacks title, specific performance is not an available remedy for the buyer. As to the remedies of damages and restitution, what limits does the English rule impose on the buyer?

2. **The principal case.** Did the seller in the principal case breach because he lacked title to the condo? Assuming that the rule of Flureau v. Thornhill applies, in what circumstances is the buyer entitled to recover expectation damages? Why did the seller in the principal case not get the benefit of the rule of Flureau v. Thornhill?

3. **The American rule.** Is there any reason to retain the English rule in modern American law? *See* Donovan v. Bachstadt, 453 A.2d 160, 164 (N.J. 1982):

We are satisfied that the American rule [allowing the buyer to recover expectation damages] is preferable. The English principle developed because of the uncertainties of title due to the complexity of the rules governing title to land during the eighteenth and nineteenth centuries. At that time the only evidence of title was contained in deeds which were in a phrase attributed to Lord Westbury, "difficult to read, disgusting to touch, and impossible to understand." The reason for the English principle that creates an exception to the law governing damages for breaches of executory contracts for the sale of property is no longer valid, and the exception should be eliminated. Cessante ratione legis, cessat et ipsa lex (the reason for a law ceasing, the law itself ceases). Indeed in England the rule has been modified by placing the burden of proof on the vendor to establish that he has done everything within his power to carry out the contract.

Whether titles are clear may be ascertained by record searches. Moreover, limitation periods may be applicable. Thus, it is standard practice for title examiners to search the title back for 60 years and until a warranty deed is found in the chain of title. Further the parties may insert appropriate provisions in their agreements protecting them from title defects so that to a very large extent sellers may control the measure of redress.

There is no sound basis why benefit of the bargain damages should not be awarded whether the subject matter of the contract is realty or personalty. Serious losses should not be borne by the vendee of real estate to the benefit of the defaulting vendor. This is particularly so when an instalment purchase contract is involved that extends over a period of years during which the vendee makes substantial payments upon the principal, as well as extensive improvements to the property.

The innocent purchaser should be permitted to recover benefit of the bargain damages irrespective of the good or bad faith of the seller. Contract culpability depends on the breach of the contractual promise. Where, as here, the seller agreed that title would be marketable, the seller's liability should depend upon his breach of that promise.

4. **Breach by seller: damages.** Suppose that Seller contracts to sell Blackacre to Buyer for $10,000. Seller breaches. On the date set for closing, the fair market value of Blackacre is $11,000. If Buyer is entitled to recover expectation damages, what recovery is Buyer entitled to on these facts? Suppose Blackacre is worth $10,000; does Buyer have an expectation recovery? Suppose Blackacre is worth $9,000?

5. **The principal case.** Since the seller in the principal case could not invoke the limiting rule of Flureau v. Thornhill, the seller was liable for the buyer's expectation damages. What are those damages — the difference between the contract price of $73,000 and the resale price of $100,000?

KUTZIN v. PIRNIE
591 A.2d 932 (N.J. 1991)

Clifford, J.

This is an action on a contract for the sale of residential property. The sellers' real-estate agent prepared the contract, after which defendants, the prospective buyers, signed it, paid a deposit of nearly ten percent of the purchase price, and then decided not to go through with the purchase. In the trial court the buyers argued that the contract had been rescinded because attorneys for both parties had sought to amend it during the three-day period provided by the contract's attorney-review clause. The court found the contract to be valid and awarded the sellers compensatory damages, albeit in an amount less than the deposit. The Appellate Division agreed that the contract is binding but held that the sellers are entitled to keep the entire deposit as damages. We granted certification to determine whether the contract is enforceable and, if so, whether the sellers should be allowed to keep the deposit. We affirm the Appellate Division holding that the contract is valid but modify that court's judgment on the issue of damages and reinstate the damage award of the trial court.

I

On September 1, 1987, defendants, Duncan and Gertrude Pirnie, and plaintiffs, Milton and Ruth Kutzin, signed a contract for the sale of the Kutzins' house in Haworth for $365,000. The contract, which is the standard form real estate sales contract adopted by the New Jersey Association of Realtors, had been prepared by Weichert Realtors (Weichert), the sellers' real-estate agent. Under its terms, the Pirnies agreed to pay a partial deposit of $1,000 on signing the contract and the remainder of the deposit, $35,000, within seven days. In compliance therewith, the Pirnies made out a check for $1,000 to the trust account of Russo Real Estate (Russo), their real-estate agent. The contract does not contain a "forfeiture" or "liquidated damages" clause; with reference to the disposition of the deposit should the sale not take place, the contract merely states, "If this contract is voided by either party, the escrow monies shall be disbursed pursuant to the written direction of both parties."

The contract also contains the following attorney-review provision:

1. Study by Attorney

The Buyer or the Seller may choose to have an attorney study this contract. If an attorney is consulted, the attorney must complete his or her review of the contract within a three-day period. This contract will be legally binding at the end of this three-day period unless an attorney for the Buyer or the Seller reviews and disapproves of the contract.

The Kutzins' attorney, Marshall Kozinn, telephoned Russo on September 2nd to communicate his approval of the contract with one exception: he wanted to hold the deposit in his trust account pending closing. Kozinn followed up that conversation by mailing a letter to Russo dated September 3, 1987, with a copy to Joseph Maccarone, the Pirnies' attorney. Russo had already complied with Kozinn's request (without discussing the matter with Maccarone) by endorsing the Pirnies' check to Kozinn's trust account and sending it to him on September 2nd.

In a telephone conversation with Kozinn on September 4th, Maccarone agreed to allow Kozinn to hold the deposit but expressed his opinion that the contract prepared by Weichert did not provide adequate protection for the buyers. That same day Maccarone mailed to Kozinn [a letter with] his standard rider for protection of buyers of real estate. Significantly, the rider was silent on the issue of what would happen to the deposit if the sale were not completed.

On September 10th, Maccarone telephoned Kozinn to inquire if the terms of the rider were acceptable. When Kozinn indicated that they were not, the attorneys discussed their differences and eventually agreed on certain changes. During that conversation, Kozinn mentioned that he had not yet received the additional deposit of $35,000 and questioned whether the Pirnies intended to proceed with the purchase. Maccarone assured Kozinn of the Pirnies' intention to buy the house, stating that "if the deposit was to be any demonstration of good faith or what have you [Kozinn] would have the deposit." Kozinn received the Pirnies' check for the balance of the deposit the next day. Thus assured that the sale would occur, the Kutzins left for their Florida home on the 13th of September.

Maccarone revised the rider and on September 21st sent to Kozinn two copies, already signed by the Pirnies, for execution by the Kutzins. Kozinn received the copies of the modified rider on September 22nd and forwarded them to the Kutzins that same day. A letter accompanied the riders requesting, among other things, that the Kutzins sign and return the riders to Kozinn as soon as the couple returned from Florida. The Kutzins apparently received the letter when they returned to New Jersey on September 24th.

Shortly thereafter the Pirnies instructed their new attorney, Harold Goldman, to write Kozinn the following letter, which was mailed on September 28th:

> Be advised the Purnies [sic: "Pirnies" or "Pirnie" throughout] have retained my office to represent them in their effort to negotiate the purchase of a home in Haworth owned by your client, Milton Kutzin. Mrs. Purnie has indicated to me that the Purnies are no longer interested in purchasing the subject property. Therefore, please treat this letter as formal notice to withdraw the offer to purchase by the Purnies. I must add that the desire to withdraw the offer to purchase was communicated to Joan Harrison, the listing broker, yesterday by both Mrs. Purnie and [myself]. It is my understanding that you are presently holding in trust deposit monies remitted by the Purnies in regard to the proposed purchase. Please call [me] to arrange for the return of said monies.

The Kutzins refused to return the deposit and promptly sued for specific performance of the contract. The Pirnies counterclaimed for return of their $36,000 deposit, contending that the contract had been validly rescinded either pursuant to the attorney-review provision or by agreement of the parties. Because the Kutzins sold the house to another buyer for $352,500 while the case was pending, they amended their complaint to seek only damages.

The trial court ruled that the parties had entered into a binding contract that had not been rescinded either by agreement or pursuant to the attorney-review clause. Consequently, the court held that the sellers were entitled to $17,325 in damages. That amount consisted of the $12,500 difference between the $365,000 the Pirnies had contracted to pay and the $352,500 for which the house eventually sold; $3,825 in utilities, real-estate taxes, and insurance expenses the Kutzins had incurred during the six-month period between the originally-anticipated closing date and the date of actual sale; and $1,000 the Kutzins had paid for a new basement carpet, which their realtor had recommended they buy to enhance the attractiveness of their house to prospective buyers. The court denied recovery of interest the Kutzins contended they would have earned on the purchase price had the sale to the Pirnies gone through. It also refused to award damages for the increased capital-gains tax the Kutzins had paid as a result of the breach. The court ordered the Kutzins to return the $18,675 balance of the deposit to the Pirnies.

On appeal, the Kutzins argued that they should recover the lost interest and the increased capital-gains tax they had incurred, or, alternatively, that they should be allowed to retain the deposit. On cross-appeal the Pirnies claimed entitlement to the entire deposit, again asserting that the contract had been validly rescinded. In an unreported opinion, the Appellate Division found that the contract between the parties "was enforceable according to its terms" but that "the Kutzins' claims to compensation for their allegedly increased tax liability and lost interest were too speculative to be compensable." The court then noted that "the Kutzins' loss as determined by the trial court was less than the Pirnies' $36,000 deposit," and concluded that "the Kutzins are entitled to retain the [entire] deposit, but they may not recover any additional amount as damages."

II

[The court concluded that the buyer had not validly terminated the contract pursuant to the attorney-review provision, and hence was liable for damages for breach of contract.]

III

The issue of whether a seller should be entitled to retain a deposit when a buyer breaches a contract that does not contain a liquidated-damages or forfeiture clause has long troubled courts. As Professor Williston has observed,

> Few questions in the law have given rise to more discussion and difference of opinion than that concerning the right of one who has materially broken his contract without legal excuse to recover for such benefit [here, the deposit] as he may have conferred on the other party

12 S. Williston, A Treatise on the Law of Contracts § 1473 at 220 (3d ed. 1961).

-A-

"[T]he common-law rule, which has been very generally followed [was] that where the vendee of real property makes a part payment on the purchase price, but fails to fulfill the contract without lawful excuse, he cannot recover the payment even though the vendor may have made a profit by reason of the default." Quillen v. Kelley, 140 A.2d 517, 520 (Md. 1958); see, e.g., Annotation, *Modern Status of Defaulting Vendee's Right to Recover Contractual Payments Withheld by Vendor as Forfeited*, 4 A.L.R.4th 993, 997 (1981) (The general rule is that "a vendee in default cannot recover back the money he has paid on an executory contract to his vendor who is not himself in default."). The thought behind that rule is that "restitution should always be refused, for the good and sufficient reason that the [buyer] is guilty of a breach of contract and should never be allowed to have advantage from his own wrong." 5A A. Corbin, Corbin on Contracts § 1129 at 37 (1964); see, e.g., Haslack v. Mayers, 26 N.J.L. 284, 290-91 (Sup. Ct. 1857) ("The plaintiff here has deliberately broken his covenant with the defendant. For the court to aid him would be to lend its aid to an act of bad faith. Let him perform his contract or the loss is the consequence of his own act.").

New Jersey traditionally has adhered to the common-law rule. Following a long line of cases, the Appellate Division held that the Kutzins are entitled to retain the deposit even though the court was "sympathetic to the trial judge's ruling that the Pirnies were entitled to the return of the balance of their $36,000 contract deposit in excess of the Kutzins' actual damages."

-B-

Despite the ample authority supporting the Appellate Division's disposition of the damages question, "there has been a growing recognition of the injustice that often results from the application of the rule permitting total forfeiture of part payments under a contract of sale." Great United Realty Co. v. Lewis, 101 A.2d 881, 883 (Md. 1954). Professor Corbin led the movement favoring departure from the strict common-law rule. In [his article] *The Right of a Defaulting Vendee to the Restitution of Instalments Paid*, 40 Yale L.J. 1013, 1013 (1931), he stated:

> If a contractor has committed a total breach of his contract, having rendered no performance whatever thereunder, no penalty or forfeiture will be enforced against him; he will be required to do no more than to make the injured party whole by paying full compensatory damages. In like manner, a contractor who commits a breach after he has rendered part performance must also make the injured party whole by payment of full compensatory damages. The part performance rendered, however, may be much more valuable to the defendant than the amount of the injury caused by the breach; and in such case, to allow the injured party to retain the benefit of the part performance so rendered, without making restitution of any part of such value, is the enforcement of a penalty or forfeiture against the contract-breaker.

Corbin went on to declare that if a plaintiff "can and does show by proper evidence that the defendant is holding an amount of money as a penalty rather than as compensation for injury, he should be given judgment for restitution of that amount." *Id.* at 1025-26. He then concluded that

> [t]he cases denying restitution can be justified on one or more of the following grounds: (1) The defendant has not rescinded and remains ready and willing to perform, and still has a right to specific performance by the vendee; (2) the plaintiff has not shown that the injury caused by his breach is less than the instalments received by the defendant; (3) there is an express provision that the money may be retained by the vendor and the facts are such as to make this a genuine provision for liquidated damages,

and not one for a penalty or forfeiture. *If the facts are such that none of these justifications exists, restitution should be allowed.*

Id. at 1032-33 (emphasis added).

Professor Corbin's article formed the basis for sections 1122 to 1135 of his treatise, Corbin on Contracts (see especially section 1129 on restitution of installments in favor of a defaulting purchaser of land), and also was used in the formulation of section 357 of the Restatement of Contracts (1932). Section 357 states:

(1) Where the defendant fails or refuses to perform his contract and is justified therein by the plaintiff's own breach of duty or non-performance of a condition, but the plaintiff has rendered a part performance under the contract that is a net benefit to the defendant, the plaintiff can get judgment, except as stated in Subsection (2), for the amount of such benefit in excess of the harm that he has caused to the defendant by his own breach, in no case exceeding a ratable proportion of the agreed compensation, if

(a) the plaintiff's breach or non-performance is not willful and deliberate; or

(b) the defendant, with knowledge that the plaintiff's breach of duty or non-performance of condition has occurred or will thereafter occur, assents to the rendition of the part performance, or accepts the benefit of it, or retains property received although its return in specie is still not unreasonably difficult or injurious.

(2) The plaintiff has no right to compensation for his part performance if it is merely a payment of earnest money, or if the contract provides that it may be retained and it is not so greatly in excess of the defendant's harm that the provision is rejected as imposing a penalty.

(3) The measure of the defendant's benefit from the plaintiff's part performance is the amount by which he has been enriched as a result of such performance unless the facts are those stated in Subsection (1b), in which case it is the price fixed by the contract for such part performance, or, if no price is so fixed, a ratable proportion of the total contract price.

That section was adopted by the Appellate Division in Power-Matics, Inc. v. Ligotti, 191 A.2d 483 (N.J. Super. Ct. App. Div. 1963), in which the plaintiff sought recovery for its part performance after it had breached a contract to build a porch. The court concluded that the "plaintiff should have been allowed to offer evidence to establish, if it could, a right to recover the amount of the benefit it conferred upon defendants in excess of the harm it had caused defendants by its own breach — rather than be compelled to suffer a complete forfeiture."

Section 374(1) of the Restatement (Second) of Contracts is based on section 357 but "is more liberal in allowing recovery in accord with the policy behind Uniform Commercial Code § 2-718(2)." Restatement (Second) of Contracts § 374 Reporter's Note (1981). That section sets forth the rule as follows:

[I]f a party justifiably refuses to perform on the ground that his remaining duties of performance have been discharged by the other party's breach, the party in breach is entitled to restitution for any benefit that he has conferred by way of part performance or reliance in excess of the loss that he has caused by his own breach.

Id. § 374(1). Particularly relevant to this case is the following illustration:

A contracts to sell land to B for $100,000, which B promises to pay in $10,000 installments before transfer of title. After B has paid $30,000 he fails to pay the remaining installments and A sells the land to another buyer for $95,000. B can recover $30,000 from A in restitution less $5,000 damages for B's breach of contract, or $25,000. If A does not sell the land to another buyer and obtains a decree of specific performance against B, B has no right to restitution.

Id. § 374 illustration 1.

Since publication of the first Restatement of Contracts in 1932, few courts have followed the common-law rule refusing restitution. See 5A Corbin, § 1129, at 37-38. The Restatement approach of allowing recovery "has steadily increased in favor and probably represents the weight of authority." 12 Williston, § 1473 at 222. [I]n Wilkins v. Birnbaum, 278 A.2d 829, 831 (Del. 1971), the Supreme Court of Delaware recognized that "a defaulting buyer [who] can prove that the deposit exceeds in amount the actual damages resulting from the breach [can] recover back the excess, but the burden of proving this is placed on him." *See also* Annotation, 4 A.L.R.4th at 1026-27 (citing "cases containing no forfeiture provision [that] support or recognize the principle that in view of equitable considerations, a defaulting vendee may recover payments made to the extent that they exceed the damages sustained by the vendor as a result of the breach").

With the issue squarely presented in this case, we overrule those New Jersey cases adhering to the common-law rule and adopt the modern approach set forth in section 374(1) of the Restatement (Second) of Contracts. In Professor Williston's words, "to deny recovery [in this situation] often gives the [seller] more than fair compensation for the injury he has sustained and imposes a forfeiture (which the law abhors) on the [breaching buyer]." 12 Williston, § 1473 at 222. The approach that we adopt is suggested to have the added benefit of promoting economic efficiency: penalties deter "efficient" breaches of contract "by making the cost of the breach to the contract breaker greater than the cost of the breach to the victim." R. Posner, Economic Analysis of Law § 4.10 at 116 (3d ed. 1986).

-C-

We conclude that the Pirnies are entitled, under the Restatement formulation of damages, to restitution for any benefit that they conferred by way of part performance or reliance in excess of the loss that they caused by their own breach. See Restatement (Second) of Contracts, § 374(1). We stress, however, that "[o]ne who charges an unjust enrichment has the burden of proving it." Oliver v. Lawson, 223 A.2d 355 (citing 5A Corbin, § 1132 at 64). As Professor Corbin stated:

Whether the vendor has "rescinded" for the vendee's breach or not, and whether there is an express provision for forfeiture or not, it is clear that the vendee in default should in no case be given restitution of money paid unless it affirmatively appears that the money so paid is in excess of the injury caused to the vendor by the breach. The vendee sues because he asserts that retention of the money is unjust enrichment; but there is no injustice if the defendant is retaining no more than the amount of injury caused by the plaintiff's breach. In cases where the plaintiff may have a right of restitution, he should be permitted to show that the defendant's injury is less than the installments paid; but unless he successfully shows this, he should recover nothing.

The Defaulting Vendee, 40 Yale L.J. at 1023.

The trial court found that the Kutzins had suffered $17,325 in damages, a figure that we accept because it is not challenged in this Court. The Pirnies' deposit of $36,000 exceeded the injury caused by their breach by $18,675, and they are thus entitled to recovery of that amount.

Our holding is not affected by the fact that the $36,000 deposit was less than ten percent of the $365,000 purchase price. Whenever the breaching buyer proves that the deposit exceeds the seller's actual damages suffered as a result of the breach, the buyer may recover the difference.

III

To ensure that our opinion not be misread, we emphasize that the contract at issue does not contain a forfeiture or liquidated-damages clause; it merely states, "If this contract is voided by either party, the escrow monies shall be disbursed pursuant to the written direction of both parties." The contract is otherwise silent on the subject of what would happen to the deposit were the sale not to occur. Had the contract contained a liquidated-damages clause, this case would have been governed by section 374(2) of the Restatement (Second) of Contracts, which states:

To the extent that, under the manifested assent of the parties, a party's performance is to be retained in the case of breach, that party is not entitled to restitution if the value of the performance as liquidated damages is reasonable in the light of the anticipated loss caused by the breach and the difficulties of proof of loss.

Although we do not consider the validity or enforceability of a liquidated-damages clause in this case, we are reminded of Professor Corbin's warning: "Penalties and forfeitures are not favored; and calling an outrageous penalty by the more kindly name of liquidated damages does not absolve it from its sin." *Defaulting Vendee*, 40 Yale L.J. at 1016.

IV

[T]he contract between the Kutzins and the Pirnies was not rescinded under the terms of its attorney-review clause. Thus, the Pirnies' refusal to proceed constituted a breach of contract entitling the Kutzins to recover compensatory damages for the loss they suffered as a result of the breach. We hold that the Kutzins cannot retain the entire deposit as damages. The Pirnies are entitled to restitution of their deposit less the amount of the injury to the Kutzins caused by the Pirnies' breach. To allow retention of the entire deposit would unjustly enrich the Kutzins and would penalize the Pirnies contrary to the policy behind our law of contracts.

The judgment of the Appellate Division is modified to reinstate the trial court's damage award. As modified the judgment is:

Affirmed.

NOTES AND QUESTIONS

1. **Buyer in breach.** When the buyer breaches the contract of sale, the seller's expectation damages are the difference between the contract price and the (lower) market value of the property on the date of breach. In the principal case, the contract price was $365,000, and the market value at the time of breach (accepting the resale contract price as good evidence of market value) was $352,500; the $12,500 difference represented the benefit of the seller's bargain with the defendant buyer.

2. **Consequential damages.** The seller's additional damages of $4,825 in the principal case represent what most lawyers would call special (or consequential) damages: damages that are not based on the value of the subject matter of the contract (see Note 1), but that represent collateral losses caused by the breach. Special damages are subject to the Hadley v. Baxendale requirement that they be foreseeable by the party in breach at the time of contracting, and the requirement of certainty. *See* Restatement Second of Contracts §§ 351 (foreseeability), 352 (certainty). In the principal case, were any of the items of special damages contestable on the grounds of foreseeability or certainty?

3. **The buyer's claim in Kutzin v. Pirnie.** How would you characterize the buyer's claim in the principal case? Since the seller didn't breach, the buyer's claim is not one for damages is it? The traditional obstacle to the buyer's recovery in the principal case is the rule that a party in breach cannot recover in restitution for the value of benefits conferred on the nonbreaching party. Why does the court reject the traditional rule? For a contrary view, see Maxton Builders, Inc. v. Lo Galbo, 502 N.E.2d 184 (N.Y. 1986) (under a longstanding usage in New York, seller is entitled to retain buyer's deposit not exceeding 10% of purchase price when buyer breaches unless the contract denies seller that right).

4. **Liquidated damages clauses.** The court in the principal case emphasizes the contract's omission of a liquidated damages clause — a clause in which the parties specify that the buyer's down payment can be retained as damages in the event that the buyer breaches. Suppose that the contract had specified that the down payment could be retained as liquidated damages. Would the seller have been able to retain the entire deposit in that case? What is the rule applicable to liquidated damages provisions? Does *Maxton Builders* (Note 3) provide a judicially-created liquidated damages provision? In New Jersey, which party — buyer or seller — has the burden of securing a contract term regarding the seller's entitlement to retain the buyer's deposit? In New York, which party has that burden?

b.   Specific Performance

CENTEX HOMES CORP. v. BOAG
320 A.2d 194 (N.J. Super. Ct. Ch. 1974)

GELMAN, J.S.C.

Plaintiff Centex Homes Corporation is engaged in the development and construction of a luxury high-rise condominium project in the Boroughs of Cliffside Park and Fort Lee. The project when completed will consist of six 31-story buildings containing in excess of 3600 condominium apartment units, together with recreational buildings and facilities, parking garages and other common elements associated with this form of residential development. As sponsor of the project Centex offers the condominium apartment units for sale to the public and has filed an offering plan covering such sales with the appropriate regulatory agencies of the States of New Jersey and New York.

On September 13, 1972 defendants Mr. & Mrs. Eugene Boag executed a contract for the purchase of apartment unit No. 2019 in the building under construction and known as "Winston Towers 200." The contract purchase price was $73,700, and prior to signing the contract defendants had given Centex a deposit in the amount of $525. At or shortly after signing the contract defendants delivered to Centex a check in the amount of $6,870 which, together with the deposit, represented approximately 10% of the total purchase of the apartment unit. Shortly thereafter Boag was notified by his employer that he was to be transferred to the Chicago, Illinois, area. Under date of September 27, 1972 he advised Centex that he "would be unable to complete the purchase" agreement and stopped payment on the $6,870, check. Centex deposited the check for collection approximately two weeks after receiving notice from defendant, but the check was not honored by defendants' bank. On August 8, 1973 Centex instituted this action in Chancery Division for specific performance of the purchase agreement or, in the alternative, for liquidated damages in the amount of $6,870. The matter is presently before this court on the motion of Centex for summary judgment.

Both parties acknowledge, and our research has confirmed, that no court in this State or in the United States has determined in any reported decision whether the equitable remedy of specific performance will lie for the enforcement of a contract for the sale of a condominium apartment. [U]nder a condominium housing scheme each condominium apartment unit constitutes a separate parcel of real property which may be dealt with in the same manner as any real estate. Upon closing of title the apartment unit owner receives a recordable deed which confers upon him the same rights and subjects him to the same obligations as in the case of traditional forms of real estate ownership, the only difference being that the condominium owner receives in addition an undivided interest in the common elements associated with the building and assigned to each unit.

Centex urges that since the subject matter of the contract is the transfer of a fee interest in real estate, the remedy of specific performance is available to enforce the agreement under principles of equity which are well-settled in this state.

The principle underlying the specific performance remedy is equity's jurisdiction to grant relief where the damage remedy at law is inadequate. The text writers generally agree that at the time this branch of equity jurisdiction was evolving in England, the presumed uniqueness of land as well as its importance to the social order of that era led to the conclusion that damages at law could never be adequate to compensate for the breach of a contract to transfer an interest in land. Hence specific performance became a fixed remedy in this class of transactions. The judicial attitude has remained substantially unchanged and is expressed in Pomeroy as follows:

> in applying this doctrine the courts of equity have established the further rule that in general the legal remedy of damages is inadequate in all agreements for the sale or letting of land, or of any estate therein; and therefore in such class of contracts the jurisdiction is always exercised, and a specific performance granted, unless prevented by other and independent equitable considerations which directly affect the remedial right of the complaining party.

1 Pomeroy, Equity Jurisprudence (5th ed. 1941), § 221(b).

While the inadequacy of the damage remedy suffices to explain the origin of the vendee's right to obtain specific performance in equity, it does not provide a rationale for the availability of the remedy at the instance of the vendor of real estate. Except upon a showing of unusual circumstances or a change in the vendor's position, such as where the vendee has entered into possession, the vendor's damages are usually measurable, his remedy at law is adequate and there is no jurisdictional basis for equitable relief. But see Restatement, Contracts § 360, comment c.[2] The early English precedents suggest that the availability of the remedy in a suit by a vendor was an outgrowth of the equitable concept of mutuality, i.e., that equity would not specifically enforce an agreement unless the remedy was available to both parties.

So far as can be determined from our decisional law, the mutuality of remedy concept has been the prop which has supported equitable jurisdiction to grant specific performance in actions by vendors of real estate. The first reported discussion of the question occurs in Hopper v. Hopper, 16 N.J.Eq. 147 (Ch.1863), which was an action by a vendor to compel specific performance of a contract for the sale of land. In answer to the contention that equity lacked jurisdiction because the vendor had an adequate legal remedy, Chancellor Green said (at p. 148):

> It constitutes no objection to the relief prayed for, that the application is made by the vendor to enforce the payment of the purchase money, and not

---

[2] The Restatement's reasoning, as expressed in § 360, comment c, amounts to the inconsistent propositions that (1) because the vendor may not have sustained any damage which is actionable at law, specific performance should be granted, and (2) he would otherwise sustain damage equal to the loss of interest on the proceeds of the sale. Yet loss of interest is readily measurable and can be recovered in an action at law, and to the extent that the vendor has sustained no economic injury, there is no compelling reason for equity to grant to him the otherwise extraordinary remedy of specific performance. At the end of the comment, the author suggests that the vendor is entitled to specific performance because that remedy should be mutual, a concept which is substantially rejected as a decisional basis in §§ 372 and 373 of the Restatement.

by the vendee to compel a delivery of the title. The vendor has not a complete remedy at law. Pecuniary damages for the breach of the contract is not what the complainant asks, or is entitled to receive at the hands of a court of equity. He asks to receive the price stipulated to be paid in lieu of the land. The doctrine is well established that the remedy is mutual, and that the vendor may maintain his bill in all cases where the purchaser could sue for a specific performance of the agreement.

No other rationale has been offered by our decisions subsequent to *Hopper*, and specific performance has been routinely granted to vendors without further discussion of the underlying jurisdictional issue.

Our present Supreme Court has squarely held, however, that mutuality of remedy is not an appropriate basis for granting or denying specific performance. Fleischer v. James Drug Stores, 62 A.2d 383 (N.J. 1948). The test is whether the obligations of the contract are mutual and not whether each is entitled to precisely the same remedy in the event of a breach. In *Fleischer* plaintiff sought specific performance against a cooperative buying and selling association although his membership contract was terminable by him on 60 days' notice. Justice Heher said:

And the requisite mutuality is not wanting. The contention contra rests upon the premise that, although the corporation can terminate the contract only in certain restricted and unusual circumstances, any member may withdraw at any time by merely giving notice.

Clearly, there is mutuality of obligation, for until his withdrawal complainant is under a continuing obligation of performance in the event of performance by the corporation. It is not essential that the remedy of specific performance be mutual. The modern view is that the rule of mutuality of remedy is satisfied if the decree of specific performance operates effectively against both parties and gives to each the benefit of a mutual obligation.

The fact that the remedy of specific enforcement is available to one party to a contract is not in itself a sufficient reason for making the remedy available to the other; but it may be decisive when the adequacy of damages is difficult to determine and there is no other reason for refusing specific enforcement. Restatement, Contracts (1932), sections 372, 373. It is not necessary, to serve the ends of equal justice, that the parties shall have identical remedies in case of breach.

62 A.2d at 388.

The disappearance of the mutuality of remedy doctrine from our law dictates the conclusion that specific performance relief should no longer be automatically available to a vendor of real estate, but should be confined to those special instances where a vendor will otherwise suffer an economic injury for which his damage remedy at law will not be adequate, or where other equitable considerations require that the relief be granted. As Chancellor Vroom noted in King v. Morford, 1 N.J.Eq. 274, 281-282 (Ch.Div.1831), whether a contract should be specifically enforced is always a matter resting in the sound discretion of the court and considerable caution should be used in decreeing the specific performance of agreements, and the court is bound to see that it really does the complete justice which it aims at, and which is the ground of its jurisdiction.

Here the subject matter of the real estate transaction — a condominium apartment unit — has no unique quality but is one of hundreds of virtually identical units being offered by a developer for sale to the public. The units are sold by means of sample, in this case model apartments, in much the same manner as items of personal property are sold in the market place. The sales prices for the units are fixed in accordance with a schedule filed by Centex as part of its offering plan, and the only variance as between apartments having the same floor plan (of which six plans are available) is the floor level or the bulding location within the project. In actuality, the condominium apartment units, regardless of their realty label, share the same characteristics as personal property.

From the foregoing one must conclude that the damages sustained by a condominium sponsor resulting from the breach of the sales agreement are readily measurable and the damage remedy at law is wholly adequate. No compelling reasons have been shown by Centex for the granting of specific performance relief and its complaint is therefore dismissed as to the first count.

Centex also seeks money damages pursuant to a liquidated damage clause in its contract with the defendants. It is sufficient to note only that under the language of that clause (which was authored by Centex) liquidated damages are limited to such moneys as were paid by defendant at the time the default occurred. Since the default here consisted of the defendant's stopping payment of his check for the balance of the down-payment, Centex's liquidated damages are limited to the retention of the moneys paid prior to that date, or the initial $525 deposit. Accordingly, the second count of the complaint for damage relief will also be dismissed.

NOTES AND QUESTIONS

1. **Specific performance: buyer.** The buyer's right to specific performance follows from the property view that each parcel of land is unique; damages are inadequate to protect the buyer's expectancy interest because no comparable parcels are available for the buyer to purchase with the damages award. Does the principal case suggest that at least in some cases, the buyer might not be able to get specific performance? Other courts have found condominiums sufficiently unique and have awarded specific performance to a buyer. *See, e.g.*, Schwinder v. Austin Bank of Chicago, 809 N.E.2d 180 (Ill. App. 2004).

2. **Specific performance: seller.** The seller's expectancy is different: seller expects to get a certain price for the property. If the buyer breaches, that price can be obtained by resale of the property and recovery of damages from the buyer for any shortfall in the resale price. According to the court in the principal case, the seller's right to specific performance rests not on the inadequacy of the seller's damages remedy, but rather on the idea that remedies must be mutual; since the buyer is entitled to specific performance, the seller must also be entitled to it. A better reason for awarding specific performance to a seller is the illiquidity of real estate and the difficulty of proving its value. *See* Stoebuck & Whitman § 10.5, at 739. Courts routinely award specific performance to sellers.

3. **Mutuality of obligation and of remedy.** Mutuality of obligation is a requirement in contracts, but it means no more than that each party must give consideration for the contract to be binding. As the principal case notes, there is no requirement that each party must have identical or comparable remedies.

C. THE CLOSING

At the closing, the seller will deliver a deed to the buyer (Section C.1). Usually the delivery of the deed is not to the buyer directly, but rather to an escrow agent who will hold the deed pending payment of the purchase price and satisfaction of other conditions of closing (Section C.2). Under the doctrine of merger (Section C.3), the closing marks the start of a new set of legal relations between buyer and seller, determined by the terms of the deed rather than by the contract of sale.

The closing marks the point at which the parties become grantor and grantee. The seller tenders a deed conveying an estate to the buyer, who tenders payment of the purchase price. If the purchase is being financed by a loan, the buyer will execute the promissory note and mortgage in favor of the lender at this point.

1. Delivery of a Deed

A deed is effective to transfer legal title to the grantee only when it is signed and delivered, although a few states retain the requirement of a seal (usually just the word "seal" or another notation printed at the bottom of the deed). Acceptance is also required, but is rarely an issue. The following case will shed some light on the delivery requirement.

SALTER v. HAMITER
887 So. 2d 230 (Ala. 2004)

LYONS, JUSTICE.

Frank T. Salter appeals from the trial court's April 25, 2003, judgment declaring void three warranty deeds from Mary Ellen Knowles to Salter. We reverse the trial court's judgment and render a judgment for Salter.

I. Facts and Procedural History

The evidence in the record reveals the following facts. Frank T. Salter first met Mary Ellen Knowles in the early 1960s; the two became business associates and good friends. They engaged in many business ventures together in which Knowles acted as the bookkeeper. In October 1966, Knowles gave Salter power of attorney over all of her assets. On March 13, 1967, Knowles executed a will leaving everything she owned to Salter. At some point after she had executed the will, Knowles deeded all of the real property she owned in Choctaw County, Escambia County, Dale County, Conecuh County, and Covington County to Salter. The only deeds that are of issue in this case cover the real property located in Conecuh County and Covington County, totaling approximately 1,000 acres.

In an attempt to effectuate the transfer of the three parcels of property located in Conecuh County and Covington County, Knowles executed three deeds in November 1967. After executing the deeds, Knowles presented them to her attorney and told him that it was her desire to transfer title of the described properties to Salter, and she wanted to know if the deeds "looked alright." According to her attorney, Knowles, not wanting any trouble with her family, also asked her attorney what would happen if the deeds were not recorded until after her death. Knowles's attorney told her that the deeds "looked fine." Her attorney testified that he explained to Knowles the consequences of not recording the deeds and further explained that "delivery" of the deeds to the grantee was an essential element for the conveyance of real property.

A couple of months after Knowles met with her attorney to discuss the deeds, she was admitted to the hospital to undergo some tests. While at the hospital, she telephoned her attorney and asked him to come to the hospital to witness her delivery of the deeds to Salter and to make sure that the delivery of the deeds was a "good delivery." When Salter and Knowles's attorney arrived at the hospital, Knowles retrieved the deeds from her purse and handed them to Salter. Once Salter had the deeds in his hand, Knowles's attorney advised her that what had just transpired was "a sufficient delivery of the deeds." Knowles requested at this time that Salter not record the deeds until after her death. Salter retained physical possession of the deeds. After the delivery of the deeds, Salter managed the timber property on the lands conveyed to him by the deeds, possessed keys to all of the gates located on the properties, and hunted on the properties. The properties remained in Knowles's name for purposes of ad valorem tax assessments; however, the invoices for those taxes were mailed to one of two businesses operated jointly by Salter and Knowles — Salter Truck and Tractor and Salter and Knowles's Brooklyn farming operation — and many of the invoices were paid from one of the joint business bank accounts maintained by Salter and Knowles. There is also evidence indicating that, following the delivery of the deeds to Salter, Knowles sold timber off and leased mineral rights to the properties described in the deeds; she also sold parcels of land included in the properties described in the deeds. Nevertheless, several of the purchasers testified that Salter knew of and consented to those transactions and even stated that Knowles would not make a decision concerning a sale without Salter's consent.

In September 1985, Knowles executed another will; the will contained no reference to the real property located in Conecuh County and Covington County. During the consultation with her attorney in preparation for drafting this will, Knowles told her attorney that she had already deeded most of her property to Salter and that she was aware that she did not have title to any of the real property she had previously conveyed to Salter.

All three deeds remained in the exclusive possession and control of Salter until Salter recorded them several days after Knowles's death on May 28, 2000.

In October 2000, the representatives of Knowles's estate, Harold Hamiter and Gillis Ralls ("the Hamiter appellees"), filed the present action seeking to have the three deeds declared void because, they argued, (1) the deeds were not properly delivered, (2) the deeds violated the statute of wills, and (3) Salter was barred by the doctrine of laches because he had failed to assert his claim to ownership within 20 years of the date of the execution of the three deeds. The complaint was subsequently amended to assert additional claims based upon the rule of repose and the Statute of Frauds. After conducting a bench trial, the trial court on April 25, 2003, declared all three deeds void. The trial court specifically found (1) that the three deeds "were intended to be the equivalent of a will" and that, "as a will, none of the three deeds [met] the requirements of the statute of wills"; (2) that "there was no intent by Knowles to vest title, ownership and control of her lands in Salter at the time of the purported delivery of the deeds at issue"; and (3) that "Salter's lack of action until after the death of Knowles [indicated] lack of present acceptance of the delivery." Salter appeals.

III. Analysis

A. Deeds or Will

Salter first argues that the trial court erred by finding that Knowles intended the three deeds to be a will. Salter points out that Knowles knew the difference between a deed and a will as evidenced by the many deeds she had executed before she executed the deeds at issue here and by the three wills she had executed. Because Knowles knew the difference between the two types of documents, Salter argues, Knowles intended the documents here to be deeds as evidenced by the fact that she consulted with her attorney on how to transfer a valid present interest in the properties to Salter and by the fact that, after the deeds were delivered, she executed another will, in which she made no provision for the real property located in either Conecuh County or Covington County. Salter further argues that because deeds are irrevocable documents and wills cannot be irrevocable, it was Knowles's intent that the three documents be deeds.

The Hamiter appellees respond by arguing that Knowles did not intend the documents to be deeds, which would convey a present interest in the properties to Salter, as evidenced by the fact that Knowles remained in possession and control of the properties located in Conecuh County and Covington County for 33 years following the alleged delivery of the documents. The Hamiter appellees point out that, between the time of the alleged delivery of the documents and her death, Knowles built a new house on one of the properties and resided there, mortgaged a portion of the properties, sold timber from the properties, leased mineral rights to the properties, executed a hunting lease on the properties, and sold portions of the properties to third parties. The Hamiter appellees contend that Knowles's conduct indicated that she did not intend to convey a present, irrevocable interest in the properties to Salter, but instead intended the documents to be a will. The Hamiter appellees point out that the trial court, when addressing this issue in its judgment, used language identical to the language in Randolph v. Randolph, 18 So.2d 555 (Ala. 1944), a case in which the court found a deed to be the equivalent of a will. The Hamiter appellees further argue that, because the purported will did not meet the requirements of the statute of wills, title to the properties located in Conecuh County and Covington County vested in Knowles's devisees immediately upon her death.

As this Court stated in Henderson v. Henderson, 97 So. 353 (Ala. 1923):

> In determining whether an instrument be a deed or a will, the controlling question is:
>
>> Did the [grantor] intend any estate or interest whatever to vest before his death, and by the execution of the paper? Or did he intend that all the interest and estate should take effect only after his death? If the former, it is a deed; if the latter, a will; and it is immaterial whether he calls it a will or a deed; the instrument will have operation according to its legal effect.

97 So. at 372. The grantor's intent must, if possible, be gathered from the language in the instrument.

The three documents themselves evidence that Knowles intended the documents to be deeds. Each of the three documents states that Knowles "do[es] grant, bargain, sell, and convey" the properties described therein to Salter in exchange for $10. The use of the present tense in this statement evidences Knowles's intention to convey title to the properties immediately rather than upon her death. The documents do not contain any words of revocation or condition. The Hamiter appellees even concede in their brief to this Court that the documents are unconditional on their face. Thus, there is no indication from the face of the documents that Knowles did not intend for Salter to enjoy the incidents of ownership of the properties as he did before her death. Because we can discern the grantor's intent from the documents, there is no need to consider parol evidence. See Sipple v. Ogden, 628 So.2d 569, 571 (Ala. 1993) ("In examining the four corners of the conveyance, it is clear to the Court that the instrument is unambiguous and, therefore, the Court is not required to resort to arbitrary rules of construction nor to receive extrinsic evidence in order to ascertain the intention of the parties, especially that of the grantor."). Evidence as to Knowles's continued transactions with third parties with respect to the properties is not relevant to determinating that these documents are deeds and thus not subject to the statute of wills.

Furthermore, the Hamiter appellees' reliance on Randolph v. Randolph, *supra*, is misplaced. In *Randolph*, this Court held that a request for the cancellation of a deed was due to be granted because the grantor had been induced by fraud to convey the property. 18 So.2d at 560. Such fraud negated the grantor's intent to convey a present interest in the property. Unlike *Randolph*, no fraud claim is presented in the case before us.

The trial court erred to the extent it based its finding that the documents were invalid on noncompliance with the statute of wills.

B. Delivery and Acceptance of the Deeds

Salter next argues that the trial court erred in its conclusion that the deeds were neither validly delivered to him nor accepted by him. Salter quotes the undisputed testimony of Knowles's attorney in which he detailed all of the events that transpired before the delivery of the deeds, during the delivery of the deeds at the hospital, and after the delivery of the deeds. Most notably, Knowles's attorney explained that Knowles physically delivered the deeds to Salter, that she desired to effectuate an absolute transfer of title to Salter, and that she placed no conditions upon the conveyance. Salter points out that the trial court acknowledged the delivery of the deeds when it stated in its order that "the deeds were given to Salter [by Knowles] at the Evergreen hospital where Mrs. Knowles was having tests" performed. Salter argues that the trial court, having made this finding, erred by applying case law dealing with the delivery of a deed by a grantor to a third party, instead of case law addressing the delivery of a deed from a grantor to a grantee.

[To be effective, a] deed must be delivered to the grantee. Delivery "may be actual, by a transfer of the conveyance from the manual possession of the grantor, to the manual possession of the grantee, though not a word is spoken; or it may be by saying something and doing nothing." Gulf Red Cedar Co. v. Crenshaw, 53 So. 812, 813 (Ala. 1910). Nevertheless, to meet the delivery requirement, it must be clear from the evidence that the grantor intended to divest himself or herself of title to the property and that the grantor relinquished control and dominion over the property. The intention of the grantor is "of paramount importance" in determining whether a deed has been delivered and is to be ascertained from all the circumstances surrounding the delivery. Boohaker v. Brashier, 428 So.2d 627, 629 (Ala.1983). Furthermore, when "a deed is found in the possession of a grantee, the presumption arises that it was duly delivered to him." Williams v. Higgins, 69 Ala. 517, 522 (1881). The burden is on the complainant to rebut this presumption.

The evidence without dispute indicates Knowles's intention to deliver the deeds to Salter during her hospitalization. Most convincing of her intention, as the trial court noted in its order, is the undisputed evidence that Knowles physically delivered the deeds to Salter and that minutes before doing so, Knowles told her attorney, "I want to deliver these deeds to Mr. Salter." Knowles was adamant that this delivery be valid as evidenced by her insistence that her attorney orchestrate and witness the delivery and her consultations with her attorney concerning the steps that needed to be taken in order to vest title to the properties in Salter. Knowles, an astute businesswoman, knew the operative legal effect of delivering a deed as evidenced by her past conveyances of title in other properties to Salter and to third parties. It is apparent through the undisputed evidence of her actions and words on the occasion of her hospitalization that Knowles made a deliberate decision to transfer to Salter her title to the properties located in Conecuh County and Covington County.

In order for a deed purporting to convey title to real property to be effective for that purpose, it not only must be delivered or tendered to the grantee or the grantee's representative, but also must be accepted by or on behalf of the grantee. "When a deed is for the benefit of the grantee, imposing on him no burdens or duties, the presumption is of his acceptance." Fitzpatrick v. Brigman, 30 So. 500, 502 (Ala. 1900). In the present case, the deeds did not impose any burdens or duties upon Salter, and there is, therefore, a presumption of Salter's acceptance.

While the Hamiter appellees rely upon Salter's failure to record the deeds until after Knowles's death to overcome the presumption of his acceptance, Salter argues that he was not obligated to record the deeds, as the trial court suggested in its order when it stated that Salter's "lack of action" indicated his lack of acceptance.

The fact that Salter did not record the deeds until after Knowles's death does not defeat the undisputed evidence of his acceptance of the deeds. It is a familiar rule of law in Alabama that "the validity of a deed, as between the grantor and grantee therein, is not dependent upon its timely recordation." Murphree v. Smith, 277 So.2d 327, 329 (Ala. 1973). The recording statute, § 35-4-90, Ala.Code 1975, does not render void an unrecorded deed except for the benefit of those particular classes of persons named in the statute.[1] The recording statute does not include one's heirs within the class of persons the statute is designed to protect. As Salter testified, he was merely following Knowles's wishes by not recording the deeds until after her death; there is nothing to the contrary in the record to indicate that Knowles's request amounted to a condition of the conveyance.

The presumption that Salter accepted the deeds is corroborated by the fact that he took physical possession of the deeds upon delivery and by the fact that he executed a codicil to his will after the deeds were delivered to him, in which he declared that in the event he predeceased Knowles he devised to her "all real property which ha[d] heretofore been conveyed to [him] by the said Mary Ellen Knowles."

The Hamiter appellees contend that Knowles's continued possession and control of the properties for 33 years *after* the alleged delivery of the deeds was hostile to Salter's claim. The facts that Knowles remained in possession of the properties, that she possibly paid taxes on the property occasionally, and that she sold several parcels that were included within the properties described in the deeds after she had delivered the deeds to Salter does not affect the validity of the original delivery of the deeds and the contemporaneous transfer of title to Salter. Knowles's subsequent conduct is relevant only as to the issue whether the rule of repose barred Salter's claim to the properties.

The trial court erred in its finding that the deeds were neither validly delivered by Knowles nor accepted by Salter. The factual determinations on which the trial court based that finding were inconsistent with the undisputed testimony concerning the delivery and acceptance of the deeds and are therefore not binding on this Court.

[The court then discussed and rejected the Hamiter appellees' defenses of rule of repose and doctrine of laches. The rule of repose is an Alabama doctrine that is "similar to, but broader than" adverse possession.]

IV. Conclusion

Knowles properly conveyed the properties located in Conecuh County and Covington County to Salter by three separate deeds. We hold that the trial court's findings of fact were clearly erroneous and that the trial court improperly applied

---

[1] Section 35-4-90, Ala.Code 1975, states:

(a) All conveyances of real property, deeds, mortgages, deeds of trust or instruments in the nature of mortgages to secure any debts are inoperative and void as to purchasers for a valuable consideration, mortgagees and judgment creditors without notice, unless the same have been recorded before the accrual of the right of such purchasers, mortgagees or judgment creditors.

the law to undisputed facts. We, therefore, reverse the trial court's judgment declaring void the three warranty deeds conveying such properties, and we render a declaratory judgment recognizing Salter's title.

REVERSED AND JUDGMENT RENDERED.

NOTES AND QUESTIONS

1. **Effect of an undelivered deed.** The effect of nondelivery of a deed is that the deed is void — totally ineffective to convey title to the grantee. A forged deed is also void.

2. **The delivery requirement.** What is required for a deed to be delivered? Why does the court find a valid delivery in the principal case? What is the effect of Knowles's possession of the property after she handed Salter the deed in the hospital? It is possible for a deed to be handed over to a grantee but not be "delivered" because of a lack of intent. For example, if a deed is given to a grantee for the grantee to inspect it or for the grantee to take it to an escrow agent, the deed is not effective to transfer title. *See, e.g.,* Martinez v. Martinez, 678 P.2d 1163 (N.M. 1984). Furthermore, physical transfer of the deed to the grantee is not always necessary if the deed is intended to be operative as a present conveyance. *See* Stoebuck & Whitman § 11.3, at 828.

3. **Conditional delivery to the grantee.** If a grantor delivers a deed to the grantee but imposes an oral condition on its effectiveness, most courts hold that the condition is ineffective and the deed passes title to the grantee. *See* Stoebuck & Whitman § 11.3, at 830. In some cases (particularly where the condition is the grantor's death), courts may find the deed ineffective to pass title, and in a few cases courts will enforce the condition. *Id.* at 830-31.

4. **Conditional delivery to an escrow agent.** Although a grantor cannot make a conditional delivery to the grantee, grantors can and very frequently do deliver a deed on condition to an escrow agent.

2.   Escrow

Most sales of real estate are not accomplished by a delivery of the deed directly from seller to purchaser and of the purchase price directly from purchaser to seller. Generally, the seller delivers the deed to an escrow agent on the condition that the purchaser pay the purchase price and possibly on other conditions.

FERGUSON v. CASPAR
359 A.2d 17 (D.C. 1976)

REILLY, CHIEF JUDGE.

One of the most formal transactions known to the law is the transfer of title to real estate. In order to insure finality to such transactions, the practice in this jurisdiction is for the contracting parties, including the lienors and lienees, after they are satisfied with the report on title search, to meet with one another in the office of a title company, agree on the apportionment of outstanding taxes and other charges, and execute and deliver the conveyances (deeds) necessary to close the transaction. Such a meeting, popularly called a "closing" or a "settlement," precedes the transmission by the title company of the conveyancing instruments to the Recorder of Deeds for permanent entry into the official land records.

Although hundreds of such settlements occur every year in the District of Columbia, it is seldom indeed that the parties conduct themselves in such a way as to taint the finality of the "closing." The case before us stems from one of these uncommon situations and raises the question as to what point in a settlement proceeding finality attaches.

Appellee Mrs. Ida Caspar was the owner of an unrestored row house in the Capitol Hill area. On November 18, 1972, she entered into a contract for the sale of the premises to the appellants for the sum of $23,000.00 payment of the purchase price to be made in cash at the time of settlement. Settlement was to be made at the office of the Lawyers Title Insurance Corporation on or before February 1, 1973. The contract of sale included a provision that the seller would convey the premises free of all notices of municipal violations existing at the date of the contract, such provision to survive the delivery of the deed. On October 13, 1972, Mrs. Caspar had been personally served with a deficiency notice by a District of Columbia housing inspector informing her that there existed 126 Housing Code violations upon the premises and calling for their correction within 60 days. Subsequently, Mrs. Caspar, upon her written request, obtained an extension of time for compliance to January 25, 1973.

Early in January, 1973, the appellants became aware of the existence of the Housing Code violations but did not bring this matter to the attention of the seller. Instead, they obtained an estimate of $6,125.00 from a housing contractor as the cost of correcting the deficiencies. The notice of violations was still outstanding at the time of settlement.

By agreement, the parties met at the office of the Lawyers Title Insurance Corporation for settlement on the afternoon of February 1, 1973. Mrs. Caspar was attended by her son and daughter who assisted their mother in business matters. The appellants were present with their attorney. The settlement officer, an employee of the title company, prepared settlement statements for the respective parties which each of them signed. In addition, the parties signed the requisite District of Columbia tax recordation forms. Mrs. Caspar executed and delivered her deed to the property to the settlement officer. The purchasers delivered to the settlement officer the personal check of Mr. Ferguson in the sum of $12,924.42 payable to the order of the title company, representing the balance due as set forth in the settlement statement.

After the documents had been delivered to the settlement officer and as the parties were rising to leave, the attorney for the appellants handed separate letters to the settlement officer and to Mrs. Caspar's son. The letter addressed to the title company, after referring to the clause in the contract of sale requiring Mrs. Caspar to convey the premises free of any municipal violation notices, advised the title company that as of January 26, 1973, the outstanding Housing Code violations had not been corrected and that the purchasers had obtained an estimate in the amount of $6,125.00 to bring the premises into compliance. The letter concluded by stating:

This is to put you on notice that purchasers are paying $6,125.00 of the purchase price to you as escrow agent to hold until seller has complied with the outstanding violation notices on this property. Written notice signed by the purchaser shall be sufficient to discharge you from any further obligations with respect to this sum.

The letter directed to Mrs. Caspar informed her of the existence of the notice of the Housing Code violations and her obligation under the agreement to comply with the notice. It went on to state that the Fergusons had obtained an estimate of approximately $6,125.00 as the cost of repairing the premises and concluded as follows:

This is to advise you that Fergusons intend to enforce the requirement that these violations be corrected. Accordingly, I have written Lawyers Title requesting that they withhold the above amount from the purchase price in an escrow account until you and the Fergusons have reached a final understanding as to the cost of making these corrections.

Upon receiving the letter directed to the title company, the settlement officer advised the parties that the company could not record the deed or withhold any funds without formal authority to hold any funds in escrow. He informed the parties that he could not proceed with the settlement since the contract of sale provided for payment in cash and there was no provision for withholding any funds in escrow. Mrs. Caspar's son suggested that the parties complete the settlement, have the deed recorded, and thereafter "work out or litigate" the question of the Housing Code violations. The attorney for the appellants recommended that Mrs. Caspar seek the advice of an attorney. The parties then dispersed without the matter being resolved.

On February 13, 1973, not having received any further word or instructions from the parties, the settlement officer wrote to the Fergusons, returning the personal check which had been presented at the settlement and informing them that the deed could not be recorded in view of their attorney's letter directing the title company to withhold certain monies in escrow. Two days later, the Fergusons' attorney replied, returning the personal check to the settlement officer and insisting that the deed be recorded. This letter was received by the title company on February 16 and on the same day, the deed executed by Mrs. Caspar was returned to her son. on February 17, Mrs. Caspar signed a contract of sale for the premises to the appellees, John and Mary McAteer, and her deed to them was executed and recorded on February 23.

On February 21, 1973, appellants filed a complaint against Mrs. Caspar seeking a declaratory judgment and specific performance of the contract of sale entered into between the parties. Subsequently, the complaint was amended to include the McAteers as parties-defendant. In her answer to the amended complaint, Mrs. Caspar alleged inter alia that the appellants had breached the contract of sale and were not entitled to specific performance. The case was tried before the court without a jury. At the close of all the evidence, the court granted appellees' motion to dismiss the complaint on the ground that the plaintiffs, by imposing conditions on their tender of payment of the purchase price, had failed to make an unconditional tender of full performance of the contract on their part and had forfeited their right to specific performance. On June 15, 1973, the trial court entered its Judgment and Order of Dismissal setting forth its Findings of Fact and Conclusions of Law.

On this appeal, appellants' principal contentions are that legal title to the property in question passed to them upon the settlement between the seller and purchasers and that the trial court erred in concluding that the appellants were not entitled to specific performance of the contract of sale by reason of their failure to tender the full purchase price for the property as required by the contract. We agree with the determination of the trial court and affirm.

The initial contention of appellants is based upon the erroneous conclusion that legal title to the property in question passed to them when the settlement statements were signed by the respective parties, the seller's deed delivered to the settlement officer, and the personal check of the purchasers for the balance due delivered to the settlement officer. In this conclusion, appellants misconstrue the nature and effect of the settlement proceedings engaged in between the various parties at the meeting. In their briefs on appeal, the appellants and appellees both infer that under the circumstances of this case the title company's position in the transaction was that of an escrow agent. Our study of the contract of sale and the proceedings which ensued at the settlement meeting confirms our understanding that, as is the usual and customary practice in real estate transactions in the District of Columbia where the parties employ a third party to accept their respective tenders of performance under the contract, a valid escrow arrangement is created and the title company serves in the capacity of an escrow agent in the transaction.

Generally, an escrow agreement is created in a formal contract between the parties, setting forth the conditions and contingencies under which the instruments deposited in escrow are to be delivered and to take effect. However, no precise form of words is necessary to create an escrow but it must appear from all the facts and circumstances surrounding the execution and delivery of the instruments that they were not to take effect until certain conditions are performed.

A valid escrow agreement is a triangular arrangement. First there must be a contract between the seller and the buyer agreeing to the conditions of a deposit, then there must be delivery of the items on deposit to the escrow agent, and he must agree to perform the function of receiving and dispersing the items. The agreement by the seller and buyer to all the terms of the escrow instructions and the acceptance by the escrow agent of the position of depository create the escrow.

In the case at bar, the seller and the purchasers agreed to make full settlement in accordance with the terms of the contract of sale at the office of Lawyers Title Insurance Corporation, the title company searching the title, and that "deposit with the Title Company of the purchase money, the deed of conveyance for execution and such other papers as are required of either party by the terms of this contract shall be considered good and sufficient tender of performance of the terms hereof." Significantly, the deed executed by the seller was delivered to the settlement officer. The purchasers' personal check, which included the balance of the purchase price, was made payable to the title company and delivered to the settlement officer. The deed was deposited with the settlement officer as an escrow agent with the implied understanding that delivery to the purchasers was not to be effected until the purchasers had complied with their obligation under the contract of sale to pay the amount due the seller as purchase money. On the other hand, the settlement officer was not free to disburse any of the funds deposited by the purchasers until the title company was assured that the seller's deed conveyed title "good of record and in fact." Thus, the settlement meeting was only the initial step in the transaction and until all the conditions of the contract had been fulfilled, the settlement was not complete.[9] Where a deed is deposited as an escrow, title does not pass to the grantee unless and until the condition of its delivery is performed. Although the purchasers tendered their personal check for the balance due from them at the settlement in ostensible payment of the purchase price, their subsequent direction to the title company to withhold from the seller a substantial portion of the purchase money to which she was entitled created a deviation from the condition upon which delivery of the deed to them could be effected. The settlement officer informed the purchasers that the settlement could not be completed and the deed could not be recorded. Since the condition precedent to the delivery of the deed had not been fulfilled, legal title to the property did not pass to the purchasers.

Appellants point to the fact that settlement statements were signed by the respective parties as indicative that settlement between the parties had been completed. Each of these statements was a separate and distinct document, one being the seller's statement establishing the "AMOUNT TO BE PAID SELLER" and the other, the purchasers' statement indicating the "BALANCE REQUIRED TO COMPLETE SETTLEMENT." The seller's statement contained an itemization of charges to be borne by the seller, including a charge for the apportionment of unpaid taxes, the brokerage fee to be paid to the real estate broker, disbursements to be paid to the broker for the costs of evicting the tenants, one-half of the recordation tax, and a charge of $50 to be held for water charges. These charges and anticipated disbursements were applied against the purchase price of the property and a balance struck, establishing the net amount which would be paid to the seller by the title company as the proceeds of the sale after the disbursements had been made and the settlement completed. The seller's signature on the statement noted her approval and acceptance of the statement as correct.

The purchasers' statement itemized the credits to their account, consisting of a credit for apportionment of unpaid taxes, the amount deposited with the broker as earnest money, and a credit to the purchasers of the sum to be received by the title company as the proceeds of the refinancing of other property owned by the purchasers. Against these credits, the purchasers were charged with the purchase price of the property and miscellaneous closing costs to be paid by them, including examination of title, title insurance, settlement fee, conveyancing fees, recording fees, and their share of the recordation tax. Offsetting the credits against the charges established a balance to be paid by the purchasers to the title company at settlement.

---

[9] The customary practice in settlements of this nature is for the title company to deposit the purchaser's check to assure that the check is honored. After the check clears and before recording the deed, the title company brings the title down to date by making a continuation title search from the date of its initial search to the date of recordation of the deed to assure that no liens or encumbrances have been filed against the property in the interim.

We do not attribute to these documents the significance which appellants attach to them. In effect, the seller's statement merely indicated what the seller would receive as the net proceeds of the sale after the settlement had been fully completed. The purchasers' statement was a statement of account of what remained to be paid by the purchasers to the title company, including the closing costs to be paid to the title company, after crediting the purchasers for the earnest money paid to the real estate broker and the sum anticipated to be received from the refinancing settlement. The incidental charges set forth on each statement were the concern solely of the party charged. Neither party bound himself to the settlement statement of the other. Neither statement constituted an acknowledgment that either the seller or the title company had received the purchase money which the purchasers were obligated to pay. The individual settlement statements were in effect an account stated separately between the title company and the seller and between the title company and the purchasers. Thus we reject the contention that the signing of the individual settlement statements by each of the parties signified that the transaction had been completed.

The appellants, contending that the settlement proceeding was completed, argue further that when the legal title to the premises passed to them the title to the purchase money vested in the seller and the subsequent demand by the purchasers that the title company withhold a portion of the seller's money was a "legal nullity" and "obviously unenforceable." In an escrow arrangement, the escrow holder is the dual agent of both parties until the performance of the conditions of the escrow agreement, whereupon he becomes the agent of each of the parties to the transaction in respect to those things placed in escrow to which each party has thus become entitled. Thus, when the conditions specified in the escrow agreement have been fully performed, the title to the premises passes to the purchaser and title to the purchase money passes to the seller. Thereupon, the escrow holder becomes the agent of the purchaser as to the deed and of the seller as to the money. However, as we have pointed out supra, the settlement was not completed and since the conditions upon which the seller's deed was to be delivered to the purchasers had not been performed, legal title to the property did not pass to the purchasers and title to the purchase money deposited with the settlement officer did not vest in the seller.

Furthermore, we find it difficult to comprehend appellants' present contention that their written demand upon the title company was a "legal nullity" in view of their contrary position at the settlement meeting. Upon receipt of the written demand from appellants' attorney, the settlement officer notified the parties that under the circumstances he could not proceed with the settlement. At the same time, Mrs. Caspar's son suggested that the appellants permit the settlement to proceed and that thereafter the parties "work out" the question of the Housing Code violations. Nevertheless, the appellants persisted in their demand that a portion of the purchase money be retained in escrow by the title company. The impasse was not resolved and the meeting broke up. By making the demand upon the title company, appellants placed the company in the difficult position of having to determine the rights of the respective parties. If the company honored appellants' demand, the seller could complain that the company had breached its duty to her. If the company refused to comply with the demand, the appellants would charge the title company with having disbursed the purchase money contrary to their express direction. In either event, the title company would have risked being subject to legal action by the party aggrieved. After waiting a reasonable period for the parties to adjust their differences and not having received any further word from either of them, the title company terminated its escrow agency and returned the escrow instruments to the respective parties. This turn of events was brought about by appellants' actions in serving the demand upon the title company and in persisting in their position. They cannot escape the consequences of their action by now claiming that their demand was a "nullity."

There is no dispute that a substantial number of violations of Housing Code regulations were duly noted against the premises and were in existance at the time the contract of sale was executed. Nor is there any dispute that Mrs. Caspar, as record owner of the property, was officially notified of the violations. Prior to the time for settlement, none of these violations had been corrected. Under these circumstances, the purchasers could have refused to consummate settlement and then have brought an action at law against the seller for such damages as they may have sustained. Alternatively, the purchasers could have elected to complete the settlement, and under the survival provisions of the contract, could have sued to recover from the seller such damages as they may have sustained by reason of her failure to correct the outstanding violations. The appellants here made no effort to rescind the contract but instead gave every indication of their intention to go forward with the transaction. Thus, despite the breach of the contract by the seller, the purchasers elected to proceed with the contract and obligated themselves to continue their performance of its terms.

To sustain the right to specific performance of their contract, the purchasers must show that they have performed or have offered to perform all of the obligations required of them by the contract.

It is the fundamental doctrine upon which the specific enforcement of contracts in equity depends, that either of the parties seeking to obtain the equitable remedy against the other must, as a condition precedent to the existence of his remedial right, show that he has done or offered to do, or is then ready and willing to do, all the essential and material acts required of him by the agreement at the time of commencing the suit, and also that he is ready and willing to do all such acts as shall be required of him in the specific execution of the contract according to its terms.

Thus, [in a case] where the purchaser under a contract for the sale of property instructed the escrow agent to hold the purchase money deposited with it until further notice and not to pay out any money to the seller, it was held that the purchaser had failed to perform his obligation under the contract to pay the purchase price to the seller and hence was not entitled to specific performance. And where an escrow contract required the purchaser to deposit a specific sum for the account of the vendor, a deposit of such sum with conditions that it could not and would not be paid to the seller did not constitute compliance with stance or a subsequently-formed decision the contract. Similarly, where the purchase money was paid into escrow by the purchaser with instructions not agreed to by the seller, and which instructions went beyond reasonable requirements for securing the concurrent exchange of the deed for the purchase price, it was held that there was not a sufficient tender of performance on the part of the purchaser. A tender of performance by the purchaser which contains conditions other than those specified in the contract between the parties is ineffectual, and a tender of payment by the purchaser is ineffective where the purchaser has made arbitrary deductions therefrom for unliquidated claims against the seller.

In the case at bar, the trial court concluded that the appellants "were not ready or willing to perform in accordance with the terms of the agreement" and that their "effort to impose conditions other than those specified in the contract resulted in a breach of their contractual duty, and a forfeiture of their right to specific performance of the contract." Appellants dispute this conclusion, pointing to the delivery of their personal check in the amount found to be due in accordance with the settlement sheet signed by them as proof that they were in fact ready and willing to perform their obligations under the contract. However, the evidence of record belies their contention. Appellants appeared at the settlement meeting armed with the letter demanding that a substantial portion of the purchase money be withheld from the seller. This was a preconceived plan by them to compel the seller to accept a lesser sum in payment for the property. The delivery of their check in ostensible payment of the amount due was a mere pretense since appellants never intended to have the seller receive the full amount due her upon settlement. The conclusion that appellants were not ready or willing to perform their obligation under the contract to pay the purchase price in cash is adequately supported by the record. By their own conduct, the appellants precluded their right to obtain specific performance of the contract.

Affirmed.

NOTES AND QUESTIONS

1. **The principal case.** What did the purchaser do wrong in the principal case? Wasn't the seller the party in breach because of the housing code violations? What would you have advised the purchaser to do at the closing?

2. **The careless or dishonest escrow agent.** What if the escrow agent delivers the deed to the purchaser before the required conditions are met, either mistakenly or in conspiracy with the grantee? As between the grantor and the grantee, the deed is not effective to transfer title. *See* Stoebuck & Whitman § 11.4, at 837. But if the grantee records the deed and transfers the property to a bona fide purchaser for value, courts are split. Some courts treat the deed as undelivered, which means title is still in the grantor. *See, e.g.,* Watts v. Archer, 107 N.W.2d 549 (Iowa 1961). Others hold for the bona fide purchaser on the basis that the grantor chose the escrow agent. *See* Stoebuck & Whitman § 11.4, at 837. Compare the policy behind U.C.C. § 2-403(2), the "entrusting" exception to the general rule that a party may not transfer a greater interest in personal property than the party owns, as set forth in Note 1 after O'Keeffe v. Snyder in Chapter 1, Section B.3.d.

What if the escrow agent steals the settlement funds? The party who bears the loss is the one who would have been entitled to the money. Thus, before conditions for closing are met, the buyer bears the loss, and after closing, the seller bears the loss. *See generally* Robert L. Flores, *A Comparison of the Rules and Rationales for Allocating Risks Arising in Realty Sales Using Executory Sale Contracts and Escrows*, 59 Mo. L. Rev. 307 (1994) (comparing loss of escrow funds with casualty losses of the property).

3.   The Merger Doctrine

SECOR v. KNIGHT
716 P.2d 790 (Utah 1986)

Durham, Justice.

Defendants Jesse and Michele Knight appeal from an order which enjoined the operation of a basement rental apartment in the Knights' home. Plaintiffs, who are residents of the subdivision, brought the action for injunction on the ground that defendants were violating a restrictive covenant limiting buildings in the subdivision to single-family dwellings. Plaintiffs alleged that defendants' lot was subject to that restriction. Defendants answered and filed third-party complaints against the developers of the subdivision, alleging fraud, and against the title company which handled the closing on the sale of the lot, alleging breach of fiduciary duty. The trial court entered judgment for plaintiffs, enjoining defendants from further operation of any apartment in their home. The court also ordered judgment in favor of the developers on the basis of no cause of action and dismissed with prejudice the complaint against the title company. We affirm.

In 1978, the Knights purchased a lot in the Manor Estates subdivision from the Petersons, the developers of the project. Before purchasing the lot, the Knights met with a sales agent for the subdivision, David Goates, and discussed their interest in purchasing a lot. In that discussion, the Knights specifically indicated their desire and intent to build a house with a basement apartment. Friends of the Knights, Mr. and Mrs. Erickson, were also present at that meeting and expressed the same interest. Both couples ultimately bought lots in the subdivision.

The evidence, which is conflicting, appears to indicate that at the meeting between the Knights, the Ericksons, and Mr. Goates on April 3, 1978, Mr. Goates stated that the developer wanted homes with 1,500 square feet and attached garages. Goates further stated that the developer had originally considered multiple units such as apartments and condominiums as a possible use in the subdivision, but that it had been decided that duplexes would not be allowed. The evidence also indicates, however, that the exact nature of the restrictions to be imposed was unclear and that Mr. Goates implied that there would be no problem with having a separate apartment in the basement. Further, he told the Knights and their friends that he was aware of situations in which people in other subdivisions had built basement apartments, despite restrictions prohibiting them, and that there were no problems because the neighbors took no action. At trial, Mr. Goates testified that he had specifically told defendants that if they built an apartment to be used for nonfamily members, defendants would do so at their own risk. The trial court ultimately determined that as a result of this conversation the Knights were on notice that duplexes would not be allowed, although the court also found that the statements made by the agent were misleading and were made in order to accomplish the sale.

At the conclusion of the meeting with Mr. Goates, the Knights decided to buy a lot and entered into an earnest money agreement on April 3, 1978. The earnest money agreement made no reference to restrictive covenants, although it did contain a statement which provided "that execution of the final contract shall abrogate this Earnest Money Receipt and Offer to Purchase."

At the time the earnest money agreement was signed, the area was zoned for multiple units, and neither the subdivision plat nor the restrictive covenants had been recorded. More than two months later, on June 10, 1978, the subdivision plat was recorded, and on June 20, 1978, the restrictive covenants were recorded whereby land use in Manor Estates was restricted to single-family dwellings. The Knights were not notified of these actions. On June 27, 1978, the Knights attended a closing at the offices of third-party defendant Guardian Title Company. There was no discussion regarding restrictive covenants at that time. Although there was some testimony that the Knights did not see or read the deed at the closing and that they did not receive a copy of the restrictive covenants, the trial court found, based on other testimony, that at the closing the Knights received a warranty deed which referred to "restrictions of record." The deed was recorded on July 5, 1978.

Subsequently, the Knights obtained financing and a building permit for a home. They later obtained a building permit for the basement apartment, apparently after the construction of the apartment. During this period, the Knights never inquired into the existence of any restrictions on the use of their land. The Knights began rental of the apartment in the summer of 1980. In October 1980, plaintiffs filed this suit asking for an injunction against further violation of the restrictive covenants by operation of the basement apartment.

The primary issue before this Court is whether, under the circumstances of this case, the restrictive covenant limiting use to a single-family dwelling is enforceable as to the Knights. For the reasons stated below, we hold that it is.

In their appeal, the Knights claim that based on the earnest money agreement they had acquired a vested equitable interest in the property and that any modification in that interest, i.e., the imposition of restrictive covenants, required their express consent. In opposing the Knights' claim, the Secors, plaintiffs below, and the Petersons, third-party defendants, assert the doctrine of merger, which this Court recognizes. They correctly state the general rule, which is that on delivery and acceptance of a deed the provisions of the underlying contract for the conveyance are deemed extinguished or superseded by the deed. 3 Corbin, Contracts § 604, at 627 (1960); Annot., 38 A.L.R.2d 1310, 1312-13 (1954); Annot., 84 A.L.R. 1008, 1009 (1933). The basis for imposing the doctrine of merger is "not due to any peculiar sanctity attaching to the deed itself, but because it is regarded as the final repository of the agreement which led to its execution." 84 A.L.R. at 1009.

> The defense of so severe a rule [merger] must rest on the ground that in conveyances of land, the parties habitually put their full agreement in the deed, at least with reference to title, and that if it is intended that the vendor shall be responsible for defective title, a warranty is inserted.

S. Williston, Contracts § 926, at 783 (3d ed.1961). There are, however, certain exceptions to this doctrine, including fraud, mistake, and the existence of collateral rights in the contract of sale. In cases relating to collateral terms, courts generally find that the execution and delivery of a deed is not the intended performance of those specific terms and that therefore the terms are not extinguished by acceptance of the deed. For example, in Stubbs v. Hemmert, 567 P.2d 168 (Utah. 1977), this Court found that the terms in the underlying contract relating to the removal of air compressors from a piece of property were collateral to the agreement to convey the property and were therefore not extinguished by the deed. In this regard, covenants relating to title and encumbrances are not considered to be collateral because they relate to the same subject matter as does the deed.

In arguing against the application of the merger doctrine in this case, the Knights claim that the intent of the parties must be examined. The Knights further assert that the evidence clearly indicates that merger would be inconsistent with their intent. While the latter assertion may be correct, the Knights misconstrue the significance of intent as it generally relates to merger. Although intent may be an issue where a specific term in the original contract of sale is omitted in the deed, the intent issue arises primarily in cases focusing on terms which involve a different subject matter or are collateral to the conveyance. In such cases the question of whether a specific term is or is not collateral, and hence whether the term will or will not merge into the deed, is determined by the intent of the parties. In Stubbs v. Hemmert, this Court explained the operation of the merger doctrine and the significance of the intent of the parties in cases involving the collateral terms exception:

> The doctrine of merger is applicable when the acts to be performed by the seller in a contract relate only to the delivery of title to the buyer. Execution and delivery of a deed by the seller then usually constitute full performance on his part, and acceptance of the deed by the buyer manifests his acceptance of that performance even though the estate conveyed may differ from that promised in the antecedent agreement. Therefore, in such a case, the deed is the final agreement and all prior terms, whether written or verbal, are extinguished and unenforceable.

> However, if the original contract calls for performance by the seller of some act collateral to conveyance of title, his obligations with respect thereto survive the deed and are not extinguished by it. Whether the terms of the contract are collateral, or are part of the obligation to convey and therefore unenforceable after delivery of the deed, depends to a great extent on the intent of the parties with respect thereto.

567 P.2d at 169. As this case involves terms relating to title, which are not collateral, the Knights' reliance on intent is misplaced.

The major justification for adherence to the merger doctrine is that upholding merger, in all but the exceptional cases involving fraud, mistake or collateral terms, preserves the integrity of the final document of conveyance and encourages the diligence of the parties. That diligence involves a duty on the part of both parties to make certain that their agreements have in fact been fully included in the final document. In this regard, the Knights may have been less than diligent in failing to protect their rights by reading their deed and inquiring about its provisions. Such lack of diligence on the part of the Knights had the effect of exposing them to the harsh result we reach today.

[The court concluded that the Knights had not proved the elements of a fraud claim.] In the absence of fraud, the merger doctrine applies, and we hold that the restrictive covenants are enforceable against the Knights.

In reaching this holding, however, we do not condone the manner in which this transaction was conducted by the developers/sellers, the Petersons, and their agent, Mr. Goates. On execution of the earnest money agreement, the parties entered into a binding contract, and pursuant to that contract both parties acquired rights and duties. On that basis, the developers should have notified the Knights on or prior to delivery of the deed [of the prohibition against duplexes]. The failure to so notify the Knights cannot change the result in this case because of the operation of the merger doctrine, an admittedly harsh rule of law, but in our view such action on the part of the developers would have prevented the dispute and would therefore have averted this litigation.

Furthermore, we believe it appropriate to censure the developers on other grounds as well, although the application of the merger doctrine in this case is likewise not affected by the following observations. [T]he [Knights'] lack of diligence does not negate the fact that both Mr. Peterson, a licensed real estate broker, and Mr. Goates, a licensed real estate sales agent, had a duty to conduct the sales transaction honestly and fairly. By obfuscating the nature of the restriction to be imposed, by unilaterally inserting the reference in the deed to restrictions of record which had only been recorded a few days before closing, and then by failing in any way to point out the modification inserted in the deed, the sellers' actions were seriously deficient in relation to the duty owed to the public in general and to the Knights in particular. In our view, the entire course of dealing in this transaction was substandard.

Notwithstanding the deficiencies in the sellers' course of dealing, the Knights failed to establish fraud in this case, and in the absence of fraud the merger doctrine applies. Therefore we affirm the judgment of no cause of action against the Petersons, and we uphold the injunction ordered by the trial court.

Finally, the Knights have appealed from the dismissal of the breach of fiduciary duty action against Guardian Title. The trial court found no fiduciary relationship existed between the Knights and Guardian, and our review of the record indicates ample evidentiary support for that finding. We therefore also affirm the dismissal of the action against Guardian Title Company.

NOTES AND QUESTIONS

1. **The parol evidence rule in contract law.** A partially integrated written contract can be supplemented by proof of prior or contemporaneous negotiations or agreements of the parties, but it cannot be contradicted by such proof. A fully integrated contract can neither be contradicted nor supplemented. The rationale is that the subsequent agreement supersedes the earlier negotiations or agreements. *See* E. Allan Farnsworth, Contracts § 7.2 (3d ed. 1999). Doctrinally, the prior

negotiations or agreements are said to "merge" into (be discharged by) the later written agreement.

2. **Merger.** Suppose that the seller promises in the contract of sale to deliver marketable title, and conveys the property by a quitclaim deed. If after closing a defect in the seller's title comes to light, is the buyer entitled to sue on the promise contained in the contract of sale? If not, does that result make sense? What is the relationship between the merger doctrine in sales of land and the parol evidence rule in contracts? *See* Paul Teich, *A Second Call for Abolition of the Rule of Merger by Deed*, 71 U. Det. Mercy L. Rev. 543 (1994) (excellent review and critique of the doctrine). The merger doctrine is said to be unpopular with modern courts. *See* Stoebuck & Whitman § 10.12, at 785. Can you surmise why?

In the principal case, the buyers argued against application of the merger doctrine. In some cases, it may be the seller who makes such an argument. *See* Weiss v. Old Republic Nat'l Title Ins. Co., 584 S.E.2d 710, 713 (Ga. Ct. App. 2003) (warranty deed superseded provision in sales agreement requiring that objection to marketable title be made within thirty days of date of agreement).

3. **Collateral agreements.** A collateral agreement between the contracting parties is not discharged by a subsequent writing, either in contract law generally or in sales of land. That exception provides the basis for the merger rule's undoing in cases involving sales of land, although courts apply the exception erratically. A fair generalization — perhaps not worth very much — is that the modern trend is to restrict merger doctrine to covenants in the contract of sale that "relate to title." *See* Caparrelli v. Rolling Greens, Inc., 190 A.2d 369 (N.J. 1963) (seller's warranty regarding the condition of the premises did not merge into subsequent deed); Rouse v. Brooks, 383 N.E.2d 666 (Ill. App. Ct. 1978) (express warranty that home was "in good, proper, satisfactory and functional working order and condition" did not merge into deed); Teich, 7 U. Det. Mercy L. Rev. at 556-59; Stoebuck & Whitman § 10.12, at 786. *But see* Embassy Group, Inc. v. Hatch, 865 P.2d 1366 (Utah Ct. App. 1993) (disputed size and price of lot "cannot be viewed as collateral because those terms relate directly to title and conveyance").

4. **The principal case.** How is merger doctrine relevant in the principal case? Is the deed provision that the conveyance was made subject to "restrictions of record" relevant to the court's conclusion on merger? *See* Teich, 7 U. Det. Mercy L. Rev. at 556-59. Might the court have reached the same conclusion without the provision in the deed? How does the court define the scope of the collateral agreement exception?

4. **Agreement of the parties.** In order to avoid the application of the merger doctrine or to avoid the collateral agreement exception, the parties sometimes agree that contract provisions will or will not "survive" the closing. In Ferguson v. Casper, in subsection 2 above, the contract provided that the provision regarding municipal violations would "survive the delivery of the deed."

D. DISPUTES AFTER CLOSING

A sale is completed when the seller/grantor gets paid and the buyer/grantee receives a deed to and possession of the property. Typically, grantor and grantee go their separate ways after the closing, and if everything goes well, further contact between them is unnecessary.

But as we know, things do not always go well. Perhaps a defect in the grantor's title comes to light after the closing. As discussed in Secor v. Knight (Section C.3), the grantee's remedy against the grantor for title defects is now based on title covenants contained in the deed (Section D.2). The grantee may also have a cause of action against a title insurer (Section D.3) if the defect is within the coverage of the title policy.

We learned in Section B.1.b that the implied covenant of marketable title protects the buyer against an unreasonable risk of litigation. Title covenants in deeds do not. For the grantee to prevail against the grantor, there must be more than a risk of a third party claim. Claims by third parties are resolved in many cases based on the operation of the recording act, which is the first topic that we will address in this section. Under the recording acts that exist in all states, a grantee will take title free of prior unrecorded transactions, and conversely will be charged with knowledge, within the limits of the required search, of documents that are on record (Section D.1.b).

Perhaps the grantee's title is perfectly good, but the passage of time reveals that the *condition* of the home is less than the grantee expected. If the grantee's expectations are based on representations made by the grantor, the grantee may have a claim against the grantor in fraud if the representations were knowingly false. What if the grantor made no misrepresentations, but failed to disclose pertinent information about the condition of the premises? (Fraud and nondisclosure are considered in Section D.4.a.) Similarly, courts are now widely recognizing an implied warranty by builder-sellers of new homes that the subject property is free of defects in workmanship (Section D.4.b).

1. Title Disputes with Third Party Claimants — The Recording System

a. Title Search

One way in which a defect in the seller's title may come to light is through a title search conducted by the buyer before the closing. More often the title search is conducted by a title company and results in the issuance of a title commitment (discussed in Section D.3). The following excerpt describes how a title search to determine the status of the seller's title is conducted.

WILLIAM B. STOEBUCK & DALE A. WHITMAN
THE LAW OF PROPERTY 869-70, 892-93
(3d ed. 1999)*

Ownership of land can exist only because it is recognized and enforced by the legal institution of the state. Hence, it is not surprising that virtually all modern governments have developed and operate systems of records designed to permit

---

* Reprinted with permission of the West Group.

interested persons to discover who owns any given parcel. In America, every state maintains a *recording* system.

In fundamental concept, each recording system is much like a library of title-related documents. These documents include all of the instruments which have been employed in prior legal transactions affecting the land, and which someone has taken the trouble to "record," or add to the library's collection. The searcher is expected to visit the library, use an official index system to identify and read the documents which relate to the land in question, and then to decide, by the application of his or her knowledge of real estate law and practice, who owns the land and to what encumbrances it is subject. This system is frugal in its expenditure of public funds and personnel. The government employees' only tasks are to receive, copy, index, and return the documents and to maintain the collection. The more demanding work of searching, analyzing, and reaching of legal conclusions from the instruments is left to the private users.

Since the typical recorder's office may contain thousands of volumes and millions of documents, some form of index is essential so that searchers can locate instruments that affect the land whose title is being searched. Thus the office contains two types of volumes: index books and books which hold the actual copies of the legal instruments. The latter are sometimes called "deed books," even though they include other types of documents, such as leases, mortgages, and releases in addition to deeds.

There are two dominant methods of indexing. The oldest and most common is based on the names of the parties to each instrument. Under this "name index" system, two separate alphabetical indexes are maintained: one by the names of the grantors or other persons against whom the document operates, and the other by the names of the grantees or other persons in whose favor it operates. A separate set of these indexes is typically constructed each year, and they may be consolidated periodically into index books covering, say, 5-year or 10-year time spans. A few counties employ computers to produce and regularly update a consolidated set of grantor and grantee indexes for the entire time covered by the records.

An alternative and far superior approach to indexing is the tract or parcel index, but it is available in only a handful of states. Here a separate page or set of pages in the index books is devoted to each tract of land, such as a quarter-quarter section, a specific block in a subdivision, or even an individual parcel of land. This page reflects the history of the tract's title from the time of the original conveyance from the sovereign. In both name and tract index systems, the index books do not contain copies of the actual documents. Instead, they merely give the names of the parties, the recording date, the book and page number of the deed book in which the full copy of each instrument is to be found, and sometimes a brief legal description of the land affected. The searcher must jot down the book and page number and must then pull down and open the relevant deed book to read the instrument itself.

In a name index system the search procedure is generally as follows. The searcher begins by looking for the name of the putative present owner in the grantee index, working backward from the present date. When it is found, the searcher notes the name of the corresponding grantor of that instrument, and then seeks his or her name in the grantee index. This process is repeated until the searcher has worked backward in time through a chain of successive conveyances extending back to the sovereign. The second phase of the search is to look up the name of each of the prior owners, as discovered by the foregoing process, in the grantor index to determine whether any of them made an "adverse" conveyance — that is, one to a person outside the chain of title. In the third phase, the searcher must pull down the relevant deed books and read carefully each instrument which has been identified from both the grantee and grantor indexes, to determine that it is in regular order, is properly executed, and purports to transfer the land in question. Finally, the searcher must check whatever public records are maintained separately from the indexes to the deed books, such as court dockets and probate indexes, tax and assessment records, and the like.

A search in a jurisdiction using a tract index is much simpler, since all instruments affecting a given parcel will be indexed on a single page or a set of consecutive pages in the index book. It is easy to construct the chain of title and to identify potentially adverse conveyances merely by running one's eye down the appropriate column. Of course, the instruments themselves must still be read and the other public records checked.

PROBLEM 5-A. Chain of Title. Your client has signed a contract to buy Blackacre from its owner Frank. Assume the following chain of title to Blackacre: Abel (who owned in fee simple absolute) sold Blackacre to Bonnie, who sold it to Charles, who sold it to Dominique, who sold it to Elwood, who sold it to Frank. Using the excerpt from Stoebuck & Whitman, describe how a title search would be conducted in the office of the recorder of deeds. Assume that the recorder's office maintains a name index (grantor-grantee) rather than a tract index.

b.   Operation of Recording Acts

BURRIS v. McDOUGALD
832 S.W.2d 707 (Tex. App. 1992)

SEERDEN, JUSTICE.

This is a trespass to try title suit. Trial was to the court. The judgment ordered that the parties were tenants in common of the disputed property. The trial court made findings of fact and conclusions of law. By a single point of error, appellant contends that the trial court erred in declaring her to be a tenant in common with appellee and that the facts found by the trial court entitled her to judgment declaring her the owner of the entire property as a matter of law. We agree and reverse the judgment of the trial court.

Shannon McDougald, grandson of Winnie Elizabeth Stone, brought suit against Erna Mae Burris, daughter of Winnie Elizabeth Stone, claiming ownership in the property, basing his position on adverse possession and delay in recording appellant's deed. Appellant Burris filed a counterclaim based on the fact that she had a deed to the property. The trial court found that on September 21, 1951, a valid deed was executed and delivered to appellant and another person whose interest was subsequently conveyed to appellant, and this deed was not recorded until 1985. It further found that Winnie Elizabeth Stone, the grantor in the 1951 deed, died in the 1970's, with a will that left all of her estate to her son, appellee's father, and that the occupancy of the land by Winnie Elizabeth Stone was not hostile to or inconsistent with the claim of appellant. Neither appellee nor anyone under whom he claimed was a creditor or good faith purchaser.

In its conclusions of law, the trial court first concluded that the appellee had not acquired title to the property by adverse possession. Secondly, the trial court concluded that the equities in this case — the long delay in recording the deed, and the use of the property by appellee and the persons under whom he claims title — justify making Erna Mae Burris and Shannon Dan McDougald tenants in common.

By her single point of error, appellant contends that she is entitled to be declared the sole owner, in fee simple, of the property in dispute because the trial court properly found that she had a valid deed to that property, delay in recording the deed does not affect the title and there was no adverse possession. Appellee argues for affirmance on the theory that the execution of a deed does not estop an individual from seeking equitable relief.

The issue before us is whether appellee's claim of equity can defeat appellant's title. The trial court found that legal title was established in appellant by the deed delivered to her in 1951. Appellee first sought to defeat legal title through adverse possession. The trial court found that appellee had not established title through adverse possession. To establish title by adverse possession, a party must show possession, use, a hostile claim, exclusive domination, and appropriation for the statutory period. Pierce v. Gillespie, 761 S.W.2d 390, 396 (Tex.App. — Corpus Christi 1988, no writ). The evidence at trial showed that Winnie Stone's occupancy of the land was not hostile. In failing to show hostile possession, appellee failed to establish a vital element of his cause of action, and we agree with the trial court that appellee cannot claim title through adverse possession.

Appellee next sought to establish an interest in the land through the length of time between receipt of the deed by appellant and the time that she recorded the deed. Appellee argues that the lapse of time in appellant's recording of the deed supports the trial court's judgment. In Texas the recording of a deed is not essential to an effective conveyance of title. An unrecorded conveyance is binding on the parties to the instrument, the parties' heirs, and all of those who have knowledge of the conveyance. The law requires the recording of title to land for the protection of innocent purchasers and creditors. Appellee here was neither an interested purchaser nor a creditor entitled to notice under the statute. The delay in recording the deed is not a reason to divest appellant of her ownership in the property.

Winnie Elizabeth Stone transferred title to appellant in 1951. The evidence conclusively established that since 1951 appellant has retained title in the property. Therefore, we find that the trial court erred as a matter of law in attempting to divest Erna Mae Burris of title. There was no evidence presented to show that Shannon McDougald had an ownership interest in the property. Appellant's point of error is sustained.

We reverse the judgment of the trial court and render judgment for the appellant.

NOTES AND QUESTIONS

1. **Consequence of failure to record.** In most states, a purchaser's failure to record does not affect the validity of the conveyance as between grantor and grantee. However, recording acts provide a strong incentive to a grantee to record for other reasons.

2. **Common law priority.** Under the common law, the first transferee of an interest in land had priority over a subsequent transferee. "First in time is first in right." There was no recording system.

3. **Operation of the recording acts.** Every state has a recording act that reverses the priorities established by the common law if the requirements of the act are met and allows a subsequent purchaser to take title free of an earlier adverse conveyance that is not recorded. In all but a handful of states, only a bona fide purchaser is protected by the recording acts. Bona fide purchaser status has two parts: the purchaser must give value and must lack knowledge or notice of the prior adverse claim. A donee, including an heir or devisee, is bound regardless of notice of a prior claim. As the principal case holds, the purchaser who fails to qualify for protection under the local recording act is governed by the common law rule of first in time, first in right.

4. **Types of notice.** Three types of notice will bar a buyer of the servient estate from enjoying bona fide purchaser status. Terminology is not uniform in the cases and literature, but we will use the terms as follows: *Actual notice*: The purchaser has subjective knowledge of the existence of the prior claim burdening the land. *Constructive (or record) notice*: If the prior adverse claim is properly recorded, the purchaser is deemed aware of the information that a search of the record would reveal, regardless of whether the purchaser searches the record. *Inquiry notice*: When a purchaser is aware or should be aware of facts that a reasonable person would investigate and, if investigated, would reveal the existence of an adverse claim, the purchaser is deemed to be aware of the claim. *See* Methonen v. Stone 941 P.2d 1248, 1252 (Alaska 1997) ("It is well established that a purchaser will be charged with notice of an interest adverse to his title when he is aware of facts which would lead a reasonably prudent person to a course of investigation which, properly executed, would lead to knowledge of the servitude. The purchaser is considered apprised of those facts obvious from an inspection of the property."); Martinez v. Affordable Housing Network, Inc., 123 P.3d 1201, 1207 (Colo. 2005) ("[W]ith certain exceptions, possession of real estate is sufficient to put an interested person on inquiry notice of any legal or equitable claim the person or persons in open, notorious, and exclusive possession of the property may have.").

5. **Three types of recording acts.** Notice statutes, adopted in about half of the states, provide that a subsequent purchaser takes free of prior unrecorded interests in the land simply by qualifying as a bona fide purchaser for value. Race-notice statutes, also adopted in about half the states, require that the subsequent interest holder must be a bona fide purchaser *and* must record his interest before the earlier interest holder records. In three states with race statutes, the subsequent interest holder's knowledge or notice of a prior adverse interest is

irrelevant; a subsequent purchaser prevails over a prior interest holder by recording first. These differences follow from the language of the recording acts as illustrated below.

> a. *A notice statute.* "No conveyance, transfer, or mortgage of real property shall be good and effectual in law or equity against creditors or subsequent purchasers for a valuable consideration and without notice, unless the same be recorded." Raymond E. Sweat, *Understanding the Recording Systems, in* Real Property Practice and Litigation 99, at 102 (Beverly J. Quail ed. 1990).

> b. *A race-notice statute.* "Every conveyance of real estate which shall not be recorded shall be void as against any subsequent purchaser in good faith, and for a valuable consideration of the same real estate or any portion thereof, whose conveyance shall be first duly recorded." *Id.*

> c. *A race statute.* "No conveyance of land shall be valid to pass any property interest as against a purchaser for valuable consideration but from the time of recording." *Id.* (Note that the subsequent purchaser must give value to qualify for the statute's protection, but that notice of a prior claim is irrelevant.)

See generally John H. Scheid, *Down Labyrinthine Ways: A Recording Acts Guide for First Year Law Students*, 80 U. Det. Mercy L. Rev. 91 (2002).

6. **Determining the type of recording statute.** The recording statute for the state of Alabama is set out in a footnote to Salter v. Hamiter, *supra* Section C.1. What type of recording statute is it? What type of recording statute does your state have?

7. **The shelter principle.** The "shelter" principle provides that "[o]nce a bona fide purchaser has perfected title by operation of the recording acts, he or she can pass that perfected status along to a chain of future grantees even if they do not qualify as BFPs." Stoebuck & Whitman § 11.10, at 889. Can you think of a reason for the shelter principle?

8. **More on the BFP.** A purchaser who lacks record notice of a prior adverse claim is nevertheless not a bona fide purchaser if the purchaser has knowledge or inquiry notice of the existence of the prior claim. At least, that is the situation in most states. In some states, however, the language of the recording act can be read to eliminate inquiry notice as a disqualification on bona fide purchaser status. The Ohio statute, for example, provides as follows:

> All deeds and instruments of writing properly executed for the conveyance or encumbrance of lands, shall be recorded in the office of the county recorder of the county in which the premises are situated, and until so recorded or filed for record, they are fraudulent, so far as relates to a subsequent bona fide purchaser having, at the time of purchase, no *knowledge* of the existence of such former deed or land contract or instrument.

Ohio Rev. Code Ann. § 5301.25 (emphasis added). In Emrick v. Multicon Builders, Inc., 566 N.E.2d 1189 (Ohio 1991), the court held that a purchaser for value takes free of a prior adverse claim that is not recorded, unless the purchaser has actual *knowledge* of it. "When the document containing the restriction is unrecorded, an actual knowledge standard [rather than an inquiry or constructive notice standard] must be applied." Suppose the recording statute provides that an unrecorded deed is invalid against a subsequent purchaser who lacks "actual *notice*" of it. Does that language likewise eliminate the doctrine of inquiry notice? *See* Johnson v. Bell, 666 P.2d 308 (Utah 1983).

9. **Interests outside of the recording act.** Many recording acts contain exemptions: interests that do not need to be recorded to enjoy protection against subsequent purchasers. An example is a short-term lease. (Statutory assessments of what is "short" term for this purpose vary, as you might expect.) What do you suppose is the reason for protecting such an interest without the necessity of recordation? Another interest that falls outside the recording act is title by adverse possession. *See* Mugaas v. Smith, 206 P.2d 332 (Wash. 1949) (holding for the adverse possessor because to hold otherwise would have the effect of requiring an adverse possessor to continue in open and notorious possession even after the statute of limitations had run).

PROBLEM 5-B. What result in the following cases under the common law first-in-time rule, and under notice, race-notice, and race statutes? Assume that O owns in fee simple, that the stated events occur in the sequence stated, and that all grantees give value for the transfers to them.

a. O conveys Blackacre to A, who does not record. O conveys to B, who knows of the conveyance to A. B records.

b. O conveys Blackacre to A, who does not record. O conveys to B, who does not know of the conveyance to A. B does not record.

c. O conveys Blackacre to A, who does not record. O conveys to B, who lacks knowledge of the conveyance to A. Subsequently, A records, then B records.

d. O conveys to A, who does not record. O dies. O's heir H conveys to B, who does not know of the deed to A. B records. *See* Earle v. Fiske, 103 Mass. 491 (1870).

c. The Index

HOWARD SAVINGS BANK v. BRUNSON
582 A.2d 1305 (N.J. Super. Ct. Ch. Div. 1990)

Margolis, J.S.C.

This matter involves cross motions for summary judgment on a priority dispute between mortgage holders. The essential facts are undisputed.

In January 1986, defendant Burl Brunson (Brunson) purchased a parcel of property in Newark, New Jersey. The deed for the property was properly recorded pursuant to N.J.S.A. 46:21-1 and indexed pursuant to N.J.S.A. 46:20-4 on January 24, 1986. In March 1986, Brunson borrowed $50,000 from plaintiff Howard Savings Bank (Howard) secured by a mortgage which was properly recorded on May 1, 1986. This mortgage was *not* properly indexed until February 3, 1988.

On October 6, 1987, Brunson executed and delivered a deed for the property to defendants Jesus Ijalba and Celeste Ijalba (Ijalba), which deed was properly recorded in the office of the register of Essex County on November 4, 1987. On October 6, 1987, Ijalba executed and delivered a mortgage covering the subject premises to defendant Chrysler First Financial Services Corporation (Chrysler). This mortgage was also properly recorded on November 4, 1987.

On the basis of a thorough title search and an affidavit of title executed by Brunson on October 5, 1987, representing that he had not allowed any legal interest to be created which would affect the ownership or use of the property, defendant Chicago Title Insurance Company (Chicago Title) issued a title insurance policy to Chrysler.

On May 19, 1988, Howard brought a foreclosure action against Chrysler and Ijalba, claiming that the proceeds of Brunson's sale of the premises to Ijalba were not applied to the mortgage held by Howard, and that its mortgage had priority over all subsequent encumbrancers of the property. The central issue before the court is whether Howard's prior interest in the property, which was recorded but misindexed, has priority over the interests of Ijalba and Chrysler, subsequent lienors who failed to discover Howard's interest due to the misindexing.

Our inquiry begins with the New Jersey Recording Act. N.J.S.A. 46:21-1 provides:

> Except as otherwise provided herein, whenever any deed or instrument of the nature or description set forth in section 46:16-1 of this title, which shall have been or shall be duly acknowledged or proved and certified, shall have been or shall be duly recorded or lodged for record with the county recording officer of the county in which the real estate or other property affected thereby is situated or located such record shall, from that time, be notice to all subsequent judgment creditors, purchasers and mortgagees of the execution of the deed or instrument so recorded and of the contents thereof.

Howard contends that, because its mortgage from Brunson was properly recorded pursuant to the Recording Act, its interest has priority over all subsequent encumbrancers. Plaintiff further argues that valid recordation of a mortgage *alone* serves as constructive notice to interested parties; thus, defendants had constructive notice of Howard's interest because the mortgage was properly recorded over 17 months before defendants obtained an interest in the property.

N.J.S.A. 46:20-1 and 46:20-4 provide in pertinent part:

> The county recording officer of each county shall provide, at the expense of their respective counties, a book or books, and shall, in case it is not already done, make and therein enter indexes, in alphabetical order, to all the various books of record, called and backed "deeds" and called and backed "mortgages," heretofore or hereafter recorded in their respective offices, distinguishing the book in which each deed or mortgage is recorded.

> The indexes herein required to be kept shall contain the names of the several grantors and grantees of deeds, and the names of the several

mortgagors of mortgages.

> The county recording officer of each county shall keep, in addition to the daily entries of the same, an alphabetical index of all the names of the grantors in deeds, parties to instruments and mortgagors in mortgages that may be presented to him for record, which alphabetical index shall be made of all such deeds and instruments by the county recording officer on the same day, or on the day following, that they are received for record.

Plaintiff discounts the significance of N.J.S.A. 46:20-1, the indexing statute, arguing that although it imposes a duty on the county register to maintain an alphabetized index of the chronological record, it places no duty upon the mortgagee with regard to providing notice to subsequent parties in interest because it is not part of the record.

Howard relies on Semon v. Terhune, 40 N.J.Eq. 364, 2 A. 18 (Ch. 1885) and its progeny in support of its argument. *Semon*, like the case at bar, involved the effect of misindexing a mortgage on a subsequent purchaser's constructive notice of its existence. The court held that the misindexing had no effect on the initial party's priority because only the record is necessary to provide notice and the index is not a part of that record. See also Schwartz v. Grunwald, 415 A.2d 1203 (N.J. Super. Ct. Ch. Div. 1980) (proper filing of notice of lis pendens is effective, regardless of indexing omission or mistake).

Defendants maintain that N.J.S.A. 46:21-1 must be read in conjunction with the indexing statute in order that the spirit and intent of the Recording Act be met. Chief among the cases and articles cited to support their argument is Jones, *The New Jersey Recording Act — A Study of its Policy*, 12 Rutgers L.Rev. 328 (1957). In an exhaustive and definitive treatment of the subject, Jones discusses the history and intent of the Recording Act.

> An historical study of the [Recording] Act, as well as an analysis of the cases interpreting it, leads to the conclusion that it was designed to compel the recording of instruments affecting title, for the ultimate purpose of permitting purchasers to rely upon the record title and to purchase and hold title to lands within this state with confidence.

Id. at 329-330.

Clearly, the fundamental purpose of the Recording Act is to provide notice to subsequent parties in interest and "[to protect] purchasers and encumbrancers of real property against undisclosed titles and liens." Solomon v. Canter, 113 N.J.Eq. 43, 45, 166 A. 158 (E. & A.1933). See Van Dyke v. Carol Building Co., 36 N.J.Super. 281, 286, 115 A.2d 607 (App.Div.1955) (Purchasers and encumbrancers "may rely upon the public records and in the absence of actual knowledge or of facts to put them on inquiry, are chargeable only with such facts as may be ascertained by reference thereto."). Once a mortgagee provides notice, a corresponding protection against subsequent titles and liens arises, ensuring that he may safely rely upon the statutes to establish the validity and priority of his mortgage. The issue which this court faces is whether the requisite notice is achieved through the mere recordation of a mortgage or whether notice is achieved only if the mortgage is also properly indexed.

Jones points out that *Semon* was decided in 1885, before a legislative require-ment even existed for a mortgage index. At that time, mortgage entries were few and infrequent, and title searchers were able to thumb through the record books to ascertain the contents with little trouble. As the number of entries grew, however, there also grew a practical need for indices to the mortgage books to provide the means for efficient title searches. Jones, *supra* at 341-342. This need was codified in essentially its present form in 1898, but the Legislature has not since amended the recording statute or the indexing statute to reflect the extraordinary changes that have occurred in the custom and practice of title searching since then. Yet the New Jersey Supreme Court, in Palamarg Realty Co. v. Rehac, 80 N.J. 446, 461, 404 A.2d 21 (1979), emphasized the fact that "title searching, upon which so much of our conveyancing practice rests, has been created in very large part without the aid of legislation," and that an investigation of the custom and practice of title searching is essential to determine current disputes in that area of law.

For these reasons, and because this court is not bound by courts of equal jurisdiction, this court chooses to reexamine the *Semon* rule that the index is not considered in practice to be a part of the record. For purposes of this analysis, it is necessary to determine, from the evidence currently before the court, whether the current custom and practice of title searching require that the index be interpreted to be an integral part of the record.

In this regard, this court has had the benefit of the uncontroverted certification of Lawrance J. Fineberg, resident vice-president and associate regional counsel of defendant Chicago Title, an attorney fully familiar with the custom, practice and procedure of title searching in New Jersey. Fineberg states that the "customary period for title searching is to go back 60 years to a warranty deed" in order to establish an unbroken chain of title for the premises in question. Once the searcher has gone back at least 60 years, he "adverses" each successive owner in the chain of title for the time period during which that owner held title in order to discover liens, restrictions, conveyances to third parties and the like which would encumber title. In performing the adversing task, Fineberg continues, "[i]t has long been the practice of New Jersey title searchers to check the alphabetical indices under the name of each owner of record to see whether he executed any instruments which would create adverse interests in the particular property."

Furthermore, "the only way to perform a search *without* relying on the indices is to turn each page of each record book in the county during the entire period of time that each individual appeared of record to be the owner until one discovers a particular instrument creating an adverse interest. There are literally thousands of record books in each county and each Mortgage Book contains at least 1,000 pages." (Emphasis supplied.)

Fineberg's certification unequivocally supports the title searchers' practice of relying solely upon the statutorily required alphabetical indices in performing title searches. This practice, and the resulting necessity of considering the index to be a part of the record so as to protect title searchers who rely upon it, is discussed favorably by several commentators. See Jones, *supra* at 340 ("[T]oday the index *must* be considered as part of the record, and an instrument which is not properly indexed is not 'duly recorded.'"); 29 N.J.Practice (Cunningham & Tischler, Law of

Mortgages) (1975) at 106. Cunningham & Tischler explain: "A mortgage can hardly be deemed 'duly recorded' unless it is properly indexed, if we are to take seriously the many statements by New Jersey courts to the effect that the object of the recording statutes is to prevent imposition upon subsequent bona fide purchasers and mortgagees; for without an index, searching for a mortgage in the public records would be like looking for the proverbial needle in a haystack." See also Security Pacific Finance Corp. v. Taylor, 193 N.J.Super. 434, 442, 474 A.2d 1096 (Ch.Div.1984) (although the court declined to make a finding that a search of the index is required in order to avail subsequent purchasers or mortgagees of the protection of the Recording Act, it stated that "[i]t cannot seriously be disputed that the index is a part of the record and that a purchaser or mortgagee has a duty to see to it that his instrument is properly recorded *and indexed.*").

As Jones pointed out, "what is reasonable under the circumstances existing in one generation may be unreasonable under those existing in a subsequent generation." Jones, *supra* at 330. It would be unreasonable to saddle a purchaser with the obligation of thumbing through every page of every record book in the county register's office, representing the entire period of time that an individual appeared of record to be the owner, in order to overcome the risk of improper indexing, given the enormous number of real estate transactions which occur and are recorded daily in our state. A rule prohibiting title searchers from depending upon the alphabetical index would unduly hinder the commercial transactions in the State: lengthy title searches would cost more and would cause unreasonably long closings; potential purchasers, mortgagors and lenders would hesitate to be involved in commercial transactions where they could not be confident that a reasonable search of the record would reveal prior interests or where they feared being held liable for a clerk's misindexing error; and the cost of title insurance would increase.

The solution is that the recording and indexing statutes must be read *in pari materia* such that they are "construed together as a unitary and harmonious whole in order that each may be fully effective." Clifton v. Passaic County Bd. of Taxation, 28 N.J. 411, 421, 147 A.2d 1 (1958). The indices must be construed to be part of the record so as to reflect the current custom and practice of title searching and to provide stability and certainty in real estate transactions so that subsequent parties in interest may safely rely upon the record.

Obviously, one effect of finding a duty in the mortgagee to see that his instrument is properly indexed will be that the mortgagee will be required to conduct "run down" searches or to employ some other similar mechanism for ensuring that his interest is properly indexed. Yet such a practice is seen as making good business sense anyway. See Jones, *supra* at 344 n.76. Furthermore, placing the burden upon the mortgagee to ensure that the requisite notice has been given is not out of step with the equitable maxim that where a loss must be borne by one of two innocent parties, equity will impose the loss on the party whose first act would have prevented the loss.

Plaintiff cites several cases from other courts in support of its contention that a valid recordation alone serves as constructive notice to all interested parties of an encumbrancer's interest in the property. These cases are distinguishable from the facts of the case at bar, but because they address similar issues, they merit consideration. In New Jersey Bank v. Azco Realty Co., Inc., 372 A.2d 356 (N.J. Super. Ct. App. Div. 1977), a foreclosure action, the court held that plaintiff was entitled to priority over defendant, regardless of whether defendant had actual notice of the prior recording. While this court does not disagree with the decision in *Azco*, the facts clearly distinguish it from the case at bar. *Azco* involved a bank which waited over a year to properly record its mortgage, and then did so three days before defendant recorded its mortgage in the same property. Due to the two-day time lag in the recording clerk's office, defendant could not have had actual notice of plaintiff's prior interest.

Unlike the *Azco* plaintiff, which was unable to check for errors in indexing because its interest had not yet been recorded, plaintiff in the present case had 21 months after the recording of its interest to ascertain whether its mortgage was properly indexed. More importantly, unlike the facts in *Azco*, where neither party could have avoided the notice problem which occurred (it was due to the recording of plaintiff's interest on a Friday, and defendant's closing occurring on the following Monday, leaving less than one business day for the county clerk's office to record the interest), in the present case, plaintiff *could have* avoided the error in indexing by doing a "run down" subsequent to the recording, but failed to do so.

Plaintiff also cites to Lakewood Township v. Block 251, Parcel 34, 138 A.2d 768 (N.J. Super. Ct. App. Div. 1958) in support of its argument. In *Lakewood*, a clerk failed to index the township's tax foreclosure action in the name of the last record owner of property and the court held that the error did not render the tax foreclosure judgment invalid for the subsequent purchaser's lack of notice. This case is easily distinguishable because the court found that defendant had alternative means of obtaining notice of the impending sale of the property (defendant could have done a tax search, notices were placed in the newspaper and a foreclosure complaint was filed in the clerk's office) and was therefore properly held to have had constructive notice. In the case at bar, however, defendants did not have any reasonable means of obtaining notice other than checking the indices.

For the reasons set forth above, the court is satisfied that defendants made a reasonable search of the chain of title by searching the indices alone, the deed and mortgage of Ijalba and Chrysler have priority over Howard's lien, and defendants' cross motion for summary judgment is granted.

NOTES AND QUESTIONS

1. **Claimants in the principal case.** The principal case involves competing priority claims by successive mortgagees. The priority principles we are discussing apply as between competing owners in fee (O conveys Blackacre to A one day, and to B the next day); between competing holders of lesser interests (like the prior and later mortgagees in the principal case); and between a fee owner on one side and the holder of a lesser interest on the other (e.g., Witter v. Taggart, Section D.1.d).

2. **Two innocent parties.** In the principal case, note that both the prior and subsequent mortgagees are innocent: each has recorded his mortgage. In this situation, one view is that the prior conveyance, although misindexed, is

nevertheless recorded as required by the recording acts, and imparts constructive notice to successors of the burdened land. *See* Luthi v. Evans, 576 P.2d 1064 (Kan. 1978) (fact that deed is improperly indexed does not prevent subsequent purchaser from having constructive notice of the deed). Another view, taken in the principal case, is that a misindexed deed is effectively lost, imposes an impossibly high search burden on subsequent purchasers, and thus imparts no constructive notice. Which view do you think is better? Is the presence or absence of a statutory provision making the index an official part of the record relevant? *See* 4 A.L.P. § 17.25. If both parties are innocent, what is the tiebreaker? Which of the two innocent parties can avoid the problem at the least cost?

3. **Other protections.** As the principal cases reprinted above indicate, the recording acts are far from foolproof. What other protections might the purchaser seek against a loss resulting from a prior effective adverse claim?

d.   Chain of Title Problems

WITTER v. TAGGART
577 N.E.2d 338 (N.Y. 1991)

BELLACOSA, JUDGE.

Plaintiff Witter and defendants Taggarts are East Islip neighboring property owners. Their homes are on opposite sides of a canal on the south shore of Long Island. Witter's home is north of the canal and the Taggarts' home and dock are across the canal on the south side. The Winganhauppauge or Champlin's Creek lies immediately west of both parcels. Their property dispute arose when the Taggarts erected a 70-foot long dock on their canal-side frontage. This was done after a title search revealed that their deed expressly permitted building the dock and reflected no recorded restrictions in their direct property chain against doing so. Witter complained of a violation of his scenic easement to an unobstructed view of the creek and an adjacent nature preserve, which he claims is protected by a restrictive covenant contained in his chain of title. He sued to compel the Taggarts to dismantle and remove the dock and to permanently enjoin any such building in the future.

Supreme Court granted the Taggarts' motion for summary judgment dismissing Witter's complaint and denied Witter's cross motion for summary judgment. Relying principally on Buffalo Academy of Sacred Heart v. Boehm Bros., 196 N.E. 42 (N.Y. 1935), the trial court held that the Taggarts are not bound by or charged with constructive notice of a restrictive covenant which does not appear in their direct chain of title to the allegedly burdened land. Although it noted a possible conflict between *Buffalo Academy* and our affirmance of the result in Ammirati v. Wire Forms, 78 N.Y. S.2d 844 (N.Y. App. Div. 1948), the court distinguished and explained away the conflict.

The Appellate Division affirmed the instant case, reasoning that under *Buffalo Academy*, the restrictive covenant contained in the chain of deeds to Witter's allegedly benefited parcel was outside the chain of title to the Taggarts' land and did not constitute binding notice to them. We granted Witter's motion for leave to appeal to decide whether the covenant recited in Witter's chain of title to his purported "dominant" land, which appears nowhere in the direct chain of title to the Taggarts' purported "servient" land, burdens the Taggarts' property. We agree with the lower courts that it does not, and therefore affirm the order of the Appellate Division.

The homes of these neighbors are located on lots which have been separately deeded through a series of conveyances, originally severed and conveyed out by a common grantor, Lawrance. Lawrance conveyed one parcel of his land to Witter's predecessor in title in 1951. The deed contained the restrictive covenant providing that "no docks, buildings, or other structures [or trees or plants] shall be erected [or grown]" on the grantor's (Lawrance's) retained servient lands to the south "which shall obstruct or interfere with the outlook or view from the [dominant] premises" over the Winganhauppauge Creek. That deed provided that the covenant expressly ran with the *dominant* land. William and Susan Witter purchased the dominant parcel in 1963 by deed granting them all the rights of their grantor, which included the restrictive covenant. In 1984, Susan Witter transferred her interest to William Witter alone.

After common grantor Lawrance died, his heirs in 1962 conveyed his retained, allegedly servient, land to the Taggarts' predecessor in title. Lawrance's deed made no reference to the restrictive covenant benefiting the Witter property and neither did the heirs' deed to the Taggarts' predecessors. The restrictive covenant was also not included or referenced in any of the several subsequent mesne conveyances of that allegedly servient parcel or in the deed ultimately to the Taggarts in 1984. Quite to the contrary, the Taggarts' deed specifically permitted them to build a dock on their parcel.

Restrictive covenants are also commonly categorized as negative easements. They restrain servient landowners from making otherwise lawful uses of their property. However, the law has long favored free and unencumbered use of real property, and covenants restricting use are strictly construed against those seeking to enforce them. Courts will enforce restraints only where their existence has been established with clear and convincing proof by the dominant landowner.

The guiding principle for determining the ultimate binding effect of a restrictive covenant is that "[i]n the absence of actual notice before or at the time of purchase or of other exceptional circumstances, an owner of land is only bound by restrictions if they appear in some deed of record in the conveyance to [that owner] or [that owner's] direct predecessors in title." Buffalo Academy of Sacred Heart v. Boehm Bros., 196 N.E. at 45. Courts have consistently recognized and applied this principle, which provides reliability and certainty in land ownership and use.

In *Buffalo Academy*, we held that a restrictive covenant did not run with the dominant land, but added that even if it did, the servient landowners were not bound because the deed to the servient land did not reflect the covenant. We noted that this rule is "implicit in the acts providing for the recording of conveyances." *Id.* The recording act (Real Property Law art. 9) was enacted to accomplish a twofold purpose: to protect the rights of innocent purchasers who acquire an interest in property without knowledge of prior encumbrances, and to establish a public record which will furnish potential purchasers with actual or at least constructive notice of previous conveyances and encumbrances that might affect their interests and uses.

The recording statutes in a grantor-grantee indexing system charge a purchaser with notice of matters only in the record of the purchased land's chain of title back to the original grantor. *Buffalo Academy* recognized that a "purchaser is not normally required to search *outside* the chain of title" (emphasis added) and is not chargeable with constructive notice of conveyances recorded outside of that purchaser's direct chain of title where, as in Suffolk County, the grantor-grantee system of indexing is used. This is true even if covenants are included in a deed to another lot conveyed by the same grantor.

To impute legal notice for failing to search each chain of title or "deed out" from a common grantor "would seem to negative the beneficent purposes of the recording acts" and would place too great a burden on prospective purchasers. *Id.* Therefore, purchasers like the Taggarts should not be penalized for failing to search every chain of title branching out from a common grantor's roots in order to unearth potential restrictive covenants. They are legally bound to search only within their own tree trunk line and are bound by constructive or inquiry notice only of restrictions which appear in deeds or other instruments of conveyance in that primary stem. Property law principles and practice have long established that a deed conveyed by a common grantor to a dominant landowner does *not* form part of the chain of title to the servient land retained by the common grantor.

A grantor may effectively extinguish or terminate a covenant when, as here, the grantor conveys retained servient land to a bona fide purchaser who takes title without actual or constructive notice of the covenant because the grantor and dominant owner failed to record the covenant in the servient land's chain of title. One way the dominant landowner or grantor can prevent this result is by recording in the servient chain the conveyance creating the covenant rights so as to impose notice on subsequent purchasers of the servient land.

It goes almost without repeating that definiteness, certainty, alienability and unencumbered use of property are highly desirable objectives of property law. To restrict the Taggarts because of Lawrance's failure to include the covenant in the deed to his retained servient land, or for the failure by Witter's predecessors to insist that it be protected and recorded so as to be enforceable against the burdened property, would seriously undermine these paramount values, as well as the recording acts.

Ammirati v. Wire Forms, 76 N.Y.S.2d 379, *rev'd*, 78 N.Y.S.2d 844 (N.Y. App. Div.) *aff'd without opn.* 82 N.E.2d 789 (N.Y. 1948), on which Witter principally relies, is readily harmonized with *Buffalo Academy*'s "exceptional circumstances" qualifying clause. In *Ammirati*, the common grantor conveyed a *landlocked* dominant estate. The recorded dominant deed and subsequent deeds in that chain of title recited an *affirmative easement* for ingress and egress over the grantor's *adjoining* retained servient land. The Appellate Division held that the servient land was burdened even though the easement was not included in its chain of title, reasoning that *Buffalo Academy* was inapplicable because "[i]t deals only with a covenant imposing building restrictions upon the use to which the property may be put."

Our affirmance only of the result reached in *Ammirati*, did not alter the general principles articulated in *Buffalo Academy* and is readily supportable in view of the sui generis features in *Ammirati*, i.e., a landlocked dominant parcel with an affirmative easement by necessity. The circumstances constituting the "necessity" ordinarily also constitute inquiry notice of the easement, which limits the common grantor servient owner's ability to extinguish the easement. In this case, the Taggarts did not have inquiry notice of a covenant in the deed to Witter's fully accessible parcel located *across* the canal.

Although the context of this restrictive covenant case parallels the situation of *Buffalo Academy*, we note further that the general rule of that case does not turn on the distinction between an affirmative or negative easement, and to the extent that the Appellate Division memorandum in *Ammirati* may be read inconsistently with *Buffalo Academy* in that respect, we add that it should not be followed.

We emphasize that our affirmance in *Ammirati* does *not*, as Witter would have us now hold, stand for the proposition that where a deed from a common grantor separates parcels into dominant and servient properties, the deed conveying the dominant parcel is considered part of the chain of title of the *retained servient* land. Rather, we hold that, consistent with long-standing precedents and property principles, the Taggarts did not have actual or constructive notice of this restrictive covenant because it was never included in their deed or direct chain of title. There being no other imputable constructive or inquiry notice, they are not bound by that covenant.

Accordingly, the order of the Appellate Division should be affirmed, with costs.

NOTES AND QUESTIONS

1. **Notice.** In the principal case, there is no indication that Taggart had actual knowledge of the restriction on his lot (actual notice) or that he had or should have had any information which, if pursued, would have led him to find the restriction (inquiry notice). And although the 1951 deed to Witter's predecessor, which contained the restriction on Lawrance's retained land, was recorded, Taggart lacked constructive notice of the restriction because it was contained in a deed that was outside the scope of the record search chargeable to Taggart. There is disagreement among the states over how extensive the purchaser's search of the record must be.

2. **Scope of record search: deeds in the chain of title.** In every state, a purchaser is charged with notice of the contents of prior recorded deeds that transfer title to the land that the purchaser is buying. In the principal case, that land is the lot south of the canal. Is the scenic restriction contained in any deed that transfers title to the south lot?

3. **Deeds out of the chain of title: one view.** Lawrance created the restriction on the south lot in 1951 when he transferred the lot north of the canal to Witter's predecessor. That 1951 deed would not have shown up in a search of the grantee index under Lawrance's name. (In the grantee index, the 1951 sale would have been indexed under the name of Witter's predecessor.) As the principal case notes, the extent of a purchaser's title search would be expanded considerably if the purchaser were charged with notice of the contents of all deeds to other parcels

executed by each owner in the chain of title to the subject property. The name of *every* owner in the chain of title to the subject land would have to be run in the grantor index to see what transfers of other land each owner might have made, and the deed for every such transfer would have to be pulled and inspected in its entirety to see if the owner created any restrictions on the subject land. In the principal case, for example, the grantor index entry for Lawrance's sale of the north lot would show up in the grantor index as a sale of the north lot, but it probably would not identify any restriction on the south lot buried in the language of the sale deed. To find the restriction, the deed to Witter's predecessor would have to be read in its entirety. *See* Stoebuck & Whitman § 11.11, at 897 (such a search task "can be monumental").

4. **Deeds out of the chain of title: another view.** Despite the potential burden to subsequent purchasers, some states charge the purchaser with knowledge of the contents of deeds of other parcels executed by owners in the chain of title to the subject property. *See* Finley v. Glenn, 154 A. 299, 301 (Pa. 1931):

> When [the subsequent purchasers] came to examine the title which was tendered to them, it was of primary consequence that they should know whether their grantors held title to the land which they were to convey. They could determine that question only by searching the records for grants from them [the grantors]. Coming upon this conveyance, it was their duty to read it, *not to read only the description* of the property to see what was conveyed, but to read the deed *in its entirety*, to note *anything else* which might be set forth in it. The deed was notice to them of *all* it contained; otherwise the purpose of the recording acts would be frustrated.

Accord, Rowland Family Trust v. Pelletier, 673 A.2d 1081 (R.I. 1996). The cases are "about evenly divided" between the Witter v. Taggart and Finley v. Glenn views. *See* Stoebuck & Whitman § 11.11, at 897.

5. **Proper recordation.** The court in the principal case says that Witter's predecessor could have protected himself against a subsequent purchaser of Lawrance's retained land by recording the restriction in the chain of title of the retained land. How would Witter's predecessor (P) have done that? Would P request two instruments from the grantor: one to transfer fee simple title to the land and the other to evidence the restriction? Or would P request that Lawrance deed both lots to P, who would then deed back the south lot with the restriction? (The former would put an unmistakable reference in the grantor index that the indexed transfer contains a servitude affecting the retained land. The latter would put the restriction in the direct chain of title.) Or would P accept one deed containing the grant of the fee and creating the restriction, and request that the recording clerk record the deed under Lawrances's name twice, both as a seller of the north lot and as creating a restriction on the south lot? In states that take the Finley v. Glenn view (Note 4) are two instruments — or a special request to the recordation clerk — necessary?

6. **Review.** New York's statute is the race-notice type. *See* N.Y. Real Prop. Law § 291 (McKinney). Review the race-notice language quoted in Note 5 after Burris v. McDougald (Section D.1.b above), and see if you can explain the court's result in terms of that language. Did Taggart record his deed? Was Taggart a bona

fide purchaser? Did Witter's predecessor fail to record his deed? Be careful on this last one. Did Witter's predecessor fail to record, or fail to record in such a way as to give Taggart notice of the easement? If the latter, isn't it necessary to treat the deed creating the restriction as unrecorded? If not, could Taggart prevail under the language of a race-notice statute ("every conveyance *which shall not be recorded* shall be void," etc.)? *See* Stoebuck & Whitman § 11.11, at 894 n.7.

7. **Wild deeds.** The principal case presents one type of adverse interest that is "difficult or impossible [for the title searcher] to find even though extant in the deed books and accurately indexed." Stoebuck & Whitman § 11.11, at 894. The same problem is presented by a "wild deed." Suppose that Alice transfers Blackacre to Xanthes, who does not record the deed. Xanthes transfers to Yoakum, who records. If Alice subsequently contracts to sell Blackacre to Paul, will Paul have record notice of Yoakum's adverse claim to Blackacre? How extensive a search of the record would be required to uncover the deed from Xanthes to Yoakum? In order for Paul to qualify as a BFP under a notice or race-notice statute, is it necessary to treat the deed from Xanthes to Yoakum *as though* it were unrecorded? *See* Stoebuck & Whitman § 11.11, at 894-95.

8. **More on the chain of title: early and late recording.** Who wins in each of the following situations? What is the issue in each?

a. Arnie contracts to buy Blackacre from Oliver. Closing is delayed. Before closing occurs, Arnie deeds Blackacre to his grandson Barry by warranty deed as a wedding present. Barry records the deed. Subsequently Oliver conveys to Arnie, and Arnie records the deed. (Under the doctrine of estoppel by deed, discussed later, the effect of Oliver's conveyance to Arnie is to vest title in Arnie's grantee, Barry.) Subsequently, Charles makes Arnie an offer on Blackacre that Arnie can't refuse, and Arnie conveys Blackacre to Charles, who does not know about Arnie's deed to Barry. Is Charles a purchaser for value without notice?

b. Orville conveys Blackacre to Alan, who does not record the deed. Orville then conveys Blackacre to Bart, who knows of the conveyance to Alan. Bart records. Then Alan records. Then Bart conveys Blackacre to Chastity, who does not know of the deed from Orville to Alan. Chastity records. Is Chastity a purchaser for value without notice? *Compare* Woods v. Garnett, 16 So. 390 (Miss. 1894) (Alan wins), *with* Morse v. Curtis, 2 N.E. 929 (Mass. 1885) (Chastity wins). What result if Bart had not known of the conveyance to Alan?

The classic article discussing chain of title problems is Harry M. Cross, *The Record "Chain of Title" Hypocrisy*, 57 Colum. L. Rev. 787 (1957). For a recent study, see John W. Fisher, II, *The Scope of Title Examination in West Virginia: Can Reasonable Minds Differ?*, 98 W. Va. L. Rev. 449 (1996).

9. **Tract indexes.** Review the chain of title problems we have considered: deeds from a common grantor (Witter v. Taggart); wild deeds (Note 7); deeds recorded early (Note 8.a) and deeds recorded late (Note 8.b). Would any of those problems disappear if deeds were indexed under a tract rather than a grantor-grantee index? Most title companies use a title plant with a tract index for title searches.

e.   Marketable Title Legislation

H & F LAND, INC. v. PANAMA CITY-BAY COUNTY AIRPORT
736 So. 2d 1167 (Fla. 1999)

ANSTEAD, J.

We have for review a decision on the following question certified [by the intermediate appellate court] to be of great public importance:

> DOES THE MARKETABLE RECORD TITLE ACT, CHAPTER 712, FLORIDA STATUTES, OPERATE TO EXTINGUISH AN OTHER-WISE VALID CLAIM OF A COMMON LAW WAY OF NECESSITY WHEN SUCH CLAIM WAS NOT ASSERTED WITHIN THIRTY YEARS?

For the reasons that follow, we answer the certified question in the affirmative and hold that statutory or common law ways of necessity are subject to the provisions of the Marketable Record Title to Real Property Act ("MRTA").

FACTS AND PROCEEDINGS TO DATE

Coastal Lands Inc. ("Coastal") once owned all of the land now owned by the parties in this case. On October 4, 1940, Coastal conveyed 390 acres of land it owned to Bay County, which in turn conveyed this acreage to the Panama City Airport Board on July 23, 1947. This land is now owned by respondent, Panama City-Bay County Airport and Industrial District, with the Panama City-Bay County International Airport currently operating on it. As a result of the 1940 transfer, a small piece of land retained by Coastal became both water- and landlocked. This small parcel of land, approximately eight-tenths of an acre, is located on a peninsula that abuts the Airport District's property. The parties agree that an implied common law way of necessity from this small parcel and over the Airport District's property was created as a result of the 1940 transaction between Coastal and Bay County. However, no notice of a claim to such a way of necessity was ever filed in the public records or asserted by use.

This small parcel was conveyed by Coastal to O.E. Hobbs on June 15, 1943, along with the remainder of the land originally retained by Coastal when it sold part of its property to Bay County. H & F Land, Inc. ("H & F") acquired this small parcel in 1992.

In 1996, some fifty-six years after any way of necessity would have been created, H & F filed a lawsuit and asserted for the first time that along with its acquisition of the small parcel, it also acquired a right to a way of necessity across the Airport District's land. In turn, Panama City filed a motion for summary judgment in that action, asserting that by operation of law, specifically Chapter 712, Florida Statutes (1993), MRTA, the way of necessity claimed by H & F had long been extinguished because the owners of the easement had failed to publicly assert a claim thereto. The trial court agreed and granted the motion. On appeal, the First District affirmed the grant of summary judgment, but certified the question set out above.

ANALYSIS

As noted above, the parties are in agreement that H & F and its predecessors in title were at one time entitled to a way of necessity by reason of the 1940 transaction, which left the small parcel now owned by H & F water- and landlocked. At issue today is the effect of MRTA on this way of necessity, now codified under the provisions of section 704.01(1), Florida Statutes (1995).[2] While numerous other states have adopted acts similar to MRTA, no other case has specifically addressed this issue. To analyze the issue, we must address two questions. First, whether a claim under a common law way of necessity is an interest in land subject to MRTA? And, second, if so, are there any exceptions in MRTA that apply to preserve the way of necessity despite the failure to assert a claim to this right within the time limitations provided in MRTA?

BACKGROUND OF MRTA AND SECTION 704.01

In landmark legislation fundamentally revamping Florida property law, the Florida Legislature adopted MRTA in 1963 for the purpose of simplifying and facilitating land title transactions. See § 712.10, Fla. Stat. (1995). MRTA was designed to simplify conveyances of real property, stabilize titles, and give certainty to land ownership.

MRTA is based on the Model Marketable Title Act, which was proposed in 1960 with multiple objectives: (1) to limit title searches to recently recorded instruments only; (2) to clear old defects of record; (3) to establish perimeters within which marketability can be determined; (4) to reduce the number of quiet title actions; and (5) to reduce the costs of abstracts and closings. See Lori Tofflemire Moorhouse, Note, *Marketable Record Title Act and Recording Act: Is Harmonic Coexistence Possible?*, 29 U.Fla.L.Rev. 916, 923-24 (1977). In its essence, the Model Act sought to accomplish these objectives by providing that when a person has a record title to land for a designated duration, claims and interests in the property that stem from transactions before that period are extinguished unless the claimant seasonably records a notice to preserve his interest. See *id.* at 924. In much the same manner as the Model Act, MRTA's provisions contain a scheme to accomplish the same objective of stabilizing property law by clearing old defects from land titles, limiting the period of record search, and clearly defining marketability by extinguishing old interests of record not specifically claimed or reserved.

Section 712.02 of MRTA expressly provides that any person vested with any estate in land of record for thirty years or more shall have a marketable record title

---

[2] Section 704.01(1) in relevant part provides:

Such an implied grant [an implied grant of a way of necessity] exists where a person has heretofore granted or hereafter grants lands to which there is no accessible right-of-way except over his land, or has heretofore retained or hereafter retains land which is inaccessible except over the land which he conveys.

Fla. Stat. (1995).

free and clear of all claims of an interest in land except those preserved by section 712.03:

> Any person having the legal capacity to own land in this state, who, alone or together with his predecessors in title, has been vested with any estate in land of record for 30 years or more, shall have a marketable record title to such estate in said land, which shall be *free and clear of all claims except the matters set forth as exceptions* to marketability in § 712.03.

§ 712.02, Fla. Stat. (1995) (emphasis added). In construing this provision in Marshall v. Hollywood, Inc., 236 So.2d 114 (Fla.1970), this Court stated: "By the Marketable Record Title Act, *any claim or interest*, vested or contingent, present or future, is cut off unless the claimant preserves his claim by filing a notice within a 30-year period. If a notice is not filed, the claim is lost." *Id.* at 119 (quoting Catsman, *The Marketable Record Title Act and Uniform Title Standards*, § 6.2, in III Florida Real Property Practice (1965) (emphasis added). We must determine whether a claim to a common law way of necessity falls within the "all claims" language used in the statute and as interpreted expansively in *Marshall*.

WAY OF NECESSITY

A way of necessity is an easement that arises from an implied grant or implied reservation of an interest in land. It is based upon the principle and assumption that whenever a party conveys property, he conveys whatever is necessary for the beneficial use of that property, but retains whatever is necessary for the beneficial use of the land he still holds. It is also important to note that an easement is more than a mere personal privilege; it is an interest in land. Hence, it is an interest in the Airport District's land that H & F seeks to have recognized and enforced in these legal proceedings.

EFFECT OF MRTA

Based upon the unambiguous language in MRTA referring to "all claims" and the clear policy underlying MRTA, both of which clearly mandate that "any claim or interest" in property be publicly asserted and recorded, we find that MRTA indeed encompasses all claims to an interest in property, including ways of necessity, unless such claims are expressly excepted from MRTA's provisions. In fact, Florida appellate courts have consistently applied MRTA to easements and rights of way in situations similar to the one involved herein.

Importantly, this Court has upheld the extinguishment of interests in land under MRTA even where those interests were more clearly established and defined than those in question here. In *Marshall*, we held that MRTA operates to confer marketability to a recorded chain of title in land, even if the chain originates from a forged or a wild deed, so long as the strict recording requirements of MRTA are met. As a result, we concluded that a root of title based upon a forged deed would prevail even over an otherwise entirely valid deed recorded earlier in the chain of title. *Id.* In so holding, we refused to create an exception to MRTA and its clear policy favoring recording, even for legitimate interests in real property that had been lost only by reason of the existence of a recorded, but otherwise ordinarily invalid transfer. This holding, of course, was predicated upon the clear policy announced in MRTA favoring the recordation of instruments while also providing a generous time period for the assertion of any claims of an interest in land.

Having refused to look behind the recorded wild deed in *Marshall* to establish that it was based on a forgery or was otherwise invalid, it would make little sense for us to go behind the legitimate deed of the Airport District in this case to discover an unclaimed easement against the Airport District's property and except it from MRTA's recording requirements. A core concern of MRTA was that there be no "hidden" interests in property that could be asserted without limitation against a record property owner. In other words, MRTA shifted the burden to those claiming "any claim or interest" in property to come forward in a timely fashion and assert that interest publicly. Creating judicial exceptions to this comprehensive legislative scheme would undermine the core purpose of MRTA of providing stability to property law by requiring that all claims to an interest in property be recorded. As in *Marshall*, our conclusion today is predicated upon the unambiguous provisions of MRTA as well as the fundamental policy concerns underlying its enactment.

EXCEPTIONS

Having concluded that MRTA does apply to the asserted way of necessity, we must next consider the exceptions provided in section 712.03 of MRTA, only the first two of which merit discussion.[4]

The first exception preserves "[e]states or interests, easements and use restrictions disclosed by and defects inherent in the muniments of title[5] on which an estate is based beginning with the root of title." § 712.03(1), Fla. Stat. (1995). This exception has been narrowly construed. See, e.g., ITT Rayonier, Inc. v. Wadsworth, 346 So.2d 1004 (Fla.1977). In addition, the portion dealing with "defects inherent in the muniments of title" has been strictly limited to the "face of the instrument" instead of to an examination of the circumstances surrounding the deed. *Id.*

Initially, we note that the term "root of title" refers to the last title transaction creating the estate in question and which was recorded at least thirty years ago.[6] See § 712.01(2), Fla. Stat. (1995). In this case, the root of title is the 1947 conveyance from Bay County to the Panama City Airport Board. For this exception to apply in the instant case, the 1947 deed from Bay County to the Panama City Airport Board would have had to disclose on its face the common law way of necessity, or the common law way of necessity would have had to constitute a defect in that title, which was reflected on the face of the title instrument.

In the instant case, the 1947 transfer to Panama City never mentioned or referenced the common law way of necessity; therefore, it was not "disclosed by"

---

[4] The remaining five exceptions of MRTA clearly do not apply to the case at bar. Moreover, there is no claim that ways of necessity are expressly made the subject of a specific exception to MRTA.

[5] "Muniments of title" means the written evidence which a land owner can use to defend title to his estate. See Black's Law Dictionary 1019 (6th ed. 1990).

[6] Section 712.01(2) defines "root of title" as the "title transaction purporting to create or transfer the estate claimed by any person and which is the last title transaction to have been recorded at least 30 years prior to the time when marketability is being determined."

the muniments of title as provided for in section 712.03(1). Indeed, we acknowledge that no deed would ordinarily reflect the way of necessity because by its very nature, a common law way of necessity is implied from the circumstances surrounding its creation. If such an easement was expressly provided for, there would be no common law way of necessity created.[7]

Further, we conclude that the common law way of necessity does not qualify as a defect inherent in the title because it constitutes a recognized legal interest in land and not a defect in title as this Court has interpreted that term. In *ITT Rayonier, Inc.*, this Court dealt specifically with this exception in answering a series of certified questions from the United States Court of Appeals. The Court explained that "[t]he terms 'defects inherent in the muniments of title' do not refer to defects or failures in the transmission of title, as the plaintiff's argument suggests, but refer to defects in the make-up or constitution of the deed or other muniments of title on which such transmission depends." 346 So.2d at 1011.[8] Similarly, we conclude there has been no showing here of any "defects in the make-up or constitution of the deed or other muniments of title" by which the Panama City Airport Board acquired its property. The deed was in regular form and simply conveyed the title to the property that the County intended to convey and the Panama City Airport Board intended to receive. Hence, we conclude that the exception under section 712.03(1) does not apply to a common law way of necessity.

FILING OF NOTICE

As for the second exception, the statute preserves estates, interests, claims or charges filed with a proper notice in accordance with the provisions of MRTA. See § 712.03(2), Fla. Stat. (1995). In this regard, section 712.05 of MRTA specifically provides:

> Any person claiming an interest in land may preserve and protect the same from extinguishment by the operation of this act by filing for record, during the 30-year period immediately following the effective date of the root of title, a notice, in writing, in accordance with the provisions hereof, which notice shall have the effect of so preserving such claim of right for a period of not longer than 30 years after filing the same unless again filed as required herein.

§ 712.05, Fla. Stat. (1995). In City of Miami v. St. Joe Paper Co., 364 So.2d 439, 442 (Fla.1978), the court explained this provision:

> The Marketable Record Title Act is also a recording act in that it provides for a simple and easy method by which the owner of an existing old interest may preserve it. If he fails to take the step of filing the notice as provided, he has only himself to blame if his interest is extinguished. The legislature

---

[7] Obviously, the better practice in any land transaction is to expressly provide for all easements. Nevertheless, this case illustrates the difficulty in enforcing a way of necessity even if timely asserted and the difficulty of determining where it would be located and in establishing conditions on its use.

[8] The Court cited as an example of an inherent defect, a deed purporting to convey homestead property but only executed by a husband when the constitution required execution by both husband and wife. See Reid v. Bradshaw, 302 So. 180 (Fla. 1st DCA 1974).

did not intend to arbitrarily wipe out old claims and interests without affording a means of preserving them and giving a reasonable period of time within which to take the necessary steps to accomplish that purpose.

Similarly, in Cunningham v. Haley, 501 So.2d 649, 652-53 (Fla. 5th DCA 1986), the court explained:

It is the intent of sections 712.02(1) and 712.03(1), that easements and use restrictions and other estates, interests, and claims created prior to the root of title be extinguished by section 712.03(1), Florida Statutes, unless those matters are filed under section 712.05(1) or unless, as provided in section 712.03(1), after the date of the root of title, some muniment of title refers specifically to a recorded title transaction which imposed, transferred, or continued such easement, use restrictions, estate, interest, or claim.

In other words, "[a] claimant will not be cut off if he has been a party to any title transaction recorded within a period of not less than thirty years or if he files a simple notice prescribed by the Act during the time allowed for this purpose." Wilson v. Kelley, 226 So.2d 123, 127 (Fla. 2d DCA 1969). We conclude that this exception does apply, but H & F has not demonstrated compliance with its conditions.

H & F contends it could not and should not have had to file a claim under section 712.05 or otherwise as to the common law way of necessity because such right was already created in a prior transaction. Again, we disagree. We conclude that section 712.05 clearly mandates and H & F's predecessors had the opportunity to record their claim to an easement, i.e., to a common law way of necessity across the Airport District's property. In fact, it would appear that the very nature of the property right claimed here, one inferred by the law but otherwise hidden to the public, would make it especially important under MRTA's scheme to have it recorded. H & F also contends that it is difficult and impracticable to file a notice of a common law way of necessity because of the uncertainty in determining its location, especially when a servient estate is subdivided. However, it is apparent that H & F's predecessors had access to all the information that must be contained in a recorded notice as required by section 702.06. As such, they could and should have properly filed the notice.[9] Since they failed to do so, H & F cannot avail itself of this exception.

H & F further asserts that a common law way of necessity should not be subject to any recording requirement, including that of MRTA, because such an interest in land is not subject to the recording requirements of section 695.01, Florida Statutes (1995), Florida's general recording statute. However, section 712.07 provides that courts should construe MRTA independent of any other recording act. It provides:

---

[9] Moreover, as soon as a claimant makes a claim and begins to use the claimed way of necessity, the location becomes presumptively established. See Sapp v. General Dev. Corp., 472 So. 2d 544 (Fla. 2d DCA 1985). However, as we noted earlier, no public claim by attempted use was established here. Moreover, in response to H & F's concern over the difficulty and impracticability of filing a common law way of necessity, we note that filing the notice in this case would have only affected one parcel of land, Section 19, because it has never been subdivided.

Nothing contained in this law shall be construed to extend the period for the bringing of an action or for the doing of any other act required under any statute of limitations or to affect the operation of any statute governing the effect of the recording or the failure to record any instrument affecting land.

§ 712.07, Fla. Stat. (1995). We conclude that MRTA's broad recording provision is not limited to interests subject to section 695.01 and does include the easement claimed here.

LIMITATIONS EFFECT

As a final point, we recognize that MRTA also functions much as "a statute of limitations in that it requires stale demands to be asserted within a reasonable time after a cause of action has accrued. It prescribes a period within which a right may be enforced." *St. Joe Paper Co.*, 364 So.2d at 442. Although MRTA can produce harsh results, in upholding its constitutionality, this Court has declared: "We are committed to the rule that statutes of this nature [statute of limitations] are good where a reasonable time is allowed to prosecute an asserted right." *Id.* at 443 (quoting Buck v. Triplett, 32 So.2d 753, 754 (Fla. 1947)). "The law is well settled by decisions of the Supreme Court of the United States, and in other jurisdictions, that statutes of limitation affecting existing rights are not unconstitutional if a reasonable time is given for the enforcement of the right before the bar takes effect." Campbell v. Horne, 3 So.2d 125, 126 (Fla. 1941). As noted above, MRTA's provisions provide reasonable time periods for claims to be asserted. Even for those who choose to wait, the Legislature has been gracious in allowing a thirty-year period in which to record a claim.

CONCLUSION

Our decision today is predicated upon the strong public policy concerns underlying the enactment of MRTA. The Legislature clearly stated the purpose of MRTA and the exclusivity of its exceptions by adopting section 712.10. It provides: "This law shall be liberally construed to effect the legislative purpose of simplifying and facilitating land title transactions by allowing persons to rely on a record title as described in § 712.02 subject only to such limitations as appear in § 712.03." § 712.10, Fla. Stat. (1995).[11] While we also recognize the public policy concerns behind section 704.01, we conclude that it is important for the overall stability of property law under MRTA that claimants assert their interests in property in a reasonable and timely manner.[12] As we noted earlier, subject to some limited exceptions, MRTA has essentially shifted the burden to those claiming an interest in land to publicly assert these claims so that all interests in land will be a matter

---

[11] We recognize that section 704.08, Florida Statutes (1995), allows an easement for ingress and egress for the relatives and descendants of persons buried in a cemetery to visit the cemetery at reasonable times and in a reasonable manner. However, we conclude that this provision is not relevant to our analysis and we express no opinion on its interplay with MRTA.

[12] Of course, nothing in this opinion prevents H & F from seeking an easement from the Airport District to gain access to its property.

of public record. The circumstances of this case serve as a vivid illustration of the legislature's concerns in seeking to provide stability in property law while still providing a reasonable opportunity for the assertion of legitimate but unrecorded claims.

In the instant case, H & F's predecessor in title to the implied right now asserted could have recorded a notice of claim any time within the approximately fourteen years following the adoption of MRTA in 1963 until 1977, the end of the thirty-year period following the effective date of the root of the Airport District's title. Because H & F's predecessor failed to use or record its way of necessity or publicly assert it in any way, MRTA mandates the extinguishment of such an interest in property in favor of the record title owner of the property. Recognition of an implied but untimely asserted right of way over the record title holder's interest would undermine the clear purpose and effect of MRTA.

We therefore answer the certified question in the affirmative and approve the decision below.

It is so ordered.

2.   The Seller's Deed Covenants

SEYMOUR v. EVANS
608 So. 2d 1141 (Miss. 1992)

McRae, Justice.

This is an appeal from a judgment of the Chancery Court of Jackson County, dated March 30, 1989. Appellees are purchasers of real property who, after accepting deeds and obligating themselves to pay, discovered that zoning ordinances prevented them from using the property as they had intended. The chancellor set aside the deeds, finding that they violated the seller's implied warranties. He further ordered the return of the appellees' purchase payments and awarded consequential damages and attorney's fees to the appellees. We reverse and render on grounds that the deeds by which the appellees obtained their properties were valid and did not give rise to a breach of implied covenants.

FACTS AND PROCEEDINGS

The events leading up to this appeal began when appellant Edna C. Seymour decided to sell part of the land she owned in Jackson County, Mississippi. On August 22, 1983, she conveyed by warranty deed a three-acre parcel to John M. and Katherine McDonnell. The McDonnells executed a promissory note and deed of trust in favor of Seymour for the deferred portion of the purchase price. On September 13, 1983, the McDonnells conveyed by warranty deed this same three-acre tract to Jerry W. and Bonnie Ann Coleman. The Colemans assumed the McDonnells' indebtedness to Seymour.

Two couples, Larry and Gina Evans, and Dudley and Lori Cruse, expressed an interest in purchasing another tract containing five and one half acres which

Seymour offered for sale. They requested that the property be divided equally and conveyed to them separately. Accordingly, Seymour executed two warranty deeds on April 20, 1984. One conveyed to the Evanses a parcel of land containing about 2.75 acres; the other conveyed to the Cruses a parcel of equal size. Seymour also conveyed to each couple an easement across her unsold property for purposes of ingress and egress. The Evanses and the Cruses executed promissory notes and deeds of trust in favor of Seymour.

The Colemans, the Evanses, and the Cruses all intended to use their newly-conveyed properties for residential purposes. The land was unimproved, so, after receiving their deeds, the grantees cleared the property of underbrush and began to make improvements thereon.

On May 14, 1986, about two years later, the Cruses filed an application with the Jackson County Planning Department for a permit to locate a mobile home on their tract. Roger Clark, then Assistant Director of the Jackson County Planning Department, told them that a permit could not be issued because the division of April 20, 1984 violated the Jackson County subdivision ordinances. As Clark explained it, the property could be brought into compliance only by procuring plat approval and by paving a road for ingress and egress. The Cruses informed the Evanses of their difficulties, and both couples contacted Seymour. Seymour said there was nothing she could do.

The appellees subsequently met on several occasions with officials of the Jackson County Planning Department and the Planning Commission. At each meeting, they were told that no permits could be issued until the properties were brought into compliance with the subdivision regulations. The appellees also approached Jackson County Supervisor Tommy Brodnax. Brodnax also advised them that the subdivision regulations would have to be satisfied before permits would issue. Finally, appellees appeared informally before the Jackson County Board of Supervisors. They received the same advice there. The Colemans and the Evanses took the various county officials at their word and never filed for permits. The parties agree that Seymour was unaware of the subdivision regulations at the time when she conveyed the subject properties.

On April 13, 1988, the appellees filed a complaint in chancery court against Seymour, John Phillips and Associates (Seymour's realtor), Century 21-K Realty (the Evanses' and the Cruses' realtor), the McDonnells, and Jackson County. The two real estate agencies were subsequently dismissed as part of a negotiated settlement. The county was dismissed with prejudice on March 3, 1989. The chancellor entered judgment against Seymour and the McDonnells on March 30, 1989. The decree set aside the warranty deed from Seymour to the Evanses, the warranty deed from Seymour to the Cruses, and the warranty deed from the McDonnells to the Colemans. The decree also required Seymour to reimburse the Evanses and the Cruses for all payments made on the property together with their down payments, taxes, surveyors fees, forestry fees, loss of wages, closing costs, and attorney's fees.

The Evanses, the Cruses, and the Colemans each received their respective tracts by warranty deed. According to Miss.Code Ann. § 89-1-33:

The word "warrant" without restrictive words in a conveyance shall have the effect of embracing all of the five covenants known to common law, to wit: seisin, power to sell, freedom from encumbrance, quiet enjoyment and warranty of title.

The chancellor found that the conveyances by which appellees acquired their interests in the subject properties "violate[d] the common law covenants of warranty granted under section 89-1-33, especially power to sell." His Findings of Fact and Conclusions of Law does not disclose the analysis he employed in reaching this outcome. In order to determine whether the chancellor correctly applied the law of implied warranties, we must therefore consider each covenant separately.

Covenants of Seisin and Power to Sell

First are the covenants of seisin and power to sell. The distinction between these two warranties is largely one of only historical significance. As a practical matter, they are identical in content and scope. See 6A R. Powell, Real Property ¶ 900[2][b] (P. Rohan rev. ed. 1989); 7 G. Thompson, Real Property § 3178 at 242 (1962). The purpose of both is to provide assurance that the grantor has the estate he purports to convey. The record before us contains nothing to indicate that Seymour's estate in the property she conveyed was anything less than fee simple absolute. No third party has ever asserted a conflicting claim or interest. More to the point, the Jackson County subdivision regulations did not in any wise diminish Seymour's estate. Accordingly, they cannot be regarded as either a restriction on Seymour's power to sell or as a limitation on the estate with which Seymour was seised.

Appellees concede that Seymour's title was impeccable, but they insist that the conveyances nevertheless violated Seymour's warranty of power to sell because Seymour did not have the "power" to sell land in violation of the county subdivision ordinances. This novel argument must fail for two reasons. First, to define "power to sell" in such terms expands the scope of the warranty beyond its traditional focus on the estate of the grantor. Secondly, a deed which runs afoul of subdivision regulations is perfectly valid despite the violation. In Sienkiewicz v. Smith, 649 P.2d 112 (Wash. 1982), a trial court ruled that an earnest money contract was unenforceable since the conveyance it secured would violate a subdivision platting statute. On appeal, the Supreme Court of Washington disagreed:

Although we have long held that generally an agreement violating a statute or municipal ordinance is void, this is not necessarily true where the agreement is neither immoral nor criminal in nature and the statute or ordinance subjects violators merely to a penalty without more. In Marriott Financial Services, Inc. v. Capitol Funds, Inc., 217 S.E.2d 551 (N.C. 1975), the North Carolina Supreme Court refused to grant rescission to a purchaser on the grounds that the vendor had not complied with a city platting ordinance. In so ruling, the court looked to the language and purpose of the statute and asserted that since the contract was neither immoral nor criminal, the penalty for violation is limited to the penalties expressly provided for in the statute. Rescission was not included among those penalties. This sentiment is echoed in Gilmore v. Hershaw, 521 P.2d 934 (Wash. 1974), wherein we refused to grant rescission for a violation of [a subdivision statute] on the grounds that the Legislature specifically provided remedies other than rescission for violation of that platting and subdivision statute.

Id. at 115.

The holdings of the Washington and North Carolina courts appear to represent the majority view. Further, the propositions set out in *Sienkiewicz* and *Marriott* harmonize with this Court's position on analogous points of law. In Rast v. Sorrell, 127 So.2d 435 (Miss. 1961), the seller of a pool hall sued for damages after the buyer refused to go through with the contract. The buyer argued that the contract was void since the business had been operated in violation of a licensing statute. We held:

> The contract here involved is not declared void and unenforceable by the statute. It is not a contract malum in se, it is a contract malum prohibitum, and the penalty, which is alone a criminal penalty, is imposed for the sole purpose of protecting the public revenue. There is no inherent infirmity or illegality in such a contract. The Legislature intended to rely alone on the penalty provided in the statute for the protection of the revenue of the state.

Id. at 437.

We addressed a similar matter in Gardner v. Reed, 42 So.2d 206 (Miss. 1949). In *Gardner*, a buyer defended against the enforcement of a contract for the sale of fertilizer on grounds that the seller, a commercial fertilizer dealer, had not complied with statutory registration, inspection, and notice requirements. In holding for the buyer, we noted that "[t]he contract covered the purchase of a lawful commodity, and was not malum in se but merely malum prohibitum." The contract was deemed enforceable "since the contract was to cover the sale of a commodity, the sale of which is not prohibited by law, and there is no statutory provision declaring such a contact void and unenforceable for failure to comply with the provisions thereof, but makes such failure a criminal offense instead." *Id.* at 208.

Rast and *Gardner* implicate that the conveyances from Seymour to appellees are valid and enforceable so long as the ordinances they are alleged to violate regulate actions which are merely malum in prohibitum. In Mississippi State Highway Commission v. Wagley, 231 So.2d 507 (Miss.1970), we noted that the violation of a zoning restriction is malum prohibitum so long as the proscribed use does not involve "inherent evil." *Id.* at 509. There is nothing inherently evil about selling small tracts of land without platting them and without constructing paved streets for ingress and egress. Accordingly, Seymour's conveyances were not invalid even though they conflicted with Jackson County's subdivision ordinances. There is no question that Seymour had the "power" to sell the land as she did.

Covenant Against Encumbrances

Appellees additionally argue that Seymour breached her warranty of freedom from encumbrances by conveying the land in violation of the Jackson County subdivision regulations.

As a general rule, zoning and other public restrictions on the use of land do not in and of themselves constitute breaches of a covenant against encumbrances. This is true even though the regulation renders one's title unmarketable. Professor Powell cogently explains the state of the law:

> Encumbrances can usually be classified as one of three types: (1) servitudes, (2) liens or charges on the land, and (3) present or future estates which may be carved out of the estate conveyed. A servitude generally affects the land or its use and enjoyment in some physical way. It reduces the value of the land because a purchaser will not pay as much for a parcel of land which is limited in its usage as he or she would for an unencumbered one. Thus, easements and covenants are encumbrances. However, the existence of a zoning ordinance which limits the use of the land, even though its effect may be substantially similar to that of a restrictive covenant, is not considered a violation of the covenant. The attitude of the courts seems to be that these restrictions are public regulations equally applicable to all land in the district and are equally open for the grantor and grantee to investigate. Therefore, the purchaser takes title with the risk that such a regulation may exist.

Powell on Real Property, ¶ 900[2].

The law becomes a bit murky where property is not merely subject to a zoning restriction but is actually in violation of the restriction at the time of conveyance. The jurisdictions are not in agreement, but a majority seems generally to regard an existing violation as a breach of the covenant against encumbrances. Professor Powell explains:

> [C]ourts will not presume that a purchaser intended to use land in violation of a regulation. This interpretation of the distinction is supported by the fact that where construction on, or use of, the premises at the time of the conveyance already violates a restriction, the purchaser may assume that it is permitted and a breach of the covenant will occur.

Powell, Real Property ¶ 900[2][c].[3]

---

[3] The Powell rationale is, of course, inapplicable where the violation is not apparent. If the purchaser cannot discern the violation, then he cannot logically "assume" that the nonconformity is permitted. Many courts have therefore recognized an exception to the general rule where latent violations exist. See, e.g., Frimberger v. Anzellotti, 25 Conn. App. 401, 594 A.2d 1029 (Conn. App. Ct. 1991); Fahmie v. Wulster, 81 N.J. 391, 408 A.2d 789 (1979); Domer v. Sleeper, 533 P.2d 9 (Alaska 1975); McCrae v. Giteles, 253 So. 2d 260 (Fla. Dist. Ct. App. 1971); Silverblatt v. Livadas, 340 Mass. 474, 164 N.E.2d 875 (1960). *Frimberger* concludes that such an exception is justified since

> a conceptual enlargement of the covenant against encumbrances [to include latent, existing violations of restrictive land use ordinances] would create uncertainty and confusion in the law of conveyancing and title insurance because neither a title search nor a physical examination of the premises would disclose the violation.

Frimberger, 594 A.2d at 1033; accord *Feit*, slip op at 3; see also Comment, *Public Land Use Regulations & Marketability of Title*, 1958 Wis. L. Rev. 128.

A few courts have recognized a second exception to the general rule where an extant violation of a land use ordinance is easily remediable. See FFG, Inc. v. Jones, 6 Haw. App. 35, 708 P.2d 836 (Hawaii Ct. App. 1985) (zoning law violation which merely required the redesigning and repainting or parking lot on commercial property did not constitute encumbrance); see also Feit, slip op. at 4 (noting existence of

The Seymour conveyances obviously do not fall within the scope of the general rule that existing violations breach the implied covenant against encumbrances: The purported violations were not "existing" at the time of the conveyance. Rather, the conveyances themselves gave rise to the violations. The purchaser is not entitled to assume that a violation is permissible where there has been no history of tacit assent. We therefore find that the alleged violations of the Jackson County subdivision ordinances do not abridge Seymour's covenant against encumbrances.

Covenant of Quiet Enjoyment

The appellees further maintain that Seymour breached her warranty of quiet enjoyment. According to Bridges v. Heimburger, 360 So.2d 929, 931 (Miss.1978), the warranty of quiet enjoyment is breached where "there ha[s] been a judicial determination of loss of title or some other hostile action equivalent to eviction." The appellees claim that the county's refusal to grant permits was an action "equivalent to eviction."

The law does not precisely define the "equivalent" of eviction, but at least in the context of conveyance by warranty deed, it is clear that a grantee may claim constructive eviction only where his title suffers from an infirmity which endangers his right to possess the property. According to Powell, the covenant of quiet enjoyment "assures the grantee that his or her quiet possession or enjoyment will not be disrupted by the grantor or anyone else with paramount title." Powell on Real Property ¶ 900[2][e]. Cf. Bridges, 360 So.2d at 931 (covenant of quiet enjoyment not breached where grantee had good title and where grantee's "possession was never disturbed or even threatened"). In practical effect, therefore, this covenant operates "as the fraternal, if not identical, twin of the covenant of warranty." Powell on Real Property ¶ 900[2][e]. In the instant case, the record reveals no blemish on the appellees' title. Further, the appellees have demonstrated no infringement upon their right to possess the tracts in question; they merely assert that the violations of the subdivision ordinance prevent them from using the properties in the manner they intended.[6] In the absence of an impediment to good

---

exception). The rationale for this exception is that minor non-conformities do not substantially diminish the value of the property and thus do not qualify as encumbrances. See *Jones*, 708 P.2d at 48-49.

[6] The appellees cite no authority to support their proposition that a frustration of intended use amounts to a breach of the covenant of quiet enjoyment. Courts in other jurisdictions have regarded "constructive eviction" as included the legal inability to use a leasehold as one intended. See Park West Mgmt. Corp. v. Mitchell, 47 N.Y.2d 316, 418 N.Y.S.2d 310, 391 N.E.2d 1288 (1979) (covenant of quiet enjoyment includes a duty to refrain from act or omission which would render premises unusable by leasehold tenant); Polk v. Armstrong, 91 Nev. 557, 540 P.2d 96 (1975) (commercial tenant's inability to obtain operating license due to landlord's failure to bring premises into compliance with law amounted to constructive eviction). These cases as readily distinguishable from the instant case, however. First and most obviously, the case sub judice does not involve a leasehold. Seymour retained no control over the parcels she conveyed and assumed no responsibility for facilitating the appellees' use thereof. Secondly, unlike the litigants in *Mitchell* and *Polk*, the parties here entered no agreement contemplating the appellees' intended use of the properties. There is nothing in either the contracts of sale or the warranty deeds to indicate that the appellees intended to use the tracts for any particular purpose. Where the parties do not specify the purpose for which property is to be used, the grantor certainly cannot be viewed as having guaranteed the property's suitability for a particular use. Cf. Pursue Energy Corp. v. Perkins, 558 So. 2d 349, 352 (Miss. 1990) (court must look to language of instrument when determining

title or the right to possession, there can be no breach of the covenant of quiet enjoyment.

We hold that Seymour did not breach the warranties implied in her deeds to the appellees by conveying the subject properties in contravention to county subdivision ordinances.

The record does not clearly and conclusively indicate that the appellees could not have obtained the permits or variances they needed in order to use their properties in the manner they intended. We find, however, that even if the county had officially denied the appellees both permits and variances, the denials would not have given rise to breaches of Seymour's implied warranties. The covenants of seisen, power to sell, title, and quiet enjoyment all require some infringement on title or the right to possess. No such infringement occurred here. The violation of a subdivision ordinance breaches a covenant against encumbrances only where the violation already exists at the time of conveyance. The violation at issue here did not preexist the conveyance.

Given the facts contained in the record, we hold that the ability of the appellees to obtain permits or variances does not affect Seymour's implied warranties.

REVERSED AND RENDERED.

NOTES AND QUESTIONS

1. **Types of deeds.** There are three types of deeds, which differ in the amount of protection they extend to the grantee. A general warranty deed confers the most protection to the buyer; the seller in a general warranty deed warrants to the buyer that the seller's title is free of defects arising either during the seller's period of ownership of the property or before. *See, e.g.,* Tanglewood Land Co. v. Wood, 252 S.E.2d 546, 552 (N.C. Ct. App. 1979) (unlike special warranty deed, general warranty deed warrants seller's title "against the claims and demands of all persons whomsoever"). A special warranty deed protects the buyer only against defects arising during the seller's ownership of the property. *See, e.g.,* Dillow v. Magraw, 649 A.2d 1157, 1168 (Md. Ct. Spec. App. 1994) (special warranty deed includes "any act impairing the title during the holding of the property by the grantor," but "makes no covenant as to the status of title prior to title actually vesting in the grantor"). A quitclaim deed contains no protections for the grantee; the seller transfers whatever title the seller has, without purporting to say that the seller has anything.

2. **Deed covenants.** The common law recognized five title covenants and one covenant in aid of the others.

a. *Seisin.* The seller represents that seller owns the title that the deed purports to transfer. The seller who purports to convey a fee simple absolute breaches the covenant of seisin if the seller owns only a defeasible fee or a life estate in the land.

b. *Right to convey.* The seller represents that seller has the right to convey the title that the deed purports to convey. The principal case indicates that the

intent of parties to a conveyance); Deason v. Cox, 527 So. 2d 624, 627 (Miss. 1988) (same).

covenants of seisin and right to convey are virtually indistinguishable; both "focus on the estate of the grantor." *See also* Wright v. Hinnenkamp, 687 P.2d 163 (Or. Ct. App. 1984) (seller breached covenants of seisin and right to convey in statutory warranty deed when adverse possessor had already perfected title before seller's conveyance to buyer). In rare instances, however, the seller may breach one but not the other. Suppose that the seller is subject to a valid restraint on alienation; would a transfer by the seller violate the covenant of seisin or the covenant of right to convey? Suppose that seller has a power of attorney to sell someone else's land, and purports to sell it in the seller's own name; breach of the covenant of seisin or right to convey? In the principal case, what was the buyer's argument that the seller lacked power to convey? What is the court's answer?

c. *Against encumbrances.* Seller warrants that the subject property is free of encumbrances such as liens, leases, or easements, which "diminish the value of the estate even though they are consistent with the passage of the fee in the estate." Marathon Builders, Inc. v. Polinger, 283 A.2d 617, 621 (Md. 1971). In general, what you learned about encumbrances that impair marketability in connection with the contract of sale applies here. *See, e.g.,* Magun v. Bombaci, 492 A.2d 235, 236 (Conn. Super. Ct. 1985) (location of driveway and sewer lines partially on adjoining property was not an encumbrance and did not violate deed covenant against encumbrances); In re Country World Casinos, 181 F.3d 1146, 1153-54 (10th Cir. 1999) (environmental contamination was not "encumbrance" for purposes of warranty against encumbrances in warranty deed). One trouble spot concerns encumbrances such as easements that are discoverable by or known to the buyer. *See* Richitt v. Southern Pine Plantations, Inc., 491 S.E.2d 528, 529 (Ga. Ct. App. 1997) (public road did not constitute an encumbrance in breach of deed covenant where buyer knew that road existed and was being used and thus had duty to inquire about the interest possessed by those using the road); Stoebuck & Whitman § 11.13, at 909 (cases are "badly divided" as to whether a known defect violates seller's deed covenant against encumbrances). Another trouble spot concerns existing violations of zoning or related ordinances. Assuming that the court in Seymour v. Evans is right that the majority rule in this "murky" area is that a zoning violation breaches the seller's covenant against encumbrances, is the exception for latent violations (see footnote 3) sensible? Or should the exception become the general rule? *See* Hoffer v. Callister, 47 P.3d 1261 (Idaho 2002) (holding that a zoning violation was not a breach of the seller's warranty against encumbrances) ("Neither a title search nor a physical examination of the premises would have disclosed the alleged violation. The better way to deal with violations of zoning regulations is by contract provision."). *See generally* Adam Forman, Comment, *What You Can't See Can Hurt You: Do Latent Violations of a Restrictive Land Use Ordinance, Existing Upon Conveyance, Constitute a Breach of the Covenant Against Encumbrances?*, 64 Alb. L. Rev. 803 (2000).

d. *Quiet enjoyment.* The seller promises that the grantee will not be evicted or substantially disturbed in possession by the grantor or anyone with a paramount title.

e. *Warranty.* The seller promises to defend against lawful title claims against the buyer, and to indemnify the buyer for any loss resulting from an eviction or disturbance of possession. The quiet enjoyment and general warranty covenants are essentially identical. The seller's promise to defend against *lawful* claims covers only a successful suit against the grantee by a paramount title holder; the covenant is not breached, and the costs of defense are not recoverable, when the grantee's defense of his title is successful. *See* Black v. Patel, 594 S.E.2d 162, 164-65 (S.C. 2004). In Bloom v. Hendricks, 804 P.2d 1069, 1074-75 (N.M. 1991), the court recognized the general rule, but applied the following exception:

> [W]e believe a grantor should have limited liability under our statutory warranty covenants for the costs of a grantee's [successful] defense of an adverse claim. Whether the grantor may be held responsible should depend upon whether the grantor in fact has assumed the risk of those costs. Determinative of that assumption of risk are two factors: (1) whether the grantor bears some responsibility for the substance of an adverse claim, or had actual or constructive knowledge of a potential adverse claim at the time he warranted his title and agreed to defend it, and (2) whether the grantee has made demand of the grantor to defend the title. By "actual or constructive knowledge of a potential claim" we mean awareness of facts that later give rise to the adverse claim, or the existence of recorded title documents that, under NMSA 1978, Section 14-9-2, constitute "notice to all the world." By "demand" we mean notification to the grantor of a suit and specific request that he appear and conduct the defense.

The court denied recovery against the buyer's immediate grantor, on whom no demand to defend had been made, and granted recovery against a remote grantor, who had actual knowledge of the third party claim at the time he warranted title.

f. *Further assurances.* The seller promises to execute any necessary additional documents to perfect the title that the seller purports to convey to the buyer.

The first three covenants are present covenants, and the last three are future covenants. The significance of this distinction will be addressed in the next principal case.

3. **Statutory deeds.** In older warranty deeds, the covenants specified in Note 2 are spelled out in so many words. In many states, however, the seller conveys by a short form deed authorized by statute. The statute either provides the appropriate language or indicates the significance that particular language has. Notice that the Mississippi statute in the principal case provides that the word "warrant," without qualification, implies the common law covenants into the deed. *See also* Holmes Development, LLC v. Cook, 48 P.3d 895, 904 (Utah 2002) (by statute, the title covenants of seisin, right to convey, no encumbrances, quiet enjoyment, and warranty inhere in a warranty deed, even if not expressly set forth therein).

4. **Estoppel by deed.** *See* Wood v. Sympson, 833 P.2d 1239, 1243 (Okla. 1992):

> The doctrine of after-acquired title or estoppel by deed, although of common law origin, is part of our statutory law. [Okla. Stat. tit. 16, § 17] provides:

> > All rights of a mortgagor or grantor in and to the premises described in the instrument and existing at the time or subsequently accruing, shall accrue to the benefit of the mortgagee or grantee, and be covered by his

mortgage or conveyed by his deed, as the case may be.

Where a grantor conveys by warranty deed an interest he does not then own, but thereafter acquires, the reacquired interest inures to the benefit of the grantee. The vesting of title in the grantee, upon his grantor's reentry into the chain of title, passes by operation of law without any intervention of any court. The initial conveyance from a grantor who does not then own an interest in the property vests in the grantee equitable title to the interest purportedly conveyed in the warranty deed, so that when the grantor later acquires legal title it will instantly and immediately pass to the grantee. The purpose of the doctrine is to assure a grantor's or encumbrancer's warranty is effectuated.

But see Dalessio v. Baggia, 783 N.E.2d 890 (Mass. App. Ct. 2003) (doctrine of estoppel by deed did not apply when grantor conveyed by quitclaim deed).

BRIDGES v. HEIMBURGER
360 So. 2d 929 (Miss. 1978)

William H. Bizzell, J.

This is an appeal from a decree of the Chancery Court which awarded damages for breach of warranty of title to a lot in Jackson County.

Appellants (Defendants) Bridges and Deweese formerly owned the lot. In 1967 they agreed to sell this and other lots to one Hugh H. Moore. Through mutual error the grantee in the deed was Moore Homes, Inc. but the purchase money deed of trust was executed by Moore individually. On Moore's failure to make payment Appellants foreclosed in 1968 and repurchased at the foreclosure sale. The legal title of course remained in Moore Homes, Inc. Appellants were not aware of the error and it was not discovered by any of the successive owners and lien holders until 1974.

In 1969 Appellants conveyed this lot by general warranty deed to Doyle Homes, Inc. The record does not show either the sale price or the value of the lot at that time. Doyle Homes, Inc. constructed a home on the lot and in 1970 conveyed by general warranty deed to Appellee (Complainant) Heimburger and his wife. On the same day the Heimburgers executed a deed of trust securing an installment note in the principal sum of $30,250. Heimburger later testified that he paid $200 at closing, so apparently $30,450 represented the total purchase price of house and lot including closing costs. Thereafter and prior to this litigation his wife conveyed to Heimburger all her interest in the lot.

In February 1974 Heimburger contracted to sell the house for $36,500. A closing statement prepared for the proposed sale indicated that after mortgage pay-off, real estate commission and other closing costs his net from the sale would have been $3,493.81. The title defect was discovered in April 1974, just before the scheduled closing, and the sale was not completed. Heimburger employed an attorney and paid him a fee of $1250. The Attorney wrote a demand letter in May and filed a damage suit in June. The Bill of Complaint prayed for a judgment for money damages and attorney fees against Doyle Homes, Inc. and against Appellants Bridges and Deweese. Appellants filed a demurrer which was overruled, and then filed their answer. Doyle Homes, Inc. did not answer or appear.

The cause was not heard until November 1975. Meanwhile, in November 1974 a quitclaim deed was executed by Moore Homes, Inc. and Hugh H. Moore individually to Doyle Homes, Inc., thus curing the defect in title. At no time was Appellee's possession disturbed or threatened. After the title problem arose he rented the house for a time and collected a net rental of $2600 but made no further mortgage payments. He apparently made no further serious effort to sell the house. Although at trial he gave the excuse that the lawsuit would have interfered with a sale, it is obvious that his suit for damages could not have affected the sale, rental or occupancy of the property, and after November 1974 there was no title problem. In September 1975 the property was sold at foreclosure for $33,391.00, apparently the total then owing under the deed of trust.

The evidence at the November 1975 hearing is summarized above and was not in substantial conflict. The Chancellor was of the opinion that Appellee Heimburger should recover the amount which he would have netted from the sale except for failure of title, plus reasonable attorney fee. A money judgment was entered against Defendants Doyle Homes, Inc., W. P. Bridges, Jr. and Dewitt Deweese in the amount of $3,493.81 damages plus $1,250.00 attorney fee plus court costs. Defendants Bridges and Deweese appealed.

Any liability of Appellants Bridges and Deweese necessarily springs from their 1969 general warranty deed to Doyle Homes, Inc. Mississippi Code Section 89-1-33 (1972) provides that the word "warrant" embraces all of the five common law covenants: seisin, power to sell, freedom from incumbrance, quiet enjoyment and warranty of title. The covenant of freedom from incumbrance is not applicable here. The rules as to liability and damages for breach of the other four covenants are relatively well settled.

The covenant of seisin and the covenant of power to sell (good right to convey) are an assurance that grantor has the estate he purports to convey. These covenants technically were breached when Appellants conveyed to Doyle Homes, Inc., since the legal title was then in a third person. These covenants however are generally regarded as personal covenants, which do not run with the land. Accordingly, Appellants as remote grantors were not liable to Appellee for breach of these covenants.

The other two covenants, quiet enjoyment and warranty of title, are generally held to run with the land, so that a remote grantor may be held liable for their breach. But these two covenants are broken only by eviction or the equivalent of eviction. Accordingly, if Appellee had been evicted, or if there had been a judicial determination of loss of title or some other hostile action equivalent to eviction, he might have a claim against Appellants Bridges and Deweese as remote grantors. But Appellee's possession was never disturbed or even threatened. The evidence at trial not only showed that the flaw had been cured, but showed further that Appellee had originally acquired a good equitable title with right to reformation of the 1967 transaction which created the flaw. Accordingly, because there was no eviction or its equivalent, there was no breach here of the covenants of quiet enjoyment or warranty of title.

Under the foregoing general rules it appears that Appellee had no right to recover against Appellants for breach of warranty. Two other principles should be mentioned, however, which would prevent our affirming this decree. First, in all events, any liability of Appellants Bridges and Deweese would be limited to the value of the property, usually determined by sale price, at the time their 1969 deed was executed. Apparently the lot was vacant at the time Appellants conveyed it to Doyle Homes, Inc.; there is no evidence as to value or as to consideration paid at that time.

A second reason this decree could not be upheld is that profits lost through a failure of resale, on account of some breach of a covenant, are not recoverable. Appellee did not lose any part of his purchase money. The house cost him $30,450; its sale price at foreclosure prior to the trial was $33,391. This represents an actual gain in the total transaction, even without considering the rentals collected by him during litigation.

The decree of the trial court is reversed and the Bill of Complaint is dismissed on its merits as to Defendants (Appellants) Bridges and Deweese.

REVERSED AND RENDERED.

NOTES AND QUESTIONS

1. **Present and future covenants and why it matters.** The seller's covenants of seisin, right to convey, and against encumbrances are present covenants; they are breached, if at all, when the seller executes and delivers the deed. *See e.g.*, Marathon Builders, Inc. v. Polinger, 283 A.2d 617 (Md. 1971). Two consequences follow: the statute of limitations begins to run from the delivery of the deed, and the seller is liable only to the buyer, not to more remote owners of the property. The covenants of quiet enjoyment and warranty are future covenants; they are breached only when the grantee is evicted, and a breach can be asserted by remote grantees. *See* Stoebuck & Whitman § 11.13, at 910-11. Notice the difficulties for both buyer and seller posed by the temporal dimension of the deed covenants: the buyer might not discover a breach of the present covenants until years after the conveyance, when the statute of limitations has run; the seller remains liable on the future covenants for years after delivering the deed. *See* Brown v. Lober, 389 N.E.2d 1188 (Ill. 1979).

2. **Damages.** The basic rule of damages for breach of deed covenants is that the seller's liability is capped at the price the seller received for the land. What problems does that rule pose for the buyer? If the rule were that the buyer could recover damages based on the land's value at the time of eviction, what problem would that pose for the seller? Does the buyer have an alternative means to protect against losses that exceed the cap on seller's damages? In most transactions today, the buyer obtains title insurance, which will be addressed in Section D.3.

PROBLEM 5-C. In 1974, Profitt sells Blackacre to Atkinson, who resells it in 1978 to Carter, who resells it in 1980 to Isley. Two months after buying, Isley discovers that Profitt had mortgaged the land and that the mortgage still had an outstanding balance of $4,300. Assume that the statute of limitations for the covenant against encumbrances is ten years and that the mortgagee has made no effort to evict Isley or to foreclose on the mortgage. What remedy does Isley have, and against whom? *See* Proffitt v. Isley, 683 S.W.2d 243 (Ark. Ct. App. 1985). *Cf.* Benton v. Gaudry, 496 S.E.2d 507 (Ga. Ct. App. 1998).

3.   Claims Against the Title Insurer

BEAR FRITZ LAND CO. v. KACHEMAK BAY TITLE AGENCY, INC.
920 P.2d 759 (Alaska 1996)

Compton, Chief Justice.

I. FACTS AND PROCEEDINGS

In 1984 Robert Cooper and Virginia Cooper owned a parcel of property in Homer known as Fritz Subdivision, Unit 2. While the Coopers were making improvements on the parcel, a representative of the Army Corps of Engineers (Corps) inspected the site and ordered the Coopers to stop construction. The Corps believed the parcel included wetlands which the Coopers needed a permit to fill.

The Coopers applied for a wetlands permit in October 1984. On April 23, 1985, the Corps sent the Coopers copies of a proposed permit which allowed them to fill certain areas in the subdivision. The permit became effective on May 2, 1985, the date on which it was signed by the Chief of the Corps' Regulatory Branch. It was valid for three years from the date of issuance. The Coopers never recorded the permit.

During the permitting process, the Coopers apparently were negotiating the sale of the subdivision to Bear Fritz Land Company (Bear Fritz). On May 1, 1985, Bear Fritz obtained from Kachemak Bay Title Agency, Inc. and Ticor Title Insurance Company (collectively, Ticor) a preliminary commitment for title insurance on the property. On May 8, Bear Fritz executed an agreement to purchase the lots. At the end of May the parties closed the sale. The Coopers financed the transaction. On August 22, Ticor sent Bear Fritz a title insurance policy.

Bear Fritz claims it first learned of the wetlands permit in 1989 or 1990 while negotiating the sale of two lots in the subdivision. The permit already had expired. Bear Fritz stopped making payments on the purchase money note.

The Coopers sued Bear Fritz on the note. Bear Fritz filed a third-party complaint against Ticor, claiming that Ticor's failure to disclose the permit in the title policy and the preliminary commitment was a breach of its contract with Bear Fritz, and negligence on which Bear Fritz reasonably had relied in closing the deal.[3] Ticor moved for summary judgment. The superior court granted the motion,

---

[3] The Coopers and Bear Fritz settled their dispute.

primarily on the basis of its conclusion that the permit and the property's wetlands status were not defects in the title. Bear Fritz appeals. We affirm.

II. DISCUSSION

A. Standard of Review.

We will uphold summary judgment only if the record presents no genuine issues of material fact and the moving party is entitled to judgment on the law applicable to the established facts. When making this determination, we will draw all reasonable inferences in favor of the non-moving party.

B. The Policy Language Is Not Ambiguous.

The policy Ticor issued states:

> Ticor, subject to the conditions and stipulations of this policy, does hereby insure the person or persons named against loss or damage sustained by reason of:

> 1. Title to the estate, lien or interest being vested, at the date hereof, otherwise than as stated or

> 2. Any defect in, or lien or encumbrance on, said title existing at the date hereof, not shown in Schedule B.

Schedule B provides that "defects, liens, encumbrances and other matters against which the company does not insure" include:

> Any laws, governmental acts or regulations, including but not limited to zoning ordinances, restricting, regulating or prohibiting the occupancy, use or enjoyment of the land or any improvement thereon, or any zoning ordinances prohibiting a reduction in the dimensions or area, or separation in ownership, of any lot or parcel of land; or the effect of any violation of any such restrictions, regulations or prohibitions.

Bear Fritz devotes a significant portion of its briefing to a discussion of the general principles of insurance contract construction. According to Bear Fritz, both the general insuring clause and the governmental regulation exception are vague and ambiguous. It argues that the general insuring clause should be construed in favor of coverage, and that "[t]he general exception for laws and ordinances is void because it is not intelligible to a lay person." Bear Fritz further argues that "had Appellee Ticor not intended to cover wetlands designations it should have expressly stated so in the Title Policy to avoid any possible ambiguity or misunderstanding by its policy holder."

Bear Fritz's arguments are not persuasive. The policy language is reasonably clear and unambiguous. See Somerset Sav. Bank v. Chicago Title Ins. Co., 420 Mass. 422, 649 N.E.2d 1123, 1126-28 (1995) (finding unambiguous a title insurance policy virtually identical to that presented here); Lick Mill Creek Apartments v. Chicago Title Ins. Co., 231 Cal.App.3d 1654, 283 Cal.Rptr. 231, 234-38 & n. 3 (1991) (same). Therefore, the principles of construction favoring the insured are not material. See Jarvis v. Aetna Casualty and Sur. Co., 633 P.2d 1359, 1363 (Alaska 1981) ("This rule [that ambiguity and uncertainty in an insurance policy is resolved in favor of the insured] is not applied whenever two parties to a contract simply disagree over the interpretation of any of its terms. Rather, ambiguity is found to exist only when the contract, taken as a whole, is reasonably subject to differing interpretations." (internal quotations omitted)). The general rule is that "[a]n insurance company has the right to limit the coverage of a policy issued by it and when it has done so, the plain language of the limitation must be respected." *Id.* The rule applies here; it negates Bear Fritz's contention that coverage for wetlands designation cannot be excluded because the policy exception does not mention it expressly and specifically.

C. The Property's Wetlands Status and the Permit Restrictions Are Not a "Defect in, or Lien or Encumbrance on" the Title.

Bear Fritz contends that the property's wetlands classification and the restrictions of the wetlands permit are a defect, lien or encumbrance covered by the title policy. Ticor responds:

> Bear Fritz loses its coverage argument at the very first level of insurance policy analysis: as the permit in question did not affect title, it never came within the type of risk that this insurance purported to cover in the first place. . . . Title insurance does not cover all risks involved in the purchase or ownership of property. As the name implies, title insurance provides protection against defects in *title*. [A] title policy identifies the party in whom title vests, and insures against defects in that vested party's title. It does *not* insure that the new owner will be able to develop the property without restriction.

(Emphasis in the original.)

Ticor is correct. The law amply supports the distinction Ticor draws between defects or encumbrances affecting the marketability of title and defects affecting only the market value of the property. The law also supports Ticor's contention that the wetlands designation and permit are in the latter category.

In Domer v. Sleeper, we accepted the Washington Supreme Court's definition of "encumbrance" as

> any right to, or interest in, land which may subsist in third persons, to the diminution of the value of the estate of the tenant, but consistent with the passing of the fee; and, also, a burden upon the land depreciative of its value, such as a lien, easement, or servitude, which, though adverse to the interest of the landowner, does not conflict with his conveyance of the land in fee.

533 P.2d 9, 11 (Alaska 1975) (quoting Hebb v. Severson, 201 P.2d 156, 160 (Wash. 1948)). In *Domer* we held that building and fire code violations discovered by the buyer of a building were not encumbrances affecting the marketability of title. "[A] contrary rule would," we said, "generate considerable uncertainty as to the buyer's

title." *Id.* at 13.

The requirement that the property in this case comply with wetlands-protection provisions is similar to the requirement that the building in *Domer* comply with the building and fire codes. As with the building and fire code violations in *Domer*, the wetlands designation here is not an encumbrance: it does not give any third person a right to or interest in the property, nor does it burden the property with a lien, interest or servitude.

Cases from other jurisdictions further support Ticor's position. In Hocking v. Title Ins. & Trust Co., 234 P.2d 625 (Cal. 1951), the buyer of two lots in a subdivision found that she could not build on the lots without considerable unforeseen expense, because the seller had not complied with various local ordinances regarding subdivision of the land. She claimed the title was defective and sought damages from the title insurer. The California Supreme Court denied her claim:

> Although it is unfortunate that plaintiff has been unable to use her lots for the building purposes she contemplated, it is our view that the facts which she pleads do not affect the marketability of her *title* to the land, but merely impair the market *value* of the property. She appears to possess fee simple title to the property for whatever it may be worth; if she has been damaged by false representations in respect to the condition and value of the land her remedy would seem to be against others than the insurers of the title she acquired.

234 P.2d at 629-30 (emphasis in original). Faced with similar facts forty years later, the Supreme Court of Mississippi reached the same result in Seymour v. Evans, 608 So.2d 1141, 1144-47 (Miss. 1992).

In *Frimberger v. Anzellotti*, the Appellate Court of Connecticut held that wetlands designation does not affect the marketability of title or rise to the level of an encumbrance, even where the property had been improved in violation of the wetlands provisions. 594 A.2d 1029, 1031-32 (Conn. App. Ct. 1991) (citing *Domer*, 533 P.2d 9). In *Lick Mill Creek Apartments*, the California Court of Appeals held that a title insurance company whose representative had physically inspected a property prior to issuing a title insurance policy was not responsible for the costs associated with the cleanup of hazardous wastes on the insured property. The court found that although the wastes may have affected the market value of the property, they did not affect the marketability of title.

Finally, in *Somerset Savings*, the Massachusetts Supreme Judicial Court held that a restriction which required the consent of the state's Executive Office of Transportation and Construction (EOTC) to build on land formerly used as a railroad right-of-way did not come within the general coverage of title insurance. It wrote:

> It is well established that building or zoning laws are not encumbrances or defects affecting title to property. Such restrictions are concerned with the use of land. There is a difference between economic lack of market-ability, which concerns conditions that affect the use of the land, and title marketability, which relates to defects affecting the legally recognized rights and incidents of ownership. An individual can hold clear title to a

parcel of land, although the same parcel is valueless or considered economically unmarketable because of some restriction or regulation on its use. A title insurance policy provides protection against defects in, or liens or encumbrances on, title. Such coverage affords no protection for governmentally imposed impediments on the use of the land or for impairments in the value of the land.

The requirement of [EOTC] approval, prior to the issuance of a building permit, is a restriction on the use of the property, but it does not affect the owner's title to the property. It is a restriction that may affect the value of the property and the marketability of the parcel, but it has no bearing on the title to the property.

The insurance policy provided coverage for losses sustained as the result of a defect in or lien or encumbrance on the title to the property and for unmarketability of the title. Although they may have impaired the property's market value or caused a halt to construction on the property, the requirements of [the railroad right-of-way restriction] have no effect on the marketability of the title nor did they create a defect, lien, or encumbrance on the title. The existence of the statutory restriction, therefore, does not give rise to coverage under the policy.

649 N.E.2d at 1127-28. With a few minor changes, the reasoning and language of the *Somerset Savings* opinion could be applied to this case. We conclude that *Somerset Savings* and the other cited precedents are a correct statement of the law, and hold that neither the property's wetlands status nor the existence of the permit is an insured event or circumstance covered by Ticor's policy.

In light of this conclusion, it is unnecessary for us to address Bear Fritz's claim that the policy's governmental regulation exception is inapplicable or its claim that Ticor had a duty to disclose the permit in the preliminary commitment. See Bank of California v. First Am. Title Ins. Co., 826 P.2d 1126 (Alaska 1992) (establishing potential tort liability for misrepresentations made in preliminary commitments for title insurance).

III. CONCLUSION

The judgment of the superior court is AFFIRMED.

GREENBERG v. STEWART TITLE GUARANTY CO.
492 N.W.2d 147 (Wis. 1992)

BABLITCH, JUSTICE.

The issue presented is whether the issuance of title commitments and subsequently issued title insurance policies give rise in Wisconsin to a tort cause of action against the title insurer and/or its issuing agent separate and apart from the contractual obligations of the title policy. Martin J. Greenberg, the appellant, obtained from Stewart Title Guaranty Company, through its agent, Southeastern Wisconsin Title Company, four owner's title insurance policies in the amount of $250,000 each, which insured the interest in title in four condominiums. When Greenberg was unable to sell the condominiums because of an alleged defect in title, he contended that Stewart and Southeastern were liable not only under the contract, but in addition, for damage in tort for negligence. The circuit court held that the relationship between the parties involved a contract of indemnity and that no tort liability existed in Wisconsin law. We agree, and affirm the judgment of the circuit court.

The relevant facts follow. Martin Greenberg, the appellant, and John Huber (Huber) purchased four condominium units in Lake Geneva, Wisconsin. Before acquiring the condominiums, Greenberg and Huber contacted Stewart Title Guaranty Company (Stewart) through its agent, Southeastern Wisconsin Title Company (Southeastern). Title commitments were provided to Greenberg and Huber. A title commitment is a document which describes the property as the title insurer is willing to insure it and contains the same exclusions and general and specific exceptions as later appear in the title insurance policy. Joyce Dickey Palomar, *Title Insurance Companies' Liability For Failure to Search Title and Disclose Record Title*, 20 Creighton L.Rev. 455, 462 n. 39 (1986-87). Greenberg stated in his deposition that he received the title commitments from either Stewart or Southeastern.

Stewart, through its agent, Southeastern, then issued owner's title insurance policies insuring Huber's and Greenberg's title interest in the condominiums. Huber and Greenberg purchased the condominiums and, after acquisition, used the units to secure loans from several banks. Huber quitclaimed his interest in the condominiums to Greenberg, who decided to sell the units. Greenberg alleges that he was unable to sell the units because certain liens and encumbrances against the property made it impossible for him to transfer marketable title. He further alleges that, as a result, his lending institutions obtained a foreclosure judgment, and, after a sheriff's sale of the units, deficiency judgments were entered against him in the amount of $564,771.71.

Greenberg made a claim to Stewart alleging that the titles were unmarketable. Stewart denied the claim and Greenberg brought suit against Stewart and Southeastern. His complaint alleged five claims for relief: (1) negligent misrepresentation; (2) negligence; (3) breach of fiduciary duty; (4) breach of contract; (5) lack of good-faith and fair dealing. Specifically, as to the first cause of action, Greenberg's complaint alleges that Southeastern and Stewart "breached the duties they owed to Greenberg under common law by failing to disclose liens and encumbrances and facts relating to same which were known to [them]." Under the second cause of action the complaint alleges that Stewart and Southeastern "owed Greenberg a duty to base the title insurance commitments and policies for the Units on reasonably diligent searches of the public records," and that they "breached their duties to Greenberg by failing to make reasonably diligent searches which would have disclosed liens and encumbrances of record showing title to the Units to be unmarketable." The circuit court dismissed the first two claims holding that the relationship between the parties involved a contract of indemnity and that no tort liability existed in Wisconsin law. The circuit court dismissed the third claim because Greenberg's complaint did not allege any facts from which the court could find a fiduciary duty. The circuit court ordered further briefing on the breach of contract claim and Greenberg voluntarily dismissed the fifth claim. In addition, the circuit court dismissed Southeastern as a party to the action because the only claim remaining in the lawsuit was the breach of contract claim and, as the agent, Southeastern was not a party to the contract.

Greenberg appealed from the judgment dismissing Southeastern as a party, and the court of appeals certified the following issue to this court: "Is a title insurance company liable in tort for failure to discover a title defect or does such liability sound in contract only?" We accepted certification from the court of appeals.

Greenberg maintains that he can sue a title insurance company for negligence because the issuance of a title commitment and a title insurance policy places a common law duty on a title company to search and disclose any reasonably discoverable defects in title. According to Greenberg, this duty is separate and distinct from the title company's contractual duties under the title insurance policy. We disagree.

Courts in other jurisdictions are split on the question of whether a title insurance company can be exposed to liability in tort for negligence in searching records. Some courts and commentators have concluded that a title company should be liable in tort as well as in contract if it negligently fails to discover and disclose a defect. "The underlying notion [of these opinions] is that the insured has the reasonable expectation that the title company will search the title." Walker Rogge, Inc. v. Chelsea Title & Guar. Co., 562 A.2d 208, 218 (N.J.1989).

Other jurisdictions have refused to impose tort liability on title insurance companies. These courts reason that because a title insurer does not purport to act as anything other than an insurance company, no tort liability exists unless the insurer has voluntarily assumed a duty of searching title for the insured's benefit in addition to the contract to insure title. They further conclude that the issuance of a preliminary report or title commitment is not an independent assumption of a duty to search and disclose reasonably discoverable defects. We find this reasoning, particularly the reasoning of Justice Pollock of the New Jersey Supreme Court in *Walker Rogge*, persuasive.

In *Rogge*, the insured, Walker Rogge, Inc., sued a title insurance company when it discovered that the acreage of the tract of land it purchased was approximately 12 acres, instead of the approximate 19 acres Rogge thought it had purchased. In support of its negligence claim, Rogge pointed to the title company's separate charge for a title examination and to its reliance on the title company to conduct a reasonable search. In response to Rogge's arguments, Justice Pollock, writing for the majority, stated:

> Although we recognize that an insured expects that a title company will conduct a reasonable title examination, the relationship between the company and the insured is essentially contractual. The end result of the relationship between the title company and the insured is the issuance of the policy. To this extent, the relationship differs from other relationships

conceivably sounding in both tort and contract, such as the relationship between physician and patient, to which plaintiff alludes. Although the relationship between physician and patient is contractual in its origins, the purpose of the relationship is to obtain the services of the physician in treating the patient. The patient reasonably expects the physician to follow the appropriate standard of care when providing those services. By contrast, the title company is providing not services, but a policy of insurance. That policy appropriately limits the rights and duties of the parties.

From this perspective, the insured expects that in consideration for payment of the premium, it will receive a policy of insurance. The insurer's expectation is that in exchange for that premium it will insure against certain risks subject to the terms of the policy. If the title company fails to conduct a reasonable title examination or, having conducted such an examination, fails to disclose the results to the insured, then it runs the risk of liability under the policy. In many, if not most, cases conduct that would constitute the failure to make a reasonable title search would also result in a breach of the terms of the policy.

562 A.2d at 220.

We also find instructive the Texas Court of Appeals' discussion of title insurance in Houston Title Co. v. Ojeda de Toca, 733 S.W.2d 325, 327 (Tex. App. 1987), rev'd on other grounds Ojeda de Toca v. Wise, 748 S.W.2d 449 (Tex. 1988). "The title insurance company is not, as is an abstract company, employed to examine title; rather, the title insurance company is employed to guarantee the status of title and to insure against existing defects. Thus, the relationship between the parties is limited to that of indemnitor and indemnitee."

In Blackhawk Prod. v. Chicago Ins., 423 N.W.2d 521 (Wis. 1988), we explained:

Title insurance has been described as a contract of indemnity. Its purpose is to indemnify the insured for impairment of its interest due to failure of title as guaranteed in the title insurance report. That is, it protects against losses sustained in the event that a specific contingency, such as the discovery of an unexcepted lien affecting title, occurs.

This language and the language quoted above from other jurisdictions indicate that a title insurance company is not an abstractor of title employed to examine title. Rather, a title insurance company guarantees the status of title and insures up to the policy limits against existing defects. Thus, the only duty undertaken by a title insurance company in issuing a policy of insurance is to indemnify the insured up to the policy limits against loss suffered by the insured if the title is not as stated in the policy.

Similarly, the issuance of a title commitment does not, as Greenberg suggests, constitute an independent undertaking by the insurer to search the title for the benefit of the insured. Rather, the title commitment "generally constitutes no more than a statement of the terms and conditions upon which the insurer is willing to issue its title policy." Lawrence v. Chicago Title Ins. Co., 237 Cal.Rptr. 264 (Cal. Ct. App. 1987). Any search done by an insurer in preparation for preparing a title commitment is done to protect itself in deciding whether to insure the property and to protect against losses covered in the policy.

Greenberg also argues that, even if the title commitment did not constitute a duty separate and distinct from the title company's contractual duties, accompanying every contract is a common law duty to perform with care, skill, reasonable diligence and faithfulness the thing they agreed to be done. He contends that the duty that accompanies his contract is for the insurance company to search and disclose reasonable defects.

Southeastern disputes this contention. Southeastern contends that in order for a cause of action to arise in tort in a contractual setting, the plaintiff must show an assumption of a duty that exists independent of the contract. We agree.

Furthermore, even were we to agree with Greenberg's contention that an independent duty need not exist in order to bring a claim in tort because every contract contains a duty to perform with care, skill, reasonable diligence and faithfulness the thing they agreed to be done, we would conclude that no action against Southeastern can be brought in tort. There was no obligation under the contract to search the title, thus no duty could arise to search the title with due care and skill.

We therefore hold that a title insurance company and/or its agent is not liable in negligence for an alleged defect in title when it issues a title insurance policy unless it has voluntarily assumed a duty to conduct a reasonable search in addition to the mere contract to insure title.

We further hold that the issuance of a title commitment is not an assumption of an independent duty to search. Greenberg himself acknowledged the lack of such a duty in his deposition testimony:

> Q — Can you produce any documents, including either the title commitments or title policies, whereby any of the defendants took on the obligation to warranty title to these four units?
>
> A — I don't understand what warranty title means. Are you talking about insuring title? Are you talking about warranty against certain exceptions? Are your talking about a warranty as to marketability? I don't understand your question.
>
> Q — Okay. As a real estate lawyer and professor, you're generally aware of the content of standard title policies and title commitments; correct?
>
> A — Correct.
>
> Q — And nowhere in those documents is there any warranty of title; is there?
>
> A — There is not a warranty of title, but there is an insurance of marketable title.

Accordingly, we agree with the decision of the circuit court dismissing Greenberg's tort claims and its judgment is affirmed.

Lastly, Greenberg contends that even if the title insurance company (Stewart) did not have a duty to make a reasonable title search, the title insurer's agent (Southeastern) should be liable in tort. He reasons that Southeastern owes a duty by virtue of its actions in allegedly negligently searching the record because its liability is not limited by the terms of a contract, as Southeastern was not a party to the contract. We disagree.

An agent of an insurance company owes a duty only to the insurance company. In the present case, Southeastern, the agent, performed its services solely for the benefit of the insurance company and owed no duty to Greenberg. Thus, no action in tort may be brought against Southeastern.

For the reasons set forth in this opinion, we affirm the judgment of the circuit court.

NOTES AND QUESTIONS

1. **Review.** To what extent do courts treat marketability of title differently when the buyer's claim is against the title insurance company rather than against the seller? In addition to the *Bear Fritz* case, see Radovanov v. Land Title Co. of America, 545 N.E.2d 351 (Ill. App. Ct. 1989) (despite exception in policy for "any law, ordinance or governmental regulation, including but not limited to building and zoning ordinances, restricting or regulating or prohibiting occupancy, use or enjoyment of land, or the effect of any violation of any such law," pending housing code violation lawsuit predating the title policy was covered by the insured's commitment to indemnify for unmarketable title); Camp v. Commonwealth Land Title Ins. Co., 787 F.2d 1258 (8th Cir. 1986) (applying Arkansas law) (violation of a restrictive covenant due to construction of house below specified grade did not render buyer's title unmarketable and was not covered by policy). If there is a difference, what argument(s) might be made in support of it?

2. **Comparisons.** What are the advantages and disadvantages of title insurance compared to the seller's warranties of title? *See* Jerome J. Curtis, Jr., *Title Assurance in Sales of California Residential Realty: A Critique of Title Insurance and Title Covenants With Suggested Reforms*, 7 Pac. L.J. 1 (1976).

3. **Tort and contract.** Why might an insured seek to recover against a title insurer in tort rather than in contract? *See generally* James Bruce Davis, *More Than They Bargained For: Are Title Insurance Companies Liable in Tort for Undisclosed Title Defects?*, 45 Cath. U. L. Rev. 71 (1995).

4. **Independent duty.** In *Greenberg* and *Walter Rogge* (discussed in *Greenberg*), the courts held that the issuance of a title policy does not itself constitute an independent undertaking by the insurer to search the title for the benefit of the insured. What might constitute an independent undertaking? In *Walter Rogge*, the court suggested some possibly relevant facts:

Notwithstanding the essentially contractual nature of the relationship between a title company and its insured, the company could be subject to a negligence action if the "act complained of was the direct result of duties voluntarily assumed by the insurer in addition to the mere contract to insure title." *Brown's Tie & Lumber Co. v. Chi. Title Co.*, , 764 P.2d 423, at

426. As support for its negligence claim against Chelsea, Walker Rogge points to various facts. For example, Chelsea had twice insured the property in question and on four other occasions it had opened files on the property. In addition, Chelsea's own back title plant reflected that the tract comprised twelve, not eighteen, acres. One of Chelsea's employees, moreover, supervised the closing, at which time the purchase price was computed on that basis. Because it restricted plaintiff's claim to the policy, the trial court did not determine whether Chelsea knew or should have known of the difference in acreage and of its materiality to the transaction. The court did not, therefore, determine whether Chelsea assumed an independent duty to assure the quantity of acreage, whether it breached that duty, or whether the breach caused any damage to Walker Rogge. Consequently, we are obliged to remand the matter to the trial court for a determination of those issues. In remanding, we do not decide whether Chelsea was obligated to bring the difference in acreage to the attention of its insured under an implied duty of fair dealing. That issue has played no role at the trial or appellate level. We leave to the discretion of the trial court whether the matter should be resolved on the present record or should be supplemented by additional testimony.

4.   Condition of the Premises

a.   Fraud and Nondisclosure

The following two cases are best considered as a unit. In reading them, consider the following questions: (1) How is nondisclosure different from fraud? (2) Should the duty to disclose defects, if it exists, be limited to disclosure of known defects, or should it include a duty to investigate for latent defects in order to be able to disclose them? (3) What *types* of conditions require disclosure (e.g., physical condition of the property, value, desirability)? (4) Who should bear the duty to disclose — the seller alone, or also the real estate broker? (5) What remedies does the buyer have when the seller (or broker) is guilty of an actionable nondisclosure?

STAMBOVSKY v. ACKLEY
572 N.Y.S.2d 672 (N.Y. App. Div. 1991)

RUBIN, JUSTICE.

Plaintiff, to his horror, discovered that the house he had recently contracted to purchase was widely reputed to be possessed by poltergeists, reportedly seen by defendant seller and members of her family on numerous occasions over the last nine years. Plaintiff promptly commenced this action seeking rescission of the contract of sale. Supreme Court reluctantly dismissed the complaint, holding that plaintiff has no remedy at law in this jurisdiction.

The unusual facts of this case, as disclosed by the record, clearly warrant a grant of equitable relief to the buyer who, as a resident of New York City, cannot be expected to have any familiarity with the folklore of the Village of Nyack. Not being a "local," plaintiff could not readily learn that the home he had contracted to purchase is haunted. Whether the source of the spectral apparitions seen by defendant seller are parapsychic or psychogenic, having reported their presence in both a national publication ("Readers' Digest") and the local press (in 1977 and 1982, respectively), defendant is estopped to deny their existence and, as a matter of law, the house is haunted. More to the point, however, no divination is required to conclude that it is defendant's promotional efforts in publicizing her close encounters with these spirits which fostered the home's reputation in the community. In 1989, the house was included in a five-home walking tour of Nyack and described in a November 27th newspaper article as "a riverfront Victorian (with ghost)." The impact of the reputation thus created goes to the very essence of the bargain between the parties, greatly impairing both the value of the property and its potential for resale. The extent of this impairment may be presumed for the purpose of reviewing the disposition of this motion to dismiss the cause of action for rescission and represents merely an issue of fact for resolution at trial.

While I agree with Supreme Court that the real estate broker, as agent for the seller, is under no duty to disclose to a potential buyer the phantasmal reputation of the premises and that, in his pursuit of a legal remedy for fraudulent misrepresentation against the seller, plaintiff hasn't a ghost of a chance, I am nevertheless moved by the spirit of equity to allow the buyer to seek rescission of the contract of sale and recovery of his down payment. New York law fails to recognize any remedy for damages incurred as a result of the seller's mere silence, applying instead the strict rule of caveat emptor. Therefore, the theoretical basis for granting relief, even under the extraordinary facts of this case, is elusive if not ephemeral.

> "Pity me not but lend thy serious hearing to what I shall unfold" (William Shakespeare, Hamlet, Act I, Scene V [Ghost]).

From the perspective of a person in the position of plaintiff herein, a very practical problem arises with respect to the discovery of a paranormal phenomenon: "Who you gonna' call?" as the title song to the movie "Ghostbusters" asks. Applying the strict rule of caveat emptor to a contract involving a house possessed by poltergeists conjures up visions of a psychic or medium routinely accompanying the structural engineer and Terminix man on an inspection of every home subject to a contract of sale. It portends that the prudent attorney will establish an escrow account lest the subject of the transaction come back to haunt him and his client — or pray that his malpractice insurance coverage extends to supernatural disasters. In the interest of avoiding such untenable consequences, the notion that a haunting is a condition which can and should be ascertained upon reasonable inspection of the premises is a hobgoblin which should be exorcised from the body of legal precedent and laid quietly to rest.

It has been suggested by a leading authority that the ancient rule which holds that mere non-disclosure does not constitute actionable misrepresentation "finds proper application in cases where the fact undisclosed is patent, or the plaintiff has equal opportunities for obtaining information which he may be expected to utilize, or the defendant has no reason to think that he is acting under any misapprehension" (Prosser, Law of Torts § 106, at 696 [4th ed., 1971]). However, with respect to transactions in real estate, New York adheres to the doctrine of caveat emptor and imposes no duty upon the vendor to disclose any information concerning the premises unless there is a confidential or fiduciary relationship between the parties or some conduct on the part of the seller which constitutes "active concealment," e.g., foundation cracks covered by seller. Normally, some affirmative misrepresentation, e.g., industrial waste on land allegedly used only as farm, or partial disclosure, e.g., existence of third unopened street concealed, is required to impose upon the seller a duty to communicate undisclosed conditions affecting the premises

Caveat emptor is not so all-encompassing a doctrine of common law as to render every act of non-disclosure immune from redress, whether legal or equitable. Common law is not moribund. Ex facto jus oritur (law arises out of facts). Where fairness and common sense dictate that an exception should be created, the evolution of the law should not be stifled by rigid application of a legal maxim.

The doctrine of caveat emptor requires that a buyer act prudently to assess the fitness and value of his purchase and operates to bar the purchaser who fails to exercise due care from seeking the equitable remedy of rescission. For the purposes of the instant motion to dismiss the action, plaintiff is entitled to every favorable inference which may reasonably be drawn from the pleadings, specifically, in this instance, that he met his obligation to conduct an inspection of the premises and a search of available public records with respect to title. It should be apparent, however, that the most meticulous inspection and the search would not reveal the presence of poltergeists at the premises or unearth the property's ghoulish reputation in the community. Therefore, there is no sound policy reason to deny plaintiff relief for failing to discover a state of affairs which the most prudent purchaser would not be expected to even contemplate.

The case law in this jurisdiction dealing with the duty of a vendor of real property to disclose information to the buyer is distinguishable from the matter under review. The most salient distinction is that existing cases invariably deal with the physical condition of the premises, defects in title, liens against the property, expenses or income, and other factors affecting its operation. No case has been brought to this court's attention in which the property value was impaired as the result of the reputation created by information disseminated to the public by the seller (or, for that matter, as a result of possession by poltergeists).

Where a condition which has been created by the seller materially impairs the value of the contract and is peculiarly within the knowledge of the seller or unlikely to be discovered by a prudent purchaser exercising due care with respect to the subject transaction, nondisclosure constitutes a basis for rescission as a matter of equity. Any other outcome places upon the buyer not merely the obligation to exercise care in his purchase but rather to be omniscient with respect to any fact which may affect the bargain. No practical purpose is served by imposing such a burden upon a purchaser. To the contrary, it encourages predatory business practice and offends the principle that equity will suffer no wrong to be without a remedy.

Defendant's contention that the contract of sale, particularly the merger or "as is" clause, bars recovery of the buyer's deposit is unavailing. Even an express disclaimer will not be given effect where the facts are peculiarly within the knowledge of the party invoking it. Moreover, a fair reading of the merger clause reveals that it expressly disclaims only representations made with respect to the physical condition of the premises and merely makes general reference to representations concerning "any other matter or things affecting or relating to the aforesaid premises." As broad as this language may be, a reasonable interpretation is that its effect is limited to tangible or physical matters and does not extend to paranormal phenomena. Finally, if the language of the contract is to be construed as broadly as defendant urges to encompass the presence of poltergeists in the house, it cannot be said that she has delivered the premises "vacant" in accordance with her obligation under the provisions of the contract rider.

To the extent New York law may be said to require something more than "mere concealment" to apply even the equitable remedy of rescission, the case of Junius Construction Corporation v. Cohen, 257 N.Y. 393, 178 N.E. 672, while not precisely on point, provides some guidance. In that case, the seller disclosed that an official map indicated two as yet unopened streets which were planned for construction at the edges of the parcel. What was not disclosed was that the same map indicated a third street which, if opened, would divide the plot in half. The court held that, while the seller was under no duty to mention the planned streets at all, having undertaken to disclose two of them, he was obliged to reveal the third.

In the case at bar, defendant seller deliberately fostered the public belief that her home was possessed. Having undertaken to inform the public at large, to whom she has no legal relationship, about the supernatural occurrences on her property, she may be said to owe no less a duty to her contract vendee. It has been remarked that the occasional modern cases which permit a seller to take unfair advantage of a buyer's ignorance so long as he is not actively misled are "singularly unappetizing" (Prosser, Law of Torts § 106, at 696 [4th ed. 1971]). Where, as here, the seller not only takes unfair advantage of the buyer's ignorance but has created and perpetuated a condition about which he is unlikely to even inquire, enforcement of the contract (in whole or in part) is offensive to the court's sense of equity. Application of the remedy of rescission, within the bounds of the narrow exception to the doctrine of caveat emptor set forth herein, is entirely appropriate to relieve the unwitting purchaser from the consequences of a most unnatural bargain.

Accordingly, the judgment of the Supreme Court, New York County, entered April 9, 1990, which dismissed the complaint, should be modified, on the law and the facts and in the exercise of discretion, and the first cause of action seeking rescission of the contract reinstated, without costs.

SMITH, JUSTICE (dissenting).

The parties herein were represented by counsel and dealt at arm's length. This is evidenced by the contract of sale which contained various riders and a specific provision that all prior understandings and agreements between the parties were merged into the contract, that the contract completely expressed their full agreement and that neither had relied upon any statement by anyone else not set forth in the contract. There is no allegation that defendants, by some specific act, other than the failure to speak, deceived the plaintiff. Nevertheless, a cause of action may be sufficiently stated where there is a confidential or fiduciary relationship creating a duty to disclose and there was a failure to disclose a material fact, calculated to induce a false belief. However, plaintiff herein has not alleged and there is no basis for concluding that a confidential or fiduciary relationship existed between these parties to an arm's length transaction such as to give rise to a duty to disclose. In addition, there is no allegation that defendants thwarted plaintiff's efforts to fulfill his responsibilities fixed by the doctrine of caveat emptor.

[I]f the doctrine of caveat emptor is to be discarded, it should be for a reason more substantive than a poltergeist. The existence of a poltergeist is no more binding upon the defendants than it is upon this court.

JOHNSON v. DAVIS
480 So. 2d 625 (Fla. 1985)

ADKINS, JUSTICE.

In May of 1982, the Davises entered into a contract to buy for $310,000 the Johnsons' home, which at the time was three years old. The contract required a $5,000 deposit payment, an additional $26,000 deposit payment within five days and a closing by June 21, 1982. The crucial provision of the contract, for the purposes of the case at bar, is Paragraph F which provided:

> F. Roof Inspection: Prior to closing at Buyer's expense, Buyer shall have the right to obtain a written report from a licensed roofer stating that the roof is in a watertight condition. In the event repairs are required either to correct leaks or to replace damage to facia or soffit, seller shall pay for said repairs which shall be performed by a licensed roofing contractor.

Before the Davises made the additional $26,000 deposit payment, Mrs. Davis noticed some buckling and peeling plaster around the corner of a window frame in the family room and stains on the ceilings in the family room and kitchen of the home. Upon inquiring, Mrs. Davis was told by Mr. Johnson that the window had had a minor problem that had long since been corrected and that the stains were wallpaper glue and the result of ceiling beams being moved. There is disagreement among the parties as to whether Mr. Johnson also told Mrs. Davis at this time that there had never been any problems with the roof or ceilings. The Davises thereafter paid the remainder of their deposit and the Johnsons vacated the home. Several days later, following a heavy rain, Mrs. Davis entered the home and discovered water "gushing" in from around the window frame, the ceiling of the family room, the light fixtures, the glass doors, and the stove in the kitchen.

Two roofers hired by the Johnsons' broker concluded that for under $1,000 they could "fix" certain leaks in the roof and by doing so make the roof "watertight." Three roofers hired by the Davises found that the roof was inherently defective, that any repairs would be temporary because the roof was "slipping," and that only a new $15,000 roof could be "watertight."

The Davises filed a complaint alleging breach of contract, fraud and misrepresentation, and sought recission of the contract and return of their deposit. The Johnsons counterclaimed seeking the deposit as liquidated damages.

The trial court entered its final judgment on May 27, 1983. The court awarded the Davises $26,000 plus interest and awarded the Johnsons $5,000 plus interest. Each party was to bear their own attorneys' fees.

The Johnsons appealed and the Davises cross-appealed from the final judgment. The Third District found for the Davises affirming the trial court's return of the majority of the deposit to the Davises ($26,000), and reversing the award of $5,000 to the Johnsons as well as the court's failure to award the Davises costs and fees. Accordingly, the court remanded with directions to return to the Davises the balance of their deposit and to award them costs and fees.

The contract contemplated the possibility that the roof may not be watertight at the time of inspection and provided a remedy if it was not in such a condition. The roof inspection provision of the contract did not impose any obligation beyond the seller correcting the leaks and replacing damage to the facia or soffit. The record is devoid of any evidence that the seller refused to make needed repairs to the roof. In fact, the record reflects that the Davises' never even demanded that the areas of leakage be repaired either by way of repair or replacement. Yet the Davises insist that the Johnsons breached the contract justifying recission. We find this contention to be without merit.

We also agree with the district court's conclusions under a theory of fraud and find that the Johnsons' statements to the Davises regarding the condition of the roof constituted a fraudulent misrepresentation entitling respondents to the return of their $26,000 deposit payment. In the state of Florida, relief for a fraudulent misrepresentation may be granted only when the following elements are present: (1) a false statement concerning a material fact; (2) the representor's knowledge that the representation is false; (3) an intention that the representation induce another to act on it; and, (4) consequent injury by the party acting in reliance on the representation.

The evidence adduced at trial shows that after the buyer and the seller signed the purchase and sales agreement and after receiving the $5,000 initial deposit payment the Johnsons affirmatively repeated to the Davises that there were no problems with the roof. The Johnsons subsequently received the additional $26,000 deposit payment from the Davises. The record reflects that the statement made by the Johnsons was a false representation of material fact, made with knowledge of its falsity, upon which the Davises relied to their detriment as evidenced by the $26,000 paid to the Johnsons.

The doctrine of caveat emptor does not exempt a seller from responsibility for the statements and representations which he makes to induce the buyer to act, when under the circumstances these amount to fraud in the legal sense. To be grounds for relief, the false representations need not have been made at the time of the signing of the purchase and sales agreement in order for the element of reliance to be present. The fact that the false statements as to the quality of the roof were made after the signing of the purchase and sales agreement does not excuse the seller from liability when the misrepresentations were made prior to the execution of the contract by conveyance of the property. It would be contrary to all notions of fairness and justice for this Court to place its stamp of approval on an affirmative misrepresentation by a wrongdoer just because it was made after the signing of the executory contract when all of the necessary elements for actionable fraud are present. Furthermore, the Davises' reliance on the truth of the Johnsons' representation was justified and is supported by this Court's decision in Besett v. Basnett, 389 So.2d 995 (1980), where we held "that a recipient may rely on the truth of a representation, even though its falsity could have been ascertained had he made an investigation, unless he knows the representation to be false or its falsity is obvious to him." *Id.* at 998.

In determining whether a seller of a home has a duty to disclose latent material defects to a buyer, the established tort law distinction between misfeasance and nonfeasance, action and inaction must carefully be analyzed. The highly individualistic philosophy of the earlier common law consistently imposed liability upon the commission of affirmative acts of harm, but shrank from converting the courts into an institution for forcing men to help one another. This distinction is deeply rooted in our case law. Liability for nonfeasance has therefore been slow to receive recognition in the evolution of tort law.

In theory, the difference between misfeasance and nonfeasance, action and inaction, is quite simple and obvious; however, in practice it is not always easy to draw the line and determine whether conduct is active or passive. That is, where failure to disclose a material fact is calculated to induce a false belief, the distinction between concealment and affirmative representations is tenuous. Both proceed from the same motives and are attended with the same consequences; both are violative of the principles of fair dealing and good faith; both are calculated to produce the same result; and, in fact, both essentially have the same effect.

Still there exists in much of our case law the old tort notion that there can be no liability for nonfeasance. The courts in some jurisdictions, including Florida, hold that where the parties are dealing at arms's length and the facts lie equally open to both parties, with equal opportunity of examination, mere nondisclosure does not constitute a fraudulent concealment. The Fourth District affirmed that rule of law in Banks v. Salina, 413 So.2d 851 (Fla. 4th DCA 1982), and found that although the sellers had sold a home without disclosing the presence of a defective roof and swimming pool of which the sellers had knowledge, "[i]n Florida, there is no duty to disclose when parties are dealing at arms length." *Id.* at 852.

These unappetizing cases are not in tune with the times and do not conform with current notions of justice, equity and fair dealing. One should not be able to stand behind the impervious shield of caveat emptor and take advantage of another's ignorance. Our courts have taken great strides since the days when the judicial emphasis was on rigid rules and ancient precedents. Modern concepts of justice and fair dealing have given our courts the opportunity and latitude to change legal precepts in order to conform to society's needs. Thus, the tendency of the more recent cases has been to restrict rather than extend the doctrine of caveat emptor. The law appears to be working toward the ultimate conclusion that full disclosure of all material facts must be made whenever elementary fair conduct demands it.

The harness placed on the doctrine of caveat emptor in a number of other jurisdictions has resulted in the seller of a home being liable for failing to disclose material defects of which he is aware. This philosophy was succinctly expressed in Lingsch v. Savage, 213 Cal.App.2d 729, 29 Cal.Rptr. 201 (1963):

It is now settled in California that where the seller knows of facts materially affecting the value or desirability of the property which are known or accessible only to him and also knows that such facts are not known to or within the reach of the diligent attention and observation of the buyer, the seller is under a duty to disclose them to the buyer.

In Posner v. Davis, 395 N.E.2d 133 (Ill. App. Ct. 1979), buyers brought an action alleging that the sellers of a home fraudulently concealed certain defects in the home which included a leaking roof and basement flooding. Relying on *Lingsch*, the court concluded that the sellers knew of and failed to disclose latent material defects and thus were liable for fraudulent concealment. Numerous other jurisdictions have followed this view in formulating law involving the sale of homes. See Flakus v. Schug, 329 N.W.2d 859 (Neb. 1983) (basement flooding); Thacker v. Tyree, 297 S.E.2d 885 (W.Va.1982) (cracked walls and foundation problems); Maguire v. Masino, 325 So.2d 844 (La.Ct.App.1975) (termite infestation); Weintraub v. Krobatsch, 64 N.J. 445, 317 A.2d 68 (1974) (roach infestation); Cohen v. Vivian, 349 P.2d 366 (Colo. 1960) (soil defect).

We are of the opinion, in view of the reasoning and results in *Lingsch*, *Posner* and the aforementioned cases decided in other jurisdictions, that the same philosophy regarding the sale of homes should also be the law in the state of Florida. Accordingly, we hold that where the seller of a home knows of facts materially affecting the value of the property which are not readily observable and are not known to the buyer, the seller is under a duty to disclose them to the buyer. This duty is equally applicable to all forms of real property, new and used.

In the case at bar, the evidence shows that the Johnsons knew of and failed to disclose that there had been problems with the roof of the house. Mr. Johnson admitted during his testimony that the Johnsons were aware of roof problems prior to entering into the contract of sale and receiving the $5,000 deposit payment. Thus, we agree with the district court and find that the Johnsons' fraudulent concealment also entitles the Davises to the return of the $5,000 deposit payment plus interest. We further find that the Davises should be awarded costs and fees.

The decision of the Third District Court of Appeals is hereby approved.

It is so ordered.

NOTES AND QUESTIONS

1. **Fraud.** On what traditional basis did the court in Johnson v. Davis find that the sellers had committed fraud?

2. **Nondisclosure: the tradional view.** How does nondisclosure differ from classic common law fraud? Under what (limited) circumstances, discussed in Stambovsky v. Ackley, could nondisclosure amount to fraud? Were those limited circumstances present in Johnson v. Davis or in Stambovsky v. Ackley?

3. **Nondisclosure: the modern view.** Johnson v. Davis represents the weight of modern authority, which imposes on sellers of real estate the duty

> to disclose latent defects, known to the seller, which substantially affect the value or habitability of the property, but which are unknown to the purchaser, and would not be discovered by a reasonably diligent inspection.

Denis Binder, *The Duty to Disclose Geologic Hazards in Real Estate Transactions*, 1 Chapman L. Rev. 13, 21 (1998). What is the basis for the imposition of that duty on sellers? Should the duty also extend to the seller's broker? *See id.* at 28-33.

4. **Disclosure of what?** What is the difference between the undisclosed condition in Stambovsky v. Ackley and in Johnson v. Davis? Why is disclosure required in *Stambovsky*? Is a seller required to disclose that the home had been the site of a multiple murder ten years before? *See* Reed v. King, 193 Cal. Rptr. 130 (Cal. Ct. App. 1983).

5. **Statutes.** By one count, approximately half the states have now enacted mandatory statutes, requiring that residential sellers communicate to potential buyers their knowledge of the condition of the premises.

> These state disclosure statutes accomplish two objectives. First, they allocate to property sellers the burden of providing a detailed accounting of their knowledge about defective conditions to prospective purchasers. Second, they protect sellers from liability for failing to disclose psychologically stigmatizing conditions, such as when a homicide, suicide, felony, or death by AIDS occurred on the property. This is the case because the statutes limit the scope of disclosure to defects that are physical in nature and material in significance. Disclosure laws thereby constitute a brake on the erosion of the doctrine of caveat emptor.

Alan M. Weinberger, *Let the Buyer Be Well Informed? Doubting the Demise of Caveat Emptor*, 55 Md. L. Rev. 387, 414 (1996). *See also* Robert M. Washburn, *Residential Real Estate Condition Disclosure Legislation*, 44 DePaul L. Rev. 381 (1995) (comprehensive discussion of judicially-created disclosure obligations and of statutes requiring disclosure); Ronald Benton Brown, *Buyers Beware: Statutes Shield Real Estate Brokers and Sellers Who Do Not Disclose That Properties Are Psychologically Tainted*, 49 Okla. L. Rev. 625 (1996).

6. **Megan's Law.** Many states have now enacted laws requiring law enforcement officials to notify communities when convicted sex offenders move into the locale. If a seller knows about the presence of such an offender, must the seller disclose the information to a prospective buyer? See Thomas D. Larson, Comment, *To Disclose or Not to Disclose: The Dilemma of Homeowners and Real Estate Brokers under Wisconsin's "Megan's Law,"* 81 Marq. L. Rev. 1161 (1998); Lori A. Polonchak, Comment, *Surprise! You Just Moved Next to a Sexual Predator: The Duty of Residential Sellers and Real Estate Brokers to Disclose the Presence of Sexual Predators to Prospective Purchasers*, 102 Dick. L. Rev. 169 (1997).

7. **Off-site conditions.** "[T]he issue in this case is whether a builder-developer of new homes and the brokers marketing those homes have a duty to disclose to prospective buyers that the homes have been constructed near an abandoned hazardous-waste dump." How should the court answer the question? Construct arguments on both sides of the issue. If the court decides in favor of a disclosure duty, can you think of any appropriate limitations on the holding? *See* Strawn v. Canuso, 657 A.2d 420 (N.J. 1995). *See generally* Robert Kwong,

Comment, *Fraud and the Duty to Disclose Off-Site Land Conditions: Actual Knowledge vs. Seller Status*, 24 B.C. Envtl. Aff. L. Rev. 897 (1997).

8. **Remedies.** What remedy for the seller's nondisclosure does the court in Stambovsky v. Ackley authorize? Consider Nystrom v. Cabada, 652 So. 2d 1266 (Fla. Dist. Ct. App. 1995), in which the court found that Nystrom, the seller, "knew or should have known of [the complained of] defects and had a duty to disclose them" to Cabada, the buyer. The trial court found in favor of the plaintiff on the issues of breach of warranty, contract, fraud, and rescission. The appellate court disagreed with the trial court's remedy, stating:

> In rescission, Cabada could return the property to the Nystroms in return for a refund of the purchase price, but could not elect that remedy and recover damages also. Niesz v. Gehris, 418 So.2d 445 (Fla. D. Ct. App. 1982), *review denied*, 427 So.2d 736 (Fla. 1983). In fraud, damages are determined by the "benefit of the bargain" rule which awards as damages the difference between the actual value of the property and its value had the alleged facts regarding it been true, or the "out-of-pocket" rule, which awards as damages the difference between the purchase price and the real or actual value of the property. Martin v. Brown, 566 So.2d 890 (Fla. D. Ct. App. 1990). As for breach of contract or warranty arising from construction defects, the measure of damages is that set forth in Grossman Holdings Ltd. v. Hourihan, 414 So.2d 1037 (Fla. 1982). In *Hourihan*, our supreme court adopted section 346(1)(a) of the Restatement (First) on Contracts (1932), which in pertinent part provides:

> (a) For defective or unfinished construction [the contracting party] can get judgment [from the builder] for either

> (i) the reasonable cost of construction and completion in accordance with the contract, if this is possible and does not involve unreasonable economic waste; or

> (ii) the difference between the value that the product contracted for would have had and the value of the performance that has been received by the plaintiff, if construction and completion in accordance with the contract would involve unreasonable economic waste.

> Cabada was offered the option of rescission, but opted for the more attractive remedy of keeping the residence together with what amounts to a full refund of the purchase price.[1] Such a remedy is not supported by any authority which has come to our attention, applying either the measure of damages available in fraud or breach of contract.

Id. at 1268.

9. **Breach of Warranty?** In Nystrom v. Cabada discussed in Note 8 above, the seller, although not a licensed general contractor, had acted as his own general contractor in constructing the home, which he then lived in for a year before selling it. Does the builder of a home owe any special duty to a buyer?

---

[1] An appraisal in evidence, made one month before closing, reflects a land value of $32,000 and a value of the structure itself in the amount of $89,212.

10. **Unfair Trade Practice Acts.** An unfair trade practices act, if a state has one, offers a disappointed buyer the prospect of recovering augmented damages and attorney's fees in cases of the seller's fraud or actionable nondisclosure. *See, e.g.*, Tanpiengco v. Tasto, 806 A.2d 1080 (Conn. App. Ct. 2002) (per curiam) (punitive damages and attorney's fees awarded under Connecticut Unfair Trade Practices Act where broker knew that property adjoined a former municipal landfill and that part of property was located on landfill, but made "deliberate nondisclosures" by saying that property was open space owned by municipality and would never be built on). In *Tanpiengco*, the buyers, in addition to the penalties noted, sought rescission of the contract of sale.

b. Implied Warranty

In most states, a builder-seller makes an implied warranty of habitability or workmanlike quality in the sale of a home. The warranty does not apply to ordinary sellers or to sellers of nonresidential properties. Who may assert this warranty against the builder-seller?

LEMPKE v. DAGENAIS
547 A.2d 290 (N.H. 1988)

THAYER, JUSTICE.

This is an appeal from the trial court's dismissal of the plaintiffs' complaint alleging breach of implied warranty of workmanlike quality and negligence. The primary issue before this court is whether a subsequent purchaser of real property may sue the builder/contractor on the theory of implied warranty of workmanlike quality for latent defects which cause economic loss, absent privity of contract.

We hold that privity of contract is not necessary for a subsequent purchaser to sue a builder or contractor under an implied warranty theory for latent defects which manifest themselves within a reasonable time after purchase and which cause economic harm. Accordingly, we reverse the dismissal by the trial court, and remand.

In 1977, the plaintiffs' predecessors in title contracted with the defendant, Dagenais, to build a garage. In April, 1978, within six months after the garage's construction, the original owners sold the property to plaintiffs, Elaine and Larry Lempke. Shortly after they purchased the property, the plaintiffs began to notice structural problems with the garage — the roof line was uneven and the roof trusses were bowing out. The plaintiffs contend that the separation of the trusses from the roof was a latent defect which could not be discovered until the separation and bowing became noticeable from the exterior of the structure. Fearing a cave-in of the roof, the plaintiffs contacted the defendant and asked him to repair the defects. The defendant initially agreed to do so, but never completed the necessary repairs. The plaintiffs then brought suit against the builder. In turn, the builder filed a motion to dismiss, which the superior court granted based on our holding in Ellis v. Morris, 513 A.2d 951 (N.H. 1986). This appeal followed.

The plaintiffs set forth three claims in their brief: one for breach of implied warranty of workmanlike quality; one for negligence; and one, in the alternative, for breach of assigned contract rights. We need address only the first two claims.

We have previously denied aggrieved subsequent purchasers recovery in tort for economic loss and denied them recovery under an implied warranty theory for economic loss. The court in *Ellis* acknowledged the problems a subsequent purchaser faces, but declined to follow the examples of those cases which allow recovery. The policy arguments relied upon in *Ellis* for precluding tort recovery for economic loss, in these circumstances, accurately reflect New Hampshire law and present judicial scholarship, and, as such, remain controlling on the negligence claim. However, the denial of relief to subsequent purchasers on an implied warranty theory was predicated on the court's adherence to the requirement of privity in a contract action and on the fear that to allow recovery without privity would impose unlimited liability on builders and contractors. Thus we need only discuss the implied warranty issue.

I. Privity

This case affords us an opportunity to review and reassess the issue of privity as it relates to implied warranties of workmanlike quality. In Norton v. Burleaud, 342 A.2d 629 (N.H. 1975), this court held that an implied warranty of workmanlike quality applied between the builder of a house and the first purchaser. The *Norton* court so held based on the facts before it, and did not explicitly or impliedly limit the benefit of implied warranties solely to the first purchaser. The question before us today is whether this implied warranty may be relied upon by subsequent purchasers and, if so, whether recovery may be had for solely economic loss.

There has been much judicial debate on the basis of implied warranty. Some courts find that it is premised on tort concepts. Other courts find that implied warranty is based in contract. Other authorities find implied warranty neither a tort nor a contract concept, but "a freak hybrid born of the illicit intercourse of tort and contract. Originally sounding in tort, yet arising out of the warrantor's consent to be bound, it later ceased necessarily to be consensual, and at the same time came to lie mainly in contract." Prosser, *The Assault Upon the Citadel*, 69 Yale L.J. 1099, 1126 (1960).

Regardless of whether courts have found the implied warranty to be based in contract or tort, many have found that it exists independently, imposed by operation of law, the imposition of which is a matter of public policy. See 67A Am.Jur.2d § 690 ("Implied warranties arise by operation of law and not by agreement of the parties, their purpose being to protect the buyer from loss."). We continue to agree with our statement in Elliott v. Lachance, 109 N.H. 481, 483, 256 A.2d 153, 155 (1969), that "[implied] warranties are not created by an agreement between the parties but are said to be imposed by law on the basis of public policy. They arise by operation of law because of the relationship between the parties, the nature of the transaction, and the surrounding circumstances," and agree with other courts that find implied warranties, in circumstances similar to those presented here, to be creatures of public policy "that ha[ve] evolved to protect purchasers of homes upon the discovery of latent defects," Redarowicz v.

Ohlendorf, 441 N.E.2d 324 (Ill. 1982), and that, regardless of their theoretical origins, "exist independently."

There are jurisdictions which have refused to extend the implied warranty to subsequent purchasers, finding privity necessary. However, numerous jurisdictions have now found privity of contract unnecessary for implied warranty. Despite the *Ellis* ruling, New Hampshire has generally disfavored privity in certain situations. See, e.g., RSA 382-A:2-318 (Supp.1986) (New Hampshire adoption of UCC Alternative C which abolishes privity in implied warranty suits); Spherex, Inc. v. Alexander Grant & Co., 451 A.2d 1308, 1311 (N.H. 1982). In *Spherex*, the court found privity of contract unnecessary for negligent misrepresentation by an accountant. "Our reluctance to applying the privity rule has been extended to allowing the proper plaintiff to recover for mere financial loss resulting from negligent performance of services." We likened an accountant to a manufacturer and found that an accountant was in the best position to regulate the effects of his conduct by controlling the degree of care exercised in his professional duties.

In keeping with judicial trends and the spirit of the law in New Hampshire, we now hold that the privity requirement should be abandoned in suits by subsequent purchasers against a builder or contractor for breach of an implied warranty of good workmanship for latent defects. "To require privity between the contractor and the home owner in such a situation would defeat the purpose of the implied warranty of good workmanship and could leave innocent homeowners without a remedy." Aronsohn v. Mandara, 484 A.2d 675 (N.J. 1984).

Numerous practical and policy reasons justify our holding. First, "[c]ommon experience teaches that latent defects in a house will not manifest themselves for a considerable period of time after the original purchaser has sold the property to a subsequent unsuspecting buyer." Terlinde v. Neely, 275 S.C. 395, 271 S.E.2d 768, 769 (1980).

Second, our society is rapidly changing. "We are an increasingly mobile people; a builder-vendor should know that a house he builds might be resold within a relatively short period of time and should not expect that the warranty will be limited by the number of days that the original owner holds onto the property." *Redarowicz*, 441 N.E.2d at 330. Furthermore, "the character of society has changed such that the ordinary buyer is not in a position to discover hidden defects." *Terlinde*, 271 S.E.2d at 769.

Third, like an initial buyer, the subsequent purchaser has little opportunity to inspect and little experience and knowledge about construction. "Consumer protection demands that those who buy homes are entitled to rely on the skill of a builder and that the house is constructed so as to be reasonably fit for its intended use." Moxley v. Laramie Builders, Inc., 600 P.2d 733, 735 (Wyo. 1979).

Fourth, the builder/contractor will not be unduly taken unaware by the extension of the warranty to a subsequent purchaser. "The builder already owes a duty to construct the home in a workmanlike manner." Keyes v. Guy Bailey Homes, Inc., 439 So. 2d 670, 673 (Miss. 1983). And extension to a subsequent purchaser, within a reasonable time, will not change this basic obligation.

Fifth, arbitrarily interposing a first purchaser as a bar to recovery "might encourage sham first sales to insulate builders from liability." Richards v. Powercraft Homes, Inc., 139 Ariz. 242, 678 P.2d 427, 430 (1984).

Economic policies influence our decision as well. "[B]y virtue of superior knowledge, skill, and experience in the construction of houses, a builder-vendor is generally better positioned than the purchaser to evaluate and guard against the financial risk posed by a [latent defect]." George v. Veach, 313 S.E.2d 920, 923 (N.C. Ct. App. 1984).

Not only do policy and economic reasons convince us that a privity requirement in this situation is unwarranted, but analogous situations show us the soundness of this extension. Public policy has compelled a change in the law of personal property and goods, as witnessed by the adoption of the UCC. As one law review commentator said: the "[a]pplication of such a warranty is similar to that of implied warranty of fitness and merchantability under the Uniform Commercial Code." Comment, *Builder's Liability for Latent Defects in Used Homes*, 32 Stan.L.Rev. 607 (1980) (author urged that regardless of method employed, liability for latent defects occurring within a reasonable time should be placed on builder).

II. Economic Loss

Finally, we address the issue of whether we should allow recovery for purely economic harm, which generally is that loss resulting from the failure of the product to perform to the level expected by the buyer and is commonly measured by the cost of repairing or replacing the product. Much theoretical debate has taken place on whether to allow economic recovery and whether tort or contract is the most appropriate vehicle for such recovery.

It is clear that the majority of courts do not allow economic loss recovery in tort, but that economic loss is recoverable in contract, and that economic loss recovery "is consistent with the policy of warranty law to protect expectations of suitability and quality." Moorman Manufacturing Co. v. National Tank Co., 435 N.E.2d 443, 449 (Ill. 1982) (distinguishing between strict liability in tort and warranty). However, what is less clear is whether courts allow recovery for economic loss on an implied warranty theory, without privity, in situations such as ours. Some courts do not. Other courts implicitly allow recovery for economic loss, and other courts that have dealt directly with the issue of economic harm in implied warranty have found that an aggrieved party can recover.

The courts which have allowed economic loss recovery in situations similar to ours have done so basically because the line between property damage and economic loss is not always easy to draw. Bertschy, *The Economic Loss Doctrine in Illinois After Moorman*, 71 Ill.B.J. 346, 355 (1983). In his article, Bertschy states that the *Redarowicz* decision, the UCC commentary, and Justice Simon's comment in Moorman Mfg. Co. v. National Tank Co., 435 N.E.2d 443 at 456, that economic loss should be recoverable out of privity in some circumstances, make a "strong argument for extending policy-based warranties to subsequent purchasers in the case of economic loss."

We agree with the courts that allow economic recovery in implied warranty for subsequent purchasers, finding as they have that "the contention that a distinction should be drawn between mere 'economic loss' and personal injury is without merit."

> Why there should be a difference between an economic loss resulting from injury to property and an economic loss resulting from personal injury has not been revealed to us. When one is personally injured from a defect, he recovers mainly for his economic loss. Similarly, if a wife loses a husband because of injury resulting from a defect in construction, the measure of damages is totally economic loss. We fail to see any rational reason for such a distinction.
>
> If there is a defect in a stairway and the purchaser repairs the defect and suffers an economic loss, should he fail to recover because he did not wait until he or some member of his family fell down the stairs and broke his neck? Does the law penalize those who are alert and prevent injury? Should it not put those who prevent personal injury on the same level as those who fail to anticipate it?

Barnes v. Mac Brown & Co., Inc., 264 Ind. 227, 342 N.E.2d 619, 621 (1976). The vendee has a right to expect to receive that for which he has bargained.

Permitting recovery for economic loss in implied warranty to subsequent purchasers of property is compelling.

> In the sale of a home the transaction usually involves an individual owner who sells to an individual buyer. In such cases there ordinarily would be no implied warranty as to latent defects. Since the UCC applies to "transactions in goods," no implied warranty of merchantability or fitness for a particular purpose would be created by the Unified Commercial Code.

Szajna v. General Motors Corp., 503 N.E.2d 760, 765 (Ill. 1986) (case distinguishing between implied warranty in real estate as opposed to goods).

III. Limitations

We are, however, aware of the concerns that this court in *Ellis* raised about unlimited liability. As with any rule, there must be built-in limitations, which in this case would act as a barrier to the possibility of unlimited liability.

Therefore, our extension of the implied warranty of workmanlike quality is not unlimited; it does not force the builder to act as an insurer, in all respects, to a subsequent purchaser. Our extension is limited to latent defects "which become manifest after the subsequent owner's purchase and which were not discoverable had a reasonable inspection of the structure been made prior to the purchase." *Richards*, 678 P.2d at 430.

The implied warranty of workmanlike quality for latent defects is limited to a reasonable period of time. "The length of time for latent defects to surface, so as to place subsequent purchasers on equal footing should be controlled by the standard of reasonableness and not an arbitrary time limit created by the Court." *Terlinde*,

271 S.E.2d at 769.

Furthermore, the plaintiff still has the burden to show that the defect was caused by the defendant's workmanship, and defenses are also available to the builder. "The builder can demonstrate that the defects were not attributable to him, that they are the result of age or ordinary wear and tear, or that previous owners have made substantial changes." *Richards*, 678 P.2d at 430.

Finally, we want to clarify that the duty inherent in an implied warranty of workmanlike quality is to perform in "a workmanlike manner and in accordance with accepted standards." Norton v. Burleaud, 342 A.2d at 630. "The law recognizes an implied warranty that the contractor or builder will use the customary standard of skill and care." Kenney v. Medlin Const. & Realty Co., 315 S.E.2d 311, 314 (N.C. Ct. App. 1984).

In conclusion, to the extent Ellis v. Morris suggests otherwise, we overrule it, and therefore reverse and remand this case for further proceedings.

REVERSED AND REMANDED.

NOTES AND QUESTIONS

1. **Comparisons.** What is the difference between a fraud claim (Section D.4.a above) and a breach of warranty claim?

2. **Caveat emptor?** Recall the implied warranty of habitability in residential landlord-tenant law. (*See* Chapter 4.B.3.a.) Are the arguments for imposing a warranty in residential leases applicable to sales of residential real estate? *See* Paul G. Haskell, *The Case for an Implied Warranty of Quality in Sales of Real Property*, 53 Geo. L.J. 633 (1965).

3. **The implied warranty.** What is the content of the implied warranty recognized in the principal case? What protections does it afford the buyer? What are the limitations on the warranty recognized in the principal case?

4. **Parties.** What are the arguments for allowing recovery on the implied warranty by a subsequent purchaser from the original buyer? Against allowing such recovery?

5. **Contract and tort.** What is the difference between a contract theory and a tort (negligence) theory of recovery against a builder-seller?

6. **The defendant.** If you sell your home to a buyer, do you impliedly warrant its condition to the buyer? If not, on what basis might you be liable to your buyer for defects in the condition of the home?

7. **Waiver.** Can the implied warranty of habitability or workmanlike quality be waived? *Compare* Albrecht v. Clifford, 767 N.E.2d 42, 47 (Mass. 2002) (implied warranty of habitability cannot be waived), *with* Greeves v. Rosenbaum, 965 P.2d 669, 673 (Wyo. 1998) ("as is" clause effective to waive implied warranty of habitability), *and* Board of Managers of Village Centre Condominium Ass'n v. Wilmette Partners, 760 N.E.2d 976, 981 (Ill. 2001) ("any disclaimer that does not reference the implied warranty of habitability by name is not a valid disclaimer of that warranty"). Which approach is the best?

Chapter 6

EASEMENTS

Consider three agreements between neighbors: Landowner A agrees (1) that his neighbor B may use a portion of A's land for a more convenient access to a public street; (2) that B may operate a piggery, with its attendant noises and odors, on B's land; and (3) that A will not build too close to the boundary separating their land so as to obstruct B's access to light for B's solar conductor. All three agreements provide that their terms bind A and his heirs and assigns, and benefit B and her heirs and assigns. These examples are all illustrations of easements, which, in turn, are part of a family of interests in land that the law calls "servitudes." Servitudes are *private* restrictions on the uses that a landowner (in our examples, A) is privileged to make of his land, in contrast to such public regulation as zoning, which also limits what a landowner can do with or on his land. Unlike estates, servitudes confer a right in the holder to use, rather than to possess (exclude others from), the land subject to the servitude.

The following excerpt indicates why servitudes are important:

> "Servitude" is the generic term that describes legal devices private parties can use to create rights and obligations that run with land. Rights and obligations that run with land are useful because they create land-use arrangements that remain intact despite changes in ownership of the land. Servitudes permit the creation of neighborhoods restricted to particular uses, providing a private alternative to zoning; they permit property to be used as a basis for financing infrastructure, providing a private alternative to taxation; and they permit the creation of stable arrangements for shared use of land, providing an alternative to acquisition of fee-simple interests for transportation corridors and natural-resource exploitation. Servitudes are widely used in land development because they can be individually tailored to meet the needs of particular projects. They are widely used for roads, utilities, pipelines, and natural-resource exploitation because they are less expensive than acquisition of a fee simple.

Restatement Third of Property (Servitudes) § 1.1 cmt. a (2000). *See also* Timberstone Homeowner's Association, Inc. v. Summerlin, 467 S.E.2d 330, 332 (Ga. 1996) ("The effect of invalidating mandatory payments for maintenance of amenities in a [subdivision] without affirmative acceptance [by each successive owner of a subdivision lot] would render the provision of services or facilities in a community an impossibility because it would permit property owners to determine for themselves what portion of the amenities they would be willing to accept or reject.").

There are three major categories of servitudes: easements, real covenants, and equitable servitudes. We begin our study of servitudes with easements, the simplest of the three categories to master. In Chapter 7, we deal with real covenants and equitable servitudes.

A. CREATION OF EASEMENTS

1. Express Creation

An easement is often created by a written agreement between the parties to the easement — in the examples given above, between A (the party burdened by the easement) and B (the beneficiary of the easement). We consider these express, formal easements in this section. An easement may also be created by informal methods, without a writing. We consider informal easements in Section A.3.

a. Theory: Possession and Use

The right to possession includes the rights to use and to exclude others from using a resource. A *nonpossessory* interest in land, such as an easement, confers only use rights on the beneficiary, not the right to exclude others from the servitude area. The next case and the Notes after it show how courts respond when the parties express themselves ambiguously on the all-important issue of use vs. possession.

WALTON v. CAPITAL LAND, INC.
477 S.E.2d 499 (Va. 1996)

LACY, JUSTICE.

In this appeal, we determine the scope of an easement described as an "exclusive easement of right of way."

In 1980, Willow Investment Corporation conveyed a tract of land east of Overhill Lake in Hanover County to Norman E. Walton. The grantor reserved an easement in gross described as

> AN EXCLUSIVE EASEMENT OF RIGHT OF WAY FOR PURPOSE OF INGRESS AND EGRESS TO STATE ROUTE 33, FIFTY FOOT IN WIDTH ALONG THE ENTIRE NORTHERN BOUNDARY OF THE PROPERTY HEREIN CONVEYED.

Capital Land, Inc. (Capital) subsequently acquired an adjacent tract consisting of 34.028 acres including Overhill Lake and acquired the easement in gross over Walton's land. Capital operates a recreational facility on its tract and approximately 30,000 patrons use the easement each year.

In 1990, Capital filed this action against Walton, alleging that Walton erected a barricade across the easement, harassed those trying to use the easement, and blocked drainage through his property in order to flood the easement. Capital sought to enjoin Walton from interfering with the free and unfettered access of Capital and its patrons to its property. Capital also sought a declaratory judgment that it had the exclusive right to use the easement, including the ability to exclude Walton's use of the easement.

The trial court granted a temporary injunction and referred the matter to a commissioner in chancery to determine the rights and interests of the parties. The commissioner concluded that the easement gave Capital the exclusive right to grant to anyone it chose the authority to use the easement for ingress and egress, but that the easement was not a grant of a fee. The commissioner found that Walton, as the owner of the fee, retained the right to use the easement area but could not use it in a manner which interfered with Capital's rights in the easement.

Capital filed exceptions to the commissioner's report, challenging his determination that Walton could continue to use the area encumbered by the exclusive easement. The trial court sustained Capital's exceptions and entered an order declaring that Capital has the exclusive right to determine who may use the exclusive easement and may exclude the owner of the servient estate, Walton. We awarded Walton an appeal to consider the scope of the easement.

In determining the scope of an easement, we have repeatedly held that the owner of the servient estate retains the right to use his land in any manner which does not unreasonably interfere with the use granted in the easement. None of our prior cases, however, specifically addresses the legal right of the easement owner to exclude the servient owner's use of the land based on the phrase "exclusive easement" in the language creating the easement.

Ruling that the language creating the easement was unambiguous, the trial court looked to the dictionary definition of "exclusive" and concluded that the phrase "exclusive easement" gives the easement owner the legal right to control who may use the easement, including the legal right to exclude the servient landowner from using the easement. The trial court's resolution of the issue effectively transmuted a grant of an easement into the grant of a possessory interest or an estate by allowing the owner of the easement to deprive the servient estate owner of the use of his land.

If a conveyance grants the right to exclusive use of all or part of the servient estate for all purposes, the owner of the servient estate is stripped of his right to use the land. Conveyances of this sort are generally considered to effectively transfer an interest in fee, not an easement, and are not favored. If, however, the conveyance limits exclusive use of all or part of the servient estate to a particular purpose, the conveyance is an easement and the servient landowner retains the right to use the land in ways not inconsistent with the uses granted in the easement. Restatement of Property § 471, cmt. a, b, e (1944); 7 Thompson on Real Property (David A. Thomas ed. (1994) § 60.04(b)(1)-(2)).

In this case, the language creating the easement limited its use in two ways. First, the easement is limited to use as a "right of way" and second, the right of way can only be used for the "purpose of ingress and egress to State Route 33." This limiting language is consistent with the category of conveyances which are true easements and leaves the servient owner with the right to use his land in a manner not inconsistent with the nature of the uses granted to the owner of the easement.

Accordingly, we will reverse that portion of the judgment of the trial court sustaining Capital's exceptions to the report of the commissioner and its holding that Capital has the right to exclude the owner of the servient tract from using the easement. We will enter final judgment here specifying that Walton retains the right to use the easement but in a manner that does not interfere with Capital's right to use the easement for the purpose of ingress and egress to State Route 33.

Reversed in part, and final judgment.

NOTES AND QUESTIONS

1. **Easements appurtenant and in gross: substance and terminology.** Willow Investment reserved an "easement in gross" when it sold the land near the lake to Walton. An easement in gross is one in which the benefit "is not tied to ownership or occupancy of a particular unit or parcel of land." Restatement Third of Property, Servitudes, § 1.5(2). An easement is "appurtenant" when the benefit *is* tied to the ownership or occupancy of a particular parcel. The parcel that enjoys the benefit of an appurtenant easement is called the dominant estate. If the benefit is in gross, there is no dominant estate. Whether the benefit is appurtenant or in gross, the parcel that is subject to the easement is called the servient estate.

2. **Applications.** The easements illustrated at the outset of this chapter are appurtenant easements; why is that? A typical example of an easement in gross is landowner A's grant to Company B of a right to run a utility line above or under A's land. Why is the benefit of such an easement held in gross? In the principal case, why was Willow Investment's benefit held in gross? Why do you suppose that Willow Investment retained an easement in the parcel it sold to Walton, rather than simply selling the parcel without an encumbrance? (*See* O'Donovan v. McIntosh in Section A.2.c below for one possible answer to this last question.)

3. **Exclusive and nonexclusive easements.** The parties to an easement in gross usually intend the easement to be exclusive: the phone (or gas, or electric) company doesn't want the servient owner to be able to use its utility poles or other apparatus. *See* Restatement Third § 1.2 cmt. c. An appurtenant easement — a typical right of way, for example — is usually nonexclusive; the servient owner retains the right to use the road and to grant additional use rights to others:

> Ordinarily, when a tract of land is subjected to an easement, the servient owner may make any use of the land that does not unreasonably interfere with the use and enjoyment of the easement. The servient owner's right reasonably to use the land includes the right to grant additional easements in the same land to other persons. If the first easement is not exclusive, subsequent concurrent easements that are not unreasonably burdensome or inconsistent with the original easement are valid.

Preshlock v. Brenner, 362 S.E.2d 696, 698 (Va. 1987). *See also* Restatement (Third) of Property, Servitudes § 4.9 cmt. e (2000) (servient owner may create additional servitudes that do not unreasonably interfere with beneficiary's use). These common understandings are usually indicated by the language of the creating instrument: an appurtenant easement will *lack* language of exclusivity, while an easement in gross will often provide that the benefit granted is "exclusive." *See, e.g.,* Baseball Publishing Co. v. Bruton, 18 N.E.2d 362 (Mass. 1938) (easement in gross: "exclusive right and privilege to maintain advertising sign" on building); Pratte v. Balatsos, 113 A.2d 492 (N.H. 1955) (same: "no similar equipment nor any other kind of coin-operated machine will be installed or operated on said premises by anyone else").

4. **An "exclusive" easement in the principal case.** The easement in the principal case serviced 30,000 patrons yearly at the time of the dispute; is it plausible that Willow Investment intended to preclude Walton from granting additional, and potentially conflicting, rights to use the roadway to other users? Is it plausible that Willow Investment intended to bar Walton himself from using the strip of land designated as the right of way? Isn't the drafting moral of the *Walton* case that the designation of an easement as "exclusive," with no further elaboration, is ambiguous? Willow Investment might have intended to reserve a fee, or simply a right to bar Walton from granting additional easement or license rights in the roadway. *See* Latham v. Garner, 673 P.2d 1048 (Idaho 1983) ("exclusive" easement does not sufficiently express intent to bar servient owner from using roadway).

5. **Fee or easement: other cases.** There are numerous cases in which A grants a "right of way" in a designated strip of A's land to B, perhaps adding that the purpose of the grant is to facilitate "access for ingress and egress." These cases also raise the issue debated in the principal case: the question is whether A has granted B fee ownership of the strip, with the quoted language merely stating the motive or reason for the transfer, or whether A has granted B an easement, the quoted language indicating the substance of what the parties intended — use rights rather than possessory rights. The cases go both ways. *See, e.g.,* King Associates v. Bechtler Development, 632 S.E.2d 243 (N.C. Ct. App. 2006) (deed which granted railroad a "right of way in, over and upon" land, to have and to hold "all and singular the aforesaid lands, rights and privileges" created a fee simple rather than an easement); Bockelman v. MCI Worldcom, Inc., 403 F.3d 528 (8th Cir. 2005) (sum of $350 paid by railroad in 1902 for strip of land, which was equivalent to $7400 in 2003 dollars, constituted valuable consideration, and supported the determination that the railroad acquired a fee simple interest in the strip); Northwest Realty Co. v. Jacobs, 273 N.W.2d 141 (S.D. 1978) (easement, not fee). *See generally* Annotation, *Conveyance of "Right of Way" in Connection with Conveyance of Another Tract, as Passing Fee or Easement,* 89 A.L.R.3d 767. In Northwest Realty Co. v. Jacob, the court listed the relevant factors on the easement or fee question:

> The resolution of the problem of determining whether a deed intended to convey a fee simple title or an easement involves the consideration of the following factors: (1) the amount of consideration; (2) the particularity of the description of the property conveyed; (3) the extent of the limitation upon the use of the property; (4) the type of interest which best serves the manifested purpose of the parties; (5) the peculiarities of wording used in the conveyance document; (6) to whom the property was assessed and who paid the taxes on the property; and (7) how the parties to the conveyance, or the heirs or assigns, have treated the property.

273 N.W.2d at 145. What does each of those factors tell us about the parties' intent on the fee vs. easement question?

6. **Creation of easements in gross: common law and American law.** The easement in the principal case could not have been created at common law. The burdening of land with a use restriction that would bind subsequent owners (that is, the creation of a servient estate) required that some other land be benefitted (i.e., it required a dominant estate). "The policy is strong against hindering the alienability of one property where no corresponding enhancement accrues to surrounding lands." Caullett v. Stanley Stilwell & Sons, Inc., 170 A.2d 52, 56 (N.J. Super. Ct. App. Div. 1961). In this country, the rule against the creation of a servitude with a benefit in gross does not apply to easements, but it may apply to real covenants, equitable servitudes, or both; *Caullett* is reprinted in Chapter 7, and we will assess the scope and merits of the rule when we reach that case. In American law, the distinction between appurtenant and in-gross easement benefits is important on the question of transferability of the benefit, not creation of the easement; we address transferability of in-gross benefits in Section A.2.c.

NOTES ON ISSUES IN SERVITUDES CASES AND ON THE NEW RESTATEMENT OF PROPERTY

1. **Issues in servitudes cases.** Servitudes cases usually present one or more of the issues listed below (be alert for multiple issues as you read the cases in this and the next chapter, even if the court does not address all of them). Because easements provide the simplest rules on these issues, we begin our study of servitudes in this chapter with easements. In Chapter 7, we turn to the two other major categories of servitudes: real covenants and equitable servitudes. You should read the following list now to get the general ideas, then refer to it periodically as we work through the cases in this chapter and the next.

(1) *Creation of a servitude.* In cases of an express agreement between A and B, a variety of questions might arise. One question is whether the parties intended to create a servitude or only a simple contractual relationship; sometimes, as in Walton v. Capital Land, Inc., the issue is whether the parties intended to create a servitude (granting use rights to the beneficiary) or an estate (granting possessory rights to the beneficiary); sometimes the question is whether the benefit of a servitude can be created in a third party, which is addressed in Garza v. Grayson, below. Some types of servitude can also be created informally, without a writing documenting its existence; in those cases, the creation of the servitude depends on compliance with the law's requirements for informal servitudes. Cases of informal easements are considered in Section A.3 below.

(2) *Running of the burden of the servitude.* Whether the servitude is created formally or informally, the burden that it imposes on the burdened party's land has the capacity to "run" with the land and bind subsequent owners of that land, if certain requirements are met. We will see what those requirements are as we work through this chapter and the next. A useful habit to acquire is that of diagramming the facts of a case to show whether a running burden issue is presented by the facts. In the following diagrams, as in the text and Notes accompanying the cases in this chapter and the next, let A represent the party who originally incurs the

servitude obligation, and let B represent the beneficiary of the servitude. You would diagram a running burden issue as follows:

A (promisor) ——— B (promisee)

|

X (successor to promisor's land)

(3) *Running of the benefit.* In your analysis of servitudes, it is important to separate the question of running burden from that of running of the benefit; the latter question asks whether a successor to the *beneficiary* of the servitude obligation is entitled to enforce the servitude against the burdened party or the burdened party's successor. Diagram a running benefit case as follows:

A (promisor) ——— B (promisee)

|

Y (successor to promisee's land)

Land might change hands frequently, so it is not unusual for a case to present questions of both the running of the burden and the benefit to the successors of the parties who originally created the servitude; in such a case, your diagram will include both X and Y. If the benefit of the servitude is held in gross, there cannot be a running benefit question; the issue would be whether the in-gross benefit may be *assigned* to Y. A servitude is not created at all unless either the benefit or the burden is appurtenant to land; if the transaction creates "in gross" burdens and benefits, it is a simple contract, not a servitude. *See* Restatement Third § 1.1 cmt. c ("Although both benefit and burden frequently run with land, a servitude is created if either one runs with land.").

(4) *Validity.* You learned, or will learn, in your Contracts course that a contract that satisfies the formal requirements of validity (e.g., consideration, statute of frauds) may still fail because of a substantive barrier such as unconscionability, illegality or violation of public policy. Although the terminology differs in the law of servitudes, the same idea applies: the capacity of A and B to fashion restrictions on the use of land is fettered to some extent by the larger interests of society. In the servitudes you will encounter in Chapter 7, the issue of substantive validity has traditionally been conducted by asking whether the burden or benefit "touches and concerns" the land of the respective parties. In easements cases, the question is usually phrased as an inquiry whether "novel" burdens may be imposed on, or novel benefits accorded to, landowners.

(5) *Scope and interpretation.* Parties who create a servitude often fail to express themselves with clarity or completeness on important aspects of their relationship. Does a right of way created during the horse and buggy era allow automotive use?

Does a restriction on the use of land to "single-family residential" purposes allow a group residential home for the mentally ill? If an easement is "exclusive," exactly who or what can the easement beneficiary exclude? In these cases, and in the case of servitudes created by implication — where the parties haven't bargained expressly over the servitude — the law establishes rules of construction to determine what burdens and benefits the parties must bear or may enjoy. Questions on the scope of easements are considered in Section 6.B below.

(6) *Termination.* A plaintiff may be unable to enforce a servitude because it is no longer in effect. It may have ended by the terms of the original agreement, or it may have come to an end by some other — sometimes unintended — means. On the termination of easements, see Section 6.C below.

2. **Servitude categories and issues.** There are important differences among easements, real covenants and equitable servitudes on some of the issues canvassed in Note 1. There is also, thankfully, a fair amount of similarity, so that you need not totally reinvent the wheel as you move in your studies from one category of servitude to the next. As noted, we treat the easement category first. Its doctrines on the questions presented in Note 1 are straightforward, allowing it to serve as a useful model for comparison to the real covenant and the equitable servitude.

3. **The Restatement Third of Property.** An important new development on the servitudes scene is the Restatement Third of Property, Servitudes (2000). The Restatement Third is a major attempt by scholars and practitioners of property law to clarify and simplify the law of servitudes. (The first Restatement's treatment of servitudes, in 1944, unfortunately reinvigorated many ancient servitude rules of unnecessary and obfuscating technicality, thus complicating the creating and running of servitude burdens and benefits. There is no second Restatement on the subject.) Instead of organizing the topic by category of servitude (easement, real covenant, equitable servitude), the third Restatement treats servitudes as a unitary category, and organizes functionally, addressing questions of the creation of servitudes, succession to benefits and burdens, validity, interpretation, and termination. With few exceptions, the new Restatement applies the same rules to each of those questions regardless whether the servitude would have been dealt with at common law as an easement, a real covenant, or an equitable servitude. Since easements have the simplest rules on most questions, the Restatement's approach is to generalize the easement rules to the other types of servitudes. *See generally* Susan F. French, *Highlights of the New Restatement (Third) of Property: Servitudes*, 35 Real Prop., Prob. & Tr. J. 225 (2000). Although the present casebook organizes servitudes by the traditional categories in accordance with the existing law that you will encounter in practice, you will be referred to the third Restatement repeatedly in the following materials, along with comparisons to the first Restatement's treatment of the subject. In this way, we hope you will enjoy the best of both worlds: an understanding of the weaknesses (and occasional strengths) of the traditional tripartite division of servitudes as well as of the strengths (and occasional weaknesses) of the best of modern thinking on the subject of servitudes.

b.   Intent and Form: Grant, Reservation, and Promise

Although a servitude allows the beneficiary to use rather than to possess the servitude area, the right to use is nevertheless a property interest held by the beneficiary in the burdened owner's land. As an interest in land covered by the statute of frauds, an easement should be created by a written document (usually a deed), and the deed should contain proper conveyancing language. Language that expresses the parties' intent ambiguously or improperly — especially the use of words of contract (promise), by which the servient owner A "agrees" to allow B to use A's land — can send the parties or their successors to court, as in the following case. The case discusses the appropriate language of conveyance that should avoid litigation over the parties' intent.

FITZSTEPHENS v. WATSON
344 P.2d 221 (Or. 1959)

O'CONNELL, JUSTICE.

This is an appeal by the defendants from a decree permanently enjoining the defendants from interfering with the flow of water in a pipeline running from a reservoir on defendants' land to the land of the plaintiff. The decree also enjoined the defendants from violating the terms of an "Easement Deed" in which the defendants covenanted to maintain the water system through which the water was conveyed to the grantee's land.

We shall refer to the defendants' and the plaintiff's lands as the servient and dominant tracts respectively. Both of these tracts originally constituted one large parcel known as the "Davies Ranch." Various seeps and springs rise on the servient tract now owned by the defendants. The water from these sources forms a small creek with well defined banks which runs southwesterly a distance of approximately 1800 feet where it empties into the Rogue River. The creek never wholly leaves the tract referred to as the "Davies Ranch" although for a few feet just north of the river a part of the creek flows over the land of an adjoining owner, the center of the creek marking the boundary between the contiguous parcels.

While Davies was still the owner of the entire tract known as the Davies Ranch he installed a water system to make use of the spring water on his land. He placed a pipe in the creek bed near the springs from which the water was permitted to flow by gravity to a large redwood storage tank. The intake pipe leading to the tank was originally either three-fourths or one inch in diameter, the evidence on this point being in dispute. A two-inch pipe conveyed the water from the reservoir for use on the ranch.

On November 20, 1946 Davies and his wife conveyed the dominant tract, consisting of approximately three acres, to Robert W. Mairs and Harriet B. Mairs. This tract was bounded on the west by the creek described above. According to the plaintiff's testimony a part of the consideration for the sale of the dominant parcel was an oral agreement between the parties by which the grantors promised to supply to the grantees water from the system on the grantor's land. Soon after the conveyance Mairs connected a two-inch pipe to the pipeline on the land retained by the grantors and used the water on the dominant tract. Thereafter, Davies and his wife executed and delivered to the Mairses an instrument entitled "Easement Deed," which was dated "_____ January, 1947," acknowledged October 8, 1947 and recorded on October 25, 1947. The relevant parts of this instrument are as follows:

> Whereas the grantors have agreed to furnished [sic] to the grantees water for use on the above described premises to the extent of three-eighths of the volume now presently flowing through the pipe line connecting a reservoir situated on the property of the grantors and running to the property above described owned by the grantees, and

> Whereas the grantors further agree to maintain an adequate reservoir and pipe line to furnish said water,

> Now this Indenture Witnesseth that the grantors hereby covenant that they, their heirs or assigns will maintain a reservoir on the property now known as the Davies Ranch and a pipe line leading from the said premises to the above described premises owned by the grantees and will furnish to the grantees, their heirs or assigns, water equal to three-eighths of the volume now flowing through the pipe line presently carrying water from the Davies Ranch premises to the above described premises owned by the grantees.

On November 4, 1947 Davies and his wife conveyed the servient tract to the defendants L.W. Watson and Anna May Watson and two other grantees whose interest the Watsons later acquired. The deed effecting this conveyance contained the following exception: "Also excepting a certain water right appertaining to a portion of said excepted Tract 1." A portion of Tract 1 constituted a part of the dominant tract.

The Mairses developed a part of the dominant tract as a fishing resort which was serviced by water from the pipeline. On April 27, 1948 they sold the eastern two-thirds of the dominant tract, including the resort buildings, to the plaintiff and his wife. No mention was made in the deed of the water right described in the "Easement Deed." Upon the death of his wife the plaintiff became the sole owner of this parcel. The plaintiff made improvements on his tract, including the construction of additional cabins, a trailer camp and laundry failities, all of which used water from the pipeline.

The remaining one-third of the dominant tract was conveyed on August 25, 1950 by the Mairses to Edgar B. Spear and wife, the deed including a grant of "all water right pertaining" to the land conveyed.

The defendants likewise have developed the servient tract as a fishing resort which is in competition with the plaintiff's business. The defendant Inell Bobo is the daughter of the Watsons. She and her husband, the defendant R.B. Bobo, live on the servient tract. The water from the system was used on dominant and servient tracts by the various owners without a water permit from the State Engineer until June 17, 1949 when the Watsons obtained a permit, followed by a "Certificate of Water Right" dated July 6, 1954.

On numerous occasions from 1949 until this suit was filed the plaintiff's water supply was interrupted for periods ranging from five minutes to five hours. The interruptions resulted from the defendants' conduct in closing a valve in the pipe leading to the plaintiff's land. The plaintiff's pipeline ran downhill and the defendants' slightly uphill, as a consequence of which the defendants were the first to suffer in the event of a water shortage. The defendants contend that the water was shut off on the occasions referred to in order to obtain a flow of water in the pipeline leading to their buildings when the water supply was short. It was also contended by the defendants that the shortage of water in the system was due in part to the plaintiff's wasteful use of the water. The plaintiff accuses the defendants of cutting off the water supply for the purpose of harassing the plaintiff and interfering with his resort business.

In 1950, shortly after the interruptions in his water supply had begun the plaintiff obtained a revocable license to draw water from a spring on the property of a landowner on the opposite side of the Rogue River. The water was pumped across the river through plastic pipe which had to be removed from time to time to prevent its being swept away by the destructive force of the river current. The plaintiff has included the cost of installing and operating this system as a part of the damage alleged to be attributable to defendants' unlawful conduct in cutting off the plaintiff's water supply.

The controversy between the parties was finally brought to a head by a letter written on October 9, 1954 by the defendants' attorney informing the plaintiff that the defendants would need all of the water during the following spring season and that the plaintiff would not be permitted to use any water from the system from that time forward. On February 15, 1955 the plaintiff filed the present suit. The trial court held that the "Easement Deed" referred to above created "a valid and perpetual easement and is binding and effective as to all its terms and covenants therein contained"; that the rights and duties thus created ran with the land both as to benefit and burden; and that the defendants were permanently enjoined from interfering with the plaintiff's use of the water and from violating the covenants in the deed.

The interest which the plaintiff acquired was an easement. The instrument by which the transfer of Davies' riparian rights was effected was entitled "Easement Deed." However, it is cast in the language of covenant as well as grant. Its title indicates that the draftsman regarded the transaction as conveyancesory rather than contractual. So also with the reference to the parties as "grantors" and "grantees." On the other hand, the instrument recites that the parties "agree" and "covenant" to supply a certain volume of water and to perform other acts necessary to provide the grantees with water from the grantors' premises. The instrument recites that "the grantors have agreed" to furnish water to the grantees, undoubtedly referring to the oral arrangement for water previously entered into between them contemporaneous with the conveyance of the land. The fact that the instrument was intended to memorialize what the parties regarded as an earlier executed transfer of water rights may have influenced the use of language describing what the parties had already settled or "agreed upon" as a part of the previous conveyance of the land. As pointed out in Conard, *Words Which Will Create an Easement*, 6 Mo.L.Rev. 245, 254 (1941):

We can, and sometimes do, grant an affirmative easement, but it is also possible to think of its creation as an undertaking by one's neighbor that he will allow the use of his land and that he will refrain from obstructing such use. In fact, the cases disclose that many laymen and many lawyers thoughtlessly employ words of promise rather than words of grant when they want to set up easement relationships.

Further, it is obvious that the parties were attempting to create in the Mairses two interests; viz., (1) the privilege of using water, an interest ordinarily created as an easement, and (2) the right to require the "grantors" and their successors to maintain the water system including the reservoir and pipeline, a type of interest which usually arises by way of covenant. Although the "Easement Deed" in the present case is not artfully drawn it may be regarded as creating these two forms of interest, granting to the Mairses an easement entitling them to the use of water from the Davies land and at the same time creating in them a contract right to have the water supplied and the water system maintained.

The fact that the Easement Deed in the present case expressed the rights and duties of the parties in contractual terms does not preclude the construction that an easement was created. As Justice Holmes stated in Hogan v. Barry, 10 N.E. 253, 254 (Mass. 1887), "There is no doubt that an easement may be created by words sounding in covenant."

Where the instrument describes the type of right in the promisor's land which has been recognized traditionally by the courts as an easement (such as the right to a supply of water from the promisor's land) words of covenant describing such rights have been construed as words of grant. 2 American Law of Property, § 9.12, p. 372; Note, 29 N.C.L.Rev. 455 (1951). In the instant case the grantors agreed "to furnish to the grantees, their heirs or assigns, water equal to three-eighths of the volume now flowing through the pipe line presently carrying water from the Davies Ranch premises to the above described premises owned by the grantees." We construe this language as creating an easement appurtenant to the land of Mairs, a part of which is now owned by the plaintiff. In addition to this easement, the instrument also created a covenant on the part of the grantors to maintain a reservoir and pipeline on their premises for the purpose of furnishing such water. The conclusion we have reached is supported by the better reasoned cases. There is authority for the proposition that a "covenant" or an "agreement" to furnish water may be construed as an easement. Murphy v. Kerr, 5 F.2d 908 (8th Cir. 1925). Cases to the contrary may be found in 3 Powell on Real Property, § 407, p. 401.

The right to use water from a spring or stream on another person's land has been recognized as an easement in many adjudicated cases. We think that the parties to the "Easement Deed" intended to create such an interest. The designation of the interest as an easement and the reference to the parties as "grantors" and "grantees" lends support to this interpretation. The instrument purports to bind not only the grantors but their "heirs or assigns" and to inure to the grantees and their "heirs or assigns." This further evidences an intent to create an interest, whether as an easement or covenant, which would be more than a personal contract between the parties to the instrument. Considering the other language in the instrument and the circumstances attending its execution we are of the opinion that the reference to the "heirs or assigns" of the grantors and grantees, respectively, indicates an intent to create a perpetual easement.

The "Easement Deed" having been recorded gave notice of plaintiff's interest to subsequent purchasers of the servient estate, including the defendants. In fact, the deed to the defendants Watson expressly excepted the interest created by the "Easement Deed." Even though the instrument had not been recorded the defendants would have had notice of plaintiff's interest from the presence of the pipeline running from the water source on defendants' land to the land of the plaintiff. Having purchased the servient land subject to the easement and covenant the defendants could not vitiate those interests by obtaining a water permit from the State Engineer.

The plaintiff's easement is limited to three-eighths of the volume of water which was flowing through the pipeline from the reservoir to the grantee's land at the time the "Easement Deed" was delivered. Since the defendants took the position in their pleadings that the plaintiff had no right to the water whatsoever, the evidence was not developed by either the plaintiff or the defendants to show that the plaintiff was entitled only to the specified quantity of water but that he took more than his share. Not having raised the issue, the defendants cannot now prevent the plaintiff from obtaining the relief which he prayed for in his complaint, namely, that the defendants be restrained from interfering with the plaintiff's rightful water supply.

The decree of the lower court is affirmed.

NOTES AND QUESTIONS

1. **Issues.** Fitzstephens v. Watson is a touchstone case, and we will recall it several times in our discussion of servitudes. How many of the issues in servitudes cases listed earlier in this chapter does the case present?

2. **Creation of easements by grant and reservation.** When Davies deeded the fee to the dominant tract in November 1946, he could have included language in the deed expressly "granting" to Mairs the water easement; instead, he granted the easement in a separate writing, the later January 1947 "Easement Deed." The *grant* of an easement can be part of a fee transaction, but it can also stand alone. The *reservation* of an easement cannot stand alone; it always involves the transfer of a possessory interest, from which the easement rights are held back. Had Davies retained the dominant tract and deeded the servient tract to Mairs, he could have "reserved" the water easement, in effect holding back some of the total bundle of sticks transferred to Mairs.

3. **Creation by contract.** Although good form requires the use of appropriate language of grant or reservation to create an easement, an easement may be created by contract as well as by conveyance. *See* Restatement Third § 2.1. Language of promise, however, invites confusion with the real covenant and the equitable servitude, whose rules sometimes differ from those applicable to easements. *See* Chapter 7. Why does the court in *Fitzstephens* conclude that the language of promise created an easement? How would you rewrite the "Easement Deed" in Fitzstephens v. Watson to remove the issue addressed in the case?

4. **Intent to create a servitude: language and circumstances.** "The intent to create a servitude may be express or implied. No particular form of expression is required." Restatement Third § 2.2. What language in the "Easement Deed" in Fitzstephens v. Watson indicates that Davies and Mairs intended to create a servitude rather than a mere contract binding only themselves? Did they intend that both the burden and the benefit of the easement run with the land of the creating parties? Had the "Easement Deed" not specifically expressed the parties' intent to create a servitude, might the court nevertheless have found an implied intent for a servitude from the nature and purposes of the arrangement? *See* Restatement Third § 2.2 cmt. i. How would you make the argument for such an implied intent?

5. **Consideration: gift of an easement.** The servient owner loses property rights by the creation of an easement, and may insist on compensation. As a property interest, however, an easement is capable of being tranferred as a gift. *See* Kuhlman v. Rivera, 701 P.2d 982, 985 (Mont. 1985) ("While Kuhlman could have entered into a contract to sell the easement, the record establishes she gave it away.").

6. **Creation by will.** Although easements are often created by deed, they may also be created by will. For example, the owner of Blackacre, O, might devise his neighbor B a right of way over Blackacre. *See* Restatement Third § 2.1 cmt. a.

7. **Requirement of a writing: the statute of frauds.** See Bob Daniels & Sons v. Weaver, 681 P.2d 1010, 1016 (Idaho Ct. App. 1984):

> [E]asements are interests in real property. [T]he statute of frauds pro-
> vides, with exceptions not applicable here, that interests in real property
> must be transferred by written instrument. An oral agreement must be
> evidenced by a written memorandum. No such memorandum appears in
> this record. Failure to comply with the statute renders an oral agreement
> unenforceable both in law and in equity. An easement established by
> unwritten agreement is merely a license, revocable by the licensor.

See also Restatement Third § 2.8 (if servitude does not comply with statute of frauds "the burden of the servitude is not enforceable and the benefit is terminable at will"). The exceptions to the statute of frauds mentioned in *Bob Daniels* are also adopted by the Restatement, and are considered in our discussion of informal easements in Section 6.B.3.

8. **Profit.** A profit (short for "profit a prendre") is a special type of easement. It authorizes its holder "to enter and remove timber, minerals, oil, gas, fish, game, or other substances from land in the possession of another." Restatement Third § 1.2. *See, e.g.,* Goss v. Wildlife Trust, Inc., 852 A.2d 996 (Md. Ct. Spec. App. 2004) (profit a prendre to hunt and fish on adjacent land). Did the agreement in Fitzstephens v. Watson create a profit? *See* Restatement Third § 1.2, Reporter's Note, at 19 ("Rights to take water and cut ice may be characterized as easements rather than profits."); *id.* 18 ("The term ["profit"] is used for descriptive purposes only; there are no doctrinal differences between [easements and profits].").

9. **Remedies to protect easement rights.** An easement creates in the beneficiary an interest in the servient owner's land. Interference with the easement constitutes a tort, for which the plaintiff is entitled to damages for harm

suffered. *See* American Metal Co. v. Fluid Chemical Co., 296 A.2d 348, 350-51 (N.J. Super. Ct. L. Div. 1972) ("Once the easement has been granted, any interference with it is a violation of the vested property rights of the easement's owner as those rights are defined in the contract, and such interference constitutes a tort."). The easement holder is also entitled to an injunction to prevent future harm. *See* William B. Stoebuck & Dale A. Whitman, The Law of Property 490 (3d ed. 2000) (injunction available to protect property interests). In some cases, the easement holder is also entitled to restitution of any benefits obtained by the defendant who interferes with the easement. *See generally* Section B below (further discussion of remedies to protect easement rights).

c.   Third-Party Beneficiaries

Easements are typically created, as they were in Walton v. Capital Land and Fitzstephens v. Watson, in a transaction between the easement beneficiary and the burdened landowner, just as contracts are made between promisor and promisee. However, it is also possible for parties to a simple contract to create rights under the contract in a third party. The comparable power of a servient landowner to create easement rights in a third party, although recognized in the following case, remains controversial in the law of property.

GARZA v. GRAYSON
467 P.2d 960 (Or. 1970)

O'CONNELL, JUSTICE.

This is a declaratory judgment proceeding in which plaintiffs seek a declaration establishing the existence of an easement over defendants' land for the construction and maintenance of a service line serving plaintiff's adjoining land. The case was tried without a jury. Defendants appeal from a decree granting the relief sought by plaintiffs.

Bjorn Gadeholt was the owner of Lots 579 and 580 in Lake View Villas, a subdivision in Lake Oswego then in the process of development. Gadeholt's lots were not served by an existing sewer system. The city was in the process of providing a sewer system for the area.

On June 28, 1963, Gadeholt conveyed Lot 579 to plaintiffs. The deed made no mention of an easement. On December 19, 1963, Gadeholt conveyed Lot 580, which adjoined Lot 579, to William Leer and wife, who are defendants' predecessors in title. The Leer deed contained the following reservation:

> RESERVING, however, an easement for public utility purposes over and across the northeasterly five feet of the above described property, consti-tuting a strip five feet in width laying adjacent to the northeast boundary of the above described tract and extending from Blue Heron Road to the most easterly corner of said tract.

Defendants [contend that] the Leer deed could not create an easement benefiting plaintiffs' land because an easement cannot be reserved in favor of a third person.

The rule adopted in most jurisdictions is that in a deed creating an estate in one person, the grantor cannot reserve an easement or other interest in a third person. There is language in our own cases supporting this view. This rule is derived from a narrow and highly technical interpretation of the meaning of the terms "reservation" and "exception" when employed in a deed.[3] It is said that a person other than the grantor "has no interest in the land to be excepted from the grant, and likewise none from which a reservation can be carved out."[4]

We do not regard this as a satisfactory reason for defeating the grantor's intention to create an easement in a person other than the grantee of the estate conveyed in the deed, if the intention to create the easement is adequately expressed in the deed. The view we take is supported by most if not all the legal commentators and by the better reasoned cases.[5] It is also adopted by the [first] Restatement of Property, § 472, p. 2966 (1944), which states the rule as follows: "By a single instrument of conveyance, there may be created an estate in land in one person and an easement in another."[6] The contrary view expressed in our previous cases is repudiated.

It will be noted that the reservation in the Leer deed did not name the person or property to be benefited by the easement. The intention to benefit the land of a prior grantee can likewise be derived from the circumstances attendant upon the grant. In the present case there was sufficient evidence to establish the grantor's intention to impose the servitude upon defendants' land for the benefit of the land previously conveyed to plaintiffs. The grantor himself testified that this was his purpose. Considering the location of the easement in relation to the surrounding land, it is difficult to conceive of the easement as having any other purpose than to benefit plaintiffs' land.

The judgment of the trial court is affirmed.

---

[3] "Theoretically, an 'exception' exists when some part of the ownership of the grantor is never parted with; while a 'reservation' is the term applicable when the instrument transfers all the grantor had but recreates in the grantor some specified interest with respect to land transferred." 6 Powell on Real Property § 892, pp. 224–225 (1968).

[4] 88 A.L.R.2d 1199, 1202 (1963).

[5] See, e.g., Townsend v. Cable, 378 S.W.2d 806, 808 (Ky. 1964); 2 American Law of Property, § 8.29, p. 254 (1952); Harris, *Reservations in Favor of Strangers to the Title*, 6 Okla.L.Rev. 127 (1953); 4 Tiffany, Law of Real Property, § 974, pp. 51–52 (3d ed. 1939); Note, *Can a Reservation or Exception of an Easement be Made in Favor of a Third Person in Pennsylvania*, 53 Dick.L.Rev. 151 (1949); Hollosy v. Gershkowitz, 98 N.E.2d 314 (Ohio Ct. App. 1950) (relying on 2 Restatement of Property, § 472).

[6] Comment b to § 472 adds the following explanation:

Concurrent conveyances of incorporeal and corporeal interests by single instrument of conveyance. It is possible in a single instrument of conveyance to convey corporeal interests to one while conveying incorporeal interests to another. Thus, conveyances may be made of a life estate to one and of a remainder in fee to another. Likewise, it is possible to convey an estate in fee to one conveyee and at the same time and by the same instrument of conveyance convey an easement in the same land to another conveyee. This result is not prevented by the fact that the conveyance of the easement is, in terms, a reservtion to the person to whom it is conveyed. Thus an easement may be created in C by a deed by A which purports to convey Blackacre to B in fee reserving an easement to C. If, in other respects, the necessary formalities for the creation of an easement are complied with, such a reservation operates as an effective conveyance to the person in whose favor the reservation is, in terms, made.

NOTES AND QUESTIONS

1. **The benefit side: a new issue.** In the principal case, the beneficiary of the easement (Garza) was not a party to the transaction that created the easement (the sale of lot 580 from Gadeholt to Leer). Nor was Garza the successor to a previously-created dominant estate, suing on running benefit theory: Garza did not acquire lot 579 after Gadeholt had attached an appurtenant benefit to it. Instead, Garza was a prior purchaser from Gadeholt. Generalizing, we can say that the beneficiary of a servitude, and hence the proper plaintiff in a servitude dispute, will be either (1) the originally benefitted party in the transaction that creates the servitude, or (2) a *successor* to the original beneficiary (who takes either by the running of an appurtenant benefit or the assignment of an in-gross benefit), or (3) a *prior purchaser* from the servient landowner who later creates the servitude in favor of the prior purchaser. This last — and for us, new — situation is the one in Garza v. Grayson. In Chapter 7, we will consider the companion question of the permissibility of a third-party beneficiary of a real covenant and an equitable servitude.

2. **Identification of the third-party beneficiary.** As the principal case indicates, if a third-party beneficiary easement is permissible, it is not a requirement that the "person or property to be benefited" by the easement be identified in the instrument of creation (although such explicit identification is good practice). *See* Kopetsky v. Crews, 838 N.E.2d 1118, 1125 (Ind. Ct. App. 2005) ("[W]here, as here, the physical situation of two parcels leads to only one reasonable conclusion as to the identity of the dominant tenement, it is appropriate to consider that physical layout in construing a grantor's express reservation of an access easement."). When a benefit is held in gross, there is no dominant estate. Is a third party easement in gross permissible? *See* Restatement Third § 2.6 cmt. a, at 103 ("The third-party doctrine provides the basis for recognizing that servitude benefits of all types can be created in favor of persons, either in gross or as holders of interests in land, who are not otherwise parties to the transaction."). If so, would the beneficiary have to be identified in the transaction creating the easement?

3. **The common law rule.** How do the *definitions* of reservation and exception discussed in the principal case rule out the possibility of creation of an easement in a third-party beneficiary? What is the court's response?

4. **Stranger to the deed: policy.** The third-party beneficiary of an easement is a "stranger to the deed" that creates the easement. The leading case against the result in *Garza* offers the following policy bases for the traditional rule that an easement benefit cannot be created in a stranger:

> Although application of the stranger-to-the-deed rule may, at times, frustrate a grantor's intent, any such frustration can readily be avoided by the direct conveyance of an easement of record from the grantor to the third party. The overriding considerations of the public policy favoring certainty in title to real property, both to protect bona fide purchasers and to avoid conflicts of ownership, which may engender needless litigation, persuade us to decline to depart from our settled rule. We have previously noted that in this area of law, where it can reasonably be assumed that settled rules are necessary and necessarily relied upon, stability and

adherence to precedent are generally more important than a better or even a correct rule of law.

In re Estate of Thomson, 509 N.E.2d 309 (N.Y. 1987). The court's statement is succinct; read it closely and make a list of the arguments that the court recites for its "stranger to the deed" rule. (We will be in a better position to analyze the court's concerns — particularly its concern for bona fide purchasers — a little later on, when we have studied bona fide purchaser doctrine.) What argument in favor of the rule adopted in Garza v. Grayson does the *Thompson* court suggest? Does the *Thomson* court's requirement that Gadeholt execute two deeds to avoid the stranger to the deed rule suggest a further objection to that rule?

5. **Reservation of an estate in a third party.** Suppose that O conveys Blackacre to "B and his heirs, reserving a life estate to A." Is the purported life estate in A valid? *See* Nelson v. Parker, 687 N.E.2d 187 (Ind. 1997) (deed to grantee "subject to a life estate" in a third person created a valid life estate: stranger-to-the-deed rule rejected because "[i]t is a trap for the unwary and if enforced serves only to frustrate the intent of the grantor.").

6. **The Third Restatement and other authority.** The Restatement Third § 2.6(2) adopts a rule allowing the benefit of any servitude to be created in a third party, but the Reporter's Note cites authority from fourteen states following the common law rule against third-party easements. *Id.* at 112. *See also* Simpson v. Kistler Investment Co., 713 P.2d 751 (Wyo. 1986) (extensive review of the case authority on creation of benefit of easement in third party). *See generally* John E. Lansche, Jr., Note, *Ancient, Antiquated, and Archaic: South Carolina Fails to Embrace the Rule That a Grantor May Reserve an Easement in Favor of a Third Party*, 52 S.C. L. Rev. 269 (2000) (discussing Springob v. Farrar, 514 S.E.2d 135 (S.C. Ct. App. 1999)).

2.   Running of Burden and Benefit

Servitudes are unique. A contract between A and B binds only them. The promisee may assign his or her contract rights to another party, but the assignment usually has to be explicit. Contract *duties* generally are not unilaterally assignable (delegable) at all; the promisee and the delegate must agree to the delegation. The rules are different in servitudes. Benefits attached to land by the agreement of the parties run freely with transfers of the benefited land (the dominant estate), without the need for a specific assignment of the easement rights. Duties attached to land run with transfers of the servient land, without the need for the transferee's independent agreement to be bound. Granting, however, that servitude burdens and benefits can "run" with the land burdened and benefited by the servitude, questions remain: what are the conditions under which a burden runs with the servient estate; how do the parties establish a benefit that is appurtenant to land, rather than limited to the original beneficiary; how does an in-gross benefit, which by definition cannot run with land, get transferred, if at all? To these questions we now turn.

a.   Running of the Burden

A successor owner of the servient estate who takes the land with notice of the existence of a servitude is bound by the servitude, without the need for independent agreement by the successor. Witter v. Taggart, discussed in Chapter 5, shows that a purchaser for value *without* notice takes free of the servitude. The case also shows that there is room for disagreement about whether a subsequent purchaser should be deemed to have notice of an earlier recorded deed creating an adverse interest. Prior to reading the principal case below, you should read (or re-read) the excerpt on title searches from Chapter 5, Section D.1.a.

WITTER v. TAGGART

[For the report of this case, see Section 5.D.1.d above.]

NOTES AND QUESTIONS

1. **Common law priority.**   Under the common law, the first transferee of an interest in land had priority over a subsequent transferee. "First in time is first in right." There was no recording system. Under common law priorities, Witter would have won the case. Why is that?

2. **Operation of the recording acts; bona fide purchasers.**   Every state has a recording act that reverses the priorities established by the common law and allows a subsequent purchaser to take title free of an earlier adverse conveyance that is not recorded, if the requirements of the recording act are met. In all but a handful of states, only a bona fide purchaser is protected by the recording acts. Bona fide purchaser status has two parts: the purchaser must give value, and must lack notice of a prior adverse interest. A donee, including an heir or devisee, is bound regardless of notice. In the principal case, was Taggart a bona fide purchaser?

3. **Types of notice.**   Three types of notice will bar a buyer of the servient estate from enjoying bona fide purchaser status. Terminology is not uniform in the cases and literature; here is how we use the terms. *Actual notice*: The purchaser has subjective knowledge of the existence of the prior claim burdening the land. *Constructive (or record) notice:* If the prior adverse claim is properly recorded, the purchaser is deemed aware of the information that a search of the records would reveal, whether the purchaser searches the record or not. *Inquiry notice*: When a purchaser is aware or should be aware of facts which a reasonable person would investigate and which, if investigated, would reveal the existence of an adverse claim, the purchaser is deemed to be aware of the claim. *See* Methonen v. Stone, 941 P.2d 1248, 1252 (Alaska 1997) ("It is well established that a purchaser will be charged with notice of an interest adverse to his title when he is aware of facts which would lead a reasonably prudent person to a course of investigation which, properly executed, would lead to knowledge of the servitude. The purchaser is considered apprised of those facts obvious from an inspection of the property."); Martinez v. Affordable Housing Network, Inc., 123 P.3d 1201, 1207 (Colo. 2005) ("[W]ith certain exceptions, possession of real estate is sufficient to put an interested person on inquiry notice of any legal or equitable claim the person or

persons in open, notorious, and exclusive possession of the property may have."). A statement in the deed to the purchaser of the servient estate that the sale is "subject to" a previously-created servitude would also constitute inquiry notice. *See* Restatement Third § 2.2 cmt. d, at 63-64; Davis v. Henning, 462 S.E.2d 106, 108 (Va. 1995); Guilbault v. Bowley, 498 A.2d 1033 (Vt. 1985); McGuire v. Bell, 761 S.W.2d 904 (Ark. 1988) ("subject to" language need only be in a deed in the chain of title to the servient estate, not in each buyer's deed).

4. **Notice in the principal case.** In the principal case, there is no indication that Taggart had actual knowledge of the restriction on his lot (actual notice) or that he had or should have had any information that, if pursued, would have led him to find the restriction (inquiry notice). And although the 1951 deed to Witter's predecessor, which contained the restriction on Lawrance's retained land, was recorded, Taggart lacked constructive notice of the restriction because it was contained in a deed that was outside of the scope of the record search chargeable to Taggart. There is disagreement among the states over how extensive the purchaser's search of the record must be.

5. **Scope of record search: deeds in the chain of title.** In every state, a purchaser is charged with knowledge of the contents of prior recorded deeds that transfer title to the land that the purchaser is buying. In the principal case, that land is the lot south of the canal. Is the scenic restriction contained in any deed transferring title to the south lot?

6. **Deeds out of the chain of title: one view.** Lawrance created the restriction on the south lot in 1951 when he transferred the lot *north* of the canal to Witter's predecessor. That 1951 deed would not have shown up in Taggart's search of the *grantee* index under Lawrance's name; it would have shown up under Lawrance's name only in the *grantor* index. (In the grantee index, the 1951 sale would have been indexed under the name of Witter's predecessor.) As the principal case notes, the extent of a purchaser's title search might be expanded considerably if the purchaser were charged with knowledge of the contents of all deeds to other property executed by every purchaser in the chain of title to the servient land. The name of *every* prior owner of the servient land would have to be run in the grantor index for the period of time that each purchaser owned the servient land, to see what transfers of other land each owner of the servient estate might have made; then the deed for every such transfer would have to be pulled and inspected in its entirety to see if the owner created any restrictions on the subject land. In the principal case, for example, the grantor index for Lawrence's transfer of the north lot would describe the 1951 transaction as a *sale* of the north lot, but the index probably would not identify the *easement* restriction on the south lot buried in the language of the sale deed. To find the easement, the title searcher would have had to read the 1951 deed in its entirety. *See* Stoebuck & Whitman, The Law of Property 897 (such a search task "can be monumental").

7. **Deeds out of the chain of title: another view.** Despite the potential burden to subsequent purchasers, some states charge the purchaser with knowledge of the contents of deeds of other parcels executed by owners in the chain of title to the subject property. *See* Finley v. Glenn, 154 A. 299, 301 (Pa. 1931) (emphasis added):

When [the subsequent purchasers] came to examine the title which was tendered to them, it was of primary consequence that they should know whether their grantors held title to the land which they were to convey. They could determine that question only by searching the records for grants from them [the grantors]. Coming upon this conveyance [a deed out of the servient owner's chain of tite], it was their duty to read it, *not to read only the description* of the property to see what was conveyed, but to read the deed *in its entirety*, to note *anything else* which might be set forth in it. The deed was notice to them of *all* it contained; otherwise the purpose of the recording acts would be frustrated.

Accord, Rowland Fanily Trust v. Pelletier, 673 A.2d 1081 (R.I. 1996). The cases are "about evenly divided" between the Witter v. Taggart and Finley v. Glenn views. *See* William B. Stoebuck & Dale A. Whitman, The Law of Property § 11.11, at 897 (3d ed. 2000).

8. **Proper recordation.** The court in the principal case says that Witter's predecessor could have protected himself against a subsequent purchaser like Taggart by recording the easement in the servient owner's chain of title. How would Witter's predecessor (P) have done that? Would P request that Lawrance execute two deeds: one to transfer fee simple title to the land purchased by P and another to grant P the easement over the grantor's land? Or would P request that Lawrance deed both lots to P, who would then deed back the south lot with the restriction? (The former procedure would put an unmistakeable reference in the grantor index that the indexed transfer contains a servitude affecting the retained land. The latter procedure would put the restriction in the direct chain of title to Lawrance's lot.) Or would P accept one deed containing the grant of the fee and creating the restriction, and request that the recording clerk index the deed under Lawrance's name twice, both as a seller and as the grantor of an easement in the south lot? In states that take the Finley v. Glenn view (Note 7) are two deeds — or a special request to the recordation clerk — necessary?

9. **Review.** In Fitzstephens v. Watson, did the defendant have notice of the easement burdening defendant's land, and if so, what kind of notice? In Garza v. Grayson, did defendant (Grayson) have notice of the easement burdening the lot he bought? In Walton v. Capital Land, would a buyer from Walton have had notice of the easement over Walton's land?

b.   Running of the Benefit

If the benefit of the servitude is appurtenant to the beneficiary's land, the benefit usually runs automatically with transfers of that land; no separate assignment of the benefit (or even mention of it) needs to be made in the instrument of transfer of the dominant estate. *See* Restatement Third § 5.1. The principal case states that rule, and announces a corollary: an appurtenant benefit "is unassignable in the absence of a transfer of the dominant estate." In short, an appurtenant benefit passes with, and only with, transfers of the dominant estate.

LUEVANO v. GROUP ONE
779 P.2d 552 (N.M. Ct. App. 1989)

Apodaca, Judge.

John and Marilyn Luevano (plaintiffs) appeal the trial court's order granting summary judgment to a group of landowners (Group Five) and ordering plaintiffs to tear down a fence between their property and adjoining properties owned by Group Five. The trial court held that Group Five possessed a valid easement as the result of an assignment. Because we conclude the subject easement was an easement appurtenant and not an easement in gross, we hold it was not assignable. We thus reverse the trial court and remand for consideration and disposition of other issues not previously reached.

Plaintiffs own a tract of land of which the northern strip consists of a road running east and west, known as Los Poblanos Ranch Road. Group Five owns land abutting the north side of the west portion of the road. Another group of defendants (Group One) owns three tracts of land to the east of plaintiffs' tract, bounded on the north by the east portion of the road. In 1953, Albert G. Simms (Simms), plaintiffs' predecessor in title, granted a right-of-way over Los Poblanos Ranch Road to Group One, including William and Sophia Padilla (the Padillas). This easement included the entire road and was not limited to only the east portion of the road abutting the properties owned by Group One. That is, the easement extended beyond the Group One properties.

In 1987 plaintiffs constructed a fence along the northern boundary of the road, thus blocking Group Five's access to the rear of the homes belonging respectively to the members of that group. Plaintiffs then filed a quiet title action seeking to extinguish the western portion of the road easement. After suit was filed, Group Five obtained an assignment of the right-of-way from the Padillas. The trial court held this assignment was valid, granted summary judgment to Group Five, and ordered plaintiffs to remove the fence.[11]

The specific issue before us is whether the easement was assignable. The answer to this question in turn depends on whether the easement granted to Group One by Simms was an easement appurtenant or an easement in gross. If it was an easement appurtenant, it is deemed to run with the land and is unassignable in the absence of a transfer of the dominant estate. Kikta v. Hughes, 766 P.2d 321 (N.M. Ct.App.1988). An easement in gross, however, may be assignable. See 3 R. Powell, The Law of Real Property ¶ 419 (P. Rohan rev. ed. 1987).

---

[11] The facts of this case are classic hornbook law. In his property law textbook, Professor Rabin gives the following example:

> EXAMPLE: X, owner of Blackacre, grants Y, owner of Whiteacre, an adjoining parcel, an easement of ingress and egress across a road on Blackacre.

> RESULT: Unless the granting instrument clearly specifies that the easement is personal to Y, it will be assumed that it is an easement appurtenant to Whiteacre.

E. Rabin, Fundamentals of Modern Real Property Law 434 (2d ed. 1982).

Plaintiffs argue that the law favors easements appurtenant and that ambiguous grants should be resolved in favor of finding them appurtenant. On the other hand, defendants argue that the grant was not related to any particular land and was therefore an easement in gross, capable of being assigned. The trial court specifically concluded that the easement was clearly alienable, assignable, devisable and inheritable and that the Padillas consequently had authority to assign their right-of-way to Group Five.

The grant does not expressly refer to any land owned by the grantees. In construing a grant, however, a court must consider the circumstances surrounding it. "If the granting instrument does not specify whether the easement is appurtenant or in gross, the court decides from the surrounding circumstances, but generally begins with the presumption that it is appurtenant." E. Rabin, Fundamentals of Modern Real Property Law 434 (2d ed. 1982). See Restatement of Property § 453 (1944); 28 C.J.S. Easements § 4 (1941). See also Siferd v. Stambor, 214 N.E.2d 106 (Ohio Ct. App. 1966) (whether easement is appurtenant must be determined from language used in deed, the surrounding circumstances at the time the right was created, and the intention of the parties at the time the deed was executed); Ernst v. Allen, 184 P. 827 (Utah 1919) (an instrument attempting to create an easement should be read in light of surrounding circumstances, the situation of the parties and property involved; if the grant refers to no land to which the easement can be appurtenant, but such land in fact exists, that fact may be established to give effect to the words used).

The record reflects that the grantees of the easement, Blas and Eloisa Gutierrez, Benjamin Gutierrez, and the Padillas, owned the three tracts of land adjoining the property of Simms, the grantor. All properties abutted the east portion of the road over which the easement was granted. Although the grant does not expressly refer to the grantees as landowners, it may be inferred from these particular circumstances that Simms intended the easement to benefit the grantees as owners of adjoining property, giving them convenient access to their respective land and not access in general as to any other lands. In the event that any of the grantees were to sell their respective land, the record does not reflect any benefit to be derived by them in retaining any interest in the right-of-way. There would be considerable benefit, on the other hand, to any party succeeding to their interests in the particular land. In view of these circumstances, we believe it is reasonable to conclude that Simms' intent was to create an easement appurtenant to the adjoining three tracts of land belonging to Group One.

Our conclusion is reinforced by the presumption favoring easements appurtenant over easements in gross. Easements are presumed appurtenant unless there is clear evidence to the contrary. See E. Rabin, *supra*; R. Powell, *supra*, at ¶ 405; C.J.S., *supra*, at 637 ("An easement is appurtenant to the land, if it is so in fact, although it is not declared to be so in the deed or instrument creating it; and an easement, which in its nature is appropriate and a useful adjunct of land owned by the grantee of the easement, will be declared an 'easement appurtenant,' and not 'in gross,' in the absence of a showing that the parties intended it to be a mere personal right."). See also Brooks v. Tanner, 680 P.2d 343 (N.M. 1984) (there is a strong constructional preference for appurtenant easements over easements in gross); Allingham v. Nelson, 627 P.2d 1179 (Kan. Ct.

App. 1981) (quoting 25 Am.Jur.2d, Easements and Licenses § 13 (1966) to the effect that an easement will never be presumed as personal when it may fairly be construed as appurtenant to some other estate); Hall v. Meyer, 527 P.2d 722 (Or. 1974) (extremely strong preference for finding an easement appurtenant rather than in gross).

We believe there are good policy reasons for the presumption that an easement is appurtenant. Construing doubtful easements as easements in gross would allow assignment of the easement to strangers to the area who could then control the use of the property. Such construction could also result in increased burdens on land beyond that contemplated by the original grantor. See Brooks v. Tanner, *supra* (burden on a servient estate cannot be increased without the owner's consent). Permitting the Padillas to assign their rights to the Group Five defendants clearly would result in an increased burden on plaintiffs' land.

Defendants emphasize the repeated use of the phrase "heirs and assigns" in the grant. They argue that this indicates the grantor intended to convey an assignable interest. We believe, however, that these words were traditionally used at common law merely to create an estate in land and not necessarily intended to create an assignable interest in land. On the contrary, the phrase could be interpreted to signify that the easement was tied to land. "The use of 'heirs or assigns,' or other similar words, in designating the person to whom the right is granted or reserved, is generally held to create an appurtenant easement." C.J.S., *supra*, at 637 (footnote omitted).

> The wording of the deed purports to grant the property to [grantee] and "its successors and assigns forever." These words of inheritance and succession, although not required by statutes, were considered at common law equally necessary to create either a fee simple title or a perpetual easement. The use of this phrase is of no assistance in determining the intent of the grantor.

Northwest Realty Co. v. Jacobs, 273 N.W.2d 141, 145 (S.D.1978).

In light of inferences that may be drawn from the circumstances surrounding the grant from Simms to Group One, as well as the preference for easements appurtenant and the policy against increasing the burden on a servient estate without the owner's consent, we hold that the grant in this appeal created an easement appurtenant that cannot exist separately from the dominant estate. Any attempt, therefore, to assign the easement, without transferring the land to which it attached, must necessarily fail.

In conclusion, because the attempted assignment of the easement to Group Five was not valid, we reverse the grant of summary judgment. The case is remanded to the trial court for a determination of whether Group Five has acquired rights to the road by prescription or dedication. Plaintiffs are awarded costs on appeal.

IT IS SO ORDERED.

NOTES AND QUESTIONS

1. **Presumption.** As *Luevano* notes, there is a presumption in favor of appurtenancy. *See also* Restatement Third § 4.5(2) ("In cases of doubt, a benefit should be construed to be appurtenant rather than in gross."). Why does this presumption exist, do you suppose?

2. **Other authority; effect of invalid transfer.** In addition to the authority cited in the principal case, see Goss v. Wildlife Trust, Inc., 852 A.2d 996 (Md. Ct. Spec. App. 2004) (appurtenant profit a prendre could not be transferred without transfer of the dominant estate); Town of Moorcroft v. Lang, 779 P.2d 1180 (Wyo. 1989) (appurtenant benefit cannot be separated from the dominant estate); Restatement Third § 5.6 (subject to a few specified exceptions, "an appurtenant benefit may not be severed and transferred separately from all or part of the benefited property. An attempted severance that is not effective to transfer the benefit does not extinguish the benefit unless manifestly intended to do so."). In transferring to Group Five, did the Padillas intend simply to enlarge the class of users of the servitude or to relinquish their own rights to use the servitude?

c.   Transferability of In-Gross Benefits

An in-gross benefit accrues to its holder as an individual rather than as a landowner; it therefore cannot run with land. That is not to say, however, that an in-gross benefit can only be enjoyed by its original beneficiary; it rather means that the mechanism of transfer of an in-gross benefit to a successor beneficiary is not the transfer of land. If you surmise that the beneficiary of in-gross benefit is much like the promisee of an ordinary contract right, you are correct. From that, it follows that an in-gross benefit arrives in the hands of a successor beneficiary by an explicit *assignment* of the right. There are two questions: Is the benefit of an in-gross easement assignable at all (a legal question), and if so, has the beneficiary in fact assigned it to the person who is claiming the benefit of it? On the first question, the common law was unrelenting in its opposition to the assignability of in-gross benefits. The trend today is toward free assignability of the benefit, unless the creating parties restrict transferability.

O'DONOVAN v. McINTOSH
728 A.2d 681 (Me. 1999)

Dana, J.

Timothy P. O'Donovan and John A. McIntosh Jr. appeal from a partial summary judgment entered in the Superior Court (Cumberland County, Cole, J.) in favor of Susan Huggins. O'Donovan and McIntosh argue that the court erred when it declared that an easement in gross held by McIntosh over Huggins's property was not assignable. We agree and vacate the judgment.

In 1987, McIntosh purchased real property at 184 Foreside Road in Falmouth. The property is adjacent to the Fish parcel [so named because the Fish family owned this land], and separates the Fish parcel from Foreside Road. McIntosh also purchased an option on the Fish parcel and then optioned both 184 Foreside

Road and his option on the Fish parcel to Casco Partners, Inc., which sought to construct a multiple lot subdivision on the Fish parcel. When Casco Partners did not proceed with the subdivision and McIntosh's option on the Fish parcel lapsed, McIntosh decided to sell 184 Foreside Road to Huggins and retain a right of way and an easement across it that would allow access to and the development of the Fish parcel.

On May 30, 1989, McIntosh conveyed the property to Huggins by warranty deed, reserving an easement for access to the Fish parcel. Concerning the easement, the deed stated:

> Excepting and reserving for the benefit of the Grantor and his heirs and assigns, a right of way and easement for access (50) feet in width to be used in common with the Grantee, her heirs and assigns, extending northerly from Foreside Road. Said right of way and easement shall (1) be for the purpose of ingress and egress to and from the lot herein conveyed and other land adjacent to and behind the above described parcel, commonly known as the "Fish parcel" and (2) not be located any closer to the house now standing on the property than 27 feet. The assigns of the Grantor herein shall be limited to those building and/or occupying a subdivision located on the above-mentioned "Fish parcel." Also reserving the right to install utilities over and under said right of way for the use and benefit of said other land. The foregoing right of way and easement shall also include the right of Grantor to enter on Grantee's land as is reasonably necessary to maintain, repair, and replace said utilities. The foregoing right of way and easement shall be subject to a duty owed by the Grantor to the Grantee, her heirs and assigns, to maintain, replace and repair the Grantee's property in the event of any disruption or damage caused to that property by the use of this right of way and easement.
>
> By acceptance of this deed the Grantor and Grantee agree to convey the right of way above mentioned to the Town of Falmouth in the event that it shall be accepted as a public way.

The deed also incorporated by reference an attached side agreement that would be "binding on subsequent owners" of the easement and in which Huggins agreed not to actively oppose any application for development permits for the Fish parcel.

In April 1995, O'Donovan, the president of Black Bear Development, Inc., entered into a purchase and sale agreement with the owners of the Fish parcel. On January 1, 1996, O'Donovan entered into a purchase and sale agreement with McIntosh for the easement.

Black Bear filed an application for subdivision approval with the Town of Falmouth Planning Board. In January 1996, the Board held the first in a series of open public meetings to address the application. The Board eventually suspended the application after a dispute arose regarding the transferability of the easement.

After the Board suspended the proposal, O'Donovan, in May 1997, filed a complaint against McIntosh and Huggins seeking, inter alia, a declaratory judgment pursuant to 14 M.R.S.A. §§ 5951-5963 (1980 & Supp.1998) concerning his right to purchase and sell the easement. McIntosh and O'Donovan filed a joint motion for a partial summary judgment, arguing that the easement may be transferred, conveyed, or otherwise assigned to O'Donovan. Huggins objected to the motion and filed a cross-motion for a summary judgment. The court granted Huggins's motion, concluding that the easement was not assignable. The court certified the judgment to allow O'Donovan and McIntosh to appeal.

An easement is a right of use over the property of another. See Restatement of Property § 450 (1944); Black's Law Dictionary 509 (6th ed.1990). The law recognizes two different types of easements: an easement in gross and an easement appurtenant. An easement appurtenant is created to benefit the dominant tenement and runs with the land. To be appurtenant, however, the easement must also be attached to or related to a dominant estate of the grantor. Here, because McIntosh owned no dominant estate to which the easement could be appurtenant, the easement is in gross. Consequently, the question becomes whether the easement in gross is assignable. We hold that the easement is assignable because the parties clearly expressed that intent in the language of the deed.

Although we have categorically stated that an easement in gross is not assignable, see, e.g., O'Neill v. Williams, 527 A.2d 322, 323 (Me.1987), we have also suggested that such an easement may be assignable in certain circumstances. See Davis v. Briggs, 105 A. 128, 130 (Me. 1918); see also White v. Crawford, 10 Mass. 183, 188 (1813) ("As to ways in gross, that they may be granted, or may accrue, in various forms, to one and his heirs and assigns, there can be no doubt."). Most important, we have never applied the rule — that an easement in gross is not assignable — to frustrate the parties' clear intent, as set forth in the deed, that the holder may assign the easement.

Our focus on the intent of the parties in this case is in accord with those courts that assess the parties' intent to determine the alienability of an easement in gross. See, e.g., Lindley v. Maggert, 645 P.2d 430, 431 (Mont. 1982) (easement freely alienable when no language in the deed exists to limit right to alienate); Weber v. Dockray, 64 A.2d 631, 633 (N.J. Super. Ct. Ch. Div. 1949) (assignability depends on intention of the parties, the nature of the burden on the servient tenant, and circumstances existing at time the grant was made); Miller v. Lutheran Conference & Camp Ass'n, 200 A. 646, 651 (Pa. 1938) ("There does not seem to be any reason why the law should prohibit the assignment of an easement in gross if the parties to its creation evidence their intention to make it assignable."); Farmer's Marine Copper Works, Inc. v. City of Galveston, 757 S.W.2d 148, 151 (Tex.Ct.App.1988) ("Although easements 'in gross' are personal to the grantee only, and are generally not assignable or transferable, the parties may create an assignable easement in gross through an express assignment provision.").

Moreover, such an approach is consistent with those authorities that increasingly recognize and advocate the free alienability of easements in gross. See Restatement of Property §§ 491, 492 (1944) (alienability of noncommercial easement determined by the manner and terms of its creation); 2 American Law of Property § 8.82 (1952) ("There seems to be no reason to deny to parties who create easements in gross the privilege of making them alienable if they wish to do so."); 4 Richard R. Powell, Powell on Real Property § 34.16, at 34-218 (1998) (noting only barriers to alienability of easement in gross is finding of creator's manifest intent to bar alienation and courts' misplaced fear of "resultant surcharge" on the land); 3 Herbert Thorndike Tiffany, Tiffany on Real Property § 761 (Supp.1998) ("[T]here is a growing recognition of the assignability of all easements in gross except those demonstrably intended to benefit only the individual who is its first recipient.").

The conclusion that an easement in gross is assignable when the parties intend is consistent with our general policy favoring the free alienability of property. The alienability of an easement in gross promotes the free alienability of land, a general policy of property law. See Restatement of Property § 489 cmt. a (1944). The Restatement explains that "[t]his policy arises from a belief that the social interest is promoted by the greater utilization of the subject matter of property resulting from the freedom of alienation of interests in it." In furtherance of this policy, we have adhered to the traditional rule of construction that whenever possible an easement is construed to be appurtenant to the land of the person for whose use the easement is created, thereby ensuring that the easement is alienable. Similarly, we have held that a profit a prendre — the right to take from the land something that is a product of the soil — is freely assignable even when that right is in gross. In addition, to give effect to the intent of the parties and promote alienability, we have abolished the technical requirement that the word "heirs" be used to preserve an interest of perpetual duration. It is consistent with the policy of promoting a high degree of alienability that we hold an easement in gross may be assignable.

Finally, we reject Huggins's argument that stare decisis compels us to hold that the easement in gross is not alienable despite the parties' contrary intent. Although we appreciate the need for uniformity and certainty produced by stare decisis, we have also recognized that "where the authorities supporting the prior rule have been drastically eroded, [and] the suppositions on which it rested are disapproved in the better-considered recent cases and in authoritative scholarly writings, and the holding of the [prior] case is counterproductive to its purposes, the situation is appropriate for legal change by the court's decision." Myrick v. James, 444 A.2d 987, 998-99 (Me. 1982). With respect to the nontransferability of an easement in gross, the primary argument proffered to support the rule is that alienability will unfairly burden the servient estate. The servient tenement holder, however, is protected because an easement holder may only use the easement in a manner consistent with the intent of the parties that created the easement. Moreover, modern authority almost unanimously rejects the restrictive rule against alienability. See, e.g., Jon W. Bruce & James W. Ely Jr., The Law of Easements and Licenses in Land ¶ 9.03[3] (1995) ("[C]ommentators have unanimously supported judicial recognition that easements in gross may be transferred."). Because the reasons supporting the rule against alienability are no longer compelling and because modern authorities disapprove of the unduly restrictive nature of the rule, we conclude that the rule against alienability cannot be used to frustrate the parties' intent that an easement be alienable.

The easement created by McIntosh and Huggins is alienable because the parties demonstrated their intent that the easement be alienable in the clear language of the deed. We construe the deed to give effect to the grantor's intent. Here, the deed created an easement "[e]xcepting and reserving the benefit of the Grantor and his heirs and assigns" and limited the assigns "to those building and/or occupying" the Fish parcel. McIntosh and Huggins also agreed to convey the right of way to the

Town of Falmouth if the Town accepted it as a public way. Moreover, the side agreement referenced in and attached to the deed bound the "subsequent owners" of the easement and prohibited Huggins from opposing development of the Fish parcel. As expressed by the clear language of the deed, McIntosh and Huggins intended that McIntosh would be free to assign the easement. The court, therefore, erred when it concluded that the easement was not assignable.[2]

The entry is:

Judgment vacated. Remanded to the Superior Court for further proceedings consistent with this opinion.

WATHEN, C.J., with whom CLIFFORD, J., joins, dissenting.

I respectfully dissent. The intent of the parties is relevant in clarifying whether an easement is appurtenant or in gross. Once that is determined, however, there is no proposition of Maine decisional law more firmly settled than the principle that an easement in gross is personal and not assignable. See O'Neill v. Williams, 527 A.2d 322, 323 (Me. 1987) ("An easement in gross is a purely personal right, is not assignable, and terminates upon the death of the individual for whom it was created.").

Stare decisis embodies the "important social policy of continuity in law" and we have expressed our particular reluctance to abandon past precedent when to do so would "interfere with the valid reliance interests of litigants arising from contract rights, real property rights or rights to property by descent." Adams v. Buffalo Forge Co., 443 A.2d 932, 935 (Me. 1982). If there is a need for changing the law, it is better addressed by the Legislature. Our ruling necessarily acts on the past as well as the future and is capable of resurrecting long forgotten easements to dash the settled expectations of landowners and title examiners. I would affirm the judgment.

---

[2] O'Donovan and McIntosh also argue that the easement is alienable because it is commercial in character. The Restatement of Property provides that "[e]asements in gross, if of a commercial character, are alienable property interests." Restatement of Property § 489 (1944). "An easement in gross is of a commercial character when the use authorized by it results primarily in economic benefit rather than personal satisfaction." Id. cmt. c. Common commercial easements in gross include easements for railroads, telephone and telegraph lines, and pipelines. See Restatement of Property § 491 cmt. b (1944). Other commercial easements include the use of land for parking lots, when the agreement between the parties granted use of lots "in connection with the operation" of a mass transportation bus line, Kansas City Area Transp. Auth. v. Ashley, 485 S.W.2d 641, 645 (Mo.Ct.App.1972), the use of land to drive a herd of cattle, which were raised for profit rather than for personal use, Crane v. Crane, 683 P.2d 1062, 1067 (Utah 1984), and a driveway leading to a commercial property, when the driveway "has been used exclusively for commercial purposes since its creation," Douglas v. Medical Investors, Inc., 182 S.E.2d 720, 723 (S.C. 1971). O'Donovan and McIntosh argue that the easement is commercial in character because the easement was intended to facilitate a proposed commercial enterprise — the development of the Fish parcel — and because McIntosh created the easement with the intent to sell it for profit. Because we conclude that the easement is alienable on the basis of the parties' intent, we need not address this issue.

NOTES AND QUESTIONS

1. **Three views on transferability.** There are three views on the question of the transferability of the benefit of an easement in gross.

a. The common law flatly prohibited the transfer of the benefit of an easement in gross, even if the parties who created the benefit intended assignability. *See* Stockdale v. Yerden, 190 N.W. 225, 226 (Mich. 1922) (easements in gross are "not assignable or inheritable, nor can they be made so by any terms of the grant"). The third Restatement attributes the common law's hostility to the transfer of in-gross benefits to a concern that "difficulty in locating the beneficiaries [if transfer were possible] would make it difficult or impossible to rid the land of obsolete or inconvenient servitudes." Restatement Third § 7.13 cmt. a. However, the common law did allow transfers of benefits that produced economic value: the benefit of an in-gross profit a prendre was transferable at common law. *Id.* § 4.6 cmt. b, at 549.

b. As footnote 2 of the principal case indicates, the first Restatement of Property distinguished "commercial" from "noncommercial" in-gross benefits, and created a default rule of transferability for commercial benefits only. *See* Restatement of Property §§ 489, 491, 492. A commercial benefit produces economic advantage rather than personal satisfaction. *Id.* § 489 cmt. c. An example is a right of way for a utility line. Personal satisfaction "contributes to pleasure rather than to financial well-being," and may include "either physical or spiritual gratification." *Id.* § 491 cmt. a. Examples of personal satisfaction are easements for boating, hunting, or fishing.

c. The third Restatement creates a presumption (in effect, a default rule) that a benefit in gross "is freely transferable." Restatement Third § 4.6(1)(c). The absence of "assigns" language or of a commercial benefit does not prevent transferability. *Id.* cmt. d. The presumption is rebutted if "the relationship of the parties, consideration paid, nature of the servitude, or other circumstances" indicate that the parties did not intend or reasonably expect transferability. *Id.* § 4.6(2).

2. **The principal case.** Which view of the transferability of an easement in gross does the *O'Donovan* court take? For a critique of the principal case, see Michael J. Polak, Case Note, O'Donovan v. McIntosh: *Changing the Contours of Maine's Easement Law*, 52 Me. L. Rev. 447 (2000).

3. **Review.** In Walton v. Capital Land, Inc. (the first case in this chapter), Willow Investment retained the benefit of an easement in gross when it transferred its parcel to Walton. The plaintiff was Capital Land, Inc. How did Capital Land get the right to enjoy the benefit? (A later Virginia case, United States v. Blackman, appearing in Section D below, holds that the benefit of an in-gross easement is transferable.)

4. **Terminology: "personal" benefits.** Courts and writers often use "personal" as a synonym for "in gross." The word "personal," however, is ambiguous. It can describe a benefit that is enjoyable individually ("personally") rather than as a landowner. In that sense, an in-gross benefit is always, by definition, personal. The word, however, can also describe a benefit that is limited ("personal") to the original holder only and therefore not transferable. In this second sense, in-gross benefits are always personal only under the common law rule; under the first and third Restatements, some in-gross benefits are personal

and some aren't. To avoid having terminology confuse substance, the third Restatement reserves the terms "appurtenant" and "in gross" to discuss the question whether enjoyment of the benefit does or does not require ownership or possession of land, and it uses the terms "personal" and "transferable" to discuss the separate question whether the benefit of a servitude is transferable. *See* Restatement Third § 1.5(3) (" 'Personal' means that a servitude benefit or burden is not transferable and does not run with land. Whether appurtenant or in gross, a servitude benefit or burden may be personal."). This is a real contribution to the clarity of analysis, and one hopes that the Restatement's usages will catch on among the courts and the profession.

PROBLEMS

6-A. Characterize the benefit in the following examples as appurtenant or in gross, and as personal or transferable.

a. A grants to his nephew B, with whom A has a close relationship, the right to dock and moor a boat on Blackacre, A's lakefront parcel. B owns no land in the vicinity, and pays nothing for the easement. *See* Restatement Third § 4.6, illus. 2.

b. Same facts, but B owns Whiteacre, adjacent to Blackacre, with no lake access. A grants the access easement "to B, for use on A's property so long as B owns Whiteacre." *See* Restatement Third § 2.6, illus. 2 (T.D. No. 1, 1989); first Restatement § 487 & cmt. d, at 3032.

c. A, owner of Blackacre, grants to "the Teddy Roosevelt Hunting Club and its assigns" the exclusive right to hunt on Blackacre for 20 years. The club owns no land in the vicinity. *See* Restatement Third § 2.6, illus. 3 (T.D. No. 1, 1989).

d. Landowner A grants an easement "to B and his heirs and assigns." If the benefit is appurtenant, what is the significance of the "heirs and assigns" language? What is its significance if the benefit is in gross?

6-B. In Martin v. Music, 254 S.W.2d 701 (Ky. 1953), the parties entered into the following agreement:

> Party of the first part [Music] gives and grants to second party [Martin] the right to construct and maintain a sewer line under and through his [Music's] property located in the Layne Heirs addition to the City of Prestonburg, Kentucky, and being lots No. 17 through 24 inclusive of said addition.
>
> In consideration of said right, second party agrees to lay said sewer line at sufficient depth to not interfere with first party's use and enjoyment of said property; and to place an intake connection in said line for use of said party at a point to be designated by him; and further agrees to pay to first party any damage which may result to his property be reason of the laying, maintaining, repairing and operation of said sewer line.

Martin constructed the sewer line and the intake connection. Music subsequently transferred some of his lots to Wells and Allen, each of whom started to construct a dwelling house and to connect to Martin's sewer. Martin sued for a declaration of rights, maintaining, in the court's words, "that the right to connect with the sewer was personal to Music alone, for the purpose of serving a dwelling house which Music planned to build, and that the right did not accrue to Wells and Allen." In determining whether Wells and Allen could connect to the sewer line, is the issue whether the benefit is appurtenant or in gross (the court's approach), or is there a more precise way to state the issue? Would the hookup benefit be of use to anyone other than an owner of land under which the sewer line ran? Does the language of the agreement indicate anything about the transferability of the hook-up benefit?

6-C. Citizens Jewelers granted to its neighbor Scales Corporation "a non-exclusive easement over and across the property of [Citizens Jewelers], which easement extends to the western boundary of property now owned by [Scales]." Unfortunately, Scales no longer owned the would-be dominant estate, having sold it to Series V. Later, Scales attempted to convey the easement to Series V by a "corrective warranty deed." When Barnes and Noble, the successor to Citizens Jewelers, interferred with use of the easement by Yaali, Ltd., the successor to the land owned by Series V, Yaali sued. The court held that the agreement between Citizens Jewelers and Scales did not create an easement in gross because the parties intended to create an easement appurtenant; it held that an easement appurtenant was not created because Scales didn't own the dominant estate at the time of the transfer of the easement. Yaali, Ltd. v. Barnes & Noble, Inc., 506 S.E.2d 116 (Ga.1998). Two judges dissented, arguing that the deed to Scales created an easement in gross, which Scales had subsequently transferred to Series V:

> According to the majority, a conveyance for [ingress and egress] generally is construed as an easement appurtenant, rather than in gross. However, no authority is cited for the proposition that, as a matter of law, such a conveyance can never be construed as an easement in gross. Indeed, as the majority acknowledges, the "surrounding circumstances" must be considered in determining whether an easement in gross was conveyed. One of the circumstances surrounding the conveyance in this case is that it appears that, at the time it was made, the property was already exclusively commercial. The grant of the right of ingress and egress to commercial property, which was not owned by the grantee on the date of the execution of the deed or other instrument, can constitute the conveyance of an easement in gross primarily for the economic benefit of the grantee. Compare Bosworth v. Nelson, 152 S.E. 575 (Ga. 1930) (boating and fishing privileges as profits a prendre). The right of ingress and egress to commercial property is, in effect, similar to the typical easement in gross granted to a railroad, utility line, or pipeline to pass over or through property of the grantor so as to facilitate the commercial purposes of the grantee. Although this conveyance did not provide that it was assignable by Yaali's predecessor, a commercial easement in gross is alienable as a matter of law, and requires no express language authorizing its assignment. Restatement of the Law of Property § 489.

Who has the better argument, the majority or dissent? If Scales held an easement in gross, would it become an appurtenant easement after it was reunited with the dominant estate, or could Series V transfer it apart from that estate, as Padilla attempted to do in the *Luevano* case? What alternatives might Scales have pursued instead of the "corrective warranty deed"?

3.   Informal Easements

All of the easements encountered up until now have been express, formal easements, their terms hammered out in a bargain between the parties and documented in a writing. But the law also recognizes informal (unwritten) easements, which the creating parties don't specifically negotiate. These may be created by estoppel, prior use, necessity, and adverse use of the servient estate for the period of the statute of limitations. Because these categories overlap, and because inconsistent causes of action may be pleaded in the alternative under modern codes of procedure, it is not unusual for one case to allow the assertion of more than one of these bases for the creation of an easement. *See, e.g.*, Pickett v. Whipple, 629 N.Y.S.2d 489 (N.Y. App. Div. 1995) (considers estoppel, prior use, necessity, and prescription); Guilbault v. Bowley, 498 A.2d 1033 (Vt. 1985) (considers estoppel and prescription). Be alert for that possibility as you read the materials. We begin by looking at a case dealing with an informal arrangement that is *not* a servitude because neither its benefit nor its burden runs with the land. But the category of *licenses* is important in its own right, and because an understanding of the category paves the way for consideration of the so-called "irrevocable license" and its doctrinal companion, the easement created by estoppel.

a.   Easements at Will: Licenses

A license in land is, essentially, the nonpossessory equivalent of a tenancy at will estate, which we saw in Chapter 4. In both, the interest that one party holds in the land of another is held at the will of both the landowner and the beneficiary of the interest. In addition to easy revocability between A and B, a license terminates by operation of law upon the death of either party or upon the licensor's transferor of the "burdened" land, *see* Doyle v. Peabody, 781 P.2d 957 (Alaska 1989) (license revoked by transfer of servient estate), limitations that apply to the tenancy at will also. And while the parties may expressly create a license, the license category, like the tenancy at will category, performs a significant catch-all function, covering situations in which the parties' intent for a revocable relationship is not expressly stated.

MANDIA v. APPLEGATE
708 A.2d 1211 (N.J. Super. Ct. App. Div. 1998)

SKILLMAN, J.A.D.

In June 1976 plaintiffs Frank Mandia and Mike Brown purchased a tract of land in Seaside Park, New Jersey, known as Funtown Pier. At the time of the purchase, Funtown Pier consisted of a small, ocean-front amusement park occupied by various concessionaires. In order to raise money to buy the property, plaintiffs approached a number of the concessionaires and proposed that they purchase ninety-nine year leases instead of continuing to rent their premises on a short term basis. Plaintiffs' financing plan was successful and prior to the closing they obtained commitments for fourteen 99-year leases, consisting of about 20% of the total property. Since that time plaintiffs have maintained and managed Funtown Pier, buying back some of the 99-year leases and selling others, while renting the remaining concession stands to short-term tenants. The area has generally improved over the years and is now completely covered with boardwalk.

The first of the concessionaires to agree to enter into a 99-year lease were defendants Applegate and Dagostino, who acquired their property for $184,505. Defendants tore down an old luncheonette that was on the site and replaced it with a two-story steel and concrete building. The building traced the "footprint" of the space defendants had leased and had a second floor overhang which extended over the walkway areas of the boardwalk approximately five feet on the east, south, and west. Defendants operated several business ventures from this building over the years, the latest and most successful being the Silver Apple Surf Shop which sells upscale beach wear.

Shortly after opening his business on the Funtown Pier, Applegate[1] asked Brown if he could display some clothing items under the overhang on the south side of the building for an end of season clearance sale. Brown agreed to the request as a special favor, telling Applegate that he was grateful to him for being the first person to enter into a 99-year lease. From that time forward, Applegate displayed merchandise on the boardwalk under the building overhang without ever again asking Brown's permission. As time went by Applegate made greater and greater use of the overhang area, displaying racks of clothing and other merchandise on a more-or-less permanent basis.

In 1994 Applegate telephoned Brown in Florida and told him that he was planning to install an electrically-operated awning which would extend over some eight feet of boardwalk beyond the southerly overhang to his building. Upon returning to New Jersey, Brown had lunch with Applegate and told him that the awning represented more use of the boardwalk area than Applegate's previous displays of merchandise and that he expected to be compensated for it. When Brown said that he felt that $10,000 was a fair seasonal rent for the area, Applegate replied "how about $5,000, how about $2,000, whatever." Brown laughed and "said, well how about $5,000." The two agreed on $5,000 and decided to let Mandia, who is an attorney, draw up a written agreement concerning Applegate's use of the boardwalk.

After consulting with an attorney who advised him that the proposed agreement gave him nothing, Applegate told Brown that he would not sign it. Nevertheless, Applegate continued to display his merchandise under the overhang and awning during the 1994, 1995 and 1996 seasons, during which time he refused to make any payment to plaintiffs for this use.

On June 19, 1995, plaintiffs' counsel sent defendants a formal demand that they cease using the boardwalk for the display of merchandise. The letter reminded the defendants that their lease provided that he could not encumber or obstruct the boardwalk or entrance to their building and warned that the lease also provided

---

[1] Although the property owners are listed as Applegate and Dagostino, there is little in the record concerning the extent of Dagostino's involvement in the business venture. Applegate seems to have managed the businesses and to have made all of the decisions that are the subject of this lawsuit.

that "if the tenant defaults in any of its obligations and fails to cure said default after 30 days' notice from the landlord, the landlord may reclaim the premises and the lease will be at an end." On July 27, 1995, plaintiffs' counsel sent defendants another letter which formally notified them that because of his continued use of the boardwalk area, plaintiffs were invoking the forfeiture clause of the lease and declaring defendants' leasehold to be at an end. Defendants ignored both of these letters and continued to operate the Silver Apple Surf Shop as before, including the unauthorized use of the boardwalk under the overhang and awning.

Plaintiffs then brought the present lawsuit seeking an order enjoining defendants' use of the boardwalk area adjoining their property for the display of merchandise, compensating plaintiffs for defendants' past unauthorized use of this property and declaring that defendants had forfeited their leasehold. The case was tried over four days, at the conclusion of which the court issued an oral opinion. The court concluded that even though plaintiffs own the boardwalk under the overhang to defendants' building, they "waived" their right to prevent defendants from displaying merchandise in this area because they had previously permitted this use. However, because defendants did not show a similar pattern of permissive use of the area under the newly installed awning, the court concluded that they had no right to continue displaying merchandise in that area. Accordingly, the court entered judgment declaring that defendants have the "right to display merchandise on the boardwalk beneath the existing overhang on the defendants' building, without having to pay rent or other compensation for such usage," but enjoining defendants from displaying any merchandise "and from making any other use of any portion of the boardwalk area to the south of the existing overhang on the southerly side of defendants' leased premises." In addition, the court awarded plaintiffs $5,000 as total compensation for defendants' unauthorized use of the area beyond the overhang to their building during the 1994, 1995 and 1996 seasons. Finally, the court dismissed the count of plaintiffs' complaint which sought a declaration that defendants had forfeited their leasehold interest. The court subsequently entered an order denying plaintiffs' motion for a new trial and/or reconsideration.

Plaintiffs appeal from the judgment and the order denying their motion for a new trial and/or reconsideration. We conclude that the trial court erred in ruling that defendants have a right to display merchandise outside their leased premises without plaintiffs' consent and in refusing to grant an injunction prohibiting that use. We also conclude that the court awarded plaintiffs inadequate damages for the unauthorized use of the boardwalk area during the 1994, 1995 and 1996 seasons. Accordingly, we reverse in some respects and modify in other respects the parts of the judgment dealing with those claims. We affirm the part of the judgment denying plaintiffs' demand for a declaration that defendants' leasehold interest has been forfeited.

I

It is undisputed that plaintiffs own the entire area of the boardwalk underneath the overhang to defendants' building and that the lease does not expressly grant defendants any interest in that area. To the contrary, the lease provides that "[the lessee] shall neither encumber or obstruct the sidewalk and front of, or any entrance to, the building on the leased premises," and that "[a]ll sidewalks, walkways and entrances in or around the demised premises shall be kept 'as is' with no further construction or encumbrances thereon." Nevertheless, because plaintiffs permitted defendants to display merchandise in certain areas underneath the overhang from 1977 or 1978 to 1993, the trial court concluded that plaintiffs had "waived" their right to prevent defendants from continuing this activity, thereby in effect holding that defendants had acquired a perpetual easement for the display of merchandise over this part of plaintiffs' property.

Reasoning

Defendants' permissive use of plaintiffs' property resulted in a revocable license rather than an easement. "A parol consent to enter upon land amounts only to a license." Eileen T. Quigley, Inc. v. Miller Family Farms, Inc., 266 N.J.Super. 283, 295, 629 A.2d 110 (App.Div.1993). "A license is simply a personal privilege to use the land of another in some specific way or for some particular purpose or act." Township of Sandyston v. Angerman, 134 N.J.Super. 448, 451, 341 A.2d 682 (App.Div.1975). Plaintiffs gave defendants consent to use the part of the boardwalk under the overhang to their building for the display of merchandise. Because defendants provided no consideration for this consent and did not expend any significant amount of money or worsen their position in any other way in reliance upon their belief that they had a right to continue this use, they only had a revocable license to display their merchandise under the overhang. See Restatement (Third) of Property (Servitudes) § 4.1, comment f (Tentative Draft No. 4, 1994); 4 Powell, Real Property § 34.26 at 34–315 to 34–318 (1997).

Although the trial court did not find that defendants had established an easement, it nevertheless concluded that plaintiffs had "waived" their right to prevent defendants' use of the boardwalk for display of merchandise by permitting this use to continue over a period of sixteen or seventeen years. However, the establishment of an interest in land is governed by the previously discussed principles of real property law rather than any amorphous concept of waiver. In any event, there is no factual foundation for a finding that plaintiffs relinquished their right to prevent defendants from using the area of the boardwalk underneath the overhang for the display of merchandise. The record only shows that plaintiffs granted defendants and certain other lessees permission to display merchandise or make other use of some areas of the boardwalk.[3] There is no evidence plaintiffs ever indicated this permission was permanent and could not be revoked. Permission to make a transitory use of property is the hallmark of a revocable license. Such permission does not constitute a permanent waiver of the property owner's right to prevent others from using his property. Therefore, the trial court erred in granting defendants what amounts to a perpetual easement for the display of merchandise on the boardwalk area underneath the overhang to their building.

---

[3] The record also indicates that plaintiffs refused to allow many lessees to make such uses of the boardwalk area. In fact, plaintiffs brought two prior lawsuits to enjoin lessees under ninety-nine year leases from obstructing the boardwalk.

II

We turn next to the trial court's award of only $5,000 in damages for defendants' unauthorized use of the boardwalk area over the three year period from 1994 to 1996. Initially, we note that because the trial court concluded that defendants were entitled to display their merchandise in the area underneath the overhang, the damage award apparently was based solely on defendants' unauthorized use of the area underneath their newly installed awning. Consequently, we ordinarily would remand the case for a redetermination of damages in light of our conclusion that defendants' display of merchandise on the entire boardwalk area, including the portion under the overhang, was unauthorized. However, because the trial record clearly indicates that the fair value of this use of the boardwalk is at least $5,000 per year and plaintiffs have limited their damages claim to this amount, we conclude that the interest of justice would be served by our finally deciding the issue. [The court concluded that $5,000 per year for the disputed boardwalk area was reasonable, and modified the lower court judgment to award plaintiff $15,000.]

III

Finally, we consider plaintiffs' argument that the trial court erred in refusing to declare a forfeiture of defendants' leasehold interest. [E]ven if the forfeiture clause could be construed to apply to the wilful maintenance of an obstruction on the boardwalk, we are satisfied that it was not triggered by defendants' display of merchandise during the 1994, 1995 and 1996 summer seasons because, when viewed in light of the prior business and personal relationship between the parties, defendants' compliance with their other obligations, and the good faith dispute between the parties as to their rights and obligations under the lease, that activity only constituted a minor breach of defendants' lease obligations. Cf. Johnson v. City of Hackensack, 200 N.J.Super. 185, 190, 491 A.2d 14 ("Where a forfeiture results from the failure to use property for the purpose specified in the deed, a minor deviation from that use will not effect the forfeiture as long as the specified use is substantially carried out"); see also 49 Am.Jur.2d Landlord and Tenant § 339 (1995) ("[A] lessee who has breached a covenant of the lease providing for its termination because of such breach may, under some circumstances, avoid the forfeiture of the lease through intervention of equity, where it clearly appears necessary to prevent an unduly oppressive result, or to prevent an unconscionable advantage to the lessor or an unconscionable disadvantage to the lessee.").

Accordingly, paragraph one of the judgment is modified to enjoin defendants from placing any merchandise, clothing, tables, or similar articles upon or in any other way obstructing any of the boardwalk area outside of their premises; paragraph two is modified to award plaintiffs $15,000 in damages for the unauthorized use of the area described in paragraph one during the 1994-96 seasons; paragraph three is affirmed; and paragraph four is reversed.

lost the right
to hang stuff
on the awning

NOTES AND QUESTIONS

1. **The wisdom of Applegate's actions.** Because Applegate was willing to pay the price asked by plaintiffs for use of the additional boardwalk space, why didn't he make a deal and avoid this lawsuit? What did Applegate lose as a result of the litigation? What else did he risk losing, had the court ruled differently?

no consideration -
never indicated
permanent?

2. **License in the principal case.** Why did the court conclude that Applegate had only a license? Do you think the court's conclusion was correct? Why did the court conclude that plaintiffs hadn't "waived" the right to revoke the permission?

3. **Licenses in general.** Since both parties may unburden themselves easily, a license is exempt from the requirement of a writing for the creation of more substantial interests in land, such as estates and easements. Although it is usually studied in connection with easements, a license is not a servitude, because it has no capacity to "run" to successors. But as the next case indicates, in some states it can become the basis for a servitude created by estoppel.

4. **Tickets.** When you buy a ticket to the opera or a rock concert, you are a licensee of your specified seat. The law treats the ticket not as a conveyance of an interest in the impresario's premises, but as a revocable permission to you to occupy a portion of those premises. For a famous and typically terse opinion to that effect by Justice Holmes, see Marrone v. Washington Jockey Club, 227 U.S. 633, 636-637 (1913):

> The fact that the purchase of the ticket made a contract is not enough. A contract binds the person of the maker, but does not create an interest in the property that it may concern, unless it also operates as a conveyance. The ticket was not a conveyance of an interest in the race track, not only because it was not under seal, but because by common understanding it did not purport to have that effect. There would be obvious inconveniences if it were construed otherwise. But if it did not create such an interest, that is to say, a right in rem, valid against the landowner and third persons, the holder had no right to enforce specific performance by self-help [plaintiff had tried to enter the race track, been turned away, and sued for damages for being forcibly prevented from entering]. His only right was to sue upon the contract for breach. It is true that if the contract were incidental to a right of property either in the land or in goods upon the land, there might be an irrevocable right of entry; but when the contract stands by itself, it must be either a conveyance or a license, subject to being revoked.

Why would it be "inconvenient" to treat a ticket as a conveyance? What remedy would a conveyance give the ticket holder? What remedies does the license (contract) holder have?

5. **Law and social practices.** Under the rule stated in *Marrone*, the proprietors of the race track (theater, opera house, baseball stadium) can refuse to admit, or can evict, a patron arbitrarily. What does "arbitrary" mean in this context? Should the law provide a ticket holder with more protection than damages for arbitrary eviction? The leading article on the ticket cases suggests a negative answer to the second question, and also sheds some light on the first question:

> Amusement proprietors do not arbitrarily eject their patrons. They do refuse admittance more or less arbitrarily. Occasionally they eject patrons

whom they believe to be disorderly or to have violated the rules of admittance. In such cases their belief is honest, but not always reasonable. If a proprietor should eject a patron whom he did not believe to be violating established rules of admittance or of conduct, he would be considered unfair by his fellow-tradesmen as well as by the public.

The law as commonly stated permits the proprietor to eject arbitrarily as well as for cause. But the privilege is illusory, because the jury may find the proprietor liable for use of excessive force or incivility. If the law were restated to forbid arbitrary or unreasonable ejections, the principal effects would be to give the jury an additional opportunity for holding proprietors liable who act reasonably or in good faith, and to impede performance of the proprietor's duty to keep his premises safe for others.

Alfred Conard, *The Privilege of Forcibly Ejecting an Amusement Patron*, 90 U. Pa. L. Rev. 809, 823 (1942).

b.   Estoppel

If A creates an easement in her land in favor of B, and the parties do not reduce the arrangement to writing, the easement is unenforceable because of the statute of frauds. However, estoppel (of A) can create a nonpossessory interest in B just as it can create an estate, as we saw in considering estoppel to assert the statute of frauds in lease cases. If A grants B a revocable permission to use A's land (a license), the license can, by estoppel (of A), grow up into an irrevocable permission in B. Such "irrevocable licenses," as they are sometimes called, are analytically indistinguishable from easements. Neither the enforcement of an agreed-upon oral easement, nor the recognition of an irrevocable license, is uncontroversial, especially the latter.

HENRY v. DALTON
151 A.2d 362 (R.I. 1959)

Powers, Justice.

This bill in equity was brought to establish an irrevocable right in the land of the respondent for use as a driveway to the garage of the complainants. [A] decree was entered denying and dismissing the bill of complaint.

The testimony discloses that on May 27, 1922 the complainants purchased a house on Carver Street in the city of Pawtucket and that within a month thereafter respondent's husband purchased the adjoining property. It further appears that the distance between the foundations of both houses is approximately 14.5 feet, only 5.8 feet of which is the property of complainants. It is mutually agreed that at the time the parties purchased their respective properties a wooden fence separated the properties along the boundary lines. A few years later this fence was taken down and replaced by a hedge, which although planted by respondent's husband was a joint venture and Henry and Dalton each contributed one half of its cost.

In 1938 complainant William E. Henry spoke to respondent's husband about removing the hedge from the boundary line and making common use of their respective properties as a driveway. Henry explained that he wished to construct a two-car garage at the rear of his property since he and his son each had a car. It is undisputed that William Dalton, husband of respondent, readily gave his permission and respondent states in her deposition that her husband advised her of the request and of his consent. The hedge was removed and complainants filled in their own strip to bring it up to grade with their neighbors' land. At the same time the Henrys constructed a two-car garage at the rear of their property.

Although there is conflicting testimony as to whether or not thereafter the Daltons were careful to drive only over the strip which constituted their exclusive property, it is undisputed that until sometime in 1957 the Henrys and the Daltons and their friends used the driveway freely without incident and relations between the parties were friendly and harmonious. In 1954 respondent and her husband placed two posts in the driveway with a chain between them to prevent strangers from backing in and out. It appears that this was done because the Daltons were concerned for the safety of their grandchildren. This measure was taken without consulting the Henrys, but complainant William Henry testified that relations remained as friendly as ever.

In November 1956 complainants negotiated for the sale of their home in Pawtucket intending to purchase a home in the town of Cumberland, which property they had visited with the Daltons in June of that year. The complainant husband testified that in June 1956 he told William Dalton of this intention. He stated that both Mr. and Mrs. Dalton accompanied them on a visit to the Cumberland property and at that time Mr. Dalton assured him that there would be no trouble about the driveway in the sale of the Pawtucket property.

It is undisputed that about the second week in November 1956 Mr. Henry called on the Daltons and requested that they execute an instrument which would have granted an easement in the driveway, with covenants for each of the parties to maintain one-half thereof and binding on them, their heirs and assigns forever. William Dalton, who at that time was seriously ill and died the following January, refused to execute the agreement stating that signing it was out of the question and he intended to close the driveway.

After the death of William Dalton in January 1957 relations between complainants and respondent apparently became strained. It appears from the testimony of complainants' daughter Dorothy L. Henry that until September 1957 complainants continued to use the driveway despite admitted differences, but in that month she and Mrs. Dalton exchanged words and two days thereafter complainants were notified by Mrs. Dalton's attorney that, unless the wishes of his client regarding the use of the driveway were respected, permission for its use by complainants would be withdrawn. It does not appear in the record whether any discussions or conferences were had between the parties following receipt of this communication, but on December 4, 1957, complainants brought their bill of complaint.

The testimony of complainant William E. Henry was substantially corroborated by that of his wife and their daughter. Because of illness, respondent Jane E.

Dalton was unable to testify at the trial, but her testimony was taken by deposition and was substantially corroborated by her son Raymond.

[The complainants] contend that a license even though orally granted becomes irrevocable when the licensee, relying on the parol agreement, changes his position by making alterations on his property. They argue that in such circumstances withdrawal of the permission by the licensor would constitute "fraud" within the meaning of proceedings in equity.

The complainants maintain that when they expended money and labor in bringing the grade of their property up to respondent's property and constructed a garage, ingress and egress to which depended upon the permanence of the license, they had changed their position in reliance upon their understanding with Mr. Dalton and by implication with respondent, so that the license became executed and by the rule adopted in some jurisdictions was irrevocable. They rely on a line of cases apparently beginning with Rerick v. Kern, 14 Serge. & R., Pa., 267. In that case the respondent gave oral permission to the complainant to divert a stream of water and thus permit the complainant to construct a mill which after considerable expense apparently became very profitable. The Pennsylvania court held that, when the complainant relying on the respondent's permission expended money and labor, the license became executed and on the theory of estoppel could not be revoked.

[The complainants] acknowledge that the authorities are divided on the question, but contend that this court indicated commendation of their contention in Foster v. Browning, 4 R.I. 47. That was an action of trespass for breaking and entering the plaintiff's close in which the court reversed the trial justice for instructing the jury that if the plaintiff's predecessor in title had orally licensed a right of way to Browning, and the latter relying on said license had expended moneys in opening and building the way, the license thereby became irrevocable.

It appears from the discussion by Ames, C.J., that the license to Browning, although parol, was to him and his heirs in perpetuity. In the instant case there was no definiteness as to time. We are persuaded that the rule contended for is in the minority and should not be adopted by this court.

We are of the opinion that in reason and justice the better rule is expressed in the case of Crosdale v. Lanigan, 29 N.E. 824. There the plaintiff was required to remove a wall built on the property of the defendant pursuant to a license. The court stated the rule as follows:

[A] parol license to do an act on the land of the licensor, while it justifies anything done by the licensee before revocation, is, nevertheless, revocable at the option of the licensor, and this, although the intention was to confer a continuing right and money had been expended by the licensee upon the faith of the license. This is plainly the rule of the statute [of frauds]. It is also, we believe, the rule required by public policy. It prevents the burdening of lands with restrictions founded upon oral agreements, easily misunderstood. It gives security and certainty to titles, which are most important to be preserved against defects and qualifications not founded upon solemn instruments. The jurisdiction of courts to enforce oral contracts for the sale of land, is clearly defined and well understood, and is indisputable; but to change what commenced in a license into an irrevocable right, on the ground of equitable estoppel, is another and quite different matter. It is far better, we think, that the law requiring interests in land to be evidenced by deed, should be observed, than to leave it to the chancellor to construe an executed license as a grant, depending upon what, in his view, may be equity in the special case.

29 N.E. at 825.

Counsel for the complainants urge that the statute of frauds was conceived and is designed to protect against fraud and should not be used to assist in the perpetration of fraud. We are in accord with this contention, but are not convinced that in the circumstances of the instant case the respondent's revocation of the complainants' license is fraudulent within any acceptable definition of that term. The right which complainants seek to establish in the land of the respondent is essentially an easement and should be the subject of a grant, expressed in the solemnity of a written instrument. It is no hardship for one in the position of these complainants either to secure an easement in perpetuity in the manner provided by the statute, or, such being refused, to weigh the advantages inuring to them as against the uncertainty implicit in the making of expenditures on the basis of a revocable license.

The complainants' appeal is denied and dismissed, the decree appealed from is affirmed, and the cause is remanded to the superior court for further proceedings.

NOTES AND QUESTIONS

1. **Two functions of estoppel.** The third Restatement of Property recognizes servitudes created by estoppel, and distinguishes two functions performed by detrimental reliance. In the *oral grant of an easement*, A and B orally agree that B can use A's land as a passageway either in perpetuity or for a specified term and B relies on the agreement; B's detrimental reliance on the grant may estop (preclude) A from invoking the Statute of Frauds to repudiate the grant. *See* Restatement Third § 2.9 (imperfectly formalized grant or contract for easement is enforceable on basis of detrimental reliance by grantee or promisee). In cases of *permission to use land*, landowner A gives B permission to make some use of A's land, and no duration is stated by the parties or inferable from the facts of the case. B detrimentally relies on the permission. *See* Restatement Third § 2.10 & cmt. b (servitude may be created by operation of law through beneficiary's foreseeable and reasonable reliance on permission to use landowner's land). What different function does estoppel perform in the two situations identified by the Restatement? Can you think of any comparisons from your Contracts course? *Compare* Restatement Second of Contracts § 90 *with id.* § 139.

2. **Significance of detrimental reliance; two views.** Croasdale v. Lanigan, quoted and followed in Henry v. Dalton, is the leading statement against the effectuation of oral easement or the creation of irrevocable licenses. What reasons does the court give for its view? What are the arguments on the other side, in favor of use rights created by estoppel? *See generally* Stewart E. Sterk, *Estoppel in Property Law*, 77 Neb. L. Rev. 756 (1998).

3. **Neighbors and the statute of frauds.** Suppose the parties to the claimed easement or irrevocable license are neighbors, as in the principal case. Is that a factor in favor of, or against, the creation of rights by estoppel? Compare the following views.

a. Shepard v. Purvine, 248 P.2d 352, 361 (Or. 1952): "These people were close friends and neighbors, and were not dealing at arms' length. One's word was considered as good as his bond. [F]or plaintiff to have insisted upon a deed would have been embarrassing; in effect it would have been expressing a doubt about his friend's integrity."

b. Charles E. Clark, Real Covenants and Other Interests Which "Run With Land" 61 (2d ed. 1947): "It is a rule of good sense, sound morality, and hence good law that one ought not to expect something for nothing. It is to be noticed that here the ungracious neighbor who refuses to yield to the blandishments of anyone is the one who best protects his property. Surely the law ought not to penalize one for acts of neighborliness."

4. **Estoppel; implementation.** Because oral easements and irrevocable licenses are created without a writing, they should be recognized only when the trier of fact is satisfied that the *evidentiary* function of the statute of frauds is satisfied (that A in fact made the oral grant or gave the oral permission to use), and when the conduct of both parties "provides a basis for *substantive* relief sufficient to justify overriding the [s]tatute's protective and channeling functions." Restatement Third § 2.9 cmt. b, at 134-35. The grantee's "investment in improvements either to the servient estate or to other land of the investor" usually satisfies the evidentiary requirement. *Id.* § 2.10 cmt. e, at 146. Why is that? *See* Harber v. Jensen, 97 P.3d 57, 63 (Wyo. 2004) ("[O]ne claiming an irrevocable license must prove the licensor had knowledge of the licensee's improvements and acted in some way to induce the licensee's reliance on the permissive use to make such improvements. Additionally, the improvements themselves must have required the use of the licensor's property.").

With respect to the grantee's reliance, the Restatement Third indicates that "[t]he sophistication of the parties, the complexity of the servitude, the potential economic impact on the burdened estate, and the residential or commercial character of the benefitted estate are factors that bear on the reasonableness of relying on an oral transaction." *Id.* § 2.9 cmt. e, at 137. In addition, "consideration should always be given to the question whether restitution would adequately serve the interests of justice." *Id.* cmt. e, at 138.

5. **Application.** Applying the Restatement Third's criteria, was the court correct to deny a servitude in Henry v. Dalton? Should Applegate have been awarded an irrevocable license in Mandia v. Applegate in Section A.3?

6. **Counseling.** In 1965, Taylor built a $25,000 house on his property, using (with permission) a roadway over Holbrook's land during the construction and afterwards. In 1970, Holbrook demands that their agreement concerning the roadway be put in writing; Taylor refuses, and testifies that Holbrook is trying to force him to buy an easement for $500. Holbrook blocks off the road with a steel cable. Taylor sues to remove the cable and for a declaration of rights. Assume that your state adopts the doctrine of estoppel to create irrevocable rights in land; if

Taylor had consulted you about filing suit, what would you have advised? (Bear in mind that litigation is costly, in money, time, and irritation. Some monetary costs can be collected from the losing party, but one big cost item — the winning party's attorney's fees — ordinarily cannot.) *See* Holbrook v. Taylor, 532 S.W.2d 763 (Ky. 1976).

7. **Duration.** What is the duration of a servitude created by estoppel? *Compare* Restatement of Property § 519 cmt. g (1944) (license "is irrevocable to the extent necessary to prevent the licensee from being unfairly deprived of the fruits of expenditures made by him"), *with* Restatement Third § 4.3 cmt. e (duration is indeterminate; servitude lasts until terminated under the generally applicable rules for termination of servitudes).

8. **Intended licenses.** If A and B expressly agree, or the surrounding circumstances show, that the parties intended to create only a license, is recognition of an easement by estoppel or an irrevocable license appropriate? *See* Woods v. Libby, 635 A.2d 960 (Me. 1993).

c. Prior Use

An easement may be created by implication when an owner divides her land into separate parcels and conveys one of the parcels away. The easement is created on the basis of the circumstances existing prior to or at the time of the owner's severance of title. In one class of cases, the easement is implied from the circumstance that the owner, prior to the severance of title, used one portion of her property for the benefit of another portion; this is the appropriately-named "prior use" easement, considered here. In another class of cases, the easement arises by implication from the circumstance that the owner divides his land in a way that leaves either the owner or the transferee without access to his or her parcel; this is the so-called "easement by necessity," considered in the next principal case after Otero v. Pacheco.

OTERO v. PACHECO
612 P.2d 1335 (N.M. Ct. App. 1980)

HERNANDEZ, JUDGE.

Plaintiffs-Appellants [Otero] sued Defendants-Appellees alleging fraud and unjust enrichment due to plaintiffs' payment of ad valorem taxes which were owed by defendants. They further alleged that the sewer line which serviced both of their homes had backed up on various occasions, causing damage to their home. Defendants answered and counterclaimed, alleging that they had an easement across plaintiffs' property for the maintenance of the sewer line. The trial court, sitting without a jury, entered judgment for the plaintiffs on their claim for payment of taxes owed by defendants, and entered judgment for defendants on their counterclaim. The plaintiffs appeal the judgment entered for defendants.

The undisputed facts are these. The defendants acquired title to two lots in 1944, lots 4 and 5 of Block 5 of the Indian School Addition in the City of Santa Fe. Lot 5 fronted on Cochiti Street, and lot 4, a corner lot, sided on Taos Street.

Defendants' home was constructed partly on lot 5 and partly on lot 4, and originally had a septic tank which was situated on lot 4. In 1950 the City of Santa Fe notified defendants that they had to abandon the use of their septic tank, and connect to the sanitary sewer line which had just been installed along Taos Street.

Defendants installed a sewer line running from their home across lot 4 to the Taos Street sewer line. There is no evidence that there existed any alternative way to connect to the Taos Street sewer, and there was no sanitary sewer line along Cochiti Street at that time. In 1951 the defendants built another house on the remaining part of lot 4, and connected it to the same sewer line. Defendants in 1953 sold this house to a Mrs. McAfoos. The deed to Mrs. McAfoos did not contain a reservation of an easement. However, defendant Alexandro Pacheco testified that he told Mrs. McAfoos of the sewer line's existence and that it provided service to his home. The title passed from Mrs. McAfoos through several intervening owners and ultimately came to the plaintiffs in 1965. The first owner after Mrs. McAfoos testified that he was never told, and did not know, that the sewer line serviced defendants' home during the approximately eight years that he owned that property. Plaintiff Severo Otero testified that he did not learn until 1974 that the sewer line which serviced his house also serviced that of the defendants.

[Plaintiff contends] that the trial court erred in deciding that the defendants had an easement across lot 4. The pertinent findings of the trial court, all of which are supported by substantial evidence in the record, are: that the defendants acquired title to both lots 4 and 5 in 1944; that the sewer line was reasonably necessary to the use and enjoyment of lot 5 at the time of the sale of lot 4, and that it continues to be reasonably necessary to the use and enjoyment of lot 5; and "that the sewer line was and now is an improvement of a permanent and substantial character, actually and apparently intended to be preserved as a servitude for the necessary [and] convenient use and enjoyment of the Pacheco lot and residence." The trial court went on to conclude that the defendants had an easement across lot 4 for a sewer line for the benefit of lot 5 and that the plaintiffs took title to lot 4 subject to that easement.

Although the trial court did not characterize the type of easement, it is readily apparent from the findings that the court was speaking of an easement by implied reservation. Whether such an easement is recognized by the appellate courts of this State is a matter of first impression. However, the converse, i.e., an easement by implied grant, was recognized by our Supreme Court in Venegas v. Luby, 164 P.2d 584 (N.M. 1945):

> It seems well settled that if the owner of land subjects one part of it to a visible servitude in favor of another and then conveys away the dominant portion while it is enjoying the servitude of the portion retained, and the use is reasonably necessary for the full enjoyment of the part granted, an implied easement arises in favor of the premises conveyed and passes by the conveyance without mention.

The nature of and rationale for these two types of easements was very ably set forth by the Supreme Court of Texas in Mitchell v. Castellaw, 246 S.W.2d 163 (Tex. 1952):

It is universally recognized that where the owner of a single area of land conveys away part of it, the circumstances attending the conveyance may themselves, without aid of language in the deed, and indeed sometimes in spite of such language, cause an easement to arise as between the two parcels thus created, not only in favor of the parcel granted ("implied grant") but also in favor of the one remaining in the ownership of the grantor ("implied reservation"). The basis of the doctrine is that the law reads into the instrument that which the circumstances show both grantor and grantee must have intended, had they given the obvious facts of the transaction proper consideration. And in the case of an implied reservation it is not necessarily a bar to its creation that the grantor's deed, into which the law reads it, actually warrants the servient tract thereby conveyed to be free of incumbrance.

There is a split in authority over the question of the degree of necessity that is required to imply the retention of an easement. According to one view, an easement is implied by reservation only where there is strict necessity. The other view was set forth by the Supreme Court of Oregon in Jack v. Hunt, 264 P.2d 461 (Or. 1953):

The majority rule makes no distinction between the degree of necessity in the granting or the retaining of an implied easement. In either circumstances the degree of necessity is answered if [the easement is] necessary to the reasonable enjoyment of the property.

The trial court thought that reasonable necessity was the better view, and so do we. This view is more in harmony with Venegas v. Luby, *supra*, than is strict necessity. However, in *Venegas*, it is clearly indicated that reasonable necessity is not synonymous with mere convenience.

Applying the foregoing to the facts of this case, the trial court was correct in deciding that the defendants had an easement by implied reservation as the result of a reasonable necessity which continues to exist.

The plaintiffs' third point of error is that they were allegedly bona fide purchasers for value of lot 4, and that they took free and clear of any easement of which they had no notice. The general rule is that a bona fide purchaser does not take subject to an easement unless he has actual or constructive knowledge of its existence. However, the law charges a person with notice of facts which inquiry would have disclosed where the circumstances are such that a reasonably prudent person would have inquired.

While there is come conflict of authority as to whether existing drains, pipes, and sewers may be properly characterized as apparent, within the rule as to apparent or visible easements, the majority of the cases which have considered the question have taken the view that appearance and visibility are not synonymous, and that the fact that the pipe, sewer, or drain may be hidden underground does not negative its character as an apparent condition; at least, where the appliances connected with and leading to it are obvious. The circumstances in this situation were such that a reasonably prudent person would have inquired.

The judgment is affirmed.

ANDREWS, Judge (dissenting).

I dissent. I cannot agree with the majority that the circumstances were such as to put the Oteros on constructive notice of the existence of the sewer line.

> The purchaser of property may assume that no easements are attached to the property purchased which are not of record except those which are open and visible, and he cannot otherwise be bound with notice. There should be such a connection between the use and the thing as to suggest to the purchaser that the one estate is servient to the other.

Southern Union Gas Co. v. Cantrell, 241 P.2d 1209, 1213 (N.M. 1952).

The facts in this case do not support the inference that the Oteros had constructive notice of the existence of the sewer line. While the appearance of the adjoining Pacheco property was such as to suggest that it was connected to a sewer line, there is nothing in the record to indicate that it was in any way apparent that it, at one time, had been necessary to lay such a line under the Oteros' land. The history of the development of the sewer system in the area is not apparent to the average purchaser, and the Oteros were justified in assuming that the Pachecos' sewer connections did not impinge on the property rights of the surrounding landholders.

I would reverse.

NOTES AND QUESTIONS

1. **Parties.** When was the easement created in the principal case and between which parties? Who was the lawsuit between? Were there any issues in the case besides creation of an easement?

2. **Basis of prior use easements.** What is the theoretical basis for the law's recognition of a prior-use easement? If the parties intended an easement, but didn't express one, why should the law do for them what they didn't do for themselves? *See* Restatement Third § 2.12 cmts. a & g. Does recognition of the implied easement further policies of fairness and efficiency? *See id. See also* Gray v. Norwest Bank Wyoming, 984 P.2d 1088, 1091 (Wyo. 1999):

> The creation of easements by implication is an attempt to infer the intention of the parties to a conveyance of land. This inference drawn from the circumstances surrounding the conveyance represents an attempt to determine the intention of parties who had not thought or had not bothered to put the intention into words, or perhaps more often, to parties who actually had formed no intention conscious to themselves.

3. **A leading case.** In a leading older case, Van Sandt v. Royster, 83 P.2d 698 (Kan. 1938), Laura Bailey owned lots 19 and 20, and constructed a sewer line from her home on lot 20 across lot 19; she then conveyed lot 19 to John J. Jones, who knew about the installation of the sewer line and paid Bailey one-third of the cost of its installation. In a dispute between the successor owners of lots 19 and 20, the court held that an implied easement for the sewer line was created in the Bailey-to-Jones conveyance. In *Van Sandt*, does recognition of the implied easement fulfill the actual intent of the parties? Was it an implied-in-fact easement?

4. **Doctrine.** "It is commonly said that three things are essential to create an easement by implication upon severance of unity of ownership: (1) a separation of title; (2) the use [prior to severance of title] which gives rise to the easement shall have been so long continued and apparent as to show that it was intended to be permanent; and (3) that the easement is necessary to the beneficial enjoyment of the land granted." Romanchuk v. Plotkin, 9 N.W.2d 421, 424 (Minn. 1943). How do these doctrinal requirements express the underlying theory of easements implied from prior use?

5. **"Apparency."** Is there a difference between an easement that leaves a visible mark on the servient land (e.g., a depression in the ground along a sewer line) and one whose only evidence is a plumbing facility on the servient estate? *Compare* Wolek v. DiFeo, 159 A.2d 127 (N.J. Super. Ct. App. Div. 1960) (apparency requires visible mark on servient land), *with* Romanchuk v. Plotkin, 9 N.W.2d 421, 425 (Minn. 1943) ("An underground drainpipe, even though it is buried and invisible, connected with and forming the only means of draining waste from plumbing fixtures and appliances of a dwelling house, is apparent, because a *plumber* could see the fixtures and appliances and readily determine the location and course of the sewer drain.") (emphasis added). Why would (should) a court charge an ordinary purchaser with the knowledge of an expert? The Restatement Third § 2.12(4) dispenses with apparency for a sewer line easement created by prior use. What can be said in favor of that approach?

6. **Necessity.** What does "necessity" mean in a prior-use easement? Is a cost-benefit analysis (weighing the costs, including possible waste, to the dominant owner of having to reroute the easement or to negotiate a new easement with the servient owner) a useful way to determine whether the easement is necessary? *See* Restatement Third § 2.12 cmt. e; Reed v. Luzny, 627 N.E.2d 1362 (Ind. Ct. App. 1994) (where separate water and sewer connections were readily obtainable by dominant estate, receipt of utility services without cost from servient estate was not reasonably necessary). Apply that analysis to support the outcome in the principal case.

7. **Grant and reservation.** Had Pacheco sold his original home straddling lots 4 and 5 to McAfoos, would the implied easement have arisen by grant or reservation? Why might it be easier to justify the implied grant of an easement? (Note that a warranty deed will contain a covenant by the grantor that the land conveyed is free of encumbrances. See Chapter 5.) Is it sensible to treat the grant and reservation situations the same, as *Otero* does?

8. **Negating intent.** If the implied easement is based on the parties' actual or presumed intent, it should not be implied when the parties expressly negate an easement. The easiest case is an express agreement by the common owner and the grantee to discontinue the prior use. *See* Gray v. Norwest Bank Wyoming, 984 P.2d 1088 (Wyo. 1999) ("Seller at Seller's expense agrees to close off tunnels at property line of properties being purchased."). Suppose that the Otero-to-McAfoos deed had contained express easements for various purposes other than a sewer line; would that negate the implied easement for the sewer line? In the case of an easement by implied grant, suppose the common owner inserts a provision that the privilege of use is revocable at the common owner's will?

9. **Other issues.** In the principal case, do you agree with the majority or the dissent's resolution of the issue of the running of the burden? *See* Restatement Third § 7.14(2) (appurtenant easement for underground utilities created by prior use cannot be extinguished under the local recording act "unless the statute requires a different result"). *See generally* Joel Eichengrun, *The Problem of Hidden Easements and the Subsequent Purchaser Without Notice*, 40 Okla. L. Rev. 3 (1987). Is there a running benefit issue in *Otero*? Would you expect the benefit of an implied sewer line easement to be appurtenant or in gross? Is the importance of the benefit to the landowner part of the reason for implying the easement in the first place?

10. **Easements implied from map.** See Restatement Third § 2.13:

§ 2.13 Servitudes Implied from Map or Boundary Reference

In a conveyance or contract to convey an estate in land, description of the land conveyed by reference to a map or boundary may imply the creation of a servitude, if the grantor has the power to create the servitude, and if a different intent is not expressed or implied by the circumstances:

(1) A description of the land conveyed that refers to a plat or map showing streets, ways, parks, open space, beaches, or other areas for common use or benefit, implies creation of a servitude restricting use of the land shown on the map to the indicated uses.

(2) A description of the land conveyed that uses a street, or other way, as a boundary implies that the conveyance includes an easement to use the street or other way.

See also Patterson v. Powell, 571 S.E.2d 400 (Ga. Ct. App. 2002) (landowners acquired permanent irrevocable easement in lake as appurtenance to the purchase of their property in accordance with subdivision plat).

d. Necessity

The following case contains some (useful) repetition on the prior use easement, and also introduces a closely-related easement, one implied on the basis of necessity.

CANALI v. SATRE
688 N.E.2d 351 (Ill. App. Ct. 1997)

INGLIS, J.

Plaintiff, Charles F. Canali, appeals the decision of the circuit court of Du Page County granting defendants Daniel A. Satre and Gwendolyn J. Satre summary judgment. We reverse.

Plaintiff filed a complaint asserting that he had acquired an "easement of necessity by implication" to a driveway located on defendants' adjacent property. Defendants counterclaimed to quiet title. Thereafter, both parties filed motions for summary judgment. Plaintiff argues, as he argued below, that he acquired an implied easement because his parcel and defendants' parcel were commonly owned and the parcels were then severed, leaving plaintiff's parcel landlocked. Defendants argue that plaintiff fails to satisfy all of the requirements for finding an implied easement and that the statute of limitations barred plaintiff from bringing this action.

The parcels that are the subject of this appeal are adjoining tracts located to the north of Plank Road in Du Page County. Defendants now own parcel D, including the long narrow strip from their property to Plank Road. Plaintiff now owns parcel E. Previously, William and Ida Schultz owned all of the subject properties. Between 1931 and 1936, three parcels were conveyed to separate purchasers: parcel A in 1931, parcel B in 1932, and parcel C in July 1936. On December 9, 1936, William Schultz conveyed parcel D, retaining parcel E for himself until it was sold in 1941. The parties agree that parcel E was landlocked at the time Schultz conveyed parcel D.

The trial court granted defendants' motion for summary judgment and counterclaim to quiet title, finding that at the time of the severance of the two properties in 1936 there was no evidence or claim that the driveway was the sole method of ingress and egress. The court believed plaintiff bought the parcel as is from the bankruptcy court and must take it as he found it, with or without access, and held that there had been no proof that this was a property subject to an easement by necessity.

On appeal, plaintiff contends that the trial court erred in granting summary judgment to defendants. Since the parties filed cross-motions for summary judgment, only a question of law is involved and the court decides the issue based on the record. On appeal from the entry of summary judgment, we review the matter de novo.

There are two types of implied easements, an easement implied from a preexisting use and an easement by necessity. In either case, easements created by implication arise as an inference of the intention of the parties to a conveyance of land. Granite Properties Ltd. Partnership v. Manns, 512 N.E.2d 1230 (Ill. 1987). The courts attempt to ascribe an intention to parties who, for some reason, failed to set forth their intention at the time of conveyance. To fill the gaps resulting from the parties' failure to set forth their intention, courts look to particular facts suggestive of that intent.

An easement implied from a prior existing use arises by law when one portion of an estate derives a benefit and advantage from another, of a permanent, open, and visible character; when that portion is severed, the grantee takes that portion with all the benefits and burdens that appear to belong to it. Absent an express agreement to the contrary, the conveyance or transfer imparts a grant of the right to continue such use. To establish an easement by prior use (1) there must be common ownership of the land followed by a separation of title; (2) before the separation occurs, the use giving rise to the easement must have been long continued, obvious, or manifest, to a degree that shows permanency; and (3) the use of the claimed easement must be necessary to the beneficial enjoyment of the land granted or retained.

An easement by necessity usually arises when a grantor conveys an inner portion of land that has no access to a public highway except over the remaining lands of either the grantor or the grantor plus strangers. In such a situation, an easement over the remaining lands of the grantor is implied in the grant. Similarly, an easement by necessity is implied when the grantor retains the inner portion, conveying the balance to another.

Defendants contend that there is no implied easement by necessity because plaintiff failed to prove two of the three required elements. Defendants argue that plaintiff failed to show that, before the conveyance or transfer, the common owner's use of the parcel was apparent, obvious, continuous, and permanent and that plaintiff failed to prove that the claimed easement is necessary and beneficial to the enjoyment of the parcel. Defendants, however, confuse the requirements for easements created by necessity with those created by prior use.

Where an easement arises from a preexisting use, proof of the prior use is evidence that the parties probably intended an easement. The theory is that the parties would have intended to continue a known, apparent, continuous, and permanent use of the land. On the other hand, an easement by necessity requires no proof of a known existing use from which to infer the parties' intent, but only requires proof of necessity. In such a case, it is presumed that the parties did not intend to render the land unfit for occupancy. Because questions regarding easements of necessity do not rest on a preexisting use, but on the need for a way across the granted or reserved premises, we agree with plaintiff that the question of a preexisting use is irrelevant.

Further, contrary to defendants' argument, the supreme court recognized that, while "necessity" applies to both types of implied easements, "the necessity requirement will have a different meaning and significance in the case involving proof of prior use than it will in a case in which necessity alone supports the implication." *Granite*, 117 Ill.2d at 440, 512 N.E.2d 1230. The court held that when circumstances such as an apparent prior use of land supports the inference of the parties' intention, the required extent of the claimed easement's necessity will be less than when necessity is the only circumstance from which the inference of intention will be drawn. *Granite*, 117 Ill.2d at 440, 512 N.E.2d 1230.

Applying the above principles, we find an easement by necessity can be drawn from the circumstances of this case. The record shows that Schultz conveyed that portion of his land abutting Plank Road to strangers, retaining lots D and E. The only means of ingress and egress to Plank Road was through that portion of lot D leading to Plank Road. Thereafter, Schultz conveyed lot D, retaining lot E, thereby landlocking lot E at the time of severance. This proof permits the presumption that the parties intended an easement to be created at the time of severance. Moreover, where such a situation exists, the easement need not be for continuous use but may lay dormant through successive grantees to be used at any time by a subsequent titleholder.

The court will not create an implied easement, however, if there are other reasonable alternatives allowing access. Here, the configuration of plaintiff's and defendants' parcels and the narrow strip leading to the roadway, logically, as well as logistically, creates a reasonable means of ingress and egress for both properties. There is no proof that allowing plaintiff to use the driveway would adversely impact defendants. Nor is there evidence that defendants' property would be impaired or reduced.

Defendants contend that the statute of limitations regarding claims to real estate bars plaintiff's claim to an easement. We fail to see how the statute applies to a case such as this, where plaintiff claims an implied easement by necessity. While the time of severance is important to establish the presumption that the grantee and grantor did not intend to render the land unfit for occupancy, the interest in the easement did not arise until its use became necessary. See Finn v. Williams, 33 N.E.2d 226 (Ill. 1941) (the easement by necessity may lie dormant through several transfers of title, yet pass with each transfer as appurtenant to the dominant estate and be exercised at any time by the titleholder). To find otherwise would frustrate the purpose of an easement by necessity, which is to put land to its highest and best use. Further, we must exercise great care not to construe a statute in a way that is contrary to its intent and that works a hardship.

Accordingly, we reverse the order granting summary judgment and the counterclaim to quiet title to defendants and enter summary judgment for plaintiff.

Reversed.

NOTES AND QUESTIONS

1. **Comparisons: prior use and necessity.** What factual showing is required for a prior use easement that is not required for an easement based solely on necessity? Does "necessity" have a different meaning in easements by necessity than in prior use easements? *See* Peter G. Glenn, *Implied Easements in the North Carolina Courts: An Essay on the Meaning of "Necessary,"* 58 N.C. L. Rev. 223 (1980). If the facts showed a prior roadway use over the servient parcel by the former common owner, could the claimant of an easement argue *both* prior use and necessity? What would be the advantage of joining the two claims?

2. **Strict and reasonable necessity.** Strict necessity, the common law formulation, is still required for an easement by necessity in some states. Other states and the third Restatement accept "reasonable" necessity. *See* Restatement Third § 2.15 cmt. d ("disproportionate effort or expense"). How strict is strict necessity? If a parcel had water but not land access (or land access only over a rugged mountain road), would an easement by strict necessity be recognized? *Compare* Kingsley v. Gouldsborough Land Improvement Co., 29 A. 1074 (Me. 1894) (denying easement by necessity when dominant estate had "navigable waters on three sides of it"), *with* Morrell v. Rice, 622 A.2d 1156 (Me. 1993) (recognizing easement by necessity when dominant estate was otherwise accessible only over a tidal flat, which would have cost $300,000 to dredge out for boat access). If any alternative access defeats strict necessity, would an easement *ever* be implied on the basis of necessity? *See* Chandler Flyers, Inc. v. Stellar Dev. Corp., 592 P.2d 387 (Ariz. Ct. App. 1979) ("in an age of helicopters and parachutes, virtually all property is accessible in some manner"). If strict necessity does not mean "no other way in or out," how does it differ from reasonable necessity? (Incidentally, does *Chandler Flyers* assume that flying over the servient estate is not a trespass, or at least not an actionable one? *See* Section A.3.e below.)

3. **Necessity and convenience.** Is there a difference between necessity (of whatever strength) and "convenience"? *See* Turner v. Baisley, 602 N.Y.S.2d 907 (N.Y. App. Div. 1993) (plaintiff's claimed easement by necessity over his sister's parcel failed because plaintiff's land fronted on a public road, making use of his sister's land "a mere convenience, which is insufficient to establish the element of reasonable necessity, an essential element to create an implied easement by necessity"). What is the test of "necessity" for a prior use easement in a state that uses a test of reasonable necessity for an easement by necessity?

4. **Other access.** If, at the time of severance, the dominant owner enjoys another access route, should an easement by necessity be implied? Does it matter whether the alternative access exists under a revocable or irrevocable permission? *See* Herrera v. Roman Catholic Church, 819 P.2d 264 (N.M. Ct. App. 1991).

5. **Unity of title and severance.** In the principal case, why was it important for the plaintiff to establish the sequence of conveyances from the common owner to the buyers of parcels A through E? Suppose plaintiff had not been able to show the sequence of conveyances? *See* Othen v. Rosier, 226 S.W.2d 622 (Tex. 1950) (no easement by necessity when claimant could not establish sequence of conveyances); Scott v. Cannon, 959 S.W.2d 712 (Tex. App. 1998) (easement by necessity requires proof that both parcels were once owned by single grantor); Leach v. Anderl, 526 A.2d 1096 (N.J. Super. Ct. App. Div. 1987) (no easement by necessity).

6. **Theories of easement by necessity.** *Canali* bases the easement by necessity on the presumed intent of the parties to the transaction that landlocks one of the parcels. Other courts have expressed a different view. *See* Bob Daniels and Sons v. Weaver, 681 P.2d 1010 (Idaho Ct. App. 1984) ("An easement by necessity is not a creature of contract; it is a creature of public policy. Such an easement arises independently from any contract and may even thwart the intent of the sellers or purchasers."). Either theory will produce the same result in many cases. Some possible differences: Might any disclaimer of the easement in the deed between the parties have to be clear and unequivocal? Should unity of title be required? If unity of title is not required, should the claimant of the easement have to pay compensation for the recognition of the easement? Must necessity exist at the time of severance, or at the time the easement is claimed, or both? Despite these possible differences, the Restatement Third's treatment is probably typical: it notes that both the intent and public policy theories "have force," and does not otherwise distinguish them. *See* Restatement Third § 2.15 cmt. a.

7. **Dormancy.** How far-reaching is the dormancy principle of Finn v. Williams (used by the *Canali* court to answer defendant's statute of limitations claim)? Does it imply an answer to the question of the duration of an easement by necessity? *See* Restatement Third § 4.3(1). To the question whether a bona fide purchaser of the servient estate takes subject to the easement? *See* Restatement Third § 7.14(1).

8. **Affirmative easements: necessity for uses other than roads.** Does the common law standard of necessity suggest why most cases involve roadways? What else is "necessary" today: is the dominant owner entitled to run utility or cable TV lines over or under the servient estate? *See* Restatement Third § 2.15 cmt. d & illus. 12.

9. **Statutory easements by necessity.** More than half the states have statutes allowing private owners of landlocked parcels to acquire an easement by necessity over the land of a neighbor. *See* Restatement Third § 2.15, Statutory Note, at 220-21; Perkins v. Smith, 794 So. 2d 647 (Fla. D. Ct. App. 2001) (landowner was entitled to statutory way of necessity over abutting landowner's land even though a shorter, but more costly, route was available over other land); Atlanta-East, Inc. v. Tate Mountain Assoc., Inc., 462 S.E.2d 613 (Ga. 1995) (in absence of evidence that dominant owner could build roadway over mountainous area at reasonable expense, owner was entitled to statutory easement over neighbor's land); Davis v. Forsyth County, 453 S.E.2d 231 (N.C. Ct. App. 1995) (statutory easement by necessity may be granted against county). These statutes are useful when the claimant of an easement by necessity cannot establish unity of title and severance to obtain an easement under common law doctrine. Since the creation of the easement constitutes a statutory taking of the servient owner's property, the statutes usually provide for compensation to the servient owner. Might such a statute be objectionable on the ground that it takes property for private rather than public use? *See* Estate of Waggoner v. Gleghorn, 378 S.W.2d 47 (Tex. 1964). See also Chapter 8.C infra.

e.   Adverse Use

Just as possessory rights may be created in another's lands by adverse possession, use rights may be created by adverse use for the period of the statute of limitations. An easement acquired by adverse use of the owner's land is called a "prescriptive easement."

FIESE v. SITORIUS
526 N.W.2d 86 (Neb. 1995)

LANPHIER, JUSTICE.

Plaintiff-appellant, Larry Fiese, who operates an airport, brought this action in the district court for Dawson County to enjoin defendants-appellees, George R. and Marcia E. Sitorius, who own land next to the airport, from placing any obstruction in airspace over the Sitoriuses' land. Fiese claimed he has acquired an avigation easement by prescription to take off and land over the Sitoriuses' farm. After a trial, the district court dismissed the action with prejudice, concluding that an avigation easement by prescription has never been recognized in Nebraska. Fiese then filed a motion for new trial, which was denied. Fiese appeals from the judgment of the district court overruling his motion. We affirm the judgment of the district court because we conclude that under the circumstances of this case, Fiese could not obtain an avigation easement by prescription. To obtain an easement by prescription, use must be adverse, under a claim of right, continuous and uninterrupted, open and notorious, exclusive, and with the knowledge and acquiescence of the owner of the servient tenement for the full prescriptive period. Federal law prohibits landowners from interfering with aircraft flying in the navigable airspace of the United States. Since the Sitoriuses had no right to prohibit flights in the navigable airspace overlying their property, Fiese's use of the navigable airspace was not adverse for the purpose of obtaining an easement by prescription.

BACKGROUND

Fiese alleged in his second amended petition that he and his predecessor in interest, his father, have operated a private airstrip on his property continuously since 1969. The grass airstrip, roughly 160 feet wide and 2,400 feet long, runs from the south to the northernmost edge of Fiese's property. At the northernmost edge of Fiese's property, where the airstrip ends, is a county road. Across the county road, to the north, lies the Sitoriuses' farm and dwelling.

The evidence adduced at trial showed that Fiese's father commenced the operation of the airstrip in 1969. Fiese testified that his father typically took off toward and landed from the north, except when wind conditions required doing otherwise. In 1981, Fiese bought the airstrip and the agricultural spraying business from his father. Fiese testified that during the time his father owned the business, and continuously since 1981, there has never been a year during which they have not taken off and landed on the north end of the airstrip. Fiese testified that neither he nor his father ever received permission from the Sitoriuses to fly over their land.

Fiese alleged that on August 6, 1992, the Sitoriuses placed on their own property a stack of hay, approximately 30 feet wide and 15 feet high, to prevent Fiese and others from safely using the airstrip. The hay was admittedly placed directly on the other side of the road, approximately 60 feet from the northern end of Fiese's airstrip. Fiese also alleged that the Sitoriuses had previously erected a pole 20 to 25 feet tall directly across the road from the northern end of his airstrip.

On February 5, 1993, Fiese filed a lawsuit in which he sought an injunction to prevent the Sitoriuses from placing any obstruction in the airspace overlying the Sitoriuses' land. He claimed an avigation easement and contended that he and his predecessor in interest, his father, used the airspace overlying the Sitoriuses' land since 1969. Fiese alleged that he and his father had used the airspace "openly, notoriously, adversely, continuously, and under claim of right and without interruption, all with the knowledge and acquiescence of Defendants and Defendants' predecessors in interest." After the trial, the suit was dismissed, and this appeal followed.

AVIGATION EASEMENT

The primary issue raised by this appeal is whether Nebraska law allows a private party to obtain by prescription an avigation easement. An avigation easement grants the holder of the easement the right to navigate aircraft in the designated airspace overlying another's land. Johnson v. Airport Authority, 115 N.W.2d 426 (Neb. 1962). The Legislature has acknowledged the existence of avigation easements and the right of certain political subdivisions to acquire such easements through eminent domain. See Neb.Rev.Stat. § 3-204. This court has ruled that the condemnation of an avigation easement is a taking, as that term is defined within the context of Fifth Amendment jurisprudence. Johnson v. Airport

Authority, *supra*. However, we have never ruled on whether a private party may obtain an avigation easement by prescription.

There is no clear trend among the jurisdictions which have considered the issue. Though no court has apparently ever upheld an avigation easement, some have determined that an avigation easement may be acquired by prescription under the right circumstances. Petersen v. Port of Seattle, 618 P.2d 67 (Wash. 1980); Drennen v. County of Ventura, 112 Cal.Rptr. 907 (Cal. Dist. Ct. App. 1974); Shipp v. Louisville and Jefferson County Air Board, 431 S.W.2d 867 (Ky. 1968). In other jurisdictions, courts have held that an avigation easement may not be acquired by prescription. Sticklen v. Kittle, 287 S.E.2d 148 (W. Va. 1981); Hinman v. Pacific Air Transport, 84 F.2d 755 (9th Cir.1936)

The issue has been addressed most recently by the Supreme Court of Connecticut. In County of Westchester, N.Y. v. Town of Greenwich, 629 A.2d 1084 (Conn. 1993), the plaintiff, Westchester County, owned and operated an airport. The defendants owned land beneath the air approach zone for one of the airport's runways. Trees on the defendants' land had grown into the air approach zone. Their growth reduced the buffer of airspace around the airport referred to as a "clear zone." Due to the reduction in the clear zone, the Federal Aviation Administration reduced the usable length of the airport's runway. Consequently, the plaintiff asserted that it had acquired, by prescription, an avigation easement. Additionally, the plaintiff sought an injunction authorizing it to top or cut down, as necessary, the defendants' trees which had penetrated into the clear zone.

The Connecticut Supreme Court refused to decide generally whether an avigation easement may be acquired by prescription. Relying on federal law, 49 U.S.C. §§ 1301(29) and 1304 (1988), the Connecticut Supreme Court concluded that the defendants had no right to stop the plaintiff's overflights. In relevant part, § 1304 provides that "[t]here is recognized and declared to exist in behalf of any citizen of the United States a public right of freedom of transit through the navigable airspace of the United States." " 'Navigable airspace' means airspace above the minimum altitudes of flight prescribed by regulations issued under this chapter, and shall include airspace needed to insure safety in take-off and landing of aircraft." § 1301(29). The Connecticut Supreme Court determined that since the defendants could not prevent the overflights, the plaintiff's use of the airspace could not be considered adverse. It therefore held that the use could not ripen into a prescriptive easement.

In this, we are controlled by the advancing juggernaut of seemingly ubiquitous preemptive federal legislation. "It would be difficult to visualize a more comprehensive scheme of combined regulation, subsidization and operational participation than that which the Congress has provided in the field of aviation." American Airlines, Inc. v. Town of Hempstead, 272 F. Supp. 226, 232 (E.D.N.Y. 1967), *aff'd*, 398 F.2d 369 (2d Cir. 1968). In particular with respect to the regulation of "navigable airspace," Congress has legislated so pervasively that state provisions inhibiting that regulation, whether in the form of legislation or judicial decision, must be declared invalid under the supremacy clause.

When Congress legislated "navigable airspace," it was apparently not done with a "soft hand" with due regard in mind for the rights of those owning property adjoining or near airports. Relevant federal law dictates the answer as to whether the private airstrip which is the subject of this litigation can obtain an easement of prescription over adjoining land. Sections 1301(29) and 1304 of the United States Code prohibit landowners from obtaining injunctive relief against aircraft using the navigable airspace of the United States. Therefore, the Sitoriuses could not enjoin Fiese from using the airspace above the Sitoriuses' property to safely take off and land. Fiese had a right to use the airspace overlying the Sitoriuses' land to safely take off and land. The right was not granted by the Sitoriuses, but by the U.S. government. The statutory right of freedom of transit through the navigable airspace of the United States is, in effect, a license. Fiese's use of the airspace, therefore, was not adverse, but permissive. See Drennen v. County of Ventura, *supra* (no prescriptive easement where overflights did not interfere with owner's actual use and enjoyment of land); City of Statesville v. Credit and Loan Co., 294 S.E.2d 405 (N.C. Ct. App. 1982) (flights over land of another were not adverse for purpose of obtaining prescriptive easement where state law prohibited owner from preventing overflight).

A permissive use of the land of another is not adverse and cannot give an easement by prescription no matter how long it may be continued. The use and enjoyment which will create an easement by prescription must be adverse, under a claim of right, continuous and uninterrupted, open and notorious, exclusive, and with the knowledge and acquiescence of the owner of the servient tenement for the full prescriptive period. Since Fiese's use of the airspace necessary to safely take off and land was permissive, pursuant to a license from the U.S. government, it could not ripen into an easement by prescription. Fiese has no easement.

Fiese also seeks an injunction, and since this is a suit in equity, we must determine whether Fiese has any other legal basis entitling him to enjoin Sitoriuses from placing obstructions on their own land. An injunction will not lie unless the right is clear, the damage is irreparable, and the remedy at law is inadequate. Although Congress has granted Fiese a right of freedom of transit through the navigable airspace of the United States pursuant to 49 U.S.C.App. § 1304, Congress has not provided an attendant remedy for protection of that right. The section of the Federal Aviation Act recognizing a public right of freedom of transit through navigable airspace of the United States, 49 U.S.C.App. § 1304, does not create a private right of action in favor of airport owners. Hence, Fiese cannot base his request for an injunction on the provision of federal law granting him the right of freedom of transit through navigable airspace. The Federal Aviation Act merely permits the filing of a complaint with the Secretary of Transportation or the Civil Aeronautics Board for acts or omissions in contravention of the provisions of the act. 49 U.S.C.App. § 1482(a) (1988). As explained above, since the federal government has comprehensively occupied the field of navigable airspace regulation, our determination is controlled by federal law.

CONCLUSION

In light of the foregoing, the judgment of the district court dismissing the action was proper and is, therefore, affirmed.

NOTES AND QUESTIONS

1. **The mailbox by prescription.** In Gajewski v. Taylor, 536 N.W.2d 360 (N.D. 1995), Gajewski maintained his mailbox across the public road on Taylor's side, in accordance with U.S. Postal Service requirements, for at least twenty years. Taylor, who said he almost ran into the mailbox while avoiding a collision with an oncoming truck, asked Gajewski to move the mailbox to Gadjewski's side of the road. The postal authorities objected, citing safety concerns. Gadjewski sued to enjoin Taylor from moving or removing the mailbox. Judgment for Gadjewski was affirmed; Gadjewski had acquired an easement by prescription. Query: doesn't this case raise the same issue as the principal case? Should Gajewski have been denied an easement by prescription or should Fiese have been granted one?

2. **Possession and use.** American legal theory places prescription on the same theoretical footing as adverse possession: just as B's adverse possession of A's land may ripen into fee simple ownership, B's adverse *use* of A's land may ripen into an easement. What element of adverse use was absent in Fiese v. Sitorius? Was the flyer's use of the farmer's air space permissive, or did the farmer lack a cause of action to prevent that use? Are those the same thing?

3. **Lost grant theory.** In English as in American law, B's use of A's land for the period of the statute of limitations gives B a prescriptive easement, but the English theory is different. After several centuries of development, the English courts settled on the theory that a claimant's use of the servient estate continuously for the limitations period raises an irrebutable presumption that the use originated in a grant, which has unfortunately been lost (or mislaid?). *See* Robert Megarry & H.W.R. Wade, The Law of Property 876-878 (5th ed. 1984). The lost grant theory pretty violently forces the facts to conform to available concepts, doesn't it? Since easements are typically created by grant, every easement must be attributed to a grant. Thus, the servient owner's "acquiescence" in B's use, indicated by failure to sue within the limitations period, becomes evidence of an affirmative *consent* to B's use.

4. **Consequences of theory.** Although American courts subscribe to the adverse possession analogy, doctrinal traces of the common law lost grant theory linger on in references to "acquiescence" in statements of the doctrinal requirements for acquisition of a prescriptive easement. *See, e.g.,* Burns v. Plachecki, 223 N.W.2d 133, 135-36 (Minn. 1974) (proof of use that is inconsistent with the owner's rights, "under circumstances from which the owner's knowledge and acquiescence may be inferred," raises presumption of hostility); *see also* Garrett v. Jackson, 20 Pa. 331, 335-36 (1853) ("enjoyment [of the servient estate] without evidence to explain how it began, is presumed to have been in pursuance of a full and unqualified grant"), quoted in Loudenslager v. Mosteller, 307 A.2d 286, 287 (Pa. 1973). Theories matter. If the servient owner demonstrates *non* acquiescence during the statutory period (for example, by sending a letter to the adverse user objecting to the trespass), is the prescription interrupted? The leading case is Dartnell v. Bidwell, 98 A. 743, 744-45 (Me. 1916), in which the court held that prescription *was* interrupted:

> [T]he question is whether the plaintiff's acquiescence was interrupted in law by the letter from which we have quoted. It is not claimed that the defendant's use was interrupted by it. If acquiescence is consent by silence,

to break the silence by denials and remonstrances ought to afford evidence of nonqacquiesence, rebutting the presumption of a grant.

Under the analogy of adverse use to adverse possession, what would happen if B failed to act after A ignored the letter? Under that analogy, what is the significance of A's "acquiesence" in B's use; is it a basis for presuming consent, defeating the adverse claimant?

5. **Doctrine: exclusivity.** Note that the *Fiese* court states "exclusivity" as an element of a prescriptive easement. The third Restatement agrees with the cases omitting that requirement, noting that an exclusivity requirement "causes confusion in prescription cases because servitudes are generally not exclusive." Restatement Third § 2.17 cmt. g. Does the distinction between possession and use suggest anything about the appropriateness of an exclusivity requirement for prescriptive easements? *See* Scott v. Cannon, 959 S.W.2d 712 (Tex. App. 1998) (joint use of roadway by dominant and servient owners did not preclude finding of easement by prescription). Does the "exclusivity" requirement say anything that cannot be said under some other requirement?

6. **Presumption of hostility.** As in the case of adverse possession, the claimant's use of the servient estate for the prescriptive period may create a presumption of adversity. But some states observe an exception:

> [W]hen unenclosed and unimproved wildlands or woodlands are involved, the presumption is that the use was permissive, and the burden of proving that the use was adverse or under a claim of right is upon the one asserting these rights. The states that have adopted this exception have explained that in the case of unenclosed woodlands, permission is presumed because, otherwise, "[a]n owner could not allow his neighbor to pass and repass over a trail, upon his open, unenclosed land without danger of having an adverse title successfully set against him." Larue v. Kosich, 187 P.2d 642, 645 (Ariz. 1947). Moreover, "[a] landowner who quietly acquiesces in the use of a path, or road, across his uncultivated land, resulting in no injury to him, but in great convenience to his neighbor, ought not to have thereby lost his rights." Weaver v. Pitts, 133 S.E. 2, 3 (N.C. 1926).

Forrester v. Kiler, 633 A.2d 913, 915 (Md. Ct. Spec. App. 1993). *See also* Boldt v. Roth, 618 N.W.2d 393 (Minn. 2000) (inference of permissive use arising from family relationship between owners of servient and dominant estates ceases when servient estate is transferred to nonfamily member).

7. **Acquisition by the state.** Can the state or a town acquire an easement by prescription? *See* Restatement Third § 2.18(1) ("[g]overnmental bodies may acquire servitudes by dedication and condemnation, as well as by the methods set forth in §§ 2.1 through 2.17 [estoppel, prior use, necessity, plat or map, prescription]. The public may acquire servitudes by dedication and prescription."); McIntyre v. Board of County Commissioners, 86 P.3d 402 (Colo. 2004) (easement denied under statute permitting county to acquire a public road by prescription; county "must have taken some overt claim of right action, formal or informal, giving notice to the landowner of the public's claim of right and demonstrating that it considered the footpath across the land to be a public road, for example, by performing maintenance or including the footpath on its county road system

during the prescriptive period"); Bockstiegel v. Board of County Commissioners, 97 P.3d 324 (Colo. Ct. App. 2004) (county acquired public way over historic stagecoach road); Koontz v. Town of Superior, 746 P.2d 1264 (Wyo. 1987) (town acquired prescriptive easement for a roadway). If so, does such acquisition constitute a taking requiring compensation? *See* Weidner v. State Dept. of Transp., 860 P.2d 1205 (Alaska 1993) (landowner must sue to recover compensation within limitations period; thereafter, right to sue is extinguished and title is vested in the adverse user).

8. **Public easements.** Can the public acquire an easement by prescription? *See* Restatement Third § 2.18(1), (2) and cmt. b ("public may acquire servitudes by prescription," but "control rights are lodged in the state" if it chooses to exercise those rights); Scoville v. Fisher, 149 N.W.2d 339 (Neb. 1967) (yes, but ordinary presumption of hostile use does not apply in cases of use of owner's unenclosed and unimproved land); Bustillos v. Murphy, 117 Cal. Rptr. 2d 895, 898 (Cal. Ct. App. 2002) (recreational use statute barred claim by individual for easement over landowner's land; "Bustillos does not have any use or interest in the property that is distinguishable from the public generally."). Could public prescriptive easements be denied on the basis of the "adversity" requirement?

9. **Beach access: the public trust doctrine.** "The prescriptive easement doctrine has not been notably successful in providing public access [to beaches], largely because most courts presume that public use of beaches is with the permission of the owner, and the burden of proving adverse use cannot be met." Jesse Dukeminier & James E. Krier, Property 814 (4th ed. 1998). A viable alternative in some states is the public trust doctrine:

> The public trust doctrine acknowledges that the ownership, dominion and sovereignty over land flowed by tidal waters, which extend to the mean high water mark, is vested in the State in trust for the people. The public's right to use the land and water encompasses navigation, fishing and recreational uses, including bathing, swimming and other shore activities.

Matthews v. Bay Head Improvement Association, 471 A.2d 355 (N.J. 1984) (holding that the public has the right to reasonable access over privately held dry sand beach to reach the ocean, and right to sunbathe on and otherwise enjoy such privately held land in connection with use of the beach). *See generally* Joseph Sax, *The Public Trust Doctrine in Natural Resource Law: Effective Judicial Interventio* n, 68 Mich. L. Rev. 471 (1970); Richard J. Lazarus, *Changing Conceptions of Property and Sovereignty in Natural Resources: Questioning the Public Trust Doctrine,* 71 Iowa L. Rev. 631 (1986).

PROBLEM 6-D. Assume a ten year statute of limitations. Does the claimant acquire an easement by prescription in the following cases? What is the issue in each case? (As a refresher on relevant issues, you may want to review adverse possession in Chapter 1.)

a. B owns an express ten-foot right of way easement across the land of C, a neighbor. The grant locates the easement along the boundary separating C's land from that of A. B uses a ten foot right of way for the statutory period, but on A's side of the boundary. Is B entitled to a prescriptive easement against A? *See* Biegert v. Dudgeon, 330 N.W.2d 897 (Neb. 1983) (allowing the easement). *But see*

Chaney v. Haynes, 458 S.E.2d 451 (Va. 1995) (denying the easement). Suppose instead that B uses a roadway on A's land, believing (incorrectly) that it is a public roadway. *See* Cardenas v. Kurpjuweit, 779 P.2d 414 (Idaho 1989) (allowing the easement).

b. B uses a pathway across A's land for the statutory period, knowing that the land belongs to A. *See* Foster v. Sumner, 378 S.E.2d 659 (W. Va. 1989) (per curiam).

c. B owns Blackacre, situated next to Whiteacre, which is owned by A. B uses a pathway across A's land for five years without permission. B then transfers Blackacre to Y, who continues to use the pathway for five years. *See* Johnston v. Bates, 778 S.W.2d 357 (Mo. Ct. App. 1989).

d. A and B share a common driveway. Neither A nor B knows that the driveway is almost entirely on A's land. B subsequently sells his land to Y, by a deed that does not mention the driveway. After the statute of limitations has run, the truth comes out at a time when A and Y are fighting over several unrelated matters. A tries to bar Y's use of that part of the driveway on A's land. Assume that B's and Y's periods of possession are both necessary to satisfy the statutory period. *See* Jacobs v. Lewicki, 208 N.Y.S.2d 140 (N.Y. App. Div. 1960).

e. A grants B an express license allowing B to use a right of way across A's land. After five years' use under the license, B transfers his land to Y, who uses the right of way for eight more years, at which time a dispute erupts between A and Y, and A blocks off the right of way. *See* Waltimyer v. Smith, 556 A.2d 912 (Pa. Super. Ct. 1989). Suppose Y used the right of way for ten years *after* the transfer from B?

f. A knows about B's use of A's land for a roadway, and testifies "it was o.k. with me that he used the land, I just didn't want him to acquire any rights by doing so." *See* Kellison v. McIsaac, 559 A.2d 834, 836 (N.H. 1989) ("the requisite continuous nature of the trespassory use can be broken if the actual owner *communicates* permission to the adverse user to cross the owner's land") (emphasis added).

g. A erects barriers — posts and cables — over the roadway used by B; B drives around or pushes down the barriers; A replaces them, B ignores them, and so on. Has A interrupted B's prescriptive use? *See* Pittman v. Lowther, 610 S.E.2d 479 (S.C. 2005) (case of first impression; good discussion of the authorities, concluding that "[t]o adopt an interpretation of 'effective interruption' which requires a servient landowner to take actions in addition to erecting barriers like fences and cables, would encourage wrongful or potentially violent behavior that is contrary to sound public policy considerations and the peaceful resolution of disputes").

h. A *possesses* a portion of B's land for the limitations period but doesn't pay taxes as required for adverse possession; does B acquire an easement by prescription? *See* Kapner v. Meadowlark Ranch, 11 Cal. Rptr. 3d 138 (Cal. Ct. App. 2004) ("Here we hold, among other things, that adverse possession may not masquerade as a prescriptive easement.").

B. SCOPE OF EASEMENTS

Suppose that in the late 19th century, landowner A grants a perpetual right of way over his land to his neighbor B, who occupies a single-family dwelling on adjacent land. B uses the easement for horse-and-buggy or foot access over the easement space. Consider the following sets of questions that may arise about the easement as the years pass: (1) If B acquires an automobile, may B drive it over the easement area? If B builds an apartment house on his land, may all of the occupants of the apartments use the right of way? If the right of way area is unpaved or unimproved, may B improve it? (2) If the agreement between A and B didn't locate the easement on a specific area of A's land, or indicate its width, what part and how much of A's land is subject to the easement? (3) If either A or B, but not both, subsequently decides that the easement should be located elsewhere on A's land, may either party unilaterally impose the change in location? (4) Who has the responsibility to keep the easement area in repair?

These questions of the intensity of use, the initial location and subsequent relocation, and the repair and maintenance of the easement get treated in the law under the heading of the "scope" of the easement. When the easement agreement is embodied in a written document, such scope questions should be addressed therein. (As an example, rather than a model, of drafting on the scope question, see O'Donova. v. McIntosh in Section A.2.c above.) When the questions aren't addressed by the parties, default rules apply. The default rules are usually fuzzy (rife with adjectives like "reasonable" use), suggesting that one important reason for express terms, at least on the major scope questions, is to give a measure of certainty to the parties' bargain and thereby eliminate litigation.

If the scope questions arise early in the life of the easement, the dispute may be between A and B, the parties who created the easement. But scope questions tend to be generated by the passage of time, which brings changes that the parties might have foreseen and provided for, but didn't. In that case, the dispute is commonly between successors in ownership of the dominant and servient land.

SCHERGER v. NORTHERN NATURAL GAS CO.
575 N.W.2d 578 (Minn. 1998)

PAGE, JUSTICE.

Norbert and Delores Scherger (the "Schergers") petitioned the Dodge County District Court for [an order] requiring Northern Natural Gas Co. ("Northern") to initiate condemnation proceedings in order to replace an existing Northern pipeline located within an easement on the Schergers' property. After cross-motions for summary judgment on stipulated facts, the district court denied the Schergers' motion seeking to require Northern to initiate condemnation proceedings and granted Northern's motion, which sought to have the Schergers' action dismissed. On appeal, the court of appeals reversed and remanded, holding that the location of Northern's replacement pipeline easement on the Schergers' property "must be within the scope of the easement as defined by construction of the original 1932 pipeline." We reverse and reinstate the summary judgment entered in favor of Northern.

The stipulated facts are as follows: Northern is a Delaware corporation engaged in the transportation of natural gas in interstate commerce through a pipeline system it owns, operates, and maintains. The Schergers are the owners of farm property located in Dodge County, Minnesota. On November 3, 1931, the Schergers' predecessors in title granted an easement in favor of Northern. Among other things, the agreement granting the easement gave Northern a "blanket" easement[2] over and through a portion of the Schergers' property "together with the right of ingress to and egress from said premises, for the purpose of constructing, inspecting, repairing, maintaining and replacing the property of the grantee located thereon, or the removal thereof, in whole or in part, at the will of the grantee." The easement agreement also provides for the payment of "the sum of Fifty Cents (50 cents) per lineal rod which is to be paid when and as the location of pipe lines over and through the lands hereinafter described shall be established, surveyed and measured." In 1932, pursuant to this agreement, Northern constructed a natural gas pipeline through the Schergers' property, which it has operated and maintained since.

By letter dated October 26, 1995, Northern informed the Schergers that, pursuant to the 1931 easement agreement, it intended to "replace" the pipeline running through the Schergers' property. At that time, Northern tendered a check to the Schergers for $905 as compensation for installing the replacement pipeline.[3] The replacement pipeline was to run alongside the original pipeline, 50 feet away at its closest point and 300 feet at its most distant. The Schergers responded to Northern's letter by demanding, pursuant to Minn.Stat. § 300.045 (1996), "a definite and specific description of [Northern's] present gas pipeline easement on their property." Further, the Schergers demanded that a new easement agreement be negotiated and that if negotiations were unsuccessful, "then [Northern] should use [its] eminent domain powers" to acquire a new easement. In response, Northern indicated that it was willing to define the "present pipe line easement" across the property when construction of the replacement pipeline was completed, but asserted that the original easement agreement gave it the right to put the replacement pipeline anywhere on the property within the boundaries of the original easement grant.[4]

In denying the Schergers' motion for summary judgment and granting Northern's motion, the district court found that "there is no ambiguity in the terms of the easement, and that the easement grants [Northern] the right to replace the pipeline." In addition, the district court found that Minn.Stat. § 300.045 was inapplicable. [T]he court of appeals reversed, holding that the location of the replacement pipeline must be within the scope of the easement "as defined by construction of the original 1932 pipeline." Scherger v. Northern Natural Gas Co.,

---

[2] A "blanket" easement is an easement granted over a large defined area of property.

[3] Although the original easement established that the Schergers were only to receive 50 cents per lineal rod, Northern, on its own initiative, paid the Schergers $5.00 per lineal rod.

[4] While initially refusing to allow Northern on to their property to replace the pipeline prior to the resolution of this matter, the Schergers, by letter dated November 7, 1995, permitted Northern to proceed with construction of the replacement pipeline pending the outcome of judicial proceedings.

562 N.W.2d 328, 331 (Minn. Ct. App. 1997) (citing Mielke v. Yellowstone Pipeline Co., 870 P.2d 1005 (Wash. Ct. App. 1994)). It remanded for a determination of whether or not Northern's replacement pipeline was "within the 'line of reasonable enjoyment' of the original easement or within 'the minimum necessary for the safe conduct of [Northern's] business'" (quoting *Mielke* and Minn.Stat. § 300.045). While using the statute's language, the court of appeals declined to reach the issue of the applicability of Minn.Stat. § 300.045.

We are presented with two issues: (1) whether Northern, as grantee, under a blanket easement, has the right under the terms of the 1931 easement agreement to replace the pipeline constructed on the Schergers' property in 1932, with a new pipeline, at a different location within the easement; and (2) whether a demand under Minn.Stat. § 300.045 for a legal description of an older, existing easement legally restricts Northern's easement to the location of the original pipeline.

An easement is an interest in land possessed by another which entitles the grantee of the interest to a limited use or enjoyment of that land. The extent of an easement depends entirely upon the construction of the terms of the agreement granting the easement. "When the terms of an easement grant are unclear, extrinsic evidence may be used to aid in the interpretation of the easement grant; however, when the language granting the easement is clear and unambiguous, the court's power to determine the extent of the easement granted is limited." Bergh and Misson Farms, Inc. v. Great Lakes Transmission Co., 565 N.W.2d 23, 26 (Minn. 1997). While ambiguities in contract agreements are resolved against the drafter, "[g]enerally, an easement grant is to be strictly construed against the grantor." *Bergh*, 565 N.W.2d at 26.

The Schergers contend that under the terms of the 1931 easement agreement, the parties intended that the location of the pipeline easement was to be "fixed" once the pipeline was installed within the boundaries of the blanket easement. In support of this contention, the Schergers note that the original pipeline has been undisturbed for over 60 years and that the easement agreement failed to include an inflationary escalator for additional lineal rods of pipeline. The Schergers also contend that Northern's interpretation of the easement agreement is absurd in that it would allow Northern to "fully occupy the farm, or critical portions of it, with pipelines at any time." Northern asserts that the plain language of the 1931 easement agreement, in essence, entitles it to replace the original pipeline by placing it anywhere within the blanket easement.

Our review of the parties' easement agreement leads us to conclude that the agreement is clear and unambiguous and that it supports Northern's contention that Northern may replace the original pipeline by placing it anywhere within the blanket easement granted by the agreement. The agreement states that Northern may "construct, maintain, and operate pipe lines" within the easement and gives Northern the "right of ingress to and egress from [the easement] for the purpose of constructing, inspecting, repairing, maintaining and replacing" its pipelines. This language, without question, contemplates that in the future additional and/or replacement pipelines could be constructed. We can find nothing in the easement agreement which limits or restricts in any way the location within the easement of any additional or replacement pipelines. Therefore, based on the plain language of the agreement, we reverse the court of appeals and hold that Northern is entitled to replace the original pipeline at any location within the grant of the 1931 blanket easement on the Schergers' property.

Next, we turn to the issue of the applicability of Minn.Stat. § 300.045 to these proceedings whereby, on demand, the Schergers sought to restrict or limit the pipeline location to its original path. The Schergers claim that Minn.Stat. § 300.045 prevents Northern from replacing its pipeline outside the confines of the easement "fixed" by the location of the original pipeline. The legislature enacted Minn.Stat. § 300.045 in 1973. Section 300.045 currently reads as follows:

> When public service corporations, including pipeline companies, acquire easements over private property by purchase, gift, or eminent domain proceedings, except temporary easements for construction, they must definitely and specifically describe the easement being acquired, and may not acquire an easement greater than the minimum necessary for the safe conduct of their business.

This language has not been substantively altered over the years. However, Minn.Stat. § 300.045 was amended in 1993 by the addition of language intended to protect landowners from marketability of title problems caused by easements covering large tracts of land. The 1993 amendment provides, in pertinent part:

> When a question arises as to the location of an easement across specific property and the recorded description of the easement does not include a definite and specific description of the easement by a method identified [herein], the public service corporation holding the easement shall, upon written request by the specific property owner, produce and record in a timely manner a definite and specific description using a method described [herein].

A plain reading of the language "when public service corporations acquire easements" contained in the first paragraph of Minn.Stat. § 300.045, leads inescapably to the conclusion that that provision of the statute applies to easements acquired after the statute's effective date. There simply is nothing in this statute to suggest that the legislature intended the language to apply to easements acquired before its enactment. Thus, because Northern acquired its easement over the Schergers' property before the enactment of the statute in 1973, neither provision of Minn.Stat. § 300.045 is applicable to this case.

Reversed and summary judgment for Northern reinstated.

NOTES AND QUESTIONS

A. Intensity of B's Use of A's Land

1. **Another case.** In Bergh & Mission Farms, Inc. v. Great Lakes Transmission Co., 565 N.W.2d 23 (Minn. 1997), Great Lakes decided to recoat a 350 foot section of the buried pipeline located within the easement. Without asking permission of the servient owner, Great Lakes entered the servient estate, "brought two bulldozers, a backhoe, and a pickup truck onto the field," and

proceeded to spend six weeks on the recoating project during the local monsoon season. In the servient owner's suit for damages for negligent and intentional trespass, the court held that the question of the reasonableness of the repair route chosen by Great Lakes was irrelevant:

> We read the provisions of the right-of-way agreement between the Berghs and Great Lakes granting Great Lakes the right of "ingress and egress to and from the right of way" and to temporarily use work space as needed for "maintenance" of the pipeline in conjunction with Great Lakes' obligation to pay for damages caused by the exercise of its rights under the right-of-way agreement as specifically defining all of Great Lakes' rights and responsibilities with respect to accessing the pipeline easement. Because the right-of-way agreement specifically defines Great Lakes' rights and responsibilities with respect to accessing the pipeline easement, we have no occasion to read a reasonableness requirement into the easement grant.

Id. at 26-27.

2. **Interpretation and drafting.** Were the easement grants in *Scherger* and *Bergh* unambiguous, or were they simply silent on the questions at issue in the cases? What appealing means of interpreting the easements in favor of the landowner in each case did the Minnesota court bypass? *See* Christopher R. Duggan, Note, *Property Owners Beware: The Minnesota Supreme Court has Twice "Misconstrued" Express Easements,* 25 Wm. Mitchell L. Rev. 1545 (1999) (critical analysis of both cases). The two Minnesota cases highlight the importance of foresight and precision at the time easements are drafted. As the cases indicate, the absence of stated restrictions on the beneficiary's use of the servient estate causes courts to favor expansive interpretations of the rights of the easement holder. The remainder of the Notes highlight the most common issues.

3. **Use rights of dominant estate owner.** See Restatement Third § 4.10:

> § 4.10 Use Rights Conferred by a Servitude

> Except as limited by the terms of the servitude, the holder of an easement or profit is entitled to use the servient estate in a manner that is reasonably necessary for the convenient enjoyment of the servitude. The manner, frequency, and intensity of the use may change over time to take advantage of developments in technology and to accommodate normal development of the dominant estate or enterprise benefited by the servitude. Unless authorized by the terms of the servitude, the holder is not entitled to cause unreasonable damage to the servient estate or interfere unreasonably with its enjoyment.

See Hayes v. Aquia Marina, Inc., 414 S.E.2d 820 (Va. 1992) (expansion of marina from 84 to 280 boat slips did not unreasonably burden servient owner whose land provided sole means of land access to marina). *See also* Note 5 following Frenning v. Dow, the next principal case.

4. **Use rights of servient owner.** Adopting the widely-followed judicial rule, as well as the rule of the first Restatement § 486 (1944), the third Restatement provides that the holder of the servient estate "is entitled to make any use of the

servient estate that does not unreasonably interfere with enjoyment of the easement or profit for its intended purpose." Restatement Third § 4.9. *See* Figliuzzi v. Carcajou Shooting Club of Lake Koshkonong, 516 N.W.2d 410 (Wis. 1994) (servient owner barred from constructing four-building, twenty-six unit condominium that would interfere with dominant owner's easement to fish, shoot, and hunt on servient estate; servient owner "may not unreasonably interfere with the use by the easement holder").

B. Location and Relocation of the Easement

5. **Initial location of the easement.** *See* Hall v. Allen, 771 S.W.2d 50 (Mo. 1989) (grantee of express easement is entitled to "convenient, reasonable and accessible use" if location of easement is not specified by the creating parties); Annotation, *Location of Easement of Way Created by Grant Which Does Not Specify Location*, 24 A.L.R.4th 1053, 1067-81 (1983) (discussion of cases locating easement in position established by dominant owner's use after creation of the easement); Restatement Third § 4.8(1) (servient owner has the right "within a reasonable time to specify a location that is reasonably suited to carry out the purpose of the servitude").

6. **Relocation.** The traditional rule is that the location of an easement, once fixed on the servient estate, cannot be altered under a rule of reasonableness by either the dominant or servient owner. *See* Sakansky v. Wein, 169 A. 1, 3 (N.H. 1933):

> In the case at bar the parties are bound by a contract which not only gave the dominant owner a way across the servient estate for the purpose of access to the rear of its premises, but also gave that way definite location upon the ground. [The dominant owner] has no right to insist upon the use of any other land of the defendants for a way, regardless of how necessary such other use may be to it and regardless of how little damage or inconvenience such use of the defendants' land might occasion to them. No more may the [servient owner] compel the [dominant owner] to detour over other land of theirs.

What is the basis for the court's refusal to consider the reasonableness of the dominant owner's request? Is the refusal more justified in *Sakansky* than in the *Bergh* case (Note 1 above) and in *Scherger*?

7. **Relocation: the Third Restatement.** In a departure from established law, the third Restatement grants the servient owner the unilateral power to make reasonable and necessary changes in the location or dimensions of an affirmative easement, if the changes do not "significantly lessen the utility" of the servitude, or increase the burdens on the beneficiary of the servitude, or frustrate the servitude's purpose, and if the servient estate owner pays the expenses of making the changes. *See* Restatement Third § 4.8(3). The Restatement's position was adopted by the New York Court of Appeals in Lewis v. Young, 705 N.E.2d 649 (N.Y. 1998):

> Traditionally, reasons given for denying easement holders the right to make changes in location are that "treating the location as variable would depreciate the value of the servient estate, discourage its improvement, and

incite litigation" (Restatement [Third] of Property [Servitudes], Tentative Draft No. 4, § 4.8[3], comment f). Those same policy reasons, however, do not justify denying a landowner's (or "servient owner's") limited authority to move an unlocated right of way. Indeed, recognizing that authority likely increases the value of the servient estate, and encourages the landowner to make improvements. Moreover, because a landowner's authority to relocate a right of way without consent is limited — in that relocation may not impair the easement holder's rights — both parties have an incentive to resolve any dispute prior to relocation. The easement holder has an interest in influencing the landowner's choice of a new location, and the landowner will want to avoid the risk and cost of allowing a court to make an after-the-fact determination as to the propriety of the relocation.

Recognition of a relocation right in landowners raises its own policy concerns: that landowners (whose purchase price reflected the existence of the easement) will receive a windfall, that easement holders may be rendered vulnerable to harassment by the landowner and that the settled expectations of the easement holder will be disrupted (see, Note, *The Right of Owners of Servient Estates to Relocate Easements Unilaterally*, 109 Harv.L.Rev. 1693 [1996]; but see, Note, *Balancing the Equities: Is Missouri Adopting a Progressive Rule for Relocation of Easements?*, 61 Mo.L.Rev. 1039 [1996]). We conclude, however, that these concerns are adequately addressed by the limitation that a landowner may not unilaterally change a right of way if that change impairs enjoyment of the easement holder's rights.

Thus, based on our precedents and their underlying policy considerations, we conclude that — as in the easement alteration cases — a balancing test is also appropriate as to relocation of an undefined right of way. In the absence of a demonstrated intent to provide otherwise, a landowner, consonant with the beneficial use and development of its property, can move that right of way, so long as the landowner bears the expense of the relocation, and so long as the change does not frustrate the parties' intent or object in creating the right of way, does not increase the burden on the easement holder, and does not significantly lessen the utility of the right of way (see, Restatement [Third] of Property [Servitudes], Tentative Draft No. 4, § 4.8[3]).

8. **Commentary.** For a detailed and searching analysis of the cases and commentary on both sides of the relocation issue, culminating in approval (with important modifications) of the third Restatement's position, see John A. Lovett, *A Bend in the Road: Easement Relocation and Pliability in the New Restatement (Third) of Property: Servitudes*, 38 Conn. L. Rev. 1 (2005). The Reporter's views and a criticism are found, respectively, in Susan F. French, *Relocating Easements: Restatement (Third) Servitudes, § 4.8(3)*, 38 Real Prop., Prob. & Tr. J. 1 (2003); John V. Orth, *Relocating Easements: A Response to Professor French*, 38 Real Prop., Prob. & Tr. J. 643 (2004).

C. Repairs and Maintenance

9. **Repairs.** The servient owner owes no duty to the easement beneficiary to maintain or repair the servient estate, unless failure to do so would unreasonably interfere with the beneficiary's use of the easement. *See* Restatement Third §§ 4.9, 4.13; Bransford v. International Paper Timberlands Operating Co., 750 So. 2d 424 (La. Ct. App. 2000) (servient owner's failure to remove beaver dams on its property that caused flooding and loss of timber on dominant estate was not breach of duty; "[g]enerally, the owner of the servient estate is not required to do anything. His obligation is to abstain from doing something, or to permit something to be done, on his estate."). The servient owner's joint use with the easement beneficiary of an improvement on the servient estate (e.g., a paved road), however, obligates the servient owner to contribute to reasonable repair and maintenance costs. Restatement Third § 4.13(3).

10. **Improvements.** "When reasonably necessary to the convenient enjoyment of an easement, the holder of the easement may make improvements and construct improvements on the servient estate for enjoyment of the easement." Restatement Third § 4.10 cmt. e, at 597. *See id.* § 4.9 cmt. d, at 585 (specifying situations in which servient owner may use improvements constructed by the holder of the easement).

D. Informal easements

11. **Scope of informal easements.** In general, the scope of an easement created by estoppel, prior use, or necessity tracks that of an expressly created easement on the matters covered in the preceding Notes. An exception is commonly stated for prescriptive easements, which "are generally less capable of expansion to meet changing needs and technologies than express or implied easements." Restatement Third § 4.8 cmt. e, at 561. *See, e.g.,* Han Farms, Inc. v. Molitor, 70 P.3d 1238 (Mont. 2003) (scope of easement by prescription is limited to the use that created the easement); McNeil v. Kingrey, 377 S.E.2d 430 (Va. 1989). The Restatement Third, however, points out that courts "generally permit changes necessary to maintain the utility of the [prescriptive] easement, if the change does not significantly increase the burden on the servient estate," and notes that changes in height and depth are permitted more readily than changes in width, which may be permitted only if "necessary for safety and if the burden on the servient estate is not thereby unreasonably increased." Restatement Third § 4.8 cmt. e, at 562-563. Is the more restrictive treatment of prescriptive easements sensible, or does it illustrate that prescription, like adverse possession, is perhaps a disfavored doctrine?

FRENNING v. DOW
544 A.2d 145 (R.I. 1988)

WEISBERGER, JUSTICE.

This case comes before us on appeal by the plaintiffs from a judgment entered in the Superior Court extinguishing an easement that had been in existence since 1838 on the ground of excessive use. We vacate the judgment. The facts in the case insofar as pertinent to this appeal are as follows.

The defendants' predecessor in title (Gray) granted to plaintiffs' predecessor (Shaw) an easement to cross defendants' land "with teams loaded or not, caragies [sic] of any kind, Stock, on Horse back, or on foot, doing as little damage as may be to him his heirs & assigns forever." At the time of the granting of the easement the dominant tenement consisted of 102 acres of land in the town of Little Compton. Since that time, plaintiffs' predecessor and plaintiffs have acquired contiguous parcels of land so that the total holdings of plaintiffs at the time of trial consisted of 257 acres.

The trial justice made the following additional findings of fact:

[A] Plaintiff has used the way to service with farm equipment not just the original parcel but additional contiguous land.

[B] The way has been used for the benefit of another house on an adjoining parcel, recently built.

[C] Plaintiffs' guests have used the way on social occasions, and on one occasion, in 25 automobiles, they entered her property over her right of way from West Main Road and exited over the way here in litigation.

[D] The use of the way by the plaintiff has materially increased, and has burdened defendants' property far more heavily than the right granted.

[E] The use of the way to service some 150 additional acres, to service the house recently built, and to [accommodate] plaintiffs' social guests constitutes an actual trespass for which money damages lie. Brightman v. Chapin, 15 R.I. 166 [1 A. 412].

[F] There is no way here to sever the increased burden (and thus stop the trespass) so as to preserve the original rights and servitude, there being no practical way to monitor and police the user.

[G] Injunctive relief to limit the use to that which was granted would be unenforceable.

As a result of these findings, the trial justice concluded that the easement had been extinguished or forfeited.

The plaintiffs argue in support of their appeal that the additional intensity of use was insufficient to justify a forfeiture or extinguishment of the easement. Generally courts have not favored extinguishing an easement unless injunctive relief would be ineffective to relieve the servient tenement. The cases in support of this proposition are legion and are set forth in an annotation in 16 A.L.R.2d 609 (1951). The principal case upon which this annotation is based is Penn Bowling Recreation Center, Inc. v. Hot Shoppes, Inc., 179 F.2d 64 (D.C. Cir. 1949), in which the Court of Appeals for the District of Columbia Circuit set aside a summary judgment extinguishing an easement in circumstances wherein a building had been constructed partly on the dominant parcel and partly upon contiguous land that was not entitled to be benefited by the easement. Moreover the building in question built in part upon land not entitled to the easement consisted of a large bowling alley and restaurant to which the plaintiff had brought fuel oil, food, equipment, and supplies over the right of way, and the plaintiff also used the same right of way to remove trash, garbage, and other material. The court observed:

> Misuse of an easement right is not sufficient to constitute a forfeiture, waiver, or abandonment of such right. The right to an easement is not lost by using it in an unauthorized manner or to an unauthorized extent, unless it is impossible to sever the increased burden so as to preserve to the owner of the dominant tenement that to which he is entitled, and impose upon the servient tenement only that burden which was originally imposed upon it.

179 F.2d at 66.

The court ultimately determined that there was an insufficient basis for the granting of summary judgment of extinguishment, even though it was apparent that difficulties would be encountered in supervising the use of the easement by the dominant and nondominant portion of the plaintiff's premises.

Courts have stated in this type of context that equity abhors a forfeiture. However, this only begins the inquiry. We recognize that it is the well-established rule in this jurisdiction that findings of fact of a trial justice will not be disturbed on appeal unless they are clearly wrong or unless the trial justice has overlooked material evidence on a controlling issue. We also give great deference to the drawing of factual inferences by the trial justice as long as the inferences drawn are logical and flow from the established facts. In the case at bar we accept the trial justice's finding of fact as valid and binding; we accept his inferences, save for the ultimate conclusion that this easement must be extinguished because it is impossible to sever the increased burden from that which rightfully adheres to the dominant tenement.

During the past quarter-century, we believe, courts of equity have surmounted problems far greater than that posed by the monitoring of the use of this easement. Without belaboring the point unduly, courts of equity have redistricted legislatures throughout the land. Courts have administered correctional institutions, desegregated school systems, supervised environmental rehabilitation, and undertaken the disposition of complex litigation beyond the wildest dreams of the ancient English chancellors. We are of the opinion that the problem posed by the contiguous acreage owned by the plaintiffs is not beyond the powers of a court of equity to resolve. We may suggest, however, that in accordance with methods established in more complex litigation, it is the burden of the plaintiffs here to propose to the trial justice a plan that may be subject to monitoring by the defendants and ultimate enforcement by the court. We believe that the plaintiffs should be given this opportunity before the easement is totally extinguished.

For the reasons stated, the appeal of the plaintiffs is sustained. The judgment of extinguishment of the easement is vacated, and the papers in the case may be remanded to the Superior Court for further proceedings consistent with this opinion.

NOTES AND QUESTIONS

1. **Termination or injunction?** The authorities are in agreement that "an appurtenant easement or profit may not be used for the benefit of property other than the dominant estate." Restatement Third § 4.11. *Frenning* states the orthodox view that the appropriate remedy is an injunction to bar the unauthorized use rather than a decree terminating the easement. Termination is appropriate only when it is impossible to sever the authorized and tortious uses. *See* Lutheran High School Association v. Woodlands III Holdings, LLC, 81 P.3d 792 (Utah Ct. App. 2003) (injunction requiring dominant owner to prohibit tenants and patrons of dominant owner's adjacent non-dominant tract from using easement, rather than "extreme" remedy of termination, was proper when servient owner failed to show that trial court was incapable of separating proper from improper use of servient estate); Crimmins v. Gould, 308 P.2d 786 (Cal. Dist. Ct. App. 1957) (termination allowed when dominant owner extended servitude to non-dominant parcels accessible by public road; impossible to separate public use of servient estate from use by non-dominant owners).

2. **Injunction or damages?** In Brown v. Voss, 715 P.2d 514 (Wash. 1986), the dominant owner extended the easement to non-dominant property; instead of enjoining the unauthorized use, the court relegated the servient owner to a claim for damages. The third Restatement notes that damages should be substituted for coercive relief "only if extension of the easement does not increase the burden on the servient estate, and if future use of the easement is restricted to limit the risk of future increases in the burden on the servient estate." Restatement Third § 4.11 cmt. b, at 621. Is it sensible to protect the servient owner's entitlement to freedom from unauthorized use by a liability rule (as Brown v. Voss does) rather than a property rule? What problems do you see with the substitution of damages for injunctive relief?

3. **Frenning in Rhode Island.** In Burke-Tarr Co. v. Ferland Corp., 724 A.2d 1014 (R.I. 1999), the court reaffirmed the *Frenning* principle that injunction rather than extinguishment is the normal remedy for unauthorized extension of the benefit to non-dominant property. Surprisingly, however, the court refused to grant an injunction to the servient estate owner, on the ground that the grant of the easement was unrestricted and the non-dominant use was "an increase in degree and not in kind." The court affirmed an award of damages to the servient owner. Did the court confuse two separate issues? Is the case a roundabout way of accomplishing the same result as in Brown v. Voss?

4. **Estoppel to enlarge scope of easement.** Can an easement for use of nondominant property be created in the dominant owner on the basis of estoppel? What would be the requirements? *See* Storms v. Tuck, 579 S.W.2d 447 (Tex. 1979).

5. **Subdivision of dominant estate.** Suppose that B, owner of Whiteacre, has an appurtenant right of way easement across Blackacre; B then subdivides Whiteacre into three parcels and sells two of them. Each buyer builds an apartment complex. Are all the tenants of the apartments entitled to use the easement? What do you think the test should be? *See* Martin v. Music, 254 S.W.2d 701 (Ky. 1953); Restatement Third § 5.7. How do the hypotheticals in this Note differ from the situation in Frenning v. Dow?

6. **Subdivision of profit à prendre.** B enjoys a profit à prendre to take sand and gravel from A's land. Is B entitled to divide the benefit among C, D, and E? Would it matter whether A granted B an "exclusive" right to the sand and gravel? *See* Restatement Third § 5.9 & cmt. b ("exclusive benefits are more likely to be divisible than nonexclusive benefits"); Heydon v. Mediaone of Southeast Michigan, Inc., 739 N.W.2d 373 (Mich. Ct. App. 2007) (utility company holding exclusive prescriptive easement in gross over servient land could authorize cable company to place cable television lines on the utility poles); Gressette v. South Carolina Electric Co., 635 S.E.2d 538 (S.C. 2006) (remand to determine whether electric company's easement to install fiber optic cables allowed company to convey excess capacity on the cables to third-party companies); Lighthouse Tennis Club v. South Island Public Service District, 586 S.E.2d 146 (S.C. Ct. App. 2003) (public service district's access easement was limited to use of servient estate to service water and sewer lines, and did not authorize district to allow access across easement to telecommunications companies); Bogart v. Caprock Communications Corp., 69 P.3d 266 (Okla. 2003) (telecommunications' company's installation of fiber optic cable on public road easement did not impose any increased servitude on private owner's land requiring additional compensation to owner); Centel Cable Television Co. v. Cook, 567 N.E.2d 1010 (Ohio 1991) (public utility's authorization to cable company to string coaxial cable lines in easement was authorized where grant was silent about grantor's intent regarding apportionment and cable lines imposed no extra burden on the easement); Abbott v. Nampa School District, 808 P.2d 1289 (Idaho 1991) (easement holder may grant license to stranger to easement so long as licensee's use is consistent with the easement and imposes no unreasonable increased burden). *Cf.* Patel v. Southern California Water Company, 119 Cal. Rptr. 2d 119 (Cal. Ct. App. 2002) (water company's easement for access to its adjacent land was limited to water-related activities; company's sale of right to use the land to telecommunications companies was unauthorized, but was not inverse condemnation).

RAVEN RED ASH COAL CO. v. BALL
39 S.E.2d 231 (Va. 1946)

Hudgins, Justice.

Plaintiff, Estil Ball, stated, in his notice of motion, that he was entitled to recover $5,000 from the defendant for the use and occupation of an easement across [Ball's] land. Defendant denied any liability. The trial court entered judgment for plaintiff in the sum of $500 on the verdict returned by the jury. From that judgment, defendant obtained this writ of error.

There is no substantial conflict in the evidence. Plaintiff proved that he is the present owner of approximately 100 acres of land lying in Russell county which was a part of a 265-acre tract formerly owned by Reuben Sparks, and that Reuben Sparks and his wife, by deed dated November 19, 1887, conveyed the coal and mineral rights on the 265-acre tract to Joseph I. Doran and William A. Dick. The deed conveying the mineral rights to Doran and Dick, their heirs and assigns, conveyed an easement expressed in the following language: "The right to pass through, over and upon said tract of land by railway or otherwise to reach any other lands belonging to the said Joseph I. Doran and Wm. A. Dick or those claiming such other lands by, through or under them, for the purpose of digging for, mining, or otherwise securing the coal and other things hereinbefore specified, and removing same from such other land."

[The easement extended 2800 feet across plaintiff's hundred acres. Doran and Dick used the easement to transport coal from their adjacent 3,000 acres. Raven Red Ash leased the mineral interests from Doran and Dick, and built a tramway over the easement. Subsequently, Raven acquired mineral rights on five additional tracts totalling about 80 acres.]

The testimony reveals that, during the past five years, defendant transported 49,016 tons of coal mined from the five small tracts over the tramway erected across plaintiff's land and transported 950,000 tons of coal mined from [the 3000 acres] formerly owned by Doran and Dick. There remains to be mined approximately 8,000,000 tons of coal on the tracts formerly owned by Doran and Dick and 180,000 tons of coal on the other small tracts.

Ball concedes that defendant exercised its right in transporting across plaintiff's land the 950,000 tons of coal mined from tracts of land formerly owned by Doran and Dick, but contends that it violated the property rights of plaintiff in transporting the 49,016 tons of coal mined from the five small tracts described above across plaintiff's land to defendant's tipple.

Clayborn v. Camilla Red Ash Coal Co., 105 S.E. 117 (Va. 1920), holds that every use of an easement not necessarily included in the grant is a trespass to realty and renders the owner of the dominant tenement liable in a tort action to the owner of the servient tenement for all damages proven to have resulted therefrom, and, in the absence of proof of special damage, the owner of the servient tenement may recover nominal damages only.

Plaintiff did not prove any specific damage to the realty by the illegal use of the easement, and admitted that "that's the reason we have sued for use and occupancy [a restitutionary claim, rather than a claim for damages]." It thus appears that plaintiff bases his sole ground of recovery on the right to maintain assumpsit for use and occupation.

Since plaintiff failed to prove that he gave express permission for the additional use of the easement or that defendant promised to pay for such use, it became necessary for the plaintiff to establish facts and circumstances from which the law will imply the promise to pay for use and occupancy.

Where a naked trespass is committed, whether upon the person or property, assumpsit will not lie. If one commits an assault and battery upon another, it is absurd to imply a promise by the defendant to pay the victim a reasonable compensation. There is no basis for an implication of a contract where cattle inadvertently invade a neighbor's premises and trample down and destroy his crops. In each instance, a wrong and nothing more and nothing less has been committed. On the other hand, if a trespasser invades the premises of his neighbor, cuts and removes timbers or severs minerals from the land and converts them to his own use, the owner may waive the tort and sue in assumpsit for the value of the materials converted. Such a person has depleted the value of the owner's property and materially enhanced his own possessions.

The general rule stated in the majority of cases we have found is that, in an action for use and occupation, or for damages to realty, based on assumpsit, the plaintiff must prove that the defendant occupied the premises with his permission, either express or implied, or that the trespasser obtained something from the soil, such as growing crops, timber or ore, and appropriated the same to his own use.

In the Notes on Restatement of Restitution by Warren A. Seavey and Austin W. Scott, pp. 193-194, this is said: "The reasons for denying an action of assumpsit against the trespasser for the value of land acquired by a trespass or for the value of its use are largely historical. Like many other rules originating at an early period, the reasons for its existence have largely disappeared but, except in a few jurisdictions, the rule remains."

To hold that a trespasser who benefits himself by cutting and removing trees from another's land is liable on an implied contract, and that another trespasser who benefits himself by the illegal use of another's land is not liable on an implied contract is illogical. The only distinction is that in one case the benefit he received is the diminution of another's property. In the other case, he still receives the benefit but does not thereby diminish the value of the owner's property. In both cases, he has received substantial benefit by his own wrong. As the gist of the action is to prevent the unjust enrichment of a wrongdoer from the illegal use of another's property, such wrongdoer should be held [liable] on an implied promise in both cases.

The facts in Edwards v. Lee, 96 S.W.2d 1028 (Ky. 1936), were that Edwards discovered a cave on the land belonging to himself and his wife, which he developed and advertised as the "Great Onyx Cave." Later, Lee, the owner of an adjoining tract, filed suit against Edwards and the heirs of his wife, claiming that a portion of the cave was under his land. He asked for an accounting of the profits which resulted from the operation of the cave and for an injunction prohibiting Edwards and his associates from further trespassing or using that part of the cave under his land. It was said that the action was based on repeated trespasses to land and that, although no damage or injury was shown to plaintiff's land, plaintiff was entitled to recover on the ground of an implied promise to pay. The measure of recovery was fixed at one-third of the net profits inasmuch as one-third of the cave was under plaintiff's land. It was contended that the use of the cave by the trespasser did not damage or diminish Lee's property, but the court held that the gist of the action was the unjust enrichment of the wrongdoer, which would support an implied promise to pay.

In the Notes on Restatement of Restitution, *supra*, commenting on Edwards v. Lee, this is said at p. 194: "The decision is a welcomed departure from the result in Phillips v. Homfray (1883), 24 Chan.Div. 439, where recovery was denied against a person who had used a passageway under the plaintiff's land for the removal of coal."

The illegal transportation of the coal in question across plaintiff's land was intentional, deliberate and repeated from time to time for a period of years.

Defendant had no moral or legal right to enrich itself by this illegal use of plaintiff's property. To limit plaintiff to the recovery of nominal damages for the repeated trespasses will enable defendant, as a trespasser, to obtain a more favorable position than a party contracting for the same right. Natural justice plainly requires the law to imply a promise to pay a fair value of the benefits received. Defendant's estate has been enhanced by just this much.

While plaintiff offered no evidence to establish the value of the illegal use of the easement, we, as reasonable men, know that the transportation of 49,016 tons of coal over the tramroad across the plaintiff's land was a benefit to defendant. However, in the absence of proof of the value of the benefit, the court could enter no judgment for plaintiff. This proof is supplied by the testimony of the general manager on his cross-examination. The substance of his testimony on this point is that the prevailing rate of payment, or purchase of a right of way for transportation of coal across another's land, is one cent per ton, and that this purchase includes the right to construct and maintain a tramway for distances varying up to 2 1/2 miles; but that, where the owner of the easement has already entered upon the land, and has constructed and is maintaining a tramroad for the transportation of coal from certain specified tracts, the purchase price should be much less — a small fraction of a cent per ton. The jury were instructed that they should fix the amount of damages, if any, at such as would fairly compensate plaintiff for the use and occupation of this strip of land in the hauling and transportation of 49,016 tons of coal over the same.

While the evidence on the value of the benefits retained by defendant is not as clear and full as it could be, and perhaps should have been, the jury had all the facts and circumstances before it and evidently concluded that the value of the benefit to the defendant for the illegal use of the easement should be computed at one cent per ton. Viewing the case as a whole, we find no reversible error, and the judgment of the trial court is affirmed.

Affirmed.

NOTES AND QUESTIONS

1. **Restitution.** Restitution sometimes functions as a plaintiff's alternative remedy for the defendant's breach of contract or, as in the principal case, the defendant's tort. You may encounter it in your courses on those subjects. Sometimes, however, restitution serves as an independent *source* of a defendant's liability (example: you provide a security deposit to your landlord under an oral lease that violates the statute of frauds; your landlord repudiates the lease and refuses to return your deposit; you have no contract claim under the unenforceable lease, but it is unjust for your landlord to refuse to honor the agreement and keep your money). In this latter function, Restitution is on a theoretical par with Tort and Contract as one of the major bases of civil liability. Given the independent importance of restitution, and the reality that omitting a restitutionary cause of action is probably malpractice, it is regrettable that students aren't given more exposure to it in the first year of study. For superb introductions to the law of restitution, see Douglas Laycock, *The Scope and Significance of Restitution*, 67 Tex. L. Rev. 1277 (1989); Andrew Kull, *Rationalizing Restitution*, 83 Calif. L. Rev.

1191 (1995); 1 George E. Palmer, The Law of Restitution §§ 1.1-1.8 (1978).

2. **Damages and restitution.** What injury did Ball suffer as a result of the coal company's tort? What benefit did the company derive from that tort? Which one is Ball seeking to recover? Does the case suggest why an attorney's awareness of a possible restitutionary cause of action is important?

3. **Restitution for tortious use of land.** The Restatement of Restitution § 129 (1937) followed the generally-accepted rule (which traces to Phillips v. Homfray, cited in the principal case), that restitution is not available for a defendant's tortious use of the plaintiff's land, unless the defendant had "tortiously severed and taken possession of anything in or upon the land." There are historical explanations for that rule, but no convincing modern ones. The court in the principal case did not follow it.

4. **Explanations: waiving the tort.** Think about this catchy phrase. If Estil Ball really "waived" the tort in order to sue in restitution, on what basis could he claim any remedy? Speaking more accurately, what did Ball do if he didn't really waive the tort?

5. **Comparisons.** Would restitution have been an available cause of action in Frenning v. Dow? How about in Mandia v. Applegate, Section A.3 above?

C. TERMINATION OF EASEMENTS

An easement may end according to its terms, or when its purpose has been fulfilled. It may end through the conduct of either or both of the parties to it: the easement holder may relinquish the benefit (sometimes voluntarily, often not); or the burdened party may re-acquire the rights surrendered by the creation of the easement; or both parties may act to end it. In some states, statutes terminate an easement after a specified period of time, under specified circumstances.

1. Expiration

HOWELL v. CLYDE
493 S.E.2d 323 (N.C. Ct. App. 1997)

JOHN, JUDGE.

In this controversy regarding an easement granted to plaintiff's predecessors in title, defendant contends the court erroneously concluded that the recording statute, N.C.G.S. § 47-18 (1984), protected plaintiff as a bona fide purchaser for value from oral termination of the easement. We reverse the trial court.

In an agreement dated 15 September 1969 and recorded 22 September 1969, Ray A. Warren and spouse Hazel Warren (the Warrens) granted to Scenic Views, Inc. (Scenic Views), a 30 foot wide access easement (the easement) across certain property the couple owned in Watauga County. The instrument granting the easement provided, inter alia, as follows:

As a substantial part of the consideration, for this easement, the party of the second part, its successors and assigns, agrees to faithfully perform the following conditions:

   1. That legally binding restrictions will be imposed upon the property owned by the party of the second part, its successors and assigns, and to which the easement is granting access, limiting said property to residential use, and that no trailers, trailer park, campground, shacks, or outside toilets, shall be erected thereon.

   It is specifically agreed that the party of the second part, its successors and assigns will faithfully perform the foregoing conditions and that if all or any one part thereof is violated, this instrument shall be void and the parties of the first part or their heirs and assigns, may re-enter and take possession of the above described access route.

By a series of mesne conveyances, plaintiff acquired the property benefitted by the easement and previously owned by Scenic Views. Likewise by a series of mesne conveyances, defendant acquired the property previously owned by the Warrens. The deeds of both plaintiff and defendant specifically refer to the easement. Neither the respective chains of title nor validity of the various deeds are in dispute.

Defendant asserts that conditions contained in the instrument granting the easement were breached when plaintiff's predecessors in title, Norbert F. Goode and Myra V. Mayse, raised goats for commercial purposes and located a trailer on the property. Defendant allegedly informed Goode and Mayse that the easement was terminated, and thereafter locked the gates located at either end of the easement. No instrument terminating the easement was recorded.

Plaintiff purchased the Scenic View property and recorded the conveyance 21 June 1995. At about the same time, he went to defendant's home and obtained the combination for the locks on the gates controlling the easement. The parties do not agree as to whether this occurred prior or subsequent to plaintiff's purchase of the property. Similarly disputed is whether plaintiff took possession of the property subject to notice that defendant believed the easement was terminated.

On 19 February 1996, plaintiff initiated the instant declaratory judgment action seeking interpretation of the instrument granting the easement. Plaintiff's complaint included a prayer for both preliminary and permanent injunctions precluding defendant from denying plaintiff access to the easement. Plaintiff also sought damages for the alleged wrongful denial of his access to the easement. A preliminary injunction issued 4 March 1996 in Watauga County District Court.

Defendant answered, and by means of counterclaim, asserted the easement granted to plaintiff's predecessors in title was a defeasible easement which had been terminated:

   The easement was either a determinable easement, which terminated automatically when the express conditions were violated, or an easement subject to conditions subsequent, which terminated when the defendant re-entered and took possession of the easement after the conditions were violated by informing the owners of the property of the termination and locking the gate to the property.

By way of the counterclaim, defendant sought the court's directive quieting title to his property. Plaintiff's reply alleged that any purported termination of the easement was unrecorded, and that plaintiff's continued rights in the easement as a bona fide purchaser for value were thus superior to those of defendant.

The court entered summary judgment in favor of plaintiff and permanently enjoined defendant from interfering with the recorded easement. Defendant timely appealed.

N.C.G.S. § 47-27 (1984) provides as follows:

> No deed, agreement for right-of-way, or easement of any character shall be valid as against any creditor or purchaser for a valuable consideration but from the registration thereof within the county where the land affected thereby lies.

The question presented herein is whether defendant's failure to record the alleged termination of the easement accorded plaintiff a superior interest therein. This Court was confronted with a similar problem in Price v. Bunn, 187 S.E.2d 423 (N.C. Ct. App. 1972).

In *Price*, we considered the effect of a deed granting an easement to flood and impound water upon the grantor's lands "forever or so long as" the grantee or successors used the easement, and providing that in the event the grantee

> should fail to keep up and maintain the dam across Moccasin Creek, and should fail to use the rights and privileges for the period of five years, the terms of this easement shall become null and void and of no effect, and the property and rights herein given, granted, and conveyed, shall revert to [the grantor].

We held the language of the deed accorded to the grantee a determinable, or defeasible, easement, and noted that:

> [t]he estate known as the fee simple determinable is created when apt and appropriate language is used by a grantor or devisor indicative of an intent on the part of the grantor or devisor that a fee simple estate conveyed or devised will expire automatically upon the happening of a certain event or upon the discontinuance of certain existing facts. Typical language creating such estates may specify that the grantee or devisee shall have land "until" some event occurs, or "while," "during," or "for so long as" some state of facts continues to exist. Upon the happening of the specified event, the fee simple determinable automatically terminates, and reverts to the grantor or to his heirs. . . . When the specified event occurs, the possessory estate of the grantee or devisee ends by operation of law automatically and without the necessity of any act or re-entry, without the institution of any lawsuit, or the intervention of any court.

Id. at 427.

The dam at issue in *Price* had washed out prior to 1951, and was not rebuilt until 1966. We held that the failure of the grantee or his successors to exercise the rights granted by the easement for a period of five years following grant thereof caused automatic termination of the easement and reversion of the rights and interests previously created to the grantor and his successors. *Price*, 187 S.E.2d at 428.

We conclude the instrument granting the easement sub judice contained certain conditions upon the occurrence of which the easement was defeasible. Whether the defeasible easement conveyed by the instrument was a determinable easement as in *Price* or an easement subject to a condition subsequent, as defendant pleads alternatively, is an issue we need not resolve at this juncture. The trial court entered summary judgment in favor of plaintiff solely in consequence of its determination that the undisputed facts showed defendant had failed to record any purported termination of the easement. The court thus considered plaintiff's duly recorded interest in the easement to be superior as a matter of law to that of defendant.

However, *Price* indicates that recordation of termination of the easement, whether determinable or subject to conditions subsequent, was not required to make such termination effective as against plaintiff. Plaintiff has cited no authority, nor have we located any, requiring the further step of recordation to terminate a defeasible easement under the circumstances sub judice. We therefore reverse the trial court's judgment grounded exclusively upon defendant's failure to record the alleged termination of the easement and remand this case for further proceedings.

Reversed and remanded.

NOTES AND QUESTIONS

1. **Duration of easements.** Although an easement creates a nonpossessory interest in the servient land rather than an estate, the available durations of an easement track the permissible estates that we studied in Chapter 2: an easement may be perpetual (equivalent to a fee simple estate), for life, or for a term. (May an easement be held at the will of the grantor and grantee? What would it be called?) As indicated in the principal case, an easement may also be defeasible. *See* Richard R. Powell & Patrick J. Rohan, Powell on Real Property 572 (Abr. ed. 1968) ("easements can run the gamut of durability," just as estates). In the principal case, why wasn't it necessary for the court to determine whether Howell's claimed easement was determinable or subject to a condition subsequent? After reviewing the relevant materials in Chapter 2, how would you classify the easement?

2. **Easements for a special purpose.** An easement for a specific purpose is implicitly defeasible; it terminates when the purpose "ceases to exist [i.e., is accomplished], is abandoned, or is rendered impossible of accomplishment." Sasser v. Spartan Food System, Inc., 452 So. 2d 475, 478 (Ala. 1984). The termination of an easement by necessity when the dominant owner acquires a permanent alternative access route is a special illustration of this broader point. *See* Restatement Third § 4.3(1). In which of the following cases would the easement end under the facts stated:

a. A, owner of Whiteacre, grants "to B and his heirs," an easement across Whiteacre "for ingress and egress to and from Blackacre," owned by B. Subsequently, B acquires another easement to Blackacre from C. Does the acquisition of the subsequent easement terminate the easement granted by A? *See*

McClendon v. Hollis, 730 So. 2d 229 (Ala. Ct. App. 1998) ("The deed is unambiguous, contains no conditions, and makes no reference to a specific purpose.").

b. A, owner of Whiteacre, grants B an easement "for the purpose of facilitating access to Blackacre for the construction of a home on same." Is B entitled to use the easement after completion of construction?

3. **Faulty analysis?** In Thar v. Edwin N. Moran Revocable Trust, 905 P.2d 413 (Wyo. 1995), Moran granted an easement across his land to Thar, providing access to a landlocked parcel that Thar leased from the state. Subsequently Thar acquired fee simple title to the landlocked parcel and leased it to a tenant. When Thar's tenant used the easement, Moran sued for trespass. Moran's counsel argued that the easement was in gross, and nontransferable. A dissenting judge agreed that the easement was in gross but argued that it was assignable either because it was a "commercial" easement or because Moran and Thar had provided that the agreement was binding on their heirs, executors and assigns. The court declined to address assignability, and held that the easement *expired* when Thar acquired the fee title: "Moran granted an easement to serve leased lands, not an easement to serve lands held in fee." Who has the better analysis in the case?

4. **My neighbor's keeper?** A granted B an easement for access to B's land. B also enjoyed access directly from a public street. The agreement provided that the easement would "cease, terminate and be extinguished at any time when any building is erected on any part of the land now owned by the Grantee in addition to the buildings now on said land, or when any building on said land is enlarged." Twenty years later, Y purchased the dominant estate with knowledge of the terms of the easement. During "a chance meeting," Y informed A of plans to renovate his house by constructing an addition to the kitchen; A, who was "consciously aware that the construction would be in violation of the easement, did not respond nor react when she was told of the plans." After Y built a 230 square foot addition, A notified Y of intent to block off the easement. Y sued to enjoin A, claiming that A was estopped to enforce termination of the easement. Result? *See* Eis v. Meyer, 566 A.2d 422 (Conn. 1989).

2.   Extinguishment

a.   Conduct of Easement Holder

STRAHIN v. LANTZ
456 S.E.2d 12 (W. Va. 1995)

CLECKLEY, JUSTICE.

In this property case involving the use of an easement by prescription, the appellants and plaintiffs below, James Strahin, et al., brought suit to enjoin the appellee and defendant below, Vonda Lee Lantz, from locking a gate to the road which accesses their property. They appeal an order of the Circuit Court of Barbour County entered June 30, 1993, which held the prescriptive easement was extinguished due to abandonment. The plaintiffs argue that this Court should adopt the majority view and hold abandonment must be shown by clear and convincing evidence of nonuse coupled with evidence of intent to abandon. They contend no evidence of such intent was introduced below and request this Court to reverse the judgment.

I.

The defendant owns approximately sixty acres of land in Barbour County, a portion of which is adjacent to County Route 5/10. The plaintiff James Strahin purchased a 5.75 acre tract of land from the plaintiff Richard Newman in August of 1992.[2] To access the property, it is necessary to take Miner Road which is a dirt roadway off Route 5/10 that travels over the defendant's property and leads to Miner Hollow.

In the early 1900s, when the local coal mine was in operation, many houses were located up Miner Hollow. Persons living up the hollow would travel Miner Road across the defendant's property without her permission. The evidence is undisputed that a prescriptive easement was created across Miner Road.[3] When the coal mine closed, the families moved away and the houses deteriorated. In 1985, the defendant placed a gate across the road. The owners of the property up Miner Hollow continued to pass through the gate on occasion to access their property to cut grass, care for gardens, and hunt game.

From the middle 1940s to the middle 1950s, the defendant's cousin, Mr. Sandridge, owned a home on the 5.75 acre tract now owned by James Strahin. The home was abandoned in the early 1960s and was later destroyed by fire. The issue in this case is whether the prescriptive easement created by the driveway leading from Miner Road to the homesite was extinguished by abandonment.

James Strahin plans to construct a home on the tract. The defendant maintains she suffered property damage when a gas line leading to her home was broken and certain trees were cut down from her side of the property line as a result of bulldozing the road in preparation for construction of the home. This lawsuit was initiated after she placed a lock on the gate and would not allow persons to travel on Miner Road.

The case was tried upon the facts without a jury. After hearing arguments, testimony from the parties and witnesses who had lived up Miner Hollow, and a view of the area, the circuit court issued specific findings of fact and conclusions of law. The circuit court found the prescriptive easement over the defendant's land from Miner Road to the 5.75 acre tract was extinguished by abandonment.

---

[2] The property was transferred by quitclaim deed. A second deed of general warranty was later prepared and entered.

[3] Syllabus Point 1 of Jamison v. Waldeck United Methodist Church, 445 S.E.2d 229 (W. Va. 1994), sets forth the factors necessary for the creation of a prescriptive easement:

> The open, continuous and uninterrupted use of a road over the land of another, under bona fide claim of right, and without objection from the owner, for a period of ten years, creates in the user of such road a right by prescription to the continued use thereof. In the absence of any one or all of such requisites, the claimant of a private way does not acquire such way by prescription over the lands of another.

Accordingly, it held that James Strahin was not entitled to travel over the driveway in question to access the land. This appeal ensued.

II.

This Court has never directly addressed the factors necessary to show termination of a prescriptive easement by abandonment. In an analogous situation addressed in Moyer v. Martin, 131 S.E. 859, 861 (W. Va. 1926), we set forth the situations in which an owner of an easement by grant may lose his rights.[5]

> Having once been granted to him, he cannot lose it by mere non-user. He may lose it by adverse possession by the owner of the servient estate for the proper length of time, or by abandonment, not by mere non-user, but by proofs of an intention to abandon; or, of course, by deed or other instrument in writing.

Section 504 (Easements) of the Restatement of Property states the majority rule that abandonment must be shown by evidence of intent to discontinue the use and that evidence of nonuse, without more, is insufficient to extinguish the right. "Abandonment is a question of intention and may be proved by a cessation of use coupled with circumstances clearly showing an intention to abandon the right." 6B Michie's Jurisprudence, Easements § 18, at 166-67 (1985).

This rule is in keeping with public policy considerations which revere vested property rights. Courts should not interfere with the rights of an owner of a prescriptive easement absent a clear showing that the owner does not intend to exercise his rights in the future.

We hereby adopt the foregoing rule and hold that abandonment of an easement by prescription is a question of intention that may be proved by nonuse combined with circumstances which evidence an intent to abandon the right. It is the burden of the party asserting the absence of an easement by prescription to prove abandonment by clear and convincing evidence.

What particular actions would constitute proof of intent to abandon an easement by prescription would necessarily depend on the unique facts of each case. In Downing House Realty v. Hampe, 497 A.2d 862 (N.H. 1985), the Supreme Court of New Hampshire addressed the issue of intent to abandon an easement when faced with similar facts to this case. The easement was not frequently used in the past, a fence was erected over a portion of the easement and remained there for approximately thirty years, and large trees grew where the easement existed. Nevertheless, the court found the evidence insufficient to establish abandonment

---

[5] We find the criteria listed in *Moyer* persuasive because it has been argued that prescriptive easements should be treated the same as easements created by deed:

> An easement established by prescription is just as well established as one originating in the most formal deed. The methods of extinguishment of prescriptive easements and easements created by deed should be identical. Either nonuser should be effective as to both, or as to neither. The Restatement of Property § 504 takes the position that nonuser alone is never sufficient to prove abandonment as to any variety of easement, but constitutes relevant evidence which, with other accompanying facts, can justify a finding of abandonment.

3 Richard R. Powell, Powell on Property, Easements and Licenses § 34.20 (1994).

because of the lack of permanency of the nonuse. Had the owner of the easement chosen to exercise control of the land, the fence and trees could easily be removed.

In the case at bar, testimony was heard from thirty-nine-year-old Eric Lantz that a fence existed over the driveway for as long as he could remember. A gas line ran across the driveway and the area was grown over with small trees. Despite this evidence of nonuse, no evidence was introduced to show the intent to abandon the prescriptive easement. To the contrary, the evidence showed that Mr. Strahin invested money to improve the land to construct a residence.

In Norman v. Belcher, 378 S.E.2d 446, 448 (W. Va. 1989), this Court held that "[a] private easement may be extinguished by adverse possession wholly inconsistent with the use of the easement." Significantly, the defendant did not introduce evidence or assert the easement was extinguished by adverse possession. The record evidence is insufficient to determine if the elements for adverse possession were met. Accordingly, this Court cannot conclude the prescriptive easement was extinguished based only on the existence of the fence and gas line.

Based on the foregoing, we find the prescriptive easement was not extinguished and the plaintiffs have the right to travel across the driveway to access the 5.75 acre tract.[8] Furthermore, because the parties agree a prescriptive easement exists across Miner Road, the lock on the gate preventing the plaintiffs access to the road must be removed. The decision of the Circuit Court of Barbour County is hereby reversed, and this case is remanded for entry of an order consistent with this opinion.

Reversed and remanded.

NOTES AND QUESTIONS

1. **Possession and use.** Why is abandonment of an easement possible, but not abandonment of a fee simple title? (Recall the *Pocono Springs* case in Ch. 2.) Do the different rules promote the same, or similar, policies? *See* Restatement of Property § 504 cmt. a.

2. **Nonuse and intent.** Nonuse by the easement beneficiary, "even for a lengthy period," usually does not constitute abandonment; independent proof of the beneficiary's intent to abandon is also required. Restatement Third § 7.4 cmt. c, at 354. The longer the nonuse, however, the less evidence of intent to abandon is required. *Id.*

3. **Rails to trails.** In the Rails-to-Trails Act, 16 U.S.C. §§ 1241 et seq., Congress authorized the Surface Transportation Board (the successor to the Interstate Commerce Commission) to allow railroads to abandon a railroad line, in which case the Act provided for the "railbanking" of the line for possible future railroad use, or to discontinue a rail line and transfer the right of way to a public or private entity willing to maintain the right of way as a trail for public hiking. The

---

[8] We note that James Strahin's proposed use of the driveway does not place an additional burden upon the road outside the parameters of the creation of the prescriptive easement. The use of the driveway during the prescriptive period was for vehicular traffic to a residence. Crane v. Hayes, 417 S.E.2d 117 (W. Va. 1992), states: "The character and purpose of an easement acquired by prescription are determined by the use made of it during the prescriptive period."

effect of either railbanking or trailmaking is to prevent the re-acquisition of unencumbered ownership by the underlying fee owner of the former right of way. Does that constitute a taking of the fee owner's property, requiring compensation? Does the answer depend on whether railbanking or trailmaking falls within the scope of uses allowed by the original easement grant? *See* Glosemeyer v. United States, 45 Fed. Cl. 771, 777-78 (Fed. Cl. 2000):

> In all of these [consolidated] cases, the railroads' applications to the ICC for authority to abandon are clear evidence of intent to abandon their easements. The applications are full of statements which unequivocally signify an intent to abandon. When a railroad's application for abandonment states that there is "no feasible alternative" to abandonment, that it seeks to "physically" abandon a rail line, or that it is "not possible to operate [a] line profitably in the future," a reader is left with no choice but to conclude that the railroad intends to abandon the rail line.

> This intent was confirmed by conduct. The railroads here removed their tracks [rails, ties, and rail bed] and ceased all operations. The fact that no trains have been run over these easements for years is strong evidence of abandonment. Finally, the railroads in these cases actually rid themselves by conveyance of their entire legal interests in these easements [to the trail providers].

> These facts compel the court to find that the railroads intended to abandon, and in fact did abandon, their easements. The remaining question, then, is whether, under Missouri law, the interception of the fee owners' right to possession by conversion of the railbeds to trail use precludes an abandonment — i.e., is either trail use or railbanking, or their combination, sufficient under state law to forestall plaintiffs' right to immediate possession? Only if this question is answered in the negative is the possibility of a taking presented.

> [T]rail use, by itself, would not constitute a railroad purpose. The transportation use contemplated by a railroad purpose would clearly be the movement of trains over rails. Recreational hiking, jogging and cycling are not connected with railroad use in any meaningful way.

> The Government argues, however, that railbanking is a railroad purpose under state law and that the easements thus should not be deemed abandoned. It contends that holding out the possibility of a reactivation, even if remote and indefinite, is a railroad purpose in and of itself. This future potentiality thus becomes a present railroad purpose in the view of the Government. There is no question that this potentiality, insofar as these particular easements are concerned, exists purely in the realm of the hypothetical. No evidence was offered of a present intent to reinstate rail service in the future. In sum, neither component of railbanking — the preservation of the rail line for future use nor the "interim" use of the easement as a recreational trail — constitutes a railroad purpose under Missouri law. These easements, therefore, would have been extinguished except for federal preemption of Missouri law.

Having established that the easements would have been extinguished, and thus that, but for the application of the Rails-to-Trails Act, the plaintiffs would have been seised in their lands without any restrictions, we have little difficulty concluding that a taking has occurred.

See also Preseault v. United States, 100 F.3d 1525 (Fed. Cir. 1996). *But see* Restatement Third § 4.10 cmt. d, at 595 (purpose of easement for "railroad right of way" may be "narrowly defined as transportation by railroad, or more generally defined as transportation or movement of people and goods"). If the latter interpretation indicated by the Restatement is adopted, would railbanking constitute a taking? Would trailmaking?

4. **Abandonment and prescription.** Suppose that B acquires an easement over A's land by prescription. Subsequently, B ceases to use the easement for the prescriptive period. Does B's nonuse constitute abandonment? *See* Restatement Third § 7.4 cmt. d. *But see* Jon W. Bruce & James W. Ely, Jr., The Law of Easements and Licenses § 905 (1988) (discussing cases holding that nonuse of prescriptive easement for prescriptive period extinguishes easement or creates presumption of intent to abandon).

5. **Reliance.** A minority of courts holds that reliance by the servient owner on the easement beneficiary's abandonment is a necessary element of abandonment doctrine. Does that view confuse abandonment with some other doctrine? *See* Lague, Inc. v. Royea, 568 A.2d 357, 359 (Vt. 1989) (overruling cases requiring reliance: "Even without a requirement of reliance, the difficulty of proving intent to abandon an easement is such that its application is often impractical."). If reliance by the servient owner *were* present, would that offer an alternative basis for termination of an easement?

6. **Release.** Abandonment focuses on the conduct of the holder of the benefit of the easement. So, too, does *release*, a transaction in which the benefit holder transfers the benefit to the servient owner. *See* Restatement Third § 7.3. Although the release should be in writing, *id.* cmt. a, the traditional exceptions to the statute of frauds apply. *See, e.g.*, Romberg v. Slemon, 778 P.2d 315, 317 (Colo. Ct. App. 1989) (in exchange for an alternative access, dominant owner orally agreed to vacate the easement; servient owner performed the agreement by "grading, improving, and dedicating a road and driveway that provided an alternative access").

b. Conduct of the Servient Owner

ESTOJAK v. MAZSA
562 A.2d 271 (Pa. 1989)

Larsen, Justice.

This appeal presents a single issue: whether the appellants' easement, a right of ingress and egress over appellees' property, was extinguished by adverse possession. We answer in the negative.

Appellants, Andrew and Michael Estojak, own and operate a business known as Andy's Auto Body on Jennings Street in Bethlehem, Northampton County. The property on which this business is located is situated in a plan known as the Minsi Trail Farm, the plan of which was recorded in the Northampton County Recorder's Office on August 13, 1925.

On July 16, 1985, appellants purchased two additional lots in the Minsi Trail Farm Plan which lots (designated Lots Nos. 3 and 4) are located at the intersection of Yeates Street and East Union Street, two streets that were dedicated for public use on the recorded plan, but which were never accepted by the municipality for public use and were never opened to the public. On July 22, 1985, appellants bulldozed and graded a roadway over East Union Street from Yeates Street through to its intersection with Jennings Street in order to gain ingress and egress to their newly purchased lots, and to facilitate travel from their business on Jennings Street to said lots.

Appellees are owners of certain lots adjacent to appellants' newly purchased lots on East Union Street. Appellees John and Sarah Mazsa own the lot east of appellants' lot no. 3 on the north side of East Union Street and fronting on Jennings Street (appellees Mazsas' lot is designated lot no. 1); appellees A. Derwood and Elizabeth A. Johnson own the lot east of appellants' lot no. 4 on the south side of East Union Street and fronting on Jennings Street (appellees Johnsons' lot is designated lot no. 2). Shortly after appellants bulldozed and graded the roadway across East Union Street, appellees Mazsa and Johnson erected a fence on East Union Street between their respective lots in order to prevent appellants from using said roadway for ingress and egress to their property.

On August 26, 1985, appellants filed a declaratory judgment action pursuant to 42 Pa.C.S.A. §§ 7531-7541 asking the Court of Common Pleas of Northampton County to declare and establish their right of access over the unopened portions of East Union Street and Yeates Street, and requesting the court to restrain and enjoin appellees from blocking said access. In their complaint for a declaratory judgment and other relief, appellants alleged, inter alia, that when the City of Bethlehem failed to accept the unopened portions of East Union and Yeates Streets within twenty-one years after their dedication, the city's rights to said streets lapsed and ownership of the property dedicated for use as a public street "reverted" to appellees as owners of the adjacent land. The complaint further alleged, however, that "this ownership is subject to the private rights of owners of land within the Minsi Trail Farm Subdivision to use the land for access in and about the Subdivision."

Appellees' answer and counterclaim admitted that the ownership of the unopened portions of East Union and Yeates Streets had "reverted" to the appellees as abutting landowners, but denied that appellants had any right of access over said property. To the contrary, appellees claimed that any right of access over said unopened streets had been extinguished by appellees' adverse possession of the land for a period in excess of twenty-one years. Appellees requested that appellants be denied any right of access over East Union and Yeates Streets and, further, that the appellants be ordered to restore the property to its original condition and to pay damages for the unlawful removal of trees and shrubs.

Trial was conducted on April 2, 1986 and the parties stipulated that ownership of the disputed property was as set forth in the complaint, i.e. that ownership of the disputed portions of East Union and Yeates Streets had "reverted" to the adjoining property owners, the appellees Mazsa and Johnson. It was further stipulated that the disputed portions of East Union and Yeates Streets are laid out on the recorded Minsi Trail Farm Plan as being fifty feet in width and that the City of Bethlehem had never owned said unopened streets. Further, the parties "agree that the only legal issue which is to be addressed in this matter is whether or not the various [appellees] have extinguished the [appellants'] right of easement over the disputed portions of the unowned streets by adverse possession." Notes of Testimony (N.T.), April 2, 1986, at 4.

As it was also agreed that the parties claiming the benefit of adverse possession had the burden of proof, appellees Mazsa and Johnson presented their evidence on this issue. A. Derwood Johnson and his wife, Elizabeth A. Johnson, testified that they had lived at 745 Jennings Street (lot no. 2) since 1958, and that they had continuously maintained the adjoining portions of East Union Street as a yard and play area for the enjoyment of their family since that time. Shortly after they moved into this residence, Mr. Johnson put in a driveway, laid with stone, alongside his house and located eight to ten feet within East Union Street which was just a grassy area with a few cherry trees and an apricot tree thereon when the Johnsons moved in. Mr. Johnson cut the grass and maintained the East Union Street property as an extension of his yard, and never saw anyone drive through or over this property. Mr. Johnson testified that in July, 1985, a cherry tree was cut down without his permission which was in the path of the appellants' roadway.

The Johnsons never erected or placed anything on the disputed property that would block access to and over East Union Street, i.e., no fence, walls, gates, buildings, plants or shrubs were ever built or planted that would block access or would indicate that access was restricted. There was a hurricane fence alongside the Johnson house, but that was inside their property line as were hedges and trees planted by the Johnsons. Mr. Johnson testified that there was never a need to erect any sort of barrier to block access over East Union Street because the natural contour of the land formed an embankment along Jennings Street which acted as a natural barrier to prevent the passage of vehicular traffic. Other than their neighbors, the Mazsas, no one walked over this East Union Street property.

Appellees John Mazsa and his wife, Sarah Mazsa, testified that they had bought their property at 803 Jennings Street (lot no. 1) in 1950 and immediately built and moved into a house thereon. The Mazsas also testified that they and their family used East Union Street as an extension of their yard for family gatherings, play, and gardening. (Mr. Mazsa had an organic garden which extended into East Street about ten feet, but which was not disturbed by appellees' bulldozing/grading.) Mr. Mazsa planted some willow trees on East Union Street, but there was no testimony as to their location, or whether they were still alive in 1985. The Mazsas had also cut the grass on East Union Street and continually maintained it as a lawn or yard since they moved in.

The Mazsas never erected or placed anything on the disputed property to restrict access over East Union Street or to indicate to the public that access was restricted. Their testimony was that no barriers were necessary because it was "impossible" to gain access to East Union Street because of the natural embankment along Jennings Street (although pedestrian traffic was possible).

Appellant Andrew Estojak testified that he graded and bulldozed the disputed portions of East Union Street in order to gain access to his property located adjacent thereto (lots no. 3 and 4). Mr. Estojak never knew of anything done by appellees to give the impression that access over East Union Street was restricted, and he stated that on several occasions he had walked or driven a small all-terrain vehicle (ATV) over said property without being told to stop.

Messers. Johnson and Mazsa testified on rebuttal that they had seen or were aware that Andrew Estojak had driven ATVs over East Union Street on several occasions and had not complained to him or asked him to stop, although Mr. Mazsa did give him a "dirty look" one time.

The trial court ruled in favor of appellees. The court correctly recognized that, where a municipality fails to accept or open a dedicated street in a plan within twenty-years, the owners of property within the plan or subdivision retain private rights of easement by implication over the unopened streets. However, the court held that such an easement may be extinguished by adverse possession, stating that to "claim title by adverse possession, one must prove actual, visible, notorious, exclusive and distinct, hostile and continuous use for 21 years. Dunlap v. Larkin, 493 A.2d 750 (Pa. Super. Ct. 1985)." Opinion in Support of Decree Nisi dated August 27, 1986, Slip op. at 3. Relying on *Dunlap* and Reed v. Wolyniec, 471 A.2d 80 (Pa. Super. Ct. 1983), the trial court concluded "that all of the elements of adverse possession [by appellees] have been established as to the unopened portion of East Union Street." Accordingly, the court rendered the following conclusions of law:

> 1. Failure of a municipality to open a street for 21 years does not extinguish the private easement of abutting property owners.

> 2. Use of a piece of land for lawn purposes in connection with the residence, together with continued maintenance of the lawn, is sufficient to establish adverse possession.

On October 24, 1986, the trial court entered its final order in this case, an Amended Decree Nisi which stated that appellant's private easement rights to the unopened portion of East Union Street from the intersection with Jennings Street to the intersection with Bryan Street (i.e., that portion adjacent to the property owned by appellees Johnson and Mazsa) had been extinguished by the adverse possession of appellees Johnson and Mazsa. On appeal to the Superior Court, this final order was affirmed by memorandum opinion. 534 A.2d 137.

Appellants asserted on appeal that the trial court applied the wrong legal standards to determine whether the appellants' easement had been extinguished by adverse possession, and that the record did not support a finding of extinguishment by adverse possession under the appropriate standards. The Superior Court agreed with appellants that the trial court applied the wrong legal standards to the issue, namely the standards applicable to the acquisition of title to property by adverse possession as opposed to the standards for extinguishing an easement over a servient tenement. Nevertheless, Superior Court affirmed on the grounds that the record evidence was sufficient to establish extinguishment of appellants' easement over East Union Street under the appropriate legal standards. In Superior Court's view, the acts of appellees in maintaining the property as a lawn/yard coupled with the "natural topographical surface" of the property sufficiently obstructed ingress and egress over East Union Street for the prescriptive period to extinguish the easement by adverse possession.

We granted appellants' petition for allowance of appeal from Superior Court, and we now reverse. Superior Court was correct in its identification of the proper legal standards governing this case, but it clearly erred in its application of those standards to the record evidence.

The standards for determining the acquisition of title to land by adverse possession and for determining whether an easement over property has been extinguished by adverse possession contain the same basic elements — in each situation, the possession that will acquire title or extinguish an easement must be actual, continuous, adverse, visible, notorious and hostile possession of the land in question for the prescriptive period of twenty-one years. However, the focus of these standards is markedly different in the two situations, for conduct that is sufficient to acquire title to land may not be sufficient to extinguish someone else's easement over (or use of) that land. To extinguish an easement over (or use of) the servient tenements, the servient tenement owner must demonstrate a visible, notorious and continuous adverse and hostile use of said land which is inconsistent with the use made and rights held by the easement holder, not merely possession which is inconsistent with another's claim of title.

Fairly recent decisions of this Court illustrate the above distinction between claim of title versus extinguishment of an easement by adverse possession, and are dispositive of the instant case. In Mellace v. Armstrong, 365 A.2d 850 (Pa. 1976), appellant landowners claimed that they had extinguished appellee adjacent property owner's easement by adverse possession over a period of twenty-one years, as they had erected a fence for some eighteen years, and had planted a "victory garden," hemlocks and other trees and plants in the common alleyway. In rejecting appellants assertions, we stated:

> Appellants contend that use of the alley as a passageway by appellees or other persons despite the growing grass, the victory garden, or the low stone wall around the iris bed, is immaterial to appellants' claim of adverse possession. We do not agree. Such facts might be immaterial if the issue were whether the appellants acquired the fee by adverse possession, since one may acquire title to the fee by adverse possession even though many other persons used the land as guests or trespassers. The same is not true, however, when we are considering whether or not an easement by deed has been extinguished. Even the nonuse of an easement acquired by deed will not cause the easement to be extinguished when an adverse possessor of the land for twenty-one years has not acted adversely to the easement.

As we said in Stozenski v. Borough of Forty Fort, Luzerne County, 317 A.2d 602, 605 (Pa. 1974): "The repudiation of the rights of other persons in a right-of-way must be manifested by words or acts which are inconsistent with or infringe upon the other persons' right to pass across the land whenever the necessity to do so arises."

In Stozenski v. Borough of Forty Fort, 456 Pa. 5, 317 A.2d 602 (1974). property owners on either side of a dedicated but unopened street as laid out in a subdivision plan had maintained the "street" area for more than twenty-one years as a lawn or yard, by cutting grass on either side of the area and by the existence of a low concrete curb running lengthwise through the middle of the street area. Another landowner in the subdivision (which happened to be the municipality, as a grantee of land therein) sought to use the "street" area as a private easement. In rejecting the plaintiff property owners' (servient tenement owners') claim of extinguishment of easement by adverse possession, we stated:

> [T]he adverse possession that will bar easements must be actual, continuous, adverse, visible, notorious, and hostile possession of the land in question for twenty-one years. [T]here must be shown, by word or act, an express repudiation of the interests acquired by others, and an intention to set up a hostile claim. The repudiation of the rights of other persons in a right-of-way must be manifested by words or acts which are inconsistent with or infringe upon the other persons' right to pass across the land whenever the necessity to do so arises. No particular conduct is required, but the obstructing conduct must be inconsistent with one's right to use and enjoy the easement. In the present case, nothing was done which interfered with the use and enjoyment of the twenty foot wide road easement by the defendant or any of its predecessors in title. The grass and the low curbing did not in any way obstruct or inhibit ingress and egress from Wyoming Avenue, over the road easement, to defendant's property. Plaintiffs' use of a two foot strip and an eight foot strip on either side of the road as part of their yards was not inconsistent with the defendant's easement rights. The plaintiffs erected no fences, planted no trees or shrubbery, constructed no walls or gates — did nothing, from which an inference can be drawn that they disclaimed any of the defendant's right-of-way interest in the land. Moreover, it is irrelevant that defendant and its predecessors in title may never have improved, maintained, or used the road as a means of ingress or egress to their property. Nonuse, no matter for what duration of time, will not extinguish an easement. We conclude that the plaintiffs' use of the road easement was permissive — not adverse. The trial court did not err in denying plaintiffs' claim of adverse possession.

See also Piper v. Mowris, 351 A.2d 635 (Pa. 1976) (erection of a gate and fence which did not actually obstruct right of way and planting of nonobstructing trees did not establish adverse possession adequate to extinguish easement).

Applying the appropriate standards to the instant case, it is clear that appellees failed to meet their burden of establishing adverse possession of the disputed portion of East Union Street sufficient to extinguish the private right of ingress and egress held by other land owners within the Minsi Trail Farm Plan. As these appellees admitted on cross-examination, they took no action and erected no barriers that obstructed the East Union Street right of way in any manner, nor did they take any action or erect any structure or plant any trees, shrubs, etc. that would give the impression that access to the right of way was restricted.

It is true that these appellees did maintain, care for and use the disputed portions of East Union Street as extensions of their own yards over an extended period of time and may have considered said property their own. Indeed, we sympathize with these neighbors who saw their children grow up enjoying their extended yard which they maintained continuously in a labor of love and who watched the unannounced bulldozer rip its way through their yard and through their tranquility. However, the law is clear on this issue — because appellees did nothing which could remotely be deemed to be inconsistent with the right of ingress and egress over East Union Street until after appellants graded the roadway and did not repudiate such right of way by word or deed, the private easement for ingress and egress held by appellants and other landowners within the Plan was not extinguished and remains intact.

Appellees and Superior Court improperly relied upon the existence of a "natural obstruction," i.e., an embankment, to the use of the easement for ingress and egress over East Union Street. Appellees have offered no authority, and our research has found none, for the proposition that the existence of a "natural barrier" to use of an easement which existed when the easement was created may supply the elements of adverse, hostile and notorious use by the servient tenement owners so as to extinguish the easement. Regardless of any natural embankment barrier to vehicular traffic which existed when the easement was created by operation of law, or of the cherry tree which existed when appellees acquired their property and which was removed to clear the roadway, the dispositive fact is that appellees did nothing to restrict access over East Union Street or to indicate to the world that they repudiated the private rights of easement held by the landowners in the Minsi Trail Farm Plan.

We hold, therefore, that appellants' easement over the disputed portions of East Union Street for ingress and egress to their property has not been extinguished by adverse possession by appellees.[3]

Accordingly, the order of Superior Court affirming the decree of the Court of Common Pleas of Northampton County is reversed.

NIX, CHIEF JUSTICE, concurring.

I join in the majority opinion holding that extinguishment of an easement by deed can only be accomplished by acts hostile to the use encompassed by the

---

[3] As noted, this case presented only the single issue of whether adverse possession had extinguished appellants' private easement for ingress and egress. We were not asked to decide whether the "improvements" to said easement by appellants, i.e., the bulldozing and grading of the roadway, unduly burdened the servient tenement owners' property, nor have we been asked to determine whether use by vehicular traffic for operation of an auto body repair business exceeded the scope of the easement over East Union Street. The parties have narrowly confined the issue as stated, and we have correspondingly confined our decision.

easement. I write separately only to note that I would not foreclose the possibility of reliance on a natural barrier, coupled with acts adverse to the easement, in an appropriate case.

NOTES AND QUESTIONS

1. **The third Restatement.** A servitude is extinguished "[t]o the extent that a use of property violates a servitude burdening the property and the use is maintained adversely to a person entitled to enforce the servitude for the prescriptive period." Restatement Third § 7.7.

2. **A disfavored doctrine?** In Bentz v. McDaniel, 872 So. 2d 978 (Fla. Dist. Ct. App. 2004), the court stated that prescription is not favored in the law, and that any doubt as to the acquisition of prescriptive rights must be resolved in favor of the owner. The court applied the same principles to *extinguishment* of an easement by prescription, holding that the servient owner had not offered clear and convincing proof of his adverse use of the easement area.

c.   Conduct of Both Parties

PERGAMENT v. LORING PROPERTIES, LTD.
599 N.W.2d 146 (Minn. 1999)

Heard, considered, and decided by the court en banc.

We are asked to determine when the mortgage exception to the merger doctrine prevents an easement from being extinguished. We conclude that at the time fee title to the dominant estate is united with fee title to the servient estate, the easement is extinguished with this exception: a mortgagee of the dominant estate will be entitled to the benefit of the easement should the mortgagee's interest become possessory.

In this case, respondent, Brian A. Pergament, brought an action in district court seeking declaratory judgment that he was entitled to an easement to eight parking spaces in the parking lot of appellant, Loring Properties, Ltd. Relying on the mortgage exception to the merger doctrine, the district court granted Pergament's motion for summary judgment, concluding that Pergament was entitled to the easement, and the court of appeals affirmed the district court. We conclude that the easement had been extinguished and we reverse.

On September 19, 1986, BSR Properties entered into a contract for deed with Willow Street Properties to purchase property that included an apartment building, an office building and a parking lot. On November 20, 1987, the City of Minneapolis approved a plan to subdivide the property into two separate parcels, one parcel containing the apartment building, the other parcel containing the office building and parking lot. On December 22, 1987, BSR acquired fee title to the apartment building. To obtain the purchase money for this transaction, BSR obtained a loan from Midwest Federal Savings and Loan and agreed to secure the loan with a mortgage to the apartment building.

Before lending BSR the money, Midwest Federal required that BSR obtain from Willow, the contract-vendor, a parking easement for the benefit of the apartment building, allowing use of eight parking spaces in the parking lot adjacent to the office building. This easement was created by a declaration dated December 22, 1987.

On July 28, 1988, BSR paid to Willow the balance due on the contract for deed and acquired fee title to the remaining property, the office building and parking lot. BSR financed the transaction with a loan from Canada Life Assurance Company and, to secure the loan, BSR gave Canada Life a mortgage to the office building and parking lot. By becoming fee owner of the office building/parking lot, as well as the apartment building, BSR united title to the easement's dominant and servient estates.

On December 20, 1990, BSR conveyed the office building/parking lot to Canada Life by deed in lieu of foreclosure. The parking easement was mentioned in the deed. On September 30, 1993, Canada Life sold the office building/parking lot to Loring Properties. The easement was not mentioned in the deed but was referred to in the title insurance policy.

On February 28, 1997, BSR sold the apartment property to Pergament and, incidental to the transaction, Midwest Federal's mortgage was satisfied. Although the deed from BSR to Pergament mentioned the easement, Pergament admitted that he was unaware of it when he purchased the apartment building. From the date the easement was created, all parking spaces in the parking lot were used exclusively in conjunction with the office building and were never assigned to nor used by apartment residents.

When Pergament discovered that the easement was mentioned in his deed, he requested that Loring Properties designate eight of the parking spaces in its parking lot for use by apartment residents. Pergament's request was denied and he brought an action in district court for a judgment declaring that he was entitled to an easement for the parking spaces. The district court granted Pergament's motion for summary judgment and the court of appeals affirmed. See Pergament v. Loring Properties, Ltd., 586 N.W.2d 778 (Minn. App. 1998).

The Merger Doctrine

Under the merger doctrine, an easement that benefits the dominant estate and burdens the servient estate is extinguished when fee title to each estate is united in one owner.[1] In his treatise, The Law Of Real Property, Professor Powell explains

---

[1] The merger doctrine is defined in the Restatement (First) of Property, Servitudes § 497 (1944):

> An easement appurtenant is extinguished by unity of ownership of estates in the dominant and servient tenements to the extent to which the uses which could have been made prior to the unity by virtue of ownership of the estate in the dominant tenement can be made after the unity by virtue of ownership of the estate in the servient tenement.

The comment to this section explains:

> If the two tracts come into common ownership they cannot continue to be dominant and servient, and the easement appurtenant ceases to exist because, though the privileges of use once authorized by it still exist, they are no longer incidental to the ownership of the dominant

that the reason for the doctrine is that one cannot have, indeed has no need for, an easement in property one owns in fee. See 4 Richard R. Powell, The Law of Real Property § 34.22 (Patrick J. Rohan ed., 1997). Thus, in July 1988 when BSR obtained fee title to the servient estate (the office building/parking lot), BSR held fee title to both the dominant estate (the apartment building) and the servient estate and, under the merger doctrine, the parking easement was extinguished as to BSR and its successors in interest. See Sorkil v. Strom, 194 N.W. 333, 334 (Minn. 1923) (stating that "when an owner of an estate enjoys an easement over another estate and acquires title to the latter the easement is thereby extinguished").

Once extinguished, an easement is not revived or reinstated when referred to in a subsequent conveyance. See Caroga Realty Co. v. Tapper, 143 N.W.2d 215, 226 n. 3 (Minn. 1966); see also Werner v. Sample, 107 N.W.2d 43, 44 (Minn. 1961) (concluding that reference to an extinguished easement does not create or revive an easement, "it presupposes an existing easement"); United Parking Stations, Inc. v. Calvary Temple, 101 N.W.2d 208, 212 (Minn. 1960) (holding that a recital in a contract for deed does not reinstate or recreate a previously extinguished easement). Therefore, the extinguished parking easement was not revived as to BSR or its successors simply because the deeds conveying the property mentioned the easement.

The Mortgage Exception

Under the mortgage exception to the merger doctrine, the mortgagee of the dominant estate is protected from losing its interest in an easement otherwise extinguished when fee title to the dominant estate and fee title to the servient estate have been united in one fee owner.[2] This exception is grounded in equity and is intended to protect the mortgagee of the dominant estate from losing the value of its interest in an easement that is otherwise extinguished. See Duval v. Becker, 32 A. 308, 309-10 (Md. 1895) (stating that allowing an extinguishment of the mortgagee's interest "would jeopardize, if not wholly destroy the stability of every mortgage as security"). Thus, even though fee ownership of the dominant and servient estates was eventually merged in BSR, Midwest Federal's interest in the

---

tenement but have become incidents of the ownership of what was formerly the servient tenement.

Restatement (First) of Property, Servitudes § 497 cmt. a. The proposed Restatement (Third) of Property, Servitudes § 7.5, would clarify this rule. It states:

A servitude is terminated when all the benefits and burdens come into a single ownership. Transfer of a previously benefited or burdened parcel into separate ownership does not revive a servitude terminated under the rule of this section.

Restatement (Third) of Property, Servitudes § 7.5 (Tentative Draft No. 6, 1997).

[2] The mortgage exception to the merger doctrine is defined in the Restatement (First) of Property, Servitudes § 497 cmt. d:

[I]f either a dominant or servient tenement held in fee is subject to a power of termination or to an executory interest, and the fee ownership in the dominant tenement is united with the fee ownership in the servient tenement, the power of termination or the executory interest remains unaffected by such unity. Accordingly, if the power of termination or the executory interest becomes possessory, the possessory estate is entitled to the benefit, or remains subject to the burden, of the easement.

parking easement was not extinguished. If Midwest Federal's mortgagee interest[3] in the apartment building would have become possessory, Midwest Federal would have had the benefit of the parking easement and the servient estate, the office building/parking lot, would have had the burden of the easement. Therefore, under the mortgage exception, Midwest Federal retained its inchoate interest in the parking easement until the mortgage was satisfied.

Pergament argues, however, that the mortgage exception to the merger doctrine prevented BSR's interest in the easement from being extinguished and therefore prevents his interest, as BSR's successor, from being extinguished. Pergament would extend the mortgage exception to the merger doctrine so that as long as Midwest Federal had a protected mortgage interest in the parking easement, the easement could not be extinguished as to anyone who later acquired the apartment property. Under Pergament's theory, a mortgage acts as a shield to defeat the merger doctrine. Relying on Schwoyer v. Smith, 131 A.2d 385 (Pa. 1957), both the district court and the court of appeals agreed with Pergament that the mortgagee's interest in the easement prevented the merger doctrine from extinguishing the easement even as to the fee owner and its successors.

Upon close reading, however, *Schwoyer* does not support the lower courts' expansion of the mortgage exception to the merger doctrine. In *Schwoyer*, as in our case, the dominant and servient estates were united in one ownership, then sold to separate owners. *Id.* at 386. One of the owners sought to enforce an easement running to the benefit of the dominant estate and burdening the servient estate. The owner of the servient estate argued that the merger doctrine extinguished the easement because the previous owner of the servient estate had acquired the dominant estate. The Pennsylvania Supreme Court rejected the merger argument and held that the easement was not extinguished. The critical distinction between *Schwoyer* and our case is that in *Schwoyer*, the dominant estate was acquired by mortgage foreclosure. Therefore, the party that acquired the dominant estate by mortgage foreclosure obtained all the rights and interests the mortgagee held, including the rights and interests in the easement. By contrast, Pergament acquired the apartment property from the mortgagor, BSR, and therefore acquired only those interests BSR held at the time of the conveyance. Under the doctrine of merger, BSR's interest in the easement was extinguished and therefore BSR's successor in interest, Pergament, could not have acquired any interest in the easement from BSR.

Conclusion

The merger doctrine is intended to extinguish easements when title to the dominant and servient estates are united in one fee owner simply because one has no need for an easement in property one owns in fee. By concluding that an easement may never be extinguished while there is a mortgage on the dominant estate, the lower court decisions have distorted the mortgage exception to the

---

[3] In Minnesota a mortgage is a lien on property and not an estate in property. See Minn.Stat. § 559.17, subd. 1 (1998); Mutual Benefit Life Ins. Co. v. Frantz Klodt & Son, 237 N.W.2d 350, 353 (Minn. 1975).

merger doctrine. This exception is intended only to protect the mortgagee of the dominant estate, should its interest become possessory, from losing the full value of its security interests, including the benefit of any easement.

We conclude that the easement was extinguished as to BSR and its assigns and successors, including Pergament, when BSR united fee title to the dominant and servient estates and we reverse and remand to the district court and direct that judgment be entered accordingly.

Reversed.

NOTE

See Sarah Stolpman, Case Note, *To Merge or Not to Merge: Determining the Scope of the Mortgage Exception to the Merger Doctrine*, 27 Wm. Mitchell L. Rev. 1331 (2000).

d.   Termination Pursuant to Statute

H & F LAND, INC., v. PANAMA CITY-BAY COUNTY AIRPORT
736 So. 2d 1167 (Fla. 1999)

[For the report of this case, see Section 5.D.1.e, above.]

D. NEGATIVE EASEMENTS

Return to the examples of easements given at the beginning of this chapter. The first two examples illustrate *affirmative* easements — servitudes that give the benefitted party the right either to physically enter the servient land, or to transmit noises, smoke, odors, and the like onto the servient land. Were it not for the servitude, B's physical intrusion onto A's land would be barred by the law of trespass (recall Jacque v. Steenburg Homes in Chapter 1), and B's use of A's land as a dump for the objectionable particulate or other matter would be prohibited by the law of nuisance (recall Adams v. Cleveland Cliffs Iron Co. in Chapter 1). Except for the easement in Witter v. Taggart, the easements in all of our principal cases up to this point have been affirmative easements.

The third example given at the beginning of the chapter illustrates a *negative* easement. In a negative easement, the beneficiary does not acquire the right to make a physical or "constructive" intrusion onto the servient estate; rather, the beneficiary acquires a right to prevent the servient owner from using the servient owner's own land in some way that, were it not for the servitude, the servient owner would be privileged to make. *See* Prospect Dev. Co. v. Bershader, 515 S.E.2d 291, 299 (Va. 1999) ("[A] negative easement does not bestow upon the owner of the dominant tract the right to travel physically upon the servient estate, but rather requires that the owner of the servient estate refrain from undertaking certain activities on the servient estate which the owner would otherwise be entitled to perform."). The terms "affirmative" and "negative" focus on the *beneficiary* of the easement, and identify the different kind of right or power over the servient estate that the easement beneficiary holds.

As the principal case below notes, the common law was restrictive towards negative easements, recognizing only four. The case also shows that at least some American courts do not regard themselves bound by the limitations of the inherited common law of easements. The question of the expandability of the negative easement category is important. An obligation that cannot be enforced as an easement will be enforced, if at all, as a real covenant or equitable servitude (Chapter 7). Generally, it is advantageous for a plaintiff to be able to present his or her case as an easement. In addition to its elaboration of the importance of the negative easement category, the principal case also furthers our understanding of an easement "in gross," which we introduced in Note 6 after Walton v. Capital Land Co., at the beginning of this chapter.

UNITED STATES v. BLACKMAN
613 S.E.2d 442 (Va. 2005)

KOONTZ, JUSTICE.

[T]he United States District Court for the Western District of Virginia ("district court"), by its order entered October 21, 2004, certified to this Court the following question of law: In Virginia in 1973, would a conveyance of a negative easement in gross by a private property owner to a private party for the purpose of land conservation and historic preservation be valid? By order entered January 3, 2005, we accepted the certified question.

BACKGROUND

The Green Springs Historic District (the "District") is an area of roughly 14,000 acres in Louisa County that was settled in the 1700s. Much of the land in this area has historically been used for agricultural purposes, and this agricultural setting remains today. Because the land has been continuously farmed for almost three centuries, many of the homes and farms have been preserved in their original context with little alteration. In the early 1970s, the Commonwealth of Virginia bought two hundred acres of land in the Green Springs area with the intention of building a prison. There was much local opposition, and some landowners expressed the belief that the prison would damage the character of their historic community. Reacting to this opposition, the then-governor of Virginia announced in 1972 that the state would not build the prison facility in the area if that area could be preserved. In response to the governor's challenge, local citizens organized a non-profit group dubbed Historic Green Springs, Inc. ("HGSI"), which obtained donations of easements for land conservation and historic preservation from landowners and initiated an effort to have the area designated as a National Historic Landmark District. The Green Springs Historic District was listed on the National Register of Historic Places in March of 1973, and was ultimately designated as a National Historic Landmark in 1974.

By a "Deed of Easement" dated March 19, 1973 (the "Easement"), D.L. Atkins and Frances Atkins granted to HGSI an assignable easement over several parcels of their property, including Eastern View Farm. The Easement states in part that "in consideration of the grant to the Grantee of similar easements in gross by other owners of land in the said Green Springs Historic District for similar purposes, the Grantors [D.L. Atkins and Frances Atkins] do hereby grant and convey to the Grantee [HGSI] an easement in gross restricting in perpetuity, in the manner hereinafter set forth, the use of the following described tracts of land, together with the improvements erected thereon." In 1978, HGSI decided to convey its entire portfolio of easements to the United States. In the resulting deed of easement to the United States, all of the original grantors of similar easements within the District acknowledged their agreement to the conveyance by affixing their signatures to the deed. The National Park Service ("NPS") now administers these easements, including the Easement at issue, on behalf of the United States as part of the Green Springs National Historic Landmark District. The Easement at issue provides that the manor house on Eastern View Farm:

> will be maintained and preserved in its present state as nearly as practicable, though structural changes, alterations, additions, or improvements as would not in the opinion of the Grantee fundamentally alter its historic character or its setting may be made thereto by the owner, provided that the prior written approval of the Grantee to such change, alteration, addition, or improvements shall have been obtained. This provision applies as well to those 18th and 19th Century outbuildings located on the described property.

Peter F. Blackman ("Blackman") purchased Eastern View Farm on July 1, 2002. Blackman wishes to renovate and rehabilitate the manor house. Specifically, Blackman seeks to remove the existing front porch on the manor house, replace the siding, and create an addition. In support of these intended alterations, Blackman submitted several sets of renovation plans to the NPS for review, but the NPS repeatedly denied certain aspects of his plans. Rather than working with the NPS for final approval of his plan, Blackman's attorney stated in a latter dated January 13, 2004 that Blackman would "commence the Rehabilitation at a time of his choosing, without further notice to [NPS], in accordance with the attached elevations." Subsequently, Blackman removed the porch from his house. The United States filed the complaint in this case June 14, 2004, and on June 16, 2004 Judge James C. Turk issued a temporary restraining order restraining Blackman from "commencing and/or continuing renovation work to the manor house located on the Eastern View Parcel, in the Green Springs National Historic Landmark District, unless he has first obtained written approval from the National Park Service." In defense of his actions, Blackman argues that the original deed of easement granted to HGSI was invalid because at the time it was purportedly created, Virginia law did not recognize any kind of negative easement in gross, including such easements for the purpose of land conservation and historic preservation.

DISCUSSION

The question certified by the district court presents the issue of law whether, in 1973, the law of Virginia permitted an individual landowner to grant a negative easement in gross to a third party for the purpose of land conservation and historic preservation. As indicated by the district court, if the law of this Commonwealth did not recognize the validity of such an easement at that time, then the purported property restrictions granted to HGSI are invalid and would be unenforceable by HGSI's transferee, the United States. Although previously we have not addressed the issue of the validity of a negative easement in gross under the law existing in 1973, the issue is of considerable significance beyond the specific historic district involved in this case. By the brief of *amici curiae* filed in this case, we are advised that at least seven other charitable entities hold conservation or historic preservation easements, many of them easements in gross, conveyed prior to 1973, [and] that thousands of acres and numerous historically significant sites and buildings located in this Commonwealth are currently protected by easements of the type at issue in this case. Underlying the issue is a degree of apparent conflict between the common law preference for unrestricted rights of ownership of real property and the public policy of this Commonwealth as expressed in Article XI of the Constitution of Virginia, ratified by the people of this Commonwealth in 1970, that "it shall be the policy of this Commonwealth to conserve its historical sites and buildings." Accordingly, we take this opportunity to discuss in some detail the relevant law.

"An easement is a privilege without profit, which the owner of one tenement has a right to enjoy in respect of that tenement in or over the tenement of another person; by reason whereof the latter is obliged to suffer, or refrain from doing something on his own tenement for the advantage of the former." Amstutz v. Everett Jones Lumber Corp., 604 S.E.2d 437, 441 (Va. 2004). Easements are described as being "affirmative" easements when they convey privileges on the part of one person or owner of land (the "dominant tract") to use the land of another (the "servient tract") in a particular manner or for a particular purpose. Easements are described as being "negative" when they convey rights to demand that the owner of the servient tract refrain from certain otherwise permissible uses of his own land. Negative easements do not bestow upon the owner of the dominant tract the right to travel physically upon the servient tract, which is the feature common to all affirmative easements, but only the legal right to object to a use of the servient tract by its owner inconsistent with the terms of the easement. In this sense, negative easements have been described as consisting solely of "a veto power." Prospect Dev. Co. v. Bershader, 515 S.E.2d 291, 299 (Va. 1999).

At common law, an owner of land was not permitted at his pleasure to create easements of every novel character and annex them to the land so that the land would be burdened with the easement when the land was conveyed to subsequent grantees. Rather, the landowner was limited to the creation of easements permitted by the common law or by statute. The traditional negative easements recognized at common law were those created to protect the flow of air, light, and artificial streams of water, and to ensure the subjacent and lateral support of buildings or land. See Andrew Dana & Michael Ramsey, *Conservation Easements and the Common Law*, 8 Stan. Envtl. L.J. 2, 13 (1989).

Easements, whether affirmative or negative, are classified as either "appurtenant" or "in gross." An easement appurtenant has both a dominant and a servient tract and is capable of being transferred or inherited. It frequently is said that an easement appurtenant "runs with the land," which is to say that the benefit conveyed by or the duty owed under the easement passes with the ownership of the land to which it is appurtenant. The four negative easements traditionally recognized at common law are, by their nature, easements appurtenant, as their intent is to benefit an adjoining or nearby parcel of land. See Federico Cheever, *Environmental Law: Public Good and Private Magic in the Law of Land Trusts and Conservation Easements: A Happy Present and a Troubled Future*, 73 Denv. U.L.Rev. 1077, 1081 (1996).

In contrast, an easement in gross is an easement "which is not appurtenant to any estate in land, but in which the servitude is imposed upon land with the benefit thereof running to an individual." Lester Coal Corp. v. Lester, 122 S.E.2d 901, 904 (Va. 1961). At common law, easements in gross were strongly disfavored because they were viewed as interfering with the free use of land. Thus, the common law rule of long standing is that an easement is "never presumed to be in gross when it [can] fairly be construed to be appurtenant to land." French v. Williams, 4 S.E. 591, 594 (Va. 1886). For an easement to be treated as being in gross, the deed or other instrument granting the easement must plainly manifest that the parties so intended.

Because easements in gross were disfavored by the common law, they could neither be transferred by the original grantee nor pass by inheritance. By statute, however, Virginia long ago abrogated common law restrictions on the transfer of interests in land "by declaring that any interest in or claim to real estate may be disposed of by deed or will." Carrington v. Goddin, 54 Va. (13 Gratt.) 587, 599-600 (1857). Pursuant to this statutory change in the common law rule, currently embodied in Code § 55-6, we have recognized that an affirmative easement in gross is an interest in land that may be disposed of by deed or will. City of Richmond v. Richmond Sand & Gravel Co., 96 S.E. 204, 207 (Va. 1918). Following this Court's decision in *Lester Coal Corp., supra*, 122 S.E.2d at 904, which in dictum made reference to the common law rule that easements in gross remained nontransferable by deed or will, Code § 55-6 was amended "to make clear the transferability of easements in gross." Since 1962, Code § 55-6, in pertinent part, has expressly provided that "[a]ny interest in or claim to real estate, *including easements in gross*, may be disposed of by deed or will." (Emphasis added.)

Code § 55-6 unambiguously speaks to "easements in gross" as interests in real estate capable of disposition by deed or will. There is no suggestion in this language that the statute was intended to apply only to affirmative easements in gross and not to negative easements in gross. The significance of this statutory change in the common law is manifest. Easements in gross, whether affirmative or negative, are now recognized interests in real property, rather than merely personal covenants not capable of being disposed of by deed or will as was the case under common law. Moreover, as pertinent to the present inquiry, such was the case well before 1973 in this Commonwealth.

The 1962 amendment and clarification of Code § 55-6 with regard to the transferability of easements in gross has facilitated, in part, Virginia's long recognition of the value of conserving and preserving the natural beauty and historic sites and buildings in which it richly abounds. In 1966, the General Assembly enacted the Open-Space Land Act. This Act, currently found in Code §§ 10.1-1700 through -1705, is intended to encourage the acquisition by certain public bodies of fee simple title or "easements in gross or such other interests in real estate" that are designed to maintain the preservation or provision of open-space land. Code § 10.1-1703. By definition, open-space land includes land that is preserved for "historic or scenic purposes." Code § 10.1-1700. Additionally, in 1966, the General Assembly enacted statutes creating the Virginia Outdoors Foundation, and the Virginia Historic Landmarks Commission. As currently expressed in Code § 10.1-1800, the purpose of the Virginia Outdoors Foundation is "to promote the preservation of open-space lands." The Virginia Historic Landmarks Commission, now known as the Virginia Board of Historic Resources, was charged with the designation of historic landmarks and districts. 1966 Va. Acts ch. 632, § 4(A). These statutes evince a strong public policy in favor of land conservation and preservation of historic sites and buildings. [T]his public policy was expressly embodied in Article XI of the Constitution of Virginia which, since 1970, has provided:

> § 1. To the end that the people have clean air, pure water, and the use and enjoyment for recreation of adequate public lands, waters, and other natural resources, it shall be the policy of the Commonwealth to conserve, develop, and utilize its natural resources, its public lands, and its historical sites and buildings. Further, it shall be the Commonwealth's policy to protect its atmosphere, lands, and waters from pollution, impairment, or destruction, for the benefit, enjoyment, and general welfare of the people of the Commonwealth.

> § 2. In the furtherance of such policy, the General Assembly may undertake the conservation, development, or utilization of lands or natural resources of the Commonwealth, the acquisition and protection of historical sites and buildings, and the protection of its atmosphere, lands, and waters from pollution, impairment, or destruction, by agencies of the Commonwealth or by the creation of public authorities, or by leases or other contracts with agencies of the United States, with other states, with units of government in the Commonwealth, or with private persons or corporations.

In further support of this public policy, the General Assembly in 1988 enacted the Virginia Conservation Easement Act ("VCEA"), Code §§ 10.1-1009 through 10.1-1016. In pertinent part, as defined in the VCEA a conservation easement is "a nonpossessory interest of a holder in real property, whether easement appurtenant or in gross, the purposes of which include retaining or protecting natural or open-space values of real property or preserving the historical, architectural or archaeological aspects of real property." Code § 10.1-1009.

Mindful of this background, we now consider the validity of the negative easement in gross granted to HGSI by the Atkinses in the 1973 deed and subsequently conveyed, with the Atkinses' concurrence, to the United States in

1978. The validity of that easement is dependent upon whether it was a type of negative easement that would have been recognized by the law of Virginia in 1973. For the reasons that follow, we conclude that the 1973 deed created a valid easement.

Blackman contends that a negative easement in gross for the purpose of land conservation and historic preservation was not valid in this Commonwealth until 1988 with the enactment of the VCEA. The thrust of this contention is that the VCEA would have been unnecessary if such easements were already valid. We are not persuaded by this contention.

Blackman's contention suggests an analysis devoid of due consideration of the pertinent statutory and constitutional provisions in effect in the Commonwealth long before the 1988 enactment of the VCEA. As discussed above, Code § 55-6 since at least 1962 has recognized easements in gross, whether affirmative or negative, as interests in real property capable of being transferred by deed or will. Because easements in gross were not transferable at common law and, indeed, were strongly disfavored, it is self-evident that this statute materially changed the common law and recognized "interest[s] in or claim[s] to real estate" beyond those traditionally recognized at common law. Moreover, in the subsequent 1966 enactment of the Open-Space Land Act, the General Assembly specifically recognized easements in gross when it authorized acquisition by certain public bodies of easements in gross in real property which is preserved for historic purposes. Such easements under that Act, under certain circumstances, would be negative easements in gross. Accordingly, while we continue to be of opinion that "the law will not permit a land-owner to create easements of every novel character and attach them to the soil," Tardy v. Creasey, 81 Va. (6 Hans.) 553, 557 (Va. 1886), the easement at issue in the present case is not of a novel character and is consistent with the statutory recognition of negative easements in gross for conservation and historic purposes.

More specifically, it does not necessarily follow that conservation easements were not valid in this Commonwealth prior to the enactment of the VCEA. There is ample evidence that similar interests in land were already recognized by statute under the Open-Space Land Act. Moreover, as referenced by the *amici curiae* in their brief, it is a matter of public record that conservation easements or similar interests in land, far from being unique to the Historic Green Springs conservation effort, have been in common use in Virginia for many years before the adoption of the VCEA.

In enacting the VCEA, the General Assembly undertook to comprehensively address various land interests that can be used for conserving and preserving the natural and historical nature of property. In so doing, the General Assembly addressed the use of such easements in a manner consistent with Code § 55-6, the Open-Space Land Act, and the public policy favoring land conservation and preservation of historic sites and buildings in the Commonwealth as expressed in the Constitution of Virginia. The readily apparent purpose of the VCEA was to codify and consolidate the law of conservation easements to promote the granting of such easements to charitable organizations. When so viewed, it is clear that the VCEA did not create a new right to burden land by a negative easement in gross for the purpose of land conservation and historic preservation. Rather, it facilitated the continued creation of such easements by providing a clear statutory framework under which tax exemptions are made available to charitable organizations devoted to those purposes and tax benefits and incentives are provided to the grantors of such easements.

The fact that such easements were being conveyed without these benefits and incentives prior to the enactment of the VCEA does not support Blackman's contention that these easements were invalid at that time. To the contrary, Virginia not only was committed to encouraging and supporting land conservation and the preservation of historic sites and buildings in the Commonwealth, as evidenced by the constitutional and statutory expressions of that public policy discussed *supra*, but also recognized negative easements in gross created for these purposes as valid in 1973. Indeed, as noted by the district court, the granting of conservation easements by the landowners in the Historic Green Springs District was the direct result of the encouragement by the Governor for the express purpose of preserving the historic and natural beauty of that unique area.

For these reasons, we hold that the law of Virginia in 1973 did recognize as valid a negative easement in gross created for the purpose of land conservation and historic preservation. Accordingly, we answer the first certified question in the affirmative.

NOTES AND QUESTIONS

1. **Easements in gross; transferability.** The court uses Virginia's recognition in the 1960s of a *transferable* easement in gross — an interest not recognized at common law — as partial support for its conclusion that another new interest — a *negative* easement outside of the common law four — was also recognized in Virginia at the time of the Atkinses' transfer of an easement to HGSI. We considered the transferability of in-gross easement benefits in Section A.2.c above. Our present concern is with the expandability of the category of negative easements.

2. **Negative easements: common law and American law.** As the principal case notes, the common law category of negative easements was "strictly limited" to the following four: easements for light, air, flow from a stream, and support for buildings. *See* F.H. Lawson & Bernard Rudden, The Law of Property 129-30 (2d ed. 1982). *See also* 2 American Law of Property § 9.13, at 373 (suggesting that the negative easement category is limited to those recognized at common law). The easement recognized in the principal case is not one of the common law four, nor are the easements recognized in the following cases: Prospect Dev. Co. v. Bershader, 515 S.E.2d 291 (Va. 1999) (recognizing easement barring developer from building on land that developer represented to be "preserved land"); Petersen v. Friedman, 328 P.2d 264 (Cal. Ct. App. 1958) (recognizing a negative easement of view created by reservation when owner of two hillside lots transferred the lower lot). (Question: although an easement of view resembles an easement for light and air, how does it differ?) Witter v. Taggart, reprinted in Section 5.D.1.d and discussed in Section A.2.a above, also illustrates a negative easement of view, but the question of its validity under common law doctrine was not raised. The principal case shows that the question of the elasticity of the

negative easement category remains a live issue in American easement law.

3. **Negative easements: policy.** The common law restriction on new types of negative easements was based in part on public policy. Because England lacked a recording system until the 20th century, a purchaser of land could discover servitudes only by inspection; unlike an affirmative easement, a negative easement leaves no physical traces on the servient estate and thus is difficult to discover. In addition, since negative easements could be created by prescription (adverse use for the period of the statute of limitations), any enlargement of the negative easement category would have increased the opportunity for unbargained-for restrictions on the development of the servient estate. *See* Jesse Dukeminier, James E. Krier, Gregory S. Alexander & Michael H. Schill, Property 736-737 (6th ed. 2006). These policy objections are unpersuasive in American law, which protects bona fide purchasers against unrecorded and undiscoverable easements, and which protects the servient owner's freedom to use the land by refusing to recognize the creation of negative easements by prescription.

4. **Negative easements: concepts.** Professors Dukeminier and Krier also note that the common law prohibition against new negative easements had a conceptual basis. Unlike possessory interests, which were created by physical livery of seisin, easements at common law were created by a written conveyance containing the grant or reservation of the easement. To the common law mind, an easement right had to be one that the judges could regard as capable of creation by a conveyance, and English judges had difficulty imagining the conveyance of a negative right. *Id.* at 737. *See also* Restatement of Property § 450(e) (1944) (easement must be "capable of creation by conveyance"). To elaborate the "conveyability" point, consider an affirmative easement: an owner, A, has a right to use A's own land; in granting a right of way to B, A transfers to B the same right that A has, the right to use A's land. In the case of a negative easement, however, although A "relinquishes his right to use his land or a portion of it in a certain specified manner," the grantee "does not acquire the right relinquished but instead obtains the power to enforce the restriction against the landowner." D. Gregory, *The Easement as a Conservation Technique* 19 (International Union for Conservation of Nature and Natural Resources, Environmental Law Paper No. 1, 1972).

One would not expect this metaphysical difficulty to trouble modern American courts, and it has not. *See* Reichert v. Weeden, 618 P.2d 1216, 1219 (Mont. 1980) (servient owner's agreement to refrain from using his land as a tavern after a specified date created a negative easement; servient owners "took away from the land [the right to sell liquor or operate a bar] and conveyed it to defendants by means of a written, recorded agreement. They gave away an interest in the land by creating a negative easement binding not only themselves, but [also] their heirs and assigns"). *See also* Fuller v. Arms, 45 Vt. 400 (1873) (grantor's right of view over the servient estate was the proper subject for a reservation in the deed to the servient estate).

5. **Environmental easements.** Solar and conservation easements are important modern examples of negative easements: in the former, landowner A agrees not to obstruct B's access to sunlight; in the latter, landowner A agrees, usually with a state agency or conservation organization, to leave the land in its

natural (undeveloped) condition. *See generally* John Wiley, *Private Land Use Controls as Barriers to Solar Development: The Need for State Legislation*, 1 Solar L. Rptr. 281 (1979); Jeffrey A. Blackie, Note, *Conservation Easements and the Doctrine of Changed Conditions*, 40 Hastings L.J. 1187 (1989). Because of the modern importance of conservation of land and the development of alternative energy sources, the question of the possibility of new negative easements is critically important. To avoid doubts, legislation in many states expressly validates conservation and solar easements, and provides the criteria for their creation. For a listing of statutes validating conservation easements, see Restatement Third § 1.6, Statutory Note, at 39-44.

6. **Informal negative easements.** A negative easement cannot be created by prior use, necessity, or prescription. *See* Restatement Third § 2.12 cmt. b (prior use); Maiorellora v. Arlotta, (necessity); *cf.* Restatement Third § 2.12 cmt. b (necessity); Hefazi v. Stiglitz, 862 A.2d 901, 911 (D.C. 2004) (prescription: "[I]t is well settled that a *negative* easement [here, for light and air] cannot be created by prescription."); Fontainebleau Hotel Corp. v. Forty-Five Twenty-Five Inc., 114 So. 2d 357 (Fla. Dist. Ct. App. 1959) (prescription); Walter Henry Cook, *Legal Analysis in the Law of Prescriptive Easements*, 15 S. Cal. L. Rev. 44, 50-51 (1941) (prescription). However, a negative easement can be created by estoppel. *See* Prospect Dev. Co. v. Bershader, 515 S.E.2d 291 (Va. 1999). What might be the reasons for the general refusal of courts to recognize informal negative easements, and for the exception for easements by estoppel?

NOTES ON ANCIENT LIGHTS AND SPITE FENCES

1. **An easement for light and air: the doctrine of "ancient lights."** Under the English lost grant theory of prescriptive easements, landowner B's "acquiescence" in A's adverse use of B's land for the period of the statute of limitations raises an irrebutable presumption that the use originated in the express grant of the easement to A. Since a negative easement may be created by express grant, it follows from the lost grant theory of prescription that a negative easement may be acquired by prescription. Accordingly, the English doctrine of "ancient lights" recognized B's right to a prescriptive negative easement if B maintained a window near A's boundary line for the period of the statute of limitations; A's acquiescence in B's access to light and air for the statutory period created a right in B to bar A from building too close to the boundary line so as to diminish the pre-existing quantity of light and air. American courts have uniformly rejected the English doctrine of ancient lights; B may not acquire a negative easement by prescription. *See* Fontainebleau Hotel Corp. v. Forty-Five Twenty-Five, Inc., 114 So. 2d 357 (Fla. Dist. Ct. App. 1959).

2. **Corollary doctrine: spite fences.** To protect herself from B's acquisition of a prescriptive easement, A had to build a fence or wall obstructing B's window before the prescriptive period expired. Since such a wall always served at least one good purpose — prevention of B's acquisition of a negative easement — the English courts, as "a useful corollary to the doctrine of ancient lights," Curtis Berger, Land Ownership and Use 547 (3d ed. 1983), took the view that an inquiry into the fence builder's motives was improper. *That* refusal led to the English doctrine of "spite fences," under which a court will not enjoin a structure on B's

land erected purely to harass or spite B's neighbor. Although American courts have uniformly rejected the English doctrine of ancient lights, the corollary spite fence doctrine — no inquiry into the fence builder's motive is allowed — exists in American law in a minority of states. The majority view is that a court of equity, "even in the absence of a statute, will usually enjoin as a private nuisance a spite structure serving no useful purpose." *Id.* at 548. Statutes barring the erection of structures intended to harass a neighbor exist; the statutes, as you might expect, leave questions of interpretation for the courts. *See, e.g.,* Dalton v. Bua, 822 A.2d 392 (Conn. Super. Ct. 2003) (hedge was not a "structure" under malicious structure statute):

> The walls and fences at issue in the malicious structure cases decided since 1867 have been constructions built by persons. Hedges, however, grow naturally. There is no suggestion that the hedge in question here was maliciously planted. The suggestion, rather, is that it has maliciously been allowed to grow [blocking the plaintiffs' view of Long Island Sound]. Rather than, "Don't build it," the Daltons want the law to say, "You must trim it." This is a significant difference. The complaint is not that the Buas have *done* something. Whatever the problems of the action/inaction distinction in the tort or criminal law, that distinction lies at the heart of the malicious structure statutes in question here. These statutes prohibit malicious "structures" from being "erected." They do not require naturally growing plantings to be affirmatively trimmed.

> The law is reluctant to compel possessors of land to alter the natural condition of their property; and the courts should be reluctant to interpret ancient statutes like those before it now to impose such a new duty. A statutory duty potentially extending to every tree owner in the state must be imposed by the legislature.

NOTE: WHAT IS AN EASEMENT?

In Chapter 7, we will encounter servitudes that are not easements — they are, instead, either "real covenants" or "equitable servitudes." As you will see, real covenants are analyzed under rules as to running of burden and benefit that differ substantially from the easement rules that we have studied in this chapter. Equitable servitudes, although analytically indistinguishable from easements on most questions, are nevertheless not identical, so that some of their rules also differ from easement rules. As a result, under present American law, the determination of which rules apply in a particular case requires classification of the parties' transaction. On the basis of what we have said so far, and as a transition into Chapter 7, we can offer the following criteria for the identification of an easement.

First, focus on the interest of the beneficiary of the servitude. If the bargain between A and B allows B to go onto A's land (actually or constructively), courts will most likely not experience any difficulty in classifying the transaction as an easement. In other words, the category of affirmative easements is potentially quite large. If the parties' bargain allows B to veto A's use of A's land, *and the veto power falls within the four negative easements recognized at common law,* an

American court should also find little difficulty classifying the servitude as an easement. However, if the veto power is novel (that is, outside of the common law four), a court may conclude that the servitude is not an easement. That, at least, is the suggestion of the venerable American Law of Property treatise. *See* 2 A.L.P. § 9.12, at 373 (possibility of construing a servitude obligation as a negative easement "seems to be limited to those [situations] where the character of the negative duties fits into one of the recognized types of negative easements" at common law). Conversely, the court may allow the new negative easement; you have read one case, United States v. Blackman, and have been cited to several other American cases, doing so. The point is that a negative servitude falling outside of the common law negative easement category is at least a *potential* candidate for treatment as a real covenant or equitable servitude rather than an easement.

Second, focus on the servient owner. Whether B, the benefitted party, is entitled to go onto A's land (affirmative easement) or entitled to veto A's use of that land (negative easement), the *duty* is the same from A's standpoint: it is a negative duty, to refrain either from interfering with B's use of A's land, or from using A's own land in a way that B is entitled to veto. That is to say, neither an affirmative nor a negative easement creates an affirmative *duty* in A. So important is this conceptual point that it is included in the legislative statement of fundamental principles in Article 651 of the Louisiana Civil Code: "The owner of the servient estate is not required to do anything. His obligation is to abstain from doing something on his estate or to permit something to be done on it." *See also id.* cmt. (b) ("servitudes may not involve affirmative duties for the owner of the servient estate").

To summarize: in the present state of American law, some veto powers held by B over A's land use may not qualify as easements, and all affirmative duties imposed on A probably will not qualify as easements. To the extent, however, that the Restatement Third of Property (Servitudes) influences the development of the law, the importance of classification of servitudes will fade, to be replaced with an emphasis on the substantive law.

Chapter 7

PROMISES RUNNING WITH THE LAND

Suppose that you're a developer in the early 19th century. You want to build a residential enclave, entirely free of commercial or industrial uses. You want your enclave to be self-sustaining, capable of paying for the maintenance and repair of the common areas (parks and playgrounds) that you plan to provide in your development. How can you realize your plans? The answer seems simple: make each purchaser agree to use his land only for residential uses, and further agree to shoulder a portion of the cost of upkeep of the common areas. But in order for your plan to endure, those obligations must be capable of running with the land to successors from each of your original buyers. And therein lies the problem.

Negative obligations as easements. Easements create durable obligations, and your residential-use-only restriction resembles a negative easement. But recall that the common law recognized only four negative easements, and yours isn't one of the permissible ones. Although we saw cases (e.g., United States v. Blackman) in which American courts have rejected that limitation, the question of the scope of the negative easement category was certainly an open question in the 19th century and may still be an open question in many American states. *See, e.g.,* 2 A.L.P. § 9.12, at 373 (possibility of construing a servitude obligation as a negative easement "seems to be limited to those covenants where the character of the negative duties fit into one of the recognized types of negative easements" at common law).

Affirmative obligations as easements. Moreover, notice that your buyer's promise to pay maintenance costs creates an *affirmative* obligation. Return again to the easement examples that opened Chapter 6. Recall that the first and second examples are classic "affirmative" easements, while the third example is a classic common law "negative" easement. The terms "affirmative" and "negative" easement, however, refer to the right or power bestowed on the *beneficiary* by the easement — to enter upon or to veto A's use of A's own land, respectively. If we changed the focus to the *servient* owner, we would have to say that the *duty* imposed on that owner by all three easements is a negative duty, not an affirmative one: the servient owner must either refrain from interfering with the beneficiary's use of his land (the affirmative easement examples) or must refrain from making the use of his own land that is prohibited by the terms of the easement (negative easement). In contrast to its tentative statement regarding the exclusivity of the negative easement category, the American Law of Property states unequivocally that "where the [servitude] imposes any affirmative duties upon the covenantor, it is impossible for the court to construe the [servitude] as an easement." 2 A.L.P. § 9.12, at 373. *See also id.* § 9.36, at 438 ("affirmative duties cannot exist" as easements).

In short, from a doctrinal standpoint, you need help if your planned development is to be realized. As this chapter indicates, you will first turn to something called a "real covenant," a category that was established at common law in leases in the 16th century, but hardly used outside of that area since then. For reasons to be indicated, that category will prove ineffective for your purposes. (The category does retain considerable importance, however, in its original setting: covenants made between landlord and tenant.) Then, with the help of the equity courts, you will turn to a much more flexible and easement-like arrangement called an "equitable servitude."

In addition to distinguishing real covenants and equitable servitudes from each other and from easements, this chapter will also ask whether unification of the law of servitudes is not only desirable but also long overdue, a question that comes into particularly sharp focus when consideration is paid to the absurd consequences (considered in Section 7.B) that follow from the law's retention of multiple categories to address functionally similar transactions.

A. ENFORCEMENT OF PROMISES RUNNING WITH THE LAND

Any obligation undertaken between landowners A and B that does not qualify as an easement will be enforceable against A's successor only as a promise running with the land. Traditionally, there are two categories of such promises: real covenants and equitable servitudes. Each category has its own requirements. Determining which requirements apply is relatively simple: if the beneficiary of the promise seeks a damages remedy for breach, the real covenant requirements apply; if the beneficiary seeks equitable relief, the equitable servitude requirements apply. The two categories differ because they originated in different courts — real covenants in the law courts and equitable servitudes in the English Chancery Court.

1. Real Covenants: Enforcement by the Damages Remedy

a. Creation of Covenants

As an interest affecting land use, a real covenant, at least by the better view, must be created in a writing (deed, easement, lease) that complies with the Statute of Frauds, and most covenants in fact are created that way. *See* William B. Stoebuck & Dale A. Whitman, The Law of Property § 8.14, at 474 (3d ed. 2000). Even when the statute requires that an obligation be signed by the party to be charged, the courts have held that a grantee's covenant contained in a deed is enforceable. *Id.* at 474 n.7. The first Restatement of Property explains that result doctrinally on the ground that a promise contained in such a "deed poll" (one not signed by the grantee) is not subject to the Statute of Frauds, and in policy terms on the ground that a transaction consummated by deed "contains the elements of deliberation and certainty of proof the Statute was designed to secure." Restatement of Property § 522(2) & cmt. d, at 3168 (1944).

Although easements, as we have seen, may be created by estoppel, implication, or prescription, it is often stated that real covenants may not. *See, e.g.*, Dukeminier, Krier, Alexander & Schill, Property 868 (6th ed. 2006). The first Restatement of Property, however, does recognize that an "oral promise or representation that certain land will be used in a particular way, though otherwise unenforceable, is enforceable to the extent necessary to protect expenditures made in reasonable reliance upon it." Restatement of Property § 524. The question whether the benefit of a covenant may be created in a third party is considered in Section A.3 below.

Moving from creation to running, you will note from the following case that we enter into a new and strange realm of inquiry.

b.   Running of Burden and Benefit

GALLAGHER v. BELL
516 A.2d 1028 (Md. Ct. Spec. App. 1986)

WILNER, JUDGE.

In 1960, appellants George and Judith Gallagher bought a charming eighteenth century tenant house situated on about a half acre of land in Montgomery County. It was, unfortunately, in the middle of a larger tract owned by appellees [F. Meade Bell and David P. Bell] that was intended for eventual development. [The Bells bought the larger tract in 1959 from the Sisters of Mercy of the Union, who retained the half-acre tract; the Gallaghers bought the half-acre tract from the Sisters a year later. In 1961, in return for the Bells' grant of a temporary right of way easement, the Gallaghers "covenanted and agreed, for themselves, their heirs and assigns, that they will dedicate one-half the streets bounding on their said property and shall share pro rata the cost of installation of said streets and the utilities" by the Bells.]

Years passed without further contact between the parties. The Bells were small developers, building only a few homes a year. [I]n October, 1979, the Gallaghers sold their property to Deborah Camalier. Ms. Camalier, who became aware of the recorded 1961 agreement between the Gallaghers and the Bells, apparently insisted on an indemnity from the Gallaghers. The Gallaghers thereupon signed and delivered to Ms. Camalier this agreement:

> Consonant with the contract of sale of the residence at 9703 Kentsdale Drive, Potomac, Maryland, entered into between George R. and Judith K. Gallagher (sellers) and Deborah Camalier (buyer), on October 22, 1979, sellers agree to indemnify and to save the purchaser harmless against any agreement on file in the courthouse in regard to the expense of the road construction along the property lines of the above residence.

The Bells finally got started on the roads in the area of the Gallagher/Camalier property in 1983. In July of that year, they made demand on Ms. Camalier for some $18,000. When Ms. Camalier refused payment, relying on her indemnity agreement, the Bells made demand on the Gallaghers, and, when they rejected the demand, the Bells filed this lawsuit. It is undisputed that, at the time the suit was filed, the streets for which contribution was sought had not yet been completed.

The Gallaghers defended the action on the basis that the covenant they made in 1961 was a covenant running with the land and that their liability on it terminated when they conveyed the property to Ms. Camalier. If there is any continuing liability on the covenant, they argued, it is that either of Ms. Camalier or Mr. and Mrs. Sindelar, to whom Ms. Camalier conveyed the property in December, 1983. Regarding the nature of the covenant to be a factual matter, however, the court submitted the issue to a jury, which returned a verdict for the Bells in the amount of $7,000.

From the judgment entered on that verdict and the court's refusal to grant a judgment n.o.v., the Gallaghers have brought this appeal. The principal issue before us is whether the Gallaghers have any continuing liability on their promise to pay; that, in turn, depends on whether the promise is to be regarded as a covenant "running with the land" or as a personal promise on their part.

Nature of the Covenant

Covenants made by parties to the conveyance of an interest in land may be regarded as being either personal in nature or as running with the land. The difference, as observed in 5 R. Powell, The Law of Real Property, § 673[1], "hinges upon whether the original covenanting parties' respective rights or duties can devolve upon their successors."

The earliest source generally cited for the concept of a covenant running with the land and being enforceable by or against persons other than the original contracting parties is Spencer's Case, 5 Co.Rep. 16a, 77 Eng.Rep. 72 (QB 1583). The plaintiff there leased certain property to S for a term of 21 years. S, for himself and his executors and administrators, promised in the lease that he, his executors, administrators, or assigns would build a brick wall on the premises. S assigned his leasehold interest to J, who then assigned it to Clark. When the wall was not built, Spencer sued Clark on the covenant. Although the Court denied recovery, it set out in its opinion a number of principles for determining when such extended liability would accrue.

Powell notes that "[t]he elements most often said to be required for covenants to run at law are that: (1) the covenant 'touch and concern' the land; (2) the original covenanting parties intend the covenant to run; and (3) there be some form of privity of estate." A fourth requirement, "sometimes mentioned," is that the covenant be in writing. Powell § 673[1].

(a) Touch and Concern

The "touch and concern" test is a key one. As early as Glenn v. Canby, 24 Md. 127, 130 (1866), the Court announced as "established doctrine" that "a covenant to run with the land must extend to the land, so that the thing required to be done will affect the quality, value, or mode of enjoying the estate conveyed, and thus constitute a condition annexed, or appurtenent to it." See also Whalen v. Baltimore & Ohio R. Co., 108 Md. 11, 20, 69 A. 390 (1908): "The question as to whether the covenant runs with the land does not depend on its being performed on the land itself, but its performance must touch and concern the land, or some right or easement annexed or appurtenant thereto."

Each covenant carries with it a burden (to the covenantor) and a benefit (to the covenantee), and the language used to determine whether the covenant "touches and concerns" the land sometimes depends on whether the assignee in question is the plaintiff or the defendant. The Maryland Court of Appeals, on several occasions, has defined the "touch and concern" test in terms of whether performance of the covenant will "tend necessarily to enhance [the] value [of the land] or render it more convenient or beneficial to the owners or occupants." Whalen v. Baltimore & Ohio R. Co., *supra*, 108 Md. at 20, 69 A. 390. That, of course, looks at the issue essentially from the benefit point of view. Powell, at § 673[2], states that the generally accepted test for the "touch and concern" test is that proposed by Dean Harry Bigelow; i.e.,

> [I]f the covenantor's legal interest in land is rendered less valuable by the covenant's performance, then the burden of the covenant satisfies the requirement that the covenant touch and concern land. If, on the other hand, the covenantee's legal interest in land is rendered more valuable by the covenant's performance, then the benefit of the covenant satisfies the requirement that the covenant touch and concern land.

Both Tiffany (3 H. Tiffany, The Law of Real Property, (3d ed. 1939)) and the Restatement of Property (§ 537 (1944)) generally adopt this more complete way of viewing the criterion. Tiffany states, at § 854, p. 455,

> Ordinarily, a covenant is regarded as touching and concerning the land if it is of value to the covenantee by reason of his occupation of the land or by reason of an easement which he has in the land, or if it is a burden on the covenantor by reason of his occupation of the land.

The [first] Restatement test is not quite the same as that espoused by Dean Bigelow or Tiffany. It provides, in § 537:

> The successors in title to land respecting the use of which the owner has made a promise can be bound as promisors only if
>
>> (a) the performance of the promise will benefit the promisee or other beneficiary of the promise in the physical use or enjoyment of the land possessed by him, or
>>
>> (b) the consummation of the transaction of which the promise is a part will operate to benefit and is for the benefit of the promisor in the physical use or enjoyment of land possessed by him, and the burden on the land of the promisor bears a reasonable relation to the benefit received by the person benefited.

This requires that some aspect of the promise be of benefit in the use and enjoyment of land. Either the promisee must be benefited in the enjoyment of his land or the transaction spawning the promise must benefit the promisor in the enjoyment of the servient land. It would seem that subsection (a) concerns the running of the benefit, whereas subsection (b) sets the standard for the running of the burden. Comment b, for example, states, in relevant part, that "[f]or the burden of a promise to run the promise must be one respecting the use of the land of the promisor." Restatement, *supra*, at p. 3219.

Here, of course, we are concerned only with the running of the burden, for the party seeking to enforce the covenant is the original covenantee. There is no doubt that the covenantees would be benefited by performance of the promise; their interest in their land is obviously rendered more valuable by it. It is equally true that, in terms of Dean Bigelow's test, the Gallaghers' interest in their property was immediately and continually rendered less valuable by the covenant. Even under the Restatement benefit-oriented test, the fact is that, while the particular covenant was a detriment to the Gallaghers, the transaction from which that covenant arose was of benefit to them. In return for their promise, they received a right-of-way that, at least arguably, they did not otherwise have and that was essential to avoid their being landlocked. Appellees throughout have regarded the extension of that right-of-way as valuable consideration and have not suggested that it does not bear a reasonable relation to the burden imposed on the Gallaghers.

Covenants to pay money have often been found to run with the land. See Chesapeake Ranch Club v. CRC Members, 483 A.2d 1334 (Md.App.1984); Powell, *supra*, § 675[2]; American Law of Property, *supra*, § 9.13, pp. 380-82. [T]he Court of Appeals has found covenants to pay rent and taxes, to keep demised or mortgaged property insured, to repair or rebuild such premises, and to build and maintain railroad depots and facilities on conveyed land to "touch and concern" the land. Certainly, this covenant has no lesser connection to the land. Under any of the tests noted, it clearly "touches and concerns" the land owned by the Gallaghers.

(b) Intent

The second factor mentioned by Powell is whether the parties intended the covenant to run with the land. Both the [first] Restatement § 531 and Powell § 673[2][b] make clear that the benefit or the burden of a covenant will not pass to a successor in interest unless the parties intended that result.[9] Unlike the "touch and concern" test, which looks objectively at the nature and quality of the covenant and seeks to measure the relationship between its performance and someone's enjoyment of land, the intention requirement "focuses on the subjective state of mind of the original covenanting parties." Powell, *supra*, § 673[2][b].

The intention of the parties, as to whether a covenant is personal to the covenanting parties or extends to their assignees, "may be ascertained from the language of the conveyances alone or from that language together with other evidence of intent." Gnau v. Kinlein, 217 Md. 43, 48, 141 A.2d 492 (1958). Powell concurs that intent is "sought in the language of [the] transaction, read in the light of the circumstances of its formulation," adding that "[t]echnical words are not generally vital; however, the presence of the word 'assigns' constitutes strong

---

[9] The parties' intent is a co-equal factor with the "touch and concern" criterion. Tiffany states that "[t]he correct rule appears to be that the parties to the covenant may, by indicating an intention to that effect, prevent the covenant from running, although it is such that otherwise it would run, while if the covenant is one which does not touch and concern the land, the parties cannot make it run by indicating an intention or desire that it shall run." 3 Tiffany, *supra*, § 854, p. 461.

evidence of the devolutive intent." Powell, *supra*, at p. 60-51. He continues:

> Judicial decisions as to whether a covenant was intended to be "personal" or to possess the quality of devolution have often relied on particular factors to justify a finding that a covenant was not personal. Factors, for example, strongly favoring the running of the benefit include: (1) the retention of adjacent land by a grantor-convenantee; (2) the benefiting of retained land as a result of the agreement; and (3) the establishment of a common plan of development which includes land retained by the grantor. In some instances, the nature of the covenant may require the conclusion that the requisite intention for the running of the benefit is present. The factors which favor an inference that the burden shall run include the permanent nature of the situation to be produced by the performance of the covenant and the fact that the covenant was made against a background of a common plan of development.

Powell, *supra* at pp. 60-54, -56.

The record here reveals the following: (1) by inserting this same requirement in their contract with the Sisters, appellees made clear their intent to impose the obligation on whoever purchased the half-acre lot, not the Gallaghers in particular; (2) the covenant at issue was in conformance with that requirement and simply confirmed the obligation imposed on Mr. Gallagher by his contract with the Sisters; (3) the covenant at issue expressly extends to the assigns of the Gallaghers; (4) that covenant was intended to benefit adjacent land retained by the covenantee; (5) the time for performance was uncertain and would not necessarily occur while the Gallaghers were in title; (6) the Gallaghers have consistently maintained that the covenant ran with the land; (7) on July 20, 1983 — before commencement of this litigation — appellees filed among the Land Records of Montgomery County a Declaration of Covenant reciting the Gallaghers' sale to Ms. Camalier, asserting that "by virtue of said conveyance, Deborah N. Camalier became the assignee of the Gallaghers *and bound by the aforesaid Agreement regarding pro rata payment of the cost of installation of streets and utilities*" and attesting that the purpose of the Declaration was "to memorialize the pro rata costs *attributable to the Property now owned by the said Deborah N. Camalier*" (emphasis added); (8) at trial, counsel for appellees specifically characterized the 1961 agreement as "a document that constitutes a covenant and runs with the land"; and (9) also at trial, F. Meade Bell, one of the appellees, acknowledged that, because of the inclusion of "heirs and assigns" in the 1961 agreement, he initially sought recovery from Ms. Camalier and that he set his sight on the Gallaghers only because of the indemnity agreement between her and the Gallaghers.

Each of these facts indicates that the covenant was intended to run with the land. Indeed, the last three enumerated above, taken together, constitute a virtual concession by appellees to that effect. Against that, appellees seek to draw an inference that the 1961 covenant was a personal one from (1) the "fact" that they already had a similar covenant running with the land by virtue of the clause in Mr. Gallagher's contract with the Sisters, and (2) the indemnity agreement between the Gallaghers and Ms. Camalier.

We do not regard such an inference as a *reasonable* one. As noted, the contract with the Sisters was not signed by Mrs. Gallagher, and the covenant therein was not included in the deed. It therefore did not directly bind her or her assigns. She became directly bound only by virtue of the 1961 agreement with appellees. If there is an inference to be drawn from the indemnity agreement, it seems to us that it is an unfavorable one to appellees. On this record, the only reasonable inference that can be drawn from the agreement is that Ms. Camalier recognized that, by taking title with knowledge of the recorded 1961 agreement, she would become liable on the covenant and that she desired to have recourse to the original covenantors. As noted, appellees, in their 1983 Declaration of Covenant, shared that view.

On this record, therefore, we think it clear as a matter of law that the parties intended the covenant at issue to run with the land and to bind the assigns of the Gallaghers.

(c) Privity

The requirement that there be privity of estate between the parties in order that a covenant run with the land appears to stem not from Spencer's Case, which mentions the concept of privity only in passing and in connection with leases and conveyances of personalty, but rather from Webb v. Russell, 100 Eng.Rep. 639 (K.B. 1789). The facts of that case were a bit complex and are not especially germane to what is now before us; what is important is Lord Kenyon's pronouncement that "[i]t is not sufficient that a covenant is concerning the land, but, in order to make it run with the land, there must be privity of estate between the covenanting parties." *Webb*, 100 Eng.Rep. at 644. That requirement of privity, which in fact was present in Spencer's Case, became firmly ingrained in the Maryland law. The question is, what kind of privity is required?

Powell points out that there are at least three kinds of privity of estate that have been mentioned by the courts — mutual privity, requiring that the original parties have had a mutual and continuing interest in the same land; [successive] privity, requiring that the covenant be made in connection with the conveyance of an estate in fee from one of the [original] parties to the other; and vertical privity, requiring only that "the person presently claiming the benefit, or being subjected to the burden, is a successor to the estate of the original person so benefited or burdened." Powell, § 673[2]. He further observes that:

> Many modern cases still require some type of privity for covenants to run at law. Unfortunately, there is frequently no consistency as to the type of privity required even within a jurisdiction, and many courts just do not state which type of privity they require. According to one authority, as of 1970, six states which formerly required horizontal privity had abolished the requirement, and it had been expressly adopted in only one state in the twenty-seven years previous to 1970. Modern legal writers unanimously favor the abolition of at least mutual and [successive] privity.

The modern view, rather clearly, is that no more than vertical privity is required. That is also the view of Judge Charles E. Clark, formerly of the Court of Appeals for the Second Circuit and one of the preeminent authorities on the law of covenants. See Clark, Covenants and Interests Running with Land 117 (2d ed. 1947); 165 Broadway Building v. City Investing Co., 120 F.2d 813, 816-17 (2d Cir.) (opinion by Clark, J.).

We see nothing in the Maryland cases heretofore decided precluding our adoption of this modern and, to us, more rational view. Focusing on the precise relationship of the original contracting parties can create artificial results, causing covenants to be regarded as personal (and thus binding on persons who have long since conveyed the land or, conversely, unenforceable by successors to the covenantee) when the covenant touches and concerns the land and the parties clearly intended for it to run with the land. The "vertical privity" concept avoids that problem and focuses instead on the devolutional relationships, where, we think, the focus should be.

(d) Conclusion

Upon this analysis, we conclude that the covenant in question — to pay a pro rata share of the cost of installing the streets adjacent to the property — was one that runs with the land.

Consequence

Noting that the question [of a promisor's continuing liability after transfer] has "not been extensively litigated," Powell observes, at § 673[3], that

> A liability continuing after the original covenantor had lost control of the burdened land would be harsh, and might well lessen the willingness of people to utilize covenants. It is not surprising, therefore, to find several courts holding that the conveyance of the burdened land ends the covenantor's liability. A few states have enacted statutes to this same effect. This result normally embodies the intention of the original parties reasonably inferable from the circumstances of the original covenant, giving due emphasis to the nature of the conduct promised. This is particularly true with respect to covenants to render services or to curtail the use of the burdened land; but is less likely to be true in the case of covenants to pay money, where the personal credit of the original covenantor is an important factor.

[T]he record here clearly indicates that the Bells were not relying especially upon the credit of the Gallaghers in extracting the covenant. They wanted, and insisted upon, the undertaking from whomever purchased the burdened tract, and indeed turned to the Gallaghers only when they mistakenly concluded that Ms. Camalier was not liable because of her indemnity agreement. In a case similar on its facts to this one, the Pennsylvania Court concluded in Leh v. Burke, 231 Pa. Super. 98, 331 A.2d 755 (1974), that:

> When a promise to do an affirmative act, such as in this case to make a monetary payment, is found to run with the land, the person in possession at the time the obligation matures is responsible for discharging it.

Conversely, prior or subsequent owners of the property, including the original covenantor, are relieved of responsibility not arising contemporaneously with their interest in the land.

We need not, in this case, go so far as to announce such a rule as a matter of law, or indeed as to every kind of covenant that may run with the land. It will suffice to conclude only that the continuing liability of an original covenantor on a covenant of the type involved here will end upon his conveyance of the burdened property if the parties intended for that to be the case, and that the record here demonstrates such an intent. Compare, however, the uncritical and unsupported statement in a casenote to McKenrick v. Savings Bank, 197 A. 580 (Md. 1938), in 2 Md. L. Rev. 265, 268 (1938), that "[a]s the covenantor's obligation is contractual, he always remains liable for any breaches whenever they occur."

It is evident that the liability of the Gallaghers to appellees on the 1961 covenant ended in 1980 when they conveyed their property to Ms. Camalier. Any liability they may have under their indemnity agreement — a matter not now before us and upon which we express no opinion — would flow to Ms. Camalier and not to appellees. The court therefore erred in not entering judgment in favor of the Gallaghers.

Judgment reversed.

NOTES AND QUESTIONS

1. **Parties.** Under the court's holding in the principal case, did the plaintiff sue the wrong party? Who should the Bells have sued? Does the decision in the principal case mean that the Gallaghers entirely escape liability for the costs of installing the streets and sewers?

2. **Liability of promisor after transfer.** Under the third Restatement, a promisor is liable only for performances that accrue while the promisor holds the burdened property, unless the parties creating the servitude provide otherwise. *See* Restatement (Third) of Property (Servitudes) § 4.4(1) & cmt. a; § 4.7(3) (2000). How does that view compare with the position of the court in the principal case? *See generally* William B. Stoebuck & Dale A. Whitman § 8.21 (3d ed. 2000).

3. **Enforcement after transfer of benefitted land.** If the benefit runs with the land, the promisee loses the right to enforce the servitude after transfer of the dominant estate. *See* Restatement of Property §§ 549, 550 (1944).

4. **Old and new requirements.** Which requirements for the running of the burden of a real covenant track the easement requirements? What are the additional requirements for the running of the burden of a real covenant? Which of the parties involved in a servitude — the creating parties and their successors — do the additional real covenant requirements focus on? What does touch and concern focus on?

5. **Why not an easement?** Could the Bells have avoided the complexities of real covenant analysis by seeking to enforce the Gallaghers' promise against Camalier as an easement?

6. **Why a real covenant?** Why does the court discuss the requirements for the running of the burden of a real covenant rather than an equitable servitude?

What relief are the Bells seeking?

A. Touch and Concern

7. **The touch and concern requirement.** In order to run to a successor of the promisee, the benefit of a real covenant must touch and concern the land of the promisee, and in order to run to a successor of the promisor, the burden of a real covenant must touch and concern the land of the promisor. Is there any relationship between the touch and concern inquiry in covenants and the appurtenancy question in easements?

8. **Policy.** Should courts be able to *prevent* enforcement of the promise against the promisor's successor because of the court's assessment of the burdensomeness of the covenant? The following excerpts, taken from works that justify reading in full, present the opposing views on that question.

a. Richard A. Epstein, *Notice and Freedom of Contract in the Law of Servitudes*, 55 S. Cal. L. Rev. 1353, 1359-60 (1982):

> There is no need to filter the private arrangements that should be respected [enforced] from those that should not. Parties who wish to create a servitude can just as easily enter into personal arrangements as real property arrangements; in other words, they can negate the intention to make the servitude run. The very fact that parties unambiguously tie a servitude to the land suggests that they think it should touch and concern the land. Insistence upon the touch and concern requirement denies the original parties their contractual freedom by subordinating their desires to the interests of future third parties, who by definition have no proprietary claim to the subject property.

b. Stewart E. Sterk, *Freedom from Freedom of Contract: The Enduring Value of Servitude Restrictions*, 70 Iowa L. Rev. 615, 617 (1985):

> [T]o leave landowners unrestricted in their right to impose by contract obligations that run to successors-in-interest of land would be to ignore, or to subordinate as unworthy of decisive consideration, at least two problems. First, a number of servitudes create externalities. They affect not only the owners of burdened and benefited land, but third parties whose interests are not represented in the negotiation process. Second, many servitudes, particularly those that bind or benefit multiple parties, are difficult to remove because of high transaction costs. Even when parties to the original agreement consider the costs of removing the restrictions and take steps to reduce those costs, their actions do not eliminate the need for subsequent consideration. Current landowners have limited foresight; permitting their restrictions to govern land use for long periods or periods of unlimited duration might frustrate even their own preferences for the future. More important, even if current landowners possessed perfect foresight, to permit their preferences to govern for long periods or forever would be to resolve against future generations difficult questions of intergenerational fairness.

9. **Doctrine.** Whether a court should intervene to bar the running of covenants intended by the parties to run is one question; the interventionists have

clearly carried the day on that one. How to identify the proper cases for intervention is a separate question, on which the overwhelming consensus, at least among academic writers, is that the common law "touch and concern" formulation is unsatisfactory. Do you see any flaw in Dean Bigelow's version of the touch and concern test, discussed in Gallagher v. Bell? How about the test of the first Restatement of Property § 537?

10. **Negative covenants.** As you might expect, courts seem to have little difficulty concluding that a negative covenant touches and concerns the land. *See, e.g.*, Sloan v. Johnson, 491 S.E.2d 725, 729 (Va. 1997) ("The covenant 'touches and concerns' the land because it limits the number of houses that may be constructed upon each lot."). However, promises by A not to use his land in competition with a business conducted by his neighbor have been problematic. *See* 2 A.L.P. § 9.13, at 378-80. Would the burden of such a covenant run with the land under the first Restatement of Property § 537, quoted in the principal case?

Recent cases dealing with noncompetition promises tend to focus on the reasonableness of the covenant (area restricted; duration of the restriction), and to uphold those that are reasonable. *See, e.g.*, Whitinsville Plaza, Inc. v. Kotseas, 390 N.E.2d 243 (Mass. 1979); Davidson Bros., Inc. v. D. Katz & Sons, Inc., 579 A.2d 288 (N.J. 1990) (remand for determination whether covenant barring supermarket or grocery store from urban renewal area serviced only by two high-priced convenience stores was reasonable).

11. **Affirmative covenants.** Suppose a covenant requires the promisor to build or maintain something on his land; would you expect such a covenant to touch and concern the promisor's land? *See* 2 A.L.P. § 9.13. Suppose the covenant requires the promisor to pay money, as in the principal case; would that covenant run under the first Restatement's test? The court in Neponsit Property Owners' Association, Inc. v. Emigrant Indus. Sav. Bank, 15 N.E.2d 793, 796 (N.Y. 1938), concluded that it may, stating:

> A promise to pay for something to be done in connection with the promisor's land does not differ essentially from a promise by the promisor to do the thing himself, and both promises constitute, in a substantial sense, a restriction upon the owner's right to use the land, and a burden upon the legal interest of the owner. On the other hand, a covenant to perform or pay for the performance of an affirmative act disconnected with the use of the land cannot ordinarily touch or concern the land in any substantial degree.

For a controversial case in which the court concluded that a covenant to pay money did not touch and concern the land of the promisor, see Eagle Enterprises, Inc. v. Gross, 349 N.E.2d 816 (N.Y. 1976) (lot buyer's promise to buy water for seasonal use from developer held not to touch and concern land in suit against buyer's successor, who converted from seasonal to year-round use of the land and dug a well).

12. **Benefits touching and concerning the land.** The first Restatement of Property § 543(2) provided that a promise touches and concerns the promisee's land only if performance of the promise would (a) produce an advantage "in a physical sense" to the beneficiary; or (b) decrease competition in the beneficiary's use of his land; or (c) constitute a return to the beneficiary for the promisor's use

of the beneficiary's land. Under the first Restatement, would the benefit of A's noncompetition promise run to B's successor Y? Could Y or B enforce A's noncompetition promise against A's successor X under the first Restatement? Recall § 537, discussed above.

13. **The third Restatement.** The third Restatement adopts the view that a court has the power to bar the running of a covenant that the parties intend to run, but it "supersedes" touch and concern as the doctrinal formula for the judicial screening of covenants. *See* Restatement Third § 3.2. Instead, the Restatement substitutes a series of more specific policy inquiries for determining whether a servitude creates a valid obligation:

§ 3.1 Validity of Servitudes: General Rule

A servitude created under the rules set forth in Chapter 2 is valid unless it is illegal or unconstitutional or violates public policy.

Servitudes that are invalid because they violate public policy include, but are not limited to:

(1) a servitude that is arbitrary, spiteful, or capricious;

(2) a servitude that unreasonably burdens a fundamental constitutional right;

(3) a servitude that imposes an unreasonable restraint on alienation under § 3.4 or § 3.5;

(4) a servitude that imposes an unreasonable restraint on trade or competition under § 3.6; and

(5) a servitude that is unconscionable under § 3.7.

For a recent defense and a recent criticism of the third Restatement's new formulation, see Susan F. French, *The Touch and Concern Doctrine and the Restatement (Third) of Servitudes*, 77 Neb. L. Rev. 653 (1998); A. Dan Tarlock, *Touch and Concern is Dead, Long Live the Doctrine*, 77 Neb. L. Rev. 804 (1998).

B. Intent That the Covenant Run

14. **Old and new Restatements.** For the burden of a covenant to run, the parties must intend that the burden run, and for the benefit of the covenant to run, the parties must intend that the benefit run. *See* Restatement of Property § 544; Restatement Third § 2.2. The intent requirement is usually satisfied by language in the document creating the covenant. For example, the instrument creating a covenant may expressly state that the covenant runs with the land of the promisor or promisee, or both, or it may state that the burden or benefit runs to "successors and assigns" of the promisor or promisee, or both. On what basis did the court in Gallagher v. Bell find that the parties intended the burden of the covenant to run to the Gallaghers' successors?

15. **Touch and concern and intent.** If the parties do not expressly state their intent that the burden or benefit of a covenant run, courts may look to the nature and circumstances of the covenant. If the covenant touches and concerns the burdened or benefitted land, a court may take that as an indication that the

parties intended the burden or benefit to run to successors to that land. *See* Restatement Third § 2.2, cmts. b, I; Susan F. French, *Toward a Modern Law of Servitudes: Reweaving the Ancient Strands*, 55 S. Cal. L. Rev. 1261, 1289 (1982). A few courts, however, refuse to glean intent for a running burden from circumstances and require the creating parties to expressly bind the successors of the promisor. *See* Lowe v. Wilson, 250 S.W.2d 366, 368 (Tenn. 1952) (Tennessee law requires express language binding heirs and assigns for the burden of a covenant to run.). *See also* Inwood North Homeowners' Association, Inc. v. Harris, 736 S.W.2d 632, 635 (1987) (in Texas, the "in esse" rule requires that a covenant that relates to something not yet in existence must expressly bind assigns in order to run).

C. Privity
1. Running of the Burden: Horizontal Privity

16. **Horizontal privity: property and contract.** The parties to the creation of a covenant always stand in privity of contract: the relationship of rights and duties created by the covenant itself. Horizontal privity requires an additional, property relationship between the parties *at the time the covenant is created*. What two versions of horizontal privity does Professor Powell's treatise, cited in *Gallagher v. Bell*, identify? Are they the same as the two versions indicated in the first Restatement of Property § 534?

§ 534. Privity Between Promisee and Promisor.

The successors in title to land respecting the use of which the owner has made a promise are not bound as promisors upon the promise unless

(a) the transaction of which the promise is a part includes a transfer of an interest either in the land benefitted by or in the land burdened by the performance of the promise; or

(b) the promise is made in the adjustment of the mutual relationships arising out of the existence of an easement held by one of the parties to the promise in the land of the other.

The English courts restricted horizontal privity to situations in which the promising parties stood in a mutual estate relationship with each other (e.g., a landlord-tenant relationship). How does § 534 liberalize the English common law of horizontal privity?

17. **The third Restatement: abolition of horizontal privity.** Finding no good reason for the horizontal privity requirement, the third Restatement abolishes it. *See* Restatement Third § 2.4.

18. **Reform?** Despite the modern view adopted by the court in *Gallagher* and the view of the third Restatement, some courts, including state supreme courts, continue to list horizontal privity as a requirement for the running of a covenant. *See, e.g.*, Kaanapali Hillside Homeowners' Association v. Doran, 162 P.3d 1277, 1289-90 (Hawai'i 2007); Barner v. Chappell, 585 S.E.2d 590, 594 (Va. 2003); Columbia Club, Inc. v. American Fletcher Realty Corp., 720 N.E.2d 411 (Ind. App. 1999); Lake Limerick Country Club v. Hunt Mfg. Homes, Inc., 84 P.3d 295, 299 (Wash. App. 2004). In some cases, these courts question the continued validity of

the requirement. *See Kaanapali*, 162 P.3d at 1290 n.13 ("We express no opinion regarding the view that horizontal and mutual privity should not be required for a covenant to run. Rather we only note that horizontal and mutual privity exist here."); *Lake Limerick*, 84 P.3d at 302 ("To whatever extent 'horizontal privity' might still be required, it is easily met here."). Why does reform come slowly?

19. **Living with horizontal privity.** Would you surmise that horizontal privity is most often present or absent when parties enter into a covenant? *See* Restatement Third § 1.4 cmt. a, at 29 ("American courts removed all significance from the horizontal privity requirement by finding privity in a grantor-grantee relationship."). In cases in which horizontal privity is absent (e.g., Problem 7-A.c below), might you be able to avoid the requirement by classification? If the obligation in Problem 7-A.c were not an easement, what remedy do you think that the plaintiff would seek for its enforcement, damages or an injunction? If the plaintiff sought an injunction, the case would fall under the equitable servitude category (Section A.2 below) and (as we shall see), horizontal privity would not be a requirement.

2. Running Burden: Vertical Privity

20. **Vertical privity: meaning.** The first Restatement of Property § 535 defined vertical privity as follows:

> § 535. Privity as Between Promisor and Successor. The successors in title to land respecting the use of which the owner has made a promise are not bound as promisors upon the promise unless by their succession they hold (a) the estate or interest held by the promisor at the time the promise was made, or (b) an estate or interest corresponding in duration to the estate or interest held by the promisor at that time.

21. **Review: easements.** Does an adverse possessor bear the burden of an *easement* on the servient estate? Does a tenant of the servient estate? *See* 2 A.L.P. § 8.14 (subjection to burden of easement "is due merely to the fact of possession").

22. **Vertical privity: the third Restatement.** The third Restatement eschews vertical privity, adopting instead a general rule that an appurtenant burden runs "automatically with the property interest to which it is appurtenant." Restatement Third § 5.1. There are two exceptions, both applicable to affirmative burdens. An affirmative burden does not run to a tenant of the servient owner unless the obligation "can more reasonably be performed by a person in possession than by the holder of the reversion." *Id.* § 5.3(2). Examples: T leases lot 10 in Green Acres Subdivision from A; T is not required to pay assessments levied by the property owners' association (*id.* cmt. d, illus. 5), but *is* obligated to perform covenants requiring that residents recycle newspapers and bottles and use special containers for garbage (*id.*, illus. 7). The other exception applies to life tenants: "the life tenant's liability for performance of affirmative covenants is limited to the value of the life estate." *Id.* § 5.4. Notice that neither exception applies to the adverse possessor, who is liable for breach of a covenant burdening the property under the basic rule of § 5.1.

3. Running of the Benefit of a Real Covenant

23. **Horizontal privity not required.** We saw earlier that the Restatement Third dispenses with horizontal privity for the running of the burden of a covenant. It was never required for the running of the benefit. *See* Restatement of Property § 548.

24. **Vertical privity.** Vertical privity *is* required, however, for the running of the benefit of a real covenant. In a departure from its test for the running of the burden, the first Restatement required only that the plaintiff "*succeed* to some interest of the [original] beneficiary in the land respecting the use of which the promise was made." Restatement of Property § 547 (emphasis added). However, in 165 Broadway Building v. City Investing Co., 120 F.2d 813, 816 (2d Cir. 1941), Judge (former Professor and Dean) Clark stated that "[t]he parties to an action to enforce a covenant, if not themselves makers of the contract, must each have succeeded by privity to *the* estate of one of such makers" (emphasis added). How do the two formulations differ? Is a tenant of the promisee entitled to enforce the promise under the Restatement test? *See* Restatement of Property § 547 cmt. c, at 3269. Under Judge Clark's test? Is an adverse possessor of the promisee's land entitled to enforce the promise under either test? *See* Restatement of Property § 547 cmt. d.

25. **Review: easements.** Again, compare easements: Does the benefit of an appurtenant easement run to an adverse possessor? Does the benefit run to a tenant of the dominant estate? *See* 2 A.L.P. §§ 8.7, 8.71; Restatement of Property § 487 cmt. e & illus. 5.

26. **The third Restatement.** *See* Restatement Third of Property, Servitudes, § 5.2 (appurtenant benefit "runs to all subsequent owners and possessors of the benefited property"); 5.3(1) (tenant of promisee of benefitted estate gets benefit of covenants to repair, maintain, or render services to the property, and any benefit "that can be enjoyed by the lessee without diminishing its value to the lessor and without materially increasing the burden of performance on the person obligated to perform the covenant"). Examples: T leases lot 10 in Greenacre from B; T is entitled to the benefit of a covenant requiring the owner of lot 9 to trim trees to protect the view from other lots (§ 5.3, cmt. c, illus. 2), but not to receive the benefit of an arrangement entitling all lot owners to receive royalties from oil wells located on the property belonging to the homeowners' association (*id.*, illus. 3). Does an adverse possessor enjoy the benefit of a servitude under the third Restatement formulation?

PROBLEMS

7-A. In which of the following cases is horizontal privity present under the test of the first Restatement?

a. In 1990, A grants a roadway easement to B. In 1995, A and B execute a covenant in which A agrees to maintain the easement to facilitate B's passage. If A conveyed to X, would X be bound to pay for maintenance? *See* Morse v. Aldrich, 19 Pick. 449 (Mass. 1837). (Morse v. Aldrich originated the American version of mutual privity: the substitution of a mutual interest between the parties to the promise for the mutual estate required by the English view of horizontal privity.)

b. In 1990, B conveys Blackacre to A. The deed contains a covenant by A to maintain a fence along the boundary between the land conveyed and land retained by B. When A transfers to X, is X bound?

c. A and B are neighbors, both concerned about approaching commercialization of their area. A and B agree to restrict their respective parcels to residential use only. When A transfers to X, is X bound? *Compare* Wheeler v. Schad, 7 Nev. 204 (1871) (no horizontal privity when covenant was made six days after deed conveying fee interest between the covenanting parties), *with* Sonoma Dev., Inc. v. Miller, 515 S.E.2d 577 (Va. 1999) (covenant executed in different, earlier document, but on same day as deed, satisfied horizontal privity; earlier document was recorded). The *Sonoma Development* case based its decision on Restatement § 534(a); can you see how?

d. Did the court require horizontal privity in Gallagher v. Bell? Was it present in that case?

e. Was horizontal privity present to support the promises made by Davies to Mairs in Fitzstephens v. Watson in Chapter 6?

7-B. Vertical privity. B owns a ten acre parcel of land and sells five acres to A, who promises to use the parcel only for residential purposes and to keep a fence along the boundary between the parcels in good repair. X adversely possesses against A. Do A's promises run to X? (Hint: If A had also been an adverse possessor, would X have been able to tack A's time of possession onto his own?) What requirement stated in § 535 excludes the adverse possessor from the burden of covenants running with the land? Does it matter whether plaintiff sues X before the statute of limitations has run? *See* Restatement Third, Introductory Note to Chapter 5, at 4-5. Change the facts: if X is a tenant of A rather than an adverse possessor, what element of the privity specified in Restatement § 535 is lacking?

2. Equitable Servitudes: Enforcement by Equitable Remedies

a. Running Requirements

In order to get immediately to the most dramatic difference between real covenants and equitable servitudes, we modify slightly our usual order of presentation. Here, we address first the requirements for the running of the burden and benefit of an equitable servitude. Then we address two, by-now familiar, problems of the creation of such servitudes: May an equitable servitude be implied, and may an equitable servitude be created in a third-party beneficiary?

In Keppell v. Bailey, 39 Eng. Rep. 1042 (Ch. 1834), the English Court of Chancery applied the same requirements to the running of a burden of a promise in equity that the law courts applied to real covenants. Fourteen years later, in the landmark case of Tulk v. Moxhay, Chancery took an entirely different tack and launched the category of "equitable servitudes."

TULK v. MOXHAY
41 Eng. Rep. 1143 (Court of Chancery 1848)

In the year 1808 the Plaintiff, being then the owner in fee of the vacant piece of ground in Leicester Square, as well as of several of the houses forming the Square, sold the piece of ground by the description of "Leicester Square garden or pleasure ground, with the equestrian statue then standing in the centre thereof, and the iron railing and stone work round the same," to one Elms in fee: and the deed of conveyance contained a covenant by Elms, for himself, his heirs, and assigns, with the Plaintiff, his heirs, executors, and administrators,

> that Elms, his heirs, and assigns should, and would from time to time, and at all times thereafter at his and their own costs and charges, keep and maintain the said piece of ground and square garden, and the iron railing round the same in its then form, and in sufficient and proper repair as a square garden and pleasure ground, in an open state, uncovered with any buildings, in neat and ornamental order; and that it should be lawful for the inhabitants of Leicester Square, tenants of the Plaintiff, on payment of a reasonable rent for the same, to have keys at their own expense and the privilege of admission therewith at any time or times into the said square garden and pleasure ground.

The piece of land so conveyed passed by divers mesne conveyances into the hands of the Defendant, whose purchase deed contained no similar covenant with his vendor: but he admitted that he had purchased with notice of the covenant in the deed of 1808.

The Defendant having manifested an intention to alter the character of the square garden, and asserted a right, if he thought fit, to build upon it; the Plaintiff, who still remained owner of several houses in the square, filed this bill for an injunction; and an injunction was granted by the Master of the Rolls to restrain the Defendant from converting or using the piece of ground and square garden, and the iron railing round the same, to or for any other purpose than as a square garden and pleasure ground in an open state, and uncovered with buildings.

On a motion, now made, to discharge that order.

THE LORD CHANCELLOR [Cottenham].

That this Court has jurisdiction to enforce a contract between the owner of land and his neighbour purchasing a part of it, that the latter shall either use or abstain from using the land purchased in a particular way, is what I never knew disputed. Here there is no question about the contract: the owner of certain houses in the square sells the land adjoining, with a covenant from the purchaser not to use it for any other purpose than as a square garden. And it is now contended, not that the vendee could violate the contract, but that he might sell the piece of land, and that the purchaser from him may violate it without this Court having any power to interfere. If that were so, it would be impossible for an owner of land to sell part of it without incurring the risk of rendering what he retains worthless. It is said that, the covenant being one which does not run with the land, this court cannot enforce it; but the question is, not whether the covenant runs with the land, but whether a party shall be permitted to use the land in a manner inconsistent with the contract entered into by his vendor, and with notice of which he purchased. Of course, the price would be affected by the covenant, and nothing could be more inequitable than the original purchaser should be able to sell the property the next day for a greater price, in consideration of the assignee being allowed to escape from the liability which he had himself undertaken.

That the question does not depend upon whether the covenant runs with the land is evident from this, that if there was a mere agreement and no covenant, this Court would enforce it against a party purchasing with notice of it; for if an equity is attached to the property by the owner, no one purchasing with notice of that equity can stand in a different situation from the party from who he purchased.

I think the cases cited before the Vice-Chancellor and this decision of the Master of the Rolls perfectly right, and, therefore, that this motion must be refused, with costs.

NOTES AND QUESTIONS

1. **Existing law.** Would Elms's promise to refrain from building on the square have run to Moxhay as a negative easement in England? Had Tulk sought damages, would the covenant have run to Moxhay as a real covenant? If the answer to these questions is no, what is the significance of the case?

2. **Rationale.** Why does the court allow enforcement? In explaining its result, does the court rely on the concept of a servitude at all? What requirement(s) does the court impose for the running of the covenant?

3. **Later rationale.** Many a case becomes important not for what it says, but for what later courts understand it to mean. Although *Tulk* speaks only in terms of contract rights and remedies, later English cases decided that the case really recognized a new kind of servitude enforceable in equity, hence "equitable servitude." This development is traced in London County Council v. Allen, 3 K.B. 642 (1914). Analogizing to easements, the English courts decided that only negative promises could run to a successor as an equitable servitude. *See* Haywood v. Brunswick Permanent Building Soc'y, 8 Q.B. 403 (1881). In American law, by contrast, "the decided weight of authority favors the enforcement in equity against purchasers with notice of affirmative agreements as equitable servitudes." 2 A.L.P. § 9.36, at 438-39.

4. **Running of the burden.** On the analogy to easements, what should the requirements be for the running of the burden of an equitable servitude? Touch and concern is a requirement. Why is it a requirement?

5. **Running of the benefit.** On the analogy to easements, what would you expect the requirements to be for the running of the benefit of an equitable servitude?

6. **Variations on a theme: what is a real covenant?** If both affirmative and negative obligations can be enforced in American law as equitable servitudes (Note 3 above), why would a plaintiff ever try to enforce an obligation as a real covenant, with the latter's formidable set of running requirements? Can you think of situations in which damages will be the plaintiff's only possible recovery? Is

Gallagher v. Bell, section A.1.b above, suggestive on this question? With regard to affirmative covenants in general, the American Law of Property notes that it is "very common" for the plaintiff to seek damages rather than an injunction for breach. *See* 2 A.L.P. § 9.13, at 377. Can you think of a reason why?

7. **Money in equity.** Damages is the quintessential legal remedy, just as specific performance decrees and injunctions are the primary equitable remedies. Nevertheless, courts sitting in equity do grant money judgments, particularly when the substantive area in dispute was originally created by equity courts. An award of damages for a trustee's breach of fiduciary obligations owed to the trust beneficiaries is one example (trusts were created in equity.). Closer to the point, courts in equity generally enforce the obligation of a lot owner in a subdivision to pay maintenance assessments. *See, e.g.*, Timberstone Homeowner's Association v. Summerlin, 467 S.E.2d 330, 332 (1996) ("Whether the assessment obligation is a covenant running with the land or an equitable servitude, it is clear that [it] is an enforceable covenant against a purchaser with notice."). It is also widely agreed that a court sitting in equity can grant "clean up" damages incident to the award of an injunction, to avoid multiplicity of actions. With these observations in mind, revisit Note 6 above: In what cases will a plaintiff *have* to employ real covenant theory to get a judgment?

8. **The third Restatement.** The third Restatement avoids the doctrinal puzzles raised in Notes 6 and 7. It abandons the requirements of horizontal and vertical privity for the running of the burden of a servitude. Since these two privities are what distinguish real covenants from equitable servitudes, the new Restatement accordingly drops the labels "real covenant" and "equitable servitude," except when discussing the historical development of the law. The Restatement merges the former real covenant and equitable servitude into a unitary category of "covenants that run with the land," *see* Restatement Third § 1.4, and allows such covenants to be enforced by any remedy. *Id.* § 8.3.

9. **The notice requirement and real covenants.** Notice of the burden is not listed among the common law requirements for the running of a real covenant. Does that mean that a real covenant can be enforced against a successor owner of the burdened tract without notice? Although the common law did not require notice, recording statutes protect subsequent purchasers for value against unrecorded covenants. *See* Chapter 5, Section D.1.

NOTES ON RUNNING COVENANTS IN LEASES

A. Real Covenants in Leases

1. **Running burden: requirements.** When the promisee of a lease covenant seeks damages against a transferee of the promisor, the running requirements are those specified in the Restatement Second of Property (Landlord and Tenant) § 16.1(2): intent, notice, touch and concern, and vertical privity. (Horizontal privity is not specified separately because it is always present between the landlord and the tenant.) These running requirements trace back to the sixteenth-century decision in Spencer's Case, 77 Eng. Rep. 72 (K.B. 1583), in which the landlord sought damages for an assignee's breach of the tenant's promise to construct a wall on the leased premises. As we have seen, the requirements of Spencer's Case

subsequently were applied to promises made between landowners in fee, and the requirement of "privity" was expanded to mean both horizontal privity between promisor and promisee and vertical privity between the promisor and his transferee.

2. **Transferee's liability: intent and notice.** In a well-drafted lease, the parties' intent that lease promises run to successors will be clearly manifested (e.g., "tenant promises, for himself, his successors and assigns," to pay the rent specified in the lease, or "landlord promises, for herself, her successors and assigns" to return a security deposit to the tenant). But intent may also be inferred from the nature of the promise or the circumstances of the leasing transaction; for example, the fact that a covenant touches and concerns the promisor's interest in the leased premises (see Note 3) suggests that the parties intended that it run to subsequent transferees of that interest. Why is that? As with covenants between owners in fee, a successor for value of either the landlord or tenant who lacks notice of a burden has no obligation to perform it. *See, e.g.,* J.C. Penney Co. v. Giant Eagle, Inc. 85 F.3d 120 (3d Cir. 1996). The transferee's awareness of the burden may take the form of actual, inquiry or record notice.

3. **Transferee's liability: touch and concern.** The Restatement Second § 16.1(2)(a) elaborates the "touch and concern" requirement for a running burden as follows:

> A promise by the landlord touches and concerns his interest in the leased property to the extent its performance is not related to other property and affects the use and enjoyment of the leased property by the tenant. A promise by the tenant touches and concerns his interest in the leased property if its performance affects the use and enjoyment of the leased property by the tenant or enhances the reversionary interest of the landlord.

Restatement Second § 16.1 cmt. b, at 117-118.

a. Apply the Restatement's tests to the following promises by the tenant: to repair the leased premises; not to use the premises for other than residential purposes; not to use the leased premises to compete with the landlord's business conducted on neighboring land; to pay rent; to pay taxes on the leased premises; to pay the cost of insurance on the buildings on the leased premises. *See id.* cmt. b, and illustrations 1-13.

b. Apply the Restatement test to the following promises by the landlord: to repair the leased premises; to supply utilities to the leased premises.

4. **Vertical privity on the landlord's side.** We discussed the distinction between assignment and sublease on the tenant's side in Chapter 4.D. The landlord's transfer of the entire reversion is the equivalent of the tenant's assignment of the lease; the landlord's transferee steps into privity of estate with the landlord, and consequently into privity with the tenant. It is possible, however, for the landlord to make transfers that are the equivalent of subleases. The Restatement Second § 16.1 cmt. e, at 123, states that the landlord's transferee is in privity of estate with the tenant if the landlord's transferee is the first in line to succeed the tenant should the tenant's interest be terminated immediately.

5. **Running benefit.** We have spoken mostly of running burdens. An assignee of the tenant enjoys the benefit of the landlord's promises that run with the land; an assignee of the landlord enjoys the benefit of the tenant's promises that run with the land. In each case, the running requirements are intent, touch and concern, and privity. *See* Restatement Second § 16.2. Notice is not required for the running of the benefit; why?

B. Equitable Servitudes in Leases

6. **Running burdens.** The requirements for the running in equity of the burden of a lease promise are intent, notice and touch and concern. The absence of a requirement that the promisor and the transferee be in privity of estate means that the landlord is entitled to enforce the burden of an equitable servitude against a sublessee as well as an assignee. So too may the tenant enforce the burden of an equitable servitude against any transferee of the landlord's interest.

7. **Running benefit.** An assignee of the tenant or landlord may enjoin breach by the promisor if the landlord and tenant intended the benefit to run and the benefit touches and concerns the transferred estate.

PROBLEMS

7-C. Landlord's noncompetition promise; running of burden. In a ten year lease of Blackacre, L promises not to use Whiteacre (owned by L and located near the leased premises) in competition with the business conducted by T on Blackacre. During the term of the lease, L transfers the reversion in Blackacre to L-1, who owns Greenacre, also located near Blackacre. L also transfers Whiteacre to L-2. Both L-1 and L-2 open competing businesses. Is T entitled to enjoin L-1? L-2?

7-D. L's promise to return T's security deposits; running of burden. L promises to return T's security deposit at the end of the lease. L subsequently assigns the reversion to L-1, but does not turn over the security deposit. At the end of the term, is L-1 liable to T for the amount of the security deposit? *See* Mullendore Theatres, Inc. v. Growth Realty Investors Co., 691 P.2d 970 (Wash. Ct. App. 1984):

> A lease covenant does not run with the land unless it touches or concerns the land. To do so, it must be so related to the land as to enhance its value and confer a benefit upon it. Otherwise, it is a collateral and personal obligation of the original lessor. In order to be a running covenant, a promise to pay money must restrict the use of the funds to the benefit of the property. There was no such restriction in this covenant. The landlord was not required to spend the money for repairs or maintenance, or in any other way related to the property. He was not even required to transfer it to his successors. The covenant was not directly related to, and did not touch and concern, the property. This proposition is supported by the weight of authority from other jurisdictions. Almost all courts that have considered the question have held that a promise to return a security deposit does not run with the land.

But see Restatement Second § 16.1 cmt. b, illus. 13 (landlord's promise to return a security deposit touches and concerns the landlord's interest so as to run to the landlord's successor). Which view is better — that of *Mullendore Theatres* or the Restatement Second?

7-E. Running of burden of equitable servitude. L leases to T for five years. The lease contains a promise by T to use the premises for residential purposes only. T subleases to T-1 for 3 years. T-1 opens a professional office on the premises. Assuming intent and notice, is L entitled to enjoin T-1 from violation of T's promise?

7-F. Transfer by L. Is L-1 in privity of estate with T in the following examples (assume a ten year lease)?

a. After five years, L transfers to L-1 for the remainder of the lease term. *See* Restatement Second § 15.1 cmt. h, illus. 14.

b. L transfers the reversion to L-1 for L's life. *Id.*, illus. 10.

c. L transfers to L-1 from and after L's death. *Id.*, illus. 12.

b.   Implied Creation

As indicated earlier, a covenant is usually created by an express agreement between the parties. However, as with easements, equitable servitudes may be created by implication. The next case, though dated, remains a classic text in the field of property law.

SANBORN v. McLEAN
206 N.W. 496 (Mich. 1925)

WIEST, J.

Defendant Christina McLean owns the west 35 feet of lot 86 of Green Lawn subdivision, at the northeast corner of Collingwood avenue and Second boulevard, in the city of Detroit, upon which there is a dwelling house, occupied by herself and her husband, defendant John A. McLean. The house fronts Collingwood avenue. At the rear of the lot is an alley. Mrs. McLean derived title from her husband, and, in the course of the opinion, we will speak of both as defendants. Mr. and Mrs. McLean started to erect a gasoline filling station at the rear end of their lot, and they and their contractor, William S. Weir, were enjoined by decree from doing so and bring the issues before us by appeal. Mr. Weir will not be further mentioned in the opinion.

Collingwood avenue is a high grade residence street between Woodward avenue and Hamilton boulevard, with single, double, and apartment houses, and plaintiffs, who are owners of land adjoining and in the vicinity of defendants' land, and who trace title, as do defendants, to the proprietors of the subdivision, claim that the proposed gasoline station will be a nuisance *per se*, is in violation of the general plan fixed for use of all lots on the street for residence purposes only, as evidenced by restrictions upon 53 of the 91 lots fronting on Collingwood avenue, and that defendants' lot is subject to a reciprocal negative easement barring a use so detrimental to the enjoyment and value of its neighbors. Defendants insist that no restrictions appear in their chain of title and they purchased without notice of any reciprocal negative easement, and deny that a gasoline station is a nuisance *per se*. We find no occasion to pass upon the question of nuisance, as the case can be decided under the rule of reciprocal negative easement.

This subdivision was planned strictly for residence purposes, except lots fronting Woodward avenue and Hamilton boulevard. The 91 lots on Collingwood avenue were platted in 1891, designed for and each one sold solely for residence purposes, and residences have been erected upon all of the lots. Is defendants' lot subject to a reciprocal negative easement? If the owner of two or more lots, so situated as to bear the relation, sells one with restrictions of benefit to the land retained, the servitude becomes mutual, and, during the period of restraint, the owner of the lot or lots retained can do nothing forbidden to the owner of the lot sold. For want of a better descriptive term this is styled a reciprocal negative easement. It runs with the land sold by virtue of express fastening and abides with the land retained until loosened by expiration of its period of service or by events working its destruction. It is not personal to owners, but operative upon use of the land by any owner having actual or constructive notice thereof. It is an easement passing its benefits and carrying its obligations to all purchasers of land, subject to its affirmative or negative mandates. It originates for mutual benefit and exists with vigor sufficient to work its ends. It must start with a common owner. Reciprocal negative easements are never retroactive; the very nature of their origin forbids. They arise, if at all, out of a benefit accorded land retained, by restrictions upon neighboring land sold by a common owner. Such a scheme of restriction must start with a common owner; it cannot arise and fasten upon one lot by reason of other lot owners conforming to a general plan. If a reciprocal negative easement attached to defendants' lot, it was fastened thereto while in the hands of the common owner of it and neighboring lots by way of sale of other lots with restrictions beneficial at that time to it. This leads to inquiry as to what lots, if any, were sold with restrictions by the common owner before the sale of defendants' lot. While the proofs cover another avenue, we need consider sales only on Collingwood.

December 28, 1892, Robert J. and Joseph R. McLaughlin, who were then evidently owners of the lots on Collingwood avenue, deeded lots 37 to 41 and 58 to 62, inclusive, with the following restrictions:

> No residence shall be erected upon said premises which shall cost less than $2,500, and nothing but residences shall be erected upon said premises. Said residences shall front on Helene (now Collingwood) avenue and be placed no nearer than 20 feet from the front street line.

July 24, 1893, the McLaughlins conveyed lots 17 to 21 and 78 to 82, both inclusive, and lot 98 with the same restrictions. Such restrictions were imposed for the benefit of the lands held by the grantors to carry out the scheme of a residential district, and a restrictive negative easement attached to the lots retained, and title to lot 86 was then in the McLaughlins. Defendants' title, through mesne conveyances, runs back to a deed by the McLaughlins dated September 7, 1893, without restrictions mentioned therein. Subsequent deeds to other lots were executed by the McLaughlins, some with restrictions and some without. Previous to September 7, 1893, a reciprocal negative easement had attached to lot 86 by acts of the owners, as before mentioned, and such easement is still attached and may now be enforced by plaintiffs, provided defendants, at the time of their purchase, had knowledge, actual or constructive, thereof. The plaintiffs run back with their title, as do defendants, to a common owner. This common owner, as before stated, by restrictions upon lots sold, had burdened all the lots retained with reciprocal restrictions. Defendants' lot and plaintiff Sanborn's lot, next thereto, were held by such common owner, burdened with a reciprocal negative easement, and, when later sold to separate parties, remained burdened therewith, and right to demand observance thereof passed to each purchaser with notice of the easement. The restrictions were upon defendants' lot while it was in the hands of the common owners, and abstract of title to defendants' lot showed the common owners, and the record showed deeds of lots in the plat restricted to perfect and carry out the general plan and resulting in a reciprocal negative easement upon defendants' lot and all lots within its scope, and defendants and their predecessors in title were bound by constructive notice under our recording acts. The original plan was repeatedly declared in subsequent sales of lots by restrictions in the deeds, and, while some lots sold were not so restricted, the purchasers thereof, in every instance, observed the general plan and purpose of the restrictions in building residences. For upward of 30 years the united efforts of all persons interested have carried out the common purpose of making and keeping all the lots strictly for residences, and defendants are the first to depart therefrom.

When Mr. McLean purchased on contract in 1910 or 1911, there was a partly built dwelling house on lot 86, which he completed and now occupies. He had an abstract of title which he examined and claims he was told by the grantor that the lot was unrestricted. Considering the character of use made of all the lots open to a view of Mr. McLean when he purchased, we think, he was put thereby to inquiry, beyond asking his grantor, whether there were restrictions. He had an abstract showing the subdivision and that lot 86 had 97 companions. He could not avoid noticing the strictly uniform residence character given the lots by the expensive dwellings thereon, and the least inquiry would have quickly developed the fact that lot 86 was subjected to a reciprocal negative easement, and he could finish his house, and, like the others, enjoy the benefits of the easement. We do not say Mr. McLean should have asked his neighbors about restrictions, but we do say that with the notice he had from a view of the premises on the street, clearly indicating the residences were built and the lots occupied in strict accordance with a general plan, he was put to inquiry, and, had he inquired, he would have found of record the reason for such general conformation, and the benefits thereof serving the owners of lot 86 and the obligations running with such service and available to adjacent lot owners to prevent a departure from the general plan by an owner of lot 86.

While no case appears to be on all fours with the one at bar, the principles we have stated, and the conclusions announced, are supported by Allen v. City of Detroit, 167 Mich. 464, 133 N.W. 317; McQuade v. Wilcox, 215 Mich. 302, 183 N.W. 771; French v. White Star Refining Co., 229 Mich. 474, 201 N.W. 444; Silberman v. Uhrlaub, 116 App. Div. 869, 102 N.Y.S. 299; Boyden v. Roberts, 131 Wis. 659, 111 N.W. 701; Howland v. Andrus, 80 N.J. Eq. 276, 83 A. 982.

We notice the decree in the circuit directed that the work done on the building be torn down. If the portion of the building constructed can be utilized for any purpose within the restrictions, it need not be destroyed.

With this modification, the decree in the circuit is affirmed, with costs to plaintiffs.

NOTES AND QUESTIONS

1. **History.** See Schovee v. Mikolasko, 737 A.2d 578, 586 (Md. 1999):

> [T]he implied negative reciprocal easement or servitude doctrine arose before the advent of comprehensive zoning in order to provide a measure of protection for those who bought lots in what they reasonably expected was a general development in which all of the lots would be equally burdened and benefitted. In those early days, it was uncommon for the developer to evidence the development or impose uniform restrictions through a recorded Declaration that would later be incorporated in individual deeds. They often filed subdivision plats of one kind or another but did not take the extra step of using one instrument to impose the restrictions. The common, almost universal, practice, instead, was for the developer to place the restrictions in the deeds to individual lots and, sometimes, to represent to the purchasers of those lots that the same restrictions would be placed in subsequent deeds to the other lots. Litigation arose most frequently when the developer then neglected to include the restrictions in one or more of the subsequent deeds and those buyers proceeded or proposed to use their property in a manner that would not be allowed by the restrictions.

2. **Theory of the case.** Defendant McLean didn't agree to the restriction against nonresidential uses that the court imposes on lot 86. Nor is McLean the successor to an express promise made by McLaughlin, since McLaughlin made no promises in any of the sales in the subdivision. Where does the servitude that plaintiff is enforcing come from?

3. **Common plan: theory.** Why is proof of the developer's common plan for the subdivision required in *Sanborn*? (Hint: For which requirement of a covenant running with the land does the plan requirement substitute?) What is the analogous requirement in prior use easement cases? Why is it important to be reasonably sure that the developer *had* a common plan? See Shoney's, Inc. v. Cooke, 353 S.E.2d 300 (S.C. Ct. App. 1987) ("[T]he omission of such a restriction from each of the seven deeds tends to show either that no general scheme exists or that, if a general scheme did exist, the grantor abandoned it.").

4. **Common plan: proof.** See Warren v. Detlefsen, 663 S.W.2d 710, 711-12 (Ark. 1984):

> While parol evidence is generally inadmissible to vary or contradict the language of a restrictive covenant, such evidence is admissible to establish a general building plan or scheme of development and improvement. Such plan or scheme can be proven by express covenant, by implication from a field map, or by parol representation made in sales brochures, maps, advertising, or oral statements upon which the purchaser relied in making his decision to purchase.

See also Mid-State Equipment Co. v. Bell, 225 S.E.2d 877, 884 (Va. 1976):

In ascertaining the parties' intention, we examine the words used in the restriction, the plats, the deeds, such surrounding circumstances as the parties are presumed to have considered when their minds met, the purpose to be achieved by the covenant, and the use of the property, keeping in mind that such a restriction is not merely for the grantor's benefit but that it assures purchasers that property will be devoted in a specified manner to the intended purpose.

5. **Common plan in *Sanborn*.** What is the evidence in *Sanborn* of the McLaughlins' common plan for the subdivision? Was all of the evidence of a common plan available at the time of sale of the first subdivision lot? If not, should the reciprocal servitude have arisen with the first sale, or later? If the servitude arose later, would earlier buyers have been protected?

6. **Notice.** Does McLean have inquiry notice of a restriction on lot 86? How is McLean's position different from that of a purchaser of land burdened with an affirmative easement? Does McLean have record notice of the restriction on lot 86 (i.e., can McLean find a restriction *on lot 86* in the direct chain of title to lot 86 or in any deed from McLaughlin to any other purchaser)? Does the court's attribution of notice to McLean hide the fact that the court has to choose which of two innocent parties to sacrifice: the innocent subsequent purchaser (McLean), or the innocent original purchaser from the developer (Sanborn)? Would you choose differently?

3.   Third-Party Beneficiaries of Promises

In Chapter 6, we saw that the courts are divided on the question of whether the benefit of an easement may be created in a third party. We now address the same issue with respect to promises running with the land.

SNOW v. VAN DAM
197 N.E. 224 (Mass. 1935)

Lummus, Justice.

This suit relates to land on the seashore at Brier Neck, title to which [was held in 1907 by] one Shackelford. [The tract was divided by Thatcher Road, a county road running east and west.] The entrance to the tract was at the northwesterly corner, where is situated the lot now owned by the defendant Van Dam. The northerly part of the tract, including the lot of the defendant Van Dam, is low and marshy. From Thatcher Road, going south, there is a fairly sharp ascent to the top of a low hill, from which there is a gentle slope southward to the beach. This hill and slope were in 1906, and still are, well adapted to summer residences. In 1907 the whole tract, except the part north of Thatcher Road, was divided into building lots. In all, about a hundred building lots were laid out. Each of the plaintiffs owns one of these building lots, either on the hill or on the southerly slope, on which he has built a summer residence.

Between July 8, 1907, and January 23, 1923, almost all the lots into which the part of the tract south of Thatcher Road was divided, including the lots of most of the plaintiffs, were sold at various times by the general owner of the tract to various persons. With negligible exceptions, the deeds contained uniform restrictions, of which the material one is that "only one dwelling house shall be erected or maintained thereon at any given time which building shall cost not less than $2500 and no outbuilding containing a privy shall be erected or maintained on said parcel without the consent in writing of the grantor or their [sic] heirs."

The low and marshy land north of Thatcher Road was first divided, on a revised plan of 1919, into three parcels, called C, D and E. On January 23, 1923, Shackelford conveyed lots C, D and E to one Robert C. Clark, subject to the following restrictions:

> Only one dwelling house may be maintained on each of said parcels of land at any given time, which dwelling house shall cost not less than Twenty-Five Hundred Dollars ($2500) unless plans and specifications for a dwelling house of less cost shall be approved in writing by the grantor of said parcels of land, and no outbuilding containing a privy shall be maintained on either of said parcels of land without the consent in writing of the grantor.

Lot D is now owned by the defendant Van Dam, having been conveyed to him by Robert C. Clark on February 18, 1933, subject to the restrictions contained in the deed to him "in so far as the same may be now in force and applicable." This phrase did not purport to create any new restriction, and could have no such effect. The defendants have erected on lot D a large building to be used for the sale of ice cream and dairy products and the conducting of the business of a common victualler. The plaintiffs bring this suit for an injunction, claiming a violation of the restrictions. We think that the erection of a building to be used for business purposes was a violation of the language of the restriction. The zoning of the land for business in 1927 by the city of Gloucester could not operate to remove existing restrictions.

Prior to the conveyance from Shackelford to Robert C. Clark on January 23, 1923, there could not have been, under the law of this commonwealth, any enforceable restriction upon lot D. If any now exists in favor of the lands of the plaintiffs, it must have been created by that deed.

A restriction, to be attached to land by way of benefit, must not only tend to benefit that land itself, but must also be intended to be appurtenant to that land. If not intended to benefit an ascertainable dominant estate, the restriction will not burden the supposed servient estate, but will be a mere personal contract on both sides.

In the absence of express statement, an intention that a restriction upon one lot shall be appurtenant to a neighboring lot is sometimes inferred from the relation of the lots to each other. But in many cases there has been a scheme or plan for restricting the lots in a tract undergoing development to obtain substantial uniformity in building and use. The existence of such a building scheme has often been relied on to show an intention that the restrictions imposed upon the several lots shall be appurtenant to every other lot in the tract included in the scheme. In some cases the absence of such a scheme has made it impossible to show that the burden of the restriction was intended to be appurtenant to neighboring land. In the present case, unless the lots of the plaintiffs and the defendant Van Dam were included in one scheme of restrictions, there is nothing to show that the restrictions upon the lot of the defendant Van Dam were intended to be appurtenant to the lots of the plaintiffs.

What is meant by a "scheme" of this sort? In England, where the idea has been most fully developed, it is established that the area covered by the scheme and the restrictions imposed within that area must be apparent to the several purchasers when the sales begin. The purchasers must know the extent of their reciprocal rights and obligations, or, in other words, the "local law" imposed by the vendor upon a definite tract. Where such a scheme exists, it appears to be the law of England and some American jurisdictions that a grantee subject to restrictions acquires by implication an enforceable right to have the remaining land of the vendor, within the limits of the scheme, bound by similar restrictions. But it was settled in this commonwealth by Sprague v. Kimball, 213 Mass. 380, 100 N.E. 622, that the statute of frauds prevents the enforcement against the vendor, or any purchaser from him of a lot not expressly restricted, of any implied or oral agreement that the vendor's remaining land shall be bound by restrictions similar to those imposed upon lots conveyed. Only where the vendor binds his remaining land by writing, can reciprocity of restriction between the vendor and the vendee be enforced.

Nevertheless, the existence of a "scheme" continues to be important in Massachusetts for the purpose of determining the land to which the restrictions are appurtenant. Sometimes the scheme has been established by preliminary statements of intention to restrict the tract, particularly in documents of a public nature. More often it is shown by the substantial uniformity of the restrictions upon the lots included in the tract. In some jurisdictions the logic of the English rule, that the extent and character of the scheme must be apparent when the sale of the lots begins, had led to rulings that the restrictions imposed in later deeds are not evidence of the existence or nature of the scheme. In the present case there is no evidence of a scheme except a list of conveyances of different lots from 1907 to 1923 with substantially uniform restrictions. [However,] in Massachusetts a "scheme" has legal effect if definitely settled by the common vendor when the sale of lots begins, even though at that time evidence of such settlement is lacking and a series of subsequent conveyances is needed to supply it. In Bacon v. Sandberg, 179 Mass. 396, 398, 60 N.E. 936, 937, it was said, "the criterion in this class of cases is the intent of the grantor in imposing the restrictions."

Neither the restricting of every lot within the area covered, nor absolute identity of restrictions upon different lots, is essential to the existence of a scheme. But extensive omissions or variations tend to show that no scheme exists, and that the restrictions are only personal contracts.

The existence of a "scheme" is important in the law of restrictions for another purpose, namely, to enable the restrictions to be made appurtenant to a lot within the scheme which has been earlier conveyed by the common vendor. In the present case the lots of some of the plaintiffs were sold before, and the lots of others after, the conveyance from Shackelford to Robert C. Clark on January 23, 1923, which first imposed a restriction upon the lot now owned by the defendant Van Dam. The plaintiffs whose lots were sold before January 23, 1923, cannot claim succession to any rights of Shackelford or of land then retained by him. In general, an equitable easement or restriction cannot be created in favor of land owned by a stranger. Nevertheless an earlier purchaser in a land development has long been allowed to enforce against a later purchaser the restrictions imposed upon the latter by the deed to him in pursuance of a scheme of restrictions. Earlier as well as later purchasers of lots within the area covered by the scheme acquire such an interest in the restrictions that the common vendor cannot release them.

The rationale of the rule allowing an earlier purchaser to enforce restrictions in a deed to a later one pursuant to a building scheme, is not easy to find. The simple explanation that the deed to the earlier purchaser, subject to restrictions, implied an enforceable agreement on the part of the vendor to restrict in like manner all the remaining land included in the scheme (Dean Stone, now Mr. Justice Stone, in 19 Colum. L. Rev., 177, 187), cannot be accepted in Massachusetts without conflict with Sprague v. Kimball, [*supra*]. In Bristol v. Woodward, 251 N.Y. 275, 288, 167 N.E. 441, 446, Cardozo, C.J., said,

> If we regard the restriction from the point of view of contract, there is trouble in understanding how the purchaser of lot A can gain a right to enforce the restriction against the later purchaser of lot B without an extraordinary extension of Lawrence v. Fox, 20 N.Y. 268. Perhaps it is enough to say that the extension of the doctrine, even if illogical, has been made too often and too consistently to permit withdrawal or retreat.

It follows from what has been said, that if there was a scheme of restrictions, existing when the sale of lots began in 1907, which scheme included the lands of the plaintiffs and of the defendant Van Dam, and if the restrictions imposed upon the land of the defendant Van Dam in 1923 were imposed in pursuance of that scheme, then all the plaintiffs are entitled to relief. The burden is upon the plaintiffs to show the existence of such a scheme. In our opinion they have done so. Unquestionably there was a scheme which included all the land south of Thatcher Road. The real question is, whether in its origin it included the land north of that road, where is situated the lot of the defendant Van Dam. That lot lies at the gateway of the whole development. One must pass it to visit any part of Brier Neck. The use made of that lot tends strongly to fix the character of the entire tract. It is true, that the land north of Thatcher Road was not divided into lots until 1919, but it was shown on all the plans from the beginning. The failure to divide it sooner was apparently due to a belief that it could not be sold, not to an intent to reserve it for other than residential purposes. We think that the scheme from the beginning contemplated that no part of the Brier Neck tract should be used for commercial purposes. When the lot of the defendant Van Dam was restricted in 1923, the restriction was in pursuance of the original scheme and gave rights to earlier as well as to later purchasers.

[The court affirmed the lower court order enjoining defendant from using Lot D for any purpose other than a dwelling house.]

NOTES AND QUESTIONS

1. **Review.** On what theory would the plaintiffs who bought their lots from Shackelford *after* Shackelford sold Lot D to Robert C. Clark be entitled to enforce the residential use restriction against Van Dam?

2. *Sanborn* **in Massachusetts.** Are the plaintiffs who bought their lots *before* Shackelford sold Lot D to Clark entitled to sue Van Dam on the theory that Van Dam is the successor to an express promise made by Shackelford to restrict Lot D to residential use only? If not, would the theory adopted by the court in Sanborn v. McLean provide a cause of action? Is the *Sanborn* theory available in Massachusetts? *See* Sprague v. Kimball, 100 N.E. 622 (Mass. 1913) (requiring a writing to create an equitable servitude).

3. **Theory in *Snow*.** On what theory does the court in Snow v. Van Dam allow the plaintiffs who bought their lots from Shackelford before Clark to enforce the residential use only restriction against Van Dam? Does the court identify the theory? Do you see any relationship between the plaintiffs who bought before Clark and the plaintiff in Garza v. Grayson (Chapter 6)?

4. **Common plan.** In the principal case, is a common plan of development important to plaintiffs who bought before Clark, after Clark, or both?

5. **Notice.** Insofar as Van Dam is concerned, why is notice of the promise relating to Lot D a relevant question? Why does Van Dam have notice of the restriction on his lot? Is Van Dam's difficulty in finding the restriction comparable to the difficulty faced by McLean in Sanborn v. McLean?

6. **Third party beneficiary theory in real covenants.** In Nicholson v. 300 Broadway Realty Corp., 164 N.E.2d 832 (N.Y. 1959), the Embossing Co. in 1929 promised to supply steam heat to Aaron Nicholson's building and to maintain all necessary piping apparatus for that purpose. Embossing performed under the agreement for almost 30 years, then sold its building to Jack Spitzer, who transferred it to Betty Thompson, who then transferred it to the defendant 300 Broadway Realty Corporation, which balked at continuing to perform the agreement. Both Spitzer and Thompson allegedly were acting as defendant's agents in taking title to the property, and both expressly agreed to perform Embossing's obligations to Nicholson under the 1929 agreement. In a suit by Nicholson's successor against the realty corporation for damages, the court held that Embossing's promise was capable of running to defendant as a real covenant. In addition, the court said the following:

> However, the complaint may also be upheld upon the simpler and equally compelling ground that it spells out a cause of action for breach of contract. [T]he complaint here alleges that the defendant, initially through its agent Spitzer and then through its agent Thompson, expressly assumed the performance of Embossing's contract duty to furnish steam heat to the plaintiffs' building. Although Embossing could not relieve itself of its obligation on the covenant in the absence of a complete novation, it may be inferred from the complaint that Embossing would not have sold its property on the terms fixed had it not been assured that the grantee, the real grantee, of its property would assume its obligation to furnish heat. The complaint alleges that the conveyance procedure employed by the defendant was designed solely to enable it "to avoid performance of [its]

obligation." If such was the defendant's purpose, it must be condemned; to approve what was here attempted would be to sanction an evasion which offends against concepts of fair dealing and falls far below permissible standards of business morality. Be this as it may, though, any purpose or intent that the defendant may have had to avoid performance of the obligation will be wholly ineffectual if the plaintiffs are able to prove their allegations of agency and express assumption of duty.

Accepting, as on this appeal we must, the truth of the allegations that the express provisions of assumption were actually made by Spitzer and Thompson, as agents, "acting for and on behalf of the defendant," there can be no doubt that the plaintiffs have a direct right of action against the latter to enforce the contract duty explicitly assumed by it through agents. The assumption agreement between Embossing and the defendant is supported by manifest consideration and constitutes a creditor beneficiary contract in which Embossing is promisee, the defendant is promisor and the plaintiffs are third-party beneficiaries.

Questions: Under the plaintiff's running covenant theory, what promise would plaintiff be enforcing against the defendant? Under the alternative theory discussed in the excerpt reprinted above, what additional promise is required to support plaintiff's cause of action? Do you see any connection between Nicholson v. 300 Broadway Realty Corp. and Snow v. Van Dam?

7. **Running burden.** The third party beneficiaries of Robert Clark's promise regarding Lot D were the lot buyers from Shackelford who bought before Shackelford sold to Clark. The defendant Van Dam bought Lot D from Clark. On what theory is Van Dam bound by Clark's promise restricting Lot D? Was Van Dam in a better position than Christina McLean to know about the restrictions burdening the respective lots that they bought?

8. **Modern subdivisions.** Suppose that the developer of a subdivision records a declaration of restrictions, and extracts a promise from *every* buyer in the subdivision to comply with the restrictions. Is every lot owner in the subdivision entitled to sue (and be sued) for violation of the restrictions? On what theory or theories?

PROBLEM 7-G. Both Sanborn v. McLean (Section A.2.b above) and Snow v. Van Dam deal with servitudes in residential subdivisions. To see the relationship between the theories of the two cases, suppose that Dan Developer subdivides and sells 50 lots, numbered in the order of sale. Developer includes a restriction requiring "residential use only" in almost all of the deeds, but not in a few. In the following cases, on what theory might plaintiff enforce the restriction against defendant?

a. Lot 1 promises, lot 25 doesn't. Lot 1 sues to enjoin lot 25. Result under Sanborn v. McLean? Under Snow v. Van Dam? Does plaintiff need to prove a common plan? Y, N

b. Same facts; can lot 25 enjoin lot 1? Does plaintiff need to prove a common plan? *See* Sloan v. Johnson, 491 S.E.2d 725 (Va. 1997).

Y

c. Lot 1 doesn't promise, but lot 25 does. Can lot 1 sue lot 25 under the *Sanborn* theory? Under Snow v. Van Dam? Is proof of a common plan required? *No*

d. Same facts as c; can lot 25 sue lot 1? *No*

e. Neither lot 25 nor lot 1 promises. Can either lot owner prevail against the other?

In Problem 7-C.d and e some courts would say that lot 25 can sue lot 1 *if* enough deeds in the subdivision contain covenants to suggest that the developer had a plan for uniform development of the subdivision; the rationale is that it is unfair for lot 25 to be liable to lot 1 but be barred from suing lot 1. If courts find a common plan, they allow enforcement of the restriction without the showing of a connection between plaintiff's lot and defendant's: plaintiff need not demonstrate that he is the owner of a lot benefitted by an express or implied servitude, or the third party beneficiary of a promise made by defendant or a predecessor of defendant. A leading treatise on property law calls this approach "second-generation theory," to distinguish it from the first-generation cases, *Sanborn* and *Snow*. *See* Stoebuck & Whitman, the Law of Property § 8.33 (3d ed. 2000). *See also* Restatement Third § 2.14(1) ("Each lot included within the general plan is the implied beneficiary of all express and implied servitudes imposed to carry out the general plan."). (The third Restatement's *Sanborn* provision is § 2.14(2)(b).)

B.   (SOME FURTHER) CONSEQUENCES OF CLASSIFICATION

You have already seen (e.g., future interests) that property law is burdened with more than its share of classifications that produce different substantive results for functionally similar interests. With respect to servitudes — second only to future interests in its adherence to historical distinctions that have outlived their usefulness — now is a good time to see what *further* consequences, in addition to the requirements for the running of the benefit and burden, might turn on the classification of a servitude as an easement or a covenant. And as a review, it is also useful to consider again how servitudes differ from ordinary contracts and licenses, and (going ever further back in the materials in this book) how promises respecting land use differ from land use restrictions imposed by way of defeasible fees. In short, let's play the classification game.

1. Covenants and Easements

a. Third-Party Beneficiaries

NATURE CONSERVANCY v. CONGEL
689 N.Y.S.2d 317 (N.Y. App. Div. 1999)

CALLAHAN, J.

Madalyn Eisenberg, Henry Eisenberg, M.D., Carol Dana and Sidney T. Dana, M.D. (plaintiffs) are the owners of real property for whose benefit a restrictive covenant was imposed in a deed from the predecessor in title of Scott Congel and Milestone Materials (Milestone) (collectively defendants). At issue on this appeal is whether plaintiffs may enforce the covenant as third-party beneficiaries despite the absence of any privity between the grantor and plaintiffs. Supreme Court concluded that plaintiffs are "strangers to the deed" and could not enforce the restrictive covenant. We disagree.

Plaintiffs' residential property is located on Woodchuck Hill Road in the Town of DeWitt. It is adjacent to a picturesque rural area known as the "Buffer Lands," containing White Lake swamp, wetlands and forest with some rare and endangered species. The area was previously owned by the Allied Corporation (Allied), which operated a quarry that was separated from the residential lots on Woodchuck Hill Road by the undeveloped Buffer Lands. In 1986 Allied sold its property to General Crushed Stone Company (General Crushed Stone), which subsequently became Milestone by merger. The deed from Allied to General Crushed Stone contained the following restrictive covenant that is at issue on appeal:

> Buffer Lands. The "Buffer Lands" are that part of the premises hereby conveyed lying northerly of the "Approx. Escarpment Line" as shown on a map entitled "The Solvay Process Company, New York, Syracuse Plant, Inventory Map — Jamesville Quarry, Land in Towns of Dewitt and Manlius, 31949" (said map to be filed in the Office of the Onondaga Clerk simultaneously with the recording of this deed). The Grantee covenants on behalf of itself, its successors and assigns, that so long as any part of the premises hereby conveyed is used as a quarry, the Buffer Lands will remain in their natural state. This covenant shall be a covenant running with the land, binding on and enforceable against the Grantee, its successors and assigns. This covenant is for the benefit of and enforceable by all parties owning property adjoining the premises hereby conveyed and the Grantor, its successors and assigns. This covenant is also enforceable by Nature Conservancy.

In 1997 Congel purchased 461.45 acres of the Buffer Lands from Milestone. Congel intended to develop the property by constructing thereon a personal residence and erecting a perimeter fence. The deed conveying the premises to Congel recited that it was "[s]ubject to all other title matters of record."

Plaintiffs commenced this action to enforce the restrictive covenant in the Allied deed and to enjoin Congel from destroying the "natural state" of the Buffer Lands by constructing a residence and erecting barriers thereon. Plaintiffs moved for a preliminary injunction, and each defendant cross-moved to dismiss the complaint.

In a lengthy written decision, Supreme Court agreed with defendants that plaintiffs could not enforce the restrictive covenant because they are strangers to the deed. In declining to follow this Court's holding in Zamiarski v. Kozial, 239 N.Y.S.2d 221, the court noted that "in the subsequent thirty-four years no other appellate court has cited *Zamiarski* to reaffirm support for said legal position" and concluded that such decision "appears to be in direct contravention to the Court of Appeals' holding in [Matter of Estate of Thomson v. Wade, 69 N.Y.2d 570, 509 N.E.2d 309]." We conclude that the order should be reversed, plaintiffs' motion granted, defendants' cross motions denied and the complaint reinstated.

In this case, the court declined to follow the third-party beneficiary doctrine set forth in *Zamiarski*, concluding that it was in direct contravention to the long-accepted rule [stated in the *Thomson* case]. We note, however, that *Thomson* concerned the enforceability of an easement, not a restrictive covenant. Although restrictive covenants have been commonly categorized as "negative easements" because they restrain servient landowners from making otherwise lawful uses of their property, a negative easement is not a true easement. An easement entitles the owner of land to use the land of another for some purpose. Indeed, the parties concede that the restrictive covenant in this case is not a conservation easement. Furthermore, we note no cases following *Thomson* that apply to restrictive covenants; rather, they apply only to easements. This suggests that the rule enunciated in *Thomson* is limited to easements (a reservation or exception), and is not applicable to restrictive covenants, which do not constitute a reservation or exception.

Contrary to the court's conclusion, this Court's decision in *Zamiarski* remains good law, as recognized by the leading treatises. Plaintiffs, as owners of the property adjoining the Buffer Lands, for whose benefit the restrictive covenant was included in the deed from Allied to defendants' predecessor in title, may enforce the covenant as third-party beneficiaries despite the absence of any privity between the original grantor and plaintiffs. The covenant states that it is "for the benefit of and enforceable by all parties owning property adjoining the premises hereby conveyed." In addition, plaintiffs submitted evidentiary proof establishing the original grantor's intent to benefit them as the adjoining property owners.

Accordingly, the order should be reversed, plaintiffs' motion for a preliminary injunction granted, defendants' cross motions denied and the complaint reinstated.

Order unanimously reversed on the law with costs, motion granted, cross motions denied and complaint reinstated.

NOTES AND QUESTIONS

1. **Not an easement.**   Is the restriction in the principal case not an easement because (1) it does not entitle the beneficiary to use the servient owner's land, or (2) it is a negative easement outside of the common law four, or (3) it is created by

language of promise? Why is the court trying to avoid classifying the servitude as an easement?

2. **Policy.** Is it better to determine the validity of third-party servitudes on policy grounds or by classifying the servitude as an easement or a covenant? Consider the law of New York at present: a third-party beneficiary easement is not permitted, Estate of Thomson, 509 N.E.2d 309 (N.Y. 1987), but a third-party equitable servitude, Zamiarski v. Kozial, 239 N.Y.S.2d 221 (N.Y. App. Div. 1963); Nature Conservancy v. Congel, or real covenant, Nicholson v. 300 Broadway Realty Corp., section A.3 note 6 above, is permitted. Does that make sense?

3. **The third Restatement.** As part of its effort to simplify concepts and vocabulary, the third Restatement recognizes affirmative easements, affirmative covenants, and negative (restrictive) covenants. *See* Restatement Third §§ 1.2 (easement defined), 1.3 (affirmative and negative covenants defined). It abolishes the negative easement: "A 'negative easement' is a restrictive covenant." *Id.* § 1.3(3). But the third Restatement recognizes the validity of *all* third-party servitudes, not just third-party covenants. *See id.* § 2.6(2).

4. **Third-party beneficiaries and privity.** The American Law of Property states that it is a "commonly accepted principle that the enforcement of an equitable servitude is limited to those landowners who can trace title to the promisee either prior to or subsequent to the date of the agreement" that the plaintiff seeks to enforce. 2 A.L.P. § 9.30, at 425. Did the plaintiffs in Snow v. Van Dam satisfy that requirement? In the principal case, is the plaintiff in privity with the promisee of General Crushed Stone's promise? If not, why is plaintiff entitled to sue as a third-party beneficiary of that promise? Does the *Nature Conservancy* court apply the contract version of third-party beneficiary theory? *See* Restatement Second of Contracts § 302 & cmt. a (1981) (distinguishing intended and incidental beneficiaries of a promise; enforcement limited to intended beneficiaries).

b.   Running Burdens with Benefits in Gross

CAULLETT v. STANLEY STILWELL & SONS, INC.
170 A.2d 52 (N.J. Super. Ct. App. Div. 1961)

FREUND, J.A.D.

This is an action in the nature of a bill to quiet title to a parcel of land in the Township of Holmdel. Defendant appeals from the entry of summary judgment in favor of plaintiffs.

Defendant, a developer, by warranty deed conveyed the subject property, consisting of a lot approximately one acre in size, to the plaintiffs for a consideration of $4,000. The deed was delivered on January 13, 1959. Following the collapse of negotiations directed towards agreement on the construction by defendant of a dwelling on the transferred premises, the present suit was instituted.

The focal point of the action is a recital in the deed, inserted under the heading of "covenants, agreements and restrictions," to the effect that: "(i) The grantors reserve the right to build or construct the original dwelling or building on said premises." The item is one of those designated in the instrument as "covenants running with the land [which] shall bind the purchasers, their heirs, executors, administrators and assigns."

In support of their motion for summary judgment, plaintiffs set forth that no contract exists or ever did exist between the parties for the construction of a dwelling or building on the premises. The principal officer of the defendant corporation, in a countering affidavit, stated that one of the foremost considerations in fixing the price of the lot, and one of the primary conditions of the sale as it was effected, was the understanding that when the purchasers declared themselves ready and able to build, defendant would act as general contractor.

The trial judge held that the provision in question was unenforceable and should properly be stricken from the deed. He granted plaintiffs the relief demanded in their complaint, namely, an adjudication that: (1) defendant has no claim, right or interest in and to the lands by virtue of the clause in question; (2) defendant has no interest, right or cause of action against plaintiffs by virtue of the covenant; and (3) the clause in question is stricken from the deed and declared null, void and of no further force and effect.

The central issue argued on the appeal is whether the recital constitutes an enforceable covenant restricting the use of plaintiffs' land. Defendant urges that it comprises an ordinary property restriction, entered into for the benefit of the grantor and his retained lands. Plaintiff maintains that the clause is too vague to be capable of enforcement and that, in any event, it amounts to no more than a personal covenant which in no way affects or burdens the realty and has no place in an instrument establishing and delimiting the title to same.

While restrictive covenants are to be construed realistically in the light of the circumstances under which they were created, counter considerations, favoring the free transferability of land, have produced the rule that incursions on the use of property will not be enforced unless their meaning is clear and free from doubt. Thus, if the covenants or restrictions are vague or ambiguous, they should not be construed to impair the alienability of the subject property.

Approached from a direction compatible with the constructional principles set forth above, it is clear that the deed item in question is incapable of enforcement and is therefore not restrictive of plaintiffs' title. The clause is descriptive of neither the type of structure to be built, the cost thereof, or the duration of the grantees' obligation. While it might conceivably have been intended to grant to defendant a right of first refusal on construction bids on the property, this is by no means its palpable design. What, for example, would be its effect were plaintiffs to erect a structure by their own hands?

It must be remembered that a restrictive covenant is in its inception a mere contract, subject to the interpretative doctrines of contract law which focus on the parties' mutual purpose. See 3 Williston, Contracts (rev. ed. 1936), § 620, pp. 1787-88, nn. 5 and 6. A purported contract so obscure that no one can be sure of its meaning is incapable of remedy at law or equity for its alleged breach, and therefore cannot constitute a valid impediment to title.

Moreover, assuming arguendo that the clause is sufficiently definite to give defendant a primary option to build whenever plaintiffs should decide to construct a dwelling or building on the premises, it still cannot operate either as a covenant running with the land at law, or as an equitable servitude enforceable against the original grantee and all successors, having notice, to his interest.

In the first place, it is clear to us that the item in question does not satisfy the primary requirement of covenants directly restrictive of title to land — that they "touch and concern" the subject property. To constitute a real rather than a personal covenant, the promise must exercise direct influence on the occupation, use or enjoyment of the premises. It must be a promise "respecting the use of the land," that is, "a use of identified land which is not merely casual and which is not merely an incident in the performance of the promise." 5 Restatement, Property, Scope Note to Part III, pp. 3147-48 (1944).

The provision here in issue is not of the variety described above. It pertains to the use of plaintiffs' land only in the very incidental fashion that refusal to allow defendant to build the original structure would seemingly preclude plaintiffs from constructing at all. This is at best a personal arrangement between the two parties, designed to insure defendant a profit on the erection of a dwelling in return, allegedly, for a comparatively low sales price on the land. While there is nothing in our law precluding such an arrangement as a [simple] contract, this form of contract, contemplating a single personal service upon the property, does not affect the title. And the stipulation between the parties in their instrument to the effect that this was a covenant running with the land cannot override the inherently personal nature of their arrangement under established legal principles. We note, in addition, that even if the deed clause were to be construed as directly restricting plaintiffs' use of their land, i.e., prohibiting erection of a structure until such time as the owner shall permit such construction to be performed by the grantor, the clause would nonetheless comprise neither a legal restriction nor an equitable servitude upon the estate. This is so because whatever the effect of the burden of the covenant, its benefit is clearly personal to the grantor, securing to him a mere commercial advantage in the operation of his business and not enhancing or otherwise affecting the use or value of any retained lands.

Generally prerequisite to a conclusion that a covenant runs with the land at law is a finding that both burdened and benefited properties exist and were intended to be so affected by the contracting parties. Where, however, the benefit attaches to the property of one of the parties, the fact that the burden is in gross, i.e., personal, does not preclude the covenant from running with the land conveyed. There is no public policy opposed to the running of a benefit, since a continuing benefit is presumed to help rather than hinder the alienability of the property to which it is attached. Restatement of Property § 543, comment (c). When, however, as here, the burden is placed upon the land, and the benefit is personal to one of the parties and does not extend to his or other lands, the burden is generally held not to run with the land at law. The policy is strong against hindering the alienability of one property where no corresponding enhancement accrues to surrounding lands. See

Restatement of Property § 537; 2 American Law of Property § 9.13, pp. 373-76 (1952).

Nor can the covenant be enforced as an equitable servitude where the benefit is in gross and neither affects retained land of the grantor nor is part of a neighborhood scheme of similar restrictions. Purporting to follow the case of Tulk v. Moxhay, 41 Eng.Rep. 1143 (Ch.1848), our courts have consistently enforced the covenantal rights of an owner of benefited property against a successor, with notice, to the burdened land, even though the covenant did not run with the land at law. However, the right to urge enforcement of a servitude against the burdened land "depends primarily on the covenant's having been made for the benefit" of other land, either retained by the grantor or part of a perceptible neighborhood scheme. Hayes v. Waverly & Passaic R.R. Co., 51 N.J.Eq. 345, 348, 27 A. 648 (Ch. 1893). Where the benefit is purely personal to the grantor, and has not been directed towards the improvement of neighboring properties, it cannot pass as an incident to any of his retained land and therefore is not considered to burden the conveyed premises but only, at best, to obligate the grantee personally.

The latter doctrine has recently come under considerable criticism, see 2 American Law of Property § 9.32, pp. 428-430, and has even been rejected in some jurisdictions, thus permitting attachment of an equitable servitude even though the benefit is in gross. See, e.g., Pratte v. Balatsos, 113 A.2d 492 (N.H. 1955). But the law in this jurisdiction, as last authoritatively declared, is that "from the very nature of the equitable restriction arising from a restrictive covenant," the "existence of the dominant estate is essential to the validity of the servitude granted." Welitoff v. Kohl, 147 A. 390, 393 (N.J. 1929).

We therefore conclude that the clause in question, even were we to assume both its clarity and its direct operation upon the use of plaintiffs' land, cannot comprise an impairment of plaintiffs' title, because of the indisputably personal nature of the benefit conferred thereby. An intention to dispense broader land use benefits, in the form of a neighborhood scheme, cannot here be found, as in effect conceded by defendant and as expressly stipulated in the parties' deed.

The right of plaintiffs to bring an action to quiet title, where the alleged restriction is in reality unenforceable, is questioned. But it is clear that such actions may be instituted to clear the title instrument of excess verbiage having the practical effect of inhibiting the transferability of the estate. Courts will not be blind to the understandable reluctance of title companies to insure in the face of a questionable and somewhat anomalous deed provision, and to the even greater unwillingness of prospective purchasers to accept an uninsurable title. The action was a proper one under the statute.

Defendant asserts that this action is basically one for rescission of the contract and that plaintiffs should restore defendant to the status quo by reconveying the property in return for the consideration paid therefor. But we do not analyze the action as one for rescission. It purports to be, and is, in the nature of a bill to quiet title. Nor can we entertain defendant's alternative request for leave to amend its answer to seek rescission. No such request was made below and there is no proper basis for permitting it at this stage of the litigation.

The judgment of the trial court is affirmed.

NOTES AND QUESTIONS

1. **Common law.** By analogizing equitable servitudes to easements, the English courts imposed on equitable servitudes the English easement rule against the running of the burden when the benefit is held in gross. On the analogy to easements, what should the rule be in this country regarding the running of the burden of an equitable servitude in gross? *See* 2 A.L.P. § 9.32, at 430 (although some American courts have denied enforcement of equitable servitudes in gross, it is "illogical" to do so considering "that practically all of the American courts have now recognized the validity of legal easements in gross against subsequent owners of the servient land"). Note the interesting question of legal process involved here: should a court follow a rule only when doing so furthers the reason or purpose underlying the rule?

2. **Authority.** The American Law of Property indicates that the rule against running burdens when the benefit is held in gross applies only to equitable servitudes. *See* 2 A.L.P. § 9.13, at 374-76; § 9.32. The first Restatement of Property indicates that the rule applies only to real covenants. *See* Restatement of Property § 537 & cmt. c; § 539 cmt. k. (Review § 537 of the first Restatement, considered in connection with Gallager v. Bell, Section A.1.b, *supra*. Do you see how that section provides that the burden of a real covenant cannot run when the benefit is held in gross?) The third Restatement adopts the view that benefits can be created in gross. *See* Restatement Third § 2.6(1). What does the court in the principal case say?

3. **Policy.** The major objection to the running of burdens when the benefit is held in gross is the difficulty of freeing the burdened land from the restriction by negotiating a release: the holder of an appurtenant benefit can be located by inquiry or inspection of the land records; an in-gross benefit, not being tied to land use, migrates with its owner. *See* Restatement Third § 7.13 cmt. a. Is that convincing? Suppose that the defendant in Snow v. Van Dam wanted to buy the right to sell ice cream on Lot D. Could he find the relevant benefitted owners? Do you think that a release would otherwise be difficult to negotiate successfully in that case? Suppose that in Walton v. Capital Land Co. (Chapter 6), Walton wanted to buy back the right to exclude other users from the right of way across his land. Although the benefit was held in gross, it was held by a corporation; would it have been difficult for Walton to identify the party with whom he had to negotiate? Should the relevant question (difficulty or ease of securing a release) be addressed directly, or through classification of the benefit? *See* Restatement Third § 7.13 (court may modify or terminate a servitude held in gross with the consent of beneficiaries who can be located, "subject to suitable provisions for protection of the interests of those who have not been located").

4. **A few other questions.** Consider the following further possible differences between the easement and covenant categories.

a. An easement is a property interest, and like all property, it can be the subject of a gift. *See* Chapter 6. Can I give you a real covenant or an equitable servitude?

b. A court will refuse to enforce an equitable servitude when neighborhood conditions have so changed that the benefitted party ceases to enjoy any substantial benefit from performance of the obligation. (The analogy is to the doctrine of frustration of purpose in the law of contracts.) Is an easement subject to termination under the doctrine of changed conditions? *See* Section C.2 below.

2.   Leases, Licenses, Contracts, and Servitudes

TODD v. KROLICK
466 N.Y.S.2d 788 (N.Y. App. Div. 1983)

MEMORANDUM DECISION.

Appeal from an order of the Supreme Court at Special Term, entered October 18, 1982 in Schenectady County, which granted plaintiff's motion for a preliminary injunction and denied defendants' cross motion to dismiss the complaint.

Plaintiff is the operator of a business that provides laundry machines for use in apartment complexes pursuant to agreements under which the owners of the apartments receive a share of the revenues generated by the coin operated machines. On August 10, 1979, plaintiff entered into a written agreement with Monarch Associates, defendants' predecessor in title, giving plaintiff a sole and exclusive right to install and maintain laundry machines in the apartment complex presently owned by defendants. The contract was for a period of 10 years and purported to be binding "on the heirs, successors and assigns of the parties and the rights hereunder shall not be disturbed or affected by foreclosure, acquisition, merger or any change of ownership."

In 1980, Monarch Associates, in lieu of foreclosure, transferred the property by deed to Marine Midland Bank. In February, 1981, the bank conveyed the property to defendants. During negotiations for the purchase of the property, defendants inquired about the laundry machines on the property and were advised by Marine Midland Bank that there was no existing agreement concerning any laundry machines located on the subject premises. In response to several written requests from defendants to remove the machines, plaintiff commenced this action seeking a permanent injunction preventing the removal of the machines during the term of its contract with Monarch Associates and, by order to show cause, moved for a preliminary injunction. Defendants opposed the motion and cross-moved to dismiss the complaint. Special Term granted plaintiff's motion for a preliminary injunction and denied defendants' cross motion. This appeal by defendants ensued.

[T]he contract between plaintiff and Monarch Associates was in the nature of a license rather than a lease or an easement. The agreement did not give plaintiff exclusive possession and control of any definite space in the apartment complex, the only requirement being that tenants have access to the machines. Accordingly, defendants are not bound by the terms of the contract merely because they had knowledge of the agreement and may have accepted benefits thereunder. While it is difficult to distinguish an easement from a license in real property, they are distinct in principle. An easement always implies an interest in the land in and over which it is to be enjoyed, whereas a license merely confers a personal privilege to do some act or acts on the land without possessing any interest therein. Further, since an easement creates an interest in land, it is normally created by grant or prescription. While the grant need not contain all the formalities of a deed, it must contain a description of the land that is to be subject to the easement with sufficient clarity to locate it with reasonable certainty. Here, the contract between plaintiff and defendants' predecessor in title did not purport to create any interest in plaintiff in the apartment complex. Instead, it merely conferred upon plaintiff the right or privilege to install laundry machines on the property and to service the same. Accordingly, we conclude that the agreement did no more than create a revocable license which was extinguished by the conveyance of the property to defendants.

Order reversed, on the law, with costs, and complaint dismissed.

LEVINE, JUSTICE (dissenting).

I respectfully dissent. The agreement between plaintiff and defendants' predecessor in interest created more than a revocable license. It gave plaintiff the right, exclusive against the owner of the fee and third persons, to install and maintain coin-operated washing and drying machines at a specifically designated apartment building in the City of Saratoga Springs. Incidental thereto, it also gave plaintiff the right to draw water and electricity from the building's power and water lines and to connect with its sewer line for waste disposal. These property-related benefits conferred in favor of plaintiff and burdens on the property interest of the owner were sufficient, under both past and recent precedent, to create an interest in the nature either of an easement in gross or arising out of a covenant "running with the land." As such, plaintiff's interest was enforceable against the original owner and any successors with notice. Rather than merely being given a privilege to do one or more acts on the real property for a specific purpose, plaintiff essentially was granted the right to commercial exploitation of, and permanent possession and occupancy of space in, the servient realty during a fixed period of time. [T]hese are the basic characteristics which distinguish an easement in gross from a license. Certainly, the exclusive rights to occupy a portion of the realty and to draw water and power therefrom conferred a greater estate in the land than the right to take water from a spring on the property in Historic Estates v. United Paper Board Co., 21 N.Y.S.2d 819 (N.Y. App. Div.), aff'd 33 N.E.2d 866 (N.Y.), or to maintain equipment on the subject property in Arvay v. New York Tel. Co., 434 N.Y.S.2d 480 (N.Y. App. Div.).

Nor does the absence of a more complete description of the subject land negate the existence of an easement here. The building in which the machines were to be placed was clearly identified in the agreement. The agreement's description of the servient realty was no less specific here than it was in the agreement in Borough Bill Posting Co. v. Levy, 129 N.Y.S. 740 (N.Y. App. Div.). That no definite location for plaintiff's machines was designated in the agreement is likewise not fatal to an easement. The failure to specify a definite space for the location of the signs in Borough Bill Posting Co. or the location of the machines to be maintained on the land in Arvay did not negate the existence of easements in those cases. Bermann v.

Windale Properties, 164 N.Y.S.2d 817 (N.Y. App. Div.), relied upon by the majority for this point, should not be controlling. In *Bermann* and the cases cited therein, the competing contentions were restricted to whether the agreements created a license or a lease. Since the agreements in those cases did not describe specifically demised premises, it was proper to hold that no leases had been created. However, in none of these cases was there consideration of whether an easement in gross had been granted.

Equally, in my view, the rights plaintiff acquired in the contract are enforceable against a purchaser with notice as a covenant "running with the land." The provision of the agreement expressly binding the owner, his heirs and successors in interest establishes the parties' intent to have the covenant run. Undeniably, there was an unbroken line of succession of conveyances between defendants and plaintiff's convenator sufficient to establish privity of estate. Under the agreement, the owner was prevented from excluding plaintiff's machines from the property, from otherwise using the area to be devoted to the machines, and from installing on the property his own machines and those of third persons. Defendants' predecessor's covenants in the agreement thus seriously impinged upon the covenantor's rights of ownership and beneficial enjoyment of the property. Therefore, the agreement substantially "touched and concerned" the subject property. Since there were sufficient allegations that defendants were purchasers with notice and establishing plaintiff's rights as either an easement in gross or a covenant running with the land, Special Term properly denied defendants' cross motion to dismiss the complaint.

Moreover, in view of the serious questions regarding the adequacy of plaintiff's remedy at law, Special Term was also correct in granting a preliminary injunction. Therefore, its order should be affirmed.

NOTES AND QUESTIONS

1. **The last appeal.** New York's highest court, without dissent, affirmed the Appellate Division. *See* Todd v. Krolick, 466 N.E.2d 149 (N.Y. 1984):

> The complaint does not state a cause of action because, as the Appellate Division held, the washing machine agreement between plaintiff and Monarch Associates which plaintiff seeks to enforce against defendants, Monarch's successor in title, is a license, not a lease or easement. The complaint is insufficient for the further reason that it fails to allege that the agreement, which purported to bind Monarch and its successors for a period of 10 years, was recorded. Under sections 290 and 291 of the Real Property Law the agreement, whether a license, lease, easement or covenant running with the land, because it creates an interest in real property for longer than three years, "is void as against any person who subsequently purchases or acquires the same real property in good faith for a valuable consideration" (Real Property Law, § 291). The complaint alleges no more than that defendants had notice of the washing machines, not that they had notice of the agreement. There is, therefore, no allegation of constructive notice of the agreement sufficient to make section 291 inapplicable.

Do you agree with either of the reasons given by the court? On notice, is the case distinguishable from Weiman v. Butterman in Chapter 4, Section A.3?

2. **Categories and consequences.** In *Todd*, would wrongful termination of the contract prior to its stated end have given plaintiff a damages claim against Monarch for breach of contract? Would that remedy have been satisfactory to the plaintiff do you think? What remedies does B have against X (the purchaser of the apartment complex), if the A-B transaction is: a contract; a lease; a license; an easement?

3. **Easement.** If a lease for a fixed period isn't a tenancy at will, why is a nonpossessory interest for a fixed period (as in *Todd*) a license? Why isn't it an easement or a running covenant? Shouldn't the whole classification question — possessory vs. nonpossessory interest — be irrelevant in *Todd*? If X has notice, shouldn't B win under either classification? Isn't the dissent in *Todd* right?

4. **Policy.** To call a nonpossessory term arrangement a license is essentially to call it a simple contract right, enforceable against the promisor by damages only, and not enforceable at all against the promisor's successor. What policy reasons might influence a court to call the arrangement a license? Is it better to discuss those policy objections openly, or to decide whether the arrangement in the principal case runs or not by categorizing the transaction?

ARONSOHN v. MANDARA
484 A.2d 675 (N.J. 1984)

SCHREIBER, J.

Edward Kawash and Theresa A. Kawash, who owned a home at 479 Weymouth Drive, Wyckoff, New Jersey, decided to add a patio to the rear of their house. They entered into a contract with the Mandara Masonry Corporation for the construction of that patio at a cost of $5,000. The Corporation was owned by William S. Mandara, who constructed the addition with his father, Salvatore Mandara, and three other employees. According to the complaint, the patio was constructed in 1974.

Plaintiffs, Richard F. Aronsohn and Deborah Aronsohn, purchased the home from Mr. and Mrs. Kawash in August 1975. The purchase agreement provided that the contract was subject to "a satisfactory engineering inspection," that the agreement was made "upon the knowledge of the parties as to the value of whatever buildings are upon the [land] and not on any representations made as to character or quality," and that "no representations have been made by any of the parties except as set forth herein."

In 1978, plaintiffs noticed that the patio was beginning to separate from the wall of the house; that some of the slate slabs that formed the patio floor were beginning to rise; and that the outside patio wall was beginning to buckle. Plaintiffs then commenced this action against the defendant Corporation and Salvatore Mandara alleging breaches of express and implied warranties [plaintiffs' other claims are omitted].

At the trial plaintiffs introduced evidence establishing the aforementioned facts and also produced as their expert a building contractor who had made visual inspections of the patio. The patio floor consisted of slate slabs resting on concrete, which had been poured over a dirt foundation. The patio extended along the entire rear of the house, and since the land sloped sharply down away from the house, it had been necessary to build up the ground. The patio was surrounded by a cinder-block wall with brick facing.

The expert's ultimate conclusion was that the construction was improper, in part because the ground supporting the patio had not been adequately compacted. The expert asserted that because the dirt had been improperly compacted, it had pushed out the wall. He also testified that the penetration of water beneath the slabs had contributed to the problem. The water was unable to escape, according to him, because no weepholes had been provided to permit drainage. He estimated that it would cost $16,000 to remove the existing patio and install a new one.

Salvatore Mandara testified on behalf of defendants. He explained how the patio had been built and stated that the construction method accorded with industry standards. He also stated that the patio could have been built in another fashion, but that cost had been a factor for Mr. and Mrs. Kawash. In his opinion the problem was due to the owners' failure to patch up cracks as they appeared; had they done so, he said, water would not have seeped beneath the slabs into the ground, causing the slabs to rise and the wall to buckle.

The trial court granted defendants' motion to dismiss. It found that plaintiffs' claim on express warranty was flawed because defendants' contract to construct the patio had been with Edward and Theresa Kawash and not the plaintiffs. The trial court also held that no implied warranty of habitability applied because the philosophy of the law with respect to mass producers of goods or homes was inapplicable to a situation like this one, which involved a service contract. The Appellate Division affirmed. It found that neither express nor implied warranty was justified since there was no privity of contract, though it disagreed with the trial court that this was a service contract. We granted plaintiffs' petition for certification.

I

Plaintiffs are seeking the benefit of the bargain they made in their agreement to purchase the home. That benefit is based on the previous owners' contract with defendants to construct the patio.

When, as in this case, there is no express contractual provision concerning workmanship, the law implies a covenant that the contract will be performed in a reasonably good and workmanlike manner. The agreement between defendant and the Kawashes concerning the building of the patio thus contained an implied promise by defendant to construct the patio in a workmanlike fashion. If the Kawashes, while they still owned the property, had discovered that the patio had been negligently built, defendants would have been liable to them for damage to the property flowing from a breach of that implied promise of reasonable workmanship. The question in this case is whether the contractor should be immunized from his contractual obligation to have performed his work in a workmanlike, non-negligent manner simply because the original owner or buyer transferred the property to a successor. We think not, at least in the absence of a nonassignability clause in the contract.

Ordinarily, rights for breach of contract are assignable. There would certainly be no problem with enforcing such an assignment if the contract between the contractor and the homeowner contained an express provision authorizing assignment to a successor owner of the homeowner's rights against the contractor. See Restatement (Second) of the Law of Contracts § 317 (1981). If the contract contains no prohibition on assignment, such rights may be assigned in the absence of any public policy reason to the contrary. See 4 A. Corbin, On Contracts § 857, at 410; § 872, at 485-86; § 873, at 494 (1951). Here, there has been no proof of any provision in the Kawashes' contract with defendant prohibiting assignment of the Kawashes' contractual rights, and there are no compelling policy reasons justifying a bar to the assignment of those rights.

Moreover, one can infer from the circumstances that the Kawashes did in fact assign those rights to plaintiffs. Once they sold their house to plaintiffs, the Kawashes no longer had any interest in retaining for themselves the right to have had their patio built in a non-negligent manner. Rather, it is reasonable to infer that they transferred any such claim to plaintiffs. The transfer or conveyance of their property is indicative of their intent to assign to the buyers their right of action to enforce promises made with respect to that property. See 3 H. Tiffany, Real Property § 849, at 444 (3d ed. 1939). Defendants' contention that the provision in the purchase agreement that "[t]his contract contains the entire agreement of the parties" impliedly negates any assignment of the contract between defendants and the Kawashes misses the point. The implied covenants and terms of a contract are as effective components of the agreement as those expressed.

Defendants' implied promise to construct the patio in a workmanlike manner may also be analogized to a real property covenant that runs with the land. What happens when a vendor has had a new roof installed, accompanied by a ten-year warranty, and the vendor sells the home within one year after the installation? Should not covenants of this type, which benefit the property, continue to run with the land? Although the technical elements of covenants that run with the land may not be satisfied, the policy reasons for not requiring contractual privity are fully applicable to promises by contractors properly to perform their work on residential homes. The benefits of such covenants touch and concern the property and should flow with the ownership despite the absence of privity between the contractor and the present owner. This policy was expressed in Horn v. Miller, 20 A. 706, 708 (1890), as follows:

> The obligation of contracts is, in general, limited to the parties making them. Where privity of contract is dispensed with, there must ordinarily be privity of estate; but justice sometimes even requires that the right to enjoy such contracts should extend to all who have a beneficial interest in their fulfillment, not to impose a burden upon an ignorant and innocent third person, but to enable purchasers of land to avail themselves of the benefit to which they are in justice entitled.

There is some precedent for extending the contractual liability of a home builder to a third person who may buy that home despite the absence of contractual privity between the contractor and the buyer. We agree with the Mississippi Supreme Court [in Keyes v. Guy Bailey Homes, Inc., 439 So.2d 670 (Miss. 1983)] that the privity requirement should be abandoned in suits brought by a homeowner against a contractor for violation of an implied promise of good workmanship. To require privity between the contractor and the homeowner in such a situation would defeat the purpose of the implied warranty of good workmanship and could leave innocent homeowners without a remedy for negligently built structures in their home. The contractor should not be relieved of liability for unworkmanlike construction simply because of the fortuity that the property on which he did the construction has changed hands. Nor should an innocent buyer of property be deprived of recourse against a contractor who made improvements on the property if the buyer suffers financial loss as a result of the contractor's negligent workmanship. This is not to say that a contractor, in his agreement with the owner, could not have imposed limitations or restrictions on his obligations that could be binding on a subsequent purchaser, provided they did not contravene public policy. Such a distribution of risks comports with the original negotiation. See Epstein, *Commentary on Product Liability — Passage of Time*, 58 N.Y.U. L. Rev. 930, 933 (1983).

II

Although we find that defendants may be liable to plaintiffs for violating an implied provision of their contract with the Kawashes, we agree with the trial court and the Appellate Division that plaintiffs may not sustain a cause of action against defendants on any express provision in that contract. Plaintiffs did not establish that defendants had violated any express provisions in the Kawashes' agreement.

IV

There was conflicting evidence in the instant case as to whether the defendant Corporation built the patio in a workmanlike manner. Since the evidence should have been judged in the light most favorable to the plaintiffs on the defendant's motion for judgment, we are of the opinion, for the reasons stated, that plaintiffs made a prima facie showing of a cause of action. Therefore, the matter should be remanded for a new trial.

On retrial several other matters will undoubtedly be clarified. Plaintiffs' purchase contract provided that they could have an engineering inspection of the premises. The record does not disclose the nature and extent of that inspection. If a defective condition had been readily apparent or discoverable upon a reasonable inspection before or at the time plaintiffs took title, then recovery for the defective condition would not be appropriate. For example, plaintiffs' complaint about the lack of weepholes, a condition that was readily apparent on visual inspection, is not well founded.

The record is not clear whether the other allegedly defective condition, inadequate compaction of the ground, was apparent or discoverable upon a reasonable inspection. It is also uncertain whether plaintiffs might have prevented the damage if they had acted promptly when cracks first appeared. In addition, there was some evidence of the cost of a new patio, but that evidence did not take into account depreciation. These and other matters to which we have referred should be explored on the retrial.

The case is reversed and remanded for a new trial, with costs to abide the event.

NOTES AND QUESTIONS

1. **Contract law.** How does the court explain its result in terms of contract law? Do you see a possible flaw in any step in the court's argument? If you represented the building contractor, what term might you insert in future contracts to avoid the liability imposed by the court?

2. **Property law.** The court also supports its result by an analogy to the law of promises running with the land. What "technical elements" of that law might stand in the way of the imposition of liability on the defendant? Treating the defendant's promise as a real covenant, is it relevant that the breach occurred *before* the Kawashes sold the land to the plaintiffs? *See* Restatement of Property § 552 cmt. a (1944) ("The benefit which is capable of running is that of future performance of the promise. If the promise has been broken, the cause of action which may have arisen out of the breach is incapable of running."). Would the Kawashes' cause of action on the breached real covenant have been assignable? *See id.* What would an assignment require? *See id.* cmt. c (assignment of cause of action on breached promise "requires something more than a mere transfer of the land. There must in addition be a manifestation of an intention to assign."). Is the court's real covenant analogy subject to the same potential flaw that besets its contract analysis? Is the court's result a good one?

3. **The contractor's warranty as a running covenant.** What is the content of the masonry contractor's promise in the principal case? When is that promise breached? In order for the contractor's promise to run to a subsequent purchaser of the dominant estate as a real covenant, is it necessary to treat the contractor's obligation as both a warranty and an implied promise to repair (along the lines of the implied warranty of habitability now widely recognized in lease cases)? If the contractor's warranty creates a servitude, is the burden in gross?

3. Covenants and Defeasible Fees Compared

You recall from Chapter 2 that a transferor may impose a land use restriction by way of a defeasible fee ("to the A Church so long as the land is used for church purposes") as well as by a covenant ("to the A Church, which covenants that the land shall be used only for church purposes"). The following case allows us to review the important distinction between the two forms of restriction. It is also, if you pay attention to the extended metaphor that the writer of the opinion exploits, a fun read — quite refreshing at this point. (To appreciate the metaphor, it helps to know that Carl G. Jung [1875-1961] was a friend and early collaborator of Freud, who later broke with Freud, founded his own school of analytical psychology, and developed the concept of the collective unconscious. *See* Alasdair MacIntyre, *Carl Gustav Jung, in* 4 The Encyclopedia of Philosophy 294 (1967)).

HUMPHREY v. C.G. JUNG EDUCATIONAL CENTER
714 F.2d 477 (5th Cir. 1983)

JOHN R. BROWN, CIRCUIT JUDGE.

Very rarely does a Texas trespass to try a title suit disturb the collective consciousness of this court. As diversity jurisdiction sometimes manifests itself in unusual ways, however, we consider such a suit today. By interpreting past decisions, we must probe the psyche of the Texas courts to determine whether those courts would enforce the deed clause in question as a condition subsequent with right of re-entry, and so allow the plaintiffs to claim an undivided one-half interest in an improved lot in the museum district of Houston. Finding the clause to be ambiguous, the district court in a bench trial held that the Texas courts would construe the clause as a mere covenant, and so deny the plaintiffs' claim. Accordingly, the court rendered judgment in favor of the defendants. We agree and affirm.

Case History

The case was submitted to the district court for decision on stipulated facts which we briefly summarize. The disputed property is located in Lot F, in Block 8, of the Turner Addition to the City of Houston, on Montrose Boulevard. Block 8 is divided into six lots of approximately equal size, which were sold by the owners, the Trustees of the Hermann Hospital Estate, on March 20, 1919. Each deed contained various restrictions, which expired by their terms on January 1, 1935. Lot F was conveyed to Herbert Humphrey and Robert Caldwell. Herbert and Blanche Humphrey also purchased Lot D, while Robert and Edith Caldwell also purchased Lot A. On February 11, 1920, the Humphreys and Caldwells conveyed Lot F to Tom Randolph. That general warranty deed contains the following provisions:

> It is agreed by the vendee herein, as part of the consideration herein and as a covenant running with the land hereby conveyed, that the said land should be used for residence purposes only, and that no dwelling house shallever be erected thereon, the original cost of which shall be less than $10,000.00 and that no portion of same, other than galleries and steps, shall be erected nearer than 28 feet to the property line on Montrose Blvd., nor nearer than 15 feet to the property line on 16th Street and that no outhouses shall be erected nearer than 35 feet to any street or avenue line, and no part of same shall ever be conveyed, transferred or demised to any person other than of the Caucasian race, and the vendee covenants that he will not use or permit to be used the property hereby conveyed for the purpose of erecting, establishing or conducting thereon any store or shop for the sale of merchandise or any other commodity, and should the owner of the land hereby conveyed at any time fail to comply with any of the provisions of this covenant, Grantors herein, or any owner of property in Block 8, Turner Addition, may by instituting suit, enforce a compliance therewith, or restrain the further violation thereof, or said land shall revert to the Grantors herein, should they so elect.

Resolution of this suit depends entirely upon the interpretation given to those provisions.

The Caldwells sold Lot A in 1941. The Humphreys sold Lot D in 1942. Neither deed placed any restrictions on the use of the property. None of the Humphreys have owned property in or resided in the Turner Addition since 1942.

None of the restrictions set forth in the deed to Lot F were violated prior to August, 1972, when that property was conveyed to Jasper Galleries, Inc. Jasper Galleries demolished the existing residence and built an art gallery building on Lots F and E. The gallery grandly opened in May, 1973. In July, 1975, Jasper Galleries conveyed Lots F and E to Carolyn Grant Fay.[3]

No other lot in Block 8 is still being used for residential purposes. Lots A, B and C are the site of the contemporary Arts Museum, while Lot D is the site of the offices of an architectural firm.

Plaintiffs Robert K. Humphrey and Elizabeth Humphrey Murphy are children of Blanche and Herbert Humphrey, while plaintiff Marjorie Hunter Humphrey is the widow of a third child of Blanche and Herbert Humphrey. The Humphreys instituted this suit in September, 1976. The parties agree that Lot F is being used for nonresidential purposes, in violation of the restrictions contained in the 1920 deed. They differ as to whether under Texas law the Humphreys can enforce those restrictions as conditions subsequent and so reenter the property.

Analytical Jurisprudence

Fay and her tenants argued below that the Texas courts would construe the residential-use-only restriction as a covenant, the remedies for a breach of which would be limited to injunctive relief and damages, rather than as a condition subsequent, the breach of which would allow the plaintiffs to reclaim title to the property. The district court concluded that even when a deed contains express language of reverter or reentry, a Texas court may construe the deed restriction as a covenant. Such covenants are enforceable only by injunctive relief or damages, not by forfeiture of the estate. Relying on W.F. White Land Co. v. Christenson, 14 S.W.2d 369 (Tex.Civ.App.—Fort Worth 1928, no writ), the court held that the provisions in this deed were ambiguous in their meaning. Citing settled Texas rules of construction, which look with disfavor upon forfeitures, the court then concluded that the Texas courts would resolve that ambiguity in favor of the grantee, Fay, and construe the provisions as covenants. As the plaintiffs sought neither injunctive relief nor damages, they could recover nothing. The court held, moreover, that any recovery under the residential-use covenant would be precluded by the neighborhood's drastic change in character over the years. The court rendered judgment in favor of the defendants.

---

[3] The other appellees, the C.G. Jung Educational Center of Houston and Archway Galleries are lessees of Carolyn Grant Fay.

Second Opinion

We consider the issue of whether the Texas courts would find these deed provisions to be ambiguous and so construe them as creating mere covenants rather than conditions subsequent enforceable by forfeiture of the estate. As did the district court, we must determine how Texas' courts would resolve this question. While the diagnosis is difficult, we are convinced that the district court's analysis was correct.

Forfeitures are not favored under the law. "If the terms of a contract are fairly susceptible of an interpretation which will prevent a forfeiture, they will be so construed." Henshaw v. Texas Natural Resources Foundation, 216 S.W.2d 566, 570 (Tex. 1949). "The courts will not declare a forfeiture, unless they are compelled to do so, by language which will admit of but one construction, and that construction is such as compels a forfeiture." Link v. Texas Pharmacal Co., 276 S.W.2d 903, 906 (Tex.Civ.App.—San Antonio 1955 no writ), quoting Automobile Ins. Co. v. Teague, 37 S.W.2d 151, 153 (Tex. Comm. App. 1931).

> Forfeitures clauses fail in the event they are ambiguously expressed. As stated in Decker v. Kirlicks, 216 S.W. 385, 386, 110 Tex. 90: "If the provision is ambiguous, that alone condemns it as a forfeiture provision. The forfeiture should rest upon surer ground."

Link, 276 S.W.2d at 906.

However, although conditions subsequent are not favored, "Where the language creating the condition is clear and specific it will be enforced." Hudson v. Caffey, 179 S.W.2d 1017, 1019 (Tex. Civ. App.—Texarkana 1944, writ ref'd w.o.m.).

The fundamental issue before us, then, is whether the Texas courts would find the language of the 1920 deed to be ambiguous as to whether it creates conditions subsequent with right of reentry or merely a number of covenants. If the courts would consider the language to be at all ambiguous, under Texas law we must decline to enforce the residential-use restriction as a condition subsequent and construe it as a covenant. If there is no ambiguity, however, the Humphreys may reenter and reclaim their share of the property.

We agree with the district court that the Texas courts would find the language in the deed to be ambiguous. In *White Land Company*, the Court of Civil Appeals construed a deed which contained the following two provisions:

> [I]n case the said grantee, or his heirs, as executors, administrators or assigns shall ever violate any one of said conditions contained herein and made a part of the covenants of this deed, the said land and all improvements therein shall immediately revert to and become the property of the grantor herein and its successors or assigns, and it shall be lawful for said grantor and its successors or assigns to re-enter said premises as in its first and former estate.

> [T]he conditions herein contained are intended to and shall run with the land, and should the grantee, his heirs, executors, administrators or assigns, or any person claiming under him, violate any of the foregoing covenants, then W.F. White Land Company, or its successors, or any owner

of any lot conveyed herein, shall have the right to enjoin the doing of same, and in the event the violation has already taken place, then such remedy shall extend to the removal of the improvements placed on said premises in violation of any covenant herein.

14 S.W.2d at 370.

Although that deed contained express language of both reverter and reentry, the court concluded "that what purported to be conditions subsequent in the deed are merely building restrictions denoting covenants, for the violation of which injunctive relief was provided in the instrument." 14 S.W.2d at 371. The court held that the provision for alternative remedies short of forfeiture and the single reference to the restrictions as "covenants" created ambiguity sufficient to require the court to adopt that interpretation of the instrument.

The Humphreys seek to distinguish *White Land Company* by contending that that case was decided by the application of the "election of remedies" doctrine. That doctrine holds that where two inconsistent remedies are available to a complaining party, the selection of one remedy acts as a waiver of the other. In *White Land Company* the plaintiffs had sought injunctive relief in the alternative to the court's declaration of a forfeiture of the property. The Humphreys claim that the *White Land Company* court declined to order a forfeiture because the plaintiffs had chosen to invoke the less harsh remedy of injunctive relief. *White Land Company* contains language to support the Humphreys' view. At the same time, however, the opinion places great emphasis upon the fact that a deed must be unambiguous and unequivocal in its language if it is to be construed as creating a condition subsequent. *White Land Company* quite plainly holds that the language in question in that particular deed was not sufficiently clear. The provision for alternative relief and the reference to the restrictions as covenants rendered the deed sufficiently ambiguous to lead the court to interpret it as indeed creating covenants rather than conditions subsequent.

The Humphreys also seek to distinguish *White Land Company* from the present case by pointing to differences in the language of the two deeds concerned. In particular, the Humphreys emphasize that the deed here specifically provides that the land shall "revert" to the grantors "should they so elect." In *White Land Company*, there was no such language in the deed. The similarities between the instruments far outweigh any differences, however. In making its decision, the court in *White Land Company* relied at least in part on the fact that the restrictions in question were expressly referred to in the deed as "covenants." To [the] court, the use of that term rendered the deed less than unequivocal in its meaning. Here, the restrictions are consistently described as a "covenant," and never as a condition. As the district court pointed out, the deed contains neither the customary language of a conditional limitation nor that of a condition subsequent. The use of the language of reversion at the end of the provisions does not dispel the ambiguity inherent in the language of the deed.

White Land Company stands firmly for the proposition that the Texas courts will construe anything less than clear, plain and unequivocal language as creating merely a restrictive covenant, despite the fact that the deed contains provisions for reverter or right of reentry upon the breach of those covenants. We are convinced that the Texas courts would consider this language to be less than unequivocal. Given that fact, the district court was correct in concluding that the deed was ambiguous and in applying Texas' strong constructional preference for restrictive covenants as opposed to conditions subsequent.

The Humphreys argue that the Texas Supreme Court would not follow *White Land Company*. As they point out, the case has been criticized by one commentator. Goldstein, *Rights of Entry and Possibilities of Reverter as Devices to Restrict the Use of Land*, 54 Harv.L.Rev. 248, 260-62 (1940). We have seen no indication, however, that the Texas Supreme Court would disapprove of or decline to follow *White Land Company*. Absent a clear signal to that effect, we are bound to follow these decisions of the highest Texas courts which have expressed themselves on this issue.

Once we have determined that the Texas courts would find these deed provisions to be ambiguous, the case is decided. Under Texas law, such ambiguity must be resolved in favor of the grantee, and the provisions construed as mere restrictive covenants enforceable via injunctive relief or suit for damages. The plaintiffs thus cannot regain the estate via forfeiture. As the plaintiffs have asked for neither an injunction nor damages they are entitled to no relief. Moreover, as the district court found, the plaintiffs would in any event be precluded from enforcing the covenants because of the drastically changed character of the neighborhood in which the disputed property is located.

The district court correctly entered judgment for the defendants.

AFFIRMED.

NOTES AND QUESTIONS

1. **The relevant issue.** The Goldstein article cited by the court called the *White Land Company* case "the high water mark of constructional aversion" to the defeasible fee estate. 54 Harv. L. Rev. at 261. Given the unmistakable language of forfeiture in both that case and in *Humphrey*, what should the constructional question have been? (Review the Notes after Forsgren v. Sollie in Chapter 2.)

2. **The third Restatement.** Section 8.4 of the third Restatement provides:

§ 8.4 Remedy for Condition Broken by Violation of General-Plan Restrictions

Land-use restrictions created to implement a general plan of development in a residential community may be enforced by any remedy available for enforcement of a restrictive covenant. A provision for forfeiture of the burdened estate to the common grantor on breach of condition or termination of a fee-simple determinable caused by violation of the restriction is not enforceable.

See also *id.* § 2.2 cmt. e, at 66-67 (defeasible fees "were widely used to create subdivision restrictons in the first half of the 20th century because of the doctrinal uncertainties and limitations of servitudes law," but were completely abandoned "when doctrinal uncertainties in servitudes law abated"). Was the *White Land Company* case ahead of its time? See generally Gerald Korngold, *For Unifying*

Servitudes and Defeasible Fees: Property Law's Functional Equivalents, 66 Tex. L. Rev. 533 (1988).

3. **Review.** What "doctrinal uncertainties" of the law of servitudes are avoided by a grantor's imposition of a land use restriction in the form of a defeasible fee estate?

C. SCOPE AND TERMINATION OF COVENANTS

Much of what we have said earlier about the scope and termination of easements applies as well to running covenants. *See, e.g.*, Peckham v. Milroy, 17 P.3d 1256 (Wash. Ct. App. 2001) (discussing abandonment of, and estoppel to assert, benefit of restrictive covenant prohibiting home businesses). Accordingly, we compress the scope and termination questions here, focusing primarily on new issues.

1. Scope

The question of the uses allowed or restricted by a covenant usually turns on the language of the document at issue; the problems are essentially those of the interpretation of contract language. *See generally* E. Allan Farnsworth, Contracts §§ 7.1-7.17 (3d ed. 1999). Some unambiguous restrictions, however, are invalid because they violate public policy, or a statutory or constitutional provision. The following case deals with both an intepretation and a validity question.

HILL v. COMMUNITY OF DAMIEN OF MOLOKAI
911 P.2d 861 (N.M. 1996)

FROST, JUSTICE.

Defendant-Appellant Community of Damien of Molokai (Community) appeals from the district court's ruling in favor of Plaintiffs-Appellees, enjoining the further use of the property at 716 Rio Arriba, S.E., Albuquerque, as a group home for individuals with AIDS. Plaintiffs-Appellees argue that the group home violates a restrictive covenant. The Community contends that the group home is a permitted use under the covenant and, alternatively, that enforcing the restrictive covenant against the group home would violate the Federal Fair Housing Act, 42 U.S.C. §§ 3601-3631 (1988) [hereinafter FHA]. We reverse.

I. FACTS

The underlying facts of this case are not in dispute. The Community is a private, nonprofit corporation which provides homes to people with AIDS as well as other terminal illnesses. In December 1992 the Community leased the residence at 716 Rio Arriba, S.E., Albuquerque, located in a planned subdivision called Four Hills Village, for use as a group home for four individuals with AIDS. The four residents who subsequently moved into the Community's group home were unrelated, and each required some degree of in-home nursing care.

Plaintiffs-Appellees, William Hill, III, Derek Head, Charlene Leamons, and Bernard Dueto (hereinafter Neighbors) live in Four Hills Village on the same dead-end street as the group home. Shortly after the group home opened, the Neighbors noticed an increase in traffic on Rio Arriba street, going to and from the group home. The Neighbors believed that the Community's use of its house as a group home for people with AIDS violated one of the restrictive covenants applicable to all the homes in the sixteenth installment of Four Hills Village. Installment sixteen encompasses the Community's group home and the Neighbors' houses. The applicable covenant provides in relevant part:

2. USE OF LAND

No lot shall ever be used for any purpose other than single family residence purposes. No dwelling house located thereon shall ever be used for other than single family residence purposes, nor shall any outbuildings or structure located thereon be used in a manner other than incidental to such family residence purposes. The erection or maintenance or use of any building, or the use of any lot for other purposes, including, but not restricted to such examples as stores, shops, flats, duplex houses, apartment houses, rooming houses, tourist courts, schools, churches, hospitals, and filling stations is hereby expressly prohibited.

The Neighbors specifically argue that the term "single family residence" does not include group homes in which unrelated people live together.

On August 12, 1993, the Neighbors filed for an injunction to enforce the covenant and to prevent further use of the Community's house as a group home. After hearing evidence at two separate hearings, the trial court held that the restrictive covenant prevented the use of the Community's house as a group home for people with AIDS and issued a permanent injunction against the Community. The trial court entered specific findings that the Community's use of the home generated a significant number of vehicle trips up and down the street and that the increased traffic had detrimentally altered the character of the neighborhood.

The Community appealed the trial court's order, and we granted a stay of the permanent injunction pending this appeal. We now review, first, the Community's claims regarding the proper interpretation of the restrictive covenant, and second, the applicability of the FHA.

II. FOUR HILLS RESTRICTIVE COVENANTS

The first issue before us is the applicability of the Four Hills restrictive covenant to the Community's group home. As this Court noted in Cain v. Powers, 668 P.2d 300, 302 (N.M. 1983), in determining whether to enforce a restrictive covenant, we are guided by certain general rules of construction. First, if the language is unclear or ambiguous, we will resolve the restrictive covenant in favor of the free enjoyment of the property and against restrictions. Second, we will not read restrictions on the use and enjoyment of the land into the covenant by implication. Third, we must interpret the covenant reasonably, but strictly, so as not to create an illogical, unnatural, or strained construction. Fourth, we must give words in the restrictive covenant their ordinary and intended meaning.

A. Operating a Group Home Constitutes Residential Use

In reaching its conclusion that the group home violated the residential use restriction, the trial court made two specific findings regarding the nature of the current use of the home. The court found that the "Community uses the house as a non-profit hostel for providing services to handicapped individuals" and that the "Community uses of the residence are much closer to the uses commonly associated with health care facilities, apartment houses, and rooming houses than uses which are commonly associated with single family residences." Thus the trial court apparently concluded that the property was being used for commercial purposes rather than residential purposes. However, we find that the trial court's conclusions are incorrect as a matter of law.

It is undisputed that the group home is designed to provide the four individuals who live in the house with a traditional family structure, setting, and atmosphere, and that the individuals who reside there use the home much as would any family with a disabled family member. The four residents share communal meals. They provide support for each other socially, emotionally, and financially. They also receive spiritual guidance together from religious leaders who visit them on Tuesday evenings.

To provide for their health care needs, the residents contract with a private nursing service for health-care workers. These health-care workers do not reside at the home, and they are not affiliated with the Community in any way. The number of hours of service provided by the health-care workers is determined by a case-management group assigned by the state pursuant to a state program. The in-home health services that the residents receive from the health-care workers are precisely the same services to which any disabled individual would be entitled regardless of whether he or she lived in a group home or alone in a private residence. The health-care workers do most of the cooking and cleaning. The residents do their own shopping unless they are physically unable to leave the home.

The Community's role in the group home is to provide oversight and administrative assistance. It organizes the health-care workers' schedules to ensure that a nurse is present twenty-four hours per day, and it provides oversight to ensure that the workers are doing their jobs properly. It also receives donations of food and furniture on behalf of the residents. The Community provides additional assistance for the residents at times when they are unable to perform tasks themselves. A Community worker remains at the house during the afternoon and evening but does not reside at the home. The Community, in turn, collects rent from the residents based on the amount of social security income the residents receive, and it enforces a policy of no drinking or drug use in the home.

The Community's activities in providing the group home for the residents do not render the home a nonresidential operation such as a hospice or boarding house. As the South Carolina Supreme Court noted when faced with a similar situation involving a group home for mentally impaired individuals:

> This Court finds persuasive the reasoning of other jurisdictions which have held that the incident necessities of operating a group home such as

maintaining records, filing accounting reports, managing, supervising, and providing care for individuals in exchange for monetary compensation are collateral to the prime purpose and function of a family housekeeping unit. Hence, these activities do not, in and of themselves, change the character of a residence from private to commercial.

Rhodes v. Palmetto Pathway Homes, Inc., 400 S.E.2d 484, 485-486 (S.C. 1991). In Jackson v. Williams, 714 P.2d 1017, 1022 (Okla.1985), the Oklahoma Supreme Court similarly concluded:

> The essential purpose of the group home is to create a normal family atmosphere dissimilar from that found in traditional institutional care for the mentally handicapped. The operation of a group home is thus distinguishable from a use that is commercial — i.e., a boarding house that provides food and lodging only — or is institutional in character.

We agree. Accordingly, we conclude as a matter of law that, given the undisputed facts regarding how the Community operates the group home and regarding the nature of the family life in the home, the home is used for residential purposes in compliance with the restrictive covenant.

B. Residents of Group Home Meet Single Family Requirement

The Neighbors also argue on appeal that the four, unrelated residents of the group home do not constitute a "single family" as required by the restrictive covenant. The Neighbors contend that the restrictive covenant should be interpreted such that the term "family" encompasses only individuals related by blood or by law. We disagree.

The word "family" is not defined in the restrictive covenant and nothing in the covenant suggests that it was the intent of the framers to limit the term to a discrete family unit comprised only of individuals related by blood or by law. Accordingly, the use of the term "family" in the covenant is ambiguous. As we noted above, we must resolve any ambiguity in the restrictive covenant in favor of the free enjoyment of the property. This rule of construction therefore militates in favor of a conclusion that the term "family" encompasses a broader group than just related individuals and against restricting the use of the property solely to a traditional nuclear family.

In addition, there are several other factors that lead us to define the term "family" as including unrelated individuals. First, the Albuquerque municipal zoning ordinance provides a definition of family that is at odds with the restrictive definition suggested by the Neighbors. The Albuquerque zoning ordinance includes within the definition of the term "family," "[a]ny group of not more than five [unrelated] persons living together in a dwelling." Albuquerque, N.M., Rev. Ordinances, art. XIV, § 7-14-5(B) (41) (1974 & Supp.1991). Second, there is a strong public policy in favor of including small group homes within the definition of the term "family." The federal government has expressed a clear policy in favor of removing barriers preventing individuals with physical and mental disabilities from living in group homes in residential settings and against restrictive definitions of "families" that serve to exclude congregate living arrangements for the disabled.

The FHA squarely sets out this important public policy. The Developmental Disabilities Assistance and Bill of Rights Act, 42 U.S.C. § 6000 (1988 & Supp. II 1990), and the Rehabilitation Act of 1973, 29 U.S.C. § 701 (1988 & Supp. IV 1992), also identify a national policy favoring persons with disabilities living independently in normal communities and opposing barriers to this goal.

In New Mexico, the Developmental Disabilities Act, NMSA 1978, § 28-16A-2 expresses a clear state policy in favor of integrating disabled individuals into communities. The Act provides in relevant part:

> It is the purpose of the legislature in enacting the Developmental Disabilities Act to promote opportunities for all persons with developmental disabilities to live, work and participate with their peers in New Mexico communities. Priority shall be given to the development and implementation of support and services for persons with developmental disabilities that will enable and encourage them to achieve their greatest potential for independent and productive living by participating in inclusive community activities; and live in their own homes and apartments or in facilities located within their own communities and in contact with other persons living in their communities.

Section 28-16A-2(A). Although this act is directed at assisting individuals with developmental disabilities, such as autism or mental retardation, we find that this important state policy applies with equal force to individuals with any form of disability or handicap.

This overwhelming public policy is extremely persuasive in directing us toward an expansive interpretation of the term "family." See Crane Neck Ass'n v. New York City, 61 N.Y.2d 154, 460 N.E.2d 1336, 1339 (refusing to enforce restrictive covenant that contravened long-standing public policy favoring the establishment of group homes for the mentally disabled); Craig v. Bossenbery, 351 N.W.2d 596, 599 (Mich. Ct. App. 1984) (noting that strong public policy favoring group homes overrides enforcement even of unambiguous restrictive covenant).

Third, other jurisdictions have consistently held that restrictive covenants mandating single-family residences do not bar group homes in which the occupants live as a family unit.

Accordingly, we reject the Neighbors' claim that the term "family" in the restrictive covenants should be read to include only individuals related by blood or by law. We therefore conclude that the Community's use of the property as a group home does not violate the Four Hills restrictive covenant.

C. Findings Regarding Increased Traffic

The Neighbors strenuously argue that the covenant should be interpreted to exclude the group home because the group home's operation has an adverse impact on the neighborhood. In support of this claim, the Neighbors point to the trial court's findings that "[t]he amount of vehicular traffic generated by [the] Community's use of the house greatly exceeds what is expected in an average residential area" and that, as a result, "the character of [the] residential neighborhood relative to traffic and to parked vehicles has been significantly altered to the detriment of this residential neighborhood and is [sic] residents." However, the Neighbors fail to appreciate that the amount of traffic generated by the group home simply is not relevant to determining whether the use of the house as a group home violated the covenant in this case. A review of all the provisions in the covenant reveals that the restrictive covenants for the Four Hills Village are not directed at controlling either traffic or on-street parking. The various covenants and restrictions that attach to the neighborhood homes merely regulate the structural appearance and use of the homes. For example, the covenants regulate building architecture, views, frontage, setback, visible fences and walls, signs and billboards, trash and weeds, trailers and campers parked in yards, maintaining livestock, and of course nonresidential uses of homes. However, not one of the fifteen provisions and numerous paragraphs of the covenants attempts to control the number of automobiles that a resident may accommodate on or off the property nor the amount of traffic a resident may generate.

Accordingly, because the covenants do not regulate traffic or off-street parking, and because the amount of traffic generated by the group home is irrelevant to whether the home is used for single-family residential purposes, we conclude that the Neighbors' argument is without merit.

III. FAIR HOUSING ACT

The Community's second contention is that the trial court erred in concluding that the FHA did not apply in the present case. Although we have already agreed with the Community on its first argument that it did not violate the restrictive covenants, given the importance of the issues raised, we review the Community's second claim in order to correct the trial court's erroneous ruling on the legal effect of the FHA. We find that, even if we were to adopt the Neighbors' proposed definition that the term "family" only included individuals related by blood or by law, we would still find for the Community because such a restriction would violate the FHA.

Section 3604(f)(1) of the FHA provides in relevant part that it is unlawful "[t]o discriminate in the sale or rental, or to otherwise make unavailable or deny, a dwelling to any buyer or renter because of a handicap of a person residing in or intending to reside in that dwelling after it is sold, rented, or made available." Section 3604(f)(3)(B) states, "For purposes of this subsection, discrimination includes a refusal to make reasonable accommodations in rules, policies, practices, or services, when such accommodations may be necessary to afford such person equal opportunity to use and enjoy a dwelling."

Courts have interpreted these provisions as creating three distinct claims for violations of § 3604(f) of the FHA: discriminatory intent, disparate impact, and reasonable accommodation. The first two are based on § 3604(f)(1), whereas the third arises out of § 3604(f)(3). The Community has raised each of these claims and we will address each of them in turn.

At the outset, we note that the Neighbors do not contest that persons with AIDS are considered handicapped under the FHA. Nor do they challenge the Community's standing to bring suit under the FHA.

A. Discriminatory Intent

A discriminatory-intent claim focuses on whether a defendant has treated handicapped individuals differently from other similarly situated individuals. Stewart B. McKinney Foundation, Inc. v. Town Plan & Zoning Comm'n, 790 F. Supp. 1197, 1211 (D. Conn. 1992). "To prevail on its claim of discriminatory [intent], the plaintiff is not required to show the defendants were motivated by some purposeful, malicious desire to discriminate against HIV-infected persons." *Id.* "[The] plaintiff need only show that the handicap of the potential residents [of a group home], a protected group under the FHA, was in some part the basis for the policy being challenged." Potomac Group Home Corp. v. Montgomery County, 823 F.Supp. 1285, 1295 (D.Md. 1993).

[T]he Community argues that the Neighbors were aware of the Community's use of the property as a group home and decided to enforce the covenants, in part, because of antagonism to that use. The Community presented evidence that the Neighbors' traffic complaints began a few days after a newspaper article was published that described the group home and that the Neighbors inquired into the availability of other possible sites for the home outside of their neighborhood. The Community also identified several covenant violations by other landowners in the neighborhood that were not being prosecuted. However, this evidence is equivocal at best. Absent further evidence of an intent to enforce the covenant because of some animus toward the use of the property as a group home because the residents have AIDS, the Community's allegations are insufficient to support a claim for discriminatory enforcement of the covenant.

B. Disparate Impact

To demonstrate a violation of the FHA under the disparate-impact analysis, a plaintiff need only prove that the defendant's conduct actually or predictably results in discrimination or has a discriminatory effect. "The plaintiff need make no showing whatsoever that the action resulting in discrimination in housing was motivated [by a desire to discriminate against the handicapped]. Effect, and not motivation, is the touchstone." *McKinney Foundation*, 790 F.Supp. at 1216.

[W]e find that the Community has proved that enforcing the covenant as interpreted by the Neighbors would violate the FHA. [T]he covenant, which attempts to limit group homes, has the discriminatory effect of denying housing to the handicapped. Individuals with disabling handicaps, such as the one suffered by the Community's residents, frequently require congregate living arrangements for physical assistance and psychological and emotional support in order to live outside of an institution and in a residential community. Without congregate living arrangements many disabled individuals would be unable to reside in traditional neighborhoods or communities and would be forced into hospitals and institutions. [T]he negative effects of covenants that restrict congregate living arrangements are substantially more onerous for the disabled than for others.

A covenant that restricts occupancy only to related individuals or that bars group homes has a disparate impact not only on the current residents of the Community's group home who have AIDS but also on all disabled individuals who need congregate living arrangements in order to live in traditional neighborhoods and communities. As we noted above, there is a very strong public policy favoring placement of disabled individuals in congregate living arrangements located in traditional residential community settings such as Four Hills. Of course, one possible consequence of congregate living arrangements is that they have the potential to generate more traffic than a typical nuclear family. In the present case the trial court made a finding that the increased traffic generated by the Community's group home has negatively affected the residential character of the neighborhood. However, we find it significant that the trial court rejected the Neighbors' proposed finding of fact that this additional traffic posed any increased safety hazard to the neighborhood.

Accordingly, we conclude that the negative effects of increased traffic, without any additional harms, are outweighed by the Community's interest in maintaining its congregate home for individuals with AIDS. Because the Community has proved a "disparate impact" under the FHA, the Neighbors cannot enforce the covenant against the Community.

C. Reasonable Accommodation

The Community's third claim under the FHA is that the Neighbors failed to make reasonable accommodations under § 3604(f)(3)(B). This section provides that "discrimination includes a refusal to make reasonable accommodations in rules, policies, practices or services when such accommodations may be necessary to afford [a handicapped] person equal opportunity to use and enjoy a dwelling." "Reasonable accommodation" has been defined to include "changing some rule that is generally applicable so as to make its burden less onerous on the handicapped individual." North Shore-Chicago Rehabilitation, Inc. v. Village of Skokie, 827 F.Supp. 497, 508 (N.D. Ill. 1993). [T]he restriction does not need to be directed at the handicapped. It does not even need to have a disparate impact on handicapped groups in general. The restriction need only serve as an impediment to an individual plaintiff who is handicapped and is denied access to housing in order to implicate the "reasonable accommodation" requirement of the FHA.

In the present case, the proposed interpretation of the Four Hills restrictive covenant also has the effect of denying housing access to the handicapped residents. Accordingly, § 3604(f)(3)(B) of the FHA is implicated, and the Neighbors would be required to reasonably accommodate the group home provided it would not require a fundamental alteration in the nature of the restrictions or impose undue financial or administrative burdens on the Neighbors.

The Neighbors do not suggest that allowing the group home to operate would impose any financial or administrative burdens on them. The Neighbors are not responsible for operating or maintaining the group home in any way, nor do they have to pay any additional costs as a result of the group home. Furthermore, nonenforcement of the single-family residence requirement against the Community's group home would not fundamentally alter the nature of the restrictions. As discussed above, the Four Hills restrictive covenants as a whole were designed to regulate the structural appearance of houses and to prevent the use of houses for business purposes. The Community's use of the property for a group home does not affect its structural appearance and is not a business use. The residents use the house like a traditional residential home and act as a second family for one another. Indeed, the Neighbors' stated reason for enforcing the restrictive covenant is not because of the nonresidential nature of the occupancy, but because of the additional traffic generated by the group home. However, traffic regulation is not a fundamental aspect of the Four Hills restrictive covenants.

Accordingly, we conclude that nonenforcement of the Four Hills restrictive covenants against the Community's group home would not impose an undue hardship or burden on the Neighbors and would not interfere with the plain purpose of the covenants. "A reasonable accommodation would have been not to seek enforcement of the covenant." Martin v. Constance, 843 F.Supp. 1321, 1326 (E.D. Mo. 1994). Therefore, the reasonable accomodation prong of the FHA would also bar enforcement of the restrictive covenant if it prevented the Community's use of the house as a congregate living arrangement for people with AIDS.

CONCLUSION

We conclude that the Community is entitled to continue operating its group home for individuals with AIDS both under the Four Hills restrictive covenants and under the Fair Housing Act. Accordingly, for the reasons discussed above, the trial court's ruling is reversed and the injunction is vacated.

NOTES AND QUESTIONS

1. **Article.** For an insightful article on "the meaning problem" in the interpretation of covenants, see Robert D. Brussack, *Group Homes, Families, and Meaning in the Law of Subdivision Covenants*, 16 Ga. L. Rev. 33 (1981).

2. **Another case.** In Rhodes v. Palmetto Pathway Homes, Inc., 400 S.E.2d 484 (S.C. 1991), the court held that a covenant restricting lot uses to "private residence purposes" was not violated by plaintiff's use of her lot as a group residence for mentally impaired adults, and that enforcement of the covenant against plaintiff would violate the Fair Housing Act. *Compare* Laursen v. Giolli, 549 So. 2d 1174 (Fla. Dist. Ct. App. 1989) (owner's use of residential property as licensed adult congregate living facility, "housing three elderly ladies and a nighttime caretaker" was a commercial use that violated residential use only restriction). How is *Laursen* different from *Rhodes* and the principal case?

3. **Other "single family residential" covenant cases.** Both the "single family" and the "residential" language in covenants can provoke litigation. *See, e.g.*, Berry v. Teves, 752 So. 2d 112 (Fla. Dist. Ct. App. 2000) (covenant allowed "residential purposes only" and prohibited "trade, traffic or business of any kind"; latent ambiguity precluded summary judgment on question whether covenant prohibited *rentals* of owner's residence); Martellini v. Little Angels Day Care, Inc., 847 A.2d 838 (R.I. 2004) (covenant limiting use to "single family private residence purposes" prohibited day care center); Isbrandtsen v. North Branch Corp., 556 A.2d 81 (Vt. 1988) (grantee could not rent her property to paying guests); Hanley

v. Misischi, 302 A.2d 79 (R.I. 1973) (owner of lot in subdivision could not use lot solely to construct street to give access to homes outside of the subdivision); Holbrook v. Davison, 375 S.E.2d 840 (Ga. 1989) (lot owner not prohibited from keeping livestock on vacant lot since other provisions in document allowing barns contemplated livestock); Hillcrest Homeowners Association v. Wiley, 778 P.2d 421 (Mont. 1989) (building of garage on lot without building home violated covenant). *See generally* Annotation, *Use of Property for Multiple Dwellings as Violating Restrictive Covenant Permitting Property to be Used for Residential Purposes Only*, 99 A.L.R.3d 985; Annotation, *Children's Day Care Use as Violation of Restrictive Covenant*, 81 A.L.R.5th 345; Annotation, *Construction and Application of "Residential Purposes Only" or Similar Covenant Restriction to Incidental Use of Dwelling for Business, Professional, or Other Purposes*, 1 A.L.R.6th 135; Annotation, *Hospital, Sanitarium, Home for Aged, Nursing Home, or the Like as Violation of Restrictive Covenant*, 94 A.L.R.2d 726.

4. **Other scope questions.** To get the flavor of issues that are litigated under the language of restrictive covenants, and also a sense of the value of foresight at the drafting stage, consider the following cases:

a. *"One dwelling house." See* 5011 Community Organization v. Harris, 548 A.2d 9 (Conn. App. Ct. 1988) (covenant limited quality and type of dwelling, not use of lot; construction of parking lot to serve restaurant was allowed); Albino v. Pacific First Federal Savings & Loan Ass'n, 479 P.2d 760 (Or. 1971) (covenant bars multiple family or apartment building); Shapiro v. Levin, 302 A.2d 417 (Pa. Super. Ct. 1973) (covenant prohibits erection of eight-unit townhouse); Leverich v. Roy, 87 N.E.2d 226 (Ill. App. Ct. 1949) (covenant does not bar two families living separate and apart in one house).

b. *Satellite dishes. See* Breeling v. Churchill, 423 N.W.2d 469 (Neb. 1988) (satellite dish violated covenant prohibiting any "outside radio, television, Ham broadcasting, or other electronic antenna or aerial"); Greek Peak, Inc. v. Grodner, 547 N.Y.S.2d 944 (N.Y. App. Div. 1989) (evidence was insufficient to establish that homeowner's satellite dish on pole outside house, anchored in concrete and attached to house by brackets was a "free standing TV, FM, ham radio or aerial tower" in violation of covenant), *aff'd*, 556 N.Y.S.2d 509 (N.Y. 1990). *See generally* Annotation, *Radio or Television Aerials, Antennas, Towers, or Satellite Dishes or Discs as within Terms of Covenant Restricting Use, Erection, or Maintenance of Such Structures Upon Residential Property*, 76 A.L.R.4th 498.

c. *"Structures."* A covenant bars any "building, fence or other structure on any lot" until the proposed construction shall have been approved by the subdivision developer. *See* Sea Pines Plantation Co. v. Wells, 363 S.E.2d 891 (S.C. 1987) (flagpole, satellite dish, and Jacuzzi on the roof of residence were "structures" prohibited by the covenant); Black Horse Run Property Owners Assoc. v. Kaleel, 362 S.E.2d 619 (N.C. Ct. App. 1987) (radio tower with supporting guy wires was "structure" requiring approval of architectural control committee). *See generally* Annotation, *What Constitutes a "Structure" Within Restrictive Covenant*, 75 A.L.R.3d 1095.

d. *Mobile homes.* Starr v. Thompson, 385 S.E.2d 535 (N.C. Ct. App. 1989) (factory-built modular unit was "mobile home" in violation of covenant, even though axles, wheels, and tongue were removed, and even though it was not a mobile home for zoning purposes); Garland v. Carnes, 379 S.E.2d 782 (Ga. 1989) (mobile home with shingle roof and hardboard siding was prohibited under covenant barring "mobile homes and trailers and buildings with metal roofs or metal siding"; error to admit parol evidence to show that grantor intended to prohibit only mobile homes with metal roofs or sidings because restriction was not ambiguous); Fischer v. Driesen, 446 N.W.2d 84 (Iowa Ct. App. 1989) (double-wide trailer was permanent structure and not mobile home under restrictive covenant); Williams v. Brooks, 383 S.E.2d 712 (Va. 1989) (covenant prohibiting any "structure of a temporary character, that is, a trailer, basement, tent, shack, garage, barn, or other outbuilding" held not to prohibit mobile home permanently affixed to land). *See generally* Annotation, *What is "Mobile Home," "House Trailer," "Trailer House," or "Trailer" Within Meaning of Restrictive Covenant*, 83 A.L.R.5th 651.

2. Termination

COWLING v. COLLIGAN
312 S.W.2d 943 (Tex. 1958)

CALVERT, JUSTICE.

This class suit was brought by R.E. Cowling and some seventeen other owners of lots in Post Oak Gardens Subdivision, an addition to the City of Houston, against Mrs. R.M. Colligan as owner and J. Terry Falkenbury as tenant or lessee of Tract No. 2 in the subdivision. The purpose of the suit was to obtain a declaratory judgment that certain restrictive covenants, and particularly a covenant restricting use of the lots in the subdivision 'for residence purposes only' were still valid, binding and enforceable restrictions on the use of all lots or tracts in the subdivision and to enjoin the defendants from using Tract No. 2 for business or commercial purposes. Falkenbury died before trial and his interest, if any, went out of the case.

The case was tried without a jury. Judgment was entered declaring the restrictive covenants contained in a certain instrument of record, including the covenant limiting the use of the lots for residence purposes only, to be 'valid, subsisting and enforceable restrictive covenants' which had 'not been waived, breached or abandoned to such an extent that they are no longer enforceable.' However, the court recited in its judgment that there had been such a change of conditions and of uses of lands in the vicinity of Tract No. 2 as to make it unjust and inequitable to enforce the covenants against that tract and ordered it removed from their effect. The Court of Civil Appeals affirmed.

The findings of fact pertinent to the issue before us establish that the subdivision contains 49 tracts or lots ranging in size from 4 to 7.81 acres; that a church is located on the east three acres of Tract No. 1, to the west of Tract No. 2, and immediately across Bering Drive; that churches have been built upon two other tracts in the subdivision, and several other tracts have been sold to church bodies who contemplate the erection of church buildings; that one-half of the remaining building sites on the subdivision have residences erected upon them;

that Tract No. 2, owned by the defendant, contains 5 acres, is bounded on the south by Westheimer Road and on the west by Bering Drive, has no improvements upon it except for one small frame building which is easily removable, and has never been devoted to any business or commercial use except for the storage of pipe and related items upon it; that the property adjoining Tract No. 2 on the east also fronts on Westheimer Road, is outside of the subdivision, is unrestricted, and is devoted to business and commercial uses; that the property abutting Westheimer Road on the south is outside the subdivision, is unrestricted, and is devoted to business and commercial uses; that Westheimer Road was a quiet country road at the time the subdivision was platted and the restrictions laid, but is now a heavily-traveled main thoroughfare; that the reasonable market value of Tract No. 2, restricted, is $10,000 per acre, whereas, if unrestricted, it is from $35,000 to $43,000 per acre. What may be said to be an 'ultimate' fact finding of the trial court is as follows: "Tract No. 2, by reason of all of said matters, is no longer suitable for exclusively residential purposes."

The trial court concluded that the restrictions laid by the instrument of record are "valid, subsisting and enforceable restrictive covenants, and the same have not been waived, breached and abandoned to such an extent that the same are no longer enforceable in accordance with their terms." The trial court further concluded, however, that "it is no longer just and equitable to enforce said restrictive covenants against Tract No. 2 and to prevent the use of it for business and commercial purposes."

The plaintiffs contended in the Court of Civil Appeals, and contend here, that, as a matter of law, the facts found by the trial court do not support its second conclusion and that the court erred in removing Tract No. 2 from the effect of the restrictive covenant. We agree.

There are certain rules of law by which a court of equity must be guided in determining whether to enforce a residential-only restriction. It may refuse to enforce it because of the acquiescence of the lot owners in such substantial violations within the restricted area as to amount to an abandonment of the covenant or a waiver of the right to enforce it. 5 Restatement of the Law of Property § 561. It may also refuse to enforce it because there has been such a change of conditions in the restricted area or surrounding it that it is no longer possible to secure in a substantial degree the benefits sought to be realized through the covenant. 5 Restatement of the Law of Property § 564.

As heretofore indicated, the trial court found that the restrictions in Post Oak Gardens had not been waived or abandoned. Whether that conclusion be treated as an ultimate finding of fact or as a conclusion of law, the only contrary evidentiary fact found by the trial court is the erection and existence of churches in the subdivision. In the absence of a statement of facts we must presume that the other evidence heard supports the finding or conclusion.

The authorities are uniform in declaring that the erection of a church violates a covenant restricting the use of property for residential purposes. 14 Am.Jur., Pocket Part 97, Covenants, Conditions and Restrictions, § 225. It has been held, however, that the violation is so trivial in character that the failure of other property owners in the restricted area to complain does not operate as a waiver of their right to enforce the covenant against business or commercial development, or as an abandonment of the covenant. Mechling v. Dawson, 28 S.W.2d 18, 19 (Ky. App. 1930). We approve that holding.

A court may not refuse to enforce a residential-only restriction against a particular lot on the sole ground that a change of conditions has rendered the lot unsuitable for residential purposes and it would therefore be inequitable to enforce it. The equities favoring the particular owner is only one facet of the judicial inquiry. Those equities must be weighed against the equities favoring the lot owners who, having acquired their property on the strength of the restriction, wish to preserve the residential character of the area. The judgment must arise out of a balancing of equities or of relative hardships. 5 Restatement of the Law of Property § 563. In paragraph c of § 563 it is said: "It is not sufficient to create the disproportion (of harm) that will justify refusing to grant injunctive relief that the harm ensuing from granting such relief will be greater than the benefit gained thereby. When the disproportion between harm and benefit is the sole reason for refusing relief, the disproportion must be one of considerable magnitude."

The trial court made no finding that the removal of Tract No. 2 from the restriction would not prove harmful to the plaintiffs who wish to preserve the residential character of the subdivision, and we may not presume such a finding. Other than the advent of churches into the subdivision the only changed conditions found by the court lie outside the subdivision. Tract No. 2 is a border tract and is openly exposed to those changed conditions, but the majority view is that "if the benefits of the original plan for a restricted subdivision can still be realized for the protection of the interior lots, the restriction should be enforced against the border lots, notwithstanding that such lot owners are deprived of the most valuable use of their lots." 2 American Law of Property 447. We are committed to that view.

The reasoning of the courts is that if because of changed conditions outside the restricted area one lot or tract were permitted to drop from under the protective cover of residential-only restrictions, the owner of the adjoining lot would then have an equal claim on the conscience of the court, and, in due course, all other lots would fall like ten-pins, thus circumventing and nullifying the restriction and destroying the essentially residential character of the entire area. It is no answer to that reasoning to say that the trial court's judgment has declared the restriction enforceable against all other lots and thus will prevent such a disastrous result. The judgment is res adjudicata only of present and not of future conditions.

We can see no reason why our normal procedure should not be followed in this case. Accordingly, the judgment of the Court of Civil Appeals is reversed and the judgment of the trial court is reformed by striking from it the following:

> provided, however, by reason of the change of conditions and uses of lands in the vicinity of Tract Two (2) Post Oak Gardens, both in the immediate area within said subdivision, as well as adjoining and abutting lands without, it is no longer just and equitable to enforce said restrictive covenants against said Tract Two (2), and the said Tract Two (2) is hereby ordered removed from the effect of such restrictive covenants.

As reformed the judgment of the trial court is affirmed, and that court is directed to issue a writ of injunction in appropriate terms restraining and enjoining the defendant from devoting Tract No. 2 to business or commercial uses.

NOTES AND QUESTIONS

1. **A different scenario.** What would have been the result in the principal case if the owner of Tract No. 2 had wanted to construct a church?

2. **Abandonment and waiver.** The court in Cowling v. Colligan discusses the doctrines of abandonment and waiver as if they are the same. The third Restatement differentiates the two. It provides that a servitude is extinguished by abandonment. Restatement Third § 7.4. Recall that abandonment requires intent to abandon. Waiver may result in denial of remedies for a particular violation, but the beneficiary of the servitude may still enforce it against different types of violations or violations that have a larger impact. *Id.* § 7.4 comment b; § 8.3 comment e. Which doctrine more appropriately applies in the principal case?

3. **Contract law.** To what contract doctrine does the doctrine of changed conditions bear an obvious affinity? *See* Section B.1.b. note 4 above.

4. **The third Restatement.** See Restatement Third § 7.10:

§ 7.10 Modification and Termination of a Servitude Because of Changed Conditions

(1) When a change has taken place since the creation of a servitude that makes it impossible as a practical matter to accomplish the purpose for which the servitude was created, a court may modify the servitude to permit the purpose to be accomplished. If modification is not practicable, or would not be effective, a court may terminate the servitude. Compensation for resulting harm to the beneficiaries may be awarded as a condition of modifying or terminating the servitude.

(2) If the purpose of a servitude can be accomplished, but because of changed conditions the servient estate is no longer suitable for uses permitted by the servitude, a court may modify the servitude to permit other uses under conditions designed to preserve the benefits of the original servitude.

Section 7.11 of the third Restatement provides separate rules for the modification and termination of conservation servitudes. *See generally* Jeffrey A. Blackie, Note, *Conservation Easements and the Doctrine of Changed Conditions*, 40 Hastings L.J. 1187 (1989).

5. **The principal case.** Though Cowling v. Colligan is an older case, its result is typical. "The test [for changed conditions] is stringent: relief is granted only if the purpose of the servitude can no longer be accomplished." Restatement Third § 7.10 cmt. a. In the principal case, why did the owner of Tract No. 2 fail to get the restrictive covenant cancelled? Compare Chesterfield Meadows Shopping Center Associates v. Smith, 568 S.E.2d 676 (Va. 2002), in which the court applied the doctrine of changed conditions to invalidate a restrictive covenant adopted primarily for the purpose of protecting a historic home after the historic home was moved to another location.

6. **Zoning and covenants.** All lots in a subdivision are restricted to single-family use. Defendant buys a vacant lot with notice of the restriction. Subsequently, the township changes its zoning ordinance to limit construction on defendant's lot to office buildings and to prohibit the construction of single-family residences. Defendant plans to build an office building on his lot; neighbors sue to enjoin defendant. Result? *See* Rofe v. Robinson, 329 N.W.2d 704, 707–08 (Mich. 1982):

> Economic impracticability does not itself justify lifting building restrictions. Plaintiffs purchased their property, in apparent reliance on the deed restrictions, and defendants were on notice of the restrictions when they purchased their lots. "The right to live in a district uninvaded by stores, garages, business and apartment houses is a valuable right." Signaigo v. Begun, 234 Mich. 246, 250, 207 N.W. 709 (1926).

> The change in zoning does not support defendants' challenge to the validity of the deed restriction. If, as the defendants contend, the property as restricted is substantially valueless regardless of the zoning, then it is the deed restriction and not the zoning which brought about the loss of value.

> Even if the zoning were relevant, it is well established in this state that a change in zoning cannot, by itself, override prior restrictions placed in deeds. Zoning laws determine property owners' obligations to the community at large but do not determine the rights and obligations of parties to a private contract. These are separate obligations, both of which may be enforceable.

> A change in zoning is not sufficient evidence of a change in the character of an area to require lifting residential restrictions. "Such change is only a factor to be considered in determining whether a change of circumstances has occurred that an equity court will not enforce the restriction." Brideau v. Grissom, 369 Mich. 661, 668, 120 N.W.2d 829 (1963). A change in zoning is thus only relevant if it is indicative of a change in the character of the area. Rezoning itself is not such a change.

Most zoning ordinances are "cumulative," meaning that uses permitted in more restrictive zones are also permitted in less restrictive zones. *See* Village of Euclid v. Ambler Realty Co. in Chapter 8, Section B.1, for an example of such an ordinance. With a cumulative zoning ordinance, a home would be a permitted use in a district zoned for commercial use. Therefore, actual conflicts between zoning and restrictive covenants are rare.

7. **Categories: easements.** Does (should) the doctrine of changed conditions apply to easements? The traditional answer is that it does not. *See* Waldrop v. Town of Brevard, 62 S.E.2d 512, 515 (N.C. 1950) ("Changed conditions may, under certain circumstances, justify the non-enforcement of restrictive covenants, but a change, such as that suggested by the plaintiffs here, will not in any manner affect a duly recorded easement previously granted."). But Restatement Third § 7.10, quoted in note 2 above, applies the doctrine of changed conditions to easements as well as to covenants. In rejecting the Restatement view, the Wisconsin Supreme

Court in *AKG Real Estate, LLC v. Kosterman*, 717 N.W.2d 835, 847 (Wis. 2006), stated:

> [V]igorous academic debate persists over whether wise public policy warrants the extension of the changed conditions doctrine to easements. On one hand, proponents of the *Restatement* position argue that judicial intervention is necessary to rectify the problem of holdouts, who could otherwise single-handedly impede economic development. *See e.g.*, Uriel Reichman, *Toward a Unified Concept of Servitudes*, 55 S. Cal. L.Rev. 1177, 1233 (1982); Susan F. French, *Toward a Modern Law of Servitudes: Reweaving the Ancient Strands*, 55 S. Cal. L.Rev. 1261, 1265, 1300 (1982). Conversely, opponents of the *Restatement* position contend that the uncertainty caused by judicial modification of easements does more to hamper economic development than does current law because the *Restatement* discourages investment by rendering property rights uncertain. *See e.g.*, Richard A. Epstein, *Covenants and Constitutions*, 73 Cornell L.Rev. 906, 914 (1987); Carol M. Rose, *Servitudes, Security, and Assent: Some Comments on Professors French and Reichman*, 55 S. Cal. L.Rev. 1403, 1412-13 (1982).

> Given the lack of consensus and lack of evidence that the changed-conditions doctrine produces superior economic and legal consequences, we reject the *Restatement's* departure from the general rule that express easements cannot be unilaterally modified. We are not persuaded that the policy arguments are sufficiently compelling to justify overturning more than a century of precedent and upsetting the settled expectations of thousands of easement holders.

8. **Categories: defeasible fees.** Does (should) the doctrine of changed conditions apply to defeasible fees? *Cf.* Humphrey v. C.G. Jung Educational Center (Section B.3 above).

9. **Covenants to pay money.** The third Restatement provides that a covenant to pay money terminates after a reasonable time unless the covenant specifies the total amount due or the duration of the obligation; the rule does not apply to an "obligation to pay for services or facilities concurrently provided to the burdened estate." Restatement Third § 7.12(1).

D.   COMMON INTEREST COMMUNITIES

Section 1.8 of the Restatement Third defines a common-interest community as follows:

> A "common-interest community" is a real-estate development or neighborhood in which individually owned lots or units are burdened by a servitude that imposes an obligation that cannot be avoided by nonuse or withdrawal.

The Introductory Note to Chapter 6 of the third Restatement elaborates on the importance of, and the concerns raised by, common-interest communities:

> Buyers of residential property, particularly first-time buyers in common interest communities, tend to focus on price, location, schools, and physical

characteristics of the property, rather than on the details of the documents that impose servitudes on the property and create the governing association. Even if the buyer carefully reads the documents, however, there is usually no realistic opportunity to negotiate changes. Once the first lot has been sold subject to a declaration of servitudes for the development, the provisions bind all property subject to the declaration. Unless the developer has reserved a power to modify its terms unilaterally, changes require consent of all owners, or the percentage specified for amendment of the declaration.

Another important factor in determining rules appropriate for residential common interest communities is the importance accorded the home in American society. The home is not only a haven of personal autonomy, liberty, and security, but, for many, it is also a major financial investment. Through their control of maintenance and assessment levels, rulemaking powers, and enforcement efforts, community associations often have substantial power to affect both the quality of life and financial health of their members.

There are [also] important public interests at stake in the law governing common interest communities. They provide an increasing share of the housing available to Americans at all income levels. Their popularity is due to many factors, but important among them is their ability to increase the amenities available to residents by providing a workable mechanism for sharing enjoyment and spreading the costs across a stable base of contributors. Another important factor is the mechanism they provide for controlling the community environment through provision of services, imposition of design controls, enactment of rules and regulations, and enforcement of servitudes. The size and scope of common interest communities vary widely, from those that have little power to affect the lives of their members or others to those that take the place of traditional towns. Many associations provide services that complement or provide a substitute for government services. Parks and other recreational facilities, street maintenance, security, and utilities may be provided by associations. Assumption of otherwise public responsibilities like maintenance of drainage channels by the common interest community may be required as a condition of development approval. The public not only has an interest in the availability of the kinds of housing opportunities made available through the common interest community, but also has direct financial interests in the successful functioning of these communities. If the association fails, the public may have to take over the streets and parks and provide some of the other "public" services previously provided by the association.

Restatement Third of Property, Servitudes, Introductory Note to Chapter 6, at 67-68.

NAHRSTEDT v. LAKESIDE VILLAGE CONDOMINIUM ASSOC., INC.

878 P.2d 1275 (Cal. 1994)

KENNARD, JUSTICE.

A homeowner in a 530-unit condominium complex sued to prevent the homeowners association from enforcing a restriction against keeping cats, dogs, and other animals in the condominium development. [In a condominium, each apartment owner has fee simple title to his or her unit, while the common areas are owned by all residents of the condominium as tenants in common.] The owner asserted that the restriction, which was contained in the project's declaration[1] recorded by the condominium project's developer, was "unreasonable" as applied to her because she kept her three cats indoors and because her cats were "noiseless" and "created no nuisance." Agreeing with the premise underlying the owner's complaint, the Court of Appeal concluded that the homeowners association could enforce the restriction only upon proof that plaintiff's cats would be likely to interfere with the right of other homeowners "to the peaceful and quiet enjoyment of their property."

[W]e reverse the judgment of the Court of Appeal and remand for further proceedings consistent with the views expressed in this opinion.

I

Lakeside Village is a large condominium development in Culver City, Los Angeles County. It consists of 530 units spread throughout 12 separate 3-story buildings. The residents share common lobbies and hallways, in addition to laundry and trash facilities.

The Lakeside Village project is subject to certain covenants, conditions and restrictions (hereafter CC&R's) that were included in the developer's declaration recorded with the Los Angeles County Recorder on April 17, 1978, at the inception of the development project. Ownership of a unit includes membership in the project's homeowners association, the Lakeside Village Condominium Association (hereafter Association), the body that enforces the project's CC&R's, including the pet restriction, which provides in relevant part: "No animals (which shall mean dogs and cats), livestock, reptiles or poultry shall be kept in any unit."[3]

In January 1988, plaintiff Natore Nahrstedt purchased a Lakeside Village condominium and moved in with her three cats. When the Association learned of the cats' presence, it demanded their removal and assessed fines against Nahrstedt for each successive month that she remained in violation of the condominium project's pet restriction.

---

[1] The declaration is the operative document for a common interest development, setting forth, among other things, the restrictions on the use or enjoyment of any portion of the development. (Civ. Code, §§ 1351, 1353.) In some states, the declaration is also referred to as the "master deed."

[3] The CC&R's permit residents to keep "domestic fish and birds."

Nahrstedt then brought this lawsuit against the Association, its officers, and two of its employees, asking the trial court to invalidate the assessments, to enjoin future assessments, to award damages for violation of her privacy when the Association "peered" into her condominium unit, to award damages for infliction of emotional distress, and to declare the pet restriction "unreasonable" as applied to indoor cats (such as hers) that are not allowed free run of the project's common areas. Nahrstedt also alleged she did not know of the pet restriction when she bought her condominium. The complaint incorporated by reference the grant deed, the declaration of CC&R's, and the condominium plan for the Lakeside Village condominium project.

The Association demurred to the complaint. In its supporting points and authorities, the Association argued that the pet restriction furthers the collective "health, happiness and peace of mind" of persons living in close proximity within the Lakeside Village condominium development, and therefore is reasonable as a matter of law. The trial court sustained the demurrer as to each cause of action and dismissed Nahrstedt's complaint. Nahrstedt appealed.

A divided Court of Appeal reversed the trial court's judgment of dismissal. In the majority's view, the complaint stated a claim for declaratory relief based on its allegations that Nahrstedt's three cats are kept inside her condominium unit and do not bother her neighbors. According to the majority, whether a condominium use restriction is "unreasonable," as that term is used in section 1354, hinges on the facts of a particular homeowner's case. Thus, the majority reasoned, Nahrstedt would be entitled to declaratory relief if application of the pet restriction in her case would not be reasonable. The Court of Appeal also revived Nahrstedt's causes of action for invasion of privacy, invalidation of the assessments, and injunctive relief, as well as her action for emotional distress based on a theory of negligence.

The dissenting justice took the view that enforcement of the Lakeside Village pet restriction against Nahrstedt should not depend on the "reasonableness" of the restriction as applied to Nahrstedt. To evaluate on a case-by-case basis the reasonableness of a recorded use restriction included in the declaration of a condominium project, the dissent said, would be at odds with the Legislature's intent that such restrictions be regarded as presumptively reasonable and subject to enforcement under the rules governing equitable servitudes. Application of those rules, the dissenting justice concluded, would render a recorded use restriction valid unless "there are constitutional principles at stake, enforcement is arbitrary, or the association fails to follow its own procedures."

On the Association's petition, we granted review to decide when a condominium owner can prevent enforcement of a use restriction that the project's developer has included in the recorded declaration of CC&R's.

II

Use restrictions are an inherent part of any common interest development and are crucial to the stable, planned environment of any shared ownership arrangement. The viability of shared ownership of improved real property rests on the existence of extensive reciprocal servitudes, together with the ability of each co-owner to prevent the property's partition. The restrictions on the use of property in any common interest development may limit activities conducted in the common areas as well as in the confines of the home itself. Commonly, use restrictions preclude alteration of building exteriors, limit the number of persons that can occupy each unit, and place limitations on — or prohibit altogether — the keeping of pets.

Restrictions on property use are not the only characteristic of common interest ownership. Ordinarily, such ownership also entails mandatory membership in an owners association, which, through an elected board of directors, is empowered to enforce any use restrictions contained in the project's declaration or master deed and to enact new rules governing the use and occupancy of property within the project. Because of its considerable power in managing and regulating a common interest development, the governing board of an owners association must guard against the potential for the abuse of that power.[6] Generally, courts will uphold decisions made by the governing board of an owners association so long as they represent good faith efforts to further the purposes of the common interest development, are consistent with the development's governing documents, and comply with public policy.

Thus, subordination of individual property rights to the collective judgment of the owners association together with restrictions on the use of real property comprise the chief attributes of owning property in a common interest development. As the Florida District Court of Appeal observed in Hidden Harbour Estates, Inc. v. Norman (Fla. Dist. Ct. App. 1975) 309 So.2d 180, a decision frequently cited in condominium cases:

> [I]nherent in the condominium concept is the principle that to promote the health, happiness, and peace of mind of the majority of the unit owners since they are living in such close proximity and using facilities in common, each unit owner must give up a certain degree of freedom of choice which he [or she] might otherwise enjoy in separate, privately owned property. Condominium unit owners comprise a little democratic sub-society of necessity more restrictive as it pertains to use of condominium property than may be existent outside the condominium organization.

(*Id.* at 181-182.)

Notwithstanding the limitations on personal autonomy that are inherent in the concept of shared ownership of residential property, common interest developments have increased in popularity in recent years, in part because they generally provide a more affordable alternative to ownership of a single-family home. One significant factor in the continued popularity of the common interest form of property ownership is the ability of homeowners to enforce restrictive CC&R's against other owners (including future purchasers) of project units. Generally, however, such enforcement is possible only if the restriction that is sought to be

---

[6] The power to regulate pertains to a "wide spectrum of activities," such as the volume of playing music, hours of social gatherings, use of patio furniture and barbecues, and rental of units. (Note, *Community Association Use Restrictions: Applying the Business Judgment Doctrine, supra,* 64 Chi.Kent L.Rev. 653, 669.)

enforced meets the requirements of equitable servitudes or of covenants running with the land.

When restrictions limiting the use of property within a common interest development satisfy the requirements of covenants running with the land or of equitable servitudes, what standard or test governs their enforceability? In California, our Legislature has made common interest development use restrictions contained in a project's recorded declaration "enforceable *unless unreasonable*." (§ 1354, subd. (a), italics added.)

In states lacking such legislative guidance, some courts have adopted a standard under which a common interest development's recorded use restrictions will be enforced so long as they are "reasonable." (See Riley v. Stoves (1974) 22 Ariz.App. 223, 228, 526 P.2d 747, 752 [asking whether the challenged restriction provided "a reasonable means to accomplish the private objective"].) Others would limit the "reasonableness" standard only to those restrictions adopted by majority vote of the homeowners or enacted under the rulemaking power of an association's governing board, and would not apply this test to restrictions included in a planned development project's recorded declaration or master deed. Because such restrictions are presumptively valid, these authorities would enforce them regardless of reasonableness. The first court to articulate this view was the Florida Fourth District Court of Appeal.

In Hidden Harbour Estates v. Basso (Fla. Dist. Ct. App. 1981) 393 So.2d 637, the Florida court distinguished two categories of use restrictions: use restrictions set forth in the declaration or master deed of the condominium project itself, and rules promulgated by the governing board of the condominium owners association or the board's interpretation of a rule. The latter category of use restrictions, the court said, should be subject to a "reasonableness" test, so as to "somewhat fetter the discretion of the board of directors." (*Id.* at p. 640.) Such a standard, the court explained, best assures that governing boards will "enact rules and make decisions that are reasonably related to the promotion of the health, happiness and peace of mind" of the project owners, considered collectively.

By contrast, restrictions contained in the declaration or master deed of the condominium complex, the Florida court concluded, should not be evaluated under a "reasonableness" standard. Rather, such use restrictions are "clothed with a very strong presumption of validity" and should be upheld even if they exhibit some degree of unreasonableness. Nonenforcement would be proper only if such restrictions were arbitrary or in violation of public policy or some fundamental constitutional right.

Indeed, giving deference to use restrictions contained in a condominium project's originating documents protects the general expectations of condominium owners "that restrictions in place at the time they purchase their units will be enforceable." (Note, *Judicial Review of Condominium Rulemaking*, (1981), 94 Harv.L.Rev. 647, 653; Ellickson, *Cities and Homeowners' Associations* (1982) 130 U.Pa.L.Rev. 1519, 1526-1527 [stating that association members "unanimously consent to the provisions in the association's original documents" and courts therefore should not scrutinize such documents for "reasonableness."].) This in turn encourages the development of shared ownership housing — generally a less costly alternative to single-dwelling ownership — by attracting buyers who prefer a stable, planned environment. It also protects buyers who have paid a premium for condominium units in reliance on a particular restrictive scheme.

III

[E]quitable servitudes permit courts to enforce promises restricting land use when there is no privity of contract between the party seeking to enforce the promise and the party resisting enforcement. Like any promise given in exchange for consideration, an agreement to refrain from a particular use of land is subject to contract principles, under which courts try "to effectuate the legitimate desires of the covenanting parties." (Hannula v. Hacienda Homes (1949) 34 Cal.2d 442, 444-445, 211 P.2d 302.) When landowners express the intention to limit land use, "that intention should be carried out." (*Id.* at p. 444, 211 P.2d 302; Epstein, *Notice and Freedom of Contract in the Law of Servitudes* (1982) 55 So.Cal.L.Rev. 1353, 1359 ["We may not understand why property owners want certain obligations to run with the land, but as it is their land some very strong reason should be advanced" before courts should override those obligations.])

Thus, when enforcing equitable servitudes, courts are generally disinclined to question the wisdom of agreed-to restrictions. This rule does not apply, however, when the restriction does not comport with public policy. Equity will not enforce any restrictive covenant that violates public policy. Nor will courts enforce as equitable servitudes those restrictions that are arbitrary, that is, bearing no rational relationship to the protection, preservation, operation or purpose of the affected land.

These limitations on the equitable enforcement of restrictive servitudes that are either arbitrary or violate fundamental public policy are specific applications of the general rule that courts will not enforce a restrictive covenant when "the harm caused by the restriction is so disproportionate to the benefit produced" by its enforcement that the restriction "ought not to be enforced." (Rest., Property, § 539, com. f.) When a use restriction bears no relationship to the land it burdens, or violates a fundamental policy inuring to the public at large, the resulting harm will always be disproportionate to any benefit.

With these principles of equitable servitude law to guide us, we now turn to section 1354. As mentioned earlier, under subdivision (a) of section 1354 the use restrictions for a common interest development that are set forth in the recorded declaration are "enforceable equitable servitudes, unless unreasonable." In other words, such restrictions should be enforced unless they are wholly arbitrary, violate a fundamental public policy, or impose a burden on the use of affected land that far outweighs any benefit.

When courts accord a presumption of validity to all such recorded use restrictions and measure them against deferential standards of equitable servitude law, it discourages lawsuits by owners of individual units seeking personal exemptions from the restrictions. This also promotes stability and predictability in two ways. It provides substantial assurance to prospective condominium purchasers that they may rely with confidence on the promises embodied in the project's recorded

CC&R's. And it protects all owners in the planned development from unanticipated increases in association fees to fund the defense of legal challenges to recorded restrictions.

How courts enforce recorded use restrictions affects not only those who have made their homes in planned developments, but also the owners associations charged with the fiduciary obligation to enforce those restrictions. When courts treat recorded use restrictions as presumptively valid, and place on the challenger the burden of proving the restriction "unreasonable" under the deferential standards applicable to equitable servitudes, associations can proceed to enforce reasonable restrictive covenants without fear that their actions will embroil them in costly and prolonged legal proceedings. Of course, when an association determines that a unit owner has violated a use restriction, the association must do so in good faith, not in an arbitrary or capricious manner, and its enforcement procedures must be fair and applied uniformly.

There is an additional beneficiary of legal rules that are protective of recorded use restrictions: the judicial system. Fewer lawsuits challenging such restrictions will be brought, and those that are filed may be disposed of more expeditiously, if the rules courts use in evaluating such restrictions are clear, simple, and not subject to exceptions based on the peculiar circumstances or hardships of individual residents in condominiums and other shared-ownership developments.

Contrary to the dissent's accusations that the majority's decision "fray[s]" the "social fabric," we are of the view that our social fabric is best preserved if courts uphold and enforce solemn written instruments that embody the expectations of the parties rather than treat them as "worthless paper" as the dissent would. Our social fabric is founded on the stability of expectation and obligation that arises from the consistent enforcement of the terms of deeds, contracts, wills, statutes, and other writings. To allow one person to escape obligations under a written instrument upsets the expectations of all the other parties governed by that instrument (here, the owners of the other 529 units) that the instrument will be uniformly and predictably enforced.

The salutary effect of enforcing written instruments and the statutes that apply to them is particularly true in the case of the declaration of a common interest development. As we have discussed, common interest developments are a more intensive and efficient form of land use that greatly benefits society and expands opportunities for home ownership. In turn, however, a common interest development creates a community of property owners living in close proximity to each other, typically much closer than if each owned his or her separate plot of land. This proximity is feasible, and units in a common interest development are marketable, largely because the recorded declaration of CC&R's assures owners of a stable and predictable environment.

Refusing to enforce the CC&R's contained in a recorded declaration, or enforcing them only after protracted litigation that would require justification of their application on a case-by-case basis, would impose great strain on the social fabric of the common interest development. It would frustrate owners who had purchased their units in reliance on the CC&R's. It would put the owners and the homeowners association in the difficult and divisive position of deciding whether particular CC&R's should be applied to a particular owner. Here, for example, deciding whether a particular animal is "confined to an owner's unit and create[s] no noise, odor, or nuisance" is a fact-intensive determination that can only be made by examining in detail the behavior of the particular animal and the behavior of the particular owner. Homeowners associations are ill-equipped to make such investigations, and any decision they might make in a particular case could be divisive or subject to claims of partiality.

Enforcing the CC&R's contained in a recorded declaration only after protracted case-by-case litigation would impose substantial litigation costs on the owners through their homeowners association, which would have to defend not only against owners contesting the application of the CC&R's to them, but also against owners contesting any case-by-case exceptions the homeowners association might make. In short, it is difficult to imagine what could more disrupt the harmony of a common interest development than the course proposed by the dissent.

V

We conclude, as a matter of law, that the recorded pet restriction of the Lakeside Village condominium development prohibiting cats or dogs but allowing some other pets is not arbitrary, but is rationally related to health, sanitation and noise concerns legitimately held by residents of a high-density condominium project such as Lakeside Village, which includes 530 units in 12 separate 3-story buildings.

Nahrstedt's complaint alleges no facts that could possibly support a finding that the burden of the restriction on the affected property is so disproportionate to its benefit that the restriction is unreasonable and should not be enforced. Also, the complaint's allegations center on Nahrstedt and her cats (that she keeps them inside her condominium unit and that they do not bother her neighbors), without any reference to the effect on the condominium development as a whole, thus rendering the allegations legally insufficient to overcome section 1354's presumption of the restriction's validity.

[W]e discern no fundamental public policy that would favor the keeping of pets in a condominium project. There is no federal or state constitutional provision or any California statute that confers a general right to keep household pets in condominiums or other common interest developments. Nor does case law offer any support for the position that the recognized scope of autonomy privacy encompasses the right to keep pets: courts that have considered condominium pet restrictions have uniformly upheld them.

CONCLUSION

In this case, the pet restriction was contained in the project's declaration or governing document, which was recorded with the county recorder before any of the 530 units was sold. For many owners, the pet restriction may have been an important inducement to purchase into the development. Because the homeowners collectively have the power to repeal the pet restriction, its continued existence reflects their desire to retain it.

Plaintiff's allegations, even if true, are insufficient to show that the pet restriction's harmful effects substantially outweigh its benefits to the condominium development as a whole, that it bears no rational relationship to the purpose or function of the development, or that it violates public policy. We reverse the judgment of the Court of Appeal, and remand for further proceedings consistent with the views expressed in this opinion.

ARABIN, JUSTICE, dissenting.

"There are two means of refuge from the misery of life: music and cats."[1]

I respectfully dissent. I find the provision known as the "pet restriction" contained in the covenants, conditions, and restrictions (CC&R's) governing the Lakeside Village project patently arbitrary and unreasonable within the meaning of Civil Code section 1354. Given the substantial benefits derived from pet ownership, the undue burden on the use of property imposed on condominium owners who can maintain pets within the confines of their units without creating a nuisance or disturbing the quiet enjoyment of others substantially outweighs whatever meager utility the restriction may serve in the abstract. It certainly does not promote "health, happiness [or] peace of mind" commensurate with its tariff on the quality of life for those who value the companionship of animals. Worse, it contributes to the fraying of our social fabric.

What is gained from an uncompromising prohibition against pets that are confined to an owner's unit and create no noise, odor, or nuisance? To the extent such animals are not seen, heard, or smelled any more than if they were not kept in the first place, there is no corresponding or concomitant benefit. Pets that remain within the four corners of their owners' condominium space can have no deleterious or offensive effect on the project's common areas or any neighboring unit. Certainly, if other owners and residents are totally unaware of their presence, prohibiting pets does not in any respect foster the "health, happiness [or] peace of mind" of anyone except the homeowners association's board of directors, who are thereby able to promote a form of sophisticated bigotry. In light of the substantial and disproportionate burden imposed for those who must forego virtually any and all association with pets, this lack of benefit renders a categorical ban unreasonable under Civil Code section 1354.

The proffered justification is all the more spurious when measured against the terms of the pet restriction itself, which contains an exception for domestic fish and birds. A squawking bird can readily create the very kind of disturbance supposedly prevented by banning other types of pets. At the same time, many animals prohibited by the restriction, such as hamsters and the like, turtles, and small reptiles, make no sound whatsoever. Disposal of bird droppings in common trash areas poses as much of a health concern as cat litter or rabbit pellets, which likewise can be handled in a manner that avoids potential problems. Birds are also known to carry disease and provoke allergies. Neither is maintaining fish without possible risk of interfering with the quiet enjoyment of condominium neighbors. Aquarium

---

[1] Albert Schweitzer.

water must be changed and disposed of in the common drainage system. Leakage from a fish tank could cause serious water damage to the owner's unit, those below, and common areas. Defendants and the majority purport such solicitude for the "health, sanitation and noise concerns" of other unit owners, but fail to explain how the possession of pets, such as plaintiff's cats, under the circumstances alleged in her complaint, jeopardizes that goal any more than the fish and birds expressly allowed by the pet restriction. This inconsistency underscores its unreasonableness and discriminatory impact.

From the statement of the facts through the conclusion, the majority's analysis gives scant acknowledgment to any of the foregoing considerations but simply takes refuge behind the "presumption of validity" now accorded all CC&R's irrespective of subject matter. They never objectively scrutinize defendants' blandishments of protecting "health and happiness" or realistically assess the substantial impact on affected unit owners and their use of their property.

Here, such inquiry should start with an evaluation of the interest that will suffer upon enforcement of the pet restriction. In determining the "burden on the use of land," due recognition must be given to the fact that this particular "use" transcends the impersonal and mundane matters typically regulated by condominium CC&R's, such as whether someone can place a doormat in the hallway or hang a towel on the patio rail or have food in the pool area, and reaches the very quality of life of hundreds of owners and residents. Nonetheless, the majority accept uncritically the proffered justification of preserving "health and happiness" and essentially consider only one criterion to determine enforceability: was the restriction recorded in the original declaration? If so, it is "presumptively valid," unless in violation of public policy. Given the application of the law to the facts alleged and by an inversion of relative interests, it is difficult to hypothesize any CC&R's that would not pass muster. Such sanctity has not been afforded any writing save the commandments delivered to Moses on Mount Sinai, and they were set in stone, not upon worthless paper.

Moreover, unlike most conduct controlled by CC&R's, the activity at issue here is strictly confined to the owner's interior space; it does not in any manner invade other units or the common areas. Owning a home of one's own has always epitomized the American dream. More than simply embodying the notion of having "one's castle," it represents the sense of freedom and self-determination emblematic of our national character. Granted, those who live in multi-unit developments cannot exercise this freedom to the same extent possible on a large estate. But owning pets that do not disturb the quiet enjoyment of others does not reasonably come within this compromise. Nevertheless, with no demonstrated or discernible benefit, the majority arbitrarily sacrifice the dream to the tyranny of the "commonality."

Our true task in this turmoil is to strike a balance between the governing rights accorded a condominium association and the individual freedom of its members. To fulfill that function, a reviewing court must view with a skeptic's eye restrictions driven by fear, anxiety, or intolerance. In any community, we do not exist in vacuo. There are many annoyances which we tolerate because not to do so would be repressive and place the freedom of others at risk.

In contravention, the majority's failure to consider the real burden imposed by the pet restriction unfortunately belittles and trivializes the interest at stake here. Pet ownership substantially enhances the quality of life for those who desire it. When others are not only undisturbed by, but completely unaware of, the presence of pets being enjoyed by their neighbors, the balance of benefit and burden is rendered disproportionate and unreasonable, rebutting any presumption of validity. Their view, shorn of grace and guiding philosophy, is devoid of the humanity that must temper the interpretation and application of all laws, for in a civilized society that is the source of their authority. As judicial architects of the rules of life, we better serve when we construct halls of harmony rather than walls of wrath.

I would affirm the judgment of the Court of Appeal.

NOTES AND QUESTIONS

1. **General-plan developments compared.** Restatement Third § 1.8 cmt. a:

> Common-interest communities are usually also general-plan developments because they are usually developed according to a general plan of land-use restrictions. However, general-plan developments are not common-interest communities unless they also include common property that all lot owners are required to support or an association supported by mandatory assessments.

2. **The pet restriction.** The Restatement Third § 3.4 tests a direct restraint on alienation by the standard of reasonableness. An indirect restraint, however, must only have a rational justification. *See id.* § 3.5 & cmt. a. An indirect restraint is one that "reduces the desirability of the property to prospective transferees," or otherwise "affects the value or marketability" of the property. *Id.* § 3.4 cmt. b, at 441. Is the pet restriction in the principal case a restraint on alienation? If so, is it valid? Does the Restatement Third agree with the principal case? Several years after the principal case, the California legislature enacted a statute prohibiting common interest communities from prohibiting an owner from keeping at least one pet. *See* Cal. Civ. Code § 1360.5.

3. **Association rules.** Suppose that the restriction in the principal case had been contained in a set of rules promulgated by the governing board of the condominium owners' association rather than in the recorded declaration of restrictions. Would a different standard of review have applied in that case, and if so, what is that standard? Would the pet restriction have violated that other standard?

4. **Discretionary association decisions.** What do you think the answer should be to the question posed in the case of Lamden v. La Jolla Shores Clubdominium Homeowners Assoc., 980 P.2d 940, 940, 942-943 (Cal. 1999):

> [Plaintiff's] building in a condominium development suffered from termite infestation. The board of directors of the development's community association decided to treat the infestation locally ("spot-treat"), rather than fumigate. Alleging the board's decision diminished the value of her unit, the owner of a condominium in the development sued the community association. In adjudicating her claims, under what standard should a court

evaluate the board's decision?

[T]ermite inspection reports recommend[ed] fumigation, but the Association's Board decided against that approach. [T]he Board based its decision not to fumigate on concerns about the cost of fumigation, logistical problems with temporarily relocating residents, concern that fumigation residue could affect residents' health and safety, awareness that upcoming walkway renovations would include replacement of damaged areas, pet moving expenses, anticipated breakage by the termite company, lost rental income and the likelihood that termite infestation would recur even if primary treatment were utilized. The Board decided to continue to rely on secondary treatment until a more widespread problem was demonstrated.

The court held for the board, adopting the following rule, analogous to the common law "business judgment rule:"

Where a duly constituted community association board, upon reasonable investigation, in good faith and with regard for the best interests of the community association and its members, exercises discretion within the scope of its authority under relevant statutes, covenants and restrictions to select among means for discharging an obligation to maintain and repair a development's common areas, courts should defer to the board's authority and presumed expertise.

Id. at 942. The court distinguished *Nahrstedt* on the basis that *Nahrstedt* determined "the standard of judicial review for recorded use restrictions" while it was deciding "the standard of judicial review of discretionary economic decisions by community association boards." *Id.* at 949. Other courts have applied the business judgment rule to business decisions of homeowners' association boards. *See, e.g.,* Lake Monticello Owners' Association v. Lake, 463 S.E.2d 652, 656 (Va. 1995); Mueller v. Zimmer, 124 P.3d 340, 352 (Wyo. 2005).

5. **Creation of a common interest community.** A developer who wishes to develop a common interest community with covenants, conditions, and restrictions (CC&Rs) that run with the land as real covenants and equitable servitudes should properly record a declaration of the CC&Rs then include in each initial deed of a lot in the community a covenant by the purchaser to comply with the CC&Rs. But see Citizens for Covenant Compliance v. Anderson, 906 P.2d 1314, 1315-16 (Cal. 1995):

The Andersons want to plant and harvest grapes, operate a winery, and keep llamas on their property in Woodside. Some neighbors object, and claim such activities are prohibited by covenants, conditions and restrictions (CC&R's) that limit the Andersons' property, and theirs, to residential use. The Andersons counter, thus far successfully, that the CC&R's are not enforceable because they are not mentioned in any deed to their property. The dispute is now before us.

The CC&R's of this case were recorded before any of the properties they purport to govern were sold, thus giving all buyers constructive notice of their existence. They state they are to bind and benefit each parcel of property as part of a planned community. Nevertheless, the Court of

Appeal held they are not enforceable because they were not also mentioned in a deed or other document when the property was sold. We disagree, and adopt the following rule: if a declaration establishing a common plan for the ownership of property in a subdivision and containing restrictions upon the use of the property as part of the common plan is recorded before the execution of the contract of sale, describes the property it is to govern, and states that it is to bind all purchasers and their successors, subsequent purchasers who have constructive notice of the recorded declaration are deemed to intend and agree to be bound by, and to accept the benefits of, the common plan; the restrictions, therefore, are not unenforceable merely because they are not additionally cited in a deed or other document at the time of the sale.

6. **The common interest community as a choice.** Developers may create common interest communities with comprehensive declarations of covenants, conditions and restrictions (CC&Rs) because they believe that the restrictions and amenities that such regimes provide will make the homes in their residential subdivisions more attractive to purchasers. However, substantial debate continues over whether homeowners who purchase homes in common interest communities in fact make a meaningful choice. *Compare* Robert C. Ellickson, *Cities and Homeowners Associations*, 130 U. Pa. L. Rev. 1519, 1520 (1982) (characterizing membership in a homeowners' association as "perfectly voluntary"); Robert H. Nelson, *Privatizing the Neighborhood: A Proposal to Replace Zoning with Private Collective Property Rights in Existing Neighborhoods*, 7 Geo. Mason L. Rev. 827, 828 (1999) (characterizing homeowners' associations as "the choice for millions of people for their residential property"); Laura T. Rahe, *The Right to Exclude: Preserving the Auonomy of the Homeowners' Association*, 34 Urb. Law. 521, 552 (2002) (describing homeowners' associations as "the product of individual choices"); *with* Gregory S. Alexander, *Freedom, Coercion and the Law of Servitudes*, 73 Cornell L. Rev. 883, 902 (1988) (discussing the "coercive nature of membership in" homeowners' associations); Paula A. Franzese & Steven Siegel, *Trust and Community: The Common Interest Community as Metaphor and Paradox*, 72 Mo. L. Rev. 1111, 1112 (2007) (arguing that common interest communities are "the product of distorted market forces"); Paula A Franzese, *Does It Take a Village? Privatization, Patterns of Restriciveness and the Demise of Community*, 47 Vill. L. Rev. 553 (2002).

7. **The common interest community as "local government."** In many communities, the homeowners association now takes on many of the functions previously undertaken by local governments. *See* Robert C. Ellickson, *Cities and Homeowners Associations*, 130 U. Pa. L. Rev. 1519, 1520 (1982); Paula A. Franzese & Steven Siegel, *Trust and Community: The Common Interest Community as Metaphor and Paradox*, 72 Mo. L. Rev. 1111, 1112 (2007). For example, homeowners' associations may pay for maintenance of streets and parks within the subdivision and provide private security. When homeowners' associations take on governmental functions, the issue arises as to whether they become subject to constitutional limitations. The New Jersey Supreme Court recently found that a homeowners' association had not violated the free speech and assembly rights of residents. Committee for a Better Twin Rivers v. Twin Rivers Community Trust, 929 A.2d 1060, 1072-74 (N.J. 2007). The holding was based on the New Jersey

constitution, which the court had earlier held could apply to private actors in some circumstances, rather than on the federal Constitution. *Id.* at 1066.

8. **Amendment of CC&Rs.** Unless a declaration of CC&Rs provides for amendment by vote of a specified percentage of homeowners, most courts hold that it cannot be amended except by unanimous decision of all of the homeowners within the common interest community. Many CC&Rs, however, do provide for amendment by a majority or a super-majority of homeowners.

ARMSTRONG v. LEDGES HOMEOWNERS ASSOCIATION, INC.
633 S.E.2d 78 (N.C. 2006)

WAINWRIGHT, JUSTICE.

This is a declaratory judgment action brought by subdivision property owners against their homeowners' association. The dispositive question before the Court is *to what extent* the homeowners' association may amend a declaration of restrictive covenants. There are no disputed questions of fact.

We hold that amendments to a declaration of restrictive covenants must be reasonable. Reasonableness may be ascertained from the language of the declaration, deeds, and plats, together with other objective circumstances surrounding the parties' bargain, including the nature and character of the community. Because we determine that the amendment to the declaration *sub judice*, which authorizes broad assessments "for the general purposes of promoting the safety, welfare, recreation, health, common benefit, and enjoyment of the residents of Lots in The Ledges as may be more specifically authorized from time to time by the Board," is unreasonable, we conclude that the amendment is invalid and unenforceable.

Petitioners own lots in The Ledges of Hidden Hills subdivision (the Ledges) in Henderson County. The Ledges was developed in 1988 by Vogel Development Corporation (Vogel) pursuant to a plat recorded in the Henderson County Public Registry. Forty-nine lots are set out along two main roads that form a Y shape. There are four *cul de sacs*. The plat designates the roads as "public roads," which are maintained by the State, and shows no common areas or amenities.

Before selling any lots, Vogel recorded a Declaration of Limitations, Restrictions and Uses (Declaration). The Declaration contained thirty-six provisions which restricted the lots to single family residential use; established setbacks, side building lines, minimum square footage, and architectural controls; and otherwise ensured a sanitary and aesthetically pleasing neighborhood. The Declaration emphasized that roads in the Ledges are "dedicated to public use forever" and that Vogel may "dedicate the roads to the North Carolina Department of Transportation." Finally, the Declaration provided for the establishment of a homeowners' association.

The Declaration did not contain any provision for the collection of dues or assessments, and it appears that formation of a homeowners' association was primarily intended to relieve Vogel from the ongoing responsibility to enforce the architectural control covenants.

Vogel began conveying lots in the Ledges after recording the Declaration and plat. Later, Vogel decided to construct a lighted sign on private property in the Sunlight Ridge Drive right of way. Sunlight Ridge Drive is the entry road to the Ledges. Because lighting the sign required ongoing payment of a utility bill, Vogel included the following additional language in subsequent conveyances:

> The grantor herein contemplates the establishment of a non-profit corporation to be known as The Ledges of Hidden Hills Homeowners Association, and by acceptance of this deed the grantees agree to become and shall automatically so become members of said Homeowners Association when so formed by said grantor; and said grantees agree to abide by the corporate charter, bylaws, and rules and regulations of said Homeowners Association and *agree to pay prorata [sic] charges and assessments which may be levied by said Homeowners Association when so formed.* Until the above contemplated Homeowners Association is formed or in the event the same is not formed, the grantor reserves the right to assess the above-described lot and the owners thereof an equal pro-rata [sic] share of the common expense *for electrical street lights and electrical subdivision entrance sign lights* and any other *common utility expense* for various lots within the Subdivision.

(Emphasis added.) This language appears in each petitioner's deed, together with a reference to the previously recorded Declaration. Because specific language in a deed governs related general language, we determine that assessments for "common expense" for "electrical" service are the kind of assessments that the deed provides "may be levied by the Homeowners Association." See Smith v. Mitchell, 269 S.E.2d 608, 614 (N.C. 1980) (applying the maxim "the specific controls the general" to construction of a restrictive deed covenant). Our conclusion is supported by the deposition of Edward T. Vogel, President of Vogel Development Corporation, taken during this action. In his deposition, Mr. Vogel agreed that the assessment provision was added so that Vogel would not be responsible for paying the electric bill indefinitely.

Articles of Incorporation for the Ledges Homeowners' Association (Association) were not filed with the Secretary of State until 20 September 1994. The Articles provide that the Association is incorporated for the purposes of "upkeep, maintenance and beautification of the common amenities of [the Ledges]," "enforcement of the restrictive covenants of [the Ledges]," and "engag[ing] in any other lawful activities allowed for non-profit corporations under the laws of the State of North Carolina."

Sometime before the Association's first annual meeting in 1995, the Association's three-member Board of Directors adopted by-laws. These by-laws set forth the Association's powers and duties, which included the operation, improvement, and maintenance of common areas; determination of funds needed for operation, administration, maintenance, and management of the Ledges; collection of assessments and common expenses; and employment and dismissal of personnel.

Such bylaws are "administrative provisions" adopted for the "internal governance" of the Association. Black's Law Dictionary 193 (7th ed.1999) [hereinafter Black's]. "The bylaws [of a nonprofit corporation] may contain any provision for "regulating and managing the affairs of the corporation," but no bylaw may be "*inconsistent with law.*" N.C.G.S. § 55A-2-06 (2005). [T]he powers of a homeowners' association are contractual and limited to those powers granted to it by the declaration. Therefore, to be consistent with law, an association's by-laws must necessarily also be consistent with the declaration.

At the first annual meeting, the by-laws were amended to provide that the Association would have a lien on the lot of any owner who failed to pay an assessment. Thereafter, the Association began assessing lot owners for the bills incurred for lighting the Ledges entrance sign. Additionally, the Association assessed owners for mowing the roadside on individual private lots along Sunlight Ridge Drive, for snow removal from subdivision roads, and for operating and legal expenses. By affidavit submitted in support of petitioners' motion for summary judgment, petitioner Vivian Armstrong stated that the annual electrical bill for the sign is less than sixty cents per lot per month or approximately seven dollars and twenty cents per year; however, the Association has billed lot owners total assessments of approximately eighty to one hundred dollars per year.

On 18 June 2003, Armstrong sent an e-mail to the President of the Association, Marvin Katz, challenging the validity of these assessments:

> Since purchasing property here, we've received two invoices from the Ledges homeowner's [sic] association. In good faith, we relied upon the representation that the money was legitimately owed. We've recently learned that the nature of the homeowner's [sic] association has been misrepresented. Therefore, we ask for a full and immediate refund of $160.

Armstrong requested that the matter be placed on the agenda of the officers' next meeting.

At a meeting held on 16 July 2003, the board amended the Association by-laws again, greatly expanding the entity's enumerated powers and duties. In particular, the amended by-laws provided that the Association shall have the power to "[i]mpose charges for late payment of assessments and, after notice and an opportunity to be heard, levy reasonable fines not to exceed One Hundred Fifty Dollars ($150.00) per violation (on a daily basis for continuing violations) of the Restrictive Covenants, Bylaws, and Rules and Regulations of the Association.

On 1 August 2003, petitioners Robert and Vivian Armstrong sent a letter to the Association requesting termination of their membership. On 8 August 2003, petitioners L.A. and E. Ann Moore requested termination of their Association membership as well. In their letter, the Moores stated:

> We chose this particular property last year for several reasons. After a thorough search of Western North Carolina and the Hendersonville/ Brevard area, in particular, we decided expressly against living in a gated community with "all the amenities." Golf courses, swimming pools and clubhouses are not our choice for daily living. Walking trails, while

enjoyable and convenient, are but another source of assessment we don't need.

The Ledges appeared to be the answer to our desires, and until recent events we've been sure of it. The current Covenants are more restrictive than any other area in which we've resided, but not unreasonably so. While receptive to OPEN discussion of a small change or two, *we are adamant in our opposition to the expressed plan of The Board to turn us into a Planned Community.*

(Emphasis added.)

On 17 October 2003, petitioners filed a declaratory judgment action in Superior Court, Henderson County, seeking, among other relief, a declaration that the amended by-laws are unenforceable.

On 24 November 2003, a majority of the Association members adopted "Amended and Restated Restrictive Covenants of the Ledges of the Hidden Hills" (Amended Declaration). The Amended Declaration contains substantially different covenants from the originally recorded Declaration, including a clause requiring Association membership, a clause restricting rentals to terms of six months or greater, and clauses conferring powers and duties on the Association which correspond to the powers and duties previously adopted in the Association's amended by-laws.

Additionally, the Amended Declaration imposes new affirmative obligations on lot owners. It contains provisions authorizing the assessment of fees and the entry of a lien against any property whose owner has failed to pay assessed fees for a period of ninety days. According to the Amended Declaration, such fees are to be "assessed for common expenses" and "shall be used for the general purposes of promoting the safety, welfare, recreation, health, common benefit, and enjoyment of the residents of Lots in The Ledges as may be more specifically authorized from time to time by the Board." Special assessments may be made if the annual fee is inadequate in any year; however, surplus funds are to be retained by the Association. Unpaid assessments bear twelve percent interest per annum.

Petitioners amended their complaint in early December 2003 to reflect the November changes to the Association by-laws and original Declaration. Petitioners asserted five claims for relief, seeking: (1) a declaration that the Ledges is not subject to the Planned Community Act, (2) a declaration that the amended Association by-laws are invalid and unenforceable, (3) a declaration that lot owners are not required to join the Association or otherwise be bound by actions of the Association, (4) a declaration that the Amended Declaration is invalid and unenforceable, and (5) a permanent injunction preventing the Association from enforcing the amended by-laws or recording the Amended Declaration. In their answer to the amended complaint, respondents admitted that neither the amended by-laws nor the Amended Declaration subjected the Ledges to North Carolina's Planned Community Act.

Both petitioners and respondents moved for summary judgment, submitting multiple affidavits and exhibits in support of their positions. Following a hearing, the trial court granted respondents' motion for summary judgment, denied petitioners' motion for summary judgment, and dismissed petitioners' claims with prejudice. In so doing, the court found that the Amended Declaration was valid and enforceable. Petitioners then appealed to the North Carolina Court of Appeals.

The Court of Appeals determined that the plain language of the Declaration is sufficient to support *any* amendment thereto made by a majority vote of Association members. Accordingly, the Court of Appeals affirmed the trial court's order of summary judgment in favor of respondents.

Robert and Vivian Armstrong then filed a petition for discretionary review in this Court, arguing that the Court of Appeals erred by determining that the scope of the disputed amendment does not exceed the authority granted to the Association in the covenants contained in the original Declaration. Petitioners did not seek discretionary review of remaining issues resolved by the Court of Appeals. This Court granted the Armstrongs' petition on 26 January 2006.

Because covenants originate in contract, the primary purpose of a court when interpreting a covenant is to give effect to the *original* intent of the parties; however, covenants are strictly construed in favor of the *free use of land* whenever strict construction does not contradict the plain and obvious purpose of the contracting parties. Moreover, the North Carolina Court of Appeals has held that affirmative covenants are unenforceable "unless the obligation [is] imposed in clear and unambiguous language which is sufficiently definite to guide the courts in its application." Beech Mountain Prop. Owners' Ass'n v. Seifart, 269 S.E.2d 178, 179-80, 183 (N.C. App. 1980). The existence of definite and certain assessment provisions in a declaration does not imply that subsequent additional assessments were contemplated by the parties.

Developers of subdivisions and other common interest communities establish and maintain the character of a community, in part, by recording a declaration listing multiple covenants to which all community residents agree to abide. Lot owners take their property subject to the recorded declaration, as well as any additional covenants contained in their deeds. Because covenants impose continuing obligations on the lot owners, the recorded declaration usually provides for the creation of a homeowners' association to enforce the declaration of covenants and manage land for the common benefit of all lot owners, thereby preserving the character of the community and neighborhood property values. In a community that is not subject to the North Carolina Planned Community Act, the powers of a homeowners' association are contractual and are limited to those powers granted to it by the declaration. Although individual lot owners may voluntarily undertake additional responsibilities that are not set forth in the declaration, or undertake additional responsibilities by mistake, lot owners are not *contractually bound* to perform or continue to perform such tasks.

Declarations of covenants that are intended to govern communities over long periods of time are necessarily unable to resolve every question or community concern that may arise during the term of years. This is especially true for luxury communities in which residents enjoy multiple common areas, private roads, gates, and other amenities, many of which are staffed and maintained by third parties. For this reason, most declarations contain specific provisions authorizing the homeowners' association to amend the covenants contained therein.

The term amend means to improve, make right, remedy, correct an error, or repair. See generally Black's at 80. Amendment provisions are enforceable; however, such provisions give rise to a serious question about the permissible scope of amendment, which results from a conflict between the legitimate desire of a homeowners' association to respond to new and unanticipated circumstances and the need to protect minority or dissenting homeowners by preserving the original nature of their bargain. In the same way that the powers of a homeowners' association are limited to those powers granted to it by the original declaration, an amendment should not exceed the purpose of the original declaration.

In the case *sub judice*, petitioners argue that the affirmative covenants contained in their deeds authorize only nominal assessments for the maintenance of a lighted sign at the subdivision entrance; thus, the Association's subsequent amendment of the Declaration to authorize broad general assessments to "promot[e] the safety, welfare, recreation, health, common benefit, and enjoyment of the residents of Lots in The Ledges as may be more specifically authorized from time to time by the Board" is invalid and unenforceable. Respondents contend that the Declaration of Restrictive Covenants expressly permits the homeowners' association to amend the covenants; thus, *any* amendment that is adopted in accordance with association by-laws and is neither illegal nor against public policy is valid and enforceable, regardless of its breadth or subject matter. We hold that a provision authorizing a homeowners' association to amend a declaration of covenants does not permit amendments of unlimited scope; rather, every amendment must be *reasonable* in light of the contracting parties' original intent.

A disputing party will necessarily argue that an amendment is reasonable if he believes that it benefits him and unreasonable if he believes that it harms him. However, the court may ascertain reasonableness from the language of the original declaration of covenants, deeds, and plats, together with other objective circumstances surrounding the parties' bargain, including the nature and character of the community. For example, it may be relevant that a particular geographic area is known for its resort, retirement, or seasonal "snowbird" population. Thus, it may not be reasonable to retroactively prohibit rentals in a mountain community during ski season or in a beach community during the summer. Similarly, it may not be reasonable to continually raise assessments in a retirement community where residents live primarily on a fixed income. Finally, a homeowners' association cannot unreasonably restrict property rental by implementing a garnishment or "taking" of rents (which is essentially an assessment); although it may be reasonable to restrict the frequency of rentals to prevent rented property from becoming like a motel.

Correspondingly, restrictions are generally enforceable when clearly set forth in the original declaration. Thus, rentals may be prohibited by the original declaration. In this way, the declaration may prevent a simple majority of association members from turning established non-rental property into a rental complex, and vice-versa.

In all such cases, a court reviewing the disputed declaration amendment must consider both the legitimate needs of the homeowners' association and the legitimate expectations of lot owners. A court may determine that an amendment is unreasonable, and, therefore, invalid and unenforceable against *existing* owners who purchased their property before the amendment was passed; however, the same court may also find that the amendment is binding as to *subsequent* purchasers who buy their property with notice of a recorded amended declaration.

Here, petitioners purchased lots in a small residential neighborhood with public roads, no common areas, and no amenities. The neighborhood consists simply of forty-nine private lots set out along two main roads and four *cul de sacs*. Given the nature of this community, it makes sense that the Declaration itself did not contain any affirmative covenants authorizing assessments. Neither the Declaration nor the plat shows any source of common expense.

Although petitioners' deeds contain an additional covenant requiring lot owners to pay a pro rata share of the utility bills incurred from lighting the entrance sign, it is clear from the language of this provision, together with the Declaration, the plat, and the circumstances surrounding installation of the sign, that the parties did not intend this provision to confer *unlimited* powers of assessment on the Association. The sole purpose of this additional deed covenant was to ensure that the developer did not remain responsible for lighting the entrance sign after the lots were conveyed. Payment of the utility bill is the single shared obligation contained in petitioners' deeds, and each lot owner's pro rata share of this expense totals approximately seven dollars and twenty cents per year.

For these reasons, we determine that the Association's amendment to the Declaration which authorizes broad assessments "for the general purposes of promoting the safety, welfare, recreation, health, common benefit, and enjoyment of the residents of Lots in The Ledges as may be more specifically authorized from time to time by the Board" is unreasonable. The amendment grants the Association practically unlimited power to assess lot owners and is contrary to the original intent of the contracting parties. Indeed, the purposes for which the Association has billed additional assessments of approximately eighty to one hundred dollars per year are unrelated to all other provisions of the deeds, Declaration, and plat: for example, assessments for mowing land that the plat clearly designates as private property and assessments for snow removal from roads that the plat clearly designates as public.

For the reasons stated above, we conclude that the disputed amendment is invalid and unenforceable. In so doing, we echo the rationale of the Supreme Court of Nebraska in Boyles v. Hausmann, 517 N.W.2d 610, 617 (Neb. 1994): "The law will not subject a minority of landowners to unlimited and unexpected restrictions on the use of their land merely because the covenant agreement permitted a majority to make changes in existing covenants." Here, petitioners purchased their lots without notice that they would be subjected to additional restrictions on use of the lots and responsible for additional affirmative monetary obligations imposed by a homeowners' association. This Court will not permit the Association to use the Declaration's amendment provision as a vehicle for imposing a new and different set of covenants, thereby substituting a new obligation for the original bargain of the covenanting parties. Accordingly, we reverse the opinion of the North Carolina Court of Appeals and remand this case to that court for further remand to the trial court for additional proceedings not inconsistent with this opinion.

Reversed and remanded.

NOTES AND QUESTIONS

1. **The "reasonableness" standard.** How does the standard of reasonableness applied by the court in the principal case to amendments of CC&Rs compare to the standard applied by the California court in *Nahrstedt* to original restrictions? Would the assessments adopted by the residents of The Ledges have been reasonable in an original declaration of CC&Rs?

2. **Other possibilities.** Evergreen Highlands Association v. West, 73 P.3d 1 (Colo. 2003), involved facts similar to those in the principal case. The majority of lot owners voted to amend subdivision covenants to require all owners to join the homeowners association and to pay dues for maintenance of common areas. The court held that the amendment "was valid and binding because its terms were within the scope of the modification clause of the original covenants" without discussion of reasonableness. *Id.* at 9. The court in the *Boyles* case, cited in the principal case, held that a provision in CC&Rs permitting a "change" by a majority of the homeowners did not give them "authority to adopt new and different covenants." Boyles v. Hausmann, 517 N.W.2d 610, 613, 618 (Neb. 1994). As discussed in the principal case, courts may enforce an amendment against subsequent purchasers with notice of the amendment but not against owners who purchased before the amendment. *See generally* Patrick A. Randolph, *Changing the Rules: Should Courts Limit the Power of Common Interest Communities to Alter Unit Owners' Privileges In the Face of Vested Expectations?*, 38 Santa Clara L. Rev. 1081 (1998).

Chapter 8

GOVERNMENT REGULATION AND TAKING OF LAND

Covenants and easements illustrate the regulation of land use by private agreement. In this chapter, we turn to *government* regulation of land use. The law of nuisance, considered in Section A, illustrates one kind of government — i.e., judicial — regulation of land use, but this "judicial zoning" (as the law of nuisance is sometimes called) is necessarily ad hoc and piecemeal. In Section B of this chapter, we turn to government regulation of land use that differs in source and aspiration from the regulation involved in servitudes and in nuisance: it originates in legislation that seeks to be systematic and comprehensive. Thus, in Section B, we consider zoning, the prototype of such comprehensive regulatory legislation, which offers insights into the purposes behind land use regulation and the legitimate means of accomplishing those purposes.

Zoning is an example of *regulation* of the use of land that remains in private hands. It differs from the alternative management technique of government *expropriation* of land, which can be accomplished through the inherent sovereign (federal and state) power of eminent domain. The power of eminent domain is considered in Section C. However, as you would expect having come this far in this book, these categories — regulation and taking — are not separated by a bright line. In a typically cryptic and intriguing utterance, Justice Holmes noted in Pennsylvania Coal Co. v. Mahon, 260 U.S. 393 (1922), that government regulation of land use that "goes too far" constitutes a taking of private property in violation of the Constitution. Launched early in the 20th century, this doctrine of "regulatory takings" remained a minor theme in the Supreme Court's takings jurisprudence until it was revived in the 1970s and '80s, for purposes and with implications that are explored in Section D.

A. NUISANCE

We touched on the law of nuisance in Chapter 1 in a comparison with the law of trespass and an introduction to our discussion of what is property. Now we consider the details.

BURCH v. NEDPOWER MOUNT STORM, LLC
647 S.E.2d 879 (W. Va. 2007)

MAYNARD, JUSTICE.

The appellants appeal the April 7, 2006, order of the Circuit Court of Grant County that dismissed their nuisance claim in which they sought an injunction against the appellees, NedPower Mount Storm, LLC and Shell WindEnergy, Inc., to enjoin the appellees from constructing a wind power electric generating facility in close proximity to the appellants' property. For the reasons that follow, we reverse the circuit court and remand for proceedings consistent with this opinion.

FACTS

By final order dated April 2, 2003, the Public Service Commission ("the PSC") granted NedPower Mount Storm LLC, an appellee herein, a certificate of convenience and necessity to construct and operate a wind power electric generating facility along the Allegheny Front in Grant County. NedPower has entered into a contract with appellee Shell WindEnergy, Inc., to sell the entire facility to Shell upon its completion. It is contemplated that the wind power facility will be located on a site approximately 14 miles long with an average width of one-half mile. The facility is to include up to 200 wind turbines. Each turbine is to be mounted on a steel tower approximately 15 feet in diameter and 210 to 450 feet in height, and have three blades of approximately 115 feet.

The appellants are seven homeowners who live from about one-half mile to two miles from the projected wind turbines. On November 23, 2005, the appellants filed a complaint in the Circuit Court of Grant County seeking to permanently enjoin NedPower and Shell WindEnergy, Inc., from constructing and operating the wind power facility on the basis that it would create a private nuisance. Specifically, the appellants asserted that they will be negatively impacted by noise from the wind turbines; the turbines will create a "flicker" or "strobe" effect when the sun is near the horizon; the turbines will pose a significant danger from broken blades, ice throws, and collapsing towers; and the wind power facility will cause a reduction in the appellants' property values.

The appellees subsequently filed a joint motion for judgment on the pleadings in which they essentially argued that a circuit court has no jurisdiction to enjoin, as a prospective private nuisance, projects authorized by the PSC, and that a private party cannot collaterally attack a final order of the PSC by means of bringing an injunction action in circuit court.

By order of April 7, 2006, the circuit court granted the appellees' motion for judgment on the pleadings and dismissed the appellants' action with prejudice. The circuit court based its ruling on the following grounds: it has no jurisdiction to enjoin the construction of a project that was approved by the PSC; most of the assertions made by the appellants concern activities that constitute a public rather than a private nuisance; a prospective injunction is not a proper remedy in this case because the wind facility is not a nuisance *per se* and does not constitute an impending or imminent danger of certain effect; and the PSC's approval of the facility collaterally estops the appellants from challenging it in circuit court.

The appellants now appeal the circuit court's order.

DISCUSSION

1. *Jurisdiction*

The circuit court first found that because the Legislature granted the PSC the power to decide the siting of electric generating facilities that are designated under federal law as exempt wholesale generators, the circuit court lacks jurisdiction to enjoin the construction and operation of these facilities under our law of nuisance.

We begin our discussion with the recognition that our common law has always provided a remedy for a nuisance. This Court has explained that

> "nuisance is a flexible area of the law that is adaptable to a wide variety of factual situations." Sharon Steel Corp. v. City of Fairmont, 334 S.E.2d 616, 621 (W.Va. 1985). In fact, "[i]t has been said that the term 'nuisance' is incapable of an exact and exhaustive definition which will fit all cases, because the controlling facts are seldom alike, and each case stands on its own footing." Harless v. Workman, 114 S.E.2d 548, 552 (W.Va. 1960). Nonetheless, "the term ['nuisance'] is generally 'applied to that class of wrongs which arises from the unreasonable, unwarrantable or unlawful use by a person of his own property and produces such material annoyance, inconvenience, discomfort, or hurt that the law will presume a consequent damage.' " *Harless*, 114 S.E.2d at 552. Stated another way, "nuisance is the unreasonable, unusual, or unnatural use of one's property so that it substantially impairs the right of another to peacefully enjoy his or her property." 58 Am.Jur.2d Nuisances § 2 (2002).

Booker v. Foose, 613 S.E.2d 94, 97 (W.Va. 2005). In the past, we described a nuisance as

> anything which annoys or disturbs the free use of one's property, or which renders its ordinary use or physical occupation uncomfortable. A nuisance is anything which interferes with the rights of a citizen, either in person, property, the enjoyment of his property, or his comfort. A condition is a nuisance when it clearly appears that enjoyment of property is materially lessened, and physical comfort of persons in their homes is materially interfered with thereby.

Martin v. Williams, 93 S.E.2d 835, 844 (W.Va. 1956). More recently, we held that "[a] private nuisance is a substantial and unreasonable interference with the private use and enjoyment of another's land." Syllabus Point 1, Hendricks v. Stalnaker, 380 S.E.2d 198 (W.Va. 1989). The test to determine unreasonableness has been stated by this Court as follows: "An interference with the private use and enjoyment of another's land is unreasonable when the gravity of the harm outweighs the social value of the activity alleged to cause the harm." Syllabus Point 2, *Hendricks*, *supra*. With regard to remedying a nuisance, it has long been understood that "[j]urisdiction in equity to abate nuisances is undoubted and of universal recognition." State v. Ehrlick, 64 S.E. 935, 937 (W.Va. 1909).

Our examination of the express language of the statutes reveals no specific language indicating the Legislature's intent to disregard or abrogate the common law doctrine of nuisance as it applies to electric generating facilities designated as exempt wholesale generators. Therefore, this Court will presume that the Legislature left intact the circuit court's jurisdiction in equity over electric generating facilities like the one at issue.

Contrary to the arguments of the appellees, we do not believe that a nuisance action to enjoin the construction of an electric generating facility conflicts with the role of the PSC in granting siting certificates to these facilities. The Legislature has charged the PSC with the responsibility for "appraising and balancing the interests of current and future utility service customers, the general interests of the state's economy and the interests of the utilities subject to its jurisdiction in its deliberations and decisions." W.Va.Code § 24-1-1(b). Specific to deciding whether to grant or refuse a siting certificate to an electric generating facility, W.Va.Code § 24-2-11c(c) (2003) provides that "[t]he commission shall appraise and balance the interests of the public, the general interests of the state and local economy, and the interests of the applicant." Notably absent in this balancing of interests are the interests of nearby landowners whose use and enjoyment of their properties may be substantially interfered with by the operation of an electric generating facility. Because the rights of nearby landowners are not a primary consideration in the PSC's siting determinations, we believe it is necessary to preserve the traditional rights of these landowners to seek appropriate remedies in the circuit courts.

Accordingly, we now hold that the right of a person under the common law to bring in circuit court a nuisance claim to enjoin the construction and/or operation of an electric generating facility that is designated under federal law as an exempt wholesale generator is not precluded by the fact that the Public Service Commission of West Virginia has granted a siting certificate to the owner or operator of the facility.

2. Private Nuisance Claim for a Prospective Injunction

In addition to finding that it had no jurisdiction to hear the appellants' nuisance claim for an injunction, the circuit court ruled that the appellants failed to set forth sufficient facts in their complaint alleging a private nuisance that would support the granting of a prospective injunction against the appellees. Specifically, the circuit court found that even if the appellants' alleged injuries for which remedies are available in nuisance, these alleged injuries do not support a prospective injunction because the injuries are speculative and contingent.

Our reading of the appellants' complaint indicates that the appellants allege, as private nuisances, that the wind turbines will cause constant noise when the wind is blowing and an increase in noise as the wind velocity increases; the turbines will create an eyesore as a result of the turbines' "flicker" or "strobe" effect when the sun is near the horizon; and proximity of the appellants' property to the turbines will result in a diminution in the appellants' property values. We will now determine the legal effect of each of these allegations under our settled law of nuisance.

First, the appellants allege that the noise from the turbines will constitute a nuisance. This Court has held that "[n]oise alone may create a nuisance, depending on time, locality and degree." Syllabus, Point 1, Ritz v. Woman's Club of Charleston,

173 S.E. 564 (W.Va. 1934). We have further held that "[w]here an unusual and recurring noise is introduced in a residential district, and the noise prevents sleep or otherwise disturbs materially the rest and comfort of the residents, the noise may be inhibited by a court of equity." Syllabus Point 2, *Ritz, supra.* See also Snyder v. Cabell, 1 S.E. 241 (W.Va. 1886) (affirming injunction against skating rink's operation where it was found that noise from the rink materially interfered with the comfort and enjoyment of nearby residents.). These holdings are grounded on a principle that is essential to a civil society which is that "every person . . . has the right not to be disturbed in his house; he has the right to rest and quiet and not to be materially disturbed in his rest and enjoyment of home by loud noises." *Snyder*, 1 S.E. at 251. Thus, we find that the appellants' allegation of noise is cognizable under our law as an abatable nuisance.

Second, the appellants allege that a "flicker" or "strobe" effect from the turbines will create an eyesore. Traditionally "courts of equity have hesitated to exercise authority in the abatement of nuisances where the subject matter is objected to by the complainants merely because it is offensive to the sight." Parkersburg Builders Material Co. v. Barrack, 191 S.E. 368, 369 (W.Va. 1937). This Court has explained in further detail that

> [e]quity should act only where there is presented a situation which is offensive to the view of average persons of the community. And, even where there is a situation which the average person would deem offensive to the sight, such fact alone will not justify interference by a court of equity. The surroundings must be considered. Unsightly things are not to be banned solely on that account. Many of them are necessary in carrying on the proper activities of organized society. But such things should be properly placed, and not so located as to be unduly offensive to neighbors or to the public.

Barrack, 191 S.E. at 371. When an unsightly activity is not properly placed, when it is unduly offensive to its neighbors, and when it is accompanied by other interferences to the use and enjoyment of another's property, this Court has shown a willingness to abate the activity as a nuisance. For example, in Syllabus Point 3 of Mahoney v. Walter, 205 S.E.2d 692 (W.Va. 1974), it was held:

> The establishment of an automobile salvage yard with its incident noise, unsightliness, hazards from the presence of flammable materials, open vehicles, rodents and insects, and resultant depreciation of adjoining residential property values in an area which, though unrestricted and containing some commercial businesses, is primarily residential, together with the interference with the use, comfort and enjoyment of the surrounding properties caused by its operation, may be a nuisance and may be abated by a court of competent jurisdiction.

We hold, therefore, that while unsightliness alone rarely justifies interference by a circuit court applying equitable principles, an unsightly activity may be abated when it occurs in a residential area and is accompanied by other nuisances.

Third, the appellants allege that construction of the wind turbines will cause a reduction in their property values. With regard to the legal effect of mere diminution in the value of property, this Court has explained:

> Upon the question of reduction in value of the plaintiffs' properties, as the result of the establishment of the used car lot nearby, we find this statement in Wood on Nuisances, 3rd Edition, § 640: "Mere diminution of the value of the property, in consequence of the use to which adjoining premises are devoted, unaccompanied with other ill-results, is *damnum absque injuria*." Also in 66 C.J.S., Nuisances, § 19, P. 771, it is stated that: "However, a use of property which does not create a nuisance cannot be enjoined or a lawful structure abated merely because it renders neighboring property less valuable."

Martin, 93 S.E.2d at 843-844. However, the appellants in this case do not rely merely upon diminution of property values to support their nuisance claim, but also noise and unsightliness. According to *Martin, supra,*

> The establishment of what is commonly known as a "used car lot" with its incident noise, light, unsightliness and resultant depreciation of adjoining residential property values in an area which, though unrestricted and without the corporate limits of a town or city, was across a highway from zoned residential property lying within the corporate limits, and which area had previously been exclusively residential on both sides of the highway for a distance of approximately one-fourth of a mile, and which "used car lot" greatly interferes with the use, comfort and enjoyment of such surrounding residential properties, constitutes a nuisance in fact, and may be abated by a court of equity.

See also *Mahoney, supra* (holding that automobile salvage yard with noise, unsightliness, flammable materials hazards, rodents and insects, and resultant depreciation of adjoining residential property values may be a nuisance and may be abated). We hold, therefore, that an activity that diminishes the value of nearby property and also creates interferences to the use and enjoyment of the nearby property may be abated by a circuit court applying equitable principles. In addition, the landowners may seek compensation for any diminution in the value of their property caused by the nuisance.

Finally, the remedy sought by the appellants is an injunction against the construction and operation of the wind power facility.

> It is a general rule that when the thing complained of is not a nuisance *per se*, but may or may not become so, according to circumstances, and the injury apprehended is eventual or contingent, equity will not interfere; the presumption being that a person entering into a legitimate business will conduct it in a proper way, so that it will not constitute a nuisance.

Syllabus Point 2, Chambers v. Cramer, 38 S.E. 691 (W.Va. 1901). We have recognized that a lawful business or a business authorized to be conducted by the government cannot constitute a nuisance *per se*. In the early case of McGregor v. Camden, 34 S.E. 936, 937 (W.Va. 1899), this Court succinctly stated that "[a] lawful business cannot be a nuisance *per se*, but from its surrounding places and circumstances, or the manner in which it is conducted it may become a nuisance." See also, Martin, 93 S.E.2d at 838 ("The operation of a used car lot is a lawful business, and, as a general rule, it cannot be a nuisance *per se*."); Frye v. McCrory Corp., 107 S.E.2d 378, 382 (W.Va. 1959), quoting 66 C.J.S., Nuisances, Section 9 ("The lawful and proper use of property or conduct of business does not ordinarily create an actionable nuisance, and is never a 'nuisance *per se*' in the strict sense of that term.").[9] Further, according to Syllabus Point 6 of Watson v. Fairmont & S. Ry. Co., 39 S.E. 193 (W.Va. 1901),

> When a person or corporation is authorized by the legislature by an express statute to do an act, or by the council of a city or town to which the power to authorize it has been delegated by a legislative act, such person or corporation cannot be regarded as committing a nuisance in the execution of such act nor proceeded against merely upon the theory that it is a nuisance, either at law or in equity.

See also, Syllabus Point 1, *Frye, supra* ("The maintaining of a vault under a public sidewalk of a municipality, by authority of law, does not constitute a nuisance *per se*."). Therefore, when we apply these holdings to the instant facts, we must conclude that, as a lawful business which has been granted a siting certificate by the PSC, the appellees' wind power facility cannot be considered a nuisance *per se*.

However, the fact that the appellees' electric generating facility does not constitute a nuisance *per se* does not mean that it cannot be abated as a nuisance. It is also true that a business that is not a nuisance *per se* may still constitute a nuisance in light of the surrounding circumstances. In Syllabus Point 2 of *Mahoney, supra*, this Court held,

> As a general rule, a fair test as to whether a business or a particular use of a property in connection with the operation of the business constitutes a nuisance, is the reasonableness or unreasonableness of the operation or use in relation to the particular locality and under all the existing circumstances.

Specifically, "[t]o sustain a [prospective] injunction inhibiting [a] business, not *per se* constituting a nuisance, it must be shown that the danger of injury from it is impending and imminent, and the effect certain." Syllabus Point 1, Pope v. Bridgewater Gas Co., 43 S.E. 87 (W.Va. 1903). With regard to whether an injury in nuisance is certain, this Court has explained that "[m]ere possible, eventual or contingent danger is not enough. That injury will result must be shown beyond question not resting on hypothesis or conjecture, but established by conclusive evidence. If the injury be doubtful, eventual, or contingent an injunction will not be granted." *Pope*, 43 S.E. at 89. Essentially, the proper test to determine whether a proposed activity should be enjoined on the basis that the activity will constitute a nuisance has been stated as follows: "To warrant the perpetuation of an injunction restraining, as a threatened nuisance, the erection of a building proposed to be used for legitimate purposes, the fact that it will be a nuisance if so used must be made clearly to appear, beyond all ground of fair questioning." Syllabus Point 3, *Chambers, supra*.

---

[9] The classic example of an unlawful business that constitutes a nuisance *per se* that can be abated by injunction is a brothel. See State v. Navy, 123 W.Va. 722, 725, 17 S.E.2d 626, 628 (1941) ("A bawdy house is a public nuisance *per se* that may be abated by injunction").

Applying the above law to the allegations in the appellants' complaint, and taking these allegations as true, we conclude that the allegations are legally sufficient to state a claim to prospectively enjoin a nuisance. Stated differently, it does not definitively appear to us that the appellants can prove no set of facts in support of their claim. The appellants have alleged certain injury to the use and enjoyment of their properties as a result of constant loud noise from the wind turbines, the turbines' unsightliness, and reduction in the appellants' property values. If the appellants are able to adduce sufficient evidence to prove these allegations beyond all ground of fair questioning, abatement would be appropriate. Therefore, we find that the circuit court erred in ruling that the appellants failed to assert any facts of a private nuisance that would support a prospective injunction.

The appellees argue, however, that under this Court's holding in Severt v. Beckley Coals, Inc., 170 S.E.2d 577 (W.Va. 1969), the appellants do not have a cognizable nuisance claim because they have an adequate remedy at law. In *Severt*, the defendant began a coal mining operation within 120 feet of the plaintiffs' home. The defendant installed an exhaust fan, a crusher, and a belt carrier, and used trucks to transport coal. The defendant's facility was in constant operation from approximately 6:00 a.m. until 2:00 a.m. the following morning, and continued six days a week. The plaintiffs sued the defendant and produced evidence at trial that the defendant's facility deposited large quantities of dust on the plaintiffs' property, and that constant loud noise from the facility disturbed the plaintiffs' peace and disrupted their sleep. The plaintiffs also produced evidence of a reduction in the value of their property. The jury awarded the plaintiffs for damages to real estate and personal injury, but the circuit court refused the plaintiffs' request for injunctive relief to prevent the defendant from operating its coal mining facility.

This Court affirmed the circuit court's denial of injunctive relief. In Syllabus Point 3 of *Severt*, the Court held that "[e]quity does not have jurisdiction of a case in which the plaintiff has a full, complete and adequate remedy at law, unless some peculiar feature of the case comes within the province of a court of equity." The Court explained that "[i]t clearly appears from the evidence disclosed by the record that the plaintiffs have an adequate remedy at law for the recovery of damages to compensate them fully for the injuries and damages caused by the defendant." *Severt*, 170 S.E.2d at 581.

After careful consideration of the reasoning in *Severt*, we do not find *Severt* to be governing precedent. Frankly, *Severt* is inconsistent with this Court's line of nuisance cases which clearly hold that continual substantial interferences with a person's use and enjoyment of property by things such as noise and unsightliness can best be abated by courts applying equitable principles. This is due to the fact that constant loud noise and unsightliness that interferes with the use and enjoyment of property simply are not susceptible to computation. Thus, money damages alone are an insufficient remedy. Moreover, the fact that the appellants may have an adequate legal remedy for reduction in property values does not bar equity claims to abate other alleged nuisances. This Court held in Syllabus Point 1, Lyons v. Viglianco, 8 S.E.2d 801 (W.Va. 1940), that " '[c]ourts of equity exercise a very salutary jurisdiction in matters of nuisances.' Moundsville v. Ohio River Rr. Co., 16 S.E. 514. Where equity jurisdiction is rightfully invoked in such a matter, the enforcement also of a legal demand is ancillary." Thus, for these reasons, we decline to apply *Severt* to the instant case.

3. Collateral Estoppel

Last, the circuit court ruled that even if the appellants could assert facts sufficient to allege a nuisance claim for a prospective injunction and the circuit court had jurisdiction to hear it, the appellants are collaterally estopped from bringing such a claim.

We find that collateral estoppel does not bar the appellants from bringing a nuisance claim for a prospective injunction in circuit court because the issues previously decided by the PSC in granting the appellees a siting certificate are not identical to the issues in a nuisance claim.

The PSC, in determining the propriety of constructing and operating the wind power facility, was charged with appraising and balancing the interests of the public, the general interests of the state and local economy, and the interests of the applicant. The issue in a nuisance claim, however, is whether an interference with the private use and enjoyment of another's land is unreasonable, *i.e.*, whether the gravity of the harm outweighs the social value of the activity alleged to cause the harm. The PSC did not specifically decide the issue of whether the social utility of the wind power facility outweighs any interference with the appellants' private use and enjoyment of their properties. Accordingly, we find that the circuit court erred in ruling that the appellants' nuisance claims are barred by collateral estoppel.

Finally, prior to closing, we wish to emphasize several important points. First, in considering the appellants' claim for a permanent injunction, the circuit court has great latitude in fashioning an appropriate remedy. Certainly, the court has the power to completely enjoin the construction of the wind power facility. The circuit court may also fashion an equitable remedy short of a complete injunction. We have held that "[i]n the matter of a private nuisance, the relief granted should be such as to cause the defendant no more injury than is necessary to protect the plaintiff's rights." Syllabus Point 2, *Lyons, supra.* Second, although the PSC's grant of a siting certificate to the appellees does not abrogate the circuit court's jurisdiction to hear the appellants' claim, the siting certificate is persuasive evidence of the reasonableness and social utility of the appellees' use of the property to operate a wind power facility. Finally, our decision in this case is merely that the appellants have alleged sufficient facts in their complaint to avoid a dismissal on the pleadings. In other words, the appellants should have their day in court. Beyond this, we offer no opinion on the ultimate success or failure of the appellants' claim.

CONCLUSION

In conclusion, having found no basis in law for the circuit court's ruling that dismissed on the pleadings the appellants' nuisance claim for an injunction, we reverse the April 7, 2006, order of the Circuit Court of Grant County, and we remand this case to the circuit court for proceedings consistent with this opinion.

Reversed and remanded.

BENJAMIN, JUSTICE, dissenting.

The appellant landowners conceded, and the Court apparently agreed, that if appellee NedPower were a public utility with the power of eminent domain, they could not have the construction and operation of its wind-turbine facilities enjoined as a private nuisance. Rather, they would be limited to a claim for money damages in an eminent domain or inverse condemnation proceeding[2] for noise, unsightliness, and any diminution in the value of their property caused by the facilities.

I am of the opinion that NedPower, with respect to its EWGs, possesses the power of eminent domain. The Court should, therefore, have denied the relief sought by the appellant landowners because, as the appellants conceded, if NedPower were a public utility with the power of eminent domain they could not enjoin the construction and operation of its wind turbines as a private nuisance. Accordingly, I dissent.

NOTES AND QUESTIONS

1. **A definition and examples.** How does the court define nuisance? What examples does the court give of nuisances? According to the court, is something that is merely unsightly a nuisance?

2. **A balancing test.** The court suggests a balancing of the gravity of harm caused by conduct against its social value (or utility). The Restatement (Second) of Torts sets forth factors to consider in balancing:

§ 827. **Gravity of Harm — Factors Involved.** In determining the gravity of the harm from an intentional invasion of another's interest in the use and enjoyment of land, the following factors are important:

(a) the extent of the harm involved;

(b) the character of the harm involved;

(c) the social value that the law attaches to the type of use or enjoyment invaded;

(d) the suitability of the particular use or enjoyment invaded to the character of the locality; and

(e) the burden on the person harmed of avoiding the harm.

---

[2] Recently, this Court recognized the distinction between condemnation and inverse condemnation proceedings, noting that:

The United States Supreme Court drew the following distinction between "inverse condemnation" and condemnation proceedings in United States v. Clarke, 445 U.S. 253, 100 S. Ct., 1127, 63 L. Ed. 2d 373 (1980). "[A] landowner's action to recover just compensation for a taking by physical intrusion has come to be referred to as 'inverse' or 'reverse' condemnation. . . . [A] 'condemnation' proceeding is commonly understood to be an action brought by a condemning authority such as the Government in the exercise of its power of eminent domain." Id. at 255, 100 S.Ct. at 1129.

West Virginia Department of Transportation v. Dodson Mobile Home Sales and Services, Inc., 218 W. Va. 121, 123, n.2, 624 S.E.2d 468, 470, n.2, (2005).

§ 828. Utility of Conduct — Factors Involved. In determining the utility of conduct that causes an intentional invasion of another's interest in the use and enjoyment of land, the following factors are important:

(a) the social value that the law attaches to the primary purpose of the conduct;

(b) the suitability of the conduct to the character of the locality; and

(c) the impracticability of preventing or avoiding the invasion.

Restatement (Second) of Torts (1977).

3. **Public nuisance.** In Armory Park Neighborhood Assoc. v. Episcopal Community Services in Arizona, 712 P.2d 914, 917 (Ariz. 1985), the court discussed the difference between public and private nuisances:

> [A] private nuisance is strictly limited to an interference with a person's interest in the enjoyment of real property. The Restatement defines a private nuisance as "a nontrespassory invasion of another's interest in the private use and enjoyment of land." Restatement (Second) of Torts § 821D. A public nuisance, to the contrary, is not limited to an interference with the use and enjoyment of the plaintiff's land. It encompasses any unreasonable interference with a right common to the general public.
>
> We have previously distinguished public and private nuisances. In City of Phoenix v. Johnson, 75 P.2d 30, 34 (Ariz. 1938), we noted that a nuisance is public when it affects rights of "citizens as part of the public, while a private nuisance is one which affects a single individual or a definite number of persons in the enjoyment of some private right which is not common to the public." A public nuisance must also affect a considerable number of people.

See also City of Virginia Beach v. Murphy, 389 S.E.2d 462, 462, 464 (Va. 1990) (municipal ordinance prohibiting playing of audio or video equipment, or musical instrument, in manner or volume to annoy "any person" was valid; right to be free of unreasonably loud, disturbing and unnecessary noise was common to all members of the public); State v. Hafner, 587 N.W.2d 177, 179 (N.D. 1998) (farmer's runaway hogs and cattle were public nuisance).

4. **Nuisance per se.** In Wernke v. Halas, 600 N.E.2d 117, 120 (Ind. Ct. App. 1992), the court distinguished nuisance *per se* and nuisance in fact:

> Both public and private nuisances are further subdivided into nuisances *per se*, or nuisances at law, and nuisances *per accidens*, or nuisances in fact. "A nuisance *per se*, as the term implies, is that which is a nuisance in itself, and which, therefore, cannot be so conducted or maintained as to be lawfully carried on or permitted to exist." Windfall Manufacturing Co. v. Patterson, 47 N.E. 2, 4 (Ind. 1897). Thus, for example, a house of prostitution and an obstruction that encroaches on the right-of-way of a public highway are nuisances *per se*. *Id.* On the other hand, an otherwise lawful use may become a nuisance *per accidens* by virtue of the circumstances surrounding the use.

Logically, therefore, the determination that something is a nuisance *per se* is a question of law for the court, and the determination of "whether that which is not in itself a nuisance is a nuisance in fact" is a question for the jury or the judge as trier of fact.

5. **Remedies.** For additional discussion of remedies, see the casebook favorites, Boomer v. Atlantic Cement Co., 257 N.E.2d 870 (N.Y. 1970) (denying injunction but requiring cement company to pay permanent damages to injured property owners), and Spur Indus., Inc. v. Del E. Webb Development Co., 494 P.2d 700, 708 (Ariz. 1972) (enjoining cattle feedlot but requiring developer who "brought people to the nuisance" to indemnify feedlot owner for the cost of moving or shutting down).

B. ZONING

Virtually unknown in the 19th century, zoning was widely established in the American states by the 1930s, a dramatic turnabout that is largely attributable to three factors. First, plagued by the encroachment of industrialization on residential Manhattan, the City of New York showed how government could respond, by adopting the first comprehensive zoning ordinance in 1916. Second, influenced by the New York ordinance, the United States Commerce Department promulgated the Standard State Zoning Enabling Act in 1926 (SZEA), thus offering a model statute for states choosing to follow New York's lead. Finally, in the same fruitful year of 1926, the landmark Supreme Court decision in Village of Euclid v. Ambler Realty Co., 272 U.S. 365 (1926), *infra*, established that a zoning ordinance of the kind envisioned by the SZEA was not an unconstitutional infringement on the rights of property owners subject to the ordinance.

1.   Validity

U.S. DEPARTMENT OF COMMERCE
A STANDARD STATE ZONING ENABLING ACT (1926)

SEC. 1. Grant of Power. — For the purpose of promoting health, safety, morals, or the general welfare of the community, the legislative body of cities and incorporated villages is hereby empowered to regulate and restrict the height, number of stories, and size of buildings and other structures, the percentage of a lot that may be occupied, the size of yards, courts, and other open spaces, the density of population, and the location and use of buildings, structures, and land for trade, industry, residence, or other purposes.

SEC. 2. Districts. — For any or all of said purposes the local legislative body may divide the municipality into districts of such number, shape, and area as may be deemed best suited to carry out the purposes of this act; and within such districts it may regulate and restrict the erection, construction, reconstruction, alteration, repair, or use of buildings, structures, or land. All such regulations shall be uniform for each class or kind of building throughout each district, but the regulations in one district may differ from those in other districts.

SEC. 3. Purposes in View. — Such regulations shall be made in accordance with a comprehensive plan and designed to lessen congestion in the streets; to secure safety from fire, panic, and other dangers; to promote health and the general welfare; to provide adequate light and air; to prevent the overcrowding of land; to avoid undue concentration of population; and to facilitate the adequate provision of transportation, water, sewerage, schools, parks, and other public requirements. Such regulations shall be made with reasonable consideration, among other things, to the character of the district and its peculiar suitability for particular uses, and with a view to conserving the value of buildings and encouraging the most appropriate use of land throughout such municipality.

SEC. 4. Method of Procedure. — The legislative body of such municipality shall provide for the manner in which such regulations and restrictions and the boundaries of such districts shall be determined, established, and enforced, and from time to time amended, supplemented, or changed. However, no regulation, restriction, or boundary shall become effective until after a public hearing in relation thereto, at which parties in interest and citizens shall have an opportunity to be heard. At least 15 days' notice of the time and place of such hearing shall be published in an official paper, or a paper of general circulation, in such municipality.

SEC. 5. Changes. — Such regulations, restrictions, and boundaries may from time to time be amended, supplemented, changed, modified, or repealed. In case, however, of a protest against such change, signed by the owners of 20 percent or more either of the area of the lots included in such proposed change, or of those immediately adjacent in the rear thereof extending _____ feet therefrom, or of those directly opposite thereto extending _____ feet from the street frontage of such opposite lots, such amendment shall not become effective except by the favorable vote of three-fourths of all the members of the legislative body of such municipality. The provisions of the previous section relative to public hearings and official notice shall apply equally to all changes or amendments.

SEC. 6. Zoning Commission. — In order to avail itself of the powers conferred by this act, such legislative body shall appoint a commission, to be known as the zoning commission, to recommend the boundaries of the various original districts and appropriate regulations to be enforced therein. Such commission shall make a preliminary report and hold public hearings thereon before submitting its final report, and such legislative body shall not hold its public hearings or take action until it has received the final report of such commission. Where a city planning commission already exists, it may be appointed as the zoning commission.

SEC. 7. Board of Adjustment. — Such local legislative body may provide for the appointment of a board of adjustment, and in the regulations and restrictions adopted pursuant to the authority of this act, may provide that the said board of adjustment may, in appropriate cases and subject to appropriate conditions and safeguards, make special exceptions to the terms of the ordinance in harmony with its general purpose and intent and in accordance with general or specific rules therein contained.

The board of adjustment shall consist of five members, each to be appointed to a term of three years and removable for cause by the appointing authority upon written charges and after a public hearing. Vacancies shall be filled for the unexpired term of any member whose term becomes vacant.

The board shall adopt rules in accordance with the provisions of any ordinance adopted pursuant to this act. Meetings of the board shall be held at the call of the chairman and at such other times as the board may determine. Such chairman, or in his absence the acting chairman, may administer oaths and compel the attendance of witnesses. All meetings of the board shall be open to the public. The board shall keep minutes of its proceedings, showing the vote of each member upon each question, or if absent or failing to vote, indicating such fact, and shall keep records of its examinations and other official actions, all of which shall be immediately filed in the office of the board and shall be a public record.

Appeals to the board of adjustment may be taken by any person aggrieved or by any officer, department, board, or bureau of the municipality affected by any decision of the adminstrative officer. Such appeal shall be taken within a reasonable time, as provided by the rules of the board, by filing with the officer from whom the appeal is taken, and with the board of adjustment, a notice of appeal specifying the grounds thereof. The officer from whom the appeal is taken shall forthwith transmit to the board all the papers constituting the record upon which the action appealed from was taken.

An appeal stays all proceedings in furtherance of the action appealed from, unless the officer from whom the appeal is taken certifies to the board of adjustment after the notice of appeal shall have been filed with him that by reason of facts stated in the certificate a stay would, in his opinion, cause imminent peril to life or property. In such case, proceedings shall not be stayed otherwise than by a restraining order which may be granted by the board of adjustment or by a court of record on application on notice to the officer from whom the appeal is taken and on due cause shown.

The board of adjustment shall fix a reasonable time for the hearing of the appeal, give public notice thereof, as well as due notice to the parties in interest, and decide the same within a reasonable time. Upon the hearing any party may appear in person or by agent or attorney.

The board of adjustment shall have the following powers:

1. To hear and decide appeals where it is alleged that there is error in any order, requirement, decision, or determination made by an administrative official in the enforcement of this act or of any ordinance adopted pursuant thereto.

2. To hear and decide special exceptions to the terms of the ordinance upon which such board is required to pass under such ordinance.

3. To authorize, upon appeal in specific cases, such variance from the terms of the ordinance as will not be contrary to the public interest, where, owing to special conditions, a literal enforcement of the provisions of the ordinance will result in unnecessary hardship, and so that the spirit of the ordinance shall be observed and substantial justice done.

In exercising the above-mentioned powers, such board may, in conformity with the provisions of this act, reverse or affirm, wholly or partly, or may modify, the order, requirement, decision, or determination appealed from and may make such order, requirement, decision, or determination as ought to be made, and to that end shall have all the powers of the officer from whom the appeal is taken.

The concurring vote of four members of the board shall be necessary to reverse any order, requirement, decision, or determination of any such administrative official, or to decide in favor of the applicant on any matter upon which it is required to pass under any such ordinance, or to effect any variation in such ordinance.

Any person or persons, jointly or severally, aggrieved by any decision of the board of adjustment, or any taxpayer, or any officer, department, board, or bureau of the municipality, may present to a court of record a petition, duly verified, setting forth that such decision is illegal, in whole or in part, specifying the grounds of the illegality. Such petition shall be presented to the court within 30 days after the filing of the decision in the office of the board.

SEC. 8. Enforcement and Remedies. — The local legislative body may provide by ordinance for the enforcement of this act and of any ordinance or regulation made thereunder. A violation of this act or of such ordinance or regulation is hereby declared to be a misdemeanor, and such local legislative body may provide for the punishment thereof by fine or imprisonment or both. It is also empowered to provide civil penalties for such violation.

In case any building or structure is erected, constructed, reconstructed, altered, repaired, converted, or maintained, or any building, structure, or land is used in violation of this act or of any ordinance or other regulation made under authority conferred hereby, the proper local authorities of the municipality, in addition to other remedies, may institute any appropriate action or proceedings to prevent such unlawful erection, construction, reconstruction, alteration, repair, conversion, maintenance, or use, to restrain, correct, or abate such violation, to prevent the occupancy of said building, structure, or land, or to prevent any illegal act, conduct, business, or use in or about such premises.

NOTES

1. **Necessity for the enabling act.** Unlike the federal government, which is one of enumerated powers, state governments enjoy an inherent police power to provide for the general welfare, and state governments may also authorize county and municipal governments to exercise the police power. However, because the state's grant of the police power to municipalities and counties is generally understood not to authorize a power to zone, an enabling act is necessary. *See* William B. Stoebuck & Dale A. Whitman, The Law of Property § 9.10, at 568-69 (3d ed. 2000).

2. **SZEA.** For a recent proposal for improving the SZEA, see Michael J. McCormack, Comment, *Applying the Basic Principles of Cognitive Science to the Standard State Zoning Enabling Act*, 27 B.C. Envtl. Aff. L. Rev. 519, 563-65 (2000).

3. **The comprehensive plan.** Notice the dictate of Section 3 that zoning regulations "shall be made in accordance with a comprehensive plan." Despite that mandatory language, most courts have held that a comprehensive zoning ordinance can itself constitute a comprehensive plan and need not be preceded by one. *See generally* Charles Haar, *"In Accordance With a Comprehensive Plan,"* 68 Harv. L. Rev. 1154 (1955); Stuart Meck, *The Legislative Requirement That Zoning and Land Use Controls be Consistent With an Independently Adopted Local Comprehensive Plan: A Model Statute*, 3 Wash. U. J.L. & Pol'y 295 (2000).

4. **Commentary.** Some planners and commentators believe that the SZEA of the 1920s is outdated and untenable for the twenty-first century. *See* American Planning Association, Growing Smart Legislative Guidebook (2002), available at www.planning.org/guidebook/Guidebook.htm; Michael Lewyn, *Twenty-First Century Planning and the Constitution*, 74 Colo. L. Rev. 651, 659-60 (2003).

VILLAGE OF EUCLID v. AMBLER REALTY CO.
272 U.S. 365 (1926)

JUSTICE SUTHERLAND delivered the opinion of the Court.

The village of Euclid is an Ohio municipal corporation. It adjoins and practically is a suburb of the city of Cleveland. Its estimated population is between 5,000 and 10,000, and its area from 12 to 14 square miles, the greater part of which is farm lands or unimproved acreage. It lies, roughly, in the form of a parallelogram measuring approximately 3 1/2 miles each way. East and west it is traversed by three principal highways: Euclid avenue, through the southerly border, St. Clair avenue, through the central portion, and Lake Shore boulevard, through the northerly border, in close proximity to the shore of Lake Erie. The Nickel Plate Railroad lies from 1,500 to 1,800 feet north of Euclid avenue, and the Lake Shore Railroad 1,600 feet farther to the north. The three highways and the two railroads are substantially parallel.

Appellee is the owner of a tract of land containing 68 acres, situated in the westerly end of the village, abutting on Euclid avenue to the south and the Nickel Plate Railroad to the north. Adjoining this tract, both on the east and on the west, there have been laid out restricted residential plats upon which residences have been erected.

On November 13, 1922, an ordinance was adopted by the village council, establishing a comprehensive zoning plan for regulating and restricting the location of trades, industries, apartment houses, two-family houses, single family houses, etc., the lot area to be built upon, the size and height of buildings, etc.

The entire area of the village is divided by the ordinance into six classes of use districts, denominated U-1 to U-6, inclusive; three classes of height districts, denominated H-1 to H-3, inclusive; and four classes of area districts, denominated A-1 to A-4, inclusive. The use districts are classified in respect of the buildings which may be erected within their respective limits, as follows: U-1 is restricted to single family dwellings, public parks, water towers and reservoirs, suburban and interurban electric railway passenger stations and rights of way, and farming, noncommercial greenhouse nurseries, and truck gardening; U-2 is extended to include two-family dwellings; U-3 is further extended to include apartment houses, hotels, churches, schools, public libraries, museums, private clubs, community center buildings, hospitals, sanitariums, public playgrounds, and recreation buildings, and a city hall and courthouse; U-4 is further extended to include banks, offices, studios, telephone exchanges, fire and police stations, restaurants, theaters and moving picture shows, retail stores and shops, sales offices, sample rooms, wholesale stores for hardware, drugs, and groceries, stations for gasoline and oil (not exceeding 1,000 gallons storage) and for ice delivery, skating rinks and dance halls, electric substations, job and newspaper printing, public garages for motor vehicles, stables and wagon sheds (not exceeding five horses, wagons or motor trucks), and distributing stations for central store and commercial enterprises; U-5 is further extended to include billboards and advertising signs (if permitted), warehouses, ice and ice cream manufacturing and cold storage plants, bottling works, milk bottling and central distribution stations, laundries, carpet cleaning, dry cleaning, and dyeing establishments, blacksmith, horseshoeing, wagon and motor vehicle repair shops, freight stations, street car barns, stables and wagon sheds (for more than five horses, wagons or motor trucks), and wholesale produce markets and salesroom; U-6 is further extended to include plants for sewage disposal and for producing gas, garbage and refuse incineration, scrap iron, junk, scrap paper, and rag storage, aviation fields, cemeteries, crematories, penal and correctional institutions, insane and feeble-minded institutions, storage of oil and gasoline (not to exceed 25,000 gallons), and manufacturing and industrial operations of any kind other than, and any public utility not included in, a class U-1, U-2, U-3, U-4, or U-5 use. There is a seventh class of uses which is prohibited altogether.

Class U-1 is the only district in which buildings are restricted to those enumerated. In the other classes the uses are cumulative — that is to say, uses in class U-2 include those enumerated in the preceding class U-1; class U-3 includes uses enumerated in the preceding classes, U-2, and U-1; and so on. In addition to the enumerated uses, the ordinance provides for accessory uses; that is, for uses customarily incident to the principal use, such as private garages. Many regulations are provided in respect of such accessory uses.

The height districts are classified as follows: In class H-1, buildings are limited to a height of 2 1/2 stories, or 35 feet; in class H-2, to 4 stories, or 50 feet; in class H-3, to 80 feet. To all of these, certain exceptions are made, as in the case of church spires, water tanks, etc.

The classification of area districts is: In A-1 districts, dwellings or apartment houses to accommodate more than one family must have at least 5,000 square feet for interior lots and at least 4,000 square feet for corner lots; in A-2 districts, the area must be at least 2,500 square feet for interior lots, and 2,000 square feet for corner lots; in A-3 districts, the limits are 1,250 and 1,000 square feet, respectively; in A-4 districts, the limits are 900 and 700 square feet, respectively. The ordinance contains, in great variety and detail, provisions in respect of width of lots, front, side, and rear yards, and other matters, including restrictions and regulations as to the use of billboards, signboards, and advertising signs.

A single family dwelling consists of a basement and not less than three rooms and a bathroom. A two-family dwelling consists of a basement and not less than four living rooms and a bathroom for each family, and is further described as a detached dwelling for the occupation of two families, one having its principal living rooms on the first floor and the other on the second floor.

Appellee's tract of land comes under U-2, U-3 and U-6. The first strip of 620 feet immediately north of Euclid avenue falls in class U-2, the next 130 feet to the north, in U-3, and the remainder in U-6. The uses of the first 620 feet, therefore, do not include apartment houses, hotels, churches, schools, or other public and semipublic buildings, or other uses enumerated in respect of U-3 to U-6, inclusive. The uses of the next 130 feet include all of these, but exclude industries, theaters, banks, shops, and the various other uses set forth in respect of U-4 to U-6, inclusive.

Annexed to the ordinance, and made a part of it, is a zone map, showing the location and limits of the various use, height, and area districts, from which it appears that the three classes overlap one another; that is to say, for example, both U-5 and U-6 use districts are in A-4 area district, but the former is in H-2 and the latter in H-3 height districts.

The lands lying between the two railroads for the entire length of the village area and extending some distance on either side to the north and south, having an average width of about 1,600 feet, are left open, with slight exceptions, for industrial and all other uses. This includes the larger part of appellee's tract. Approximately one-sixth of the area of the entire village is included in U-5 and U-6 use districts. That part of the village lying south of Euclid avenue is principally in U-1 districts. The lands lying north of Euclid avenue and bordering on the long strip just described are included in U-1, U-2, U-3, and U-4 districts, principally in U-2.

The enforcement of the ordinance is intrusted to the inspector of buildings, under rules and regulations of the board of zoning appeals. Meetings of the board are public, and minutes of its proceedings are kept. It is authorized to adopt rules and regulations to carry into effect provisions of the ordinance. Decisions of the inspector of buildings may be appealed to the board by any person claiming to be adversely affected by any such decision. The board is given power in specific cases of practical difficulty or unnecessary hardship to interpret the ordinance in harmony with its general purpose and intent, so that the public health, safety and general welfare may be secure and substantial justice done. Penalties are prescribed for violations, and it is provided that the various provisions are to be regarded as independent and the holding of any provision to be unconstitutional, void or ineffective shall not affect any of the others.

The ordinance is assailed on the grounds that it is in derogation of section 1 of the Fourteenth Amendment to the federal Constitution in that it deprives appellee of liberty and property without due process of law and denies it the equal protection of the law, and that it offends against certain provisions of the Constitution of the state of Ohio. The prayer of the bill is for an injunction restraining the enforcement of the ordinance and all attempts to impose or maintain as to appellee's property any of the restrictions, limitations or conditions.

The court below held the ordinance to be unconstitutional and void, and enjoined its enforcement.

Before proceeding to a consideration of the case, it is necessary to determine the scope of the inquiry. The bill alleges that the tract of land in question is vacant and has been held for years for the purpose of selling and developing it for industrial uses, for which it is especially adapted, being immediately in the path or progressive industrial development; that for such uses it has a market value of about $10,000 per acre, but if the use be limited to residential purposes the market value is not in excess of $2,500 per acre; that the first 200 feet of the parcel back from Euclid avenue, if unrestricted in respect of use, has a value of $150 per front foot, but if limited to residential uses, and ordinary mercantile business be excluded therefrom, its value is not in excess of $50 per front foot.

It is specifically averred that the ordinance attempts to restrict and control the lawful uses of appellee's land, so as to confiscate and destroy a great part of its value; that it is being enforced in accordance with its terms; that propective buyers of land for industrial, commercial, and residential uses in the metropolitan district of Cleveland are deterred from buying any part of this land because of the existence of the ordinance and the necessity thereby entailed of conducting burdensome and expensive litigation in order to vindicate the right to use the land for lawful and legitimate purposes; that the ordinance constitutes a cloud upon the land, reduces and destroys its value, and has the effect of diverting the normal industrial, commercial, and residential development thereof to other and less favorable locations.

The record goes no farther than to show, as the lower court found, that the normal and reasonably to be expected use and development of that part of appellee's land adjoining Euclid avenue is for general trade and commercial purposes, particularly retail stores and like establishments, and that the normal and reasonably to be expected use and development of the residue of the land is for industrial and trade purposes. Whatever injury is inflicted by the mere existence and threatened enforcement of the ordinance is due to restrictions in respect of these and similar uses, to which perhaps should be added — if not included in the foregoing — restrictions in respect of apartment houses.

A motion was made in the court below to dismiss the bill on the ground that, because complainant (appellee) had made no effort to obtain a building permit or apply to the zoning board of appeals for relief, as it might have done under the terms of the ordinance, the suit was premature. The motion was properly overruled. The effect of the allegations of the bill is that the ordinance of its own force operates greatly to reduce the value of appellee's lands and destroy their marketability for industrial, commercial and residential uses, and the attack is directed, not against any specific provision or provisions, but against the ordinance as an entirety. Assuming the premises, the existence and maintenance of the ordinance in effect constitutes a present invasion of appellee's property rights and a threat to continue it. Under these circumstances, the equitable jurisdiction is clear.

It is not necessary to set forth the provisions of the Ohio Constitution which are thought to be infringed. The question is the same under both Constitutions, namely, as stated by appellee: Is the ordinance invalid, in that it violates the constitutional protection "to the right of property in the appellee by attempted regulations under the guise of the police power, which are unreasonable and confiscatory?"

Building zone laws are of modern origin. They began in this country about 25 years ago. Until recent years, urban life was comparatively simple; but, with the great increase and concentration of population, problems have developed, and constantly are developing, which require, and will continue to require, additional restrictions in respect of the use and occupation of private lands in urban communities. Regulations, the wisdom, necessity, and validity of which, as applied to existing conditions, are so apparent that they are now uniformly sustained, a century ago, or even half a century ago, probably would have been rejected as arbitrary and oppressive. Such regulations are sustained, under the complex conditions of our day, for reasons analogous to those which justify traffic regulations, which, before the advent of automobiles and rapid transit street railways, would have been condemned as fatally arbitrary and unreasonable. And in this there is no inconsistency, for, while the meaning of constitutional guaranties never varies, the scope of their application must expand or contract to meet the new and different conditions which are constantly coming within the field of their operation. In a changing world it is impossible that it should be otherwise. But although a degree of elasticity is thus imparted, not to the meaning, but to the application of constitutional principles, statutes and ordinances, which, after giving due weight to the new conditions, are found clearly not to conform to the Constitution, of course, must fall.

The ordinance now under review, and all similar laws and regulations, must find their justification in some aspect of the police power, asserted for the public welfare. The line which in this field separates the legitimate from the illegitimate assumption of power is not capable of precise delimitation. It varies with circumstances and conditions. A regulatory zoning ordinance, which would be clearly valid as applied to the great cities, might be clearly invalid as applied to rural communities. In solving doubts, the maxim "sic utere tuo ut alienum non laedas," which lies at the foundation of so much of the common [law] of nuisances, ordinarily will furnish a fairly helpful clew. And the law of nuisances, likewise, may be consulted, not for the purpose of controlling, but for the helpful aid of its analogies in the process of ascertaining the scope of, the power. Thus the question whether the power exists to forbid the erection of a building of a particular kind or for a particular use, like the question whether a particular thing is a nuisance, is to be determined, not by an abstract consideration of the building or of the thing considered apart, but by considering it in connection with the circumstances and the locality. A nuisance may be merely a right thing in the wrong place, like a pig in the parlor instead of the barnyard. If the validity of the legislative classification for zoning purposes be fairly debatable, the legislative judgment must be allowed to control.

There is no serious difference of opinion in respect of the validity of laws and regulations fixing the height of buildings within reasonable limits, the character of materials and methods of construction, and the adjoining area which must be left open, in order to minimize the danger of fire or collapse, the evils of overcrowding and the like, and excluding from residential sections offensive trades, industries and structures likely to create nuisances.

Here, however, the exclusion is in general terms of all industrial establishments, and it may thereby happen that not only offensive or dangerous industries will be excluded, but those which are neither offensive nor dangerous will share the same fate. But this is no more than happens in respect of many practice-forbidding laws which this court has upheld, although drawn in general terms so as to include individual cases that may turn out to be innocuous in themselves. The inclusion of a reasonable margin, to insure effective enforcement, will not put upon a law, otherwise valid, the stamp of invalidity. Such laws may also find their justification in the fact that, in some fields, the bad fades into the good by such insensible degrees that the two are not capable of being readily distinguished and separated in terms of legislation. In the light of these considerations, we are not prepared to say that the end in view was not sufficient to justify the general rule of the ordinance, although some industries of an innocent character might fall within the proscribed class. It cannot be said that the ordinance in this respect "passes the bounds of reason and assumes the character of a merely arbitrary fiat." Purity Extract Co. v. Lynch, 226 U. S. 192, 204. Moreover, the restrictive provisions of the ordinance in this particular may be sustained upon the principles applicable to the broader exclusion from residential districts of all business and trade structures, presently to be discussed.

It is said that the village of Euclid is a mere suburb of the city of Cleveland; that the industrial development of that city has now reached and in some degree extended into the village, and in the obvious course of things will soon absorb the entire area for industrial enterprises; that the effect of the ordinance is to divert this natural development elsewhere, with the consequent loss of increased values to the owners of the lands within the village borders. But the village, though physically a suburb of Cleveland, is politically a separate municipality, with powers of its own and authority to govern itself as it sees fit, within the limits of the organic law of its creation and the state and federal Constitutions. Its governing authorities, presumably representing a majority of its inhabitants and voicing their will, have determined, not that industrial development shall cease at its boundaries, but that the course of such development shall proceed within definitely fixed lines. If it be a proper exercise of the police power to relegate industrial establishments to localities separated from residential sections, it is not easy to find a sufficient reason for denying the power because the effect of its exercise is to divert an industrial flow from the course which it would follow, to the injury of the residential public, if left alone, to another course where such injury will be obviated. It is not meant by this, however, to exclude the possibility of cases where the general public interest would so far outweigh the interest of the municipality that the municipality would not be allowed to stand in the way.

We find no difficulty in sustaining restrictions of the kind thus far reviewed. The serious question in the case arises over the provisions of the ordinance excluding from residential districts apartment houses, business houses, retail stores and shops, and other like establishments. This question involves the validity of what is really the crux of the more recent zoning legislation, namely, the creation and maintenance of residential districts, from which business and trade of every sort, including hotels and apartment houses, are excluded. Upon that question this Court has not thus far spoken. The decisions of the state courts are numerous and conflicting; but those which broadly sustain the power greatly outnumber those which deny it altogether or narrowly limit it, and it is very apparent that there is a constantly increasing tendency in the direction of the broader view.

The decisions [sustaining the zoning power] agree that the exclusion of buildings devoted to business, trade, etc., from residential districts, bears a rational relation to the health and safety of the community. Some of the grounds for this conclusion are promotion of the health and security from injury of children and others by separating dwelling houses from territory devoted to trade and industry; suppression and prevention of disorder; facilitating the extinguishment of fires, and the enforcement of street traffic regulations and other general welfare ordinances; aiding the health and safety of the community, by excluding from residential areas the confusion and danger of fire, contagion, and disorder, which in greater or less degree attach to the location of stores, shops, and factories. Another ground is that the construction and repair of streets may be rendered easier and less expensive, by confining the greater part of the heavy traffic to the streets where business is carried on.

The matter of zoning has received much attention at the hands of commissions and experts, and the results of their investigations have been set forth in comprehensive reports. These reports, which bear every evidence of painstaking consideration, concur in the view that the segregation of residential, business and industrial buildings will make it easier to provide fire apparatus suitable for the character and intensity of the development in each section; that it will increase the safety and security of home life, greatly tend to prevent street accidents, especially to children, by reducing the traffic and resulting confusion in residential sections, decrease noise and other conditions which produce or intensify nervous disorders, preserve a more favorable environment in which to rear children, etc. With particular reference to apartment houses, it is pointed out that the development of detached house sections is greatly retarded by the coming of apartment houses, which has sometimes resulted in destroying the entire section for private house purposes; that in such sections very often the apartment house is a mere parasite, constructed in order to take advantage of the open spaces and attractive surroundings created by the residential character of the district. Moreover, the coming of one apartment house is followed by others, interfering by their height and bulk with the free circulation of air and monopolizing the rays of the sun which otherwise would fall upon the smaller homes, and bringing, as their necessary accompaniments, the disturbing noises incident to increased traffic and business, and the occupation, by means of moving and parked automobiles, of larger portions of the streets, thus detracting from their safety and depriving children of the privilege of quiet and open spaces for play, enjoyed by those in more favored localities — until, finally, the residential character of the neighborhood and its desirability as a place of detached residences are utterly destroyed. Under these circumstances, apartment houses, which in a different environment would be not only entirely unobjectionable but highly desirable, come very near to being nuisances.

If these reasons, thus summarized, do not demonstrate the wisdom or sound policy in all respects of those restrictions which we have indicated as pertinent to the inquiry, at least, the reasons are sufficiently cogent to preclude us from saying, as it must be said before the ordinance can be declared unconstitutional, that such provisions are clearly arbitrary and unreasonable, having no substantial relation to the public health, safety, morals, or general welfare.

It is true that when, if ever, the provisions set forth in the ordinance in tedious and minute detail, come to be concretely applied to particular premises, including those of the appellee, or to particular conditions, or to be considered in connection with specific complaints, some of them, or even many of them, may be found to be clearly arbitrary and unreasonable. But where the equitable remedy of injunction is sought, as it is here, not upon the ground of a present infringement or denial of a specific right, or of a particular injury in process of actual execution, but upon the broad ground that the mere existence and threatened enforcement of the ordinance, by materially and adversely affecting values and curtailing the opportunities of the market, constitute a present and irreparable injury, the court will not scrutinize its provisions, sentence by sentence, to ascertain by a process of piecemeal dissection whether there may be, here and there, provisions of a minor character, or relating to matters of administration, or not shown to contribute to the injury complained of, which, if attacked separately, might not withstand the test of constitutionality. In respect of such provisions, of which specific complaint is not made, it cannot be said that the landowner has suffered or is threatened with an injury which entitles him to challenge their constitutionality.

The relief sought here is an injunction against the enforcement of any of the restrictions, limitations, or conditions of the ordinance. And the gravamen of the complaint is that a portion of the land of the appellee cannot be sold for certain enumerated uses because of the general and broad restraints of the ordinance. What would be the effect of a restraint imposed by one or more or the innumerable provisions of the ordinance, considered apart, upon the value or marketability of the lands, is neither disclosed by the bill nor by the evidence, and we are afforded no basis, apart from mere speculation, upon which to rest a conclusion that it or they would have any appreciable effect upon those matters. Under these circumstances, therefore, it is enough for us to determine, as we do, that the ordinance in its general scope and dominant features, so far as its provisions are here involved, is a valid exercise of authority, leaving other provisions to be dealt with as cases arise directly involving them.

Decree reversed.

NOTES AND QUESTIONS

1. **Prelude to *Euclid*.** For a discussion of the Court's land use decisions prior to the principal case, see Joseph Gordon Hylton, *Prelude to* Euclid: *The United States Supreme Court and the Constitutionality of Land Use Regulation, 1900-1920,* 3 Wash. U. J.L. & Pol'y 1 (2000).

2. **Euclidean zoning: the pyramid.** Fittingly enough, the central metaphor for the kind of zoning validated in the principal case comes from geometry: the pyramid. The "highest" use zone, authorizing single-family residential use only (U-

1 in *Euclid*), sits at the top. Each lower zone on the pyramid incorporates the allowed uses of the higher zones and adds new authorized uses. At the bottom of the pyramid sits the heavy industry zone (U-6 in *Euclid*), which allows all uses. Euclidean zoning is also called "cumulative" zoning. Note that in addition to allocating and restricting land *uses*, the zoning ordinance in the case also, as is typical of zoning ordinances, specifies height and bulk restrictions on structures.

3. **Rationale in *Euclid*.** What purpose or purposes of the city's exercise of the police power through its zoning ordinance did the Court emphasize? What is the connection between the public nuisance doctrine and the rationale of *Euclid*?

4. **Pigs in parlors.** It's easy to see why a factory next to a single-family residence would be a nuisance, and consequently why an ordinance excluding factories from residential zones is a valid exercise of the police power. How did the Court in *Euclid* justify the exclusion of *apartment buildings* from the U-1 zone? Although the Court did not address the issue, does the same rationale justify the exclusion of duplexes from the U-1 zone: would a duplex be a "parasite" on single-family residences? Can you identify a broader rationale to justify the various exclusions of the Euclid ordinance?

5. **Elements of judicial review.** What positions does the Court indicate on the questions of the presumptive validity of the city's zoning ordinance; the required relationship between the terms of the ordinance and the police power goals addressed by the ordinance; and the final authority as to the wisdom of a legislative zoning classification? *See* John G. Sprankling, Understanding Property Law § 36.05[B][2], at 614 (2d ed. 2007).

6. **Procedures.** Why wasn't Ambler Realty's failure to seek a building permit or apply to the zoning board for a variance (*see* § 7 of the SZEA) fatal to its lawsuit? What *did* Ambler Realty have to establish in order to bring its challenge to the ordinance, and how did it make that showing?

7. **The *Nectow* case.** Two years after *Euclid*, the Court showed the importance of the distinction between a challenge to the general validity of a zoning ordinance and a challenge of its validity as applied to a specific parcel. In Nectow v. City of Cambridge, 277 U.S. 183 (1928) (opinion by Sutherland, J.), the city's ordinance placed 100 feet of plaintiff's 29,000 square-foot parcel in a residential district (R-3). A master appointed by the lower court found that "no practical use can be made of the land" for residential purposes, in part, as the Court noted, "because of the industrial and railroad purposes to which the immediately adjoining lands to the south and east have been devoted." The Court held that the ordinance was unconstitutional as applied to plaintiff's parcel.

> The boundary line of the residential district before reaching [plaintiff's] locus runs for some distance along the streets, and to exclude the locus from the residential district requires only that such line shall be continued 100 feet further along Henry street and thence south along Brookline street. There does not appear to be any reason why this should not be done. Nevertheless, if that were all, we should not be warranted in substituting our judgment for that of the zoning authorities primarily charged with the duty and responsibility of determining the question. But that is not all. The government power to interfere by zoning regulations with the general rights of the land owner by restricting the character of his use, is not

unlimited, and such restriction cannot be imposed if it does not bear a substantial relation to the public health, safety, morals, or general welfare. Here, the express finding of the master is that the health, safety, convenience, and general welfare of the inhabitants of the part of the city affected will not be promoted by the disposition made by the ordinance of the locus in question. This finding of the master, after a hearing and an inspection of the entire area affected, is determinative of the case. That the invasion of the property of plaintiff was serious and highly injurious is clearly established, and, since a necessary basis for the support of that invasion is wanting, the action of the zoning authorities comes within the ban of the Fourteenth Amendment and cannot be sustained.

277 U.S. at 188. If, as the Court indicates, an arguably more rational drawing of the R-3 district was possible, why wasn't that fact alone enough to establish a violation of Nectow's constitutional rights? Does *Euclid* indicate the answer?

8. **Remedies.** When a zoning ordinance is unconstitutional as applied to a landowner's parcel, what is the landowner's appropriate remedy? If the landowner is deprived of a valuable use of the land pending resolution of the dispute, should the landowner be entitled to damages? *Cf.* First English Evangelical Lutheran Church v. County of Los Angeles, 482 U.S. 304 (1987), discussed in note 4 following Tahoe Sierra Preservation Council, Inc. v. Tahoe Regional Planning Agency, in Section D.2.c below.

9. **The downside of Euclidean zoning.** Note two potentially troubling aspects of the Euclid ordinance, and of all ordinances modeled on the SZEA (which is to say, most of the zoning ordinances adopted in the 1930s): the emphasis on uniformity of use within each zone, and the emphasis on regulation in advance by general rules. Does it follow from the desirability of separating incompatible land uses that allowed uses must be uniform? Does rational planning mandate general legislative rules as opposed to regulation by administrative agency? For another critique of Euclidean zoning, see Joel Kosman, *Toward an Inclusionary Jurisprudence: A Reconceptualization of Zoning*, 43 Cath. U. L. Rev. 59, 61-62 (1993).

2. Nonconforming Uses and "Vested Rights"

It is difficult to write a zoning ordinance on a clean slate. Some use that the planner excludes from a particular zone for the *future* may already exist in that zone on the effective date of the ordinance. The law of such "nonconforming uses" reflects the tension between the planner's desire to allocate land uses rationally and comprehensively, and the planner's fear that immediate elimination of extant conflicting uses would be unconstitutional. The principal case and Notes indicate the issues generated by this tension, and the strategies and techniques adopted by zoning ordinances to deal with it.

VILLAGE OF VALATIE v. SMITH
632 N.E.2d 1264 (N.Y. 1994)

SIMONS, JUDGE.

This appeal challenges the facial validity of chapter 85 of the Village Code of the Village of Valatie, a local law that terminates the nonconforming use of a mobile home upon the transfer of ownership of either the mobile home or the land upon which it sits. Defendant argues that it is unconstitutional for the Village to use a change in ownership as the termination date for a nonconforming use. We conclude, however, that defendant has failed to carry her burden of showing that the local law is unreasonable on its face. Accordingly, we modify the order of the Appellate Division by denying defendant's cross motion for summary judgment.

In 1968, the Village enacted chapter 85 to prohibit the placement of mobile homes outside mobile home parks. Under the law, any existing mobile home located outside a park which met certain health standards was allowed to remain as a nonconforming use until either ownership of the land or ownership of the mobile home changed. According to the Village, six mobile homes, including one owned by defendant's father, fell within this exception at the time the law was passed.

In 1989, defendant inherited the mobile home from her father and the Village instituted this action to enforce the law and have the unit removed. Both the Village and defendant moved before Supreme Court for summary judgment. The court granted defendant's motion and denied the Village's. The court characterized defendant's mobile home as a lawful nonconforming use — i.e., a use that was legally in place at the time the municipality enacted legislation prohibiting the use. Reasoning that the right to continue a nonconforming use runs with the land, the court held that the portion of the ordinance setting termination at the transfer of ownership was unconstitutional. The Appellate Division affirmed. The Court acknowledged that a municipality had the authority to phase out a nonconforming use with an "amortization period," but it concluded that this particular law was unreasonable, and therefore unconstitutional, because the period of time allowed "bears no relationship to the use of the land or the investment in that use." 596 N.Y.S.2d 581, 583 (1993).

Preliminarily, it is important to note that the question presented is the facial validity of the local law. The Court is not called upon to decide whether the local law as applied so deprived defendant of the value of her property as to constitute a governmental taking under the Fifth Amendment. Nor does defendant challenge the power of a municipality to regulate land use, including the placement of mobile homes, as a valid exercise of the police power. Finally, there is no question that municipalities may enact laws reasonably limiting the duration of nonconforming uses.[8] Thus, the narrow issue is whether the Village acted unreasonably by establishing an amortization period that uses the transfer of ownership as an end point.

---

[8] Though the difference between a nonconforming use and a nonconforming structure will at times be relevant (see Matter of Harbison v. City of Buffalo, 4 N.Y.2d 553, 561-562, 152 N.E.2d 42), our reasoning in this case applies equally whether the mobile home is characterized as a use or a structure.

The policy of allowing nonconforming uses to continue originated in concerns that the application of land use regulations to uses existing prior to the regulations' enactment might be construed as confiscatory and unconstitutional (4 Rathkopf, Zoning and Planning § 51.01[2][b], at 51-6 [Ziegler 4th ed]). While it was initially assumed that nonconforming uses would disappear with time, just the opposite proved to be true in many instances, with the nonconforming use thriving in the absence of any new lawful competition. In light of the problems presented by continuing nonconforming uses, this Court has characterized the law's allowance of such uses as a "grudging tolerance," and we have recognized the right of municipalities to take reasonable measures to eliminate them. See Matter of Pelham Esplanade v. Board of Trustees, 565 N.E.2d 508, 510 (N.Y. 1990).

Most often, elimination has been effected by establishing amortization periods, at the conclusion of which the nonconforming use must end. As commentators have noted, the term "amortization period" is somewhat misleading. See, e.g., 4 Rathkopf, Zoning and Planning § 51B.05[1], at 51B-44, n.3 (Ziegler 4th ed). "Amortization" properly refers to a liquidation, but in this context the owner is not required to take any particular financial step. "Amortization period" simply designates a period of time granted to owners of nonconforming uses during which they may phase out their operations as they see fit and make other arrangements. It is, in effect, a grace period, putting owners on fair notice of the law and giving them a fair opportunity to recoup their investment. Though the amortization period is typically discussed in terms of protecting the owners' financial interests, it serves more generally to protect "an individual's interest in maintaining the present use" of the property. Modjeska Sign Studios v. Berle, 373 N.E.2d 255, 261 (N.Y. 1977).

The validity of an amortization period depends on its reasonableness. We have avoided any fixed formula for determining what constitutes a reasonable period. Instead, we have held that an amortization period is presumed valid, and the owner must carry the heavy burden of overcoming that presumption by demonstrating that the loss suffered is so substantial that it outweighs the public benefit to be gained by the exercise of the police power. Using this approach, courts have declared valid a variety of amortization periods. Indeed, in some circumstances, no amortization period at all is required. In other circumstances, the amortization period may vary in duration among the affected properties. We have also held that an amortization period may validly come to an end at the occurrence of an event as unpredictable as the destruction of the nonconforming use by fire.

Defendant here does not challenge the local law's constitutionality under our established balancing test for amortization periods — i.e., whether the individual loss outweighs the public benefit. Instead, the challenge is a more basic due process claim: that the means of eliminating nonconforming uses is not reasonably related to the Village's legitimate interest in land use planning. More particularly, defendant makes two arguments: first, that the length of an amortization period must be related either to land use objectives or to the financial recoupment needs of the owner and, second, that the local law violates the principle that zoning is to regulate land use rather than ownership. Neither argument withstands analysis.

We have never required that the length of the amortization period be based on a municipality's land use objectives. To the contrary, the periods are routinely calculated to protect the rights of individual owners at the temporary expense of public land use objectives. Typically, the period of time allowed has been measured for reasonableness by considering whether the owners had adequate time to recoup their investment in the use. Patently, such protection of an individual's interest is unrelated to land use objectives. Indeed, were land use objectives the only permissible criteria for scheduling amortization, the law would require immediate elimination of nonconforming uses in all instances. Instead, the setting of the amortization period involves balancing the interests of the individual and those of the public. Thus, the real issue here is whether it was irrational for the Village, in striking that balance, to consider a nonfinancial interest of the individual owners — specifically, the individual's interest in not being displaced involuntarily.

It is significant that the six properties involved here are residential. In our previous cases dealing with amortization, we have focused almost exclusively on commercial properties, where the owner's interest is easily reduced to financial considerations. The same may not be true for the owners of residential properties, especially in instances where the property is the primary residence of the owner. Simply being able to recoup one's financial investment may be a secondary concern to staying in a neighborhood or remaining on a particular piece of land. Indeed, when mobile homes are involved, there may actually be little or no financial loss, given that the owner often will be able to relocate the structure and sell the land for legal development. Here, rather than focusing solely on financial recoupment, the Village apparently took a broader view of "an individual's interest in maintaining the present use" of the property. It enacted a law that allowed owners to keep their mobile homes in place until they decided to sell, even though they may have recouped their investment long ago. By doing so, it saved the owners from a forced relocation at the end of a predetermined amortization period set by the Village. Defendant has not demonstrated why such an approach is irrational or explained why a municipality should be barred constitutionally from considering the nonfinancial interests of the owners in setting an amortization schedule. Thus, on this motion for summary judgment and the present record, defendant has failed to overcome the presumption of the law's validity and prove, as she must, unconstitutionality beyond a reasonable doubt.

Equally unavailing on this facial challenge is defendant's contention that the law might prevent some owners from recouping their investment. Defendant raises the hypothetical concern that in some circumstances owners might not have adequate time to recoup — for instance, if a sale took place shortly after the law's enactment. Whatever the validity of that concern, it is not relevant to this facial challenge to the law. Defendant has not claimed that she was so injured, and her argument must fall to the general principle that a litigant cannot sustain a facial challenge to a law when that law is constitutional in its application to that litigant.

Defendant's second argument is premised on the "fundamental rule that zoning deals basically with land use and not with the person who owns or occupies it."

Matter of Dexter v. Town Bd., 324 N.E.2d 870, 871 (N.Y. 1975).[9] In essence, the rule is a prohibition against ad hominem zoning decisions. In *Dexter*, for instance, a zoning change needed to allow a supermarket was to be effective only if a certain corporation developed the site. We voided the action on the ground that the identity of the site's owner was irrelevant to its suitability for a certain type of development. Likewise, variances to accommodate the personal physical needs of the occupants have been denied on the basis that such needs are unrelated to land use. See Matter of Fuhst v. Foley, 382 N.E.2d 756 (N.Y. 1978). In the present case, defendant claims that the Village's amortization scheme is similarly personal in that the right to the nonconforming use is enjoyed only by those who owned the property in 1968 and cannot be transferred.

Defendant misconstrues the nature of the prohibition against ad hominem zoning. The hallmark of cases like *Dexter* and *Fuhst* is that an identifiable individual is singled out for special treatment in land use regulation. No such individualized treatment is involved in the present case. All similarly situated owners are treated identically. The same is true for all prospective buyers. The only preferential treatment identified by defendant is that the owner in 1968 has rights that no future owner will enjoy. But the law has long recognized the special status of those who have a preexisting use at the time land controls are adopted. Indeed, the allowance of a nonconforming use in the first instance is based on that recognition. To the extent that defendant's argument is an attack on special treatment for the owners of nonconforming uses it flies in the face of established law. In fact, what defendant is actually arguing is that the Village should not be allowed to infringe on an owner's ability to transfer the right to continue a nonconforming use. It is true that, in the absence of amortization legislation, the right to continue a nonconforming use runs with the land. However, once a valid amortization scheme is enacted, the right ends at the termination of the amortization period. As a practical matter, that means the owner of record during the amortization period will enjoy a right that cannot be transferred to a subsequent owner once the period passes. In such circumstances, the law is not rendered invalid because the original owner no longer has a right to transfer or because the original owner and subsequent owners have received disparate treatment under the land use regulations.

Here, of course, the absence of the right at the time of transfer is not left to the happenstance of when the owner decides to sell but is an explicit part of the legislative plan. But that difference does not change the test for the validity of an amortization period. The test remains whether the period unreasonably inflicts a substantial loss on the owner or fails to comport to the reasonableness required by due process. Put simply, there is no independent requirement that the right to continue the nonconforming use be available for transfer at a given time. That is true whether the right to continue the nonconforming use is terminated by the passage of time, destruction of the use, abandonment or, as here, transfer of ownership. Thus, the mere fact that the right cannot be transferred or that later owners are treated disparately from the original owner is insufficient to sustain

---

[9] In attempting to distinguish *Dexter*, the Village notes that its local law was simply an exercise of its police power and not "zoning." The distinction is irrelevant in this context.

defendant's facial challenge to the ordinance.

Nor can we subscribe to the Appellate Division's theory that the amortization period here is unreasonable because it may be too long. In the Appellate Division's view, an open-ended amortization schedule does not reasonably advance land use objectives. The Appellate Division noted that if a corporation owned one of the mobile homes here, the amortization period would be limitless in theory. The Village answers by stating that all six mobile homes were owned by individuals, and thus amortization would end, at the latest, upon their deaths. Because the class of nonconforming users became closed at the law's enactment and will never contain more than those six, the concern about corporate ownership is unfounded, the Village argues. At this point in the litigation, defendant has not demonstrated that the Village is factually in error as to the ownership of the six units.

Of greater concern to us, the Appellate Division's rationale would seriously undermine the law of nonconforming uses. Amortization periods are the exceptions; in the absence of such schemes, owners of nonconforming uses are free to continue the uses indefinitely and transfer them to successor owners. Were the Appellate Division's rationale accepted, amortization periods would be required to avoid the problem of indefinite continuation of nonconforming uses. Amortization periods have never been mandatory as a matter of constitutional law, and consequently we must reject the Appellate Division's reasoning.

Thus, we conclude that defendant has failed to prevail on her facial challenge to the Village law. As to the remaining issues raised, further factual development is necessary.

Accordingly, the order of the Appellate Division should be modified, without costs, by denying defendant's cross motion for summary judgment and, as so modified, affirmed.

Order modified, without costs, by denying defendant's cross motion for summary judgment and, as so modified, affirmed.

NOTES AND QUESTIONS

1. **SZEA and nonconforming uses.** Does the SZEA address the issue of nonconforming uses? *See* Douglas W. Kmiec, *Deregulating Land Use: An Alternative Free Enterprise Development System*, 130 U. Pa. L. Rev. 28, 50 n.81 (1981) (citing "the omission of any reference to nonconforming uses in the SZEA"). What is the source of the restrictions on nonconforming uses in the principal case?

2. **Restricting the nonconforming use.** One way that zoning ordinances may deal with a nonconforming use is to use a strategy of attrition: to allow the use to continue, but to hedge it about with restrictions to bring about its demise. *See* Rhod-A-Zalea & 35th, Inc. v. Snohomish County, 959 P.2d 1024, 1027-1028 (Wash. 1998) (holder of the nonconforming use is usually denied the right to "significantly change, alter, extend, or enlarge" the use). *See also* Hansen Bros. Enterprises v. Board of Supervisors, 907 P.2d 1324, 1336-1337 (Cal. 1996) (distinguishing intensification of use from expansion of use); William B. Stoebuck & Dale A. Whitman, The Law of Property § 9.17, at 594 (3d ed. 2000) (typical zoning

restrictions on extension or expansion of nonconforming uses "has caused no end of litigation").

3. **Terminating the nonconforming use: destruction, abandonment and discontinuance.** An additional strategy is to provide in the zoning ordinance for termination of the nonconforming use. One method of termination focuses on acts of God: zoning ordinances often provide that *destruction* of the nonconforming use by fire or other casualty ends the use. Another method of terminating the use focuses on the actions of the owner: under many ordinances, an *abandoned* use cannot be resumed. Abandonment is tricky, however, for the same reason highlighted in servitudes: the difficulty of proving the owner's intent to abandon, if intent is required. *See* Boles v. City of Chattanooga, 892 S.W.2d 416, 420-22 (Tenn. Ct. App. 1994) (ordinance provided for termination of nonconforming use if use "is discontinued for 100 consecutive days"):

> The word "discontinued" as used in a zoning ordinance is generally construed to be synonymous with the term "abandoned." Douglas Hale Gross, Annotation, *Zoning: Right to Resume Nonconforming Use of Premises After Involuntary Break in the Continuity of Nonconforming Use Caused by Governmental Activity*, 56 A.L.R.3d, 138, 151 (1974). The meaning of the word "abandoned," in the zoning context, generally includes an intention by the landowner to abandon as well as an overt act of abandonment. In seeking to determine whether the word "discontinued" includes an element of voluntariness, we look to appellate court decisions of other states.
>
> We believe that the term "discontinued" or words of similar import, as utilized in zoning ordinances with specific time limitations, should be construed to include an element of intent, combined with some act — or failure to act — indicative of abandonment. Landowners who have enjoyed a non-conforming use on their properties, often for many years, no doubt come to rely economically on those non-conforming uses. Moreover, discontinuances of non-conforming uses can occur for a wide variety of involuntary reasons, not all of which stem from alleged violations of the law and some of which may be laudable. To hold that a non-conforming use can be cut off automatically by time limits on discontinuance, regardless of the reason for that discontinuance, strikes us as intrinsically unfair. Such a holding also seems contrary to the underlying concern for private property rights. Accordingly, we hold that the term "discontinued" as found in the Chattanooga Zoning Ordinance does not apply if the discontinuance of the non-conforming use is purely involuntary in nature.

But see Canada's Tavern, Inc. v. Town of Glen Echo, 271 A.2d 664, 666 (Md. 1970) (under ordinance defining "abandoned" as "the cessation of a nonconforming use for a period of six months or more," intent to abandon was not required under the plain language of the statute; court dismissed the landowner's contrary argument as "sophistic"). Do you agree with *Boles* or with *Canada's Tavern*? Does the answer to the question whether "abandonment" or "discontinuance" should be read to include an intent requirement depend on the importance the interpreter places on private property rights?

4. **Drafting.** If you were drafting a zoning ordinance addressing nonconforming uses, would you add any bases of termination other than abandonment and destruction? For what reason might those two methods of termination be regarded as inadequate to deal with the problem of nonconforming uses?

5. **Termination: amortization.** A third, and direct, method of termination is imposed by the zoning ordinance itself: under *amortization* provisions, the nonconforming use is given a specified period of time to operate, after which it must be discontinued. What is the theory underlying the doctrine of amortization? Is it responsive to the reasons for the recognition of nonconforming uses?

6. **Amortization, pro and con.** Some states reject the doctrine of amortization. See PA Northwestern Distributors v. Zoning Hearing Board of the Twp. of Moon, 584 A.2d 1372, 1375-76 (Pa. 1991), invalidating a ninety-day amortization period applicable to plaintiff's adult book store:

> A lawful nonconforming use establishes in the property owner a vested property right which cannot be abrogated or destroyed, unless it is a nuisance, it is abandoned, or it is extinguished by eminent domain. The Pennsylvania Constitution protects the right of a property owner to use his or her property in any lawful way that he or she so chooses. If government desires to interfere with the owner's use, where the use is lawful and is not a nuisance nor is it abandoned, it must compensate the owner for the resulting loss. A gradual phasing out of nonconforming uses which occurs when an ordinance only restricts future uses differs in significant measure from an amortization provision which restricts future uses and extinguishes a lawful nonconforming use on a timetable which is not of the property owner's choosing. Thus, we hold that the amortization and discontinuance of a lawful pre-existing nonconforming use is *per se* confiscatory and violative of the Pennsylvania Constitution.

One justice concurred on the ground that the amortization period was unreasonable as applied to plaintiff's land. One justice dissented. What problems does the *per se* rule of invalidity adopted in Pennsylvania pose? Does it have any advantages? *See generally* Margaret Collins, *Methods of Determining Amortization Periods for Nonconforming Uses*, 3 Wash. U. J.L. & Pol'y 215 (2000).

7. **More on the principal case.** Why did the defendant's facial challenge to the ordinance fail in Village of Valatie v. Smith? Under what circumstances might the defendant have made a successful challenge to the application of the ordinance to her? Can you think of any circumstances under which a nonconforming use could be terminated immediately without constitutional infirmity?

8. **Nonconforming uses and structures.** Footnote 1 in the principal case suggests that the distinction between a nonconforming use and a nonconforming structure might be relevant to the question of its restriction or termination. Why?

9. **Vested rights: two applications.** Courts and litigants often invoke the concept of "vested rights" in cases involving nonconforming uses; the nonconforming user is said to have a *right* to continue to make the preexisting (i.e., vested) use. *See PA Northwestern Distributors* (Note 6 above). The doctrine is sometimes also applied to a builder who secures a building permit for a use

subsequently made unlawful by the adoption or amendment of a zoning ordinance. The issue is what if anything is required in addition to acquisition of the permit to vest in the builder a right to proceed with the nonconforming project. Most states hold that the granting of a building permit does not immunize the developer from a subsequent adoption of or change in the zoning law that renders the approved use unlawful. What the majority *does* require is much harder to say. The expenditure of money, even substantial sums, on plans and specifications may not be enough. *See* John G. Sprankling, Understanding Property Law § 36.07 at 619 (2d ed. 2007) (noting that "[s]tates vary widely on the extent of the required reliance" to establish a vested right, and that many states require that the developer actually begin construction, as opposed to spending money on plans, to constitute reliance). Why might the beginning of construction constitute a sensible test for vesting the developer's rights? *See* H.R.D.E., Inc. v. Zoning Officer of the City of Romney, 430 S.E.2d 341, 345 (W. Va. 1993) ("In those cases where the courts have found a vested right to exist where something less than actual use has occurred, the courts have usually also found that substantial costs toward the completion of the project have been incurred or that there has been a change in position relative to the erection of a building or establishment of a business.").

10. **Vested rights and estoppel.** Whatever the test for the vesting of a builder's rights, would the majority doctrine perhaps more accurately be labeled "estoppel" rather than vested rights? *See* Stoebuck & Whitman, The Law of Property § 9.22, at 613-14 (estoppel is "analytically distinct" from vested rights, and applies when the builder detrimentally relies on a building permit).

11. **Minority and majority views compared.** The minority view is that the builder's rights vest upon acquisition of the building permit; further acts in reliance on the permission are unnecessary. *See* Rhod-A-Zalea & 35th, Inc. v. Snohomish County, Note 2 above. Are you persuaded by the following argument in support of the minority view?

> The minority rule, vesting rights under the then-existing regulations as of the time when proper application [for a building permit] is filed, is not without substantial support. The minority rule is, we feel, the more practical one to administer. It serves to avoid a great deal of extended litigation. It makes for greater certainty in the law and its administration.

Smith v. Winhall Planning Comm'n, 436 A.2d 760, 761 (Vt. 1981). Is the majority or minority view more responsive to the legislative goal of restricting and phasing out nonconforming uses? *See generally* Gregory Overstreet & Diana M. Kirchheim, *The Quest for the Best Test to Vest: Washington's Vested Rights Doctrine Beats the Rest*, 23 Seattle U. L. Rev. 1043, 1045 (2000).

3. Zoning Flexibility

Zoning is legislation, and it is commonplace that the kind of general rules established by legislation can cause hardship when applied in concrete instances. The Standard State Zoning Enabling Act anticipated this problem, and established three devices to provide flexibility in the administration of the zoning ordinance: amendments, variances, and special exceptions. These devices are the subject of the present section.

a.   Amendments: Rezoning

GRISWOLD v. CITY OF HOMER
925 P.2d 1015 (Alaska 1996)

EASTAUGH, JUSTICE.

In 1992 the Homer City Council adopted Ordinance 92-18 amending Homer's zoning and planning code to allow motor vehicle sales and services on thirteen lots in Homer's Central Business District. Frank Griswold claims Ordinance 92-18 is invalid because it constitutes spot zoning. We affirm the superior court's rejection of that claim.

FACTS AND PROCEEDINGS

Alaska Statute 29.40.020 requires that each first class borough establish a planning commission which will prepare, submit, and implement a comprehensive plan.[1] This plan must be adopted before the local government can adopt a zoning ordinance.

The City adopted a comprehensive land use plan in 1983 and revised it in 1989. The City Council enacted zoning ordinances to implement the plans. Motor vehicle sales and services were not a permissible use within the Central Business District (CBD). Several businesses provided automobile services in the CBD before the City adopted the zoning ordinances. Those businesses were "grandfathered" into the zoning district and allowed to continue to provide those services as nonconforming uses, so long as those uses did not extend beyond the original lot boundaries and the property owners did not discontinue their nonconforming uses for more than one year.

Guy Rosi Sr. owns a parcel (Lot 13) in the CBD. Rosi Sr. has continuously operated an automobile repair service on Lot 13. His repair business remains a valid nonconforming use in the CBD. Rosi Sr. also operated an automobile dealership on Lot 13 until sometime prior to 1990, but lost the right to continue that nonconforming use on that lot by discontinuing the vehicle sales business for more than one year.

Guy Rosi Jr. owns Lot 12, which is adjacent to his father's lot. Lot 12 is also in the CBD; because it had never been used for automobile sales or services, these

---

[1] AS 29.40.030 defines a comprehensive plan as follows:

> [A] compilation of policy statements, goals, standards, and maps for guiding the physical, social, and economic development, both private and public, of the first or second class borough, and may include, but is not limited to, the following:
>
> (1) statements of policies, goals, and standards;
>
> (2) a land use plan;
>
> (3) a community facilities plan;
>
> (4) a transportation plan; and
>
> (5) recommendations for implementation of the comprehensive plan.

uses were not grandfathered for Lot 12.

In 1986 the City received complaints that Lot 12 was being used for vehicle sales in violation of the zoning ordinance. In May 1986 Rosi Jr. applied to the Homer Advisory Planning Commission for a conditional use permit for Lot 12. The commission denied the application. It found that public services and facilities were adequate to serve the proposed use. The commission also found that automobile sales were not consistent with the purpose of the CBD; were not in harmony with the Comprehensive Plan; would negatively impact neighborhood character; but might not negatively impact the value of adjoining property more than permitted uses.

Rosi Jr. then applied for a contract rezone under Homer City Code (HCC) 21.63.020(c). The City granted the application in 1986, rezoning Rosi Jr.'s lot to General Commercial 1(GC1) and restricting its use to vehicle sales. Griswold does not challenge the Lot 12 contract rezone in this litigation.

Rosi Sr.'s Lot 13 was not affected by the Lot 12 contract rezone. In September 1990 Rosi Sr. requested that the CBD be rezoned to allow vehicle sales and related services. In August 1991 Rosi Sr., stating that he had not received any response to his earlier request, asked that Lot 13 be rezoned to allow vehicle sales and related services. During this period, there were numerous zoning proposals and public hearings regarding automobile-related services in the CBD, but some people spoke in favor of rezoning the area.

In January 1992 a commission memorandum informed the City Manager that the commission had been wrestling with several possible amendments to the zoning code since 1990, and that "[c]entral to the issue is the Commission's desire to rezone the Guy Rosi property to allow for vehicle sales." The commission noted that a proposed ordinance would allow automobile-related services in the CBD only on Main Street from Pioneer Avenue to the Homer Bypass, excluding corner lots with frontage on Pioneer Avenue and the Homer Bypass Road. However, the commission staff recommended that the council pass an ordinance which would allow automobile-related services "everywhere in the Central Business District or nowhere." The memo stated that the City Attorney felt the proposed ordinance would be difficult to enforce and defend.

In April the City Council adopted Ordinance 92-18, which amended HCC 21.48.020 by adding the following section:

> *hh.* Automobile and vehicle repair, vehicle maintenance, public garage, and motor vehicle sales, showrooms and sales lots, but only on Main Street from Pioneer Avenue to the Homer Bypass Road, excluding corner lots with frontage on Pioneer Avenue or the Homer Bypass Road, be allowed as a permitted use.

Frank Griswold, the plaintiff in this case, owns an automobile repair shop in the CBD. Its operation was grandfathered in under the zoning code. He also lives in the CBD. Griswold's lot was not one of the thirteen lots directly affected by Ordinance 92-18. Griswold brought suit against the City, alleging that Ordinance 92-18 is an invalid exercise of the City's zoning power. Following a bench trial, the superior court found against Griswold on all issues.

DISCUSSION

We have repeatedly held that it is the role of elected representatives rather than the courts to decide whether a particular statute or ordinance is a wise one. In *Concerned Citizens of S. Kenai Peninsula v. Kenai Peninsula Borough*, 527 P.2d 447, 452 (Alaska 1974), we stated:

> A court's inquiry into arbitrariness begins with the presumption that the action of the legislature is proper. The party claiming a denial of substantive due process has the burden of demonstrating that no rational basis for the challenged legislation exists. This burden is a heavy one, for if any conceivable legitimate public policy for the enactment is apparent on its face or is offered by those defending the enactment, the opponents of the measure must disprove the factual basis for such a justification.

See also 6 Eugene McQuillan, Municipal Corporations § 20.05, at 12 (3d ed. 1988) ("The validity of an ordinance will be upheld where there is room for a difference of opinion even though the correctness of the legislative judgment is doubtful.").

However, we will invalidate zoning decisions which are the result of prejudice, arbitrary decision-making, or improper motives. Similarly, a legislative body's zoning decision violates substantive due process if it has no reasonable relationship to a legitimate government purpose. Moreover, another court has noted, "The dividing line between mere difference in opinion and what is arbitrary is the line between zoning based on objective factual evidence and zoning without a rational basis." *Smith v. County of Washington*, 406 P.2d 545, 548 (Or. 1965).[4] In this case, Griswold argues that the City's Ordinance does not have a legitimate basis but rather is arbitrary spot zoning.[5]

We have not previously had the opportunity to consider whether a municipality's planning and zoning enactment is invalid because it constitutes "spot zoning." The City states that "this is not a case of 'spot zoning' at all" because the area in question remains zoned CBD. However, treatise discussions of spot zoning appear to make no distinction between cases where a zoning district has been reclassified and those where a new use without district reclassification is at issue. See, e.g., 1 Robert M. Anderson American Law of Zoning 3d § 5.12, at 358 (1986) ("The common [spot zoning] situation is one in which an amendment is initiated at the request of an owner or owners who seek to establish a use prohibited by the existing regulations."). See also *Ballenger v. Door County*, 388 N.W.2d 624, 627 (Wis. Ct. App. 1986) (applying spot zoning analysis in a case where the zoning district remained the same but the permitted uses within the district were expanded); *Concerned Citizens of S. Kenai Peninsula*, 527 P.2d at 452 (whether zoning decision violates substantive due process depends on whether it has a reasonable relationship to a legitimate public purpose).

---

[4] We have held that, although a planning commission is not required to make specific findings supporting its decisions, it must articulate reasons for its decisions sufficient to assist the parties preparing for review and to restrain agencies within the bounds of their jurisdiction.

[5] Griswold also argues that the Ordinance is invalid because it is inconsistent with the City's zoning code and comprehensive plan. We consider this argument in conjunction with our discussion of spot zoning.

A. Claim of Spot Zoning

The "classic" definition of spot zoning is "the process of singling out a small parcel of land for a use classification totally different from that of the surrounding area, for the benefit of the owner of such property and to the detriment of other owners." Anderson, *supra*, § 5.12, at 359 (quoting Jones v. Zoning Bd. of Adjustment of Long Beach, 108 A.2d 498 (N.J. Super. Ct. 1954)). Spot zoning "is the very antithesis of planned zoning." *Id.*[6] Courts have developed numerous variations of this definition. These variations have but minor differences and describe any zoning amendment which "reclassifies a small parcel in a manner inconsistent with existing zoning patterns, for the benefit of the owner and to the detriment of the community, or without any substantial public purpose." Anderson, *supra*, § 5.12, at 362.

Professor Ziegler states:

> Faced with an allegation of spot zoning, courts determine first whether the rezoning is compatible with the comprehensive plan or, where no plan exists, with surrounding uses. Courts then examine the degree of public benefit gained and the characteristics of land, including parcel size and other factors indicating that any reclassification should have embraced a larger area containing the subject parcel rather than that parcel alone. No one particular characteristic associated with spot zoning, except a failure to comply with at least the spirit of a comprehensive plan, is necessarily fatal to the amendment. Spot zoning analysis depends primarily on the facts and circumstances of the particular case. Therefore, the criteria are flexible and provide guidelines for judicial balancing of interests.

3 Edward H. Ziegler Jr., Rathkoph's The Law of Zoning and Planning § 28.01, at 28-3 (4th ed.1995).

In accord with the guidance offered by Professor Ziegler, in determining whether Ordinance 92-18 constitutes spot zoning, we will consider (1) the consistency of the amendment with the comprehensive plan; (2) the benefits and detriments of the amendment to the owners, adjacent landowners, and community; and (3) the size of the area "rezoned."

1. Consistency with the comprehensive plan

Just as an ordinance which complies with a comprehensive plan may still constitute an arbitrary exercise of a city's zoning power, nonconformance with a comprehensive plan does not necessarily render a zoning action illegal. However, consistency with a comprehensive plan is one indication that the zoning action in question has a rational basis and is not an arbitrary exercise of the City's zoning power.

---

[6] The City argues that spot zoning should not be considered per se illegal, but merely descriptive. Thus, whether spot zoning is valid or invalid would depend upon the facts of each case. However, we will follow the vast majority of jurisdictions which hold that, while not all small-parcel zoning is illegal, spot zoning is per se illegal. Thus, spot zoning is simply the legal term of art for a zoning decision which affects a small parcel of land and which is found to be an arbitrary exercise of legislative power.

Homer's comprehensive plan divides the city into several zoning areas. By its own terms, Homer's comprehensive plan is not intended to set specific land use standards and boundaries; specific standards and boundaries are instead implemented through the City's zoning ordinance. The plan states, "The City shall encourage a mix of business/commercial and public/governmental activities in areas zoned or planned as central business district." The plan states that the CBD is "intended primarily for retail sales and services occurring within enclosed structures." The plan's objectives for the CBD are (1) to guide growth and development to provide a centrally located business and commercial area and focal point for the community; (2) to encourage infilling of the area already designated CBD before expanding the area; (3) to promote a safe, attractive, and easily accessible business and commercial core for pedestrian and vehicular visitors and residents; (4) to attract and accommodate a variety of uses to fill the business and commercial needs of downtown Homer; and (5) to tie into state and federal programs that beautify the business and commercial core.

Griswold does not dispute that the CBD is intended to allow commercial uses. He notes however, that although auto-related services are explicitly permitted in the General Commercial 1 District under HCC 21.49.020(d), the planning commission previously denied a conditional use permit for auto-related services on Main Street, specifically finding, inter alia, that automobile sales were not consistent with the purpose of the CBD and were not in harmony with the comprehensive plan. He also notes that the comprehensive plan provides that the CBD was meant primarily for retail sales and services occurring within enclosed structures. Further, the fact that the City began phasing out auto-related services in the CBD when it adopted the comprehensive plan, while simultaneously specifically permitting these services in the General Commercial I District, indicates to Griswold that auto-related sales and services were, at least at one time, considered incompatible with the CBD.

The superior court concluded that the Ordinance was consistent with the comprehensive plan. In so concluding, it considered the policy statement implementing the Ordinance, and found that the Ordinance "encourages private investment and infilling" and "enhances convenient access to other parts of the CBD which are designated for other uses." It noted that Policy 4.1 provided: "The City shall research the nature of land uses and CBD land use needs and evaluate the need for subzones in the CBD."

Griswold points to trial evidence that the expansion of auto-related services in the CBD does not further all the goals of the comprehensive plan, but he fails to demonstrate that the superior court's finding — that the Ordinance is consistent with the plan — is clearly erroneous. Although the evidence presented by Griswold would permit a finding that the City Council had believed in 1986 that auto-related uses were incompatible with the CBD and the zoning ordinance as it then read, that evidence does not compel a finding that auto-related uses are in fact incompatible with the CBD or comprehensive plan, or that the City Council's 1992 change of opinion is unsupportable and arbitrary.

The superior court did not clearly err in making the findings discussed above. The court permissibly relied on Policy 4.1, which anticipates the type of action at issue here. The comprehensive plan does not expressly prohibit automobile sales or service establishments in the CBD. As the City notes, motor vehicle sales are most appropriately classified as a business and commercial use, for which the CBD was intended under the plan. Homer's city planner testified at trial that the Ordinance is in accordance with Homer's comprehensive plan. We conclude that the superior court did not err in holding that Ordinance 92-18 is consistent with the City's comprehensive plan.

2. Effect of small-parcel zoning on owner and community

Perhaps the most important factor in determining whether a small-parcel zoning amendment will be upheld is whether the amendment provides a benefit to the public, rather than primarily a benefit to a private owner. See Anderson, *supra*, §§ 5.13-5.14; Ziegler, *supra*, § 28.03, § 28.04, at 28-19 (calling an amendment intended only to benefit the owner of the rezoned tract the "classic case" of spot zoning). Courts generally do not assume that a zoning amendment is primarily for the benefit of a landowner merely because the amendment was adopted at the request of the landowner. Anderson, *supra*, § 5.13, at 368. If the owner's benefit is merely incidental to the general community's benefit, the amendment will be upheld. Ziegler, *supra*, § 28.04, at 28-19 to 28-20. The City argues that Ordinance 92-18 serves the interests of the general community rather than primarily the interests of the Rosis. We agree.

a. Benefits and detriments to the community

Griswold argues that there are many negative aspects of the City's decision to allow auto-related uses in the CBD. Griswold presented evidence that the neighborhood character would be harmed by the zoning amendment. He presented evidence that a newspaper article quoted Planning Commissioner Cushing as saying that public opinion was overwhelmingly against allowing auto-related services in the CBD and that many Homer citizens expressed the opinion that their homes and businesses would be harmed by introducing auto-related services into the area. A real estate agent testified that property in the CBD has a higher value than property in the GC1 District.

Many jurisdictions, including this one, have held that interests such as the preservation of neighborhood character, traffic safety, and aesthetics are legitimate concerns. Barber v. Municipality of Anchorage, 776 P.2d 1035, 1037 (Alaska 1989) (holding the government's interest in aesthetics is substantial and should be accorded respect); Cadoux v. Planning and Zoning Comm'n of Weston, 294 A.2d 582, 584 (Conn. 1972) (holding increased traffic a valid reason to deny application for rezone). Contrary to the implication of the City's argument[7] these are tangible harms. Moreover, the City itself appears to be concerned about the effects of auto-related services on property values and aesthetics, as evidenced by the council's findings supporting its confinement of the zoning change to Main Street,[8]

---

[7] The City argues that Griswold could not show any "concrete detriment" but instead "could only argue that car lots were not pleasant to look at, they didn't alleviate traffic, and other similar arguments."

[8] At trial the City's planner testified that the Ordinance was restricted to Main Street to avoid certain

and the commission's earlier finding that use for automobile sales would negatively impact neighborhood character.

However, despite this negative aspect of Ordinance 92-18, it appears that the Ordinance will result in genuine benefits for the City of Homer. The City notes that before adopting Ordinance 92-18, for a year and a half it deliberated proposals which would allow auto-related uses in the CBD and delineated the many benefits which it believed the Ordinance will confer upon the community. These benefits include encouraging filling in vacant places in the CBD; increasing the tax base and employment in the CBD; increasing convenience and accessibility for local and regional customers for vehicle repairs or purchases; and promoting orderly growth and development in the CBD.[9] Homer's city planner testified that the Ordinance provides a convenience to the public and guides growth and development to a centrally located area, while restricting such uses to areas away from tourists or to areas for visitors and pedestrians.

The superior court stated that Ordinance 92-18 advances legitimate legislative goals articulated in HCC 21.28.020 including but not limited to regulating and limiting the density of populations; conserving and stabilizing the value of properties; providing adequate open spaces for light and air; preventing undue concentration of population; lessening congestion on streets and highways; and promoting health, safety and general welfare. The court found "as a matter of fact and law that Ordinance No. 92-18 bears a substantial relationship between legitimate legislative goals and the means chosen to achieve those goals."

Griswold has demonstrated that there are some negative aspects of allowing auto-related uses in the CBD. Nonetheless, giving proper deference to the City Council as legislative policymaker and to the superior court as finder of fact, we cannot conclude that these detriments so outweigh the benefits of Ordinance 92-18 that we must hold the Ordinance was arbitrarily and capriciously adopted.

b. Benefit to the landowner

It appears that initially the City was primarily concerned with Rosi Sr.'s interests.[10] Rosi Sr. initiated the inquiry into rezoning the CBD. Before the City amended the zoning code, the planning commission chair stated that "[c]entral to

---

negative impacts in more tourist-oriented areas. These negative impacts include traffic congestion, visual blight, detraction from the pleasing aesthetic nature of Pioneer Avenue, and conflict with the comprehensive plan's goal of promoting sidewalks, pocket parks, and pedestrian amenities in the CBD.

[9] Not all of the goals articulated by the City can be considered legitimate per se. For example, any zoning change which eases restrictions on property use could be said to further the goal of "filling in vacant places." Similarly, increasing the tax base and the employment of a community is not automatically a legitimate zoning goal. Thus, the goal of increasing the tax base and employment opportunities is usually legitimate only if the ordinance is otherwise reasonable and in accordance with the comprehensive plan. Some courts have allowed inconsistent small or single parcel rezoning in order to raise tax revenues or stimulate needed industry if the public receives higher tax revenue or employment industries. Generally, the facility being built must be indisputably needed, and the city must have secured assurance as to the existence and amount of increased employment and tax revenue.

[10] Currently, Rosi Jr.'s lot is not affected by Ordinance 92-18 since that lot has been contract rezoned to GC1.

the issue is the Commission's desire to rezone the Guy Rosi property to allow for vehicle sales." In 1991 commissioners "voiced their dislike for spot zoning but felt it important to right a wrong [done to Mr. Rosi]." The City planning staff stated that " 'spot zoning' is not good planning; however there are extenuating circumstances that support the proposed change in zone." The commission supported these conclusions with the following findings of fact: (1) the property owner had owned and operated a business on the property since the early 1950's; (2) public testimony and response to staff were positive; (3) the City Attorney's response was positive; and (4) the business was an expensive business to establish and maintain. This desire to accommodate the needs of a businessman who had been in the community for decades is understandable. Nevertheless, small-parcel zoning designed merely to benefit one owner constitutes unwarranted discrimination and arbitrary decision-making, unless the ordinance amendment is designed to achieve the statutory objectives of the City's own zoning scheme, even where the purpose of the change is to bring a nonconforming use into conformance or allow it to expand. Otherwise, the City would be forced either to discriminate arbitrarily among landowners seeking relaxed restrictions or to abandon the concept of planned zoning altogether. Thus, if assisting Guy Rosi Sr. was the primary purpose of the Ordinance, we would invalidate it even if it was not the product of discriminatory animus.

However, it appears that the City Council was ultimately motivated to pass the Ordinance because of the community benefits the council perceived rather than because of the benefit the Ordinance would confer upon Rosi Sr. The Ordinance restricted auto-related uses to one street not because its real intent was to benefit Rosi Sr.'s property, but, as Homer's city planner testified, because the City desired to minimize the negative impact of auto-related uses, especially the impact of such uses on more pedestrian and tourist-oriented areas such as Pioneer Avenue. Similarly, it appears that vacant lots located farther from Pioneer Avenue were excluded not because Rosi did not own these lots, but in an attempt to prevent urban sprawl by filling in vacant places in developed areas before expanding development. These reasons are legitimate, nondiscriminatory justifications for enacting the Ordinance.

3. Size of "rezoned" area

Ordinance 92-18 directly affects 7.29 acres.[11] The size of the area reclassified has been called "more significant [than all other factors] in determining the presence of spot zoning." Anderson, *supra*, § 5.15, at 378. The rationale for that statement is that "[i]t is inherently difficult to relate a reclassification of a single lot to the comprehensive plan; it is less troublesome to demonstrate that a change which affects a larger area is in accordance with a plan to control development for the benefit of all." *Id.* at 379.

---

[11] There may be an immaterial discrepancy about the size of the reclassified area. There was testimony Ordinance 92-18 affected 7.29 acres, but the trial court's memorandum decision stated the affected lots contained about 7.44 acres. That decision did not state that the exact size of the parcel was significant to its determination that the amendment does not constitute illegal spot zoning.

We believe that the relationship between the size of reclassification and a finding of spot zoning is properly seen as symptomatic rather than causal, and thus that the size of the area rezoned should not be considered more significant than other factors in determining whether spot zoning has occurred. A parcel cannot be too large per se to preclude a finding of spot zoning, nor can it be so small that it mandates a finding of spot zoning. Although Anderson notes that reclassifications of parcels under three acres are nearly always found invalid, while reclassifications of parcels over thirteen acres are nearly always found valid, as Ziegler notes, the relative size of the parcel is invariably considered by courts. Ziegler, *supra*, § 28.04, at 28-14. One court found spot zoning where the reclassified parcel was 635 acres in an affected area of 7,680 acres. Chrobuck v. Snohomish County, 480 P.2d 489, 497 (Wash. 1971).

Nor does the reclassification of more than one parcel negate the possibility of finding spot zoning. Ziegler, *supra*, § 28.04, at 28-15. In this case, there was some evidence that the reclassified area may have been expanded to avoid a charge of spot zoning. Other courts have invalidated zoning amendments after finding that a multiple-parcel reclassification was a subterfuge to obscure the actual purpose of special treatment for a particular landowner. See Atherton v. Selectmen of Bourne, 149 N.E.2d 232, 235 (Mass. 1958) (holding that the amendment is "no less 'spot zoning' by the inclusion of the additional six lots than it would be without them" where proponents of a zoning change apparently anticipated a charge of spot zoning and enlarged the area to include the three lots on either side of the lot in question).

Homer's CBD is over 400 acres; the reclassified area is 7.29 acres. The CBD appears to contain approximately 500 lots; the reclassified area contains 13 lots. A comparison of the size of the area rezoned and the size of the entire CBD is not in itself sufficient to persuade us that the City's decision was the product of prejudice, arbitrary decision-making, or improper motives.

Further, it is not necessarily appropriate to compare the area of the affected lots with that of the entire CBD. The comprehensive plan recognized the possibility of subzones. The City considered significant portions of the CBD to be inappropriate for automobile sales and services, particularly Pioneer Avenue and the Bypass. Subtracting those areas from the entire CBD, the reclassified area on Main Street is a relatively larger part of the remaining CBD.

Thus, having considered the relative size of the rezoned area in determining whether Ordinance 92-18 constituted spot zoning, we hold that the size of the area rezoned does not require a finding of spot zoning given other factors supporting a contrary conclusion. We conclude that the superior court did not err in finding that Ordinance 92-18 does not constitute spot zoning.

IV. CONCLUSION

We hold that Ordinance 92-18 does not constitute spot zoning, and consequently AFFIRM the judgment below.

NOTES AND QUESTIONS

1. **Two types of amendments.** A "text amendment" leaves existing zones in place but changes the terms of the ordinance to expand or contract the permitted uses or the applicable height and bulk restrictions, or both. A "map amendment" leaves the wording of the ordinance intact, but re-draws the zoning lines on the municipality's zoning map, in effect rezoning the parcels in the redrawn district. Which type of amendment was presented in the principal case?

2. **Amendment and nonconforming uses.** Text amendments can create new nonconforming uses, which are "grandfathered" in just as are nonconforming uses generated by the municipality's original zoning. (Review question: why did Rosi Sr. lose the right under the original Homer zoning ordinance to continue his nonconforming automobile dealership on Lot 13 in the CBD?) Building projects that are under way when an amendment occurs may be allowed to continue under the doctrines of vested rights or estoppel. See Section B.2 above.

3. **Zoning amendment: promulgation and challenge; standing.** Most zoning amendments, as in the principal case, occur at the behest of a landowner desiring to make a different, usually more intensive and more remunerative, use than allowed by the ordinance. Challenges to a zoning amendment, as in the principal case, are typically made by some landowner in the zone aggrieved by the amendment. The rules on standing to bring a challenge vary; the "general concept is that the rezoning must have caused a third-party challenger a loss that is (significantly?) different from that suffered by the public." William B. Stoebuck & Dale A. Whitman, The Law of Property § 9.22, at 615 (3d ed. 2000). Why did Frank Griswold have standing to challenge the Homer amendment? In what way is his position as an "aggrieved" party vulnerable?

4. **Spot zoning.** When the number of parcels affected by the amendment is small, and the extent of the incompatibility between the existing and the changed uses is wide, a conclusion that the amendment constitutes invalid "spot zoning" usually follows. *See, e.g.*, Fritts v. City of Ashland, 348 S.W.2d 712, 713 (Ky. 1961) (invalidating rezoning of four-acre tract in residential zone to industrial use, to prevent threatened loss of jobs and taxes provided by local garment factory). What is the *legal* basis for that conclusion? Can you identify two or more bases for the challenge mounted in the principal case against the Homer amendment? *See* Stoebuck & Whitman, The Law of Property § 9.22, at 617-18.

5. **"Change or mistake" doctrine.** In spot zoning cases, a few courts take the position that an amendment is invalid unless it is based on a change in neighborhood conditions or a mistake in original zoning:

> Before a zoning board rezones property, there should be proof either that there was some mistake in the original zoning or that the character of the neighborhood has changed to such an extent that a reclassification ought properly to be made. Those who buy property in a zoned district have the right to expect that the classification made in the ordinance will not be changed unless a change is required for the public good.

Zoning Comm'n of Town of New Canaan v. New Canaan Building Co., 148 A.2d 330, 333 (Conn. 1959) (invalidating map amendment placing parcel previously in apartment zone in single-family residential zone). Would the amendment in the principal case have been valid under the *New Canaan* test?

6. **Deference or not?**   If a zoning amendment is regarded — as it typically is — as a legislative act, what presumptions will a challenger have to overcome? Were these presumptions applied in the principal case? For the proposition that zoning is an exercise of legislative rather than judicial power, see Town of Tyrone v. Tyrone, 565 S.E.2d 806, 808 (Ga. 2002) (reversing trial court's order to municipality to rezone a parcel from agricultural-residential to commercial) ("[C]ourts have no power to zone or rezone property. Once the trial court concluded that the current zoning was unconstitutional, it should have ordered the town council to rezone the property to a constitutional designation."). *See also* Emmett McLoughlin Realty, Inc. v. Pima County, 58 P.3d 39, 41 (Ariz. Ct. App. 2002) (holding that a state statute requiring a zoning authority to secure an affected landowner's "express written consent" before rezoning a parcel was an unconstitutional delegation of legislative authority). *Emmett McLoughlin* is notable for the number of points made in support of the statute by the landowner, as well as the court's well-reasoned responses — in short it shows craftsmanship in advocacy and in judging.

7. **Contract rezoning.**   In the principal case, Rosi Jr. applied for and received a contract rezoning of Lot 12 to permit automobile sales and only such sales. Under contract rezoning, the applicant agrees to restrict use of the rezoned parcel to only one of the several uses that would be allowed if the rezoning were made without restrictions. The technique is controversial, the major objection being that the municipality cannot validly contract away the discretion it enjoys under the police power to refuse to amend its zoning ordinance. Against that (undoubtedly correct) objection, the distinction, which eludes many of the objecting courts, between a unilateral and a bilateral contract is critical. A unilateral contract imposes no obligation on the city, and thus avoids the objection: the applicant promises to observe the restricted use *if* the city rezones the applicant's parcel, leaving the city free to rezone or not. Some authorities refer to unilateral contract rezoning as *conditional* rezoning, a usage that orthodox contracts scholars would presumably avoid because the condition — that the city rezone — is more precisely the acceptance of the applicant's offer rather than a condition of performance to be rendered after the contract is formed. For a convincing argument in favor of the technique of unilateral contract (or "conditional") rezoning, see Stoebuck & Whitman, The Law of Property § 9.25, at 625-29.

b.   Variances

MATTHEW v. SMITH
707 S.W.2d 411 (Mo. 1986)

WELLIVER, JUDGE.

This is an appeal from a circuit court judgment affirming the Board of Zoning Adjustment's decision to grant Jim and Susan Brandt a variance. The Brandts purchased a residential lot containing two separate houses upon a tract of land zoned for a single-family use. The court of appeals reversed the circuit court judgment, and the case was then certified to this Court by a dissenting judge. We reverse and remand.

The Brandts own a tract of land comprising one and one-half plotted lots. When they purchased the property in March of 1980, there already were two houses on the land, one toward the front of Erie Street and one in the rear. Each of the buildings is occupied by one residential family as tenants of the Brandts. The two houses apparently have been used as separate residences for the past thirty years, with only intermittent vacancies. The property is zoned for Single Family Residences. At the suggestion of a city official, the Brandts applied for a variance which would allow them to rent both houses with a single family in each house. After some delay, including two hearings by the Board of Zoning Adjustment of Kansas City, the Board granted the application. Appellant, Jon Matthew, a neighboring landowner challenged the grant of the variance and sought a petition for certiorari from the Board's action. The circuit court affirmed the Board's order; on appeal, the court of appeals held that the Board was without authority to grant the requested variance. A dissenting judge certified the case to this Court. Prompted by the persuasive opinions of both the majority of the Western District and the dissenting judge who certified the case to this Court, we believe that a review of the applicable law is warranted.

Zoning law developed during the early part of this century as a mechanism for channeling growth. Zoning acts authorize municipalities to pass ordinances, which designate the boundaries for districts and which define the allowable land uses in such districts. Board of Zoning Adjustments (Appeals) were created to review specific applications of the zoning ordinances.

Under most zoning acts, these boards have the authority to grant variances from the strict letter of the zoning ordinance. The variance procedure "fulfil[s] a sort of 'escape hatch' or 'safety valve' function for individual landowners who would suffer special hardship from the literal application of the zoning ordinance." City & Borough of Juneau v. Thibodeau, 595 P.2d 626, 633 (Alaska 1979). See also A. Rathkopf, 3 The Law of Zoning and Planning § 38 (1979); N. Williams, 5 American Planning Law § 129.05 (1985). It is often said that "[t]he variance provides an administrative alternative for individual relief that can avoid the damage that can occur to a zoning ordinance as a result of as applied taking litigation." D. Mandelker, Land Use Law, at 169 (1982). The general rule is that the authority to grant a variance should be exercised sparingly and only under exceptional circumstances.

Both the majority of courts and the commentators recognize two types of variances: an area (nonuse) variance and a use variance.

> The two types of variances with which cases are customarily concerned are "use" variances and "nonuse variances." The latter consist mostly of variances of bulk restrictions, of area, height, density, setback, side line restrictions, and restrictions covering miscellaneous subjects, including the right to enlarge nonconforming uses or to alter nonconforming structures.
>
> As the name indicates, a use variance is one which permits a use other than one of those prescribed by the zoning ordinance in the particular

district; it permits a use which the ordinance prohibits. A nonuse variance authorizes deviations from restrictions which relate to a permitted use, rather than limitations on the use itself, that is, restrictions on the bulk of buildings, or relating to their height, size, and extent of lot coverage, or minimum habitable area therein, or on the placement of buildings and structures on the lot with respect to required yards. Variances made necessary by the physical characteristics of the lot itself are nonuse variances of a kind commonly termed "area variances."

A. Rathkopf, *supra*, § 38.01. Many zoning acts or ordinances expressly distinguish between the two types of variances. When the distinction is not statutory, "the courts have always distinguished use from area variances." D. Mandelker, Land Use Law, at 167 (1982). Some jurisdictions, whether by express statutory directive or by court interpretation, do not permit the grant of a use variance. D. Mandelker, Land Use Law, at 168; N. Williams, *supra*, § 132, at 31.

Past decisions in this State have placed Missouri within those jurisdictions not permitting a use variance.[2] This line of cases would suggest that the Brandts are not entitled to the variance. They seek a variance to use the property in a manner not permitted under the permissible uses established by the ordinance. The ordinance clearly permits only the use of the property for a single family residence. The applicant is not seeking a variance from the area and yard restrictions which are no doubt violated because of the existence of the second residence. Such an area variance is not necessary because the applicant has a permissible nonconforming structure under the ordinance.

Commentators, however, have questioned the rationale underlying the Missouri cases. See e.g., A. Rathkopf, *supra*, § 37.02, at 25 n. 4; N. Williams, *supra*, § 132.02, at 33-4. These past cases, beginning with State ex rel. Nigro v. Kansas City, 27 S.W.2d 1030 (Mo. 1930), are based upon the premise that the granting of a use variance would be an unconstitutional delegation of power to the Board to amend the ordinance. See generally Mandelker, "Delegation of Power and Function In Zoning Administration," 1963 Wash. U.L.Q. 60, 68-71. This view has long since been repudiated by most jurisdictions, and it is contrary to the express language of § 89.090, RSMo 1978, which grants the Board the "power to vary or modify the application of any of the regulations or provisions of such ordinance relating to the *use*, construction or alteration of buildings or structures, or the *use* of land" (emphasis added). We, therefore, hold that under the proper circumstances an applicant may obtain a use variance.

Section 89.090, RSMo 1978 delegates to the Board of Adjustment the power to grant a variance when the applicant establishes "practical difficulties or unnecessary hardship in the way of carrying out the strict letter of such ordinance so that the spirit of the ordinance shall be observed, public safety and welfare secured and substantial justice done." Missouri lifted this language out of the 1920 amendment to the General City Law of New York, which provided:

---

[2] Treatise writers observe that Missouri cases establish that a use variance is not authorized. A. Rathkopf, *supra*, § 37.02 at 25; N. Williams, *supra*, § 132.02, at 33. See e.g., State ex rel. Nigro v. Kansas City, 27 S.W.2d 1030 (Mo. 1930); Rosedale-Skinker Imp. Ass'n v. Bd. of Adj. of St. Louis, 425 S.W.2d 929 (Mo. 1968).

Where there are practical difficulties in the way of carrying out the strict letter of such ordinance, the board of zoning appeals shall have the power to vary or modify the application of any of the regulations or provisions of such ordinance relating to the use, construction or alteration of buildings or structures, or the use of land, so that the spirit of the ordinance shall be observed, public safety and welfare secured and substantial justice done.

The New York statute served as the first general model for other jurisdictions; soon thereafter, however, many states adopted the Standard Zoning Act that had been prepared in the early 1920's under the aegis of the United States Department of Commerce. Section 7 of the Act provides:

To authorize upon appeal in specific cases such variance from the terms of the ordinance as will not be contrary to the public interest, where, owing to special conditions, a literal enforcement of the provisions of the ordinance will result in unnecessary hardship, and so that the spirit of the ordinance shall be observed and substantial justice done.

The standards set forth in these two models, however, only became meaningful after being interpreted by the courts.

Almost all jurisdictions embellished the general concepts of "unnecessary hardship" or "practical difficulties" by further defining the conditions an applicant must satisfy before obtaining a variance. Quite often, local zoning ordinances "summarize that case law by spelling out the same more specific standards in the ordinance, for the convenience of everybody." N. Williams, *supra*, § 131.02, at 28. The North Kansas City Ordinance, for example, provides in part:

Section 27. Board of Adjustment.

A. *Purpose.* The board of adjustment may grant variances from the provisions of this ordinance in harmony with its general purpose and intent and may vary them only in specific instances hereinafter set forth. The board of adjustment, based on standards hereafter prescribed and after hearing, may decide that there are practical difficulties or particular hardship in the way of carrying out the strict letter of these regulations. The concurring vote of four members of the board shall be necessary to reverse any order, requirement or decision of the party appealed from or to issue an order or variance or to decide in favor of an appellant.

B. *Standards.*

1. The board of adjustment may vary the provisions of this ordinance as authorized in this section, but only when it shall have made findings based upon evidence presented to it in the following specific cases:

(a) That the property in question cannot yield a reasonable return if permitted to be used only under the conditions allowed by the regulations governing the district in which it is located;

(b) That the plight of the owner is due to unique circumstances; and

(c) That the variance, if granted, will not alter the essential character of the locality.

Local ordinances may further define the power of the Board of Adjustment to grant a variance, but they may not conflict with the statutory criteria and how courts have interpreted those criteria. This explains why courts examine a Board's decision under the standard expressed in the statute and established through case law.

Unfortunately, any attempt to set forth a unified structure illustrating how all the courts have treated these conditions would, according to Professor Williams, prove unsuccessful. Williams observes that the law of variances is in "great confusion" and that aside from general themes any further attempt at unifying the law indicates "either (a) [one] has not read the case law, or (b) [one] has simply not understood it. Here far more than elsewhere in American planning law, muddle reigns supreme." N. Williams, *supra*, § 129.01, at 12. Yet, four general themes can be distilled from variance law and indicate what an applicant for a variance must prove: (1) relief is necessary because of the unique character of the property rather than for personal considerations; and (2) applying the strict letter of the ordinance would result in unnecessary hardship; and the (3) imposition of such a hardship is not necessary for the preservation of the plan; and (4) granting the variance will result in substantial justice to all. See A. Rathkopf, *supra*, § 37.06; N. Williams, *supra*, § 129.06. Although all the requirements must be satisfied, it is generally held that " '[u]nnecessary hardship' is the principal basis on which a variance is granted." D. Mandelker, Land Use Law, at 167.

Before further examining the contours of unnecessary hardship, jurisdictions such as Missouri that follow the New York model rather than the Standard Act need to address the significance of the statutory dual standard of "unnecessary hardship" or "practical difficulties." Generally, this dual standard has been treated in one of two ways. On the one hand, many courts view the two terms as interchangeable. D. Hagman, Urban Planning & Land Development Control Law § 111, at 205 (1975). On the other hand, a number of jurisdictions follow the approach of New York, the jurisdiction where the language originated, and hold that "practical difficulties" is a slightly lesser standard than "unnecessary hardship" and only applies to the granting of an area variance and not a use variance.[5] D. Mandelker, Land Use Law, at 167; A. Rathkopf, *supra*, § 38.01, at § 38.05. The rationale for this approach is that an area variance is a relaxation of one or more incidental limitations to a permitted use and does not alter the character of the district as much as a use not permitted by the ordinance.

In light of our decision to permit the granting of a use variance, we are persuaded that the New York rule reflects the sound approach for treating the distinction between area and use variances. To obtain a use variance, an applicant must demonstrate, inter alia, unnecessary hardship; and, to obtain an area variance, an applicant must establish, inter alia, the existence of conditions slightly less rigorous than unnecessary hardship.[6]

---

[5] In City & Borough of Juneau v. Thibodeau, 595 P.2d 626 (Alaska 1979), the court observed that in those cases adopting the "practical difficulties" test for area variances, the standards (practical difficulties or unnecessary hardship) were phrased in the disjunctive, but when phrased in the conjunctive both standards must be satisfied.

[6] Because the case law in this state focuses on the granting of area variances and does not reflect the widely held approach for defining unnecessary hardship, these cases still establish the guidelines for

While today we enter a field not yet developed by case law in our own jurisdiction, other jurisdictions provide some guidance for determining what is required to establish unnecessary hardship when granting a use variance. It is generally said that Otto v. Steinhilber, 24 N.E.2d 851, 853 (N.Y. 1939) contains the classic definition of unnecessary hardship:

> Before the Board may exercise its discretion and grant a variance upon the ground of unnecessary hardship, the record must show that (1) the land in question cannot yield a reasonable return if used only for a purpose allowed in that zone; (2) that the plight of the owner is due to unique circumstances and not to the general conditions in the neighborhood which may reflect the unreasonableness of the zoning ordinance itself; and (3) that the use to be authorized by the variance will not alter the essential character of the locality.

Quite often the existence of unnecessary hardship depends upon whether the landowner can establish that without the variance the property cannot yield a reasonable return. "Reasonable return is not maximum return." Curtis v. Main, 482 A.2d 1253, 1257 (Me.1984). Rather, the landowner must demonstrate that he or she will be deprived of all beneficial use of the property under any of the permitted uses:

> A zoning regulation imposes unnecessary hardship if property to which it applies cannot yield a reasonable return from any permitted use. Lack of a reasonable return may be shown by proof that the owner has been deprived of all beneficial use of his land. All beneficial use is said to have been lost where the land is not suitable for any use permitted by the zoning ordinance.

Greenawalt v. Zoning Bd. of Adj. of Davenport, 345 N.W.2d 537, 542-43 (Iowa 1984). Most courts agree that mere conclusory and lay opinion concerning the lack of any reasonable return is not sufficient; there must be actual proof, often in the form of dollars and cents evidence. In a well-reasoned opinion, Judge Meyer of the New York Court of Appeals stated:

> Whether the existing zoning permits of a reasonable return requires proof from which can be determined the rate of return earned by like property in the community and proof in dollars and cents form of the owner's investment in the property as well as the return that the property will produce from the various uses permissible under the existing classification.

North Westchester Prof. Park v. Town of Bedford, 458 N.E.2d 809, 814 (N.Y. 1983). Such pronouncements and requirements of the vast majority of jurisdictions illustrate that, if the law of variances is to have any viability, only in the exceptional case will a use variance be justified.

The record before this Court is fraught with personality conflicts and charges of bias on the part of one of the Board members.[7] Also, the record is without sufficient

---

when an area variance may be granted due to "practical difficulties," regardless of the language used therein. E.g., Brown v. Beuc, 384 S.W.2d 845 (Mo. Ct. App.1964).

[7] We need not reach appellant's charge of bias. Suffice it to say, that the Board acts as a quasi-judicial body and must assure a fair and impartial hearing. See generally D. Mandelker, Land Use Law, at

evidence to establish unnecessary hardship.[8] The only evidence in the record is the conclusory opinion of Brandt that they would be deprived of a reasonable return if not allowed to rent both houses. No evidence of land values was offered; and, no dollars and cents proof was presented to demonstrate that they would be deprived of all beneficial use of their property. Appellant, in fact, was not permitted to introduce such evidence. The Board, therefore, was without authority to grant a use variance upon this record.

The record, however, indicates that the Brandts may be entitled to a nonconforming use under the ordinance. A nonconforming use differs from a variance. Nonconforming uses are those that are in existence prior to and at the time of adoption of the zoning ordinance and which have been maintained from that time to the present. The North Kansas City Zoning Ordinance provides:

> Any nonconforming building, structure or use which existed lawfully at the time of the adoption of this ordinance and which remains nonconforming, and only such building, structure or use which shall become nonconforming upon the adoption of this ordinance or any subsequent amendment thereto, may be continued in accordance with the regulations which follow.

§ 5.B North Kansas City Zoning Ordinance. The ordinance further provides that one loses the right to a nonconforming use if the property is abandoned as a nonconforming use for a period of more than six months. The record indicates that a city official, based upon what was apparently scant evidence, suggested to the Brandts that they may have lost their right to a nonconforming use. There is no substantial evidence in this record indicating the length of time the property may have been unoccupied. Nothing in the record indicates whether the Brandts may have been refurbishing the property or looking for tenants during any such time. Nothing suggests that the Brandts intended to abandon their nonconforming use during the period of time the property may have been unoccupied. Both the trial court and counsel for the Board suggest that the Brandts "may very well have a valid nonconforming use of the premises in question." We do not believe that anything in the record indicates that the Brandts have waived their right to or abandoned their claim of a nonconforming use.

The judgment of the circuit court is reversed and the cause is remanded back to the circuit court with directions that the cause be remanded back to the Board of Adjustment with directions that the applicants be permitted to present evidence warranting the grant of a variance and to amend their application to claim a

---

184-85; A. Rathkopf, *supra*, § 37.02, at 35; § 37.07, at 90.

[8] The Constitution requires that the decision of the Board be reviewed to determine if it is authorized by law and supported by competent and substantial evidence. Mo. Const. art. V, § 18. When the Brandts initially applied for a variance and a hearing was held, there were no minutes of the proceeding and the circuit court had to send the case back to the Board before it could review the Board's order. Nothing in the record indicates why this occurred, but the statute expressly requires that such minutes be transcribed: "All meetings of the board shall be open to the public. The board shall keep minutes of its proceedings. All testimony, objections thereto and rulings thereon, shall be taken down by a reporter employed by the board for that purpose." § 89.080, RSMo 1978. Compliance with this requirement is necessary if there is to be any meaningful review exercised by the circuit court upon the issuance of a writ of certiorari.

nonconforming use of the premises and for such hearing and decision as may be required consistent with this opinion.

ROBERTSON, Judge, concurring in result.

I concur in the result reached by the principal opinion; however, I disagree with the reasoning by which the opinion reaches that result.

The property for which the variance is sought in the present case is improved with two single-family dwellings. The house nearest the street is the original dwelling on the parcel. The other house is a renovation of, and addition to, the former garage, located on the back of the parcel. The zoning ordinance in question defines "lot" as follows: "A parcel of land occupied by, or intended for occupancy by, one principal building, unified groups [sic] of buildings for principal use, and having access to a public street. A lot may be one or more platted lots, or tracts as conveyed, or parts thereof." North Kansas City Code, Appendix A § 3(7).

> In the applicable zone, the "permitted uses" are defined to include "dwellings, one-family." *Id.* §§ 7, 8. The zoning ordinance defines the pertinent "[l]ot area per family" as: "Every dwelling hereafter constructed, reconstructed, moved or altered shall provide a lot area of not less than three thousand eight hundred fifty square feet per family."

Id. § 8. The property on which the two houses are situated apparently contains approximately one and one-half times the number of square feet required for a single one-family residence.[1] The back house was built several decades prior to the enactment of the zoning ordinance. However, there is some question whether occupancy of both houses as single-family dwellings would be acceptable under the ordinance as a pre-existing nonconforming use, since there may have been a lapse in occupancy terminating that status. The property owner therefore requested and obtained a variance to excuse strict compliance with the requirements of the zoning ordinance.

In its analysis prefatory to concluding that the judgment must be reversed, the principal opinion proceeds on the assumption that the variance requested here would be characterized under the "New York model" as a "use" variance, rather than a "non-use" or "area" variance. In distinguishing between the two, the discussion quoted by the principal opinion from Rathkopf's Law of Zoning and Planning is apropos, with the addition of the sentence which follows the quoted language.

> The two types of variances with which cases are customarily concerned are "use" variances and "nonuse variances." The latter consist mostly of variances of bulk restrictions, of area, height, density, setback, side line

---

[1] The testimony and the parties refer to the property as constituting one and one-half "lots." The ordinance contains a provision that, in single-family zoning districts, dwellings are to be "located on a lot," and that "there shall be no more than one principal building on one lot except as may be approved in the planned zoning process." *Id.* § 4(C). Since the definition of "lot" applicable under the zoning ordinance has no relation to platted lots, and pertains only to parcels occupied by "one principal building," this provision is superfluous and adds nothing to the pertinent zoning restrictions. Furthermore, since the term "lot" refers to no other particular standard, it may be presumed that the "lot" referred to is the "lot area" required for a single-family dwelling.

restrictions, and restrictions covering miscellaneous subjects, including the right to enlarge nonconforming uses or to alter nonconforming structures. As the name indicates, a use variance is one which permits a use other than the one of those prescribed by the zoning ordinance in the particular district; it permits a use which the ordinance prohibits. A nonuse variance authorizes deviations from restrictions which relate to a permitted use, rather than limitations on the use itself, that is, restrictions on the bulk of buildings, or relating to their height, size, and extent of lot coverage, or minimum habitable area therein, or on the placement of buildings and structures on the lot with respect to required yards. Variance made necessary by the physical characteristics of the lot itself are nonuse variances of a kind commonly termed "area variances." *These may consist of a variance of the minimum required area of lot for a permitted use, (the most common "area" variance) or a variance of the required width of the lot or its frontage on a street.*

Rathkopf, 3, The Law of Zoning and Planning, § 38.01, pp. 38-1, -2 (1979) (emphasis added).

That part of the variance which alters the requirement imposed by § 3 that each lot on which principal residences are located have "access to a public street" is equivalent to a requirement that a lot have "frontage on a street." Such a variance is therefore an "area" variance. That part of the variance which alters the requirement that principal residences in the zone occupy a minimum of 3,850 square feet is also clearly an area variance.

The North Kansas City Zoning Ordinance defines "use" as "The purpose or activity for which the land or building thereon is designed, arranged or intended, or for which it is occupied or maintained." North Kansas City Code, Appendix A § 3(7), p. 481. In the context of multiple-family dwellings, the New York Court of Appeals stated that "in an area zoned for apartment houses, to seek a variance of height, floor area, and density is to seek an area variance because the essential use of a land is not being changed. In such a situation, the essential use remains the same (apartments), although the particulars (height, lot area, floor area ratio) of said use may be different." Wilcox v. Zoning Board of Appeals, 217 N.E.2d 633 (N.Y. 1966).

In Hoffman v. Harris, 216 N.E.2d 326 (N.Y. 1966), two residences were situated on one parcel of land comprising just over two acres. The land was zoned for single-family residences, with a lot area requirement of two acres per residence. One of the residences had been the main house of a larger estate, and the other had been the "gatehouse." At the time the zoning ordinance came into effect, the gatehouse had been occupied by the gardener for the main house, a permitted "accessory" use in the zoning district. Subsequently, however, the gatehouse was rented to a family who were not employed in the main house. Such a use was not a pre-existing nonconforming use, and a variance was therefore requested to excuse compliance with the zoning ordinance. The Board of Zoning Appeals granted the variance and the Court of Appeals affirmed, holding that the variance sought was an "area" variance rather than a "use" variance, and that proof of "practical difficulties" alone was therefore sufficient. *Id.* at 330; see also Rathkopf, *supra*, at p. 38-47 (citing *Hoffman* as a case to be "looked to for guidance" on the question of establishing "practical difficulties"). *Hoffman* is indistinguishable from the present case, and clearly establishes that the variance involved here is an "area" variance under the New York model.[2]

Because the present case does not involve a "use" variance, it is not necessary to address, as the principal opinion does, whether Missouri has historically rejected variances of that type. This Court has never held that "use" variances are prohibited, notwithstanding proof of "unnecessary hardship," although two Court of Appeals cases have arguably so held. State ex rel. Meyer v. Kinealy, 402 S.W.2d 1 (Mo. Ct. App.1966); State ex rel. Sheridan v. Hudson, 400 S.W.2d 425 (Mo. Ct. App.1966); contra, Beckmeyer v. Beuc, 367 S.W.2d 9 (Mo. Ct. App. 1963).

Both the *Meyer* and *Sheridan* cases attribute their holdings to this Court's opinion in State ex rel. Nigro v. Kansas City, 27 S.W.2d 1030 (Mo. 1930). In that case, a variance was sought to construct and use for retail business purposes a new building, to be situated on one corner of an intersection, on property zoned for residential purposes. The basis for the owner's request was that the other three corners of the intersection were zoned for businesses, that new residential development in the area would create more need for retail businesses, and that denial of the variance would deprive him of potential profits. The circuit court reversed the zoning board's denial of the variance, and this Court reversed the circuit court's judgment, holding that the evidence did not demonstrate "practical difficulties" or "unnecessary hardship" within the meaning of both the zoning ordinance and the relevant statute, so as to authorize a variance. This Court also commented that

> if in a specific case the enforcement of a regulation according to its strict letter would cause unnecessary hardship and the board can by varying or modifying the application of the regulation obviate the hardship and at the same time fully effectuate the spirit and purpose of the ordinance, they are authorized to so vary or modify the application. But the board can in no case relieve from a substantial compliance with the ordinance; their administrative discretion is limited to the narrow compass of the statute; they cannot merely pick and choose as the individuals of whom they will or will not require a strict compliance with the ordinance.

Id. at 1032. This Court also stated that, rather than seeking to establish the statutory standards for a variance, the landowner was in fact asking the board of zoning appeals to "rezone" property, which the board was not empowered to do. Nothing in the *Nigro* opinion requires the conclusion that "use" variances are categorically prohibited under the statutory standard.[3]

---

[2] Were the variance involved here actually a "use" variance, the ordinance would appear to prohibit it under any circumstance. The ordinance conditions the authority of the board to grant a variance on proof "[t]hat the variance, if granted, will not alter the essential character of the locality." North Kansas City Code, Appendix A § 27(B)(1)(c). This language is presumably derived from *Wilcox, supra,* which described an "area" variance as one involving "no change in the essential character of the zoned district." *Id.* at 634. However, since the variance here is not a "use" variance, this problem is not before us.

[3] The remaining cases cited by the principal opinion in footnote 2 do not address the prohibition of "use" variances. Two of them concern "area" variances. Rosedale-Skinker Improvement Assn., Inc. v. Bd. of Adj. of St. Louis, 425 S.W.2d 929 (Mo. 1968); Brown v. Beuc, 384 S.W.2d 845 (Mo. Ct. App. 1964).

Notwithstanding that the variance involved here is an "area" variance rather than a "use" variance, the ordinance itself requires proof which is similar to the "unnecessary hardship" standard as it is described by the principal opinion. Under the ordinance, the board is authorized to grant a variance only if it is demonstrated "[t]hat the property in question cannot yield a reasonable return if permitted to be used only under the conditions allowed by the regulations governing the district in which it is located." North Kansas City Ordinance, Appendix A, § 27(B)(1)(a). It is the application of this standard that requires that the judgment in the present case be reversed and remanded.

As the principal opinion notes, proof under the "reasonable return" standard cannot be made by mere lay opinion, without a showing of the facts upon which such an opinion could be based. Such evidence was not before the board in the present case, and was in fact rejected when offered. In light of this deficiency, the board's decision was unlawful, and the judgment affirming that decision must be reversed. Remand is advisable, however, to permit the landowners to submit proof under this standard if available. I therefore concur in the principal opinion only to the extent of the result reached.

BLACKMAR, Judge, concurring.

The property owner has laid the foundation for the grant of a variance by showing that two separate houses were located on a single lot at the time the zoning ordinance was adopted. There would be a substantial waste if habitable structures were required to be torn down. This showing should permit the Board to find, in its discretion, after hearing all evidence, that the tests of "unnecessary hardship" and "practical difficulties" are met.

Rate of return is an important consideration. Although initial cost may not be a controlling circumstance in determining the base from which reasonable return is to be calculated, it is a starting point. The Board was plainly wrong in denying the plaintiff the right to inquire about the initial cost. This error taints the hearing, and the order based on it cannot stand. I concur, therefore, in the judgment of reversal and remand to the Board.

NOTES AND QUESTIONS

1. **Amendment compared.** How are amendments and variances similar? How do they differ? What considerations would affect your advice to a client on whether to seek a variance or to push for an amendment?

2. **Nonconforming use compared.** How does a variance differ from a nonconforming use?

3. **Empirical studies and recommendations.** For empirical studies documenting the damage that the variance procedure can do to the goal of uniformity underlying zoning acts, see Jesse Dukeminier, Jr. & Clyde L. Stapleton, *The Zoning Board of Adjustment: A Case Study in Misrule*, 50 Ky. L.J. 273

The third held that a board of zoning adjustment was not authorized to grant a "use" variance on the ground of financial hardship. Bartholomew v. Bd. of Adj. of Kansas City, 307 S.W.2d 730, 733 (Mo. Ct. App. 1957).

(1962); Note, *Zoning Variances and Exceptions: The Philadelphia Experience*, 103 U. Pa. L. Rev. 516 (1955). For a discussion of possible reform, see David W. Owens, *The Zoning Variance: Reappraisal and Recommendations for Reform of a Much-Maligned Tool*, 29 Colum. J. Envtl. L. 279, 322 (2004).

c.   Special Exceptions

TRUSTEES OF UNION COLLEGE v. MEMBERS OF THE SCHENECTADY CITY COUNCIL
690 N.E.2d 862 (N.Y. 1997)

KAYE, CHIEF JUDGE.

In Cornell University v. Bagnardi, 503 N.E.2d 509 (N.Y. 1986), involving the application of local zoning regulations, we considered the correct balance to be struck when educational institutions seek expansion into a residential zone. Today we consider the novel, but related, question whether a municipality has acted lawfully in excluding educational institutions from a residential historic district. Like Supreme Court and the Appellate Division, we conclude that the City law denying educational institutions the opportunity to apply for special use permits in a Single Family Historic District was unauthorized and therefore unconstitutional.

Respondent Union College is the owner of seven properties located in an area known as the General Electric Realty Plot in the City of Schenectady. The area was established in 1899 and developed as an "ideal residential section" to attract General Electric managers, scientists and others to Schenectady. Over the years, the Realty Plot matured into a distinctive, turn of the century residential neighborhood encompassing a nine block area adjacent to respondent's campus. Today, the Realty Plot is listed on the National Register of Historic Places.

In 1978, the City adopted Ordinance No. 78-45, which established an A-2 Single Family Historic District incorporating the Realty Plot. In an effort to preserve the historical sense of the area, the ordinance limited property uses to large, single-family residences. Educational, religious, philanthropic and eleemosynary institutions could, however, apply for special use permits within the Historic District.

The City amended its zoning provisions in 1984, adopting Schenectady City Code § 264-8, which limited permitted uses within the A-2 Historic District to single-family dwellings and for the first time restricted special permit uses to public utility facilities, substations and structures. Thus, all other special uses permitted from 1978 to 1984 — including, most particularly, educational uses — were foreclosed. Before and after the amendment, the ordinance allowed a property owner who could show "practical difficulties" or "unnecessary hardships" to obtain a variance. The Code also allowed a private party unable or unwilling to pursue a variance or special use permit to seek an amendment to the Code itself.

In November 1992, respondent proposed that City Code § 264-8[C] be amended to include any nonresidential educational use as a special permit use within the District, but then confined its proposal to "faculty offices, administrative offices and homes for visiting dignitaries and guests of the College." Over the next two years, respondent pressed for the amendment. The City's Historic Districts Commission and the New York State Office of Parks, Recreation and Historic Preservation, however, both projected that the proposed amendment would have a deleterious effect on the historic preservation values of the Realty Plot.

In January 1995, Union College discontinued its pursuit of an amendment and instead commenced this declaratory judgment action against the City, its Mayor and the Schenectady City Council, seeking a declaration that City Code § 264-8 was unconstitutional on its face. Following joinder of issue, both sides moved for summary judgment. In comprehensive opinions, Supreme Court granted the College's motion and denied the cross-motion, and the Appellate Division unanimously affirmed.

Discussion

The presumption of constitutionality enjoyed by a legislative enactment, such as the zoning ordinance at issue here, is formidable but not conclusive. With the police power as the predicate for the State's delegation of municipal zoning authority, a zoning ordinance will be struck down if it bears no substantial relation to the police power objective of promoting the public health, safety, morals or general welfare.

Unquestionably, municipalities can "enact land-use restrictions or controls to enhance the quality of life by preserving the character and desirable aesthetic features of a city." Penn Cent. Transp. Co. v. New York City, 438 U.S. 104, 129 (1978). In support of City Code § 264-8, appellants point both to the Constitution's general grant of authority to adopt local laws and to the Legislature's specific grants of authority to localities to "manage the historical and cultural properties under their jurisdiction in a spirit of stewardship and trusteeship for future generations." General Municipal Law art. 5-K ("Historic Preservation"), § 119-aa. Appellants underscore that, as a matter of public policy, "the historical, archeological, architectural and cultural heritage of the state is among the most important environmental assets of the state and that it should be preserved." Parks, Recreation and Historic Preservation Law § 14.01.

The preservation of structures and areas with special historic, architectural or cultural significance is surely an important governmental objective. But the public interest in historical preservation does not as a matter of law override competing educational interests, which by their very nature also are "clearly in furtherance of the public morals and general welfare." Matter of Diocese of Rochester v. Planning Bd. of Town of Brighton, 136 N.E.2d 827, 836 (1956).

As a consequence of their inherently beneficial nature, educational institutions have long "enjoyed special treatment with respect to residential zoning ordinances and have been permitted to expand into neighborhoods where nonconforming uses would otherwise not have been allowed." Cornell, 503 N.E.2d at 513. Indeed, we have held that as a general rule "the total exclusion of [educational] institutions from a residential district serves no end that is reasonably related to the morals, health, welfare and safety of the community [and] is beyond the scope of the localities' zoning authority." Cornell, 503 N.E.2d at 514 N.Y.2d at 514.

The decision to restrict a proposed educational use can only be made after the intended use is evaluated against other legitimate interests, with primary consideration given to the over-all impact on the public welfare. A municipality's pursuit of other legitimate objectives, such as historic preservation, does not diminish the importance of striking a balance between the important contribution made to society by educational institutions and the inimical consequences of their presence in residential neighborhoods. Thus, like traditional residential zoning ordinances, those designed to further an historic preservation purpose are not immune from the deliberative process that must precede the restriction of educational uses. Rather, proposed educational uses must be weighed against the interest in historical preservation, as well as other legitimate, competing interests, to determine how best to serve the public welfare.

Here, the issue is whether Union College may be denied the opportunity to submit its proposed educational use to the zoning board for such an evaluation. Although appellants argue that section 264-8 itself represents a deliberative balancing of interests, the ordinance merely reflects the City's sweeping policy decision that historical preservation interests will, in all cases, outweigh educational interests. In practical effect, the ordinance wholly excludes educational uses from the Historical District by improperly eliminating any opportunity for the balancing of individual educational uses against the public's historical preservation interests.

The importance of evaluating proposed educational uses on a case-by-case basis is clearly illustrated here, where the City's conclusion that the presence of an educational use in the District will, in all instances, undermine the ordinance's purpose of promoting, maintaining and enhancing the historically significant buildings within the Realty Plot is completely unsupported. Plainly stated, depriving respondent of the opportunity to have its presumptively beneficial educational use weighed against competing interests, and thereby wholly excluding educational uses from the District, bears no substantial relation to the public health, safety, morals or general welfare, and is therefore beyond the City's zoning authority.

Appellants urge that, although educational uses are not included in the category of special permit uses allowed in the District, anyone seeking to use District property for an educational or other nonresidential purpose can apply for a variance or seek to amend the law. Neither the variance process — which requires a showing of practical difficulties or unnecessary hardships — nor the amendment process allows the zoning board to conduct the proper inquiry, which is to balance a particular applicant's educational use against the public interest in historical preservation.

As we noted in *Cornell*, a special permit application "affords zoning boards an opportunity to weigh the proposed use in relation to neighboring land uses and to cushion any adverse effects by the imposition of conditions designed to mitigate them." 503 N.E.2d at 516. Indeed, if educational uses were included in the category of special permit uses allowed in Schenectady's Historical District, the reviewing body could determine the appropriateness of Union College's proposed use relative to the District's historical preservation goals "by weighing the public need and benefit against the local impact and effect" (City Code, art. XI ["Special Permit Uses"]). The board could, if necessary, then impose reasonable conditions to mitigate any anticipated negative impacts on the historical character of the area — so long as those conditions do not operate indirectly to exclude the use altogether — thereby accommodating the public interest both in historical preservation and in education.

In failing to provide any means whereby Union College's proposed educational uses might be balanced against the public's interest in historical preservation, City Code § 264-8 serves no end that is substantially related to the promotion of the public health, safety, morals or general welfare, and as such is unconstitutional.

Accordingly, the order of the Appellate Division should be affirmed, with costs.

NOTES AND QUESTIONS

1. **Theory of the special exception.**   See Tullo v. Township of Millburn, 149 A.2d 620, 624-25 (N.J. Super. Ct. App. Div. 1959):

> The theory is that certain uses, considered by the local legislative body to be essential or desirable for the welfare of the community and its citizenry or substantial segments of it, are entirely appropriate and not essentially incompatible with the basic uses in any zone (or in certain particular zones), but not at every or any location therein or without restrictions or conditions being imposed by reason of special problems the use or its particular location in relation to neighboring properties presents from a zoning standpoint, such as traffic congestion, safety, health, noise, and the like. The enabling act therefore permits the local ordinance to require approval of the local administrative agency as to the location of such use within the zone. If the board finds compliance with the standards or requisites set forth in the ordinance, the right to the exception exists, subject to such specific safeguarding conditions as the agency may impose by reason of the nature, location and incidents of the particular use. Without intending here to be inclusive or to prescribe limits, the uses so treated are generally those serving considerable numbers of people, such as private schools, clubs, hospitals and even churches, as distinguished from governmental structures or activities on the one hand and strictly individual residences or businesses on the other. This method of zoning treatment is also frequently extended to certain unusual kinds of strictly private business or activity which, though desirable and compatible, may by their nature present peculiar zoning problems or have unduly unfavorable effect on their neighbors if not specially regulated. Gasoline stations are an example of this second category. The point is that such special uses are permissive in the particular zone under the ordinance and neither non-conforming nor akin to a variance. The latter must be especially clearly distinguished. In the sense here discussed it relates primarily to the allowance of a use of a particular property prohibited in the particular zone for special reasons.

2. **Standards.**   See Nani v. Zoning Bd. of Review, 242 A.2d 403, 404-06 (R.I. 1968):

In a long line of cases this court, equating the "public convenience" requirement in zoning ordinances with "public need," has held that a zoning board should make a special exception to the terms of an ordinance where the showing has been that the use proposed to be established will serve a community need; conversely, it has also held that an applicant will not qualify for an exception where the proof is that there is no public need at the specific location for the use requested. Along with these decisions, and neither overruling those which precede nor being overruled by those which follow, are the two opinions in Center Realty Corp. v. Zoning Board of Review, 189 A.2d 347, and 194 A.2d 671. In each, the court without reference to the "public need" cases, rejects the notion that an exception should be refused on the ground that the public has no need for more of what it already has in sufficiency, or that entitlement to an exception requires a showing that members of the public would be convenienced thereby. The standard they fix for satisfying the "public convenience and welfare" requirement is proof that the location of the use proposed at the site selected will not be detrimental to the public health, safety, morals or welfare.

There is a basic difference between the two approaches. The cases which follow the "public need" concept find a dual standard in the "public convenience and welfare" requirement. While they read the word "welfare" as though it had police power overtones, they consider the word "convenience" as though it were used in a "public utility" context, and thus as demanding that the use proposed be reasonably necessary for the public accommodation. The *Center Realty* view treats the words "convenience" and "welfare" as though they are synonymous, and reading them as if the legislative intention had been to use them in a strict police power sense, in effect, considers them as if they were a substitute for the phrase "the public health, safety, morals or general welfare." To construe them as imposing a "public need" criterion, the *Center Realty* view says, smacks of licensing and the regulation of competition, and, as such, is beyond the ken of what is permissible in zoning.

Rathkopf, in urging [the *Center Realty*] rationale, says: "The denial of a permit to establish a use which has been legislatively found to be compatible with other permitted uses, only on the ground that it does not serve public convenience, or conversely, the grant of a permit on the ground that it would serve public convenience, without, in either case, consideration of public health, safety and general welfare as related to zoning considerations, seem to be entirely inconsistent with the purposes of zoning and the device of a special exception use. A particular use should not be permitted, although incompatible in a particular location, on the sole justification of convenience to the public, nor should it be excluded for lack of proof that there is a public demand (as distinguished from public necessity, as in the case of utilities) for its establishment." 2 Rathkopf, The Law of Zoning and Planning (3d ed.) 1967 Cumulative Supplement, 54-18, p. 158.

It is important, and indeed essential, that we decide between the two. The public, the zoning boards and the bar are entitled to know how the "public convenience and welfare" precondition will be construed and what are to be the guidelines for the grant of an exception. We hold that an application for an exception for a particular use should not be denied either for lack of proof that there is a community or a neighborhood need for its establishment or because the proof is that there is no such need; nor should such a use be permitted on the sole ground that it will serve the community or neighborhood needs or accommodate the public. The rule, henceforth, shall be that satisfaction of a "public convenience and welfare" precondition will hinge on a showing that a proposed use will not result in conditions that will be inimical to the public health, safety, morals and welfare.

4. Zoning Purposes and Means: Selected Issues

a. Aesthetics

ANDERSON v. CITY OF ISSAQUAH
851 P.2d 744 (Wash. Ct. App. 1993)

Kennedy, Judge.

Appellants M. Bruce Anderson, Gary D. LaChance, and M. Bruce Anderson, Inc. (hereinafter referred to as "Anderson"), challenge the denial of their application for a land use certification, arguing, inter alia, that the building design requirements contained in Issaquah Municipal Code (IMC) 16.16.060 are unconstitutionally vague. The superior court rejected this constitutional challenge. We reverse and direct that Anderson's land use certification be issued.

FACTS

Anderson owns property located at 145 N.W. Gilman Boulevard in the City of Issaquah. In 1988, Anderson applied to the City for a land use certification to develop the property. The property is zoned for general commercial use. Anderson desired to build a 6800 square foot commercial building for several retail tenants.

After obtaining architectural plans, Anderson submitted the project to various City departments for the necessary approvals. The process went smoothly until the approval of the Issaquah Development Commission (Development Commission) was sought. This commission was created to administer and enforce the City's land use regulations. It has the authority to approve or deny applications for land use certification.

Chapter 16.16.060 of the IMC enumerates various building design objectives which the Development Commission is required to administer and enforce. Insofar as is relevant to this appeal, the Development Commission is to be guided by the following criteria:

IMC 16.16.060(B). Relationship of Building and Site to Adjoining Area.

1. Buildings and structures shall be made compatible with adjacent buildings of conflicting architectural styles by such means as screens and site breaks, or other suitable methods and materials.

2. Harmony in texture, lines, and masses shall be encouraged.

IMC 16.16.060(D). Building Design.

1. Evaluation of a project shall be based on quality of its design and relationship to the natural setting of the valley and surrounding mountains.

2. Building components, such as windows, doors, eaves and parapets, shall have appropriate proportions and relationship to each other, expressing themselves as a part of the overall design.

3. Colors shall be harmonious, with bright or brilliant colors used only for minimal accent.

4. Design attention shall be given to screening from public view all mechanical equipment, including refuse enclosures, electrical transformer pads and vaults, communication equipment, and other utility hardware on roofs, grounds or buildings.

5. Exterior lighting shall be part of the architectural concept. Fixtures, standards and all exposed accessories shall be harmonious with the building design.

6. Monotony of design in single or multiple building projects shall be avoided. Efforts should be made to create an interesting project by use of complimentary details, functional orientation of buildings, parking and access provisions and relating the development to the site. In multiple building projects, variable siting of individual buildings, heights of buildings, or other methods shall be used to prevent a monotonous design.

As initially designed, Anderson's proposed structure was to be faced with off-white stucco and was to have a blue metal roof. It was designed in a "modern" style with an unbroken "warehouse" appearance in the rear, and large retail style windows in the front. The City moved a Victorian era residence, the "Alexander House," onto the neighboring property to serve as a visitors' center. Across the street from the Anderson site is a gasoline station that looks like a gasoline station. Located nearby and within view from the proposed building site are two more gasoline stations, the First Mutual Bank Building built in the "Issaquah territorial style," an Elk's hall which is described in the record by the Mayor of Issaquah as a "box building," an auto repair shop, and a veterinary clinic with a cyclone-fenced dog run. The area is described in the record as "a natural transition area between old downtown Issaquah and the new village style construction of Gilman [Boulevard]."

The Development Commission reviewed Anderson's application for the first time at a public hearing on December 21, 1988. Commissioner Nash commented that "the facade did not fit with the concept of the surrounding area." Commissioner McGinnis agreed. Commissioner Nash expressed concern about the building color and stated that he did not think the building was compatible with the image of

Issaquah. Commissioner Larson said that he would like to see more depth to the building facade. Commissioner Nash said there should be some interest created along the blank back wall. Commissioner Garrison suggested that the rear facade needed to be redesigned. At the conclusion of the meeting, the Development Commission voted to continue the hearing to give Anderson an opportunity to modify the building design.

On January 18, 1989, Anderson came back before the Development Commission with modified plans which included changing the roofing from metal to tile, changing the color of the structure from off-white to "Cape Cod" gray with "Tahoe" blue trim, and adding brick to the front facade. During the ensuing discussion among the commissioners, Commissioner Larson stated that the revisions to the front facade had not satisfied his concerns from the last meeting. In response to Anderson's request for more specific design guidelines, Commissioner McGinnis stated that the Development Commission had "been giving direction; it is the applicant's responsibility to take the direction/suggestions and incorporate them into a revised plan that reflects the changes." Commissioner Larson then suggested that "[t]he facade can be broken up with sculptures, benches, fountains, etc." Commissioner Nash suggested that Anderson "drive up and down Gilman and look at both good and bad examples of what has been done with flat facades."

As the discussion continued, Commissioner Larson stated that Anderson "should present a [plan] that achieves what the Commission is trying to achieve through its comments/suggestions at these meetings" and stated that "architectural screens, fountains, paving of brick, wood or other similar method[s] of screening in lieu of vegetative landscaping are examples of design suggestions that can be used to break up the front facade." Commissioner Davis objected to the front facade, stating that he could not see putting an expanse of glass facing Gilman Boulevard. "The building is not compatible with Gilman." Commissioner O'Shea agreed. Commissioner Nash stated that "the application needs major changes to be acceptable." Commissioner O'Shea agreed. Commissioner Nash stated that "this facade does not create the same feeling as the building/environment around this site."

Commissioner Nash continued, stating that he "personally like[d] the introduction of brick and the use of tiles rather than metal on the roof." Commissioner Larson stated that he would like to see a review of the blue to be used: "Tahoe blue may be too dark." Commissioner Steinwachs agreed. Commissioner Larson noted that "the front of the building could be modulated [to] have other design techniques employed to make the front facade more interesting." With this, the Development Commission voted to continue the discussion to a future hearing.

On February 15, 1989, Anderson came back before the Development Commission. In the meantime, Anderson's architects had added a 5-foot overhang and a 7-foot accent overhang to the plans for the front of the building. More brick had been added to the front of the building. Wood trim and accent colors had been added to the back of the building and trees were added to the landscaping to further break up the rear facade.

Anderson explained that the plans still called for large, floor to ceiling windows as this was to be a retail premises: "[A] glass front is necessary to rent the space."

Commissioner Steinwachs stated that he had driven Gilman Boulevard and taken notes. The following verbatim statements by Steinwachs was placed into the minutes:

My General Observation From Driving Up and Down Gilman Boulevard.

I see certain design elements and techniques used in various combinations in various locations to achieve a visual effect that is sensitive to the unique character of our Signature Street. I see heavy use of brick, wood, and tile. I see minimal use of stucco. I see colors that are mostly earthtones, avoiding extreme contrasts. I see various methods used to provide modulation in both horizontal and vertical lines, such as gables, bay windows, recesses in front faces, porches, rails, many vertical columns, and breaks in roof lines. I see long, sloping, conspicuous roofs with large overhangs. I see windows with panels above and below windows. I see no windows that extend down to floor level. This is the impression I have of Gilman Boulevard as it relates to building design.

Commissioner Nash agreed stating, "[T]here is a certain feeling you get when you drive along Gilman Boulevard, and this building does not give this same feeling." Commissioner Steinwachs wondered if the applicant had any option but to start "from scratch." Anderson responded that he would be willing to change from stucco to wood facing but that, after working on the project for 9 months and experiencing total frustration, he was not willing to make additional design changes.

At that point, the Development Commission denied Anderson's application, giving four reasons:

1. After four [sic] lengthy review meetings of the Development Commission, the applicant has not been sufficiently responsive to concerns expressed by the Commission to warrant approval or an additional continuance of the review.

2. The primary concerns expressed relate to the building architecture as it relates to Gilman Boulevard in general, and the immediate neighborhood in particular.

3. The Development Commission is charged with protecting, preserving and enhancing the aesthetic values that have established the desirable quality and unique character of Issaquah, reference IMC 16.16.010C.[3]

4. We see certain design elements and techniques used in various combinations in various locations to achieve a visual effect that is sensitive to the unique character of our Signature Street. On Gilman Boulevard we see heavy use of brick, wood and tile. We see minimal use of stucco. We see various methods used to provide both horizontal and vertical modulation, including gables, breaks in rooflines, bay windows, recesses and protru-

---

[3] IMC 16.16.010(C) provides that one of the purposes of the code is "[t]o protect, preserve and enhance the social, cultural, economic, environmental and aesthetic values that have established the desirable quality and unique character of Issaquah."

sions in front face. We see long, sloping, conspicuous roofs with large overhangs. We see no windows that extend to ground level. We see brick and wood panels at intervals between windows. We see earthtone colors avoiding extreme contrast.

Anderson, who by this time had an estimated $250,000 into the project, timely appealed the adverse ruling to the Issaquah City Council. After a lengthy hearing and much debate, the City Council decided to affirm the Development Commission's decision.

The City Council considered formal written findings and conclusions on April 3, 1989. The City Council verbally adopted its action on that date but required that certain changes be made to the proposed findings and conclusions. Those changes were made and the final findings and conclusions were signed on April 5, 1989 (backdated to April 3). On April 5, a notice of action was issued to Anderson, stating that he had 14 days from the date of that notice in which to file any appeal.

Thirteen days later, on April 18, 1989, Anderson filed a complaint in King County Superior Court. Following trial, the court dismissed Anderson's complaint, rejecting the same claims now raised in this appeal.

DISCUSSION
Constitutionality of IMC 16.16.060 (Building Design Provisions)

[A] statute which either forbids or requires the doing of an act in terms so vague that men [and women] of common intelligence must necessarily guess at its meaning and differ as to its application, violates the first essential of due process of law.

Connally v. General Constr. Co., 269 U.S. 385, 391 (1926). In the field of regulatory statutes governing business activities, statutes which employ technical words which are commonly understood within an industry, or which employ words with a well-settled common law meaning generally will be sustained against a charge of vagueness. The vagueness test does not require a statute to meet impossible standards of specificity.

In the area of land use, a court looks not only at the face of the ordinance but also at its application to the person who has sought to comply with the ordinance and/or who is alleged to have failed to comply. The purpose of the void for vagueness doctrine is to limit arbitrary and discretionary enforcements of the law.

Looking first at the face of the building design sections of IMC 16.16.060, we note that an ordinary citizen reading these sections would learn only that a given building project should bear a good relationship with the Issaquah Valley and surrounding mountains; its windows, doors, eaves and parapets should be of "appropriate proportions," its colors should be "harmonious" and seldom "bright" or "brilliant"; its mechanical equipment should be screened from public view; its exterior lighting should be "harmonious" with the building design and "monotony should be avoided." The project should also be "interesting." IMC 16.16.060(D)(1)-(6). If the building is not "compatible" with adjacent buildings, it should be "made compatible" by the use of screens and site breaks "or other suitable methods and materials." "Harmony in texture, lines, and masses [is] encouraged." The landscaping should provide an "attractive transition" to adjoining properties. IMC 16.16.060(B)(1)-(3).

As is stated in the brief of amici curiae,[9] we conclude that these code sections "do not give effective or meaningful guidance" to applicants, to design professionals, or to the public officials of Issaquah who are responsible for enforcing the code. Brief of Amici Curiae, at 1. Although it is clear from the code sections here at issue that mechanical equipment must be screened from public view and that, probably, earth tones or pastels located within the cool and muted ranges of the color wheel are going to be preferred, there is nothing in the code from which an applicant can determine whether his or her project is going to be seen by the Development Commission as "interesting" versus "monotonous" and as "harmonious" with the valley and the mountains. Neither is it clear from the code just what else, besides the valley and the mountains, a particular project is supposed to be harmonious with, although "[h]armony in texture, lines, and masses" is certainly encouraged. IMC 16.16.060(B)(2).[10]

In attempting to interpret and apply this code, the commissioners charged with that task were left with only their own individual, subjective "feelings" about the "image of Issaquah" and as to whether this project was "compatible" or "interesting." The commissioners stated that the City was "making a statement" on its "signature street"[11] and invited Anderson to take a drive up and down Gilman Boulevard and "look at good and bad examples of what has been done with flat facades." One commissioner drove up and down Gilman, taking notes, in a no doubt sincere effort to define that which is left undefined in the code.[12]

The point we make here is that neither Anderson nor the commissioners may constitutionally be required or allowed to guess at the meaning of the code's building design requirements by driving up and down Gilman Boulevard looking at "good and bad" examples of what has been done with other buildings, recently or in the past. We hold that the code sections here at issue are unconstitutionally vague on their face. The words employed are not technical words which are commonly understood within the professional building design industry. Neither do these words have a settled common law meaning.

---

[9] The amici curiae are the Seattle Chapter of the American Institute of Architects, the Washington Council of the American Institute of Architects, and the Washington Chapter of the American Society of Landscape Architects.

[10] Apparently a particular building need not be particularly compatible with the design of an adjacent building in that it can be "made compatible" by the use of "screens and site breaks." IMC 16.16.060(B)(1).

[11] The term "signature street" is not defined in the ordinance here at issue.

[12] Although Commissioner Steinwachs stated that he saw heavy use of brick, wood and tile, minimal use of stucco, many gables, bay windows, and long, sloping vertical roofs, it is clear from the record that also to be seen on Gilman Boulevard are a number of approved and completed projects that do not bear these characteristics. Examples include a Shuck's Auto Supply store at 607 N.W. Gilman Boulevard; a strip mall known as Town and County Square at 1135 Gilman Boulevard; a Mobil gasoline station located at 55 N.W. Gilman Boulevard and a Skipper's Restaurant located at the southeast corner of Front Street and Gilman Boulevard.

As they were applied to Anderson, it is also clear the code sections at issue fail to pass constitutional muster. Because the commissioners themselves had no objective guidelines to follow, they necessarily had to resort to their own subjective "feelings." The "statement" Issaquah is apparently trying to make on its "signature street" is not written in the code. In order to be enforceable, that "statement" must be written down in the code, in understandable terms.[13] The unacceptable alternative is what happened here. The commissioners enforced not a building design code but their own arbitrary concept of the provisions of an unwritten "statement" to be made on Gilman Boulevard. The commissioners' individual concepts were as vague and undefined as those written in the code. This is the very epitome of discretionary, arbitrary enforcement of the law.

Councilwoman McHenry said it very well during the appeal to the City Council:

> [M]aybe we haven't done a good job in communicating what kind of image we want. We all want an image. I bet you if I stated my image it would be certainly different from everyone of you here and everyone in the audience. [I]f we want a specific design, I agree with proponent's counsel, and that is that we come up with a specific district design. We don't have such a design requirement. So we all have to rely on some gut feel. And often times this gut feel gets us into trouble because it could be misinterpreted or misconstrued.

Although the City argues that its code is not unconstitutionally vague, it primarily relies upon the procedural safeguards contained in the code. Because aesthetic considerations are subjective in concept, the City argues that they cannot be reduced to a formula or a number. The vagueness test does not require a statute to meet impossible standards of specificity.

As well illustrated by the appendices to the brief of amici curiae, aesthetic considerations are not impossible to define in a code or ordinance.[14] Moreover, the procedural safeguards contained in the Issaquah Municipal Code (providing for appeal to the city council and to the courts) do not cure the constitutional defects here apparent.

Certainly, the IMC grants Anderson the right to appeal the adverse decision of the Development Commission. But just as IMC 16.16.060 provides no standards by which an applicant or the Development Commission or the City Council can determine whether a given building design passes muster under the code, it provides no ascertainable criteria by which a court can review a decision at issue, regardless of whether the court applies the arbitrary and capricious standard as the

---

[13] We reject the City's argument that Issaquah's comprehensive plan and its I-90 subarea amendment when read in conjunction with IMC 16.16.060 fills in the constitutional gap. The comprehensive plan contains only very general statements of policy, criteria, and goals. By the terms of the plan, the City stated its intention to enact and enforce specific regulations in order to carry out the comprehensive plan. It is one of these regulations that is at issue here.

[14] Appendix A to the brief of amici curiae is a portion of the design objectives plan for entry way corridors for Bozeman, Montana. Appendix B is a portion of the development code for San Bernardino, California. Both codes contain extensive written criteria illustrated by schematic drawings and photographs. The illustrations clarify a number of concepts which otherwise might be difficult to describe with the requisite degree of clarity.

City argues is appropriate or the clearly erroneous standard as Anderson argues is appropriate. Under either standard of review, the appellate process is to no avail where the statute at issue contains no ascertainable standards and where, as here, the Development Commission was not empowered to adopt clearly ascertainable standards of its own.[15] The procedural safeguards provided here do not save the ordinance.

Anderson has argued strenuously in this appeal that a municipality has no power to deny a proposed development for aesthetic reasons alone. Anderson argues this issue is "settled" by Washington case law. See, e.g., Polygon Corp. v. Seattle, 578 P.2d 1309 (Wash. 1978). Relying on these same cases, the City argues that, although Anderson's land use certification admittedly was denied solely on the basis of aesthetics, IMC 16.16 is valid because aesthetic concerns are only one of the bases contained in the code for the exercise of police power relating to land use. The amici point out that the modern view is that aesthetics alone will justify a regulation, provided that there are adequate standards and they are appropriately applied. See 1 A. & D. Rathkopf, Zoning and Planning § 14.02[4] (1986).

We believe the issue of whether a community can exert control over design issues based solely on accepted community aesthetic values is far from "settled" in Washington case law. The possibility certainly has not been foreclosed by our Supreme Court. See *Polygon*, 578 P.2d 1309 ("While this court has not held that aesthetic factors alone will support an exercise of the police power, such considerations taken together with other factors can support such action."). Clearly, however, aesthetic standards are an appropriate component of land use governance. Whenever a community adopts such standards they can and must be drafted to give clear guidance to all parties concerned. Applicants must have an understandable statement of what is expected from new construction. Design professionals need to know in advance what standards will be acceptable in a given community. It is unreasonable to expect applicants to pay for repetitive revisions of plans in an effort to comply with the unarticulated, unpublished "statements" a given community may wish to make on or off its "signature street." It is equally unreasonable, and a deprivation of due process, to expect or allow a design review board such as the Issaquah Development Commission to create standards on an ad hoc basis, during the design review process.

CONCLUSION

It is not disputed that Anderson's project meets all of the City's land use requirements except for those unwritten and therefore unenforceable requirements relating to building design which the Development Commission unsuccessfully tried to articulate during the course of several hearings. We order that Anderson's land use certification be issued, provided however, that those changes which Anderson agreed to through the hearing before the City Council may validly be imposed.

---

[15] We do not decide whether such authority could have been delegated to this commission. Such authority was not delegated here.

LAMAR CORP. v. CITY OF TWIN FALLS
981 P.2d 1146 (Idaho 1999)

KIDWELL, JUSTICE.

The City Council of the City of Twin Falls and City of Twin Falls appeal a decision of the district court reversing a zoning decision of the City Council. The City Council had denied the application of Idaho Outdoor Advertising for a special use permit to erect a billboard. The district court reversed, ruling that the Twin Falls zoning ordinance unconstitutionally limited commercial speech. The City also appeals the district court's denial of its request to delete certain materials from the transcript and record on appeal. Idaho Outdoor cross-appeals the district court's decision that sufficient evidence supported the City's action, as well as the district court's denial of its motion for attorney fees. The decision of the district court is affirmed in part and reversed in part.

I.
FACTS AND PROCEDURAL HISTORY

The City of Twin Falls has adopted a Comprehensive Plan to guide future development. The Comprehensive Plan identifies Addison Avenue as an "entryway corridor" into the city and states goals that include "promot[ing] and encourag[ing] aesthetically pleasing approaches to the City" and "[e]ncourag[ing] area beautification through sign design that enhances the community."

The Twin Falls Zoning Code (TFZC) regulates signs in conformance with the City's Comprehensive Plan and its Building Code. Billboards are allowed only by special use permit. In order to issue a permit, the Planning and Zoning Commission (P&Z) must find that the billboards, in addition to meeting measurable size, height, and spacing requirements, meet six additional criteria listed in TFZC § 10-9-2(M)(4)(c) relating to traffic safety and visual impact.

In March 1995, Idaho Outdoor applied for a special use permit to erect a twelve by twenty-four foot, illuminated, double-faced billboard at 468 Addison Avenue West. P&Z held a hearing on the application the following month. Planning and Zoning staff recommended that the permit be denied, or, in the alternative, that a permit be issued subject to the condition that Idaho Outdoor remove two nonconforming billboards several hundred yards away. By a 5-2 vote, P&Z granted the special use permit conditioned on the removal of two other billboards.

Idaho Outdoor appealed to the City Council. The City Council initially voted 4-3 to deny the special use permit. Later, the City Council upheld P&Z's decision to issue a special use permit conditioned on the removal of the two nonconforming billboards.

Idaho Outdoor appealed the permit denial to the district court. In July 1996, the district court reversed the City Council's decision and remanded for new hearings. Citing Nollan v. California Coastal Comm'n, 483 U.S. 825 (1987), it held that any conditions on the special use permit must relate to the same property or the same billboard for which the permit was sought.

P&Z held a new hearing in September 1996. P&Z Staff used overhead projections to review the request from a planning and zoning perspective. Although finding that the area had many signs related to on-site businesses, P&Z members noted that the proposed billboard was larger than existing signs and not harmonious to the area. P&Z voted 5-1 to deny the special use permit.

Idaho Outdoor appealed to the City Council. At the hearing, staff showed pictures of the site and an Idaho Outdoor executive circulated competing computer-generated photographs. Two speakers representing Idaho Outdoor suggested that nearby on-site signs, as well as a building across the street, were taller than the proposed billboard. Two neighbors spoke against the proposed billboard, opposing it on the basis of visual blight, size, and potentially lowering property values. One specifically noted the visual effect at an entrance to the city.

Affirming P&Z's action, the City Council unanimously voted to deny the permit on the basis that it did not meet the visual impact requirements of TFZC § 10-9-2(M)(4)(c). The City Council found:

> The proposed sign will be twenty-two (22) to twenty-four (24) feet in height and twenty-four (24) feet in width, in an area where there are low level single story buildings and very few projections above the building lines. The proposed sign would stand out high above the existing skyline on property with only 106 feet of frontage on Addison Avenue West.

It concluded: "The sign is not compatible with building heights of the existing neighborhood and imposes a foreign and inharmonious element to the existing skyline. In addition, the proposed sign is inconsistent with the adopted Comprehensive Plan regarding gateway arterials."

Idaho Outdoor appealed to the district court. In October 1997, the district court reversed the City Council's decision and ordered the City to issue a special use permit. Although holding that there was sufficient evidence to support the City Council's findings of fact and that the City Council's denial of the special use permit was not arbitrary, capricious, or an abuse of discretion, the district court concluded that TFZC § 10-9-2(M)(4)(c) "contain[ed] insufficient objective and definite standards to guide the licensing authority in its decision" and thus was an unconstitutional prior restraint on commercial speech. The district court denied attorney fees to Idaho Outdoor.

The City appealed and Idaho Outdoor cross-appealed. In its notice of cross-appeal, Idaho Outdoor requested that the transcript and record include enumerated materials before the district court in the first district court proceeding. The City moved the district court to delete materials relating to the first district court proceeding. The district court denied the City's request.

II.
STANDARD OF REVIEW

The district court reviewed the City Council's permit denial in its appellate capacity pursuant to I.C. §§ 67-5279 and 67-6521(1)(d). This Court reviews the record independently of the district court's decision made in its appellate capacity.

We defer to the City Council's findings of fact unless those findings are clearly erroneous and unsupported by evidence in the record. We may not substitute our judgment for that of the City Council as to the weight of the evidence on factual matters.

A strong presumption of validity favors the actions of zoning authorities when applying and interpreting their own zoning ordinances. However, the City Council's zoning decision may be set aside if it (a) violates constitutional or statutory provisions; (b) exceeds the City Council's statutory authority; (c) is made upon unlawful procedure; (d) is not supported by substantial evidence on the record as a whole; or (e) is arbitrary, capricious, or an abuse of discretion. I.C. § 67-5279(3). Even if the City Council erred as above, this Court will affirm its action unless a substantial right of Idaho Outdoor has been prejudiced.

III.
ANALYSIS

The Permit Requirement of Twin Falls Zoning Code § 10-9-2(M)(4)(c)
Is Not an Unconstitutional Prior Restraint on Commercial Free Speech.

A court may set aside a zoning decision if it concludes that the decision violates constitutional provisions. I.C. § 67-5279(3)(a). The City Council denied Idaho Outdoor a special use permit, finding that the proposed billboard violated TFZC § 10-9-2(M)(4)(c)(5) because it was not compatible with building heights in the existing neighborhood and it imposed a foreign or inharmonious element to the existing skyline. The district court held that TFZC § 10-9-2(M)(4)(c) "contain[ed] insufficient objective and definite standards to guide the licensing authority in its decision" and was therefore an unconstitutional prior restraint on commercial speech in violation of the First Amendment.

Billboard advertising is a form of commercial free speech protected under the First Amendment. See Metromedia, Inc. v. City of San Diego, 453 U.S. 490, 501 (1981). When a medium is used for speech or expression, even content-neutral governmental restrictions on the medium are analyzed for their impact on the potential exercise of First Amendment rights. See City of Ladue v. Gilleo, 512 U.S. 43, 48 (1994); City of Lakewood v. Plain Dealer Publ'g Co., 486 U.S. 750, 769 (1988). As the U.S. Supreme Court has explained:

> Billboards combine communicative and noncommunicative aspects. As with other media, the government has legitimate interests in controlling the noncommunicative aspects of the medium but the First and Fourteenth Amendments foreclose a similar interest in controlling the communicative aspects. Because regulation of the noncommunicative aspects of a medium often impinges to some degree on the communicative aspects, it has been necessary for the courts to reconcile the government's regulatory interests with the individual's right to expression.

Metromedia, 453 U.S. at 502.

Governments may regulate commercial speech to implement a substantial governmental interest if the regulation directly advances that interest and reaches no further than necessary to accomplish the given objective. A city's appearance is a substantial government interest, *Metromedia*, 453 U.S. at 507-08, and cities may enact zoning ordinances to preserve aesthetics. A city may regulate the construction and placement of billboards for the purpose of preserving aesthetics even though aesthetic judgments are "necessarily subjective." *Metromedia*, 453 U.S. at 510. In addition, cities may place restrictions on billboards even if they permit identical on-site commercial advertising. *Metromedia*, 453 U.S. at 511.

Any restrictions placed on billboards, like all ordinances "subjecting the exercise of First Amendment freedoms to the prior restraint of a license," must have "narrow, objective, and definite standards to guide the licensing authority." Shuttlesworth v. City of Birmingham, 394 U.S. 147, 150-51 (1969). The regulations must be narrowly drawn so that zoning officials do not have "unbridled discretion" to permit or deny the exercise of First Amendment rights. *City of Lakewood*, 486 U.S. at 755.

In *Desert Outdoor Advertising*, 103 F.3d 814 (9th Cir. 1996), Moreno Valley city officials enacted zoning ordinances regulating billboards to improve community aesthetics. As in Twin Falls, billboards could not be erected until city officials issued a conditional use permit. Along with locational and structural considerations, Moreno Valley officials had to make findings of fact that "such a display will not have a harmful effect upon the health or welfare of the general public and will not be detrimental to the welfare of the general public and will not be detrimental to the aesthetic quality of the community or the surrounding land uses." *Id.* at 817. There is little similarity between the general standards promulgated by the Moreno Valley ordinance and the narrowly tailored standards of TFZC § 10-9-2(M)(4)(c). The Moreno Valley standards, such as "detrimental to the aesthetic quality of the community,"are even broader than the deliberately general standards promulgated by the City in its Comprehensive Plan (e.g., "[p]romote and encourage aesthetically pleasing approaches to the city."). They stand in sharp contrast to the specific findings required by TFZC § 10-9-2(M)(4)(c):

(1) That the location and placement of the sign will not endanger motorists.

(2) That the sign will not cover or blanket any prominent view of a structure or facade of historical or architectural significance.

(3) That the sign will not obstruct views of users of adjacent buildings to side yards, front yards or to open space.

(4) That the sign will not negatively impact the visual quality of a public open space as a public recreation facility, square, plaza, courtyard and the like.

(5) That the sign is compatible with building heights of the existing neighborhood and does not impose a foreign or inharmonious element to an existing skyline.

(6) That the sign's lighting will not cause hazardous or unsafe driving conditions for motorists.

When interpreting statutes or ordinances, this Court construes words and phrases according to context. Words must be given their plain, obvious, and rational meanings. The ordinance should be construed as a whole to give effect to the City's intent.

TFZC § 10-9-2(M)(4)(c) contains six provisions that require the Commission to exercise judgment in accordance with narrow and definite standards. The phrase "foreign or inharmonious element" in the ordinance is tied to language about the existing skyline and existing building heights of a neighborhood, and therefore provides a basis for reasoned judgment. The City Council's findings of fact illustrate that it was guided in its discretion by the language and context of the ordinance. The City Council found that the sign was incompatible with existing building heights and imposed a foreign and inharmonious element because: "[I]n an area where there are low level single story buildings and very few projections above the building lines, [t]he proposed sign would stand out high above the existing skyline on property with only 106 feet of frontage on Addison Avenue West."

We hold that TFZC § 10-9-2(M)(4)(c) contains sufficiently objective and definite standards to guide zoning officials in making zoning decisions, and is therefore not an unconstitutional prior restraint on commercial speech. Therefore, we reverse the judgment of the district court reversing the City Council's denial of a special use permit.

The City's Denial of the Special Use Permit Was Supported by Substantial Evidence, and Was Not Arbitrary, Capricious, or an Abuse of Discretion.

The district court held that there was sufficient evidence to support the City Council's factual finding that "[t]he proposed sign will be twenty-two (22) to twenty-four (24) feet in height in an area where there are low level single story buildings and very few projections above the building lines. The proposed sign would stand out high above the existing skyline." On cross-appeal, Idaho Outdoor contends that this finding was unsupported by substantial evidence. In addition, Idaho Outdoor contends that bias on the part of City Council members predisposed them to deny Idaho Outdoor's application regardless of facts in the record, and thus the City Council's permit denial was arbitrary, capricious, and an abuse of discretion.

This Court may set aside the decision of a zoning agency if the Court concludes that its findings, inferences, conclusions or decisions are not supported by substantial evidence on the record as a whole, or are arbitrary, capricious, or an abuse of discretion. I.C. § 67-5279(3)(d), (e). "Substantial and competent evidence" is "relevant evidence which a reasonable mind might accept to support a conclusion." Mancilla v. Greg, 963 P.2d 368, 370 (Idaho 1998).

The record establishes substantial evidence to support the City Council's decision. Staff introduced photographs and sketches showing the area with the proposed billboard superimposed on the view. One City Council member specifically challenged an Idaho Outdoor representative about his competing visual representation of the billboard, suggesting that it was drawn to look smaller than twelve feet by twenty-four feet. Objecting that a billboard of the proposed size was out of place, a neighbor noted that Addison Avenue property owners were not allowed to put even four-foot by eight-foot signs on their own properties. Another City Council member noted that, from the photographs, the sign could be considered harmonious when looking to the east, but not when looking to the west. Although no one challenged Idaho Outdoor's assertion that a building across the street exceeded the billboard's height, City Council members were free to draw their own conclusions by looking at the photographs.

Moreover, the hearing record does not support Idaho Outdoor's charge of arbitrary and capricious action. Staff originally recommended against granting the permit, but felt that its negative character would be outweighed if the company removed two nonconforming signs several hundred yards away. The City Council agreed. On remand from the first district court proceeding, the City Council denied the permit after holding hearings and discussing the evidence. Although a few comments by City Council members indicated an antipathy against billboards, the record indicates that City Council members viewed the photographs supplied both by staff and Idaho Outdoor and applied their reasoned judgment in denying the permit.

We affirm the district court's holding that the City Council's action was not arbitrary, capricious, an abuse of discretion, or unsupported by substantial evidence.

IV.
CONCLUSION

Twin Falls Zoning Code § 10-9-2(M)(4)(c) is not an unconstitutional prior restraint on commercial free speech; therefore, the district court's judgment setting aside the City Council's denial of the special use permit and ordering the City to issue a special use permit is reversed. We affirm the district court's ruling that substantial evidence supported the City Council's action.

Costs are awarded to the appellants.

NOTES AND QUESTIONS

1. **Zoning for aesthetics.** What are the arguments for and against, regarding aesthetics as a valid police power purpose?

2. **Challenges.** What are the possible constitutional bases of a challenge to an ordinance that regulates on the basis of aesthetic considerations? See Kenneth Regan, *You Can't Build That Here: The Constitutionality of Aesthetic Zoning and Architectural Review*, 58 Fordham L. Rev. 1013, 1024 (1990).

b. Exclusionary Zoning

Euclidean zoning is inherently exclusionary, barring commercial uses from preferred residential zones, and industrial uses from commercial zones. "Exclusionary zoning" as used in this section, however, has become something of a term of art, referring not to the exclusion of uses accomplished by the typical Euclidean zoning ordinance, but rather to the exclusion of individuals or groups from residential zones. The various zoning requirements that can have that effect, intended or not, are the subject of the next principal cases.

CASPERSEN v. TOWN OF LYME
661 A.2d 759 (N.H. 1995)

HORTON, JUSTICE.

The plaintiffs, Finn M.W. Caspersen and Barbara M. Caspersen, trustees, appeal a decision of the Superior Court upholding the validity of a zoning ordinance enacted by the defendant, Town of Lyme. On appeal, the plaintiffs argue that a provision in the ordinance that prohibits lot sizes of less than fifty acres in a mountain and forest district: (1) violates their substantive due process and equal protection rights under the State and Federal Constitutions; (2) is exclusionary; (3) violates New Hampshire's controlled growth statutes; and (4) was improperly adopted. We affirm.

The town is a rural community situated on the western edge of the State, roughly at the midpoint of the border between New Hampshire and Vermont. It is bounded on the west by the Connecticut River and on the east by mountainous, undeveloped terrain.

The plaintiffs own roughly 800 acres of land in the southeast corner of town, which they purchased between 1962 and 1990. They manage the property for forestry. For tax purposes, they keep all but a few acres classified as open space land. The plaintiffs have never attempted to develop their land and have no plans to do so.

In 1989, the town adopted a comprehensive zoning ordinance which is the subject of this appeal. In the years preceding the town's adoption of the zoning ordinance, the town passed numerous general ordinances regulating certain land uses. During the early 1980's, the town's planning board began developing a master plan pursuant to RSA 674:1-:4 (1986 & Supp.1994). In 1985, having completed the master plan, the town began work on a comprehensive zoning ordinance.

The first ordinance proposal was rejected by the voters. This proposal allowed only one dwelling per lot and prohibited subdivision. The voters were concerned about these provisions. The planning board, in the words of one of its members, "went back to the drawing board."

The present version of the zoning ordinance permits forestry and single family dwellings within the mountain and forest district. It establishes a minimum conforming lot size of fifty acres. The stated objectives of the mountain and forest district include: (1) encouraging the continuation of large tracts of forest land; (2) encouraging "forestry and timber harvesting," while permitting other compatible uses including low density development; (3) protecting wildlife habitat and natural area; and (4) avoiding unreasonable town expenses.

Two public hearings on the revised ordinance were held in January and February 1989. On March 6, 1989, the plaintiffs and other landowners from the proposed mountain and forest district submitted a protest petition to the town pursuant to RSA 675:5 (1986) (current version at RSA 675:5 (1986 & Supp.1994)). The revised ordinance was passed at a regular town meeting. Less than a two-thirds majority voted for its passage.

The plaintiffs challenged the ordinance. The town's board of selectmen held a rehearing but did not sustain the plaintiffs' challenge. The plaintiffs appealed to the superior court. Several town residents intervened in the action in support of the town. The superior court upheld the validity of the ordinance. This appeal followed.

Standing to Challenge Exclusionary Zoning

In their appeal to the superior court, the plaintiffs complained that the zoning ordinance is exclusionary because it effectively precludes development of low or moderate-income housing on their property in the mountain and forest district. The trial court ruled that the plaintiffs lacked standing to challenge the ordinance on that basis. We agree. The plaintiffs appealed to the superior court under the provisions of RSA 677:4. To have standing to take a direct statutory appeal from a zoning action of a legislative body, the appealing party must have been "aggrieved" by that action. RSA 677:4 (1986). Aggrievement is found when the appellant shows a direct definite interest in the outcome of the proceedings. The existence of this interest, and the resultant standing to appeal, is a factual determination in each case.

The plaintiffs own land in the mountain and forest district and, therefore, themselves, are not excluded from the area by the alleged exclusionary effect of the ordinance. Although they allege that the ordinance "makes it financially impracticable for developers to build affordable housing," they admit that they are not in the construction business and have no present or future intention to provide low or moderate-income housing on their own land. The plaintiffs' general interest in a diverse community is not sufficient to sustain their standing on this issue. Warth v. Seldin, 422 U.S. 490, 512-14 (1975). Based on the record below, we affirm the trial court's factual finding that the plaintiffs are not sufficiently aggrieved by the ordinance to challenge the alleged exclusionary effect of the ordinance on others.

Equal Protection and Substantive Due Process

The plaintiffs argue that the ordinance violates their substantive due process and equal protection rights under the State and Federal Constitutions without distinguishing between the two arguments. Consideration of the plaintiffs' substantive due process claim is appropriate. The plaintiffs' amended petition to appeal to the superior court, although not using the words, states a substantive due process claim and asserts an unconstitutional action. Further, a substantial portion of the trial record is devoted to the merits of a substantive due process claim. Such is not the case with any claim of equal protection. Other than under the subject of exclusionary zoning, which is dealt with above, there is no claim articulated, either in the amended petition to appeal or in the trial record, that the ordinance fails to provide equal protection to any person or class. There are passing and undeveloped references to equal protection in the plaintiffs' requests for findings of fact and rulings of law and a passing reference to equal protection in the order of the trial court. The plaintiffs' notice of appeal includes equal protection in its general challenge to the constitutionality of the ordinance, and the plaintiffs' brief makes a general claim that the equal protection clauses "protect individuals' property rights from unrestrained intrusion by the government in the form of zoning." Such a broad statement may be true of substantive due process, but it is hardly true of equal protection, in the case where the unrestrained intrusion is equally applied to all persons and classes. Therefore, we will address only whether the ordinance violates the plaintiffs' substantive due process rights.

In deciding this case, we first look to our own State Constitution, and then, if necessary, to the Federal Constitution to determine whether it provides the plaintiffs greater rights, citing decisions of federal courts and courts of other jurisdictions when helpful in analyzing and deciding the State issue. Because federal law is not more favorable to the plaintiffs in this case, we make no separate federal analysis. See Resolution Trust Corp. v. Town of Highland Beach, 18 F.3d 1536, 1549 (11th Cir.1994).

A substantive due process challenge questions the fundamental fairness of "local zoning ordinances both generally and in the relationship of the particular ordinance to particular property under particular conditions existing at the time of litigation." 1 E. Ziegler, Jr., Rathkopf's The Law of Zoning and Planning, § 3.01[1], at 3-3 (1994). "The appropriate inquiry for reviewing [a] substantive due process claim is whether the claimants proved that the provision constitutes a restriction on property rights that is not rationally related to the town's legitimate goals." Asselin v. Town of Conway, 628 A.2d 247, 250 (N.H. 1993). Given the presumption that a properly enacted zoning ordinance is valid, our analysis focuses on whether the record supports the trial court's decision upholding the ordinance.

The plaintiffs concede that the ordinance was passed for legitimate purposes, including to encourage forestry and timber harvesting in the mountain and forest district. Nevertheless, the plaintiffs maintain that the ordinance is constitutionally infirm because the record does not support the conclusion that the fifty-acre minimum lot size in the mountain and forest district is rationally related to the accomplishment of those goals. We disagree.

Robert Burke, an expert in forestry, testified that small lots create access problems because of the necessity to gain permission to cross abutting lots. He testified that "on small properties you don't have many opportunities for harvesting," and therefore "size has an important effect" on the profitability of forestry enterprises. Burke noted that on fifty acres, there are more opportunities for harvesting because you have the potential to grow enough different kinds of trees. He concluded that fifty acres is the minimum lot size where forestry becomes profitable. The evidence supports a finding that the fifty-acre minimum lot size in the mountain and forest district is rationally related to the town's legitimate goals of encouraging forestry and timber harvesting in that district. There is no arbitrary maximum lot size controlling a substantive due process analysis. The constitutionality of a lot size must be assessed in light of the town's zoning goals. See, e.g., Gisler v. County of Madera, 112 Cal.Rptr. 919, 921-22 (Cal. Ct. App. 1974) (eighteen acres for agricultural use); D & R Pipeline Const. Co. v. Greene County, 630 S.W.2d 236, 237 (Mo.Ct.App.1982) (ten acres for reservoir protection); Southern Burlington Cty. N.A.A.C.P. v. Mt. Laurel Tp., 456 A.2d 390, 471 (N.J. 1975) (five acres for open space); Oregonians in Action v. LCDC, 854 P.2d 1010, 1014-15 (Or. Ct. App. 1993) (eighty acres for new farm parcels); Codorus Tp. v. Rodgers, 492 A.2d 73, 75 (Pa. Commw. Ct. 1985) (fifty acres for agricultural use); see also Wis.Stat. § 91.75(1) (1992) (legislatively created thirty-five acre minimum for farmland preservation); National Agricultural Lands Study, The Protection of Farmland: A Reference Guidebook for State and Local Governments 114-16 (1981) (forty-five selected communities with agricultural minimum lot sizes ranging from ten to 640 acres, average being sixty-three acres). If a town's goals are legitimate, and a large minimum lot size a reasonable means of accomplishing those goals, then there is no constitutional violation.

Nor do we find support in the record for the plaintiffs' argument that the fifty-acre minimum is unreasonable when considered in a regional context. The plaintiffs did not offer evidence comparing the means and objectives of other towns with similar geographic characteristics. The mere fact that other towns in the state have minimum lot sizes less than fifty acres does not render the Lyme ordinance unconstitutional. Many of those zoning districts are, no doubt, residential or commercial in character. The fifty-acre minimum lot size would probably be invalid as applied to a residential or commercial zoning district. The primary objective of the mountain and forest district is the encouragement of the continuation of large tracts of forest land to promote "forestry and timber harvesting." Town of Lyme Zoning Ordinance, art. III, § 3.257 (1989).

Finally, we note that the plaintiffs have argued that the fifty-acre minimum lot size is unconstitutional because better alternatives exist to accomplish the town's goals of encouraging forestry and timber harvesting. An analysis of least restrictive alternatives is not part of a rational basis analysis. Heller v. Doe by Doe, 509 U.S. 312 (1993). We will not second-guess the town's choice of means to accomplish its legitimate goals, so long as the means chosen is rationally related to those goals.

Growth Control

The plaintiffs' final argument is that the ordinance is a growth control ordinance that did not comply with RSA 674:22 (1986). They maintain that the fifty-acre minimum operates as a growth control because it effectively halts development in one-half of the town's area, thereby restricting growth in the town as a whole.

RSA 674:22 provides:

The local legislative body may further exercise the powers granted under this subdivision to regulate and control the timing of development. Any ordinance imposing such a control may be adopted only after preparation and adoption by the planning board of a master plan and a capital improvement program and shall be based upon a growth control management process intended to assess and balance community development needs and consider regional development needs.

Growth control ordinances are intended "to regulate and control the timing of development." RSA 674:22. Applying this definition to this case, we hold that the Lyme ordinance is not a growth control ordinance pursuant to RSA 674:22. The ordinance places no time-related controls on the mountain and forest district. See, e.g., Stoney-Brook Dev. Corp. v. Town of Fremont, 474 A.2d 561 (N.H. 1984) (annual limits on building permits); Beck v. Town of Raymond, 394 A.2d 847 (N.H. 1978) (number of annual building permits based on town-wide annual growth rates). Nothing in the ordinance prevents development of the district to its full capacity immediately, albeit the density of such development would be lower in the mountain and forest district than in the other districts. "Any denial of subdivision approval will naturally have the secondary effect of limiting growth." Zukis v. Town of Fitzwilliam, 604 A.2d 956, 958 (N.H. 1992). RSA 674:22, however, does not apply to a zoning action merely because the zoning action has an effect on growth. The Lyme ordinance is not designed to "regulate and control the timing" of development in the town. We hold that RSA 674:22 is not applicable to this case and affirm the trial court's refusal to find that the "ordinance is an invalidly enacted growth control ordinance."

In summary, we hold that the plaintiffs lack standing to bring an exclusionary zoning claim, that the Lyme zoning ordinance was properly enacted under RSA chapter 675, that the provisions of the ordinance do not violate the plaintiffs' substantive due process rights, and that the ordinance is not a growth control ordinance pursuant to RSA 674:22. The trial court's decision is affirmed.

Affirmed.

BROCK, CHIEF JUSTICE, concurring specially.

I concur in the result reached by the majority in this case. I would reach a different result under the substantive due process analysis had the plaintiffs not conceded, at the trial court and on appeal, that the ordinance was passed for legitimate purposes. I would have a difficult time finding the "primary objective" of the ordinance, preserving and protecting a "heritage" of "large tracts of undeveloped forest land," to be a legitimate zoning purpose. I also fail to understand how a fifty-acre minimum lot size requirement on residential land relates to the encouragement of commercial forestry.

Further, I believe that, given an appropriate occasion, we should review our holding in Asselin v. Town of Conway, 628 A.2d 247 (N.H. 1993), that substantive due process challenges to zoning ordinances are evaluated under the rational basis standard, while equal protection challenges to those same ordinances are reviewed with heightened scrutiny. The constitutional guarantees of substantive due process and equal protection involve complementary concepts: If a challenged law burdens all persons equally when they exercise a particular right, we review the law under the due process clause, but if the law distinguishes between who may and may not exercise a particular right, then we review it under the equal protection guarantee. E.g., 2 R. Rotunda & J. Nowak, Treatise on Constitutional Law: Substance and Procedure § 15.4, at 400 (2d ed. 1992). The difference in analysis is not based on the individual right being exercised or infringed upon; it is, rather, based on the way that the challenged law or action operates on individuals. Under the United States Constitution, the identity of scrutiny seems never to have been challenged: "Analysis under the equal protection clause of the fourteenth amendment is identical to that used under the due process clauses." *Id.* § 14.7, at 370.

Ownership, use, and enjoyment of property are fundamental rights protected by both the State and Federal Constitutions. Zoning ordinances should be reviewed with heightened scrutiny, regardless of the nature of the constitutional challenge made to them.

ENGLISH v. AUGUSTA TOWNSHIP
514 N.W.2d 172 (Mich. Ct. App. 1994)

SHEPHERD, PRESIDING JUDGE.

Defendant appeals as of right from a judgment of the trial court ordering defendant to rezone plaintiffs' property from agricultural/residential (AR) to manufactured housing park (MHP). We affirm the trial court's conclusion that defendant engaged in exclusionary zoning, but vacate its order of rezoning and replace it with an injunction that defendant not interfere with plaintiffs' proposed use.

Plaintiffs own a forty-nine acre parcel of land on Whittaker Road in Augusta Township. In 1989, plaintiffs filed a petition with defendant seeking a change in the zoning classification of their property from AR to MHP for the purpose of constructing a mobile-home park. Defendant township denied plaintiffs' petition for rezoning. In response, plaintiffs filed a lawsuit in the Washtenaw Circuit Court against defendant, seeking monetary damages and a writ of mandamus to compel defendant to rezone their property to MHP.

At a bench trial, testimony revealed that while the township had no existing mobile-home parks, the township had zoned a ninety-six acre area for mobile homes. However, a former township zoning official testified that that particular area was chosen by the township board for MHP zoning because the board believed that it would never be developed. The township supervisor who owned eighty of the ninety-six acres in the MHP zone intended to have his family continue to operate the parcel as a farm. The MHP zone was located in the extreme southwest corner of the township, away from available water and sewer systems. A toxic-waste landfill was located immediately adjacent to the MHP zone, and a federal prison at Milan was just three-quarters of a mile away. The former township zoning official testified that he was pressured by the township board to keep manufactured housing out of the township, despite inquiries by a number of developers. There was also testimony that the building department was under pressure to limit the issuance of permits for low-cost housing in general. The township planner who examined plaintiffs' application for rezoning testified that the township considered itself a rural residential and agricultural community, and it did not need a mobile-home park.

With respect to plaintiffs' proposed development, there was testimony that a nearby water line could provide adequate pressure and volume for a mobile-home park via an extension. The nearby sewer system was not capable of handling the additional volume; however, the system could handle the additional volume with an expansion of two pump stations. Topographically, plaintiffs' property is suitable for development, with the exception of a lowland swale that cuts roughly across the middle. According to the township's master plan, the larger portion of plaintiffs' property north of the swale was to have a density of five to seven units an acre, while the southern portion was to remain agricultural. Plaintiffs' proposal to the township was for approximately five to seven units an acre over the entire parcel, excluding the wetlands area. Roadways would have to be built for the mobile-home development; however, the construction of roads would also be necessary for any other development of similar density. The local roads were found sufficient to handle the proposed development.

Following the bench trial, the trial court issued its written findings of fact and conclusions of law. The trial court found that defendant had, in effect, unconstitutionally excluded mobile-home parks from the township by relegating mobile homes to an undevelopable area. Further, the trial court found that plaintiffs had demonstrated a demand for their proposed use, and that plaintiffs' parcel was suitable for a mobile-home park. Subsequently, the trial court ordered defendant to rezone plaintiffs' property from AR to MHP. Herein, defendant appeals as of right from that order.

I. EXCLUSIONARY ZONING

The Legislature addressed the problem of exclusionary zoning with the enactment of § 27a of the Township Rural Zoning Act, M.C.L. § 125.297a; M.S.A. § 5.2963(27a), which provides:

> A zoning ordinance or zoning decision shall not have the effect of totally prohibiting the establishment of a land use within a township in the presence of a demonstrated need for that land use within either the township or surrounding area within the state, unless there is no location within the township where the use may be appropriately located, or the use is unlawful.

An ordinance that has the effect of totally prohibiting a particular land use within a township is impermissible in the absence of special circumstances. M.C.L. § 125.297a; M.S.A. § 5.2963(27a). A zoning ordinance that totally excludes an otherwise legitimate use carries with it a strong taint of unlawful discrimination and a denial of equal protection of the law with regard to the excluded use.

A zoning ordinance may not totally exclude a lawful land use where (1) there is a demonstrated need for the land use in the township or surrounding area, and (2) the use is appropriate for the location. Eveline Twp. v. H & D Trucking Co., 448 N.W.2d 727 (Mich. Ct. App. 1989). Applying the rule to the facts of the case at bar, we agree with the trial court's conclusion that defendant engaged in exclusionary zoning.

Defendant argues that the existence of the site presently zoned MHP requires a finding that mobile-home parks are not totally excluded from the township. However, there was ample evidence that the zoning of that parcel for mobile homes was nothing less than a subterfuge for the township's unwritten policy of excluding mobile-home parks altogether. As noted above, the township board chose the site because they believed that it would never be developed. The township supervisor owned the vast majority of the site, fully intending to continue to operate the property as a family farm. In addition, the site was inappropriate for its zoned use because of the unavailability of water and sewer service and its proximity to a toxic-waste landfill and a federal prison. Thus, in effect, the township has designated no appropriate site for a mobile-home park.[1]

Under the first prong of the test set forth in *Eveline Twp.*, there was evidence of the need for a mobile-home park in the township. There was testimony that numerous developers inquired about developing a mobile-home park, but they were turned away because of the township's unwritten policy of exclusion. There was also testimony that township officials exerted pressure to limit low-cost housing in general. Thus, we will not disturb the trial court's finding that there was a need or demand for the use within the township.

Further, under the second factor outlined in *Eveline Twp.*, there was evidence that the use was appropriate for the proposed location. Plaintiffs' proposed development was near an existing water line with sufficient pressure and volume. Sewer service was feasible with an upgrade of two pumping stations. With respect to the larger portion of the property north of the swale, the proposed development would have the same density as previously contemplated by the township under the AR zoning classification. With respect to the southern portion of plaintiffs' property that was slated by the township for agricultural use, there is no discernible reason for the distinction other than to create an arbitrary boundary along the path of the swale.[2] The southern portion is similar in all other respects to the northern portion. Further, local roads were found sufficient. Again, we agree with the conclusion of the trial court that the proposed use was appropriate for the location. Thus, there was evidence to support both prongs of the test set out in *Eveline Twp.*

In summary, we agree with the decision of the trial court that defendant engaged in exclusionary zoning in violation of M.C.L. § 125.297a; M.S.A. § 5.2963(27a).

II. REMEDY

Having determined that defendant has improperly engaged in exclusionary zoning, the question of plaintiffs' remedy remains. The trial court ordered

---

[1] Currently, there are no mobile-home parks in the township.

[2] The swale does not appear to be such a significant topographical feature that a well-designed site plan could not work around it.

defendant to rezone plaintiffs' property from AR to MHP. However, we believe that the trial court went too far in fashioning a remedy.

It is not a novel proposition that zoning cases often present issues concerning the doctrine of separation of powers, because zoning classifications are determined by local legislative bodies. In the past, our Supreme Court has cautioned against judicial zoning or rezoning as infringing upon the separation of powers. Most recently, in Schwartz v. City of Flint, 395 N.W.2d 678 (Mich. 1986), our Supreme Court overruled its decision in Ed Zaagman, Inc. v. City of Kentwood, 277 N.W.2d 475 (Mich. 1979), which had allowed courts to determine and implement the most equitable or "midsatisfactory use" of a parcel of land. Our Supreme Court in *Schwartz* expressed strong sentiments against judicial zoning of any kind.

We recognize that the *Schwartz* decision was limited to cases involving an unconstitutional application of a zoning ordinance to a particular parcel. The Supreme Court noted that cases of exclusionary zoning involved "an entirely different type of determination, necessitating potentially broader relief." However, the Supreme Court did not explain what that "potentially broader relief" might be.

Accordingly, in light of the strong language in *Schwartz* prohibiting any form of judicial zoning, we conclude that the trial court went too far when it ordered defendant to change the zoning classification of plaintiffs' property. Thus, we vacate the trial court's order requiring defendant to rezone plaintiffs' property from AR to MHP.

However, while we vacate the trial court's order, we do not leave plaintiffs without any relief. Instead, we fashion a remedy in accordance with *Schwartz*. The abundant record in this case not only supports the trial court's finding that plaintiffs' property was suitable for the proposed use under the test for exclusionary zoning, *Eveline Twp.*, but also that plaintiffs' proposal was a "specific reasonable use" under the standard adopted in *Schwartz*. Stated differently, while the trial court did not specifically analyze the present case in light of *Schwartz*, the trial court's findings nevertheless make it clear that plaintiffs have satisfied the burden of demonstrating that the mobile-home park was a "specific reasonable use." Notably, while a proposed use must be specific, "it need not amount to a 'plan,' " according to *Schwartz*.

Thus, we remand this matter to the trial court with instructions to enter an injunction prohibiting defendant from interfering with plaintiffs' reasonable, proposed use of their property as a mobile-home park. However, we note that our decision does not exempt plaintiffs from complying with all applicable federal, state, and local regulations governing mobile-home parks. In particular, plaintiffs are not exempt from the site-plan review process. Further, plaintiffs may be required to contribute to certain costs for the construction and maintenance of the development's infrastructure. We express no opinion regarding such details, which may necessitate additional public hearings in the township and in the trial court.

The decision of the trial court that defendant engaged in exclusionary zoning is affirmed. The trial court's order of rezoning is vacated, with instructions to enter an injunction preventing defendant from interfering with plaintiffs' specific reasonable use of their property as a mobile-home park.

NOTES AND QUESTIONS

1. **An influential dissent.** In Vickers v. Gloucester Twp., 181 A.2d 129 (N.J. 1962), the court upheld an ordinance relegating trailer camps to the industrial district, which had the effect of prohibiting trailer camps throughout the township. The case is famous for the vigorous dissent of Justice Hall:

> In my opinion legitimate use of the zoning power by municipalities does not encompass the right to erect barricades on their boundaries through exclusion or too tight restriction of uses where the real purpose is to prevent feared disruption with a so-called way of life. Nor does it encompass provisions designed to let in as new residents only certain kinds of people, or those who can afford to live in favored kinds of housing, or to keep down tax bills of present property owners. When one of the above is the true situation deeper considerations intrinsic to a free society gain the ascendancy and courts must not be hesitant to strike down purely selfish and undemocratic enactments. The opportunity to live in the open spaces in decent housing one can afford and in the manner one desires is a vital one in a democracy.

> Trailer living is a perfectly respectable, healthy and useful kind of housing, adopted by choice by several million people in this country today. Municipalities and courts can no longer refuse to recognize its proper and significant place in today's society and should stop acting on the basis of old wives' tales.

Id. at 147-48.

2. **"Certain kinds of people."** Who is excluded from living in a community when mobile homes are banned? How does the exclusion of mobile homes keep down the tax bills of present property owners?

BRITTON v. TOWN OF CHESTER
595 A.2d 492 (N.H. 1991)

BATCHELDER, JUSTICE.

In this appeal, the defendant, the Town of Chester (the town), challenges a ruling by the Master approved by the Superior Court, that the Chester Zoning Ordinance is invalid and unconstitutional. In addition, the town argues that the relief granted to plaintiff Remillard, permitting him to construct multi-family housing on a parcel not currently zoned for such development, violates the separation of powers provision of the New Hampshire Constitution, N.H. Const. pt. I, art. 37, and creates an unreasonable use for this parcel. We modify the trial court's ruling that the ordinance as a whole is invalid, but we affirm the granting of specific relief to plaintiff Remillard as well as the court's ruling that the ordinance, on the facts of this case, is unlawful as applied.

The plaintiffs brought a petition in 1985, for declaratory and injunctive relief, challenging the validity of the multi-family housing provisions of the Chester Zoning Ordinance. The master's report, filed after a hearing, contains extensive factual findings which we summarize here. The town of Chester lies in the west-central portion of Rockingham County, thirteen miles east of the city of Manchester. Primary highway access is provided by New Hampshire Routes 102 and 121. The available housing stock is principally single-family homes. There is no municipal sewer or water service, and other municipal services remain modest. The town has not encouraged industrial or commercial development; it is a "bedroom community," with the majority of its labor force commuting to Manchester. Because of its close proximity to job centers and the ready availability of vacant land, the town is projected to have among the highest growth rates in New Hampshire over the next two decades.

The United States Department of Housing and Urban Development, having settled upon the median income for non-metropolitan Rockingham County as a yardstick, has determined that a low-income family in Chester is a household with annual earnings of $16,500 or less, and a moderate-income family has annual earnings of $16,501 to $25,680. Various federal and State government agencies have also determined that low- and moderate-income families should not pay in excess of 30% of their gross income for rent. Thus, a low-income family in Chester should pay less than $4,950 annually, and a moderate-income family in Chester should pay between $4,951 and $7,704 annually, for housing.

The plaintiffs in this case are a group of low- and moderate-income people who have been unsuccessful in finding affordable, adequate housing in the town, and a builder who, the master found, is committed to the construction of such housing. At trial, two plaintiffs testified as representative members of the group of low- and moderate-income people. Plaintiff George Edwards is a woodcutter who grew up in the town. He lives in Chester with his wife and three minor children in a one-bedroom, thirty-foot by eight-foot camper trailer with no running water. Their annual income is $14,040, which places them in the low-income category. Roger McFarland grew up and works in the town. He lives in Derry with his wife and three teenage children in a two-bedroom apartment which is too small to meet their needs. He and his wife both work, and their combined annual income is $24,000. Under the area standards, the McFarlands are a moderate-income family. Raymond Remillard is the plaintiff home builder. A long-time resident of the town, he owns an undeveloped twenty-three-acre parcel of land on Route 102 in the town's eastern section. Since 1979, he has attempted to obtain permission from the town to build a moderate-sized multi-family housing development on his land.

The zoning ordinance in effect at the beginning of this action in 1985 provided for a single-family home on a two-acre lot or a duplex on a three-acre lot, and it excluded multi-family housing from all five zoning districts in the town. In July, 1986, the town amended its zoning ordinance to allow multi-family housing. Article six of the amended ordinance now permits multi-family housing as part of a "planned residential development" (PRD), a form of multi-family housing required to include a variety of housing types, such as single-family homes, duplexes, and multi-family structures.

After a hearing, the master recommended that judgment be ordered for the plaintiffs; that the town's land use ordinances, including the zoning ordinance, be ruled invalid; and that plaintiff Remillard be awarded a "builder's remedy." We will uphold the findings and rulings of a court-approved master's recommendation unless they are unsupported by the evidence or are erroneous as a matter of law. "The test on appeal is not whether we would have found as the master did, but whether there was evidence on which he could reasonably base his finding." Lake Sunapee Protective Assoc. v. N.H. Wetlands Bd., 574 A.2d 1368, 1373 (N.H. 1990).

We first turn to the ordinance itself, because it does, on its face, permit the type of development that the plaintiffs argue is being prohibited. The master found, however, that the ordinance placed an unreasonable barrier to the development of affordable housing for low- and moderate-income families. Under the ordinance, PRDs are allowed on tracts of not less than twenty acres in two designated "R-2" (medium-density residential) zoning districts. Due to existing home construction and environmental considerations, such as wetlands and steep slopes, only slightly more than half of all the land in the two R-2 districts could reasonably be used for multi-family development. This constitutes only 1.73% of the land in the town. This fact standing alone does not, in the confines of this case, give rise to an entitlement to a legal remedy for those who seek to provide multi-family housing. However, it does serve to point out that the two R-2 districts are, in reality, less likely to be developed than would appear from a reading of the ordinance. A reviewing court must read the entire ordinance in the light of these facts.

Article six of the ordinance also imposes several subjective requirements and restrictions on the developer of a PRD. Any project must first receive the approval of the town planning board as to "whether in its judgment the proposal meets the objectives and purposes set forth [in the ordinance] in which event the Administrator [i.e., the planning board] may grant approval to [the] proposal subject to reasonable conditions and limitations." Consequently, the ordinance allows the planning board to control various aspects of a PRD without reference to any objective criteria. One potentially onerous section permits the planning board to "retain, at the applicant's expense, a registered professional engineer, hydrologist, and any other applicable professional to represent the [planning board] and assist the [planning board] in determining compliance with [the] ordinance and other applicable regulations." The master found such subjective review for developing multi-family housing to be a substantial disincentive to the creation of such units, because it would escalate the economic risks of developing affordable housing to the point where these projects would not be realistically feasible. In addition, we question the availability of bank financing for such projects, where the developer is required to submit a "blank check" to the planning board along with his proposal, and where to do so could halt, change the character of, or even bankrupt the project.

The defendant first argues that the trial court erred in ruling that the zoning ordinance exceeds the powers delegated to the town by the zoning enabling legislation, RSA 674:16-30. In support of this argument, the town asserts that the zoning enabling act does not require it to zone for the low-income housing needs of the region beyond its boundaries. Further, the town maintains that even if it were required to consider regional housing needs when enacting its zoning ordinance, the Chester Zoning Ordinance is valid because it provides for an adequate range of housing types. These arguments fail to persuade us of any error in the master's proposed order.

RSA 674:16 authorizes the local legislative body of any city or town to adopt or amend a zoning ordinance "[f]or the purpose of promoting the health, safety, or *the general welfare of the community*." (Emphasis added.) The defendant asserts that the term "community" as used in the statute refers only to the municipality itself and not to some broader region in which the municipality is situated. We disagree.

The possibility that a municipality might be obligated to consider the needs of the region outside its boundaries was addressed early on in our land use jurisprudence by the United States Supreme Court, paving the way for the term "community" to be used in the broader sense. In Village of Euclid v. Ambler Realty Co., 272 U.S. 365 (1926), the Court recognized "the possibility of cases where the general public interest would so far outweigh the interest of the municipality that the municipality would not be allowed to stand in the way." *Id.* at 390. When an ordinance will have an impact beyond the boundaries of the municipality, the welfare of the entire affected region must be considered in determining the ordinance's validity.

We have previously addressed the issue of whether municipalities are required to consider regional needs when enacting zoning ordinances which control growth. In Beck v. Town of Raymond, 394 A.2d 847, 852 (N.H. 1978), we held that "[growth] controls must not be imposed simply to exclude outsiders, especially outsiders of any disadvantaged social or economic group, see Southern Burlington County N.A.A.C.P. v. Township of Mount Laurel, 336 A.2d 713 (N.J. 1975) [*Mt. Laurel I*]." We reasoned that "each municipality [should] bear its fair share of the burden of increased growth." Today, we pursue the logical extension of the reasoning in *Beck* and apply its rationale and high purpose to zoning regulations which wrongfully exclude persons of low-income or moderate-income from the zoning municipality.

In *Beck*, this court sent a message to zoning bodies that "[t]owns may not refuse to confront the future by building a moat around themselves and pulling up the drawbridge." The town of Chester appears willing to lower that bridge only for people who can afford a single-family home on a two-acre lot or a duplex on a three-acre lot. Others are realistically prohibited from crossing.

Municipalities are not isolated enclaves, far removed from the concerns of the area in which they are situated. As subdivisions of the State, they do not exist solely to serve their own residents, and their regulations should promote the general welfare, both within and without their boundaries. Therefore, we interpret the general welfare provision of the zoning enabling statute, RSA 674:16, to include the welfare of the "community," as defined in this case, in which a municipality is located and of which it forms a part.

A municipality's power to zone property to promote the health, safety, and general welfare of the community is delegated to it by the State, and the municipality must, therefore, exercise this power in conformance with the enabling legislation. Because the Chester Zoning Ordinance does not provide for the lawful needs of the community, in that it flies in the face of the general welfare provision of RSA 674:16 and is, therefore, at odds with the statute upon which it is grounded, we hold that, as applied to the facts of this case, the ordinance is an invalid exercise of the power delegated to the town pursuant to RSA 674:16-30. We so hold because of the master's finding that "there are no substantial and compelling reasons that would warrant the Town of Chester, through its land use ordinances, from fulfilling its obligation to provide low-income and moderate-income families within the community and a proportionate share of same within its region from a realistic opportunity to obtain affordable housing."

The town further asserts that the trial court erred in ruling that the zoning ordinance is repugnant to the New Hampshire Constitution, part I, articles 2 and 12, and part II, article 5. In keeping with our longstanding policy against reaching a constitutional issue in a case that can be decided on other grounds, however, we do not reach the defendant's constitutional arguments. The trial court's order declared the Chester Zoning Ordinance invalid and unconstitutional; as a result, but for this appeal, the town has been left "unzoned." To leave the town with no land use controls would be incompatible with the orderly development of the general community, and the court erred when it ruled the ordinance invalid. It is not, however, within the power of this court to act as a super zoning board. "Zoning is properly a legislative function, and courts are prevented by the doctrine of separation of powers from invasion of this field." Godfrey v. Zoning Bd. of Adjustment, 344 S.E.2d 272, 276 (N.C. 1986). Moreover, our decision today is limited to those sections of the zoning ordinance which hinder the construction of multi-family housing units. Accordingly, we defer to the legislative body of the town, within a reasonable time period, to bring these sections of its zoning ordinance into line with the zoning enabling legislation and with this opinion. Consequently, we will temporarily allow the zoning ordinance to remain in effect.

As to the specific relief granted to plaintiff Remillard, the town contends that the court's order effectively rezones the parcel in violation of the separation of powers provision found in part I, article 37 of the New Hampshire Constitution. It further asserts that, even if it were lawful for a court to rezone or grant specific relief, plaintiff Remillard's proposed development does not qualify for such a remedy.

The master found that the requirement that multi-family housing may be built only as part of a PRD containing a variety of housing types violated plaintiff Remillard's rights under the equal protection clause of the New Hampshire Constitution, part I, article 2. The master also found that plaintiff Remillard was "unalterably committed to develop [his] tract to accommodate low- and moderate-income families." Accordingly, he granted specific relief to plaintiff Remillard, ordering that the town allow him to build his development as proposed.

The trial court has the power, subject to our review for abuse of discretion, to order definitive relief for plaintiff Remillard. In Soares v. Town of Atkinson, 529 A.2d 867 (N.H. 1987), we upheld the master's finding that granting a "builder's remedy," i.e., allowing the plaintiff builder to complete his project as proposed, is discretionary. Although we there upheld the decision that such relief was inappropriate, noting that the master determined that the ordered revision of the town ordinances would permit the building of the plaintiff's project, we did not reject such relief as a proper remedy in appropriate zoning cases. In this appeal, the master found such relief to be appropriate, and the town has not carried its burden on appeal to persuade us to the contrary. A successful plaintiff is entitled to relief which rewards his or her efforts in testing the legality of the ordinance and prevents retributive action by the municipality, such as correcting the illegality but taking pains to leave the plaintiff unbenefitted. The Pennsylvania Supreme Court reasoned in Casey v. Zoning Board of Warwick Township, 328 A.2d 464, 469 (Pa. 1974), that "[t]o forsake a challenger's reasonable development plans after all the time, effort and capital invested in such a challenge is grossly inequitable."

The master relied on Southern Burlington County N.A.A.C.P. v. Township of Mount Laurel, 456 A.2d 390 (N.J. 1983), (*Mt. Laurel II*), in determining that plaintiff Remillard was entitled to build his development as proposed. In *Mount Laurel I*, the New Jersey Supreme Court held that the municipality's zoning ordinance violated the general welfare provision of its State Constitution by not affording a realistic opportunity for the construction of its "fair share" of the present and prospective regional need for low- and moderate-income housing. *Mt. Laurel II* was a return to the New Jersey Supreme Court, eight years later, prompted by the realization that *Mt. Laurel I* had not resulted in realistic housing opportunities for low- and moderate-income people, but in "paper, process, witnesses, trials and appeals." *Mt. Laurel II*, 456 A.2d at 410. The court noted that the "builder's remedy," which effectively grants a building permit to a plaintiff/developer, based on the development proposal, as long as other local regulations are followed, should be made more readily available to insure that low- and moderate-income housing is actually built.

Since 1979, plaintiff Remillard has attempted to obtain permission to build a moderate-sized multi-family housing development on his land in Chester. He is committed to setting aside a minimum of ten of the forty-eight units for low- and moderate-income tenants for twenty years. "Equity will not suffer a wrong without a remedy." 2 Pomeroy's Equity Jurisprudence § 423 (5th ed. 1941). Hence, we hold that the "builder's remedy" is appropriate in this case, both to compensate the developer who has invested substantial time and resources in pursuing this litigation, and as the most likely means of insuring that low- and moderate-income housing is actually built.

Although we determine that the "builder's remedy" is appropriate in this case, we do not adopt the *Mt. Laurel* analysis for determining whether such a remedy will be granted. Instead, we find the rule developed in Sinclair Pipe Line Co. v. Richton Park, 167 N.E.2d 406 (Ill. 1960), is the better rule as it eliminates the calculation of arbitrary mathematical quotas which *Mt. Laurel* requires. That rule is followed with some variation by the supreme courts of several other states, and awards relief to the plaintiff builder if his development is found to be reasonable, i.e., providing a realistic opportunity for the construction of low- and moderate-income housing and consistent with sound zoning concepts and environmental concerns. Once an existing zoning ordinance is found invalid in whole or in part, whether on constitutional grounds or, as here, on grounds of statutory construction and application, the court may provide relief in the form of a declaration that the plaintiff builder's proposed use is reasonable, and the municipality may not interfere with it. The plaintiff must bear the burden of proving reasonable use by a preponderance of the evidence. Once the plaintiff's burden has been met, he will be permitted to proceed with the proposed development, provided he complies with all other applicable regulations.

The town's argument that the specific relief granted to plaintiff Remillard violates the separation of powers provision found in part I, article 37 of the New Hampshire Constitution, to the extent that the trial court exercised legislative power specifically delegated to the local zoning authority, is without merit. The rule we adopt today does not produce this result. See Opinion of the Justices, 431 A.2d 783, 785-86 (N.H. 1981) ("complete separation of powers would interfere with the efficient operation of government consequently there must be some overlapping of the power of each branch"). This rule will permit the municipality to continue to control its own development, so long as it does so for the general welfare of the community. It will also accommodate the construction of low- and moderate-income housing that had been unlawfully excluded.

The town argues that plaintiff Remillard's proposed use of his property is not reasonable, and that the master erred in implicitly finding to the contrary, as it would be constructed atop a potential high-yield aquifer. During the hearing before the master, plaintiff Remillard's expert concluded that the proposed development would not adversely affect any aquifer, and the town's engineering expert agreed. The master made a specific finding that any wells, streams, and aquifers would be protected by the project as proposed. Because we determine that the master did not abuse his discretion or err as a matter of law, we uphold his finding with respect to the reasonableness of the proposed project.

The zoning ordinance evolved as an innovative means to counter the problems of uncontrolled growth. It was never conceived to be a device to facilitate the use of governmental power to prevent access to a municipality by "outsiders of any disadvantaged social or economic group." *Beck*, 394 A.2d at 852. The town of Chester has adopted a zoning ordinance which is blatantly exclusionary. This court will not condone the town's conduct.

Affirmed in part and reversed in part.

NOTES AND QUESTIONS

1. **Challenges to an exclusionary ordinance.** What are some possible constitutional arguments against an ordinance that is allegedly exclusionary? *See* Village of Arlington Heights v. Metropolitan Housing Development Corp., 429 U.S. 252, 265 (1977) (holding that a violation of the federal Equal Protection Clause requires proof of "discriminatory intent or purpose").

2. **Federal and state challenges.** What are some differences between a challenge to an allegedly exclusionary zoning ordinance based on the federal Constitution and on a state constitution? Is it significant that the federal Constitution limits federal jurisdiction to "cases or controversies"? That there is no federal constutitional right to housing? *See* Lindsey v. Normet, 405 U.S. 56, 68-69 (1972).

3. **Remedies.** What remedies are available if a court finds that an ordinance is exclusionary? (Think in particular of Britton v. Town of Chester, and its discussion of the New Jersey *Mt. Laurel* cases.)

4. **Conclusion of the Mt. Laurel litigation.** The principal case discusses the *Mt. Laurel I* and *Mt. Laurel II* decisions. "Finally, in 1997, Mount Laurel

approved a rental complex of 140 town houses for low- and moderate-income families, apparently ending the twenty-six year legal battle." Keith Sealing, *Dear Landlord: Please Don't Put a Price on My Soul: Teaching Property Law Students that "Property Rights Serve Human Values,"* 5 N.Y. City L. Rev. 35, 82 (2002) (citing Ronald Smothers, *Ending Battle, Suburb Allows Home for Poor*, New York Times, Apr. 12, 1997, at A-21).

c.   Restrictions on the "Family"

This section continues the topic of the previous one, in that the definition of "family" in ordinances establishing single-family use zones can also have an exclusionary effect on unwanted individuals or groups. Perhaps because of the attention that the Supreme Court has given to the area, "family" restrictions are something of a recognized subset of exclusionary zoning cases, and are treated as such here. (The relevant Supreme Court cases are reviewed in the principal case below.)

DINAN v. BOARD OF ZONING APPEALS
595 A.2d 864 (Conn. 1991)

SHEA, ASSOCIATE JUSTICE.

The plaintiffs, James and Darlene Dinan, appealed from a decision of the defendant board of zoning appeals of the town of Stratford (board) sustaining a cease and desist order of the zoning enforcement officer that directed them to terminate the use of their property, which is located in a single-family residence zone of Stratford, as a rooming house. The trial court sustained the appeal, holding, inter alia, that the definition of "family" in § 1.18 of the Stratford zoning regulations as "[a]ny number of individuals related by blood, marriage or adoption, living together as a single housekeeping unit" was invalid because: (1) it exceeded the authority conferred on municipalities to establish zoning districts; and (2) violated the due process and equal protection clauses of our state constitution "in that [it] discriminate[s] against individuals based on biological or legal relationships."

In its appeal from that judgment, the defendant board presents as the principal issue the propriety of the ruling that a zoning restriction limiting the use of residences in single-family zones solely to families composed of persons related by blood, marriage or adoption is not authorized by the enabling act and violates our state constitutional provisions concerning due process of law and equal protection. We conclude that, as applied in this instance to the occupancy of each floor of the plaintiffs' two-family house by a group of five unrelated persons, § 1.18 of the Stratford zoning regulations is not ultra vires of the zoning authority given to towns by the enabling act and does not offend our state constitution. We also resolve the remaining issues in favor of the board. Accordingly, we reverse the judgment and remand the case with direction to dismiss the plaintiffs' appeal.

The memorandum of decision contains no finding of subordinate facts, but the statements of facts in the briefs are unchallenged and we rely upon them. The plaintiffs own a two-family house located in a single-family residence zone, which, as the board concedes, satisfies the requirements for a legal nonconforming use as a residence for two families. Each of the two floors of the house is occupied by five unrelated persons, each occupant having a separate rental arrangement with the plaintiffs, who do not reside on the premises. The two floors of the building constitute separate apartments or housekeeping units within which the occupants share common cooking and bathroom facilities. There are eleven striped parking spaces on the property which are available to the ten occupants.

On January 20, 1989, the Stratford zoning enforcement officer ordered the plaintiffs to cease using their property as a rooming house rather than as a residence for two families. The plaintiffs appealed from this order to the board, claiming that the definition of "family" in § 1.18 of the zoning regulations is unauthorized by the enabling act and violates our state and federal constitutions. The board denied the appeal and upheld the zoning enforcement officer in his interpretation of the regulations.

The plaintiffs appealed from the decision of the board to the Superior Court, raising the ultra vires and constitutional issues set forth in their application to the board as well as some additional issues. The trial court sustained the appeal, declaring the definition of "family" in § 1.18 to be invalid as beyond the statutory zoning authority given to municipalities and violative of our state constitution. The court also concluded that § 4.1.4[2] of the zoning regulations, which allows "[t]he letting of rooms to not more than two persons in addition to the family of the occupant of the family dwelling unit" and "a total of not more than five persons" as roomers "without table board" with the permission of the planning and zoning commission, was inapplicable to the property of the plaintiffs, who do not reside on the premises. On this basis the actions of the board were characterized as "arbitrary, capricious and illegal."

On the grant of certification by the Appellate Court pursuant to General Statutes § 8-8(o), the board filed an appeal in that court, which we have transferred to this court. General Statutes § 51-199(c); Practice Book § 4023. In addition to the principal issue of the validity of the provision of the regulation defining "family" to include only related persons, the board also challenges certain conclusions that the court may have reached, not contained in the memorandum of decision, which relate to whether the plaintiffs' property is being operated as a rooming house.

I

The trial court concluded that the definition of "family" in § 1.18 of the zoning regulations "is invalid in that it is not related to any objective established" by

---

[2] "[Stratford Zoning Regulations §] 4.1.4. The letting of rooms to not more than two persons in addition to the family of the occupant of the family dwelling unit, provided that the commission, may with the approval of the health officer, grant permission for the letting of rooms without table board, to a total of not more than five persons. All dwelling units legally occupied by more than 5 but not more than 8 roomers at the time of adoption of these regulations may be continued as nonconforming uses at the same locations."

General Statutes § 8-2,[3] which sets forth the subjects that a zoning commission of a municipality may regulate, estalishes standards for such regulations and states various objectives and concerns to be weighed in their enactment. "Under our law, a municipality, as a creation of the state, has no inherent powers of its own." Capalbo v. Planning & Zoning Board of Appeals, 547 A.2d 528 (Conn. 1988). The power to enact a particular zoning regulation must be found in the zoning enabling statute, § 8-2.

The plaintiffs do not challenge the authority of the town to establish districts or zones to be used only for single-family residences, such as the zone in which their property is located. "The limitation that a residence may not be used by more than one family is not uncommon in zoning jurisprudence" and has been upheld implicitly by this court. Planning & Zoning Commission v. Synanon Foundation, Inc., 216 A.2d 442 (Conn. 1966). Their attack upon the validity of § 1.18 is confined for the most part to its restriction of the term "family" to persons "related by blood, marriage or adoption," thus excluding groups of unrelated persons that may possibly function in the same manner as a traditional family of related persons so far as the community is concerned. This claim, however, is more directly related to due process concerns involving the rationality of zoning classifications than to the ultra vires question of the scope of the enabling act. If there is a reasonable basis to support the separate treatment for zoning purposes of families of related individuals as compared to groups of unrelated individuals, the broad grant of authority conferred by § 8-2 to adopt regulations "designed to promote the general welfare" must be deemed to sanction a zoning regulation reflecting that distinction

---

[3] General Statutes § 8-2 provides in part:

The zoning commission of each city, town or borough is authorized to regulate, within the limits of such municipality, the height, number of stories and size of buildings and other structures; the percentage of the area of the lot that may be occupied; the size of yards, courts and other open spaces; the density of population and the location and use of buildings, structures and land for trade, industry, residence or other purposes, including water-dependent uses as defined in section 22a-93, and the height, size and location of advertising signs and billboards. Such zoning commission may divide the municipality into districts of such number, shape and area as may be best suited to carry out the purposes of this chapter; and, within such districts, it may regulate the erection, construction, reconstruction, alteration or use of buildings or structures and the use of land. All such regulations shall be uniform for each class or kind of buildings, structures or use of land throughout each district, but the regulations in one district may differ from those in another district, and may provide that certain classes or kinds of buildings, structures or uses of land are permitted only after obtaining a special permit or special exception from a zoning commission, planning commission, combined planning and zoning commission or zoning board of appeals, whichever commission or board the regulations may, notwithstanding any special act to the contrary, designate, subject to standards set forth in the regulations and to conditions necessary to protect the public health, safety, convenience and property values. Such regulations shall be made in accordance with a comprehensive plan and shall be designed to lessen congestion in the streets; to secure safety from fire, panic, flood and other dangers; to promote health and the general welfare; to provide adequate light and air; to prevent the overcrowding of land; to avoid undue concentration of population and to facilitate the adequate provision for transportation, water, sewerage, schools, parks and other public requirements. Such regulations shall be made with reasonable consideration as to the character of the district and its peculiar suitability for particular uses and with a view to conserving the value of buildings and encouraging the most appropriate use of land throughout such municipality. Such regulations shall also encourage the development of housing opportunities for all citizens of the municipality consistent with soil types, terrain and infrastructure capacity. Zoning regulations shall be made with reasonable consideration for their impact on agriculture.

in the uses permitted in different zoning districts.

Single-family residence districts have been justified as "manifestly in furtherance" of the zoning objective of controlling population density in residential districts. Planning & Zoning Commission v. Synanon Foundation, Inc., *supra.* Section 8-2 expressly authorizes regulation of "the density of population" and the adoption of provisions "designed to avoid undue concentration of population." The creation of single-family residence districts is one method of achieving this objective and, therefore, is within the authority granted by § 8-2. It can hardly be disputed that some definition of the term family is appropriate and is implicitly authorized by the statute. Whether the definition of "family" in a zoning regulation can be limited to include only related persons, therefore, involves the enabling act only in the sense that the legislature must be presumed never to have intended to authorize irrational classifications wholly unrelated to zoning objectives or violative of constitutional rights. Accordingly, we conclude that the ultra vires question of whether § 1.18 exceeds the grant of authority contained in § 8-2 depends upon our resolution of the issue of the reasonableness of the distinction made between a traditional family and any other group occupying a residence, which is similar to the constitutional question of equal protection of the law.

II

The plaintiffs limit their constitutional attack upon § 1.18 to the claim that its restriction of the term "family" to include only traditional families of related persons violates the due process clause of article first, § 8[5] and the equal protection clause of article first, § 20[6] of the Connecticut constitution. They do not invoke the parallel provisions of our federal constitution because authoritative precedent construing those provisions appears unfavorable to their position. Although the plaintiffs claim no significant difference in the text of the pertinent clauses of our state and federal constitutions, it is well established that federal precedent is not controlling when this court undertakes the interpretation of similar language in our state constitution. "Federal law, whether based upon statute or constitution, establishes a minimum national standard for the exercise of individual rights and does not inhibit state governments from affording higher levels of protection for such rights." Cologne v. Westfarms Associates, 469 A.2d 1201 (Conn. 1984). In construing our state constitution, however, it is useful to consider the judicial gloss placed upon the corresponding language of article fourteen, § 1 of the amendments to our federal constitution, even though it is not dispositive of the issue before us.

The United States Supreme Court has considered zoning ordinances restricting the use of residences to families of related persons in two significant cases. In Belle Terre v. Boraas, 416 U.S. 1 (1974), the court upheld an ordinance restricting land use to single-family dwellings and defining "family" to mean only persons related

---

[5] Article first, § 8 of the Connecticut constitution provides in part: "No person shall be deprived of life, liberty or property without due process of law."

[6] Article first, § 20 of the Connecticut constitution provides in part: "No person shall be denied the equal protection of the law.'"

by blood, marriage or adoption unless the occupants number two or less.[7] The court concluded, in the context of the application of the ordinance to prohibit the use of a house by six unrelated students at a nearby college, that the restriction of property for use by a single traditional family was a permissible exercise of the legislative line drawing function that falls within the police power. "The police power is not confined to elimination of filth, stench, and unhealthy places. It is ample to lay out zones where family values, youth values, and the blessings of quiet seclusion and clean air make the area a sanctuary for people." *Id.* at 9.

In Moore v. East Cleveland, 431 U.S. 494 (1977), the zoning ordinance defined "family" to include some traditional family relationships but not others. As applied to prevent a grandchild, after his mother's death, from living with his grandmother, the court invalidated the ordinance as violating due process "by slicing deeply into the family itself." *Id.* at 498. "Ours is by no means a tradition limited to respect for the bonds uniting the members of the nuclear family. The tradition of uncles, aunts, cousins and especially grandparents sharing a household along with parents and children has roots equally venerable and equally deserving of constitutional recognition."[8] *Id.* at 504.

"This court does not embark upon the resolution of questions involving the validity of [legislation] in the absence of a practical necessity for their determination in the case presented and a sufficient factual background for their adjudication." State v. Madera, 503 A.2d 136 (Conn. 1985). In deciding the case before us, therefore, we need consider the application of the definition of "family" in § 1.18 only with respect to the constitutional rights of the plaintiffs as owners of a two-family house, each floor of which is rented to five unrelated persons who have made separate rental arrangements with the plaintiffs. A party "cannot mount a constitutional challenge to a statute on the basis of its possible applications in circumstances not presented by his own case, unless first amendment freedoms are affected, a situation not claimed to exist here." 503 A.2d 136. The plaintiffs, therefore, can assert only their own right to constitutional protection of their economic interest in maximizing the income from their property, and may not raise such interests as the ten occupants of the property may have arising possibly from some undisclosed associational bond among them. "[J]udicial power is to be exercised to strike down legislation, whether state or federal, only at the instance of one who is himself immediately harmed, or immediately threatened with harm, by the challenged action." Poe v. Ullman, 367 U.S. 497, 504 (1961). "We have uniformly resisted the efforts of litigants to assert constitutional claims of others

---

[7] The ordinance in *Belle Terre* defined "family" to mean " '[o]ne or more persons related by blood, adoption, or marriage, living and cooking together as a single housekeeping unit, exclusive of household servants. A number of persons but not exceeding two (2) living and cooking together as a single housekeeping unit though not related by blood, adoption, or marriage shall be deemed to constitute a family.' "

[8] The special status given to traditional families, both extended and nuclear, by Moore v. East Cleveland raises a federal constitutional question of the validity of proposals for zoning regulations that restrict the number of occupants of a building on the basis of floor area as applied to such families. This method of controlling population density has been advocated by some courts and commentators as an alternative to zoning restrictions based on occupancy by a single traditional family. See Note, *Single Family Zoning: The Ramifications of State Court Rejection of* Belle Terre *on Use and Density Control,* 32 Hastings L.J. 1687, 1708-1709 (1981).

not in a direct adversarial posture before the court." Southern Connecticut Gas Co. v. Housing Authority, 468 A.2d 574 (Conn. 1983).

In affirming the cease and desist order, the board implicitly adopted the characterization by the zoning enforcement officer of the existing use of the plaintiffs' property as a "rooming house." At the hearing before the board, the plaintiffs contended that they were not operating a rooming house because they did not reside in the house and each floor constituted a separate housekeeping unit of five occupants, who share such common facilities as the kitchen, the bathroom and a common storage area in the cellar, but have exclusive possession of a bedroom. Our decision does not turn upon whether the cease and desist order employed the appropriate nomenclature in referring to the plaintiffs' property. The five persons who occupy one floor of the plaintiffs' two-family house may well constitute a single housekeeping unit within the meaning of § 1.18, an issue we need not decide. Nevertheless, we perceive little distinction in the impact on a neighborhood of single-family homes from the plaintiffs' use of their property and that from a rooming house, or a dwelling such as that in *Belle Terre* leased to six college students, which the United States Supreme Court regarded as sufficiently objectionable to justify its exclusion from a single-family zone. "The regimes of boarding houses and the like present urban problems. More people occupy a given space; more cars rather continuously pass by; more cars are parked; noise travels with crowds." Belle Terre v. Boraas, 416 U.S. at 9.

Although the record does not contain any indication that the plaintiffs use their property as a boarding house or fraternity house, their provision for eleven parking spaces available to their tenants suggests the likelihood that more cars are parked on their property than are ordinarily found on the site of a single-family or two-family house. Apart from this difference in the physical appearance of their property as compared to other homes in the neighborhood, the separate rental arrangements that the plaintiffs make with each tenant indicate a lack of cohesion within both five person groups that negates the claim that each group constitutes a family of five unrelated individuals. Even though common facilities are shared, and possibly even meals, there is no indication of any tie among the plaintiffs' tenants that is likely to outlast their separate occupancies of the premises.

Traditional families are united not merely by the legal relationships among them but also by the deep affection that arises from a lifetime of sharing not just common facilities or meals in a home, but every aspect of experience. Nontraditional families may have a similar basis for their unity. Such lasting relationships are likely to generate the interest of a family not only in the home it occupies, but in the neighborhood, its schools, parks and other accouterments of urban living. The transient and separate character of residency by the plaintiffs' tenants is not as likely to stimulate on their part similar concerns about the quality of living in the neighborhood for the long term.

The municipal legislative body empowered to adopt zoning regulations in Stratford could reasonably have concluded that roomers or such occupants as the plaintiffs' tenants are less likely to develop the kind of friendly relationships with neighbors that abound in residential districts occupied by traditional families. While the plaintiffs' tenants continue to reside on the property, they are not likely to have children who would become playmates of other children living in the area. Neighbors are not so likely to call upon them to borrow a cup of sugar, provide a ride to the store, mind the family pets, water the plants or perform any of the countless services that families, both traditional and nontraditional, provide to each other as a result of longtime acquaintance and mutual self-interest. The fact that both families and individuals differ with respect to their habits and conduct in relation to the community does not render invalid the legislative judgment that the probable effect of the kind of occupancy the plaintiffs seek to maintain would be detrimental in a neighborhood of single-family homes.

We agree with *Belle Terre* that the police power may be used constitutionally to promote "family values" and "youth values" that contribute to creating "a sanctuary for people." In authorizing municipalities to adopt zoning regulations "designed to promote the general welfare," § 8-2 permits the consideration of all factors relevant to the quality of living when classifying the uses to be allowed in various zones. In this instance Stratford has chosen to create a zoning district permitting "one-family dwellings" to be occupied by "[a]ny number of individuals related by blood, marriage or adoption, living together as a single housekeeping unit," but allowing also two roomers in addition to the family of the occupant or, with the necessary approval, a total of not more than five roomers. Stratford Zoning Regs. §§ 4.1.1, 1.18, 4.1.4. "A boarding or rooming house" is a permitted use in a two-family zone. Stratford Zoning Regs. § 5.1.

The restriction of the definition of "family" to related persons is an exercise in legislative line drawing that serves to provide an element of cohesion not to be found in the occupancy of the plaintiffs' property by ten individuals with separate rental agreements and no common bond of significant duration. That the line is imperfect in that it may exclude some unrelated groups that may function in the community in essentially the same manner as a traditional family, insofar as zoning objectives are concerned, does not render it invalid. "[E]very line drawn by a legislature leaves some out that might well have been included." Belle Terre v. Boraas, 416 U.S. at 8. As previously noted, the plaintiffs can prevail only if their own constitutional rights as property owners are violated and cannot rely on possible applications of the regulation to other groups that may possess characteristics relevant to zoning objectives in substantially the same degree as traditional families.

The only constitutional rights the plaintiffs can assert in this case are economic in nature and do not involve such suspect classifications as race or gender. "We deal with economic and social legislation where legislatures have historically drawn lines which we respect against the charge of violation of the Equal Protection Clause." *Id.* Section 1.18 is valid as applied to the plaintiffs, if there is a rational basis for excluding from a zone established for occupancy by single families a group of ten unrelated individuals with no mutual link other than their occupancy of the same dwelling under separate rental arrangements with the plaintiffs. We conclude that there are sufficient reasons relevant to the objectives of zoning set forth in § 8-2 to justify the distinction made by § 1.18 between a family of related persons and the group of ten unrelated individuals who occupy the plaintiffs' property.

The judgment is reversed and the case is remanded with direction to dismiss the plaintiffs' appeal.

NOTES AND QUESTIONS

1. ***Euclid* again.** In a sense, we have come back to where we started our study. What justifications can be offered for single-family residential zones? Are definitions of "family" the most precise way to address whatever concerns underlie the zoning ordinance?

2. **Challenges.** What constitutional arguments can be made against an ordinance that defines "family" in an allegedly exclusionary way?

3. ***Belle Terre* and *Moore*.** Are Village of Belle Terre v. Boraas and Moore v. City of East Cleveland distinguishable? Or does *Moore* substantially undercut or limit *Belle Terre*?

C. EMINENT DOMAIN

The federal government, the states, and local governments, through the states, have the power of eminent domain. The Takings Clause of the Fifth Amendment to the Constitution provides: "[N]or shall private property be taken for public use, without just compensation." This clause is made applicable to the states by the Fourteenth Amendment. Therefore, the eminent domain power is subject to the requirements that just compensation be paid and that a taking must be for "public use." The public use requirement of the Constitution has been the subject of many court cases.

KELO v. CITY OF NEW LONDON, CONNECTICUT
545 U.S. 469 (2005)

JUSTICE STEVENS delivered the opinion of the Court.

In 2000, the city of New London approved a development plan that, in the words of the Supreme Court of Connecticut, was "projected to create in excess of 1,000 jobs, to increase tax and other revenues, and to revitalize an economically distressed city, including its downtown and waterfront areas." 843 A.2d 500, 507 (2004). In assembling the land needed for this project, the city's development agent has purchased property from willing sellers and proposes to use the power of eminent domain to acquire the remainder of the property from unwilling owners in exchange for just compensation. The question presented is whether the city's proposed disposition of this property qualifies as a "public use" within the meaning of the Takings Clause of the Fifth Amendment to the Constitution.

I

The city of New London (hereinafter City) sits at the junction of the Thames River and the Long Island Sound in southeastern Connecticut. Decades of economic decline led a state agency in 1990 to designate the City a "distressed municipality." In 1996, the Federal Government closed the Naval Undersea

Warfare Center, which had been located in the Fort Trumbull area of the City and had employed over 1,500 people. In 1998, the City's unemployment rate was nearly double that of the State, and its population of just under 24,000 residents was at its lowest since 1920.

These conditions prompted state and local officials to target New London, and particularly its Fort Trumbull area, for economic revitalization. To this end, respondent New London Development Corporation (NLDC), a private nonprofit entity established some years earlier to assist the City in planning economic development, was reactivated. In January 1998, the State authorized a $5.35 million bond issue to support the NLDC's planning activities and a $10 million bond issue toward the creation of a Fort Trumbull State Park. In February, the pharmaceutical company Pfizer Inc. announced that it would build a $300 million research facility on a site immediately adjacent to Fort Trumbull; local planners hoped that Pfizer would draw new business to the area, thereby serving as a catalyst to the area's rejuvenation. After receiving initial approval from the city council, the NLDC continued its planning activities and held a series of neighborhood meetings to educate the public about the process. In May, the city council authorized the NLDC to formally submit its plans to the relevant state agencies for review. Upon obtaining state-level approval, the NLDC finalized an integrated development plan focused on 90 acres of the Fort Trumbull area.

The Fort Trumbull area is situated on a peninsula that juts into the Thames River. The area comprises approximately 115 privately owned properties, as well as the 32 acres of land formerly occupied by the naval facility (Trumbull State Park now occupies 18 of those 32 acres). The development plan encompasses seven parcels. Parcel 1 is designated for a waterfront conference hotel at the center of a "small urban village" that will include restaurants and shopping. This parcel will also have marinas for both recreational and commercial uses. A pedestrian "riverwalk" will originate here and continue down the coast, connecting the waterfront areas of the development. Parcel 2 will be the site of approximately 80 new residences organized into an urban neighborhood and linked by public walkway to the remainder of the development, including the state park. This parcel also includes space reserved for a new U.S. Coast Guard Museum. Parcel 3, which is located immediately north of the Pfizer facility, will contain at least 90,000 square feet of research and development office space. Parcel 4A is a 2.4-acre site that will be used either to support the adjacent state park, by providing parking or retail services for visitors, or to support the nearby marina. Parcel 4B will include a renovated marina, as well as the final stretch of the riverwalk. Parcels 5, 6, and 7 will provide land for office and retail space, parking, and water-dependent commercial uses.

The NLDC intended the development plan to capitalize on the arrival of the Pfizer facility and the new commerce it was expected to attract. In addition to creating jobs, generating tax revenue, and helping to "build momentum for the revitalization of downtown New London," the plan was also designed to make the City more attractive and to create leisure and recreational opportunities on the waterfront and in the park.

The city council approved the plan in January 2000, and designated the NLDC as its development agent in charge of implementation. The city council also authorized the NLDC to purchase property or to acquire property by exercising eminent domain in the City's name. The NLDC successfully negotiated the purchase of most of the real estate in the 90-acre area, but its negotiations with petitioners failed. As a consequence, in November 2000, the NLDC initiated the condemnation proceedings that gave rise to this case.

II

Petitioner Susette Kelo has lived in the Fort Trumbull area since 1997. She has made extensive improvements to her house, which she prizes for its water view. Petitioner Wilhelmina Dery was born in her Fort Trumbull house in 1918 and has lived there her entire life. Her husband Charles (also a petitioner) has lived in the house since they married some 60 years ago. In all, the nine petitioners own 15 properties in Fort Trumbull — 4 in parcel 3 of the development plan and 11 in parcel 4A. Ten of the parcels are occupied by the owner or a family member; the other five are held as investment properties. There is no allegation that any of these properties is blighted or otherwise in poor condition; rather, they were condemned only because they happen to be located in the development area.

In December 2000, petitioners brought this action in the New London Superior Court. They claimed, among other things, that the taking of their properties would violate the "public use" restriction in the Fifth Amendment. After a 7-day bench trial, the Superior Court granted a permanent restraining order prohibiting the taking of the properties located in parcel 4A (park or marina support). It, however, denied petitioners relief as to the properties located in parcel 3 (office space).

After the Superior Court ruled, both sides took appeals to the Supreme Court of Connecticut. That court held, over a dissent, that all of the City's proposed takings were valid. It began by upholding the lower court's determination that the takings were authorized by the State's municipal development statute. That statute expresses a legislative determination that the taking of land, even developed land, as part of an economic development project is a "public use" and in the "public interest." Next, relying on cases such as Hawaii Housing Authority v. Midkiff, 467 U.S. 229 (1984), and Berman v. Parker, 348 U.S. 26 (1954), the court held that such economic development qualified as a valid public use under both the Federal and State Constitutions.

We granted certiorari to determine whether a city's decision to take property for the purpose of economic development satisfies the "public use" requirement of the Fifth Amendment.

III

Two polar propositions are perfectly clear. On the one hand, it has long been accepted that the sovereign may not take the property of A for the sole purpose of transferring it to another private party B, even though A is paid just compensation. On the other hand, it is equally clear that a State may transfer property from one private party to another if future "use by the public" is the purpose of the taking; the condemnation of land for a railroad with common-carrier duties is a familiar example. Neither of these propositions, however, determines the disposition of this case.

As for the first proposition, the City would no doubt be forbidden from taking petitioners' land for the purpose of conferring a private benefit on a particular private party. Nor would the City be allowed to take property under the mere pretext of a public purpose, when its actual purpose was to bestow a private benefit. The takings before us, however, would be executed pursuant to a "carefully considered" development plan. The trial judge and all the members of the Supreme Court of Connecticut agreed that there was no evidence of an illegitimate purpose in this case.[6] Therefore, as was true of the statute challenged in *Midkiff*, 467 U.S. at 245, the City's development plan was not adopted "to benefit a particular class of identifiable individuals."

On the other hand, this is not a case in which the City is planning to open the condemned land — at least not in its entirety — to use by the general public. Nor will the private lessees of the land in any sense be required to operate like common carriers, making their services available to all comers. But although such a projected use would be sufficient to satisfy the public use requirement, this "Court long ago rejected any literal requirement that condemned property be put into use for the general public." *Id.* at 244. Indeed, while many state courts in the mid-19th century endorsed "use by the public" as the proper definition of public use, that narrow view steadily eroded over time. Not only was the "use by the public" test difficult to administer (*e.g.*, what proportion of the public need have access to the property? at what price?), but it proved to be impractical given the diverse and always evolving needs of society. Accordingly, when this Court began applying the Fifth Amendment to the States at the close of the 19th century, it embraced the broader and more natural interpretation of public use as "public purpose."

The disposition of this case therefore turns on the question whether the City's development plan serves a "public purpose." Without exception, our cases have defined that concept broadly, reflecting our longstanding policy of deference to legislative judgments in this field.

In Berman v. Parker, 348 U.S. 26 (1954), this Court upheld a redevelopment plan targeting a blighted area of Washington, D.C., in which most of the housing for the area's 5,000 inhabitants was beyond repair. Under the plan, the area would be condemned and part of it utilized for the construction of streets, schools, and other public facilities. The remainder of the land would be leased or sold to private

---

[6] See 843 A. 2d, at 595 (Zarella, J., concurring in part and dissenting in part) ("The record clearly demonstrates that the development plan was not intended to serve the interests of Pfizer, Inc., or any other private entity, but rather, to revitalize the local economy by creating temporary and permanent jobs, generating a significant increase in tax revenue, encouraging spin-off economic activities and maximizing public access to the waterfront"). And while the City intends to transfer certain of the parcels to a private developer in a long-term lease — which developer, in turn, is expected to lease the office space and so forth to other private tenants — the identities of those private parties were not known when the plan was adopted. It is, of course, difficult to accuse the government of having taken A's property to benefit the private interests of B when the identity of B was unknown.

parties for the purpose of redevelopment, including the construction of low-cost housing.

The owner of a department store located in the area challenged the condemnation, pointing out that his store was not itself blighted and arguing that the creation of a "better balanced, more attractive community" was not a valid public use. *Id.* at 31. Writing for a unanimous Court, Justice Douglas refused to evaluate this claim in isolation, deferring instead to the legislative and agency judgment that the area "must be planned as a whole" for the plan to be successful. *Id.* at 34. The Court explained that "community redevelopment programs need not, by force of the Constitution, be on a piecemeal basis — lot by lot, building by building." *Id.* at 35. The public use underlying the taking was unequivocally affirmed:

> We do not sit to determine whether a particular housing project is or is not desirable. The concept of the public welfare is broad and inclusive. The values it represents are spiritual as well as physical, aesthetic as well as monetary. It is within the power of the legislature to determine that the community should be beautiful as well as healthy, spacious as well as clean, well-balanced as well as carefully patrolled. In the present case, the Congress and its authorized agencies have made determinations that take into account a wide variety of values. It is not for us to reappraise them. If those who govern the District of Columbia decide that the Nation's Capital should be beautiful as well as sanitary, there is nothing in the Fifth Amendment that stands in the way.

Id. at 33.

In Hawaii Housing Authority v. Midkiff, 467 U.S. 229 (1984), the Court considered a Hawaii statute whereby fee title was taken from lessors and transferred to lessees (for just compensation) in order to reduce the concentration of land ownership. We unanimously upheld the statute and rejected the Ninth Circuit's view that it was "a naked attempt on the part of the state of Hawaii to take the property of A and transfer it to B solely for B's private use and benefit." *Id.* at 235. Reaffirming *Berman*'s deferential approach to legislative judgments in this field, we concluded that the State's purpose of eliminating the "social and economic evils of a land oligopoly" qualified as a valid public use. 467 U.S. at 241-242. Our opinion also rejected the contention that the mere fact that the State immediately transferred the properties to private individuals upon condemnation somehow diminished the public character of the taking. "It is only the taking's purpose, and not its mechanics," we explained, that matters in determining public use. *Id.* at 244.

Viewed as a whole, our jurisprudence has recognized that the needs of society have varied between different parts of the Nation, just as they have evolved over time in response to changed circumstances. Our earliest cases in particular embodied a strong theme of federalism, emphasizing the "great respect" that we owe to state legislatures and state courts in discerning local public needs. See Hairston v. Danville & Western R. Co., 208 U.S. 598 (1908) (noting that these needs were likely to vary depending on a State's "resources, the capacity of the soil, the relative importance of industries to the general public welfare, and the long-established methods and habits of the people"). For more than a century, our public use jurisprudence has wisely eschewed rigid formulas and intrusive scrutiny in favor of affording legislatures broad latitude in determining what public needs justify the use of the takings power.

IV

Those who govern the City were not confronted with the need to remove blight in the Fort Trumbull area, but their determination that the area was sufficiently distressed to justify a program of economic rejuvenation is entitled to our deference. The City has carefully formulated an economic development plan that it believes will provide appreciable benefits to the community, including — but by no means limited to — new jobs and increased tax revenue. As with other exercises in urban planning and development, the City is endeavoring to coordinate a variety of commercial, residential, and recreational uses of land, with the hope that they will form a whole greater than the sum of its parts. To effectuate this plan, the City has invoked a state statute that specifically authorizes the use of eminent domain to promote economic development. Given the comprehensive character of the plan, the thorough deliberation that preceded its adoption, and the limited scope of our review, it is appropriate for us, as it was in *Berman*, to resolve the challenges of the individual owners, not on a piecemeal basis, but rather in light of the entire plan. Because that plan unquestionably serves a public purpose, the takings challenged here satisfy the public use requirement of the Fifth Amendment.

To avoid this result, petitioners urge us to adopt a new bright-line rule that economic development does not qualify as a public use. Putting aside the unpersuasive suggestion that the City's plan will provide only purely economic benefits, neither precedent nor logic supports petitioners' proposal. Promoting economic development is a traditional and long accepted function of government. There is, moreover, no principled way of distinguishing economic development from the other public purposes that we have recognized. In our cases upholding takings that facilitated agriculture and mining, for example, we emphasized the importance of those industries to the welfare of the States in question; in *Berman*, we endorsed the purpose of transforming a blighted area into a "well-balanced" community through redevelopment, 348 U.S. at 33; in *Midkiff*, we upheld the interest in breaking up a land oligopoly that "created artificial deterrents to the normal functioning of the State's residential land market," 467 U.S. at 242. It would be incongruous to hold that the City's interest in the economic benefits to be derived from the development of the Fort Trumbull area less of a public character than any of those other interests. Clearly, there is no basis for exempting economic development from our traditionally broad understanding of public purpose.

Petitioners contend that using eminent domain for economic development impermissibly blurs the boundary between public and private takings. Again, our cases foreclose this objection. Quite simply, the government's pursuit of a public purpose will often benefit individual private parties. For example, in *Midkiff*, the forced transfer of property conferred a direct and significant benefit on those lessees who were previously unable to purchase their homes. The owner of the department store in *Berman* objected to "taking from one businessman for the benefit of another businessman," 348 U.S. at 33, referring to the fact that under the redevelopment plan land would be leased or sold to private developers for redevelopment. Our rejection of that contention has particular relevance to the instant case: "The public end may be as well or better served through an agency of private enterprise than through a department of government — or so the Congress might conclude. We cannot say that public ownership is the sole method of promoting the public purposes of community redevelopment projects." *Id.* at 34.

It is further argued that without a bright-line rule nothing would stop a city from transferring citizen *A*'s property to citizen *B* for the sole reason that citizen *B* will put the property to a more productive use and thus pay more taxes. Such a one-to-one transfer of property, executed outside the confines of an integrated development plan, is not presented in this case. While such an unusual exercise of government power would certainly raise a suspicion that a private purpose was afoot, the hypothetical cases posited by petitioners can be confronted if and when they arise. They do not warrant the crafting of an artificial restriction on the concept of public use.

Alternatively, petitioners maintain that for takings of this kind we should require a "reasonable certainty" that the expected public benefits will actually accrue. Such a rule, however, would represent an even greater departure from our precedent. "When the legislature's purpose is legitimate and its means are not irrational, our cases make clear that empirical debates over the wisdom of takings — no less than debates over the wisdom of other kinds of socioeconomic legislation — are not to be carried out in the federal courts." *Midkiff*, 467 U.S. at 242. The disadvantages of a heightened form of review are especially pronounced in this type of case. Orderly implementation of a comprehensive redevelopment plan obviously requires that the legal rights of all interested parties be established before new construction can be commenced. A constitutional rule that required postponement of the judicial approval of every condemnation until the likelihood of success of the plan had been assured would unquestionably impose a significant impediment to the successful consummation of many such plans.

Just as we decline to second-guess the City's considered judgments about the efficacy of its development plan, we also decline to second-guess the City's determinations as to what lands it needs to acquire in order to effectuate the project. "It is not for the courts to oversee the choice of the boundary line nor to sit in review on the size of a particular project area. Once the question of the public purpose has been decided, the amount and character of land to be taken for the project and the need for a particular tract to complete the integrated plan rests in the discretion of the legislative branch." *Berman*, 348 U.S. at 35-36.

In affirming the City's authority to take petitioners' properties, we do not minimize the hardship that condemnations may entail, notwithstanding the payment of just compensation. We emphasize that nothing in our opinion precludes any State from placing further restrictions on its exercise of the takings power. Indeed, many States already impose "public use" requirements that are stricter than the federal baseline. Some of these requirements have been established as a matter of state constitutional law, while others are expressed in state eminent domain statutes that carefully limit the grounds upon which takings may be exercised. As the submissions of the parties and their *amici* make clear, the necessity and wisdom of using eminent domain to promote economic development are certainly matters of legitimate public debate. This Court's authority, however, extends only to determining whether the City's proposed condemnations are for a "public use" within the meaning of the Fifth Amendment to the Federal Constitution. Because over a century of our case law interpreting that provision dictates an affirmative answer to that question, we may not grant petitioners the relief that they seek.

The judgment of the Supreme Court of Connecticut is affirmed.

Justice O'CONNOR, with whom THE CHIEF JUSTICE, Justice SCALIA, and Justice THOMAS join, dissenting.

Today the Court abandons [a] long-held, basic limitation on government power. Under the banner of economic development, all private property is now vulnerable to being taken and transferred to another private owner, so long as it might be upgraded — *i.e.*, given to an owner who will use it in a way that the legislature deems more beneficial to the public — in the process. To reason, as the Court does, that the incidental public benefits resulting from the subsequent ordinary use of private property render economic development takings "for public use" is to wash out any distinction between private and public use of property — and thereby effectively to delete the words "for public use" from the Takings Clause of the Fifth Amendment. Accordingly I respectfully dissent.

Our cases have generally identified three categories of takings that comply with the public use requirement, though it is in the nature of things that the boundaries between these categories are not always firm. Two are relatively straightforward and uncontroversial. First, the sovereign may transfer private property to public ownership — such as for a road, a hospital, or a military base. Second, the sovereign may transfer private property to private parties, often common carriers, who make the property available for the public's use — such as with a railroad, a public utility, or a stadium. But "public ownership" and "use-by-the-public" are sometimes too constricting and impractical ways to define the scope of the Public Use Clause. Thus we have allowed that, in certain circumstances and to meet certain exigencies, takings that serve a public purpose also satisfy the Constitution even if the property is destined for subsequent private use. See, e.g., Berman v. Parker, 348 U.S. 26 (1954); Hawaii Housing Authority v. Midkiff, 467 U.S. 229 (1984).

[T]he Court today significantly expands the meaning of public use. It holds that the sovereign may take private property currently put to ordinary private use, and give it over for new, ordinary private use, so long as the new use is predicted to generate some secondary benefit for the public — such as increased tax revenue, more jobs, maybe even aesthetic pleasure. But nearly any lawful use of real private property can be said to generate some incidental benefit to the public. Thus, if predicted (or even guaranteed) positive side-effects are enough to render transfer from one private party to another constitutional, then the words "for public use" do not realistically exclude *any* takings, and thus do not exert any constraint on the eminent domain power.

Any property may now be taken for the benefit of another private party, but the fallout from this decision will not be random. The beneficiaries are likely to be those citizens with disproportionate influence and power in the political process, including large corporations and development firms. As for the victims, the government now has license to transfer property from those with fewer resources to those with more.

I would hold that the takings in both Parcel 3 and Parcel 4A are unconstitutional, reverse the judgment of the Supreme Court of Connecticut, and remand for further proceedings.

NOTES AND QUESTIONS

1. **Controversy.** The *Kelo* decision generated much debate in newspapers, state legislatures, and legal journals. For a sampling of the legal scholarship, see David L. Callies, *Public Use: What Should Replace the Rational Basis Test?*, Probate and Property, Mar./Apr. 2005; Charles H. Cohen, *Eminent Domain After* Kelo v. City of New London: *An Argument for Banning Economic Development Takings*, 29 Harv. J.L. & Pub. Pol'y 491 (2006); Daniel H. Cole, *Why Kelo is Not Good News for Local Planners and Developers*, Ga. St. L. Rev. 803 (2006); Wendell E. Pritchett, *Beyond* Kelo: *Thinking About Urban Development in the 21st Century*, 22 Ga. St. U. L. Rev. 895 (2006); Debra Pogrund Stark, *How Do You Solve a Problem Like in* Kelo?, 40 J. Marshall L. Rev. 609 (2007); Symposium, *Federalism Issues Following* Kelo v. City of New London, 28 U. Haw. L. Rev. 327 (2006); Symposium, *Perspectives on* Kelo v. City of New London, 38 McGeorge L. Rev. 369 (2007).

2. **Legislative reaction.** The Court suggests that states may impose more stringent public use requirements than the Constitution. Many legislatures in fact reacted to *Kelo* with bills designed to limit the eminent domain power. *See* Donald E. Sanders & Patricia Pattison, *The Aftermath of* Kelo, 34 Real Est. L.J. 157 (2005). Congress also has considered legislation addressing the issues of *Kelo*.

3. **Recent news.** Pfizer recently announced that it is leaving New London and moving most of the employees who had occupied its offices there to nearby Groton, Connecticut. *See* N.Y. Times, Nov. 13, 2009, at A1.

4. **Just compensation.** In addition to public use, the Fifth Amendment requires just compensation. For a discussion of just compensation issues, see Lee Anne Fennell, *Taking Eminent Domain Apart*, 2004 Mich. St. L. Rev. 957; Christopher Serkin, *The Meaning of Value: Assessing Just Compensation for Regulatory Takings*, 99 Nw. U. L. Rev. 677 (2005).

D. REGULATORY TAKINGS: INVERSE CONDEMNATION

When government exercises the power of eminent domain to take or transfer outright ownership of private property, a "taking" of the property has clearly occurred. What if government leaves ownership as it is, however, but regulates the use of the property? Can regulation constitute a taking? The case below was the first in which the Supreme Court held that it can.

When does a land use regulation "go too far" and thus accomplish an unconstitutional taking of private property? The answer, as this Section shows, is that no one knows for sure. The leading Supreme Court decisions, which are many and increasing with just about each Term of the Court, are for the most part suggestive rather than canonical, and just about all conclusions you draw must be regarded as tentative. To borrow Professor Rose's metaphors, takings jurisprudence consists not of crystals but rather mud. *See* Carol M. Rose, *Crystals and Mud in Property Law*, 40 Stanford L. Rev. 577 (1988).

There is perhaps a certain amount of necessity in all of this uncertainty, given the sensitiveness, durability, and magnitude of the underlying issues (state power vs. individual freedom, individual rights vs. community needs, etc.). In any event, our goal in this Section is modest: to consider the methodological approaches to determining whether a regulation constitutes a taking, and to identify the major substantive themes that are important to the Court or to significant voting blocs on the Court.

1.   Origins of the Doctrine

PENNSYLVANIA COAL CO. v. MAHON
260 U.S. 393 (1922)

JUSTICE HOLMES delivered the opinion of the Court.

This is a bill in equity brought by the defendants in error to prevent the Pennsylvania Coal Company from mining under their property in such way as to remove the supports and cause a subsidence of the surface and of their house. The bill sets out a deed executed by the Coal Company in 1878, under which the plaintiffs claim. The deed conveys the surface but in express terms reserves the right to remove all the coal under the same and the grantee takes the premises with the risk and waives all claim for damages that may arise from mining out the coal. But the plaintiffs say that whatever may have been the Coal Company's rights, they were taken away by an Act of Pennsylvania, approved May 27, 1921, commonly known there as the Kohler Act. The Court of Common Pleas found that if not restrained the defendant would cause the damage to prevent which the bill was brought but denied an injunction, holding that the statute if applied to this case would be unconstitutional. On appeal the Supreme Court of the State agreed that the defendant had contract and property rights protected by the Constitution of the United States, but held that the statute was a legitimate exercise of the police power and directed a decree for the plaintiffs. A writ of error was granted bringing the case to this Court.

The statute forbids the mining of anthracite coal in such way as to cause the subsidence of, among other things, any structure used as a human habitation, with certain exceptions, including among them land where the surface is owned by the owner of the underlying coal and is distant more than one hundred and fifty feet from any improved property belonging to any other person. As applied to this case the statute is admitted to destroy previously existing rights of property and contract. The question is whether the police power can be stretched so far.

Government hardly could go on if to some extent values incident to property could not be diminished without paying for every such change in the general law. As long recognized some values are enjoyed under an implied limitation and must yield to the police power. But obviously the implied limitation must have its limits or the contract and due process clauses are gone. One fact for consideration in determining such limits is the extent of the diminution. When it reaches a certain magnitude, in most if not in all cases there must be an exercise of eminent domain and compensation to sustain the act. So the question depends upon the particular facts. The greatest weight is given to the judgment of the legislature but it always is open to interested parties to contend that the legislature has gone beyond its constitutional power.

This is the case of a single private house. No doubt there is a public interest even in this, as there is in every purchase and sale and in all that happens within the commonwealth. Some existing rights may be modified even in such a case. But usually in ordinary private affairs the public interest does not warrant much of this kind of interference. A source of damage to such a house is not a public nuisance even if similar damage is inflicted on others in different places. The damage is not common or public. The extent of the public interest is shown by the statute to be limited, since the statute ordinarily does not apply to land when the surface is owned by the owner of the coal. Furthermore, it is not justified as a protection of personal safety. That could be provided for by notice. Indeed the very foundation of this bill is that the defendant gave timely notice of its intent to mine under the house. On the other hand the extent of the taking is great. It purports to abolish what is recognized in Pennsylvania as an estate in land — a very valuable estate — and what is declared by the Court below to be a contract hitherto binding the plaintiffs. If we were called upon to deal with the plaintiffs' position alone we should think it clear that the statute does not disclose a public interest sufficient to warrant so extensive a destruction of the defendant's constitutionally protected rights.

But the case has been treated as one in which the general validity of the act should be discussed. The Attorney General of the State, the City of Scranton and the representatives of other extensive interests were allowed to take part in the argument below and have submitted their contentions here. It seems, therefore, to be our duty to go farther in the statement of our opinion, in order that it may be known at once, and that further suits should not be brought in vain.

It is our opinion that the act cannot be sustained as an exercise of the police power, so far as it affects the mining of coal under streets or cities in places where the right to mine such coal has been reserved. As said in a Pennsylvania case, "For practical purposes, the right to coal consists in the right to mine it." Commonwealth v. Clearview Coal Co., 256 Pa. 328, 331, 100 Atl. 820. What makes the right to mine coal valuable is that it can be exercised with profit. To make it commercially impracticable to mine certain coal has very nearly the same effect for constitutional purposes as appropriating or destroying it. Thus, we think that we are warranted in assuming that the statute does.

It is true that in Plymouth Coal Co. v. Pennsylvania, 232 U.S. 531, it was held competent for the legislature to require a pillar of coal to the left along the line of adjoining property, that with the pillar on the other side of the line would be a barrier sufficient for the safety of the employees of either mine in case the other should be abandoned and allowed to fill with water. But that was a requirement for the safety of employees invited into the mine, and secured an average reciprocity of advantage that has been recognized as a justification of various laws.

The rights of the public in a street purchased or laid out by eminent domain are those that it has paid for. If in any case its representatives have been so short sighted as to acquire only surface rights without the right of support we see no more authority for supplying the latter without compensation than there was for taking the right of way in the first place and refusing to pay for it because the public wanted it very much. The protection of private property in the Fifth Amendment presupposes that it is wanted for public use, but provides that it shall not be taken for such use without compensation. A similar assumption is made in the decisions upon the Fourteenth Amendment. When this seemingly absolute protection is found to be qualified by the police power, the natural tendency of human nature is to extend the qualification more and more until at last private property disappears. But that cannot be accomplished in this way under the Constitution of the United States.

The general rule at least is that while property may be regulated to a certain extent, if regulation goes too far it will be recognized as a taking. It may be doubted how far exceptional cases, like the blowing up of a house to stop a conflagration, go — and if they go beyond the general rule, whether they do not stand as much upon tradition as upon principle. In general it is not plain that a man's misfortunes or necessities will justify his shifting the damages to his neighbor's shoulders. We are in danger of forgetting that a strong public desire to improve the public condition is not enough to warrant achieving the desire by a shorter cut than the constitutional way of paying for the change. As we already have said this is a question of degree — and therefore cannot be disposed of by general propositions. But we regard this as going beyond any of the cases decided by this Court.

We assume, of course, that the statute was passed upon the conviction that an exigency existed that would warrant it, and we assume that an exigency exists that would warrant the exercise of eminent domain. But the question at bottom is upon whom the loss of the changes desired should fall. So far as private persons or communities have seen fit to take the risk of acquiring only surface rights, we cannot see that the fact that their risk has become a danger warrants the giving to them greater rights than they bought.

Decree reversed.

JUSTICE BRANDEIS dissenting.

Coal in place is land, and the right of the owner to use his land is not absolute. He may not so use it as to create a public nuisance, and uses, once harmless, may, owing to changed conditions, seriously threaten the public welfare. Whenever they do, the Legislature has power to prohibit such uses without paying compensation; and the power to prohibit extends alike to the manner, the character and the purpose of the use. Are we justified in declaring that the Legislature of Pennsylvania has, in restricting the right to mine anthracite, exercised this power so arbitrarily as to violate the Fourteenth Amendment?

Every restriction upon the use of property imposed in the exercise of the police power deprives the owner of some right theretofore enjoyed, and is, in that sense, an abridgment by the state of rights in property without making compensation. But restriction imposed to protect the public health, safety or morals from dangers threatened is not a taking. The restriction here in question is merely the prohibition of a noxious use. The property so restricted remains in the possession of its owner. The state does not appropriate it or make any use of it. The state merely prevents the owner from making a use which interferes with paramount rights of the public. Whenever the use prohibited ceases to be noxious — as it may because of further change in local or social conditions — the restriction will have to be removed and the owner will again be free to enjoy his property as heretofore.

The restriction upon the use of this property cannot, of course, be lawfully imposed, unless its purpose is to protect the public. But the purpose of a restriction does not cease to be public, because incidentally some private persons may thereby receive gratuitously valuable special benefits. Thus, owners of low buildings may obtain, through statutory restrictions upon the height of neighboring structures, benefits equivalent to an easement of light and air. Furthermore, a restriction, though imposed for a public purpose, will not be lawful, unless the restriction is an appropriate means to the public end. But to keep coal in place is surely an appropriate means of preventing subsidence of the surface; and ordinarily it is the only available means. Restriction upon use does not become inappropriate as a means, merely because it deprives the owner of the only use to which the property can then be profitably put. Nor is a restriction imposed through exercise of the police power inappropriate as a means, merely because the same end might be effected through exercise of the power of eminent domain, or otherwise at public expense. Every restriction upon the height of buildings might be secured through acquiring by eminent domain the right of each owner to build above the limiting height; but it is settled that the state need not resort to that power. If by mining anthracite coal the owner would necessarily unloose poisonous gases, I suppose no one would doubt the power of the state to prevent the mining, without buying his coal fields. And why may not the state, likewise, without paying compensation, prohibit one from digging so deep or excavating so near the surface, as to expose the community to like dangers? In the latter case, as in the former, carrying on the business would be a public nuisance.

It is said that one fact for consideration in determining whether the limits of the police power have been exceeded is the extent of the resulting diminution in value, and that here the restriction destroys existing rights of property and contract. But values are relative. If we are to consider the value of the coal kept in place by the restriction, we should compare it with the value of all other parts of the land. That is, with the value not of the coal alone, but with the value of the whole property. The rights of an owner as against the public are not increased by dividing the interests in his property into surface and subsoil. The sum of the rights in the parts can not be greater than the rights in the whole. The estate of an owner in land is grandiloquently described as extending ab orco usque ad coelum. But I suppose no one would contend that by selling his interest above 100 feet from the surface he could prevent the state from limiting, by the police power, the height of structures in a city. And why should a sale of underground rights bar the state's power? For aught that appears the value of the coal kept in place by the restriction may be negligible as compared with the value of the whole property, or even as compared with that part of it which is represented by the coal remaining in place and which may be extracted despite the statute. Where the surface and the coal belong to the same person, self-interest would ordinarily prevent mining to such an extent as to cause a subsidence. It was, doubtless, for this reason that the Legislature, estimating the degrees of danger, deemed statutory restriction unnecessary for the public safety under such conditions.

It is said that this is a case of a single dwelling house, that the restriction upon mining abolishes a valuable estate hitherto secured by a contract with the plaintiffs, and that the restriction upon mining cannot be justified as a protection of personal safety, since that could be provided for by notice. The propriety of deferring a good deal to tribunals on the spot has been repeatedly recognized. May we say that notice would afford adequate protection of the public safety where the Legislature and the highest court of the state, with greater knowledge of local conditions, have declared, in effect, that it would not? If the public safety is imperiled, surely neither grant, nor contract, can prevail against the exercise of the police power.

This case involves only mining which causes subsidence of a dwelling house. But the Kohler Act contains additional provisions; and as to these, also, an opinion is expressed. These provisions deal with mining under cities to such an extent as to cause subsidence of [public buildings, streets, and railway tracks]. A prohibition of mining which causes subsidence of such structures and facilities is obviously enacted for a public purpose; and it seems, likewise, clear that mere notice of intention to mine would not in this connection secure the public safety. Yet it is said that these provisions of the act cannot be sustained as an exercise of the police power where the right to mine such coal has been reserved. The conclusion seems to rest upon the assumption that in order to justify such exercise of the police power there must be "an average reciprocity of advantage" as between the owner of the property restricted and the rest of the community; and that here such reciprocity is absent. Reciprocity of advantage is an important consideration, and may even be an essential, where the state's power is exercised for the purpose of conferring benefits upon the property of a neighborhood. But where the police power is exercised, not to confer benefits upon property owners but to protect the public from detriment and danger, there is in my opinion, no room for considering reciprocity of advantage.

NOTES AND QUESTIONS

1. **Another case.** In 1966, Pennsylvania again enacted a statute (the Bituminous Mine Subsidence and Land Conservation Act) aimed at mining practices that caused subsidence damage to public buildings and private dwellings. As implemented by the state's environmental protection agency, the Act required 50% of the coal beneath protected structures to be kept in place to provide surface support. A case challenging the Act as an unconstitutional taking of property again reached the Supreme Court, but this time the decision went in favor of the legislation. The Court found that the Subsidence Act differed from the Kohler Act

in two important ways:

First, unlike the Kohler Act, the character of the governmental action involved here leans heavily against finding a taking; the Commonwealth of Pennsylvania has acted to arrest what it perceives to be a significant threat to the common welfare. Second, there is no record in this case to support a finding, similar to the one the Court made in *Pennsylvania Coal*, that the Subsidence Act makes it impossible for petitioners to profitably engage in their business, or that there has been undue interference with their investment-backed expectations.

The Public Purpose

Unlike the Kohler Act, the Subsidence Act does not merely involve a balancing of the private economic interests of coal companies against the private interests of the surface owners. The Pennsylvania Legislature specifically found that important public interests are served by enforcing a policy that is designed to minimize subsidence in certain areas.

Thus, the Subsidence Act differs from the Kohler Act in critical and dispositive respects. With regard to the Kohler Act, the Court believed that the Commonwealth had acted only to ensure against damage to some private landowners' homes. Justice Holmes stated that if the private individuals needed support for their structures, they should not have "take[n] the risk of acquiring only surface rights." Here, by contrast, the Commonwealth is acting to protect the public interest in health, the environment, and the fiscal integrity of the area. That private individuals erred in taking a risk cannot estop the Commonwealth from exercising its police power to abate activity akin to a public nuisance. The Subsidence Act is a prime example that "circumstances may so change in time as to clothe with a [public] interest what at other times would be a matter of purely private concern." Block v. Hirsh, 256 U.S. 135, 155 (1921).

Diminution of Value and Investment-Backed Expectations

The second factor that distinguishes this case from *Pennsylvania Coal* is the finding in that case that the Kohler Act made mining of "certain coal" commercially impracticable. In this case, by contrast, petitioners have not shown any deprivation significant enough to satisfy the heavy burden placed upon one alleging a regulatory taking. [P]etitioners have not claimed, at this stage, that the Act makes it commercially impracticable for them to continue mining their bituminous coal interests in western Pennsylvania. Indeed, petitioners have not even pointed to a single mine that can no longer be mined for profit. Petitioners described the effect that the Subsidence Act had from 1966-1982 on 13 mines that the various companies operate, and claimed that they have been required to leave a bit less than 27 million tons of coal in place [for] support. The total coal in those 13 mines amounts to over 1.46 billion tons. Thus [the Act] requires them to leave less than 2% of their coal in place. We do know, however, that petitioners have never claimed that their mining operations, or even any specific mines, have been unprofitable since the Subsidence Act was passed.

Keystone Bituminous Coal Association v. DeBenedictis, 480 U.S. 470, 485, 487-488, 493, 495-496 (1987). Although Pennsylvania Coal Co. v. Mahon is no longer authoritative on the question of the regulation of subsidence mining, it remains (as you will see) a seminal case, frequently cited and quoted in the Court's takings cases.

2. **Factors.** In the principal case, what factors does Justice Holmes find important in determining that the Kohler Act caused a taking of Pennsylvania Coal Company's property? What factors are important to Justice Brandeis's argument upholding the Act?

3. **Nuisance law.** How important is nuisance law to the majority and the dissent? How does characterization of the conduct regulated by a statute as a nuisance affect the analysis of the question whether the legislation effects a taking of property?

4. **Literature.** Some of the leading articles on regulatory takings are cited in the cases that follow. For recent commentary on the topic, see the following: Nestor M. Davidson, *The Problem of Equality in Takings*, 102 Nw. U. L. Rev. 1 (2008); Carol M. Rose, *What Federalism Tells Us About Takings Jurisprudence*, 54 UCLA L. Rev. 1681 (2007); Jeffrey M. Gaba, *John Locke and the Meaning of the Takings Clause*, 72 Mo. L. Rev. 525 (2007); Abraham Bell & Gideon Parchomovsky, *Takings Reassessed*, 87 Va. L. Rev. 277 (2001); Hanoch Dagan, *Just Compensation, Incentives, and Social Meanings*, 99 Mich. L. Rev. 134 (2000); Glynn S. Lunney, Jr., *Takings, Efficiency, and Distributive Justice: A Response to Professor Dagan*, 99 Mich. L. Rev. 157 (2000); Susan Rose-Ackerman & Jim Rossi, *Disentangling Deregulatory Takings*, 86 Va. L. Rev. 1435 (2000); Julie Patterson Forrester, *Bankruptcy Takings*, 51 Fla. L. Rev. 851 (1999); Michael A. Heller & James E. Krier, *Deterrence and Distribution in the Law of Takings*, 112 Harv. L. Rev. 997 (1999).

2. The Search for Method

a. "Ad hoc, factual inquiries"

PENN CENTRAL TRANSPORTATION CO. v.
CITY OF NEW YORK
438 U.S. 104 (1978)

MR. JUSTICE BRENNAN delivered the opinion of the Court.

The question presented is whether a city may, as part of a comprehensive program to preserve historic landmarks and historic districts, place restrictions on the development of individual historic landmarks — in addition to those imposed by applicable zoning ordinances — without effecting a "taking" requiring the payment of "just compensation." Specifically, we must decide whether the application of New York City's Landmarks Preservation Law to the parcel of land occupied by Grand Central Terminal has "taken" its owners' property in violation of the Fifth and Fourteenth Amendments.

I

A

Over the past 50 years, all 50 States and over 500 municipalities have enacted laws to encourage or require the preservation of buildings and areas with historic or aesthetic importance. These nationwide legislative efforts have been precipitated by two concerns. The first is recognition that, in recent years, large numbers of historic structures, landmarks, and areas have been destroyed without adequate consideration of either the values represented therein or the possibility of preserving the destroyed properties for use in economically productive ways. The second is a widely shared belief that structures with special historic, cultural, or architectural significance enhance the quality of life for all. Not only do these buildings and their workmanship represent the lessons of the past and embody precious features of our heritage, they serve as examples of quality for today. "[H]istoric conservation is but one aspect of the much larger problem, basically an environmental one, of enhancing — or perhaps developing for the first time — the quality of life for people."[4]

New York City, responding to similar concerns and acting pursuant to a New York State enabling Act,[5] adopted its Landmarks Preservation Law in 1965. The city acted from the conviction that "the standing of [New York City] as a world-wide tourist center and world capital of business, culture and government" would be threatened if legislation were not enacted to protect historic landmarks and neighborhoods from precipitate decisions to destroy or fundamentally alter their character. The city believed that comprehensive measures to safeguard desirable features of the existing urban fabric would benefit its citizens in a variety of ways: e.g., fostering "civic pride in the beauty and noble accomplishments of the past"; protecting and enhancing "the city's attractions to tourists and visitors"; "support[ing] and stimul[ating] business and industry"; "strengthen[ing] the economy of the city"; and promoting "the use of historic districts, landmarks, interior landmarks and scenic landmarks for the education, pleasure and welfare of the people of the city."

The New York City law is typical of many urban landmark laws in that its primary method of achieving its goals is not by acquisitions of historic properties,[6] but rather by involving public entities in land-use decisions affecting these properties and providing services, standards, controls, and incentives that will encourage preservation by private owners and users. While the law does place

---

[4] Gilbert, *Introduction, Precedents for the Future*, 36 Law & Contemp. Prob. 311, 312 (1971), quoting address by Robert Stipe, 1971 Conference on Preservation Law, Washington, D. C., May 1, 1971 (unpublished text, pp. 6-7).

[5] See N.Y.Gen.Mun.Law § 96-a (McKinney 1977). It declares that it is the public policy of the State of New York to preserve structures and areas with special historical or aesthetic interest or value and authorizes local governments to impose reasonable restrictions to perpetuate such structures and areas.

[6] The consensus is that widespread public ownership of historic properties in urban settings is neither feasible nor wise. Public ownership reduces the tax base, burdens the public budget with costs of acquisitions and maintenance, and results in the preservation of public buildings as museums and similar facilities, rather than as economically productive features of the urban scene. See Wilson & Winkler, *The Response of State Legislation to Historic Preservation*, 36 Law & Contemp. Prob. 329, 330-331, 339-340 (1971).

special restrictions on landmark properties as a necessary feature to the attainment of its larger objectives, the major theme of the law is to ensure the owners of any such properties both a "reasonable return" on their investments and maximum latitude to use their parcels for purposes not inconsistent with the preservation goals.

The operation of the law can be briefly summarized. The primary responsibility for administering the law is vested in the Landmarks Preservation Commission (Commission), a broad based, 11-member agency assisted by a technical staff. The Commission first performs the function, critical to any landmark preservation effort, of identifying properties and areas that have "a special character or special historical or aesthetic interest or value as part of the development, heritage or cultural characteristics of the city, state or nation." If the Commission determines, after giving all interested parties an opportunity to be heard, that a building or area satisfies the ordinance's criteria, it will designate a building to be a "landmark," situated on a particular "landmark site," or will designate an area to be a "historic district." Thus far, 31 historic districts and over 400 individual landmarks have been finally designated, and the process is a continuing one.

Final designation as a landmark results in restrictions upon the property owner's options concerning use of the landmark site. First, the law imposes a duty upon the owner to keep the exterior features of the building "in good repair" to assure that the law's objectives not be defeated by the landmark's falling into a state of irremediable disrepair. Second, the Commission must approve in advance any proposal to alter the exterior architectural features of the landmark or to construct any exterior improvement on the landmark site, thus ensuring that decisions concerning construction on the landmark site are made with due consideration of both the public interest in the maintenance of the structure and the landowner's interest in use of the property.

In the event an owner wishes to alter a landmark site, three separate procedures are available through which administrative approval may be obtained. First, the owner may apply to the Commission for a "certificate of no effect on protected architectural features," that is, for an order approving the improvement or alteration on the ground that it will not change or affect any architectural feature of the landmark and will be in harmony therewith. Denial of the certificate is subject to judicial review.

Second, the owner may apply to the Commission for a certificate of "appropriateness." Such certificates will be granted if the Commission concludes — focusing upon aesthetic, historical, and architectural values — that the proposed construction on the landmark site would not unduly hinder the protection, enhancement, perpetuation, and use of the landmark. Again, denial of the certificate is subject to judicial review. Moreover, the owner who is denied either a certificate of no exterior effect or a certificate of appropriateness may submit an alternative or modified plan for approval. The final procedure — seeking a certificate of appropriateness on the ground of "insufficient return" — provides special mechanisms, which vary depending on whether or not the landmark enjoys a tax exemption, to ensure that designation does not cause economic hardship.

Although the designation of a landmark and landmark site restricts the owner's control over the parcel, designation also enhances the economic position of the landmark owner in one significant respect. Under New York City's zoning laws, owners of real property who have not developed their property to the full extent permitted by the applicable zoning laws are allowed to transfer development rights to contiguous parcels on the same city block. A 1968 ordinance gave the owners of landmark sites additional opportunities to transfer development rights to other parcels. Subject to a restriction that the floor area of the transferee lot may not be increased by more than 20% above its authorized level, the ordinance permitted transfers from a landmark parcel to property across the street or across a street intersection. In 1969, the class of recipient lots was expanded to include lots "across a street and opposite to another lot or lots which except for the intervention of streets or street intersections f[or]m a series extending to the lot occupied by the landmark building[, provided that] all lots [are] in the same ownership." In addition, the 1969 amendment permits, in highly commercialized areas like midtown Manhattan, the transfer of all unused development rights to a single parcel.

B

This case involves the application of New York City's Landmarks Preservation Law to Grand Central Terminal (Terminal). The Terminal, which is owned by the Penn Central Transportation Co. and its affiliates (Penn Central), is one of New York City's most famous buildings. Opened in 1913, it is regarded not only as providing an ingenious engineering solution to the problems presented by urban railroad stations, but also as a magnificent example of the French beaux-arts style.

The Terminal is located in midtown Manhattan. Its south facade faces 42d Street and that street's intersection with Park Avenue. At street level, the Terminal is bounded on the west by Vanderbilt Avenue, on the east by the Commodore Hotel, and on the north by the Pan-American Building. Although a 20-story office tower, to have been located above the Terminal, was part of the original design, the planned tower was never constructed. The Terminal itself is an eight-story structure which Penn Central uses as a railroad station and in which it rents space not needed for railroad purposes to a variety of commercial interests. The Terminal is one of a number of properties owned by appellant Penn Central in this area of midtown Manhattan. The others include the Barclay, Biltmore, Commodore, Roosevelt, and Waldorf-Astoria Hotels, the Pan-American Building and other office buildings along Park Avenue, and the Yale Club. At least eight of these are eligible to be recipients of development rights afforded the Terminal by virtue of landmark designation.

On August 2, 1967, following a public hearing, the Commission designated the Terminal a "landmark" and designated the "city tax block" it occupies a "landmark site." The Board of Estimate confirmed this action on September 21, 1967. Although appellant Penn Central had opposed the designation before the Commission, it did not seek judicial review of the final designation decision.

On January 22, 1968, appellant Penn Central, to increase its income, entered into a renewable 50-year lease and sublease agreement with appellant UGP

Properties, Inc. (UGP), a wholly owned subsidiary of Union General Properties, Ltd., a United Kingdom corporation. Under the terms of the agreement, UGP was to construct a multistory office building above the Terminal. UGP promised to pay Penn Central $1 million annually during construction and at least $3 million annually thereafter. The rentals would be offset in part by a loss of some $700,000 to $1 million in net rentals presently received from concessionaires displaced by the new building.

Appellants UGP and Penn Central then applied to the Commission for permission to construct an office building atop the Terminal. Two separate plans, both designed by architect Marcel Breuer and both apparently satisfying the terms of the applicable zoning ordinance, were submitted to the Commission for approval. The first, Breuer I, provided for the construction of a 55-story office building, to be cantilevered above the existing facade and to rest on the roof of the Terminal. The second, Breuer II Revised, called for tearing down a portion of the Terminal that included the 42d Street facade, stripping off some of the remaining features of the Terminal's facade, and constructing a 53-story office building. The Commission denied a certificate of no exterior effect on September 20, 1968. Appellants then applied for a certificate of "appropriateness" as to both proposals. After four days of hearings at which over 80 witnesses testified, the Commission denied this application as to both proposals.

The Commission's reasons for rejecting certificates respecting Breuer II Revised are summarized in the following statement: "To protect a Landmark, one does not tear it down. To perpetuate its architectural features, one does not strip them off." Record 2255. Breuer I, which would have preserved the existing vertical facades of the present structure, received more sympathetic consideration. The Commission first focused on the effect that the proposed tower would have on one desirable feature created by the present structure and its surroundings: the dramatic view of the Terminal from Park Avenue South. Although appellants had contended that the Pan-American Building had already destroyed the silhouette of the south facade and that one additional tower could do no further damage and might even provide a better background for the facade, the Commission disagreed, stating that it found the majestic approach from the south to be still unique in the city and that a 55-story tower atop the Terminal would be far more detrimental to its south facade than the Pan-American Building 375 feet away. Moreover, the Commission found that from closer vantage points the Pan Am Building and the other towers were largely cut off from view, which would not be the case of the mass on top of the Terminal planned under Breuer I. In conclusion, the Commission stated:

> [We have] no fixed rule against making additions to designated buildings — it all depends on how they are done. But to balance a 55-story office tower above a flamboyant Beaux-Arts facade seems nothing more than an aesthetic joke. Quite simply, the tower would overwhelm the Terminal by its sheer mass. The "addition" would be four times as high as the existing structure and would reduce the Landmark itself to the status of a curiosity.

> Landmarks cannot be divorced from their settings — particularly when the setting is a dramatic and integral part of the original concept. The

Terminal, in its setting, is a great example of urban design. Such examples are not so plentiful in New York City that we can afford to lose any of the few we have. And we must preserve them in a meaningful way — with alterations and additions of such character, scale, materials and mass as will protect, enhance and perpetuate the original design rather than overwhelm it.

Id. at 2251.

Appellants did not seek judicial review of the denial of either certificate. Because the Terminal site enjoyed a tax exemption, remained suitable for its present and future uses, and was not the subject of a contract of sale, there were no further administrative remedies available to appellants as to the Breuer I and Breuer II Revised plans. Further, appellants did not avail themselves of the opportunity to develop and submit other plans for the Commission's consideration and approval. Instead, appellants filed suit in New York Supreme Court, Trial Term, claiming, inter alia, that the application of the Landmarks Preservation Law had "taken" their property without just compensation in violation of the Fifth and Fourteenth Amendments and arbitrarily deprived them of their property without due process of law in violation of the Fourteenth Amendment. Appellants sought a declaratory judgment, injunctive relief barring the city from using the Landmarks Law to impede the construction of any structure that might otherwise lawfully be constructed on the Terminal site, and damages for the "temporary taking" that occurred between August 2, 1967, the designation date, and the date when the restrictions arising from the Landmarks Law would be lifted. The trial court granted the injunctive and declaratory relief, but severed the question of damages for a "temporary taking."

Appellees appealed, and the New York Supreme Court, Appellate Division, reversed. 377 N.Y.S.2d 20 (1975). The New York Court of Appeals affirmed. 366 N.E.2d 1271 (N.Y. 1977). That court summarily rejected any claim that the Landmarks Law had "taken" property without "just compensation," indicating that there could be no "taking" since the law had not transferred control of the property to the city, but only restricted appellants' exploitation of it. In that circumstance, the Court of Appeals held that appellants' attack on the law could prevail only if the law deprived appellants of their property in violation of the Due Process Clause of the Fourteenth Amendment. Whether or not there was a denial of substantive due process turned on whether the restrictions deprived Penn Central of a "reasonable return" on the "privately created and privately managed ingredient" of the Terminal. *Id.* at 1273.[23] The Court of Appeals concluded that the Landmarks Law

---

[23] The Court of Appeals suggested that in calculating the value of the property upon which appellants were entitled to earn a reasonable return, the "publicly created" components of the value of the property — i.e., those elements of its value attributable to the "efforts of organized society" or to the "social complex" in which the Terminal is located — had to be excluded. However, since the record upon which the Court of Appeals decided the case did not, as that court recognized, contain a basis for segregating the privately created from the publicly created elements of the value of the Terminal site and since the judgment of the Court of Appeals in any event rests upon bases that support our affirmance, see *infra*, this page, we have no occasion to address the question whether it is permissible or feasible to separate out the "social increments" of the value of property. See Costonis, *The Disparity Issue: A Context for the Grand Central Terminal Decision*, 91 Harv.L.Rev. 402, 416-417 (1977).

had not effected a denial of due process because: (1) the landmark regulation permitted the same use as had been made of the Terminal for more than half a century; (2) the appellants had failed to show that they could not earn a reasonable return on their investment in the Terminal itself; (3) even if the Terminal proper could never operate at a reasonable profit some of the income from Penn Central's extensive real estate holdings in the area, which include hotels and office buildings, must realistically be imputed to the Terminal; and (4) the development rights above the Terminal, which had been made transferable to numerous sites in the vicinity of the Terminal, one or two of which were suitable for the construction of office buildings, were valuable to appellants and provided "significant, perhaps 'fair,' compensation for the loss of rights above the terminal itself." *Id.* at 1276-1278.

We noted probable jurisdiction. We affirm.

II

The issues presented by appellants are (1) whether the restrictions imposed by New York City's law upon appellants' exploitation of the Terminal site effect a "taking" of appellants' property for a public use within the meaning of the Fifth Amendment, which of course is made applicable to the States through the Fourteenth Amendment, and, (2), if so, whether the transferable development rights afforded appellants constitute "just compensation" within the meaning of the Fifth Amendment. We need only address the question whether a "taking" has occurred.[25]

Before considering appellants' specific contentions, it will be useful to review the factors that have shaped the jurisprudence of the Fifth Amendment injunction "nor shall private property be taken for public use, without just compensation." The question of what constitutes a "taking" for purposes of the Fifth Amendment has proved to be a problem of considerable difficulty. While this Court has recognized that the "Fifth Amendment's guarantee [is] designed to bar Government from forcing some people alone to bear public burdens which, in all fairness and justice, should be borne by the public as a whole," Armstrong v. United States, 364 U.S. 40, 49 (1960), this Court, quite simply, has been unable to develop any "set formula" for determining when "justice and fairness" require that economic injuries caused by public action be compensated by the government, rather than remain disproportionately concentrated on a few persons. See Goldblatt v. Hempstead, 369 U.S. 590, 594 (1962). Indeed, we have frequently observed that whether a particular restriction will be rendered invalid by the government's failure to pay for any losses proximately caused by it depends largely "upon the particular circumstances [in that] case." United States v. Central Eureka Mining Co., 357 U.S. 155, 168 (1958).

In engaging in these essentially ad hoc, factual inquiries, the Court's decisions have identified several factors that have particular significance. The economic impact of the regulation on the claimant and, particularly, the extent to which the regulation has interfered with distinct investment-backed expectations are, of course, relevant considerations. So, too, is the character of the governmental action.

---

[25] As is implicit in our opinion, we do not embrace the proposition that a "taking" can never occur unless government has transferred physical control over a portion of a parcel.

A "taking" may more readily be found when the interference with property can be characterized as a physical invasion by government, than when interference arises from some public program adjusting the benefits and burdens of economic life to promote the common good.

"Government hardly could go on if to some extent values incident to property could not be diminished without paying for every such change in the general law," Pennsylvania Coal Co. v. Mahon, 260 U.S. 393, 413 (1922), and this Court has accordingly recognized, in a wide variety of contexts, that government may execute laws or programs that adversely affect recognized economic values. Exercises of the taxing power are one obvious example. More importantly for the present case, in instances in which a state tribunal reasonably concluded that "the health, safety, morals, or general welfare" would be promoted by prohibiting particular contemplated uses of land, this Court has upheld land-use regulations that destroyed or adversely affected recognized real property interests. See Nectow v. Cambridge, 277 U.S. 183, 188 (1928). Zoning laws are, of course, the classic example, see Euclid v. Ambler Realty Co., 272 U.S. 365 (1926) (prohibition of industrial use); Gorieb v. Fox, 274 U.S. 603, 608 (1927) (requirement that portions of parcels be left unbuilt); Welch v. Swasey, 214 U.S. 91 (1909) (height restriction), which have been viewed as permissible governmental action even when prohibiting the most beneficial use of the property.

Zoning laws generally do not affect existing uses of real property, but "taking" challenges have also been held to be without merit in a wide variety of situations when the challenged governmental actions prohibited a beneficial use to which individual parcels had previously been devoted and thus caused substantial individualized harm. Miller v. Schoene, 276 U.S. 272 (1928), is illustrative. In that case, a state entomologist, acting pursuant to a state statute, ordered the claimants to cut down a large number of ornamental red cedar trees because they produced cedar rust fatal to apple trees cultivated nearby. Although the statute provided for recovery of any expense incurred in removing the cedars, and permitted claimants to use the felled trees, it did not provide compensation for the value of the standing trees or for the resulting decrease in market value of the properties as a whole. A unanimous Court held that this latter omission did not render the statute invalid. The Court held that the State might properly make "a choice between the preservation of one class of property and that of the other" and since the apple industry was important in the State involved, concluded that the State had not exceeded "its constitutional powers by deciding upon the destruction of one class of property [without compensation] in order to save another which, in the judgment of the legislature, is of greater value to the public." Id. at 279. Again, Hadacheck v. Sebastian, 239 U.S. 394 (1915), upheld a law prohibiting the claimant from continuing his otherwise lawful business of operating a brickyard in a particular physical community on the ground that the legislature had reasonably concluded that the presence of the brickyard was inconsistent with neighboring uses. See also United States v. Central Eureka Mining Co., supra (government order closing gold mines so that skilled miners would be available for other mining work held not a taking); Atchison, T. & S. F. R. Co. v. Public Utilities Comm'n, 346 U.S. 346 (1953) (railroad may be required to share cost of constructing railroad grade improvement); Walls v. Midland Carbon Co., 254 U.S. 300 (1920) (law prohibiting manufacture of carbon black upheld); Reinman v. Little Rock, 237 U.S. 171 (1915) (law prohibiting livery stable upheld); Mugler v. Kansas, 123 U.S. 623 (1887) (law prohibiting liquor business upheld).

Goldblatt v. Hempstead is a recent example. There, a 1958 city safety ordinance banned any excavations below the water table and effectively prohibited the claimant from continuing a sand and gravel mining business that had been operated on the particular parcel since 1927. The Court upheld the ordinance against a "taking" challenge, although the ordinance prohibited the present and presumably most beneficial use of the property and had, like the regulations in *Miller* and *Hadacheck*, severely affected a particular owner. The Court assumed that the ordinance did not prevent the owner's reasonable use of the property since the owner made no showing of an adverse effect on the value of the land. Because the restriction served a substantial public purpose, the Court thus held no taking had occurred.

Pennsylvania Coal Co. v. Mahon is the leading case for the proposition that a state statute that substantially furthers important public policies may so frustrate distinct investment-backed expectations as to amount to a "taking." See also Armstrong v. United States, 364 U.S. 40 (1960) (government's complete destruction of a materialman's lien in certain property held a "taking"); Hudson Water Co. v. McCarter, 209 U.S. 349, 355 (1908) (if height restriction makes property wholly useless "the rights of property prevail over the other public interest" and compensation is required). See generally Michelman, *Property, Utility, and Fairness: Comments on the Ethical Foundations of "Just Compensation" Law,* 80 Harv.L.Rev. 1165, 1229-1234 (1967).

Finally, government actions that may be characterized as acquisitions of resources to permit or facilitate uniquely public functions have often been held to constitute "takings." United States v. Causby, 328 U.S. 256 (1946), is illustrative. In holding that direct overflights above the claimant's land, that destroyed the present use of the land as a chicken farm, constituted a "taking," *Causby* emphasized that Government had not "merely destroyed property [but was] using a part of it for the flight of its planes." *Id.* at 262-263 n. 7. See also Griggs v. Allegheny County, 369 U.S. 84 (1962) (overflights held a taking); Portsmouth Co. v. United States, 260 U.S. 327 (1922) (United States military installations' repeated firing of guns over claimant's land is a taking); United States v. Cress, 243 U.S. 316 (1917) (repeated floodings of land caused by water project is taking). See generally Michelman, *supra* at 1226-1229; Sax, Takings and the Police Power, 74 Yale L.J. 36 (1964).

B

In contending that the New York City law has "taken" their property in violation of the Fifth and Fourteenth Amendments, appellants make a series of arguments, which, while tailored to the facts of this case, essentially urge that any substantial restriction imposed pursuant to a landmark law must be accompanied by just compensation if it is to be constitutional.

They first observe that the airspace above the Terminal is a valuable property interest, citing United States v. Causby, *supra*. They urge that the Landmarks Law has deprived them of any gainful use of their "air rights" above the Terminal and that, irrespective of the value of the remainder of their parcel, the city has "taken" their right to this superadjacent airspace, thus entitling them to "just compensation" measured by the fair market value of these air rights.

Apart from our own disagreement with appellants' characterization of the effect of the New York City law, the submission that appellants may establish a "taking" simply by showing that they have been denied the ability to exploit a property interest that they heretofore had believed was available for development is quite simply untenable. Were this the rule, this Court would have erred not only in upholding laws restricting the development of air rights, see Welch v. Swasey, *supra*, but also in approving those prohibiting both the subjacent, see Goldblatt v. Hempstead, 369 U.S. 590 (1962), and the lateral, see Gorieb v. Fox, 274 U.S. 603 (1927), development of particular parcels.[27] "Taking" jurisprudence does not divide a single parcel into discrete segments and attempt to determine whether rights in a particular segment have been entirely abrogated. In deciding whether a particular governmental action has effected a taking, this Court rather focuses both on the character of the action and on the nature and extent of the interference with rights in the parcel as a whole — here, the city tax block designated as the "landmark site."

Secondly, focusing on the character and impact of the New York City law, appellants argue that it effects a "taking" because its operation has significantly diminished the value of the Terminal site. Appellants concede that the decisions sustaining other land-use regulations uniformly reject the proposition that diminution in property value, standing alone, can establish a "taking," see Euclid v. Ambler Realty Co., 272 U.S. 365 (1926) (75% diminution in value caused by zoning law); Hadacheck v. Sebastian, 239 U.S. 394 (1915) (87 1/2% diminution in value), and that the "taking" issue in these contexts is resolved by focusing on the uses the regulations permit. Appellants, moreover, also do not dispute that a showing of diminution in property value would not establish a taking if the restriction had been imposed as a result of historic-district legislation, but appellants argue that New York City's regulation of individual landmarks is fundamentally different from zoning or from historic-district legislation because the controls imposed by New York City's law apply only to individuals who own selected properties.

Stated baldly, appellants' position appears to be that the only means of ensuring that selected owners are not singled out to endure financial hardship for no reason is to hold that any restriction imposed on individual landmarks pursuant to the New York City scheme is a "taking" requiring the payment of "just compensation." Agreement with this argument would, of course, invalidate not just New York City's law, but all comparable landmark legislation in the Nation. We find no merit in it.

---

[27] These cases dispose of any contention that might be based on Pennsylvania Coal Co. v. Mahon that full use of air rights is so bound up with the investment-backed expectations of appellants that governmental deprivation of these rights invariably — i.e., irrespective of the impact of the restriction on the value of the parcel as a whole — constitutes a "taking." Similarly, *Welch, Goldblatt,* and *Gorieb* illustrate the fallacy of appellants' related contention that a "taking" must be found to have occurred whenever the land-use restriction may be characterized as imposing a "servitude" on the claimant's parcel.

It is true, as appellants emphasize, that both historic-district legislation and zoning laws regulate all properties within given physical communities whereas landmark laws apply only to selected parcels. But, contrary to appellants' suggestions, landmark laws are not like discriminatory, or "reverse spot," zoning: that is, a land-use decision which arbitrarily singles out a particular parcel for different, less favorable treatment than the neighboring ones. In contrast to discriminatory zoning, which is the antithesis of land-use control as part of some comprehensive plan, the New York City law embodies a comprehensive plan to preserve structures of historic or aesthetic interest wherever they might be found in the city,[28] and as noted, over 400 landmarks and 31 historic districts have been designated pursuant to this plan.

Equally without merit is the related argument that the decision to designate a structure as a landmark "is inevitably arbitrary or at least subjective, because it is basically a matter of taste," Reply Brief for Appellants 22, thus unavoidably singling out individual landowners for disparate and unfair treatment. The argument has a particularly hollow ring in this case. For appellants not only did not seek judicial review of either the designation or of the denials of the certificates of appropriateness and of no exterior effect, but do not even now suggest that the Commission's decisions concerning the Terminal were in any sense arbitrary or unprincipled. But, in any event, a landmark owner has a right to judicial review of any Commission decision, and, quite simply, there is no basis whatsoever for a conclusion that courts will have any greater difficulty identifying arbitrary or discriminatory action in the context of landmark regulation than in the context of classic zoning or indeed in any other context.[29]

Next, appellants observe that New York City's law differs from zoning laws and historic-district ordinances in that the Landmarks Law does not impose identical or similar restrictions on all structures located in particular physical communities. It follows, they argue, that New York City's law is inherently incapable of producing the fair and equitable distribution of benefits and burdens of governmental action which is characteristic of zoning laws and historic-district legislation and which they maintain is a constitutional requirement if "just compensation" is not to be afforded. It is, of course, true that the Landmarks Law has a more severe impact on some landowners than on others, but that in itself does not mean that the law effects a "taking." Legislation designed to promote the general welfare commonly burdens some more than others. The owners of the brickyard in *Hadacheck*, of the cedar trees in Miller v. Schoene, and of the gravel and sand mine in Goldblatt v.

---

[28] Although the New York Court of Appeals contrasted the New York City Landmarks Law with both zoning and historic-district legislation and stated at one point that landmark laws do not "further a general community plan," 366 N.E.2d 1271, 1274 (N.Y. 1977), it also emphasized that the implementation of the objectives of the Landmarks Law constitutes an "acceptable reason for singling out one particular parcel for different and less favorable treatment." 366 N.E.2d at 1275. Therefore, we do not understand the New York Court of Appeals to disagree with our characterization of the law.

[29] When a property owner challenges the application of a zoning ordinance to his property, the judicial inquiry focuses upon whether the challenged restriction can reasonably be deemed to promote the objectives of the community land-use plan, and will include consideration of the treatment of similar parcels. See generally Nectow v. Cambridge, 277 U.S. 183 (1928). When a property owner challenges a landmark designation or restriction as arbitrary or discriminatory, a similar inquiry presumably will occur.

Hempstead, were uniquely burdened by the legislation sustained in those cases.[30] Similarly, zoning laws often affect some property owners more severely than others but have not been held to be invalid on that account. For example, the property owner in *Euclid* who wished to use its property for industrial purposes was affected far more severely by the ordinance than its neighbors who wished to use their land for residences.

In any event, appellants' repeated suggestions that they are solely burdened and unbenefited is factually inaccurate. This contention overlooks the fact that the New York City law applies to vast numbers of structures in the city in addition to the Terminal — all the structures contained in the 31 historic districts and over 400 individual landmarks, many of which are close to the Terminal. Unless we are to reject the judgment of the New York City Council that the preservation of landmarks benefits all New York citizens and all structures, both economically and by improving the quality of life in the city as a whole — which we are unwilling to do — we cannot conclude that the owners of the Terminal have in no sense been benefited by the Landmarks Law. Doubtless appellants believe they are more burdened than benefited by the law, but that must have been true, too, of the property owners in *Miller*, *Hadacheck*, *Euclid*, and *Goldblatt*.[32]

Appellants' final broad-based attack would have us treat the law as an instance, like that in United States v. Causby, in which government, acting in an enterprise capacity, has appropriated part of their property for some strictly governmental purpose. Apart from the fact that Causby was a case of invasion of airspace that destroyed the use of the farm beneath and this New York City law has in nowise impaired the present use of the Terminal, the Landmarks Law neither exploits appellants' parcel for city purposes nor facilitates nor arises from any entrepreneurial operations of the city. The situation is not remotely like that in *Causby* where the airspace above the property was in the flight pattern for military aircraft. The Landmarks Law's effect is simply to prohibit appellants or anyone else from occupying portions of the airspace above the Terminal, while permitting appellants to use the remainder of the parcel in a gainful fashion. This is no more an appropriation of property by government for its own uses than is a zoning law

---

[30] Appellants attempt to distinguish these cases on the ground that, in each, government was prohibiting a "noxious" use of land and that in the present case, in contrast, appellants' proposed construction above the Terminal would be beneficial. We observe that the uses in issue in *Hadacheck*, *Miller*, and *Goldblatt* were perfectly lawful in themselves. They involved no "blameworthiness, moral wrongdoing or conscious act of dangerous risk-taking which induce[d society] to shift the cost to a pa[rt]icular individual." Sax, *Takings and the Police Power*, 74 Yale L.J. 36, 50 (1964). These cases are better understood as resting not on any supposed "noxious" quality of the prohibited uses but rather on the ground that the restrictions were reasonably related to the implementation of a policy — not unlike historic preservation — expected to produce a widespread public benefit and applicable to all similarly situated property. Nor, correlatively, can it be asserted that the destruction or fundamental alteration of a historic landmark is not harmful. The suggestion that the beneficial quality of appellants' proposed construction is established by the fact that the construction would have been consistent with applicable zoning laws ignores the development in sensibilities and ideals reflected in landmark legislation like New York City's.

[32] It is, of course, true that the fact the duties imposed by zoning and historic-district legislation apply throughout particular physical communities provides assurances against arbitrariness, but the applicability of the Landmarks Law to a large number of parcels in the city, in our view, provides comparable, if not identical, assurances.

prohibiting, for "aesthetic" reasons, two or more adult theaters within a specified area or a safety regulation prohibiting excavations below a certain level. See Goldblatt v. Hempstead.

C

Rejection of appellants' broad arguments is not, however, the end of our inquiry, for all we thus far have established is that the New York City law is not rendered invalid by its failure to provide "just compensation" whenever a landmark owner is restricted in the exploitation of property interests, such as air rights, to a greater extent than provided for under applicable zoning laws. We now must consider whether the interference with appellants' property is of such a magnitude that "there must be an exercise of eminent domain and compensation to sustain [it]." Pennsylvania Coal Co. v. Mahon, 260 U.S. at 413. That inquiry may be narrowed to the question of the severity of the impact of the law on appellants' parcel, and its resolution in turn requires a careful assessment of the impact of the regulation on the Terminal site.

Unlike the governmental acts in *Goldblatt*, *Miller*, *Causby*, *Griggs*, and *Hadacheck*, the New York City law does not interfere in any way with the present uses of the Terminal. Its designation as a landmark not only permits but contemplates that appellants may continue to use the property precisely as it has been used for the past 65 years: as a railroad terminal containing office space and concessions. So the law does not interfere with what must be regarded as Penn Central's primary expectation concerning the use of the parcel. More importantly, on this record, we must regard the New York City law as permitting Penn Central not only to profit from the Terminal but also to obtain a "reasonable return" on its investment.

Appellants, moreover, exaggerate the effect of the law on their ability to make use of the air rights above the Terminal in two respects.[33] First, it simply cannot be maintained, on this record, that appellants have been prohibited from occupying any portion of the airspace above the Terminal. While the Commission's actions in denying applications to construct an office building in excess of 50 stories above the Terminal may indicate that it will refuse to issue a certificate of appropriateness for any comparably sized structure, nothing the Commission has said or done suggests an intention to prohibit any construction above the Terminal. The Commission's report emphasized that whether any construction would be allowed depended upon whether the proposed addition "would harmonize in scale, material and character with [the Terminal]." Record 2251. Since appellants have not sought approval for the construction of a smaller structure, we do not know that appellants will be denied any use of any portion of the airspace above the Terminal.[34]

Second, to the extent appellants have been denied the right to build above the Terminal, it is not literally accurate to say that they have been denied all use of even

---

[33] Appellants, of course, argue at length that the transferable development rights, while valuable, do not constitute "just compensation." Brief for Appellants 36-43.

[34] Counsel for appellants admitted at oral argument that the Commission has not suggested that it would not, for example, approve a 20-story office tower along the lines of that which was part of the original plan for the Terminal. See Tr. of Oral Arg. 19.

those pre-existing air rights. Their ability to use these rights has not been abrogated; they are made transferable to at least eight parcels in the vicinity of the Terminal, one or two of which have been found suitable for the construction of new office buildings. Although appellants and others have argued that New York City's transferable development-rights program is far from ideal, the New York courts here supportably found that, at least in the case of the Terminal, the rights afforded are valuable. While these rights may well not have constituted "just compensation" if a "taking" had occurred, the rights nevertheless undoubtedly mitigate whatever financial burdens the law has imposed on appellants and, for that reason, are to be taken into account in considering the impact of regulation.

On this record, we conclude that the application of New York City's Landmarks Law has not effected a "taking" of appellants' property. The restrictions imposed are substantially related to the promotion of the general welfare and not only permit reasonable beneficial use of the landmark site but also afford appellants opportunities further to enhance not only the Terminal site proper but also other properties.[36]

Affirmed.

Mr. Justice REHNQUIST, with whom THE CHIEF JUSTICE and Mr. Justice STEVENS join, dissenting.

Of the over one million buildings and structures in the city of New York, appellees have singled out 400 for designation as official landmarks. The question in this case is whether the cost associated with the city of New York's desire to preserve a limited number of "landmarks" within its borders must be borne by all of its taxpayers or whether it can instead be imposed entirely on the owners of the individual properties.

I

A

Appellees do not dispute that valuable property rights have been destroyed. And the Court has frequently emphasized that the term "property" as used in the Taking Clause includes the entire "group of rights inhering in the citizen's [ownership]." United States v. General Motors Corp., 323 U.S. 373 (1945). The term is not used in the

> vulgar and untechnical sense of the physical thing with respect to which the citizen exercises rights recognized by law. [Instead, it] denote[s] the group of rights inhering in the citizen's relation to the physical *thing, as the right to possess, use and dispose of it.* [T]he constitutional provision is addressed to every sort of interest the citizen may possess.

Id., at 377-378 (emphasis added).

---

[36] We emphasize that our holding today is on the present record, which in turn is based on Penn Central's present ability to use the Terminal for its intended purposes and in a gainful fashion. The city conceded at oral argument that if appellants can demonstrate at some point in the future that circumstances have so changed that the Terminal ceases to be "economically viable," appellants may obtain relief. See Tr. of Oral Arg. 42-43.

While neighboring landowners are free to use their land and "air rights" in any way consistent with the broad boundaries of New York zoning, Penn Central, absent the permission of appellees, must forever maintain its property in its present state. The property has been thus subjected to a nonconsensual servitude not borne by any neighboring or similar properties.

B

[A]n examination of the two exceptions where the destruction of property does not constitute a taking demonstrates that a compensable taking has occurred here.

1

As early as 1887, the Court recognized that the government can prevent a property owner from using his property to injure others without having to compensate the owner for the value of the forbidden use. Mugler v. Kansas, 123 U.S. 623 (1887). Appellees are not prohibiting a nuisance. The record is clear that the proposed addition to the Grand Central Terminal would be in full compliance with zoning, height limitations, and other health and safety requirements. Instead, appellees are seeking to preserve what they believe to be an outstanding example of beaux-arts architecture. Penn Central is prevented from further developing its property basically because too good a job was done in designing and building it. The city of New York, because of its unadorned admiration for the design, has decided that the owners of the building must preserve it unchanged for the benefit of sightseeing New Yorkers and tourists.

Unlike land-use regulations, appellees' actions do not merely prohibit Penn Central from using its property in a narrow set of noxious ways. Instead, appellees have placed an affirmative duty on Penn Central to maintain the Terminal in its present state and in "good repair." Appellants are not free to use their property as they see fit within broad outer boundaries but must strictly adhere to their past use except where appellees conclude that alternative uses would not detract from the landmark. While Penn Central may continue to use the Terminal as it is presently designed, appellees otherwise "exercise complete dominion and control over the surface of the land," United States v. Causby, 328 U.S. 256, 262 (1946), and must compensate the owner for his loss.

2

Even where the government prohibits a noninjurious use, the Court has ruled that a taking does not take place if the prohibition applies over a broad cross section of land and thereby "secure[s] an average reciprocity of advantage." Pennsylvania Coal Co. v. Mahon. It is for this reason that zoning does not constitute a "taking." While zoning at times reduces individual property values, the burden is shared relatively evenly and it is reasonable to conclude that on the whole an individual who is harmed by one aspect of the zoning will be benefited by another.

Here, however, a multimillion dollar loss has been imposed on appellants; it is uniquely felt and is not offset by any benefits flowing from the preservation of some

400 other "landmarks" in New York City. Appellees have imposed a substantial cost on less than one one-tenth of one percent of the buildings in New York City for the general benefit of all its people. It is exactly this imposition of general costs on a few individuals at which the "taking" protection is directed.

C

Appellees contend that, even if they have "taken" appellants' property, TDR's constitute "just compensation." Appellants, of course, argue that TDR's are highly imperfect compensation. Because the lower courts held that there was no "taking," they did not have to reach the question of whether or not just compensation has already been awarded. The New York Court of Appeals' discussion of TDR's gives some support to appellants. On the other hand, there is evidence in the record that Penn Central has been offered substantial amounts for its TDR's. Because the record on appeal is relatively slim, I would remand to the Court of Appeals for a determination of whether TDR's constitute a "full and perfect equivalent for the property taken." Monongahela Navigation Co. v. United States, 148 U.S. 312, 326 (1893).

NOTES AND QUESTIONS

1. **Procedural protections.** What procedural protections did the New York landmarks statute provide for landowners? Did the landowner take advantage of those protections? Should the landowner have done so?

2. **A test?** Does Justice Brennan state a test for determining when a regulation constitutes a taking, or does he rather suggest that alleged "takings" challenges do not lend themselves to a clear test?

3. **Factors.** To what extent is the economic impact of the regulation on the landowner an important factor in regulatory takings analysis? What is a "distinct, investment-backed expectation," and what is its relevance in regulatory takings analysis? *See* Steven J. Eagle, *The Rise and Rise of "Investment-Backed Expectations,"* 32 Urb. Law. 437 (2000).

4. **Conceptual severance.** Professor Margaret Jane Radin, in *The Liberal Conception of Property: Cross Currents in the Jurisprudence of Takings*, 88 Colum. L. Rev. 1667 (1988), has identified a "conceptual severance" argument at work in the opinions of some members of the Court in regulatory takings cases: whether a regulation amounts to a taking may depend on how the landowner's relevant "property" is defined. What is Justice Rehnquist's assessment of the impact of the regulation on the landowner's bundle of sticks?

5. **Reciprocity of advantage.** Does the landowner in the principal case derive any offsetting advantage from the burden that the regulation imposes on it?

b.   Categorical Tests

LUCAS v. SOUTH CAROLINA COASTAL COUNCIL
505 U.S. 1003 (1992)

JUSTICE SCALIA delivered the opinion of the Court.

In 1986, petitioner David H. Lucas paid $975,000 for two residential lots on the Isle of Palms in Charleston County, South Carolina, on which he intended to build single-family homes. In 1988, however, the South Carolina Legislature enacted the Beachfront Management Act which had the direct effect of barring petitioner from erecting any permanent habitable structures on his two parcels. A state trial court found that this prohibition rendered Lucas's parcels "valueless." This case requires us to decide whether the Act's dramatic effect on the economic value of Lucas's lots accomplished a taking of private property under the Fifth and Fourteenth Amendments requiring the payment of "just compensation."

I

A

South Carolina's expressed interest in intensively managing development activities in the so-called "coastal zone" dates from 1977 when, in the aftermath of Congress's passage of the federal Coastal Zone Management Act of 1972, 16 U.S.C. § 1451 et seq., the legislature enacted a Coastal Zone Management Act of its own. See S.C.Code Ann. § 48-39-10 et seq. (1987). In its original form, the South Carolina Act required owners of coastal zone land that qualified as a "critical area" (defined in the legislation to include beaches and immediately adjacent sand dunes § 48-39-10(J)) to obtain a permit from the newly created South Carolina Coastal Council prior to committing the land to a "use other than the use the critical area was devoted to on [September 28, 1977]." § 48-39-130(A).

In the late 1970s, Lucas and others began extensive residential development of the Isle of Palms, a barrier island situated eastward of the city of Charleston. Toward the close of the development cycle for one residential subdivision known as "Beachwood East," Lucas in 1986 purchased the two lots at issue in this litigation for his own account. No portion of the lots, which were located approximately 300 feet from the beach, qualified as a "critical area" under the 1977 Act; accordingly, at the time Lucas acquired these parcels, he was not legally obliged to obtain a permit from the Council in advance of any development activity. His intention with respect to the lots was to do what the owners of the immediately adjacent parcels had already done: erect single-family residences. He commissioned architectural drawings for this purpose.

The Beachfront Management Act brought Lucas's plans to an abrupt end. Under that 1988 legislation, the Council was directed to establish a "baseline" connecting the landward-most "point[s] of erosion during the past forty years" in the region of the Isle of Palms that includes Lucas's lots. S.C.Code Ann. § 48-39-280(A)(2) (Supp.1988). In action not challenged here, the Council fixed this baseline landward of Lucas's parcels. That was significant, for under the Act construction of occupiable improvements was flatly prohibited seaward of a line drawn 20 feet landward of, and parallel to, the baseline. The Act provided no exceptions.

B

Lucas promptly filed suit in the South Carolina Court of Common Pleas, contending that the Beachfront Management Act's construction bar effected a taking of his property without just compensation. Lucas did not take issue with the validity of the Act as a lawful exercise of South Carolina's police power, but contended that the Act's complete extinguishment of his property's value entitled him to compensation regardless of whether the legislature had acted in furtherance of legitimate police power objectives. Following a bench trial, the court agreed. Among its factual determinations was the finding that "at the time Lucas purchased the two lots, both were zoned for single-family residential construction and there were no restrictions imposed upon such use of the property by either the State of South Carolina, the County of Charleston, or the Town of the Isle of Palms." The trial court further found that the Beachfront Management Act decreed a permanent ban on construction insofar as Lucas's lots were concerned, and that this prohibition "deprive[d] Lucas of any reasonable economic use of the lots, eliminated the unrestricted right of use, and render[ed] them valueless." The court thus concluded that Lucas's properties had been "taken" by operation of the Act, and it ordered respondent to pay "just compensation" in the amount of $1,232,387.50.

The Supreme Court of South Carolina reversed. It found dispositive what it described as Lucas's concession "that the Beachfront Management Act [was] properly and validly designed to preserve South Carolina's beaches." 404 S.E.2d 895, 896 (1991). Failing an attack on the validity of the statute as such, the court believed itself bound to accept the "uncontested findings" of the South Carolina Legislature that new construction in the coastal zone — such as petitioner intended — threatened this public resource. The court ruled that when a regulation respecting the use of property is designed "to prevent serious public harm," no compensation is owing under the Takings Clause regardless of the regulation's effect on the property's value.

III
A

Prior to Justice Holmes's exposition in Pennsylvania Coal Co. v. Mahon, it was generally thought that the Takings Clause reached only a "direct appropriation" of property, or the functional equivalent of a "practical ouster of [the owner's] possession." Justice Holmes recognized in *Mahon*, however, that if the protection against physical appropriations of private property was to be meaningfully enforced, the government's power to redefine the range of interests included in the ownership of property was necessarily constrained by constitutional limits. Nevertheless, our decision in *Mahon* offered little insight into when, and under what circumstances, a given regulation would be seen as going "too far" for purposes of the Fifth Amendment. In 70-odd years of succeeding "regulatory takings" jurisprudence, we have generally eschewed any "set formula" for determining how far is too far, preferring to "engag[e] in essentially ad hoc, factual inquiries." Penn Central Transportation Co. v. New York City, 438 U.S. 104, 124 (1978). See Epstein, *Takings: Descent and Resurrection*, 1987 S.Ct. Rev. 1, 4. We have, however, described at least two discrete categories of regulatory action as compensable without case-specific inquiry into the public interest advanced in support of the restraint. The first encompasses regulations that compel the property owner to suffer a physical "invasion" of his property. In general (at least with regard to permanent invasions), no matter how minute the intrusion, and no matter how weighty the public purpose behind it, we have required compensation. See Loretto v. Teleprompter Manhattan CATV Corp., 458 U.S. 419 (1982). In *Loretto*, we determined that New York's law requiring landlords to allow television cable companies to emplace cable facilities in their apartment buildings constituted a taking, even though the facilities occupied only 1 1/2 cubic feet of the landlords' property.

The second situation in which we have found categorical treatment appropriate is where regulation denies all economically beneficial or productive use of land. As we have said on numerous occasions, the Fifth Amendment is violated when land-use regulation "does not substantially advance legitimate state interests or *denies an owner economically viable use of his land*." *Agins v. Tiburon*, 447 U.S. at 260 (emphasis added).[7]

We have never set forth the justification for this rule. Perhaps it is simply, as Justice Brennan suggested, that total deprivation of beneficial use is, from the landowner's point of view, the equivalent of a physical appropriation. See San Diego Gas & Electric Co. v. San Diego, 450 U.S., at 652. "[F]or what is the land but the profits thereof[?]" 1 E. Coke, Institutes, ch. 1, § 1 (1st Am. ed. 1812). Surely, at least, in the extraordinary circumstance when no productive or economically beneficial use of land is permitted, it is less realistic to indulge our usual assumption that the legislature is simply "adjusting the benefits and burdens of

---

[7] Regrettably, the rhetorical force of our "deprivation of all economically feasible use" rule is greater than its precision, since the rule does not make clear the "property interest" against which the loss of value is to be measured. When, for example, a regulation requires a developer to leave 90% of a rural tract in its natural state, it is unclear whether we would analyze the situation as one in which the owner has been deprived of all economically beneficial use of the burdened portion of the tract, or as one in which the owner has suffered a mere diminution in value of the tract as a whole. (For an extreme — and, we think, unsupportable — view of the relevant calculus, see Penn Central Transportation Co. v. New York City, 366 N.E.2d 1271, 1276-1277 (N.Y. 1977), *aff'd*, 438 U.S. 104 (1978), where the state court examined the diminution in a particular parcel's value produced by a municipal ordinance in light of total value of the takings claimant's other holdings in the vicinity.) Unsurprisingly, this uncertainty regarding the composition of the denominator in our "deprivation" fraction has produced inconsistent pronouncements by the Court. Compare Pennsylvania Coal Co. v. Mahon (law restricting subsurface extraction of coal held to effect a taking), with Keystone Bituminous Coal Assn. v. DeBenedictis, 480 U.S. 470, 497-502 (1987) (nearly identical law held not to effect a taking); Rose, Mahon *Reconstructed: Why the Takings Issue is Still a Muddle*, 57 S.Cal.L.Rev. 561, 566-569 (1984). The answer to this difficult question may lie in how the owner's reasonable expectations have been shaped by the State's law of property — i.e., whether and to what degree the State's law has accorded legal recognition and protection to the particular interest in land with respect to which the takings claimant alleges a diminution in (or elimination of) value. In any event, we avoid this difficulty in the present case, since the "interest in land" that Lucas has pleaded (a fee simple interest) is an estate with a rich tradition of protection at common law, and since the South Carolina Court of Common Pleas found that the Beachfront Management Act left each of Lucas's beachfront lots without economic value.

economic life," *Penn Central Transportation Co.*, 438 U.S. at 124, in a manner that secures an "average reciprocity of advantage" to everyone concerned. And the functional basis for permitting the government, by regulation, to affect property values without compensation — that "Government hardly could go on if to some extent values incident to property could not be diminished without paying for every such change in the general law" — does not apply to the relatively rare situations where the government has deprived a landowner of all economically beneficial uses.

On the other side of the balance, affirmatively supporting a compensation requirement, is the fact that regulations that leave the owner of land without economically beneficial or productive options for its use — typically, as here, by requiring land to be left substantially in its natural state — carry with them a heightened risk that private property is being pressed into some form of public service under the guise of mitigating serious public harm. See, e.g., Annicelli v. South Kingstown, 463 A.2d 133, 140-141 (R.I.1983) (prohibition on construction adjacent to beach justified on twin grounds of safety and "conservation of open space"); Morris County Land Improvement Co. v. Parsippany-Troy Hills Township, 193 A.2d 232, 240 (N.J. 1963) (prohibition on filling marshlands imposed in order to preserve region as water detention basin and create wildlife refuge). The many statutes on the books, both state and federal, that provide for the use of eminent domain to impose servitudes on private scenic lands preventing developmental uses, or to acquire such lands altogether, suggest the practical equivalence in this setting of negative regulation and appropriation.

We think, in short, that there are good reasons for our frequently expressed belief that when the owner of real property has been called upon to sacrifice all economically beneficial uses in the name of the common good, that is, to leave his property economically idle, he has suffered a taking.[8]

---

[8] Justice STEVENS criticizes the "deprivation of all economically beneficial use" rule as "wholly arbitrary," in that "[the] landowner whose property is diminished in value 95% recovers nothing," while the landowner who suffers a complete elimination of value "recovers the land's full value." This analysis errs in its assumption that the landowner whose deprivation is one step short of complete is not entitled to compensation. Such an owner might not be able to claim the benefit of our categorical formulation, but, as we have acknowledged time and again, "[t]he economic impact of the regulation on the claimant and the extent to which the regulation has interfered with distinct investment-backed expectations" are keenly relevant to takings analysis generally. Penn Central Transportation Co. v. New York City, 438 U.S. 104 (1978). It is true that in at least some cases the landowner with 95% loss will get nothing, while the landowner with total loss will recover in full. But that occasional result is no more strange than the gross disparity between the landowner whose premises are taken for a highway (who recovers in full) and the landowner whose property is reduced to 5% of its former value by the highway (who recovers nothing). Takings law is full of these "all-or-nothing" situations. Justice STEVENS similarly misinterprets our focus on "developmental" uses of property (the uses proscribed by the Beachfront Management Act) as betraying an "assumption that the only uses of property cognizable under the Constitution are developmental uses." We make no such assumption. Though our prior takings cases evince an abiding concern for the productive use of, and economic investment in, land, there are plainly a number of noneconomic interests in land whose impairment will invite exceedingly close scrutiny under the Takings Clause. See, e.g., Loretto v. Teleprompter Manhattan CATV Corp., 458 U.S. 419, 436 (1982) (interest in excluding strangers from one's land).

B

It is correct that many of our prior opinions have suggested that "harmful or noxious uses" of property may be proscribed by government regulation without the requirement of compensation. For a number of reasons, however, we think the South Carolina Supreme Court was too quick to conclude that that principle decides the present case. The "harmful or noxious uses" principle was the Court's early attempt to describe in theoretical terms why government may, consistent with the Takings Clause, affect property values by regulation without incurring an obligation to compensate — a reality we nowadays acknowledge explicitly with respect to the full scope of the State's police power.

The transition from our early focus on control of "noxious" uses to our contemporary understanding of the broad realm within which government may regulate without compensation was an easy one, since the distinction between "harm-preventing" and "benefit-conferring" regulation is often in the eye of the beholder. It is quite possible, for example, to describe in either fashion the ecological, economic, and esthetic concerns that inspired the South Carolina Legislature in the present case. One could say that imposing a servitude on Lucas's land is necessary in order to prevent his use of it from "harming" South Carolina's ecological resources; or, instead, in order to achieve the "benefits" of an ecological preserve. Compare, e.g., Claridge v. New Hampshire Wetlands Board, 485 A.2d 287, 292 (N.H. 1984) (owner may, without compensation, be barred from filling wetlands because landfilling would deprive adjacent coastal habitats and marine fisheries of ecological support), with, e.g., Bartlett v. Zoning Comm'n of Old Lyme, 282 A.2d 907, 910 (Conn. 1971) (owner barred from filling tidal marshland must be compensated, despite municipality's "laudable" goal of "preserv[ing] marshlands from encroachment or destruction"). Whether one or the other of the competing characterizations will come to one's lips in a particular case depends primarily upon one's evaluation of the worth of competing uses of real estate. See Restatement (Second) of Torts § 822, Comment g, p. 112 (1979) ("Practically all human activities unless carried on in a wilderness interfere to some extent with others or involve some risk of interference"). A given restraint will be seen as mitigating "harm" to the adjacent parcels or securing a "benefit" for them, depending upon the observer's evaluation of the relative importance of the use that the restraint favors. See Sax, *Takings and the Police Power*, 74 Yale L.J. 36, 49 (1964) ("[T]he problem [in this area] is not one of noxiousness or harm-creating activity at all; rather it is a problem of inconsistency between perfectly innocent and independently desirable uses"). Whether Lucas's construction of single-family residences on his parcels should be described as bringing "harm" to South Carolina's adjacent ecological resources thus depends principally upon whether the describer believes that the State's use interest in nurturing those resources is so important that any competing adjacent use must yield.[12]

---

[12] In Justice BLACKMUN's view, even with respect to regulations that deprive an owner of all developmental or economically beneficial land uses, the test for required compensation is whether the legislature has recited a harm-preventing justification for its action. Since such a justification can be formulated in practically every case, this amounts to a test of whether the legislature has a stupid staff. We think the Takings Clause requires courts to do more than insist upon artful harm-preventing characterizations.

When it is understood that "prevention of harmful use" was merely our early formulation of the police power justification necessary to sustain (without compensation) any regulatory diminution in value; and that the distinction between regulation that "prevents harmful use" and that which "confers benefits" is difficult, if not impossible, to discern on an objective, value-free basis; it becomes self-evident that noxious-use logic cannot serve as a touchstone to distinguish regulatory "takings" — which require compensation — from regulatory deprivations that do not require compensation. A fortiori the legislature's recitation of a noxious-use justification cannot be the basis for departing from our categorical rule that total regulatory takings must be compensated. If it were, departure would virtually always be allowed. The South Carolina Supreme Court's approach would essentially nullify *Mahon's* affirmation of limits to the noncompensable exercise of the police power. Our cases provide no support for this: None of them that employed the logic of "harmful use" prevention to sustain a regulation involved an allegation that the regulation wholly eliminated the value of the claimant's land.[13]

Where the State seeks to sustain regulation that deprives land of all economically beneficial use, we think it may resist compensation only if the logically antecedent inquiry into the nature of the owner's estate shows that the proscribed use interests were not part of his title to begin with. This accords, we think, with our "takings" jurisprudence, which has traditionally been guided by the understandings of our citizens regarding the content of, and the State's power over, the "bundle of rights" that they acquire when they obtain title to property. It seems to us that the property owner necessarily expects the uses of his property to be restricted, from time to time, by various measures newly enacted by the State in legitimate exercise of its police powers; "[a]s long recognized, some values are enjoyed under an implied limitation and must yield to the police power." Pennsylvania Coal Co. v. Mahon, 260 U.S. at 413. And in the case of personal property, by reason of the State's traditionally high degree of control over commercial dealings, he ought to be aware of the possibility that new regulation might even render his property economically worthless (at least if the property's only economically productive use is sale or manufacture for sale). See Andrus v. Allard, 444 U.S. 51 (1979) (prohibition on sale of eagle feathers). In the case of land, however, we think the notion pressed by the Council that title is somehow held subject to the "implied limitation" that the State may subsequently eliminate all economically valuable use is inconsistent with the historical compact recorded in the Takings Clause that has become part of our constitutional culture.

Where "permanent physical occupation" of land is concerned, we have refused to allow the government to decree it anew (without compensation), no matter how weighty the asserted "public interests" involved — though we assuredly would

---

[13] E.g., Mugler v. Kansas, 123 U.S. 623 (1887) (prohibition upon use of a building as a brewery; other uses permitted); Plymouth Coal Co. v. Pennsylvania, 232 U.S. 531 (1914) (requirement that "pillar" of coal be left in ground to safeguard mine workers; mineral rights could otherwise be exploited); Reinman v. Little Rock, 237 U.S. 171 (1915) (declaration that livery stable constituted a public nuisance; other uses of the property permitted); Hadacheck v. Sebastian, 239 U.S. 394 (1915) (prohibition of brick manufacturing in residential area; other uses permitted); Goldblatt v. Hempstead, 369 U.S. 590 (1962) (prohibition on excavation; other uses permitted).

permit the government to assert a permanent easement that was a pre-existing limitation upon the landowner's title. Compare Scranton v. Wheeler, 179 U.S. 141, 163 (1900) (interests of "riparian owner in the submerged lands bordering on a public navigable water" held subject to Government's navigational servitude), with Kaiser Aetna v. United States, 444 U.S. at 178-180 (imposition of navigational servitude on marina created and rendered navigable at private expense held to constitute a taking). We believe similar treatment must be accorded confiscatory regulations, i.e., regulations that prohibit all economically beneficial use of land: Any limitation so severe cannot be newly legislated or decreed (without compensation), but must inhere in the title itself, in the restrictions that background principles of the State's law of property and nuisance already place upon land ownership. A law or decree with such an effect must, in other words, do no more than duplicate the result that could have been achieved in the courts — by adjacent landowners (or other uniquely affected persons) under the State's law of private nuisance, or by the State under its complementary power to abate nuisances that affect the public generally, or otherwise.[16]

On this analysis, the owner of a lake-bed, for example, would not be entitled to compensation when he is denied the requisite permit to engage in a landfilling operation that would have the effect of flooding others' land. Nor the corporate owner of a nuclear generating plant, when it is directed to remove all improvements from its land upon discovery that the plant sits astride an earthquake fault. Such regulatory action may well have the effect of eliminating the land's only economically productive use, but it does not proscribe a productive use that was previously permissible under relevant property and nuisance principles. The use of these properties for what are now expressly prohibited purposes was always unlawful, and (subject to other constitutional limitations) it was open to the State at any point to make the implication of those background principles of nuisance and property law explicit. See Michelman, *Property, Utility, and Fairness, Comments on the Ethical Foundations of "Just Compensation" Law*, 80 Harv.L.Rev. 1165, 1239-1241 (1967). In light of our traditional resort to "existing rules or understandings that stem from an independent source such as state law" to define the range of interests that qualify for protection as "property" under the Fifth and Fourteenth Amendments, Board of Regents of State Colleges v. Roth, 408 U.S. 564, 577 (1972), this recognition that the Takings Clause does not require compensation when an owner is barred from putting land to a use that is proscribed by those "existing rules or understandings" is surely unexceptional. When, however, a regulation that declares "off-limits" all economically productive or beneficial uses of land goes beyond what the relevant background principles would dictate, compensation must be paid to sustain it.[17]

---

[16] The principal "otherwise" that we have in mind is litigation absolving the State (or private parties) of liability for the destruction of "real and personal property, in cases of actual necessity, to prevent the spreading of a fire" or to forestall other grave threats to the lives and property of others. Bowditch v. Boston, 101 U.S. 16 (1880).

[17] Of course, the State may elect to rescind its regulation and thereby avoid having to pay compensation for a permanent deprivation. See *First English Evangelical Lutheran Church*, 482 U.S. at 321. But "where the [regulation has] already worked a taking of all use of property, no subsequent

The "total taking" inquiry we require today will ordinarily entail (as the application of state nuisance law ordinarily entails) analysis of, among other things, the degree of harm to public lands and resources, or adjacent private property, posed by the claimant's proposed activities, see, e.g., Restatement (Second) of Torts §§ 826, 827, the social value of the claimant's activities and their suitability to the locality in question, see, e.g., id. §§ 828(a) and (b), 831, and the relative ease with which the alleged harm can be avoided through measures taken by the claimant and the government (or adjacent private landowners) alike, see, e.g., id. §§ 827(e), 828(c), 830. The fact that a particular use has long been engaged in by similarly situated owners ordinarily imports a lack of any common-law prohibition (though changed circumstances or new knowledge may make what was previously permissible no longer so), see id., § 827, Comment g. So also does the fact that other landowners, similarly situated, are permitted to continue the use denied to the claimant.

It seems unlikely that common-law principles would have prevented the erection of any habitable or productive improvements on petitioner's land; they rarely support prohibition of the "essential use" of land, Curtin v. Benson, 222 U.S. 78, 86 (1911). The question, however, is one of state law to be dealt with on remand. We emphasize that to win its case South Carolina must do more than proffer the legislature's declaration that the uses Lucas desires are inconsistent with the public interest, or the conclusory assertion that they violate a common-law maxim such as sic utere tuo ut alienum non laedas. As we have said, a "State, by ipse dixit, may not transform private property into public property without compensation." Webb's Fabulous Pharmacies, Inc. v. Beckwith, 449 U.S. 155, 164 (1980). Instead, as it would be required to do if it sought to restrain Lucas in a common-law action for public nuisance, South Carolina must identify background principles of nuisance and property law that prohibit the uses he now intends in the circumstances in which the property is presently found. Only on this showing can the State fairly claim that, in proscribing all such beneficial uses, the Beachfront Management Act is taking nothing.

The judgment is reversed, and the case is remanded for proceedings not inconsistent with this opinion.

NOTES AND QUESTIONS

1. **Literature.** For studies relevant to the principal case, see Hope M. Babcock, *Should* Lucas v. South Carolina Coastal Council *Protect Where the Wild Things Are? Of Beavers, Bob-O-Links, and Other Things That Go Bump in the Night*, 85 Iowa L. Rev. 849 (2000); Andrew S. Gold, *Regulatory Takings and Original Intent: The Direct, Physical Takings Thesis "Goes Too Far,"* 49 Am. U. L. Rev. 181, 182 (1999) ("Contrary to most recent scholarship [arguing that the Framers intended the Fifth Amendment to apply only to physical takings], the text and historical record of the Takings Clause arguably support a just compensation requirement for regulatory takings.").

---

action by the government can relieve it of the duty to provide compensation for the period during which the taking was effective." *Id.*

2. **Method.** How does the Court's method for determining whether the contested South Carolina regulation constitutes a taking differ from the Court's method in the *Penn Central* case?

3. **The categorical approach.** What two discrete categories of cases require the method of analysis employed by the Court in *Lucas*? Why?

4. **Scope of the categorical approach.** Are there likely to be many cases involving total deprivation of value to the landowner? Does the answer depend on whether one uses "conceptual severance" to define the relevant property of the landowner? Does the principal case require total or nearly total deprivation of value?

5. **Review and extensions.** Review *Pennsylvania Coal* and *Penn Central*. What role do the following themes from those earlier cases play in the opinions in the principal case: distinct, investment-backed expectations; the diminution in value that Lucas's parcel suffers; conceptual severance; average reciprocity of advantage?

6. **The nuisance exception.** What is the "nuisance exception," and what is its importance in the principal case? What body of law determines whether a particular land use is a nuisance? Is the exception in fact a "nuisance exception" or is it broader? Consider the discussion of the exception in the following case.

7. **The "substantially advances" requirement.** The Court in *Lucas* cites Agins v. City of Tiburon, 447 U.S. 255, 260 (1980), for the proposition that a violation of the Fifth Amendment occurs if a regulation "does not substantially advance legitimate state interests." This requirement had raised a number of questions in recent years: Does the Takings Clause require that a regulation substantially advance a legitimate state interest? Does this test require a higher level of scrutiny than the Due Process Clause? In Lingle v. Chevron, 544 U.S. 528, 545 (2005), the Court resolved the confusion, holding that "the 'substantially advances' formula announced in *Agins* is not a valid method of identifying regulatory takings for which the Fifth Amendment requires just compensation."

c. **Refining the Tests**

PALAZZOLO v. RHODE ISLAND
533 U.S. 606 (2001)

Justice Kennedy delivered the opinion of the Court.

Petitioner Anthony Palazzolo owns a waterfront parcel of land in the town of Westerly, Rhode Island. Almost all of the property is designated as coastal wetlands under Rhode Island law. After petitioner's development proposals were rejected by respondent Rhode Island Coastal Resources Management Council (Council), he sued in state court, asserting the Council's application of its wetlands regulations took the property without compensation in violation of the Takings Clause of the Fifth Amendment, binding upon the State through the Due Process Clause of the Fourteenth Amendment. Petitioner sought review in this Court, contending the Supreme Court of Rhode Island erred in rejecting his takings claim. We granted certiorari.

I

In 1959 petitioner, a lifelong Westerly resident, decided to invest in three undeveloped, adjoining parcels along Atlantic Avenue. To the north, the property faces, and borders upon, Winnapaug Pond; the south of the property faces Atlantic Avenue and the beachfront homes abutting it on the other side, and beyond that the dunes and the beach. To purchase and hold the property, petitioner and associates formed Shore Gardens, Inc. (SGI). After SGI purchased the property petitioner bought out his associates and became the sole shareholder. In the first decade of SGI's ownership of the property the corporation submitted a plat to the town subdividing the property into 80 lots; and it engaged in various transactions that left it with 74 lots, which together encompassed about 20 acres. During the same period SGI also made initial attempts to develop the property and submitted intermittent applications to state agencies to fill substantial portions of the parcel. Most of the property was then, as it is now, salt marsh subject to tidal flooding. The wet ground and permeable soil would require considerable fill — as much as six feet in some places — before significant structures could be built. SGI's proposal, submitted in 1962 to the Rhode Island Division of Harbors and Rivers (DHR), sought to dredge from Winnapaug Pond and fill the entire property. The application was denied for lack of essential information. A second, similar proposal followed a year later. A third application, submitted in 1966 while the second application was pending, proposed more limited filling of the land for use as a private beach club. These latter two applications were referred to the Rhode Island Department of Natural Resources, which indicated initial assent. The agency later withdrew approval, however, citing adverse environmental impacts. SGI did not contest the ruling.

No further attempts to develop the property were made for over a decade. Two intervening events, however, become important to the issues presented. First, in 1971, Rhode Island enacted legislation creating the Council, an agency charged with the duty of protecting the State's coastal properties. Regulations promulgated by the Council designated salt marshes like those on SGI's property as protected "coastal wetlands," Rhode Island Coastal Resources Management Program (CRMP) § 210.3 (as amended, June 28, 1983), on which development is limited to a great extent. Second, in 1978, SGI's corporate charter was revoked for failure to pay corporate income taxes; and title to the property passed, by operation of state law, to petitioner as the corporation's sole shareholder.

In 1983, petitioner, now the owner, renewed the efforts to develop the property. An application to the Council, resembling the 1962 submission, requested permission to construct a wooden bulkhead along the shore of Winnapaug Pond and to fill the entire marshland area. The Council rejected the application.

Petitioner went back to the drawing board, this time hiring counsel and preparing a more specific and limited proposal for use of the property. The new application, submitted to the Council in 1985, echoed the 1966 request to build a private beach club.

The application fared no better with the Council than previous ones. Under the agency's regulations, a landowner wishing to fill salt marsh on Winnapaug Pond needed a "special exception" from the Council. CRMP § 130. In a short opinion the

Council said the beach club proposal conflicted with the regulatory standard for a special exception. This time petitioner appealed the decision to the Rhode Island courts, challenging the Council's conclusion as contrary to principles of state administrative law. The Council's decision was affirmed.

Petitioner filed an inverse condemnation action in Rhode Island Superior Court, asserting that the State's wetlands regulations, as applied by the Council to his parcel, had taken the property without compensation in violation of the Fifth and Fourteenth Amendments. The suit alleged the Council's action deprived him of "economically, beneficial use" of his property, resulting in a total taking requiring compensation under Lucas v. South Carolina Coastal Council, 505 U.S. 1003 (1992). He sought damages in the amount of $3,150,000, a figure derived from an appraiser's estimate as to the value of a 74-lot residential subdivision. The State countered with a host of defenses. After a bench trial, a justice of the Superior Court ruled against petitioner, accepting some of the State's theories.

The Rhode Island Supreme Court affirmed. Like the Superior Court, the State Supreme Court recited multiple grounds for rejecting petitioner's suit. The court held that petitioner had no right to challenge regulations predating 1978, when he succeeded to legal ownership of the property from SGI; and that the claim of deprivation of all economically beneficial use was contradicted by undisputed evidence that he had $200,000 in development value remaining on an upland parcel of the property. In addition to holding petitioner could not assert a takings claim based on the denial of all economic use, the court concluded he could not recover under the more general test of Penn Central Transp. Co. v. City New York, 438 U.S. 104 (1978). On this claim, too, the date of acquisition of the parcel was found determinative, and the court held he could have had "no reasonable investment-backed expectations that were affected by this regulation" because it predated his ownership, 746 A.2d, at 717.

We disagree with the Supreme Court of Rhode Island as to the first of these conclusions; and, we hold, the court was correct to conclude that the owner is not deprived of all economic use of his property because the value of upland portions is substantial. We remand for further consideration of the claim under the principles set forth in *Penn Central.*

II

The Takings Clause of the Fifth Amendment, applicable to the States through the Fourteenth Amendment, prohibits the government from taking private property for public use without just compensation. The clearest sort of taking occurs when the government encroaches upon or occupies private land for its own proposed use. Our cases establish that even a minimal "permanent physical occupation of real property" requires compensation under the Clause. Loretto v. Teleprompter Manhattan CATV Corp., 458 U.S. 419, 427 (1982). In Pennsylvania Coal Co. v. Mahon, 260 U.S. 393 (1922), the Court recognized that there will be instances when government actions do not encroach upon or occupy the property yet still affect and limit its use to such an extent that a taking occurs. In Justice Holmes' well-known, if less than self-defining, formulation, "while property may be regulated to a certain extent, if a regulation goes too far it will be recognized as a taking." *Id.* at 415.

Since *Mahon*, we have given some, but not too specific, guidance to courts confronted with deciding whether a particular government action goes too far and effects a regulatory taking. First, we have observed, with certain qualifications, that a regulation which "denies all economically beneficial or productive use of land" will require compensation under the Takings Clause. *Lucas*, 505 U.S. at 1015. Where a regulation places limitations on land that fall short of eliminating all economically beneficial use, a taking nonetheless may have occurred, depending on a complex of factors including the regulation's economic effect on the landowner, the extent to which the regulation interferes with reasonable investment-backed expectations, and the character of the government action. *Penn Central, supra*, at 124. These inquiries are informed by the purpose of the Takings Clause, which is to prevent the government from "forcing some people alone to bear public burdens which, in all fairness and justice, should be borne by the public as a whole." Armstrong v. United States, 364 U.S. 40, 49 (1960).

When the Council promulgated its wetlands regulations, the disputed parcel was owned not by petitioner but by the corporation of which he was sole shareholder. When title was transferred to petitioner by operation of law, the wetlands regulations were in force. The state court held the postregulation acquisition of title was fatal to the claim for deprivation of all economic use and to the *Penn Central* claim. While the first holding was couched in terms of background principles of state property law and the second in terms of petitioner's reasonable investment-backed expectations, the two holdings together amount to a single, sweeping, rule: A purchaser or a successive title holder like petitioner is deemed to have notice of an earlier-enacted restriction and is barred from claiming that it effects a taking.

The theory underlying the argument that postenactment purchasers cannot challenge a regulation under the Takings Clause seems to run on these lines: Property rights are created by the State. So, the argument goes, by prospective legislation the State can shape and define property rights and reasonable investment-backed expectations, and subsequent owners cannot claim any injury from lost value. After all, they purchased or took title with notice of the limitation.

The State may not put so potent a Hobbesian stick into the Lockean bundle. The right to improve property, of course, is subject to the reasonable exercise of state authority, including the enforcement of valid zoning and land-use restrictions. The Takings Clause, however, in certain circumstances allows a landowner to assert that a particular exercise of the State's regulatory power is so unreasonable or onerous as to compel compensation. Just as a prospective enactment, such as a new zoning ordinance, can limit the value of land without effecting a taking because it can be understood as reasonable by all concerned, other enactments are unreasonable and do not become less so through passage of time or title. Were we to accept the State's rule, the postenactment transfer of title would absolve the State of its obligation to defend any action restricting land use, no matter how extreme or unreasonable. A State would be allowed, in effect, to put an expiration date on the Takings Clause. This ought not to be the rule. Future generations, too, have a right to challenge unreasonable limitations on the use and value of land.

Nor does the justification of notice take into account the effect on owners at the time of enactment, who are prejudiced as well. Should an owner attempt to challenge a new regulation, but not survive the process of ripening his or her claim (which, as this case demonstrates, will often take years), under the proposed rule the right to compensation may not be asserted by an heir or successor, and so may not be asserted at all. The State's rule would work a critical alteration to the nature of property, as the newly regulated landowner is stripped of the ability to transfer the interest which was possessed prior to the regulation. The State may not by this means secure a windfall for itself. The proposed rule is, furthermore, capricious in effect. The young owner contrasted with the older owner, the owner with the resources to hold contrasted with the owner with the need to sell, would be in different positions. The Takings Clause is not so quixotic. A blanket rule that purchasers with notice have no compensation right when a claim becomes ripe is too blunt an instrument to accord with the duty to compensate for what is taken.

Direct condemnation, by invocation of the State's power of eminent domain, presents different considerations from cases alleging a taking based on a burdensome regulation. In a direct condemnation action, or when a State has physically invaded the property without filing suit, the fact and extent of the taking are known. In such an instance, it is a general rule of the law of eminent domain that any award goes to the owner at the time of the taking, and that the right to compensation is not passed to a subsequent purchaser. A challenge to the application of a land-use regulation, by contrast, does not mature until ripeness requirements have been satisfied, under principles we have discussed; until this point an inverse condemnation claim alleging a regulatory taking cannot be maintained. It would be illogical, and unfair, to bar a regulatory takings claim because of the post-enactment transfer of ownership where the steps necessary to make the claim ripe were not taken, or could not have been taken, by a previous owner.

We have no occasion to consider the precise circumstances when a legislative enactment can be deemed a background principle of state law or whether those circumstances are present here. It suffices to say that a regulation that otherwise would be unconstitutional absent compensation is not transformed into a background principle of the State's law by mere virtue of the passage of title. This relative standard would be incompatible with our description of the concept in *Lucas*, which is explained in terms of those common, shared understandings of permissible limitations derived from a State's legal tradition. A regulation or common-law rule cannot be a background principle for some owners but not for others. The determination whether an existing, general law can limit all economic use of property must turn on objective factors, such as the nature of the land use proscribed. A law does not become a background principle for subsequent owners by enactment itself.

For reasons we discuss next, the state court will not find it necessary to explore these matters on remand in connection with the claim that all economic use was deprived; it must address, however, the merits of petitioner's claim under *Penn Central*. That claim is not barred by the mere fact that title was acquired after the effective date of the state-imposed restriction.

III

As the date of transfer of title does not bar petitioner's takings claim, we have before us the alternative ground relied upon by the Rhode Island Supreme Court in ruling upon the merits of the takings claims. It held that all economically beneficial use was not deprived because the uplands portion of the property can still be improved. On this point, we agree with the court's decision. Petitioner accepts the Council's contention and the state trial court's finding that his parcel retains $200,000 in development value under the State's wetlands regulations. He asserts, nonetheless, that he has suffered a total taking and contends the Council cannot sidestep the holding in *Lucas* "by the simple expedient of leaving a landowner a few crumbs of value."

Assuming a taking is otherwise established, a State may not evade the duty to compensate on the premise that the landowner is left with a token interest. This is not the situation of the landowner in this case, however. A regulation permitting a landowner to build a substantial residence on an 18-acre parcel does not leave the property "economically idle." *Lucas, supra,* at 1019.

For the reasons we have discussed, the State Supreme Court erred in ruling that acquisition of title after the effective date of the regulations barred the takings claims. The court did not err in finding that petitioner failed to establish a deprivation of all economic value, for it is undisputed that the parcel retains significant worth for construction of a residence. The claims under the *Penn Central* analysis were not examined, and for this purpose the case should be remanded.

The judgment of the Rhode Island Supreme Court is affirmed in part and reversed in part, and the case is remanded for further proceedings not inconsistent with this opinion.

TAHOE-SIERRA PRESERVATION COUNCIL, INC. v. TAHOE REGIONAL PLANNING AGENCY
535 U.S. 302 (2002)

Justice Stevens delivered the opinion of the Court.

The question presented is whether a moratorium on development imposed during the process of devising a comprehensive land-use plan constitutes a *per se* taking of property requiring compensation under the Takings Clause of the United States Constitution. This case actually involves two moratoria ordered by respondent Tahoe Regional Planning Agency (TRPA) to maintain the status quo while studying the impact of development on Lake Tahoe and designing a strategy for environmentally sound growth. The first, Ordinance 81-5, was effective from August 24, 1981, until August 26, 1983, whereas the second more restrictive Resolution 83-21 was in effect from August 27, 1983, until April 25, 1984. As a result of these two directives, virtually all development on a substantial portion of the property subject to TRPA's jurisdiction was prohibited for a period of 32 months. Although the question we decide relates only to that 32-month period, a brief description of the events leading up to the moratoria and a comment on the two permanent plans that TRPA adopted thereafter will clarify the narrow scope of our holding.

I

The relevant facts are undisputed. The Court of Appeals, while reversing the District Court on a question of law, accepted all of its findings of fact, and no party challenges those findings. All agree that Lake Tahoe is "uniquely beautiful," 34 F.Supp.2d 1226, 1230 (D.Nev.1999), that President Clinton was right to call it a " 'national treasure that must be protected and preserved,' " *ibid.*, and that Mark Twain aptly described the clarity of its waters as " 'not *merely* transparent, but dazzlingly, brilliantly so,' " *ibid.* (quoting M. Twain, Roughing It 174-175 (1872)).

Lake Tahoe's exceptional clarity is attributed to the absence of algae that obscures the waters of most other lakes. Historically, the lack of nitrogen and phosphorous, which nourish the growth of algae, has ensured the transparency of its waters. Unfortunately, the lake's pristine state has deteriorated rapidly over the past 40 years; increased land development in the Lake Tahoe Basin (Basin) has threatened the " 'noble sheet of blue water' " beloved by Twain and countless others. 34 F.Supp.2d at 1230. As the District Court found, "[d]ramatic decreases in clarity first began to be noted in the late 1950's/early 1960's, shortly after development at the lake began in earnest." *Id.* at 1231. The lake's unsurpassed beauty, it seems, is the wellspring of its undoing.

The upsurge of development in the area has caused "increased nutrient loading of the lake largely because of the increase in impervious coverage of land in the Basin resulting from that development." *Ibid.*

> Impervious coverage — such as asphalt, concrete, buildings, and even packed dirt — prevents precipitation from being absorbed by the soil. Instead, the water is gathered and concentrated by such coverage. Larger amounts of water flowing off a driveway or a roof have more erosive force than scattered raindrops falling over a dispersed area — especially one covered with indigenous vegetation, which softens the impact of the raindrops themselves.

Ibid.

Given this trend, the District Court predicted that "unless the process is stopped, the lake will lose its clarity and its trademark blue color, becoming green and opaque for eternity."

Those areas in the Basin that have steeper slopes produce more runoff; therefore, they are usually considered "high hazard" lands. Moreover, certain areas near streams or wetlands known as "Stream Environment Zones" (SEZs) are especially vulnerable to the impact of development because, in their natural state, they act as filters for much of the debris that runoff carries. Because "[t]he most obvious response to this problem . . . is to restrict development around the lake —

especially in SEZ lands, as well as in areas already naturally prone to runoff," *id.* at 1232, conservation efforts have focused on controlling growth in these high hazard areas.

In the 1960's, when the problems associated with the burgeoning development began to receive significant attention, jurisdiction over the Basin, which occupies 501 square miles, was shared by the States of California and Nevada, five counties, several municipalities, and the Forest Service of the Federal Government. In 1968, the legislatures of the two States adopted the Tahoe Regional Planning Compact, which Congress approved in 1969. The compact set goals for the protection and preservation of the lake and created TRPA.

Pursuant to the compact, in 1972 TRPA adopted a Land Use Ordinance that divided the land in the Basin into seven "land capability districts," based largely on steepness but also taking into consideration other factors affecting runoff. Each district was assigned a "land coverage coefficient — a recommended limit on the percentage of such land that could be covered by impervious surface." Those limits ranged from 1% for districts 1 and 2 to 30% for districts 6 and 7. Land in districts 1, 2, and 3 is characterized as "high hazard" or "sensitive," while land in districts 4, 5, 6, and 7 is "low hazard" or "non-sensitive." The SEZ lands, though often treated as a separate category, were actually a subcategory of district 1.

Unfortunately, the 1972 ordinance allowed numerous exceptions and did not significantly limit the construction of new residential housing. California became so dissatisfied with TRPA that it withdrew its financial support and unilaterally imposed stricter regulations on the part of the Basin located in California. Eventually the two States, with the approval of Congress and the President, adopted an extensive amendment to the compact that became effective on December 19, 1980.

The 1980 Tahoe Regional Planning Compact (Compact) redefined the structure, functions, and voting procedures of TRPA; and directed it to develop regional "environmental threshold carrying capacities" — a term that embraced "standards for air quality, water quality, soil conservation, vegetation preservation and noise." 94 Stat. 3235, 3239. The Compact provided that TRPA "shall adopt" those standards within 18 months, and that "[w]ithin 1 year after" their adoption, it "shall" adopt an amended regional plan that achieves and maintains those carrying capacities. *Id.*, at 3240. [F]or the period prior to the adoption of the final plan, the Compact itself prohibited the development of new subdivisions, condominiums, and apartment buildings, and also prohibited each city and county in the Basin from granting any more permits in 1981, 1982, or 1983 than had been granted in 1978.

[TRPA eventually] concluded that it could not meet the deadlines in the Compact. On June 25, 1981, it therefore enacted Ordinance 81-5 imposing the first of the two moratoria on development that petitioners challenge in this proceeding. The ordinance provided that it would become effective on August 24, 1981, and remain in effect pending the adoption of the permanent plan required by the Compact.

The District Court made a detailed analysis of the ordinance, noting that it might even prohibit hiking or picnicking on SEZ lands, but construed it as essentially banning any construction or other activity that involved the removal of vegetation or the creation of land coverage on all SEZ lands, as well as on class 1, 2, and 3 lands in California. Some permits could be obtained for such construction in Nevada if certain findings were made. It is undisputed, however, that Ordinance 81-5 prohibited the construction of any new residences on SEZ lands in either State and on class 1, 2, and 3 lands in California.

Given the complexity of the task of defining "environmental threshold carrying capacities" and the division of opinion within TRPA's governing board, the District Court found that it was "unsurprising" that TRPA failed to adopt those thresholds until August 26, 1982, roughly two months after the Compact deadline. *Ibid.* Under a liberal reading of the Compact, TRPA then had until August 26, 1983, to adopt a new regional plan. "Unfortunately, but again not surprisingly, no regional plan was in place as of that date." 34 F.Supp.2d at 1235. TRPA therefore adopted Resolution 83-21, "which completely suspended all project reviews and approvals, including the acceptance of new proposals," and which remained in effect until a new regional plan was adopted on April 26, 1984. Thus, Resolution 83-21 imposed an 8-month moratorium prohibiting all construction on high hazard lands in either State. In combination, Ordinance 81-5 and Resolution 83-21 effectively prohibited all construction on sensitive lands in California and on all SEZ lands in the entire Basin for 32 months, and on sensitive lands in Nevada (other than SEZ lands) for eight months. It is these two moratoria that are at issue in this case.

II

Approximately two months after the adoption of the 1984 plan, petitioners filed parallel actions against TRPA and other defendants in federal courts in Nevada and California that were ultimately consolidated for trial in the District of Nevada. The petitioners include the Tahoe-Sierra Preservation Council, Inc., a nonprofit membership corporation representing about 2,000 owners of both improved and unimproved parcels of real estate in the Lake Tahoe Basin, and a class of some 400 individual owners of vacant lots located either on SEZ lands or in other parts of districts 1, 2, or 3. Those individuals purchased their properties prior to the effective date of the 1980 Compact, App. 34, primarily for the purpose of constructing "at a time of their choosing" a single-family home "to serve as a permanent, retirement or vacation residence," *id.*, at 36. When they made those purchases, they did so with the understanding that such construction was authorized provided that "they complied with all reasonable requirements for building." *Ibid.*

Petitioners' complaints gave rise to protracted litigation that has produced four opinions by the Court of Appeals for the Ninth Circuit and several published District Court opinions. For present purposes, however, we limit our discussion to the lower courts' disposition of the claims based on the 2-year moratorium (Ordinance 81-5) and the ensuing 8-month moratorium (Resolution 83-21).

The District Court began its constitutional analysis by identifying the distinction between a direct government appropriation of property without just compensation and a government regulation that imposes such a severe restriction on the owner's use of her property that it produces "nearly the same result as a direct appropriation." 34 F.Supp.2d, at 1238. The court noted that all of the claims in this case "are of the 'regulatory takings' variety." *Id.*, at 1239. [T]he court first considered whether the analysis adopted in Penn Central Transp. Co. v. New York City, 438 U.S. 104 (1978), would lead to the conclusion that TRPA had effected a "partial taking," and then whether those actions had effected a "total taking."

Emphasizing the temporary nature of the regulations, the testimony that the "average holding time of a lot in the Tahoe area between lot purchase and home construction is twenty-five years," and the failure of petitioners to offer specific evidence of harm, the District Court concluded that "consideration of the *Penn Central* factors clearly leads to the conclusion that there was no taking." 34 F.Supp.2d, at 1240. In the absence of evidence regarding any of the individual plaintiffs, the court evaluated the "average" purchasers' intent and found that such purchasers "did not have reasonable, investment-backed expectations that they would be able to build single-family homes on their land within the six-year period involved in this lawsuit."[11]

The District Court had more difficulty with the "total taking" issue. Although it was satisfied that petitioners' property did retain some value during the moratoria, it found that they had been temporarily deprived of "all economically viable use of their land." *Id.*, at 1245. The court concluded that those actions therefore constituted "categorical" takings under our decision in Lucas v. South Carolina Coastal Council, 505 U.S. 1003 (1992). Accordingly, it ordered TRPA to pay damages to most petitioners for the 32-month period from August 24, 1981, to April 25, 1984, and to those owning class 1, 2, or 3 property in Nevada for the 8-month period from August 27, 1983, to April 25, 1984.

Both parties appealed. TRPA successfully challenged the District Court's takings determination, and petitioners unsuccessfully challenged the dismissal of their claims based on the 1984 and 1987 plans. Petitioners did not, however, challenge the District Court's findings or conclusions concerning its application of *Penn Central.*

Contrary to the District Court, the Court of Appeals held that because the regulations had only a temporary impact on petitioners' fee interest in the properties, no categorical taking had occurred. The Court of Appeals distinguished *Lucas* as applying to the "relatively rare" case in which a regulation denies all productive use of an entire parcel, whereas the moratoria involve only a "temporal 'slice' " of the fee interest and a form of regulation that is widespread and well established. 216 F.3d at 773-774. It also rejected petitioners' argument that our decision in *First English* was controlling. Faced squarely with the question whether a taking had occurred, the court held that *Penn Central* was the appropriate framework for analysis. Petitioners, however, had failed to challenge the District Court's conclusion that they could not make out a taking claim under the *Penn Central* factors.

---

[11] 34 F. Supp. 2d at 1241. The court stated that petitioners "had plenty of time to build before the restrictions went into effect — and almost everyone in the Tahoe Basin knew in the late 1970s that a crackdown on development was in the works." In addition, the court found "the fact that no evidence was introduced regarding the specific diminution in value of any of the plaintiffs' individual properties clearly weighs against a finding that there was a partial taking of the plaintiffs' property." *Ibid.*

Over the dissent of five judges, the Ninth Circuit denied a petition for rehearing en banc. Because of the importance of the case, we granted certiorari limited to the question stated at the beginning of this opinion. We now affirm.

III

Petitioners make only a facial attack on Ordinance 81-5 and Resolution 83-21. They contend that the mere enactment of a temporary regulation that, while in effect, denies a property owner all viable economic use of her property gives rise to an unqualified constitutional obligation to compensate her for the value of its use during that period. Hence, they "face an uphill battle," Keystone Bituminous Coal Assn. v. DeBenedictis, 480 U.S. 470, 495 (1987), that is made especially steep by their desire for a categorical rule requiring compensation whenever the government imposes such a moratorium on development. Under their proposed rule, there is no need to evaluate the landowners' investment-backed expectations, the actual impact of the regulation on any individual, the importance of the public interest served by the regulation, or the reasons for imposing the temporary restriction. For petitioners, it is enough that a regulation imposes a temporary deprivation — no matter how brief — of all economically viable use to trigger a *per se* rule that a taking has occurred. Petitioners assert that our opinions in *First English* and *Lucas* have already endorsed their view, and that it is a logical application of the principle that the Takings Clause was "designed to bar Government from forcing some people alone to bear burdens which, in all fairness and justice, should be borne by the public as a whole." Armstrong v. United States, 364 U.S. 40, 49 (1960).

We shall first explain why our cases do not support their proposed categorical rule — indeed, fairly read, they implicitly reject it. Next, we shall explain why the *Armstrong* principle requires rejection of that rule as well as the less extreme position advanced by petitioners at oral argument. In our view the answer to the abstract question whether a temporary moratorium effects a taking is neither "yes, always" nor "no, never"; the answer depends upon the particular circumstances of the case. Resisting "[t]he temptation to adopt what amount to *per se* rules in either direction," Palazzolo v. Rhode Island, 533 U.S. 606, 636 (2001) (O'CONNOR, J., concurring), we conclude that the circumstances in this case are best analyzed within the *Penn Central* framework.

IV

The text of the Fifth Amendment itself provides a basis for drawing a distinction between physical takings and regulatory takings. Its plain language requires the payment of compensation whenever the government acquires private property for a public purpose, whether the acquisition is the result of a condemnation proceeding or a physical appropriation. But the Constitution contains no comparable reference to regulations that prohibit a property owner from making certain uses of her private property. Our jurisprudence involving condemnations and physical takings is as old as the Republic and, for the most part, involves the straightforward application of *per se* rules. Our regulatory takings jurisprudence, in contrast, is of more recent vintage and is characterized by "essentially ad hoc, factual inquiries," *Penn Central*, 438 U.S., at 124, designed to allow "careful examination and weighing of all the relevant circumstances." *Palazzolo*, 533 U.S. at 636 (O'CONNOR, J., concurring).

This longstanding distinction between acquisitions of property for public use, on the one hand, and regulations prohibiting private uses, on the other, makes it inappropriate to treat cases involving physical takings as controlling precedents for the evaluation of a claim that there has been a "regulatory taking," and vice versa. Land-use regulations are ubiquitous and most of them impact property values in some tangential way — often in completely unanticipated ways. Treating them all as *per se* takings would transform government regulation into a luxury few governments could afford. By contrast, physical appropriations are relatively rare, easily identified, and usually represent a greater affront to individual property rights. "This case does not present the 'classi[c] taking' in which the government directly appropriates private property for its own use," Eastern Enterprises v. Apfel, 524 U.S. 498, 522 (1998); instead the interference with property rights "arises from some public program adjusting the benefits and burdens of economic life to promote the common good," *Penn Central*, 438 U.S. at 124.

Perhaps recognizing this fundamental distinction, petitioners wisely do not place all their emphasis on analogies to physical takings cases. Instead, they rely principally on our decision in Lucas v. South Carolina Coastal Council, 505 U.S. 1003 (1992) — a regulatory takings case that, nevertheless, applied a categorical rule — to argue that the *Penn Central* framework is inapplicable here. A brief review of some of the cases that led to our decision in *Lucas*, however, will help to explain why the holding in that case does not answer the question presented here.

As we noted in *Lucas*, it was Justice Holmes' opinion in Pennsylvania Coal Co. v. Mahon, 260 U.S. 393 (1922), that gave birth to our regulatory takings jurisprudence. In subsequent opinions we have repeatedly and consistently endorsed Holmes' observation that "if regulation goes too far it will be recognized as a taking." *Id.* at 415. Justice Holmes did not provide a standard for determining when a regulation goes "too far," but he did reject the view expressed in Justice Brandeis' dissent that there could not be a taking because the property remained in the possession of the owner and had not been appropriated or used by the public. After *Mahon*, neither a physical appropriation nor a public use has ever been a necessary component of a "regulatory taking."

In the decades following that decision, we have "generally eschewed" any set formula for determining how far is too far, choosing instead to engage in " 'essentially ad hoc, factual inquiries.' " *Lucas*, 505 U.S. at 1015 (quoting *Penn Central*, 438 U.S. at 124). Indeed, we still resist the temptation to adopt *per se* rules in our cases involving partial regulatory takings, preferring to examine "a number of factors" rather than a simple "mathematically precise" formula. Justice Brennan's opinion for the Court in *Penn Central* did, however, make it clear that even though multiple factors are relevant in the analysis of regulatory takings claims, in such cases we must focus on "the parcel as a whole":

> "Taking" jurisprudence does not divide a single parcel into discrete segments and attempt to determine whether rights in a particular segment have been entirely abrogated. In deciding whether a particular governmental action has effected a taking, this Court focuses rather both on the

character of the action and on the nature and extent of the interference with rights in the parcel as a whole — here, the city tax block designated as the "landmark site."

Id. at 130-131.

This requirement that "the aggregate must be viewed in its entirety" explains why, for example, a regulation that prohibited commercial transactions in eagle feathers, but did not bar other uses or impose any physical invasion or restraint upon them, was not a taking. Andrus v. Allard, 444 U.S. 51, 66 (1979). It also clarifies why restrictions on the use of only limited portions of the parcel, such as setback ordinances, Gorieb v. Fox, 274 U.S. 603 (1927), or a requirement that coal pillars be left in place to prevent mine subsidence, Keystone Bituminous Coal Assn. v. DeBenedictis, 480 U.S., at 498, were not considered regulatory takings. In each of these cases, we affirmed that "where an owner possesses a full 'bundle' of property rights, the destruction of one 'strand' of the bundle is not a taking." *Andrus,* 444 U.S. at 65-66.

While the foregoing cases considered whether particular regulations had "gone too far" and were therefore invalid, none of them addressed the separate remedial question of how compensation is measured once a regulatory taking is established. In his dissenting opinion in San Diego Gas & Elec. Co. v. San Diego, 450 U.S. 621, 636 (1981), Justice Brennan identified that question and explained how he would answer it:

> The constitutional rule I propose requires that, once a court finds that a police power regulation has effected a "taking," the government entity must pay just compensation for the period commencing on the date the regulation first effected the "taking," and ending on the date the government entity chooses to rescind or otherwise amend the regulation.

Id. at 658.

Justice Brennan's proposed rule was subsequently endorsed by the Court in *First English*, 482 U.S. at 315, 318, 321. *First English* was certainly a significant decision, and nothing that we say today qualifies its holding. Nonetheless, it is important to recognize that we did not address in that case the quite different and logically prior question whether the temporary regulation at issue had in fact constituted a taking.

In *First English*, the Court unambiguously and repeatedly characterized the issue to be decided as a "compensation question" or a "remedial question." *Id.* at 311 ("The disposition of the case on these grounds isolates the remedial question for our consideration"). And the Court's statement of its holding was equally unambiguous: "We merely hold that where the government's activities *have already worked a taking* of all use of property, no subsequent action by the government can relieve it of the duty to provide compensation for the period during which the taking was effective." *Id.* at 321 (emphasis added). In fact, *First English* expressly disavowed any ruling on the merits of the takings issue because the California courts had decided the remedial question on the assumption that a taking had been alleged. *Id.* at 312-313 ("We reject appellee's suggestion that we must independently evaluate the adequacy of the complaint and resolve the takings claim on the merits before we can reach the remedial question"). After our remand, the California courts concluded that there had not been a taking, and we declined review of that decision.

To the extent that the Court in *First English* referenced the antecedent takings question, we identified two reasons why a regulation temporarily denying an owner all use of her property might not constitute a taking. First, we recognized that "the county might avoid the conclusion that a compensable taking had occurred by establishing that the denial of all use was insulated as a part of the State's authority to enact safety regulations." 482 U.S. at 313. Second, we limited our holding "to the facts presented" and recognized "the quite different questions that would arise in the case of normal delays in obtaining building permits, changes in zoning ordinances, variances, and the like which [were] not before us." *Id.* at 321. Thus, our decision in *First English* surely did not approve, and implicitly rejected, the categorical submission that petitioners are now advocating.

Similarly, our decision in *Lucas* is not dispositive of the question presented. Although *Lucas* endorsed and applied a categorical rule, it was not the one that petitioners propose. Lucas purchased two residential lots in 1988 for $975,000. These lots were rendered "valueless" by a statute enacted two years later. The trial court found that a taking had occurred and ordered compensation of $1,232,387.50, representing the value of the fee simple estate, plus interest. As the statute read at the time of the trial, it effected a taking that "was unconditional and permanent." 505 U.S. at 1012. While the State's appeal was pending, the statute was amended to authorize exceptions that might have allowed Lucas to obtain a building permit. Despite the fact that the amendment gave the State Supreme Court the opportunity to dispose of the appeal on ripeness grounds, it resolved the merits of the permanent takings claim and reversed. Since "Lucas had no reason to proceed on a 'temporary taking' theory at trial," we decided the case on the permanent taking theory that both the trial court and the State Supreme Court had addressed. *Ibid.*

The categorical rule that we applied in *Lucas* states that compensation is required when a regulation deprives an owner of "*all* economically beneficial uses" of his land. *Id.* at 1019. Under that rule, a statute that "wholly eliminated the value" of Lucas' fee simple title clearly qualified as a taking. But our holding was limited to "the extraordinary circumstance when *no* productive or economically beneficial use of land is permitted." *Id.* at 1017. The emphasis on the word "no" in the text of the opinion was, in effect, reiterated in a footnote explaining that the categorical rule would not apply if the diminution in value were 95% instead of 100%. *Id.* at 1019 n.8. Anything less than a "complete elimination of value," or a "total loss," the Court acknowledged, would require the kind of analysis applied in *Penn Central. Lucas,* 505 U.S. at 1019-1020 n.8.

Certainly, our holding that the permanent "obliteration of the value" of a fee simple estate constitutes a categorical taking does not answer the question whether a regulation prohibiting any economic use of land for a 32-month period has the same legal effect. Petitioners seek to bring this case under the rule announced in *Lucas* by arguing that we can effectively sever a 32-month segment from the remainder of each landowner's fee simple estate, and then ask whether that segment has been taken in its entirety by the moratoria. Of course, defining the property interest taken in terms of the very regulation being challenged is circular.

With property so divided, every delay would become a total ban; the moratorium and the normal permit process alike would constitute categorical takings. Petitioners' "conceptual severance" argument is unavailing because it ignores *Penn Central*'s admonition that in regulatory takings cases we must focus on "the parcel as a whole." 438 U.S. at 130-131. We have consistently rejected such an approach to the "denominator" question. See *Keystone*, 480 U.S. at 497. See also Concrete Pipe & Products of Cal., Inc. v. Construction Laborers Pension Trust for Southern Cal., 508 U.S. 602, 644 (1993) ("To the extent that any portion of property is taken, that portion is always taken in its entirety; the relevant question, however, is whether the property taken is all, or only a portion of, the parcel in question"). Thus, the District Court erred when it disaggregated petitioners' property into temporal segments corresponding to the regulations at issue and then analyzed whether petitioners were deprived of all economically viable use during each period. The starting point for the court's analysis should have been to ask whether there was a total taking of the entire parcel; if not, then *Penn Central* was the proper framework.

An interest in real property is defined by the metes and bounds that describe its geographic dimensions and the term of years that describes the temporal aspect of the owner's interest. Both dimensions must be considered if the interest is to be viewed in its entirety. Hence, a permanent deprivation of the owner's use of the entire area is a taking of "the parcel as a whole," whereas a temporary restriction that merely causes a diminution in value is not. Logically, a fee simple estate cannot be rendered valueless by a temporary prohibition on economic use, because the property will recover value as soon as the prohibition is lifted. Cf. Agins v. City of Tiburon, 447 U.S. at 263 n.9 ("Even if the appellants' ability to sell their property was limited during the pendency of the condemnation proceeding, the appellants were free to sell or develop their property when the proceedings ended. Mere fluctuations in value during the process of governmental decisionmaking, absent extraordinary delay, are 'incidents of ownership. They cannot be considered as a "taking" in the constitutional sense' " (quoting Danforth v. United States, 308 U.S. 271, 285 (1939))).

Neither *Lucas*, nor *First English*, nor any of our other regulatory takings cases compels us to accept petitioners' categorical submission. In fact, these cases make clear that the categorical rule in *Lucas* was carved out for the "extraordinary case" in which a regulation permanently deprives property of all value; the default rule remains that, in the regulatory taking context, we require a more fact specific inquiry. Nevertheless, we will consider whether the interest in protecting individual property owners from bearing public burdens "which, in all fairness and justice, should be borne by the public as a whole," Armstrong v. United States, 364 U.S. at 49, justifies creating a new rule for these circumstances.

V

Considerations of "fairness and justice" arguably could support the conclusion that TRPA's moratoria were takings of petitioners' property based on any of seven different theories. First, even though we have not previously done so, we might now announce a categorical rule that, in the interest of fairness and justice, compensation is required whenever government temporarily deprives an owner of all economically viable use of her property. Second, we could craft a narrower rule that would cover all temporary land-use restrictions except those "normal delays in obtaining building permits, changes in zoning ordinances, variances, and the like" which were put to one side in our opinion in *First English*, 482 U.S. at 321. Third, we could adopt a rule like the one suggested by an *amicus* supporting petitioners that would "allow a short fixed period for deliberations to take place without compensation — say maximum one year — after which the just compensation requirements" would "kick in." Fourth, with the benefit of hindsight, we might characterize the successive actions of TRPA as a "series of rolling moratoria" that were the functional equivalent of a permanent taking. Fifth, were it not for the findings of the District Court that TRPA acted diligently and in good faith, we might have concluded that the agency was stalling in order to avoid promulgating the environmental threshold carrying capacities and regional plan mandated by the 1980 Compact. Sixth, apart from the District Court's finding that TRPA's actions represented a proportional response to a serious risk of harm to the lake, petitioners might have argued that the moratoria did not substantially advance a legitimate state interest. Finally, if petitioners had challenged the application of the moratoria to their individual parcels, instead of making a facial challenge, some of them might have prevailed under a *Penn Central* analysis.

As the case comes to us, however, none of the last four theories is available. The "rolling moratoria" theory was presented in the petition for certiorari, but our order granting review did not encompass that issue; the case was tried in the District Court and reviewed in the Court of Appeals on the theory that each of the two moratoria was a separate taking, one for a 2-year period and the other for an 8-month period. And, as we have already noted, recovery on either a bad faith theory or a theory that the state interests were insubstantial is foreclosed by the District Court's unchallenged findings of fact. Recovery under a *Penn Central* analysis is also foreclosed both because petitioners expressly disavowed that theory, and because they did not appeal from the District Court's conclusion that the evidence would not support it. Nonetheless, each of the three *per se* theories is fairly encompassed within the question that we decided to answer.

With respect to these theories, the ultimate constitutional question is whether the concepts of "fairness and justice" that underlie the Takings Clause will be better served by one of these categorical rules or by a *Penn Central* inquiry into all of the relevant circumstances in particular cases. From that perspective, the extreme categorical rule that any deprivation of all economic use, no matter how brief, constitutes a compensable taking surely cannot be sustained. Petitioners' broad submission would apply to numerous "normal delays in obtaining building permits, changes in zoning ordinances, variances, and the like," 482 U.S. at 321, as well as to orders temporarily prohibiting access to crime scenes, businesses that violate health codes, fire-damaged buildings, or other areas that we cannot now foresee. Such a rule would undoubtedly require changes in numerous practices that have long been considered permissible exercises of the police power. As Justice Holmes warned in *Mahon*, "[g]overnment hardly could go on if to some extent values incident to property could not be diminished without paying for every such change in the general law." 260 U.S. at 413. A rule that required compensation for every delay in the use of property would render routine government processes prohibitively expensive or encourage hasty decisionmaking. Such an important change in the law should be the product of legislative rulemaking rather than adjudication.

More importantly, for reasons set out at some length by Justice O'CONNOR in her concurring opinion in Palazzolo v. Rhode Island, 533 U.S., at 636, we are persuaded that the better approach to claims that a regulation has effected a temporary taking "requires careful examination and weighing of all the relevant circumstances." In that opinion, Justice O'CONNOR specifically considered the role that the "temporal relationship between regulatory enactment and title acquisition" should play in the analysis of a takings claim. *Id.* at 632. We have no occasion to address that particular issue in this case, because it involves a different temporal relationship — the distinction between a temporary restriction and one that is permanent. Her comments on the "fairness and justice" inquiry are, nevertheless, instructive:

> Today's holding does not mean that the timing of the regulation's enactment relative to the acquisition of title is immaterial to the *Penn Central* analysis. Indeed, it would be just as much error to expunge this consideration from the takings inquiry as it would be to accord it exclusive significance. Our polestar instead remains the principles set forth in *Penn Central* itself and our other cases that govern partial regulatory takings. Under these cases, interference with investment-backed expectations is one of a number of factors that a court must examine.
>
> The Fifth Amendment forbids the taking of private property for public use without just compensation. We have recognized that this constitutional guarantee is "designed to bar Government from forcing some people alone to bear public burdens which, in all fairness and justice, should be borne by the public as a whole." *Penn Central*, 438 U.S., at 123-124 (quoting Armstrong v. United States, 364 U.S. 40, 49 (1960)). The concepts of "fairness and justice" that underlie the Takings Clause, of course, are less than fully determinate. Accordingly, we have eschewed "any 'set formula' for determining when 'justice and fairness' require that economic injuries caused by public action be compensated by the government, rather than remain disproportionately concentrated on a few persons." *Penn Central*, *supra*, at 124 (quoting Goldblatt v. Hempstead, 369 U.S. 590, 594 (1962)). The outcome instead "depends largely 'upon the particular circumstances [in that] case.'" *Penn Central*, *supra*, at 124 (quoting United States v. Central Eureka Mining Co., 357 U.S. 155, 168 (1958)).

Id. at 633.

In rejecting petitioners' *per se* rule, we do not hold that the temporary nature of a land-use restriction precludes finding that it effects a taking; we simply recognize that it should not be given exclusive significance one way or the other.

A narrower rule that excluded the normal delays associated with processing permits, or that covered only delays of more than a year, would certainly have a less severe impact on prevailing practices, but it would still impose serious financial constraints on the planning process. Unlike the "extraordinary circumstance" in which the government deprives a property owner of all economic use, *Lucas*, 505 U.S. at 1017, moratoria like Ordinance 81-5 and Resolution 83-21 are used widely among land-use planners to preserve the status quo while formulating a more permanent development strategy. In fact, the consensus in the planning community appears to be that moratoria, or "interim development controls" as they are often called, are an essential tool of successful development. Yet even the weak version of petitioners' categorical rule would treat these interim measures as takings regardless of the good faith of the planners, the reasonable expectations of the landowners, or the actual impact of the moratorium on property values.

The interest in facilitating informed decisionmaking by regulatory agencies counsels against adopting a *per se* rule that would impose such severe costs on their deliberations. Otherwise, the financial constraints of compensating property owners during a moratorium may force officials to rush through the planning process or to abandon the practice altogether. To the extent that communities are forced to abandon using moratoria, landowners will have incentives to develop their property quickly before a comprehensive plan can be enacted, thereby fostering inefficient and ill-conceived growth. A finding in the 1980 Compact itself, which presumably was endorsed by all three legislative bodies that participated in its enactment, attests to the importance of that concern. 94 Stat. 3243 ("The legislatures of the States of California and Nevada find that in order to make effective the regional plan as revised by the agency, it is necessary to halt temporarily works of development in the region which might otherwise absorb the entire capability of the region for further development or direct it out of harmony with the ultimate plan").

As Justice KENNEDY explained in his opinion for the Court in *Palazzolo*, it is the interest in informed decisionmaking that underlies our decisions imposing a strict ripeness requirement on landowners asserting regulatory takings claims:

> These cases stand for the important principle that a landowner may not establish a taking before a land-use authority has the opportunity, using its own reasonable procedures, to decide and explain the reach of a challenged regulation. Under our ripeness rules a takings claim based on a law or regulation which is alleged to go too far in burdening property depends upon the landowner's first having followed reasonable and necessary steps to allow regulatory agencies to exercise their full discretion in considering development plans for the property, including the opportunity to grant any variances or waivers allowed by law. As a general rule, until these ordinary processes have been followed the extent of the restriction on property is not known and a regulatory taking has not yet been established.

533 U.S. at 620-621.

We would create a perverse system of incentives were we to hold that landowners must wait for a takings claim to ripen so that planners can make well-reasoned decisions while, at the same time, holding that those planners must compensate landowners for the delay.

Indeed, the interest in protecting the decisional process is even stronger when an agency is developing a regional plan than when it is considering a permit for a single parcel. In the proceedings involving the Lake Tahoe Basin, for example, the moratoria enabled TRPA to obtain the benefit of comments and criticisms from interested parties, such as the petitioners, during its deliberations. Since a categorical rule tied to the length of deliberations would likely create added pressure on decisionmakers to reach a quick resolution of land-use questions, it would only serve to disadvantage those landowners and interest groups who are not as organized or familiar with the planning process. Moreover, with a temporary ban on development there is a lesser risk that individual landowners will be "singled out" to bear a special burden that should be shared by the public as a whole. Nollan v. California Coastal Comm'n, 483 U.S. 825, 835 (1987). At least with a moratorium there is a clear "reciprocity of advantage," *Mahon*, 260 U.S. at 415, because it protects the interests of all affected landowners against immediate construction that might be inconsistent with the provisions of the plan that is ultimately adopted. "While each of us is burdened somewhat by such restrictions, we, in turn, benefit greatly from the restrictions that are placed on others." *Keystone*, 480 U.S. at 491. In fact, there is reason to believe property values often will continue to increase despite a moratorium. Such an increase makes sense in this context because property values throughout the Basin can be expected to reflect the added assurance that Lake Tahoe will remain in its pristine state. Since in some cases a 1-year moratorium may not impose a burden at all, we should not adopt a rule that assumes moratoria always force individuals to bear a special burden that should be shared by the public as a whole.

It may well be true that any moratorium that lasts for more than one year should be viewed with special skepticism. But given the fact that the District Court found that the 32 months required by TRPA to formulate the 1984 Regional Plan was not unreasonable, we could not possibly conclude that every delay of over one year is constitutionally unacceptable. Formulating a general rule of this kind is a suitable task for state legislatures. In our view, the duration of the restriction is one of the important factors that a court must consider in the appraisal of a regulatory takings claim, but with respect to that factor as with respect to other factors, the "temptation to adopt what amount to *per se* rules in either direction must be resisted." *Palazzolo*, 533 U.S. at 636 (O'CONNOR, J., concurring). There may be moratoria that last longer than one year which interfere with reasonable investment-backed expectations, but as the District Court's opinion illustrates, petitioners' proposed rule is simply "too blunt an instrument" for identifying those cases. *Id.* at 628. We conclude, therefore, that the interest in "fairness and justice" will be best served by relying on the familiar *Penn Central* approach when deciding cases like this, rather than by attempting to craft a new categorical rule.

Accordingly, the judgment of the Court of Appeals is affirmed.

NOTES AND QUESTIONS

1. **Literature.** For comment on the preceding two cases, see Thomas J. Koffer, *What to "Take" From* Palazzolo *and* Tahoe-Sierra: *A Temporary Loss for Property Rights*, 21 Va. Envtl. L.J. 503 (2003); Gregory M. Stein, *Takings in the 21st Century: Reasonable Investment-Backed Expectations After* Palazzolo *and* Tahoe-Sierra, 69 Tenn. L. Rev. 891 (2002).

2. **Background principles of state law.** What is a "background principle of state law"? What is the difference between "background principles of state law" and "reasonable investment-backed expectations"?

3. **Conceptual severance again.** What does the *Tahoe-Sierra* case add to your understanding of the conceptual severance issue?

4. **Remedies.** If a court finds a regulatory taking has occurred, is the property owner entitled to "just compensation"? In First English Evangelical Lutheran Church v. County of Los Angeles, 482 U.S. 304, 321 (1987), discussed in *Tahoe-Sierra*, the Court said:

> Once a court determines that a taking has occurred, the government retains the whole range of options already available — amendment of the regulation, withdrawal of the invalidated regulation, or exercise of eminent domain. Thus we do not, as the Solicitor General suggests, "permit a court, at the behest of a private person, to require the Government to exercise the power of eminent domain." We merely hold that where the government's activities have already worked a taking of all use of property, no subsequent action by the government can relieve it of the duty to provide compensation for the period during which the taking was effective.

For what period are the landowner's damages measured in cases of "temporary takings"? Might the period be measured in different ways? *See* Gregory M. Stein, *Pinpointing the Beginning and Ending of a Temporary Regulatory Taking*, 70 Wash. L. Rev. 953 (1995). *See generally* David Schultz, *The Price is Right! Property Valuation for Temporary Takings*, 22 Hamline L. Rev. 281 (1998).

5. **Review.** Recall Note 9 following the case of Fiese v. Sitorius in Chapter 6, discussing the public trust doctrine in Matthews v. Bay Head Improvement Association. Why doesn't the court's condemnation of an easement across private land for beach access in *Matthews* constitute a taking requiring compensation? *See generally* Barton H. Thompson, Jr., *Judicial Takings*, 76 Va. L. Rev. 1449 (1990).

d.   Exactions

In the cases set forth above, the issue is whether government regulation goes "too far." What if instead of regulating property, the government requires a property owner to dedicate land to public use as a condition of approval for development? The following case discusses this type of "exaction."

DOLAN v. CITY OF TIGARD
512 U.S. 374 (1994)

CHIEF JUSTICE REHNQUIST delivered the opinion of the Court.

Petitioner challenges the decision of the Oregon Supreme Court which held that the city of Tigard could condition the approval of her building permit on the dedication of a portion of her property for flood control and traffic improvements. 854 P.2d 437 (1993). We granted certiorari to resolve a question left open by our decision in Nollan v. California Coastal Comm'n, 483 U.S. 825 (1987), of what is the required degree of connection between the exactions imposed by the city and the projected impacts of the proposed development.

I

The State of Oregon enacted a comprehensive land use management program in 1973. The program required all Oregon cities and counties to adopt new comprehensive land use plans that were consistent with the statewide planning goals. The plans are implemented by land use regulations which are part of an integrated hierarchy of legally binding goals, plans, and regulations. Pursuant to the State's requirements, the city of Tigard, a community of some 30,000 residents on the southwest edge of Portland, developed a comprehensive plan and codified it in its Community Development Code (CDC). The CDC requires property owners in the area zoned Central Business District to comply with a 15% open space and landscaping requirement, which limits total site coverage, including all structures and paved parking, to 85% of the parcel. After the completion of a transportation study that identified congestion in the Central Business District as a particular problem, the city adopted a plan for a pedestrian/bicycle pathway intended to encourage alternatives to automobile transportation for short trips. The CDC requires that new development facilitate this plan by dedicating land for pedestrian pathways where provided for in the pedestrian/bicycle pathway plan.

The city also adopted a Master Drainage Plan. The Drainage Plan noted that flooding occurred in several areas along Fanno Creek, including areas near petitioner's property. The Drainage Plan also established that the increase in impervious surfaces associated with continued urbanization would exacerbate these flooding problems. To combat these risks, the Drainage Plan suggested a series of improvements to the Fanno Creek Basin, including channel excavation in the area next to petitioner's property. Other recommendations included ensuring that the floodplain remains free of structures and that it be preserved as greenways to minimize flood damage to structures. The Drainage Plan concluded that the cost of these improvements should be shared based on both direct and indirect benefits, with property owners along the waterways paying more due to the direct benefit that they would receive. [The] CDC and the Tigard Park Plan carry out these recommendations.

Petitioner Florence Dolan owns a plumbing and electric supply store located on Main Street in the Central Business District of the city. The store covers approximately 9,700 square feet on the eastern side of a 1.67-acre parcel, which includes a gravel parking lot. Fanno Creek flows through the southwestern corner of the lot and along its western boundary. The year-round flow of the creek renders the area within the creek's 100-year floodplain virtually unusable for commercial development. The city's comprehensive plan includes the Fanno Creek floodplain as part of the city's greenway system.

Petitioner applied to the city for a permit to redevelop the site. Her proposed plans called for nearly doubling the size of the store to 17,600 square feet and paving a 39-space parking lot. The existing store, located on the opposite side of the parcel, would be razed in sections as construction progressed on the new building. In the second phase of the project, petitioner proposed to build an additional structure on the northeast side of the site for complementary businesses and to provide more parking. The proposed expansion and intensified use are consistent with the city's zoning scheme in the Central Business District.

The City Planning Commission granted petitioner's permit application subject to conditions imposed by the city's CDC. The CDC establishes the following standard for site development review approval:

> Where landfill and/or development is allowed within and adjacent to the 100-year floodplain, the City shall require the dedication of sufficient open land area for greenway adjoining and within the floodplain. This area shall include portions at a suitable elevation for the construction of a pedestrian/ bicycle pathway within the floodplain in accordance with the adopted pedestrian/bicycle plan.

Thus, the Commission required that petitioner dedicate the portion of her property lying within the 100-year floodplain for improvement of a storm drainage system along Fanno Creek and that she dedicate an additional 15-foot strip of land adjacent to the floodplain as a pedestrian/bicycle pathway. The dedication required by that condition encompasses approximately 7,000 square feet, or roughly 10% of the property. In accordance with city practice, petitioner could rely on the dedicated property to meet the 15% open space and landscaping requirement mandated by the city's zoning scheme. The city would bear the cost of maintaining a landscaped buffer between the dedicated area and the new store.

Petitioner requested variances from the CDC standards. Variances are granted only where it can be shown that, owing to special circumstances related to a specific piece of the land, the literal interpretation of the applicable zoning provisions would cause "an undue or unnecessary hardship" unless the variance is granted. CDC § 18.134.010. Rather than posing alternative mitigating measures to offset the expected impacts of her proposed development, as allowed under the CDC, petitioner simply argued that her proposed development would not conflict with the policies of the comprehensive plan. The Commission denied the request.

Petitioner appealed to the Land Use Board of Appeals (LUBA) on the ground that the city's dedication requirements were not related to the proposed development, and, therefore, those requirements constituted an uncompensated taking of her property under the Fifth Amendment. Given the undisputed fact that the proposed larger building and paved parking area would increase the amount of impervious surfaces and the runoff into Fanno Creek, LUBA concluded that "there is a 'reasonable relationship' between the proposed development and the requirement to dedicate land along Fanno Creek for a greenway." With respect to the pedestrian/bicycle pathway, LUBA noted the Commission's finding that a significantly larger retail sales building and parking lot would attract larger numbers of customers and employees and their vehicles. It again found a "reasonable relationship" between alleviating the impacts of increased traffic from the development and facilitating the provision of a pedestrian/bicycle pathway as an alternative means of transportation.

The Oregon Court of Appeals affirmed, rejecting petitioner's contention that in Nollan v. California Coastal Comm'n, we had abandoned the "reasonable relationship" test in favor of a stricter "essential nexus" test. 832 P.2d 853 (1992). The

Oregon Supreme Court affirmed. 854 P.2d 437 (1993). The court also disagreed with petitioner's contention that the Nollan Court abandoned the "reasonably related" test. We granted certiorari because of an alleged conflict between the Oregon Supreme Court's decision and our decision in *Nollan*.

II

One of the principal purposes of the Takings Clause is "to bar Government from forcing some people alone to bear public burdens which, in all fairness and justice, should be borne by the public as a whole." Armstrong v. United States, 364 U.S. 40, 49 (1960). Without question, had the city simply required petitioner to dedicate a strip of land along Fanno Creek for public use, rather than conditioning the grant of her permit to redevelop her property on such a dedication, a taking would have occurred. Such public access would deprive petitioner of the right to exclude others, "one of the most essential sticks in the bundle of rights that are commonly characterized as property." Kaiser Aetna v. United States, 444 U.S. 164, 176 (1979).

On the other side of the ledger, the authority of state and local governments to engage in land use planning has been sustained against constitutional challenge as long ago as our decision in Village of Euclid v. Ambler Realty Co., 272 U.S. 365 (1926). A land use regulation does not effect a taking if it "substantially advance[s] legitimate state interests" and does not "den[y] an owner economically viable use of his land." Agins v. City of Tiburon, 447 U.S. 255, 260 (1980).[6]

The sort of land use regulations discussed in the cases just cited, however, differ in two relevant particulars from the present case. First, they involved essentially legislative determinations classifying entire areas of the city, whereas here the city made an adjudicative decision to condition petitioner's application for a building permit on an individual parcel. Second, the conditions imposed were not simply a limitation on the use petitioner might make of her own parcel, but a requirement that she deed portions of the property to the city. In *Nollan*, we held that governmental authority to exact such a condition was circumscribed by the Fifth and Fourteenth Amendments. Under the well-settled doctrine of "unconstitutional conditions," the government may not require a person to give up a constitutional right — here the right to receive just compensation when property is taken for a public use — in exchange for a discretionary benefit conferred by the government where the benefit sought has little or no relationship to the property.

Petitioner contends that the city has forced her to choose between the building permit and her right under the Fifth Amendment to just compensation for the public easements. Petitioner does not quarrel with the city's authority to exact some forms of dedication as a condition for the grant of a building permit, but challenges the showing made by the city to justify these exactions. She argues that the city has identified "no special benefits" conferred on her, and has not identified any "special quantifiable burdens" created by her new store that would justify the particular

---

[6] There can be no argument that the permit conditions would deprive petitioner of "economically beneficial us[e]" of her property as she currently operates a retail store on the lot. Petitioner assuredly is able to derive some economic use from her property. See, e.g., Lucas v. South Carolina Coastal Council, 505 U.S. 1003, 1019 (1992).

dedications required from her which are not required from the public at large.

III

In evaluating petitioner's claim, we must first determine whether the "essential nexus" exists between the "legitimate state interest" and the permit condition exacted by the city. *Nollan*, 483 U.S., at 837. If we find that a nexus exists, we must then decide the required degree of connection between the exactions and the projected impact of the proposed development. We were not required to reach this question in *Nollan*, because we concluded that the connection did not meet even the loosest standard. Here, however, we must decide this question.

A

We addressed the essential nexus question in *Nollan*. The California Coastal Commission demanded a lateral public easement across the Nollans' beachfront lot in exchange for a permit to demolish an existing bungalow and replace it with a three-bedroom house. The public easement was designed to connect two public beaches that were separated by the Nollan's property. The Coastal Commission had asserted that the public easement condition was imposed to promote the legitimate state interest of diminishing the "blockage of the view of the ocean" caused by construction of the larger house.

We agreed that the Coastal Commission's concern with protecting visual access to the ocean constituted a legitimate public interest. We also agreed that the permit condition would have been constitutional "even if it consisted of the requirement that the Nollans provide a viewing spot on their property for passersby with whose sighting of the ocean their new house would interfere." *Id.*, at 836. We resolved, however, that the Coastal Commission's regulatory authority was set completely adrift from its constitutional moorings when it claimed that a nexus existed between visual access to the ocean and a permit condition requiring lateral public access along the Nollans' beachfront lot. How enhancing the public's ability to "traverse to and along the shorefront" served the same governmental purpose of "visual access to the ocean" from the roadway was beyond our ability to countenance. The absence of a nexus left the Coastal Commission in the position of simply trying to obtain an easement through gimmickry, which converted a valid regulation of land use into " 'an out-and-out plan of extortion.' " *Id.* quoting J.E.D. Associates, Inc. v. Atkinson, 432 A.2d 12, 14-15 (N.H. 1981).

No such gimmicks are associated with the permit conditions imposed by the city in this case. Undoubtedly, the prevention of flooding along Fanno Creek and the reduction of traffic congestion in the Central Business District qualify as the type of legitimate public purposes we have upheld. It seems equally obvious that a nexus exists between preventing flooding along Fanno Creek and limiting development within the creek's 100-year floodplain. Petitioner proposes to double the size of her retail store and to pave her now-gravel parking lot, thereby expanding the impervious surface on the property and increasing the amount of storm water runoff into Fanno Creek.

The same may be said for the city's attempt to reduce traffic congestion by providing for alternative means of transportation. In theory, a pedestrian/bicycle pathway provides a useful alternative means of transportation for workers and shoppers: "Pedestrians and bicyclists occupying dedicated spaces for walking and/or bicycling . . . remove potential vehicles from streets, resulting in an overall improvement in total transportation system flow." A. Nelson, Public Provision of Pedestrian and Bicycle Access Ways: Public Policy Rationale and the Nature of Private Benefits 11, Center for Planning Development, Georgia Institute of Technology, Working Paper Series (Jan. 1994).

B

The second part of our analysis requires us to determine whether the degree of the exactions demanded by the city's permit conditions bears the required relationship to the projected impact of petitioner's proposed development. Here the Oregon Supreme Court deferred to what it termed the "city's unchallenged factual findings" supporting the dedication conditions and found them to be reasonably related to the impact of the expansion of petitioner's business.

The city required that petitioner dedicate "to the City as Greenway all portions of the site that fall within the existing 100-year floodplain [of Fanno Creek] and all property 15 feet above [the floodplain] boundary." In addition, the city demanded that the retail store be designed so as not to intrude into the greenway area. The city relies on the Commission's rather tentative findings that increased storm water flow from petitioner's property "can only add to the public need to manage the [floodplain] for drainage purposes" to support its conclusion that the "requirement of dedication of the floodplain area on the site is related to the applicant's plan to intensify development on the site." The question for us is whether these findings are constitutionally sufficient to justify the conditions imposed by the city on petitioner's building permit. Since state courts have been dealing with this question a good deal longer than we have, we turn to representative decisions made by them.

In some States, very generalized statements as to the necessary connection between the required dedication and the proposed development seem to suffice. We think this standard is too lax to adequately protect petitioner's right to just compensation if her property is taken for a public purpose.

Other state courts require a very exacting correspondence, described as the "specifi[c] and uniquely attributable" test. Under this standard, if the local government cannot demonstrate that its exaction is directly proportional to the specifically created need, the exaction becomes "a veiled exercise of the power of eminent domain and a confiscation of private property behind the defense of police regulations." Pioneer Trust & Savings Bank v. Mount Prospect, 176 N.E.2d 799, 802 (Ill. 1961). We do not think the Federal Constitution requires such exacting scrutiny, given the nature of the interests involved.

A number of state courts have taken an intermediate position, requiring the municipality to show a "reasonable relationship" between the required dedication and the impact of the proposed development. Typical is the Supreme Court of

Nebraska's opinion in Simpson v. North Platte, 292 N.W.2d 297, 301 (Neb. 1980), where that court stated:

> The distinction, therefore, which must be made between an appropriate exercise of the police power and an improper exercise of eminent domain is whether the requirement has some reasonable relationship or nexus to the use to which the property is being made or is merely being used as an excuse for taking property simply because at that particular moment the landowner is asking the city for some license or permit.

Thus, the court held that a city may not require a property owner to dedicate private property for some future public use as a condition of obtaining a building permit when such future use is not "occasioned by the construction sought to be permitted." 292 N.W.2d at 302.

We think the "reasonable relationship" test adopted by a majority of the state courts is closer to the federal constitutional norm than either of those previously discussed. But we do not adopt it as such, partly because the term "reasonable relationship" seems confusingly similar to the term "rational basis" which describes the minimal level of scrutiny under the Equal Protection Clause of the Fourteenth Amendment. We think a term such as "rough proportionality" best encapsulates what we hold to be the requirement of the Fifth Amendment. No precise mathematical calculation is required, but the city must make some sort of individualized determination that the required dedication is related both in nature and extent to the impact of the proposed development.[8]

It is axiomatic that increasing the amount of impervious surface will increase the quantity and rate of storm water flow from petitioner's property. Therefore, keeping the floodplain open and free from development would likely confine the pressures on Fanno Creek created by petitioner's development. In fact, because petitioner's property lies within the Central Business District, the CDC already required that petitioner leave 15% of it as open space and the undeveloped floodplain would have nearly satisfied that requirement. But the city demanded more — it not only wanted petitioner not to build in the floodplain, but it also wanted petitioner's property along Fanno Creek for its greenway system. The city has never said why a public greenway, as opposed to a private one, was required in the interest of flood control.

The difference to petitioner, of course, is the loss of her ability to exclude others. As we have noted, this right to exclude others is "one of the most essential sticks in

---

[8] Justice STEVENS' dissent takes us to task for placing the burden on the city to justify the required dedication. He is correct in arguing that in evaluating most generally applicable zoning regulations, the burden properly rests on the party challenging the regulation to prove that it constitutes an arbitrary regulation of property rights. See, e.g., Village of Euclid v. Ambler Realty Co., 272 U.S. 365 (1926). Here, by contrast, the city made an adjudicative decision to condition petitioner's application for a building permit on an individual parcel. In this situation, the burden properly rests on the city. This conclusion is not, as he suggests, undermined by our decision in Moore v. East Cleveland, 431 U.S. 494 (1977), in which we struck down a housing ordinance that limited occupancy of a dwelling unit to members of a single family as violating the Due Process Clause of the Fourteenth Amendment. The ordinance at issue in *Moore* intruded on choices concerning family living arrangements, an area in which the usual deference to the legislature was found to be inappropriate. *Id.*, at 499.

the bundle of rights that are commonly characterized as property." *Kaiser Aetna,* 444 U.S. at 176. It is difficult to see why recreational visitors trampling along petitioner's floodplain easement are sufficiently related to the city's legitimate interest in reducing flooding problems along Fanno Creek, and the city has not attempted to make any individualized determination to support this part of its request.

The city contends that the recreational easement along the greenway is only ancillary to the city's chief purpose in controlling flood hazards. It further asserts that unlike the residential property at issue in *Nollan,* petitioner's property is commercial in character, and therefore, her right to exclude others is compromised. Admittedly, petitioner wants to build a bigger store to attract members of the public to her property. She also wants, however, to be able to control the time and manner in which they enter. The recreational easement on the greenway is different in character from the exercise of state-protected rights of free expression and petition that we permitted in PruneYard Shopping Center v. Robins, 447 U.S. 74 (1980), in which we held that a major private shopping center that attracted more than 25,000 daily patrons had to provide access to persons exercising their state constitutional rights to distribute pamphlets and ask passers-by to sign their petitions. We based our decision, in part, on the fact that the shopping center "may restrict expressive activity by adopting time, place, and manner regulations that will minimize any interference with its commercial functions." *Id.* at 83. By contrast, the city wants to impose a permanent recreational easement upon petitioner's property that borders Fanno Creek. Petitioner would lose all rights to regulate the time in which the public entered onto the greenway, regardless of any interference it might pose with her retail store. Her right to exclude would not be regulated; it would be eviscerated.

If petitioner's proposed development had somehow encroached on existing greenway space in the city, it would have been reasonable to require petitioner to provide some alternative greenway space for the public either on her property or elsewhere. We conclude that the findings upon which the city relies do not show the required reasonable relationship between the floodplain easement and the petitioner's proposed new building.

With respect to the pedestrian/bicycle pathway, we have no doubt that the city was correct in finding that the larger retail sales facility proposed by petitioner will increase traffic on the streets of the Central Business District. The city estimates that the proposed development would generate roughly 435 additional trips per day. Dedications for streets, sidewalks, and other public ways are generally reasonable exactions to avoid excessive congestion from a proposed property use. But on the record before us, the city has not met its burden of demonstrating that the additional number of vehicle and bicycle trips generated by petitioner's development reasonably relate to the city's requirement for a dedication of the pedestrian/bicycle pathway easement. The city simply found that the creation of the pathway "could offset some of the traffic demand and lessen the increase in traffic congestion."[10]

---

[10] In rejecting petitioner's request for a variance from the pathway dedication condition, the city

No precise mathematical calculation is required, but the city must make some effort to quantify its findings in support of the dedication for the pedestrian/bicycle pathway beyond the conclusory statement that it could offset some of the traffic demand generated.

IV

Cities have long engaged in the commendable task of land use planning, made necessary by increasing urbanization, particularly in metropolitan areas such as Portland. The city's goals of reducing flooding hazards and traffic congestion, and providing for public greenways, are laudable, but there are outer limits to how this may be done. "A strong public desire to improve the public condition [will not] warrant achieving the desire by a shorter cut than the constitutional way of paying for the change." *Pennsylvania Coal.*

The judgment of the Supreme Court of Oregon is reversed, and the case is remanded for further proceedings not inconsistent with this opinion.

It is so ordered.

NOTES AND QUESTIONS

1. **Scope of *Dolan*.** In City of Monterey v. Del Monte Dunes at Monterey, Ltd., 526 U.S. 687, 702 (1999), the Court made clear, "we have not extended the rough-proportionality test of *Dolan* beyond the special context of exactions — land-use decisions conditioning approval of development on the dedication of property to public use." What if instead of requiring a dedication of land as a condition of development approval, the government requires or permits the developer to pay a fee in lieu of dedication? *See* Town of Flower Mound v. Stafford Estates Ltd. Partnership, 135 S.W.3d 620, 636-41 (Tex. 2004) (discussing various states' answers to this question and concluding that "[t]he Dolan standard should apply to both" situations under Texas law).

2. **Literature.** *See generally* Carlos A. Ball & Laurie Reynolds, *Exactions and Burden Distribution in Takings Law*, 47 Wm. & Mary L. Rev. 1513 (2006); Bruce W. Bringardner, *Exactions, Impact Fees, and Dedications: National and Texas Law After* Dolan *and* Del Monte Dunes, 32 Urb. Law. 561 (2000); Lee Anne Fennell, *Hard Bargains and Real Steals: Land Use Exactions Revisited*, 86 Iowa L. Rev. 1 (2000); Mark Fenster, *Takings Formalism and Regulatory Formulas: Exactions and the Consequences of Clarity*, 96 Cal. L. Rev. 609 (2004).

3. **Comparisons.** How does the principal case differ from *Nollan*? What issue does the principal case raise that was not addressed in *Nollan*?

4. **Exactions.** How are cases involving exactions from a private landowner different from cases involving simple regulation of the landowner's land use? Are you satisfied that there is a meaningful distinction? Doesn't all regulation force the

---

stated that omitting the planned section of the pathway across petitioner's property would conflict with its adopted policy of providing a continuous pathway system. But the Takings Clause requires the city to implement its policy by condemnation unless the required relationship between petitioner's development and added traffic is shown.

landowner to transfer something — some part of the bundle of sticks — to the state?

5. **Presumptions.**   Recall the presumptions regarding the constitutionality of regulatory legislation established in *Euclid* (Section B.1 above). Does *Dolan* take a different view? If so, is *Dolan*'s rule applicable to all regulations, or just to regulations that demand an exaction from the landowner?

TABLE OF CASES

[References are to pages]

[References are to pages]

[References are to pages]

[References are to pages]

D

[References are to pages]

E

[References are to pages]

[References are to pages]

[References are to pages]

[References are to pages]

N

[References are to pages]

[References are to pages]

Q

R

[References are to pages]

[References are to pages]

T

[References are to pages]

[References are to pages]

[References are to pages]

INDEX

[References are to page numbers.]

[References are to page numbers.]

[References are to page numbers.]

[References are to page numbers.]